A HISTORY OF CRIME AND THE AMERICAN CRIMINAL JUSTICE SYSTEM

This book offers a history of crime and the criminal justice system in America, written particularly for students of criminal justice and those interested in the history of crime and punishment. It follows the evolution of the criminal justice system chronologically and, when necessary, offers parallels between related criminal justice issues in different historical eras. From its antecedents in England to revolutionary times, to the American Civil War, right through the twentieth century to the age of terrorism, this book combines a wealth of resources with keen historical judgment to offer a fascinating account of the development of criminal justice in America. A new chapter brings the story up to date, looking at criminal justice through the Obama era and the early days of the Trump administration.

Each chapter is broken down into four crucial components related to the American criminal justice system from the historical perspective: lawmakers and the judiciary; law enforcement; corrections; and crime and punishment. A range of pedagogical features, including timelines of key events, learning objectives, critical thinking questions and sources, as well as a full glossary of key terms and a "Who's Who in Criminal Justice History" section, ensures that readers are well-equipped to navigate the immense body of knowledge related to criminal justice history.

Essential reading for Criminal Justice majors and historians alike, this book will be a fascinating text for anyone interested in the development of the American criminal justice system from ancient times to the present day.

Mitchel P. Roth is Professor of Criminal Justice and Criminology at Sam Houston State University, USA, and is the author of *Global Organized Crime*, 2nd ed. (Routledge, 2017).

Chapter 1-4   Test 1

Chapter 5-8   Test 2

Chapter 9-12   Test 3

Chapter 13-15   Test 4

D1613981

A HISTORY OF CRIME AND THE AMERICAN CRIMINAL JUSTICE SYSTEM

THIRD EDITION

Mitchel P. Roth

Routledge
Taylor & Francis Group

LONDON AND NEW YORK

Third edition published 2019
by Routledge
2 Park Square, Milton Park, Abingdon, Oxon, OX14 4RN

and by Routledge
711 Third Avenue, New York, NY 10017

Routledge is an imprint of the Taylor & Francis Group, an informa business

© 2019 Mitchel P. Roth

First edition published by Wadsworth Publishing 2005
Second edition published by Wadsworth/Cengage Learning 2011

British Library Cataloguing-in-Publication Data
A catalogue record for this book is available from the British Library

Library of Congress Cataloging-in-Publication Data
Names: Roth, Mitchel P., 1953– author.
Title: A history of crime and the American criminal justice system /
   Mitchel P. Roth.
Other titles: Crime and punishment.
Description: Third Edition. | New York : Routledge, 2019. | Revised edition
   of the author's Crime and punishment, c2011. | Includes bibliographical
   references and index.
Identifiers: LCCN 2018019020 | ISBN 9781138552869 (hardback) |
   ISBN 9781138552883 (pbk.) | ISBN 9781315148342 (ebook)
Subjects: LCSH: Criminal justice, Administration of—History. | Criminal justice,
   Administration of—United States—History.
Classification: LCC HV7419 .R67 2019 | DDC 364.973—dc23
LC record available at https://lccn.loc.gov/2018019020

ISBN: 978-1-138-55286-9 (hbk)
ISBN: 978-1-138-55288-3 (pbk)
ISBN: 978-1-315-14834-2 (ebk)

DOI: 10.4324/9781315148342

Typeset in Adobe Garamond and Parisine
by Apex CoVantage, LLC

This book is dedicated to my incredibly supportive wife, Ines and my son Eric, who inspires me to be a better person every day.

CONTENTS

PREFACE

This text is a history of crime and the American criminal justice system. The author has published eighteen books, many combining the disciplines of history, criminal justice, and criminology. He has taught thousands of students over the past twenty years in courses ranging from the History of Murder and the History of American Violence to the History of Organized Crime and a Global History of Crime and Punishment. With a PhD in History, the author is a tenured professor in a leading criminal justice and criminology program. While there are several texts on the market currently, this is the only one actually written by a scholar schooled in historical research methods. The author's research and academic background has allowed him to appreciate what historical lessons are most germane to modern students seeking careers in criminal justice-related careers, especially those related to corrections, law enforcement, law school, policing, counterterrorism, and organized crime suppression, to name just a few. Moreover, this book offers lessons beyond the field of criminal justice and is also geared toward courses in the humanities as well as the general reader.

On the face of it, the book takes a traditional approach to chronicling the continuum of crime and criminal justice in America, as well as historical influences from antiquity and early British history. The text is organized chronologically, and when possible, offers parallels between criminal justice issues in different historical eras. This is exemplified by various discussions of regional variations in crime and punishment, xenophobia, discrimination, and so forth. There are certain themes that resonate through the sometimes troubled history of the American criminal justice system. Among the more recurring challenges has been the federal government's sporadic curtailment of civil liberties from the early Republic to the present including the Alien and Sedition Acts under President Thomas Jefferson, the suspension of the writ of habeas corpus under President Abraham Lincoln, the Red Scare of 1919, the internment of Japanese Americans during World War II, the era of McCarthyism, and controversy over the USA PATRIOT Act. In each of these cases, the criminal justice system has responded to real or imagined threats with strategies that made controversial tradeoffs between reduced civil liberties and national security. This is just one of the historical themes that appears throughout the book.

Organization

Writing a history of the criminal justice system is a challenging task. With such a wealth of sources to draw from, it requires a certain historical judgment as to what to include and what to leave out. Since a history of all criminal justice systems[1] is beyond the scope of this book, the author draws from historical and other sources that best explain the evolution of various crimes and the current American criminal justice system, which is rooted in Old Testament ethics and morality, English antecedents, and the peculiar conditions of American history.

Each chapter is broken down into what the author considers five crucial components related to the American criminal justice system from the historical perspective, components that largely explain the evolution of a peculiarly American reaction to crime and crime control. Each chapter begins with a section on lawmakers and the judiciary, before delving into sections on law enforcement, corrections, and crime and punishment. It is the author's contention that an understanding of American criminal justice history should be rooted in the political, economic, and social patterns of American life. These are often explained in terms of race relations, immigration, economic dislocation, and certain regional predilections for violence and capital punishment (the South) or for order and capital punishment abolition (New England). When possible these issues and others are brought into play to help explain the continuum in crime and criminal justice patterns that exists in all regions of the country.

Below is a summary of each chapter:

- Chapter 1 (From Customs to Codes: Crime and Criminal Justice in the Ancient World) examines the ancient roots of criminal justice. It focuses on the development of written law codes from customs that evolved before the advent of writing. Although other societies developed legal codes and criminal justice related practices, this book focuses on those that most inspired the development of the English and American criminal justice systems. Among the civilizations covered in this chapter are the Near Eastern Hammurabic and Mosaic codes, Greek and Roman criminal justice, and the development of church law.

- Chapter 2 (Crime and Criminal Justice: English Antecedents) details the development of English criminal justice and common law. It covers the history of English criminal justice from the Anglo-Saxon period and the Viking invasions through the creation of the English Constitution and Bill of Rights. After reading the chapter, the reader will have a much better understanding of how the development of criminal justice institutions in Britain gave rise to the American criminal justice system following British colonization of America's Eastern Seaboard.

- Chapter 3 (Crime and Criminal Justice in Early America) follows the British colonization process as English criminal justice practices are modified in the New World. What's more it breaks down the development of colonial criminal justice into various regions, including the southern colonies exemplified by Virginia, New England, characterized by Massachusetts, and the Mid-Atlantic colonies featuring Pennsylvania. This is important for understanding why certain patterns existing in different regions still continue to this day.

- Chapter 4 (Crime and Criminal Justice in Revolutionary Times) examines the evolution of American criminal justice procedures during the years surrounding the American Revolution. The ratification of the American Constitution and the Bill of Rights completes the cycles of legal development spurred on by the English Constitution a century earlier.

- Chapter 5 (Crime and Criminal Justice in the New Nation) focuses on the development of the American penitentiary and various experiments in policing ranging from city guards, Texas Rangers, and the French Sûreté to city marshals and high constables.

Chapter 6 (Crime and Criminal Justice in Antebellum America) chronicles the sectional crisis taking center stage as the developing American criminal justice system is challenged on several fronts, including states' rights versus federal law, mob violence, and new sentencing procedures (good behavior and indeterminate sentencing).

Chapter 7 (Crime and Criminal Justice in the Civil War Era) follows the impact of the Civil War on the nation's criminal justice institutions. The Civil War had great consequences for the southern states when half the southern population made the transition from slavery to freedom. However, a number of obstacles were created by southern criminal justice institutions that would contradict the promises of freedom contained the Thirteenth and Fourteenth Amendments. This chapter also focuses on urban politics and corruption in New York City, attempts at prison reform, and the creation of the U.S. Secret Service.

Chapter 8 (Crime and Criminal Justice in Victorian America) examines an era marked by political and labor dissension; new identification systems, such as bertillonage and fingerprinting; and the introduction of new methods of execution (e.g., the electric chair). It is also a period when big-city police reformers finally took on the rampant corruption and political patronage, negating the effectiveness of urban police forces.

Chapter 9 (Crime and Criminal Justice in the Progressive Era) focuses attention on the reform attempts by Progressive reformers. Despite the intentions of the reformers, the Prohibition era in the Crisis Decades just on the horizon would nullify many of their reforms. World War I, together with the rise of Bolshevism in Russia, intensified many of the old fears of native-born Americans who then lashed out at immigrants, labor agitators, and anarchists, challenging civil liberties in the process. However, this was also an era of police and prison reform that introduced college cops, motorcycle patrols, and female police and national police organizations to the front lines of crime fighting.

Chapter 10 (Crime and Criminal Justice in the Crisis Decades) shows how no years had more ramifications for the evolution of the criminal justice system than the second and third decades of the twentieth century. This chapter highlights the expansion of federal criminal justice with the creation of the Bureau of Investigation and the impact of Prohibition and the Great Depression on the nation's crime problem. Other important topics include the criminalization of certain narcotics, the trend toward police professionalization, and the sensationalism of the era's crime reporting.

Chapter 11 (Criminal Justice at Midcentury) considers the impact of the world war and anticommunism on civil liberties (e.g., Japanese internment and McCarthyism); increasing racial tensions leading to riots in Los Angeles, Detroit, Harlem, and other cities; and a new focus on organized crime in America.

Chapter 12 (Nationalization of Criminal Justice) delves into the new challenges to the criminal justice system presented by the era's social unrest. This period was most notable for a number of Supreme Court decisions that expanded the rights of the accused while limiting the powers of police. Rising crime rates, urban riots, and antiwar violence would lead police executives and political leaders to examine the role of police as crime fighters. These years would also be marked by an about-face in public opinion on the death penalty.

Chapter 13 (Crime and Criminal Justice at the End of the Twentieth Century) covers criminal justice in the last two decades of the twentieth century, an era characterized by rising and falling crime rates and the implementation of a number of "get-tough" crime policies that have led to America's overcrowded prison system. The rise in crime in the 1980s signaled a more punitive era in American criminal justice, one in which lawmakers responded by rewriting laws, shifting money from schools to prisons, and locking up record numbers of people under new sentencing guidelines. Serial killers, mass murderers, FBI confrontations, police brutality, and acts of domestic terrorism dominated news coverage. But what was most unexpected was the drop in crime in cities such as New York, where old strategies of community policing borrowed from past historical experience were combined with new technologies of the approaching twenty-first century, such as Compstat, to make cities safer.

Chapter 14 (Criminal Justice in the Age of Terrorism) begins with the unexpected attacks of 9/11 and their concomitant impact on every level of the criminal justice system. This chapter is shadowed by the impact of the USA PATRIOT Act and the reorganization of federal criminal justice, as well as emerging issues such as extraordinary rendition, military tribunals, roving wiretaps, and black site prisons in foreign countries. Except for acts of international terrorism, no form of criminality garnered more headlines or had bigger national repercussions in this era than the multi-billion white-collar scandals and their accompanying impact on the nation's financial stability. These and other emerging issues are covered as well. This chapter has been expanded to include various new alternatives to imprisonment, the crisis of an aging prison population, and the emergence of prison gangs.

Chapter 15: (Crime and Criminal Justice in Contemporary America) is new to this edition of the text. It brings the story of American crime and criminal justice through the years of the administration of President Barack Obama and the first year of the presidency of Donald Trump. The 2016 presidential contest offers a perfect bookend to the chapters, focusing on a number of uniquely American leitmotifs that reflect existential fears of foreign immigration and anxieties of a country experiencing rapid demographic change.

Conclusion: Also new to this edition, it contributes some closing observations by a criminal justice historian on where America stands at the end of the second decade of the twenty-first century and some of the lessons that can be gleaned from the preceding chapters.

Learning tools

In order to navigate the immense body of knowledge related to criminal justice history each chapter is supplemented and organized with a number of learning tools. Each chapter begins with a set of seven to ten Learning Objectives. These objectives are designed to lead students to overarching themes of each chapter. This is followed by an extensive Time Line that allows the student to check which events occur at which point in the historical process and perhaps play a role as a catalyst in events to come. Each chapter, except for the final chapter, concludes with a trial that documents the legal process and offers insight into the American crime and the criminal justice system at various stages in history. This is followed by a Point–Counterpoint section, which uses primary documents and the actual words of participants in the criminal justice process to give the reader both sides of various controversies. Additional features included in the book are as follows:

"History Vignette" Boxes. Throughout this book, various vignettes/time capsules to illustrate significant moments in criminal justice history, parallels between past and present

criminal justice, and contributions to the criminal justice system made by individuals reflecting the diversity of the American people. More than fifty boxes are new to this edition. Also new is the addition of boxes that add examples of global crime and criminal justice, especially helpful in a globalized world.

- *Critical Thinking Questions*: These were conceived as a base for examining the lessons of each chapter in greater detail.

- *Key Terms*: An understanding of what are the key terms in each chapter plays an important role in the overall learning process and helps differentiate the more important names, incidents, and ideas crucial to that chapter.

- *Notable Trials*. Each chapter ends with a notable trial from the period covered. Many are not the traditional trials captured on Court TV. Some are political in nature (Sacco and Vanzetti and the Rosenbergs), while others were selected because they had a major effect on history (Zenger trial) or were of legal significance (*Gideon v. Wainwright*). As one criminal justice historian has noted, "Not much is known about the day-to-day work of the courtroom"[2] prior to 1800. To reveal the ordinary criminal process would require a painstaking examination of contemporary newspaper coverage, since only the most sensational cases bothered with trial transcripts. Several sensational cases are covered as well (O. J. Simpson and Lizzie Borden).

- *Point–Counterpoint*. These sections discuss issues important in criminal justice using primary documents and the actual words of participants in the criminal justice process to give the reader both sides of various issues and controversies.

- *Glossary*. For anyone confused by the difference between heresy and blasphemy or between treason and sedition, a handy alphabetical glossary is included at the end of the book, which has been updated and expanded as well. Here students will find definitions of unfamiliar and familiar words that make up the lexicon for the history of American criminal justice.

- *Who's Who in Criminal Justice History*. In addition, throughout the text, a number of famous people make a brief cameo. In order to guide students through this crowd of individuals, some well-known but many unfamiliar, the author has added a "Who's Who in Criminal Justice History" section that highlights the accomplishments and dates associated with each individual. It is hoped that these biographical capsules will lead students to pursue the lives of these people in more detail.

New for this edition

The reorganization and additional materials in this edition include the following:

- Replacing the section and caption in each chapter, formerly entitled **"American Violence"** and integrating it in the **"Crime and Punishment"** sections. This change also marks a substantial revision that distinguishes it from previous additions, which focused mostly on the historical development of the criminal justice and gave short shrift to crime and criminals. Readers will benefit for a more extensive examination of various types of crime and crime trends over the centuries.

- There is much more coverage of **women** and **minorities** in each chapter.

■ The **Trial of George Zimmerman** for the death of Trayvon Martin has been added as the Notable Trial in Chapter 14. There is also a new **Point–Counterpoint** on the "Stand Your Ground Defense" after the trial.

■ The addition of **Chapter 15** and a **Conclusion** bring the history up through the early Trump administration and tie together a number of themes and issues covered in the book.

■ This edition has added a substantial number of **Appendices** that include historical time lines for both prison and policing developments over the centuries. There are also lists of the police chiefs in major police departments including the NYPD and the FBI and many others.

■ The author has also corrected several errors and eliminated or at least abbreviated any repetitive information.

■ The **Who's Who** and **Glossary** sections have all been updated.

Mitchel P. Roth
Huntsville, Texas

Notes

1 See for example, Mitchel P. Roth, *An Eye for an Eye: A Global History of Crime and Punishment*, London: Reaktion Books, 2014. It is currently available in English, Croatian, and Turkish editions.
2 Lawrence M. Friedman, *Crime and Punishment in American History*, New York: Basic Books, 1993, p. 41

CHAPTER ONE

From customs to codes: Crime and criminal justice in the ancient world

Learning objectives

After finishing this chapter students should understand and be able to discuss:

- The evolution of the civil law tradition
- The impact of monotheistic religion on criminal justice and make some conclusions about its parallel impact today
- The persistence of the death penalty over the millennia
- The continued application of an "eye for an eye," or the literal view of accountability
- The continued relevance of the Ten Commandments
- Why certain capital crimes in the past are no longer considered so
- Parallels between punishment and criminal behavior in the ancient world and today

One of the most intriguing questions facing anthropologists, criminologists, sociologists, and other scholars is how the earliest preliterate societies managed to not only survive but also maintain peace and order without written law codes. There is little argument that the earliest laws were derived from folk customs, evolving from loose but unquestionable rules to fixed but more specific practices. Until relatively recently, many anthropologists scoffed at the notion of legal life in preliterate cultures but instead saw "custom as king." Thus, every society has developed rules for governing and regulating behavior. Without rules to maintain order, anarchy threatens the very existence of a community.

Before the jury, the court system, and the penitentiary, early societies relied on unwritten customs that often were more rigid than written law. French Enlightenment philosophers

	509 B.C.	451 B.C.	399 B.C.	62 B.C.	A.D. 312	A.D. 325	A.D. 518	A.D. 534
TIMELINE	Beginning of republican Rome	The Twelve Tables, first written law code of Rome	Trial and Death of Socrates	Augustus introduces organized law enforcement	Constantine converts to Christianity	Council of Nicaea	Era of Justinian begins	Publication of Code of Justinian

such as Rousseau often idealized these natural societies. But freedom from law does not necessarily mean freedom. In reality, nascent societies are ruled by customs often as definite as any law code. Individuals in preliterate society are bound together in a web of regulations enforced by thousands of **taboos.** In his study of primitive law, E. Adamson Hoebel described a taboo as a "social injunction that is sanctioned by supernatural action."[1] These unwritten rules are rigid and uncompromising and in some cultures can determine when one should stand or walk, sit or rise, and sleep or eat.

The earliest societies relied on customs, magic, and religion to maintain order prior to the advent of complex systems of law. In embryonic cultures, any breach of the customary code could expose an offending individual as well as one's corresponding social group to the wrath of the gods. Responsibility was collective in nature, as was punishment. By violating taboos, an individual was committing a serious transgression (beginning with Mosaic Code, these were equivalent to sins).[2] Hence, it was necessary for the community to punish the individual to prevent supernatural forces from taking revenge on the tribal group. When members of a society believe that consequences of a sinful act will spread to the entire group rather than just the sinner, sins become crimes. African Ashanti tribal members, for example, equated crime with sin, or *oman akyiwadie*, acts that were "hateful to the tribe," actions that were not only offensive to tribal ancestral spirits but were most likely to bring the wrath of divinities on the entire tribe. In such a case, the chief was expected to make sure the malefactor was punished; otherwise, the tribe would be punished by the wrath of its ancestors.

By most counts, "the absolutely uniform conscience does not see to exist."[3] There are few worldwide norms when it comes to crime and punishment. Taboos in primitive cultures ranged from incest and witchcraft to treason and sacrilege. The incest prohibition, however, seems to be the most universally accepted of these taboos. The Ashanti, for example, considered incest a capital crime and referred to it as *mogyadie*, or "the eating of one's own blood." That said, incest in Ashanti culture was much more complicated than in its modern context. It could include having intercourse with anyone blood-related or in the same clan. In fact, just sharing the same clan name was enough to have both parties put to death.

More recently in eighteenth-century England, the most serious secular crime was treason, and the worst religious offense was **sacrilege**, both demanding the most gruesome modes of punishment. Englishmen, one and all, saw these crimes as a threat to the state much in the way early societies saw them as threats to the existence of their meager communities. Accordingly, it should not be unexpected that these offenses remain serious charges into the twenty-first century.

In preliterate cultures, it was understood that, if members were to live together in communities comprised of a family or tribe, they must respect the rights of other members of that unit. Over time, these rights became recognized customs approved by the community. Obviously, the origins of these customs are obscure, but there is little doubt that the acceptance of certain rules of conduct enabled families and tribes to evolve into larger communities and finally into nation-states.

Courts, police, corrections, and laws are basic components of the modern criminal justice system. With the coming of personal property, which gave individuals economic authority, and the state, which defined citizenship and rights, the individual became a distinct entity. Paralleling these advances was the development of courts to levy fines and render judgments that allowed societies to make the transition from custom to law. Here, then, the broad outlines of criminal justice begin to take shape. Although formal law enforcement is nonexistent in primitive society, the development of legal procedures led to the introduction of a central authority, law codes, courts, and constables or a police presence to enforce the developing system.

Nascent cultures did not need to develop complex legal concepts until they began to congregate in communities of hundreds or thousands. It was only then that conditions necessitated the establishment of an authority to enforce sanctions, rules, and regulations. While custom emanated from the people, law was forced on the community by the decree of a master, a ruler, a monarch, or a group of elders, such as an oligarchy.

The first stage in the evolution of law was personal revenge. Without a formal apparatus to adjudicate criminal behavior, preliterate societies allowed private disputes to be settled in a personal manner. Among the Indian tribes of Lower California, every man was regarded as his own policeman and was allowed to administer justice in the form of vengeance. As individuals banded together in communities, conflict was viewed as a personal affair to be arbitrated privately between the victim and the perpetrator. It became acceptable for the victim's kin to extract revenge and not the community, clan, or tribe. Because this system was accepted by both parties, it was assumed that the killing of the perpetrator would resolve the conflict. Hence, the injured party was imbued with many of the components of today's criminal justice system, acting as judge, jury, and executioner.

Revenge or vengeance is a natural component of most criminal justice systems. Nowhere is this more obvious than when it comes to capital punishment. Today, the United States remains one of the few in the industrialized world to maintain the death penalty, but in the spirit of *lex talionis* ("an eye for an eye, a tooth for a tooth"), Hammurabi, and the Bible, although there are other capital crimes, over the past half century, the penalty has been used only to punish those who take a life: the most literal interpretation of accountability.

A community's reaction to antisocial behavior was governed by a simple basic drive: revenge. By killing a perpetrator, there would be no recurrence of that behavior. Victims initially determined the extent of retribution, which was usually not proportional to the original offense. In such instances, then, it was not unusual for the perpetrator to become the victim, leading to an indefinite cycle of violent revenge or a feud. Living on the bare margins of existence, primitive communities could ill afford the continuous destruction of life and property. The negative ramifications of an unbroken cycle of revenge led preliterate communities to place limits on vengeance, which over time became the first laws and codes of the historical era.

The first constraints on blood feuds took the form of what is better known as "blood revenge." The first step toward controlling the magnitude of vengeance was to place the responsibility for punishing the perpetrator in the hands of the group rather than allowing a specific family member to gauge the measure of revenge. In this case, an injury suffered by the member of a family, clan, or tribe was regarded as an injury to the entire community, and revenge was arbitrated in like fashion by the victim's immediate community. This was a major step in the development of law because it took the mode of revenge out of the hands of a private offender and placed it into the collective hands of the community.

Over time, the consequences of this behavior could prove devastating to a community, and a system of compensation was introduced – the next major contribution to the foundations of early criminal justice. One measure of a civilization's complexity is the distance between the feuding individuals and the administration of revenge. After measures were taken to replace vengeance with compensation, this new protocol became more complex as community leaders began to maintain order and settle conflicts through a range of activities, including adjudication, mediation, and arbitration.

The transition to the legal stage of government occurs when a society recognizes certain rules and procedures, a level of development that usually requires the knowledge of writing. The use of writing allows substantive laws to pass from the oral tradition, often the preserve of certain recognized individuals, to the society at large. For example, prior to the development of writing in Iceland in the twelfth century, the "lawspeaker" was the only authority on the country's laws, and every year, he was required to recite one-third of the laws to the common people. His term in office lasted three years, just long enough to recite the complete collection.

In order to understand the development of the Western legal tradition as well as the roots of the American criminal justice system, an understanding of historical developments pertaining to crime and punishment in classical antiquity is necessary. Readers will find many similarities between crime in the ancient world and the present with all forms of criminality surviving the transition from antiquity to the modern era. Treason, murder, **adultery**, robbery, and rape were all defined as criminal behavior in earlier eras, although the definition of some of these offenses has evolved over time.

Thanks to oral traditions and research by ethnographers and anthropologists, we do have some foundation for interpreting traditions of crime and punishment in early societies. According to African Ashanti traditions, the most common form of capital punishment was beheading with a small knife. Think of recent beheading videos by al Qaeda in Iraq and the Islamic State. Demonstrating that even the earliest cultures could be quite pragmatic when it came to punishment, the Ashanti executioner was allowed to hold the victim's head down and "slice and saw through the neck commencing from the back" if he did want to look him in the eyes. Other Ashanti punishments included strangling with a leather thong, or manually, and bludgeoning with a club.[4]

If anything has changed over the millennia, it is the individuality of punishment that existed in classical antiquity. Burning, scourging, impalement, and mutilation have fortunately been scuttled in favor of the warehousing of criminals in sterile, modern prisons and the introduction of more painless methods of capital punishment. The following is a brief survey of the earliest lawmaking advances, beginning with **Hammurabi's code** in the ancient Near East and ending with the relocation of the Roman capital to **Constantinople** following the fall of the Western Roman Empire in the fifth century.

At least sixteen different legal traditions existed at various points in history. Most scholarship focuses on the four major contemporary legal traditions – the Civil, Common, Islamic, and Socialist legal traditions. Almost ninety years ago, John Henry Wigmore[5] identified the sixteen traditions as Egyptian, Mesopotamian, Chinese, Hindu, Hebrew, Greek, Roman, Maritime,

Japanese, Mohammedan, Celtic, Germanic, Slavic, Ecclesiastical, Romanesque, and Anglican. Except for a handful of states that practice the socialist legal tradition (Cuban, China, Vietnam, North Korea), most other countries base their legal systems in some part on either the civil, common, or Islamic legal systems. Of these, most attention has been directed at the civil and common law traditions, due to a great extent to the colonial powers that spread these traditions throughout the world. The English common law traditions predominate in the British Empire's former colonies in the Caribbean, North America, Canada, Australia, and New Zealand as well as parts of Africa, India, and other areas.

Code of Hammurabi

(king made law) (king given code)

every offense had a punishment attached

Almost 4,000 years ago, the plains between the Tigris and Euphrates Rivers, in what is today Syria and Iraq, became the setting for one of the world's first great civilizations. By 5000 B.C., this region was home to large communities of people. Population pressure gave stimulus to better ways of doing things. The concentration and energies of many people living together, along with the pooling of ideas and a larger labor force, led to advances in agriculture and animal domestication. A wider variety of food sources (lentils, grapes, and olives) and a broader range of domesticated animals soon led to a transition from more nomadic hunter-gatherer cultures to more sedentary settlement patterns.

Over the ensuing centuries, life became more complex as people congregated in urban enclaves. A more stratified town life emerged in which potters, artisans, brick makers, weavers, and leather workers encouraged a transformation in methods of lawmaking. The convergence of several factors in this region of Mesopotamia gave rise to one of the greatest inventions in world history: writing. As life became more complicated and complex, some manner of record keeping was necessary to keep track of temple stores and the contributions of the citizens to the community (everyone was expected to give their share to the Gods; without writing, people could lie and say that they had already contributed). Without writing, the past and the future were indistinguishable, and opportunities for shirking responsibilities and for theft were rampant.

about 4,000 lines

Scribes invented writing in the fourth millennium B.C. using reeds to inscribe pictographs or cuneiform on flattened clumps of clay. These earliest forms of writing allowed not only record keeping but also the promulgation of laws. The oldest extant literature of most ancient cultures is in the form of laws written by scribes. In the earliest period, laws were written codes issued at the request of a royal authority. The legislation of ancient kings became written history for future scholars who have studied how the law was amended, expanded, and handed down through the generations.

The lawgivers

It has generally been accepted that the earliest written law codes were produced in **Babylonia** (part of Mesopotamia) in the ancient Near East. Hammurabi's code (ca. 1700 B.C.) is

was the first

accepted as the only substantially complete pre-Mosaic code of law. Legislators frequently borrowed from the works of other cultures, such as the Romans copying from the Greeks. Although Hammurabi (ca. 1728–1686 B.C.) is often credited with conceiving the first law code, we now know that he borrowed extensively from earlier rulers. In the 1940s, archaeologists uncovered fragments of clay tablets in Iraq that pre-dated Hammurabi's by perhaps several hundred years. Both law codes share a high proportion of technical phrases, leading some legal historians to the conclusion that Hammurabi was influenced by earlier administrators. Regardless, these laws have a familiar ring to them, dealing as they do with divorce, matrimony, savage dogs, and personal injury.

Hammurabi's code, uncovered by French archaeologists in 1901–1902, consists of 4,000 lines of laws inscribed on an eight-foot-high slab of black stone. At the top of the stone, the king is depicted looking on the sun god with adulation as authority is conferred on Hammurabi. This ancient code contains both civil and criminal law, regulating virtually every aspect of his subjects' lives. More complex and comprehensive than any law code previously attempted, Hammurabi's code is considered the apogee of legal codification prior to Roman law. Much better organized and comprehensive than biblical law, the code took a very literal view of accountability and introduced the law of retaliation, as in *lex talionis*. There were no ambiguities, and it did not take into account that circumstances change with the times. The world was viewed as part of a fixed, divine order; hence, the code was rigid and reflected absolute justice. For instance, if an architect built a structure that collapsed because of poor design and killed a client, the architect could be executed. In a similar manner, surgeons were responsible for the health of their patients. If it was determined that surgery led to the death of a patient, the surgeon could have his hand amputated.

Although Hammurabi's code is credited with attempting to protect the disenfranchised from the power of the elite, no thought was given to ending slavery or granting women equal rights. Men could divorce at will, but women had to prove they lived a blameless life before being allowed to do the same. If after petitioning for divorce her neighbors denounced her, she could be drowned in a river, a common method of execution in a land of rivers.

Egyptian civilization developed around the same time as the Sumerians. What is known about its early crime and punishment survives on a "random mixture of court documents, civil contracts, private writings, observed behavior, fictional tales and some royal decrees." Compared to modern Western standards, punishment was typically swift and severe. Crimes ranged from borrowing a donkey without permission to more familiar offenses such as burglary, robbery, fraud and tax evasion, murder, and regicide. There was a litany of punishments, including exile on work gangs, beatings, and various mutilations. Impalement was reserved for the worst crimes. Over time, more severe physical punishments were added such as various facial mutilations. When it came to the death penalty, it seemed to be rarely used compared to other ancient societies. The earliest surviving death sentence dates back to sixteenth-century B.C. Egypt. The case involved an individual condemned for practicing magic and being ordered to commit suicide. (See the death of Socrates later in this chapter.)[6]

Crime and punishment

What is most striking about this law code is the distinction of punishments by class; punishment varied according to the social status of the victim and the perpetrator. If the daughter of a gentleman was struck and suffered a miscarriage, the fine was ten shekels. However, if the daughter of an ordinary citizen was injured, the fine would only be five shekels. In like fashion, if the ordinary citizen's daughter died, the perpetrator was liable for a fine; if it was the gentleman's daughter, the wrongdoer could face execution.

Babylonia was not alone in determining punishment according to the status of victim and offenders. Ancient India's Laws of Manu punished criminal acts according to the caste of those involved. Upper-class Brahmins were usually fined or escaped punishment altogether. The harshest penal sanction that could be expected was banishment, even for murder. Conversely, lower-caste Shudra, could be corporally punished for even the most minor transgression. The Laws of Manu contained a number of sympathetic punishments, exemplified by the law "He who raises his hand or stick, shall have his hand cut off; He who in anger kicks with his foot, shall have his foot cut off."[7] Likewise, if a Brahmin was injured by a Shudra, the limb used in the assault was severed. In another instance, one who spit on a superior might have his lips cut off.

During China's Tang Dynasty (618–907), punishment was also doled out according to rank. Like their Indian and Babylonian counterparts. High-ranking offenders could expect less **punitive** punishments, while if servants and others at the bottom of the social ladder were found guilty of a crime, they could expect a punishment one degree more severe, for slaves two degrees more severe. According to this logic, a slave who assaulted a commoner and broke his leg or put out an eye would be executed. If the same actions were committed by a master, he could at worst expect one year of penal servitude.

Several ingredients of Hammurabi's code bear little resemblance to contemporary law. Besides the variation of punishment according to class, this ancient code relied on trial by ordeal in cases involving irreconcilable conflict in sworn evidence. In such cases, a judge could order the accused to jump in a river. If the individual swore falsely to the gods, it was assumed that the deities would ensure that the accused drowned. In the event that the accused survived, the accuser was liable to be put to death. This caveat was meant to discourage false testimony.

The laws of Hammurabi introduced the world to the philosophy of *lex talionis*, a concept that would reappear later in the Old Testament. This code is extremely inflexible and took a very literal view of accountability. Law was absolute and in most respects a rich man's law, but to read these laws is to gain intriguing insight into the life of the ordinary people of the ancient Near East.

While we know little about the courts and procedures preceding punishments, the codes prescribe execution by drowning for crimes including adultery, incest with a daughter-in-law, and cheating customers by watering down alcoholic beverages. Impalement was sanctioned for any woman who procured the death of her husband for the sake of her lover or for one who procured her own abortion. Individuals caught looting during fires could be cast into the flames. When it came to capital punishment, Hammurabi's code was at its most merciless. The punishment of burning could also be used to punish a priestess who ceased to live in a cloister and began frequenting inns or a man who committed incest with his mother after the death of his father. Why burning for such obvious moral taboos?

Perhaps this concept adheres to the notion of fire as a form of purification or is an attempt to avoid shedding tribal blood.

Mutilation was not uncommon under Hammurabi's code, with the amputation of hands prescribed for four offenses; ears for two different infractions; and even the removal of ears, breasts, and eyes for certain penalties. Babylonian punishments were severe and cruel, with death often inflicted and mutilations even more usual. For the student of history, it would be erroneous to assume that punishment could be no crueler, as it has been only a few centuries since European executioners supervised the boiling of prisoners alive and the hanging, quartering, and disemboweling of political offenders.

Since Hammurabi codified the law some 4,000 years ago, most societies have relied on legal principles to arbitrate between conflicting parties. Without a system of equitable laws, humanity could not transcend its primitive roots and maintain social order. By codifying both criminal and civil laws and creating specific penalties for breaking these tenets, for the first time in recorded history, a connection was established between crime and its retribution.

Mosaic Law (similar to Hammurabi)

(God made)

There are many striking parallels between the laws of Hammurabi and the Old Testament, which have been traditionally ascribed to the Jewish prophet Moses.[8] Whatever the Old Testament might have borrowed from Babylonian code, it is uncontestable that the biblical law code was something uniquely different from anything that occurred before. While this legal system does not stand in the pantheon of the great legal systems of the ancient world, its importance lies in its intrinsic connection with the national religion and its later relationship with the Christian religion. Committed to the elimination of class distinctions, it contrasted sharply with Hammurabi's code by repudiating the notion of a rich man's law by applying a uniform moral standard applicable to all people. On the other hand, Hammurabi's legislation was much more orderly and comprehensive than biblical laws.

(first 5 books of bible)

Mosaic Law, or the "Law of Moses," can be found in the first five books of the Bible and Old Testament (Genesis, Exodus, Leviticus, Numbers, and Deuteronomy). Known as the **Torah** to the Jewish people, the ancient Greeks referred to this part of the Bible as the **Pentateuch**, which means "five books" in Greek. The first five books of the Bible contain the **Ten Commandments**,[9] which are considered the foundation of law systems throughout much of the Western world.

The Ten Commandments

1 Thou shalt have no other gods before me.

2 Thou shalt not take the name of the Lord thy God in vain.

3 Thou shalt not make unto thee any graven image, or anything that is in heaven above, or that is in the earth beneath, or that is in the water under the earth. Thou shalt not bow down thyself to them, nor serve them.

> 4 Remember the Sabbath day to keep it holy.
>
> 5 Honor thy father and thy mother.
>
> 6 Thou shalt not kill.
>
> 7 Thou shalt not commit adultery.
>
> 8 Thou shalt not steal.
>
> 9 Thou shalt not bear false witness against thy neighbor.
>
> 10 Thou shalt not covet thy neighbor's house, thou shalt not covet thy neighbor's wife, nor his manservant, nor his maidservant, nor his ox, nor his ass, nor anything that is thy neighbor's.

Hebrew law evolved through discourse between the learned elders. Unlike Hammurabi's code, the Hebrew law code is not accredited to one particular individual since, according to the biblical concept, law is no more than a statement of God's will. Therefore, crime became equated with sin since every criminal offense can be considered a crime against God.

Although the Mosaic Code is rich in detail concerning the customs and moral obligations of the Jewish people – describing religious conventions such as feasting and fasting and health and sanitation – for the criminal justice scholar, the Bible offers extraordinary insight into the punishment of criminal behavior in the ancient world. The book of Exodus proclaims, "Eye for eye, tooth for tooth, hand for hand, foot for foot." While this is sometimes misconstrued to be taken literally, a more appropriate interpretation suggests that there is a set limit for punishment – that a perpetrator can be punished up to losing an eye, a tooth, a hand, or a foot for a particular offense. This concept is one of the oldest legal concepts and can be found in various incarnations in criminal codes throughout the world. There is a remarkable similarity between the Mosaic Code and that of Hammurabi in the literal interpretation of punishment. Similar to the Mosaic Code, Babylonian law asserted that a "son was forfeited for son, daughter for daughter, eye for eye, limb for limb, tooth for tooth, life for life and slave for slave."

According to the Old Testament, legal procedures seemed relatively simple. Plaintiff and defendant appeared before a judge, elder, or other authority figures sitting in the open near the main "gate of the city," and a complaint was made. The courts relied on witnesses to swing decisions either way. Unlike most legal traditions, including most present ones, two witnesses were required to prove any capital crime; therefore, a defendant could not be put to death because of the testimony of only one witness.

Mosaic crime and punishment

The Bible offers a fascinating array of criminal behavior, including the world's "first recorded murder" when Cain slew his brother Abel. God sentenced Cain not to death but to life as a "fugitive and vagabond on earth." The story of Cain and Abel would be used by generations of modern legal experts to defend alleged murderers against the death penalty during court trials. Under ancient Israeli law, murder was differentiated from **manslaughter**, a distinction that exists in the criminal law of the present day.

Murder conducted with malice aforethought, like contemporary first degree murder, was met with capital punishment. Unlike murder, which mandated death, those guilty of manslaughter were permitted to take **sanctuary** in cities of refuge. Prohibitions against taking a life were typically lifted in incidents involving self-defense, warfare, and capital punishment. Decapitation was regarded as the quickest and cleanest form of execution and was applied in cases of murder aforethought and apostasy. Banishment was meted out only in crimes of unintentional homicide or manslaughter. In these cases, the defendant was expelled from his hometown to six specific cities of refuge.

Offenses punished by death in the Old Testament

Murder: *Genesis 9:6*

Masturbation and coitus interruptus: *Genesis 38:7–10*

Working on the Sabbath: *Exodus 31:15*

Children disrespecting or cursing parents: *Leviticus 20:9*

Adultery: *Leviticus 20:10*

Incest: *Leviticus 20:11*

Sexual relations with a daughter-in-law: *Leviticus 20:14*

Homosexuality: *Leviticus 20:13*

Sexual relations with a mother-in-law: *Leviticus: 20:14*

Bestiality: *Leviticus 20:15–16*

Practicing witchcraft: *Exodus 22:18; Leviticus 20:27*

Gluttonous or drunken children: *Deuteronomy 21:18–23*

In sharp contrast to Hammurabi's code, under Mosaic Law, property offenses did not constitute a capital crime; rather, such crimes were adjudicated through the payment of fines. Since human life was considered sacred and precious because humans were made in God's image, the Mosaic Code was far more humane than previous law codes. While parts of the ancient Near East prescribed fierce physical punishments, such as facial mutilation, castration, and impalement, Mosaic Law treated the body with respect, and physical cruelty was reduced to a minimum, with even flogging being limited to forty lashes.

The Bible enumerates thirty-six capital crimes,[10] with **stoning** the most frequent method of execution. Men and women received the same punishment, as did the rich and the poor. Stoning was imposed for crimes that threatened the whole nation, including sexual crimes.

Stoning, or lapidation, is still used as a method of execution in some corners of the world where religious law predominates. Stoning requires a prisoner to be buried up to the waist if male or the shoulders if female. They are then pelted with stones by small crowd of volunteers until dead. Religious courts usually expect the stones to be small enough so that death will not occur from only several blows, but must be big enough to inflict physical harm. This extremely painful form of execution can last between ten and twenty minutes. In the twenty-first century, women have been sentenced to death by stoning for adultery by Islamic courts in a handful of majority Muslim countries, including Somalia, Iran, and Nigeria. Women are most likely to face this punishment and are more likely than men to face unfair trials. They are more vulnerable, in part, because they are most likely to be illiterate and thus be more likely to sign confessions for crimes they were innocent of committing. As recently as July 2007, a man and woman were stoned to death for adultery, despite an existing moratorium against it. In 2008, the Iranian judiciary said it planned to stop using stoning as a form of punishment but would keep it on the books as a legal form of punishment.

Adultery is considered the second most serious crime under Islamic law (the first being insulting Allah) and is considered a more serious offense than murder because "society is injured," and this act "will teach other people to do the same thing."[11] According to tradition, a stoning is carried out by digging a pit and burying the woman (or man) up to her neck before being stoned to death. A 2009 Pew survey found that 83 percent of Pakistanis believed adulterers should be stoned to death. In October 2008, a young Somalian girl was buried up to her neck and stoned to death for adultery in a stadium in front of 1,000 witnesses. Amnesty International later claimed the girl was only thirteen years old and had been raped by three men.

mosaic law has no death penalty

The Mosaic Code was stricter in sexual matters, as were most other divinely inspired codes. Prior to Mosaic Law, **bestiality**, adultery, and incest were not considered criminal offenses; however, under Mosaic Law, all forms of irregular sex were prohibited. In cases of incest and adultery, a malefactor would be strangled, and, while in his death throes, a burning torch would be thrust into his mouth to "burn his intestines." This was seen as a more humane and dignified death since it preserved the appearance of the body for burial.

Mosaic Law has been credited with introducing the foundations for the modern rule of liability. According to the **law of the goring ox**, if an owner was aware that he possessed a dangerous animal before it caused damage or injury, the owner was culpable and must pay compensatory damages. If the ox killed a man, the ox and its owner could be stoned to death. Obviously, this departs somewhat from contemporary liability law, which would not demand the death penalty for negligence.

While other cultures from the ancient Near East gave the world the wheel, cuneiform writing, and irrigation, the Jews gave the world **monotheistic religion** – the belief in one God – and in the process gave to the world a more compassionate vision of the world. Although the Mosaic Code is considered less advanced than that of Hammurabi, it was much more humanitarian in spirit. Unlike Hammurabi's code, which was inspired by a king, the Mosaic Code was inspired by a belief in God and is more people oriented.

The ancient Jewish law code later influenced the development of several future legal codes. For example, the Puritan communities of seventeenth-century New England based their law codes almost entirely on biblical law. Over the centuries, the precepts of the Old Testament have also influenced the development of law codes in continental Europe and in England. The impact of the Ten Commandments continues to resonate into the twenty-first century, bringing into question whether its display promotes one religion above others. According to Chief Justice William Rehnquist, it is not a matter of religion but "simply reflects the Ten Commandments' role in the development of our legal system." However, one opponent contends that "public buildings should display patriotic symbols that bring us together, not religious symbols that divide us."[12]

The Ten Commandments in the twenty-first century

In February 2002, the Supreme Court, for the second time that year, refused to review a lower court's ban on displaying the Ten Commandments on government property. In this particular case, the justices declined to hear an appeal by Indiana's governor, who had been prevented from placing a seven-foot stone monument of the Ten Commandments on the statehouse lawn in Indianapolis (it would have replaced one that had been previously vandalized). It was hoped that the court would resolve this murky issue since there is little consensus on this issue. While judges in Indiana, Illinois, and Wisconsin have prohibited the display of the Ten Commandments on public property, judges in Oklahoma, New Mexico, Colorado, Kansas, Wyoming, and Utah have allowed it.

Mosaic Law continued to make headlines during the first decade of the twenty-first century. Just three years after the aforementioned case, in 2005, the U.S. Supreme Court handed down two different 5–4 decisions related to the displaying of the Ten Commandments. In the Kentucky ruling, the majority ruled that public displays of two framed documents of the Ten Commandments in two courthouses violated the establishment clause of the **First Amendment** that is the foundation of the principle of separation of church and state. In the Texas case, the Court ruled in favor of allowing a six-foot high granite copy of the Ten Commandments that had been donated in 1961 to remain in place among several dozen other monuments spread across the front of the state capitol in Texas.

Ancient Greece (people made law)

Greek civilization did not invent or originate the notion of law, but the Greek law that would emerge in the seventh century B.C. differed from the earlier Mosaic and Near Eastern law codes in several respects. It was not intended to carry out the will of an omnipotent king, such as Hammurabi, or the will of God, as in the Mosaic Code. Rather, the goal was to improve the lives of ordinary human beings. Earlier law codes could be modified at the will of a king or priest, but Greek law, particularly in Athens, was based on some kind of referendum of popular consent and could be changed only with the approval of the people.

Out of the dozens of Greek city-states that made up the ancient Greek civilization, most historical ruminations focus on the city-states of Athens and Sparta. But Athens looms large and has, for the most part, become synonymous for Greece in the ancient world. While the city of Athens was dedicated to politics, entrepreneurship, and the arts, Sparta could best be compared to a military enclave, with the concomitant suppression of nonconformity and individual rights. Life in Sparta was tightly regulated, and criminal procedure tended to be

goal of law for Greece: improve the life of ordinary citizens inquisitorial in nature. With a subjugated populace, ruled by customary law and institutions, the Spartans contributed little to the evolution of the criminal justice system. Unlike the martial law of the Spartans, Athenians reveled in their political freedom in the absence of dictatorship. Unlike the divinely influenced Mosaic Law or the royally dictated Babylonian code, Greek law developed into the consensus of the people.

(people made law)

The lawgivers

a death penalty could have been written down as any punishment.

Prior to the introduction of writing, **Athenian law** and the administration of justice remained in the hands of an oligarchy, and each generation orally handed down the unwritten law codes. Over time, the underclasses demanded that the laws be recorded so that they would be known by all rather than being confined as the province of the well-born elite members of society.

The first written law code of Greek civilization is credited to the statesman Draco, who is considered the first legislator of Athens. Commissioned to write a new law code in 621 B.C. to control the masses and to eliminate blood feuds fueled by revenge, Draco attempted to suppress crime by imposing capital punishment for virtually every offense. Hence, Draco's name has become linked in perpetuity to ruthlessness, or **draconian** punishment. Citizens could be sentenced to death for stealing certain vegetables and fruit and for sacrilege, idleness, and homicide. Draco also supported the enslaving of debtors and even their families when they could not pay creditors. Draco's accomplishments are mixed from a modern vantage point. While citizens became better informed about legal procedures and protocol and forms of compensation were introduced to end the age-old cycle of private revenge, capital punishment was used to punish a wider range of crimes. In actuality, the Draconian code was no worse than customary law, but it was criticized by Athenians who were disappointed that there was no radical change in the legal system. Before passing judgment on this ancient Athenian legislator, one should remember that he did not invent these laws but simply collected and recorded the customary laws that had been unwritten until this time. But once they were recorded, Athenians could no longer ignore the need to reform such a harsh law code that then existed.

Draco wrote down all the laws and punishments.

With the introduction of **Draco's code**, Greece made the transition from the preliterate era of customary law to written code. Greek legal developments made important strides during this era. The laws recorded by Draco (and later Solon) were published on pillars of wood for religious matters and on bronze for other types of laws.

Although no fragments of Draco's code have survived, information pertaining to the laws has been passed down to us from the early Greek historians. Criminal and civil law were apparently not distinct. However, Draco's code is notable for its views on homicide. Draco's most important innovation was the establishment of the **Court of Areopagus** for murder cases, arson, and other serious crimes. Many scholars consider this the first time a distinction was made between civil and criminal law.

Since time immemorial, most killings were followed by revenge killings. To avoid revenge killings and blood feuds under Draconian law, a murderer had three choices following the commission of a murder. He could acknowledge his complicity by immediately going into exile. The perpetrator could also submit to trial and was allowed to walk free until then, as

③

long as he obeyed rules that excluded him from most sacred and public places. However, if he decided to ignore the trial process, he could be killed or immediately arrested on entering a public or sacred place by any Athenian, which was an early form of citizen's arrest.

Draco introduced radically different rules in dealing with homicide. There were voluntary, "impassioned" killings committed in the heat of the moment and involuntary or accidental ones. Justifiable homicides included accidental killings during athletic contests, the slaying of adulterers caught in **flagrante delicto**, and killings committed in war. Offenders were liable for the death penalty only in cases of voluntary or premeditated homicide. All others were punished by exile. These distinctions are significant because they mandated that only the state now had the authority to kill, eliminating the traditional blood vengeance. The state also allowed the victim's family to trade the perpetrator's punishment sentence for a fine or material compensation.[13]

Following in the footsteps of Draco, Solon built on his predecessor's achievements. Like Draco, little is known about Solon. Born into a prosperous Athenian family in 638 B.C., Solon developed a reputation for honesty and equitable judgment. After several decades of Draco's code, demands increased for a new law code. Solon was appointed to a one-year term as chief magistrate in 594 B.C. and was granted the power to rewrite the law for Athenian society.

Although it is unsubstantiated, many historians accord Solon the distinction of having created the first permanent protocol for punishing crimes against the state. A zealous proponent of the rule of law, Solon saw lawlessness as the scourge of state building and insisted that only by punishing crimes such as theft or embezzlement of public funds, **sedition**, civil disorder, enslavement of the disenfranchised, and political conspiracies could the rule of law progress. As a legal reformer, Solon is credited with taking steps to protect the marginalized population from the upper classes. Among his most noteworthy reforms was the prohibition of selling debtors and their families into slavery for failure to pay creditors. In addition, he proclaimed that all Athenians who had been sold into slavery or had fled Athens to avoid this fate could return to their former status as Athenian citizens.

Perhaps his greatest accomplishment, Solon's abolition of Draco's penal code set the stage for a much more humane criminal law as he endeavored to make the punishment fit the crime. Contrasted with Draco's code, Solon's law allowed for capital punishment only for treason and murder. However, his law protected a husband who killed his wife and her lover when caught in the act of adultery. In addition, he opened up jury service to average citizens. Solon's law reforms would last for the next 500 years. Although we have only a partial list of his laws, his reforms were much discussed by chroniclers of the ancient world. Solon's democratic conception of justice influenced not only Athens but the development of Western society as well.

The importance of Solonic law rested on the presumption that law was the will of the people or the state and therefore could be amended. Additionally, Solon stipulated that anyone could prosecute an injustice. These principles became the foundation for the future greatness of Athens. By establishing popular assemblies and a comprehensive code of laws, Solon created the environment that would allow democracy to later flourish. Claiming no divine origin, Solon's law stood as a testament to the power of human reason. But there was still much to be accomplished. Without distinction between felonies and misdemeanors and little classification of crime according to severity of penalties involved, this system of criminal justice must still be regarded as fairly primitive.

Greek crime and punishment

An examination of ancient Greek law offers some of the earliest insight into women and criminal justice. For example, women of child bearing age who married citizens were expected to observe certain rules of conduct to avoid any appearance of impropriety. But this was more to ensure the integrity of the family bloodline rather than fears about chastity. Since she was expected to produce a male heir, the husband must be sure that the infant presented to him by his wife was actually sired by him.[14]

According to the Laws of Solon, fathers, guardians, and husbands had the right to punish what he perceived as misbehavior. When adultery occurred, the male was assumed to be the aggressor, and both parties would be punished. The fear here was that an adulterous affair could produce a male heir. This could be a big concern if the father turned out to be a noncitizen. Not only would the child be introduced into the betrayed husband's home, but he would be added to the rolls of Athenian citizens.[15]

Rape and adultery law compelled husbands to seek a divorce from wife. The wife was not permitted to proclaim her innocence. Being punished for sexual conduct often included being prohibited from attending public ceremonies, wearing jewelry and, in the worst case scenario, never being allowed to marry again.[16]

The Greeks were at their most pragmatic when it came to capital punishment. While they recognized that human nature was not deterred by fear of death, at the same time, philosophers such as Plato viewed capital punishment as a form of civic purging – removing the most dangerous criminals from society in order to protect the state. Many Athenians would attest to the fact that banishment for life, not unlike life in prison, was a fate worse than death.

Death sentences were carried out in a variety of ways. At its earliest stages, stoning, or lapidation, was used as a form of community punishment, much in the manner of the ancient Israelites. This custom developed over the centuries into a more formal mode of punishment. The main principle behind stoning was that rather than a few individuals, the whole community should take part in order to remove guilt from an individual participant. Athenians did not consider stoning a legal means of execution during its historical era, but it was used in other regions of Greece. Typically, only crimes that affected the general welfare of the community were treated in this manner. These crimes included the murder of a king, sacrilege, and treason. Stoning was usually conducted outside the city so as to not injure passersby.

The ancient Greeks also developed the practice of **precipitation**, or throwing individuals from a high cliff to their deaths. This method seems to have religious origins, being that spiritual services were often conducted at high places where individuals were closer to the gods. According to some sources, this penalty is a form of the ordeal since there is a chance a person could survive the fall. In addition, the executioner is not directly shedding tribal blood in the tradition of a headsman or hangman. As law became more formalized in Greece, an excavation site known as the **Barathron** became the place of execution. This practice apparently ended by the fifth century b.c. since it is not mentioned after this date.

In addition to stoning and the Barathron, strangulation and **hemlock** were also used to punish capital crimes. The introduction of hemlock marked the transition to the most humane phase of capital punishment in Athens. In the ancient world, "hemlock" was known as "*cicuta*." The Anglo-Saxons introduced the word "hemlock" into the vocabulary of Old English in the tenth century.

Although hemlock was most famous for its use as a poison, it was also used externally as an aphrodisiac. Hemlock is a juice made from the pounding of the plant's seeds and leaves in a mortar. The poison worked only when a patient or perpetrator had a normal body temperature. Before **Socrates** took his fatal dose in 399 B.C., he was told to avoid becoming too agitated as he was prone to do because it would negate the effects of the poison. In the end, Socrates requested multiple doses of the potion. Death usually was accompanied by spasms and convulsions, but like lethal injection today, it was considered a civilized alternative to shedding blood.

Most death sentences in ancient Athens were carried out with haste. Some Greek philosophers complained that typically only one day transpired between sentence and execution. There were only two circumstances that could postpone an execution. Pregnant women could be granted a reprieve until a baby were delivered, and no one could be put to death until the return of the ship that the Athenians sent annually on a religious mission to Delos. And unlike Sparta, which conducted its executions at night, most were typically carried out during the day in Athens.

Patriotism was considered of supreme importance, and any crime directed against the state called for the maximum penalty. Traitors were executed, and their property was confiscated by the state. Treason came in a variety of incarnations: betrayal of a fortress, selling supplies, or passing information to the enemy all demanded the death penalty.

Next to treason, impiety was considered the next-greatest crime. Destruction of statues of the gods, robbing temples, or practicing magic were treated with utmost severity. The Athenian conception of filial duty brooked no mistreatment of parents, and the death penalty could be inflicted on children who assaulted their parents.

The ancient Greeks were notably less stern in their punishment of what we would regard as moral infractions. Adulterers caught in the act by an aggrieved husband could be killed with impunity. This tradition can be traced as far back as Draco's code, which proclaimed that "if one man kills another after catching him with his wife . . . he shall not go into exile for homicide on such account."[17] However, the plaintiff also had the liberty to choose between personal vengeance and monetary compensation.

Athens recognized a variety of punishments, ranging from fines and the confiscation of property to public shaming and the destruction of the homes of condemned offenders. There is some evidence that suggests that Athenians utilized imprisonment to punish debtors and to hold those waiting for torture or execution, as in the case of Socrates (see "Notable Trials" later in this chapter).

In his play, *Prometheus Bound*, Aeschylus described the epic confinement of Prometheus. The title of the Greek play, *Prometheus desmotes*, translated to "Prometheus chained." In Athens there was a prison called the **desmoterion**, or "place of chains." Prisoners in this primitive facility were given some freedom of movement, but they were probably more often chained, fettered, or held in stocks or other devices to limit movement.[18]

Solon introduced the first jury courts to Athens. Not everyone could plead their case before a jury court. Only free male citizens of full Athenian parentage on both sides of the family were allowed to address the courts. Foreigners were tried before special courts, slaves could not testify at all, and women were represented by a male relative. Judicial procedure for most crimes except for homicide relied on juries ranging in size from 201 to 2,501 jurors, depending on the importance of the case. Jurors were required to be over thirty years old. This system did not use lawyers, allowing the plaintiff and the defendant to handle their own cases and to cross-examine each other but not witnesses. Following the speeches of the contestants, jurors cast their votes in the courtroom. Each juror was given two discs: perforated for conviction and solid for acquittal. Jurors reportedly would hold the discs so as to obscure them from fellow jurors. The discs were then collected and tallied by a presiding officer.

There is fragmentary evidence that indicates that Athens had a form of institutional police known as the Scythian archers. "Scythian" meaning "northern barbarian," these trouser-wearing policemen were essentially captured warriors who were kept at the status of slave until earning freedom. Billeted in tents, the Scythians served as town guards and ushers in the Assembly and carried out routine police duties on the main roads leading into Athens. Although there are sporadic mentions of this unit in Greek historical records, little is known about their powers and protocol.

Roman law

While the Romans were ardent students of the Greeks in many endeavors, when it came to law, they were the masters. No ancient culture could match the achievements of the Romans when it came to the development of law. Today's civil law tradition is based on Roman law and is considered the oldest legal tradition in the world. Countries as diverse as Spain, France, Germany, Brazil, Argentina, and the former Yugoslavia trace their legal codes to ancient Roman law code.

The history of Rome, from its founding in 753 B.C. until the sixth century B.C., is obscured by myth and fable. Early Roman law was based on unwritten customs and the will of the gods. Romans, like the Greeks before them, were superstitious, and their gods and goddesses were based on Greek deities. The Romans borrowed liberally from Greek culture in virtually every feature of their art, culture, and national life, and like the Athenians, the aristocracy abused its power over the lower classes in Rome. Aggravating class tensions between the **patricians** and **plebeians** was the absence of a written law code. Civil unrest and dissension led the Romans to follow in the steps of Solon when they realized that adopting a written law would be the only safeguard against oppression. As long as judges were the only individuals familiar with the law and penalties for crime, they could inflict injustices without detection.

Rome was made on rape.

The lawgivers

Rape of the Sabyn women

While Solon was restructuring the laws of Athens (594 B.C.), Roman kings were expanding their mandate in both the commercial and the military realms. During the next century, Romans freed themselves from the clutches of absolute power and began experimenting with a republican form of government, necessitating a new law code. In 509 B.C., the age of the Roman kings had ended. During the subsequent years of the **Republic**, Rome was led by two magistrates, better known as consuls. It was during the period of the Republic (509 B.C.–A.D. 4) that the Roman Empire expanded throughout much of the known world.

The Twelve Tables, written in 451 B.C., are considered the first written laws of Rome. It was only when the underclasses, or plebeians, complained about the high-handed oppression of Roman officials that the law was codified. A commission of patricians was reportedly dispatched to Athens to absorb the laws of Solon and become familiar with the institutions, customs, and laws of the Greek city-state. On their return to Rome, ten men, or **decemvirs**, were appointed to fashion a new body of law. These laws would be certain and definite and accessible to everyone. Subsequently, the Twelve Tables were drafted and inscribed on twelve wood or brass tablets that were then set on display in the Roman Forum, where anyone could become familiar with the law.[19] The Twelve Tables was primitive and inadequate by modern standards, but its impact on the Roman peoples cannot be overestimated. Not only did every young Roman schoolchild reportedly learn the laws by heart, but the laws are recognized for bringing together the plebeian and patrician classes and eliminating social distinctions that formerly cleaved Rome into two hostile camps. The Twelve Tables was credited with eventually breaking down one of the last social barriers, namely, the intermarriage between the two classes.

Unfortunately, we only have fragmentary evidence concerning the actual language of the original laws passed down to us by the classical historians. However, it is clear that they were intended to be not a comprehensive law code but rather a compilation of laws that could be abused by unethical judges if the citizens were not properly informed of the law. These laws dealt mainly with private disputes among individuals. Even such transgressions against the state as abetting an enemy of Rome or accepting bribes were considered matters to be prosecuted privately before an assembly of citizens.

The drafting of the Twelve Tables was a seminal event in the history of criminal justice procedure. During the subsequent centuries, these laws were carried into almost every nation of the ancient world by the victorious Roman legions. Roman reverence for the Twelve Tables can only be compared to the English respect for the Magna Carta. Unlike the Ten Commandments, this primitive law code was not a moral code but rather was composed of legal customs borrowed from other cultures to arbitrate disputes between Rome's various classes.

Roman law was developed through the promulgation of edicts, interpretations of the law by jurists, and the issuance of statutes. The era of the **Roman Republic** (500 B.C.–A.D. 4) witnessed the expansion of the Roman Empire as well as the evolution of a distinct legal profession. However, the greatest strides in the development of Roman legal culture would take place in the eastern Roman Empire under the Christian emperors. **Emperor Constantine's** conversion to Christianity in A.D. 312 was a turning point not only in the history of the Roman Empire but in Western civilization as well. Christians had been persecuted since the reign of Nero, but despite numerous obstacles, the religion continued to gain converts among all segments of society. With the economic decline of the empire in Western Europe, Constantine built a new capital in the eastern part of the empire at Constantinople[20] (formerly Byzantium, now Istanbul, Turkey). While Rome declined in the West and was overrun by barbarian hordes in the fifth century, its greatness persisted for more than another millennium in the East. Roman civilization influenced the language, architecture, and literature of the modern world but was even more influential in its contributions to law.

Initially, church law had little impact on Roman law outside of protecting the faith. But following Constantine's conversion, virtually every emperor would be Christian as well.

In A.D. 325, church leaders from throughout the Roman Empire met for the first time to resolve disputes concerning church protocol and to settle points of church discipline. By settling such disputes as whether clergy could migrate without the permission of a bishop, the Council of Nicaea created peace in the church, at least for the time being.

The development of Roman law reached its zenith under the direction of **Emperor Justinian** (483–565). The product of over 1,000 years of juristic experimentation, the codification of earlier Roman law and its compilation during the reign of Justinian stands as one of the benchmarks of Roman civilization. Not only did he bring simplicity and equity to Roman law, but Justinian saw the need to reduce the amount of laws and to arrange them in some manageable form.

Digest =

Institutes:

Justinian's reign from 518 to 565 marks the transition from the ancient world to a medieval one, ushering in an era that would witness the development of modern Europe. Subsequent developments of social and religious institutions as well as in literature and law were shaped by Roman antecedents. Shortly after becoming emperor, Justinian entrusted the distinguished lawyer Tribonian with supervising the compilation and revision of the Roman law codes. These included not only all the edicts of previous emperors but also previous Senate statutes. Justinian added so many statutes himself in the intervening years that the final product issued in 534 became known as the Code of Justinian. Under the supervision of Tribonian, Roman law was simplified, particularly in situations concerning property and inheritance. This was necessary in order to eliminate the impact of ancient customs and the power of the extended family in property matters.

Tribonian also was charged with condensing and revising more than 3 million lines of judicial decisions into a more usable form. After eliminating obsolete and contradictory laws, in 533 the *Digest* was completed, having distilled all previous judicial decisions into a mere 150,000 lines (about one and a half times the size of the Bible). Justinian's final contributions to the updating of Roman law was twofold. Besides bringing the law closer to the teachings of the Christian church, in 533 the ***Institutes*** were published. With its publication, all other law books, including the Twelve Tables, were now officially obsolete. As a law textbook, the *Institutes* were designed to help law students digest the changes in the legal code. Combined, the *Code*, *Digest*, and *Institutes* have become known as the ***Corpus Juris Civilis***,[22] a singular achievement. Rather than a set of completely new laws, this revision of existing law would endure, and as Europeans moved out of the Dark Ages, they would turn to this work for guidance in creating a new legal system.

Roman crime and punishment

At its zenith, ancient Rome was considered a lawless city of between 750,000 and 1 million people. Without a police force, public prosecutors, or sheriffs, crime went unchecked during the last century of the Roman Republic (137–134 B.C.). One Roman satirist warned that "only a fool would go out to dinner without having made his will."[23] Robberies and house break-ins were common, and gangs of street toughs roamed the streets, giving the city the character of a town from America's Wild West era. Besides street crime, political assassinations were a common mode of replacing prominent leaders, including such legendary figures as Julius Caesar and the Gracci brothers.

The ascendance of **Augustus Caesar** to emperor in 27 B.C. signaled the beginning of organized law enforcement in the ancient world. In prior years, the Roman army functioned as police in the far-flung provinces. When crime was reported to a governor, soldiers from local legions were sent out to suppress the activity. Provincial policing efforts were inadequate because of insufficient manpower. With other non-policing duties, such as building roads and forts, protecting the outlying provinces was a challenging proposition for Rome's peacekeepers. In the Roman capital, there was little in the way of a police presence other than a small number of government-owned slaves who served in a constabulary capacity. When Augustus took the throne in 27 B.C., he made the improvement of security his first order of business. He is credited with organizing a police system comprised of several independent agencies. The most respected agency was the **Praetorian Guard**, composed of elite soldiers, replete with togas and swords. Charged with keeping order and the political peace, the Guard was commanded by two police chiefs, or prefects.

To complement the peacekeepers, Augustus established a civilian **Urban Cohort** to patrol Rome during the daytime hours. Supervised by one prefect, this constabulary group was also recruited from the military. There is still some debate over the role of the **Vigiles**. By some accounts they patrolled at night, but more recent scholarship suggests that "the evidence does not support this hypothesis and it is clear that night patrols were used for fire prevention rather than for maintaining order." Confusion over the Vigiles' duties is reportedly due to their patrolling activities which resembled those of the urban cohort.[24] In a world made of wood, firefighting became an inextricable link to policing and public order. The Augustan system of policing proved so efficient that it was adapted later in the fourth century by the Christian emperor Constantine when he built his capital of Constantinople in the eastern Roman Empire.

It is apparent from archeological excavations and historical accounts that the Romans belonged to a materialistic culture that liked to acquire property and show it off in public. Since togas had no pockets, civilians carried their valuables in a pouch or purse. Others stored precious possessions at home in strongboxes or in pagan temples where the gods could watch over them. Of sturdy construction and protected by outside guards, citizens were confident that, if temples did not dissuade thieves, then the gods would ultimately punish them. Having invented the padlock and other locking devices, the Romans are credited with raising the science of locksmithing to a level surpassed only in modern times.

Although Roman law prohibited the displaying of most weapons, for self-protection Romans wore finger rings that are considered the prototypes for brass knuckles and eye gougers. Many became proficient in self-defense skills, including boxing, wrestling, kicking, and strangling. Others gravitated toward protective associations (precursors of today's neighborhood watch groups) or hired bodyguards. The more superstitious wore amulets of the gods for protection that could range from minerals to parts of the human or animal body. A common charm worn by boys to ward off evil intentions until puberty was the phallic symbol known as the **bulla**. At home, individuals used dogs and geese as watch animals or mounted animal emblems over their doors to repel evil spirits. The progenitors of many self-defense strategies, the Romans came up with the idea of placing mannequins in their gardens to ward off criminals. Modern law enforcement has adopted similar schemes in crime-prone locations when staffing is shorthanded.

During the early Republic, the Twelve Tables prescribed definite penalties for certain crimes. Hanging would be visited on those who pastured animals at night in a neighbor's crop, while malefactors who deliberately set fire to a barn or a store of grain could be burned alive. For crimes that called for capital punishment, the method of execution was rarely left in doubt. The Romans apparently applied the same ingenuity to inflicting pain as they did to creating laws.[25] Although some penalties could be adjudicated through compensation, a host of criminal acts were met with the death penalty. Perjury was punished by precipitation, as perpetrators were tossed from the **Tarpein Cliff**. Arsonists could expect to be burned to death, crop thieves were hanged, and others met their ends being clubbed to death or hanged.

During the first two centuries of the Common Era, a number of executions took place in the Roman Colosseum. Huge crowds came to watch the gory gladiatorial games, where slaves, prisoners, and professional gladiators were pitted against each other in life and death struggles. In some cases, as a change of pace, exotic carnivorous animals were introduced into the bloody proceedings. The Roman games offered the emperors the opportunity to demonstrate their power over life and death and to reinforce his authority over his people. Condemned prisoners were typically herded into the arena at lunchtime. They were then divided into groups of either citizens or noncitizens and slaves. Citizens were usually accorded a quick death, which might include being bludgeoned about the head. Depending on the imagination and whims of the emperor, there might be other macabre executions, as in the case of two citizens being brought up to the arena floor, where only one was armed with a sword. He was then supposed to chase the other until he killed him with the sword. Once this was done, he was to turn over the sword to the next citizen, and the action was repeated until there was only one left. The survivor's victory was short-lived as he was soon executed. By contrast, the lower-level convicts met sadistic punishments following the deaths of their superiors. They were crucified, burned alive, and fed to wild animals.[26]

Considered one of the most heinous crimes by the Romans, **parricides** (children who killed a parent) were punished by being bound into a leather sack with a dog, a cock, a viper, and an ape (or some other variation) and then being tossed into a body of water. The so-called "penalty of the sack," or *culleus* dates back to at least 100 B.C. As primitive as this sounds, this special punishment lived on into the Middle Ages. Later in the first century B.C., new laws replaced the *culleus* with either burning criminals alive or being torn apart by wild animals. Regardless of the method, executions were a public occasion, but only when the convicted was male. Since victims were stripped for the occasion, women were executed in private to preserve their modesty. Since executioners were forbidden from strangling virgins, they were expected to deflower them first.[27]

By the end of the Roman Republic, capital punishment for most crimes was out of vogue. In most instances, convicts could instead accept an informal agreement to go into exile, particularly if they belonged to the elite class, but only with the caveat that, if they returned to Rome, they would be executed. In ancient Rome (64 B.C.) a series of dungeons, known as Mamertine Prison, housed offenders in large caged rooms under Rome's main sewer. One of its lower chambers dates back almost 150 years earlier. There is a lack of consensus whether Romans regularly recognized imprisonment as a penal sanction. Except for cases of debt, imprisonment was rarely used in early Rome. According to the Twelve Tables, debtors who could not or refused to pay their debts were held in private confinement by creditors for sixty days. Subsequently, the debtor's balance was announced in public on three consecutive market days. On the third and final day, the debtor might be sold into slavery or executed. One other form of imprisonment is chronicled in which Roman male heads of household were allowed to maintain their own domestic prison in which they could discipline members of the household. Called the **Ergastulum** (or "garbage pit"), the cell held immediate family members or slaves for any breach of family discipline. The works of later Roman historians describe other modes of imprisonment that ranged from chaining and quarry prisons to underground chambers similar to the prototypical dungeons of the Middle Ages.[28]

After Constantine's conversion, there was a trend toward increasingly severe punishments as the government became more autocratic. Under the Christian emperors, infractions that were formally regarded as private wrongs became public offenses and were often treated with inhuman rigor. In the time of Augustus, adulterers would be deported to separate islands. By the reign of Constantine and his successors, sexual immorality was severely punished, and the death penalty prescribed for adultery, incest, and homosexuality.

Notable trials

Socrates (399 B.C.)

The trial of the vagabond teacher and philosopher Socrates in Athens in 399 B.C. remains one of the most famous free speech trials of all time. Charged with corrupting the youth of Athens and refusing to recognize the accepted divinities of the city by a distinguished body of Athenian democrats, Socrates went on trial for his life before the Court of the Heliasts, the court that had jurisdiction over all public cases that did not involve homicide.

Socrates rose to prominence as a brave warrior during Athens' war with Sparta (431–404 B.C.) and then as an intellectual renowned for his insatiable curiosity. The charges brought against Socrates can be understood only in the context of ancient Athens. The charge of "corrupting" youth referred to Socrates' inclination of teaching young people to question the wisdom of their parents and the leaders of Athens, a charge tantamount to treason. Several of his former students were affiliated with the tyrannical oligarchy that ruled Athens for a short period before Athens returned to democratic rule in 403 B.C. To his opponents, it appeared that Socrates had been educating traitors. A well-known philosopher whose main mission in life seemed to question the wisdom of the popularly elected leaders of Athens, Socrates' political affiliations and his **Sophist** (identification as a professional philosopher) leanings earned him enemies who sought to remove him from society.

The administration of justice in the courts of Socrates' era bore little resemblance to contemporary courts. Missing from the ancient courtroom were the familiar actors of the modern courtroom. In place of judges, prosecutors, and defense attorneys was a **jury** composed of anywhere from 101 to more than 1,001. But there was always an odd number to eliminate a tie vote.

Any full Athenian citizen who was sane, over the age of thirty, and not impaired by any disabilities was qualified to become a member of the court. At the beginning of each judicial year, citizens volunteered for jury participation, and about 6,000 were selected for that year. Each juror was paid today's equivalent of nine cents per day. This leads to speculation that only members of the lower classes could be expected to participate for such low pay.

Athenian courts heard cases on about 300 days each year. In order to guard against bribery, each day juries were selected by lot and assigned to various courts. Traditionally, the more important the case, the larger the jury. Not all defendants were given the benefit of a jury trial. However, any Athenian citizen with full rights could make charges against an individual and have the case tried in the Court of the Heliasts.

While there are no independent contemporary accounts of the trial, we know many of the specifics through the writings of his disciples such as Plato. According to Plato and others, the jury hearing the case of Socrates had 501 jurors. Over the centuries, scholars have pieced together an account of the trial of Socrates. In an open-air court, a low barrier partitioned the public from the defendant and the jury. The prosecution presented its case first, followed by the defense. Each side spoke and was allowed to present its case for an hour, using a water clock as a timing device. Unlike the modern courtroom, there was no formal cross-examination.

The seventy-year-old philosopher conducted his own defense. Having never been to court before, Socrates was at a disadvantage. He had to face not only three prosecutors but also a clandestine group of accusers who had vilified his reputation in Athens for almost two decades. By the time the trial began, public opinion had already turned against Socrates. He became his own worst enemy as he delivered a long speech, punctuated with wit and defiance, but ultimately all it did was antagonize his prosecutors.

Unlike contemporary juries, Athenian juries voted twice. The first vote was whether to acquit or convict. Socrates barely lost this vote, 280 to 220. The second vote was to decide a penalty if the penalty was not prescribed by law. Under Athenian law, the jury was allowed to decide a penalty of its own and could choose between penalties proposed by the prosecution and the defense. Socrates could have avoided the death penalty if he had proposed banishment. The jury most probably would have accepted. Despite the urgings of his friends to take this way out, Socrates insisted that, if he took exile, he would betray his beliefs and would be admitting that the prosecution had spoken the truth. He was willing to die for his convictions and thus ended up facing a death sentence and took a fatal dose of hemlock.

Socrates left no writings of his own, and had he been acquitted, he might have vanished into obscurity as a harmless Athenian eccentric. Having reached the ripe old age of seventy, Socrates went to his death in Athens, a city famous for free speech, prosecuted for a philosopher's ideas and his use of free speech.

Conclusions

An examination of early law codes suggests that in complex societies, everyone is immersed in a vast network of legal rules. In less developed societies, individuals go about their daily lives unconscious of most of these legal rules. A variety of legal documents have survived to offer students insight into the legal institutions of ancient Mesopotamia, Israel, and Greece. However, evidence abounds related to Roman law. Unlike earlier societies, we have not only legislation but also juristic commentaries of the law, lay literature referring to the law, and documents of daily legal relationships.

Suffering from political, economic, and military exhaustion, by the end of the fifth century, the western Roman Empire had capitulated to the invasion of Germanic tribes. Still flourishing in the eastern half of the empire, the Byzantine Empire would not succumb until 1453. During the subsequent Middle Ages, Roman law would be resurrected and exert a lasting influence on the development of legal institutions throughout continental Europe. Events in England, including the early organization of a national common law, later gave rise to a different legal tradition.

Point – counterpoint

Ancient law codes: god-inspired v. king-inspired law

Hammurabi's Code stands out in sharp contrast to Mosaic Code, in that it was written by a king as opposed to being inspired by God. Hammurabi was the king of Babylonia in the late eighteenth and early seventeenth century B.C. The prologue to the code indicates that the king drafted the code by the command of the gods. It was the king's duty to proclaim and enforce the law and to make sure law enforcement was distributed equally. He was also imbued with the power to make amendments in order to make the code current with the needs of the day. Some of its provisions, including the disappearance of blood feuds and revenge, indicate a semi-advanced condition. On the other hand, it still preserved vestiges of a more primitive past, such as retaliatory punishments (an eye for an eye), reliance on the ordeal (#2), and liability for accidental harm. The following are several excerpts taken from the 282 sections. Although Mosaic Law is often remembered for its elucidation of the fundamental rules of social conduct contained in the Ten Commandments, it also contained strict punishments for ordinary as well as serious offenses. The following excerpts are from the Book of Exodus.

Source: *The Code of Hammurabi*, trans. by L. W. King Jr., New York, 1915); Exodus xxii

Code of laws

2. If any one bring an accusation against a man, and the accused go to the river and leap into the river, if he sink in the river his accuser shall take possession of his house. But if the river prove that the accused is not guilty, and he escape unhurt, then he who had brought the accusation shall be put to death, while he who leaped into the river shall take possession of the house that had belonged to his accuser.

3. If any one bring an accusation of any crime before the elders, and does not prove what he has charged, he shall, if it be a capital offense charged, be put to death.

5. If a judge try a case, reach a decision, and present his judgment in writing; if later error shall appear in his decision, and it be through his own fault, then he shall pay twelve times the fine set by him in the case, and he shall be publicly removed from the judge's bench, and never again shall he sit there to render judgment.

6. If any one steal the property of a temple or of the court, he shall be put to death, and also the one who receives the stolen thing from him shall be put to death. . . .

9. If any one lose an article, and find it in the possession of another: if the person in whose possession the thing is found say "A merchant sold it to me, I paid for it before

witnesses," and if the owner of the thing say, "I will bring witnesses who know my property," then shall the purchaser bring the merchant who sold it to him, and the witnesses before whom he bought it, and the owner shall bring witnesses who can identify his property. The judge shall examine their testimony – both of the witnesses before whom the price was paid, and of the witnesses who identify the lost article on oath. The merchant is then proved to be a thief and shall be put to death. The owner of the lost article receives his property, and he who bought it receives the money he paid from the estate of the merchant.

10. If the purchaser does not bring the merchant and the witnesses before whom he bought the article, but its owner bring witnesses who identify it, then the buyer is the thief and shall be put to death, and the owner receives the lost article.

11. If the owner do not bring witnesses to identify the lost article, he is an evil-doer, he has traduced, and shall be put to death.

12. If the witnesses be not at hand, then shall the judge set a limit, at the expiration of six months. If his witnesses have not appeared within the six months, he is an evil-doer, and shall bear the fine of the pending case.

[Editor's note: there is no 13th law in the code, 13 being considered and unlucky and evil number]

14. If any one steal the minor son of another, he shall be put to death.

15. If any one take a male or female slave of the court, or a male or female slave of a freed man, outside the city gates, he shall be put to death.

16. If any one receive into his house a runaway male or female slave of the court, or of a freed man, and does not bring it out at the public proclamation of the major domus, the master of the house shall be put to death.

21. If any one break a hole into a house (break in to steal), he shall be put to death before that hole and be buried.

22. If any one is committing a robbery and is caught, then he shall be put to death.

23. If the robber is not caught, then shall he who was robbed claim under oath the amount of his loss; then shall the community, and . . . on whose ground and territory and in whose domain it was compensate him for the goods stolen . . . .

108. If a tavern-keeper (feminine) does not accept corn according to gross weight in payment of drink, but takes money, and the price of the drink is less than that of the corn, she shall be convicted and thrown into the water.

109. If conspirators meet in the house of a tavern-keeper, and these conspirators are not captured and delivered to the court, the tavern-keeper shall be put to death.

110. If a "sister of a god" open a tavern, or enter a tavern to drink, then shall this woman be burned to death . . . .

195. If a son strike his father, his hands shall be hewn off.

196. If a man put out the eye of another man, his eye shall be put out. [An eye for an eye]

197. If he break another man's bone, his bone shall be broken.

198. If he put out the eye of a freed man, or break the bone of a freed man, he shall pay one gold mina.

199. If he put out the eye of a man's slave, or break the bone of a man's slave, he shall pay one-half of its value.

200. If a man knock out the teeth of his equal, his teeth shall be knocked out. [A tooth for a tooth]

201. If he knock out the teeth of a freed man, he shall pay one-third of a gold mina.

202. If any one strike the body of a man higher in rank than he, he shall receive sixty blows with an ox-whip in public.

203. If a freeborn man strike the body of another freeborn man or equal rank, he shall pay one gold mina.

204. If a freed man strike the body of another freed man, he shall pay ten shekels in money.

205. If the slave of a freed man strike the body of a freed man, his ear shall be cut off.

206. If during a quarrel one man strike another and wound him, then he shall swear, "I did not injure him wittingly," and pay the physicians.

207. If the man die of his wound, he shall swear similarly, and if he (the deceased) was a freeborn man, he shall pay half a mina in money.

208. If he was a freed man, he shall pay one-third of a mina.

209. If a man strike a freeborn woman so that she lose her unborn child, he shall pay ten shekels for her loss.

210. If the woman die, his daughter shall be put to death.

211. If a woman of the free class lose her child by a blow, he shall pay five shekels in money.

212. If this woman die, he shall pay half a mina.

213. If he strike the maidservant of a man, and she lose her child, he shall pay two shekels in money.

214. If this maidservant die, he shall pay one-third of a mina.

215. If a physician make a large incision with an operating knife and cure it, or if he open a tumor (over the eye) with an operating knife, and saves the eye, he shall receive ten shekels in money.

216. If the patient be a freed man, he receives five shekels.

217. If he be the slave of some one, his owner shall give the physician two shekels.

218. If a physician make a large incision with the operating knife, and kill him, or open a tumor with the operating knife, and cut out the eye, his hands shall be cut off.

219. If a physician make a large incision in the slave of a freed man, and kill him, he shall replace the slave with another slave.

220. If he had opened a tumor with the operating knife, and put out his eye, he shall pay half his value.

221. If a physician heal the broken bone or diseased soft part of a man, the patient shall pay the physician five shekels in money.

222. If he were a freed man he shall pay three shekels.

223. If he were a slave his owner shall pay the physician two shekels.

Exodus xxii

12 He that smiteth a man, so that he die, shall be surely put to death.

13 And if a man lie not in wait, but God deliver him into his hand; then I will appoint thee a place wither he shall flee.

14 But if a man come presumptiously upon his neighbor, to slay him with guile; thou shalt take him from mine altar, that he may die.

15 And he that smiteth his father, or his mother, shall be surely put to death.

16 And he that stealeth a man and selleth him, or if he be found in his hand, he shall surely be put to death.

17 And he that curseth his father, or mother, shall surely be put to death.

18 And if men strive together, and one smite another with a stone, or with his fist, and he die not, but keepeth his bed;

19 If he rise again, and walk abroad upon his staff, then shall he that smote him be quit; only he shall pay for the loss of his time, and shall cause him to be thoroughly healed.

20 And if a man smite his servant, or his maid, with a rod, and he die under his hand; he shall be surely punished.

21 Notwithstanding, if he continue (to live) a day or two, he shall not be punished; for he is his money.

22 If men strive, and hurt a woman with child, so that her fruit depart from her, and yet no mischief follow; he shall be surely punished, according as the woman's husband will lay upon him; and he shall pay as the judges determine.

23 And if any mischief follow, then thou shalt give life for life

24 Eye for eye, tooth for tooth, hand for hand, foot for foot

25 Burning for burning, wound for wound, stripe for stripe.

26 And if a man smite the eye of his servant, or the eye of his maid that it perish; he shall let him go free for his eye's sake.

27 And if he smite out his manservant's tooth, or his maidservant's tooth, he shall let him go free for his tooth's sake.

Key terms

Code of Hammurabi	scribes	Babylonia
lex talionis	Mosaic Law	Ten Commandments
Pentateuch	Torah	stoning
taboo	Draco's code	Athenian law
Solon's law	precipitation	hemlock
Barathron	Socrates	Twelve Tables
plebeians	Roman Republic	Constantine
Justinian	Augustus Caesar	Urban Cohort
Praetorian Guard	Vigiles	Tarpein Cliff
Ergastulum	Athenian jury	*culleus*

Critical thinking questions

1 If you were charged with committing a serious crime in the ancient world (e.g., Israel, Babylonia, Athens, or Rome), which system of law would you rather be judged under and why? Cite the negative and positive attributes of this system. Discuss in terms of one of the following types of crime: sexual offenses, homicide, or theft.

2 All ancient cultures used the death penalty in one form or another. Discuss methods of execution in the ancient world (from Hammurabi through the Roman Empire).

3 Discuss the development of law enforcement in the Roman Empire.

4 Compare and contrast court procedures in the ancient world.

5 What differences and similarities can you identify between the modern criminal justice systems and ancient criminal justice-related developments.

6 How do preliterate cultures maintain law and order without the written word? How did the invention of writing influence the development of early legal codes?

Notes

1 E. Adamson Hoebel, *The Law of Primitive Man*, Cambridge, MA: Harvard University Press, 1954.

2 Karl Menninger, *Whatever Became of Sin?*, New York: Hawthorn Boos, 1973, p. 50.

3 Jacques Barzun, *From Dawn to Decadence: 500 Years of Western Cultural Life, 1500 to the Present*, New York: Harper and Row, 2001, p. 762.

4 Robert Sutherland Rattray, *Ashanti Law and Constitution*, New York: Negro Universities Press, 1969, p. 375. To avoid mutilation or bleeding during strangulation, a leather thong or bare hands were used. If the malefactors were high-ranking, they were bludgeoned with the tusk of an elephant or some type of pestle.

5 John Henry Wigmore, *A Panorama of the World's Legal Systems*, 3 vols., St. Paul, MN: West Publishing Company, 1928.

6 Joyce Tydlesley, *Judgment of the Pharaoh: Crime and Punishment in Ancient Egypt*, London: Orion Pub, 2002, pp. 65, 72.

7 Laws of Manu, http://ww3.bergen.edu/phr/121/ManuGC.pdf

8 Hammurabi reigned at least 400 years before Moses. The Bible, however, did not connect the name of Moses with the writing of the Torah until almost ten centuries later. Although tradition has it that Moses authored the first five books of the Bible, how could Moses then have written an account of his own death? By implication, the Torah was written several centuries after the death of Moses in the thirteenth century B.C.

9 While the first four commandments are religious in nature, the remaining six are more secularly significant, including prohibitions against killing, adultery, stealing, and perjury.

10 Of the thirty-six capital offenses, eighteen were moral offenses, twelve were religious, and three were specifically for parents to control their children.

11 Richard Dowden, "Death by Stoning," *New York Times Magazine*, January 27, 2002, p. 31.

12 Patty Reinert, "Commandments Case Rejected," *Houston Chronicle*, February 26, 2002, p. A5.

13 Israel Drapkin, *Crime and Punishment in the Ancient World*, Lexington, MA: Lexington Books, 1989, pp. 181–187.

14 Sarah B. Pomeroy, *Families in Classical and Hellenistic Greece: Representations and Realities*, Oxford: Clarendon Press, 1997.

15 Sarah B. Pomeroy, *Goddesses, Whores, Wives, and Slaves: Women in Classical Antiquity*, New York: Schocken Books, 1995, p. 86.

16 Ibid., p. 86.

17 Daniel Ogden, *Greek Bastardy in the Classical and Hellenistic Periods*, Oxford: Clarendon Press, p. 33.

18 Edward M. Peters, "Prison before the Prison: The Ancient and Medieval Worlds," in *Oxford History of the Prison*, ed. Norval Morris and David Rothman, New York: Oxford University Press, 1995, pp. 3–43.

19 According to most historical accounts, the original tablets were probably destroyed by Germanic invaders during the sack of Rome in 390 B.C.

20 This strategic location on the Bosporus was formerly an ancient colony called Byzantium. Constantine enlarged the site and named it for himself.

21 Harold J. Berman, *Law and Revolution: The Formation of the Western Legal Tradition*, Cambridge, MA: Harvard University Press. According to Berman, the term medieval (or Middle Ages) came into use in the sixteenth century as a way to designate the era between early Christianity and the Protestant Reformation as well as the period between classical antiquity and the Renaissance.

22 During the Middle Ages, experts on Roman law were often referred to as "civilians."
23 Cited in John S. Dempsey, *Introduction to Private Security*, Belmont, CA: Wadsworth, 2010, p. 33.
24 Sarah Bingham, *The Praetorian Guard: A History of Rome's Elite Special Forces*, Waco: Baylor University Press, 2013, p. 107.
25 Mitchel P. Roth, *An Eye for an Eye: A Global History of Crime and Punishment*, London: Reaktion Books, 2014, p. 52.
26 Richard A. Bauman, *Crime and Punishment in Ancient Rome*, London: Routledge, 1996; Lucius Annaeus Seneca, *De Ira*, in *Moral Essays*, Vol. 1, trans. John W. Basore, Cambridge, MA: Harvard University Press, 1928.
27 Bauman, 1996, p. 18; Naphtali Lewis and Meyer Reinhold, eds., *Roman Civilization, Source Book II: Empire*, New York, 1966, pp. 548–549.
28 Peters, 1995, pp. 17–21.

Sources

Archer, Gleason L. 1928. *History of the Law*. Boston: Suffolk Law School Press.
Barzun, Jacques. 2001. *From Dawn to Decadence: 500 Years of Western Cultural Life, 1500 to the Present*. New York: Harper and Row.
Bauman, Richard A. 1996. *Crime and Punishment in Ancient Rome*. London: Routledge.
Berman, Harold J. 1983. *Law and Revolution: The Formation of the Western Legal Tradition*. Cambridge, MA: Harvard University Press.
Bingham, Sarah. 2013. *The Praetorian Guard: A History of Rome's Elite Special Forces*. Waco: Baylor University Press.
Crook, J. A. 1967. *Law and Life of Rome, 90 B.C.–A.D. 212*. Ithaca, NY: Cornell University Press.
Davies, A. Powell. 1956. *The Ten Commandments*. New York: Signet Key Books.
Diamond, A. S. 1971. *Primitive Law, Past and Present*. London: Methuen.
Dowden, Richard. 2002. "Death by Stoning." *New York Times Magazine*, January 27, pp. 28–31.
Drapkin, Israel. 1989. *Crime and Punishment in the Ancient World*. Lexington, MA: Lexington Books.
Driver, G. R. and John. C. Miles. 1952, 1955. *The Babylonian Laws*. 2 vols. Oxford: Clarendon Press.
Freeman, Charles. 1999. *The Greek Achievement: The Foundation of the Western World*. New York: Viking.
Freeman, Kathleen. 1946. *The Murder of Herodes and Other Trials from the Athenian Law Courts*. London: McDonald.
Gagarin, Michael. 1986. *Early Greek Law*. Berkeley, CA: University of California Press.
Grant, Michael. 1977. *Jesus: An Historian's Review of the Gospels*. New York: Charles Scribner's Sons.
Harries, Jill. 1999. *Law and Empire in Late Antiquity*. Cambridge: Cambridge University Press.
Hoebel, E. Adamson. 1954. *The Law of Primitive Man*. Cambridge, MA: Harvard University Press.
Jacoby, Susan. 1983. *Wild Justice: The Evolution of Revenge*. New York: Harper and Row.
Johnston, Norman. 2000. *Forms of Constraint: A History of Prison Architecture*. Urbana: University of Illinois Press.
Kelly, Martin. 1988. "Citizen Survival in Ancient Rome." *Police Studies*, 11(Winter):195–201.
Kolbert, C. F., trans. 1979. *Justinian: The Digest of Roman Law*. London: Penguin Books.
MacDowell, Douglas M. 1966. *Athenian Homicide Law in the Age of the Orators*. Manchester: Manchester University Press.
Menninger, Karl. 1973. *Whatever became of Sin?* New York: Hawthorn Books.
Morris, Norval and David Rothman, eds. 1995. *The Oxford History of the Prison*. New York: Oxford University Press.
Peters, Edward M. 1995. "Prison before the Prison." In *The Oxford History of the Prison*, ed. Norval Morris and David Rothman, pp. 17–21. New York: Oxford University Press.
Pew Global Attitudes Project. 2009. "Pakistani Public Opinion: Growing Concerns about Extremism, Continuing Discontent in the United States." http://pewglobal.org/reports/pdf/265.pdf.

Platner, Samuel and Thomas Ashby. 1929. "Mamertine Prison." In *A Topographical Dictionary of Ancient Rome*. London: Oxford University Press.

Pomeroy, Sarah B. 1995. *Goddesses, Whores, Wives, and Slaves: Women in Classical Antiquity*. New York: Schocken Books.

———. 1997. *Families in Classical and Hellenistic Greece: Representations and Realities*. Oxford: Clarendon Press.

Pound, Roscoe. 1953. *The Lawyer from Antiquity to Modern Times*. St. Paul, MN: West Publishing Company.

Rattray, Robert Sutherland. 1969. *Ashanti Law and Constitution*. New York: Negro Universities Press.

Reinert, Patty. 2002. "Commandments Case Rejected." *Houston Chronicle*, February 26, p. A5.

Reith, Charles. 1952. *The Blind Eye of History: A Study of the Origins of the Present Police Era*. London: Faber and Faber.

Robinson, O. F. 1995. *The Criminal Law of Ancient Rome*. London: Duckworth.

Roth, Mitchel P. 2014. *An Eye for an Eye: A Global History of Crime and Punishment*. London: Reaktion Books.

Saggs, H. W. F. 1962. *The Greatness That Was Babylon*. New York: Hawthorn Books.

Squatriglia, Chuck and Kevin Fagan. 2002. "Many Dog Owners Worry That Case Will Restrict Liberties." *San Francisco Chronicle*, March 22, p. A1.

Stone, I. F. 1988. *The Trial of Socrates*. Boston: Little, Brown and Company.

Tydlesley, Joyce. 2002. *Judgment of the Pharaoh: Crime and Punishment in Ancient Egypt*. London: Orion Pub.

Watson, Alan. 1985. *The Evolution of Law*. Baltimore: Johns Hopkins University Press.

White, Edward J. 1935. *The Law in the Scriptures*. St. Louis, MO: Thomas Law Book Company.

Wigmore, John Henry. 1928. *A Panorama of the World's Legal Systems*. 3 vols. St. Paul, MN: West Publishing Company.

Wolff, Hans Julius. 1951. *Roman Law: An Historical Introduction*. Norman: University of Oklahoma Press.

TIMELINE	570	860s	1066	1166	1176	1180	1194	1215
	Laws of Aethelbert of Kent	Viking invasion of British Isles	Norman invasion of England	Assize of Clarendon	Assize of Northampton	Henry II centralizes law and justice in England	Birth of coroner's office	King John signs the Magna Carta

CHAPTER TWO

Crime and criminal justice: English antecedents

Learning objectives

After finishing this chapter students should understand and be able to discuss:

- The importance of trial by ordeal as a judicial tool in the Anglo-Saxon era
- The high rates of violence and homicide in medieval England
- The impact of the Norman invasion in 1066 on the development of various criminal justice professions (bailiff, constable, and others)
- The evolution of the sheriff from shire reeve
- The development of the jury system
- The difference between the adversarial (common law) and inquisitorial (civil law) legal processes
- The impact of the Magna Carta on the development of constitutional law and political freedom

When the Romans invaded the British Isles in 55 B.C., they found a primitive island inhabited by **Celtic** tribes who had immigrated there from what today is southern Germany. There was no unity among these cultures, and the term *England* had not yet been coined. The Romans unsuccessfully attempted to put the stamp of its legal traditions on the people they came into contact with, but by the time Roman troops were withdrawn 400 years later, except for Roman roads, walls, and town sites, little had changed on the island. When the legions were removed in the early fifth century, the Romanized Britons proved ill equipped to defend their borders against marauding invaders from northern Europe. Among the Germanic and Scandinavian invaders were **Saxons, Angles**, and **Jutes**.[1] Their prolonged conquest of the island swept away any vestige of Celtic or Roman legal traditions and gave the island its

Teutonic name England, or "Land of the Angles." Out of this welter of cultures emerged the tribal foundation that would give birth to English **common law**. The three tribes that were to become known as the English would go on to conquer and prosper in most parts of England.

Anglo-Saxon England

The Saxon tribal units that migrated to England in the wake of the Roman retreat had originally lived in what is now northern Germany. These tribes fashioned iron-age weapons and tools, herded cattle, and had an extensive agricultural system. At the same time, they were warlike with a loose military organization. The most important component of their social relationship was the blood ties of the **kinship group**, a form of extended family. In many respects, the tribe functioned as a group of kinsmen.

Between the fifth and seventh centuries A.D., a succession of Saxon invasions brought these tribal kinship groups to England. Subsequently, the tribal chief would give way to a king who would function as military leader and landlord. The king was elected by the major landlords of the community, an assembly that became known as the **witan**, which is considered an early precursor to **Parliament**. In time, the witan was empowered to declare law, elect kings, and dole out lands to lords and clergy. Each kingdom was subdivided into **shires**, composed of smaller territorial subdivisions known as **hundreds**.[2] British policing can be traced to the tribal customs of these invading Germanic peoples. Each hundred was composed of 100 families and was ruled by a hundredman, or king's *reeve*, who held court every thirty days. The **shire reeve** was the forerunner of what became known as the **sheriff**. Responsible for maintaining the peace, enforcing and proclaiming laws, and collecting taxes, the shire reeve was analogous to American sheriffs who policed frontier counties in the nineteenth century.

Hundreds were divided into **tithings**, each composed of ten men, all responsible for the behavior of one another. In the event one of the tithing members committed a crime, the other members were responsible for sounding the **hue and cry** and apprehending the offender. This early peacekeeping system was based on an objective of mutual and collective responsibility in which the community was liable for keeping the peace and delivering lawbreakers to the hundred and shire courts.

The lawgivers

The earliest written laws, or **dooms**, of the Anglo-Saxons can be traced back to the **Laws of Aethelbert of Kent** (570).[3] These laws were based on local customs and are considered one of the earliest legal documents in English history. Far from comprehensive, they enumerate

1477	1530s	1556	1606	1689	1718	1725
First use of printing press in London	Protestant Reformation	The first house of correction opened at Bridewell Palace	Guy Fawkes trial	English Constitution and Bill of Rights	Thief taking elevated to a capital offense	Execution of Jonathan Wild

the punishment of various crimes, ranging from homicide to **fornication**. Each crime specified punishment and compensation. In this complex society of noblemen, commoners, freedmen, and slaves, individuals had values placed on their lives by class. Hence, in the event that a commoner was killed, his life was valued at 200 shillings, while a nobleman was worth perhaps six times that. Penalties and fines varied by class, not unlike the stark punishments of Hammurabi's code.

During the Anglo-Saxon era, there was no distinction between felonies or misdemeanors. Although it is uncertain when the concept of **felony** originated, it has been suggested that it developed at the time of the Norman Conquest as a category for more serious crimes. One of the earliest mentions of felony can be found in the *Assize of Northampton* (1176), which mentions "murder and other felony."

In the sixth century, the notion of the state had not yet evolved, and the kinship groups or family remained the chief social institution in Britain. Therefore, a crime against an individual was a crime against the family, typically resulting in a **blood feud**. Kinship members were expected to seek revenge from the perpetrators. Naturally, if the murder occurred between kinship group members, there was no bloodletting, and the perpetrator was banished.

Over time, systems of compensation were established in lieu of blood feuds. Some sources suggest that this softening of retaliation was in response to the growth of Christianity and the feudal system. Inspired by the need for collective responsibility, the ***wergild*** replaced the blood feud among Germanic tribes. Since the tribe was responsible for transgressions by clan members, a collective effort was made by the group to collect the blood money and compensate the victim's family.

During the ninth century, the British Isles endured its first recorded attacks by the Danish Vikings. Finally, in 878, King Alfred of Wessex defeated the Danish forces in battle and made peace after granting land concessions in an area that became known as the **Danelaw**. One only has to look at today's map of England to discover the widespread impact of the Scandinavian peoples on the British Isles. There are more than 700 towns that end in the suffix -*by*, which was the Scandinavian term for village or town, hence ***bylaw*** , meaning "town law."

The word *law* was introduced by the Danes in a region known as Danelaw, an area controlled by the Danes that stretched approximately from the Thames River to Liverpool. For almost half a century beginning in 886, the Danelaw was regarded as a separate political entity comprising almost half of England. Here Scandinavian settlers blended in with Anglo-Saxon neighbors, borrowing agricultural methods while contributing their own variation of legal codes and institutions.

The Danes convened local assemblies called ***Things*** , where farmers met under the supervision of a lawman to make decisions concerning the community. According to Danish legal code, the compensation to be paid for taking the life of a man, or *wergild*, was determined by the status of the victim. This contrasts with the Anglo-Saxon tradition, which was determined by the status of the victim's master. The Danes are also credited with devising a precursor to the English jury system. At local courts held at the Things, twelve freeholders were required to swear that they would not accuse an innocent man or shield a guilty one.

Anglo-Saxon legal tradition

More important to the development of criminal justice customs in England were the influences brought in by waves of Germanic invaders. Saxon tribal customs were preserved in oral traditions and were accepted and enforced by the entire society. Early Anglo-Saxon society was based on bonds of kinship and the extended family. A primitive form of social organization to be sure, the collective nature of this society diminished the importance of the individual, although each individual was responsible for the actions of his kinsmen. Whenever an individual killed or injured an individual, he brought the enmity of the victim's kin on his own family, ensuring a feud. By law, families were allowed to exact vengeance on the perpetrator's kin. Over time, attempts were made to downplay the vengeance in return for "blood money" in the form of a *wergild*, which was determined by an individual's status in society. When a defendant was charged with a crime, the only methods for determining guilt or innocence were the ordeal or **compurgation**. Considered another major precursor to the **jury trial** system, compurgation required both the defendant and the accuser to provide oath helpers to swear to the truthfulness of each party. Oath helpers were initially kinsmen and later on members of the tithing group. The number of required oath helpers depended on rank and the seriousness of the offense. Typically, an accused defendant would supply twelve relatives or close neighbors who swore to the veracity of his case.

The **bier rite** was among the earliest methods for determining guilt or innocence. First mentioned in the sixth-century Germanic poem, *Nibelungenlied*,[6] its use has been documented in European and colonial American courts between the twelfth and early nineteenth centuries.[7] The bier rite was based on the test of "cruentation." Cruentation was based on the premise that, if a murdered corpse was in the presence of its killer, the body would bleed suddenly. This evidence was sometimes used in courtrooms and accepted as "proof positive of guilt." Modern forensic science repudiates the notion of a body bleeding after livor mortis begins shortly after death due to the fact that the blood clots and settles in the bottommost part of the body shortly after expiring. However, it is possible that, if a body is poked or prodded at the time of trial, it might cause some fluid to seep from the nose or other body cavities. By most accounts, the bier rite is most closely related to other examples of "divine interventions used as tangible evidence,"[8] particularly **trial by ordeal**.

Trial by ordeal can be found in cultures throughout the world and in many time periods. As practiced in England, it was typically conducted by fire or water and was administered with the help of a priest. Considered God's judgment, the ordeal was compulsory for individuals who were caught in the act, who were formerly guilty of perjury, or who were unable to provide the appropriate number of compurgators. Built on ancient methods of determining guilt or innocence, trial by ordeal was based on the notion that the gods would protect the innocent. In Christian Britain, no less faith was placed in this method. Trial by ordeal was actually the court of last resort since it was hoped individuals would repent or confess before undergoing the ritual. There were also opportunities to stack the odds in favor of the accused for a price by corrupting officials or bribing clerics to cool off the instruments prior to the ordeal.

Trial by fire often involved the accused walking blindfolded over hot coals or plowshares or placing an arm into scalding water. In other situations, the accused might be required to take part in the "caldron dip," where he would put his hand into a cauldron of boiling water in order to pull out a stone or some other object typically weighing one pound. If the festering burns did not heal within three days, the defendant was judged guilty and faced the consequences. There were other forms of ordeal that could be adjudicated without waiting three days. Without a neutral waiting period, crowds and bystanders could have their curiosity sated by immersing heretics in cold water to see if they would float or sink. Naturally, if they sank, they were innocent. It would seem that the immediate ordeal was preferable from the community point of view. The 400 years before the Fourth Lateran Council (1215) is considered the heyday of trial by ordeal. Virtually every law code in the world in this era makes some type of reference to this procedure. Crimes ranging from murder, forgery, and witchcraft to heresy prescribed ordeals of hot iron and cold water. However, the method of ordeal was not the first resort. Since it coexisted with other methods of giving proof, it was not used until other ways for determining the truth had been exhausted.

Despite the decline of trial by ordeal in the thirteenth century, as late as the sixteenth century, England's King James placed great stock in cruentation. Not surprisingly, he had a strong affinity for the occult and the belief in witchcraft. According to recent scholarship, women "were rare in accounts of bleeding corpses – except as accused killers."[9] According to recent graduate work of historian Molly Ingram, "Female speech was less credible than male speech," and the testimony by women rarely appears in court proceedings from the era. Nonetheless, cruentation, according to Ingram, may have lasted longer because "it may have been more trusted because it was linked primarily to men rather than women."[10]

Anglo-Saxon crime and punishment

Introduced in the ninth century, **outlawry**, or the placing of an offender outside the protection of the law, was used to punish individuals who refused to appear at court, failed to pay the *wergild*, or attempted to evade the machinery of justice by fleeing. Individuals who were outlawed also forfeited their property and lost all civil rights. According to the procedure of the day, if an individual accused of a crime failed to appear at county court four consecutive times, he was pronounced an outlaw, in essence branding him an animal to be hunted down. If he was not killed while resisting capture, he could then face the hangman on proof of his sentence of outlawry. By the time of Edward III, only the sheriff had the power to kill fugitives, unless it occurred in the process of capture.

Beginning with the Laws of Aethelbert, fugitives could be accorded sanctuary at a church or other consecrated place under certain circumstances. However, a specific protocol had to be followed in which a fugitive confessed his crime to a priest, gave up any weapons, paid a fee to the church, and recounted the particulars of the offense. The perpetrator could be given sanctuary for only forty days, after which he had to appear before the coroner and promise on oath to leave the realm. Sanctuary continued through the Norman era until its abolition in 1623 under James I.

After confessing to the coroner and taking an oath to leave the country, fugitives were promised safe conduct and directed to the nearest seaport to leave the country. As an alternative to outlawry, the process of **abjuration** (the process whereby a fugitive left the country) allowed the abjurer, dressed in a simple white robe and carrying a wooden cross, to safely avoid the consequences of many crimes. Prohibited from staying for more than two nights at any stop along the way, fugitives were expected to leave quickly to avoid confrontation with the victim's families. By the sixteenth century, **Henry VIII** insisted on the branding of abjurers so that they could be easily recognized if they returned to England without being pardoned.

Norman England

The **Norman Conquest** of England by forces under William, Duke of Normandy, in 1066 is considered one of the most pivotal events in English history. Following the wishes of Edward the Confessor, who died childless in 1066, his brother-in-law Harold was appointed as his successor. However, William claimed that he had been promised the Crown earlier by Edward and, with the support of the papacy, invaded England. After his victory at the **Battle of Hastings** and the death of Harold in battle on Christmas Day 1066, William was crowned king of England at the newly completed Westminster Cathedral.

The **Normans** of northern France were descended from northern tribes (Vikings or Northmen), not unlike the Anglo-Saxons and the Danes. But during their 150 years in France, they had developed their own unique identity and a continental style of **feudalism**. This system was a military structure, strictly enforced through a structure of mutual obligation. The social classes of Norman England were divided into three general groups, with feudal lords, knights, and barons at the top. In the middle were the ordinary citizens, usually skilled workers. At the bottom were the serfs and peasants of the estates, perhaps two-thirds of the population. **Barons**, who were the highest level of Norman lords, maintained huge landholdings, or **manors**, on which lived vassals or serfs who toiled the land. In return for an oath of faithfulness and certain well-understood obligations, the lords of these estates would protect the vassals. Likewise, the peasants would heed the call to arms when the lord's interests were threatened.

A serf was tied to the land and had no right to leave his lord's estate. They could be punished for idleness, disorderly behavior, and poor workmanship. In return for working so many days a week for the lord, delivering a certain amount of lumber, or loaning his lord's horses, serfs could expect the lords to build them a new house if theirs burned down or to care for their children if they were orphaned.

In the years following the Norman Conquest, as Normans and Saxons lived more peacefully together, the authority of the sheriff was taken over by the local lord of the manor. Subsequently, the work of the hundred court was replaced by a manor court. This court chose manor officers each year, including an ale taster, bread weigher, swine ringer, and, most important, a **constable**. Responsible for helping keep the king's peace on the estate, the unpaid constable had a multitude of duties, including reporting behavior problems to the court, arresting malefactors and guarding them until trial, and calling out the hue and cry and raising **posse comitatus** (meaning "power of the county"), a posse of locals, to capture a criminal.

> Under English common law, all male persons over the age of fifteen were required to assist in law enforcement when summoned by the sheriff through the hue and cry. The term "posse" has a lasting resonance that most Americans identify with the nineteenth-century West, when county sheriffs enlisted the aid of all able-bodied men when encountering forces beyond their control. In late twentieth-century Kingston, Jamaica, gangs were so enamored with Hollywood Western movies that they adopted "posse" as the name for their organized crime gangs.

We know little about the Norman law codes, but we do know that William did not speak English, nor did he initially understand the laws of his new subjects. In order to win the allegiance of his new subjects, he compiled the laws of Edward the Confessor while at the same time introducing familiar Norman customs. Adhering to the Middle Ages custom of allowing conquered peoples to keep their legal systems, William adopted most of the Anglo-Saxon criminal justice ideas while introducing a number of customs from the European continent. Another explanation for William's reverence for the Anglo-Saxon laws was that they were evidence of a more highly developed body of jurisprudence than the unwritten customs of Normandy. William adopted the existing law-keeping systems, including the tithing system, the use of the hue and cry, the hundred courts, and the shire courts. The Normans introduced a feudal system, a system of baronial courts, as well as separate ecclesiastical or church courts. Building on existing English customs, the Norman era would give rise to the common law legal tradition. The Normans introduced the framework of a strong centralized government that would eventually lead to the development of national unity and a national system of law. Following the Norman Conquest, for the first time, all land was owned either directly or indirectly by the Crown.

The late eleventh century witnessed a recrudescence of Roman law on the European continent. The fall of the Roman Empire saw Justinian's *Corpus Juris Civilis* fall into disuse as less sophisticated versions of the Roman civil law were applied by Germanic invaders to the peoples of the Italian peninsula. The invaders introduced Germanic legal customs as well. During the **Renaissance**, which followed the so-called Dark Ages, an intellectual and scholarly interest in law emerged, beginning in Bologna, Italy. This city was home to Europe's first modern university, where law was a featured object of study. The jurists of the day recognized the high intellectual quality of Roman law in stark contrast to the "barbarized compilations" of the Germanic invaders. Subsequently, the universities of northern Italy became the center for the study of the civil legal tradition, drawing scholars and students from all over Europe. Those who studied in Bologna returned to their home nations imbued with the superiority of Justinian's civil law (including England during the reign of Henry II). Roman civil law would soon influence the development of common law, featuring a common body of law, a common legal vernacular, and a common method of instruction and scholarship.[11]

The lawgivers

With the transition to the feudal system, each lord held a special court for his tenants. The Normans adopted Saxon procedures for determining guilt and innocence: the compurgatory oath and trial by ordeal. The Normans introduced another procedure, closely related to the ordeal: **trial by battle**. A precursor to the adversarial legal system, trial by battle involved a physical contest between a defendant and a complainant. These would be fought either by the individuals directly involved in the complaint or through proxy champions. Women, children, priests, and the elderly or infirm were allowed to appoint champions to fight on their behalf. Initially, champions could be used only in disputes over land. In the case of murders, the defendant had to appear in person. These judicial duels were conducted with much formality. Knights met in battle with the accoutrements of warfare, while commoners often fought using lethal agricultural implements. The two parties then fought to a stalemate. If the loser was not killed in the battle, he was hanged. Similar to and as ancient as trial by ordeal, credence was given the notion that God gave the judgment and would not have permitted an innocent man to be defeated. Most individuals attempted to avoid this form of arbitration, fearful of the outcome. Despite its unpopularity, trial by battle remained common into the thirteenth and fourteenth centuries.

England had been Christianized for 400 years by the time William introduced separate church courts in 1066. The creation of these courts led to the separation of ecclesiastical and secular law as the church withdrew from the adjudication of secular disputes. In return, church courts controlled spiritual matters without secular interference. Initially, church, or canon, law superseded the national law of England, with the pope regarded as the supreme legislator. **Ecclesiastical courts** decided spiritual affairs, including clerical matters and decisions of marriage, legitimation, and status. The church also dealt with such offenses of morality, ranging from incest and adultery to perjury, **blasphemy**, **usury**, and **heresy**. Under this new system, all clergymen were tried by church courts, as were commoners who breached **ecclesiastical law**.

The church was particularly intrusive when it came to marriage. Ecclesiastical courts could annul a marriage if either party could not procreate children or was related by blood or matrimony. Possessing the exclusive right of annulment gave the church a heightened influence in medieval society. There were also legal consequences resulting from marriage. When a man and woman married, the woman was considered to have merged her identity with her husband. This apparently gave rise to the long-standing common law rule that one party in a marriage could not testify against the other.

Occasionally, the two systems of secular and church law overlapped. Until the twelfth century, for instance, the king insisted that sins were secular offenses. Under church rules, the harshest penalty an ecclesiastical court could pass was excommunication. Other punishments included serving penance and degradation of clerical status. In order to take advantage of the less severe penalties arbitrated by the church courts, crafty laymen claimed to be members of the cloth in order to win **benefit of clergy**. This should not be surprising in an era when secular defendants routinely faced beheading, hanging, strangulation, impalement, boiling to death, or being broken on the wheel.

Benefit of clergy surfaced at a time when clerics were subject to both secular and ecclesiastical law. The clergy were eventually given an exemption from secular rulings and would be punished only by the church. During the Middle Ages, clerics were the only members of society likely to be able to read and write. In order to separate the thief from the cleric, a sight-reading test was devised. This would be proven by the ability to read Psalm 51, or "neck verse," which, if the defendant did successfully, saved him from the gallows. But as more people learned to read, the test became obsolete. The more astute criminals often learned the psalm by heart and could recite it word for word with a book in front of them, even though they could not actually read a word.

An individual could take advantage of benefit of clergy only one time. In order to prevent a person from pleading a second time, the fatty part of the thumb was branded for future identification. By the fourteenth century, benefit of clergy was given to literate individuals outside the clergy.[12] This literacy test was not abolished until 1706.

> During the fourteenth century, it was legal to hang women in England convicted of murder. However, it was illegal to kill an unborn child. In such a case, the woman's life was spared until she gave birth. By most accounts, the first case of a condemned woman "pleading the belly" was in 1387. In most cases, once women gave birth they were given reduced sentences or pardoned.

Norman crime and punishment

With the support of the witan, or king's assembly, William became not only the Duke of Normandy but also the King of England, beginning a new line of succession. Building on the Anglo-Saxon criminal justice apparatus, the Normans introduced a variety of new law enforcement positions in order to remove some of the power from the rapacious sheriffs. In 1194, the **coroner** was introduced. Selected at the county level, the coroner was expected to conduct inquiries in cases of suspicious deaths and house break-ins. Today, the coroner is a familiar feature of the criminal justice system in most of the United States, tasked with specific duties in order to investigate cases of death where there are questionable circumstances or where there was no attending physician at the time of death. While some states have replaced the coroner with the medical examiner, most counties have one elected coroner.

By the time of the Norman invasion, the position of constable had become a position of high prestige under the French kings. Derived from the Latin *comes stabuli*, which means "head of the stables," ancient Roman constables, really just glorified servants, were given this moniker because they had demonstrated honesty while protecting the royal stables. The constable became more identifiable in a peacekeeping capacity following the conquest of England. Over time, their tasks included collecting taxes, arresting malefactors, transporting prisoners, and serving legal papers. Most first-time offenders usually became familiar with the local constable. It was the constable that was expected to make the arrest once the hue and cry was raised and then hand over the quarry to the sheriff on apprehension. However, by the fifteenth century, life was becoming increasingly complex, and inhabitants were less willing to participate in the traditional hue-and-cry process.

William I introduced the **curfew** procedure to England to "protect against the risks of fire." In a world of wood, this was a natural concern to control the spread of fire. With

Curfew = trying to control population

William wanted to deal w/ crime wave

homes heated by open fires, usually in the middle of the floor and directly under the roof, the hazards were very real. However, the curfew can be interpreted as a clever bit of subterfuge since in reality it was probably designed to keep subversive Anglo-Saxons from meeting during the hours of darkness. When the curfew bell tolled at eight o'clock each evening, inhabitants were expected to extinguish their fires and retire for the night or face harsh consequences. Within a few decades of the Norman Conquest, the curfew was relaxed to allow fires to burn after the curfew bell.

One of the more notable changes implemented by William was a movement away from capital punishment in favor of mutilation. No criminal was hanged for the next forty years. This did not mean that no one died from criminal sanctions. Indeed, scores of the convicted succumbed to mutilations after having eyes put out and testicles cut off.

Curfews have been around for hundreds of years. The word's origins can be traced back to its Latin and French roots. Curfews were traditionally created by the upper-class members of society who wanted to limit the movements of the lower class. Originally, curfews operated under the presumption that an entire class of people was guilty. In the United States, curfews were originally implemented to control African Americans in the South. During the early 1900s, curfews became popular for controlling juveniles. The ringing of the curfew bell alerted teenagers and children it was time to go home. In recent years, cities and towns across the country have expanded the use of youth curfews to address the growing concern about juvenile crime and violence, treating in like fashion an entire demographic group as if it is guilty. Curfews remain a controversial crime control strategy. There is little empirical evidence that they actually work, and according to civil libertarians, curfews violate constitutional protections.

The Domesday Book

In a time when land equaled wealth, the Domesday[13] survey was a comprehensive inquest of the English land tenure system that redistributed the land from the Saxon upper class to the Norman nobles. Although the survey was incomplete, it is still considered the high-water mark of administrative achievement for the Middle Ages for the speed and precision with which it was conducted. Twenty years after the Norman Conquest, in order to determine the extent of his landholdings and fiscal rights, William initiated a complete survey of the number of individuals who belonged to each class, including serfs, knights, barons, and so forth. In effect, this inquest reduced all social relationships to a land tenure system. The survey also enumerated the amount of arable land, water mills, meadows and pastures, and forests and fisheries and the value of the estates. The survey was conducted under mounting popular resentment, as the Saxons saw it as an attempt to strengthen the power of the invaders.

Prior to the Norman Conquest, sheriffs were drawn from the ranks of landowners and functioned as royal agents in the shires. Within five years of the conquest, Saxon sheriffs were replaced by Normans. As their duties were expanded over time, they became more oppressive as well. The stereotype of the oppressive sheriff figures prominently in the Robin Hood ballads. The Domesday survey records a number of high-handed actions in which sheriffs enriched their own coffers.

Compiled between 1085 and 1086, the Domesday Book offers an interesting picture of eleventh-century England. With a population estimated at more than 1.5 million, only 290,000 names are recorded. Of these, 9,000 settled there following the Norman Conquest. This group controlled 80 percent of the land. What becomes clear is that, following the Norman invasion, a social revolution had occurred that essentially placed a feudal Norman aristocracy between the king and the Saxon farmers, creating a national feudal system that would last for centuries. Over the next century, the Normans and Saxons coalesced into one people: the English people.

The reforms of Henry II

The reign of **Henry II**, which lasted from 1154 to 1189, signaled a turning point in the history of the English legal system. Henry and his ministers would shape many legal and administrative procedures that would determine the direction that the developing English criminal justice system would take. At the time Henry took the throne, England was well supplied with numerous courts reflecting the feudal system of twelfth-century England. Hundred courts handled petty crimes committed by the lower classes, while the shire courts were concerned with the judicial aspects of more serious offenses. Complementing the judicial arrangements of the day were courts of the manor (landlord's private estate), borough courts, honorial courts (concerned with pleas of land), and ecclesiastical courts. Despite the suggested distinctions of the various courts, the system was confusing. What actually determined to which court an individual took his plea was his status in the complicated nature of his tenure under the feudal system. The competing and overlapping jurisdictions of the old customary law (Anglo-Norman) became a source of serious trouble during the 1100s.

Under Henry II's administration, the power of the Crown increased at the expense of the clergy and the feudal barons. A chain of events led to a transition from the old tribal–feudal system of law to royal courts and to the practice of common law throughout England. During this era, the oppressive power of the sheriff diminished as it became more subordinate to the Crown. Subsequently, the sheriff would become a minor official.

In 1166, England was beset by a growing crime problem. In response, during this centennial year of the Norman Conquest, Henry II issued the **Assize of Clarendon**, which established trial by grand jury. Juries consisted of twelve men in each hundred with four from each township. Together they submitted the names of all reputed criminals in the district for trial by ordeal (similar to today's grand juries, which review the facts of a case and issue either a true bill or a no bill). When traveling judges paid a visit to a district, communities were given an efficient means for stemming the crime wave. Ten years later, the **Assize of Northampton** divided the country into six circuits, and justices in Eyre were made responsible for traveling to shires and hundreds throughout the realm. These judges superseded the local courts and were considered a means of controlling the conduct of sheriffs, bailiffs, and coroners in the Middle Ages. Henry encouraged all freemen to furnish themselves with arms and armor according to their means through the 1181 **Assize of**

Arms, trusting his subjects to heed the call to arms in event of an emergency. According to Henry's proclamation, "Whoever possesses one knight's fee shall have a shirt of mail, a helmet, a shield, and a lance." Some homicide scholars have suggested that with each man armed day and night, murder rates soon rose as well.

The introduction of itinerant judges was considered one of Henry's greatest legal innovations since their regular visits would eventually lead to a common law throughout the realm. What stifled the progress of the itinerant judges was the basic problem of how to delegate royal authority without at the same time putting too much discretionary power into the hands of the judges. This problem was resolved with the publication of *The Treatise on the Laws and Customs of England* toward the end of Henry's reign. Commonly known by its shortened title *Glanvill*, its author is unknown. According to this lawbook, there was officially a court that traveled with the king, a "chief court" that resided at Westminster, and a royal court that was periodically carried throughout the country by a group of royal justices who traversed a certain circuit of the shires.

Historian James Buchanan Given has made an extensive examination of the reports by the king's justices. The Eyre rolls offer insight into the procedure for investigating homicide in the thirteenth century. Apparently, when someone died under suspicious circumstances, the coroner was summoned to conduct an inquest. Once he arrived, he summoned an inquest jury made up of men from the vicinity where the body was found. He then examined the body and ascertained whether the homicide occurred at the scene or elsewhere. If someone was suspected of the crime, he was arrested by the coroner, who then, with the help of the jury, estimated the value of the perpetrator's property. All this was recorded on loose leaves of parchment paper. The work of Given suggests that, compared to the low homicide rates of present-day Europe, medieval England was the scene of unremitting violence.

According to one of Henry II's biographers, H. L. Warren, during his tenure as king, "criminal law did not show the same progress toward the development of rational processes" in the administration of punishment as in other areas of criminal justice reform.[14] Beginning in 1166, in the midst of a growing crime problem, criminal punishment was designed as a deterrent. After the Assize of Clarendon, anyone who failed the ordeal was sentenced to be hanged or to have a foot amputated and then be banished from the realm for forty days. The Assize of Northhampton, ten years later, introduced even more serious punishments. Mutilation, following conviction by ordeal, was extended to include the right hand and foot.

The early years of Henry II's reign witnessed great conflict between the church and the state over the jurisdiction of church law. Separate ecclesiastical courts were responsible for arbitrating cases involving church clergy. Since the shedding of blood was not allowed in church courts, the worst penalty a murderer in church court could expect was excommunication. By demanding "benefit of clergy," monks, priests, students, sextons, and others could win the right to be tried in church courts to escape severe sentences. The royal courts had no jurisdiction in these cases. Henry was troubled by the fact that almost any person with a scintilla of education or any connection with the church could take advantage of this legal loophole and wanted to end the immunity of the church from secular jurisdiction and bring it under the control of the royal courts.

Matters came to a head in 1161, when Henry II appointed **Thomas Becket** as the Archbishop of Canterbury. The assumption that Becket would continue to cooperate with the Crown would lead to one of the most famous murder cases of the Middle Ages and once again bring into question the relationship between church and state. The son of a London merchant, Becket lived a life of luxury after Henry appointed him chancellor in 1154. After the death of the current archbishop in 1161, Henry appointed Becket as the successor, confident he would remain a friend and loyal servant of the king and the state. However, things did not quite work out that way, with Becket adopting a more ascetic lifestyle. Realizing that he could not serve two masters, Becket resigned his chancellor's post under the king and was now resolute in becoming the champion of the church.

In 1164, Henry stated that he wanted to return to the customs of Henry I, which included a clause stating that, if clergymen were accused in a royal court and then tried in an ecclesiastical court, found guilty, and unfrocked, they should then be sent back to the royal court for sentencing and punishment. Henry's new rules extended the jurisdiction of the royal courts in several directions. Becket retaliated by refusing to put the archbishop's seal on any documents containing the king's proposals. The conflict between the two men intensified, leading Becket to flee to Rome and subsequently excommunicate the king and his ministers. In response, Henry confiscated Canterbury's revenues.

After Becket returned to England, relations soon worsened, leading Henry to brand Becket a "turbulent priest" as he launched into a tirade of invective that convinced several of Henry's retainers to kill Becket. Becket's martyrdom at Canterbury Cathedral at the hands of four knights forced Henry to accept an agreement with the pope by which benefit of clergy would persist. This resulted in an increase in papal authority and a check on Henry's power by the church. Over the next century, scores of monasteries would be erected in England, signifying the expanding power of the church. To Henry's credit, he was able to make peace with the church and, through a spectacular act of public contrition, was able to retain the loyalty of the middle classes.

One of the greatest English lawmakers, Henry combined Norman–French legal concepts with the ancient common law, completing the work begun by **William the Conqueror**. No less a source than F. W. Maitland noted that Henry II's reign was "a critical moment in English legal history,"[15] coinciding with an era in which customary law was no longer adequate for the needs of a rapidly changing society. With the revival of the study of Roman civil law, Henry perhaps saw the possibilities of adapting rational jurisprudence to meet the needs of an evolving criminal justice system. At his death, he could look back on numerous achievements, having made the Crown the source of all justice at the expense of the baronial courts.

The jury

The origins of jury trial are still a subject of much debate. While some authorities credit its introduction in England to Danish settlements, most evidence suggests that it was inaugurated by the Normans. A variety of prototypes for the English jury system had been suggested. As an alternative to compurgation and trial by battle or ordeal, a new form of trial was inaugurated called **inquisition**. According to this method, a judge who was selected to hear a case between two parties would order a number of men familiar with the particulars of the case, usually twelve, to investigate the case and give a sworn verdict as to who should win the dispute. These selected men became known as jurors because they had to swear to tell the truth and were required to decide in favor of one of the parties in the case. Thus, we see the beginning of trial by jury, in which jurors are peers of the defendant.

One explanation as to why the Normans extended the alternative of the jury trial was that trial by battle too often favored the omnipotent, warlike leaders over the poor and often defenseless lower classes. Unlike present-day juries, which are supposed to be unfamiliar with the case, the early Norman juries were composed of those most likely to be familiar with the proceedings.

The Fourth Lateran Council

[handwritten margin note: "There will be no more blessings by trial by ordeal"]

[handwritten margin note: Fourth Lateran Council took away trial by ordeal and move in jury trial]

The year 1215 was a pivotal one for the history of common law. That year, not only was the Magna Carta signed, but the Fourth Lateran Council convened and withdrew church support for trial by ordeal. The Fourth Lateran Council, held in Rome, was the largest assembly of its kind in the history of the Christian church. The church apparently withdrew its support for this ancient method of gathering proof because it was felt that the clergy should not be involved in taking the lives of fellow Christians. Since these trials could not be conducted without the presence of priests, trial by ordeal diminished. The abolition of the ordeal left few alternatives for determining guilt or innocence besides compurgation, jury trials, and trial by battle. Family men typically did not prefer trial by jury since, on conviction, their property would be confiscated and forfeited to the king's treasury.

In certain cases, in order to force an accused to enter a plea at arraignment, defendants were forced to undergo ***peine forte et dure***,[16] in which weighty rocks were stacked on their chests until they either agreed to a jury trial or died. In one 1605 case, Williamus Harvye was sentenced to be "thrown upon the ground and weighed down by stones," leaving his entire body, excepting his arms so he lies immobile on his back. Once covered with stones and iron, while he remained alive was entitled to "have the coarsest of bread and water. And if he eats shall not drink, and if he drinks he shall not eat."[17] Under English common law, no accused could be tried unless the accused formally entered a plea. Therefore, under the practice of *peine forte et dure*, the accused either entered a plea or died under the weights. In modern practice, if an accused stands mute at arraignment, the presiding judge will automatically enter a plea of not guilty on behalf of the accused.

Since news traveled slowly in the Middle Ages, the ruling from the Fourth Lateran Council took time to reach England and other Catholic countries from Rome. But in 1219, trial by ordeal was abolished in England. Without trial by ordeal, other methods had to become more developed for reaching resolutions in more difficult criminal cases. The demise of the ordeal led to several major developments in the quest for proof, including an increasing reliance on torture as a replacement for the ordeal procedure. But, like the ordeal, it was also meant to be the procedure of last resort. England, however, diverged from the European continental tradition at this juncture, as it made swift progress toward the trial jury, resulting in a legal tradition that became increasingly different from Roman civil legal conventions.

As England moved more toward an adversarial system characterized by a jury, continental countries went through a different evolution in criminal justice procedure. Not to be confused with the Spanish Inquisition of the fifteenth century, the European inquisitorial process placed the judges at center in the fact-gathering process (not torture). By the sixteenth century, the inquisitorial method was standardized. While the adversarial process that we are so familiar with assumes that the truth will come out after a free and open competition by two lawyers over who had the correct facts, the inquisitorial trial is more like a continuing investigation, as the judges and not the attorneys call and examine the witnesses.

Prior to the Norman Conquest, there was no legal profession in England. William introduced lawyers to Britain in the form of his "servants of the king at law." Many of the first judges were selected from their ranks. By the fourteenth century, guilds of lawyers known as **Inns of Court** could be found in London. Four of the original fourteen Inns still exist. At London's Inns of Court, the legal profession trained apprentices in the common law. Here, legal education included lectures, oral disputation, and attendance at court. Over time, the Inns made the transition from apprentice training to law school and for several centuries were more popular law schools than those at Oxford and Cambridge.

The Magna Carta

The Magna Carta is probably the best-known document in English history. Translated from Latin, it meant "Great Charter." Signed by King John at Runnymede on June 15, 1215, the Magna Carta established the fundamental principles of human rights. John ruled England from 1199 to 1216 and is considered among the least capable of the nation's kings. Violent, capricious, and vengeful, he succeeded in alienating virtually every faction of his realm. Commoners, clergy, and lords were united in their hatred for the monarch. His unpopularity was not confined to the British Isles, for in 1208 he was excommunicated by Pope Innocent III. The barons met several times prior to 1215 and decided that, before taking up arms, they would try and compel the king to sign a charter of rights. With the support of the citizens of London, John capitulated to the demands and on June 15, 1215, signed the Magna Carta at Runnymede.

Almost 300 years before the invention of the printing press, twenty to twenty-five copies of the Magna Carta were painstakingly written out by clerks for distribution around the country. Of these, only four survive. Copies were sent to various towns and read aloud so that everyone was privy to the king's concessions. In an era of almost universal illiteracy, the documents were sent to cathedrals, where the literate clergy could read the Magna Carta publicly.

Containing the basic principles that would be incorporated in the American Constitution 500 years later, the Magna Carta had great impact on subsequent developments in constitutional law and political freedom. One of the most important developments was the notion of due process found in chapter 39 of the Magna Carta: "No free man shall be taken, imprisoned, outlawed, banished, or in any way destroyed, nor will We proceed against or prosecute him, except by the lawful judgment of his equals and by the law of the land." By the seventeenth century, due process of law and habeas corpus would be united and contribute to significant constitutional developments.

Regarded as one of the foundations of modern democracy, the Magna Carta guaranteed legal tax collection (with permission of Parliament), justice to all men without fear or favor, and no imprisonment without trial. A turning point in legal history, the document set up a permanent judicial center at Westminster as well as annual assizes held by circuit judges throughout the country. Westminster became the repository for legal records and the site of the Court of Common Pleas, where suits between private individuals were held. It is during this era that one can discern the evolution of an expanded legislature comprising upper and lower houses of delegates. What would become the House of Lords was based on the hereditary right passed from father to son, while the House of Commons was filled with representatives from the commoners. This parliament sat at Westminster.

The faint origins of Parliament can be found not in law but in custom. The development of this body was spurred by the king's increasing need for revenue, which forced him to negotiate with the assorted classes of thirteenth-century England. By the early 1250s, the word *parliamentum* came into use to designate a meeting of the shire knights to consider new taxes. Although the first official Parliament convened in 1265, it would be another thirty years before Parliament was reorganized under the reign of Edward I[18] on the basis that it occupies today. By 1295, the representative nature of Parliament had been established. Often referred to as the "English Justinian," Edward became one of England's greatest lawgivers.

With the growth of towns and expanding urban areas, the prevalence of nighttime crime was increasing at an alarming rate. In order to counter the rising crime wave, King Edward I issued the **Statute of Winchester** in 1285. The position of **bailiff** was among the new criminal justice related advances introduced by the Statute, as King Edward endeavored to create a uniform law enforcement system. Initially responsible for tracking transient strangers in medieval towns after dark, today's bailiff is responsible mainly for keeping order in the court and protecting the security of jury members during deliberations.

One of the most important pieces of criminal justice legislation to come out of the Middle Ages, the Statute of Winchester required all freemen between the ages of fifteen and sixty to own armor and weapons according to their social status in order to defend the peace. These accoutrements would be inspected twice a year by constables elected from each hundred. But more important, this statute ordained that every walled town should establish a system of watch and ward, a form of day and **night watch** to maintain security. According to this statute, all large walled towns were ordered to shut their gates from sunset to sunrise. The watch was ordered to arrest any suspicious strangers and lock them up until morning. Other proactive measures included widening highways leading to market towns and eliminating potential hiding spots along the roads for thieves and **highwaymen**. The night watch and day ward would be the main police presence in English town life for almost 600 years.

The Black Death

In 1348, a trading ship reached England with an unwanted cargo of flea-ridden rats carrying the devastating bubonic plague pestilence from its origins in central Asia. The plague was usually fatal, and with no cure, perhaps 25 to 50 percent of the population perished. The impact was felt everywhere. The demographic crisis saw the clergy pared by 40 percent. According to estate records, perhaps two-thirds of the workforce perished, leading to a huge reduction in the labor force. In turn, serfs no longer felt their traditional obligations to their lords and barons and began to leave the manorial estates to take wage-paying jobs in towns. The labor shortage resulting from the Black Death made it inevitable that workers would demand rights and advantages that had been previously confined to the upper classes. However, as feudal restrictions seemed less persuasive, the state stepped in to preserve order. With the **Statute of Laborers** (1351), state control of the labor force supplanted the power of the feudal lords, leaving peasants and artisans in a stronger bargaining position with their lords and masters, with Parliament serving as an intermediary.[19] By stepping in when it did, the English government was able to ensure a continuing adequate supply of agricultural workers at rates that existed prior to the pandemic while leading to a dramatic increase in wages. Ultimately, Parliament became a more formidable presence in English society by prohibiting idleness and preventing the free movement of the menial classes under the threat of imprisonment and branding.

Statute of Laborers gave serfs the ability to work for their "rates"

Medieval crime and punishment

Late medieval England was known throughout Europe for its high crime rate. In the fourteenth century, most people lived on the bare margins of existence, as nine out of ten people still lived in the countryside. As violence escalated, English common law reacted by zealously punishing the crime of homicide. Individuals caught in a deadly encounter were cautioned that they had "a duty to retreat" in order to avoid possible bloodshed. With an increasingly centralized government, the Crown sought to maintain a monopoly on conflict resolution. It was expected that individuals would settle acrimonious disputes either amicably or in court. In the event that your adversary threatened you, you were expected to leave the scene immediately and retreat until your back was literally against the wall. At this point, it was permissible to stand and fight in self-defense. In this way, the state attempted to reduce the homicide rate by shifting the battle scene from the streets to the courts.

In response to the rise in felonies and with the escalation of organized criminal activities, **trailbaston** commissions were inaugurated *brought in to bring down crime* beginning in 1304. Because of a combination of rural unemployment, demobilized soldiers, and social unrest, several judicial innovations were introduced. The trailbaston was a special judicial commission of judges empowered to travel to crime-ridden villages and set up grand juries to help wipe out local gangs. Historians have compared the activities of this commission to twentieth-century crime commissions led by Thomas Dewey (1930s) and Rudolph Giuliani (1980s) that successfully went after organized crime in New York City. These medieval justices, like their modern-day counterparts, made headway through the use of informants who were convinced to turn state's evidence and testify against their former colleagues in return for a lighter sentence. Known as **approvers** in the Middle Ages, once a gang member was convicted, he could accuse the former gang members. But in order to prove his accusation, he was forced to vanquish each one through the ancient trial by battle. On defeating each defendant, he was pardoned. Conversely, if he was not victorious or was not killed in battle, he was executed.

For most of historical record, women have disproportionately been linked to the crimes of witchcraft, **infanticide**, and fornication. In some cases, women were excused from prosecution for certain felonies "under the assumption that she was under the guidance and direction of her husband."[20] This protection, however, was not provided in cases of treason, murder, and burglary. Women were entitled to "plead the belly" when facing imminent execution, allowing them to give birth before being put to death. In order to receive this exemption, first she had to be examined by either a midwife or a physician. When it came to pregnancy out of marriage, during the 1600s, it was considered a crime to hide one's pregnancy and subsequent delivery. According to one 1624 statute, the concealment of the death of an illegitimate infant was considered tantamount to murder. This was not applicable to men and married women delivering a legitimate child.[21]

The 1352 Statute of Treasons added the crime of "**petty treason**" for instances in which wives killed their spouses or masters were killed by servants. By some accounts, men were twice as likely as women to kill a spouse. According to one historian, when a woman killed her husband she was committing high treason, equivalent to attacking a sovereign. Most chronicles of spousal violence by women included the connivance of a lover in the commission of homicide. It was not until the sixteenth and seventeenth centuries that self-defense was considered a satisfactory explanation for the crime. Until the late eighteenth century, the penalty for husband-slaying in England was being burned at the stake. One should not overlook that the wording of the statute for petty treason left men who committed the same crime as their wives protected from this punishment. The crime of petty treason was finally abolished in 1828.[22]

Beginning in 1361, the **justice of the peace (JP)** became the cornerstone of British law and order. This peacekeeping position can be traced back to the 1260s, when it was known as the "keeper of the peace." Considered another self-help approach to maintaining rural law and order, each shire had three or four JPs who were charged with restraining the ever-present rioting. Imbued with the power to pursue and punish malefactors, they were allowed to try less serious offenders without the presence of the king's judges. In order to alleviate the caseloads of the various courts, JPs were authorized to confront most types of misdemeanors, including poaching, petty thievery, and drunken fighting. Occasionally, they were also allowed to try felony cases. In effect, London was authorizing the landed gentry to maintain law and order in their districts to reduce the pressure on the criminal justice apparatus in London. Although this was an unpaid position, wealthy landowning families saw it as a position that could lead to a better marriage or a seat in Parliament. As the powers of the JPs increased, so too did the authority of the once-mighty sheriffs erode. The JP system would persist into the late nineteenth century.

> One of the oldest criminal justice positions in the United States, contemporary justices of the peace (JPs) are state magistrates whose duties include administering justice for minor offenses and committing cases to trial at higher courts. They are usually elected within a minor civil division, but their jurisdiction usually extends throughout a county. In most states, they are compensated from fees. Most JPs have had little formal legal training, and in some states, they are allowed to conduct hearings and fix bail for future court appearance. But clearly, the position of JP has lost much of its former luster.

By the fourteenth century, the constable was still an unpaid position, recognizable only by his official staff. Over time, his duties had multiplied. While he still had to capture wrongdoers, he now had to apply unpleasant punishments as well. The constables became increasingly unpopular as they whipped vagrants and ducked **scolds** in the village pond. They also had to make regular reports of public complaints to the courts. While all adult males were responsible for serving stints as constables, those who could afford to would pay replacements. Such an odious job, then, was usually performed by the indigent, the elderly, and whomever else was in dire enough straits to accept the payoff. In William Shakespeare's time, the constable usually offered comic respite in his plays, not unlike the Keystone Kops of the silent-film era.

Introduced in the fifteenth century, the **Court of Star Chamber**[23] was created to punish wealthy supporters of organized crime activity. As organized crime declined, it was used to quell riots and other social disturbances and to punish the instigators. Procedure was rather simple. With no jury present, a defendant was ordered to stop some sort of antisocial behavior or to refrain from committing a particular offense, or else face punishment. Although the court was prohibited from imposing capital punishment, mutilation, shaming, and short imprisonment could be levied on defendants. The court remained popular through the sixteenth century. Its decline and disappearance in the seventeenth century resulted from its harsh and arbitrary sentencing and its association with the king's unpopular policies of the 1630s. Particularly glaring was its suppression of the large Puritan minority for indiscretions, real or imagined. Among the more questionable judgments of the court was the punishment in 1637 of barrister William Prynne, who had his ears cut off and was then pilloried and imprisoned for writing a book that allegedly insulted the queen. In 1642, a statute was passed in Parliament that not only abolished the court but also prohibited the procedure of making a defendant testify against himself (similar to the Fifth Amendment protection in the American Constitution).

> The Court of Star Chamber retained its sinister menace for the 1983 film *The Star Chamber*. Similar to the original court, formed in the fourteenth century to try criminals without the benefit of a jury, in this film, nine angry judges convene privately to decide the fate of criminals who have escaped retribution because of legal technicalities. Judge Hardin, played by Michael Douglas, is sick of criminals getting off because of the Fourth Amendment, which requires him to prohibit evidence obtained by unlawful search and seizures. In the tradition of the vigilante genre, this film suggests that the rule of law allows dangerous criminals back on the streets and that sometimes it is tempting for individuals to take the law into their own hands. In the case of this 1983 Star Chamber, if it votes guilty, hired killers kill the criminals. The film is ultimately a fantasy, produced at a time when America was experiencing rising crime rates (like England in 1347).

Under William the Conqueror's watch, the Normans introduced the murder fine, or **murdrum**.[24] Since there was significant resentment against the Normans, often resulting in the killing of local leaders and their servants, William instituted the murdrum. According to the law, if a Norman was found dead under suspicious circumstances, the district was required to arrest the perpetrator or pay a murder fine. However, in the event that the evidence proved the victim was not Norman, the fine was excused. By the Assize of Clarendon in 1166, there was little differentiation between Normans and Englishmen, and deliberate killings became known as murders. It is clear that, by the end of the fourteenth century, the Crown had taken a harder line toward murders, especially those committed from ambush or with "malice aforethought." In the early sixteenth century, the crime of manslaughter became distinct from murder, the difference being the presence or absence of premeditation, and in 1531, Henry VIII removed murder from benefit of clergy. From that time on, murder became synonymous with killings involving malice aforethought.

Between the fourteenth and fifteenth centuries, punishment had become somewhat less cruel, with many mutilations being abolished. But to stall recidivism, barbaric penalties were still meted out to rapists who were castrated or blinded and thieves who could be scalded to death or have an eye gouged out. Although individuals were still buried and burned alive, disemboweled, hanged, and beheaded, a movement was afoot to introduce more lenient exhibitory punishments, such as stocks and pillories, to shame individuals into reforming their criminal ways.

The popular image of the **pillory** shows the defendant spending an inexorable amount of time attached to this device, when in reality an individual might spend three hours in it every three months, often with a whetstone around his neck. However, this punishment was not altogether benign, particularly when prolonged exposure could lead to death. In the early Middle Ages, individuals were mutilated while ensconced in the pillory. Conveniently incapacitated, the law enforcer might be called on to slit a nose or cut off an upper lip or even both ears. Recidivist felons were often pinned by their ears to the pillory, and the only way to secure freedom was to pull away from the nail until the ear came off. Stocks and pillories were used to punish offenders who engaged in deceitful business practices, forgery, begging under false pretenses, and even masquerading as a king's officer. One baker appeared at court so often that he was nicknamed "pillory" for his penchant for the shaming device.

Perhaps the most glaring form of exhibitory punishment was **branding**, a punishment that could be traced back to the ancient Babylonians. During the Middle Ages, individuals were branded on either the face or the body with a mark that would be instantly identifiable with the crime committed. The letter *B* stood for blasphemer, *R* for robber, *SL* for seditious libel, and so forth. In the mid-sixteenth century, Edward VI signed a law allowing for vagrants and vagabonds to be defaced with the letter *V*. This law would not be repealed for almost a century. In an era before fingerprinting and the Bertillon system, branding was one of the few identification systems recognizable to all. One of the drawbacks for society was that, like prison tattoos today, society tended to stigmatize these individuals who were left virtually unemployable for life and therefore had no choice but a life of crime. While branding fell out of popularity by the fourteenth century, it was not outlawed in Britain until 1779.

Until the nineteenth century, virtually all felonies were punishable by death. Beginning in 1768, judges were given the prerogative of sending certain felons to the American or Australian colonies. Surely, there were plenty of felons to go around. In the case of theft, distinctions were based on the value of the stolen object. Early in the Norman era, if a felon stole an object worth twelve pence, it was considered grand larceny, a capital offense. If it was under twelve pence, it was petty larceny, which carried much less severe punishment. By the nineteenth century, juries often assigned fictitious values to stolen goods to downgrade a capital offense to petty larceny and spare the defendant from the gallows. By the late 1820s, England's Bloody Code was on the wane.

Henry VIII and the Protestant Reformation

Succeeding to the throne in 1509, the eighteen-year-old monarch who would author the song "Greensleeves," the lover of sports and music, gave no hint of the controversy and cruelty that would characterize his reign. The story of Henry's quest for a male heir that led him through six wives and into conflict with the Catholic Church is well known. For our purposes, we will concentrate on the constitutional crisis that followed Henry's establishment of the Church of England, placing himself as the supreme head of the church. Henry's determination to have a male heir led to his breach with Rome and the Act of Treason and Supremacy in 1534, which officially made him the supreme head of the Church of England. Anyone who questioned his authority, whether in public or in private, could expect a date with the headsman.

Henry was always cognizant of the fact that he ruled with the consent of Parliament. Summoning Parliament in 1529, he initiated a great social and ideological revolution that would go far toward establishing Crown and Parliament together as the foundation for the new England. He kept Parliament in session for seven years, allowing him to pass successive measures that changed the structure of the Church of England, including having the clergy accept him as head of that church. After passing a law that prohibited the clergy from convocation without his consent, **Sir Thomas More**, chancellor and author of *Utopia*, resigned. More would sign his death warrant by differing with the king over the legitimacy of his matrimonial life. He would not be alone. [According to one estimate, 72,000 people were executed during Henry's reign.]

When Henry VIII broke with the Church of Rome and declared himself supreme head of the Church of England, the resulting Reformation brought harsh punishments to anyone who stood in its way. One of the most prominent monarchs of the Renaissance era, Henry VIII was well known for his propensity for cruelty, which included the passage of an act authorizing boiling to death anyone convicted of poisoning. It would be left to his only son, Edward VI, to finally abolish this sadistic penalty.

During the sixteenth and early seventeenth centuries, numerous statutes were created targeting such crimes as robbery, burglary, and theft, reflecting the evolution of urban life. Other laws were specifically aimed at vagabondage, particularly as more and more agricultural laborers were unable to find profitable employment. By some accounts, "they were subject to the merciless cruelty of a labor and criminal code as severe and terrifying as any that had yet appeared in modern history."[25]

During the reign of Henry VIII (1509–1547) and the following Tudor sovereigns, transient vagabonds, with no visible means of support, were subject to brutal physical punishments, ranging from mutilation to execution. The lucky ones were whipped or had their ears removed, while perhaps 75,000 were hanged in the era. Conditions did not lighten up during reign of Edward VI (1547–1553), when vagabonds were branded with the letter *V* on their chests and were enslaved for two years. Under Elizabeth I, vagabonds were flagellated and either forced into galley service or a stint in the house of correction.[26]

Women were specifically targeted for witchcraft by English authorities in the sixteenth and seventeenth centuries. It has been estimated that more than 4,000 were hanged or burned as witches between 1558 and 1680. In other cases devices such as the ducking stool, the cart's tail, branding, the pillory and the branks[27] were used to torture and shame women.[28] Many of these methods would accompany English colonists to America in the seventeenth century. As we will see in the next chapter on colonial America, when a wife nagged or berated her husband, she was actually committing a common law offense. The mid-seventeenth century "was the peak period for the criminalization of women in England and throughout Europe," as exemplified by the high number of prosecutions of women for infanticide, abortion, and witchcraft.[29]

Henry said no more law School.

The invention of the printing press in the fifteenth century heralded a new era in the history of humankind. Prior to this time, manuscripts were expensive and slow to produce, and few copies of any work existed. It should not be surprising that few were literate and that education was restricted to the clergy. In 1477, the first book was printed in England. With the ability to print the Bible in English, Henry set the stage for the growth of Protestantism. At the time Henry was distancing England from the papacy, a recrudescence of Roman law was occurring across the European continent. Without Henry's break with the Vatican, Roman law might have crossed the English Channel and altered the course of criminal justice history.

Bridewells and early corrections

Poverty and lawlessness were rampant in sixteenth-century England. With the influx of destitute beggars from the rural environs to the city, upscale inhabitants feared the threat to public order, concerned that social unrest could result. In the 1550s, Edward VI, son of Henry VIII, established the first house of correction, or **Bridewell**, donating the use of Bridewell Palace, a former royal mansion, as a "hospital for moral, not physical deformities." Over the next century, Roman Catholics, nonconformists, and petty offenders would be confined here as it made the transformation from a palace for foreign dignitaries into a house of correction. By the 1630s, it was customary to issue whippings to vagrants and prostitutes on their first arrival. Adults were given twelve lashes, and children half that. With few alternatives for entertainment, the public often flocked to witness the floggings.

In 1576, Parliament mandated that Bridewells should be opened in every county. Eventually, 300 would be in operation. (These institutions would survive into the nineteenth century.) The Bridewell became an institution in which individuals had to work for their room and board. Among the more mind-numbing tasks were making nails, beating hemp, cleaning sewers, and working the treadmills. Like the modern prison, these houses of correction were designed to be self-financing while at the same time forging better citizens. Here petty criminals, transients, and the indigent were required to work while incarcerated. Some manufactured items for sale; others were involved in baking and milling. Over time, the range of occupational instructional increased to more than twenty-five trades, and as early as 1563, a system of apprenticeship was inaugurated for the children of the poor as well as young street children. By the 1770s, the house of correction, which some have compared to something between a poorhouse and a jail, had been adopted throughout much of Western Europe.

The English Bill of Rights

(The **Levellers** were among the most outspoken reformers of the seventeenth century.) While there is still debate over their long-term influence, some historians have accorded them the distinction of having anticipated some of the tenets found in the American Constitution as well as the birth of modern democracy. The Levellers originated among London's artisans and claimed that all Englishmen had the right to suffrage.

Although the Levellers' demands went unheeded in their era, much of their platform would come to fruition in America in the next century. The Levellers' prescience included the prohibition of debt imprisonment, a written constitution and bill of rights, the abolition of aristocratic titles, and a parliament elected by and for the people. Furthermore, they argued that the legal system should be simplified by purging it of Latin and French phraseology, allowing the common people to conduct their own legal affairs without the impediment of expensive legal representation. However, dissension within the Leveller ranks, together with lack of political clout, sealed their ultimate demise.

One of the most valuable legacies of the development of law in England was the **writ of habeas corpus**.[30] Originally found in article 39 of the Magna Carta, over time it had been often overlooked by those in power. But the **Habeas Corpus Amendment Act of 1679** made it impossible to secretly confine anyone. As a result of this legislation, a writ could be issued requiring that an individual accused of a crime be present in court at the time of trial and could not be convicted in absentia.

On the death of King Charles II in 1685, with no legitimate heir in sight, the Crown was passed to his Roman Catholic brother James II. Over the next three years, he retracted the denial of political and civil rights to the Roman Catholic minority. The **Glorious Revolution** that followed signaled the beginning of a new era in English criminal justice history. As the landed classes rose as one against the monarchy, James fled the country, leaving his Protestant daughter Mary and her husband, William, the throne.

In 1689, before the Parliament offered the Crown to William III and Mary II, it required their support for a bill of rights. For the first time in English history, Parliament decided who should succeed to the throne. Its impact would reach to the American colonies in the next century. Following this bloodless revolution, the power of absolute monarchy diminished in favor of a constitutional monarchy in which Parliament played an important role. In this new constitutional system, the judiciary was independent of the executive and legislative branches. The rights of all subjects would be protected regardless of one's status. Henceforth, it was illegal for the Crown to levy taxes without the consent of Parliament or to raise or keep a standing army in peacetime without the consent of Parliament. According to the English Bill of Rights, individuals had the right to a speedy trial, the right of freedom from arbitrary arrest, the right to a jury trial, and the right of petition. And almost exactly 100 years later, the American Bill of Rights repeated word for word from its British forerunner that "excessive bail ought not to be required, nor excessive fines imposed, nor cruel and unusual punishments inflicted."

[handwritten margin note: Parliment should be voted on by the people.]

Thief taking

In 1692, the profession of **thief taking** (bounty hunting) was inaugurated by the Act for Encouraging the Apprehending of Highwaymen.[31] Without a public police force and suffering a tremendous outlaw problem, the English government began offering a forty-pound reward for the arrest and successful prosecution of any highwayman. In addition, thief takers were entitled to the highwayman's horse, harness, arms, and other possessions, unless they proved to be stolen. Initially, thief takers were bandits who turned in accomplices for the promised blood money (reward). However, despite the best intentions of the Highwayman

Act, highway robbery continued unabated. Closer to medieval-style policing, thief taking was completely ineffective in tracking down criminals beyond parish boundaries. It was more effective on the local level.

In 1715, underworld boss **Jonathan Wild** (1682–1725) elevated thief taking to a science and over the next ten years was credited with sending over 100 criminals to the London gallows. His exploits earned him the title "thief taker general," even though he eventually followed his colleagues to the gallows himself in 1725. As the leading criminal of London in the first half of the eighteenth century, Jonathan Wild dominated the London underworld from 1715 until his death. During the 1720s, London suffered one of its worst crime waves. Since most powerful criminals were protected from prosecution through bribes and graft, the only response the government could muster was to begin paying rewards for the capture of robbers and prescribe the death penalty for most offenses. After a criminal apprenticeship to the London city marshal, who taught him the trade of receiving stolen goods, Wild set up an office near the Old Bailey, where he acted as agent between thief and victim.

A master at self-promotion, Wild called himself "thief taker general" by 1718. Wild exploited the law to the fullest, and his posse of thief catchers is considered by some historians as a precursor to early police departments. For ten years, he was considered the most efficient gang breaker in England. Wild improved an ingenious system for receiving stolen goods developed by Moll Cutpurse[32] in the previous century that involved getting higher prices for stolen goods by selling them back to the original owners who were willing to pay more. Wild improved on the system by posing first as a private thief taker who went after offenders to subsequently collect a reward once the objects were returned. He then organized bands of thieves whom he directed in his various schemes. Any thieves who attempted to compete with him he would set up for arrest and execution. Therefore, by aiding the law in his capacity as thief taker, Wild used the law to fatten his own coffers. Highwaymen gave London a wide berth between 1723 and 1725, as evidenced by the fact none were hanged at Tyburn during this time span.

In 1718, anti-thief taker legislation was passed, elevating thief taking to a felony – a capital offense. Over the next seven years, Wild enjoyed the protection of influential patrons, survived an assassination attempt, and had acquired extensive real estate holdings. Despite supporters who argued that he helped control the gang problem, Wild was hanged in 1725. According to one historian, "Nature intended Jonathan Wild for a sleuth, and had he been born two centuries later it is probable that he would have won a responsible position at Scotland Yard."[33]

Notable trials

Guy Fawkes (1606)

During the early seventeenth century, Protestantism was firmly entrenched as the state church in England. Under James I, both Catholics and Puritans felt the sting of oppression. When the Anglican clergy noted that their congregations were dwindling, James ordered Catholic priests to leave the country. Naturally incensed, Catholics hatched the desperate

Gunpowder Plot, hoping to reclaim the Crown and country. The Gunpowder Plot, which was probably hatched in 1604, was the brainchild of Robert Catesby, who suggested to several others that Catholics could seize power in one fell swoop by blowing up Parliament when it met on November 5, 1605. On that day, King James I and members of the House of Commons and the House of Lords would be assembled, and in the resulting chaos, the plotters hoped to establish a Catholic government.

One of the plotters traveled to the Continent to recruit aid from British Catholics in exile. Among those who jumped at the chance to restore Catholicism was a dashing, young man named Guy Fawkes (ca. 1570–1606). Having assembled their cast of conspirators, the plotters next rented a house next to Parliament and continued with their plan to detonate the building with gunpowder. In October 1605, a letter was delivered to the king warning him not to attend the forthcoming session of Parliament. The conspirators soon fled, leaving only Fawkes behind to complete the plan. He either had been assigned or had volunteered to ignite the explosion minutes before making his own escape. On November 4, Fawkes was arrested before the plan could take effect. Three days later, four conspirators were killed and several arrested, tried, and executed.

The trial of Guy Fawkes and seven others began on January 27, 1606. The conspirators stood waiting in Star Chamber waiting for the arrival of the judges. After the indictment was read out, the eight pleaded not guilty. The first lawyer to speak for the Crown noted that the matter before the court was one of treason, "but of such horror, and monstrous nature."[34] In the subsequent proceedings, every attempt was made to tarnish the Catholic Church by implicating it in the plot. All the conspirators eventually confessed to treason after lengthy torture and questioning in the Tower of London. According to protocol in treason trials in this era, it was customary for the defense not to offer any testimony. The defendants were then asked if they had anything to say as to why the sentence of death should not be pronounced against him. Several asked for mercy. In a day of quick justice and little time for appeals, on January 29, 1606, just two days after the trial, four of the men were dragged lying on their backs to the scaffold at St. Paul's churchyard for the traditional punishment for treason: being hanged, drawn, and quartered. If an individual committed murder, he was usually hanged, unless it was an aristocrat, in which case he was beheaded. The only offense considered worse than murder was high treason, which was considered the equivalent of murdering one's country, by killing or plotting to kill the nation's sovereign lord, the king. The following day, Guy Fawkes was among the last four executed.

Until the eighteenth century, convicted traitors in many parts of Western Europe were hanged, drawn, and quartered. The prisoner was typically drawn to the place of execution on a hurdle. Then he was hanged until almost dead. He was then cut down, and the real terror began. The victim, still alive and conscious in most cases, was next disemboweled. Occasionally, this was preceded by castration in order to symbolize that the traitor would be unable to sire future traitors. The bowels and entrails were then burned, and the victim was beheaded and quartered into four parts. At the conclusion of the public spectacle, the body parts were mounted on the city gates as a warning to future traitors. The head would be parboiled before being exhibited on London Bridge for deterrence value.

There is a certain mystery as to why Fawkes became a legendary figure. Perhaps it was because he did not flee with the others or had volunteered for the most dangerous task. Although the plot was never carried out, the Gunpowder Plot revived the old fear of Catholics and of papist conspiracy. Fawkes' display of courage under painful torture and his position as an almost legendary malefactor is celebrated each November 5 in Great Britain with fireworks displays and bonfires.

Conclusions

Placed in historical perspective, the signing of the Magna Carta in 1215 was preceded by Germanic invasions and followed by the Renaissance. It signaled an era that would witness the erection of the great European cathedrals and an age of faith marked by the Crusades. The growth of an urban economy gave rise to towns, commerce, markets, and fairs as European civilization expanded in all directions. The thirteenth century witnessed the birth of Parliament and rising crime rates in England. Universities flourished in Oxford, Paris, and Salerno. In a society dominated by the church and theology, craft and merchant guilds prospered; windmills, mechanical clocks, and eyeglasses soon became commonplace; and hard liquor was distilled in Salerno.

Although the Tudor era saw great strides in the development of criminal justice institutions, torture and confinement still characterized the treatment of defendants. British subjects had acquired certain basic rights, but much was ill defined and arbitrary. The Norman era introduced many of the prototypes that would become familiar components of the American criminal justice system, ranging from constables, coroners, bailiffs, and justices of the peace to the sheriff and the marshal. Meanwhile, Parliament saw a steady development from the innovations of Edward I to the Stuart Restoration in 1660, when the House of Lords and Commons began to organize as separate branches of Parliament. At this point, the power of the Commoners increased quickly as the social distinction between lords and commoners diminished. Helping bring the classes closer together was the evolution of the English language, which integrated the French of the Normans with the German of the Anglo-Saxons.

Point – counterpoint

Trial by ordeal and the Fourth Lateran Council: determining guilt or innocence (1215)

Prior to the thirteenth century, there were few methods for determining the guilt or innocence of suspected criminals. In the years leading up to the Fourth Lateran Council, most communities relied on the time-tested methods of trial by ordeal or battle or the compurgation oath. Such "judgments of God" were accepted by most members of the community, since there was little if any protocol that could be confused with trial by jury.

In 1215 church leaders convening for the Fourth Lateran Council forbade clergy members from taking part in the ordeal. Although the curtailment of such practices in most of Europe was gradual, the ordeals were almost immediately ended in England. The decline of the ordeal was a turning point in the history of adjudication procedure. Subsequently, the English common law system would adopt the adversarial jury trial, while continental

Europe leaned toward an inquisitorial system. The first passage describes the variety of ordeals popular since before the Norman Conquest of 1066. The second passage illustrates the persistence of trial by battle and oath helpers as a method of determining guilt or innocence. Notice that the "normal" number of oath helpers was twelve, a harbinger of the future jury system.

Source: Roscoe Pound, *Readings on the History and System of Common Law*, Boston: Boston Book Company, 1913, pp. 105–107; Sir Frederick Pollock and Frederic William Maitland, *The History of English Law Before the Time of Edward I*, London, 1898, 2nd edition, pp. 599–601

The ordeal was more extensively employed in the procedure of the pre-Norman period than in the later. It was the typical mode of trial among the English, contrasting English procedure with the procedure of their Norman conquerors. With them it was, until the Conquest, the only Judicium Dei so far as existing monuments bear witness.

This mode of trial finally received a fatal blow from the well-known decree of the Fourth Lateran Council of the year 1215, at which it was ordered that the ordeal should be discontinued throughout Christendom.

There were four forms of ordeal – to wit, by cold water, by hot water, by hot iron, and by morsel or "corsnaed." The first two were in the time of *Glanvill* for the poor and partly unfree classes, the "rustics"; the third was for the lay freemen, whilst the last, as we have seen, was for the clergy. The accused, however, appears to have had an election at one time between the modes by fire and by water. Whether this was true in the twelfth century is doubtful.

Each was undergone after the most solemn religious ceremonial. In the case of the cold water ordeal, a fast of three days duration was first submitted to in the presence of a priest; then the accused was brought into the church, where a mass was chanted, followed by the communion. Before communion, however, the accused was adjured by the Father, Son, and Holy Ghost, by the Christian Religion which he professed, by the only begotten Son, by the Holy Trinity, by the Holy Gospels, and by the Holy Relics, not to partake of the communion if he was guilty. Communion having been partaken, *adjuratio aquae* is made by the priest in which the water is asked to cast forth the accused if guilty and to receive him into its depths if innocent. After these ceremonies, the accused is stripped, kisses the book and the cross, is sprinkled with holy water, and then cast into the depths. If he sank, he was adjudged not guilty; if he swam, he was pronounced guilty.

Similar religious ceremonies were performed in the other forms of ordeal. If the accuser elected for the accused the trial by hot water, the water was placed in a vessel and heated to the highest degree. Then if the party were accused of an inferior crime, he plunged his arm into the water as far as the wrist and brought forth a stone suspended by a cord; if he were accused of a great crime, the stone was suspended deeper, so as to require him to plunge his arm as far as his elbow. The hand of the accused was then bandaged, and at the end of three days, the bandage was removed. If it now appeared that the wound was healed, the accused was deemed innocent, but if it had festered, he was held guilty.

If trial by hot iron was elected, a piece of iron weighing either one or three pounds, according to the nature of the crime charged, was heated under the direction of men standing by, whose duty it was to see that a proper heat was obtained, and kept until the time for the test had arrived. During the final ceremonies, the fire was left, and the iron allowed to remain in the embers. It was raised and with an invocation to the Deity, given into the naked hand of the accused, who carried it the distance of nine feet when it was dropped, and the hand bandaged as in the case of the hot water ordeal to abide by the same test.

The ordeal of the morsel, accompanied by similar ceremonials, was undergone by the accused undertaking to swallow a piece of barley bread or a piece of cheese of the weight of an ounce; if he succeeded without serious difficulty, he was deemed innocent, but if he choked and grew black in the face, he was deemed guilty.

Then came a sudden change. The Fourth Lateran Council of 1215 forbade the clergy to take part in the ceremony. Some wise churchmen had long protested against it, but perhaps the conflict with flagrant heresy and the consequent exacerbation of ecclesiastical law had something to do with the suppression of this old test. In England this decree found a prompt obedience such as it hardly found elsewhere; the ordeal was abolished at once and forever. Flourishing in the last records of John's reign, we cannot find it in any later rolls. Our criminal procedure was deprived of its handiest weapon, but to this catastrophe, we must return hereafter.

The judicial combat is an ordeal, a bilateral ordeal. The church had shown less favor to it than to the unilateral ordeals, perhaps because it had involved pagan ceremonies. Therefore, we hear nothing of it until the Normans bring it hither. In later days, English ecclesiastics had no deep dislike for it. It was a sacral process. What triumphed was not brute force but truth. The combatant who was worsted was a convicted perjurer.

The ordeal involves or is preceded by an oath, but even when the proof is to consist merely of oaths, a supernatural element is present. The swearer satisfies human justice by taking the oath. If he has sworn falsely, he is exposed to the wrath of God and in some subsequent proceeding may perhaps be convicted of perjury, but in the meantime, he has performed the task that the law set him; he has given the requisite proof. In some rare cases, a defendant was allowed to swear away a charge by his own oath; usually what was required of him was an oath supported by the oaths of oath helpers. There are good reasons for believing that, in the earliest period, he had to find kinsmen as oath helpers. When he was denying an accusation which, if not disproved, would have been cause for a blood feud, his kinsmen had a lively interest in the suit, and naturally they were called upon to assist him in freeing himself and them from the consequences of the imputed crime. The plaintiff, if he thought that there had been perjury, would have the satisfaction of knowing that some twelve of his enemies were devoted to divine vengeance. In course of time, the law no longer required kinsmen, and we see a rationalistic tendency which would convert the oath helpers into impartial "witnesses to character." Sometimes the chief swearer must choose them from among a number of men designated by the court or by his opponent; sometimes they must be his neighbors. Then again, instead of swearing positively that his oath is true, they may swear that it is true to the best of their knowledge. In some cases few, in others many helpers are demanded. A normal number is twelve, but this may be reduced to six or three or raised to twenty-four, thirty-six, or seventy-two.

Key terms

Saxons	witan	tithings
shire reeve	felony	blood feuds
trial by ordeal	*wergild*	compurgation
Battle of Hastings	hue and cry	common law
William the Conqueror	constable	posse comitatus

shires

blasphemy

neck verse

Domesday Book

Henry II

benefit of clergy

jury trial

Parliament

night watch

Court of Star Chamber

branding

Sir Thomas More

Levellers

Glorious Revolution

Guy Fawkes

hundreds

bylaw

law

feudalism

heresy

coroner

dooms

Eyres

Thomas Becket

peine forte et dure

Black Death

justice of the peace

murdrum

Henry VIII

Bridewells

Bill of Rights

highwaymen

bailiff

Anglo-Saxon

Laws of Aethelbert of Kent

Norman Conquest

trial by battle

ecclesiastical law

curfews

sheriff

Assize of Clarendon

Fourth Lateran Council

Magna Carta

Statute of Winchester

trailbaston

pillory

Protestant Reformation

thief taking

Habeas Corpus Amendment Act

Jonathan Wild

Statute of Laborers

Critical thinking questions

1 Discuss the development of law enforcement in England during the Anglo-Saxon and Norman periods. How did the Norman invasion impact the evolution of English peacekeeping?

2 Which culture had the most impact on the development of English criminal justice institutions? Discuss in terms of German, French, and Danish influence.

3 What was the role of the church in the English criminal justice system? What were some of the differences between canon and secular law?

4 Trace the evolution of the legal system in England between the Norman Conquest (1066) and the English Bill of Rights (1689).

5 Why is the reign of King Henry II considered a turning point in the history of the English legal system?

6 Discuss patterns of criminal activity and violence in England between the Norman period and the emergence of the thief takers in the seventeenth century.

7 Choose several English legal documents and discuss their impact on English criminal justice (Statute of Winchester, Magna Carta, English Bill of Rights, and so on).

8 Why were the thief takers considered progenitors of modern policing?

Notes

1 The Angles came from southern Denmark, the Saxons from continental Germany, and the Jutes from Jutland.

2 The most convincing explanation for the origin of the term *hundred* was that this unit comprised 100 households or perhaps was responsible for furnishing 100 men for the national defense.

3 Only the laws of Kent and Wessex from this era have survived.

4 The word *felony* is probably derived either from the Latin *fel,* meaning "one filled with venom," or from *fee* (property held under feudal tenure) and *lon* (price), suggesting that there is a price or loss of property if one commits a crime.

5 The *assize,* which literally means "a sitting" in Norman French, was a twice yearly royal court held in each county, normally at the county town. This procedure is credited with establishing the practice of local citizens forming grand juries to present the accused for trial by the traveling justices.

6 According to this epic poem, Siegfried, a dragon-slayer is murdered and subsequently placed on a bier. As his killer approaches the bier, the dragon-slayer's wound begins to bleed, offering proof that the killer was present.

7 Erika Engelhaupt, "How 'Talking' Corpses Were Once Used to Solve Murders," *National Geographic,* October 9, 2017, http://news.nationalgeographic.com/2017/10/how-talking-corpses-solve-murders-cruentation

8 Ibid.

9 Ibid.

10 Ibid.

11 John Henry Merryman, *The Civil Law Tradition,* Stanford: Stanford University Press, 1969, pp. 10–11.

12 In the time of Edward III, benefit of clergy was not available for highway robbers, and in 1531, it was prohibited in cases of robbery and murder. Benefit of clergy was finally abolished for all crimes in 1841.

13 There are several explanations for the title of this survey. One contemporary writer implied that the inquiry was so all-encompassing and inquisitive that it reminded people of the day of judgment, hence "Domesday." Others speculate that the hundreds convened for inquests on the Domesdays, or lawdays.

14 W. L. Warren, *Henry II,* Berkeley, CA: University of California Press, 1973, p. 354.

15 Frederick Pollock and Frederic Willian Maitland, *The History of English Law: Before the Time Edward I,* Vol. 2, Cambridge: Cambridge University Press, 1978, p. 673.

16 This phrase was misconstrued from the phrase *prison forte et dure.* According to tradition, the accused was tortured until entering a plea at arraignment. Although the last fatal use of this torture occurred in 1658, the practice was not discontinued until 1772, when it was replaced by a simple plea of guilty.

17 Evelyn Berckman, *Victims of Piracy: The Admiralty Court, 1575–1678,* London: Hamish Hamilton, 1979, p. 54.

18 A warrior as well as a lawmaker, Edward's legacy in popular culture seems to be his brutal execution of William Wallace of Hollywood's *Braveheart* fame.

19 Ernest Flagg, ed., "The Statute of Laborers (1351)," *Select Historical Documents of the Middle Ages,* Vol. 1, London: George Bell & Sons, 1892, p. 307.

20 Frankie Y. Bailey and Donna C. Hale, *Blood on Her Hands: Women Who Murder,* Belmont, CA: Wadsworth Cengage, 2004, p. 52; see also Natalie E. H. Hull, *Female Felons: Women and Serious Crime in Colonial Massachusetts,* Urbana: University of Illinois Press, 1987.

21 Bailey and Hale, 2004.

22 Frances E. Dolan, *Dangerous Familiars: Representations of Domestic Crime in England,* Ithaca, NY: Cornell University Press, 1994, pp. 24–25; Wendy Chan, *Women, Murder and Justice,* New York: Palgrave and Macmillan, 2001, pp. 10–11.

23 It got its name because of its interior design, which included a painted wooden ceiling replete with painted stars.

24 *Murdrum* is derived from *morth,* which means "secret killing."

25 Peter Linebaugh and Marcus Rediker, *The Many-Headed Hydra: Sailors, Slaves, Commoners and the Hidden History of the Revolutionary Atlantic,* Boston: Beacon Press, 2000, p. 18.

26 Ibid.

27 The origin of the term branks is unclear but is probably derived from a northern European or Viking expression. This punishment was reserved for women who publicly nagged or berated her husband. In order to control gender role conformity, communities enforced the offense of "scolding," one of the common laws directed toward defamation, gossip and slander, infractions. The branks has also been referred to as the "Gossips Bridle," a device "to hold a wagging tongue." In any case, the branks was never used as a legal punishment, but mostly as a local measure. It was typically composed of either leather or iron, or some combination, and was fixed around the jaw to prevent a woman from speaking. In some cases, an iron bit was added to depress the tongue. For more on branks, see E. J. Burford and Sandra Shulman, *Of Bridles & Burnings: The Punishment of Women*, London: Robert Hale, 1992, pp. 49–62; Karlene Faith, *Unruly Women: The Politics of Confinement & Resistance*, Vancouver: Press Gang Publishers, 1993, pp. 29–30.

28 Linebaugh and Rediker, 1994, p. 52.

29 Ibid., p. 92.

30 Meaning "you have the body," the writ of habeas corpus was designed to aid those wrongfully imprisoned. The writ ordered any official who is holding another in confinement to bring "the body" into court to establish whether the confinement is legal.

31 English highwaymen operated on horseback and usually wore masks during their robberies committed on the roads leading into London. Most sources suggest that highwaymen killed fewer victims than their horseless counterparts because of their ability to escape quickly. Although they occasionally engaged in gun battles with their victims or soldiers, treacherous accomplices and informers represented a far greater danger.

32 Born Mary Frith in 1584, from a young age she dressed like a man, carried a sword, and smoked a pipe as she made the rounds of local taverns. She became so adept at a ruse by which she cut the strings on leather purses that were used in the sixteenth century to carry valuables that she was accorded the sobriquet "Moll Cutpurse." Despite a life of crime in which she was branded four times on the hands as a thief, she lived until 1659, well into her seventies.

33 Horace Bleackley, *The Hangmen of England*, London: Chapman and Hall, 1929, p. 47.

34 http://armitstead.com/gunpowder/gunpowder_trial.html

Sources

Bailey, Frankie Y. and Donna C. Hale. 2004. *Blood on Her Hands: Women Who Murder*. Belmont, CA: Wadsworth Cengage.

Bartlett, Robert. 1986. *Trial by Fire and Water: The Medieval Judicial Ordeal*. Oxford: Clarendon Press.

Bellamy, John. 1973. *Crime and Public Order in England in the Later Middle Ages*. London: Routledge and Kegan Paul.

———. 1979. *The Tudor Law of Treason: An Introduction*. London: Routledge and Kegan Paul.

Berckman, Evelyn. 1979. *Victims of Piracy: The Admiralty Court, 1575–1678*. London: Hamish Hamilton.

Blackstone, William. 1962. *Commentaries on the Laws of England*. Boston: Beacon Press.

Bleackley, Horace. 1929. *The Hangmen of England*. London: Chapman and Hall.

Brown, Richard Maxwell. 1991. *No Duty to Retreat: Violence and Values in American History and Society*. Norman: University of Oklahoma Press.

Burford, E. J. and Sandra Shulman. 1992. *Of Bridles and Burnings: The Punishment of Women*. London: Robert Hale.

Cantor, Norman. 1997. *Imagining the Law: Common Law and the Foundations of the American Legal System*. New York: Harper Collins.

Chan, Wendy. 2001. *Women, Murder and Justice*. New York: Palgrave and Macmillan.

Cockburn, J. S., ed. 1977. *Crime in England, 1550–1800*. Princeton, NJ: Princeton University Press.

Dolan, Frances E. 1994. *Dangerous Familiars: Representations of Domestic Crime in England*. Ithaca, NY: Cornell University Press.

Engelhaupt, Erika. 2017. "How 'Talking' Corpses Were Once Used to Solve Murders." *National Geographic*, October 9. http://news.nationalgeographic.com/2017/10/how-talking-corpses-solve-murders-cruentation.

Faith, Karlene. 1993. *Unruly Women: The Politics of Confinement & Resistance*. Vancouver: Press Gang Publishers.

Flagg, Ernest, ed. 1892. "The Statute of Laborers (1351)." In *Select Historical Documents of the Middle Ages*, Vol. 1. London: George Bell and Sons.

Given, James Buchanan. 1977. *Society and Homicide in Thirteenth-Century England*. Stanford, CA: Stanford University Press.

Gladwin, Irene. 1974. *The Sheriff: The Man and His Office*. London: Victor Gollancz.

Goebel, Julius, Jr. 1976. *Felony and Misdemeanor: A Study in the History of Criminal Law*. Philadelphia: University of Pennsylvania Press.

Hamil, Frederick C. 1936. "The King's Approvers: A Chapter in the History of English Criminal Law." *Speculum*, 11(April):238–258.

———. 1937. "Presentment of Englishry and the Murder Fine." *Speculum*, 12(July):285–298.

Hamilton, Bernard. 1981. *The Medieval Inquisition*. New York: Holmes and Meier Publishers.

Hamilton, Dick. 1979. *Foul Bills and Dagger Money: 800 Years of Lawyers and Lawbreakers*. London: Cassell.

Haynes, Alan. 1994. *The Gunpowder Plot*. London: Sutton Publishing.

Hibbert, Christopher. 1957. *The Road to Tyburn: The Story of Jack Sheppard and the Eighteenth Century London Underworld*. Cleveland: World Publishing Company.

Howson, Gerald. 1971. *Thief-Taker General: The Rise and Fall of Jonathan Wild*. New York: St. Martin's Press.

Hull, Natalie E. H. 1987. *Female Felons: Women and Serious Crime in Colonial Massachusetts*. Urbana: University of Illinois Press.

Kaye, J. M. 1967. "The Early History of Murder and Manslaughter." *Law Quarterly Review*, 83:365–395.

Keeton, George W. 1966. *The Norman Conquest and the Common Law*. London: Ernest Benn.

Linebaugh, Peter and Marcus Rediker. 2000. *The Many-Headed Hydra: Sailors, Slaves, Commoners and the Hidden History of the Revolutionary Atlantic*. Boston: Beacon Press.

Maitland, Frederic William. 1965. *The Constitutional History of England*, ed. H. A. L. Fisher. Cambridge: Cambridge University Press.

McCall, Andrew. 1979. *The Medieval Underworld*. London: Hamish Hamilton.

McMullen, John L. 1984. *The Canting Crew: London's Criminal Underworld, 1550–1700*. New Brunswick, NJ: Rutgers University Press.

Merryman, John Henry. 1969. *The Civil Law Tradition*. Stanford, CA: Stanford University Press.

Pike, Luke Owen. 1968. *A History of Crime in England*. 2 vols. Montclair, NJ: Patterson Smith.

Pollock, Frederick and Frederic William Maitland. 1978. *The History of English Law: Before the Time of Edward I*. Cambridge: Cambridge University Press.

Poole, A. L. 1986. *Domesday Book to Magna Carta, 1087–1216*. 2nd ed. Oxford: Clarendon Press.

Pringle, Patrick. 1958. *The Thief-Takers*. London: Museum Press.

Sharpe, J. A. 1984. *Crime in Early Modern England*. London: Longman.

Tobias, J. J. 1979. *Crime and Police in England, 1700–1900*. New York: St. Martin's Press.

Warren, W. L. 1973. *Henry II*. Berkeley, CA: University of California Press.

CHAPTER THREE

Crime and criminal justice in early America (1597–1740)

Learning objectives

After reading this chapter students should understand and be able to discuss:

- Why different crime patterns and criminal sanctions emerged in different regions of America
- Why capital punishment varies by region in America today
- Which English criminal justice traditions were transplanted to the New World and why others were not
- The development of legal procedures in early America
- The critical role played by the Puritans and Quakers in the shaping of American values
- The underlying causes of the Salem witch trials and their uniqueness in early American criminal justice

The history of American criminal justice begins with the transplanting of European institutions to the New World. While several Spanish communities existed in parts of what is now the United States decades prior to the first permanent English settlements in Jamestown and Plymouth, they did not contribute much to the development of American criminal justice institutions. Initially, the history of colonial criminal justice is the story of thirteen separate colonies prior to the American Revolution and independence in 1776. The criminal codes, law enforcement systems, courts, and punishments resembled those of England, Holland, Spain, and France, depending on the colony. The development of American criminal justice is the story of the modification of this heritage. In order to understand the history of the

DOI: 10.4324/9781315148342-3

TIMELINE

1620	1630	1631	1640	1641	1648	1648
Mayflower Compact and settlement of Plymouth by Pilgrims	Massachusetts Bay Company and settlement of Boston by Puritans	First night watch established in Boston	Origin of the Dutch *schout*	Massachusetts *Body of Liberties* adopted	*Body of Liberties* revised and renamed *Laws and Liberties*	Dutch experiment with paid night watch in New York City

American criminal justice system, it is necessary to appreciate the remarkable diversity of colonial America.

The first steps toward English colonization of North America were taken not by the Crown but by private enterprise. Because of the high costs associated with establishing a colony, the English monarchy could not afford to colonize on its own. Instead, the Crown was content to sit back as a passive partner in the endeavor, a role that would later come back to haunt the English in the subsequent American Revolution. Except for granting charters, contracts, trade rights, and permitting migration, English officialdom let merchant entrepreneurs, Anglicans, Puritans, Catholics, and Quakers lay the foundations of early America.

An examination of the development of criminal justice in each of the thirteen colonies is beyond the scope and aim of this chapter. Instead, the focus will be on an important colony representing each of three colonial regions – regions that were culturally, politically, and socioeconomically similar – but exhibited significant regional variations in criminal codes. As will be seen, early North American colonies displayed significant differences in criminal codes from the beginning. Virginia represents the southern colonies. Pennsylvania exemplifies many of the characteristics of the middle colonies, and Massachusetts personifies the complexities of life in colonial New England. Those drawn to Virginia had economic ambitions, while mainly religious idealism motivated those who came to early New England and Pennsylvania. Each immigrant group required discipline and order to realize its goals. Since the colonists were recruited in different ways and lived in divergent conditions of climate and soil, it should not be surprising then that the laws and customs of the colonies were quite diverse.

During the 1600s, England was awash in political and religious upheaval, both of which would influence the structure of the English colonies as well as their developing criminal justice systems. Religious persecution in England proved a particularly powerful motivating force for colonization in the early years of the American colonies. Roman Catholics found a haven in Maryland, while Quakers sought refuge in Pennsylvania, southern New Jersey, and Rhode Island. Nearly 30,000 English **Puritans**, technically part of the official Church of England, immigrated to New England. Other religious minorities migrated from continental Europe seeking sanctuary from oppression as well.

Convict transportation

English colonists in the colonial era came from a country where the death penalty was mandated for a wide assortment of crimes. Capital punishment for treason, murder, manslaughter, rape, robbery, burglary, arson, counterfeiting, and theft were capital crimes in the

1651	1651–1652	1696	1661	1676	1682	1692	1704
Dutch colony of New Netherlands introduces rattle watch	New Amsterdam introduces first traffic law in New World	British Navigation Acts stimulate piracy and smuggling in colonies	Barbadian slave code provides model for southern colonies	Bacon's Rebellion	Penn's *Frame of Government*, or "Great Law"	Salem witchcraft trials	First slave patrol established in the South

American colonies at one point or another. But what most distinguished the code was the number of trivial property related capital crimes ranging from poaching deer to stealing small amounts of money.[1] The era of the so-called **Bloody Code** witnessed the number of English capital offenses increase from 50 to 225. However, there was a bit more bark than bite in the code. Prior to the passage of the 1718 Transportation Act, defendants were, more often than not, branded and dismissed. But following the Act, offenders sentenced under the Bloody Code were more likely to be transported to British colonies (except for those who committed murder, horse theft, gang crime, and other serious felonies).

Not all newcomers to America came of their own accord. In 1615, King James I introduced **transportation**, or **banishment**, as one way to rid England of its hordes of convicts and "sturdy beggars." Offenders were not shipped to places unknown or to freedom but were sent to English colonies to perform profitable service. Between 1718 and 1776, close to 30,000 British convicts were transported to the American colonies. Mostly male and in their twenties, not unlike their twentieth-century incarcerated counterparts, the majority were destined for the Chesapeake plantations of Maryland and Virginia. At only a third of the price of an African slave, white **indentured servants** were affordable to the smaller planters, much to the dismay of the large plantation owners who protested the system. An alternative to branding, hanging, mutilation, and execution at home, transportation marked an important transition in penal practice and provided a much needed labor source to the developing colonies.

Indentured servants arrived in America after signing a contract in which they agreed to work anywhere from four to seven years without wages in exchange for transportation to America. A servant's contract could be bought and sold without his consent, and he could be beaten for disobedience or running away. In the early years, on completion of their terms of indenture, servants received fifty acres of land and, later cash, clothing, and food. Beginning with the first African slaves in the early 1600s, the institution of racial slavery evolved slowly in the seventeenth-century colonies. By the 1680s, there was a shortage of white indentured servants, leading to dependence on African slavery. By the 1680s, it would be the preferred form of labor on the plantations.

The English colonists who ventured to America in the early seventeenth century were used to a rigid social system and determined to maintain order among themselves at any cost. The structure of each colony would later influence not only what crimes would be punished but also how punishment would be meted out. Early colonial communities were tiny villages, worlds to themselves where everyone knew each other's business. Some authorities suggest that you could fit the entire European population of 1650s America inside a modern sports complex. No scandal was too small to incur the wrath of the community.

Despite a number of experiments with religious laws and political compacts, the only source of government that was regarded as legitimate was one that recognized the Crown

	1705	1718	1718–1776	1727	1735	1740
TIMELINE	Virginia Slave Code passed	Quaker Code repealed and replaced by harsh English laws	Under the Transportation Act, 30,000 British convicts transported to American colonies	Virginia creates its first slave patrols	Trial of John Peter Zenger	South Carolina introduces basic slave laws of the South

as the source of all legitimate authority. Thus, colonial institutions mirrored the government in England. Each colony had a governor, usually appointed (several were elected) by the king and in a sense corresponding to the monarch, as well as a governor's council, or upper house of the legislature, that was appointed by the monarch and corresponded to the hereditary House of Lords. And each had an elected lower house of the legislature, selected by voters who had to meet various property, race, gender, and age qualifications. The variety and complexion of the colonial courts was so complicated that they almost defy description.

Virginia and the southern colonies

In 1606, King James I granted the **Virginia Company** a charter to establish a colony in the New World. According to the document, the inhabitants of the colony would enjoy "all liberties, franchises, and immunities . . . as if they had been abiding and borne within this realme of Englande."[2] On May 13, 1607, English common law dropped anchor on the banks of the James River in Virginia in the form of 104 English colonists. No one could have then imagined the degree to which the common law would be altered in the new land. The transmutation of legal codes and procedures were in part due to the new environment and harsh living conditions. Indians, disease, lack of discipline, and distance from the motherland, in time, gave birth to criminal justice procedures significantly different from those that landed on American shores with the first English colonists.

The founding of **Jamestown** was a venture financed as a short-term joint stock company, each investor sharing the costs, risks, and profits that Virginia might yield. Members of the early Virginia Company were an assortment of gentlemen, servants, and vagrants. They settled in the New World hoping to make a profit for the company and for the Crown and to improve their own prospects at the same time. After agreeing to work for the company for seven years to pay for their passage over, the servants were free to seek their own fortunes.

The Virginia colonists found neither gold nor silver as the Spanish had previously. Unprepared, ill supplied, and sickly from the confines of ship travel, survivors of the passage over continued to perish in the hostile climate. Tropical disease, poor nutrition, and outright starvation ensured that since debarking, about four in five, regardless of rank or race, died within the first year. Rations were in such short supply that one of the first recorded executions in the colonies resulted from one man's murdering of his wife and unborn child for the purposes of cannibalism.

Instead of precious metals, Virginians' wealth would come from the cultivation of tobacco. With the introduction of this moneymaking crop, settlers refused to grow anything else. A "boomtown" mentality took root in which the single men of the colony, at least the few who were healthy enough, lay about the streets in a raucous display of drinking and gambling. Before resorting to slavery in the late seventeenth century, a large labor force of white indentured male servants was required to harvest the tobacco crops, resulting in a ratio of from four to six men for every one woman. The settlement of Virginia by mostly single young men contrasted sharply with New England's settlement by families. The disparities would also be reflected in criminal justice developments in the first colonies of each region: Virginia in the South and Massachusetts in New England.

The lawgivers

Initially, Virginia was supposed to be governed by a royal council appointed by the king. Few could have predicted that the small band of settlers would fashion their own government. By the eighteenth century, all colonies, except for one, had bicameral legislatures like the English Parliament. The upper house, or council as it was known, consisted of between twelve and eighteen members appointed by the Crown or other high-ranking officials, such as the colony's governor. Usually members of the landed gentry and the elite, they were the dominant group of the colony. The lower house was an elected body, selected from the smaller, propertied class. Voting privileges were initially restricted to free white Englishmen who were heads of households. This left a large portion of inhabitants and dependents, including tenant farmers, indentured servants, laborers, blacks, artisans, and women disenfranchised with little voice in political life.

The first representative assembly held in America was convened at Jamestown's **House of Burgesses** in 1619. Each of Virginia's eleven settlements sent two representatives who sat with the governor and his Council. A miniature Parliament, the initial convocation introduced "**blue laws**" prohibiting drunkenness, gambling, idleness, "excess in apparel," absence from church, and sundry misdemeanors. During the six-day meeting of the first assembly, the Church of England was proclaimed the established church, and the Virginia Company was solicited for financial assistance to establish a college. In short order, Virginia made the transition from **martial law** (1611–1616) to a self-governing community, laying the foundation for genuine democracy. However, it would prove a false start by 1624, when the Crown revoked the Virginia Company Charter and took over Virginia as a royal colony.

The blue laws introduced in seventeenth-century colonial America to regulate activities on Sundays, were so-named after the blue paper the laws were printed on. These laws usually targeted unacceptable public behavior such as drunkenness and excesses in clothing. Modern-day blue laws are just as likely to restrict alcohol sales, auto sales, hunting, or other activities on Sunday (although you could still rent pornographic videos that same day). During the nineteenth and twentieth centuries, the Prohibition movement introduced more restrictive laws including bans on cigarette sales and entertainment, including books, movies, and plays. In 1961, the U.S. Supreme Court upheld the rights of states to enact blue laws as long as the purpose was not religious. Today there is increased support to repeal blue laws in Texas, Colorado, and elsewhere. Supporters cite the desire to boost revenues and increase consumer convenience, whereas as opponents cite religious and family concerns and believe six days a week gives plenty of time to buy liquor. The move to change blue laws related to alcohol was given a boost when New Year's Eve and Christmas both fell on Sundays in 2006. Today, thirty-eight states permit Sunday alcohol sales.

Within two decades of their arrival, Virginia colonists had adapted English criminal justice practices to the New World. Although most procedures dealing with indictment, arrest, bail, trial, judgment, and execution of sentence were familiar to any Englishman, alterations were made to these traditional processes. For example, during the early years of Virginia, the court system changed. While the county courts tried minor criminal cases, felony cases were heard at the General Court, which convened in Jamestown. But traveling to Jamestown could be a hardship for slave owners from the more far-flung reaches of the colony. A specialized type of court, called *Oyer and Terminer*, was created to handle serious criminal complaints involving slaves. These special courts were held specifically to try slaves accused of capital offenses in county courts. Here we see an example of how the institution of slavery and the widely dispersed population contributed to the modification of English criminal justice procedures in America.

Early slave codes

The status of blacks in colonial Virginia was incredibly complicated. Initially, some were indentured servants who were allowed to own property and marry and testify against whites in court once free of their indentures. In rare instances, free blacks even purchased white indentured servants. A very few arrived free, one even owning a slave himself. But most were permanently unfree. Virginia passed the first statute revealing the central position of slavery in the colonies in 1660. In a rather simple statement, the law identified a class of blacks as servants for life. Any white servant who attempted to escape with one of these servants for life was expected to serve the same amount of time as his accomplice after being captured, in essence creating a few white slaves. The subsequent passage of the **Virginia Slave Code of 1705** was one of the first slave codes in the South and established slavery as essentially race based and an integral part of the plantation economy. This Slave Code also contained provisions concerning the murder and torture of slaves, the legal status of children born to enslaved women, restrictions for interactions with non-slaves, and penalties for failing to obey commands. In perhaps the most draconian section of the code, escaped slaves could be dismembered if returned home alive.

According to Michael Stephen Hindus, although blacks were "accorded few procedural rights in the courts," a "formal system of trying slaves shows that despite plantation justice, formal law and authority reached the plantation to a considerable extent."[3] As evidence, Hindus cites the basic slave law of South Carolina. Established in 1740, it continued as the basic penal code for blacks until the end of the Civil War in the 1860s. The South Carolina code typified southern law for this era. Prohibited from offering sworn testimony, blacks were also not permitted to initiate prosecutions, unless it was done by a free third party. While all white laws applied to blacks, there were many others that only applied to blacks. Crimes such as assault with intent to rape, wounding a white man, burning crops, attempted poisoning, and insurrection were all capital crimes for black slaves. Punishment for white offenders who committed similar crimes was usually less punitive.

Blacks received some protections under the 1740 law code. Brutal treatment was prohibited, and any person who killed a slave was fined 700 pounds. By the 1820s, when the killing of slaves became more common, it became a capital offense, leading a court justice to submit that this action "elevated slaves from chattels personal to human beings."[4]

By the 1660s and 1670s, servants and slaves became more clearly defined within the legal code. Black slaves were barred from interracial marriage and sexual relations and prohibited from traveling or owning weapons without written permits. Slaves were even forbidden to learn to read or write. If a slave was caught learning to write, the slave would have a finger amputated. In 1669, Virginia won the distinction as the first colony to allow the killing of "rambunctious" slaves without fear of criminal sanctions. At that same time, slave masters were forbidden to free slaves unless they left the colony when freed. Any white person who married a nonwhite individual was banished from the colony. As the components of racial slavery became more rigid, white servants were enjoying more privileges. In contrast to their former black counterparts in bondage, white servants could no longer be stripped and publicly whipped.

Following in the footsteps of England's Bloody Code, the southern colonies followed suit, creating numerous death penalty statutes that targeted blacks only. These began in 1712, after a slave revolt struck fear into the plantation heartland, making attempted murder and rape by slaves a capital offense. "Most race dependent capital crimes," according to one historian of the death penalty, were "created in southern colonies," where in some colonies, slaves outnumbered whites. Ultimately, southern colonies such as Virginia and South Carolina found it necessary to implement more and more capital crimes in order to control the slave workforce.[5]

By some accounts, since "southern wealth was distributed more similar to England," this may have stimulated the southern "elites" to maintain capital offenses predicated on the tradition of severely punishing property crimes back in the home country. In other words, the cultural differences between the southern and New England colonies may have "reinforced southerners' preference for a greater number of capital offenses."[6]

Crime and punishment in the Chesapeake South

The early years of the Virginia colony were lean ones, rife with poor health, starvation, discord, Indian conflict, and mutinous conditions. Except for a very brief period in the early 1600s, southern colonies did not enact criminal codes the same way the New England colonies did, "but simply used English law."[7] Initially capital punishment was reserved for a litany of property crimes and crimes against morality were viewed as lesser transgressions than their counterparts in Puritan New England. Over time, the New England colonies would "decapitalize" more and more offenses while in the South there was an increase in the number of capital offenses, particularly when it came to various property offenses. According to historian Stuart Banner, this might be explained by the fact that "property tended to be distributed less evenly" than in the north.[8] Many of the capital property crimes were related to the tobacco trade. These included embezzling tobacco, fraudulently delivering it, forging inspector's stamps, smuggling, and so forth. Other death penalty offenses included being convicted for a third time for pilfering hogs, receiving stolen horses, or hiding property to swindle creditors.

Circumstances dictated law codes more severe than common law, and from its earliest days colonial authorities relied on brutal corporal punishments and hangings. When Sir Thomas Dale succeeded Captain John Smith (ca. 1580–1631) as leader of the colony in 1611, he instituted martial discipline and the law code titled *Lawes Divine, Morall, and Martiall* , known as "**Dale's Laws.**" The harshness of the law code has led some commentators to draw parallels with Draco's code of ancient Athens. Not only were the colonists expected to attend daily church services under penalty of six months' service in the galleys of Virginia company ships, but repeated absence from Sunday services could elicit the death penalty. On one occasion, a Virginia colonist was severely punished for making false charges against another colonist. As punishment, the offender was sentenced to be "disarmed and have his arms broken and his tongue bored through with an awl" and was then forced to walk-through a gauntlet of forty men and battered by each one. Finally, the unfortunate individual was kicked out of the fort and banished from the vicinity.[9]

Under Dale's Laws, capital punishment was mandated for almost two dozen offenses, including repeated blasphemy, unlicensed trading with the Indian tribes, stealing boats, embezzlement, the unlicensed killing of cattle, and the destruction of crops. Punishments for even minor violations were barbaric under the military courts, with accounts of individuals being burned at the stake, broken on the wheel, and bound to a tree with a bodkin thrust through the tongue and left to starve to death.

In 1618, a more moderate law code was introduced, but before the Enlightenment of the eighteenth century and the creation of the penitentiary system, there were few alternatives to the tradition of harsh corporal punishment and hanging. Public **shaming**, or **exhibitory punishment**, was often effective in curbing petty crime. Criminals that placed a burden on society, such as drunkards, vagrants, and other ne'er-do-wells, were treated as a serious threat to the community. Malefactors were forced to sit in the stocks or stand in pillories or offer public penance in church for violating conventional moral standards. As in the medieval past, women were often punished using local water sources. The ducking stool astride a prominent riverbank saw frequent use when women acted outside their traditional gender roles. The most frequent offenses committed by women included "bad speeches" or verbal abuse. The aegis of guilt fell more readily on women in cases of fornication and adultery since pregnancy outside the confines of marriage was sure witness to the act. Women who committed bastardy, or childbirth outside marriage, were also harshly punished in the Chesapeake colonies. If the recent mother could not afford to pay a fine, she was liable to be publicly whipped while naked to the waist. Adultery was a serious crime, but only for women because it was defined in terms of the woman's status. If she was married, illicit sex was considered adultery; if she was unmarried, it was fornication even if her partner was married. Infanticide and witchcraft were also mainly the domain of females. However, no woman was ever executed for witchcraft in Virginia and the southern colonies.

One way to contrast the punishment of sexual offenses in New England and Virginia is to examine the punishment for adultery. In Massachusetts, both parties received equal punishment, while, in the Chesapeake, women were punished more severely. In some cases, women were either flogged or dragged in the water behind a boat until almost drowned. In this case, adultery was less a threat to marriage than to bloodlines, which were important in colonial Virginia.

When it came to capital punishment, the harshest sanctions were also found in the southern colonies. In order to control a large labor force of indentured servants and slaves, the entrepreneurial planters of Virginia and other southern colonies fostered codes designed to frighten rebellious slaves and forestall any uprisings. The first twenty Africans reached Virginia in 1619, signaling more than three centuries of hardship for the black South. Slave owners were initially given free rein to punish their slaves just as they were with indentured servants. Since slaves were always a valuable commodity, punishments were designed not to incapacitate but to teach a lesson. Mutilation, whippings, and other corporal punishments were administered quickly and visibly to set an example and not interfere with agricultural work.

By the 1700s, the African slave population was soaring, and white colonists feared insurrection, real or imagined. Slave laws proscribed execution for slaves who attacked their masters. Punishments revolving around rumors of slave rebellions were always harsh and public and like their English counterparts were designed to demonstrate the power of the state.

Unlike the more religiously oriented colonies founded just a few years later, the sting of punishment fell disproportionately on the lower classes in the southern colonies. The wealthier felons were often branded with a cold iron so as not to dishonor their reputations. While the poor and the illiterate went to the gallows, their landed and more literate neighbors could plead "benefit of clergy" by reciting the age-old neck verse from the Bible and get off with a stiff reprimand and a brand on the thumb.

In the Chesapeake South, the county court played an integral part in the developing criminal justice system. Here the landed gentry presided at court much like their forefathers at their manor courts. Here accusations were leveled at defendants in front of juries composed of a cross section of the inhabitants. Run-of-the-mill offenses monopolized the court docket – fighting, swearing, failing to attend church, and slander kept the grand juries most busy. In most cases, the defendant would eventually plead guilty, and the court would arrange for two people to put up a bond of surety to guarantee against recidivism.

One July 10, 2006, Virginia Governor Timothy M. Kaine gave an informal pardon to the Grace Sherwood, who had been executed for witchcraft 300 years earlier. She was the only Virginian to be executed as a witch using evidence from trial by water. The so-called "witch of Pungo" wore men's clothes and was thought by neighbors to be responsible for their dead livestock and failing crops. Sherwood appeared in court numerous times to fight charges against her and to pursue slander charges against her neighbors.

Massachusetts and the New England colonies

A religious movement known as Puritanism emerged in sixteenth-century England. The Puritans' main goal was to purify or purge the Church of England of its Roman Catholic tendencies. In 1609, another group, later known as the **Pilgrims**, who refused to conform to the Church of England, which they felt was corrupt, actually separated from the official church. Fearing persecution, they fled to Holland, a country known for its religious toleration. After more than a decade, some of the separatist families, fearing that their children were becoming too assimilated to Dutch ways, decided to migrate to America. They were able to secure permission to settle in Virginia. Following a series of storms and misadventures, the Pilgrims aboard the *Mayflower* were blown off course and ended up founding the Plymouth colony in November 1620, the first permanent European settlement in Massachusetts. They had not disembarked blindly, having been provided with a map by the explorer and Virginia pioneer John Smith, who not only named the region "New England" but had already christened the protected harbor "Plimouth."

In order to unify the factionalized community and since they were in lands that did not have any recognized political authority (being outside the domain of the Virginia Company as well as the government of England), the Pilgrims drew up the **Mayflower Compact**, which is considered the first charter of liberties ever framed by English common people. Unlike the earlier laws of Jamestown, which were enacted under the direction of a royally appointed governor and his councilors, the Pilgrims were acting only under the authority of the 102 members of their party (many of whom were non-Pilgrims, or Strangers).

The Mayflower Compact was not actually a law code but rather a covenant signed by forty-one male company members that bound them together in a political union with the full powers of a sovereign state. Their contract established the concept that

> . for our better ordering and preservation . . . and by virtue hereof to enact, constitute, and frame such just and equal laws . . . as shall be thought most meet and convenient for the general good of the Colony.[10]

Without the aid of Crown lawyers, the signatories of this document set forth their ideal of government by the consent of the governed in a written document that anticipated the fundamental concepts of American constitutionalism. For the next seventy-one years, the Mayflower Compact was the formal mechanism for the political order of the colony. In the meantime, the governments of Connecticut, Providence, and New Haven would establish similar compacts. However, none of these would be permanent, and none was recognized under English law. Once Plymouth was absorbed by the Massachusetts Bay Colony in 1686, it came under the domain of traditional English law.

Following the establishment of Plymouth, King Charles I granted another charter to the **Massachusetts Bay Company** in 1629. The charter authorized the company to establish laws for its settlement "not contrary to the laws of our realm of England" and to inflict "lawful correction" on the spot to violators. The following year saw the establishment of the Massachusetts Bay Colony under the watchful eye of Governor John Winthrop and his Puritan colleagues. Both the Plymouth and the Massachusetts colonies would independently establish their own criminal justice statutes and procedures, reflected in the current state of Massachusetts.

During the Great Migration between 1629 and 1640, almost 80,000 English inhabitants left their Old World homes in search of religious freedom. This coincided with the era when the ill-fated Charles I ruled England without calling Parliament into session. Even more significant was the oppression faced by Puritan members of the Anglican church. Other factors for the momentous migration included widespread pestilence and economic depression. Of these immigrants, more than a quarter of them would settle in Massachusetts.

The Puritans differed from other immigrant groups in that they migrated with the highest number of family units, they had a relatively equal ratio of men to women, and their members were older than most other immigrants. The majority of them were from the middling classes, counting among their numbers artisans and craftsmen, merchants, traders, and farmers. While perhaps three-quarters of the Virginia colonists were indentured servants, less than 25 percent of the Massachusetts settlers were in this subservient position. Highly skilled and literate (for they believed that each person must know the scriptures as opposed to a priest interpreting for them) and often traveling in village or family units to the New World, this emigrant group would clearly distinguish itself from the more secular societies to the south.

Village life in Massachusetts was dominated by the family, from which much governance emanated. Consequently, in some provinces, it was illegal for single persons to live alone. In 1668, one Massachusetts court scrutinized its communities for any single people and then placed them into existing families. Failure to comply could result in a term in the local house of correction.

The lawgivers

The early northern American colonies were much more lenient than England was when it came to property crime. Crimes punished with the death penalty in England, such as robbery and burglary, were absent from the criminal statutes of the colonies in the region containing the Massachusetts Bay Colony. However, when it came to crimes against persons, punishments were more similar to English law, but in most respects less draconian.

Initially, judicial operations in early New England settlements were connected to other business of the government. Therefore, justice was administered by various executive and legislative bodies rather than by a separate judicial arm of government. Judicial power was often relegated by charter provisions. According to the Massachusetts Charter, all government power was vested in an executive council known as the assistant's court and the General Court, which was the highest regulating body in the colony. By the 1640s, most judicial functions of the General Court were turned over to other courts established by the General Court.

Typical justice procedure involved an assistant, also known as a **magistrate**, who filled a role similar to the English justice of the peace. Malefactors were brought before the assistant, who had the power to try minor cases without a jury. After the arraignment of the individual and hearing the evidence, the assistant could decide whether to press further with the case. However, before any corporal punishment could be meted out, another assistant was required to determine whether the judgment was appropriate.

The assistant's court, similar to a state supreme court, included the governor, deputy governor, and twelve assistants (magistrates) and tried cases that were punishable by banishment, dismemberment, or capital punishment. If there was disagreement between the assistants or between the assistants and the jury, the case could be appealed to the General Court. In the 1640s, Massachusetts established county governments and seven county courts. Each court was assigned five judges, and three needed to be present for there to be quorum. In the following decade, a four-tiered pyramid structure of judicial administration developed in Massachusetts. At the bottom were town courts, which conducted trials. Any appeals would go to the next level, the county courts, which also held trials but also heard appeals. County court appeals would be filed at the assistant's court, which heard trials and appeals, and at the top was the General Court, the highest court of appeal. In 1671, the General Court transferred its power to the Court of Assistants, which made it the highest trial and appellate court in the colony. While there was some variance in the judicial systems of other early New England colonies, such as Connecticut, Rhode Island, and New Haven, they were very similar in the hierarchical nature of the appeals process.

In 1685, the trial functions of the assistant's court were given over to the newly created county courts. Over time, the county courts became the most prominent ingredient in the criminal justice process. Convening as a court of common pleas, county courts heard civil suits and misdemeanors but were restricted from hearing felony cases, which were punishable by death or dismemberment.

The administration of the early Massachusetts Bay Colony criminal justice system was influenced by the teachings of the Bible. Indeed, biblical law codes superseded the English common law. Technically, there was no separation of church and state; as such, church elders tended to hold the reins of civic authority.[11] Motivated by the Old Testament, one of the early religious leaders proposed a law code based on the Mosaic Code. Known as **Moses His Judicials**, it was subsequently rejected in favor of the more formal **Body of Liberties**. The most substantial criminal code of the early Massachusetts colony, the *Body of Liberties* of 1641, subscribed to many of the notions contained in the rejected document. More important, it verified that everyone is entitled to specific rights or "liberties," including the right to plead or petition in the local courts. The *Body of Liberties* was composed of ninety-eight civil and criminal laws. Although inspired by the Mosaic Code, these laws were still considerably less severe than the ruthless laws of England. While *The Body of Liberties* recognized some property and personal rights, it perpetuated a tradition in which the colony was governed by a select few: an oligarchy of elite church members. Revised and renamed the *Laws and Liberties* in 1648, the new document is considered a turning point in colonial criminal justice. A fusion of biblical injunctions against immorality, the **Laws and Liberties of 1648** also included more secular concepts, such as due process and the right to a jury trial, and enumerated specific crimes and sanctions.

Colonial historian Peter C. Hoffer suggests that *Laws and Liberties* is written "in language reminiscent of the 'Great Charter (Magna Carta)' of English liberties."[12] According to the document,

> No mans life shall be taken away, no mans honor or good name shall be stained, no mans person shall be arrested, restrayned . . . no mans goods or estate shall be taken away from him . . . unless it be of vertue or equitie of some xpresse law of the Country warranting the same, established by a general court and sufficiently published. . . . Every person within this jurisdiction, whether inhabitant or forreiner shall enjoy the same justice and law.[13]

Although the Puritans are associated with freedom of religion, it did not mean that every religion would be tolerated in the colony; they were seeking to practice their version of Christianity. While Puritan law was equitably dispensed in the Puritan community, non-Puritans were not protected under the same laws. Deviation from the values and culture of the dominant group had a price. Particular animosity was reserved for the **Quakers**, in part because they loudly and publicly criticized the established churches and did not believe that ministers, or the symbol of church authority, were necessary. In 1658, the Massachusetts General Court passed several measures that included banishing practicing Quakers from the colony under the threat of capital punishment. The following year, in order to test the new law, several Quakers returned to Boston with twenty followers in tow. They were promptly thrown in jail, and three were selected to be executed. Prior to sentencing, one official lamented that "neither whipping nor imprisonment, nor cutting off ears, nor banishment upon pain of death, will keep you from among us . . . I desire not your deaths."[14] Two of the men were executed, with drummers drowning out their last words, while the third, a woman, was reprieved at the last moment, although she would hang in Boston for testing the authorities once again in 1660. These events did little to quiet the Quaker voice in Massachusetts, even when followed by months of suppression.

A familiar fixture in urban England, lawyers were not always available let alone wanted, so ministers often were consulted. In Puritan New England, the Bible supplied the law codes; hence, magistrates and lawyers were unnecessary for most litigation. Judges need not be schooled in the secular law, and few ordinances outside the scriptures were necessary. It was not until 1712 that an actual lawyer served as chief justice of Massachusetts. By the end of the seventeenth century, lawyers were in such disrepute in Connecticut that they were categorized along with those guilty of public drunkenness and keepers of disorderly houses.

In 1691, Great Britain granted a new charter to Massachusetts that united the colonies of Maine, Massachusetts Bay, and Plymouth into the province of Massachusetts Bay. In this new structure, the governor, with the consent and advice of his council, appointed sheriffs, marshals, justices of the peace, and the judiciary. The Puritan theocracy had governed the colony for six decades, and now with the new charter, religious freedom was granted to all Protestant denominations. This signaled a new era that allowed a transition to the common law as the colony was weaned from Mosaic Law.

Crime and punishment in Puritan New England

One historian described the myriad religious crimes of the Puritan colony as "the first colonial crime wave."[15] Within the first few years of the colony, church attendance was made compulsory under threat of fine and prison. Moreover, all work was expected to terminate between Saturday afternoon and Sunday evening; cooking was even expected to be completed the day before. As late as 1650 one ordinance in the region prohibited "doeing any servill worke" under threat of fines or a lashing, including hunting, sailing or just sitting together under a tree.[16]

The literal acceptance of the Bible led to oppressive legal measures that some saw as no better than the laws they left behind in England. No case illustrated this more than the Salem witch trials in 1692 (see "Notable Trials"). In another instance, an apparently mentally deficient denizen of the colony was whipped, had his ears cropped, and was banished from the colony for speaking critically of the local theocracy. No critic would be tolerated by the colonial elders. Originally, blasphemy was a capital crime. Although there is no accounts of executions for this offense, one could still expect six months of imprisonment, a whipping, sitting in stocks in close proximity with the gallows with a noose around the neck or enduring a hot spike driven through the tongue.

Conforming to the biblical law codes, the Puritans were least tolerant when it came to non-procreative forms of sex. Multiple convictions for masturbation was a capital offense in the New Haven colony. Colonists took to heart the Mosaic admonition, "If man lie with a beast, he shall surely be put to death." Considered the most sinister perversion, however, bestiality was punishable by a death sentence with little room for compromise. Although a capital sentence could not be passed without the testimony of two witnesses, magistrates often created loopholes in order to ensure that justice was done. Chief among community concerns was the fear "of unnatural livestock being born with human characteristics."[17] In one case, a servant with one eye and a tarnished past was believed to have committed numerous depravities. When a one-eyed pig was born in the vicinity, he was accused of siring it. The magistrates exerted considerable pressure on the suspect until he confessed and recanted twice. The magistrates ruled then that the deformed pig could be considered one witness and the withdrawn confession of the suspect would serve as another. Subsequently, the one-eyed servant was hanged.

Adultery and fornication were particularly targeted by the law. Fornication, according to one historian, "was the most common cause of legal action against women in seventeenth-century New England" and became increasingly so as the seventeenth century moved to conclusion.[18] Extramarital sex was not only a sin; if it involved a married woman, it also was considered a capital offense. Records for the seventeenth-century Puritan colonies indicate that at least three people were executed for this crime. However, for a capital punishment to be levied, it was required that there be two eyewitnesses to the actual offense. On occasions when there was only one witness, other sanctions were employed. Historian David Hackett Fischer cites a case where a man was whipped, fined, and sentenced to the house of correction while the straying wife also spent a stint in the same institution and then was instructed to wear a sign indicating her unwholesome behavior at a town meeting. According to Puritan law, fornication between an unmarried woman and a man, unmarried or married, sanctioned the man to be imprisoned, whipped, disenfranchised, and then forced to marry his partner if single.[19]

The degree to which sexual immorality was suppressed in Massachusetts was probably responsible for its having the lowest rate of premarital pregnancy in the seventeenth-century Western world. It is just as likely that many individuals charged with fornication were forced into marriage. The importance attached to female chastity prior to marriage and fidelity afterwards was, to a great extent, related to the "orderly transmission of property" down the legitimate bloodline. In the 1630s, men could be held responsible for initiating illegitimate sexual relations. The names of their female partners were not announced until a rising number of illegitimate pregnancies in the 1640s led to an ordinance that strongly encouraged the parties to marry.[20]

Rape was on the books as a capital crime, but according to one historian, it appeared that in Massachusetts, its use was left to the court's discretion. More common was a lashing followed by perhaps a humiliating hour standing under the gallows.[21] Historian Else Hambleton asserts that in the Massachusetts colony there was a pervasive belief that rape was "essentially a sterile act," that in any case where conception had occurred "consent must be inferred."[22]

Obedience within the family was considered sacrosanct. The laws of 1648 mandated the death penalty for rebellious sons over sixteen years of age. Failure to obey one's parents or any verbal or physical assault against them could lead to capital sanctions, although there is little evidence that this law was ever literally enforced. In lieu of the death penalty, several examples suggest that fines and whippings were the normal modes of punishment for such transgressions.

Infanticide has been an underreported crime throughout history since birth usually occurs in private with little fanfare. Midwives were typically present at birth to ensure a safe birth and to testify if the baby was stillborn. One of the earliest cases of infanticide was reported in Boston in 1646. Reaching back to the dark days of the Middle Ages, officials ordered the accused to undergo a form of ordeal known as "ordeal of touch." This was similar to the Germanic bier rite, in which a suspect is made to touch an alleged victim, and if the corpse bled or frothed at the mouth, the suspect was adjudged guilty. According to this relic of medieval judicial procedure, the birth mother was made to touch the face of her purported dead infant in front of a jury. When blood flushed the child's cheeks, the mother confessed. She was then hanged. Other cases of this judgment are recorded, the last apparently in 1769.

One of the main goals of Puritan punishment was to have a church member repent and return to the congregation. Although law was draconian, in reality it was rarely as punitive as the law allowed. Recent scholarship notes that Massachusetts colonists were rarely punished for Old Testament infractions and that "even those prosecuted very rarely suffered the prescribed penalty."[23] According to colonial historian Peter C. Hoffer, laws based on the Old Testament "were not meant to function in a literal way"; rather, it was hoped that they would function as a "solemn public warning to those at the edges of the Puritan community against violation of the deeper social mores that held the Puritan towns in the wilderness together."[24]

Besides punishment, another response to crime was the admonition, in which magistrates or clergymen lectured offenders privately in order to elicit a promise of reform. According to the procedures of the day, penitent reformers appeared in open court for a formal admonition by the magistrate. After a public confession of wrongdoing, there was a pronouncement of sentence, which was typically a suspended one. The admonition as it developed in Massachusetts had no precise analogue in English criminal justice practice. Its adoption followed the Puritan theology, which emphasized a "gentle correction" to impede sin, at least with the first offense.

The colonists of Massachusetts brought from England **sumptuary laws** that restricted certain fashions in favor of the more dour and drab. This tendency reflected the elite's efforts to exercise restraint in personal matters and to maintain social order in a society that witnessed significantly more social mobility. Nowhere were these laws stricter than in Massachusetts, where men and women were prohibited by law in the 1630s from displaying "new fashions, or long hair, or anything like the nature." Fashionable beaver hats were regarded as "superfluous and unnecessary" under threat of a fine.[25]

Not only were numerous other fashion statements strictly prohibited, but the mere manufacture or sale of such products was banned by statute. Over the following decades, the sumptuary laws would reflect the growing hierarchical nature of the colony. By 1651, individuals were allowed to flaunt their rank through various statements of sartorial elegance. Despite the loosening of the sumptuary prohibitions, early Puritan women continued to refrain from cosmetics, bright colors, and even false teeth.

Setting aside the periodic devastation of the Indian population, there was little in the way of violent crime in New England. Low crime rates have persisted in this region for more than 300 years. Fewer people are executed or murdered in this region than anywhere else in modern America.

According to Massachusetts court records, property crimes were more common than personal crimes. Crimes against the hierarchical social order were the most common offenses, including Sabbath violations, sexual offenses, idleness, drunkenness, and domestic disorder, all of which were apparently common.[26] Regardless of the punishment in New England, the interval between sentencing and punishment was set by law at four days.

The most prevalent form of sanctions involved fines, which was the punishment of choice for a variety of petty offenses and misdemeanors. Other public sanctions exposed offenders to an array of corporal punishments, including whippings, the stocks, and pillories. These exhibitory chastisements were administered publicly before the assembled community, usually on a market, lecture, or military training day. While public punishment and shaming was a standard response to many property and moral offenses, most of these minor offenses would have probably been tolerated back in England with perhaps a warning.

The Puritans were especially pragmatic when it came to methods of public punishment. In some instances, individuals accused of premarital sex were required to stand silently, attired in white sheets, in front of their congregation and recount their sins. Habitual drinkers wore the shame letter *D*, for "drunkard," for an entire year. An unscrupulous baker sometimes stood in the stocks supporting a lump of dough on his head. Chronic property offenders were branded on the cheek or forehead or mutilated, leaving a "mark of infamy" to warn the community of their criminal disposition.

One penalty reserved for the most serious crimes included "warning out," or banishment, which was used in New England until the eighteenth century to get rid of undesirables. Banishment was often the last resort available to longtime residents faced with patterns of criminality. In colonial Massachusetts, where labor was relatively scarce, it was impractical to run out the disorderly, though it was used in cases of heresy and political misconduct.

Particular disdain was reserved for betting, games of chance, and gambling. The General Court banned games, ranging from shuffle board to cards and dice. What most provoked the Puritan was the waste of time associated with these types of activities. In this society, a work ethic, or the notion that constant work was beneficial materially as well as spiritually because it kept one out of trouble, was revered. Time wasting, or idleness, therefore became a criminal offense in Massachusetts, punishable by fines.

Massachusetts colonists were surely familiar with England's predilection for capital punishment. In the home country, people were executed for crimes great and small, for routine theft and burglary as well as murder. However, only a fraction of the condemned were actually executed thanks to safety valves such as royal pardons, benefit of clergy, and the intercession of a jury. Among the most heinous forms of execution were burning at the stake and hanging. While hanging was the most common form of capital punishment, there are records of servants being burned at the stake for committing petty treason, defined as the killing of a master by a servant. Of the two known cases, both involved women of African descent.

Like the wearing of shame letters, which sent a message to the community, specific forms of maiming also sent a warning to potential miscreants. Among the more grotesque punishments administered by the Puritans were the amputation of ears, slitting of nostrils, and branding of faces and hands. Unlike shame letters sewn into a garment, these were permanent reminders to both offender and community. Particular ferocity was reserved for the Quakers, who were often the target of facial brandings of the letter *H*, for "heresy."

Piracy and the Navigation Acts

Between 1651 and 1696, England issued a series of **Navigation Acts** in an attempt to control colonial trade to England's benefit by prohibiting goods from being imported to England and her colonies unless on British ships manned by British crews. Other rules stipulated that certain items could only be shipped to the English market. Therefore, all goods headed to the colonies in America had to be first unloaded in England, in the process paying customs duties that pushed up prices on major staple crops of the colonies such as tobacco, sugar, and dyestuffs. These Acts created a near monopoly on British shipping and trade. It also made it difficult for colonists to receive certain luxury items such as Portuguese salt, Irish and Scottish linens, and wines from Madeira and the Azores. However, in response smugglers, black marketeers, and pirates were only too happy to challenge the English embargo and supply the goods.

The North American colonies proved to be the greatest markets for pirate plunder in the seventeenth century. Pirates engaged in a lucrative commerce with New York City and other colonial ports, and by the 1680s, pirates were familiar visitors along the Eastern coast, with their visits eagerly awaited for by merchants. New England merchants felt especially exploited by English trade rules. Forced to trade with the English at exorbitant fixed rates by its merchants prohibited American businessmen from making much profit on what had been traditionally lucrative trade goods (before the Navigation Acts). Some of America's leading families consorted with pirates as fences for pirate booty. The unwillingness of American colonists and officials to obey the Navigation Acts was not unlike the sporadic and ineffective enforcement of Prohibition laws in the 1920s. Colonists were willing to follow the letter of the law for traditional crimes such as treason, murder, and robbery, but when it came to free trade, they essentially nullified the law by creating organized smuggling ventures. New England merchants, in particular, routinely participated in trade with non-English pirates. By the Revolutionary era of the mid-1700s, the colonies were home to a number of clandestine economies, thanks to smuggling rings and black markets, which had become a way of life in America. By most accounts, New England merchants became prosperous, some making considerable fortunes smuggling Dutch linens and French brandies. According to Neville Williams, in order to avoid import taxes, British colonial businessmen probably smuggled 2 million gallons of illegal molasses into port cities between 1738 and 1750. Others have suggested that perhaps five-sixths of the tea consumed in the colonies had been smuggled. Among the parallels with the Prohibition era of the 1920s was the fact that there were not enough agents to enforce the Navigation Acts and customs officials were easily corrupted.

Under early English common law, **piracy** committed by English subjects was considered tantamount to treason, the highest felony of the era. Statutes were introduced that added trading with pirates or providing them armaments to the list of treasonous acts. The prominent English jurist William Blackstone opined that the crime of piracy, or trading with known pirates was equivalent to "robbery and depredations upon the high seas."[27] In like terms, Sir Edward Coke described pirates as enemies of mankind who "renounced all the benefits of society and government" when they came before the justice system. From the medieval era on, England hanged pirates at specific gallows erected along the Thames River.

Massachusetts lobbied colonial officials for permission to adopt England's punitive anti-piracy laws. By the end of the seventeenth century, pirates were punished as if they had committed only larceny and were only required to pay triple the damages of stolen goods. As piracy continued to flourish dozens of pirates were marched to the gallows in the coastal colonies. In just one month, close to fifty were hanged in Virginia and South Carolina.

There are a number of accounts of pirate hangings in the American colonies during the eighteenth century. The procedures for execution followed the English example, with the prisoner being led down the street in front of rubbernecking crowds. It was common for the spectators to scream crude salutations at the pirate, such as "Ye be doing the sheriff's dance!" or "You'll piss when you can't whistle!" The convict would usually have his elbows lashed together behind him, rather than his hands. Executioners recognized with experience that dying men tied only at the wrists were capable of rolling their hands free of restraints as they struggled for life. The feet were rarely tied, since this would rob the gleeful crowds who eagerly anticipated the "dance upon the air." By some accounts, executioners might purposely leave the hanging ropes too short so that the neck would not be broken and bring too quick a quick death.[28]

No form of international organized crime in the modern world illustrates the continuum of organized crime past and present like the ancient crime of sea piracy. By the Middle Ages, piracy was already an ancient occupation practiced by such groups as the Phoenicians and the Vikings.

Some of the earliest historians, such as Herodotus and Thucydides, were among the first to chronicle the exploits of pirates. More than two millennia ago, the Roman historian Dio Cassius noted that "there was never a time when piracy was not practiced. Nor may it cease as long as the nature of mankind remained the same."[29] With the commercial expansion of the sixteenth and seventeenth centuries, pirates expanded their routes from the Old World to the Americas.

Recent scholars such as Marcus Rediker suggest that the so-called "Golden Age" of piracy that lasted between 1650 and 1730 can be divided up into three distinct generations. It was the last phase between 1716 and 1726 (the most heavily documented era) that was considered the most successful era and was dominated by larger-than-life characters such as Bartholomew Roberts and Edward Teach. It was this era that has inspired most of the familiar images of popular culture, such as Long John Silver and *Treasure Island*, the sinister Blackbeard, and the Jolly Roger flag featuring a skull and crossbones.

Modern piracy tends to take place in regions with weak or failed governments and large numbers of impoverished people. Early in the twenty-first century, Somalia was the epicenter for pirate activity but has been replaced in recent years by the 900-kilometer long Strait of Malacca between Indonesia and Malaysia.[30] Today's pirates are likely to possess a combination of ancient sailing skills along with the latest in high-tech equipment, including speedboats, machine guns, and radio intercept technology capable of identifying and locating large, poorly defended vessels bearing vital raw materials such as oil and weapons. However, most evidence asserts that today's pirates are rather low-tech and are more likely to be armed with guns or knives. In any case, maritime piracy has increased at alarming rate in the twenty-first century.

Pennsylvania and the Mid-Atlantic colonies

Dutch and Swedish colonists had established settlements along the Delaware River decades before **William Penn** was granted his proprietary charter by King Charles II in 1681. The founder of Pennsylvania and a lifelong crusader for religious and civil liberty, Penn was expelled from Oxford University in his youth for his controversial and nonconforming religious views. Hoping to rid his son of his Puritan convictions, his father, an admiral in the British navy, sent him on a tour of Europe. However, this ploy backfired when, in 1667, Penn converted to Quakerism, an equally nonconformist sect, leading to a short prison sentence in England's infamous Tower of London.

What set the Quakers apart from the Puritans was their rejection of the Calvinist belief in predestination and their emphasis on the inner spirit. As a consequence of these beliefs, ministers were no longer necessary, leading Puritans to view these meetings of "Friends" as anarchy. The Quakers were a radical sect that emerged in England in the 1640s and 1650s as the Society of Friends. In their earlier days, they developed a reputation for defiance – refusing to swear oaths or remove their hats in front of magistrates and even going as far as denouncing Anglican ministers in church. Presaging their participation in nineteenth-century women's rights and antislavery reform movements, from the start, the Quakers were vehemently opposed to war and contended that women had the right to speak at public meetings.

On his father's death, Penn not only inherited the family fortune but also became the proprietor of Pennsylvania. This land had been given to Penn's father by the king as repayment for an outstanding loan to Charles II. Persecuted at home, the young Penn set about creating his vision of an ideal Christian commonwealth on the banks of the Delaware River.

The lawgivers

In December 1682, the colony's first assembly, dominated by Quakers, adopted Penn's *Frame of Government*, also known as "The Great Law or Body of Laws," the first criminal code of Pennsylvania, providing the blueprint for the colony. It laid out a political structure that was composed of a governor, council, and assembly elected by freeholders. It also laid the groundwork for trial by jury, free elections, and religious liberty. Penn came as close as anyone to allowing religious freedom in the colonies, although he excluded atheists and nonbelievers from his colony and barred non-Christians from holding office. From the start, Penn was imbued with a strong sense of English liberties. Within the first five years of his arrival, he ordered the entire text of the Magna Carta to be reprinted in Philadelphia.

The Quakers embraced an austere and ascetic mode of life once they settled in the New World. Prior to the eighteenth century, the Quakers were considerably more humane in the punishment of crime than either England or New England. Nowhere was this truer than in the use of the death penalty. At a time when Massachusetts inflicted capital punishment for offenses including adultery, man stealing, bestiality, blasphemy, burglary, cursing or smiting a parent, bearing false witness, arson, poisoning, and rape, Pennsylvania demanded death only for traitors and murderers. When Pennsylvania became a royal colony in 1718, and with Anglicans now dominating the legislature, a more severe penal code was introduced in order to bring the laws into conformity with England's Bloody Code.

Quaker punishments for deviant behavior did not range widely and were inclined to favor forfeiture of property, fines, imprisonment, and shaming over other methods. Their use of a variety of prison sentences no doubt demonstrates the influence of Enlightenment philosophy and foreshadows the birth of the penitentiary in the Quaker colony. For indiscretions such as incest and sodomy, individuals forfeited a large percentage of their estate and spent six months to one year of imprisonment at hard labor. A second offense could earn the culprit life in prison. Gambling, swearing, cursing, and drunkenness could earn malefactors a five-shilling fine or five days of imprisonment at hard labor on a bread-and-water diet. Prostitution, **bigamy**, and adultery were treated more seriously, but much less severely than in Massachusetts. Sanctions included public whippings and up to a year of imprisonment at hard labor and, for repeated offenses, life imprisonment.

Crime and punishment in Quaker Pennsylvania

Crime trends in Pennsylvania offer numerous contrasts with other British colonies. In New England, property crimes outnumbered personal crimes, and in Virginia, the reverse was true. But in Pennsylvania, these crimes tended to be distributed rather evenly among the classes. Prior to the mid-1750s, most crimes in the Quaker colony were crimes against authority, such as confronting peace officers on duty. Individuals arrested for civic disorder or physical violence were punished severely, particularly in rape cases. One individual, facing the shame and pain of a public whipping for rape, slit his own throat before the sentence could be carried out.

Paralleling the waning power of the Quakers in the Pennsylvania legislature in the eighteenth century was the increase in the number of capital crimes under more secular rule. But Pennsylvania's number of capital crimes always remained small in comparison to the other colonies. The Quaker codes were changed and became harsher by the English influence beginning in 1718. Whipping remained in fashion in Pennsylvania throughout the eighteenth century. Neighboring Delaware, heavily influenced by early Quaker code, even had a name for its permutation of this device known as "**Red Hannah**." An anachronism, Delaware authorities continued to whip prisoners into the 1940s.[31]

The development of prison reform in America can be traced back to William Penn's code. Penn and his Quaker contemporaries were adamantly opposed to the severe physical penalties exacted in England and considered imprisonment the best alternative. As previously mentioned, except for murder and treason, imprisonment at hard labor was often prescribed for crimes that typically demanded bloody retribution in the other colonies. Penn's system was the first in the colonies to put inmates to hard labor to compensate for a crime as well as to rehabilitate. Penn added other measures in an attempt to reform lawbreakers, including making all prisoners eligible for bail and allowing the wrongfully imprisoned to sue for damages. Instead of jails funded by jailers charging prisoners room and board, inmates in Pennsylvania were given free food and boarding.

Penn, a proponent of the Enlightenment philosophy that the punishment should fit the crime, enacted measures for penal reform that were considered the most humane in colonial America. In contrast to British jails, which consisted of dungeons or were often run by venal private contractors, Penn's prisons were adequately built and provided for by the government. However, like the other reforms introduced in the Quaker colony, they would endure only as long as the Quakers were in the majority. It was not long before the more tolerant Quakers were outnumbered by Anglican settlers who introduced more harsh measures based on English procedures. Penn's efforts established a tradition of institutional reform that would be reintroduced following the American Revolution.

Colonial law enforcement

Like its precursors in Europe, early American law enforcement was the bailiwick of unskilled amateurs. There was little innovation in the early colonies, with most preferring what they were familiar with: some incarnation of the English parish constable and the county sheriff. Between 1608 and the end of the revolution, most American sheriffs and constables were appointed by colonial governors and performed the same tasks as their English counterparts. In Maryland's Chesapeake settlements, the sheriff was expected not only to maintain order but also to collect taxes and fees, of which he was entitled to 10 percent.

In small-town New England, local church elders and settlement laws filled the void in law enforcement by regulating the behavior of new arrivals, townspeople, and land dealings of the citizenry. There was no clear demarcation between amateur and professional law enforcement in the colonial world. The system hinged on laypeople and on traditional institutions, including the hue and cry, sheriff, constable, night watch, magistrate, and coroner.

In New England, as need arose for peacekeepers outside the church setting, village constables were selected locally to serve processes and warrants, make arrests, collect taxes, and be on the lookout for unsavory new arrivals lurking in the community. Never wavering from the Puritan ethos, the constable was also required to visit each household in the township at least four times a year to remind the inhabitants of the Sabbath laws. When more serious situations arose, the constable could depend on his neighbors to come to his aid, harking back to the centuries-old hue and cry. According to the evidence, the system worked well in seventeenth-century Massachusetts, where the murder rate was less than half that of Maryland and Virginia, known as the Chesapeake colonies.

While the town constables were the most popular peace officers in New England, in Virginia, which was more sparsely populated, the sheriff played a more significant role. According to early custom, sheriffs were expected to reside in the county they served in and were to be members of the landowning gentry. Sheriffs were expected to fulfill a wide assortment of services, ranging from organizing courts and calling elections to running the jail and keeping county records. But they could not possibly meet their obligations without the assistance of a coterie of undersheriffs, deputies, jailers, county clerks, and whippers. Ever the most odious duties, hangmen and mutilators were often selected from the ranks of the criminal element.

In contrast to the gentry-controlled sheriff of the South and the theocratically appointed constables of New England, Pennsylvanians used a more complex method for selecting county sheriffs. Counties were required to conduct an election with multiple candidates. The names of the two men receiving the most votes would be forwarded to the governor, who would then pick one as sheriff. Sheriffs in Pennsylvania served one-year stints and were limited to three consecutive terms.

In the more urban reaches of Boston, New York, and Philadelphia, the British **night watch** system was adopted to complement the duties of the constable. During the 1630s, the dim outlines of American policing were beginning to take shape in Massachusetts. The towns were policed by the familiar English amateurs: the constable and the night watchman. In 1631, a night watch was established in Boston, the first in America. The Boston night watch was composed of six men and an officer and would form at sunset in preparation for the tasks ahead. Their duties included walking rounds crying the time of night and the state of the weather "in a moderate tone."[32] In 1634, Joshua Pratt was appointed constable of Plymouth. His duties included serving as jailer, executing punishments, sealer of weights and measures, and surveyor of lands. One problem that would remain consistent into the nineteenth century was watchmen "**cooping**" (or sleeping on duty) and drinking on the job.

The Dutch colonists of New Amsterdam became familiar with the *schout* and rattle **watch** in the 1650s.[33] The *schout fiscal* was one of the earliest peace officers in America, executing his duties in the Dutch colony of New Netherland as early as the 1620s. Officers were appointed by the colonial council in New Amsterdam, the progenitor of New York City. Their duties were typically equivalent to those of the sheriff. They were expected to enforce the law and serve court orders. Although they were not considered salaried officials, they were compensated from court fees. The early *schout* had little autonomy and was unable to pursue any action without the direction of colonial directors. By the 1650s, members of the *schout* were considered the most important police functionaries in the colony and, in most criminal cases, were responsible for county prosecution. In 1651, the Dutch colony introduced the law enforcement position of *ratel wacht*, or rattle watch, so named for the rattles used as signal mechanisms. This early alarm system was used to summon help when threatened by malefactors in the era before professional police training. By 1658, the colony boasted a paid rattle watch of eight men who functioned as night watchmen from 9 o'clock at night until sunrise. All male residents were expected to serve stints in this position and were paid the equivalent of fifty cents per night from a tax paid by property owners. When the English took over the colony and renamed New Amsterdam the more familiar New York, they introduced a new system composed of watchmen supervised by constables elected from wards and headed by a high constable.

New Amsterdam passed the first traffic law in the New World on June 27, 1652. It was designed to prevent accidents and expected all drivers and conductors to walk with their wagons, carts, and sleighs within city limits, under threat of fines and damages. After the Dutch colony passed to the English one of its earliest traffic regulations, passed in 1791, requested "Ladies and Gentlemen" to order their coachmen to conduct their carriages in the direction of the East River following performances at the John Street Theater. The New York City Police Department did not introduce its first unit specifically designed to enforce traffic regulations until 1860.

In 1700, the Philadelphia provincial council appointed a watchman, and a system was established by which all citizens, typically the heads of households, were obligated to take turns in the duty of watch and ward. By the early eighteenth century, this institution was established in most existing towns and cities.

For the next 200 years, little would change in American policing, in part because American citizens saw a standing police force as a reminder of the oppression and exploitation that they had left behind in Europe. The Dutch in New York City (1648) and the English in Boston (1663) experimented with a paid watch system but found it too expensive and abandoned it in favor of the amateur approach.

The evolution of the southern **slave patrols** in the early 1700s marked the first real advances in American policing. Slave patrolling originated not in the American colonies but in the Caribbean, where French, Spanish, Portuguese, and English slaveholders faced the same challenges as slave-owning American colonists as early as the sixteenth century. According to historian Sally E. Hadden, "The **Barbadian slave code of 1661** provided the model for several other English slaveholding colonies."[34] Many Barbadian planters would bring this code with them to South Carolina in the 1670s, where they exerted a major influence in designing the first laws governing slave law enforcement in America.

The ancient system of hue and cry was poorly suited for sparsely populated parts of Virginia. With black slavery coming to dominate southern society, the southern colonies introduced slave codes beginning with South Carolina's in 1712. The slave codes provided for the creation of brutal slave patrols, charged with protecting the plantations and punishing those responsible for serious crimes. Virginia introduced a slave patrol in 1727 in the wake of a 1721 slave revolt. Slave patrols were implemented as a proactive response to the insurrectionists. Rather than allowing bands of slaves to plot when they gathered during holidays, patrollers were ordered to break up the meetings and disperse the slaves.

While they varied in structure, many slave patrols consisted of three to five armed men on horseback who covered a prescribed beat of almost fifteen square miles. However, in South Carolina, regulations prohibited a beat from being larger than a few square miles. While making their rounds, the slave patrols were responsible for maintaining discipline, apprehending runaway slaves, and preventing slave uprisings. Routinely invading slave quarters at night and whipping and terrorizing those caught without passes after curfew, over time slave patrols became a feared presence among the black population.

Slave patrols were authorized to enforce laws against black literacy, trade, and gambling. Until recently, most historians have accepted the notion that while all white males were expected to participate in patrol service, most planters paid for substitutes, who were typically landless poor whites. However, recent research by Sally E. Hadden suggests that, in the first decades of the eighteenth century, slave patrols "frequently included men of superior social status, not just poor slaveless whites." One explanation for this was that wealthy whites lobbied for slave patrols in order to avoid serving in the militia.[35] In 1721, this practice was abolished. Despite friction between the white underclass and the owners of large plantations who controlled the best lands, the slaves became the target of the slave patrols. In response, slave communities resisted by setting up warning systems and sometimes ambushing the riders.

One of the most important American criminal justice modifications in the colonies was the "**district attorney**." There was no such analogue in England, where people were expected to prosecute criminals at their own expense, making it cost prohibitive for most farmers and small merchants. The district attorney, or county attorney, evolved as a public prosecutor in charge of prosecution in the colonies, an official paid by the government to prosecute crimes on behalf of the citizenry.

Colonial corrections

The Massachusetts Bay Colony built its first prison in Boston in 1636, the only one the colony would have for eighteen years. More jails were constructed as the population expanded into the wilderness. By the mid-1770s, the era of the American Revolution, Massachusetts was divided into twelve counties, with each required to maintain its own jail. Early jails functioned as holding facilities for debtors and others delinquent in paying taxes and fines. Initially, jails were considered a method of coercion to make someone pay rather than as a criminal sanction. Jails served as holding facilities for a variety of prisoners, including Indians and soldiers (both British and French) and Quaker, Jesuit, and Loyalist political prisoners. Serving mostly in a custodial capacity, jails were also used for presentence detention for those awaiting trial or punishment. Although jails were considered a last resort, in some cases, they performed penal functions in the late colonial period. Incarceration was an expensive investment and a loss of industrious labor, so it rarely exceeded twenty-four hours. Forgers convicted after 1692 faced the loss of an ear and imprisonment without bail for one year. Prior to 1750, incarceration by statute was rare, with mutilation and other punishments more common.

Other New England colonies developed various versions of the pre-Enlightenment prison. Connecticut confined prisoners in a copper mine named Newgate Prison, while Maine relied on small earth pits that barely measured nine and a half by four and a half by ten feet deep. Incarceration did not become an important criminal sanction until the Enlightenment of the eighteenth century.

Capital punishment

It has been several generations since the last person was executed in New England, and at this writing, only New Hampshire has prisoners actually sitting on death row. Recent attempts by Massachusetts to return the death penalty were narrowly defeated. However, for close to 400 years, capital punishment has been a transcendent feature of American criminal justice.

According to the *Body of Liberties*, capital punishment was the sanction for idolatry, witchcraft, blasphemy, murder, manslaughter, poisoning, bestiality, sodomy, adultery, kidnapping, and treason but not for property crimes. Contrary to English criminal practice, blasphemy, adultery, and other moral offenses became capital crimes in order to conform with Mosaic Law. By the eighteenth century, less moral offenses were capital crimes, as the tendency was to less vigorously enforce the death penalty. In reality, a shortage of population and other exigencies created a system in which the statutes were rarely enforced to the letter of the law. By English standards, the colonies were far from bloody. However, there were cases in which colonial law was more severe. Adultery did not demand death in England but was considered a capital crime in Massachusetts, though it was rarely carried out. After the mid-seventeenth century, no one was executed for adultery.

In contrast to Puritan New England, executions were a common occurrence in Virginia, where hundreds of crimes demanded the death penalty by the mid-1700s. According to one survey of the 164 people convicted of capital crimes between 1737 and 1772, 125 were executed without benefit of clergy. Like most English colonies, hanging was the standard method of execution. The gallows were often constructed at the scene of the crime, and the condemned individual was brought to the site in a cart. Usually surrounded by a huge crowd, the only formality was to allow the convicted to say his last words and then go to his death. Standing in the back of a cart, a noose was placed around his neck. To complete the ghastly scene, the cart was driven forward, leaving the individual to grotesquely twist in the wind as he strangled to death. It was not uncommon for bystanders to grab the legs of the culprit to facilitate an end to the macabre ceremony. As a denouement to this chain of events, the body was often given to physicians for dissection and research or was left in a public place as a warning to others. Finally, at least in the colony of Virginia, the felon's property was forfeited to the Crown.

Today the death penalty is most often used in the South; the same was true in the colonial era, when the burden was carried mostly by African slaves and indentured servants. Between 1706 and 1784, some 555 slaves, more than any northern colony, were sentenced to death in Virginia. Since the death penalty was reinstated in 1976, Virginia is second only to Texas in the number of executions carried out in America.

Colonial violence

In the 1960s, the black militant activist H. Rap Brown proclaimed that "violence is as American as cherry pie."[36] He had learned his history lessons well, for since America's earliest days the land was locked in intermittent conflicts between white colonists and indigenous cultures, between blacks and whites, and between the various religious denominations. No colony had a monopoly on violence in the colonial era. Homicide historian Randolph Roth asserted that throughout most of the 1600s the "murder rate among unrelated adults in the North American colonies surpassed the worst rates the United States experienced in the twentieth century."[37] Slave insurrections and accompanying mass executions occurred both north and south. In fact, the first mass execution of blacks occurred in New York in 1712 after a group of African slaves set buildings on fire and killed from ambush nine white colonists who responded to the conflagration. As a result, fourteen slaves went to the gallows, and five others were executed using more grisly methods. Twenty-nine years later, almost three dozen men, black and white, were charged with conspiring to torch the city. Subsequent trials led to the immolation of thirteen African Americans at the stake and the hanging of two white men and two white women. Dozens more were banished from the city for their unruly behavior.

Beginning in the eighteenth century, rioting plagued the burgeoning cities of the Eastern Seaboard. Political unrest shaped American institutions and eventually stimulated the creation of modern policing. No day occasioned unrest more than election days in Philadelphia, Boston, Baltimore, and wherever antagonistic constituents were in great numbers.

Before the silent ballot and the private voting box, opposing factions in a political contest used violence to prevent the other side from voting.

Another cause for rioting was impressment, the traditional method for keeping the British navy well stocked with young men. "Press gangs" were used to force citizens into service. Boston rioting broke out over impressment as sympathetic townsfolk violently resisted in 1747. Although the citizens resisted successfully this time, impressment continued to be an issue until after the War of 1812. In the decade leading up to the American Revolution, riots became more common. According to historian Richard Maxwell Brown, between 1641 and 1759, there were at least forty-one riots, including riots over land disputes, anti-customs riots, jailbreak riots, food riots, and even fish-dam riots. Between 1645 and 1769, there were eighteen insurgent movements by white colonists aimed at overthrowing colonial governments, the best known being Bacon's Rebellion (1676).

During the first decades of colonial America, there was little violent crime between the white colonists. What violence that did take place usually occurred in local taverns or along desolate trails. Most homicides took place between whites and the indigenous cultures. Any Indian accused of killing a white was expected to face a white court. However, if the circumstances were reversed, the whites occasionally paid compensation but were never turned over to the Indian justice system. Though subject to British law, Indians were rarely accorded the rights of white British citizens.

While hanging enjoyed popularity in America from the colonial era to the nineteenth century, colonial punishments were less severe than penal punishment in England. As previously noted, when Pennsylvania was ruled by the Quakers, most capital punishment was prohibited. Although the colonial era is best remembered by criminal justicians for the Salem **witchcraft trials**, this was an anomaly. Compared to England, which executed perhaps 30,000 for witchcraft and France 75,000, less than forty were hanged for the offense in colonial America.

Notable trials

Salem witchcraft trials (1692)

The Salem (derived from the Hebrew word *Shalom*, meaning "peace") witchcraft trials in Massachusetts were probably the most famous trials of colonial America. They have inspired books and plays such as Arthur Miller's *The Crucible*, and many parallels have been drawn with the McCarthy hearings of the 1950s (see Chapter 11). But accusations of witchcraft were hardly unique. They were much more common in Europe, where thousands were condemned to death. In New England, in the fifty years leading up to the Salem trials, dozens of people were executed for witchcraft. And after the Salem incident, trials continued to crop up. According to one source, a mob killed a suspected witch outside Philadelphia's Independence Hall as late as 1787 as the U.S. Constitution was being haggled over inside. The victims of witchcraft prosecutions were almost exclusively women, many of them old and destitute, and were perceived as a drain on the community.

Over 90 percent of witchcraft accusations and more than 90 percent of executions occurred in New England colonies where the Puritans dominated.[38] The events surrounding the outbreak of witchcraft in Salem are probably the best documented witch trials in American history. Most accounts of the Salem hysteria begin with the Reverend Samuel Parris' West Indian slave Tituba. Well versed in the superstitions of the Caribbean by the time she arrived in Salem, Tituba regaled young girls during the cloistered winter months with her knowledge of the occult. Tutoring the girls in the finer arts of palmistry, fortune-telling, necromancy, magic, and spiritualism, everything seemed rather innocent at first. Partly out of boredom, the students began to show off to neighbors. In macabre displays, they lurched into spasmodic convulsions, gesturing incoherently, and unleashed unintelligible sounds. It was not long before their sideshows came to the attention of the local arbiters of morality, of which there was a ready supply.

The diagnosis of a village doctor was that they were bewitched, and it was not long before the entire community was alarmed. The young girls continued to draw attention by interrupting church services with incongruous statements that lent credence to the charge of witchcraft; however, they were not punished but rather became objects of pity and compassion. With the assistance of local citizens, authorities embarked on a witch hunt to find the source of the bewitchment. It was not long before the young girls succumbed to pressure to name names, and warrants were served on Tituba, Sarah Good, and Sarah Osborne.[39] What ensued was a spiraling series of accusations against hundreds of persons that culminated in the hanging of nineteen individuals and the imprisonment of hundreds more.

None of the accused women was provided legal representation, and the line of questioning indicates that they were presumed guilty. Even before trial, the three accused women had attracted the community's scrutiny. Tituba, an Indian slave raised in the West Indies and schooled in the healing arts, quickly admitted her guilt and implicated the two Sarahs. The pipe-smoking Good had been deserted by her husband, which caused overwhelming and burdensome poverty. Osborne was earlier censured by her neighbors for buying out the balance of an indentured servant's contract, hiring him, and then marrying him. A subject of envy as a propertied widow, then marrying beneath her station, Osborne was soon bedridden and missed church services regularly – a scandalous situation but one that envious neighbors were happy to point out. Before the year was out, nineteen people would be executed and hundreds imprisoned.

What made the Salem witch trials so unique was the sheer number of people accused and convicted. The court in this case allowed disputed "spectral evidence" (in which witnesses claimed visions of their tormentors) and torture and encouraged the accused to confess, repent, and name names in order to gain freedom. Traditionally, a higher degree of proof was required, and the majority were eventually exonerated.

A number of refuted theories have been advanced to explain the Salem witch hunt of 1692, including mass hysteria and the hallucinogenic effects of ergotism.[40] However, is another, more sinister explanation for what happened at Salem that hinges on complicated social relations in a community in flux. As the community made the transition to a prosperous port town, earlier rivalries between the wealthier merchant class at the center of town and the struggling farmers on the periphery created an atmosphere of tension. The rural faction won a petition to form a new church. However, the faction was not sanctioned by a town charter. This unique but uncertain status, combined with old socioeconomic rivalries, ensured that all the ingredients were in place for a massive outbreak of witchcraft accusations. In the end, what was most unusual about this episode was that most accusers were from the disadvantaged rural faction, which felt left behind in the movement toward a more commercial economy, and that the majority of victims were the more prosperous members of the community.[41]

In 2001, descendants of five of the accused and executed Salem witches petitioned the Massachusetts legislature to declare them innocent. This is just the most recent attempt to clear the names of victims of the "largest witch hunt in American history." The first exonerations occurred as early as 1711, when colonial authorities absolved twenty-one of the twenty-seven (not all had been hanged) who had been convicted after family members presented petitions on their behalf. The other six, who had been hanged, had no survivors in the colony to plead for them, so their convictions stood until 1957, when all were cleared, but only one of them was cleared by name. In the pending measure, the other five women would be mentioned by name and added to the 1957 resolution.

John Peter Zenger (1735)

By most accounts, the printing trade was not much encouraged in colonial America. The colonies had incorporated the common law tradition that made it a crime to criticize someone in power, referred to as "**seditious libel**." Put another way, truth was no defense against being prosecuted for this offense.[42] John Peter Zenger was a German immigrant who arrived in the New York colony in the early 1700s as an indentured servant. Apprenticed to a printer, there was little to suggest that in a matter of years he would be embroiled in one of the most important free speech cases of his era. In 1731, Zenger was working for the *New York Weekly Gazette*. He came to public attention while covering the scandals that followed the election of William Cosby as governor of the New York colony. Zenger sought to capture readership with reports that dozens of Quakers had been illegally disqualified from voting because of their religious beliefs and that Cosby's supporters intimidated voters and had tried to stuff ballot boxes. Apprenticed to a Cosby supporter who refused to print his stories about the governor, Zenger was soon fired. Subsequently, a rival of the governor saw the chance to inflict revenge and set about financing a rival newspaper, hiring Zenger as publisher. The new paper grew in popularity as it chronicled the scandalous behavior of Governor Cosby. Cosby, in turn, ordered four issues of the paper to be condemned and publicly burned by the hangman. It was not long before Zenger himself was arrested and charged with seditious libel. Unable to raise the excessive bail, Zenger languished in jail before obtaining the services of one of the colony's leading lawyers.

The Zenger case filled the New York City courtroom to capacity as the trial got started on August 4, 1735. His attorney argued that for his client to be adjudged guilty, his words must be "false, scandalous, and seditious." The prosecutor responded that it made no difference if the libel was true because "the government is a sacred body and it was a crime to libel it." After several more skirmishes between the attorneys, the jury left the court. Ignoring instructions by Governor Cosby's handpicked judges, the jury came back with a verdict of not guilty on the charge of "publishing seditious libel." An important moment in colonial justice, the Zenger ruling did not immediately establish freedom of the press in the American colonies. No new law was promulgated in respect to seditious libel, but in the aftermath of the case, "prosecutions for seditious libel began to falter with increasing consistency."[43] According to legal scholars, legal precedents change the law, and since these come from judicial opinions that interpret the law, the outcome of the Zenger trial was not the result of a judicial opinion. However, the acquittal indicated that the public was opposed to such prosecutions. Subsequently, the threat of jury nullification would discourage similar prosecutions.

The Zenger acquittal resulted from the independent decision of the jury to ignore the instructions of the judge. Modern legal scholars view the verdict as an example of jury nullification; in other words, the jury refused to enforce the law because they thought the prosecution was unfair. Thus, while the Zenger case did not immediately change the law, it did set an important political precedent for a free press, the right of the people to criticize the government, and the right of a jury to ignore the technical requirements of the law in order to protect a defendant from an overbearing government. Legal scholar Paul Finkelman argues that the "case inspired patriots during the Revolution, supporters of a Bill of Rights during the struggle for ratification of the Constitution, and opponents of the Sedition Act of 1798" and "laid the groundwork for the evolution of the ideology of freedom of the press."[44]

During the proceedings, Zenger was never called as a witness or said a single word, but the judgment spoke volumes. Having spent ten months in jail, the case also illustrated the threat and nature of excessive bail. The Zenger case was not the first in colonial America involving jury independence, but the acquittal went a long way toward establishing a basic right that would be reaffirmed a half century later by the Constitution. One of the main contributors to the drafting of the Constitution, Governor Morris wrote, "The trial of Zenger in 1735 was the germ of American freedom, the morning star of that liberty which subsequently revolutionized America."[45]

Conclusions

The modification of English criminal justice procedures in the New World was the result of numerous abortive attempts to introduce Old World practices to America. By the mid-eighteenth century, the early religious laws of Pennsylvania and New England had been replaced by English legal precedents. Paving the road to revolutionary America, according to the historian David Rothman, "the mother country had stifled the colonists' benevolent instincts, compelling them to emulate the crude customs of the old world. The result was the predominance of archaic and punitive laws that only served to perpetuate crime."[46]

Although colonial criminal law was influenced by English criminal law, it was rarely as severe. Prior to the outbreak of the American Revolution, a distinctly American approach to criminal justice had emerged. American criminal justice was becoming more democratic than the English system and moving toward more humane and rational punishments as the number of capital crimes was reduced and defendants were provided legal rights.

Southern criminal codes more closely followed English antecedents than the northern colonies. In the South, "concern for status of offender and victim more closely paralleled the mother country's."[47]

The Puritans played a critical role in the shaping of American values. Although they have frequently been lambasted for their religious zeal and caricatured as dour prudes, recent research suggests that almost the opposite was true. Although they harshly punished fornicators and adulterers, it was because so much value was placed on the institution of marriage and the family. Perhaps this explains their low rates of premarital pregnancy compared to those of the more secularized southern colonies. Because the Puritans frowned on public drunkenness does not mean that they abstained from alcohol themselves. The Puritans left a legacy of their work ethic and moral sensibility that became the foundation of America's sense of mission. Rejecting the idea of church courts, the Puritans were committed to the separation of church and state.

At the beginning of the eighteenth century, colonial criminal law began to more closely resemble English criminal law. Concerns about labor scarcity compelled earlier lawmakers to refrain from more punitive punishments since the contributions of each settler were needed in the New World. With plenty of labor by the 1700s, there was more need for order than leniency. Legal scholars view this period as "an end of an era of leniency in punishment of crimes against property."[48]

By the 1750s, colonial cities were already teeming with gangs of thieves, robbers, and cutpurses. Ordinary crimes against property flourished. Without a professional police force, concern for crime was on the rise. For almost 150 years, the night watchman and constables were the sole protection in urban areas. While crime was much higher in London than in Philadelphia, it was only because of higher population density. Jails existed, but the concept of the penitentiary was still on the horizon. While punishment was less punitive in the New World, people still hanged for crimes ranging from murder, piracy, and arson to repeated acts of robbery. Execution day became a spectacle as crowds gathered around the gallows to listen to a felon's final words and a minister's sermon.

Point – counterpoint

Salem witchcraft trials (1692)

With few methods to ascertain guilt or innocence the Puritans of the Massachusetts Colony relied on time-tested procedures not far removed from the ordeals of the Middle Ages. In the following passages, Increase Mather (1639–1723), a prominent Puritan minister and leader supports certain grounds for convicting individuals of witchcraft. Arguing against the tests for witchcraft is Thomas Brattle (1658–1713). An opponent of the Puritan theocracy, Brattle was born into a wealthy Boston family, graduated from Harvard, and won distinction as a mathematician and astronomer.

Source: Increase Mather, *Cases of Conscience Concerning Evil Spirits Personating Men* in Cotton Mather, *The Wonders of the Invisible World* (London, 1862), pp. 277–284; Thomas Brattle, "Letter, 1692," in G. L. Burr, ed., *Narratives of the Witchcraft Cases 1648–1706*, New York, 1914., 170–190

As to the method which the Salem justices do take in their examinations, it is truly this. A warrant being issued out to apprehend the persons that are charged and complained of by the afflicted children, . . . said persons are brought before the justices (the afflicted being present). The justices ask the apprehended why they afflict those poor children; to which the apprehended answer, they do not afflict them. The justices order the apprehended to look upon the said children, which accordingly they do; and at the time of that look . . . the afflicted are cast into a fit. The apprehended are then blinded, and ordered to touch the afflicted; and at that touch, . . . the afflicted ordinarily do come out of their fits. The afflicted persons then declare and affirm, that the apprehended have afflicted them. Upon which the apprehended persons, though of never so good repute, are forthwith committed to prison, on suspicion for witchcraft. . . .

I cannot but condemn this method of the justices, of making this touch of the hand a rule to discover witchcraft; because I am fully persuaded that it is sorcery, and a superstitious method, and that which we have no role for, either from reason or religion. . . . I would fain know of these Salem gentlemen, but as yet could never know, how it comes about, that if these apprehended persons are witches, and, by a look of the eye, do cast the afflicted into their fits by poisoning them, how it comes about I say, that, by a look of their eye, they do not cast others into fits, and poison others by their looks; and in particular, tender, fearful women, who often are beheld by them, and as likely as any in the whole world to receive an ill impression from them. This Salem philosophy, some men may call the new philosophy; but I think it rather deserves the name of Salem superstition and sorcery, and it is not fit to be named in the land of such light as New England is. . . .

But furthermore, I would fain know . . . what can the jury or judges desire more, to convict any man of witchcraft, than a plain demonstration, that the said man is a witch? Now if this look and touch, circumstanced as before, be a plain demonstration, (as their philosophy teaches), what need they seek for further evidences, when, after all, it can be but a demonstration? . . . Yet certain is it, that the reasonable part of the world, when acquainted herewith, will laugh at the demonstration, and conclude that the said Salem gentlemen are actually possessed, at least, with ignorance and folly. . . .

Secondly, with respect to . . . such as confess themselves to be witches, . . . there are now about fifty of them in prison; many of which I have again and again seen and heard; and I cannot but tell you, that my faith is strong concerning them, that they are deluded, imposed upon, and under the influence of some evil spirit; and therefore unfit to be evidences either against themselves, or anyone else. . . .

These confessors . . . do very often contradict themselves, as inconsistently as is usual for any crazed, distempered person to do. . . . Even the judges themselves have, at some times, taken these confessors in flat lies, or contradictions, even in the courts; by reason of which, one would have thought, that the judges would have frowned upon the said confessors, discarded them, and not minded one tittle of any thing that they said. But instead . . . the judges vindicate these confessors, and salve their contradictions, by proclaiming, that the Devil takes away their memory, and imposes on their brain. . . .

In the next place, I proceed to the form of their indictments, and the trials thereupon.

The indictment runs for sorcery and witchcraft, acted upon the body of such an one . . . at such a particular time. . . . Now for the proof of the said sorcery and witchcraft, the prisoner at the bar pleading not guilty.

1   The afflicted persons are brought into court; and after much patience and pains taken with them, do take their oaths, that the prisoner at the bar did afflict them. . . . Often, when the afflicted do mean and intend only the appearance and shape of such an one, (say Goodwife Proctor) yet they positively swear that Goodwife Proctor did afflict them;

and they have been allowed so to do, as though there was no real difference between Goodwife Proctor and the shape of Goodwife Proctor. This . . . may readily prove a stumbling block to the jury, lead them into a very fundamental error. . . .

2   The confessors do declare what they know of the said prisoner; and some of the confessors are allowed to give their oaths; a thing which I believe was never heard of in this world; that such as confess themselves to be witches, to have renounced God and Christ, and all that is sacred, should yet be allowed and ordered to swear by the name of the great God! . . .

3   Whoever can be an evidence against the prisoner at the bar is ordered to come into court. And here it scarce ever fails but that evidences, of one nature and another, are brought in, though, I think, all of them altogether alien to the matter of indictment; for they none of them do respect witchcraft upon the bodies of the afflicted, which is the lone matter of charge in the indictment.

4   They [the accused] are searched by a jury; and as to some of them, the jury brought in, that [on] such or such a place there was a preternatural excrescence. And I wonder what person there is, whether man or woman, of whom it cannot be said but that, in some part of their body or other, there is a preternatural excrescence. The term is a very general and inclusive term. . . .

In short, the prisoner at the bar is indicted for sorcery and witchcraft acted upon the bodies of the afflicted. Now, for the proof of this, I reckon that the only pertinent evidences brought in are the evidences of the said afflicted.

It is true, that over and above the evidences of the afflicted persons, there are many evidences brought in, against the prisoner at the bar: either that he was at a witch meeting, or that he performed things which could not be done by an ordinary natural power; or that she sold butter to a sailor, which proving bad at sea, and the seamen exclaiming against her, she appeared, and soon after there was a storm, or the like. But what if there were ten thousand evidences of this nature; how do they prove the matter of indictment! And if they do not reach the matter of indictment, then I think it is clear, that the prisoner at the bar is brought in guilty, and condemned, merely from the evidences of the afflicted persons. . . .

As to the late executions, I shall only tell you, that in the opinion of many unprejudiced, considerate, and considerable spectators, some of the condemned went out of the world not only with as great protestations, but also with as good shows of innocency, as men could do.

They protested their innocency as in the presence of the great God, whom forthwith they were to appear before. They wished, and declared their wish, that their blood might be the last innocent bloodshed upon that account. With great affection they entreated Mr. C[otton] M[ather] to pray with them. They prayed that God would discover what witchcrafts were among us; they forgave their accusers; they spoke without reflection on jury and judges, for bringing them in guilty, and condemning them. They prayed earnestly for pardon for all other sins, and for an interest in the precious blood of our dear Redeemer; and seemed to be very sincere, upright, and sensible of their circumstances on all accounts. . . .

I cannot but admire that the justices, whom I think to be well-meaning men, should so far give ear to the Devil, as merely upon his authority to issue out their warrants, and apprehend people. Liberty was evermore accounted the great privilege of an Englishman; but certainly, if the Devil will be heard against us, and his testimony taken, to the seizing and apprehending of us, our liberty vanishes, and we are fools if we boast of our liberty.

Now, that the justices have thus far given ear to the Devil I think may be mathematically demonstrated to any man of common sense: And for the demonstration and proof hereof, I desire, only, that these two things may be duly considered, viz.

1 That several persons have been apprehended purely upon the complaints of these afflicted, to whom the afflicted were perfect strangers, and had not the least knowledge of imaginable, before they were apprehended.
2 That the afflicted do own and assert, and the justices do grant, that the Devil does inform and tell the afflicted the names of those persons that are thus unknown unto them. Now these two things being duly considered, I think it will appear evident to anyone, that the Devil's information is the fundamental testimony that is gone upon in the apprehending of the aforesaid people.

If I believe such or such an assertion as comes immediately from the minister of God in the pulpit, because it is the word of the everliving God, I build my faith on God's testimony: and if I practice upon it, this my practice is properly built on the word of God. Even so in the case before us, if I believe the afflicted persons as informed by the Devil, and act thereupon, this my act may properly be said to be grounded upon the testimony or information of the Devil. And now, if things are thus, I think it ought to be for a lamentation to you and me, and all such as would be accounted good Christians. . . .

The chief judge is very zealous in these proceedings, and says, he is very clear as to all that hath as yet been acted by this court, and, as far as ever I could perceive, is very impatient in hearing anything that looks another way. I very highly honor and reverence the wisdom and integrity of the said judge, and hope that this matter shall not diminish my veneration for his honor; however, I cannot but say, my great fear is, that wisdom and counsel are withheld from his honor as to this matter, which yet I look upon not so much as a judgment to his honor as to this poor land.

But although the chief judge, and some of the other judges, be very zealous in these proceedings, yet this you may take for a truth, that there are several about the Bay, men for understanding, judgment, and piety, inferior to few, (if any), in New England that do utterly condemn the said proceedings, and do freely deliver their judgment in the case to be . . . that these methods will utterly rain and undo poor New England. . . . Several of the late justices, viz. Thomas Graves, Esq., N. Byfield, Esq., Francis Foxcroft, Esq., are much dissatisfied; also several of the present justices; and in particular, some of the Boston justices, were resolved rather to throw up their commissions than be active in disturbing the liberty of Their Majesties' subjects, merely on the accusations of these afflicted, possessed children.

Finally; the principal gentlemen in Boston, and thereabout, are generally agreed that irregular and dangerous methods have been taken as to these matters. . . . Nineteen persons have now been executed, and one pressed to death for a mute: seven more are condemned; two of which are reprieved, because they pretend their being with child; one, viz. Mrs. Bradbury of Salisbury, from the intercession of some friends; and two or three more, because they are confessors.

The court is adjourned to the first Tuesday in November, then to be kept at Salem; between this and then will be [the] great assembly [the General Court], and this matter will be a peculiar matter of their agitation. I think it is matter of earnest supplication and prayer to Almighty God, that He would afford His Gracious Presence to the said assembly, and direct them aright in this weighty matter. . . . I am very sensible, that it is irksome and disagreeable to go back, when a man's doing so is an implication that he has been walking in a wrong path. However, nothing is more honorable than, upon due conviction, to retract and undo, so far as may be, what has been amiss and irregular. . . .

Many of these afflicted persons . . . do say . . . that they can see specters when their eyes are shut, as well as when they are open. This one thing I evermore accounted as very observable, and that which might serve as a good key to unlock the nature of these mysterious troubles, if duly improved by us. Can they see specters when their eyes are shut? I am sure they lie, at least speak falsely, if they say so; for the thing, in nature, is an utter impossibility. It is true, they may strongly fancy, or have things represented to their imagination, when their eyes are shut; and I think this is all which ought to be allowed to these blind, nonsensical girls. And if our officers and courts have apprehended, imprisoned, condemned, and executed our guilt-less neighbors, certainly our error is great, and we shall rue it in the conclusion.

There are two or three other things that I have observed in and by these afflicted persons, which make me strongly suspect that the Devil imposes upon their brains, and deludes their fancy and imagination; and that the Devil's book (which they say has been offered them) is a mere fancy of theirs, and no reality; that the witches' meeting, the Devil's bap-tism, and mock sacraments, which they off speak of, are nothing else but the effect of their fancy, depraved, and deluded by the Devil, and not a reality to be regarded or minded by any wise man. And whereas the confessors have owned and asserted the said meetings, the said baptism, and mock sacrament, . . . I am very apt to think, that, did you know the circumstances of the said confessors, you would not be swayed thereby, any otherwise than to be confirmed, that all is perfect devilism, and an hellish design to ruin and destroy this poor land. For whereas there are of the said confessors fifty-five in number, some of them are known to be distracted, crazed women;. . . . Others of them denied their guilt, and maintained their innocency for above eighteen hours, after most violent, distracting and dragooning methods had been used with them, to make them confess. Such methods they were, that more than one of the said confessors did since tell many, with tears in their eyes, that they thought their very lives would have gone out of their bodies; and wished that they might have been cast into the lowest dungeon, rather than be tortured with such repeated buzzings and chuckings and unreasonable urgings as they were treated withal. They soon recanted their confessions, acknowledging, with sorrow and grief, that it was an hour of great temptation with them. . . .

But, finally, as to about thirty of these fifty-five confessors, they are possessed (I reckon) with the Devil, and afflicted as the children are, and therefore not fit to be regarded as to anything they say of themselves or others. . . .

What will be the issue of these troubles, God only knows; I am afraid that his own chil-dren, to afflict and humble them, for some sin they have been guilty of before Him. . . .

This then I declare and testify, that to take away the life of anyone, merely because a specter or devil, in a bewitched or possessed person does accuse them, will bring the guilt of innocent blood on the land. . . . What does such an evidence amount unto more than this: Either such an one did afflict such an one, or the Devil in his likeness, or his eyes were bewitched. . . .

. . . . But then the inquiry is, what is sufficient proof? . . .

A free and voluntary confession of the crime made by the person suspected and accused after examination, is a sufficient ground of conviction. Indeed, if persons are distracted, or under the power of phrenetic melancholy, that alters the case; but the jurors that examine them, and their neighbors that know them, may easily determine that case; or if confession be extorted, the evidence is not so clear and convictive; but if any persons out of remorse of conscience, or from a touch of God in their spirits, confess, and show their deeds . . . nothing can be more clear. . . .

If two credible persons shall affirm upon oath that they have seen the party accused speaking such words, or doing things which none but such as have familiarity with the Devil ever did or can do, that's a sufficient ground for conviction. . . . The Devil never assists men to do supernatural things undesired. When therefore such like things shall be testified against the accused party not by specters which are devils in the shape of persons . . . but by real men or women . . ., it is proof enough that such an one has that conversation and correspondence with the Devil, as that he or she, whoever they be, ought to be exterminated from amongst men. This notwithstanding I will add. It were better that ten suspected witches should escape, than that one innocent person should be condemned. . . . I had rather judge a witch to be an honest woman, than judge an honest woman as a witch.

Key terms

blue laws	Jamestown	Virginia Company
House of Burgesses	martial law	Virginia Slave Code of 1705
Oyer and Terminer	Dale's Laws	*Lawes Divine, Morall, and Martiall*
Pilgrims	Puritans	Mayflower Compact
magistrate	*Body of Liberties*	*Moses His Judicials*
Laws and Liberties of 1648	witchcraft trials	Massachusetts Bay Company
shaming	William Penn	*Frame of Government*
Quakers	banishment	exhibitory punishment
England's Bloody Code	"Red Hannah"	night watch
schout	cooping	Barbadian slave code of 1661
slave patrols	*The Crucible*	Salem witchcraft trials
John Peter Zenger	seditious libel	Navigation Acts
piracy	rattle watch	

Critical thinking questions

1 Compare and contrast the development of criminal justice procedures in the Pennsylvania, Virginia, and Massachusetts colonies.
2 What influence did religion have on the development of colonial law?
3 How did the emergence of slavery influence criminal justice procedures? Which colonies were most influenced?
4 What impact did the acquittal of John Peter Zenger have on American freedoms?
5 Discuss variations of crime and punishment in the different colonies.

6 Why did colonial punishment become more punitive after 1700? Why was it more relaxed in the earlier period?

7 Describe the various characteristics of America's developing criminal justice system in the colonial period (i.e., police, courts, and corrections).

Notes

1 Stuart Banner, *The Death Penalty: An American History*, Cambridge, MA: Harvard University Press, 2003, p. 5.

2 https://sites.google.com/a/ridgefieldps.net/cold-case-classroom-216-unearthed/the-cold-case/the-first-virginia-charter-of-1606?tmpl=%2Fsystem%2Fapp%2Ftemplates%2Fprint%2F&showPrintDialog=1

3 Michael Stephen Hindus, *Prison and Plantation: Crime, Justice, and Authority in Massachusetts and South Carolina, 1767–1878*, Chapel Hill: University of North Carolina Press, 1980, p. 130.

4 Quoted in Hindus, 1980, p. 132.

5 Banner, 2003, p. 8.

6 Ibid., p. 7.

7 Ibid.

8 Ibid.

9 Quoted in Scott Christianson, *With Liberty for Some: 500 Years of Imprisonment in America*, Boston: Northeastern University Press, 1998, p. 7.

10 Richard L. Perry, ed., *Sources of Our Liberties: English and American Documents from Magna Carta to the Bill of Rights*, New York: McGraw-Hill, 1964, p. 60.

11 The one exception to this was the minister, who was not allowed to hold office, appointed or elected, because of the Puritan belief that politics would taint, or corrupt, the minister's soul.

12 Peter Charles Hoffer, *Law and People in Colonial America*, Baltimore: Johns Hopkins University Press, 1992, p. 18.

13 Quoted in Hoffer, 1992, p. 18.

14 Quoted in Kai T. Erikson, *Wayward Puritans: A Study in the Sociology of Deviance*, New York: John Wiley and Sons, 1966, p. 120.

15 Juliet Haines Mofford, *"The Devil Made Me Do It!" Crime and Punishment in Early New England*, Guilford: Pequot Globe Press, 2012, p. 57.

16 Ibid.

17 Richard Godbeer, *Sexual Revolution in Early America*, Baltimore: Johns Hopkins University Press, 2002.

18 Else L. Hambleton, "The Regulation of Sex in Seventeenth-Century Massachusetts," in *Sex and Sexuality in Early America*, ed. Merrill D. Smith, New York: New York University Press, 1998, pp. 97–99.

19 According to David Hackett Fisher, men were treated more harshly in New England, while the reverse was true in the Chesapeake region.

20 Hambleton, 1998.

21 Godbeer, 1998, p. 94.

22 Hambleton, 1998.

23 Hoffer, 1992, p. 19.

24 Ibid., p. 20.

25 Quoted in David Hackett Fisher, *Albion's Seed: Four British Folkways in America*, New York: Oxford University Press, 1989, pp. 141–142.

26 Ibid.

27 William Blackstone, *Commentaries on the Laws of England of Public Wrongs*, Boston: Beacon Press, 1962.

28 Richard Zacks, *The Pirate Hunter: The True Story of Captain Kidd*, New York: Hatchette Books, 2002, p. 265.

29 Naphtali Lewis and Meyer Reinhold, eds. *Roman Civilization, Sourcebook I: The Republic*, New York, Harper Torchbooks, 1966, pp. 32–45.

30 "Malacca Buccaneers," *The Economist*, June 27, 2015, p. 34.

31 Robert Graham Caldwell, *Red Hannah: Delaware's Whipping Post*, Philadelphia: University of Pennsylvania Press, 1947, pp. 69–82.

32 Raymond B. Fosdick, *American Police Systems*, New York: The Century Co., 1921, p. 60.

33 The *schout* watched for infractions of the law, and the rattle watch carried rattles to warn of their approach and functioned as night watchmen.

34 Sally E. Hadden, *Slave Patrols: Law and Violence in Virginia and the Carolinas*, Cambridge, MA: Harvard University Press, 2001, pp. 10–14.

35 Hadden, 2001, p. 21.

36 www.thisdayinquotes.com/2013/07/as-american-as-apple-pie-cherry-pie-and.html.

37 Randolph Roth, *American Homicide*, Cambridge, MA: Harvard University Press, 2009, p. 27.

38 Fisher, 1981, p. 127.

39 More than half of all girls in the Massachusetts Bay Colony were named either Mary, Elizabeth, or Sarah. These names were selected from the Bible because of their moral connotations.

40 Benjamin C. Ray, *Satan and Salem: The Witch-Hunt Crisis of 1692*, Charlottesville: University of Virginia Press, 2017.

41 Paul Boyer and Stephen Nissenbaum, *Salem Possessed: The Social Origins of Witchcraft*, Cambridge, MA: Harvard University Press, 1974; "Free the Salem Five!," *American Heritage*, December 2001.

42 Richard Kluger, *The Trials of Peter Zenger and the Birth of America's Free Press*, New York: W.W. Norton and Company, 2017.

43 Jerald Finney, "Jury Nullification: Article, Brief, and Requested Jury Instruction," July 21, 2013. https://jeraldfinney.com/tag/albert-p-blaustein-robert-l-zangrando/www.oyez.org/cases/1963/39; The principle that truth cannot be considered libel was not fully protected until the case of *New York Times v. Sullivan* (1964), which was related to a full page ad taken in the *New York Times*, accusing Martin Luther King Jr. of perjury as part of campaign to destroy his civil rights credentials; Clay Conrad, *Jury Nullification: The Evolution of a Doctrine*, Durham, NC: Carolina Academic Press, 1998, p. 38.

44 Paul Finkelman, ed., *A Brief Narrative of the Case and Tryal of John Peter Zenger, Printer of the New York Weekly Journal*, St. James: Brandywine Press, 1997, pp. 10–11.

45 Quoted by Douglas Linder, "Famous American Trials: The Trial of John Peter Zenger," http://www.famous-trials.com/zenger/87-home, p. 8.

46 David Rothman, *The Discovery of the Asylum: Social Order and Disorder in the New Republic*, Boston: Little, Brown, 1971, p. 59.

47 Hoffer, 1992, p. 82.

48 Ibid., p. 83.

Sources

Bailey, Frankie Y. and Donna C. Hale. 2004. *Blood on Her Hands: Women Who Murder*. Belmont, CA: Wadsworth Cengage.

Banner, Stuart. 2003. *The Death Penalty: An American History*. Cambridge, MA: Harvard University Press.

Beckman, Gail McKnight, comp. 1976. *The Statutes at Large of Pennsylvania in the Time of William Penn: 1680–1700*. Vol. 1. New York: Vantage Press.

Billias, George Athan, ed. 1965. *Law and Authority in Colonial America*. Barre, MA: Barre Publishers.

Blackstone, William. 1962. *Commentaries on the Laws of England of Public Wrongs*. Boston: Beacon Press.

Blumenthal, Walter Hart. 1962. *Brides from Bridewell: Female Felons Sent to Colonial America*. Rutland, VT: Charles E. Tuttle.

Boyer, Paul and Stephen Nissenbaum. 1974. *Salem Possessed: The Social Origins of Witchcraft*. Cambridge, MA: Harvard University Press.

Burford, Ephraim John and Sandra Shulman. 1992. *Of Bridles & Burnings: The Punishment of Women*. New York: St. Martin's Press.

Caldwell, Robert Graham. 1947. *Red Hannah: Delaware's Whipping Post*. Philadelphia: University of Pennsylvania Press.

Christianson, Scott. 1998. *With Liberty for Some: 500 Years of Imprisonment in America*. Boston: Northeastern University Press.

Conrad, Clay. 1998. *Jury Nullification: The Evolution of a Doctrine*. Durham, NC: Carolina Academic Press.

Dow, George Francis. 1988. *Everyday Life in the Massachusetts Bay Colony*. New York: Dover Publications.

The Economist. 2008. "Ahoy There." November 11, p. 60.

———. 2015. "Malacca Buccaneers." June 27, p. 34.

Erikson, Kai T. 1966. *Wayward Puritans: A Study in the Sociology of Deviance*. New York: John Wiley and Sons.

Faith, Karlene. 1993. *Unruly Women*. Vancouver: Press Gang Publishers.

Finkelman, Paul, ed. 1997. *A Brief Narrative of the Case and Tryal of John Peter Zenger, Printer of the New York Weekly Journal*. St. James, NY: Brandywine Press.

Fisher, David Hackett. 1989. *Albion's Seed: Four British Folkways in America*. New York: Oxford University Press.

"Free the Salem Five!" 2001. *American Heritage*, December, p. 15.

Friedman, Lawrence M. 1973. *A History of American Law*. New York: Simon and Schuster.

———. 1993. *Crime and Punishment in American History*. New York: Basic Books, 1993, p. 41.

Godbeer, Richard. 2002. *Sexual Revolution in Early America*. Baltimore: Johns Hopkins University Press.

Greenberg, Douglas. 1982. "Crime, Law Enforcement and Social Control in Colonial America." *American Journal of Legal History*, 26(October):293–325.

Hadden, Sally E. 2001. *Slave Patrols: Law and Violence in Virginia and the Carolinas*. Cambridge, MA: Harvard University Press.

Hall, Kermit L. 1989. *The Magic Mirror: Law in American History*. New York: Oxford University Press.

Hambleton, Else L. 1998. "The Regulation of Sex in Seventeenth-Century Massachusetts: The Quarterly Court of Essex County vs. Priscilla and Mr. Samuel Appleton." In *Sex and Sexuality in Early America*, ed. Merrill D. Smith, pp. 89–115. New York: New York University Press.

Hindus, Michael Stephen. 1980. *Prison and Plantation: Crime, Justice, and Authority in Massachusetts and South Carolina, 1767–1878*. Chapel Hill: University of North Carolina Press.

Hoffer, Peter Charles. 1992. *Law and People in Colonial America*. Baltimore: Johns Hopkins University Press.

Hoffer, Peter Charles and Natalie E. H Hull. 1984. *Murdering Mothers: Infanticide in England and New England, 1558–1803*. New York: New York University Press.

Jones, Ann. 1981. *Women Who Kill*. New York: Fawcett Columbine.

Kamensky, Jane. 1997. *Governing the Tongue: The Politics of Speech in Early New England*. New York: Oxford University Press.

Kluger, Richard. 2017. *The Trials of Peter Zenger and the Birth of America's Free Press*. New York: W.W. Norton and Company.

Konig, David Thomas. 1979. *Law and Society in Puritan Massachusetts: Essex County, 1629–1692*. Chapel Hill: University of North Carolina Press.

Little, Ann M. 1999. "'Shee Would Bump His Mouldy Britch': Authority, Masculinity, and the Harried Husbands of New Haven Colony, 1638–1670." In *Lethal Imagination: Violence and Brutality in American History*, ed. Michael Bellesiles, pp. 43–66. New York: New York University Press.

McManus, Edgar J. 1993. *Law and Liberty in Early New England: Criminal Justice and Due Process, 1620–1692*. Amherst: University of Massachusetts Press.

Miller, Helen Hill. 1965. *The Case for Liberty*. Chapel Hill: University of North Carolina Press.

Mofford, Juliet Haines. 2012. *"The Devil Made Me Do It!": Crime and Punishment in Early New England*. Guildford, CT: Globe Pequot Press.

Pagan, John Ruston. 2003. *Anne Orthwood's Bastard: Sex and Law in Early Virginias*. New York: Oxford University Press.

Perry, Richard L., ed. 1964. *Sources of Our Liberties: English and American Documents from Magna Carta to the Bill of Rights*. New York: McGraw-Hill.

Powers, Edwin. 1966. *Crime and Punishment in Early Massachusetts, 1620–1692: A Documentary History*. Boston: Beacon Press.

Ray, Benjamin C. 2017. *Satan and Salem: The Witch-Hunt Crisis of 1692*. Charlottesville: University of Virginia Press.

Rediker, Marcus. 2004. *Villains of All Nations: Atlantic Pirates in the Golden Age*. Boston: Beacon Press.

Reis, Elizabeth. 1997. *Damned Women: Sinners and Witches in Puritan New England*. Ithaca, NY: Cornell University Press.

Roth, Mitchel P. 2001. *Historical Dictionary of Law Enforcement*. Westport, CT: Greenwood Press.

Roth, Randolph. 2009. *American Homicide*. Cambridge, MA: Harvard University Press.

Rothman, David. 1971. *The Discovery of the Asylum: Social Order and Disorder in the New Republic*. Boston: Little, Brown and Company.

Schiff, Stacy. 2015. *The Witches: Salem, 1692: A History*. London: Weidenfeld and Nicolson.

Semmes, Raphael. 1938. *Crime and Punishment in Early Maryland*. Baltimore: Johns Hopkins University Press.

Smith, Merril D., ed. 1998. *Sex and Sexuality in Early America*. New York: New York University Press.

Webb, Jim. 2004. *Born Fighting: How the Scots-Irish Shaped America*. New York: Broadway.

Williams, Daniel E. 1993. *Pillars of Salt: An Anthology of Early American Criminal Narratives*. Madison: Madison House.

Williams, Neville. 1961. *Contraband Cargoes: Seven Centuries of Smuggling*. Brooklyn, NY: Shoe String Press, Inc.

Zacks, Richard. 2002. *The Pirate Hunter: The True Story of Captain Kidd*. New York: Hatchette Books.

CHAPTER FOUR

Crime and criminal justice in revolutionary times (1740 – 1797)

Learning objectives

After reading this chapter students should understand and be able to discuss:

- How American law enforcement was influenced by British traditions
- The impact of religion on early American criminal justice
- Which amendments in the Bill of Rights had ramifications for the fledgling criminal justice system
- Why law enforcement and criminal justice figured so little in the discussion of the founding fathers
- The impact of American reform movements on the development of the penitentiary
- How an absence of law enforcement and local government led to a strain of vigilantism and extralegal justice in America
- Traditions of violence in American history and their impact on criminal justice institutions in different regions of America

Historian Richard Maxwell Brown has suggested that "violence has accompanied virtually every stage and aspect of our national existence."[1] America was created by violence, and violence has remained part of the nation's legacy to this day. In the years leading up to the American Revolution, violence was a frequent visitor to colonial America. Relations between the colonists were often more antagonistic than their relations with Great Britain. Conflicts broke out over colonial boundaries, and tensions sometimes escalated between westerners and easterners over concerns such as representation, taxation, Indian

DOI: 10.4324/9781315148342-4

1789	1789	1790	1790	1790	1790	1791	1794	1794	1797
Creation of the office of U.S. marshal	Judiciary Act	First national census	Federal Crimes Act	Opening of Philadelphia's Walnut Street Jail	First session of U.S. Supreme Court	Bill of Rights added to Constitution	Whiskey Rebellion, first test of the American Constitution	First law enforcement officer killed following birth of Republic	Newgate Prison opens doors in New York

policy, and the delayed establishment of government institutions in frontier areas. In 1764, a group of Scotch-Irish frontier settlers from western Pennsylvania known as the Paxton Boys descended on Philadelphia, threatening to overthrow the government. The Quaker-dominated provincial assembly capitulated to their demands for better protection against Indian raids for their homes in Paxton and greater representation in the provincial assembly.

Criminal justice historian Samuel Walker noted that "the American Revolution had a major impact on criminal justice, speeding up the process of reform and accentuating the differences between American and English law."[2] According to one scholar, the era of the American Revolution saw the development of three different criminal justice systems – for whites, blacks, and Indians.[3] By the end of the eighteenth century, the influx of Europeans with non-English backgrounds found a confusing and unfamiliar criminal justice system.

Following the French and Indian War, Britain left troops in its American colonies to maintain peace between the Americans and the Indians. From the start, American citizens were hostile toward attempted peacekeeping measures by the British military because troops were not stationed along the frontiers but instead were left in important coastal cities, particularly in Boston. As the American colonies approached the revolutionary era, criminal justice procedures were still rooted in seventeenth-century British common law. Trained peace officers and the penitentiary system as we now know it did not yet exist. If there was a serious emergency in major cities such as Boston or Philadelphia, civilian authorities relied on militia who met annually and elected their own officers. But drawn from the community, they could not be counted on to repress political unrest and mob actions by such "treasonous" groups as the Sons of Liberty. Therefore, the only real alternative for peacekeeping was the soldiers of the British army stationed in important coastal cities. Sentries who perhaps challenged passersby too exuberantly sometimes faced criminal charges for assault against the peace. As the army became more visible, it tended to provoke civilians more than maintain order. Boston resistance to the presence of British soldiers would culminate in the Boston Massacre and other seminal events leading to the American Revolution.

Various historians have speculated on what might have occurred had an effective police apparatus existed at the time of the American Revolution. The breakdown of the parish constable police system was most apparent in Boston in the 1760s, as mobs of Patriots who undoubtedly included local constables ran roughshod through the cobblestone streets. According to police historian Charles Reith, if there had been an alternative to the parish constable system, "Samuel Adams would be unknown to history. There would have been no Boston mobs worthy of historical mention. Without him and his mobs there would have been no war in the American colonies."[4] There is some doubt whether the Revolution could have proceeded as smoothly had there been an effective police system in place.

The American Revolution took on many of the characteristics of a civil war, with British troops firing on British Americans and neighbor sometimes fighting neighbor. After the meeting of the first Continental Congress in September 1774, steps were taken for a planned boycott of British goods. Every county, city, and town appointed local committees called Committees of Safety to scrutinize the conduct of citizens and to publish the names of those who violated terms of the boycott. Individuals reluctant to participate in the boycott were often physically intimidated. With many citizens still loyal to the Crown, active and organized groups rapidly separated the colonies into two camps, Tories, or Loyalists, whose sympathies lay with England, and Patriots, who favored armed resistance.

The lawgivers

In 1765, protests and social unrest broke out throughout the American colonies in response to the passage of the **Stamp Act**, the first direct, or internal, tax that Parliament had ever imposed on the Americans. Previous to this, only colonial legislatures had directly taxed their citizens. Colonial leaders such as Benjamin Franklin and Patrick Henry recognized that, if this act were permitted, it would usurp the taxation functions of individual colonial legislatures, rights that Parliament had tacitly relinquished in the past. According to the Stamp Act, Americans had to purchase specially stamped paper for newspapers, pamphlets, college degrees, playing cards, liquor licenses, dice, and most legal forms, including marriage licenses, death certificates, and court documents. While the purpose of the Stamp Act was to help pay the cost for British military forces left in America for the protection of the colonists from Indian attacks, practically all colonists opposed it and resented the presence of troops in their cities, far from the Indian frontier. Attempts to circumvent the Act led to trials in vice-admiralty courts.[5]

A special Stamp Act Congress was convened and led to a systematic plan of opposition to the tax, while at the same time it still professed its subordination to the Crown. The Congress maintained that to remain a free people, no taxes could be imposed on them without their consent. This Congress was created outside the British constitutional system and functioned as an extralegal governing body, working toward a peaceful resolution of the colonists' complaints. Patrick Henry expressed this same thought in a speech delivered to Virginia's House of Burgesses in which he proclaimed, "*No taxation without representation.*" On the local level, common people in Boston and other towns formed an organization known as the "Sons of Liberty." That summer, a Boston crowd targeted the house of city stamp collector Andrew Oliver, which they destroyed in one fell swoop. This episode led to the resignation of stamp collectors throughout the colonies and exposed the inability of current criminal justice practices to enforce the peace. Although Parliament repealed the act in 1766, most historians cite the Stamp Act riots as the beginning of the colonial struggle for independence from England.

In the years leading up to the American Revolution, the court and legal systems remained rooted in British common law. Those arrested in political actions such as the Stamp Act riots faced a court system based on English common law, and little changed until the 1770s. At the time of the Declaration of Independence, the colonies were still using a variety of court systems established a half century earlier; Maryland, Massachusetts, and New York had created their courts as early as the 1690s.

The American legal profession was in its infancy, with few lawyers plying their trade in the early colonies. Some colonial legislatures even prohibited the practicing of law for fees without a special license from the local courts. Most colonies were hostile to the legal profession, with New York recording only forty-one lawyers between 1695 and 1769, and these were appointed by the governor. If one wished to study law in this era, it would have to be in England, where more than 100 sons of wealthy American families studied between 1760 and 1776. By the time of the Revolution, South Carolina and Pennsylvania could claim the greatest number of lawyers trained at the Inns of Court in England.

Prior to the American Revolution, the colonial world was moving away from its homogeneous roots. The mainly middle- and working-class English colonies would undergo a demographic transformation between 1700 and 1775, with the influx of Scots-Irish, German refugees, debtors and convicts from England, and African slaves. This feature became the new nation's greatest strength as well as a major source for social and political discord.

The U.S. Constitution and Bill of Rights

Barely 100 years elapsed between the English Bill of Rights (1689) and the American Bill of Rights. Both evolved from the insistence of the citizens on a recognition by the government of what they termed their "natural" rights. This idea of a contract between those governing and those governed can be traced back to the writings of John Locke and Montesquieu, political theorists who asserted that individuals possessed certain natural rights above and beyond the law of the state. Some of these rights were considered "inalienable" and could not be surrendered. A bill of rights was included in the new nation's Constitution, and it specifically enumerated the inalienable rights of the people on which the state was forbidden to infringe.

Prior to the War of Independence, in some of the colonies Americans enjoyed more liberties than their English counterparts. In one important study of colonial criminal justice, historian Bradley Chapin listed sixteen procedural guarantees found in colonial codes:

1 No search and seizure without warrant
2 Right to reasonable bail
3 Confessions out of court invalid
4 Right to have cause determined with reasonable speed
5 Grand jury indictment in capital cases
6 Right to know the charges
7 Straightforward pleading with double jeopardy barred
8 Right to challenge jurors
9 Process to compel witnesses for the defense
10 Right to confront accusers
11 Trial by jury
12 Limitation of punishment to the convict: no corruption of blood or forfeiture
13 No cruel or unusual punishment
14 Equal protection of the law: dependent classes – women, children, and servants – have access to the courts

15 Equal execution of the law: no capricious mitigation or application of penalties
16 [Limited] right of appeal[6]

The U.S. Constitution that was ratified in 1788 included several checks and balances to guarantee that the central government could not become omnipotent. Except for guaranteeing such rights as trial by jury and the privilege of habeas corpus, the Constitution did not specifically address individual rights. Many of the framers of the document were unhappy with the finished product, which did not offer enough protection of individual liberties, including most of those in the previous list. To remedy this deficiency, ten amendments, known as the Bill of Rights, were adopted in 1791.

It may seem surprising that these amendments identifying personal liberties were left out of the original document. However, some of the men who composed the Constitution were hoping to restrict the rights of common citizens, thus reducing the power of the ordinary American. But Americans, many of them veterans of the conflict, had anticipated these rights since the Declaration of Independence. Others at the Constitutional Convention represented this perspective and agreed to ratification of the new government only on the condition that a bill of rights be added later. Those additions are the first ten amendments to the U.S. Constitution and are known as the Bill of Rights.

Several of the amendments of the Bill of Rights have important ramifications for the study of federal criminal justice. Although the Bill of Rights applied only to the citizens' federal rights and federal law until the mid-twentieth century (see Chapter 11), the states adopted bills of rights modeled on the federal bill. As legal historians have made clear, since the Bill of Rights applied to the federal government and not the states, the amendments did not "create a national standard."[7] Criminal justice remained the bailiwick of the states until the 1950s. It would be more than a 150 years before a system was devised "for coordinating the work of the states."[8] But, according to one authority, the mere existence of these standards at this time period "marked a subtle but important shift in priorities, away from the emphasis on community order and toward a preference for individual liberty."[9]

The **First Amendment** affirmed the basic rights of freedom of religion, speech, and press and the right to assemble peacefully and to petition the government for a redress of grievances. This amendment provides perhaps the most important protections of the American democratic system. As previous chapters have demonstrated, there are few, if any, precedents for religious freedom without the interference of the state.

The **Second Amendment**, commonly known as "the right to bear arms," which protects the right of states to form militias, is today at the center of the debate over gun control. Stating that "a well-regulated militia being necessary to the security of a free state," the amendment allows for the existence of a citizen's militia. However, critics of gun control argue that it extends to every citizen the right to have arms for one's personal defense. Unlike the English right to bear arms, which limited ownership with various specifications, in America gun ownership became ingrained as both a collective duty (militia) and a personal right (protection).

The **Fourth Amendment**, prohibiting arbitrary search and seizure, is derived almost directly from an English court decision from 1765. The **Fifth Amendment**'s prohibition against self-incrimination can be traced back to the 1642 abolition of the Star Chamber.

Several amendments would figure in future constitutional challenges to the death penalty. The Fifth Amendment has been cited for its guarantee that no person shall be compelled to testify against himself and for its assurance of due process of law in a capital case. The **Sixth Amendment** has been summoned for its promise of an impartial jury in all criminal prosecutions. And the **Eighth Amendment** has been used to argue against cruel and unusual punishments (particularly in cases involving the electric chair).

Following the revolutionary era's hostilities with Great Britain and the Constitutional Conventions, the foundation for the federal criminal justice system was now in place. Along with the Bill of Rights and the U.S. Constitution, the **Federal Crimes Act of 1790** formed its nucleus. The act changed several punishments that had been popular in British common law but were prohibited by the new U.S. Constitution. It defined seventeen crimes, ranging from obstruction of process to treason. Death by hanging was prescribed for six crimes, including treason, murder, piracy, forgery, and helping individuals convicted of capital crimes escape from prison. Some aspects of the Crimes Act were rather unusual. It allowed the body of a person hanged for murder, at the discretion of the court, to be transferred to a surgeon for dissection. It was left to the marshal to carry out the postmortem part of the sentence. If an individual was apprehended while trying to rescue the body beforehand, he could be fined and imprisoned. It also permitted benefit of clergy only after a convicted defendant was branded on his right thumb. This brand denoted that the individual had made use of benefit of clergy already and guarded against repeated attempts.

The Judiciary Act of 1789

One of the most important criminal justice measures enacted by the First Congress in 1789 was the approval of the **Judiciary Act of 1789**, which established the Supreme Court, divided the country into districts, and established the parallel structure of federal and state courts. Each district had a court that was given jurisdiction over crimes that were "cognizable under the authority of the United States." Most penalties ran the gamut from small fines and short terms of imprisonment to whipping and longer prison terms.

The Judiciary Act also established the positions of **U.S. marshal** and U.S. district attorney for each district. The ratification of the Bill of Rights two years later completed the construction of the early federal criminal justice system. Although a department of justice was not initially created, the position of attorney general was initiated as legal adviser to the president.

The Judiciary Act of 1789 created the federal courts that exist almost unchanged to this day, including the Supreme Court. During its first 100 years, justices of the Supreme Court complained about their heavy workloads, particularly the requirement that they "ride circuit." Without the assistance of separate federal judges for the federal **circuit courts**, the early Supreme Court justices listened to all federal cases, whether before the U.S. Supreme Court or circuit courts. This tradition played an important role in establishing the concept of a national government and a federal judiciary. Justices were expected to travel long distances on rough roads and put up with poor accommodations, often under hazardous conditions, to sit with district court judges at circuit courts. In 1792 alone, the six justices were required to sit at a total of twenty-seven circuit courts as well as at two sessions of the Supreme Court.

The Judiciary Act of 1789 also created what became known as the "U.S. attorneys." The president was authorized to appoint "a person learned in the law" in each judicial district to act as attorney for the United States in all criminal and civil cases in which the United States had an interest. These attorneys were appointed with the consent of Congress to four-year terms (just like the marshal). The act did not give a title to this position but merely appointed an attorney in each district. Henceforth, whenever this position was mentioned in statutes or court decisions, it was referred to as either "district attorney," "attorney," or "United States attorney." Sometimes an individual would be referred to by all three terms in a single statute or legal decision. In 1870, this position became more commonly known as "United States attorney."

The position of attorney general was also introduced by the Judiciary Act. The attorney general was created to handle all lawsuits in which the United States was embroiled as well as to advise the president on questions of law. For the next eighty years (until the creation of the Department of Justice in 1870), the attorney general was assisted by only a small staff that worked together with U.S. attorneys in the states.

Slavery abolition

Despite the American Revolution's promise of natural rights and equality, there still existed widespread opposition to the emancipation of slaves in the aftermath of the war. Warfare had also interrupted the cooperative antislavery efforts of American and British **Quakers**. In 1777, Vermont's constitution became the first to specifically abolish slavery. Judicial decisions in Massachusetts (1783), Connecticut (1784), and Rhode Island (1784) would follow Vermont's example. However, other states were more reluctant, with gradual emancipation accepted in New York (1799) and New Jersey (1804). New York would finally abolish slavery in 1827.

Most systems of slavery were not race based. It was not uncommon for some societies, for example, to substitute enslavement for execution in capital cases. Slavery as a criminal sanction has been an important sources of slaves for the Ibos of West Africa and the Guarijos of northern Colombia and Venezuela. Several Asian societies adopted slavery. During China's ancient Han era, criminals and the families of individuals convicted of treason and rebellion were enslaved. According to one historian, it was possible that "At the time of Christ, an estimated five percent of the Chinese population was enslaved," many either for debt, captured in wartime, or simply family members of recently executed prisoners.[10] As late as the turn of the nineteenth century, according to Adam Hochschild, "well over three-quarters of all people were in bondage, either in correctional systems or conditions of slavery or serfdom."[11]

Law enforcement

Law enforcement, for the most part, followed the same patterns from the earliest English colony in 1607 until the end of the American Revolution in 1781. However, the **Enlightenment** and more democratic principles underlying the American Revolution gave rise to many of the basic ideas that influenced modern policing. It was in the eighteenth century that the dim outlines of American policing began to take shape. In the more rural areas, sheriffs and constables were selected from the ranks of the great landholders and performed the same functions as their counterparts across the ocean. As in medieval England, the colonial sheriff was expected to perform both police and financial duties. As chief financial officer of the county, he was entitled to 10 percent of the tax revenue he collected. From the beginning, the colonies committed themselves to this style of local peacekeeping rather than a centralized system of law enforcement. Today's decentralized police system in America, with more than 20,000 police forces and lacking a national force, is a testament to this earlier tradition.

In the eighteenth century, the theory of crime prevention was discussed by several prescient police officials in Great Britain, but little would come of it until the nineteenth century. By the late 1700s, it had become rather obvious that the traditional peacekeepers of London, such as the constable and night watch, were no match for the social and economic transformation of England. England's population doubled between 1700 and 1800, aggravating social tensions. Most English cities increased the number of constables and watchmen while at the same time making the transition from voluntary policing to a paid watch. With an ever-rising crime rate, little thought was given to innovation until the Fielding brothers came on the scene.

The Fieldings

Perhaps the most accomplished police reformers of the eighteenth century, the Fielding brothers of London laid the groundwork for the subsequent development of modern policing in nineteenth-century England and America. An impressive physical presence at over six feet tall, Henry Fielding (1707–1754) is best remembered as a novelist and playwright and as author of the novel *Tom Jones*. Because of censorship restrictions in the literary world, he left his writing career behind to become magistrate in the criminal justice system in 1748. During his six-year tenure at this post, he implemented several policies that led to increased safety on the streets of London. Fielding introduced the **Bow Street Runners**, initially called "Mr. Fielding's people," a specially formed group of constables who were expected to run to the aid of crime victims and in the pursuit of criminals. Henry Fielding demonstrated his foresight in police matters in 1749 with the publication of his essay *An Enquiry into the Causes of the Latest Increase of Robberies*, which called for the establishment of a professional full-time police force. Despite the reluctance of the public to accept a professional police force, Fielding persisted in his attempts to win the support of the government for this endeavor.

Following his death, he was succeeded by his brother John (1721–1780). Blind since birth, John served as magistrate for several years and in tribute to his brother kept the Bow Street Runners alive. His 1755 pamphlet *Plan for Preventing Robberies within Twenty Miles of London* explained his strategy for breaking up organized gangs of robbers that plagued the periphery of England's capital city. An astonishing detective in his own right, blind or sighted, Fielding was sometimes referred to as the "Blind Beak" and reportedly could identify thousands of criminals by voice alone. During his tenure as head of the Bow Street Runners, he made Bow Street the official police headquarters, where two horses were always posted at the ready to apprehend highwaymen. A police reformer like his brother Henry, he was perspicacious in his attempts to implement preventive police strategies. But it would be almost half a century before the ideas of the Fieldings became fully integrated into the London model of policing.

Patrick Colquhoun

Beginning with his appointment as London magistrate in 1792, Patrick Colquhoun (1745–1820) would focus on law enforcement reform for the next twenty-five years. He was recognized for his police acumen after the publication of several lengthy treatises on police reform. He endorsed the notion that the government should be responsible for regulating the conduct of the citizenry instead of neighborhood watch groups. This was a heretical idea at a time when local communities relied on neighborhood watchmen and local constables.

Colquhoun became interested in police reform through the work of the Fieldings, leading to the publication of his book *Treatise on the Police of the Metropolis* in 1797. Among the most important police concepts introduced in this work was the notion of crime prevention, a radical departure for the traditionally reactive police establishment. Following in the footsteps of the Fieldings, Colquhoun suggested that the police should gather information on the criminal element, keep a register of known offenders, and publish a police gazette to assist communication and apprehension of wrongdoers. To justify these reforms, he reportedly conducted research that estimated that more than 10,000 criminals resided in London.

Colquhoun was credited with the creation of the **Thames River Police** in 1789. His writings led to improved police professionalism and the first systematic examination of crime costs and origins. An advocate of paid professional policing and recruitment and management under a central authority free of political interference, he spurred police reform and introduced new solutions for maintaining public order in an era of urbanization and industrialization.

Police efforts in the colonies

Various explanations have been given for the rise in crime in the years preceding the American Revolution. Rising poverty, declining religious zeal, and urban growth all contributed to a climate of fear where robberies and burglaries became common and law-abiding citizens yearned for better law and order. Some of the earliest strides in countering the urban crime problem in the American colonies were taken in Philadelphia. Prior to 1750, the only street lighting consisted of oil lamps carried by safety-conscious citizens. In 1749, a Quaker-led citizen group initiated a street lighting campaign that included raising funds to pay someone to install and light the lamps. The following year, these efforts spurred the assembly to chip in to pay for the initiative. Over the next decade, most major colonial cities adopted this strategy. Street lighting was an important first step toward crime control.

During the revolutionary era, British troops occupied America's leading cities, which were usually important seaports. Throughout most of the war, the British occupied New York City, where they were also responsible for police protection. Dissatisfied by the British attempts at law enforcement, New York City residents harkened to the past and banded together and formed a civilian watch. In 1773, "**Centinel Boxes**" were placed around the city for the use of the watchmen. By the following year, sixteen regular watchmen were on duty every night. In extraordinary situations, the watch was augmented using different strategies. On a notoriously raucous evening, New Year's Eve, the city militia or a military garrison could be called on. The introduction of a paid night watch in the 1770s represented a great improvement over the citizen's watch but did little to stem New York City's growing crime problem. The growth of the population brought increased stratification, leading to the concomitant development of a dangerous criminal element. The night watch could not keep up with the increasing complexity of urban life. Required to be on constant vigil in the event of fire or social disorder while the city slept, the night watch was no match for the changing conditions. Without the resources or authority to maintain order, the night watch was outmatched by their criminal counterparts not only in New York City but also in most other eighteenth-century cities around the world.

Following the Revolutionary War and the evacuation of the British army from New York, the city's police problem was amplified by the diminished presence of many upper-class Loyalists who had previously provided an element of stability to the city's social structure. War historians have long noted how the ends of wars were often followed by a breakdown in morality, particularly after armies of occupation vacated sections of town that, in the case of New York, became districts notorious for vice and crime. The American army served a brief interlude as peacekeeper until the city could resume its civil authority and traditional judicial processes. Surprisingly, with few innovations in law enforcement and a burgeoning population, New York City was recognized as a peaceful law-abiding community on the cusp of the next century. But new waves of immigration would auger important changes for the criminal justice apparatus of America's cities in the next century.

Following the defeat of Britain and its German mercenaries, America's colonists were no more eager for a national police force than they had been before the outbreak of hostilities. City fathers were unable to overcome the reluctance of their citizens to support regular police through taxes. Ever vigilant against a standing army and despotism, citizens resisted any efforts in the direction of uniformed police officers. Some state constitutions even limited the number of night watchmen. The resilient night watch had clearly outlasted its initial mandate and was usually under fire for sleeping and drinking on duty while doing nothing concerning crime prevention.

The birth of federal law enforcement

After ratifying the new Constitution, in 1789, the U.S. Congress created the nation's first federal law enforcement officer late in that year. The Judiciary Act established the federal judiciary as well as the office of United States marshal. The marshal was transplanted to

America and was readily identifiable in most colonies. Following the Judiciary Act, U.S. marshals and their deputies were required to make arrests while enforcing rulings by the federal courts. Early marshals were unsalaried but were paid on the basis of the work they completed. According to most accounts, the first law enforcement officer killed in America following the birth of the Republic was U.S. Marshal Robert Forsyth, who was shot down in 1794 while trying to serve court papers in Georgia.

The decades following the American Revolution were a time of social upheaval and transformation as the political system made the transition from one based on British colonialism to an American republic. The laws set forth by the U.S. Constitution received their first test in the fall of 1794, when farmers, distillers, and artisans in southwestern Pennsylvania protested a federal excise tax on whiskey through armed demonstrations. Marshals took early action, quelling the **Whiskey Rebellion** in 1794. At issue was the federal government's early attempts to raise money by imposing an excise tax on all distilled liquors. With a depleted treasury, the government embarked on an aggressive effort to pay off the nation's staggering debt. But the tax brought the new government into conflict with western Pennsylvania farmers. Unable to afford to get their grain to market, these Scotch-Irish farmers distilled the grain into whiskey, a much easier commodity to transport. Living on the bleak margins of existence, the farmers, many of whom were Revolutionary War veterans, were reluctant to cooperate with the emerging but powerful new government. Tax collectors and supporters of the tax found themselves the target of angry farmers who would rather tar and feather the government representatives than pay their taxes. Several U.S. marshals were selected to issue summons to seventy-five distillers to appear in a Philadelphia district court, but they were no match for the 500 whiskey rebels who showed up. As a result, President Washington took steps to send in the militia. Ultimately, negotiations headed off conflict, and the militia arrested eighteen rebel leaders.

Law enforcement and criminal justice figured little in the discussion of the founding fathers over which direction the new nation would take. The only mention of law enforcement in the U.S. Constitution is the power of the president during times of national emergencies. Historian David R. Johnson suggested that "there was no debate . . . as to whether the new nation should have a national police force, because such an idea did not occur to them."[12] This would have important ramifications for future developments in American policing as it became increasingly decentralized over the next 200 years.

Corrections

By the time of the American Revolution, three major categories of confinement existed in Great Britain, including **debtors' prisons**, jails, and houses of correction (in England better known as Bridewells). According to the customs of the day, debtors and their families were often confined together until debts were absolved by creditors or Parliament. However, prisoner categories often overlapped to such an extent that jails housed together debtors, felons, children, and the insane. Complicated and confusing, penology still resembled that of the Dark Ages. While similar establishments evolved in America during the eighteenth century, new theories of incapacitation would herald the development of improved methods of confinement.

Before the advent of the nineteenth-century prison reform crusade, inmates condemned to years of unremitting idleness were often punished in British prisons and jails with various make-work strategies designed to keep them constructively occupied. These strategies included the treadmill, the crank, and oakum picking. The oakum picking regime was considered perhaps the worst of all. Prisoners were forced to unravel lengths of old tar-soaked rope and then dig out single strands, or oakum, with their bare hands. These were then tarred and used to help caulk the era's wooden ships. Although some reports indicate this procedure was terminated at the end of the wooden ship era, there was some evidence that this task lasted into the twentieth century. Other innovations applied to the British jail and workhouse regime included the treadmill, or treadwheel, a machine that probably existed in less sophisticated form back in antiquity. Picture the modern-day treadmills at your local gym and then imagine being forced to keep a steady gait, working your lower muscles, in order to power pumps and mills. The first treadmill prison device was designed by the engineer William Cubitt. During a visit to a Suffolk County jail in 1818, he saw prisoners just lounging around. Recognizing Cubitt's dismay at this scene, a local official asked him to come up with something to better occupy their days. Cubitt devised the human treadmill, which became common in British institutions into the late nineteenth century. By most accounts, its lasting popularity among prison officials was its dual function as a method of punishment and a practical strategy for grinding corn and raising water. By 1824, more than 50 prisons had adopted the device. At one Irish prison, inmates were expected to keep up a brisk pace of 48 steps per minute for ten minutes before being given a ten-minute break. Despite attempts to introduce the treadmill to America, its utilization found few supporters. In 1898, it was banned by Parliament in Britain.[13]

Prior to the American Revolution, prison reform experiments were already under way in Pennsylvania. Until the death of William Penn in 1718, few crimes were considered capital offenses. However, once the colony came back under secular leadership after his death, new capital crimes were added, including burglary, rape, sodomy, buggery, malicious maiming, and certain cases of manslaughter, arson, and witchcraft.

By the late eighteenth century, men, women, and children were still mixed together in many American jails. Before the birth of the modern penitentiary at Walnut Street (Philadelphia) in 1790, prisoners endured unimaginable squalor. In smaller facilities, inmates were tethered by chains to the floors and walls. Prisoners had to rely on charity for their most basic provisions, and seldom were beds or bedding provided.

In nascent American communities, the position of jailer was a lucrative endeavor since they derived their income from charging the inmates for most services, including removal of chains, release from jail, and the furnishing of food and bedding or even a private cell. Jailers supplemented their income by selling liquor to their charges. Eighteenth-century prison life was a raucous affair. The wealthier prisoners could afford to live in relative comfort and even leave the prison sporadically. Others might have their families with them or an occasional prostitute. In the years following the American Revolution, England's jails were bulging with criminals who could no longer be transported to America. In response, prisoners were confined in **prison hulks** (ships), which were frequently ravaged by typhus "**gaol fever**."

In prerevolutionary America, there was no real criminal class in the colonies since the labor of every colonist was considered too valuable to spend precious time and money building jails. But throughout the eighteenth century, debtors were often jailed until they could pay their creditors, a tradition dating back to ancient times. In some colonies, the creditor was made responsible for paying for a debtor's keep, and if he did not pay the debtor, he was freed. In some cases, debtors were allowed to leave their cells during the day to work or beg on the streets and then return to jail to spend the evening hours. It was in this way that the indigent sought relief and release from debt in the days prior to the modern welfare state. By the 1760s, special "debtors' prisons" were common. In 1767, Mt. Holly, New Jersey, was the site of what was reportedly the first fireproof stone structure in the country. This edifice was comprised of small cells for debtors as well as a common room where they could commiserate together during the day. In 1786, an enterprising Virginian was selected by county officials to build a log cabin especially for debtors.

The fact remained that until the nineteenth century the jail functioned as a holding facility where convicted persons waited for corporal or capital punishment or were held until trial. Considered one of America's earliest jails for felons, Connecticut officials opened the **Simsbury** underground prison in an abandoned copper mine in 1773, and in 1790, it was designated as the state prison. Little more than a mine shaft, this vestige of a more primitive era was the scene of riots and mayhem from its earliest years. The prison was hampered by severe overcrowding, so authorities secured prisoners with iron fetters around their ankles so that they could be easily guarded as they worked inside the prison.

At the local level, early county jails were more often the residence of the pauper, the ill and insane, the aged and infirm, the habitual drunkard, or deserted wives and orphans rather than of the felons we expect today. Larger cities might have poorhouses or almshouses for the relief of the poor or maybe even workhouses where vagrants could be imbued with a work ethic. However, when neither of these edifices was available, the local jail would suffice.

John Howard

It was not until the late eighteenth century that prison reformer John Howard (1726–1790) brought home to the English public the sad state of affairs in the country's prisons. Prior to the modern penitentiary, prisoners were housed in fetid **convict hulks** and jails. Initiated as a temporary measure in the late 1700s because of prison overcrowding, the British utilized broken-down war vessels and abandoned transport ships to hold inmates. These "floating hells" or "hell holds" were anchored in the rivers and bays of Britain as the prisoners died by the score from disease, malnutrition, floggings, and unsanitary conditions that were worse than the era's prisons and workhouses. After visiting some of these facilities, Howard devoted himself to prison reform to improve sanitation and to diminish abuses.

Howard would embark on an examination of continental prisons and later publicize what he saw in a series of lectures. His findings led to the removal of the insane from British prisons and separating women and children from the men. During his travels in Europe, Howard was probably most impressed by the Hospice (Asylum) of San Michele in Rome. Constructed in 1704, it contained individual cells and a system of silence. San Michele was used exclusively for delinquent boys under the age of twenty and is considered one of the first institutions in the world to exclusively house juvenile offenders. As a result of his studies, in 1777, Howard's *State of the Prisons* was published, revealing the abuses of Europe's prisons and suggestions for reforms. His campaign paid off two years later when Parliament passed the Penitentiary Act, which initiated four major reforms: provisions for a reformatory regime, secure and sanitary structures, abolition of fees for basic services, and regular inspections. In 1785, England constructed Wymondham Prison, England's first penitentiary. The prison incorporated many of Howard's reforms. Cells were furnished for separate types of offenders, and inmates worked and slept in separate cells. Solitary confinement was deemed more effective than whipping, and initially the prison was considered an overwhelming success, so much so that the Quakers would adopt many of its reforms in the construction of the Walnut Street Jail in 1790. The philosophy of separate confinement at hard labor as a mode of discipline became the model for the **Pennsylvania system** of prison discipline in the nineteenth century. Howard, a towering figure in prison reform, the reformer who introduced the word *penitentiary* and the philosophy of penitence for one's crimes, perished from "gaol fever" in 1790 while visiting Russia. Today his legacy lives on in so-called John Howard societies, which commemorate his name and reform agenda as they continue to press for prison reform throughout the world.

Benjamin Rush

The Revolutionary War had just ended four years earlier when a small group of citizens met in 1787 at Benjamin Franklin's Philadelphia home to discuss the current state of public punishment in Pennsylvania. Among those present was thirty-one-year-old Dr. Benjamin Rush. The youngest Pennsylvania signer of the Declaration of Independence, Rush was born near Philadelphia and became the most famous physician of his era. At this gathering, Rush presented a paper outlining a new program for treating criminals. His 1787 work "Enquiry into the Effects of Public Punishments upon Criminals and upon Society" criticized Pennsylvania's practice of inflicting humiliating public punishment on malefactors. Rush was a firm believer that "crimes should be punished in private or not punished at all."[14] Among Rush's other propositions were provisions for classifying prisoners for housing, a rational system of prison labor that would lead to each prison becoming self-supporting, plans for gardens for producing food, and outdoor exercise for prisoners. In addition, he proposed indeterminate periods of punishment and individualized treatment for convicts according to the nature of their crimes. Not long after this meeting, Philadelphia Quakers founded the Philadelphia Society for Alleviating the Miseries of Public Prisons, America's first prison reform organization. In 1790, the Pennsylvania assembly passed legislation that laid the groundwork for the beginning of modern prison administration in America.

Walnut Street Jail

The city of Philadelphia proved a source of disappointment for European visitors in the late eighteenth century. Philadelphia was the home of Benjamin Franklin and the American capital city (between 1790 and 1800), and visitors such as the Englishman Isaac Weld found the city tedious and blandly constructed with "heavy tasteless piles of red brick."[15] Of all the red-hued buildings, none surpassed the Walnut Street Jail as an exemplar of criminal justice experimentation in the post-revolutionary era. Intended to reform rather than to punish, few could have imagined how this facility would stimulate the development of the penitentiary in America over the next three decades. A product of Quaker benevolence and the humanitarian concerns of Cesare Beccaria, Montesquieu, Bentham, Howard, and other Enlightenment thinkers, the nineteenth-century penitentiary shunned torture and public humiliation in favor of imprisonment.

Considered the birthplace of the American penitentiary, Philadelphia's Walnut Street Jail opened in 1790. Originally used as a workhouse and debtor's prison, the Walnut Street facility contrasted sharply with the workhouses, prisons, and jails that already existed. Thanks to Quaker reformers, one wing of the jail was designated to handle all convicted felons except those sentenced to death. Unlike its predecessors, the Walnut Street Jail was used almost exclusively for the "correction" and rehabilitation of convicted felons. In time, this system of discipline became known as the "Pennsylvania system" and was heavily influenced by the efforts of reformers such as Benjamin Rush.

Contrary to existing penal protocol, Rush envisioned a prison system in which convicts were housed in a large building equipped with single cells to segregate the more dangerous and disruptive prisoners. All others were lodged in apartments. According to Rush, gardens could be provided for prisoner exercise and to grow food. One of his most prescient notions was that prison industries should provide marketable products to outsiders in order to financially support the prison system. Building on the writings of Enlightenment thinkers, Rush saw the purpose of prison punishment as a path to reformation, the prevention of future crimes, and the removal of the antisocial from society.

His influence on the design of the Walnut Street Jail is readily discernible. A precursor to the Pennsylvania system, the facility called for solitary confinement without work. It was thought that, if prisoners had nothing to do but reflect on their crimes, they would reform more quickly. However, this approach proved to be ineffective and was eventually amended. After prisoners began to suffer the debilitating physical and psychological effects of solitary confinement, work was introduced along with moral and religious instruction. In this solitary complex, each of the twenty-four cells contained

> one small window, placed high up and out of reach; the window well secured by a double iron grating, so that, provided an effort to get to it was successful, the person could perceive neither heaven nor earth, on account of the thickness of the wall. The criminal, while confined here, is permitted no convenience of bench, table, or even bed, or anything else but what is barely necessary to support life.[16]

The offenders housed at Walnut Street were divided into several classifications that were not necessarily related to the seriousness of the offense. More dangerous inmates were confined to six-by-eight-foot solitary cells, and separate compartments were provided for women and debtors, perhaps the greatest advance instituted by the new facility. In earlier years, all the prison inhabitants were kept in crowded common rooms. Promiscuous behavior was rampant, and the rooms became schools for crime as career criminals taught the neophytes the secrets of their criminal trades.

Initially, the Walnut Street Jail met with almost universal praise. Having introduced prison industries, health care, educational opportunities, and religious services to the prison environment, Walnut Street was widely lauded. But as more and more prisoners were accepted into the prison, it became overcrowded, leading to the now familiar riots and uprisings that continue to plague overtaxed and poorly run modern prisons. The early success of Walnut Street Jail led other states to implement the penitentiary idea (New York, 1796, 1816; Virginia, 1800; Massachusetts, 1804; Vermont, 1808; Maryland, 1811; and New Hampshire, 1812).

Crime and punishment

The eighteenth century is often referred to as the Age of Reason, or the Enlightenment. During this era, great thinkers, such as Beccaria, Bentham, Howard, and Penn, had a great impact on the treatment of criminals. Their efforts resulted in a transition from corporal punishment to correction and laid the groundwork for the modern penitentiary. While this rationalistic movement began in England, the most effective work in the field of criminal justice reform came from the European continent.

Some of the most convincing ideas aimed at the reform of criminal jurisprudence flowed from the pen of the Italian nobleman **Cesare Beccaria**. Unburdened by the limited perspective of a lawyer or jurist, Beccaria was free to draw his own conclusions as an informed outsider. According to Beccaria, punishment should be certain but equal for all men regardless of their station in life. He asserted that punishment "must be essentially public, prompt, necessary, the least possible in the given circumstances, proportionate to the crimes, dictated by the laws."[17]

Beccaria is considered one of the first modern writers to publicly oppose capital punishment. His celebrated treatise *On Crimes and Punishments*, published in 1764, was not only an incisive indictment of the excesses of the Italian criminal justice system; it recommended reform measures as well. His work was couched in language that indicted criminal justice in the world at large. He harshly condemned the use of torture in punishment and interrogation, the corruption of state officials, and disproportionately severe penalties for minor offenses. He reserved some of his harshest comments for the penal system, which, he argued, should exist solely to maintain law and order rather than to degrade prisoners. During the Enlightenment, his theories laid the groundwork for the subsequent reform movement of the European criminal justice system.

Beccaria argued forcefully for a humane legal system and proposed that trials be prompt and that punishments be fair and impartial and commensurate to the crime. His ideas caught the attention of numerous jurists and would have a direct influence on the penal reforms of Pennsylvania in the late eighteenth century. More than 200 years ago, Beccaria wrote,

Capital punishment cannot be useful because of the example of barbarity it presents. If human passions or the necessities of war have taught men to shed one another's blood, the laws, which are intended to moderate human conduct, ought not to extend the savage example, which in the case of a legal execution is all the more baneful in that it is carried out with studied formalities. To me it seems an absurdity that the laws, which are the expression of the public will, which abhor and which punish murder, should themselves commit one; and that, to deter citizens from private assassination, they should themselves order a public murder.[18]

These words carry weight to this day, as capital punishment in America is once again a hotly debated issue. Beccaria's ideas proved popular with some of the most prominent voices of colonial America. Thomas Jefferson cited Beccaria's influence in his composition of a "Bill for Proportioning Crimes and Punishments in Cases heretofore Capital" (1778), and Pennsylvania's Dr. Benjamin Rush claimed that Beccaria inspired his essay *Consideration of the Injustice and Impolicy of Punishing Murder by Death* (1792). Although Jefferson's bill was initially rejected, it was approved later in 1796. However, it did not eliminate the death penalty in Virginia but rather limited it to the crimes of murder and treason.

By the 1790s, hanging was considered the only legal method of execution for federal crimes. Following the lead of Enlightenment thinkers such as Beccaria, some of the leading voices of the day, including Benjamin Rush, argued for the elimination of the death penalty altogether. But Rush remained in the minority. Nevertheless, the federal government, in sharp contrast to Great Britain, retained only four capital offenses: murder, treason, rape, and arson. According to historian Roger Lane, executions decreased from almost 35 per 100,000 annually to less than 5.[19] Although no state abolished the death penalty altogether, Pennsylvania came the closest in 1794 by eliminating the death penalty for all crimes except first degree murder.

Property crime

A tradition developed in the South that tended to punish property crimes more severely than crimes of personal violence. The treatment of backcountry violence varied according to region. For example, during the eighteenth century, Virginia courts sentenced individuals to death for hog stealing and collected a one-shilling fine for the rape of an eleven-year-old girl. According to historian Edward Ayers, these values persisted into the nineteenth century, when the county courts "treated property offenders much more harshly than those accused of violence" (see Chapter 6 for more on southern violence).[20]

Mob and extralegal violence

Rioting and mob violence were common throughout the revolutionary era. Between 1750 and 1800, every one of the original thirteen states except for Virginia experienced large-scale social violence. Although most of these activities took place in a rural environment, the cities also experienced lethal violence during the revolutionary era. Without a modern police department, citizens formed bands of regulators and vigilante organizations in futile attempts to suppress disorder. On other occasions, sheriff's posses or the militia could be called in to enforce the law.

No city saw more mob violence in this era than Boston, the scene of seminal mob actions that culminated in the Stamp Act riots of 1765, the Boston Massacre, and the Boston

Tea Party of the 1770s. Revolutionary violence came in many forms. Beginning with mob violence in seaport towns, American Patriots then resorted to violence to intimidate Tory sympathizers, often utilizing the brutal method of tar and feathering, in which individuals were stripped naked and smeared with a coat of hot tar and then rolled in feathers.

Finally, large-scale bloodshed broke out with skirmishes between militia members and British regulars at Lexington and Concord, Massachusetts. Next to the American Civil War (1861–1865), the American Revolution had the second-highest ratio of casualties to population of any American military conflict. During the ensuing hostilities, bands of loosely organized Tories (Loyalists) and Whigs (Revolutionaries) fought savage guerrilla campaigns in the backcountry. The Carolinas proved a singularly bloody theater of conflict with atrocities committed by both sides. Some historians have argued the backcountry warfare between Tories and Patriots in South Carolina introduced a subculture of violence into the region that persists to this day.[21] Several British officers earned sordid reputations for violence during the conflict. For example, Sir James Beard ordered that rum privileges be revoked for every soldier who took a live prisoner, leading to the murder of captured rebels. Similarly, in 1780, Colonel Banaster Tarleton captured a Virginia regiment and showed them no quarter. "**Tarleton's Quarter**," as this killing of prisoners became known, served only to ignite patriotic passions in backcountry South Carolina and led to similar outrages by the Americans.

There is little debate that the violence of the American Revolution furnished ample justification for the use of violence against enemies for the public good. **Vigilantism, lynching**, and other methods of violence would sporadically appear in American history whenever formal mechanisms of law enforcement were absent. According to Revolution historian Gordon S. Wood, the "long tradition of extra-legislative action by the people, action that more often than not had taken the form of mob violence and crowd disturbance,"[22] ingrained in Americans a propensity to utilize extralegal devices to ensure the sovereignty of the people.

Dueling

One of the earliest examples of an extralegal device, though rare in America before the Revolution, was formal dueling. The first recorded duel took place in Plymouth, Massachusetts, in 1621. In this incident, two gentlemen had their servants serve as their stand-ins and duel with swords and daggers to a standstill. The first fatal duel was reported in Boston a little more than a century later. While cases of dueling can be found in every colony, it did not become widely accepted until the revolutionary era, when officers of the Continental armies borrowed the practice from their French allies.

> The use of the duel, from the Latin *duellum* ("war between the two"), had been an accepted practice of the Germanic Burgundians more than a half millennium before the Norman Conquest of England (1066). Also known as trial by battle or judgment of God, one early king proclaimed that "every man should be ready to defend with his sword the truth which he attests and to submit to the judgment of heaven."[23] Tradition allowed clergymen, women, and the disabled to

use proxies after they swore an oath to eschew magical spells or potions during the subsequent violent contest for the truth. If the accused adversary was able to stand his ground between sunrise and sunset, he was found innocent and the accuser would be hanged instead. Trial by combat was rather practical, and allowances were made that negated the use of proxies by levelling the playing field. In one rare case, a woman had to defend herself against a case made by a man. The man was forced to defend himself from inside a waist deep pit, while the woman warily circled him with a stone inside a leather sling. The man turned several times to hit her with the club, but missed each time. Thus, she was found innocent of the charges made against her.[24]

American vigilantism

With a virtual absence of law enforcement and local government on the colonial frontier, settlers sometimes organized themselves into vigilante groups to maintain order. In the rural South, sheriffs and slave patrols were the main exemplars of law enforcement. However, citizens occasionally resorted to taking the law into their own hands, beginning with the "**Regulators**,"[25] America's first vigilante organization, which appeared in South Carolina in 1767.

During the 1760s, organized bands of outlaws plagued the scattered settlements of the South Carolina backcountry. After a campaign of terror by the bandit gangs, which included acts of rape, theft, torture, kidnapping, and murder, the local gentry responded by organizing the Regulators to destroy the outlaw villages that shielded them on the frontier. The Regulators were organized after the governor of South Carolina pardoned five of six criminals convicted for robbery and horse stealing. This group of vigilantes tried, convicted, and punished the offenders, totally disregarding the established criminal justice system of South Carolina.

During a two-year campaign, bandit activity was eliminated, and the gangs were broken up. The Regulators, however, did not disband immediately but became the moral arbiters of the colony, waging a law-and-order crusade against the marginalized members of the colony. In the end, they disbanded when the colony agreed to establish district courts and sheriffs to maintain peace in the county backwaters. A phenomenon peculiar to America, historian Richard Maxwell Brown has documented 326 vigilante operations in the United States between 1767 and 1904.[26]

The vigilante movements of the revolutionary era were confined to the southern backcountry. In Virginia, vigilantism was legitimated by what became known as "**Lynch's law**." There is some debate as to the origins of the term since its source has been attributed to two individuals bearing the name. William L. Lynch (1724–1820) led a 1780 vigilante movement to purge Pittsylvania County, Virginia, of lawbreakers. The members of this group signed a written charter, but the document did not specifically mention hanging as the punishment, although hanging was typically the punishment for a capital offense. Virginian Charles Lynch (1736–1796) served as justice of the peace in the 1760s but is best remembered in law enforcement circles for his participation with other leading citizens in local vigilante activities. Along with other justices of the peace and militia officers, Charles Lynch arrested suspects and, following informal trials, punished anyone who threatened to upset the traditional social order. A society often on the edge of anarchy, Loyalists, slaves, Indians, and English officials were all viewed with distrust and at one time or another might find themselves tethered to the whipping post, where Lynch law was administered. Although both Lynches have been cited as the possible inspiration for the term *lynching*, the term's origins are still inconclusive.[27]

There was a darker side to American vigilante movements that essentially operated outside the boundaries of the legal system. In the case of the South Carolina Regulators, heady from their success at stifling the outlaw bands, they were not content to cease and desist once the menace was erased. Subsequently, the vigilantes aimed their "police functions" at the lower classes, whom they chastised for not living up to the Regulators' moral standards and work ethic. According to their new "Plan for Regulation," Regulators embarked on a crusade against the vagrants, idlers, and dissolute women of the backcountry, employing such violent mechanisms of social control as flogging, ducking, and various corporal punishments. In opposition, the settlers formed the "Moderators" to counter the Regulators. By 1769, peace was restored to South Carolina after Charleston's governor and assembly acquiesced to the Regulators' requests to establish circuit courts.

In the twenty-first century, vigilantism is still practiced in various under-policed corners of the world. A 2018 case in Sierra Leone illustrated the recrudescence of extralegal law when the police are corrupt and justice uncertain or slow. A man asking for directions stole a mobile device from a journalist. She, in turn, ran to a nearby cigarette kiosk and alerted the woman running it what had occurred. A crowd quickly formed and proceeded to take the law into their own hands. The thief was caught rather quickly, and the crowd beat him and returned the phone, but not before a mob participant slammed him with a gun barrel. The journalist managed to save the thief's life and get him to the police station with the assistance of several locals. However, once there, the victim realized why the police were so disrespected after they explained that the process to convict the thief would be drawn out and expensive and would require her leaving her phone as evidence and paying a large fee. In her report for *The Economist*, the journalist described a policewoman looking the wounded thief over before asking, "Why didn't you beat him more? That way he would have learned a lesson."[28]

By the 1760s and 1770s, a distinctive American identity emerged, one that reflected an increasingly "republican" society that emphasized personal independence and public virtue and that scorned the notion of concentrated power in the hands of the few. At the same time, many (though not all) Americans rejected the governing attributes of Great Britain, which hinged on its landed aristocracy, political corruption, patronage, and bureaucracy. The beginning of the imperial struggle between the colonies and Great Britain and the subsequent Declaration of Independence were the by-product of a series of British abuses of power. Initially, American leaders were not outspoken in their opposition to the new Navigation Acts. They defended the British constitution and assumed that their grievance would be resolved. By 1776, however, it was too late. When Parliament began to directly tax Americans, regulate their intercolonial trade, station troops in their cities, and prohibit settlers from moving westward, Americans saw these as efforts to deprive them of their property and freedom.

Notable trials

Boston Massacre trial (1770)

Resentment against oppressive English tax measures had declined in most colonies but was reinvigorated after the so-called Boston Massacre. In the late 1760s, British warships disembarked infantry and cannon for police duty in Boston in order to "rescue the Government from the hands of a trained mob."[29] The British "lobsterbacks" (so named for their bright red uniforms) were intended as part police force and part army of occupation. Off duty, the soldiers often supplemented their pay with daily dock work, causing deep resentment from patriotic day laborers. Deep antagonism developed between the soldiers and the local inhabitants, leading to the pivotal events of that cold March night in 1770.

Local Patriot leaders were determined to rid the city of the British army of occupation. Crowds often convened in front of the Customs House, the symbol of British oppression. It is unknown whether the crowd that showed up to taunt the solitary sentry on that March night assembled by deliberate design, but the day before there had been trouble at the docks between off-duty soldiers and local longshoremen. Alarmed, the lone sentry called for help, and Captain Preston and seven soldiers responded. In the subsequent confusion, the soldiers, apparently without any orders, fired into the crowd, killing five and wounding more than a dozen others. The Massachusetts governor called for calm, promising the outraged citizens that justice would be done. Soon the captain and eight men stood trial for murder. The ensuing trial offers a conspicuous example of Anglo-American justice in action.

No experienced lawyer would agree to defend the eight British soldiers until Patriots Josiah Quincy and John Adams, the cousin of Patriot leader Samuel Adams, offered to do so. Many Boston Patriots charged that they lacked patriotism. There was little for the lawyers to gain. Compensation for the emotionally charged case amounted to about one week's wages for a workingman.

It was decided that Captain Preston would be tried separately from his men. Despite requests by the soldiers for a joint trial, they were denied without explanation. Apparently, the soldiers felt that, if Preston were tried first and denied giving orders to fire, then the subsequent defense of the eight soldiers would be compromised.

The trial was apparently transcribed in shorthand, but no copy survives. Preston's testimony has been determined by the existing deposition that he gave before the trial. As part of the defense, thirty-four-year-old Boston attorney John Adams quoted from Beccaria's recently translated *On Crimes and Punishments*, proclaiming, "If I can but be the instrument of preserving one life, his blessing and tears of transport shall be sufficient consolation to me for the contempt of all mankind." Adams is credited with creating some doubts of Preston's culpability among the jurors. The twelve jurors, who had been sequestered on a very meager diet of "biscett and cheese and syder," deliberated quickly and two hours later returned with an acquittal on all charges.[30]

The transcripts for the trial of the soldiers, or the *Rex v. Weems* case, has survived and offers a thorough account of the proceedings. Forty witnesses would eventually testify. After deliberating three hours, the jury came back with an acquittal for six of the eight soldiers.

The other two were convicted of manslaughter. Pleading "benefit of clergy," the soldiers escaped imprisonment and were instead branded on their right thumbs.

Contemporary records indicate that the behavior of certain segments of the crowd were as responsible for the tragedy as the soldiers. No matter, for the incident was grossly exaggerated for propaganda purposes. Hundreds of colonial Americans pinned on their walls copies of master silversmith Paul Revere's rendering of the "massacre" as a constant reminder of British transgressions. Imbued with the traditional rights of Englishmen who cherished the privileges and immunities of the freeborn, the citizens of Massachusetts and elsewhere could not be assumed to relinquish their expectations. Immensely proud of his actions in the courtroom, John Adams would look back on his stellar career that would eventually take him to president and note that his involvement in the defense was

> one of the most gallant, generous, manly, and disinterested Actions of my whole Life, and one of the best Pieces of service I have ever rendered my country. Judgment of Death against those soldiers would have been as foul a Stain upon this Country as the Executions of the Quakers or Witches.

According to Boston Massacre historian Hiller B. Zobel, this incident can be remembered as "The Birth of American Justice" or perhaps "Even the Guilty Deserve a Fair Trial."[31]

Conclusions

While the emergence of the American criminal justice system was still years away, by the end of the revolutionary era, a once-beleaguered legal profession was flourishing: twenty-five of the fifty-six signers of the Declaration of Independence and thirty-one of the fifty-six members of the Constitutional Convention were practicing lawyers.

By the late eighteenth century, Pennsylvania had abolished the barbaric "Bloody Code" of Great Britain, which imposed capital and corporal punishment for a broad array of offenses. Other states followed suit so that by 1800 most states authorized capital punishment only for murder and treason. During the same period, fines and imprisonment were substituted for the punitive measures of mutilation and exhibitory forms of punishment. Between 1794 and 1814, most states had been inspired by the Walnut Street experiment to build their own model penitentiaries, launching a new era in the treatment of criminals.

The Declaration of Independence, the Articles of Confederation, and the United States Constitution signify three successive stages in the development of America and a government of laws where "law was king" and not of hereditary monarchy. The decade of the 1790s was a formative era in the nation's history. It saw the inauguration of the first periodic national census in history, the country's first federal criminal statute (which defined which crimes were subject to federal prosecution), and the construction of the first modern penitentiary. Also established in the 1790s by the First Congress was the position of attorney general. Prior to the creation of the Department of Justice, the first attorney general maintained his own legal practice while acting as a legal adviser to the president. Until the Department of Justice was created in 1870, to the detriment of federal criminal justice the attorney general was assisted by a relatively small coterie of clerks and messengers.

At the turn of the nineteenth century, America was still overwhelmingly rural, with only Philadelphia and New York possessing populations of more than 25,000. With most Americans still living along the Atlantic seaboard, the country's population was only a quarter of England's and one-sixth of France's. But from 1750 to 1800, the population would explode from 1.17 million to 5 million, creating new problems for the developing criminal justice system. The era of the American Revolution furnished the foundation for the subsequent development of more modern criminal justice institutions during the first half of the nineteenth century. But first, more effective police agencies, courts, and prisons would have to be established.

Point – counterpoint

Interpreting the Second Amendment

Few constitutional issues have been more hotly debated than the "right to bear arms" clause in the Second Amendment: "A well-regulated Militia, being necessary to the security of a free State, the right of the people to keep and bear Arms, shall not be infringed." The debate over the wording of this amendment has resulted in several popular interpretations. On one hand, gun control advocates have stressed the clause related to militias, asserting that the purpose of the amendment was to protect the formation of militias in the face of government intrusions. Opponents of gun control have focused on a "militia of the whole" made up of all healthy white males. They were expected to perform their duties with privately owned weapons. Rather than viewing the clause as a qualifying clause, many advocates cite it as more an amplification or mandate of the need for a "well-regulated militia." There is little doubt this controversy will ever be put to rest.

In the following passage, a Tennessee resident named William Aymette appealed his conviction for carrying a concealed Bowie knife in violation of state law. In 1840, the Supreme Court of Tennessee rejected Aymette's contention that the right to bear arms was not specific and that he had understood it to mean the right to carry any weapon. The Court made an important distinction here: that there is a difference between weapons useful for the common defense and those that are not (the civilized warfare test).

Source: *Aymette vs. The State* 21 Tenn. (1840), reprinted in Robert J. Cottrol, ed.
Gun Control and the Constitution: Sources and Explorations on the Second Amendment,
New York: Garland Publishing, 1994, pp. 154–162

Aymette vs. the State

1 The act of 1837–8, ch. 137, sec. 2, which prohibits any person from wearing any bowie knife, or Arkansas tooth-pick, or other knife or weapon in form, shape or size resembling a bowie knife or Arkansas tooth-pick under his clothes, or concealed about his person, does not conflict with the 26th section of the first article of the bill of rights, securing to the free white citizens the right to keep and bear arms for their common defense.

2 The arms, the right to keep and bear which is secured by the constitution, are such as are usually employed in civilized warfare, and constitute the ordinary military equipment; the legislature have the power to prohibit the keeping or wearing weapons dangerous to the peace and safety of the citizens, and which are not usual in civilized warfare.

3 The right to keep and bear arms for the common defense, is a great political right. It respects the citizens on the one hand, and the rulers on the other; and although this right must be inviolably preserved, it does not follow that the legislature is prohibited from passing laws regulating the manner in which these arms may be employed.

At the January term, 1840, of the circuit court of Giles county, Judge Dillahunty presiding, an indictment was filed against William Aymette. This indictment charged: 1st. That Aymette on the 26th day of June, 1839, in the county of Giles, "did wear a certain bowie knife under his clothes, and keep the same concealed about his person, contrary to the form of the statute," &c. 2d. "That on the same day, &c., the said Aymette did wear a certain other knife and weapon, in form, shape and size resembling a bowie knife, and under the clothes of him the said Aymette, and concealed about the person of him," &c.

The defendant pleaded not guilty, and the case was submitted to a jury at the October term, 1840, Judge Dillahunty presiding.

It appeared that Aymette, during the sitting of the circuit court in June, 1839, at Pulaski, Giles county, had fallen out with one Hamilton, and that about 10 o'clock P.M. he went in search of him to a hotel, swearing he would have his heart's blood. He had a bowie knife concealed under his vest and suspended to the waistband of his breeches, which he took out occasionally and brandished in his hand. He was put out of the hotel and proceeded from place to place in search of Hamilton, and occasionally exhibited his knife.

The jury, under the charge of the court, returned a verdict of guilty.

The defendant moved the court in arrest of judgment, but the motion was overruled and the defendant sentenced to three months imprisonment in the common jail of Giles county, and to pay a fine of two hundred dollars to the State. From this judgment defendant appealed in error.

To bear arms in defense of the State, is to employ them in war, as arms are usually employed by civilized nations. The arms, consisting of swords, muskets, rifles, &c., must necessarily be borne openly; so that a prohibition to bear them openly, would be a denial of the right altogether. And as in their constitution, the right to bear arms in defense of themselves, is coupled with the right to bear them in defense of the State, we must understand the expressions as meaning the same thing, and as relating to public, and not private; to the common, and not the individual defense.

But a prohibition to wear a spear concealed in a cane, would in no degree circumscribe the right to bear arms in defense of the State; for this weapon could in no degree contribute to its defense, and would be worse than useless in an army. And, if, as is above suggested, the wearing arms in defense of the citizens, is taken to mean, the common defense, the same observations apply.

We think, therefore, that upon either of the grounds assumed in this opinion, the legislature had the right to pass the law under which the plaintiff in error was convicted. Let the judgment be affirmed.

Key terms

Writs of Assistance

Bill of Rights

district attorneys

Bow Street Runners

Centinel Boxes

prison hulks

Stamp Act

circuit courts

The Fielding brothers

Patrick Colquhoun

U.S. marshal

debtors' prisons

U.S. Constitution

Judiciary Act of 1789

Federal Crimes Act of 1790

Thames River Police

Whiskey Rebellion

John Howard

Benjamin Rush

Age of Enlightenment

"Tarleton's Quarter"

"Lynch's law"

Quakers

Cesare Beccaria

Vigilantism

lynching

Pennsylvania system

On Crimes and Punishments

Regulators

Boston Massacre Trial

Critical thinking questions

1 How did the Judiciary Act of 1789 influence criminal justice developments in the post-colonial era?
2 Discuss the impact of the Bill of Rights on personal freedoms and criminal justice procedure.
3 What lessons about American criminal justice can be found in the events related to the Boston Massacre trial?
4 Describe the historical events surrounding the birth of the penitentiary.
5 Compare and contrast law enforcement developments in Great Britain and America during the revolutionary era.

Notes

1 Richard Maxwell Brown, *Strain of Violence: Historical Studies of American Violence and Vigilantism*, New York: Oxford University Press, 1975, p. 3.
2 Samuel Walker, *Popular Justice: A History of American Criminal Justice*, New York: Oxford University Press, 1998, p. 37.
3 Roger Lane, *Murder in America: A History*, Columbus: Ohio State University Press, 1997.
4 Charles Reith, *The Blind Eye of History: A Study of Police Origins to the Present Police Era*, London: Faber and Faber, 1952, p. 81.
5 Vice-admiralty courts were set up in each colony in 1696. Since they did not use juries, it was only natural that colonists feared that these special courts threatened their rights to trial by jury.
6 Bradley Chapin, *Criminal Justice in Colonial America, 1606–1660*, Athens: University of Georgia Press, 1983, p. 3; Quoted in David J. Bodenhamer, *Fair Trial: Rights of the Accused in American History*, New York: Oxford University Press, 1992, p. 19.
7 Lawrence M. Friedman, *Crime and Punishment in American History*, New York: Basic Books, 1993, p. 297.
8 Ibid., p. 72.
9 Walker, 1998, p. 38.
10 Karen Farrington, *Dark Justice: A History of Punishment and Torture*, New York: Smithmark Pub., 1996, p. 18.
11 Adam Hochschild, *Bury the Chains: Prophets and Rebels in the Fight to Free an Empire's Slaves*, New York: Mariners Books, 2006, p. 2.
12 David R. Johnson, *American Law Enforcement: A History*, Wheeling, IL: Forum Press, 1981, p. 9.
13 Miriam Allen Deford, *Stone Walls: Prisons from Fetters to Furloughs*, Philadelphia: Chilton, 1962; Chris Ryder, *Inside the Maze: The Untold Story of the Northern Ireland Prison Service*, London: Methuen, 2000.
14 *An Enquiry into the Effects of Public Punishment Upon Criminals and Upon Society*, Philadelphia: Joseph James, 1787, p. 12.

15 Harry Elmer Barnes, *The Evolution of Penology in Pennsylvania: A Study in American Social History*, Montclair: Patterson Smith, 1968.
16 D. L. Howard, *John Howard: Prison Reformer*, New York: Archer House, 1960, p. 61.
17 Cesare Beccaria, *On Crimes and Punishments*, Indianapolis: Bobbs-Merrill, 1963.
18 Ibid.
19 Lane, 1997.
20 Edward L. Ayers, *Vengeance and Justice: Crime and Punishment in the Nineteenth-Century American South*, New York: Oxford University Press, 1984, p. 111.
21 For an examination of the subculture of violence in Edgefield, South Carolina, from the 1760s to the twentieth century, see Fox Butterfield, *All God's Children: The Bosket Family and the American Tradition of Violence*, New York: Alfred A. Knopf, 1995.
22 Gordon S. Wood, *The Creation of the American Republic, 1776–1787*, Chapel Hill: University of North Carolina Press, 1975, pp. 319–321.
23 *The Pamphleteer*, Vol. 12, London: A.J. Valfy, Tooke's Court, Chancery Lane, 1818, p. 98.
24 Barbara Holland, *Gentleman's Blood: A History of Dueling from Swords at Dawn to Pistols Dusk*, London: Bloomsbury, 2003, pp. 9–11.
25 The term *regulator* was used generically until replaced with *vigilante* in the nineteenth century.
26 Brown, 1975.
27 The phrase "lynch law" did not enter American and English dictionaries until the 1850s.
28 "The Alternative to Bad Cops Can Be Worse," *The Economist*, May 10, 2018, https://www.economist.com/international/2018/03/10/the-alternative-to-bad-cops-can-be-worse
29 Esther Forbes, *Paul Revere and the World He Lived in*, Boston: Houghton Mifflin, 1942
30 Don Corbly, *Letters, Journals & Diaries of ye Colonial America*, 2009, p. 211, no publisher listed.
31 Hiller B. Zobel, *The Boston Massacre*, New York: W.W. Norton and Company, 1770, p. 3.

Sources

Ayers, Edward L. 1984. *Vengeance and Justice: Crime and Punishment in the Nineteenth-Century American South*. New York: Oxford University Press.
Barnes, Harry Elmer. 1968. *The Evolution of Penology in Pennsylvania: A Study in American Social History*. Montclair, NJ: Patterson Smith.
Beccaria, Cesare. 1963. *On Crimes and Punishments*. Translated with an introduction by Henry Paolucci. Indianapolis: Bobbs-Merrill.
Bodenhamer, David J. 1992. *Fair Trial: Rights of the Accused in American History*. New York: Oxford University Press.
Brown, Richard Maxwell. 1963. *The South Carolina Regulators*. Cambridge, MA: Belknap Press of Harvard University Press.
———. 1975. *Strain of Violence: Historical Studies of American Violence and Vigilantism*. New York: Oxford University Press.
Butterfield, Fox. 1995. *All God's Children: The Bosket Family and the American Tradition of Violence*. New York: Alfred A. Knopf.
Chapin, Bradley. 1983. *Criminal Justice in Colonial America, 1606–1660*. Athens: University of Georgia Press.
Ferguson, Robert A. 1994. *The American Enlightenment, 1750–1820*. Cambridge, MA: Harvard University Press.
Friedman, Lawrence M. 1993. *Crime and Punishment in American History*. New York: Basic Books.
Howard, D. L. 1958. *John Howard, Prison Reformer*. New York: Archer House.
Johnson, David R. 1981. *American Law Enforcement: A History*. Wheeling, IL: Forum Press.
Lane, Roger. 1997. *Murder in America: A History*. Columbus: Ohio State University Press.

———. 1999. "Capital Punishment." In *Violence in America*, Vol. 1, pp. 198–203. New York: Charles Scribner's Sons.

Maestro, Marcello. 1973. *Cesare Beccaria and the Origins of Penal Reform.* Philadelphia: Temple University Press.

Masur, Louis P. 1989. *Rites of Execution: Capital Punishment and the Transformation of American Culture, 1776–1865.* New York: Oxford University Press.

Miller, Helen Hill. 1965. *The Case for Liberty.* Chapel Hill: University of North Carolina Press.

Reith, Charles. 1952. *The Blind Eye of History: A Study of Police Origins to the Present Police Era.* London: Faber and Faber.

Scott, Kenneth. 1957. *Counterfeiting in Colonial America.* New York: Oxford University Press.

Walker, Samuel. 1998. *Popular Justice: A History of American Criminal Justice.* New York: Oxford University Press.

Wood, Gordon S. 1975. *The Creation of the American Republic, 1776–1787.* Chapel Hill: University of North Carolina Press.

Zobel, Hiller B. 1770. *The Boston Massacre.* New York: W.W. Norton and Company.

1798	1800	1801	1803	1807	1809	1811	1812–1814	1815
Alien and Sedition Acts	Gabriel Prosser hanged for leading failed slave revolt	New York City creates position of high constable	*Marbury v. Madison*	Aaron Burr treason trial	New Orleans City Guard	Vidocq takes command of the French Sûreté	War of 1812	Prison stripes first introduced in New York

TIMELINE

CHAPTER FIVE

Crime and criminal justice in the new nation (1797 – 1834)

Learning objectives

After reading this chapter students should understand and be able to discuss:

- How the changing population demographics contributed to increasing social tensions in urban America and what this meant for the criminal justice system
- How American justice diverged from its British traditions after American independence
- The birth of federal law enforcement
- The influence of British and French police traditions on American policing
- How the Alien and Sedition Acts provided an early test for the Bill of Rights and why national security was such an important concern in the new nation
- The evolution of the Auburn and Pennsylvania systems and their contributions to the development of modern corrections
- Why America became more violent as its population became more diverse as it moved away from its colonial roots
- How slave revolts influenced the development of southern police strategies and traditions

In the four decades following the American Revolution, experimental steps were taken toward organizing American criminal justice procedures and institutions. Post-revolutionary American criminal justice made the transition to the nineteenth century with groundwork for an organized correctional system. Meanwhile, the state of law enforcement lagged far behind, still firmly rooted in the community-oriented volunteer policing of the previous centuries. But developments in Great Britain and France would soon find voice in the

1817	1822	1823	1823	1826	1827	1829	1829
Opening of Auburn Prison	Denmark Vesey's rebellion betrayed by informers	Birth of the Texas Rangers	Boston adopts office of marshal of the city	First report of Boston's Prison Discipline Society	New York abolishes slavery	Creation of the London Metropolitan Police	Completion of Eastern State Penitentiary

emergence of organized twenty-four-hour police forces in several major American cities in the first half of the new century.

According to the first census in 1790, the nation was still rural in character, with the majority of Americans living near the Atlantic coast. Although the center of population was clustered around the Chesapeake Bay, the West was becoming the most rapidly growing part of the nation. Between 1790 and 1800, American society made incredible economic advances, measured in the growth of banks, corporations, and transportation companies. With the construction of the country's first mechanized factories, American industry was soon producing a cornucopia of items, ranging from nails and hats to firearms.

Between 1790 and 1820, at least 250,000 immigrants arrived in America, contributing to increasing social tensions in urban areas as well as mob violence. Beginning in the colonial era and continuing to this day, immigrant minorities have been victimized by those that preceded them, with established groups showing little tolerance for diversity. Recent immigrants were expected to shed their foreign traditions and quickly assimilate if they wished to prosper. In the years surrounding the American Revolution, the largest non-English immigrant groups were Irish-Catholics and Germans, immigrants who would often be targeted as scapegoats for social problems. The Protestant majority in the New World restricted their economic and political opportunities. Some colonial laws prohibited Catholics from voting or holding government offices. The years from 1790 to 1830 witnessed the economic, social, and political transformation of America. As the nation's population became more diverse and cities more populated, the developing criminal justice structures were faced with the task of coming to terms with new tensions exacerbated by the turmoil.

When the War of 1812 halted the commercial trade between America and Great Britain, a factory system began to flourish in New England, joining the American economy to the Industrial Revolution. After the War of 1812, crime increased as soldiers returned home to unemployment. A growing population and rising industrialization led to a new form of class struggle that would take its place next to the growing sectional conflict.

The lawgivers

Following the Revolution, there was an increasing willingness among Americans to disregard British precedents of criminal law. This in part was stimulated by the fact that in many new cases there were no legal precedents to rely on. After the defeat of Great Britain, America became the first modern nation to design a system of government based on certain basic philosophical principles. Most of the states designed new constitutions based on republican goals and ideals to specifically curb the abuses that provoked the Revolution. Each state

1817	1825	1830	1831	1831	1833	1834	1834
Society for the Prevention of Pauperism established	New York House of Refuge founded	Indian Removal Act	Nat Turner's rebellion	The first American bank robbery	Nullification Controversy	First major anti-Catholic riot erupts in Charlestown, Massachusetts	First private execution in the United States held behind prison walls in Pennsylvania

constitution included provisions to curb executive power and included a bill of rights guaranteeing certain freedoms, including freedom of the press, freedom of religion, and the right to a jury trial. With the fear that the new federal system might give too much power to one government body, each state constitution reflected the sovereignty of the people.

Criminal courts

After the American Revolution, the former colonies agreed to relinquish a measure of their newly won independence to a central government. But these powers were limited and clearly defined. The acceptance of the Constitution ensured that powers not specifically conferred to the federal government would remain with the states. In due course, each state created its own criminal justice system to be enforced by their own courts. For example, a New York citizen accused of keeping a disorderly house would be tried in county or local courts under the domain of New York State. However, if the charge were federal postal robbery, a federal offense, the case would come before a federal judge. As criminal justice procedures became increasingly complex during the nineteenth and twentieth centuries, criminals often found themselves wanted by both federal and state authorities, creating complicated jurisdictional issues.

Although they are now abolished in England, grand juries adopted by the new states offered an additional safeguard to accused persons. A federal grand jury was composed of between sixteen and twenty-three members, at least twelve of whom must agree that there is a prima facie case against an accused person before an indictment can be issued and a trial held before a petit jury.

John Marshall and the U.S. Supreme Court

In 1790, the Supreme Court held its first two sessions in New York City's Royal Exchange Building.[1] Elegantly attired in black and scarlet robes, the justices were little appreciated by constituents who had recently won independence from England. During its first ten years, the Court handled few matters of significance and was little considered during the construction of the new Capitol building in Washington. The low standing of the nascent Court was symbolically demonstrated by the construction of the new Capitol without any chamber reserved for the Supreme Court. When the seat of government made the transition to the banks of the Potomac River, the Supreme Court was assigned to an undignified room in the basement under the Senate Chamber. According to one visitor, "A stranger might traverse the dark avenues of the Capitol for a week, without finding the remote corner in which Justice is administered to the American Republic."[2] With the ascendance of John Marshall to chief justice in 1801, all this would change.

Born into the Virginia plantocracy in 1755, despite little formal education (tutored at home by parents), Marshall was appointed chief justice of the Supreme Court by President John Adams in 1801. Over the next thirty-five years, his decisions would lay the groundwork for American constitutional law. During his term as chief justice, Marshall was credited with writing 519 of the 1,106 decisions issued by the highest court of the land. Among his most important cases was *Marbury v. Madison* (1803), which established the principle that the Supreme Court has the final word over whether an act of Congress or a state legislature violated the U.S. Constitution. This opinion laid down the doctrine of judicial review, which to this day remains the cornerstone of constitutional law.

Marshall's imprint on constitutional law cannot be underrated. If not for his powerful intellect and direction, a lesser chief justice may have employed a more uncompromising construction of the language of the Constitution. Well versed in the legal implications of the Constitution for the solidification of the new republic, Marshall interpreted the document in the broadest national sense. Ever the proponent of a strong central government, his decisions on the court left a legacy demonstrating his support of the Constitution.

The Alien and Sedition Acts: early test for the Bill of Rights

In 1797–1798, America witnessed one of its first international scandals when it was revealed in the American press that agents of the French government had attempted to extort money from American ambassadors instead of publicly negotiating a treaty with them. The **XYZ Affair** (which alluded to three French agents known only as X, Y, and Z) resulted in a backlash of anti-French sentiment against America's former ally.

More important, this cause célèbre led to the passage of the Alien and Sedition Acts, measures that provided an early test for the Bill of Rights. A series of legislative acts passed in 1798, the Alien and Sedition Acts included the Naturalization Act, the Alien Act, the Alien Enemies Act, and the Sedition Act – legislation that targeted immigrant populations and prescribed new procedures for attaining citizenship. It also established an element that would run throughout American history: the creation of a category of aliens, outsiders who were measured or impugned for their otherness.

The Alien and Sedition Acts were promulgated in an era during which the boundaries of the new country were still being determined; thus, national security was an issue of paramount importance. Of the four laws, the most controversial was the Sedition Act, which clearly impinged on accepted civil liberties. The Alien and Sedition Acts proved an early test of the First Amendment's protection of free speech and free press. The Sedition Act was so controversial because it barred individuals from speaking or printing "any false, scandalous and malicious writing" about the president or Congress. Despite intense criticism by Thomas Jefferson and his supporters, the Sedition Act was not immediately abolished. However, what the debate over the act brought about was a wide-ranging examination of the "issues of free speech and free press in a republican society."[3] According to legal historian

John E. Semonche, "Lessons were learned, and more than a century would pass before Congress would again inhibit free political discussion."[4]

During the administration of President John Adams, this legislation targeted unpatriotic speech and brought into question the boundaries of freedom of the press and freedom of speech. According to the act, "any person [who] shall write, print, utter, or publish, or shall cause or procure to be written, printed, uttered or published . . . any false, scandalous and, malicious writing or writing against" the government could be accused of sedition. In order to regulate criticism of the presidential regime, the office was given broad powers to squelch criticism of presidential policy or the office itself. From 1798 to 1800, close to twenty-five individuals were charged with seditious offenses, and ten were convicted.

Besides official sanctions, many individuals were targeted through an informal campaign of violence and harassment as mobs of young Federalists (Anglophile supporters of the president and a strong central government) roamed the streets attacking supposed enemies of the state who often included emigrant political writers, Francophiles, and Radical Republicans (who supported the republican politics of Thomas Jefferson and were thus perceived as anti-British, hence "un-American"). Following the election of Thomas Jefferson over John Adams in 1800, the acts were allowed to essentially languish unused as Jefferson pardoned convicted defendants in an attempt to end political partisanship. His proclamation that "we are all federalists; we are all republicans," laid to rest for the time being this threat to individual liberties. However, some of the Alien and Sedition Acts would be revived sporadically under future wartime conditions.

Law enforcement

The end of the American Revolution coincided with the gradual curtailment of patronage in favor of the popular election of constables and sheriffs. By the late eighteenth century, American communities were still largely reliant on self-policing strategies. In the first decades of the nineteenth century, several cities began to incorporate a day watch to supplement the traditional night watch.

In a time before large cities, property and personal crime rates were not considered much of a problem. But by the turn of the nineteenth century, social change augured by increasing urbanization necessitated a reevaluation of the existing law enforcement systems. Prior to the American Revolution, most sheriffs and high constables were appointed by the Crown. Following the war, these positions were filled by supporters of local political leaders. Rooted in the concept of popular sovereignty, early officials of the Republic were elected by their neighbors. The history of early American policing was the history of distinctly different forces in different cities. By the early nineteenth century, American policing was still firmly rooted in the English system of part-time magistrates, sheriffs, constables, and the occasional paid watchman.

The federal government provided no direction for the construction of police forces. In rural America, it was left to elected sheriffs and their deputies to maintain peace and to arrest malefactors. As the country moved farther west, the task of policing increasingly fell under the domain of the army, federal marshals, or anyone carrying a gun.

As the nation struggled with the forces of urbanization and industrialization during the first decades of the nineteenth century, communities created civil police forces, making the transition from amateur unpaid watchmen to more formal arrangements. Port cities such as Boston, New York, and Philadelphia endured growing pains in the late eighteenth century, and the old reliance on the community consensus broke down. In the first years of the new century, Boston became the first city to require by statute the maintenance of a permanent night watch with pay fixed at fifty cents per night. In 1807, Boston established its first police districts, and by 1823, the city had selected a Harvard graduate as its first marshal.

While the United States continued to make headway in the realms of communications and transportation, American law enforcement continued to rely on outdated seventeenth century police methods. The nineteenth century saw the dawning of a more complicated urban environment, but city fathers persisted in responding to growing crime problems by adding more watchmen.

The French police system

The early development of police forces in Europe was stimulated by their affiliation with the state. France introduced the office of lieutenant of police as early as 1667. Charged with suppressing crime, this office became a political office of considerable importance in the Napoleonic era (1799–1815) under **Joseph Fouche**. Considered the father of police intelligence operations, he served as minister of police during most of Napoleon Bonaparte's tenure as emperor. An early proponent of preventive policing, Fouche is credited with establishing a centralized police force that was responsible to the national government. The French police system was considered superior to anything the British had to offer in the way of peacekeeping during the early nineteenth century. According to police historian Philip Stead, "Paris was safer for the individual than was London in the eighteenth century,"[5] noting the contrasts between London's watchmen and parish constables and Paris' centralized police system manned by armed and professional officers.

Joseph Fouche (1759–1820) was born near Nantes, France. Educated at the Nantes Oratory, he initially studied for the priesthood and taught mathematics and physics there after graduation. In 1793, he was a member of the Committee of Public Safety during the Reign of Terror following the French Revolution. His main task was regaining the support of the city of Lyons. However, he was soon vilified for using cursory trials, the guillotine, and then a mass execution with a cannon barrage to convince the city to support the revolutionary government. He was lucky to escape execution for this debacle and sank into relative obscurity for several years. In 1798, he was back on his feet. Considered rehabilitated, he was appointed to several high positions. He would make his mark in policing, beginning on July 29, 1799, when he was appointed the tenth minister of the general police of the Republic of France. He oversaw a ministry that mostly political in nature and was reportedly unconcerned about public safety issues related to traditional crime control, such as vice and street lighting. Fouche created a secret police force and won support from the emergent Napoleon Bonaparte, who confirmed him as minister of police. Fouche's career as police minister roughly coincided with Napoleon's career as emperor. He headed the police from 1799 to 1822, from 1804 to 1810, and then in 1815 following Napoleon's last return from exile. From the start, Fouche seemed well suited to police work. He is considered by many to be the father of police intelligence operations. During his tenure, he reorganized the Paris police, initiating the prefecture that exists to this day. He is also credited with establishing a centralized police force that was responsible to the national government. His administrative innovations included setting up police departments that were proportional in size to the populations of various urban units. His other accomplishments included his advocacy of preventive policing and his strategies for eliminating the country's bandit scourge.[6]

Eugene Vidocq: the first private detective

The development of the French police was given early stimulus in 1817, when the French convict Eugene Vidocq (1775–1857) was given the job of setting up a brigade of detectives that became the precursor of the modern **Sûreté**. Following a stint in the military, Vidocq fell in with some unsavory characters before winning acclaim as an escape artist after escaping from prison three times. Released from prison, he was placed in command of a group of ex-convicts who became the nucleus of the Sûreté (now the Police Judiciare). Considered the world's first private detective, Vidocq employed numerous police detection techniques considered standard procedures today, including disguises, decoys, informants, autopsies, blood tests, ballistics, criminal files, and handwriting analysis. Like Vidocq, his detectives were ex-convicts. They saw spectacular results, credited with more than 750 arrests in their first year of operation. The Sûreté would go on to earn international renown over the next century and is considered an inspiration for the creation of International Criminal Police Organization (Interpol) and the Scotland Yard Criminal Investigation Department (CID). Vidocq directed the Sûreté until his retirement in 1827. Six years later, the detective unit developed under him was incorporated as an official affiliate of the police.[7]

The London Metropolitan Police

During the early nineteenth century, London policing gradually came to grips with its growing crime problem. With the defeat of Napoleonic France in 1815, thousands of soldiers returned home to England looking for jobs and places to live. Like most wars, the Napoleonic Wars were followed by a period of unemployment. With the added transition to a factory-based economy that favored machine over man, the unemployment situation further escalated. As London grappled with the growing pains occasioned by the Industrial Revolution, pressure mounted for more professional law enforcement. To combat the rising social unrest and riots, the army was often called on to handle the situation, leading to bloody incidents such as the **Peterloo Massacre** (1819), in which government troops fired into a crowd, killing 11 and wounding 400 (including 100 women).

Although there was a growing constituency in favor of a police force, most British opposed the idea. With a tradition that ran counter to the centralized police system in vogue in continental Europe, British reformers envisioned a preventive police system rather than one in the oppressive punitive tradition of the **Napoleonic police**. One of the toughest barriers in creating a London police force was convincing the inhabitants that a police force would not be used as spies and persecutors as it was in France. It would prove a daunting mission to convince Londoners that the police could help protect the public and keep order without spilling innocent blood.

Robert Peel

By 1828, steps had been taken toward creating a professional police force. In that year, Home Secretary and future Prime Minister Robert Peel controlled almost 450 policemen, including officers of the Thames River Police, the Bow Street foot and horse patrols, and nine police offices. A rather insignificant force for a city of one and a half million people (one officer per 3,000 citizens). The London police were supplemented by 4,500 ineffective Charlies, a remnant of the seventeenth-century night watch.

Building on the innovations of the Fielding brothers and Patrick Colquhoun, chronicled in the previous chapter, in 1829, Home Secretary Robert Peel led the passage of a bill through Parliament that created the Metropolitan Police to replace the outdated watch system. A firm proponent of the adage that it was better to prevent crime than to punish and investigate in the aftermath of the crime, Peel was cautious in implementing his reforms lest he arouse the fears of his electorate.

Peel had originally hoped to create a nationwide police force, but to his constituency, this suggested oppression and totalitarianism. Peel realized that he would have to focus his ambitions on a more concentrated area. So he selected London, which at that time was awash in crime. After seven years of opposition from the public and Parliament, Peel finally got his wish with the creation of the London Metropolitan Police. A preventive rather than reactive force, it replaced the ages-old night watch with professional, paid, full-time officers. The London "**bobbies**" or "**peelers**" (in deference to Robert Peel) patrolled regular beats, wore uniforms and were paramilitary in structure and discipline.

According to the military requirements of the new force, prospective officers had to be under thirty-five years of age and at least five feet, seven inches tall. Many former army officers would make the transition from the battlefield to the streets of London, including Waterloo veteran Colonel Charles Rowan, who would serve as the first police commissioner along with barrister Richard Mayne. Under the direction of Commissioners Rowan and Mayne, the force was able to overcome the trepidation of the public about a strong police force by improving community relations and reinforcing its image as a civilian police force.

Attired in uniforms designed to look as civilian as possible, every policeman was expected to begin service as a constable and work his way through the ranks for promotion. Headquartered at 4 Whitehall Place in Westminster, the back door of the new police quarters faced **Scotland Yard**. Since this door was used mostly by constables, the headquarters became known by the moniker Scotland Yard. The police were initially regarded with disdain. However, their suppression of a riot at Cold-Bath Fields in 1833 won the public over when they were able to do it without seriously injuring anyone in the crowd despite losing one of their own to mortal injury. Within the decade, the London Metropolitan Police became the model for modern policing. Although London had made the transition, the rest of Great Britain still lagged far behind in police reform.

New York City

The dawning of modern policing in America would take place in the largest cities. By the end of the American Revolution, New York City was well on its way to becoming the country's most populated city. Between 1790 and 1820, the city's population almost quadrupled, from 33,000 to 123,000, surprisingly with little increase in crime. Historian James Richardson suggested that perhaps this was due to the homogeneous nature of its population. In the decades before tumultuous immigration, life and property remained well protected. In the early 1820s, one English visitor reported that regarding crime, "New York compared favorably with that of any English city."[8] However, this was not necessarily a compliment considering the changing environs of industrial age London. New York City was undergoing rapid changes by the 1820s but was still reliant on late eighteenth-century police strategies.

By 1800, New York City was policed by sixteen constables serving one year terms. As the chief police officer of the city, the mayor also appointed marshals (forty served in 1800 alone) who served terms at his discretion. In 1811, the legislature passed an ordinance limiting the number of city marshals to sixty. Constables and marshals alike were expected to protect courts, serve court processes, and fulfill the accepted duties of police officers, such as making arrests, maintaining order, and apprehending criminal suspects.

Early New York City marshals and constables did not wear uniforms or carry identification of their position. Instead of a salary, they depended on fees for services rendered. In 1827, night watchmen, known as "**leatherheads**" for their leather hats, were carrying thirty-three-inch clubs to dispatch the more violent elements of New York society. A figure of derision, watchmen were notorious for sleeping on duty, or "**cooping**." Widely regarded as incompetent if not corrupt, most night watchmen held day jobs, ranging from masons to cartmen. Until the 1840s, New York City policing remained fundamentally an amateur business of volunteer or poorly paid watchmen and constables. Marshals and other functionaries complemented the law enforcement apparatus, but the only true professionals in criminal justice remained the criminals themselves.

Some police problems are almost as old as the job itself. No one has come up with a solution for the "seduction of sleep," better known as "cooping." No one knows for sure where the term cooping originated, but it has been used since at least the 1930s. However, the practice of sleeping on the job was as old as the job itself. During the 1890s, while serving as NYC Police Commissioner, Theodore Roosevelt had a reputation for rousting officers asleep at their posts. In Washington, DC, this practice was referred to as "huddling," and in other areas, as "going down." It occurred in a variety of venues: some took extended breaks on a pier, at a store, or even in a Times Square theater. Today it is not uncommon for a lieutenant in each New York

City police precinct to keep an updated "integrity monitoring list" that includes popular napping locations as well as businesses that officers are prohibited from visiting while on the job. These lists are often posted inside each station house. These lieutenants are referred to as "integrity control officers" and are expected to patrol suspected locations during the early morning hours. However, by most accounts, they rarely catch violators. Modern-day cooping was more common in the 1960s, when the rumor mill had some officers carrying a pillow and alarm clock under their coats when on the midnight to 8 A.M. shift. Cooping is much less likely to take place in the modern era compared to times past, mostly due to the changes in how shifts are scheduled. For much of its history, the NYPD did not assign regular shifts and it was common for officers to be rotated among morning, evening, and nighttime shifts each week, by some accounts, as long as thirty-two hours straight. Over the past quarter century, officers have been assigned single shifts that allowed to acclimate their sleep around the hours of the job. Moreover, there are so many calls for emergency service in the course of a shift that it became almost impossible to stay out of sight for hours at a time.[9]

Jacob Hays: "terror for evil-doers"

Jacob Hays was probably the most prominent figure in early New York City policing. Born in Bedford Village, New York in 1771, he entered law enforcement as a member of New York City's "Mayor's Marshals" in 1798. Three years later, he was selected to lead the city's constables, a position he would hold for the next forty-nine years. In 1801, the position of **high constable** was created in New York City. Subservient to the mayor, this position was charged with enforcing state laws and maintaining public order. Hays earned the monikers "Old Hays" and "terror of evil-doers" for his reputation for toughness and exacting discipline. He assumed an almost mythical reputation in Europe over the years and was seldom seen without his trusty gold-headed baton. Hays was credited with introducing the police tactic of having officers patrol in pairs for protection and to guard against corruption. His other innovations included the "loss book," which led to better record keeping by requiring the recording of all thefts, criminal descriptions, and stolen goods. He also developed a network of informants. During the 1840s, Hays escorted British novelist Charles Dickens through the seamy underside of the city. As tribute to his legendary career, when the NYPD was reorganized in 1844, while Hays' position as high constable was eliminated, he was permitted to keep his title and was awarded benefits for life. He was accorded so much respect during his long life that parents warned their misbehaving children, "be good, or Old Hays will get you!" He died in 1850. (One of his descendants, Arthur Hays Sulzberger went on to become the publisher of the *New York Times*.)

Southern policing

Most southern states established surveillance systems to curb slave mobility as they struggled with the problem of runaway slaves and potential slave insurrections. According to one scholar, whites "exploited slave folk beliefs, planting rumors so that blacks would assume the '**paterollers**' (patrols) possessed more power than they actually did."[10] Night riding and terror became a legitimate means for southerners to maintain their domination of slave society.

Recent research suggests that some of the earliest law enforcement reforms occurred in the South.[11] Charleston, South Carolina, could boast a paramilitary municipal police force by the beginning of the 1780s that grew to a guard of 100 men by 1822. To one visitor in 1842, Charleston had "the best organized system of police that has ever been devised."[12]

Some scholars reject the notion that the early southern city guards constituted actual police forces, comparing them more to their slave patrol predecessors. While it is true that they walked a beat, wore uniforms, and carried weapons, the forces operated more as military slave patrols with little regard for republican society or values. Established to control the large slave population, Savannah, New Orleans, and Mobile soon followed with similar forces. Unlike the non-uniformed constables and night watchmen of the northern cities, the city guards of the southern cities, similar to the militia, wore uniforms and carried muskets or swords. Regarded as city employees decades before the northern cities had uniformed forces, the city guards were usually on duty at night, while a reserve force was available for daytime emergencies. In addition, they were salaried rather than dependent on fees.

One of the most notable police experiments of the early Republic took place in New Orleans when a city guard emerged in 1809. The very ethnic diversity of New Orleans that gave birth to the guard also had sown the seeds of its demise by the 1830s. Wearing uniforms and carrying pikes and sabers, most of the members were French speakers, and by the end of the War of 1812, few could speak English. The influx of German and Irish immigrants in the 1820s and 1830s, ever wary of armed military-style policing, would lead to friction with the native French-speaking population, and the guard dissolved in 1836.

The Texas Rangers and the mounted police tradition

While it is unknown when horses were first used in a police action, most historians can trace the utilization of mounted forces in peacekeeping operations to King Charles' *Articles of War* (1629). By 1758, the London Bow Street Runners police were established as the mounted branch of the London Metropolitan Police. In the early 1800s, the Bow Street Horse Patrol was charged with patrolling the main roads leading into London. Like later personifications of the mounted police, officers came from the military, typically the cavalry. Mounted police forces in the British tradition appeared throughout the British Empire over the next 150 years.

In the United States, the Texas Rangers exemplified the ranging tradition and are credited as America's first statewide law enforcement agency. Created prior to statehood by Stephen Austin in 1823, they did not appear in official legislation as the "Texas Rangers" until 1874. The first incarnation of state policing in American history, during the nineteenth century, the Rangers would have an off-and-on existence. A formally organized force of Texas Rangers did not appear until the outbreak of the Texas Revolution in 1835, when they were formed as an auxiliary military body. With the main goal of eliminating the bandit and Indian threat, the Rangers originally consisted of ten volunteers whose duties were to "range" over the seemingly endless Texas landscape. It was from this "ranging" activity that the Rangers derived their name. With wages of $15 a month, payable in land, these men were in a constant state of preparedness. During the fifty years between the creation of Stephen Austin's colony in Texas and the establishment of a permanent force, the functions of the Texas Rangers continued to evolve.

Corrections

In the aftermath of the American Revolution, the former colonies attempted to come to terms with rising crime rates. Philadelphia had initially implemented hard labor as a substitute for more draconian punishments. However, it was less than a rousing success. The sight of prisoners with shaved heads and in primitive garments working on public roads proved to be more exhibitory spectacle than reformative in nature. After Thomas Jefferson inaugurated a plan for hard labor in lieu of punishment in Virginia, he learned of the Walnut Street Jail experiment (see Chapter 4) in Philadelphia and backtracked. Capitalizing on Jefferson's notions combining work and punishment in 1796, Virginia authorized the construction of a penitentiary in Richmond. Opening in 1800, architect Benjamin Henry Latrobe's vision so impressed Jefferson that he selected him to design the U.S. Capitol building and to oversee its construction.

New York's Auburn system

At the dawn of the nineteenth century, New York State was grappling with its own penal obstacles. New York prison reform advocates led by **Thomas Eddy** (1758–1827), a Quaker and former Loyalist during the American Revolution visited the Walnut Street Jail in Philadelphia in 1796 and returned to New York with plans to build a new edifice that became **Newgate Prison** in 1797. Implementing many of the ideals of what would become known as the Pennsylvania system, Eddy earned a philanthropic reputation that led to his sobriquet "the John Howard of America." An advocate for humanitarian disciplinary methods, Eddy has been credited as the first American to call for separate cells for all prisoners as he helped design Newgate and lay the foundations for what became known as the Auburn model. Eddy went on to become the leading advocate of humane disciplinary methods. Among his (temporary) accomplishments was the prohibition of corporal punishment and providing food and clothing to prisoners at no cost. The jail also eschewed solitary confinement in favor of congregate housing

During its first five years, Newgate earned an enviable record for subsistence, with prison industries paying nearly all the prison's expenses. Eddy was credited with establishing a prison hospital and pharmacy and hiring the first full-time prison physician. A firm believer in rehabilitation, Newgate emphasized schooling and strict religious instruction for inmates while prohibiting corporal punishment. A proponent of individualized punishment, prisoners were classified into four categories that included juveniles under the age of eighteen, men and women, those capable of improvement, and hardened offenders.[13] But despite showing a small profit and eliminating corporal punishment in 1803, the following year, Eddy resigned as conditions in the prison deteriorated. Eddy then left Newgate to dedicate himself to building a better prison that would soon take shape at Auburn.

With the support of the New York state legislature, Auburn was selected as the site for a new prison facility, and in 1816, construction began under the direction of architect-builder John Cray. Patterned after other early American prisons with a sprinkling of solitary cells and larger night rooms, in 1823, a new plan was adopted in which all prisoners would be locked in separate cells at night but ate and worked in a congregate environment in absolute silence under threat of corporal punishment.

Unlike its Pennsylvania progenitor, which relied on solitary confinement, **Auburn Prison** would take off in another direction. Construction would hinge on providing double cells and apartments to house inmates and congregate rooms for inmates to work together during the day. In 1819, the solitary arrangements of Philadelphia influenced New York officials to construct an additional wing of the prison that provided single cells for the more uncontrollable prisoners. In 1821, a new cellblock was erected, composed of two rows of cells built on five floors. Placed back to back, the cells were much smaller than those in Pennsylvania, measuring three and a half feet wide, seven feet long, and seven feet high. However, the inauguration of solitary confinement at Auburn proved disastrous. In solitary confinement and faced with the restriction of absolute silence, five of the original eighty-three inmates died the first year.

Later in 1821, Captain **Elam Lynds** took over control of the prison and was credited with establishing the Auburn silent system. Under the new scheme, men were allowed to work in strictly supervised congregate shops during the day but were locked in individual cells at night. The Auburn design of prison, with five-tiered cellblocks containing narrow single cells for nighttime separation, would become the most influential design of American prison in the early nineteenth century. The strict code of silence was maintained under threat of flogging in an attempt to thwart the contamination of criminal behavior and put an end to the "schools for crime."

Lynds has been given credit as "inventor of the Auburn system." However, this distinction was tarnished by his darker side, which led many critics to brand him a borderline sadist. Following service in the local militia and the federal infantry, Lynds was selected principal keeper of Auburn Prison, where he rapidly gained a reputation for military discipline. He enforced lockstep marching and rigid silence with the zeal of a martinet. Any motion at the dining table that violated the prescribed protocol would elicit harsh punishment that could include solitary confinement in the "hole" or a whipping. An advocate of whipping, when Lynds was questioned by the Frenchmen Gustave de Beaumont and Alexis de Tocqueville in the 1830s as to whether he believed "that bodily chastisement might be dispensed with," Lynds responded,

> I am convinced of the contrary. I consider the chastisement by the whip, the most efficient, and, at the same time, the humane which exists; it never injures health, and obliges the prisoners to lead a life essentially healthy. . . . I consider it impossible to govern a large prison without a whip.[14]

With his penchant for corporal punishment, Lynds maintained order in Auburn until 1825, when he was authorized to take 100 inmates to the Hudson River town of Ossining to build what would become known as **Sing Sing Prison**. On his return to Auburn, his methods were finally brought into question, and in 1838, he was fired for his cruelty. Ever the disciplinarian, his acumen would soon be required at Sing Sing.

The Auburn system would flourish in the first half of the nineteenth century with thirty state prisons following this pattern, including the infamous Sing Sing Prison in 1825. New York prisons following the Auburn plan are also credited with introducing prison uniforms in 1815 using different-colored stripes (**prison stripes**) to distinguish the various categories of inmates. This was particularly helpful in the event of a prison escape where a prisoner's classification could be noted by colored stripes (striped uniforms were out of fashion by the 1950s).

The Pennsylvania system: from the Walnut Street Jail to Eastern State Penitentiary

During its short history, Walnut Street Jail was the setting for numerous correctional innovations. In 1791, better conditions for debtors were implemented, and by the following year, prison keepers were subsisting on an actual salary rather than collecting fees from prisoners. By the end of the decade, Pennsylvania witnessed the abolition of the death penalty for all crimes except premeditated murder as well as the complete revision of its penal code.

Officials soon became cognizant of one of the inherent contradictions of a prison that housed inmates in any congregate setting – that this created an environment akin to a "school for crime." In making the transition from a county jail to a state penal establishment, Walnut Street Jail was soon faced with problems of overcrowding and inadequate financing, which in turn led to riots, mass escapes, and assaults on guards.

Despite an untimely retreat from the initial attempt providing separate confinement, Quaker-inspired organizations such as the Pennsylvania Prison Society and the Philadelphia Society for Alleviating the Miseries of Public Prisons embarked on a new attempt at a separate system. Two new prisons were built in Pennsylvania following this concept. Pittsburgh's Western Penitentiary, built according to Jeremy Bentham's *Panopticon*, was completed in 1818 but was slightly regarded. However, the completion in 1829 of the **Cherry Hill Prison**, better known as **Eastern State Penitentiary**, would become the showplace for prison reform in America.

According to the noted French traveler Alexis de Tocqueville, by the 1830s, Philadelphia was still "infatuated with the prison system." This would be an oversimplification. The Quaker reform impulse was indeed still strong in Philadelphia by the 1830s as civic idealism merged with new architectural professionalism. New penal, medical, and philanthropic institutions dotted the city's landscape. Large in scale and progressive for their time, the Orphan Asylum, the House of Refuge, the Alms House, and Moyamensing Prison would all pale in comparison to Eastern State Penitentiary, America's largest federal building in 1829.

In 1829, Pennsylvania responded to the Auburn model with the opening of Eastern State Penitentiary, admitting its first prisoner on October 25. Often referred to simply as "Cherry Hill" because it was built on the site of a cherry orchard, it was the largest building project in America up to that time. Prisoners were housed in extra-large cells, each with a walled garden-exercise yard, and were expected to live and work in the cell without contact with any other prisoners. Having replaced the Walnut Jail, which was not permanently closed until 1835, the new facility was considered the nation's greatest testament to the penitentiary concept.

Architecturally, Eastern State Penitentiary resembled a medieval castle with towering thirty-foot walls surrounding seven cellblocks that branched out from a central rotunda like the spokes of a wheel. Long corridors extended through each cellblock and contained at least thirty solitary cells. Here prisoners often spent years ensconced in solitary confinement. The most expensive prison of its kind, each cell had its own private exercise yard, running water, and heat. With little provided for reading besides the Bible, it was hoped that prisoners would seek solace in the holy book and spend their lonely hours reflecting on their misspent lives. Despite the noble goals of the system's creators, many convicts became insane from the monotony of solitary confinement. After a visit to the prison in 1842, the novelist Charles Dickens lamented that "the system here is rigid, strict, and hopeless solitary confinement. I believe it, in its effects, to be cruel and wrong" and that the "slow and daily tampering with the mysteries of the brain" was "immeasurably worse than any torture to the body."[15]

The American penitentiary

While Great Britain could point to the Penitentiary Houses Act in 1799 as a universal attempt to reform the English prison system, no such umbrella of legislation came to fruition in America. The republican system of government remained a formidable obstacle to any comprehensive prison legislation and would leave it to the various states to confront the enduring problem of the American prison system.

One goal shared by the state prison building movement in the 1820s and 1830s was to make the new institutions self-sufficient. State legislators demanded that penitentiaries pay their own way, although they would be consistently at loggerheads with private businesses that worried that prison industries would flourish because of unfair business competition. The most outstanding feature of the developing Pennsylvania system, the separate/solitary system, worked against the very profitability it sought since the rigid segregation of prisoners worked against the viability of prison industries. Legislators looked for a compromise in Virginia by refraining from keeping prisoners continuously in stir as in the Pennsylvania model, allowing them to work for a time in congregate conditions while spending a good part of the day in unemployed solitude. However, when they did have the chance to work, borrowing a page from the Auburn model, they worked in silence in prison shops.

In 1826, the First Report of the Prison Discipline Society of Boston, organized under the zealous leadership of the Reverend **Louis Dwight**, was published. According to this work, there were approximately 3,500 prisoners in state penitentiaries, with 60 percent of them housed in New York, Pennsylvania, and Massachusetts. Although prison stripes were introduced in New York in 1815, prison uniforms would vary from state to state. Since different colors were used for first-time offenders and recidivists, the purpose of the different-colored stripes was to reveal at a glance the prisoner's classification in the case of an escape. The states were never consistent in the training and equipping of jail keepers. For example, prison guards in New York were initially unarmed, while early Massachusetts keepers were provided a gun and bayonet.

A lifelong advocate of the Auburn prison system, Louis Dwight is credited as one of America's first nationally known prison reformers. Having originally trained for the ministry, Louis Dwight was kept from fulfilling his ambition after a chemical laboratory accident injured his lungs so that he could not preach. By 1824, he was traversing Massachusetts dispensing Bibles to prisoners. The society would eventually distribute thousands of Bibles and religious tracts, contributing in the process to the creation of prison libraries. After discovering the abuses of the new penal institutions, he devoted his life to improving prison conditions. In 1825, he organized the Prison Discipline Society of Boston, an organization he would lead until his death in 1854. A champion of the Auburn system, Dwight led the opposition against the Pennsylvania model, but the society that he founded would die with him as others carried on his reform efforts.

Crime and punishment

The creation of the federal criminal justice system in the 1790s not only created courts but also authorized punishments such as imprisonment, corporal penalties, and, in capital cases, execution. However, while English law still recognized over 200 capital offenses in 1780 (94 percent were commuted to transportation),[16] the penal codes of the American states were far less punitive. Capital punishment was rarely meted out to whites for crimes other than murder. During the late eighteenth century, traditional punishments were clearly ineffective. With population growth, increasing mobility, and migration, the emergence of a distinct poor population made sanctions such as fines, whippings, and the pillory less effective than in the past.

While the use of capital punishment had diminished, corporal punishment was another matter, with many criminal offenses still being punished with the public infliction of pain and suffering. Most towns in New England boasted whipping posts and stocks near the commons or meetinghouse. As late as 1805, the penalty in Massachusetts for counterfeiting was the amputation of an ear after sitting in a pillory for an hour. The penalty for manslaughter consisted of having one's forehead branded in public, and many communities flogged perpetrators of petty theft. But by the 1830s, public corporal punishment began to disappear from statute books as prison became a more accepted sanction for most crimes. In 1790, Pennsylvania began the movement to prohibit flogging, and in 1805, Massachusetts followed suit. The movement to abolish corporal punishment was haphazard at best, with Connecticut constables continuing to whip petty criminals until 1828 and Delaware officials flogging black and white prisoners well into the twentieth century.

Capital punishment

Following the American Revolution and the Enlightenment, the movement to abolish the death penalty was inextricably linked with the developing penitentiary movement. But despite an emphasis on milder punishments, executions continued in the first part of the nineteenth century. With a rise in public disorder in the 1820s and 1830s, some states began to steer away from the inflammatory spectacle of public executions. Pennsylvania once again led the way in criminal justice reform as the first state to hold private executions behind prison walls beginning in 1834. During the 1830s, New York and Massachusetts would join Pennsylvania in ending public executions as sheriffs made the transition to carrying out death sentences behind prison walls.

Following the American Revolution, a new, more humanitarian age was ushered in by the protections granted by the Bill of Rights, which eliminated "cruel and unusual punishments." Hanging would predominate as the only sanctioned form of capital punishment in America for the next 100 years. Although Benjamin Rush and others were in favor of the abolition of the death penalty, they were clearly in the minority. But in sharp contrast with England's "Bloody Code," the few capital offenses in America consisted of murder, treason, arson, and rape. The rate of executions clearly fell after the colonial era, from a high of almost 35 per 100,000 to only 3 or 4 per 100,000 in the post-revolutionary years.[17] As the 1820s got under way, northern states abolished outdated traditions such as "benefit of clergy" as penitentiaries and reformatories became accepted alternatives to more punitive methods of punishment.

Until executions were hidden from the public behind prison walls, spectators would drive many miles to witness public hangings. Entertainers, vendors, and peddlers lent an air of festivity – a carnival atmosphere to what should have been a somber event. Although the gallows was the typical mode of hanging east of the Mississippi River, there are accounts during the years before the Civil War of prisoners walking up a ladder to a noose on a tree limb and then having the ladder withdrawn. The influence of the new industrial age would lead to the development of new hanging machines that were considered more humanitarian.

Juvenile delinquency

As America grew more urban during the early nineteenth century, a new class of servants, orphans, and indigents for whom no one felt responsibility began to dot the municipal landscape. As early as 1766, one of New York City's leading citizens was lamenting that "children nightly trampouze the streets with lanthorns upon poles and halloing . . . the magistry either approve of it, or do not dare suppress it."[18] More an irritant than a public crime hazard, youth gangs would gradually evolve into an urban menace by the early 1800s.

By the 1790s, the rise in wage labor and the increasing prosperity of slavery led master artisans to move away from the old system, which required apprentices. With few outlets for subsistence, once young boys left their homes, they often found themselves on the streets, stealing food and sleeping in alleys. In earlier days, the moral arbiters of the village would council the youths, but with society becoming increasingly complex, city fathers were powerless to police every street corner, with more pressing matters of public health and order taking precedence.

Groups of young homeless boys were soon congregating on the fringes of crowded cities where they could survive by robbing travelers or doing odd jobs. By the early 1820s, the **Five Points district** (derived from the intersection of five streets) of New York was a breeding ground for every kind of criminal element. It is generally conceded that some of

America's earliest organized criminal gangs were born out of this locale, where thieves, cut-throats, and pickpockets found refuge from a society intent on bringing order to the chaos that was urban America. Chief among the first Five Points gangs were the Forty Thieves, whose organization can be traced back to 1826.[19]

The gangs of New York

New York City had been a breeding ground gangs since the American Revolution. As the city grew more urban in the early nineteenth century, a new class of servants, orphans, and indigents for whom no one felt responsibility began to clamor across the municipal land-scape. The developing slums of New York City paralleled the growing disparity between the living conditions of the native-born and the more marginalized mostly Irish-Catholic immigrants. Although the Five Points tended to foster the Irish-Catholic gangs, the city's Bowery produced nativist gangs, strongly opposed to the new immigrants.

In the first decades of the nineteenth century, the Five Points district, so named for its location at the intersection of five streets, was home to an eclectic mélange of criminals. By the 1820s, overcrowding and immigration in this neighborhood created new opportunities for such gangs as the Forty Thieves, the Kerryonians, the Roach Guard, and the Plug Uglies. Belying their rather benign monikers was their propensity for brutal crimes and bellicosity. The power of these gangs would erode during the 1860s.[20]

Alcoholic republic

Virtually every American community had a village church and local tavern in the late eigh-teenth century. Diametrically opposed to one another in spirit, the tavern was the most accessible local institution for the male world of the early nineteenth century. Even the former Puritan communities of New England could boast more licensed taverns than meet-inghouses. Like their British counterparts in the medieval world, the taverns were scenes of gambling, heavy smoking, hard drinking, and even harder fighting. The winter months proved a boon to local tavern keepers with little competition for the entertainment dollars of men in the fallow months of an agricultural-based society.

Further testifying to the widespread acceptance of public drinking in early America, dur-ing one of George Washington's campaigns for a seat in the Virginia House of Burgesses, he doled out twenty-eight gallons of rum, fifty gallons of rum punch, thirty-six gallons of wine, forty-six gallons of beer, and other libations. It should be no surprise then that he won the election.

When not preoccupied by drinking, the men of the early Republic could find solace in gambling on games of chance such as dice and cards. Gambling united the classes as few other endeavors did. When weather permitted, they wagered on horse racing, cockfights, and wrestling matches. Mostly indifferent to the suffering of animals, the blood sports of dogfighting, bull and bear baiting, and cock matches were especially popular in both the North and the South.

Regardless of the social activity, alcoholic beverages were never far away, being as common as traditional victuals. The problem was not the act of drinking but the enormous quantity consumed. One estimate suggests that, during the revolutionary era, each person consumed the equivalent of three and a half gallons of pure, 200-proof alcohol. By the end of the 1790s, perhaps because of anxieties generated by rapid social and economic change, men were drinking even more, with consumption rising to an all-time high of four gallons per capita by the late 1820s.

Over the next twenty years, liquor consumption began to decline in some regions of the country. A product of **temperance crusades** by mostly New England clergymen, the campaign against drinking found a voice in the creation of the American Temperance Society in 1826. A highly charged crusade against "**demon rum**" and its accompanying social disorder was supplemented by pamphlets from medical doctors such as Benjamin Rush advising Americans of the potentially poisonous effects of alcohol. By 1840, alcohol consumption had declined from four gallons per person each year to less than one and a half gallons. And in less than a century, temperance societies would become victorious with the passage of the Volstead Act in 1920.

Violent republic

As America became more diverse as it moved from its colonial roots, so too did the relationships of its myriad citizens become more complex, often degenerating into violence. The early Republic years saw casual violence become part of the daily fabric of American life. Recreational bare-knuckle boxing and wrestling offered more acceptable outlets for male violence. For slaves, violence was part and parcel of the peculiar institution. Violence was rarely absent from any aspect of the social arena. Harsh corporal punishment was common within the family and at school. Servants, slaves, student, and children were often the target of brutal corporal and public punishments.

During the American Revolution, the southern colonies witnessed not only traditional warfare but also what has been called an "uncivil war" where vigilantes, Tories, and bands of bandits waged war against each other and the civilian populace. Following the war, the southern region's association with violence became more pronounced. During the early Republic, while northern states outlawed dueling and abandoned the institution of slavery, white southerners continued to glorify the virtues of honor, violence, and masculinity. The persistence of southern slavery guaranteed that violence would continue to be identified with southern culture. Flogging and branding and the threat of violence were emphasized for maintaining social control at a time when northern cities experimented with policing and prisons.

Slave revolts

During the 1790s, the legal status of slavery became increasingly complicated. In 1791, the former Haitian slave Pierre Dominique Toussaint Louverture led the first large-scale slave uprising in the Americas. His forces defeated troops from Spain, Britain, as well as mulatto-French forces. American slaveholders restlessly followed the subsequent events in Haiti with great interest, fearing similar uprisings in the South. Increasingly paranoid, the southern slavocracy closed ranks and suppressed even the slightest hint of insurrection. According to historian Scott Christianson, "Reported American slave revolts during the 1790s grew by 150 percent over the previous decade."[21]

In 1800, Virginia planters had reason to fear insurrection when **Gabriel Prosser** (owned by Thomas Prosser) was accused of conspiring with insurgent slaves to attack Richmond, seize the arsenal, and kill white residents. Despite the twenty-eight-year-old Gabriel's contention that he was motivated by the ideals contained in the Declaration of Independence, thirty of the accused conspirators were executed before they could put any plot into action. According to most sources, the plan came very close to succeeding if not for an informer.

In 2007, Virginia Governor Timothy M. Kaine gave Gabriel Prosser an informal pardon after he was hanged for leading a failed slave revolt in 1800. A formal pardon was not issued since these are typically reserved for the living. In the gubernatorial pardon, Kaine noted that Prosser was driven by "his devotion to the ideals of the American Revolution – it was worth risking death to secure liberty."[22]

With the slave states still dependent on slave patrols, militia, and informal methods of law enforcement, Prosser's rebellion led to the organization of a public guard in Virginia. Wary of future uprisings, General Assembly of Virginia authorized the creation of a "paid militia with its barracks in Richmond." For the next six decades, the Public Guard would patrol Richmond's penitentiary, armory, Capitol Square, and other important public places. Keepers for the new Richmond penitentiary would be selected from the ranks of the Guard as well.

Eleven years later, the largest slave insurrection in American history flared up in two isolated Louisiana parishes, but federal troops were able to suppress it before it could spread any farther. Among the more notorious near conspiracies was the **Denmark Vesey** plot in Charleston, South Carolina, led by a free black who reportedly was intent on ridding the state of its draconian slave system. Despite South Carolina's black majority, Vesey and his coconspirators were executed.[23] In retaliation for the near calamity, South Carolina's planters introduced even harsher laws prohibiting contact between freed blacks and slaves.

It was not until the 1831 **Nat Turner** revolt that a slave insurrection was allowed to come to fruition. By the end of the Virginia rebellion, Turner and his followers killed more than sixty whites. Virginia authorities took six weeks to suppress the rebellion and bring Turner and his followers to "justice." This event marked a turning point in the history of slavery in the South. Prior slave rebellions had existed in plot only. The outbreak of the Turner rebellion led southern authorities to become more aggressive in their defense of slavery and in their control of the slave population. Following the rebellions, southerners turned increasingly to slave patrols and local militia to control the slave population.

Anglo-Indian conflict

The American Revolution was a turning point in Anglo-Indian relations. Violence was formerly restrained between the indigenous peoples and Europeans because of various alliances with the French and English. Prior to the war, the British attempted to block the settlement of the western lands by American colonists while granting Indians protection of their hunting lands. But having made the irrevocable decision to side with the British late in the war, the Indians lost their protectors as the colonists rapidly invaded the Indian sanctuaries. Within several generations, military campaigns and Indian removal would reduce the Indian population east of the Mississippi River to a fraction of its prewar population.

Former Patriots saw nothing wrong with retaliating against the Indian cultures. While not all sided with the British, for the most part, the Americans branded all cultures as traitorous. Among the more lamentable examples of using broad brushstrokes to paint the diverse Indian cultures was the scandalous treatment accorded the Stockbridge Indians of Massachusetts who had so valiantly aided the Patriots but were forced from their homelands to New York.

Dueling

Prior to the American Revolution, dueling had not yet made its mark on the American consciousness. While southern gentlemen might resort to wrestling or their fists to settle matters of honor, dueling was rare before the conflict, when French and British officers introduced the tradition to American officers who helped assimilate the practice into civilian culture. Never very popular in the northern states, it soon became a fixture in the southern subculture of violence. After **Aaron Burr** killed his political adversary Alexander Hamilton in a duel in 1804, dueling was prohibited in the North but would flourish in the South among those who valued competitive self-assertion and skill with weapons as a means of maintaining personal honor. Southern towns such as New Orleans and St. Louis maintained secluded dueling grounds on the outskirts of the city as legislatures and courts turned a blind eye toward the practice. Duels were conducted under a strict protocol that found expression in books such as John L. Wilson's *The Code of Honor* (1838). While movements against dueling were sporadically organized in the South, once and future politicians, such as Andrew Jackson, Judah P. Benjamin, Thomas Hart Benton, and Sam Houston, would endear themselves to their constituents because of their participation in violent encounters at some time in their adult lives. Historian Bertram Wyatt-Brown suggested that, besides confirming the worthiness of the upper classes, dueling also "enabled lesser men" to advance into the higher echelons of society.[24]

Notable trials

Aaron Burr treason trial (1807)

On March 30, 1807, former vice president of the United States Aaron Burr was delivered to Richmond, Virginia, to stand trial for treason. In almost every civilization, treason has been viewed as the most serious secular crime, and a capital crime at that. The charges leveled at Burr included plotting to divide the Union and attempting to make himself emperor of a new nation that would encompass Mexico and most of the American territories west of the Allegheny Mountains. The Burr case is one of the most famous treason trials in American history, and the adjudication of the case would play a part in the larger drama of a young nation attempting to define itself.

No stranger to controversy, Burr today is probably best remembered for his deadly duel with Alexander Hamilton in 1804 that would not only deprive America of a great statesman and sully the reputation of another but also make dueling illegal in the northern states. Treason was the one crime defined by the U.S. Constitution. According to Article III, section 3,

> Treason against the United States shall consist only in levying War against them, or in adhering to their enemies, Giving them Aid and Comfort. No Person shall be convicted of Treason unless on the Testimony of two Witnesses to the same overt Act, or on Confession in open Court.

The charge of treason has long been used as a tool of destruction against political opposition, and the Constitution defined the limits of legal opposition to the federal government.

During the trial, Burr did not deny committing many of the acts he was accused of committing, but he denied that they were treasonable offenses. Following his indictment on murder charges for killing Hamilton in the duel in 1804, Burr's political career had effectively ended. But his controversial life had one more chapter yet to come. In the spring of 1805, Burr reportedly concocted a scheme with James Wilkinson, the military governor of Louisiana, the actual nature of which is still unclear. According to some accounts, Burr told the British minister that he would separate the states and territories west of the Appalachians from the Union and create an empire with himself as leader if the British would offer $500,000 and naval support.

As Burr and his sixty coconspirators traversed the Ohio River destined for New Orleans, his accomplice Wilkinson betrayed Burr to President Thomas Jefferson. Burr was captured and tried for treason with Chief Justice John Marshall presiding. Using the Constitution's definition of treason, it would take two witnesses to convict an individual on that charge. Unable to meet this standard, Burr was exonerated. There are still lingering questions concerning Burr's guilt or innocence, but to his dying day, Burr denied the charges. Despite having the charges against him dismissed by two grand juries, he never regained the respect of his fellow Americans, never able to escape the label of traitor.

The trial of Aaron Burr is considered the most often cited source for understanding the basic federal criminal procedure prior to the 1840s. For most of America's history, circuit courts created by the Judiciary Act of 1789 were the primary trial courts in the federal judicial system. These courts had jurisdiction over federal criminal offenses and disputes between citizens from different states that involved $500 or more. For most of the nineteenth century, except for affidavits certifying the opinion between the two judges holding the circuit court, there was no judicial review. As a result, court opinions, decisions, and especially transcripts are rare for this period.

Conclusions

There was little discussion of a crime problem before the American Revolution. However, independence from Great Britain would lead to a dramatic transformation of the country and the dawning of a crime problem that would haunt American culture for more than two centuries. By the early 1800s, various communities and cities could identify particular areas considered unsafe to the public at large. New York City, Boston, Baltimore, and Philadelphia became hotbeds for sectarian strife. The more rural parts of America were not left untouched by the growing crime problem. During the late eighteenth and early nineteenth centuries, the Natchez Trace between Nashville and Natchez was one of the most dangerous regions in the country. Among the most prolific killers of this era were brothers Micajah and Wiley **Harpe**, who were estimated to have killed dozens of innocent victims, making them probably the earliest recorded multiple murderers in American history.

During the first four decades of the American Republic, the country had grown to a manufacturing power as cities teemed with new immigrants. Peace officers in the 1820s were concerned more with issues of public health and municipal regulations than enforcing criminal laws or preventing crimes. American cities began a transformation that would not be completed until the 1840s and 1850s. Although larger cities, such as New York and Boston, contended with increasing crime and riots, only limited steps were taken toward adopting the 1829 London Metropolitan model of policing. Recent historians have concluded that "in neither Boston, New York nor any other American city was the establishment of uniformed preventive police as rapid and as dramatic as in London in 1829."[25]

Meanwhile, states struggled with the adoption of various prison designs, mainly having to decide whether to keep prisoners confined in a "solitary" environment or in a "silent" one. It was hoped the solitary system, inaugurated in Philadelphia, would give prisoners time to reflect on their crimes and become better citizens. Advocates of the silent system saw the Pennsylvania solitary system as inhumane and allowed prisoners to work with others in a congregate setting, albeit in a rigidly enforced silence. The silent system ultimately triumphed. But the main reason for the success of the Auburn model over the Pennsylvania one was the economic difference since most states would adopt the plan that saw the greatest profit. Slave states, meanwhile, had little need for large penitentiaries, reliant as they were on the punishments that accompanied slavery. Between 1790 and 1817, Pennsylvania, New York, New Jersey, Kentucky, Virginia, Massachusetts, Vermont, Maryland, New Hampshire, Ohio, and Georgia all constructed their first penitentiaries. The reform impulse remained strong in America between 1790 and 1830.

Point – counterpoint

Creating the penitentiary (1835)

During their tours of America in the 1830s, European visitors rarely failed to be impressed by the nation's new penitentiary buildings at Eastern State Penitentiary and Auburn Prison. The differences between these two systems were glaring. The Pennsylvania system, exemplified at Eastern State, was a solitary system that often led prisoners to go insane and sometimes attempt suicide. No less foreboding, the silent Auburn system, with its reliance on military discipline, became the more popular of the two systems, keeping discipline with the threat of a flogging for the slightest infraction.

The following passages are taken from William Crawford's 1835 report on American prisons. In 1831, Craw-ford (1788–1847), a London wine seller and philanthropist, was selected by the British Home Office to embark on an investigation of American prisons and to determine which system was most superior (he selected Pennsyl-vania regimen). He would eventually visit fourteen state penitentiaries and a number of local jails. The twin evils of solitary confinement and its accompanying mental health problems are chronicled in the passage on Eastern, while the issue of flogging is addressed in the Auburn selection.

Source: William Crawford, *Report of William Crawford, Esq., on the Penitentiaries of the United States*, London: Home Department, 1835, pp. 6, 25–26

The tendency of the system to produce mental disease is a subject of such vast importance that I felt it my duty to make every enquiry into the cases of the individuals who had been thus afflicted, in order to ascertain if their lamentable condition could in any degree be ascribed to the peculiar nature of their imprisonment. The information on this point contained in the following letter, addressed to me by the warden of the penitentiary, is so very satisfactory, and was so fully corroborated by other enquiries which I instituted, that no doubt whatever remains on my mind that the parties in question had suffered mental derangement before their committal to this penitentiary. It is proper to observe, that there is no state lunatic asylum in Pennsylvania, and that offenders who are afflicted with disorders of the mind, and who are considered too dangerous to be at large, are consequently sent to the penitentiary for security.

"Philadelphia, first month 20th, 1834." In reference to the subject mentioned yesterday, of the cause of the insanity of four and the idiotcy of one of our prisoners, I must refer to the several reports made annually to the Legislature. In addition to what is contained in them I may add that No. 10 appeared very strange on his admission, and told the inspectors, physician, and myself, remarkable tales of his being concerned in killing men, women, and children, in Charleston (South Carolina), who were salted up and sold for pork, and of being concerned with gangs of counterfeiters; that General Jackson was the prime mover of all this, and such a mass of nonsense that we all came to one conclusion that he was either insane, or wished us to think he was so. A two years' residence here induced us to believe that the former was the case. He was sometimes more excited than at others, but went away apparently in very much the same state of mind to that in which he came in. As he talked in the same manner on the day of his admission as on that of his discharge, no one for a moment believed that separate confinement had been the cause of his insanity, *if he was insane*. We knew nothing of him before his reception, and have never heard of him since he left the doors of the penitentiary.

There was something odd and singular in No. 48 when he arrived here, but this was attributed more to a want of education and an unbroken irritable temper than to insanity. We were told that he had ascended a chimney in the county prison at Lancaster (where he was convicted), and that he remained there three days without food, until it was supposed that he had made his escape. This feat was considered as an attempt to escape, and not attributed to insanity. He was received here Nov. 29th, 1830. On the 7th of Dec. he was set to work as a cabinet maker, at which trade he said he had served two years. We found, however, that he knew but little. On the 11th he refused to do any work, and said that he had been ordered otherwise by a higher authority than any one here. During this night the watchman found him at prayers. About eight o'clock on the morning of the 12th my attention was called to him. He was sitting with his lamp burning and a bible before him. I directed him to put out the light: this he would not do. Thomas Bradford and S. W. Crawford saw him this day, and believed him to be under the influence of religious excitement. On the contrary I thought that he was feigning insanity. He became better, but again worse, and continued so until discharged by pardon.

In the workshops the convicts are arranged in such a way as not to face each other, and to labor separately as much as possible. In each shop prisoners are selected as attendants, whose business it is to distribute the materials, hand out and grind the tools, and clean the shops, under the direction of the assistant-keeper. All this, however, is done principally by signs, so that the attention of the other convicts is not distracted. Privies are placed in the corners of the shops. Each workshop has a supply of water to which a prisoner can help himself at pleasure. In every mechanical or trade department there is at least one assistant-keeper who attends to the instruction of learners. The assistant-keeper directs the appropriation of all raw materials, keeps a daily account of the work performed by each convict, and regulates his daily task. He also superintends the removal of his men to and from their cells. A prisoner who wilfully or negligently injures his work, tools, wearing apparel, or bedding, is immediately flogged by the assistant-keeper. The prisoners are not allowed to speak to each other on any pretence, except by special direction of the officers. They are not at any time to leave their places without permission. They are never to speak to any person who does not belong to the prison, and must not look off from their work at spectators. They are not to speak even to an officer, except when absolutely necessary relative to their business. For a violation of any of these rules they are immediately flogged. A convict's word is never taken even against another convict, and much less against an officer.

The prisoners are not allowed to write nor receive any letters, or intelligence from or concerning their friends, or on any subject out of the prison. No relative, or friend, is allowed to visit or speak to a convict, except in some extraordinary case which may require a personal interview, and which can only take place in the presence of the keeper or his deputy.

The assistant-keepers are twenty in number. They are required to enforce strictly the general observance of the regulations. They are not to hold any conversation with the convicts, nor even allow them to speak on any subject except on necessary business. Each assistant-keeper must keep a list of the names of the prisoners under his charge, with the respective numbers of the cells occupied by them, and the description of work at which they are employed. If an assistant-keeper punishes a convict for misconduct, he is required within a reasonable time to make a report in writing to the keeper, or his deputy, stating the prisoner's name and offense, and the nature and extent of the punishment inflicted. The assistant-keepers are to correct convicts for every breach of discipline by stripes which are to be inflicted with a raw-hide whip, and applied to the back in such a manner as not to expose the head, face, eyes, or in any way to put the convict's health or limbs in danger. In aggravated cases, a "cat," made of six lashes of small twine, may be applied to the bare back, under the direction of the keeper or deputy. The prisoner is compelled to strip immediately on the commission of an offense, and is flogged before the other prisoners. No superior officer is required to be present on these occasions.

Source: William Crawford, *Report of William Crawford, Esq., on the Penitentiaries of the United States*, London: Home Department, 1835, pp. 6, 35–26.

Key terms

John Marshall	*Marbury v. Madison*	Alien and Sedition Acts
XYZ Affair	Joseph Fouche	Eugene Vidocq
Sûreté	Peterloo Massacre	Napoleonic policing
Robert Peel	bobbies and peelers	cooping
Jacob Hays	high constable	London Metropolitan Police
paterollers	slave patrols	mounted police tradition
Texas Rangers	Eastern State Penitentiary	Cherry Hill Prison
Louis Dwight	Newgate Prison	Auburn Prison
Elam Lynds	Thomas Eddy	prison stripes
Five Points district	temperance crusade	slave revolts
Gabriel Prosser	Nat Turner	Aaron Burr
Denmark Vesey	Harpe brothers	

Critical thinking questions

1 What impact did the development of modern police forces in Europe have on American law enforcement?
2 How did the ideas of the Enlightenment change Americans' thinking about the causes of crime? How do these ideas compare with mainstream thought about crime and punishment today?
3 What did Auburn Prison hope to achieve with its silent system of prison discipline? How does the silent system compare to today's use of boot camp prisons?
4 Did Eastern State's use of solitary confinement with labor solve the crime problem or improve prison administration? Can you make any comparisons with today's supermax or control unit prisons?
5 Discuss the trial of Aaron Burr, the Judiciary Act of 1789, and the Alien and Sedition Acts in terms of the development of federal criminal justice.

Notes

1 New York City was then the nation's capital.
2 Charles Warren, *The Supreme Court in United States History*, Boston: Little, Brown and Company, Vol. 1, 1922, p. 461.
3 Charles Warren, *The Supreme Court in United States History*, Boston: Little, Brown and Company, Vol. 1, 1922, p. 461.
4 nham, MD: Rowman and Littlefield, 1998, pp. 54–55.
5 Philip J. Stead, *The Police of Paris*, London: Staples, 1957, pp. 45–48.
6 Rand Mirante, *Medusa's Head: The Rise and Survival of Joseph Fouche: Inventor of the Modern Police State*, New York: Archway Publishing, 2014; Stead, 1957.
7 James Morton, *The First Detective, the Life and Times of Vidocq: Criminal Spy and Private Eye*, London: Random House, 2005; Stead, 1957.

8 James Richardson, *The New York Police: Colonial Times to 1901*, New York: Oxford University Press, 1970, p. 15.

9 Joseph Goldstein, "Forbidden Zone for the Police: Places Ready-Made for a Nap," *New York Times*, January 17, 2014, pp. A1, 19.

10 Patricia A. Turner, *I Heard It through the Grapevine: Rumor in African-American Culture*, Berkeley, CA: University of California Press, 1993, p. 38.

11 See Dennis C. Rousey, *Policing the Southern City: New Orleans, 1805–1889*, Baton Rouge: Louisiana State University Press, 1996.

12 Edward L. Ayers, *Vengeance and Justice: Crime and Punishment in the 19th-Century South*, New York: Oxford University Press, 1984, p. 83.

13 Larry Sullivan, *The Prison Reform Movement: Forlorn Hope*, Boston: Twayne Publishing, 1990, p. 18.

14 Gustave de Beaumont and Alexis de Tocqueville, *On the Penitentiary System in the United States and Its Application in France*, Carbondale: Southern Illinois Press, 1979, pp. 162–163.

15 Charles Dickens, *American Notes: A Journey*, New York: Fromm International Publishing, 1985, p. 99.

16 Blake McKelvey, *American Prisons: A History of Good Intentions*, Montclair, NJ: Patterson Smith, 1977, p. 2.

17 See Roger Lane, "Capital Punishment," in *Violence in America*, Vol. 1, New York: Charles Scribner's Sons, 1999, pp. 198–203.

18 Quoted in Isaac Newton Phelps Stokes, *The Iconography of Manhattan Island*, Vol. 5, New York: Robert H. Dodd, 1915, p. 760.

19 Luc Sante, *Low Life: Lures and Snares of Old New York*, New York: Vintage Books, 1992, p. 105.

20 Ibid.; Herbert Asbury, *The Gangs of New York*, New York: Capricorn Books, 1927, 1970.

21 Scott Christianson, *With Liberty for Some: 500 Years of Imprisonment in America*, Boston: Northeastern University Press, 1998, p. 92.

22 "Virginia Governor 'Pardons' Slave Who Led "Gabriel's Rebellion," https://historynewsnetwork.org/article/42380

23 David Robertson, *Denmark Vesey*, New York: Vintage, 1999.

24 Bertram Wyatt-Brown, *Honor and Violence in the Old South*, New York: Oxford University Press, 1986, p. 142.

25 Clive Emsley, *Policing and Its Context, 1750–1870*, New York: Schocken Books, 1984, p. 109. See also Roger Lane, *Policing the City: Boston, 1822–1885*, Cambridge, MA: Harvard University Press; Eric Monkkonen, *Police in Urban America, 1860–1920*, New York: Cambridge University Press, 1981.

Sources

Asbury, Herbert. 1970. *The Gangs of New York*. New York: Capricorn Books.

Attorney General's Survey of Release Procedures (1940). 1973. "State Prisons in America, 1787–1937." In *Penology: The Evolution of Corrections in America*, ed. George G. Killinger et al., pp. 23–73. St. Paul, MN: West Publishing Company.

Ayers, Edward L. 1984. *Vengeance and Justice: Crime and Punishment in the 19th-Century South*. New York: Oxford University Press.

Barnes, Harry Elmer. 1968. *The Evolution of Penology in Pennsylvania: A Study in American Social History*. Montclair, NJ: Patterson Smith.

Beaumont, Gustave de and Alexis de Tocqueville. 1979. *On the Penitentiary System in the United States and Its Application in France*. Carbondale: Southern Illinois University Press.

Christianson, Scott. 1998. *With Liberty for Some: 500 Years of Imprisonment in America*. Boston: Northeastern University Press.

Dickens, Charles. 1985. *American Notes: A Journey*. New York: Fromm International Publishing.

Emsley, Clive. 1984. *Policing and Its Context, 1750–1870*. New York: Schocken Books.

Finkel, Kenneth. 1994. "Philadelphia in the 1820s: A New Civic Consciousness." In *Eastern State Penitentiary: Crucible of Good Intentions*, ed. Norman Johnston, Philadelphia: Philadelphia Museum of Art, pp. 9–19.

Foner, Philip S. 1975. *History of Black Americans: From Africa to the Emergence of the Cotton Kingdom*. Westport, CT: Greenwood Press.

Howard, D. L. 1960. *The English Prisons*. London: Methuen.

Johnson, David R. 1979. *Policing the Urban Underworld: The Impact of Crime on the Development of the American Police, 1800–1887*. Philadelphia: Temple University Press.

Johnston, Norman. 1994. *Eastern State Penitentiary: Crucible of Good Intentions*. Philadelphia: Philadelphia Museum of Art.

Lane, Roger. 1967. *Policing the City: Boston, 1822–1885*. Cambridge, MA: Harvard University Press.

———. 1999. "Capital Punishment." In *Violence in America*. Vol. 1, pp. 198–203. New York: Charles Scribner's Sons.

Masur, Louis P. 1989. *Rites of Execution: Capital Punishment and the Transformation of American Culture, 1776–1865*. New York: Oxford University Press.

McKelvey, Blake. 1977. *American Prisons: A History of Good Intentions*. Montclair, NJ: Patterson Smith.

Miller, John C. 1951. *Crisis in Freedom: The Alien and Sedition Acts*. Boston: Little, Brown and Company.

Mintz, Steven. 1995. *Moralists and Modernizers: America's Pre-Civil War Reformers*. Baltimore: Johns Hopkins University Press.

Monkkonen, Eric. 1981. *Police in Urban America 1860–1920*. New York: Cambridge University Press.

Morton, James. 2005. *The First Detective, the Life and Times of Vidocq: Criminals, Spy and Private Eye*. London: Random House.

Reed, V. B. and James Davis Williams, eds. 1960. *The Case of Aaron Burr*. Boston: Houghton Mifflin.

Richardson, James. 1970. *The New York Police: Colonial Times to 1901*. New York: Oxford University Press.

Robertson, David. 1999. *Denmark Vesey: The Buried Story of America's Largest Slave Rebellion and the Man Who Led It*. New York: Random House.

Rorabaugh, William J. 1979. *The Alcoholic Republic: An American Tradition*. New York: Oxford University Press.

Rothman, David J. 1971. *The Discovery of the Asylum: Social Order and Disorder in the New Republic*. Boston: Little, Brown and Company.

Rousey, Dennis C. 1996. *Policing the Southern City: New Orleans, 1805–1889*. Baton Rouge: Louisiana State University Press.

Sante, Luc. 1992. *Low Life: Lures and Snares of Old New York*. New York: Vintage Books.

Semonche, John E. 1998. *Keeping the Faith: A Cultural History of the U.S. Supreme Court*. Lanham, MD: Rowman and Littlefield.

Stead, Philip J. 1957. *The Police of Paris*. London: Staples.

Stokes, Isaac Newton Phelps. 1915. *The Iconography of Manhattan Island*. Vol. 5. New York: Robert H. Dodd.

Sullivan, Larry. 1990. *The Prison Reform Movement: Forlorn Hope*. Boston: Twayne Publishing.

Teeters, Negley and John D. Shearer. 1957. *The Prison at Philadelphia, Cherry Hill: The Separate System of Penal Discipline, 1829–1913*. New York: Columbia University Press.

Turner, Patricia A. 1993. *I Heard It through the Grapevine: Rumor in African-American Culture*. Berkeley, CA: University of California Press.

Walters, Ronald G. 1978. *American Reformers, 1815–1860*. New York: Hill and Wang.

Wright, Donald R. 1993. *African Americans in the Early Republic, 1789–1831*. Arlington Heights, IL: Harlan Davidson.

Wyatt-Brown, Bertram. 1986. *Honor and Violence in the Old South*. New York: Oxford University Press.

1835	1836	1836	1837	1838	1841	1841
Rising mob violence	Tennessee introduces parole for good behavior	Congress authorizes special agents for the Postal Service	Abolitionist Elijah P. Lovejoy murdered	Temperance advocates win victory in Massachusetts	Murder of Mary Rogers spurs police reform efforts	Dorothea Dix launches reform campaign for the insane

CHAPTER SIX

Crime and criminal justice in antebellum America (1835–1857)

Learning objectives

After reading this chapter students should understand and be able to discuss:

- How the conflict between states' rights and federal law impacted the criminal justice system in the years leading to the Civil War
- The development of twenty-four-hour policing in New York City
- Why an absence in federal law enforcement led to the formation of private police and detective organizations such as the Pinkertons
- The development of indeterminate sentencing and juvenile institutions
- Why the Mary Rogers murder case inspired police reform in New York City
- The rise and fall of the death penalty abolition movement in the years leading up to the Civil War
- The rise of American gun culture and racial violence
- How patterns of crime and punishment became more recognizable along sectional lines before the Civil War

The ascendance of Andrew Jackson to the presidency in 1828 inaugurated the "**Age of the Common Man.**" Jackson's two terms in office would coincide with the dramatic transformation of American society and social institutions as he presided over a country entering the maelstrom of sectional politics, unprecedented immigration, and a criminal justice system still undergoing transition from its colonial roots.

DOI: 10.4324/9781315148342-6

1842	1845	1847	1847	1849	1850
Alexander Maconochie experiments with indeterminate sentencing	Passage of the New York City Municipal Police Act	The Colt .45 revolver enters American gun culture	Michigan abolishes the death penalty	Astor Place riot leads to improved methods of riot control	Fugitive Slave Act

A self-made man, Jackson was the first president born west of the Appalachian Mountains and the first born in a log cabin. Espousing a platform that favored the common people, he harbored a lasting animosity against the well-born and the gentry as he worked to remove the obstacles that kept ordinary white citizens from climbing the social ladder to economic prosperity. Jackson introduced an important component to urban politics by embracing a **spoils system** that opened public offices to partisan supporters. Although Jackson claimed that his goal was to prevent the development of a class of corrupt civil servants, the results of his efforts would prove otherwise.

The Jacksonian period in America coincided with the years 1820–1850, a period when Americans first perceived crime as a threat to the order and security of the Republic. In response, various constituencies turned to the developing police forces of urban America, others to the developing prison systems. Since colonial Americans felt little threatened by problems of crime, many Americans suggested that the new environment was the result of the declining authority of the church and family. With Americans on the move to the western frontier or to the new urban centers, many feared that a growing lack of community pressure had left a void in the moral center.

By the late 1820s, Irish immigration had begun to make an impact on eastern seaport cities. These towns witnessed a concomitant growth of slums as the Irish exodus continued to America over the next thirty years. The flood of immigrants into cities such as New York impacted every segment of society, particularly the development of the criminal justice system. In a time without building codes, sanitation and health services, and even professional policing, lower Manhattan reached a population density unmatched in the world. By 1855, New York was crammed with 290,000 people per square mile compared to London's 175,816. Among the most vociferous opponents to the Irish immigrants were Protestant workers who surmised that the Irish-Catholic workers represented a threat to their wages since the immigrants would work for less money. According to Protestants, the Catholic Church represented despotism and subservience to Rome; thus, nativist writers would infer that the Catholics represented a papist threat to American democratic institutions, presaging the conspirational **xenophobia** of the **Know-Nothing Party** in the 1850s.

The Irish immigration of the **antebellum** years was the first large-scale immigration to America of non–Anglo-Saxon Protestants. Most were unskilled laborers, and by 1850, they represented more than one-third of New York City's population. Restricted from upward mobility by the Protestant upper classes, they congregated in close-knit enclaves where they found that joining the Democratic Party could lead to social and economic advancement. The prevailing **nativism** of the period led to an early affinity between urban immigrants and the developing political machines of New York and Chicago.

1850	1851	1851	1853	1855	1857
Formation of nativist Know-Nothing Party	Boston creates nation's first police detection division	San Francisco Committee of Vigilance organized	New York City Police adopt complete uniforms	Allan Pinkerton founds his private detective agency	*Dred Scott* decision

By the 1830s, the nation was becoming increasingly factionalized over the issue of slavery. During the previous decade, slavery had spread west into Alabama, Mississippi, Texas (still part of Mexico), and Louisiana. Racial unrest was viewed as a continuous threat in both the North and the South. Although racial warfare was an omnipresent threat in the South with the large population of slaves, northern cities saw white mobs repeatedly attack African American neighborhoods from the 1830s into the 1850s.

One alternative to slavery and revolt that gained increasing currency in the 1830s was the abolition movement. By the late 1830s, there were 1,300 antislavery societies in the North comprised of tens of thousands of members. Foremost among the abolitionists was William Lloyd Garrison (1805–1879) of Massachusetts. Unlike British abolitionists who supported the gradual emancipation of the slaves, Garrison was of a more radical mind, insisting on immediate and unconditional emancipation. Garrison became the most reviled man in the South, and in 1831, Georgia was offering a reward of $5,000 to anyone who would transport him to Georgia for trial. Abolitionist groups drew an increasingly diverse constituency as they distributed their literature to a more receptive audience in the 1840s.

Abolitionists were often targeted by mobs in both sections of the country. Anti-abolitionist mobs were usually led by prominent members of the community, including bankers, judges, merchants, and physicians. Mobs singled out the homes and businesses of abolitionists and particularly their printing presses.

The lawgivers

The Democratic era ushered in by the Jacksonian presidency swept away many of the barriers that had reserved the legal professional as the preserve of the more respected members of society. Massachusetts was among the states leading the way in 1836, when it proclaimed that

> any citizen of this Commonwealth of the age of twenty-one years, and of good moral character, who shall have devoted three years to the study of law, in the office of some attorney within this State, shall on application to the Supreme Court or Court of Common Pleas, be admitted to practice as an attorney in any court of this Commonwealth.[1]

Within a few years, not even a high school education would be required for admission to the state bar. Over the next several years, the same "democratic" movement swept the country, and requirements to practice the law would become so lax that Abraham Lincoln was admitted to the Illinois bar in 1837 with less than a grammar school training in school credits.

Voting qualifications

One of the most profound political developments of the early nineteenth century was the gradual elimination of property qualifications for voting and holding political office. Having initially followed the English precedent during the colonial era of expecting voters to own a stake in the community by owning a certain minimum amount of land as a voting qualification, prospective officeholders were required to meet even higher property qualifications. By the 1830s, many states had discarded voting qualifications for white men. This transition from voting qualifications to universal white male suffrage was made with little dissension. One of the more notorious episodes of violence occurred in Rhode Island, where suffrage was still limited to landowners and oldest sons in the 1830s. Without a charter granting a bill of rights, in 1841, less than half the adult white males were qualified to vote. That same year, Harvard-educated attorney Thomas W. Dorr organized a campaign to draft a new state constitution that would abolish voting restrictions. Subsequently, the state militia was called out to arrest Dorr and his followers for insurrection. After an unsuccessful attempt to seize the state arsenal, Dorr was arrested and sentenced to life in prison for high treason. This turn of events unleashed a wave of popular resentment, leading the governor to pardon Dorr and Rhode Island to adopt a new constitution.

States' rights and federal law

During the Jacksonian era, states' rights came into conflict with federal law, setting the stage for numerous precedent-setting events. During the decades leading up to the Civil War, most Americans felt that they had the right to govern themselves without interference by the federal government. No real demarcation between state and federal rights had been established. No small part of the responsibility for resolving this controversy lay with the Supreme Court, which had not sufficiently settled these issues at the termination of John Marshall's career on the court. Leaders in both the North and the South, particularly those who took firm stands in favor of the rights of individual states, were left with the impression that they could leave the Union over certain grievances. While other states did not recognize the right of secession, they maintained that they had the right to nullify state laws that they found unacceptable.

South Carolina's Nullification Controversy

In one of the best-known states' rights test cases, South Carolina's John Calhoun proclaimed the right of his state to nullify any federal legislation that it disapproved of. In 1833, he was given an opportunity to test the murky waters of states' rights during the presidency of Andrew Jackson. Almost thirty years before the outbreak of the Civil War, South Carolina's resolve was tested when it attempted to nullify the "tariff of abominations," which southern states felt ruined its interests for the benefit of the North. Calhoun claimed that the tariff made southerners "the serfs of the system – out of whose labor is raised, not only the money paid into the Treasury, but the funds out of which are drawn the rich rewards of the manufacturer and his associates in interest."[2]

With South Carolina threatening to secede, Jackson, determined to uphold national authority over his leanings for the slave system, prepared for military action. The president asserted that American nationhood existed before state sovereignty and that nullification was "incompatible with the existence of the Union." Jackson denounced nullification as treason but eventually convinced Congress to pass a compromise tariff, but not before South Carolina backed down from its threat to leave the Union. In the process, this southern state learned an important lesson, namely, that successful resistance to northern "tyranny" would require the cooperation of other southern slave states.[3]

The Taney Court

Succeeding John Marshall as chief justice of the Supreme Court in 1836, Roger Taney (1777–1864) and other justices appointed by Andrew Jackson reflected the transition to a new era in which the focus of the court shifted from federal to state power. A product of a different era, Taney was the first chief justice to wear trousers rather than traditional knee breeches. Under Taney's direction, the Supreme Court would reflect Jackson's emphasis on public power in contrast to the Marshall court's constitutional protection of property rights. During his three decades at the helm, Taney increased the power of the states and limited the reach of the national government.

The Fugitive Slave Act

Since the introduction of slavery in the seventeenth century, slaves had fled from the repressive restraints of bondage. During the colonial era, most legislatures enacted laws prohibiting slaves from running away and sanctioning specific punishments for recaptured slaves. Various strategies were employed to capture runaway bondsmen, ranging from using native Indians as slave catchers to utilizing reward systems.

In the early nineteenth century, several northern states initiated programs to emancipate slaves, and abolitionists became more vocal and numerous. By the 1820s, New York, Massachusetts, and Pennsylvania had passed laws that required jury trials to convene before a master could take an alleged fugitive slave out of the state. Southerners were outraged by these "personal liberty laws" and argued that the laws violated the Constitution, which protected individual property. In 1842, the Supreme Court ruled in *Prigg v. Pennsylvania* that Pennsylvania's personal liberty laws violated the Constitution's fugitive slave clause.

In response, many northern states adopted more stringent policies for preventing the return of fugitive slaves to the South. Southerners demanded a tougher fugitive slave law, arguing that it had become virtually impossible to retrieve runaway slaves in the North. The passage of the pivotal Compromise of 1850 was accompanied by the passage of a much more uncompromising fugitive slave law.

According to the Fugitive Slave Act of 1850, alleged runaways were prohibited from testifying in court, and decision making was taken out of the hands of local officials and placed within the purview of federal officials. Most inflammatory was the use of the army and federal marshals as security forces to protect slave masters and federal officials from the violent attempts at slave rescue by abolitionists. Opposition to the law took a variety of forms, including riots, rescue attempts, and attacks on courthouses and jails.

The arrest of the slave Thomas M. Sims in 1851 demonstrates the subterfuge that was used by law enforcement to enforce the law. Reputedly a runaway from Virginia, he was arrested on a false charge of theft in Boston. Following an arraignment at the courthouse, the police commissioner overruled constitutional objections to the Fugitive Slave Act, and in the quiet of early morning, Sims was clandestinely spirited from his cell to a ship that would carry him south to slavery. This case, as did many others, served only to rouse the antislavery factions into more ardent opposition, and in 1854, a U.S. marshal was killed during a failed rescue attempt. Many Civil War historians credit the Fugitive Slave Act with escalating sectional tensions, leading to the Civil War.

The temperance movement

The transformation of American society in the first half of the nineteenth century was accompanied by growing clamor for a temperance movement and the growth of nativism. Nativism found political expression in 1843 with the formation of the American Republic Party in New York. Subsequently, the party attracted a national following as the Know-Nothing Party in 1850. Anti-Catholic and antislavery, the moral prejudices of the party found a voice in the antebellum temperance campaign of the 1840s and 1850s. Among the more vociferous temperance groups was the Sons of Temperance, which could claim 250,000 dues-paying members by 1850. Whether religious or secular in nature, reform groups soon resorted to political action to accomplish their objectives. In 1833, a resolution was introduced by an abolitionist, declaring "the traffic in ardent spirits" morally wrong.[4] The author of the resolution followed up by asking that communities be allowed to pass laws prohibiting the traffic in liquor within their jurisdictions. In 1838, temperance advocates won their first major victory when Massachusetts banned the sale of liquor in amounts under fifteen gallons. This attempt to keep distilled liquor from taverns and the poor was repealed in 1840, but not before fomenting episodes of civil disobedience.

In the mid-1840s, abolitionists joined the crusade for temperance in Maine, and in 1846, a law was passed prohibiting the sale of intoxicating beverages in less than twenty-eight-gallon increments. Enforcement of the law was added to the duties of town selectmen, who typically looked the other way when infractions occurred. Prohibitionists received their greatest victory with the passage of the **Maine Law of 1851**, which prohibited the sale and manufacture of all intoxicating beverages within the state. By 1855, thirteen states had passed similar laws, and New England, New York, and parts of the Midwest were considered dry. As a consequence, the per capita consumption of alcohol between 1830 and 1850 plummeted. Although most of the prohibition laws were repealed by the late 1850s, from the antebellum era on, the temperance crusade played an instrumental role in American politics and would offer many challenges to law enforcement on both the local and the state level in the years to come.

Murder as a capital crime

Pennsylvania introduced a statute differentiating the two degrees of murder in 1794, with only murder in the first degree a capital offense. Other states soon changed their laws to reflect the degrees of culpability in deciding on the death penalty for murder. According to Pennsylvania law, first degree included the use of poison, any premeditated murder, or murder perpetrated during the commission of an arson, a robbery, or a burglary. Other murders were classified as second degree. Virginia was the first to borrow this definition and was soon followed by Ohio (1824), New York (1827), and Missouri (1835).[5] This innovation reflected a growing movement against the death penalty during the antebellum years that saw the amount of capital crimes reduced significantly. South Carolina saw capital offenses plunge from 165 in 1813 to 22 by 1850.

Law enforcement

As American cities grappled with the problems of industrialization, urbanization, and immigration in the 1830s and 1840s, numerous experiments in policing were attempted. Southern cities such as New Orleans and Charleston tried uniformed city guards with sporadic successes. With the financial support of a wealthy local philanthropist, Philadelphia established day and night police forces in the 1830s, one of the first American cities to do so. The experiment proved only temporary, disbanding in a short time.

In 1804, New Orleans Mayor Etienne Bore introduced a mounted patrol to apprehend runaway slaves. His proposal to the form this unit was a precursor to stabling the city's first distinct police force the following year. In 1805, the city council approved the Gendarmie to continue its slave catching services while performing police duties. The following year it was disbanded and replaced. In 1809, the Gendarmie was replaced with a less militaristic version called the city guard. It was noteworthy for employing several African American members at a time when the majority of similar units were devoid of black members. However, mounting tensions led to no further recruitment of black members until after 1830, and they would not patrol the streets of New Orleans again until the Reconstruction era. The force, which was demilitarized within two decades of its inauguration, would do without uniforms and formidable weapons, such as their former swords and muskets. To this day, there is controversy over whether New Orleans played a significant part in American police evolution, but there is little doubt it was the site of police experimentation in the years leading to the creation of the New York Police force in 1845.[6]

Boston made hesitant first steps toward police reform following incessant ethnic rioting in the 1830s. After calling on the militia to suppress a riot between Irish mourners and local firemen, Marshal Francis Tukey was hired to build a proficient police force. But with a rising index of efficiency measured by the capture of several hundred criminals, the public's antagonism turned instead against the force. In 1851, Boston created the country's first police department detective division and four years later would establish a force along Robert Peel's London model.

The New York City police

With the phenomenal growth of the city in the 1840s, the old system of constables and night watchmen was soon overwhelmed by the problems accompanying the new economic and social order. Mass immigration in the 1830s and 1840s contributed to the growing juxtaposition between the well-to-do and the poor. Nowhere was this truer than in New York City.

Business entrepreneurs soon enlarged labor forces and introduced a division of labor to mass-produce goods. But while the manufacturers reaped a profit, many laborers found their status and job security on the decline. Recent immigrants were often targeted as the scapegoat for the changing environment. Much of the urban violence was directed at recent Irish-Catholic immigrants. Mobs attacked Irish communities in many northeastern cities from Philadelphia to Charlestown, Massachusetts. In fact, this mayhem was so prevalent that the nascent insurance companies would refuse to issue the Irish policies. Rioting and an increasing crime and vice problem led, by 1844, to growing sentiment for a police force in New York City based on the London model.

In 1844, New York City's traditional night watch was legislated out of existence and replaced with a new system comprised of separate day and night police forces, becoming the first city to merge the day and night forces into a uniformed police department model after Peel's English bobbies. Initially, the state authorized the hiring of 800 men to man the new force, but the city council demurred, hiring only a quarter of that number. The force quickly demonstrated its inadequacy, but the following year, the state legislature adopted the original plan for 800 uniformed municipal police officers with the passage of New York City Municipal Police Act. According to police historian Wilbur R. Miller, this act "created the first police force modeled on London's precedent outside of the British Empire."[7]

With a long-established antipathy for uniforms of any kind, many of the original officers objected to wearing specially designed uniforms, preferring to choose their own outfits. Like many Londoners in the years before the acceptance of the uniformed bobbies, there was a strong resistance to the British innovation of uniformed policing. Worried that uniforms were an infringement on American freedoms and represented the dangers of a standing army to democratic institutions, opponents compared uniformed officers to "**liveried lackeys**." Thus, a compromise was reached in which police officers wore eight-point, star-shaped copper badges over their left breasts instead of a complete uniform, hence their identification as the "**star police**," "**coppers**," or just plain "cops."[8]

The year 1845 saw the introduction of New York City's first patrol guide, which emphasized Peel's objectives of the prevention of crime, noting that "the prevention of crime being the most important object . . . the absence of crime will be considered the best proof of the efficiency of the police."[9] Responding to a fire at the Bowery Theater in 1845, wearing uniforms dignified by gleaming brass buttons, crowds of street toughs laughed at them, accusing the new police of mimicking the London Bobbies. And so the experiment with uniforms ended, and it was not revived until eight years later in 1853, when the New York City police finally adopted full uniforms.

The development of modern policing after 1845 was hampered by a lack of consensus about wearing uniforms, whether police should be armed, and the use of force. The lack of a uniform hindered the goal of policing, which was to be visible. Those against uniforms argued that it would offer criminals an advantage by immediately identifying the police. New York City was the first city to surmount the controversy by mandating that when the current officers' four-year terms of duty ended in 1853, the police commissioners would fire whoever refused to don a uniform. Boston and Chicago followed suited in a few years, and as the Civil War years approached, American men felt less insecure about wearing uniforms. In a major departure from the London model, there was little argument that American police should be armed, although it did not occur immediately.

One of the early turning points for the new force took place in May 1849, when a riot developed out of a rivalry between supporters of two leading actors at New York City's Astor Place Theater. When a mob attempted to prevent one of the performers from taking the stage, a wild melee ensued, with the mob throwing rocks at a small, outmatched police detachment. The Captain of the Eighth Ward Police, Benjamin P. Fairchild recounted

> I was directed by the Chief [Matsell] to report to him if at any time I thought it was nec-
> essary to send for the military, to sustain our position. . . . About 8 o'clock I reported to
> the Chief that I thought it would be impossible to retain our position much longer. . . .
> I was directed to rally the men and make another effort. . . . I went on the 8th street side,
> and found one or two hundred young men and boys stoning the building.[10]

Fortunately for the police, the local militia arrived on the scene just in time. Although accounts vary, the soldiers eventually fired into the crowd, killing twenty-two and wounding close to 100. A public uproar led the police force to implement riot control training and military drills for police officers, probably the first riot training in American police history. In response, the New York Police were equipped with their official first police weapon, a twenty-two-inch club, to be used only in self-defense.

From 1845 to 1853, New York City policemen were appointed by aldermen. Beginning in 1853, a board of police commissioners, made up of the mayor, the city recorder, and the city judge, took over the appointment of policemen. The new protocol ensured that a system of graft would determine the selection of police rather than any specific requirements. In the early years of the force, it cost a $40 bribe to the precinct captain to become a patrolman and at least another $150 to a political campaign. The most sought-after position was the $1,000 per year captain's position, which cost a minimum of $200 for appointment.

Federal law enforcement

For at least the first half of the nineteenth century, federal policing was mainly within the domain of the U.S. Marshals Service. Created by the Judiciary Act of 1789, marshals were originally restricted to four-year appointments by the president. During the first year of their existence, the marshals were hamstrung by a lack of direction and power. With an absence of an immediate supervisor and the political nature of their appointment, their capacity as criminal justice professionals was severely limited. Particularly vexing was their poor remuneration due to their dependence on a fee list that had been used by county sheriffs until the 1850s. But as late as 1842, legislators capped a marshal's salary at $6,000, with any additional income required to be turned over to the Treasury Department. In 1853, the outmoded fee system was discarded in favor of a more equitable pay scale.

In the years leading up to the Civil War, U.S. marshals would face the widespread counterfeiting of the skilled "**coneymen**," so named because of the wide diversity of currency issued in the years before a modern banking system. According to most estimates, one-third of the currency in circulation between 1815 and 1860 was counterfeit. With individual banks issuing various bank notes in a bewildering array of denominations, together with U.S. Treasury notes and postal currency, opportunities were many for those skilled in duplicating currencies. Although the marshals were the first line of defense, the Treasury Department occasionally hired detectives to crack the counterfeiting rings.[11] In 1865, Congress finally recognized the need for special measures to suppress counterfeiting by creating the Secret Service under the secretary of the treasury (see next chapter).

During the 1840s and following the conflict with Mexico (1846–1848), the United States increased its boundaries, adding sparsely populated territories to its domain. In these unorganized territories, the U.S. marshals provided the only formal law enforcement. According to federal law, when a population of a federal territory reached 5,000 free white males, a bicameral legislature could be elected and territorial laws promulgated. After reaching 60,000 free white males, the territory could be nominated for statehood, and the nomination would then be forwarded to Congress for final approval.

On several occasions, marshals required the army to assist them in their law enforcement functions in the vast West, and in 1854, a presidential proclamation authorized marshals to call on the army as posse comitatus. During the period before a territory became a state, any crime was considered a federal violation; hence, marshals saw continuous action as the only lawmen. As territories made the transition to statehood, marshals gave up much of their authority to territorial lawmen, such as sheriffs. As the only federal law enforcement officers prior to the Civil War, federal marshals were continually tested as America teetered on the brink of sectional conflict.

One form of federal law enforcement that has not received its proper due is the Postal Service inspectors. In 1836, Congress reorganized the Post Office and authorized it to hire full-time special agents with broad authority to investigate any aspect of the Postal Service. Imbued with arrest powers, police historian David Johnson credits the postal inspectors as "the first formal police force within the executive branch of the federal government."[12]

The Pinkertons

During the 1850s, law enforcement was often absent from the developing communities west of the Mississippi River. In 1855, **Allan J. Pinkerton** (1819–1884) founded what would become Pinkerton's National Detective Agency, which initially handled cases in communities with limited law enforcement expertise. The private detective has a rich tradition dating back to the eighteenth century thief takers of England and the exploits of Eugene François Vidocq in France. The arrival of the Pinkertons on the national stage in the 1850s heralded new developments in policing strategies and investigative techniques in America as the nation moved toward sectional conflict. Born in Glasgow, Scotland, Pinkerton found his life's calling after playing an instrumental role in the capture of a gang of counterfeiters soon after migrating to America in 1842. Pinkerton entered law enforcement in 1846 as a deputy sheriff in Illinois. In 1850, Pinkerton became the first detective hired by the Chicago Police Department and on several occasions was called on by the U.S. Treasury Department to battle counterfeiters. After opening his own detective agency in 1855, he adopted numerous investigative techniques and, according to some sources, introduced the first "**rogues' gallery**," which displayed the characteristics and idiosyncrasies of known criminals. During America's railroad expansion of the 1850s, Pinkerton was hired to create a spying system to keep railroad conductors from stealing fares. Soon after, he created an all-seeing eye as the symbol for the company, hence its motto "The Eye That Never Sleeps."

San Francisco vigilantes

San Francisco, in the wake of the 1849 California gold rush, became the center of vigilante activity[13] in America. According to historian Frank Richard Prassel, "The term regulator fell into disuse after much publicity accorded the San Francisco vigilance committees of 1851 and 1856."[14] Miner's courts dispensed justice in the gold camps of California, where formal law enforcement was almost nonexistent. According to one miner, "The marvel of marvels is, the mob-law and failure of justice were so infrequent, that society was so well and swiftly organized."[15] Forced to contend with a rapidly growing criminal element, the San Francisco Committee of Vigilance was organized in June 1851. Led by a former Mormon elder, this vigilance organization differed from other incarnations of this activity by offering those charged with crimes formal and reasonably fair trials before they were hanged. Within several months, this committee was disbanded as lawbreaking diminished.

With crime once more on the rise in 1855, a new vigilance committee was created. Under the direction of some of the town's leading citizens, hangings were soon drawing crowds by the thousands. Apologists for the vigilantes suggest that the second coming was given impetus by the collusion between corrupt city politicians and local outlaw bands. Boasting over 5,000 members, the 1856 **San Francisco Vigilance Committee** was the largest manifestation of the vigilante phenomenon in American history. With the return of the city to acceptable, honest officials, the group disbanded.[16]

Corrections

By the antebellum era, prisons had become an established part of the American criminal justice system as each year new institutions were constructed in various states. By the 1840s, many prison methods had become fixed with little room for experimentation as champions heralded the benefits of either the Pennsylvania or the Auburn system. The years 1787–1820 witnessed the initial stage of prison reform in America, which was followed by the construction of Eastern State Penitentiary and Auburn Prison between 1820 and 1830. The third wave of prison reform between 1830 and 1840 built on the foundations laid by the introduction of new prison designs. It was during this time that Auburn continued to reduce its state maintenance expenses as other New York prisons began to turn profits. Supporters of the Auburn system saw this as confirmation that the silent rigid system of discipline and security was the solution to the age-old problem of housing prisoners, while at the same time backers of the Pennsylvania system found solace in the fact that the solitary system had prevented the criminogenic contamination of prisoners through physical association.

In its 1850 report, the Boston Prison Discipline Society recorded 4,060 prisoners housed in 19 different prisons (figures for 6 other prisons were not reported in the survey). Of these, only 5 state prisons had more than 200 prisoners (New York, Massachusetts, Pennsylvania, Ohio, and Maryland), a figure that would not rise until after the Civil War. During the industrial phase of prison administration, the Auburn system prevailed over the Pennsylvania system because it produced better industrial returns and was easier to maintain.

Prison reform

During the 1840s, numerous states established prison reform societies. In 1844, the Prison Association of New York was inaugurated, and the following year saw the founding of the Massachusetts Society in Aid of Discharged Convicts and the Pennsylvania Society for the Alleviation of the Miseries of Public Prisons. Clearly, strides were being taken to counter the pervasive corruption and brutality of the contemporary prison. At the same time, a European prison congress was convened in Germany to discuss the debatable merits of the Auburn and the Pennsylvania systems.

The first critics of the Auburn system came from the ranks of the "mechanics" who saw prison industries as unfair business competition. Others pointed to the physical discipline that accompanied the silent system. Reformers maintained that the only way to maintain a system of absolute silence was by the threat of severe corporal punishments, such as flogging.

Pennsylvania prisons also came under attack since those built under the solitary system guidelines were the most costly to construct and maintain. In addition, the profits of a single individual working alone in a cell paled in comparison to New York's congregate system. In marked contrast, Eastern State Penitentiary suffered from a higher incidence of mortality, disease, and insanity. By the 1840s, many of the early efforts toward creating a functioning penitentiary had fallen on hard times, and the belief had become widespread in America that the prisons had failed to live up to earlier expectations.

Reformers such as **Dorothea Dix** visited prisons in the early 1840s and found them in deplorable condition. Born in 1802, Dix worked as a schoolteacher until 1841. She saved much of her energy for leading a reform movement to champion the rights of mentally ill prisoners. She found her calling while conducting a Sunday school lesson at a local jail in Massachusetts. On discovering the primitive and inhumane treatment of prisoners suffering from mental illness in the prison, Dix launched a one-woman humanitarian crusade that would reach across America and Europe during the antebellum years. Between 1841 and 1852, she was credited with modernizing and expanding facilities for the insane as well as helping pass reform legislation in many states and Canada. Although she persuaded the

U.S. Congress to pass a bill raising $12 million for the care of the insane, President Franklin Pierce vetoed the legislation in 1854. Over the next four years, Dix took her crusade to Europe, procuring reform legislation for the insane in several European countries. She continued to lobby on behalf of the insane and prison inmates until 1881. She died six years later in Trenton Hospital, an institution she had helped establish.

Prison conditions

Some of the most glaring examples of the divergent conditions between state prisons and local facilities were in the arena of punishment. State prisons in Massachusetts and Connecticut rarely resorted to corporal punishment, while in 1843 alone, Sing Sing Prison in New York distributed 36,000 lashes of the whip. Although records indicate that the larger the prison, the more rigorous the punishment, a clear trend toward diminished corporal punishment typified the 1840s.

Russia had a long history of using corporal punishment in the days before the penitentiary (as most countries did). No device was more notorious or feared than the knout, used in serious criminal cases. Introduced by Ivan III in the fifteenth century, it came in a variety of incarnations. There were also a number of ways of applying it. It was usually characterized as a "wooden handle about a foot long, its thongs being plaited together to give a two foot lash. At its end was fastened a further thong, eighteen inches in length, tapering to a point."[17] The extension could be detached and replaced by another length of lash. When one was sentenced to be lashed, the malefactor was sometimes stretched over the back of the executioner's assistant. One witness described a beating in which "blows tore skin from a bare back, in some places it could reach through to bones." The standard number of strokes ranged between 15 and 205, depending on the offense. In 1781, the great prison reformer John Howard visited Russia, curious to its system of punishment since he had heard that capital punishment was no longer used. However, he was much disheartened when he witnessed a knout lashing, which he described as more vicious than the English predilection for hanging and decapitation. Howard would personally witness its use on a man and a woman. He described the scene,

> The woman was taken first and stripped to the waist, hands, and feet bound by cords to the whipping post. A servant attended the executioner, both powerful men. The servant marked his ground and struck the woman with five lashes, every stroke penetrated the flesh; but his master thought him too gentle and pushed him aside and gave the remaining twenty strokes himself.[18]

The Russian author Fyodor Dostoevsky recounted his experiences in a Siberian prison camp in his 1862 novel *The House of the Dead*. After he complained about the quality of the food, he was lashed with the knout, describing the pain as "like a fire burning you; as if your back was being roasted in the very hottest of fires."[19]

CRIMINAL JUSTICE IN ANTEBELLUM AMERICA

European visitors to American prisons, ranging from Charles Dickens to Alexis de Tocqueville, commented on the solemnity and silence that characterized most prisons. However, if the same observers were to have visited in subsequent decades, they would have found a cacophony of sounds emanating from overcrowded prison cells. From the 1820s through the 1850s, corporal punishment and zealous discipline ensured obedience in prisons. Added to this was the legislative willingness to supply funds to build more prisons when cells were needed, and the overcrowding problem would be put off for several decades.

One other integral hallmark of antebellum prisons was the enforced regular labor of inmates. Prison routine required prisoners to work from eight to ten hours each day under the threat of physical punishment. Intended to impart discipline as well as a satisfactory financial windfall, those prisons that showed a profit earned the most praise from the public. Hence, the Auburn system flourished over the Pennsylvania one because it paid better returns.

By the 1840s, American prison reformers initiated paramilitary discipline to augment the already elaborate regimentation. New York prisons introduced daily routines including lockstep marching, which required inmates to move in close order and single file, moving in unison, each head inclined to the right, with each man looking over the shoulder of the man in front. In this way, guards could ensure that conversations were eliminated and prisoners could not dally from place to place. Also augmenting the increased emphasis on regimentation was the introduction of striped uniforms. Another ramification of this innovation was the adoption of prison uniforms by guards as well. It was not a huge step to designing prisons that looked like medieval fortresses, promoting security and isolation while making prisoners feel more diminutive and regulated.

Similar to other countries in the Mediterranean region, Spain has long used various forms of penal service, with some convicts forced to labor on public works projects and others working mines and rock quarries. These forms of penal servitude were tantamount to agonizingly slow death sentences. Spanish punishments were brought to its New World colonies in the sixteenth century, introducing European standards of sanctions to regions lacking strong indigenous legal traditions. In the sixteenth century, galley service was also introduced as punishment for various crimes. For example, vagabonds were require to spend four years rowing in galley service for the first offense, eight for the second, and life for the third. Typically, galley service averaged four to six years. By most accounts, it took at least a year to become adept at the oars. But like the English transportation system, most who spent sentences in the malodorous galleys would probably agree that "hitting the waves" was better than a hangman's dance on the gallows. With the popularity of new sailing technology, Spain abolished galley service in 1748. Prisoners were instead transferred to work at hard labor in Spain's North African presidios.[20]

Juvenile institutions

In 1817, the **Society for the Prevention of Pauperism** of New York became the first group in America to call attention to neglected children between the ages of ten and eighteen.

Eight years later, the **House of Refuge** opened its doors in New York City and became the earliest child-saving institution in the country. Its charges included both the destitute and the neglected and children sentenced to incarceration for criminal activity. This would be one of the first institutions to jail children and adults separately. However, discipline was anything but benign, with punishment ranging from whipping and solitary confinement to reduction in food supply. Predicting the industrial prisons of the future, the House of Refuge kept the boys busy making goods to be sold. This could occasionally lead to apprenticeships with master artisans outside the walls as long as they followed the rules. Houses of refuge were subsequently constructed in Philadelphia and Boston, where corporal punishment was banned. Although black children were initially prohibited, in 1834, New York's made plans for a "colored section."

Despite attempts to separate the children from adult prisons, many children remained behind bars in adult jails. In the late 1820s, the Boston Prison Discipline Society reported that many of these children were under the age of twelve. As late as 1845, almost a hundred children aged six to sixteen resided in the Massachusetts House of Corrections. During the 1850s, a rise in female juvenile offenders became a new concern, and reform schools were established under different guidelines from the boys. It was hoped that by offering a strong mothering environment and teaching morals, these young girls could grow up to become good mothers. In 1856, the first girl's reformatory was opened as the Massachusetts State Industrial School for Girls. Departing from the traditional dormitory-style construction, it separated children into smaller housing groups according to their offenses and backgrounds.

During the late 1850s, similar institutions were opened in Illinois and Ohio. Most avoided an urban setting in favor of a rural one. According to the theory of the day, it was presumed that city living was the root of evil and social problems and offered too many temptations to unsupervised children.

Alexander Maconochie and indeterminate sentencing

While the threat of physical punishment was omnipresent in the antebellum prison, alternative experiments to punishment were tried in several states. The main contribution of the reformatory era to American prisons was the introduction of the indeterminate sentence and parole laws. Considered the "father of parole" in the late 1830s and 1840s, Captain Alexander Maconochie of Great Britain began to conceive a new scheme for the punishment of convicts while assigned to England's prison colony at Van Diemen's Land (now Tasmania). Shortly after arriving on the island, he hatched an idea by which the convicts would be sentenced not to a specific period of time but rather to a certain amount of labor that was measured by a system of marks. According to his plan, convicts could earn marks for good conduct and work or lose them for bad behavior. Maconochie's reforms were in part spurred by the persistence of traditional methods of corporal punishment and physical intimidation. He had hoped that, by allowing prisoners to work and associate with other convicts and with the lingering threat of punishment for all, if only one convict offended, his system would encourage mutual trust and a sense of responsibility among the prisoners.

Slavery has existed as a legal business as well as penal sanction for millennia. According the psychologist Steven Pinker, for most of history, slavery was the "rule rather than the exception."[21] Slavery as a formal punishment is mentioned in both the Hebrew and Christian bibles and was even supported by ancient philosophers such as Plato and Aristotle.[22] Slave markets existed in both ancient Rome and Athens and by the 1400s was still a licit enterprise in certain areas of the world. Slavery had vanished from the European world for almost a millennium before its recrudescence in the sixteenth century as European powers, including Portugal, the Netherlands, France, England, and Spain, increasingly required slave labor for their New World colonies.

Slavery was prohibited by Islam. As a result, whenever the religion reached a new region, the odds were that it would diminish the role of slavery as a legitimate legal sanction. However, this was not always the case. Islamic states in North Africa and other Arab regions were enslaving Africans long before the Europeans. Moreover, slavery was not abolished until the twentieth century in Qatar (1952), Saudi Arabia and Yemen (1962), and Mauritania (1980).[23]

Over the next several years, Maconochie created a more elaborate system of indeterminate sentencing that would also be applicable to prisons and not just the prison colonies in Australia. Maconochie was given the opportunity to test his experimental program on Norfolk Island. Putting his **mark system** to work, he attempted to inject a certain degree of civility into what he considered a den of iniquity. He removed the bars from windows and opened prison doors, offering prisoners books and musical instruments. He tried to educate the prisoners about civilization by encouraging the planting of gardens and constructing religious sanctuaries. While he rated his experiment a success, it was not long before the colonists came into conflict with Maconochie and his charges, and after a four-year experiment, the island was returned to its former state. Although Maconochie was unsuccessful in his attempt to reform England's penal system, Walter Crofton would build on his ideas in Ireland and eventually see many of Maconochie's ideas come to fruition.

In 1817, New York's legislature passed but never applied a **good time law** by which prison sentences were reduced for good work and behavior. Beginning in 1836, Tennessee became the first state to actually implement a good time reduction of prison sentences. However, this innovation would not gain wider popularity until the late 1850s and 1860s, when twenty-three states would follow suit.

Crime and punishment

According to historian Richard Maxwell Brown, the dawning of the 1830s introduced America to "what may have been the era of the greatest urban violence that [the nation] has ever experienced."[24] The years following the war with Mexico would see violence become even more prevalent. Perhaps the preponderance of reports glamorizing the carnage in Mexico inured the younger generation to violence, a generation that would make up much of the fodder in the coming sectional conflict. Others might suggest the proliferation of handguns contributed to the growing mayhem.

By the 1830s, America's largest cities began to experience a rising fear of crime. New York City became home to burgeoning legions of gangs, including the Irish-Catholic Dead Rabbits and the nativist American Bowery Boys. The developing slums of American cities paralleled the growing disparity between the living conditions of the native-born and the marginalized denizens of urban America. On his tour of America in the early 1840s, English novelist Charles Dickens noted the "leprous houses" in the Five Points section of New York City and surmised that "in respect of filth and wretchedness,"[25] it would give the most debauched environs of London a run for the money. The rising popularity of the penny presses during the 1830s and 1840s was spurred in part by coverage of lurid, sensational crimes, such as the **Mary Rogers murder case**. The precursor to today's tabloids and mass media, the penny press hinged on selling papers, and nothing sold them like crimes of passion.

Crime stories marketed for popular consumption were not a new phenomenon. Beginning in the colonial era, crime literature was marketed in pamphlet form, usually accompanied by some religious lesson or moral warning. By the 1820s, a more secular society became increasingly acceptable of sensationalist literature without the heady dose of moralism so reminiscent of a Puritan-dominated society. By the 1820s, crime news began to steadily seep into journalism.

The Helen Jewett and Mary Rogers murder cases

The sensationalized New York City murders of Helen Jewett (1836) and Mary Rogers (1841) "illustrated the dangers and temptation of city life."[26] Both cases exemplified the changing notions of female deviance and criminality. Conversely, the crimes "became symbolic of city dangers not just for potential women victims, but for men who might be lured by their beauty into inappropriate behavior."

The New York City of the 1830s might have been a rowdy and disorderly place, but it had a low homicide rate. The 1836 murder of Helen Jewett was an outlier – a sensationally rare event. Jewett was allegedly murdered by a client in the brothel where she worked. The alleged client, a nineteen-year-old clerk, deeply immersed in the city's male sporting demi-monde, was accused of bludgeoning her to death in the brothel and setting the body on fire to cover up the crime. Both the victim and the perpetrator "typified the type of young people who were flocking"[27] to urban centers such as New York City. Signifying the increasing prominence of the penny papers and anticipating the modern fascination with the lurid, the press had a field day in the months between the crime and the trial inventing "a host of gossipy details about high life and low, judge, jurors, lawyers, and spectators." One chronicler of the case suggested that it took this "sexually infused" crime to "put a human face on prostitution."[28]

However, no murder case of the era had as much impact on the criminal justice system as the murder of Mary Rogers in 1841. This homicide morphed into "a symbol of a failed and corrupt police force . . . an emblem of the city's moral decay."[29] Like the Helen Jewett case, the fledgling penny presses covered the investigation and the trial and "competed to provide readers with the circumstances of her demise," portraying Rogers as both a "fallen woman and seductress."[30] The subsequent inept investigation of the crime has been considered by some scholars of policing to be a clarion call for police reform in New York City. A beautiful woman who clerked in a New York City tobacco shop, she reportedly had no shortage of admirers. She could count as customers leading literary figures, such as James Fenimore Cooper, Washington Irving, and **Edgar Allan Poe**. By most accounts, her murder inspired Poe to write America's first detective story, *The Mystery of Marie Roget* (1842).

The real Mary was found murdered in July 1841. Numerous theories emerged concerning her last evening. The subsequent coroner's autopsy and the inadequate police investigation that followed demonstrated to the public the limits of contemporary policing. Since the body was found just over the New Jersey border, New York City police were reluctant to investigate. Police officers traditionally did not work a homicide unless a substantial reward was offered. Since their incomes were derived from rewards and fees, police officers spent more time recovering stolen property.

In the years prior to a twenty-four-hour force, untrained and poorly paid night watchmen came under press scrutiny as newspaper editors pressed for an investigation into the murder of the famous beauty. Even New York Governor William Seward used the case to call for stronger policing. Newspapers vilified law enforcement for its zeal in pursuing robbers and thieves in order to claim reward money or worthwhile stolen property and for avoiding murders, which offered fewer financial prospects. Although the case was never solved, the murder gave impetus to a reform campaign that led to more effective policing, and within five years, the New York City police had been reorganized and made great strides toward professionalism.

Adding to the interest of the crime was its links to abortion and prostitution. It was not long before both issues, the "seductive femme fatale" and "the widely condemned but extensive practice" of abortion, became inextricably linked.[31] The aftermath of the case not only spurred calls for police reform bit also for a crackdown on abortionists. The year 1845 saw both the creation of the NYPD and the criminalization of abortion, thanks in part, to the influence of the Mary Rogers murder. That year the New York State Legislature passed the Police Reform Act, which ended the old system of night watchmen and marshals, creating a full-time salaried force in the process. Moreover, the passage of the so-called "Abortion Law" put more bite into existing statutes that outlawed treatments offered by commercial parlors.[32]

Crime fighting

The antebellum era introduced new forms of criminal enterprise to America, forcing the criminal justice system to consistently play catch-up. The first bank robbery in American history was recorded in 1831. Although it was technically a burglary since no threat of violence was used, in this case an English thief utilized duplicate keys to enter a Wall Street bank in New York City and abscond with $245,000. However, his penchant for free spending and generous tipping, together with the help of informers, led the police to his door and the remaining $185,000. The thief was sentenced to five years at hard labor in Sing Sing Prison. According to one authority, he was treated more leniently than future bank thieves because "his crime was unique and the authorities were not prepared to deal with it."[33] In the years following the Civil War, bank robberies would become much more common.

In some arenas, fresh investigative techniques heralded a new era in policing. One of the most famous murder cases of the antebellum period was the trial of Harvard professor John W. Webster for the **murder of Doctor George Parkman** in 1849.[34] A cause célèbre, this crime attracted national attention. Webster apparently struck Parkman a fatal blow while arguing in Webster's laboratory over financial matters (overdue rent).

A professor of chemistry, Webster decided to dispose of the body by dismembering it and burning it in the furnace. However, his misdeed was suspected by a college janitor who pursued his own amateur investigation and found parts of a human body. A subsequent investigation turned up a set of false teeth in the ashes. Webster's fate was sealed after Parkman's dentist identified them as belonging to the deceased, an early example of dental evidence. Webster ultimately confessed and went to the gallows.

Capital punishment

The 1850s marked the climax of the antebellum crusade to abolish execution as a criminal sanction. Michigan (1847), Rhode Island (1850s), and Wisconsin (1850s) abolished the death penalty, but opposition was barely existent in other states, although some states replaced public hangings with private executions. Once a fixture of American society, public executions on the public square were designed for maximum deterrence value. Thousands, sometimes tens of thousands, would flock to these events. In an era with little entertainment, it was not uncommon for individuals to travel great distances to attend the spectacle. While the last public execution in America took place as late as 1936, there was clearly a movement to end this medieval practice in the antebellum period. The English ended public executions in 1868 after generations of the "Bloody Code."

Pennsylvania passed a law in 1834 requiring private executions behind prison walls. During the 1830s, Massachusetts, New Hampshire, New Jersey, New York, and Connecticut also enacted laws prohibiting public executions. The thirty years before the Civil War are considered the height of America's abolitionist movement in the nineteenth century. However, the carnage of the Civil War stopped the abolitionist movement cold.

Crime and punishment: sectional variations

During the antebellum years, patterns of crime and punishment became more recognizable along sectional lines. In a study of South Carolina and Massachusetts, historian Michael Stephen Hindus contrasted the patterns of authority and criminal law in rural slaveholding South Carolina with an industrial urbanizing Massachusetts. Hindus discerned numerous conflicting patterns of crime, prosecution, and punishment in the two states of his study, patterns that reflected the difference in the two societies representing the North and the South.

The most common crimes in Massachusetts tended to be "against property and propriety." On the other hand, violent crimes among whites were the most frequent offenses in South Carolina, while crimes against property were associated with slaves. Reflecting two diametrically opposed societies, Massachusetts, particularly as it joined the industrial era, placed a high priority on order and insisted on punishment to ensure the social order. Here conviction rates were twice as high as in South Carolina, where white crime was explained away as the result of heated passions and elicited little in the way of communitarian concern. However, when it came to property crimes committed by slaves, conviction rates were much higher, and punishment was much more severe.

Most of the interracial violence between blacks and whites in the years leading up to the Civil War was disproportionately directed toward slaves and free blacks. Rarely was it the other way around. However, in 1851, the African American community of Lancaster County, Pennsylvania, took up arms against forces attempting to enforce the Fugitive Slave Law of 1850 in the town of Christiana. In the subsequent violence, black rioters killed a Maryland farmer who was attempting to reclaim several slaves. In response to this action, federal prosecutors charged thirty-eight men with taking up arms against the government, making this, according to historian Thomas P. Slaughter, "the largest mass indictment for treason in the history of our nation."[35]

Handguns and American culture

Challenging the traditional presumption that gun ownership was widespread in America between 1765 and 1850, historian Michael Bellesiles controversially suggested that guns played a "marginal role in American life prior to the Civil War."[36] Citing a study of 685 nineteenth-century murders prior to 1846, Bellesiles found that knives were the preferred weapon, with guns used in only less than 20 percent of the incidents. Others suggest that Bellesiles has over-interpreted his evidence, which is based on various data including a ten-year study of probate records and wills. While the debate continues, there is little argument that guns would be used increasingly in murders as America reached midcentury, with gun homicides almost doubling between 1846 and 1860. The years following the Civil War would demonstrate the centrality of the gun to American murder rates as soldiers returned home with their weapons in tow.

Although Samuel Colt's introduction of his 1832 revolver did not initially capture the imagination of the gun-buying public, by the 1840s, other gun companies were inspired to offer similar revolvers. Improvements in revolver construction would be reflected by a growing number of gun deaths in urban settings.

While gun ownership is common in most of rural America, the South has been most traditionally represented as a gun-owning culture. Although rifles have predominated, since the antebellum era, handguns have become an increasing presence in the South. By the late 1970s, research indicated that 40 percent of all southerners owned handguns compared to 24 percent in non-southern and mountain regions. In the nineteenth-century South, anecdotal evidence indicates that an emphasis on honor and gun ownership exacerbated the homicide rate. According to 1850 mortality reports, the South had a murder rate of 2.28 per 100,000, more than seven times the murder rates of the North.[37]

In his study on crime and punishment in the nineteenth-century American South, historian Edward L. Ayers found that slavery and the culture that propagated the institution provided an environment that allowed notions of honor to thrive. According to Ayers, honor flourished in rural societies with many opportunities for personal contacts and the existence of a "hierarchical society where one is defined by who is above or below him. Honor grows well in a society where the rationalizing power of the state is weak"[38] and where honor takes precedence overstate laws when settling personal grudges.

Gunplay was not the exclusive preserve of adults, as witnessed by an 1857 newspaper account of a young boy accidentally shooting himself in the abdomen. In an insightful editorial, the editor warned that "young America" should "take warning by accidents of this kind, and mentions having noticed several boys in the streets lately popping about with pistols." The editor closed his screed with a rhetorical flourish asking, "Is there no town ordinance forbidding the dangerous practice of shooting in the streets?"[39]

Mob rioting

America had experienced few outbreaks of mob violence prior to the 1830s. In the ensuing decade, the nation witnessed an increase in this increasingly destructive behavior. According to one estimate, there were 147 riots in 1835 alone, most related to the growing sectional rancor between abolitionists and proslavers. Another study found that almost three-quarters of America's cities with populations exceeding 20,000 experienced some type of "major disorder" between 1830 and 1865.[40]

However, the slavery issue was not the lone precipitator of this violence. Among the many explanations for the rising tide of violence was unprecedented urbanization and industrialization in a society rooted in institutions still based on rural community ideals of an earlier America. Add to this the catalyzing issues of race, **abolitionism**, the rise of party politics, and ethnic divisions, and American cities would be the setting for urban rioting for the three decades preceding the Civil War. Compounding the tensions and divisions of the era was the commercial depression of 1837 that put a squeeze on the job market at a time of increasing immigration. Between 1840 and 1860, almost 3 million Irish and half that many Germans immigrated to America, outnumbering all other immigrant groups.

Election riots were not uncommon in the days before private voting booths. Known as one of the most violent cities of the antebellum era, Baltimore, Maryland, had earned the moniker "**Mob Town**" during an 1812 anti-Federalist riot. Between 1834 and 1862, the city experienced fifteen major riots.[41] While violence often radiated from political, economic, ethnic, labor, and sectional issues, election day often led to similar strife. Baltimore was the scene of election day rioting throughout much of the 1850s, as Irish-Catholics supporting urban Democrats clashed with the nativist Protestant supporters of the Know-Nothing Party.

Ethnic and racial violence often pitted poor Irish and German immigrants against even poorer blacks and native-born Americans in a bid for unskilled jobs. In other cases, divisions were often along religious lines pitting Protestant native-born Americans against recent Catholic immigrants. Unlike other immigrant groups, the Irish preferred to live in the urban centers of the industrial Northeast. During the 1840s, poor Irish enclaves appeared in Boston, New York, Philadelphia, and Baltimore, leading to a wave of antagonism against Irish-Catholics that often ended in violence and discrimination. The first major anti-Catholic riot erupted in 1834 in Charlestown, Massachusetts, when lower-class Protestants objected to the convent school operated by the Ursuline sisters in their neighborhood. The subsequent burning of the convent provoked anti-Catholic violence throughout the country.

The 1844 **nativist riots** in Philadelphia were among the most violent incidents of the antebellum era. In his book *The Turbulent Era*, historian Michael Feldberg chronicled the cultural and religious conflict between Philadelphia's nativist Protestants and Irish-Catholic immigrants. The riots were the outcome of not simply religious intolerance but reflected the weakness of contemporary law enforcement and the social and political disorganization of the era.

Mob violence was not exclusive to the eastern states. Meanwhile, a similar epidemic of discrimination faced the Chinese immigrants who were lured to California and the West following the discovery of gold in 1848. Thousands made the journey across the Pacific seeking their fortunes. But unlike their European counterparts, the ethnic distinctiveness and competition for wages of the Chinese singled them out for racial discrimination and mob violence in the 1850s.

Most of the rioting against abolitionists occurred in the antebellum North. In some cases, early New York City gangs precipitated the violence in order to use the disorder as a cover for looting. While most assaults on abolitionists were not intended to kill, the murder of abolitionist Elijah P. Lovejoy in 1837 demonstrated the heated passions of the slavery debate. After calling for the formation of a local branch of the American Anti-Slavery Society in southern Illinois, an angry mob stormed his shop and killed him as he defended it with sixty armed abolitionists.

Notable trials

Dred Scott v. Sandford (1857)[42]

There was little to suggest in Scott's early life the mark his name would make on the brewing sectional crisis. He was born to slave parents in Virginia in the 1790s and taken to St. Louis, Missouri, by his master in 1827. After his owner's death, he was left to a series of owners, one of whom was an army surgeon who took him to the free territories of Illinois and Wisconsin before returning to St. Louis five years later. On his master's death, the surgeon's wife inherited all her husband's property, including Scott. However, the wife moved to New York and left Scott behind, and he eventually came under the care of a Missouri businessman and zealous abolitionist. With the support of the owner's widow in 1846, he initiated a suit in the Missouri courts to declare Scott free. While the wife of his former owner could have signed papers giving Scott his freedom, it was decided to fashion a deliberate test case in the fight against slavery designed to prove that a slave's bondage terminated when he was taken into free territory.

The end of the war with Mexico brought new lands into the American system and heightened the sectional conflict between pro- and antislavery supporters over whether the new lands would be free or slave states, and the issues raised by the *Dred Scott* case steadily gained importance. The case reached the Supreme Court finally in 1856 and was soon the focus of national attention as it became linked to more complicated questions, such as whether Congress had the power to prohibit slavery in a territory and whether a slave could sue in federal court.

In 1857, Chief Justice Roger B. Taney issued his stunning judgment ruling that Scott had no right to sue in federal court because neither slaves nor free blacks were citizens according to the U.S. Constitution. Taney rejected Scott's argument that he had become a free man by virtue of his residence in the free territory of Wisconsin because "the act of Congress which prohibited a citizen from holding and owning property of this kind in the territory of the United States north of the line therein mentioned, is not warranted by the Constitution, and is therefore void."[43] In one fell swoop, the Supreme Court denied citizenship to blacks and barred Congress from interfering with slaveholding in the territories. Therefore, as a national institution slavery could not be abolished without a constitutional amendment.

Taney's decision also delivered a substantive reading to the due process clause for the first time, maintaining that the due process clause limited the power of Congress to confiscate property rights no matter what procedure was set forth. Taney ruled,

> Thus the rights of property are united with the rights of person, and placed on the same ground as the Fifth Amendment to the Constitution, which provides that no person shall be deprived of life, liberty, and property, without due process of law.

The *Dred Scott* decision by the Supreme Court undermined any chances for future compromise on the issue of the expansion of slavery, as it strengthened southern resolve and heightened the sense of southern superiority over its plantation economy. Rather than quelling sectional strife, the *Dred Scott* decision turned into a catalyst that helped propel the nation into the Civil War. At the same time, the Supreme Court lost considerable standing and would subsequently play a very weak role during the Civil War. Somehow, Dred Scott the man was lost in the controversial decision. In any case, he was freed by his owners several weeks after the decision and worked as a hotel porter in St. Louis until he succumbed to tuberculosis in 1858.

Conclusions

While America had established a penal system by the mid-1830s, it did little to mitigate the growing crime rates in the antebellum years. Beginning in the 1830s, urban America endured outbreaks of mob violence over a variety of issues. Although ineffectual law enforcement has been used as the scapegoat for some of the violence, the development of professional police forces in the 1840s and 1850s does not fully explain the diminution of mob rioting in America's cities. According to Feldberg, by the 1850s, "municipal politics had absorbed much of the energies that nativist and immigrants had been investing in street violence," and local politics became an alternate but less deadly battleground.[44] Other explanations for the downturn in violence after the mid-1840s were the economic improvement following the panic of 1837 and the War with Mexico (1846–1848), which absorbed the energy of young combatants from the cities in a united war against a foreign enemy.

During the antebellum years, the groundwork for modern policing, prisons, parole and probation, and indeterminate sentencing were established. By the 1850s, small and large cities were legislating the night watch out of existence in favor of organized police forces. While their establishment did not solve all the social problems of antebellum America, urban policing began to play an integral role in maintaining order, preventing crime, and regulating public morality.

Measured by its financial successes, the Auburn system of silent confinement clearly triumphed over the solitary Pennsylvania system. One of the more important developments of the antebellum era was that an increasing number of prison inmates came from the new immigrant classes, especially the Irish. This pattern would continue from the 1830s through the 1870s.

As urban rioting continued to wreak havoc on northeastern cities, sectional violence proceeded to spread farther west following the war with Mexico and the crisis over the Kansas–Nebraska territory. It was not long before guerrilla warfare broke out in this region and the nation was preparing for war. With the Civil War on the horizon, the great strides in criminal justice experimentation and reform would suddenly become a lower priority until the reconstruction of the Union after 1865.

Point – counterpoint

Keeping the peace: vigilantes and police officers (1844, 1851)

The creation of the London Metropolitan Police Department in 1829 was a major step in the transition from medieval to modern law enforcement. It would be decades before this experiment would bear much fruit in America. The best laboratories for this experiment were the crowded eastern cities beset by urbanization and immigration. It is no wonder then that New York City passed a police bill in 1844 that would lead to the creation of the New York City Police Department the following year. That same year there was barely a handful of Anglo setters in San Francisco (then called Yerba Buena). The discovery of gold in 1848 and the subsequent avalanche of gold seekers led to rampant lawlessness in San Francisco and its environs. San Francisco would not have the time to make the transition from town to city since it became an urban center virtually overnight. The problem that was experienced in San Francisco was typical for regions where people settled in advance of police, courts, and other formal institutions of social control. In 1851, the San Francisco Vigilance Committee was convened to restore order. It was composed of city merchants and other prosperous types that had the most to lose. The following passages include a document detailing the composition of the prospective twenty-four-hour police force and then the Constitution of the San Francisco Vigilance Committee.

Source: New York City Common Council, *Report of the Special Committee of the New York City Board of Alderman on the New York City Police Department.* Document No. 53, 1844, pp. 805–810; "Papers of the San Francisco Vigilance Committee of 1851," *Publications of Pacific Coast History*, Berkeley, 1919, Vol. 4, pp. 1–3, 634–37

§ 1. The Mayor of the City of New York is, and shall continue to be, the Chief Magistrate and head of all the Police of the said City, with all the powers conferred on him and now exercised by law.

§ 2. In each of the Wards of the City of New York there shall be appointed, by the Mayor of the said City, the following number of persons to be Policemen, that is to say: 988.

§ 3. To entitle any person to be appointed such Policeman, he shall, previous to his appointed, have been a house-keeper and resident of the ward for which he shall be appointed, at least one year; shall be a person of approved discretion, integrity, courage, and moral character.

§ 9. The said Captains, Sub-Captains and Policemen shall dress in respectable citizen's dress in the daytime, and in the night with the usual watchman's cap, and the only weapon which they shall use when required shall be the usual watchman's club; they shall be known in the daytime by some proper badge, to be designated for that purpose.

§ 10. The said Captains and Assistant Captains shall, within their districts, do all the duties, as well by day as by night, that are now done by the Captains and Assistant Captains of the Watch in the nighttime, and the duties done by Foremen of engines and Engineers; shall vigilantly see that the duties of the subordinate Policemen are well performed, and in addition shall do all the duties hereinafter mentioned.

§ 13. The duties of the said Sectionmen shall be both night and day, similar to the duties which are now performed by the Roundsmen and Patrolmen of the Watch at night; they shall, while on duty, be constantly patroling their section, and see that good order is observed, and the laws enforced; and shall perform such other duties as shall be prescribed by the rules and regulations to be established by the Board of Police.

§ 17. The two-thirds of the force not on duty shall be the reserve, from which, from time to time, and in due and proportionate succession, shall be detailed, by the Captain of the Ward, a sufficient number to act as Firemen, to proceed with the Engines and Hook and Ladders to the fires, on which occasion they shall wear a fire cap and suit of fire clothes; and another sufficient number shall be detailed to attend at all public landings, theaters, and such other duties as the said Captains, Superintendent or the Mayor may direct; and when any of such reserve force shall not be required to be on any duty, they may abide and remain at their places of residence till their presence shall be required.

§ 18. In case of sickness or accident to any Policeman, by which he shall be rendered unable to attend to his duties, the Captain of the Ward to which he may be attached, may, if he deem it necessary, employ a substitute in his place, during his inability to do duty; such inability to be certified daily by a licensed Physician; and in case of any falsehood or fraud, in making or procuring such certificate, all parties concerned therein shall be deemed guilty of a misdemeanor.

§ 19. In all cases when a portion of the force shall be required to proceed to a fire, or to repress a riot, at least one Captain or one Sub-captain, a proper number of Sectionmen, and the required number of Policemen shall proceed to the scene of action; and, if occasion requires, additional force shall be added, and if needful, all the reserved force, and a part, or all of the force on duty, may be employed.

§ 20. There shall be a regular and systematic arrangement of signals for fires and riots, by which the whole Police force may be promptly apprised of the place of fire or riot, and what portion of the force is required; it shall be the duty of the Policemen detailed for that purpose, from time to time, to ring the bells and give such other signals as may be agreed on.

§ 21. It shall also be the duty of such of the Policemen as shall be detailed for the purpose, from time to time, to keep the Engines, Hose Cart and Hooks and Ladders, and apparatus attached thereto, in good order.

§ 22. The horses, or any of them, provided for the Engines or Hook and Ladder Trucks may, when not on actual duty, in proceeding to the fire, be employed on general patrol, or other duty to which they can usefully be employed for the benefit of the Police.

The San Francisco Vigilance Committee, 1851

Constitution of the San Francisco Vigilance Committee

Instituted the Eighth of June 1851

Whereas it has become apparent to the citizens of San Francisco that there is no security for life and property, either under the regulations of society as it at present exists or under the laws as now administered, therefore the citizens whose names are hereunto attached do unite themselves into an association for the maintenance of the peace and good order of society and the preservation of the lives and property of the citizens of San Francisco and do bind themselves each unto the other to do and perform every lawful act for the maintenance of law and order and to sustain the laws when faithfully and properly administered but we are determined that no thief, burglar, incendiary assassin, professed gambler, and other disturbers of the peace shall escape punishment either by the quibbles of the law, the insecurity of prisons, the carelessness or corruption of the police, or a laxity of those who pretend to administer justice.

And to secure the objects of this association we do hereby agree:

First, that the name and style of the association shall be the "Committee of Vigilance for the protection of the lives and property of the citizens and residents of the City of San Francisco."

Secondly, that there shall be a room selected for the meeting and deliberations of the Committee at which there shall be some one or more members of the Committee appointed for that purpose in constant attendance at all hours of the day and night to receive the report of any member of the association or of any other person or persons whatsoever of any act of violence done to the person or property of any citizen of San Francisco and if in the judgment of the member or members of the Committee present it be such an act as justifies the interference of this Committee either in aiding in the execution of the laws or the prompt and summary punishment of the offender the Committee shall be at once assembled for the purpose of taking such action as a majority of the Committee when assembled shall determine upon.

Thirdly, that it shall be the duty of any member or members of the Committee on duty at the Committee room whenever a general assemblage of the Committee is deemed necessary to cause a call to be made by two strokes upon a bell.

Fourthly, that when the Committee have assembled for action the decision of a majority present shall be binding upon the whole Committee and that those members of the Committee pledge their honor and hereby bind themselves to defend and sustain each other in carrying out the determined action of this Committee at the hazard of their lives and their fortunes.

Fifthly, that there shall be chosen monthly a President, Secretary, and Treasurer and it shall be the duty of the Secretary to detail the members required to be in daily attendance at the Committee room. A Sergeant-at-Arms shall be appointed whose duty it shall be to notify such members of their detail for duty. The Sergeant-at-Arms shall reside at and be in constant attendance at the Committee room.

Source: Originally entitled "Papers of the San Francisco Vigilance Committee of 1851." In *Publications of Pacific Coast History* (Berkeley, 1919), vol. 4, pp. 1–3, 634–37, 825–27.

Key terms

Age of the Common Man	Jacksonian America	Roger Taney Court
abolitionism	nullification	temperance movements
Fugitive Slave Act	Know-Nothing Party	coppers
Maine Law of 1851	star police	San Francisco Vigilance
coneymen	Allan J. Pinkerton	Committee
Dorothea Dix	House of Refuge	Alexander Maconochie
indeterminate sentencing	Mary Rogers murder case	Edgar Allan Poe
Dred Scott case	"Mob Town"	Dr. George Parkman
nativist riots	xenophobia	murder case

Critical thinking questions

1 What controversies brought the question of states' rights to center stage in the antebellum period?
2 What conditions led to the development of urban police forces in America? What role did private police and vigilantes play as peacekeepers? Why was it necessary?
3 Discuss prison reform and reformers during the antebellum era.
4 What were the goals of indeterminate sentencing?
5 Discuss the impact of the Mary Rogers murder case on American policing and popular culture.
6 What conditions led to rioting in the 1830s and 1840s?
7 What impact did the sectional crisis and the abolitionist and temperance movements have on American criminal justice? How did the *Dred Scott* decision impact the growing sectional crisis?

Notes

1 Gleason L. Archer, *History of the Law*, Boston: Suffolk Law School Press, 1928, p. 407.
2 Richard Kenner Cralle, ed., *The Works of John C. Calhoun: Reports and Letters*, Vol. VI, New York: Appleton and Co., 1864, p. 10.
3 For Jackson's views on nullification and states' rights see Jon Meacham, *American Lion: Andrew Jackson in the White House*, New York: Random House, 2008, pp. 222–237.
4 Ronald Walters, *American Reformers, 1815–1860*, New York: Hill and Wang, 1978, p. 135.
5 Lawrence M. Friedman, *A History of American Law*, New York: Simon and Schuster, 1974, p. 249.

6 Clive Emsley, *Policing and Its Context*, London: Palgrave and Macmillan, 1983; Dennis C. Rousey, *Policing the Southern City, 1805–1889*, Baton Rouge: Louisiana State University Press, 1996.

7 Wilbur R. Miller, *Cops and Bobbies: Police Authority in New York and London, 1830–1870*, Chicago: University of Chicago Press, 1973, p. 3.

8 There is some disagreement here as to the actual origins of the term *copper*. Its earliest application as a synonym for police officer appeared in George Matsell's 1859 work "A Hundred Stretches Hence." Some sources trace the shortened version *cop* to 1846 and to the books of Horatio Alger in the 1860s. Outside of Augustine Costello's *Our Police Protectors* (1885), there is little or no substantiation that the word *cop* was used earlier than the 1850s.

9 *Sir Robert Peel's Principles of Law Enforcement 1829.* https://www.durham.police.uk/About-Us/Documents/Peels_Principles_Of_Law_Enforcement.pdf

10 Quoted in Richard Moody, *Astor Place Riot*, Bloomington, IN: Indiana University Press, 1958, p. 9.

11 Ben Tarnoff, *Money-Makers: The Wicked Lives and Surprising Adventures of Three Notorious Counterfeiters*, New York: Penguin Press, 2011.

12 David R. Johnson, *American Law Enforcement: A History*, Wheeling, IL: Forum Press, 1981, p. 78.

13 Apparently, the term *vigilante* was adapted from the Spanish word for "watchman" and would eventually fine wider currency as an expression of frontier justice in the West.

14 Prassel, 1981, p. 84.

15 Bellesiles, 2000, p. 365.

16 The best account of the latter vigilance committee is Nancy J. Taniguchi, *Dirty Deeds: Land, Violence, and the 1856 Vigilance Committee*, Norman: University of Oklahoma Press, 2016.

17 Jerome Blum, *Lord and Peasant in Russia: From the Ninth to the Nineteenth Century*, Princeton, NJ: Princeton University Press, 1972.

18 Quoted in D. L. Howard, *John Howard: Prison Reformer*, New York: Archer House, 1958, p. 93.

19 Quoted in Ana Siljak, *Angel of Vengeance: The "Girl Assassin": The Governor of St. Petersburg, and Russia's Revolutionary World*, New York: St. Martin's, 2008, p. 181.

20 Ruth Pike, *Penal Servitude in Early Modern Spain*, Madison: University of Wisconsin Press, 1983, pp. 3–4.

21 Steven Pinker, *The Better Angels of Our Nature: Why Violence has Declined*, New York: Viking, 2011, p. 153. Pinker reminds us that the term "slave" is rooted in the term "Slav," referring to the fact that during the Middle Ages it was common to capture and enslave Slavic people.

22 Nayan Chanda, *Bound Together: How Traders, Preachers, Adventurers, and Warriors Shaped Globalization*, New Haven, CT: Yale University Press, 2007, p. 215.

23 Pinker, 2011, p. 153.

24 Richard Maxwell Brown, "Historical Patterns of American Violence," in *Violence in America: Historical and Comparative Perspectives*, ed. Hugh Davis Graham and Ted R. Gurr, Beverly Hills, CA: Sage Publications, 1979, p. 36.

25 Charles Dickens, *American Notes for General Circulation*, London: Chapman and Hall, 1850, p. 60.

26 Frankie Y. Bailey and Donna C. Hale, *Blood on Her Hands: Women Who Murder*, Belmont, CA: Wadsworth Cengage, 2004, p. 94.

27 Roger Lane, *Murder in America: A History*, Columbus: Ohio State University Press, 1997, p. 94.

28 Patricia Cline Cohen, *The Murder of Helen Jewett: The Life and Death of a Prostitute in Nineteenth-Century New York*, New York: Random House, 1998, pp. 21–22.

29 Daniel Stashower, *The Beautiful Cigar Girl: Mary Rogers, Edgar Allan Poe and the Invention of Murder*, New York: E. P. Dutton, 2006, p. 287.

30 Cohen, 1998.

31 Amy G. Srebnick, *The Mysterious Death of Mary Rogers: Sex and Culture in Nineteenth-Century New York*, New York: Oxford University Press, 1995, pp. 31–32.

32 Stashower, 2006, p. 288.

33 Carl Sifakis, *The Encyclopedia of American Crime*, NY: Smithmark Publishers, 1992.

34 See, for example, Robert Sullivan, *The Disappearance of Dr. Parkman*, New York: Little, Brown and Company, 1971.

35 Slaughter, 1991, p. x.

36 Michael A. Bellesiles, "The Origins of Gun Culture in the United States, 1760–1865," *Journal of American History*, 83(2), September 1996.

37 Dickson D. Bruce Jr., *Violence and Culture in the Antebellum South*, Austin: University of Texas Press, 1979, p. 242.

38 Quoted in Amy Louise Wood, ed., *The New Encyclopedia of Southern Culture*, Vol. 19, Chapel Hill: University of North Carolina Press, 2011, p. 79.

39 Wiley B. Sanders, ed., *Juvenile Offenders for a Thousand Years: Selected Readings from Anglo-Saxon Times to the Present*, Chapel Hill: University of North Carolina Press, 1970, p. 339.

40 Quoted in Michael Feldberg, *The Turbulent Era: Riot and Disorder in Jacksonian America*, New York: Oxford University Press, 1980, p. 121.

41 Richard Maxwell Brown, *American Violence*, Englewood Cliffs, NJ: Prentice Hall, 1970, p. 42.

42 Beginning in 1847, the case was known as *Scott (a man of color) v. Emerson*, after the family that owned the slave. In 1853, the case was taken up once more after a series of court decisions, but at this point, Scott's ownership was passed to John Sandford (or Sanford), Emerson's brother-in-law.

43 *Dred Scott v. Sandford*, http://www.ucl.ac.uk/USHistory/Building/docs/dred%20scott.htm

44 Feldberg, 1980, p. 121.

Sources

Archer, Gleason L. 1928. *History of the Law*. Boston: Suffolk Law School Press.

Ayers, Edward L. 1984. *Vengeance and Justice: Crime and Punishment in the 19th-Century American South*. New York: Oxford University Press.

Bailey, Frankie Y. and Donna C. Hale. 2004. *Blood on Her Hands: Women Who Murder*. Belmont, CA: Wadsworth Cengage.

Barry, John Vincent 1958. *Alexander Maconochie of Norfolk Island: A Study of a Pioneer in Penal Reform*. Melbourne: Oxford University Press.

Bellesiles, Michael A. 1996. "The Origins of Gun Culture in the United States, 1760–1865." *Journal of American History*, 83(2), September:425–455.

———. 2000. *Arming America: The Origins of a National Gun Culture*. New York: Albert A. Knopf.

Brown, Richard Maxwell. 1970. *American Violence*. Englewood Cliffs, NJ: Prentice Hall.

———. 1979. "Historical Patterns of American Violence." In *Violence in America: Historical and Comparative Perspectives*, ed. Hugh Davis Graham and Ted R. Gurr, pp. 19–48. Beverly Hills: Sage Publications.

Bruce, Dickson D., Jr. 1979. *Violence and Culture in the Antebellum South*. Austin: University of Texas Press.

Campbell, Stanley. 1968. *The Slave Catchers: Enforcement of the Fugitive Slave Law, 1850–1860*. Chapel Hill: University of North Carolina Press.

Cohen, Patricia Cline. 1998. *The Murder of Helen Jewett: The Life and Death of a Prostitute in Nineteenth-Century New York*. New York: Random House.

Courtwright, David T. 1996. *Violent Land: Single Men and Social Disorder from the Frontier to the Inner City*. Cambridge, MA: Harvard University Press.

Feldberg, Michael. 1980. *The Turbulent Era: Riot and Disorder in Jacksonian America*. New York: Oxford University Press.

Finkelman, Paul, ed. 1988. *Fugitive Slaves and American Courts*. 4 vols. New York: Garland.

Friedman, Lawrence M. 1974. *A History of American Law*. New York: Simon and Schuster.

Grimsted, David. 1998. *American Mobbing, 1828–1861: Toward Civil War*. New York: Oxford University Press.

Hindus, Michael Stephen. 1980. *Prison and Plantation: Crime, Justice and Authority in Massachusetts and South Carolina, 1767–1878*. Chapel Hill: University of North Carolina Press.

Johnson, David R. 1981. *American Law Enforcement: A History*. Wheeling, IL: Forum Press.

Jordan, Philip D. 1970. "The Wearing of Weapons in the Western Country." In *Frontier Law and Order: Ten Essays*, pp. 1–22. Lincoln: University of Nebraska Press.

Lane, Roger. 1997. *Murder in America: A History*. Columbus: Ohio State University Press.

Lewis, Orlando F. 1922. *The Development of American Prisons and Prison Customs, 1776–1845*. New York: Prison Association of New York.

Marshall, Helen E. 1937. *Forgotten Samaritan*. Chapel Hill: University of North Carolina Press.

Meacham, Jon. 2008. *American Lion: Andrew Jackson in the White House*. New York: Random House.

Miller, Wilbur R. 1973. *Cops and Bobbies: Police Authority in New York and London, 1830–1870*. Chicago: University of Chicago Press.

Moody, Richard. 1958. *The Astor Place Riot*. Bloomington, IN: Indiana University Press.

Morn, Frank. 1982. *"The Eye That Never Sleeps": A History of the Pinkerton National Detective Agency*. Bloomington, IN: Indiana University Press.

Paul, Raymond. 1971. *Who Murdered Mary Rogers?* Englewood Cliffs, NJ: Prentice Hall.

Prassel, Frank R. 1981. *The Western Peace Officer: A Legacy of Law and Order*. Norman: University of Oklahoma Press.

Sanders, Wiley B., ed. 1970. *Juvenile Offenders for a Thousand Years: Selected Readings from Anglo-Saxon Times to 1900*. Chapel Hill: University of North Carolina Press.

Senkewicz, Robert M. 1985. *Vigilantes in Gold Rush San Francisco*. Stanford, CA: Stanford University Press.

Slaughter, Thomas P. 1991. *Bloody Dawn: The Christiana Riot and Racial Violence in the Antebellum North*. New York: Oxford University Press.

Srebnick, Amy G. 1995. *The Mysterious Death of Mary Rogers: Sex and Culture in Nineteenth-Century New York*. New York: Oxford University Press.

Stashower, Daniel. 2006. *The Beautiful Cigar Girl: Mary Rogers, Edgar Allan Poe and the Invention of Murder*. New York: E. P. Dutton.

Taniguchi, Nancy J. 2016. *Dirty Deeds: Land, Violence, and the 1856 Vigilance Committee*. Norman: University of Oklahoma Press.

Tucher, Andie. 1994. *Froth and Scum: Truth, Beauty, Goodness, and the Ax Murderer in America's First Mass Medium*. Chapel Hill: University of North Carolina Press.

Walters, Ronald. 1978. *American Reformers, 1815–1860*. New York: Hill and Wang.

Williams, Jack Kenny. 1959. *Vogues in Villainy: Crime and Retribution in Ante-Bellum South Carolina*. Columbia: University of South Carolina Press.

TIMELINE	1856	1859	1861	1862	1863	1865	1865	1865
	John Brown terrorizes proslavers in Kansas	Hanging of John Brown following raid on Harper's Ferry	Civil War begins	Largest mass hanging in American history	New York City draft riots	Assassination of Abraham Lincoln	Founding of the Massachusetts "state police"	Creation of the U.S. Secret Service

CHAPTER SEVEN

Crime and criminal justice in the Civil War era (1856–1875)

Learning objectives

After reading this chapter students should understand and be able to discuss:

- The parallels between some of President Lincoln's domestic legislation during the Civil War with the current "war on terrorism"
- How the American judicial system was challenged by this crisis as never before
- Whether a state of war can justify suspending liberties guaranteed by the Constitution
- How this era witnessed changing patterns of drug addiction and led to early drug prohibition laws
- Why police reform was slowed down by the Civil War and Reconstruction in various regions
- Various efforts toward creating federal law enforcement in this era
- How an increase in the prison population and opposition to prison industries brought prison conditions to the public's attention and led to alternatives such as convict leasing
- The impact of the corruption and excesses of urban America, including political patronage on American criminal justice
- The birth of domestic terrorism in the trajectories of abolitionist John Brown and the Ku Klux Klan

The years leading up to the Civil War brought numerous critical issues dividing the nation into sharp focus, including slavery versus free labor, popular sovereignty, and the legal and political status of African Americans. The decade of the 1850s witnessed unparalleled

TIMELINE

1865	1865	1866	1866	1867	1868	1868	1870	1870
Civil War ends	First passage of black codes	Ku Klux Klan founded in Tennessee	First train robbery	Allan Pinkerton publishes manual on private policing	Fourteenth Amendment ratified by the states	The impeachment trial of President Andrew Johnson	Department of Justice organized	First meeting of National Prison Congress

urbanization, heralding an era that from 1860 to 1900 would witness city dwellers increasing from 6 million to 30 million. Whether the interior cities of St. Louis, Cleveland, Chicago, and Milwaukee or eastern urban centers such as New York City and Philadelphia, all shared the rapid growth and wealth of the Industrial Revolution. But they would also share an equally dark side, one that was characterized by racial and ethnic tensions, poverty, and an outmanned and outdated criminal justice system still playing catch-up. As sectional matters came to the fore in the 1850s, temperance reform leaders turned their attention to the impending sectional conflict. Popular interest in the crusade against "demon rum" waned as the *Dred Scott* case, "Bleeding Kansas," and John Brown's raid on Harper's Ferry dominated the day's concerns.

The Civil War years witnessed the greatest carnage in American history and ended with probably the most famous murder of the nineteenth century: the assassination of President Abraham Lincoln at Ford's Theater less than two weeks after the conclusion of the war. At the time of his murder, Lincoln was far from the respected figure that recent historians have proclaimed as the country's greatest president. Lincoln's unpopularity in the South was well known, but the loathing reserved for the president in the North has been given less coverage in history texts. Indeed, throughout the war years, his policies came under attack from all directions. Growing opposition to the war led Lincoln to suspend the constitutionally guaranteed writ of habeas corpus and authorize the arrest of hundreds of individuals for antiwar activities. His implementation by executive order of a **conscription** bill over the objections of Congress in 1862 helped precipitate riots in many cities, including the New York City draft riot of 1863, the bloodiest in American history.

As Lincoln's first term came to a close, he had infuriated Congress and was thought to have violated the Constitution by issuing executive orders creating provisional courts in conquered southern states and by installing military governors in Arkansas, Louisiana, and Tennessee without apparent constitutional authority or the approval of Congress. By the end of 1864, Lincoln's support had dwindled, as antagonists opposing emancipation, resistance to the draft, and strong criticism against the manner the war was being waged began to take its toll on his administration. This would become the historical context that would lead John Wilkes Booth to take the life of perhaps America's greatest leader in 1865.

Historian James G. Randall described the Civil War as an "eccentric period" in American history,

> a period when specious arguments and legal fictions were put forth to excuse extraordinary measures. It was a period during which the line was blurred between executive, legislative, and judicial functions; between state and federal powers; and between military and civil procedures.[1]

1870	1870s	1871	1871	1872	1873	1873	1873	1875	1876
Fifteenth Amendment	Convict leasing system established	Exposure of Tweed Ring	First National Police Convention is held in St. Louis	Credit Mobilier scandal	Congress enacts the Comstock Law	The *Slaughterhouse* cases Supreme Court decision	*Bradwell v. Illinois*	San Francisco bans opium dens	Elmira opens its doors

Until this era, the American judicial system had never faced a precedent for such a crisis as the Civil War.

While the developing cities earned a reputation for criminality and tested the developing criminal justice system, the defeated South also presented considerable obstacles in a region that had lagged far behind the rest of the nation in modernizing its criminal justice mechanisms. As Congress attempted to reconstruct the eleven former Confederate states, white supremacists swept through the night, terrorizing black communities and anyone who favored the transition to the post-slaveholding era.

Prior to the Civil War, there was little support for centralization in a society that so revered the virtues of republicanism. However, the nation that emerged from the war was a much different society, and decentralization began to give way to organization in the arenas of politics and industry. Soon reformers in the area of criminal justice engaged the public conscience over poverty, insanity, crime, corruption, and vice, leading several states to create central authorities responsible for the inspection and control of prisons. The publication of the Wines and Dwight's **Report on the Prisons and Reformatories of the United States and Canada** in 1867 jump-started the movement for the central control of state prisons.

The end of the Civil War would provide the impetus for a gradual transformation of southern criminal justice. By 1865, the South was simply too impoverished to make any advances in the realm of prisons, insane asylums, and public schools. Formerly predicated on the rules and regulations of the plantation system of slavery, states, and the federal government assumed control of the freed population from their former owners. According to historian Edward L. Ayers, the end of the Civil War saw the Ku Klux Klan and the Freedman's Bureau[2] attempt to "impose their vision of order upon the South."[3] Both sides faltered in their attempts but would leave the theoretical foundation for another century of conflict and tension between the races in the South.

As the nineteenth century moved to conclusion, a crusade was under way to create separate prison facilities for women. This movement, led by women on behalf of women, began in earnest in midcentury, when a handful of states hired matrons to oversee female inmates. By the late 1860s, Dwight and Wines, two of the leading authorities on prison reform, conceded that "carefully selected matrons . . . could provide role models" and that "matrons who exhibited characteristics of middle-class homemakers might inspire female criminals to become respectable women."[4] The campaign for separate prisons for women came to fruition in the 1870s.

Meanwhile, in the rest of the nation, the late nineteenth-century economy underwent a cycle of boom and bust, leading to a heavily contested debate over the role and rights of the industrial worker in the new economy. As liberal and progressive ideals found a national stage and a voice in organized labor, so too did big business and the so-called **robber barons** turn to private police agencies, such as the Pinkertons, to support their interests, often ending in violent confrontations.

Mirroring the growth taking place elsewhere, the federal government also began to play a more prominent role in daily life as federal courts and political parties became more influential. As citizens gained more rights thanks to the Civil Rights Act of 1866 and the Thirteenth, Fourteenth, and Fifteenth Amendments, the government took on more responsibility for protecting these rights.

In the aftermath of the Civil War, citizens were more frequently impaneled as jurors and witnesses during criminal trials. Prior to the war, the only federal criminal statutes dealt with counterfeiting, mail robbery, smuggling, embezzling federal funds, and resisting or impersonating a federal officer. With the end of hostilities in 1865, more federal crimes were added to the list. Among the new groups targeted by various criminal justice agencies were the Ku Klux Klan, Mormon settlers who practiced polygamy, and Appalachian moonshiners.

While the police became increasingly sophisticated in the late nineteenth century, professionalization and training lagged behind. Beginning in the 1850s, many forces adopted the sidearm as part of the standard equipment, but despite the improvement in revolver design, "police marksmanship proved abysmal."[5] A lack of training in safety or marksmanship characterized the use of deadly force, leading, according to one study of southern policing, to numerous accidental shootings of civilians and fellow officers.

The last half of the nineteenth century saw numerous advances in police investigation as the social sciences of anthropology, ethnology, and sociology all gained serious acceptance and photography was often used to augment studies in these disciplines. Beginning in the 1850s with the introduction of daguerreotype and the telegraph and continuing with the use of telephones in the 1880s and the Bertillon system by the 1890s, major cities in the North and the South were adopting new police technology to take the forces into the next century.

The lawgivers

One of the most important criminal justice issues to come up during the Civil War years was whether a state of war suspended the liberties guaranteed by the U.S. Constitution. Following the opening shots of the Civil War at Fort Sumter, Lincoln, and his cabinet made the preservation of what was left of the Union its highest priority. Cognizant of the fact that support for the Union cause was far from unanimous in the North, the Lincoln administration set up a strategy for dealing with opposition to the war. With members of Congress, the courts, and even the army and the government suspected of sympathizing with the South, it became paramount to maintain loyalties to the Union cause.

Lincoln suspends writ of habeas corpus

The Civil War era would see a sustained attack on constitutional liberties of freedom of speech and freedom of the press. In perhaps the greatest attack on individual liberties in

American history, President Lincoln suspended the writ of habeas corpus from areas where secession seemed imminent in 1861 to the entire country.

To justify his actions Lincoln, cited Article I, section 9, of the Constitution, which said, "The privilege of the Writ of Habeas Corpus shall not be suspended, unless when in Cases of Rebellion or Invasion the public safety may require it." Maryland, a border state with a large secessionist population, was the first state to feel the wrath of the new policy in May 1861, when several prominent state officials were "arbitrarily" arrested and imprisoned by military authorities. It was not long before a leading southern agitator who had been arrested provided the first test case for Lincoln's strategy. The last important case heard by the eighty-four-year-old Supreme Court judge Roger Taney involved a wealthy Baltimore citizen named John Merryman. In **Ex parte Merryman** , Taney ruled that only the legislative branch had the power to suspend the writ of habeas corpus and that "if the President of the United States may suspend the writ then the Constitution has conferred upon him more regal and absolute power over the liberty of the citizen than the people of England have thought its safe to entrust to the Crown,"[6] alluding to the fact that only Parliament had similar power.

While Taney had his defenders and may have been correct in his interpretation of the law, many saw him as taking sides with traitors. As the situation in Maryland abated, Merryman was eventually released. Many subsequent cases would follow a similar pattern. Individuals would be arrested on little pretext for threatening national security. After a period of time when the threat seemed to pass, the prisoners were released.

Several days after the promulgation of the Emancipation Proclamation in September 1862, Lincoln proclaimed,

> During the existing insurrection . . . all rebels and insurgents, their aiders and abettors, within the United States, and all persons discouraging voluntary enlistments, resisting military drafts, or guilty of disloyal practices . . . shall be subject to martial law and liable to trials and punishments by courts martial or military commission.

In addition, "the writ of habeas corpus" was suspended "in respect to all persons arrested" by military authority. On September 15, 1863, Lincoln suspended the writ for the duration of the war.

Throughout the Civil War, thousands of individuals were arrested by the military authorities at the direction of Secretary of State Seward and Secretary of War Stanton. But Lincoln historian David Herbert Donald suggests that "only a few were truly political prisoners," until more teeth were put into the proclamations in 1863.[7] Until then, the majority of those arrested were spies, smugglers, foreign nationals, and blockade runners. While researching arrests for this period in National Archive records, historian Mark E. Neely Jr. found many more arrests than earlier researchers but also discovered that most had "less significance in the history of civil liberties than anyone ever imagined."[8]

Although Taney would not live to see it, his position on the habeas corpus issue was upheld in 1866 in the **Ex parte Milligan** decision, which vindicated his interpretation of the Constitution. According to the *Milligan* decision, Congress had no authority to establish military commissions and ruled that the Constitution could not "be suspended during any of the great exigencies of government. Such a doctrine leads directly to anarchy and despotism."[9] Commenting on the case in the next century, Chief Justice Earl Warren noted that the case "established firmly the principle that when civil courts are open and operating resort to military tribunals for the prosecution of civilians is impermissible."[10] As the only president to suspend the writ of habeas corpus, Lincoln has drawn fire from Civil War scholars. However, recent research suggests that his actions were well-intentioned attempts to deal with an unprecedented crisis and to conduct the war more efficiently. Although the system of military justice was deeply flawed and abuses of power did take place, Lincoln's actions must be viewed in the context of the time.

Black codes

In an attempt to return to familiar antebellum social control measures, southern lawmakers framed new legal codes to regulate the former slave population. These new laws did not blatantly mention race but instead resorted to enhancing the discretionary powers of local judges and juries. For example, the range of punishments meted out for crimes considered "peculiarly 'black,'" such as vagrancy, rape, arson, and burglary,[11] were widened in the decade following the war. In 1866 in Savannah, Georgia, one of the most important cities in the South, "freedmens' courts" were sometimes influenced by local officials to sentence blacks to chain gangs or resorted to exhibitory punishments by which convicted offenders would be forced to wear a barrel with armholes and a banner announcing, "I am a thief."[12] Similar punishments were rarely accorded to white convicts.

In the aftermath of hostilities, white legislators in the southern states instituted "black codes" to replace the old slave codes, and slave patrols returned to police the rural countryside. To the informed, the new freedom looked suspiciously like the old slavery. Unable to hold office, vote, or speak to whites, former slaves were required to be employed by whites and could not change jobs without permission, were prohibited from intermarrying with whites, and were barred from carrying weapons even for self-protection. Unemployed blacks and orphaned children could be arrested for vagrancy and then assigned to work without pay. Black codes, which attempted to uphold the old racial order in the South, radicalized Congress and led congressional Republicans to try to seize control of **Reconstruction** policies from President Andrew Johnson.

There had been a long tradition of "hiring out" free blacks who did not pay taxes or failed to pay fines. The practice of temporary enslavement of free blacks existed years before the Civil War. During the 1830s, any black unable or unwilling to pay a fine in Florida could be offered for public sale by the sheriff. North Carolina extended the maximum time for hiring out to more than one year simply for siring a son outside wedlock. Several slave states had prewar laws that provided that, if a free black was hired but left before the expiration of the contract with the employer "without reasonable cause," he could be charged with a misdemeanor.

One historian has suggested that post-Civil War black codes were not imposed as an attempt to reinstate slavery but rather were the result of southern officials trying "trying to erect a legal structure that would permit the economic exploitation" of blacks by granting "them technical freedom."[13] However, any reading of individual state black codes suggest an attempt to return to the pre-Civil War status quo.

The Mississippi black code (1865)

Section 3. Be it further enacted. . . . That it shall not be lawful for any freed man, free Negro, or mulatto to intermarry with any white person; nor for any white person to intermarry with any freed man, free Negro, or mulatto; any person who shall intermarry shall be deemed guilty of felony and, on conviction thereof, shall be confined in the state penitentiary for life. . . .

Section 7. Be it further enacted, That every civil officer shall, and every person may, arrest and carry back to his or her legal employer any freed man, free Negro, or mulatto who shall have quit the service of his or her employer before the expiration of his or her term of service without good cause, and said officer and person shall be entitled to receive for arresting and carrying back every deserting employee aforesaid, the sum of five dollars, and ten cents per mile from the place of arrest to the place of delivery, and the same shall be paid by the employer, and held as a set-off for so much against the wages of said deserting employee.

Section 8. Be it further enacted, That upon affidavit made by the employer of any freed man, free Negro, or mulatto, or other credible person, before any justice of the peace or member of the board of police, that any freed man, free Negro, or mulatto, legally employed by said employer, has illegally deserted said employment, such justice of the peace or member of the board of police shall issue his warrant or warrants, returnable before himself, or other such officer, directed to any sheriff, constable, or special deputy, commanding him to arrest said deserter and return him or her to said employer, and the like proceedings shall be had as provided in the preceding section.[14]

Civil rights legislation and due process

The passage of the **Thirteenth Amendment** abolishing slavery in 1865 and then the **Fourteenth Amendment** in 1868 providing blacks with citizenship and equal protection under the law represented great strides in the nationalization of civil rights. According to the Fourteenth Amendment, no person may be deprived of life, liberty, or property without "due process of law," and all persons are to have equal protection of the laws.

In an attempt to disenfranchise the new citizens after the Civil War, white supremacist organizations such as the Ku Klux Klan waged a campaign of terror against blacks trying to exercise their rights, and southern states enacted black codes in an attempt to impose second-class citizenship on former slaves. Congress responded with various measures intended to protect the black population. Foremost among these was the Fifteenth Amendment, which specifically proclaimed that the right to vote should not be denied by reason of race, color, or previous condition of servitude. However, constitutional amendments did not apply to women; therefore, female former slaves were not covered by the Fifteenth Amendment.

Other civil rights acts followed, including the Act to Enforce the Fourteenth Amendment, better known as the Ku Klux Klan Act of 1871. This legislation outlawed conspiracies to deprive citizens of their voting rights. That same year, President Ulysses Grant declared martial law in parts of South Carolina, where the Klan was waging a terror campaign. The Supreme Court would strike down various sections of the civil rights legislation, but following the suppression of the Klan, federal protection of civil rights gradually diminished. The passage of the 1875 Civil Rights Act would prohibit discrimination by hotels, railroads, and other public facilities. But this law proved a last hurrah for civil rights protection. It too would be repudiated when in 1883 the Supreme Court ruled it unconstitutional, signaling a new era of disenfranchisement for African Americans.

Following the Civil War, the Supreme Court was faced with numerous due process challenges to state policies predicated on the Fourteenth Amendment. Ratified in 1868, this amendment had a tremendous impact on the long-term development of the law of personal status as well as the nature of the federal system. Among its most far-reaching sections was its establishment of national citizenship, declaring that all persons were guaranteed equal protection of the laws, privileges and immunities, and due process of law.

Challenges to the Fourteenth Amendment

The post-Civil War era saw a substantial number of cases dealing with criminal due process and constitutional protections of the Bill of Rights coinciding with the expansion of federal criminal law. Among the most famous of these cases were two 1873 Supreme Court decisions. In ***Bradwell v. Illinois*** , considered the "first decision under the Fourteenth Amendment,"[15] law student Myra Bradwell brought suit when she was denied admission to the Illinois bar even though the court admitted she was amply qualified. The case came before the Supreme Court, which affirmed the initial court decision that the Fourteenth Amendment did not restrict state power to limit the practice of law to males. But according to the legal concept of equality of 1870s America, as expressed by Justice Joseph P. Bradley,

> the civil law, as well as nature herself, has always recognized a wide difference in the respective spheres and destinies of man and woman. . . . The natural and proper timidity and delicacy which belongs to the female sex evidently unfits it for many of the occupations of civil life.[16]

In *Bradwell*, it became clear, at least for the moment, that the equal protection clause of the Fourteenth Amendment protected only men. Because of the efforts of *Bradwell*, Illinois passed a law in 1882 allowing women to practice any profession. However, it would be decades before women would be well represented in the legal profession. As late as 1920, only 3 percent of the nation's lawyers were women.[17]

The 1873 ***Slaughterhouse* cases** grew out of an 1869 decision by the Louisiana legislature to give a twenty-five-year monopoly to a specific New Orleans slaughterhouse to conduct its business in this city. In response, a consortium of different butchers sought an injunction against the monopoly on the grounds that it deprived them of the "privileges and immunities" guaranteed by the Fourteenth Amendment to all citizens.

After losing the case in the state supreme court, they appealed the judgment to the U.S. Supreme Court, where they were again denied by a narrow vote of five to four. According to the Supreme Court's interpretation, the amendment had been designed exclusively to grant

African Americans federal protection against discriminatory state laws (such as state laws forbidding blacks to serve on juries) but was not applicable in regard to the "privileges and immunities" of other citizens. By this ruling, states had the power then to regulate all other civil rights (including property rights and rights of contract). Although the intent of the law was actually to protect due process, the decision of the Court ignored this fact, setting a precedent that would last until the twentieth century. According to legal historian David J. Bodenhamer, in the 1870s, "the justices demonstrated a reluctance to apply any of the Bill of Rights to the states, especially in criminal matters."[18]

Birth of drug legislation

While social reformers concentrated on alcohol abuse in the nineteenth century, the United States had been plagued by a "drug problem" for decades. Drug historian H. Wayne Morgan suggests that the "public remained uninformed about it" until the communication advances of the late 1860s.[19] Indeed, the public paid little attention to drug addiction as long as it took place among the more marginalized segment of the population. When changing patterns of addiction in the 1870s introduced narcotics to the mainstream population, social and health reformers weighed in with dire predictions and warnings.

The nineteenth century saw the onset of a drug addiction problem in America beginning in the late 1840s with Chinese immigrants who popularized the smoking of **opium** in the mining towns of gold rush California and then with the wide availability of morphine products in the 1850s. The introduction of the hypodermic needle in 1856 offered a way of injecting morphine directly into the bloodstream.[20] The use of morphine rose dramatically during the Civil War period, when it was used intravenously to treat battlefield casualties. Following the war, many ex-soldiers brought the "**army disease**" of **morphine** addiction back home with them. Other factors for the growing morphine addiction problem resulted from the mass marketing of patent medicines that contained narcotics as well as the psychological trauma of the Civil War.

During the Reconstruction years, morphine was cheaper than alcohol and was widely available. Prior to the acknowledgment of the disease of addiction, doctors prescribed cheap morphine for many common complaints, leading to a substantial population of addicts. While there is no way to ascertain the number of drug addicts in Reconstruction-era America, a researcher in 1868 estimated that 80,000 to 100,000 Americans were addicted to opium.[21]

After the California gold mines were played out and the transcontinental railroad was completed, many Chinese immigrants clustered in the cities and Chinatowns along the Pacific coast. The commencement of an economic depression in California in 1875 indirectly led to America's earliest drug prohibition law (first law banning any non-alcoholic drug). The high unemployment and deterioration of living standards among the working classes brought the weight of bad times disproportionately onto the Chinese. As Chinese immigrants continued to come to California, they became the target of white frustration and despair over declining economic prospects. Into the 1870s, Anglo-Californians saw the close-knit, insular Chinese as hopelessly different and unassimilated. Sensational reports of Chinese prostitution and opium use fed the anti-Chinese sentiments of the era.

In 1875, a San Francisco ordinance was passed making it a misdemeanor to keep or visit any place where opium was smoked. America's first antidrug law prohibited the continued operation of opium dens, which were linked to vice and the mingling of white and Chinese users, a combination linked to moral degradation. Similar conditions in other parts of the West would lead to comparable anti-Chinese legislation and outright violence over the next two decades.

Abortion laws

In 1857, the recently inaugurated American Medical Association initiated a campaign to make abortion illegal throughout the country. With the controversial death of Mary Rogers (see last chapter) in 1845, New York City had already criminalized the act of abortion. One historian chronicled how the developing medical profession used this death and other cases to exercise their control over unlicensed abortionists and others who offered non-credentialed services to women. Once abortion was criminalized, the impact was felt most by working-class women who depended on unlicensed providers of services for women.

The Comstock Law

Cheap newspapers, known collectively as the "**penny press**," were filled with every manner of advertisement. Urban newspapers found abortion-related advertisements "a lucrative source of income" beginning in the 1840s and 1850s. This phenomenon accompanied the commercialization of the drug industry and reflected the desire of well-to-do women to limit their birthrate.[22] The growing abortion trade soon inspired sensationalist stories in the mass-circulation newspapers, leading to negative rhetoric and imagery that brought the entire practice of abortion into question.

Anthony Comstock (1844–1915) moved to New York in the late 1860s after serving in the Union army during the Civil War. It was not long before he was campaigning against obscenity on behalf of the YMCA. During the 1870s, the **Victorian compromise** "began to crumble."[23] His growing influence inspired Congress in 1873 to pass what became known as the Comstock Law, which prohibited the mailing of art, literature, and other materials considered obscene. The law also banned from the mail any drug, medicine, or article for abortion or contraceptive purposes (including condoms). In order to enforce the legislation, Comstock accepted a nonpaying position as a postal inspector.

In 1873, Comstock was instrumental in establishing the New York Society for the Suppression of Vice, the first organization of its kind in America. Comstock would devote the last forty-two years of his life to this society as its secretary. Later that year, a group of New England ministers organized the New England Society for the Suppression of Vice, which would become better known as the New England Watch and Ward Society. Other anti-vice societies were launched in major cities, including St. Louis, Chicago, Louisville, Cincinnati, and San Francisco. All the founders of the anti-vice societies were stalwart members of the native-born community.

Under the sway of Comstock's extremist convictions, obscenity was vaguely defined, leading to thousands of arrests. According to the *American College Dictionary*, **Comstockery** became a byword for "overzealous censorship of the fine arts and literature."[24] Margaret Sanger's books on birth control were banned, while poet Walt Whitman was fired from his job with the Department of the Interior for penning *Leaves of Grass*. Publishers removed any explicit language from their publications; for example, *pregnant* became *enceinte*.

Comstock crusaded to make birth control and abortion illegal in the United States. The new legislation enjoyed widespread support. Many native-born Americans saw contraception and abortion as a form of "race suicide," particularly in the face of mounting foreign immigration. To others, these practices "violated nature's laws, bred immorality," and "damaged health."[25] The zealous defender of morality rose to prominence by personally taking part in raids against pornography shops and abortionist offices in New York City. For his defenders, his name became a byword for morality, while his detractors regarded him as a threat to freedom of expression and the First Amendment. Comstock's campaign against birth control and abortion led to a deadly underground abortion business that was estimated to have taken the lives of thousands of women between the 1870s and the 1970s.[26]

Law enforcement

Between 1845 and 1865, major American cities established more proficient police forces that emphasized prevention over detection. As early as the 1850s, cities such as New York could boast uniformed police on the London model, while in other regions fears of a standing army led to informal vigilante groups, particularly in the trans-Mississippi West after 1850. While there is little disagreement that a breakdown in social order caused by immigration and urbanization contributed to the development of policing in urban America, historians such as Eric Monkkonen maintained that the creation of urban police forces was an attempt by municipal authorities to first control the "dangerous classes" and then to more efficiently manage their cities. He cites similar reform goals in the improvement of fire and sanitation departments in the same era.[27] Refuting the notion that modern police forces developed in response to rioting and rising crime rates, Monkkonen argued that, if this were the case, then those cities that experienced neither problem would not have established such forces.

The development of modern urban police was a slow process, one that occurred gradually in most American cities. Initially, the new police force used a syncretic approach that assimilated part of the old watch system before making the transition to totally new strategies. By 1855, Chicago had adopted a police system similar to New York City, followed by New Orleans and Cincinnati (1852), Philadelphia (1855), St. Louis (1856), Newark and Baltimore (1857), Detroit (1865), and Buffalo (1866).[28]

With few cities having established uniformed police forces by 1860, the traditional militia was still relied upon in urban areas devoid of professional police. While many police carried firearms informally, it would be decades before it was sanctioned by law in most cities.

In order to prevent the police from becoming separate and remote from the citizens they served, efforts were made in some cities to ensure that the early police were members of the community by implementing residency requirements. As immigration politics became inextricably linked with policing in cities such as New York and Boston, Irish and Irish Americans became the most common ethnocultural group in mid-nineteenth-century police forces. Cities as diverse as New York and New Orleans could claim to have a dispro-portionate number of Irish police on their forces. This can be best explained by the Irish predilection for partisan politics and the spoils system that went along with it. Although large numbers of German immigrants lived in the same cities, being better capitalized and educated than the Irish, they did not develop the same political organization at the ward level and remained underrepresented on the police forces.

While the London model of policing inspired many American police forces, it was sel-dom imitated because of the inherent differences in the two societies. In England, police officers were recruited from the military and laborers on the fringe of London. After joining the force, officers accepted the restriction of many personal liberties. Married officers were not allowed in certain parts of town, while bachelors were assigned to barracks. Barred from voting, London Bobbies were ultimately responsible to Parliament rather than their local constituents. On the other hand, the exigencies of the American system would never permit such restrictions of individual liberties, for, as the police historian Roger Lane concluded, "it was impossible in the United States to adopt the London personnel policies."[29]

Police reform was slowed in many regions by the Civil War and Reconstruction. No region of the country was more impacted by the war in terms of police reform than the South. In 1861, when New Orleans was captured by Union forces, the civil government was disbanded and replaced by martial law. With the military taking on police duties, police experimentation, which had become a hallmark of southern police reform, had ended. Although steps had been taken toward creating a professional police force in New Orleans prior to the Civil War, it would take until 1898 for the establishment of such a force.

In the West, law enforcement was inadequate for much of the nineteenth century. To contend with rising crime rates, some western states and territories authorized anti-horse thief associations, detecting societies, and vigilante groups. However, the real locus of polic-ing was typically near the county seat, town, or township. Underfinanced communities could ill afford to support constables, policemen, and sheriffs in the distant pursuit of outlaws. The additional expenditures required for capturing, trying, jailing, and sentencing could bankrupt the prototypical frontier community. Although the advent of the railroad helped transport desperadoes back to justice, law enforcement was hampered by the fixed routes of the train lines and was forced once more on horseback to navigate the patchwork of barely recognizable trails back to "civilization."

One of the more unexpected consequences of the Civil War was the decline of the U.S. militia. First used for federal peacekeeping in 1794, this ancient English tradition was trans-planted to America in an era when citizen soldiers were needed to maintain order in the days before a standing army. At the outbreak of the American Revolution, the volunteer militia was initially the only military force at the disposal of the colonists. However, "a dozen years after the Civil War the United States militia had reached its nadir."[30] Explanations for the decline of the militia vary. According to historian Robert Reinders, the decline in urban riots after the Civil War and an increasingly more professional police apparatus best explain the phenomenon. Others have suggested that the war had bred an "antimilitaristic attitude" that discouraged volunteer military service.[31] While the changing nature of urban criminal violence may have indeed led to the decline of the militia, industrial disorder and strikes beginning in the late 1870s would stimulate the return of the militia.

African American police officers

Although few records indicate the presence of black police officers in America between 1850 and the 1870s, historians have uncovered black police officers in northern cities and several in southern urban centers beginning in the 1870s and more notably in Midwestern cities such as Chicago and Cincinnati. New Orleans experimented with policing as early as the late eighteenth century. Like several other southern police forces (i.e. Charleston, South Carolina), New Orleans developed a military style municipal force as a hedge against the threat of slave insurrections. According to one chronicler of southern policing, New Orleans should be credited as having "the first racially integrated municipal police force in the United States (in 1830)."[32] In 1867, the city hired its first black officers since 1830. Historian Dennis Rousey suggests that New Orleans was "in all likelihood the first American city desegregate its police force after the Civil War."[33] During the Reconstruction era, three out of five police commissioners were black, and one-third of the police in New Orleans were African American. But this would turn out to be an ephemeral development in the postwar South.

Urban policing

While the New York City police had copied much of London's police model, including the adoption of uniforms, there were still important differences between the two forces. Not only were London police officers more inclined to military discipline, but they policed a more orderly society. However, the New York City police faced many more obstacles, in part because of the dearth of police officers. In 1856, the New York City police had one officer for every 812 and one-half citizens compared to London's one for every 351 and one-half.[34]

One of the recurring problems of nineteenth-century American policing was the influence of partisanship, which essentially allowed the police to control the election machinery. Nowhere was this better exemplified than in the debate over city versus state control of the New York City police between 1857 and 1870. According to Roger Lane, one of the spheres in which American policing sought to imitate its British counterpart was by "transferring the direction of the police from city to state, especially in a period of rising tensions."[35]

In 1857, the **New York Metropolitan Police Law** transferred control of the New York City police to state officials, citing the reluctance of Mayor Fernando Wood to suppress the vice problem and his unwillingness to enforce the 1855 Prohibition law. However, Wood defied state officials by having the city council adopt an ordinance creating a municipal police force based on the London model. Thus, for a short time New York residents were confounded by the presence of two police forces. Tension escalated between the rival forces, culminating in a riot between the two in 1857 in which the metropolitans (supported by the state) were routed by the municipals. When the state court of appeals ruled in favor of the new police law, Wood disbanded the municipal force. New York police control was finally returned to the city in 1870.

Following New York's example, other urban police forces came under state control for various time periods in the nineteenth century, including those in Baltimore, St. Louis,

Kansas City, Chicago, Detroit, New Orleans, Cleveland, Cincinnati, Indianapolis, Omaha, San Francisco, and Boston. According to police historian James Richardson, this phenomenon typically occurred where there was "significant social and political differences between the cities and their states." These cities were more likely "to be more cosmopolitan and pluralistic" and more predisposed to prostitution, gambling, and liquor. Moreover, these cities were typically dominated by a different political party than the state legislature.[36]

Federal law enforcement

During the Civil War, U.S. marshals were concerned mainly with arresting suspected traitors and Confederate sympathizers. Their role in supporting Lincoln's suspension of the writ of habeas corpus made the marshals a subject of scorn in many quarters. The passage of confiscation acts in 1861 and 1862 enlarged the marshals' powers to include confiscating the personal property of those accused of supporting the South. The government power to confiscate would not be taken away until 1868.

Following the war, marshals were confronted with protecting recently freed slaves and helping reimpose authority in the South. Ku Klux Klan groups and other white supremacists spread their campaign of terror across much of the South in defiance of the Civil Rights Act of 1866. During the early 1870s, southerners directed their efforts at regaining political control of their states. Marshals found themselves in the center of the struggle, as they were charged with supervising polling places and protecting politically active blacks from white violence. Supported by federal troops, marshals arrested almost 7,000 southerners for violating civil rights laws by 1877.

The U.S. Secret Service

Perhaps the greatest development in federal law enforcement, the formation of the U.S. Secret Service in 1865, was a last-gasp attempt to deal with the long-standing counterfeiting problem. On April 14, 1865, the very day of his assassination, Abraham Lincoln gave his approval for the formation of what would become the U.S. Secret Service. Beginning in 1863, the federal government began issuing its own currency. Prior to this time, more than 1,600 American banks printed and designed their own currency as part of a money system in which each state released its own bank notes through private banks. Indeed, this system created a counterfeiter's paradise since merchants and businessmen were oblivious to differences between legitimate and counterfeit currency. At the behest of the secretary of the treasury, Lincoln approved the Secret Service as a division of his department.

It has been estimated that anywhere between one-third to one-half of the country's paper money was illegal during the Civil War years. Chosen to lead the new federal law enforcement organization was William P. Wood, a veteran of the war with Mexico. Born in 1819, William P. Wood served as superintendent of Washington's Old Capitol Prison in 1862 and was suspected of participating in all manner of intrigue and espionage during the war years. In 1864, he focused on the counterfeiting problem, taking advantage of his prison contacts in the federal prison population. However, the Secret Service was not authorized by Congress like the Customs Service, postal inspectors, and Internal Revenue Service. In a more clandestine departure to protocol, Wood was sworn in by executive decision on July 5, 1865, in a private ceremony.

During its first year of operation, the Secret Service established field offices in 11 different cities and arrested more than 200 counterfeiters. The new branch of federal law enforcement has been credited with establishing a measure of monetary stability in the decade following the war. However, it would take two more presidential assassinations (Garfield in 1881 and McKinley in 1901) before the Secret Service was officially responsible for presidential protection in 1901.[37]

Other federal law enforcement efforts for this era included the congressional creation of the Office of Internal Revenue, which was authorized on July 1, 1862. Its main function was the enforcement of the federal taxation of distilled spirits. The origins of the Internal Revenue Service and the Bureau of Alcohol, Tobacco, and Firearms can be traced back to this office.

By the time of the Roman Empire, counterfeiters had learned their craft well, able to replicate techniques used in casting of clay molds for the melted metal in use. Over the historical record counterfeiters would be subject to some of the most brutal punishments imaginable. Emperor Constantine had them burned alive. Others who clipped precious metals from coins and then melted it down had their ears "clipped or cut off." Others had citizenship revoked. Roman counterfeiters lost their noses when they were not being castrated or being tossed into lion pits. Harsh punishment for the crime extended to other cultures as well. As Islam continued to spread in the eighth century A.D., counterfeiters sometimes had their hands amputated. In seventh century A.D., China they were punished with facial tattooing and later the death penalty. By the fourteenth century, Chinese bank notes were emblazoned with warning "To counterfeit is death."[38] Counterfeiting in seventeenth-century England was rather sophisticated. The trade in counterfeit coins had plagued England since at least the 1100s when "the penny was so bad that the man who had at market a pound could by no means buy therewith twelve pennyworths." King Henry I took a strong stand, ordering the castration and loss of the right hand for debasing coinage. Over the historical continuum, it was common for convicted counterfeiters to be either hanged or burned alive. Surprisingly, there were even more painful punishments recorded, including Russian counterfeiters occasionally having false coins melted and then poured down their throats as molten metal.[39]

State police experiments

Throughout most of the nineteenth century, there was little support for state policing. Americans favored decentralization of policing in an era that placed considerable value on a republican ideology that favored local control of policing. Massachusetts was the only state besides Texas to experiment with state policing in the nineteenth century. Beginning in 1865, Massachusetts embarked on a series of state police experiments that did not lead to a permanent force until the following century. In 1865, the state legislature passed a statute that created a state police organization comprised of close to twenty officers. According to the law, the governor was given the power to select a chief constable who would direct a force composed of all state constables and their deputies. The nascent "state police" was mandated to maintain peace and order and prevent crime by controlling vice establishments, such as brothels, taverns, and gambling establishments. The force was given police powers throughout the state.

The "state police" was reorganized several times over the next fifteen years. In 1875, it was transformed into a "state detective force" of thirty men under the direction of a chief detective chosen by the governor. Within five years, the "state detectives" were transformed into the "district police," again under the supervision of a chief appointed by the governor. Throughout the various incarnations of the force, its powers and duties remained fairly consistent and focused most of its attention on enforcing liquor laws. Following World War I, the Massachusetts State Police would be reorganized as a modern state police force.[40]

Pinkertons and U.S. marshals

In 1846, the Boston Police Department created the first municipal detective division. New York followed with a similar division in 1857 and Philadelphia two years later. Subsequent scandals would reveal that, like Britain's early thief takers, these detectives did little more than collect payoffs from amicable criminals and arrest those who failed to pay tribute. By the 1860s, municipal crime detection had been placed in the hands of private detectives, many of whom had former investigative experience.

The foremost detective agency of the nineteenth century was the Pinkertons, brainchild of Scottish immigrant Allan Pinkerton. Initially involved in railroad security, Pinkerton came to the attention of railroad lawyer Abraham Lincoln in the 1850s. Their chance meeting perhaps allowed Lincoln to survive to repeat the presidential oath in 1861. Pinkerton apparently stumbled on a plot to kill Lincoln as he passed through Maryland on his way to take office in the nation's capital. Interceding on the president-elect's behalf, Pinkerton convinced Lincoln not to leave the train in Baltimore. In 1861, Pinkerton was selected by the commanding Union general McClellan to lead the intelligence branch at the start of the Civil War.

Despite the reservations of former government detective Lafayette C. Baker, who noted that a detective bureau was "contrary to the spirit of . . . Republican institutions in time of peace,"[41] Pinkerton saw the lawlessness that punctuated the postwar years as an opportunity for earning new accolades. During the two decades following hostilities, the Pinkertons pursued (not always successfully) a virtual who's who of outlaw gangs, ranging from the Reno brothers in 1865–1866 to the James-Younger gang in the 1870s.

In the unorganized western territories, which had not yet made the transition to statehood, only federal law applied, leaving U.S. marshals as virtually the only law enforcement presence. In territories ranging from Wyoming to Arizona and New Mexico, all the governors, judges, and other officials were appointed by the president. When a territory reached 5,000 free white males, a bicameral legislature could be elected and laws promulgated. When the territory reached 60,000, it could be nominated for statehood (and then had to be approved by Congress). The position of U.S. marshal reflected the role of the federal courts. Since all criminal activities were viewed as a breech in federal law, marshals pursued a wide array of malefactors. But as the territory made the transition to statehood, the marshals saw other territorial lawmen take over their duties. As the territory came closer to statehood, federal marshals concentrated specifically on federal laws, while territorial laws were enforced by territorial county sheriffs.

Corrections

According to the federal census of 1860, the national prison population stood at 19,086. However, this figure increased by 72 percent to 32,901 in 1870, reflecting the social discord and disorganization that typically followed a war. By the late 1860s, prison overcrowding was an increasing concern. The sudden increase of the prison population after the war and a growing opposition to **prison industries** brought prison conditions to the attention of the public. In response, new institutions were built, and stimulus was given to the "reformatory" movement, an experiment in prison reform that emphasized education, trade training, a mark system, indeterminate sentencing, and parole. Building on the achievements of Captain Alexander Maconochie in Australia and Walter Crofton in Ireland, American reformatories attempted to make the transition from punitive programs to programs more reformative in nature.

According to prison historian Mark T. Carleton, the end of the Civil War was the "most decisive event in the history of southern penology."[42] With the end of hostilities, half the southern population made the transition from slavery to freedom in a region of the country where many jails and penitentiaries had been destroyed in the war.

Prior to the war, slaves who broke the law were punished on the plantation, but after 1865, new arrangements had to be made. The southern infrastructure had been destroyed during the war, and outside of prison units in several states, what little was available in the way of prison space was primitive in nature since the war had wiped out the beginnings of the penitentiary system in most states. Unprepared to handle the formidable expenses of social control by utilization of the penitentiary, southern legislatures were attracted by a cheaper alternative: convict leasing.

Convict leasing

Unable to pay and care for the burgeoning number of prisoners following the Civil War, southern states experimented with a system of convict leasing that allowed prison contractors to utilize cheap prisoner labor for an assortment of projects, including levee and railroad construction as well as agricultural work. During the 1870s and 1880s, the convict leasing system would dominate southern penology. Two different types of leasing evolved.

Under the terms of the contract system, prisoners worked behind prison walls and were fed, clothed, and guarded by prison authorities. Therefore, the lessor was only hiring the labor of the convicts behind prison walls. This system flourished in South Carolina, Texas, and Virginia by the 1880s. Other southern states and several outside the region used the lease system, in which prisoner labor was hired to work outside the confines of the prison structure.

National Prison Congress

Few Americans voiced concerns for prison conditions in 1865. The end of the Civil War and the onset of Reconstruction consumed the interest of most citizens, who had witnessed the bloodiest decade in American history. Public indifference to prison conditions was demolished in 1865 after prison reformers **Enoch Wines** (1806–1879) and **Theodore Dwight** publicized the deplorable state of several penitentiaries and reformatories they visited in the Northeast. Their tour of the prisons was chronicled and then published in seventy volumes as the *Report on the Prisons and Reformatories of the United States and Canada* in 1867.

Their conclusions offered several revealing statistics about the impact of the Civil War on the prison population. They noted that the number of male prisoners declined in state prisons anywhere from 10 to 50 percent. One explanation for this was that criminals often found refuge in the army during the war and that prison sentences were shorter in wartime. According to Wines and Dwight, the war also saw an increase in the imprisonment of women and minors. However, the years following the war saw a rapid increase in male prisoners and a general decline in female commitments.

Among their most fervent recommendations was the adoption of Sir Walter Crofton's **"Irish system."** This system was comprised of a series of graded prison stages. In the first phase, the convict spent two years in solitary confinement, followed by a period of congregate labor that would determine the prisoner's date of release and that would eventually earn a "ticket of release" during which the individual's progress on the outside would be monitored.

Wines soon envisioned the creation of a world organization in which all nations would come together to establish an ideal prison system. As a first step in this mission, Wines played a crucial role in convening the meeting of the National Prison Congress in America. In 1870, 130 delegates from 24 states, Canada, and South America met in Cincinnati. Among the most prestigious attendees were none other than Sir Walter Crofton and Enoch Wines. Both were among the forty delegates who delivered papers at the Congress. Following the delivery of various presentations, which ranged from jails and prison hygiene to executive pardon and indeterminate sentencing, the Congress joined ranks and adopted the **Declaration of Principles**, the most progressive prison reform development of the era. The "Declaration of Principles" represented an extraordinary step in the direction of progressive prison reform. Among the improvements advocated by the meeting were better sanitary conditions, the abolition of political appointment of prison administrators, the progressive classification of prisoners based on the mark system, rewards for good conduct and work, and more stress on education. The National Prison Association would eventually provide the nucleus for what would become the American Correctional Association.

Declaration of Principles adopted at the National Prison Congress

1 Reformation, not vindictive suffering, as the purpose of penal treatment of prisoners
2 Classifications made on the basis of a mark system, patterned after the Irish system
3 Rewards for good conduct
4 Prisoners recognizing that their destiny remained in their own hands
5 Acknowledgment of obstacles to prison reform, including the political appointment of prison officials
6 Job training for prison officials
7 Indeterminate sentencing replacing fixed sentences
8 The removal of gross disparities and inequities in prison sentences
9 Heightened emphasis on religion and education as part of reformation process
10 More focus on industrial training
11 Abolition of contract labor in prisons
12 More specialized institutions for different types of offenders
13 Revision of laws pertaining to the sentencing of insane criminals
14 More judicious use of pardoning power
15 Creation of a system for the collection of uniform penal statistics
16 More adequate prison architecture, providing prison hospitals, schoolrooms, and so on as well as offering more sunlight and better air ventilation
17 Centralizing prison management in each state
18 Facilitating the socialization process of prisoners through proper associations and eradicating the regimen of silence
19 Recognizing that society is in part responsible for creating crime conditions

---

Crime and punishment

Americans of the Civil War era were beset by all manner of criminal activities, some new, others harkening back to the past. Whether living in crowded cities or living on a remote frontier landscape, Americans had become accustomed to violence following the massive bloodletting of the Civil War. During the late 1870s, the cities became a crucible for criminal activity. New York City reported 80,000 crimes in 1868 and, according to historian Alexander Callow, by the early 1870s boasted 30,000 professional thieves and 2,000 gambling dens.[43]

According to David R. Johnson in his study of the development of the American police, the "ingenuity and boldness" of professional criminals made them "technically superior" to the police.[44] This was especially true in the emerging wave of bank burglaries in the 1860s.

One would be hard pressed to find a region of the country with more crime than America's large urban areas. However, the cessation of Civil War hostilities led to more complex patterns of crime and punishment in the West. While shoot-outs, cattle rustling, and robberies dominate popular mythology, criminal activity was more often confined to less violent crimes, such as embezzlement, petty theft and larceny, gambling, prostitution, drunkenness, and disorderly conduct.

Birth of organized criminal activity

The Civil War era created a variety of opportunities for organized crime activity. Abraham Lincoln's conscription law with its loophole for paying replacements presented enterprising individuals such as Chicago's Michael McDonald with an opportunity to reap a financial whirlwind from the sectional conflict cleaving America's heartland. McDonald recruited numerous sordid denizens of the underworld to work in his organized scheme by which individuals would collect bounties ranging from $100 to $1,000 to enlist in the Union army and then would promptly desert. McDonald was given a commission for each case of "**bounty jumping**" as he transported them to different regions to repeat the scheme. According to one estimate, perhaps half of the 268,000 cases of desertion during the war were the result of bounty jumping. While this cannot be substantiated, it is clear that McDonald profited enough from this business to set up several gambling dens after the cessation of hostilities.

Even New York City policemen got caught up in the **bounty racket**. In 1865, Lafayette Baker, the chief of the National Detective Police, under the War Department, uncovered a system in which police as well as other city officials colluded in a thriving business to earn fraudulent bounties. According to local newspapers, after the war an increase in robberies and burglaries was linked to many criminals who no longer had access to the bounty racket.[45]

Chicago would prove an inviting environment for underworld figures beginning in the 1830s as burglars, gamblers, prostitutes, counterfeiters, and gunmen were drawn to the city that would become synonymous with organized crime in the next century. There was little here in the way of law enforcement until the mid-1850s. By the Civil War, crime lords, such as Englishman Roger Plant, were operating enterprises offering gambling and prostitution. Gearing activities toward soldiers at nearby military outposts, Plant's operation provided a warning-and-escape system that protected customers from military patrols. Other gambling establishments operated without serious interference from the authorities, setting a pattern in Chicago that would become all too familiar in the 1920s and 1930s. By the 1860s, gambling syndicates had become a familiar presence on the urban landscape in Chicago and elsewhere.

American bandits

Outlaw gangs appeared in a variety of incarnations in the decades following the War Between the States. Some were rebel guerrilla gangs in Missouri and Kansas; others included cowboys and farmers-turned-badmen in Texas and the Oklahoma territory. In 1866, America witnessed its first organized bank robbery, thanks to ex-Confederates led by the brothers Jesse and Frank James. By most accounts, there were few protests against bank robbery in the rural hinterlands, where country folk associated the "cheating" bankers with the railroad titans constructing tracks across the cattle trails and had a hand in fencing off grazing lands to do it. It was in this atmosphere that bank robbery seemed the ultimate social protest.

Historian Eric Hobsbawm, who focused much of his work on the "social bandit" tradition, noted that banditry and lawlessness seemed most likely after a traditional social equilibrium is upset "during and after periods of abnormal hardship such as famine or wars." His thesis would fit America following the Civil War (and later World War I).[46] The best-known bandit gangs of the era appeared soon after the conflict, when the country was still cleaved and highly politicized over the sectional conflict.

The social bandit thesis has come under fire by American historians in recent years who suggest that under closer scrutiny the theory collapses. Hobsbawm suggested that social bandits in other cultures and settings were not actually criminals, since they were embroiled in a legitimate struggle against injustice and oppression on behalf of peasants against the wealthy and powerful interests that tied them to the land. Historian Richard White asserts that the social bandit tradition, at least as far as America, "tend to breakdown when measured by specific example." This was the case when one examines the second half of the nineteenth century when "there were no American peasants to champion." Moreover, the outlaws and their constituencies "came from modern, market-oriented groups and not traditional groups."[47]

According to one study, the different outlaw gangs and gunfighters could be linked to their political allegiances. Some were loyal Republicans who had supported the Unionist cost, while others remained loyal to the Democratic Party and expressed affinity for the Lost Cause. Thus, during the postwar era, those affiliated with the Republican Party, such as Wyatt Earp, James Butler Hickok, and Pat Garrett, were more likely to be standard bearers for law and order, being that they were associated with "the conservative forces consolidating the authority interest of property, order and law."[48] As a result of their political affiliation they were less likely to be labeled as outlaws. Conversely, gunfighters who were tied to the Democratic Party and the Lost Cause of the Confederacy, were regarded as "dissident resisters" of the so-called western "incorporation" and social bandits. Exemplars would include Jesse James, the Younger Brothers, Tombstone, Arizona's cowboys, and Bill "the Kid" Bonney. Violence historian Richard Maxwell Brown referred to this dichotomy as the "Western Civil War of Incorporation," in which members of outlaw gangs were more often than not resisting "civilization," and all that it represented.[49]

According to some historians these social bandits were trying to stave off the dominant trend towards an emerging class structure that favored a growing elite and rapidly rising middle-class represented by professional men, ranchers, farmers, and others who threatened "traditional values" of a threatened rural pastoral culture. The James and Younger gangs and others who had fought with Confederate guerrillas during the Civil War were regarded as heroes by many Democratic and Confederate supporters, who were alienated by the "incorporation process" that was more focused on the "consolidation of capital and centralizing of authority."[50]

Capital punishment

Beginning in colonial America, hanging was the traditional means of capital punishment. Although hanging was not designed to be a tortuous death, most were probably painful as the convict slowly strangled to death. However, if done correctly, the placement of the noose and its knot should all but guarantee a quick jerk and the sovereign of the spinal cord. But in the days of public hangings, there witnesses who would testify to the fact that the quick death was more the exception than the rule. Nonetheless, there was little discussion over this method.[51]

Abolitionist agitation against the death penalty peaked in the 1840s. According to one authority, once executions in New York State were moved indoors and other states made the transition to private hangings, reformers began to direct their energies elsewhere. Others suggest that the bloodshed of the Civil War ended the abolition movement. While anti-gallows societies persisted into the 1850s, the outbreak of the war made it difficult for Union supporters who advocated war to end slavery to support the termination of individual cases of capital punishment. Indeed, according to historian David Brion Davis, in the aftermath of the Civil War, which claimed 600,000 soldiers, "men's finer sensibilities, which had once been revolted by the execution of a fellow human being, seemed hardened and blunted."[52]

During the Civil War, soldiers were routinely executed for desertion and other crimes. According to one historian, 267 Union soldiers were executed between 1861 and 1867, more than the total of all other military executions in America's other wars.[53] This same researcher suggests that there was a certain bias toward ethnicity (Irish), race (African American), and religion (Catholic) in selecting cases of military criminals for executions. Despite Lincoln's commutation of death sentences for desertion in February 1864, the hangings and firing squads persisted until the end of hostilities.

Corruption and the city boss

The 1850s and 1860s witnessed the rise of what one urban historian has described as "an American original,"[54] the **city boss**. Before the rise of the city boss, urban concerns were the purview of the respectable gentry, whose "political credentials," according to historian Alex Callow were often established by "family fame, grandeur or fortune." But these early exemplars viewed public office as a duty rather than a calling, in an era when city services were not guaranteed, but were mostly in the hands of volunteer organizations of policemen and firemen. Until the mid-nineteenth century, cities were smaller and less diverse, both racially and ethnically. The 1850s saw a transformation in which the nation grew more urbanized and the new urban centers required new types of leaders and municipal services.

No one exemplified the corruption and excesses of urban America more than **William M. Tweed**. At the zenith of his power in the late 1860s, he controlled New York City's government, courts, and police as well as the state legislature. Best known by the sobriquet "Boss," Tweed rose to power in 1850s New York. Elected to the New York Board of Alderman in 1851 and then to an undistinguished term in the U.S. Congress, he returned home and in 1857 was elected to the Board of Supervisors, a position that audited city expenditures, appointed election inspectors, and supervised public improvements that more often than not turned into "pork barrel" spending. Over the next thirteen years, Tweed was elected president of the board four times, each time gaining more power and more access to fraud and graft. As deputy street commissioner in 1863, he had control over thousands of jobs that could be dispensed to his supporters.

While Tweed was cementing his ties to a hardy core of constituents, he also made sure to consolidate his power with the local Democratic Party organization at **Tammany Hall**. Following the Civil War, Tweed emerged as the leader of the Democratic Party. Considered the nation's first political boss, Tweed wielded tremendous power by using patronage powers to keep his supporters employed. The Tweed Ring began its reign in 1866, and over the next five years, Tweed colluded with city leaders to create a dynasty of graft unprecedented in American history up to that time. Accepting kickbacks from contractors and embellishing building costs for his own profit, Tweed was soon targeted by reformers such as *Harper's Weekly* cartoonist and social commentator Thomas Nast.

One of the most powerful urban political machines in American history, Tammany Hall was founded in 1789. Created by a Revolutionary War veteran, it was originally an organization named the Society of Saint Tammany after a legendary Indian chief. In its early years, it was a fraternal society rather than a political party. In the early 1800s, Tammany Hall's nationwide membership declined and centered only in New York City, where it would evolve into an organizational engine, or "machine," driving the Democratic Party. From 1855 to the early 1930s, Tammany Hall's political machine would dominate New York City. Often scorned for its corruption and graft, following the arrest and conviction of Boss Tweed in 1871, Tammany made a comeback just three years later and regained control of the city government.

A campaign against Tweed came to a head in 1871 when the *New York Times* obtained reports of fraud and extravagance from a disgruntled former confidant of Tweed's. Following the publication of these charges, Tweed was soon arrested for defrauding the city treasury of at least $6 million. After two trials, Tweed was sentenced to twelve years, a sentence that was subsequently reduced to one year. Rearrested after his release, he escaped from prison and fled first to Cuba and then to Spain. He was soon recognized and extradited back to the United States and died in jail in 1878.

A sign of changing times on the horizon, the year 1872 saw America's first great "robber baron" plot during the **Credit Mobilier scandal**. One of the greatest congressional scandals of the nineteenth century, a financial unit known as Credit Mobilier was created to finance the construction of the Union Pacific Railroad. In order to get the best possible terms on land grants and rights-of-way, representatives of the unit sold company stocks at a huge discount to congressmen that would "do the most good." In 1872, just one year after the Tweed Ring scandal hit the newspapers, the *New York Sun* broke the story, resulting in a congressional investigation that implicated the current vice president, Schuyler Colfax, and former Speaker of the House as well as representative and future president James A. Garfield. In the end, economic historians have estimated Credit Mobilier profits to have ranged from $13 million to $23 million.

Birth of domestic terrorism

The 1850s saw a resurgence in sectional violence over the slavery issue. Nowhere was the strife more intense than in Kansas, where rival land claims, town sites, railroad routes, and the question of slavery led to violent confrontations. Also contributing to the rising tide of violence in the 1850s was the growth in American gun production. With the increased availability of firearms, American cities for the first time thrived with gun shops offering guns and their accoutrements to a "large minority of Americans [who] found confidence their guns and longed to demonstrate their proficiency."[55]

Heralding the bloodshed that was yet to come, during the 1850s, many parts of the country witnessed the intimidation of civilians whose sectional leanings conflicted with their own. The region of Kansas, Nebraska, and Missouri was blighted by a guerrilla warfare pitting "Jayhawkers" and "Red Legs" against those they viewed as Confederate sympathizers. In reality, these gangs of bushwhackers used wartime hatreds as a cover for a campaign of horse stealing, looting, and terror. In areas such as southern Iowa, Illinois, and Indiana, southern supporters called "Copperheads" or "Butternuts" wreaked havoc against Unionists in like fashion. The weight of secession fell even harder on Unionists living in southern strongholds that dotted Kentucky, Tennessee, and Virginia.

In May 1856, proslavery forces sacked the free-soil town of Lawrence, Kansas. For **John Brown**, a failed merchant and businessman, this event marked a turning point in his life. Furious at the attack, he summoned volunteers for a "secret mission." Reviled as a terrorist fanatic and revered as a fervent abolitionist, John Brown was one of the most controversial individuals of the Civil War era. Recent scholarship traces the birth of American domestic terrorism to his attack on the proslavery hamlet along **Pottawatomie Creek**, Kansas. Recent scholarship portrays John Brown in terms similar that to those used to describe modern jihadists and religious fanatics such as Osama bin Laden, citing Brown's fanaticism and use of violence to achieve political ends in his holy war against slavery.

A puritanical Congregationalist, Brown believed that God had chosen him for a special purpose. He was convinced that only brutal action directed against slave owners would win the undeclared war over slavery. This was made particularly clear on the night of May 24, 1856 (just three days after the proslavery attack on Lawrence, Kansas) when he led seven men (including four of his sons) in an attack against proslavery settlers along Pottawatomie Creek, where they butchered five proslavery settlers with broadswords, cutting off their fingers and arms and further igniting sectional tensions.

Brown's actions on behalf of abolitionism culminated in his ill-fated attack on the federal arsenal at Harper's Ferry in 1859. Hoping to provoke a slave uprising in the South, Brown and eighteen of his acolytes captured the armory and rifle factory and waited for escaped slaves to flock to his banner. But none came, and after two days of battle, Brown was captured.

During his subsequent trial, his lawyers tried to persuade him to plead insanity, but he would have none of it, and on December 2, 1859, Brown was elevated to martyrdom by abolitionists as he mounted the gallows to his death. Prior to his death, he handed a note to his jailer that read, "I John Brown am now quite certain that the crimes of this guilty land: will never be purged away; but with Blood."[56] Never in American history, it seemed, were so many people willing to die for their beliefs. To this day, Brown remains a complex man, and opinions are split over his legacy. But at least one writer ascribes his behavior as an example of "conscious political terrorism."[57] If this is true, then his deeds continue to resonate in the misdirected terrorist campaigns of modern-day zealots, such as the John Brown Brigade (which was embroiled in violent conflict with the North Carolina Ku Klux Klan), Ted Kaczynski (the Unabomber), and Timothy McVeigh (the Oklahoma City bomber).

The New York City draft riots

The 1863 New York City anti-draft riot was probably America's greatest urban riot. Lasting from July 13 to July 16, 1863, until recently, historians have accepted the number of fatalities as close to 1,000. However, research by historians Iver Bernstein and Adrian Cook suggests that the figure was perhaps one-tenth of previous estimates, which would still make it the bloodiest in American history.

The draft riots stemmed in part from President Lincoln's conscription laws, which antagonized Irish immigrants and fueled racial hatreds. Finding themselves on the lowest rungs of the social ladder, Irish immigrants resented the fact that they should fight a war to free the blacks and worried that freedom would bring black migration north to compete for jobs. Irish gangs, on the other hand, saw an opportunity to take advantage of the situation in order to loot and pillage unimpeded. Exacerbating class tensions of the era was the fact that better capitalized draftees could pay substitutes to take their place in the ranks, while the impoverished had no other legal alternative. According to Iver Bernstein, the riot was precipitated by a variety of factors, including Confederate sympathy, resentment toward the conscription act, and ethnic hatred. However, contrary to the traditional explanations for the bloodletting, the riot should be viewed within "the context of an ongoing process of urban change beginning in the early 1850s" as well as "a new complex of social, cultural, and political relations."[58]

The New York draft riots were driven by a variety of circumstances. Poor citizens saw it as an opportunity to protest squalid living conditions and the substitute system. Northern Democrats inflamed the racist sentiments of the Irish by telling draftees that they were being sent to free southern blacks who would thank them by coming north and taking away jobs.

Much of the racial violence was directed at New York City's sizable free black population as well as the fledgling police force. In the 1860s, the police were still poorly equipped to handle riots of this magnitude. Another problem was that, while the 1850s police force was regarded as community-based, the 1863 force was viewed as instruments of the state government. With little besides batons and handguns and occasional military drills, their only response against the riots consisted of violent retribution. During the New York draft riots, as policemen found themselves targeted along with any blacks, one police commissioner ordered his men to "take no prisoners," and another wrote in his memoirs that he told his men to "kill every man who has a club."[59]

The Ku Klux Klan

The birth of the Ku Klux Klan introduced a new source of American violence in the aftermath of the Civil War. Regarded as a response to the social, cultural, and economic changes that many white southerners found so disturbing during the onset of Reconstruction, the Klan has undergone a variety of personifications over the past 140 years.

Created as a club in Pulaski, Tennessee, in 1866 by six former Confederate soldiers, few could have imagined the direction the Klan would take in its various incarnations over the next century. Well-educated members from upstanding families, the six men were inspired by Greek-letter fraternities in college to borrow the Greek word *kuklos*, meaning "circle of friends," to name their small fraternity the Ku Klux, adding "Klan" only to give it an alliterative intensity. It was not long before the name would inspire its more sinister connotations.

As the six initial members sought new members, they masked themselves in anonymity through the use of white masks with eyes cut out for the nose and eyes. This was soon complemented by a long robe. In the years of Reconstruction, it was not difficult to attract new members, especially after adopting a goal of maintaining white supremacy. Over the next decade, white terrorist groups waged an often bloody campaign to undermine the social, economic, and political reforms of the radical Republic agenda.

The main target of Klan night riders and similarly motivated standard bearers for racial supremacy were the recently freed African Americans. Lacking a formal organizational structure, individual vigilante groups attempted to violently enforce the racial codes that were threatened by the end of slavery. Striking usually at night to achieve the maximum threat, specifically targeted were blacks who defied white authority. In an attempt to restrict the free movement of blacks on local roads, open season was declared on those who attempted to move about freely. Historian James W. Clarke compared the Klan to "a uniformed, paramilitary extension of the earlier practice of slave patrols that had roamed the countryside looking for runaways."[60]

Reconstruction violence

Simmering animosities between supporters of both sides of the war often escalated into bloodshed during the Reconstruction years from 1866 to 1877. In perhaps a warning of what could be expected in the post-slavery years, on July 30, 1866, Union sympathizers and freedmen met at Mechanics' Hall in New Orleans to demand a more humiliating response to the former Confederates. It was not long before a large crowd of armed whites descended on the revelers and fired into their midst. What started as a celebration of the passage of recent civil rights legislation quickly turned into a massacre. By the time federal troops arrived, thirty-four black and three white Unionists had been murdered and dozens wounded. This incident would be repeated in other southern cities with the onset of the Reconstruction and the military occupation of the South.

Recent research indicates that continuing rivalries between Union and Confederate boosters led to the notorious Hatfield–McCoy feud, which lasted from 1873 to 1883 in the mountains of West Virginia, a region that also included the mountain communities of western Virginia and Kentucky. Mountain feuds persisted because of an absence of regular law enforcement and a tradition of people's taking law into their own hands. East Texas was perhaps the most violent region of the country during the post-Civil War era, with feuds such as the Sutton–Taylor feud of 1869–1877 rivaling the Hatfield–McCoy feud in its vitriol. The southwestern states also witnessed a host of violent conflicts in this period stemming from wartime dislocation, Reconstruction animosities, the rapid growth of the cattle industry, and the instability produced by Indian wars with the Comanches and the Kiowas.

Interracial violence

Despite the end of slavery in the South, some planters refused to recognize emancipation, and on occasion freedmen were beaten, killed, or mutilated to prevent them from leaving the plantation. Local law enforcement often supported planters by authorizing more punitive punishment for blacks than for whites. This could include public whippings, pillories, and chain gangs, clearly an attempt to send a message to the new freemen. According to Reconstruction historian George C. Rable, with little chance of a fair hearing in local courts, the Freedmen's Bureau and the army were their last resort but were rarely able to help.[61] Justice continued to be color conscious for blacks. Officials rarely heard complaints by black litigants against white defendants, nor were great attempts made to apprehend whites who killed freedmen. According to Union General Philip Sheridan, "My own opinion is that the trial of a white man for the murder of a freed man in Texas would be a farce."[62] Indeed, Texas would not execute a white man for the execution of an African American until late in the twentieth century. With little protection from local courts and law enforcement, the army was seen as the only source of protection.

America's largest mass hanging

The years following the Civil War witnessed the majority of the Indian–white confrontations in the West as settlers flocked beyond the Mississippi River to take advantage of the Homestead Act passed by congressional Republicans in 1862. That same year saw one of the worst Indian uprisings in American history when the Dakota Sioux of Minnesota revolted against inhumane treatment by government Indian agents. Following the killing of between 500 and 800 white settlers, federal troops and state militia defeated the Indians and restored order.

Following the fighting, 392 trials were held over a 30-day period (spread over 6 weeks). Of these, 250 cases were handled in just the last 10 days of trials. The Dakota warriors were tried by a military commission. However, this would be the first time that a military commission would be used "to try enemy combatants for firing shots on the battlefield." Theoretically, this type of trial was considered a wartime legal proceeding, only to be used when it was impossible to have a court martial or civil trial. Precedents for military commissions were rather thin at this time. In the course of the Mexican–American War, sixteen years earlier, General Winfield Scott introduced the commission after being frustrated at his inability to punish any of his soldiers for murdering Mexican citizens under the Articles of War. His standards followed the rules of court martial, a standard that still held in 1862. In the course of the proceedings, the defendants were entitled to hear the specific charges, make pleas, and have the sentence read out to them. The 1862 commission was the first time one was convened between whites and Indians.[63]

Ultimately, 303 death sentences were read out, as well as 69 acquittals and 16 imprisonments. Many of the trials took less than ten minutes and in some cases six to eight Dakota were brought before the court at a time, chained at the ankles. Contravening the rules of the commission the sentences were never read aloud to the defendants, which created great confusion among the convicted defendants. One witness chided the injustice of the hearings, commenting, "400 have been tried in less time than is generally taken in our courts with the trial of a single murderer." According to this son of a missionary, in many of the cases they were not allowed counsel nor any time to explain their actions during the murderous rampage. Moreover, "often not understanding the English language in which the trial was conducted, they very imperfectly understand the evidence upon which they are convicted."[64]

Before the mass execution could go forward, an appeal reached the desk of President Lincoln, who became the "first and only president ever to consider three hundred death sentences all at once."[65] With the Civil War ongoing, Lincoln was anxious about making the right call and ended up sparing the lives of 265 of the condemned. In the end, thirty-eight Indians were hanged at one time from the same gallows, the largest mass hanging in American history. According to one nineteenth-century source, "they were placed upon a platform facing inwards, and dropped by the cutting of rope all at one time."[66]

Notable trials

Trial of the Lincoln conspirators (1865)

The trial of seven coconspirators charged with assassinating President Lincoln opened on May 9, 1865, less than a month after the assassination. The proceedings would be marked by controversy and rancor from the start. Among the most celebrated of the conspirators were Mrs. Mary Surratt and Dr. Samuel Mudd, the latter charged with helping attend the injured John Wilkes Booth on his flight from Washington, DC, to sanctuary in the South.

The seven prisoners were given one to three days to prepare their cases and obtain counsel. The first day of the trial was held in a secret court session, reminiscent of the Star Chamber of Tudor England. Public demand soon opened up the proceedings to the press and the public. The court was almost immediately challenged on the grounds that it was a military tribunal. The main justification for this sort of trial was that the United States was at war and that the deceased president had been the commander in chief of the armed forces.

The defendants argued that a military court did not have jurisdiction since the accused were not members of the armed forces, but their pleas were overruled. The defendants then asked to be tried separately, and this too was denied. By most standards, the trial was extraordinary. The defendants at this time did not have the right to testify on their own behalf. To prevent the defendants from taking their own lives, great steps were taken to guard against suicide. The prisoners were kept in solitary confinement before their court appearances, and their faces were covered by canvas hoods with openings at the mouth for eating and breathing.

During the seven-week trial, the prosecution paraded a slew of witnesses, and after several more days of rebuttal and final presentations, the case went to military judges who then deliberated for two days. Conducted amid the clamor of postwar hysteria, the defendants were connected to every misdeed associated with the Confederacy, including the Anderson-ville military prison and the plot to burn New York City. Numerous witnesses who could have helped the defense were not called to testify, and little evidence connected Mary Surratt to the conspiracy outside of owning the rooming house where the plot was hatched.

At the end of June 1865, the commission reached a separate verdict for each defendant. Of the eventual eight defendants, four were sentenced to be hanged, including the only woman, Mary Surratt. An execution date was set for July 7, only twelve weeks after Lincoln's death. The public was not informed of the date until two days prior to the execution. Despite a plea for clemency on behalf of Surratt, the four mounted the gallows on a hot July day while a crowd of spectators watched. To the end, most believed that Surratt would be spared. But when all hope was lost, conspirator Lewis Paine told the executioner, "If I had two lives to give, I'd give one gladly to save Mrs. Surratt."[67] All four were then executed at the same moment.

Conclusions

The Civil War generated extraordinary problems for the American criminal justice system. By its conclusion in 1865, many of the system's components had been altered and modified. The abolition of slavery and the return of traumatized war veterans to every region of the country would lead to a rise in crime and a strain on the courts, policing, and prisons.

The end of the Civil War tested America's developing criminal justice system and introduced new forms of criminality while stimulating the development of new crime fighting strategies and institutions. Ku Klux Klan night riders, organized gambling, counterfeiters, train robbers, and bank robbery would test the ingenuity of law enforcement on both the federal and the local level.

Although there was a perceptible shift in public opinion over the death penalty between the eighteenth century and the Civil War, only Michigan, Rhode Island, and Wisconsin abolished capital punishment. The Civil War years sapped the abolitionist movement of much of its vigor as opponents to capital punishment found an array of issues and crusades that had more impact on everyday life to pour their energies into. As executions were removed from public spectacle to behind prison walls, there was less opportunity to incite activists and other opponents. Gauging the public reaction to these developments was the response to the public hanging of the Lincoln conspirators, which few disapproved of.

Slavery officially ended by constitutional action with the passage of the Thirteenth Amendment in December 1865. The end of the Civil War was followed by a period of Reconstruction lasting from 1865 to 1877, during which mob violence abated in northern cities as vigilantism seemed to grow in intensity west of the Mississippi River.

By the 1860s, urban policing had finally left its colonial roots behind, as uniformed officers patrolled beats in many major cities. Auguring a century of tremendous advances in investigation techniques, as early as the 1850s, precincts were linked to central headquarters by telegraph wires. New York City was credited with introducing a "Rogues Portrait Gallery" in the 1850s, displaying photos of hundreds of known criminals. The next decade would see the introduction of the first telegraph police boxes, by which a police officer could turn a key in a box and have his location and number be automatically recorded at headquarters. By the late 1860s, retirement pensions were available for New York police veterans, and an insurance fund was established for the families of policemen killed or disabled on duty. In 1871, 112 police officials gathered to discuss the late increase in crime, setting into motion a series of meetings that would lead to the creation of the National Chiefs of Police Union (1893), the forerunner of the International Chiefs of Police (1902).

By the 1850s, the era of correctional reform had almost ground to a halt, as focus was diverted to the prison industry. During the war years, prisons were major manufacturers of clothing, shoes, furniture, and uniforms. Following the Civil War, southern prisons were increasingly populated by black convicts. But elsewhere, prison reform would be reinvigorated in the years prior to the meeting of the National Prison Congress in 1870, and during the next decade, opposition by trade unions led to restrictions on the interstate commerce of prison goods. As the 1870s saw the arrival of the "Gilded Age," northern prisons, modeled on factories and replete with shops and contractors, stood in sharp contrast to southern prisons, which for the most part remained an anachronism. Michael Stephen Hindus' portrait of the South Carolina penitentiary, which was "almost entirely black, with its chain gangs, field hands, work songs, and white overseers, [and] resembled the plantation,"[68] remains an indelible reminder of the divergent societies in the North and the South.

The end of the Civil War was followed by one of the most dramatic events in American constitutional history when President Andrew Johnson survived impeachment by one vote in 1868. Unlike Great Britain, where impeachment is part of the political process, impeachment American style was a legal instrument since the law stated that a president may be removed from office only for "treason, bribery, or other high Crimes and misdemeanors" and only after a trial in the Senate presided over by the chief justice. Johnson's impeachment was the result of a bitter feud between the president and Congress over Reconstruction policy and over Johnson's supposedly "unconstitutional" attempt to remove Secretary of War Edwin Stanton from office against the wishes of the Senate. Following his trial, which lasted from March to April, Johnson narrowly kept his office but preserved the right to presidential independence.

Lincoln's assassination, the impeachment of Johnson, and the turmoil accompanying Reconstruction were larger-than-life episodes that captivated the nation and taxed every segment of the criminal justice system at all levels – federal, state, and local. The end of the Civil War would set the stage for the nation's greatest outbreak of outlawry in the West as the eastern cities came to grips with the complexities of the "Gilded Age" and the rise of the "robber barons."

Point – counterpoint

Ex parte Milligan: the suspension of habeas corpus (1861/66)

On March 3, 1863, Congress authorized President Abraham Lincoln to suspend the writ of habeas corpus (although Lincoln evolved his own constitutional interpretation by which he suspended the writ in 1861 without Congressional approval). On September 15, 1863, the writ was suspended in cases where officers held individuals for offenses against the military. This was considered one of Lincoln's most controversial decisions as president. Resistance to this decision resonates today in the aftermath of 9/11, 2001. In the first selection, Lincoln defends his suspension of Habeas Corpus in 1861. The second passage is from the landmark Court decision Ex parte Milligan. *In this, the Supreme Court denounced military tribunals in areas where the civil courts were open.*

Source: Richardson, ed., *Messages and Papers of the Presidents*, VI.,
pp. 24–25, 1913; *Ex parte Milligan*, 4 Wallace 2 (1866)

Soon after the first call for militia it was considered a duty to authorize the Commanding General in proper cases, according to his discretion, to suspend the privilege of the writ of habeas corpus, or, in other words, to arrest and detain without resort to the ordinary processes and forms of law such individuals as he might deem dangerous to the public safety. This authority has purposely been exercised but very sparingly. Nevertheless, the legality and propriety of what has been done under it are questioned, and the attention of the country has been called to the proposition that one who is sworn to "take care that the laws be faithfully executed" should not himself violate them. Of course some consideration was given to the questions of power and propriety before this matter was acted upon. The whole of the laws which were required to be faithfully executed were being resisted and failing of execution in nearly one-third of the States. Must they be allowed to finally fail of execution, even had it been perfectly clear that by the use of the means necessary to their execution some single law, made in such extreme tenderness of the citizen's liberty that practically it relieves more of the guilty than of the innocent, should to a very limited extent be violated? To state the question more directly, Are all the laws but one to go unexecuted, and the Government itself go to pieces lest that one be violated? Even in such a case, would not the official oath be broken if the Government should be overthrown when it was believed that disregarding the single law would tend to preserve it? But it was not believed that this question was presented. It was not believed that any law was violated. The provision of the Constitution that "the privilege of the writ of habeas corpus shall not be suspended unless when, in cases of rebellion or invasion, the public safety may require it" is equivalent to a provision – is a provision – that such privilege may be suspended when, in cases of rebellion or invasion, the public safety does require it. It was decided that we have a case of rebellion and that the public safety does require the qualified suspension of the privilege of the writ which was authorized to be made. Now it is insisted that Congress, and not the Executive, is vested with this power; but the Constitution itself is silent as to which or who is to exercise the power; and as the provision was plainly made for a dangerous emergency, it can not be believed the framers of the instrument intended that in every case the danger should run its course until Congress could be called together, the very assembling of which might be prevented, as was intended in this case, by the rebellion.

No more extended argument is now offered, as an opinion at some length will probably be presented by the Attorney General. Whether there shall be any legislation upon the subject, and, if any, what, is submitted entirely to the better judgment of Congress.

DAVIS J.: . . . The controlling question in the case is this: Upon the *facts* stated in Milligan's petition, and the exhibits filed, had the military commission mentioned in its *jurisdiction*, legally, to try and sentence him? Milligan, not a resident of one of the rebellious states, or a prisoner of war, but a citizen of Indiana for twenty years past, and never in the military or naval service, is, while at his home, arrested by the military power of the United States, imprisoned, and, on certain criminal charges preferred against him, tried, convicted, and sentenced to be hanged by a military commission, organized under the direction of the military commander of the military district of Indiana. Had this tribunal the *legal* power and authority to try and punish this man? . . .

The Constitution of the United States is a law for rulers and people, equally in war and in peace, and covers with the shield of its protection all classes of men, at all times, and under all circumstances. No doctrine, involving more pernicious consequences, was ever invented by the wit of man than that any of its provisions can be suspended during any of the great exigencies of government. Such a doctrine leads directly to anarchy or despotism, but the theory of necessity on which it is based is false; for the government, within the Constitution, has all the powers granted to it which are necessary to preserve its existence; as has been happily proved by the result of the great effort to throw off its just authority.

Have any of the rights guaranteed by the Constitution been violated in the case of Milligan? and if so, what are they?

Every trial involves the exercise of judicial power; and from what source did the military commission that tried him derive their authority? Certainly no part of the judicial power of the country was conferred on them; because the Constitution expressly vests it "in one Supreme Court and such inferior courts as the Congress may from time to time ordain and establish," and it is not pretended that the commission was a court ordained and established by Congress. They cannot justify on the mandate of the President, because he is controlled by law, and has his appropriate sphere of duty, which is to execute, not to make, the laws; and there is "no unwritten criminal code to which resort can be had as a source of jurisdiction."

But it is said that the jurisdiction is complete under the "laws and usages of war."

It can serve no useful purpose to inquire what those laws and usages are, whence they originated, where found, and on whom they operate; they can never be applied to citizens in states which have upheld the authority of the government, and where the courts are open and their process unobstructed. This Court has judicial knowledge that in Indiana the federal authority was always unopposed, and its courts always open to hear criminal accusations and redress grievances; and no usage of war would sanction a military trial there for any offense whatever of a citizen in civil life, in nowise connected with the military service. Congress could grant no such power; and to the honor of our national legislature be it said, it has never been provoked by the state of the country even to attempt its exercise. One of the plainest constitutional provisions was, therefore, infringed when Milligan was tried by a court not ordained and established by Congress, and not composed of judges appointed during good behavior.

Why was he not delivered to the circuit court of Indiana to be proceeded against according to law? . . . If it was dangerous, in the distracted condition of affairs, to leave Milligan unrestrained of his liberty, because he "conspired against the government, afforded aid and comfort to rebels, and incited the people to insurrection," the *law* said, arrest him, confine him closely, render him powerless to do further mischief; and then present his case to the grand jury of the district, with proofs of his guilt, and, if indicted, try him according to the course of the common law. If this had been done, the Constitution would have been vindicated, the law of 1863 enforced, and the securities for personal liberty preserved and defended.

Another guarantee of freedom was broken when Milligan was denied a trial by jury. . . .

It is claimed that martial law covers with its broad mantle the proceedings of this military commission. The proposition is this: that in a time of war the commander of an armed force (if, in his opinion, the exigencies of the country demand it, and of which he is to judge) has the power, within the lines of his military district, to suspend all civil rights and their remedies, and subject citizens as well as soldiers to the rule of *his will;* and in the exercise of his lawful authority cannot be restrained, except by his superior officer or the President of the United States. . . .

The statement of this proposition shows its importance; for, if true, republican government is a failure, and there is an end of liberty regulated by law. Martial law, established on such a basis, destroys every guarantee of the Constitution, and effectually renders the "military independent of, and superior to, the civil power," – the attempt to do which by the king of Great Britain was deemed by our fathers such an offense, that they assigned it to the world as one of the causes which impelled them to declare their independence. Civil liberty and this kind of martial law cannot endure together; the antagonism is irreconcilable; and, in the conflict, one or the other must perish. . . .

The necessities of the service, during the late rebellion, required that the loyal states should be placed within the limits of certain military districts and commanders appointed in them; and, it is urged, that this, in a military sense, constituted them the theater of military operations; and, as in this case, Indiana had been and was again threatened with invasion by the enemy, the occasion was furnished to establish martial law. The conclusion does not follow from the premises. If armies were collected in Indiana, they were to be employed in another locality, where the laws were obstructed and the national authority disputed. On *her* soil there was no hostile foot; if once invaded, that invasion was at an end, and with it all pretext for martial law. Martial law cannot arise from a *threatened* invasion. The necessity must be actual and present; the invasion real, such as effectually closes the courts and deposes the civil administration. . . .

Martial rule can never exist where the courts are open, and in the proper and unobstructed exercise of their jurisdiction. It is also confined to the locality of actual war. Because, during the late rebellion it could have been enforced in Virginia, where the national authority was overturned and the courts driven out, it does not follow that it should obtain in Indiana, where that authority was never disputed, and justice was always administered. And so in the case of a foreign invasion, martial rule may become a necessity in one state, when, in another, it would be "mere lawless violence." . . .

Key terms

Ex parte Merryman	*Ex parte Milligan*	writ of habeas corpus
black codes	Thirteenth Amendment	Fourteenth Amendment
Ku Klux Klan	"army disease"	morphine
opium	Chinatowns	New York Metropolitan Police Law
U.S. Secret Service	convict leasing	National Prison Congress
Enoch Wines	Theodore Dwight	Irish system
Elmira Reformatory	bounty racket	city boss
William M. Tweed	Tammany Hall	domestic terrorism
John Brown	Pottawatomie Creek	New York City draft riots
conscription	Reconstruction	Sioux mass hanging

Critical thinking questions

1 What impact did the Civil War have on corrections in the United States? Compare and contrast developments in different regions of the country.
2 Compare the development of modern policing in various regions of America between the 1850s and 1870s. Discuss the evolution of federal and state policing in the late nineteenth century.

3 What conditions necessitated the creation of private police forces such as the Pinkertons?
4 How did pre-Civil War violence differ from postwar bloodletting? Discuss the impact of race and region on violence patterns during this period.
5 Did civil rights legislation following the war have any impact on the criminal justice system? If so, at which level – state, federal, or local?

Notes

1 James G. Randall, *Constitutional Problems Under Lincoln*, Urbana: University of Illinois Press, 1964, p. 521.
2 The Freedmen's Bureau was created by Congress on March 3, 1865. Originally called the Bureau of Refugees, Freedmen, and Abandoned Lands, it was charged with the task of guiding the transition of African Americans into a life of freedom. The bureau operated in all the southern states. Among its most important responsibilities was taking over the administration of justice for freed men and women by establishing court systems responsible for the protection of civil rights. By the early 1870s, the bureau had lost most of its authority as former Confederates returned to leadership.
3 Edward L. Ayers, *Vengeance and Justice: Crime and Punishment in the 19th-Century South*, New York: Oxford University Press, 1986, p. 151.
4 Nicole H. Rafter, *Partial Justice: Women in State Prisons, 1800–1935*, Boston: Northeastern University Press, 1985, p. 14.
5 Dennis C. Rousey, *Policing the Southern City: New Orleans, 1805–1889*, Baton Rouge: Louisiana State University Press, 1991, p. 179.
6 Quoted in Randy E. Barnett and Josh Blackman, *Constitutional Law: Cases in Context*, Frederick, MD: Wolters Kluwer, 2018, p. 529
7 David Herbert Donald, *Lincoln*, New York: Simon and Schuster, 1995, p. 304.
8 Mark E. Neely, *The Fate of Liberty: Abraham Lincoln and Civil Liberties*, New York: Oxford University Press, 1991, p. 234.
9 Bernard Schwartz, *A History of the Supreme Court*, New York: Oxford, 1995, p. 139.
10 In U.S. Constitution; quoted in Stephen Dycus et al., Constitutional Law, New York: Wolters Kluwer, 2016.
11 Ayers, 1986, p. 151.
12 Ibid.
13 Theodore B. Wilson, *The Black Codes of the South*, Tuscaloosa: University of Alabama Press, 1965, p. 138.
14 *Mississippi, Laws of the State* [1865], 1896, Jackson, MS, pp. 82–86. http://wps.pearsoncustom.com/wps/media/objects/4222/4324230/documents/primarysource_16_1.html
15 Bernard Schwartz, *A Book of Legal Lists: The Best and Worst in American Law*, New York: Oxford University Press, 1997, p. 78.
16 Quoted in Ibid., p. 78.
17 Nancy Woloch, *Women and the American Experience*, Boston: McGraw-Hill, 2000, p. 78.
18 David J. Bodenhamer, *Fair Trial: Rights of the Accused in American History*, New York: Oxford University Press, 1992, p. 80.
19 H. Wayne Morgan, *Yesterday's Addicts: American Society and Drug Abuse, 1865–1920*, Norman: University of Oklahoma Press, 1974, p. 3.
20 According to Morgan, 1974, p. 7, the "first proven case of morphine addiction resulting from hypodermic medication" was reported in 1864.
21 Morgan, 1974, p. 9.

22 Carroll Smith-Rosenberg, *Disorderly Conduct: Visions of Gender in Victorian America*, New York: Oxford University Press, 1985, p. 225.

23 Lawrence M. Friedman, *Crime and Punishment in American History*, New York: Basic Books, 1993, p. 134.

24 Irish dramatist George Bernard Shaw is credited with inventing the term *Comstockery*, referring to it as "the world's outstanding joke at the expense of the United States."

25 Woloch, 2000, p. 372.

26 Smith-Rosenberg, 1985, p. 223.

27 Eric Monkkonen, *Police in Urban America, 1860–1920*, New York: Cambridge University Press, 1981, pp. 55–57.

28 Sidney L. Harring, *Policing a Class Society: The Experience of American Cities, 1865–1915*, New Brunswick, NJ: Rutgers University Press, 1983, p. 31.

29 Roger Lane, *Policing the City: Boston, 1822–1885*, Cambridge, MA: Harvard University Press, 1967, p. 119.

30 Robert Reinders, "Militia and Public Order in Nineteenth-Century America," *American Studies*, 11(2), 1977, p. 91.

31 Ibid., p. 92.

32 Rousey, 1991.

33 Ibid., p. 119. See Mitchel P. Roth and Tom Kennedy, *Houston Blue: The Story of the Houston Police Force*, Denton: University of North Texas Press, 2010, pp. 24–25, for information on first black police in Houston.

34 Richardson, 1970, p. 90.

35 Lane, 1967, p. 119.

36 Richardson, 1970, p. 123.

37 Ben Tarnoff, *Money-Makers: The Wicked Lives and Surprising Adventures of Three Notorious Counterfeiters*, New York: Penguin Press, 2011; James Mackay, *Allan Pinkerton: The First Private Eye*, New York: Wiley, 1996.

38 John K. Cooley, *Currency Wars: How Forged Money Is the New Weapon of Mass Destruction*, New York: Skyhorse Publishing, 2008, p. 55.

39 Alan Stahl, "Coin and Punishment in Medieval Venice," in *Law and the Illicit in Medieval Europe*, ed. Ruth Mazo Karras, Joel Kaye and E. Ann Matter, Philadelphia: University of Pennsylvania Press, 2010, pp. 162–179; Thomas Levenson, *Newton and the Counterfeiter: The Unknown Detective Career of the World's Greatest Scientist*, Boston: Mariner Books, 2010.

40 H. Kenneth Bechtel, *State Police in the United States: A Socio-Historical Analysis*, Westport, CT: Greenwood Press, 1995.

41 Rhodri Jeffreys-Jones, Cloak and Dollar: A History of American Intelligence, New Haven: Yale U Press, 2002, p. 35.

42 Mark T. Carleton, *Politics and Punishment: The History of the Louisiana State Penal System*, Baton Rouge, Louisiana State University Press, 1971, p. 13.

43 Alexander B. Callow Jr., *The City Boss in America: An Interpretative Reader*, New York: Oxford University Press, 1970, p. 144.

44 David R. Johnson, *Policing the Urban Underworld: The Impact of Crime on the Development of the American Police, 1800–1887*, Philadelphia: Temple University Press, 1979, p. 57.

45 Richardson, 1970, p. 126.

46 Eric Hobsbawm, *Social Bandits and Primitive Rebels*, Glencoe, IL: University of Manchester, 1960. This book was originally published as *Primitive Rebels: Studies in Archaic Forms of Social Movements in the 19th and 20th Centuries*, Manchester: University of Manchester, 1959.

47 Richard White, "Outlaw Gangs of the Middle Border: American Social Bandits," *Western Historical Quarterly*, 12, 1981, pp. 387–408, quotes on p. 394.

48 Richard Maxwell Brown, *No Duty to Retreat*, New York: Oxford University Press, 1991, p. 40.

49 Richard Maxwell Brown, *No Duty to Retreat: Violence and Values in American History and Society*, Norman: Oklahoma University Press, 1994, p. 44.

50 Ibid., pp. 44–46. See also Alan Trachtenberg, *The Incorporation of America: Culture and Society in the Gilded Age*, New York: Hill and Wang, 1982.
51 Stuart Banner, *The Death Penalty: An American History*, Cambridge, MA: Harvard University Press, 2002, p. 170.
52 Quoted in John D. Bessler, *Death in the Dark: Midnight Executions in America*, Boston: Northeastern University Press, 1997, p. 46.
53 Robert L. Alotta, *Civil War Justice: Union Army Executions Under Lincoln*, Shippensburg, PA: White Mane Publishing, 1989, p. x.
54 Callow, 1970, p. 3.
55 Michael A. Bellesiles, *Arming America: Origins of a National Gun Culture*, New York: Alfred A. Knopf, 2000, p. 387.
56 Stephen B. Oates, *To Purge This Land with Blood: A Biography of John Brown*, Amherst, University of Massachusetts Press, 1984, 2nd ed, p. 351.
57 Ken Chowder, "The Father of American Terrorism," *American Heritage*, Feb/March 2000, Vol 51, Issue 1. https://www.americanheritage.com/content/father-american-terrorism
58 Iver Bernstein, *The New York City Draft Riots: Their Significance for American Society and Politics in the Age of the Civil War*, New York: Oxford University Press, 1990, p. 6.
59 Quoted in Richardson, 1970, p. 143.
60 James W. Clarke, *The Lineaments of Wrath: Race, Violent Crime, and American Culture*, New Brunswick, NJ: Transaction Publishers, 1998, p. 84.
61 George C. Rable, *But There Was No Peace: The Role of Violence in the Politics of Reconstruction*, Athens: University of Georgia Press, 1984, p. 21.
62 Quoted in Ibid., p. 21.
63 Scott W. Berg, *38 Nooses: Lincoln, Little Crow, and the Beginning of the Frontier's End*, New York: Pantheon, 2012, pp. 190–191, 66–67.
64 Quoted in Ibid., pp. 193–194.
65 Ibid., p. 198.
66 Quoted in Richard Maxwell Brown, *American Violence*, Englewood Cliffs, NJ: Prentice Hall, 1970, p. 58.
67 Betty J. Ownsbey, *Alias 'Paine': Lewis Thornton Powell, The Mystery Man of the Lincoln Conspiracy*, Jefferson: McFarland Press, 2015, 2nd ed, p. 114.
68 Michael S. Hindus, *Prison and Plantation: Crime, Justice and Authority in Massachusetts and South Carolina, 1767–1878*, Chapel Hill: University of North Carolina Press, 1980, p. 253.

Sources

Allen, Oliver E. 1993. *The Tiger: The Rise and Fall of Tammany Hall*. New York: Addison-Wesley.
Alotta, Robert L. 1989. *Civil War Justice: Union Army Executions Under Lincoln*. Shippensburg, PA: White Mane Publishing.
Bechtel, H. Kenneth. 1995. *State Police in the United States: A Socio-Historical Analysis*. Westport, CT: Greenwood Press.
Bellesiles, Michael A. 2000. *Arming America: Origins of a National Gun Culture*. New York: Alfred A. Knopf.
Barnett, Randy E. and Josh Blackman. 2018. *Constitutional Law: Cases in Context, Frederick, MD*: Wolters Kluwer, 2018, p. 529.
Bernstein, Iver. 1990. *The New York City Draft Riots: Their Significance for American Society and Politics in the Age of the Civil War*. New York: Oxford University Press.
Bessler, John D. 1997. *Death in the Dark: Midnight Executions in America*. Boston: Northeastern University Press.

Brown, Richard Maxwell. 1970. *American Violence*. Englewood Cliffs, NJ: Prentice Hall.

Brown, Richard Maxwell. 1991. *No Duty to Retreat*. New York: Oxford University Press, p. 40.

Callow, Alexander B., Jr. 1966. *The Tweed Ring*. New York: Oxford University Press.

———. 1970. *The City Boss in America: An Interpretive Reader*. New York: Oxford University Press.

Carleton, Mark T. 1971. *Politics and Punishment: The History of the Louisiana State Penal System*. Baton Rouge: Louisiana State University Press.

Chalmers, David. 1987. *Hooded Americanism: The History of the Ku Klux Klan*. 3rd ed. Durham, NC: Duke University Press.

Chowder, Ken. 2000. "The Father of American Terrorism." *American Heritage*, February/March, Vol 51, Issue 1, pp. 81–91. https://www.admericanheritage.com/content/father-american-terrorism.

Clarke, James W. 1998. *The Lineaments of Wrath: Race, Violent Crime, and American Culture*. New Brunswick, NJ: Transaction Publishers.

Cook, Adrian. 1974. *The Armies of the Streets: The New York City Draft Riots of 1863*. Lexington, KY: University Press of Kentucky.

Donald, David Herbert. 1995. *Lincoln*. New York: Simon and Schuster.

Harring, Sidney L. 1983. *Policing a Class Society: The Experience of American Cities, 1865–1915*. New Brunswick, NJ: Rutgers University Press.

Hindus, Michael S. 1980. *Prison and Plantation: Crime, Justice, and Authority in Massachusetts and South Carolina, 1767–1878*. Chapel Hill: University of North Carolina Press.

Johnson, David R. 1979. *Policing the Urban Underworld: The Impact of Crime on the Development of the American Police, 1800–1887*. Philadelphia: Temple University Press.

———. 1995. *Illegal Tender: Counterfeiting and the Secret Service in Nineteenth-Century America*. Washington, DC: Smithsonian Institution Press.

Lane, Roger. 1967. *Policing the City: Boston, 1822–1885*. Cambridge, MA: Harvard University Press.

McPherson, James M. 1991. *Abraham Lincoln and the Second American Revolution*. New York: Oxford University Press.

Mississippi, Laws of the State [1865]. 1896. Jackson, MS, pp. 82–86. http://wps.pearsoncustom.com/wps/media/objects/4222/4324230/documents/primarysource_16_1.html

Monkkonen, Eric. 1981. *Police in Urban America, 1860–1920*. New York: Cambridge University Press.

Morgan, H. Wayne. 1974. *Yesterday's Addicts: American Society and Drug Abuse, 1865–1920*. Norman: University of Oklahoma Press.

Neely, Mark E. 1991. *The Fate of Liberty: Abraham Lincoln and Civil Liberties*. New York: Oxford University Press.

Oates, Stephen B. 1970. *To Purge This Land with Blood*. New York: Harper and Row.

Rable, George C. 1984. *But There Was No Peace: The Role of Violence in the Politics of Reconstruction*. Athens: University of Georgia Press.

Randall, James G. 1964. *Constitutional Problems under Lincoln*. Urbana: University of Illinois Press.

Reinders, Robert. 1977. "Militia and Public Order in Nineteenth-Century America." *American Studies*, 11(2):81–101.

Richardson, James. 1970. *The New York Police: Colonial Times to 1901*. New York: Oxford University Press.

Ruane, Michael E. 2009. "A Noble Cause, Reconsidered." *Houston Chronicle*, October 18, p. A8.

Steinberg, Allen. 1984. "From Private Prosecution to Plea Bargaining: Criminal Prosecution, the District Attorney, and American Legal History." *Crime & Delinquency*, 30(4), October:568–592.

Wade, Wyn Craig. 1987. *The Fiery Cross: The Ku Klux Klan in America*. New York: Simon and Schuster.

Wilson, Theodore B. 1965. *The Black Codes of the South*. Tuscaloosa: University of Alabama Press.

1876	1877	1877	1878	1878	1879
Publication of Lombroso's *Criminal Man*	End of Reconstruction as final federal troops are removed from the South	Ten Molly Maguires hanged on "Black Thursday"	First matrons hired by police departments	Massachusetts hires first paid probation officer	Supreme Court upholds execution by firing squad as constitutional

CHAPTER EIGHT

Crime and criminal justice in Victorian America (1876–1901)

Learning objectives

After reading this chapter students should understand and be able to discuss:

- How the Civil War was followed by the gradual transformation of southern criminal justice
- Why and how law enforcement coexisted with some forms of vice in the so-called Victorian compromise
- The police reform efforts of future president Theodore Roosevelt
- The changing nature of violence in various regions of the country
- The increasing visibility of women in criminal justice reform movements (juvenile justice, corrections, etc.)
- The role played by gender stereotypes in the Lizzie Borden trial and verdict
- The impact of the first National Prison Congress on the development of new alternatives to fixed sentencing
- Efforts at reforming and improving the criminal justice system for juvenile and female inmates

During the so-called **Victorian era** of the nineteenth century (which paralleled the reign of England's Queen Victoria in roughly the last half of the nineteenth century and overlapped with the American Gilded Age), a double standard existed in which certain moral offenses were tolerated as long they did "not threaten the general fabric of society."[1] According to this "Victorian compromise," gambling, prostitution, and other related forms of vice and

DOI: 10.4324/9781315148342-8

1881	1882	1886	1886	1890	1890
Assassination of President James A. Garfield by Charles Guiteau	Paris police adopt Bertillon system of identification	Publication of Thomas Byrnes' *Professional Criminals of America*	Haymarket bombing	Massacre of Sioux at Wounded Knee	First execution by electric chair

crime were tolerated under the assumption that there was little that could be officially done to eradicate them. Historian Lawrence Friedman describes this compromise as "a muddled but powerful theory of social control"[2] in which private sins could be tolerated in the "dark corners and back alleys" as long as public order was not compromised.

In earlier years, only married people could legally have sexual relations. Sexual violations were criminal acts and were equated with sin. Infractions ranged from fornication, incest, adultery, and bestiality to prostitution and homosexuality. However, in the eighteenth and early nineteenth centuries, the criminal justice system devoted less time to pursuing these behaviors. Recognizing the impossibility of purging immorality from the urban landscape, law enforcement focused on more deviant behavior while coexisting with certain "acceptable" forms of vice, such as prostitution and gambling, but with specific limits.

The lawgivers

A number of legal cases from this era hinged on interpretations of recent amendments. The Supreme Court had an overwhelming impact on a number of cases and would essentially put its stamp of approval on racial segregation. White supremacy stood triumphant in the South by the 1890s, with segregation and disenfranchisement accepted features of society south of the Mason–Dixon line. Between 1877 and the 1890s, blacks continued to vote and hold public office. But the 1890s saw the implementation of grandfather clauses, literacy tests, poll taxes, and even terror to discourage black participation in the political system. Further polarization occurred with the acceptance of current "scientific" notions of racism and criminality. Paralleling the increasing discrimination and victimization of blacks in the late nineteenth century was the mounting abuse of people of Asian descent, especially in the West.

Chinese Exclusion Act

Chinese immigrants began coming to the United State in the mid-1800s and found jobs building railroads and mining gold in the West. Many sent home money home to their families. Employers scurried to hire them as cheap labor and for their work ethic. By the 1870s, there were 70,000 Chinese in America, mostly on the Pacific Coast. It was not long before rival white laborers made the jump from resentment to violence, especially after

1892	1892	1893	1893	1893	1894	1895
Homestead strike	Publication of Sir Francis Galton's *Fingerprints*	First meeting of National Chiefs of Police Union	Trial of Lizzie Borden	Publication of Hans Gross' *Criminal Investigation*	Lexow hearings on police corruption in New York City	Theodore Roosevelt appointed New York City police commissioner

the transcontinental railroad was completed in 1869 and the Chinese began to settle in small towns and urban environs. Compared to Native Americans, Hispanics, and blacks at the end of the nineteenth century, there is little evidence that Chinese immigrants retaliated against whites. However, after a number violent incidents directed at Asians and the growing racial antagonism in 1882 the U.S. Congress passed the first of several Chinese Exclusion Laws devised to cut off further Chinese immigration. Initially the bill suspended the immigration of Chinese workers for the next twenty years. President Chester A. Arthur vetoed the bill but offered that he would approve another law that would only bar Chinese for ten years. This passed in May and was later renewed for another ten years. In 1904, President Theodore Roosevelt made it permanent.[3] Prior to the Chinese Exclusion Act of 1882, the lone law restricting immigration to America had been the Page Act of 1875, which targeted only Chinese women. Following the 1882 Exclusion Act, more and more restrictions to immigration would be added.

Over the next several years, conflict simmered until September 2, 1885, when a mob of angry white miners turned their frustrations on the Rock Springs, Wyoming, **Chinatown**. Dozens were murdered in the worst case of anti-Chinese violence in American history. No one was ever held to account for the crime. Although there was general outrage throughout the country thanks to sensational news reporting, the carnage was blamed on "the worst of our European immigrants: degraded Poles, ignorant and besotted Hungarians, and lazy convicts."[4]

Plessy v. Ferguson

In 1892, Louisiana resident Homer Plessy was riding a train out of New Orleans but was ejected from a car for whites and directed toward a car reserved for nonwhites. Light skinned and one-eighth black, Plessy claimed that a Louisiana statute that provided for separate railway carriages for whites and blacks was contrary to the **Fourteenth Amendment's** requirement of equal protection of the laws. Plessy took his case to court, reaching as high as the Supreme Court in 1896. In one fell swoop, the Court put the seal of approval on segregation by rejecting Plessy's contention and holding that segregation alone was not a constitutional violation. By a majority ruling, the Court approved a **"separate but equal" doctrine** that for more than fifty years all but nullified the Constitution's equal protection clause as an instrument of racial equality. Until 1954, *Plessy v. Ferguson*, which ruled that state-mandated segregated facilities did not violate the equal protection clause of the Fourteenth Amendment as long as facilities provided for blacks and whites were approximately equal, would serve as the constitutional cornerstone of racial discrimination in the United States.

1896	1896	1899	1901	1901
Argentina becomes first country to adopt fingerprinting as its main identification system	*Plessy v. Ferguson* Supreme Court decision	Passage of Juvenile Court Act by Illinois	Assassination of President William McKinley	Theodore Roosevelt makes Secret Service responsible for presidential protection

Law enforcement

Between 1870 and 1900, most large American cities had established professional police forces. However, for the less populated areas, a vacuum in authority led to the creation of vigilante groups, **lynchings**, and deadly feuds. While the Ku Klux Klan attempted to preserve the antebellum status quo, others took the law into their own hands to protect their newfound freedoms.

As mentioned earlier, the post-Civil War era witnessed the diminished role of the militia at a time when urban criminal violence was on the rise. Militia historian Robert Reinders suggested that the violent industrial strikes of 1877 "provided a new stimulus and role for the militia," one that demonstrated their impracticality for the industrial era.[5] In many cases, militia members sympathized with strikers, contributing to the growing disorder. In 1877, national armed forces demonstrated their superiority to the militia in quelling civil disturbances. Better trained and disciplined, the army proved better qualified at quelling riots than their militia counterparts.

The police of the 1870s and 1880s still operated by the traditional reactive styles of the past and were unlikely to capture wanted desperadoes unless they were caught in the act. Police forces saw reform efforts from local politicians, state legislatures, and chiefs of police. The New York City Police Chief George W. Walling, after having served forty years on the force, argued that police officers should work to improve their relations with the public, going beyond their mandate as keepers of the peace. In the same era, Cincinnati's George M. Roe boasted that his department had created a "gymnasium" and a "School of Instruction" for his officers in the late 1880s. According to Roe's memoir published in 1890, Cincinnati policemen were expected to "be a perfect specimen of physical manhood" and "must have a knowledge of the English language sufficient to make written reports intelligible," as well as be "versed in criminal and municipal laws to avoid making any mistakes" that could haunt them later during criminal proceedings.[6]

While police work remained a male domain well into the twentieth century, steps were taken to include women in a secondary role beginning in 1878, when some forces placed matrons in charge of female prisoners. By 1890, as a result of a campaign by several women's groups, thirty-six city police departments hired **police matrons**.

As the turn of the century approached, Irish Americans dominated the ranks of many urban police forces, with cities as diverse as Chicago, Cleveland, and San Francisco counting a disproportionate number of Irish among their ranks. Not all observers were favorable to this development, including one who wrote a diatribe in 1894 titled "The Irish Conquest of Our Cities," in which he lamented the number of Irish police chiefs in America.[7]

Police work remained a rather solitary profession in the closing decades of the nineteenth century, with most officers working either alone or in small groups. Attempts at police discipline and supervision fell short because of the limited power of police officials to enforce the rules. Outside of on-the-street supervision, there were few ways to closely supervise police on patrol. Some police commissioners sent out plainclothes patrolmen to check on colleagues. New York City police commissioner and future president Theodore Roosevelt made the rounds at night, stopping in saloons and the like. If an officer was spotted in one while on duty, he could expect a dressing down at headquarters the next morning. Some forces compiled massive rules books that included protocols for patrolling and making reports, with most violations punished with fines. According to one police historian, "Some departments' administrators punished policemen more often for violation of the rules than they did for crimes like assault and blackmail."[8]

Federal law enforcement

The South and the West continued to lag behind the North when it came to economic development. Both regions had little political clout in Washington (with smaller populations, they had less representation). Following the war, the belief that criminal law was a state and not a federal matter still persisted in the South. Congress in turn passed certain federal laws that disproportionately targeted the South and the West; hence, federal law enforcement was more inextricably tied to these regions.

According to historian Stephen Cresswell's study of federal law enforcement, for the years 1871–1890, the North had only 14 federal criminal cases per 10,000 for this time period compared to 54 per 10,000 in the South and 72 per 10,000 in the West.[9] Cresswell suggested that "certain elements in southern and western society made the violation of federal laws more common than in the North." Among the elements he cites are the get-rich mentality of the West and the prevalent dislike of the federal government in the defeated South.[10]

During **Reconstruction**, large areas of the former Confederacy were indeed relatively peaceful and could boast efficient law enforcement. With a large portion of white citizens loath to publicly denounce acts of violence against the former slaves in the 1870s, southern blacks and former Unionists often turned to the U.S. army as their only source of protection. However, the army was usually unwilling or unable to respond to such requests.

Federal law enforcement in the American West during the last half of the 1800s was the preserve of U.S. marshals. Between 1840 and 1900, marshals were elected to cover states and territories. Their main job was to uphold federal laws, which included arresting individuals for robbing the mail, deserting from the armed forces, stealing government stock, or killing Indians. Each marshal had an office deputy who was responsible for maintaining paperwork and could pass on orders to field deputies. Until 1896, only the office deputies were paid a salary, while the other federal deputies were paid through a fee system (about $2 per day) and mileage (six to ten cents per mile). Although the marshal received no salary, the position itself was considered a stepping-stone to better things. In 1896, U.S. Marshal Creighton M. Foraker assumed law enforcement responsibilities for Grants County, New Mexico, becoming the first U.S. marshal to serve under the newly implemented salary system. Foraker was instrumental in professionalizing his deputies, requiring them to be conversant in Spanish as well as act in a professional manner. In return, he gave them fixed salaries and put an end to the old **patronage system**, which saw politically motivated local sheriffs hindering investigations. He served this office until 1912.

The New York City Police Department

After the return of the New York City Police Department to city control in 1870, within a few years the force would be reorganized and a new set of standards implemented, including the requirements that police candidates be U.S. citizens and residents of the state for at least one year and not have a criminal record. In 1874, the force was rewarded with the sobriquet "The Finest." Other innovations followed: telephone links replaced the outdated telegraph system in 1880, a central office was created for the Bureau of Detectives, and four women joined the force as precinct matrons in 1888. However, a darker, more sinister side of the police force was revealed in 1894, when a New York state senate committee was appointed to investigate alleged abuses of authority by police.

The Lexow Committee

Under the leadership of Judge Clarence Lexow, a special senate committee began hearings on March 9, 1894. It went on to establish the existence of organized crime and vice rackets under the sanction and protection of the police and the city's powerful Democratic political machine operating out of Tammany Hall. The investigations, according to one historian, revealed the existence of widespread political and police malfeasance that "extended beyond simple toleration of saloons, brothels, and gambling dens."[11]

The Lexow Committee discovered a menu of bribes necessary for rising through the ranks of the New York Police Department (e.g., $300 just to be appointed to the force)[12] and an established system for shaking down illegitimate businesses. It also revealed an extensive system for shaking down prostitutes and brothel madams in order solicit business and operate. Gambling establishments were expected to pay for protection and pool halls could operate for $300 per month. Although numerous officers were dismissed and the Tammany machine was replaced by reform-minded politicians, there were no enduring achievements, and just four years later, Tammany was back in the hands of the bosses, and the police department had reverted back to its former corrupt excesses.

Theodore Roosevelt: New York City police commissioner and reformer

In 1895, future president Theodore Roosevelt (1858–1919) was appointed as one of four newly installed police commissioners. Over the next two years, he played an instrumental role in exposing departmental corruption and rooting out unscrupulous rogue police officials, including the notorious **Alexander "Clubber" Williams**. Roosevelt is credited with introducing numerous reforms, including a promotion system based on merit rather than patronage, more stringent physical and mental qualifications, and more progressive recruitment. He hired the first female civilian secretary and lobbied for Jewish officers to join the mostly Irish-Catholic rank and file. Roosevelt's term as commissioner led to better police training, a bicycle squad charged with traffic control, and more efficient call boxes, and the .32-caliber revolver became the standard on-duty sidearm.

In the late nineteenth century, police officers in major urban centers were responsible for a number of chores unrelated to law enforcement. Officers were tasked with supervising the cleaning of streets and providing shelter at the precinct houses. An old tradition and the bane of urban reformers in New York City was the continued use of precinct house basements to accommodate the homeless and the indigent. While the police referred to the basement shelters as "lodging houses," the homeless referred to them as "green-light hotels," alluding to the green lights at the entrances to the precinct houses.[13] Without bathroom facilities or beds, they were characterized by overcrowding and poor hygiene, leading Peter Conlin, a New York City police chief, to characterize them as refuges for the "lazy, dissipated, filthy, vermin-covered, disease breeding and disease-scattering scum of the city's population."[14]

Social reformer **Jacob Riis** (1849–1914) publicized these conditions as he accompanied Roosevelt on midnight excursions to the seedier police precincts with the hope of exposing police corruption and dereliction of duty. A Danish immigrant who had arrived in America only in 1877, Riis chronicled the plight of the underclasses in *The Children of the Poor* (1892) and *How the Other Half Lives* (1890). However, with few alternatives besides the city streets to seek refuge and no other social service institutions available, there were few alternatives for the homeless besides the precinct basements, where they would at least be sheltered from the elements and street crime.

Department morale improved during Roosevelt's short tenure as president of the Board of Police Commissioners from 1895 through 1897. During this period, precinct house accommodations for transients were replaced with separate lodging houses, and a system for recognizing meritorious police service was inaugurated. By 1897, New York State Republicans had apparently wearied of Roosevelt's reform campaign and, in order to get him out of office, reportedly arranged to have him appointed assistant secretary of the navy.

Civil service reform

The civil service reform taking place in New York City in the 1880s was part of a national movement led by middle- and upper-middle-class men during the era. Targeting the spoils system and political patronage, these reformers did their best to break the ties between politicians and police appointments. Some departments introduced procedures for appointments and promotions. However, politicians just as quickly found ways to sidestep medical, physical, and writing tests. Since writing tests were of the essay variety, examiners had wide latitude in grading. In New York City, there were cases of candidates' astonishingly adding inches to reach minimum height. On one occasion, a prospective candidate was rejected twice for syphilis, only to be accepted on his third try.[15]

Alexander "Clubber" Williams: corrupt cop

In an era of corrupt cops, none was more unscrupulous than Alexander "Clubber" Williams (1839–1910). Joining the New York Police Department in 1866, the physically impos-ing Williams earned the nickname "Clubber" for his dexterity with a nightstick. On one occasion, he bragged, "There is more law at the end of a policeman's nightstick than in any ruling of the Supreme Court." In 1871, he was promoted to captain and was later rewarded with a transfer to the **Tenderloin district**, leading the colorful cop to exclaim, "I've had nothing but chuck steak for a longtime and now I'm going to get a little tenderloin."[16] During his eleven years as captain in the area, he was accused and exonerated of eighteen brutality complaints. When the Lexow Committee investigated him in 1894, it found that, on an annual salary of $3,500, he had amassed more than $1 million in assets. His explana-tion for such wealth was that he made savvy real estate investments in Japan. Williams was forced to resign from the force.

Policing labor violence: the Pinkertons

During the nineteenth century, the history of private policing is closely tied to the devel-opment of the Pinkerton National Detective Agency. The Pinkertons came to national prominence during the Civil War, when they protected Lincoln from an assassination plot, and then were employed as counterespionage agents by the Union army. Following the war, Alan Pinkerton returned home to Chicago and to new challenges, ranging from pursuing train robbers to violent labor strikes.

By the 1870s, the Pinkertons claimed to have assembled the largest collection of criminal mug shots in the world as well as having created a criminal database for their agents. As the American economy struggled with the industrial upheaval of the late nineteenth century, the Pinkertons found themselves increasingly employed by corporations as strikebreakers, often leading to bloody conflict with organized labor. The most famous incident occurred in 1892 at the Carnegie Steelworks in Homestead, Pennsylvania. The veteran of more than fifty confrontations with labor by 1892, the **Homestead strike**, in which workers protested poor wages and other concerns, would prove the Pinkertons' most severe test.

When negotiations with labor leaders broke down at the Carnegie plant in June 1892, the company hired the Pinkertons to protect its factory. The Pinkertons sent 300 men by barges up the Monongahela River to the plant in July after pro-labor elements took control of the land routes from Pittsburgh. Waiting at the Homestead docks were between 3,000 and 10,000 workers. Testimony suggests that the strikers were unsure who was approach-ing, mistaking the approaching detective force for an army of strikebreaking scabs. It is unknown who fired first, but as the barges approached land, gunfire was exchanged by both groups, leaving three Pinkertons and ten workers dead. The Pinkertons were soon captured, and the strikers took over the factory until the Pennsylvania National Guard arrived several days later.

This incident was a major turning point in Pinkerton's policy for dealing with strike-breakers. Henceforth, the agency avoided taking the offensive in labor face-offs, instead opting to defend only factories. A subsequent investigation into the Homestead affair awakened Americans to the growth of the private police industry and tarnished the image of the Pinkertons. The antidetective mood that resulted from the carnage led to the passage of several **anti-Pinkerton laws** in the 1890s.[17]

Criminal identification

While fingerprinting, DNA, and serology are standard methods of police identification in the twenty-first century, before the 1880s, there was no effective system of classification or reference of criminals. Large photo collections were amassed of convicted criminals at various police headquarters, but the very size of these collections defeated their purposes. The first police forces to make use of photographic rogues' galleries included New York (1858), Danzig (1864), Moscow (1867), London (1870), and Paris (1874). According to crime historian Luc Sante, the use of crime scene photography was first reported in Switzerland in 1860.[18]

Thomas Byrnes: Chief of the New York Detective Bureau

Thomas Byrnes rose through the ranks of the NYPD between 1854 and 1895 to become "one the most celebrated detectives" in American history.[19] Like many other cops of his era, he advanced through the corrupt system of payoffs that led to various promotions. Byrnes' reputation is burnished by his contributions to criminal identification. He pioneered crime detection and revolutionized evidence collection, including the use of mug shots (these were used elsewhere as early as 1857) and criminal records. But he also had a darker side, as witnessed by his perfection of the so-called "third degree" style of interrogation. A firm believed that criminals had no civil rights, especially while he was solving a crime, he also introduced a "dead line," an invisible cordon around the Wall Street financial district that criminals would do best to avoid.

As Chief of the New York Detective Bureau in the 1880s, Byrnes is credited with creating the New York rogues' gallery, popularized with the publication of ***Professional Criminals of America*** in 1886. By disseminating his collection of 204 tintypes of celebrated criminals to the public, Byrnes hoped he could not only advertise the exploits and cunning of the New York Police Department but also help the general public in the prevention and detection of crime. Each photograph was complemented by biographical information and criminal records detailing the methods used by specific bank robbers, forgers, confidence men, shoplifters, and other crime specialists of the era. He would eventually come under scrutiny during the Lexow hearings and Commissioner Roosevelt's reform campaign, after it was disclosed he had amassed a fortune of more than a quarter million dollars on his meager police salary, and in 1895, he followed the previously mentioned "Clubber" Williams out the door. Byrnes, who reformer and Roosevelt sidekick Jacob Riis dubbed the "Big Policeman," died in 1910 at the age of 67. One recent article probably summed Byrnes up best as a "forward thinker who relied on backward techniques."[20]

The Bertillon system

First used by the police of Paris in 1882, by the following year the Bertillon system had been used to identify forty-nine criminals. Named after its creator, **Alphonse Bertillon** (1835–1914), the system required the measurement of the width and length of the head; the length of the left, middle, and little fingers; the length of the left foot, forearm, and right ear; the height of the individual; and the measurement of the person while seated from the bench to the top of the head. Other identifying characteristics included scars, birthmarks, eye and hair color, and a description of the nose. Bertillonage would be well regarded until the 1890s, when fingerprinting replaced it, to the relief of peace officers burdened by the laborious identification procedures it required. Bertillon's system did much to raise the standard of the inefficient and corrupt police methods of the nineteenth century. Born into a middle-class family, the son of a physician with a keen interest in anthropology and statistics, Alphonse Bertillon was drawn to the science at an early age. In 1878, he found employment as a records clerk for the Paris police, leading to a lifelong interest in identifications systems that would earn him the sobriquet the "Father of Modern Detection." Over the next seven years, Bertillon developed a methodology to identify recidivist offenders. Through the use of anthropometry, he created a system that became known as "bertillonage," based on human body measurements, prior to the introduction of a fingerprinting system. Subsequently, he would add photographic methods to other identification techniques and become an expert in using photography to identify forged documents.

Fingerprinting

Prior to the twentieth century, there was no reliable way to distinguish between the guilty and the innocent.[21] Perhaps the best-known system of identification, fingerprinting took decades for law enforcement to realize its value for crime investigation. With the recognition that no two fingerprints are alike in the late nineteenth century, fingerprinting became the identification method of choice in tracking an increasingly mobile population of criminals.[22]

As early as the 1820s, an anatomy professor named Johann Purkinje noted that every person's fingerprints were unique. However, without any type of classification system, this method of identification was useless. By the 1850s, fingerprints were being used by British magistrate William Herschel to prevent the wrong people from fraudulently collecting money on the dole. In 1880, Henry Faulds, a Scottish physician working in Tokyo, exonerated a suspected thief by comparing fingerprints left at the crime scene with those of the suspect.

In the late 1880s, **Sir Francis Galton** attempted to create a classification system and wrote the book ***Fingerprints*** (1892). However, it would be left to Sir Edward Richard Henry, inspector general of the Nepal police, to grapple with the problem, and in 1896, he created an identification system on fingerprinting. That same year, Argentina became the first country to base its identification system on fingerprinting. The adoption of fingerprinting finally gave crime investigators the first reliable proof of an individual's presence at a crime scene.

The early 1900s saw fingerprinting receive increased attention as the Bertillon system proved too cumbersome and unreliable. Although the Bertillon system had been widely accepted in the United States in the 1890s, most chroniclers of the history of criminal identification claim it faced its greatest challenge in 1903, when a man named **Will West** was arrested and sentenced to the federal penitentiary Leavenworth, Kansas. Despite his claims that he had never been arrested before, his photograph seemed to match that of a convicted criminal with a similar name, and apparently so did his Bertillon measurements. It turned out that there was another man named William West incarcerated in the same prison, with the same measurements, and bearing an uncanny resemblance to the other Will West. The only evidence that distinguished the two men was their fingerprints. Many historians have exaggerated the impact of this case on the transition from Bertillon to fingerprint evidence. By the time of this case, the reliability of the former system was already in question. What's more, according to one forensic expert who investigated this case, "there is ample reason to doubt the significance of the case with respect to the establishment of fingerprint identification in the United States" since Leavenworth Penitentiary officials did not install the identification system until the following year. Subsequently, fingerprinting, together with photographs, would supersede the discredited Bertillon system.

Some historians of forensic science have argued that some of "the earliest practical uses of fingerprinting" date back to the seventh century A.D., when the Chinese used them in their daily and legal enterprises "while the Western World was still in the dark ages."[23] One of earliest known European publications focused on fingerprint observation dates back to 1684. Two years later the Italian anatomy professor, Marcello Malpighi, made such an important contribution that one of the layers of the human skin now bears his name. The biggest advances in fingerprint identification came in the late 1850s when William James Hershel became "the first in British history to regularly use fingerprints officially."[24] Herschel's testing was in part inspired by an epiphany he had, when he decided that instead of using full handprints he would try borrowing from the ancient Chinese and Japanese technique of printing just fingerprints. Some experts suggest that Herschel, while stationed in India, probably borrowed the concept from Chinese individuals living near Calcutta (although he always claimed it was his sudden inspiration that led to his advance).[25] A number of years later Herschel was able to prove that fingerprints did not change with age. Research has in fact shown that they did not change from the sixth month of inter-uterine life to death.[26] Like many other scientific advances, fingerprinting would continue to evolve thanks to contributions from Dr. Henry Faulds, Francis Galton, and Juan Vucetich. But of all of the aforementioned, it took Sir Francis Galton's creating a system to identify fingerprints into a practical science.

Police professionalism

In 1893, twenty years after the first meeting of police chiefs in St. Louis (in 1871), Chicago hosted the next national meeting of police chiefs. Of the more than fifty who attended, most were from smaller communities near Chicago, although representatives from Boston, Pittsburgh, and Atlanta were among the attendees. Among the topics discussed were civil service rules for police, the adoption of police telegraphic code, and a uniform identification system. The Chicago police chief could boast having set up the first Bertillon bureau in America. The **National Chiefs of Police** laid the groundwork for what would become the International Association of Chiefs of Police in 1915. One of the more important resolutions approved at the meeting was an agreement for jurisdictional cooperation between different cities and states.

Southern policing

With few historical studies of southern police forces during the post-Civil War era, Dennis Rousey's examination of the New Orleans police is particularly valuable for making any judgments about post-Reconstruction southern policing. The end of Reconstruction in 1877 saw the Democratic governments of the South take back control of their government, political, and social institutions. But between 1868 and 1877, the percentage of African Americans on the New Orleans police force ranged from 25 to 28 percent by 1870, almost equal to its percentage of the black population. During the heyday of Reconstruction, New Orleans had the "largest integrated force in the urban South" and with its 182 black policemen "the largest contingent of black policemen."[27] Although other southern cities also were well represented with blacks during this period, this was clearly not the rule throughout the former Confederacy. For example, Charleston, South Carolina, and Petersburg, Virginia, had well-integrated forces, while Savannah and Richmond had all-white forces.

The end of Reconstruction also put an end to well-integrated policing in the South for the rest of the nineteenth century. New Orleans would see few appointments during the new era, and in 1880, its percentage of black officers had fallen to 6.6 percent. Policing in general would suffer in the South, as it reverted to antebellum conditions that favored decentralization and smaller police budgets. In New Orleans, municipal allocations fell from $325,000 in 1877 to $171,000 in 1888. A reduction in police pay was accompanied by manpower shortages contributing to a recurring crime problem in many southern cities. According to the 1870 and 1880 censuses, out of eighteen major southern cities, fifteen saw major reductions in police manpower. With the weakest police force of America's major cities, New Orleans was well on its way to becoming one of the most inefficient forces in the land, a reputation that has marked the force into the 1990s.

Compared to New York City and other northern cities in the 1880s making major strides in the direction of professionalism, "New Orleans in most ways set an example for other cities not to follow."[28] Here a patronage system continued to determine the selection of police officers, resulting in the ascendance of politically connected individuals to the higher ranks of the police organization. But New Orleans was not alone in its aversion to civil service reform. It would not be until 1895 in Chicago and 1905 in St. Louis that major steps toward nonpartisan government service reform were taken.

Policing the American West

During the 1870s, cattle towns popped up near the intersections of Texas cattle drives and railroad lines in Kansas. More primitive in most respects to urban counterparts in the Northeast, these towns soon developed similar criminal justice problems. Towns such as Dodge City, Abilene, Wichita, and Ellsworth offered liquor, prostitution, and gambling in an attempt to lure cowboy dollars at the end of the drives. Concomitant with the financial rewards were the ever-present violence and disorder that resulted. As the towns became increasingly complex and diversified, they developed police forces, usually consisting of a marshal, assistant marshal, and varying number of police officers. The town marshal's jurisdiction ended at the town limits. Harking back to Anglo-Saxon England, the county peace officer was the sheriff. Both the county sheriff and the town marshal were responsible for civil crimes, leaving federal crimes to the U.S. marshal.

During the nineteenth century, four types of law enforcement would predominate in the West, including vigilance committees (particularly in mining areas); legal citizens police, who were citizens serving brief stints as deputies with county sheriffs or town marshals; formal police; and parapolice, such as the Pinkertons, who pursued the James–Younger gang.

West of the Mississippi River, the main local law enforcement officer was the town marshal, who functioned as the chief of police, even if he was only a one-man police force. Most nineteenth-century Western towns did not appoint a marshal until the population was close to a thousand residents. Unlike the Western peace officer of popular culture, town marshals were more often expected to maintain town jails, collect taxes, serve civil papers, protect property, and arrest the drunk and disorderly rather than engage in climactic gunfights on Main Street. Over time, towns created police departments to handle local law enforcement, although the Western town marshal persists into the twenty-first century.

In the 1860s and 1870s, Indian police forces were introduced to handle crime and disorder on the growing reservation system. In 1874, John Philip Clum, probably best known for his relationship with Wyatt Earp and Tombstone, was appointed as an Indian agent and posted to the San Carlos Apache Reservation in Arizona. When he arrived, he hired four Apaches to police the reservation. As the Apache reservation grew, so did it police force, growing to twenty-five members. The U.S. government soon took notice of this successful police experiment and authorized Indian police on most reservations west of the Mississippi. By 1890, there were 59 police units, including 70 officers and 700 privates. The Indian police were chiefly responsible for keeping the peace; protecting property; discovering and returning stolen goods; and arresting the drunk and disorderly, whiskey sellers, and horse and cattle thieves. But from the start, they were poorly paid and equipped and were often, like their early New York City counterparts, unwilling to don police uniforms.[29] Indian police forces have proved effective and eventually won the respect and trust of their constituents. By the early 1900, these forces were well established, and in 1907, Congress finally budgeted more financial support for this enterprise.[30]

Corrections

According to prison historian Blake McKelvey, prison populations in the North decreased during the Civil War because of a combination of factors, explaining that "the army had absorbed the potential criminals, afforded a refuge for fugitives, or supplied a convenient commutation of sentence."[31] During this period, there were few complaints of prison over-crowding or poor accommodations.

Meanwhile in the South, the **convict lease system** continued to predominate because of a dearth in prison construction. The railroad, timber, and mining industries benefited from an agreement that often let them rent out gangs of prisoners to toil where no free man would even contemplate doing so, resulting in death rates that ran as high as 40 percent per year.

The end of the Civil War and Reconstruction witnessed a sudden increase in America's state prison populations, leading to a plethora of penal problems. Massachusetts State Prison, for example, reported that 171 of the 247 convicts entering prison in 1866 were veterans of the Civil War.[32] Between 1870 and 1904, the population of state prisons increased almost 62 percent. Shortly before the outbreak of the war, the prison population stood at almost 19,000, rising to 33,000 in 1870; 45,000 in 1890; and 57,000 in 1900. With many model prisons deteriorating badly, including those at Auburn and Eastern State, states resorted to modifying existing structures and building new ones in order to house the legions of new inmates.

Prison architecture between 1870 and 1900 continued to follow the Auburn pattern with few modifications. Improvements included the introduction of ventilating systems and steel cells that offered plumbing and running water. However, the bucket system of human waste disposal would persist in dozens of prisons into the 1930s.

Increasing resistance to prison industries by organized labor began to impact convict labor systems, causing many penal administrators to take note. Responding to claims that prison labor represented unfair competition to free labor, many states passed laws in the late 1880s prohibiting productive prison labor.

An increased emphasis on reform was a product of the times, which saw the introduction of a more therapeutic understanding of criminal behavior. Building on the efforts of reformers Maconochie, Crofton, and Wines, by 1869, twenty-three states had adopted "good time" laws, which reduced prison sentences for good work and deportment. Lasting roughly from 1870 to 1910, the reformatory movement in America saw numerous institutions adopt indeterminate sentencing, parole, and attempts at positive reform through education.

The reformatory movement

One of the most important prison reformers of his era, **Zebulon Brockway** (1827–1920) captured the attention of his fellow reformers in 1870 at the National Prison Congress (see Chapter 7). The scion of a venerable New England family, Brockway began his career in corrections as head of a New York almshouse and then of a penitentiary in Rochester. He came to prominence following the presentation of his paper "The Ideal of a True

Prison System for a State" at the 1870 National Prison Congress. His suggestions for reform would resonate for decades. Although a zealous proponent of indeterminate sentencing and the classification of prisoners according to age, sex, and offense, Brockway would not shy away from life sentences for career criminals. The subsequent adoption of a "Declaration of Principles" is testimony to the impact of Brockway's predilection for religion, education, industrious work habits, and the supervision of convicts following release.

Opening in 1876, New York's **Elmira Reformatory** initially was the benchmark for the new reformatory strategy. Formerly a Union prison camp, the state legislature consigned its notorious wartime reputation to the past and reconstructed the site as a model reformatory. Brockway was given a chance to put his proposals into action in 1877, when he was appointed as superintendent. Here, first-time offenders between the ages of sixteen and thirty were sentenced to a facility that placed more emphasis on education and trades training and offered early release through the mark system, which offered merits and demerits for progress and behavior. His tenure would allow him to incorporate his many ideas, chief among them the indeterminate sentence.

An integral part of the foundation of Elmira was its emphasis on industrial labor. Brockway found a loophole in the recent prohibitions by entering a state-supply relationship with New York that would allow his inmates to continue to produce goods, but only products that could be sold to their state facilities or departments.

Influenced by the current pseudosciences of anthropometry and heredity, by the 1880s, Brockway was ascribing the criminal tendencies of many prisoners to heredity. He also took note of the increasing population of European immigrants behind the walls, noting that they "are to a considerable extent the product of our civilization and also of emigration to our shore from the degenerated populations of crowded European marts."[33]

Despite overcoming numerous obstacles and his noble intentions, by 1893, the Elmira Reformatory was overcrowded, and Brockway's propensity for blaming criminality on low intelligence and "physical degeneracy" lost him much of his former support. An investigation the following year exposed Elmira's dirty little secret, that the worst whippings and physical punishment were administered to boys suffering from mental and physical disabilities. Brockway's experiment never regained its luster, and in 1900, he resigned his post.

Wayward sisters and the women's prison reform movement

The treatment of women in early nineteenth-century lockups were bleak, reflecting public prejudice toward female felons (more than their male counterparts). It was a time when Victorian notions of propriety meant that women were expected to exert a moral influence over society. Those that failed to live up to these expectations were regarded as particularly deserving of punishment.[34]

Some of the first advances in the treatment of female prisoners in America probably took place in police station jails. These might have been mostly all-male spaces, but a vigorous campaign by the developing women's prison reform movement led the NYPD to hire six police matrons who were assigned to two lockups, the first appointment of prison matrons in the United States. However, for the rest of the country, the hiring of matrons proceeded at a glacial pace. In 1878, Portland, Maine, hired its first matron. Between 1880 and 1886, was followed by Jersey City, Chicago, Boston, Baltimore, St. Louis, Cleveland, and Philadelphia.[35]

If there was one area that the National Prison Congress failed to address, it was the incarceration of female offenders, who until the 1870s were often housed in the same prisons as men. While it endorsed the creation of treatment-oriented prisons for women, it would take until 1874 for Indiana to open the first female-run prison in America.

During the early nineteenth century, women were incarcerated in the same prisons as men. There were few women convicts in this era, and in order to prevent sexual dalliance, women were isolated. Most women were arrested for minor crimes and were usually held in county jails or houses of correction rather than state prisons, where more serious offenders were housed. During the first half of the nineteenth century, most female arrests involved prostitution, public inebriation, and petty larceny. For example, Massachusetts did not record any women in its state prison, although local jails reported that women made up almost 20 percent of their populations.[36] In 1875, Massachusetts built the Reformatory Prison for women, the second institution of its kind in America.

According to one reformer in the 1830s, there were less than 100 women in prisons of the seven most populous states. Ten years later, Dorothea Dix counted 167.[37] With typically less than a dozen women in any prison, there were too few to devote an entire wing to them, so they were usually housed in large congregate rooms either above the guardhouse or mess hall.[38] With so much attention lavished on the more numerous men, the female prisoners were often neglected.

Mount Pleasant Female Prison

New York established the Mount Pleasant Female Prison in 1835. "Administratively dependent" of Sing Sing Prison, it welcomed its first women prisoners in 1839, becoming the first to establish a separate prison wing for women but would be the only one until the 1870s. According to historian Lawrence M. Friedman, its significance lies in the fact that it was run exclusively by female prison matrons for women.[39]

During its first decade, prisoners labored under a tedious routine of "sewing, button making, and hat-trimming." Except for a brief flurry of reform in the mid-1840s, when prison matron Eliza Wood Farnham abolished the rule of silence and initiated a less punitive regime, conditions deteriorated because of overcrowding. Farnham was hired as matron in 1844. Besides instituting a less punitive regime, Farnham introduced novels into the prison library to supplement mostly religious texts and even allowed the women to bring them back to their cells where they could take advantage of the improved lighting. Like other early reformers, Farnham saw the benefits of making the prison environment as close to traditional domesticity as possible, bringing in flowers, curtains, and even a piano. When the prison reformer Dorothea Dix visited in 1845, she described the facility as "under the direction of a matron, who, with her assistants, are much more interested in the improvement of those under their charge."[40] On the surface all seemed well; however, by 1846, a list of punishments suggests that Farnham still relied on corporal punishment, which included solitary confinement, the cropping of hair, and utilization of gags and straightjackets. The following year the conservative prison board members had had enough of her innovations, particularly the abolition of the rule of silence and forced her to resign. By 1865, Mount Pleasant was burdened with twice its capacity.[41]

The same year **Mt. Pleasant** opened, social activist Abby Hopper Gibbons helped found the Women's Prison Association of New York City in 1845, the country's oldest advocacy group for women. The association established the Isaac Hopper Home for discharged women prisoners, the first institution of its kind in the world. Gibbons advocated and lobbied for the improvement in the care of women in city prisons, as well as for the hiring of police matrons and the establishment of separate correctional facilities for women.[42]

Women penal reformers were influential in the founding of the **American Prison Association** (1870). Many supported the notion of "social feminism," arguing that women had unique needs requiring prisons that could respond to their special needs. As a result, more than twenty women's reformatories were built between 1870 and 1935. In 1874, the **Female Prison and Reformatory Institution for Girls and Women**, the first separate prison completely devoted to women, was inaugurated in Indianapolis, Indiana. The opening of the Indiana Reformatory Institution was the end result of a crusade by social feminists who campaigned for institutions suited to the specific needs of female prisoners. Prior to its opening, while both genders were confined in the same institutions, they were held in sex-segregated cells. The most troubling aspect of this era was the fact that until the 1870s males attended to both sexes.

One of the main pressures for incarcerating women in reformatories rather than prisons was the result of the changing conceptions of female criminality in the 1870s. In the past, women prisoners were often portrayed as depraved if not uncontrollable. But this image began to undergo a transition as they became increasingly viewed as "wayward girls" "who had been led astray and could, therefore, be led back to the paths of 'proper' behavior: 'childlike, domestic, and asexual.'"[43] In order to adhere to this changing interpretation, most reformatories selected first-time offenders over hardened career female criminals.

Probation

The origins of probation, or the use of a suspended sentence, can be traced back to the English "benefit of clergy," by which a member of the ordained clergy could escape the harsh penalties of the day.[44] Over time, this suspension of sentence was extended to anyone who could read Psalm 21, which acknowledged sin and promised reform.

Modern American probation has more in common with the informal practices that developed in Boston in the 1840s. Considered the oldest form of non-institutional corrections in the United States, the development of probation has generally been credited to John Augustus (1785–1859), a Boston cobbler. Augustus had an epiphany in 1841, when he observed a man being sentenced in a Boston courtroom for public drunkenness. Surmising that the man was of good character, Augustus posted bail and promised the judge he would look after the man until his hearing. Having abstained from drinking for the next three weeks, when he appeared before the judge for sentencing, the now sober citizen was given a fine in lieu of more punitive treatment. Augustus went on to spend many days in the local courts and personally arrange bail and custody for similar misdemeanants. During a 14-year period, he bailed out close to 2,000 individuals, putting up almost $250,000 of his own money as bail. His efforts would lead the Massachusetts legislature to enact the first Probation Act in 1878. By the twentieth century, every state had passed similar probation acts. Contemporary probation officers continue to follow in the footsteps of their nineteenth-century counterparts, using similar methods of investigation, screening, interviewing, and supervision.

Probation has remained popular for more than a century, mainly because it is a cheap alternative to incarceration. Some observers maintain that probation tends to "subvert the concept of fair justice."[45] There has tended to be an inherent class bias to this punishment alternative, mainly because the criminal justice system considers offenders who do not have a criminal record or who appear better socialized are better risks for probation than hardened offenders. What often tips the scales in favor of one class or another is whether someone can afford to make bail, a prior criminal record, and physical appearance at time of decision.

The Child Savers and the birth of the juvenile court system

Building on the Elmira Reformatory experiment, Massachusetts (1874) and Rhode Island (1892) passed laws authorizing separate trials for children. Except for several other hesitant steps taken elsewhere, until 1899, children in most states could be arrested, detained, tried, and sentenced to adult prisons. The establishment of the first true juvenile court in 1899 gave the criminal justice system jurisdiction over neglected and dependent children and those determined to be delinquent, the so-called dangerous classes.

Until 1899, the treatment of juveniles corresponded with that of adults. Outside of several "reform schools" and children's aid societies, juveniles were arrested, detained, tried, and imprisoned like their adult counterparts. While some states provided institutions for juveniles, it would take the "child-saving" movement at the turn of the century to use the power of the state to save children from a life of crime.

The child-saving movement was mainly the purview of a group of well-educated, politically active women from the middle and upper classes. They were instrumental in providing the impetus for the creation of a separate juvenile court system. In 1899, Illinois approved the passage of the Juvenile Court Act, establishing the first comprehensive system of juvenile justice (for children under age sixteen) and giving momentum to the development to the modern juvenile justice system.

The predominance of middle-class women in the child-saving movement coincided with an era when middle-class women were becoming better educated and enjoyed more leisure time, but because of the social circumstances of the late nineteenth century, there were few career avenues to follow. By the turn of the century, middle-class women "experienced a complex and far-reaching status revolution"[46] as they championed the interests of children, the poor, and immigrants – social outsiders whom many regarded as a threat to the new industrial order.

The child-saving movement was not without its critics. Recent scholarship suggests that these reformers were tools of the "ruling class," applying the concept of *parens patriae*[47] for their own interests, which included the control of the political system, the continuance of the child labor system, and the advancement of upper-class values.

Crime and punishment

The urbanization of America during the last forty years of the nineteenth century created new problems for urban police forces. As the ethnic makeup of cities became more diverse, police work became more complicated as well. Following the Civil War, most of the Italian, Jewish, Chinese, and African American newcomers moved into slums formerly dominated by the Irish and now policed by Irish American officers. But despite a cornucopia of endemic obstacles to keeping the peace in the 1890s, including immigration, poverty, corruption, and overcrowding, murder rates in cities such as New York were declining.

The most prominent criminals of the nineteenth century were the mythologized bad men of the West. According to recent research, these individuals were indeed men but were probably not much worse than others less well known. While poems, plays, movies, and novels have made Wyatt Earp, Billy the Kid, John Wesley Hardin, and the Jesse James Gang popular culture mainstays, the most wanted fugitives of the postwar era included Molly Maguire's assassin Thomas Hurley (according to the Pinkertons) and Mormon leader John Taylor.

As train robbery, cattle rustling, and bank robbery captured the attention of the public, the late nineteenth century introduced the nation to America's version of Jack the Ripper, except this time he had a face and a name, Herman Webster Mudgett (a.k.a. **H. H. Holmes**). As historian Roger Lane has noted in *Murder in America*, there were few known cases of multiple-sex murders (today better known as serial killings) in the nineteenth century. The thirty-four-year-old Holmes seemed a pillar of respectability during his years in Chicago. However, following a trail of missing bodies and fraudulent insurance claims, Holmes was arrested for kidnapping and murdering three children. He ultimately confessed to twenty-seven murders before being hanged in 1896.

Despite the sensational qualities of many post-Civil War crimes and murders, homicide rates declined as the country approached the 1900s.[48] This was in part a reflection of the role played by better policing, temperance groups, and public schools that led the vanguard in the battle for reform and order.

Fredericka "Marm" Mandelbaum: Queen among Thieves

Fredericka "Marm" Mandelbaum (1818–1894) was one of America's leading criminals during the second half of the nineteenth century. One historian has gone as far as labeling her "the most influential American criminal after the Civil War."[49] There is surely some exaggeration in this label, but she was one of the country's leading criminals in the Victorian era. She probably could have given Thief Taker General Jonathan Wild a run for the money when it came to fencing operations. Perhaps what was most remarkable was that an immigrant Jewish woman from Prussia was able to earn a place in the century's criminal pantheon in the first place. She was a leading fence of stolen goods and during her almost twenty-five-year reign as the country's top receiver of stolen goods, she accumulated great wealth and power inconceivable for a legitimate or illegitimate businesswoman of her era.

Arriving in America in 1850, she began her rise in the bustling New York City underworld as a street peddler and within thirty years had accumulated a fortune of more than

$1 million. Some historians have credited her as being "the head of the country's first orga-nized crime rings."[50] Similar to other Jewish criminals of the nineteenth century, she was drawn to the lucre of the garment industry. By the 1860s, she was handling so much sto-len property that she had to purchase additional warehouses in Manhattan and Brooklyn. Standing almost six feet tall, the corpulent Mandelbaum cut a striking figure in the Lower East Side criminal demimonde, leading New York newspapers to dub her "Queen among Thieves." Like other successful organized crime bosses, she was able to flourish by bribing an extensive network of judges, police officers, and politicians. As a result of her access, if anyone was looking for police protection, backing for criminal enterprises or stolen goods, Mandelbaum was the go-to contact. There were few stolen commodities that she would not handle, including stolen horses. One historian described her operation in its halcyon days as "an underworld haven for attracting the nation's most famous criminals," while the New York City police chief described her business "the Bureau for the Prevention of Convic-tion."[51] Her criminal career ended in 1884 when Pinkertons infiltrated her network. Always one step of the law, Marm managed to jump bail and get to Canada, whose extradition laws barred her from being sent back to the States. She died ten years later.

Cesare Lombroso: father of modern criminology

While still in the Italian army, the physician **Cesare Lombroso** (1835–1909) took his first steps toward the development of a highly controversial theory that would have profound influence on the world of **criminology** and criminal justice. Lombroso was consumed with resolving "the problem of the nature of the criminal." While performing a postmortem on a noted Italian brigand, Lombroso reached an epiphany that led him to build on the work of earlier writers who suggested that there was a relationship between the physical characteris-tics of a criminal and his behavior. According to Lombroso,

> At the sight of the skull, I seemed to see all of a sudden, lighted up as vast plain under a flaming sky, the problem of the nature of the criminal – an atavistic being who reproduces in his person the ferocious instincts of primitive humanity and the inferior animal.[52]

Lombroso went on to collect a mass of evidence based on the close examination of a number of criminals to support his theory that the criminal can be distinguished from the noncriminal by a variety of physical anomalies that were of an atavistic or a degenerative origin. Arguing that some individuals were born criminals, his conclusions would fly in the face of penal reformers who argued that prisoners could actually be reformed in the appropriate environment. In 1876, Lombroso's *L'Uomo delinquente* (**Criminal Man**) was published. Going beyond the theoretical, Lombroso searched for practical applications for his research. A proponent of postmortem examination of criminal brains, he is credited with providing the impetus for the study of clinical criminology and the basis for the meth-odology of cadaver identification later employed in the field of legal medicine.

Considered the founder of the positivist school of criminology and the "father of mod-ern criminology," Lombroso's theories owe much to Charles Darwin's *The Origin of Species*

(1859) and *The Descent of Man* (1871), which suggested that some men are closer to their primitive ancestors than others. Earlier speculations on degeneracy can be traced back to research conducted in France as early as the 1820s.

Much of the work by the early criminologists served as grist for the rise of racism in the nineteenth century as pseudoscience was used to explain the inequality between the races. Although Lombroso's work was not published in the United States until 1911, criminologists throughout the world had become familiar with his theories soon after their initial publication in Italy.

There exists much debate regarding what exactly Lombroso contributed to the field of criminology. No less an authority than Edwin Sutherland suggested in 1947 that "by shifting attention from crime as a social phenomenon to crime as an individual phenomenon, it delayed for forty years the work which was in progress at the time and made no lasting contribution of its own."[53] The contention that there is a criminal type, demonstrable by certain physical dimensions – that the criminal was identifiable on the basis of certain cranial, facial, and bodily measurements – may have seemed like a great advance in the late nineteenth century. However, a growing number of dissenters began to view crime as the product of certain social factors.

Lombroso was a visionary who shifted the focus of criminology toward the scientific study of the criminal and the conditions under which a crime is committed. His greatest contribution to the emerging discipline was his recognition "that it is the criminal and not the crime we should study and consider; that it is the criminal and not the crime we ought to penalize."[54]

Cesare Lombroso is best known for his 1876 book *Criminal Man*. Lesser known was his *The Female Offender*, coauthored with his son-in-law William Ferrero. Originally published in 1893, it hit the American market in 1903. In this work, the authors offered a number of observations regarding female criminality. Among their "insights," was the notion that the "criminal type" is more common among male than female offenders. *The Female Offender* begins with a study of the skulls of the sixty female offenders, which found that the lowest cranial capacity belonged to prostitutes and the highest to the poisoner. In the chapter on crimes of passion, the authors make a distinction between men and women who perpetrate crimes of passion. The woman will, according to Lombroso and Ferrero, "brood for months and years over their resentment. . . . That is to say that often premeditation in the woman is longer than the man; it is also colder and more cunning."[55] In another passage, Lombroso asserts that "greed is a moving cause of crime in women" and "will attempt or instigate the crime which promises to bring in a rich harvest of valuables."[56] These and other examples from the "science" of the era not only built on earlier theories but influenced many a courtroom outcome and criminal investigation to explain criminality in women. As early as the fifteenth century, the author Corrado Celto wrote of women, "Their perversity of mind is more fertile in new crimes than the imagination of a judge in new punishments."[57] Another observer wrote that "Feminine criminality is more cynical, more depraved, and more terrible than the criminality of the male." And according to an Italian proverb, "Rarely is a woman wicked, but when she is she surpasses the man."[58] *The Female*

Offender offers numerous observations and pages of measurements, moving through chapters on pathological anomalies, the brains of female criminals, facial anomalies, anthropometry, and related observations and theories. Ultimately, it is another example of Lombroso's late-nineteenth-century atavistic theory, now consigned to the dustbin of pseudoscience that was in vogue with the criminal anthropologists of the so-called Italian school of positive criminology.

On July 2, 1881, President James Garfield was assassinated in a train station in Washington, DC. He was the second president, and one of four American presidents, to have been assassinated. He would linger from his wounds for almost two months and, by most accounts, was expected to survive. The germ theory was not introduced until 1883, and with all the poking and prodding fingers inserted into the wound as doctors searched for the bullet, it should not be surprising that he would die from complications related to infection. His assassin, Charles Guiteau, who was under the illusion that the president had promised him the French ambassador's position and other favors, would later explain that he killed the president because he had reneged on his promises. Unprotected by a security detail, Garfield was an easy target. What distinguished this murder case was the ten-week trial in which Guiteau served as his own attorney. His performance was punctuated by tantrums, manic outbursts, and enough evidence that would suggest, at least to a modern jury, that he was insane. However, the judge and jury were bent on revenge, especially in a time of anarchists, foreign radicals, labor violence, and status anxieties about a changing America. The jury, after deliberating for only an hour, rejected extenuating circumstances related to insanity and sentenced him to hang. Many contemporary observers suggested that, if he had killed anyone else other than the president he would probably have been spared the gallows. The trial was also, in many respects, a referendum on the value of psychiatric testimony and the developing hereditary "sciences" being championed by Cesare Lombroso and others. One journalist wrote that to execute the raving assassin was as irrational "as it is to kill a cave fish for not seeing."[59]

Women and crime during the Victorian era

According to Roger Lane's study of the black criminal subculture of Philadelphia, between 1860 and 1900, women were less likely to commit homicide during this era. However, the gap was smaller between white and black women. In Philadelphia, African American women were more likely to be outside the home, "far more proportionately to be out on the streets, at work or doing dangerous things." Conversely, her white counterpart typically usually lived an overwhelmingly domestic life as housewife and mother, rather than joining the workforce. Victorian white women were more likely to be victims than killers, while black women were almost as likely to kill as to be killed.

Black women were commonly associated with various types of thievery. Being that they worked in domestic service and prostitution, the "two largest occupations open to them," they had more opportunities for more significant thefts. Many of their robberies were of white customers, the "most profitable kind of black theft" in Victorian Philadelphia.[60] Lane identified several types of stealing. One was "panel thievery," where a man would hide behind a panel when a prostitute brought her john into the room. He would then pilfer through the pockets of the man's pants which had been removed by then. Another strategy was called the "badger game," a version of an age older scam. Accordingly, after the customer and prostitute were in bed a large male associate of the prostitute would enter the room "mid-tryst," either forcing the mark to leave without his valuables or perhaps threaten blackmail. The Philadelphia incarnation of this was "badger thieving," where a single or coterie of women simply "strip rolled" or robbed the customer after he fell asleep. This was done without male accomplices. Lane has concluded that "the color bar was helpful in embarrassing married men into shutting up and slinking home."[61]

One study of Chicago from 1875–1920 suggested that the nature of woman violence was not just changing, but that they "were killing their husbands at a higher rate than in the past."[62] However, few were actually convicted of this crime. During this time period, only 16 out of 102 were convicted in Chicago. In the course of their murder trials, women were utilizing a new defense strategy. According to Adler, the women were not just getting off but were claiming that they had the right to kill abusive husbands under a "new unwritten law." This put a new spin on the historical propensity of men to claim an "unwritten law" that permitted them to kill another man who was having an affair with a family member.[63]

Like the white women who killed their allegedly abusive husbands in Chicago and were usually acquitted at trial, reputable Victorian women pinched for shoplifting in department stores remained "relatively unscathed." However, their lower-class counterparts were typically less fortunate. As one chronicler of female shoplifting put it, "middle-class women suffered from kleptomania," while lower-class women who also pilfered from stores were regarded as thieves.[64]

Prostitution

By the middle nineteenth century, urban America offered "a wide variety of commercial sexual activity." Most urban centers had brothels that would have been visible to both customers and non-customers. Indeed, prostitution had become such a successful business model that for the first time American history it "became an objective consumer commodity" in the underground economy.[65] While some states lacked laws that specifically criminalized it, was nonetheless never accepted as a respectable profession. By the 1870s, many Americans were beginning to look at the crime more as a public health problem rather than a crime. St. Louis experimented with legalization between 1870 and 1874, as local boards of health and police boards persuaded the state to give the city new powers, including the power to regulate or suppress "bawdy or disorderly houses, houses of ill-fame, or assignation." While the police might have been given licensing authority over brothels, the regulation eventually failed after it began it appeared "too much like a bargain with the devil." As historian Lawrence M. Friedman put it, "the dirty little secret of the century was not prostitution itself, but the business of prostitution. Men (and women) ran houses as a business; policemen, from patrolmen to captains, were on the take."[66]

During the last decades of the nineteenth century, a peaceful coexistence had been established in which prostitution was confined (with other vices) to specially delineated vice districts, where it supposedly would not offend the sensibilities of respectable citizens. These red light zones remained "strongholds of vice," protected from police shakedowns thanks to a covert network of police corruption, extortion, and payoff schemes.[67]

Capital punishment

Efforts to abolish the death penalty came to an abrupt halt in the 1850s as reformers diverted their attention toward slavery, the Civil War, and Reconstruction issues. Between 1865 and 1900, only Iowa, Maine, and Colorado abolished the death penalty, but all three would reinstate it within several years, and only Maine would once more don the abolitionist cloak for good beginning in 1887. During the Progressive era in the first two decades of the new century, abolition would once more gain momentum.

The electrocution of **William Kemmler** in 1890 via the **electric chair** signaled a new phase in the continuing search for a more effective and humane means of execution. Convicted of an ax murder in Buffalo, New York (which ironically prided itself as the "electric city of the future"), his execution followed a decade-long debate over America's electric future involving Thomas A. Edison and George Westinghouse. During the 1880s, both men championed two forms of electricity that they hoped would dominate homes and businesses. Edison favored direct current (DC), which was cheaper to install, and Westinghouse preferred alternating current (AC), citing the danger of DC current. With Edison on the verge of winning the marketing war, the New York legislature made New York the first state to approve electrocution as its method of capital punishment; the chair replaced the gallows. Unfortunately, for Edison, it also demonstrated the killing power of DC, and his rival's AC current was adopted.

One development that helped in the implementation of the electric chair was a movement toward the "delocalization" of executions.[68] This, along with greater discretion in death sentencing, occurred after the Civil War, when states began to require that executions be performed under state authority at one specific location. Between 1865 and 1900, twenty states made the transition from mandatory to discretionary capital punishment, permitting the jury to decide between death and alternative punishments. The movement toward state-mandated centralized execution began in 1864 in Vermont and Maine. By the 1950s, however, there were still states that continued to conduct executions under local authority (Delaware and Montana).

Few constitutional challenges were directed at the death penalty during the late nineteenth century. In *Wilkerson v. Utah* (1879), a defendant claimed that execution by firing squad violated his protection against cruel and unusual punishment. The Supreme Court upheld the death sentence, citing the fact that this method had been used for premeditated murder for years and was therefore not unconstitutional. Ax murderer William Kemmler also had his day in court (1890), citing the same grounds under the Eighth Amendment. But again the Supreme Court ruled against the defendant. In this instance, the Court noted that

> we think that the evidence is clearly in favor of the conclusion that it is within easy reach of electrical science at this day to so generate and apply to the person of the

convict a current of electricity . . . to produce instantaneous, and therefore painless, death.[69]

As a postscript, the current had to be applied two different times before Kemmler was pronounced dead.

Similar to the adoption of lethal injection in the 1970s and 1980s, a trend began following Kemmler's execution that saw other states adopt electrocution over the next twenty-five years, including Ohio (1897), Massachusetts (1901), Kentucky and New Jersey (1907), Virginia (1908), Tennessee (1909), North Carolina (1910), South Carolina (1912), Arkansas (1913), and Pennsylvania (1915). By the end of the 1920s, over half the states using the death penalty were utilizing the electric chair.

Handguns in America: the "Smith & Wesson line"

Prior to the Civil War, few states had statutes regulating the carrying of concealed handguns. By the 1920s and 1930s, some states had adopted the Uniform Act to Regulate the Sale and Possession of Firearms, a model law that prohibited unlicensed carrying of concealed weapons. Most states affirmed provisions that allowed sheriffs, judges, and police chiefs to issue concealed handgun permits to individuals who demonstrated a legitimate need for this protection. Today, all fifty states have adopted laws permitting citizens to carry concealed firearms for protection.

According to historian Michael A. Bellesiles, "The cost of firearms continued to fall after the Civil War," reaching the point where most people could "afford the so-called 'suicide special' of the 1890s."[70] Inexpensive guns were commonly used in the commission of most murders and suicides during this era and had become so ubiquitous that one religious magazine was even offering a pistol with the purchase of a subscription.[71] In marked contrast to the stereotype of the handgun-carrying South of the twentieth century, it was illegal to carry a pistol in one's pocket in Louisiana between 1856 and 1885.[72] While many citizens carried hidden weapons for personal defense, New Orleans policemen were prohibited by law from carrying concealed guns into the 1890s. However, there were no laws barring policemen and civilians from bearing arms openly. In 1932, in the first scholarly study to examine homicide from a national perspective, H. C. Brearley asserted that the South was "that part of the United States lying below the Smith and Wesson line,"[73] an assessment that holds true for the region's past and present.

Homicide in the South and West

Continuing a legacy of violence, the South and the West continued to have the highest homicide rates in the nation in the years between 1865 and 1915. A study of homicide in the Cumberland Mountains for this period found a rate of 130 per 100,000, more than 10 times the homicide rate of the 1990s.[74] In 1880, journalist Horace V. Redfield (1845–1881)[75] noted the disproportionate number of homicides in the South compared to other regions of the country. Redfield claimed that Texas had the highest homicide rate in his examination of homicide between 1865 and 1880. He suggested that this was the result of the Texas predilection for "carrying concealed weapons" and "the great laxity of carrying concealed weapons."[76]

According to Redfield's research, the "number of homicides in the Southern States is proportionately greater than in any country on earth the population of which is rated civilized."[77] While most studies of southern violence attribute it to the enduring notions of honor and a subculture of violence, more recent studies link this preference for violence to the fact that "much of the South was a lawless, frontier region settled by people whose economy was originally based on herding." The authors conclude that most herding societies are "characterized by having 'cultures of honor' in which a threat to property or reputation is dealt with by violence."[78] Homicide historian Roger Lane suggests a more convincing explanation for the high murder rates was poverty combined with "a tradition of weak government and law enforcement."[79]

Historians continue to quarrel over the levels of violence in the post-Civil War West. Scholars have long argued that violence was not common in the late nineteenth-century West. Beginning with Robert Dykstra's *Cattle Towns* (1968), which was one of the first scholarly studies to proclaim that the American West was not violent, most examinations on this theme have been based on anecdotal evidence and newspaper accounts, with little statistical sophistication. A recent study by historian Clare V. McKanna Jr. challenges earlier studies that suggest that homicide was not common in the American West. By using quantitative methods and seldom-used sources such as coroner's inquests, criminal registers, and census data, McKanna argues that lethal violence was indeed common in the American West. Not just the bailiwick of the mythical gunfighter, he found that, contrary to the prevailing belief that western violence was usually episodic, it occurred on a daily basis among "ranchers, farmers, cowboys, coal and copper miners, bartenders, cooks, butchers, gamblers, pimps, police officers, sheriff's deputies, town marshals, Baldwin-Felts detectives, coal mine guards, roisterous drunks, teenagers, old men – and occasional housewives and mothers."[80]

Southern Reconstruction was accompanied by violence on both a grand and a small scale. In some southern states, racially mixed militias banded together to protect freedmen, while whites retaliated with quasi-military organizations such as the Ku Klux Klan. White supremacist-oriented organizations fomented race riots in many parts of the South between 1868 and 1876. The end of radical Reconstruction in 1877 saw the withdrawal of Union troops from the occupied South and the dissolution of the mixed militias.

The Mafia comes to America

Despite its historical association with Chicago and New York City, the Italian Mafia first made its appearance in the New World on the docks of New Orleans. Sicilian and Old World immigrants had been debarking at New Orleans since before the Civil War. As the largest city in the post-Civil War South, with its warmer climate and Latin-Catholic culture, it was a natural destination for southern Italians. The heyday of the city's Irish gangs gave way to new immigrant gangs as the Irish were assimilated into society becoming contractors, entrepreneurs, and policemen. By the 1880s, waves of new immigrants from Italy and Sicily changed the demographics of the city. New Orleans also became embroiled in anti-Italian bias as newspapers, and city rumor mills touted the presence of sinister Italian gangs such as the Mafia and the Neapolitan Camorra. Historian John S. Kendall suggested in 1939 that the first Mafia-related crime in New Orleans dated back to 1878.

Lynching: extralegal violence

The term *lynching* evolved from its colonial era meaning, which was associated with punishment (typically not fatal) not sanctioned by law, to its more sinister connotations reflecting unlawful sentences of death by the 1890s. During the antebellum era, lynching was most often used against local whites who deviated from acceptable behaviors, such as those who beat their wives and children or subscribed to unorthodox beliefs or lifestyles. After the Civil War, a shift occurred in which the majority of lynching victims were people of color – Asians, Native Americans, Chicanos, and occasionally whites.

According to the research conducted in the 1890s by black newspaper owner **Ida B. Wells**, the overwhelming majority of cases involved the hanging of blacks in the South. Born into slavery in in Mississippi in1862, Wells was a controversial figure for most her career, or as one historian put it, a "one woman crusade for justice." She moved to Chicago in 1893, married, raised six children, and organized various women's suffrage and political clubs. She also became the city's first black female probation officers and crusaded against school segregation.[81]

While in her twenties, Wells became a leading voice in the campaign against lynchings in the last decade of the nineteenth century, Wells was drawn to the cause when three of her friends in Memphis, Tennessee, were murdered by a lynch mob. As Wells made the transition to investigative journalist and reformer, she began to make the connection between this utilization of ritualized violence and intimidation and its goal of impeding the progress of African Americans in their efforts to participate more fully in the social, political, and economic life of the nation. Violence authority Roger Lane explains that the onus of Reconstruction fell so heavily on the black population following the withdrawal of federal troops in 1877 because "the place of African-American men and women had not been fully settled."[82] Wells began writing editorials condemning the terror of lynching and according to her biographer was responsible for a "significant migration of thousands of African Americans to the West."[83]

According to her subsequent research, Wells studied white newspaper reports of lynchings and found that, during the 1890s, there was an average of 188 lynchings per year, a number exceeding legal executions by 2 to 1. In a time period when a charge of rape supplied the pretext for a lynching, she found this charge was present in only about 20 percent of the cases. A gradual decline in southern lynchings would not begin until the 1920s, when a group of white southern moderates organized the Commission on Interracial Cooperation and used their influence to improve race relations in the South.

In stark contrast to the prototypical lynching, the worst mass lynching of the century targeted Italian immigrants in New Orleans following the assassination of the city's police chief, **David Hennessey**, in 1890. In an era that found a wide audience for the theories of Lombroso, the "Italian" was assumed to display a tendency to criminal behavior. It was widely believed at the time that Hennessey had been murdered by a Mafia faction of a group of immigrant Italian dockworkers whom he had provoked for some unknown reason.

In 1890, the country was witnessing one of its periodic bouts with xenophobia that seemed to coincide with heavy immigration. Between 1870 and 1890, the Italian community grew from 3.2 to 10.5 percent of New Orleans' foreign population. Following the shooting, scores of Italian suspects were rounded up. Nineteen were indicted. In the trials that followed, suspects were acquitted, only further antagonizing local leaders. Before all the men could be freed, some more respectable members of the community organized a mob of perhaps 10,000. Reaching the jail, they unleashed their fury on the eleven Italians in custody (including three who had been acquitted). Foreign opinion cited the incident as the latest proof of American barbarism. The Italian government formerly protested the slaying of three of the men who were Italian citizens and even demanded compensation for their families. The offer to pay indemnities to the families by President Benjamin Harrison in 1891 ultimately cooled the antagonism between the two governments.

Labor violence: Molly Maguires and anarchists

Prior to the Civil War, most labor violence occurred along ethnic and racial lines. For example, Irish canal workers rioted in response to mistreatment at the hand of contractors. In other cases, Irish workers came into conflict with free blacks competing for unskilled jobs. After the war, the pattern of labor violence changed. More urban and industrialized by the 1870s, industrial conflict pitted organized labor against employers. The 1870s saw workingmen attempting to organize for collective action, igniting more than a half century of violent conflict with industrialists, their private armies, and unemployed laborers used as strikebreakers.

In the coal fields of northeastern Pennsylvania, the secret organization known as the Molly Maguires[84] rose to prominence in the 1860s and 1870s as it waged a campaign of terror against their employers. Predominantly Irish-Catholic, the so-called Mollies found themselves at odds with their Protestant bosses and neighbors over their perceived mistreatment. Unable to sustain a union organization after a labor strike was broken in 1875, the Mollies resorted to guns and dynamite and were eventually charged with killing sixteen men. Subsequently, a Pinkerton operative named James McParland (1844–1919) infiltrated the group.[85] Thanks to his testimony, forty Mollies were arrested and charged with various criminal acts. All were found guilty, and twenty were hanged, half of whom were executed on June 21, 1877, a date that became known in the region as Black Thursday. The prosecution of the Irish miners is shrouded in controversy because the defendants were arrested by private policemen and convicted on the questionable testimony of informers and McParland, who was labeled an "agent provocateur" by the defense.[86] Conducted in the most hostile of atmospheres, the prosecuting attorneys were affiliated with railroad and mining companies.

The year 1877 was a particularly violent one in American history. Following on the heels of four years of depression, the mood of the nation was volatile as labor sought to unite against the monopolistic corporations, violence, and lawlessness erupted in the nation's cities, and race riots, lynchings, and government corruption made headline news.[87] During the ongoing economic depression, unorganized railroad workers, protesting wage cuts, the use of scab labor, and the probable loss of their jobs, engaged in a series of destructive riots that hit Baltimore and Pittsburgh with particular ferocity. On the other side of the country, San Francisco workingmen rioted in sympathy with railroad strikers and engaged in hand-to-hand battles with the police and Chinese immigrants. Violence would continue to punctuate the 1880s and 1890s, culminating in the **Haymarket Square bombing** (1886) and the Homestead strike at the Carnegie steel plant (1892). In 1894, a Pullman strike led President Grover Cleveland to call in federal troops over the protest of the Illinois governor. Perhaps overstating the explosive confluence of troubles, historian Robert V. Bruce suggested that "the upheaval was perhaps our closest brush with class revolution in America."[88]

In the social unrest that accompanied the labor turmoil of the late nineteenth century, the police often found themselves targeted for defending the interests of big business and the "robber barons." Events in 1885 would precipitate one of the most notorious acts of antipolice violence in American history. That year, the Knights of Labor began a series of strikes aimed at achieving an eight-hour workday at the McCormick Harvester Works. Almost one-third of the Chicago Police Department were stationed at the picket lines trying to protect strikebreakers. At a large gathering of strikers at Chicago's Haymarket Square, an unknown anarchist tossed a bomb into the crowd, killing seven police officers and injuring seventy others. In an era of growing radical politics, the incident struck a chord with the public, who rallied to the police department. In the weeks following the tragedy, tens of thousands of dollars poured into a contribution fund for the victims. One authority has suggested that the hysteria over Haymarket "gave the signal for the law and order forces throughout the country to act."[89]

Anarchism spread to the United States in the late nineteenth century. The proponents of anarchism, or anarchists, supported the creation of cooperative societies without any centralized government. Some anarchist turned to violence and terrorism. Their most successful operations were carried out in Russia in the years leading up to the Russian Revolution (1905–1917). They were responsible for the assassination of several European leaders including Czar Alexander in 1881. American anarchism was linked to labor violence and the legions of impoverished European immigrants who felt oppressed by the nativist American elites. By the 1880s, Chicago was a hotbed of anarchism and labor violence. Home to a large population of German immigrants, many with a radical bent, the Chicago Police focused much of their counterterrorist activities on them before and after the Haymarket Bombing of 1886. The anarchists regarded them as their main adversaries. Newspapers also inflamed public opinion demonizing anarchist as "Red Ruffians," "Dynamarchists," and "bomb throwers." One newspaper even compared them to "plundering bands of Apaches." After the Haymarket Square bombing a "reign of terror swept over Chicago," according to one historian, as police staged raids in working-class districts without even producing a warrant. Suspects were arrested and subjected to the "third degree" in police stations. From then on, the word "anarchist" became synonymous with communism, terrorism, and dynamite.

Notable trials

Lizzie Borden trial (1893)

In one of the most famous murder cases in American history, thirty-two-year-old Lizzie Borden was indicted for murdering her father and stepmother with an ax in Fall River, Massachusetts. Her father was one of the wealthiest and most influential members of the community, president of the bank, and a stalwart member of the business sector. At the time of the murder, Lizzie still lived at home with her parents, her older sister, and a servant girl. Although there were no witnesses to the brutal ax slaying, attention focused almost immediately on Lizzie because of her cold and unemotional response to the incident. At the time of the killing, only Lizzie and the servant were at home, with Lizzie contending that she was in the barn at the time. Despite the conflicting evidence, the presiding judge decided that there was sufficient cause to hold Lizzie.

Lizzie was fortunate that she was rich enough to hire a substantial defense that would eventually include the Pinkerton Agency and a three-member defense team led by the state's former governor. The defense team interviewed almost 110 panelists before settling on 12 jurors: all farmers, all male, and none from the town of Fall River.

According to the prosecution, there were a number of factors that would prove their case against Lizzie, including that she did not get along with her stepmother; that she had tried to purchase a deadly poison from a drugstore the day before the murders but was rebuffed because she lacked a prescription; that there was no sign of a struggle or any property taken, so the assailant must not have seemed like a threat; that Lizzie apparently burned an ax handle and concealed the ax blade from the probable murder weapon; and that the servant was in her third-floor room and Lizzie was downstairs alone with her father and not in the barn. Without even other inconsistencies, it seemed that the prosecution had an airtight case.

The defense demonstrated how a man might have hidden in the house. The jury was taken on a walk-through of the house to become familiar with the layout of the property. In the subsequent trial, the defense was able to refute most of the evidence presented by the prosecution. During the seventh day of the trial, medical witnesses explained how Mrs. Borden was murdered at least an hour before her husband. Noting Lizzie's aloof disposition, her lawyers decided against having her testify. In their conclusions, they noted the lack of direct and circumstantial evidence – no blood, no murder weapon, no motive, and no exclusive opportunity since the prosecution could not prove that Lizzie was not in the barn as she claimed. The defense also explained that Lizzie was active in many religious and charitable groups, loved her father very much, and was not one to openly express her feelings in public.

In the end, after the thirteen-day trial, the jury deliberated for one hour and ten minutes and returned with a verdict of not guilty. Lizzie and her sister inherited the father's considerable estate and attempted to live as normal a life as possible despite an almost constant hounding by the press. Lizzie died in 1927 at the age of sixty-six.

This "crime of the century" continues to pique the interest of true crime and mystery writers. Some have offered alternative solutions, including the logical question, Why not the servant girl? And why the enduring interest in the murder? It had all the familiar hallmarks of a classic murder: there was no solution; the participants were wealthy, educated, and of a high standing in the community; the sadistic manner of the attack in an upper-class

home in small-town New England that contrasted sharply with the lower-class urban murder patterns of the day; and the fact that it was a woman accused of such a deed.

In one examination of how gender, history, and law entered into the arguments of the
trial, Janice Schuetz noted that the era of the Borden trial was a "critical period in the definition of the role of women."[90] With even the prosecutor telling the jury that it was hard
to conceive that a woman could be guilty of such a crime, Lizzie Borden owed her life to
contemporary perceptions about "true womanhood."[91] Not unlike today, patricide by an
ax-wielding woman sold newspapers. From a criminal justice perspective, the Lizzie Borden
case has several implications. The case demonstrated that an individual has the right not to
testify and that this cannot be used against the defendant. It also constitutes a case of "trial
by newspaper." However, unlike other murder cases that castigated the defendant, such as
in the Bruno Hauptmann, Sam Shepard, and Charles Manson cases, most of the papers
presented a favorable impression of Lizzie Borden.

Conclusions

Late nineteenth-century America was characterized by unprecedented social strife. Between
1861 and 1900, America was racked by the Civil War, severe economic depressions, massive
immigration, and unforeseen advances in communication, transportation, and communication. Extraordinary urbanization and industrialization transformed the country, leading
to profound challenges to the ever-evolving criminal justice system. As testimony to the
progress of police reformers of the late nineteenth century, American cities had become
much more orderly places than the antebellum period as "daily life became more predict-
able and controlled."[92] Others attributed the growing order of urban life to the socialization
skills provided by of public schools and industrialization.

Penal reformers during this era saw the implementation of indeterminate sentencing and
education at a time when the old methods of prison discipline at Auburn and Eastern State
were breaking down. While both developments met with varying degrees of success, they
helped pave the way for new reforms by modifying the thinking and the recognized objectives of the Auburn system enough to make its punitive methods of discipline more tolerable.

While penal and police reformers grappled with the new realities of late nineteenth-
century criminal justice, criminologists and scientists attempted to adapt scientific methods
to the study of criminality. Rejecting many of the legal definitions of crime, adherents of
Lombroso and others focused their attentions on the criminal act as a psychological entity,
emphasized determinism, and believed that punishment should be replaced by a scientific
treatment of criminals in order to protect society.

Point – counterpoint

Police corruption on the New York City Police Department (1894)

*In late 1894, a committee was created to investigate corruption in the New York City Police Department. What would
become known as the Lexow Commission, after chairman Clarence Lexow (1852–1910), would discover a pattern
of bribery and corruption that extended throughout the department. The most prominent target of the investigation*

was Captain Alexander "Clubber" Williams (1839–1910). The following testimony is taken from the hearings as investigators try to figure out how he amassed more than $1 million in assets on an annual salary of $3,500.

The second excerpt is taken from a 1913 investigation into the family budgets of 100 patrolmen published in 1913. The report makes clear in its summary of findings why graft and bribery might be so enticing to the underpaid police officers. What is unclear is why some officers were more susceptible to graft than others. This summary of findings suggests that the environment conducive for corruption had not measurably changed.

Source: New York State Committee, *Report and Proceedings of the Senate Committee Appointed to Investigate the Police Department of the City of New York*, Vol. V, Albany, 1895, pp. 5532–5536; Bureau of Municipal Research, *A Report on the Homes and Family Budgets of 100 Patrolmen*, March 31, 1913, pp. 4491–4494

Alexander S. Williams, recalled and further examined, testified as follows:

Q. Inspector, how much money have you in United States bonds? A. Not a dollar.

Q. Did you ever have? A. Yes, sir.

Q. How much? A. Five hundred.

Q. How much has your wife invested in United States bonds? A. None.

Q. Five hundred what; you said five hundred? A. Five hundred dollars.

Q. You are worth $500,000 altogether? A. No, sir.

Q. How near are you? A. A long ways off.

Q. How much is your place up in Cos Cob worth, Inspector? A. It is assessed; the property up there –

Q. Never mind; I am not asking what the assessment is; we know there are millions of dollars in property not properly assessed? A. It is assessed $13,000.

Q. That is no standard; we know in New York too much about assessments to take the assessment of property as an estimate of the value; what is your place worth – all your houses; how much money have you spent on that place up there? A. I could not tell you.

Q. One hundred thousand dollars? A. No, sir.

Q. Will you swear you have not spent a $100,000? A. Yes, sir.

Q. How much did the construction of the dock cost? A. That I would not tell you.

Q. Forty thousand dollars, was it not? A. No, sir.

Q. How near it? A. About $39,000 off; possibly more.

Q. How long have you been building it?

Q. How many houses have you upon your domain anyway? A. Three.

Q. Well, you have built a new house there, Queen Anne-style? A. I don't know as to Queen Anne; I don't exactly know what style it is.

Q. That is what the architect calls it; 15 rooms in the house? A. I think it contains 17.

Q. One hundred and thirty-five feet front? A. The house?

Q. Yes. A. No, sir

Q. What are the dimensions? A. Thirty-six feet front.

Q. What is the depth? A. Forty-two feet.

Q. Is that counting all the houses connected with it? A. Yes, sir.

Q. Then you have your coachman's house, near by? A. No, sir.

Q. Haven't you a coachman's house on the grounds? A. No, sir.

Q. Have you got a coachman there? A. No, sir.

Q. How long is it since you had one? A. Never had one.

Q. How are the houses occupied? A. Which?

Q. The houses on your place; you have got three houses? A. No, sir; I have not; three dwelling-houses.

Q. Those are three houses? A. Yes, sir.

Q. How are they occupied and by whom? A. The small one I gave $1,160 for, is let for $200 a year; the one I gave $3,600 for is let for $480 a year.

Q. You had dredging there, a good deal of dredging before you could build your sea wall? A. No, sir.

Q. Did you have any dredging done? A. No, sir.

Q. You had dredging done? A. Not for that sea wall.

Q. To build what? A. To make a channel.

Q. To allow your yacht to get up there? A. No, sir.

Q. What is the channel there for? A. To allow a row boat to come up.

Q. Did your yacht ever go up the channel? A. No, sir.

Q. How long have you owned that sloop-yacht, Elenor? A. One thousand eight hundred and seventy-eight, I think.

Q. Where was she built? A. Greenpoint.

Q. Have you had any craft built in Machias, Maine? A. No, sir.

Q. Directly, have you any interest there? A. No, sir.

Q. Directly or indirectly? A. Indirectly.

Q. Was there any craft built there for you? A. No, sir.

Q. What was the indirect interest you had? A. I gave a vessel a set of flags.

Q. Is that all the interest you had? A. No, sir.

Q. What other interest? A. Two thousand dollars interest in it.

Q. In what shape? A. That much ownership.

Q. In a ship or in a vessel? A. She is a brigantine.

Q. Is that the only interest you have there? A. That is all.

Q. How much did your yacht cost? A. The contract price was $4,000.

Q. How much did your yacht cost, I asked you; I did not ask you the contract price? A. It cost me something to run her since.

Q. How much did your yacht cost when she was built? A. That was the contract price.

Q. I ask the price? A. That was the cost.

Q. Who built the yacht? A. John Parmley.

Q. Over in Greenpoint? A. Yes, sir.

Q. How many did your crew consist of? A. Three.

Q. You have had her in commission ever since? A. No, sir.

Q. Every year? A. Once in a while.

Q. Every year? A, Yes, sir; I have a commission for once in a while.

Q. And you have your guests, frequently officers of the department, on your cruises? A. No, sir.

Q. Never have any? A. No, sir.

Q. Has Captain Devery never been on your yacht? A. I do not recollect that he was.

Q. You had an income of from $7,000 to $8,000 a year from the Tenderloin while you were there? A. No, sir.

Q. No income from it? A. No, sir.

Q. Of course you are prepared to swear that you never touched a dollar? A. I am prepared to swear to the truth.

Q. You are prepared to swear you never touched a dollar? A. I am prepared to swear to the truth.

Q. Are you prepared to swear you never received a dollar outside of your salary while you were captain of the Tenderloin? A. I received money, but not from the Tenderloin, as you call it.

Q. What money did you receive? A. Five or $6,000 downtown.

Q. What from? A. Stocks.

Q. From whom? A. The firm of Freece & Hoey, brokers.

Q. Freece & Hoey? A. Yes, sir.

Q. Where? A. Forty-seven Broadway.

Q. What stocks? A. I could not tell you.

Q. How much did you pay to get that $6,000? A. I didn't pay anything.

Q. Received it as a present? A. Yes, sir.

Summary of findings

1 The policemen during the first two years of service are underpaid.

The investigators' visit to the homes of the policemen who were in their first two years of service, revealed conditions, of the most convincing character in support of the contention that they are underpaid. The attached exhibits show that the average family budget for first and second year patrolmen is, for family purposes, – $871.46, and for police purposes, – $218.12, a total budget of $1,089.58; that the average patrolman's apartment consists of four rooms; that thirty-three families are without baths; that the average number of children to a family is two, and that the first year patrolman contributes $16.85 to benefit societies and $28.83 for insurance, the second year man contributing $20.07 and $27.24 respectively for benefit societies and insurance.

Attached to this report are also statements made by policemen upon certain phases of police work, such as fines, extra duties, etc.

2 Of the $800 given the patrolman for his first year's service, the minimum amount he is compelled to expend for uniform, equipment, station house charges, and contribution to the pension fund is $169.64, leaving him a balance of $630.36. From this amount again, must be subtracted approximately $73.72 which he is required to spend for meals away from home. In this connection it must be remembered that the policeman is unable to carry his luncheon with him as does the ordinary civil employee, and therefore must, buy at least one meal a day away from home. Assuming that the policeman during his first year does not become a member of any benefit or life insurance society, loses no time through sickness, and suffers no fines, he has at his disposal out of his $800 salary, $556.64 with which to support himself and family.

3 The increases in salary which accrue during the third, fourth, and fifth year of the policeman's first five years of service, do not result in a corresponding increase in income for his support and that of his family, because much of this increase usually goes toward paying the debts contracted during his first and second years of service.

4 The danger of increased indebtedness by reason of possible fines is common.

The system of taking money out of the salaries of delinquent policemen is uniformly condemned by the members of the force. In almost every instance it was the opinion of the policemen that the system of fining was one which resulted in disciplining the family rather than the policeman, in that every dollar taken from him, especially during his first year, meant an added dollar of debt to the family, and consequently an extra trip to the loan shark and more frequently a visit to the pawnshop. In fact, it was the experience of the investigators that the pawnshop furnished in sixteen cases the speedy assistance so necessary in emergencies to the policeman's little family.

In many instances patrolmen were ready to cite examples of what they regarded as gross injustices – the general complaint seemed to be inconsistency in the matter of punishment for the same type of offense. Believing the fine to be an injustice, the policemen do not give their best services to the city during the days on which in reality they are serving the City without compensation. In cases where the fine is heavy, as for example 15 days, the hardship is all the more severe, because the full amount is deducted from the next check.

About half the families run monthly accounts and pay almost entirely on the installment plan. The first of each month finds many collectors at the door of the policeman's home, and at the home where a 15-day fine has been imposed the wife is unprepared to meet the monthly bills. Next month, most of the bills have doubled. From this financial difficulty arises a natural condition of home worry and discouragement which does not add to the usefulness of the policeman to the city.

To emphasize the danger of the fining system, one has only to add the possibility of a doctor's bill, due to a sick baby or a sick wife.

The investigators also found in this connection that the families of policemen were denied treatment at the various dispensaries and hospitals when they made known that the father was a policeman.

5 "Little encouragement but plenty of discouragement," seemed to be the general feeling of the policeman during his first few years of service.

There is a widespread lack of enthusiasm among the men, due to the absence of a merit system which would reward for efficiency. At present the delinquent policeman is punished through his pocketbook, and there is no apparent reward for efficiency except in the case of demonstrations of physical courage. In other words, there is no possible chance, even by the most meritorious kind of police work, for the policeman ever to get the money which the department has taken away from him during a possible period of delinquency.

6 "No reward for over time," was another complaint. In only one instance did the policemen urge financial reward. The fact is that in the course of a policeman's work a great many hours of extra service are required, due to strikes, riots, parades, and time spent in court. At present no amount of extra duty brings with it any reward, either in salary, time off, or merits. A great many policemen ventured the opinion that, if there were some system of merits or reward for extra duty, especially with regard to presenting cases in court, a greater efficiency in the enforcement of law could be had.

In many instances, the policemen did not hesitate to say that the human element entered so strongly into the performance of their duty that they hesitated to make an arrest when this involved spending their day off in the court.

Key terms

Victorian era
Slaughterhouse cases
Anthony Comstock
Comstock Law
Theodore Roosevelt
Tenderloin district
Homestead strike
Thomas Byrnes
Bertillon system
Sir Francis Galton
National Chiefs of Police
good time laws
National Prison Congress
American Prison Association
probation
H. H. Holmes
Criminal Man
Wilkerson v. Utah
Mafia
Haymarket Square bombing

Fourteenth Amendment
Plessy v. Ferguson
penny presses
Comstockery
Lexow Committee
Jacob Riis
Pinkertons
rogues' gallery
Alphonse Bertillon
Fingerprints
Reconstruction era
Zebulon Brockway
Elmira Reformatory
Katherine Bement Davis
Child Savers
William Kemmler
lynchings
David Hennessey
Lizzie Borden trial
Bradwell v. Illinois

"separate but equal" doctrine
Victorian compromise
police matrons
Alexander "Clubber" Williams
civil service reform
anti-Pinkerton legislation
Professional Criminals of America
fingerprinting
Will West
convict lease system
Declaration of Principles
wayward sisters
Mt. Pleasant Female Prison
juvenile court system
Cesare Lombroso
electric chair
Ida B. Wells
Molly Maguires

Critical thinking questions

1 Discuss the impact of Victorian era criminal justice on women in America.
2 What upheavals in American society during the Victorian years might explain the assassination of two presidents between 1881 and 1901? What was the impact of these events on federal criminal justice agencies?
3 Contrast the development of police organizations in New York, the South, and the West.
4 What impact did the National Prison Congress have on the correctional system?
5 Discuss and compare the various reform movements of the Victorian era (e.g., juvenile court system, anti-vice societies, police professionalism, and correctional reform).
6 Examine race relations and the criminal justice system during the post-Civil War era.
7 What are the larger lessons in criminal justice and Victorian America that can be gleaned from the Lizzie Borden trial?

Notes

1 Lawrence M. Friedman, *Crime and Punishment in American History*, New York: Basic Books, 1993, p. 127.

2 Ibid.

3 Charles J. McClain Jr., *In Search of Equality: The Chinese Struggle against Discrimination in Nineteenth-Century America*, Berkeley, CA: University of California Press, 1994; Lucy Salyer, *Laws Harsh as Tigers: Chinese Immigrants and the Shaping of Modern Immigration Law*, Chapel Hill: University of North Carolina Press, 1995.

4 Quoted in Roger Lane, *Murder in America*, Columbus: Ohio State University Press, 1997, p. 173.

5 Robert C. Reinders, "Militia and Public Order in 19th Century America," *Journal of American Studies*, 11(1), 1977, p. 92.

6 George M. Roe, *Our Police: A History of the Cincinnati Police Force, from the Earliest Period until the Present Day*, Reprint of 1890 ed., New York: AMS Press, 1976, p. iii.

7 James F. Richardson, *Urban Police in the United States*, Port Washington, NY: Kennikat Press, 1974, p. 54.

8 Ibid., p. 59.

9 Stephen Cresswell, *Mormons and Cowboys, Moonshiners and Klansmen: Federal Law Enforcement in the South and the West, 1870–1893*, Tuscaloosa: University of Alabama Press, 1991, p. 4.

10 Ibid., pp. 4–5.

11 Timothy J. Gilfoyle, *A Pickpocket's Tale: The Underworld of Nineteenth Century New York*, New York: Norton, 2006, p. 244.

12 It cost another $300 to be promoted to roundsman; $1,600 to sergeant; and $14,000 to promote to captain.

13 James Lardner and Thomas Reppetto, *NYPD: A City and Its Police,* New York: Henry Holt, 2000, p. 50. The green lights supposedly were inspired by the green lamps carried by the early watchmen.

14 Quoted in Ibid.

15 Richardson, 1974, p. 63.

16 Pete Hamill, *Downtown: My Manhattan*, New York, Little, Brown and Co, 2004, p. 250.

17 Frank Morn, *"The Eye That Never Sleeps": A History of the Pinkerton National Detective Agency*, Bloomington, IN: Indiana University Press, 1982.

18 Luc Sante, *Evidence*, New York: Farrar, Straus and Giroux, 1992, p. 97.

19 J. North Conway, *The Big Policeman: The Rise and Fall of America's First, Most Ruthless and Greatest Detective*, Guildford, CT: Lyons Press, 2010; J. North Conway, *King of Heists: The Sensational Bank Robbery of 1878 That Shocked America*, Guildford, CT: Lyons Press, 2009.

20 Dan Barry, "Cheats, Swindlers and Ne'er-Do-Wells," *New York Times*, February 11, 2018, p. 24.

21 Colin Beavan, *Fingerprints: The Origins of Crime Detection and the Murder Case That Launched Forensic Science*, New York: Hyperion, 2001.

22 For a comprehensive history of criminal identification, culminating in the success of fingerprinting over rival identification systems, see Simon A. Cole, *Suspect Identities: A History of Fingerprinting and Criminal Identification*, Cambridge, MA: Harvard University Press, 2001.

23 B. C. Bridges, *Practical Fingerprinting*, New York: Funk and Wagnall's, 1942, p. 11.

24 Beavan, 2001, p. 40.

25 Ibid., pp. 42–43.

26 Brian Lane, *The Encyclopedia of Forensic Science*, London: Headline Publishing, 1992, p. 174.

27 Dennis C. Rousey, *Policing in the Southern City: New Orleans, 1805–1889*, Baton Rouge: Louisiana State University Press, 1991, p. 135.

28 Ibid., p. 188.

29 William T. Hagan, *Indian Police and Judges: Experiments in Acculturation and Control*, 1966; John P. Clum, "The San Carlos Apache Police," *New Mexico Historical Review*, July 1929.

30 Robert C. Wadman and William Thomas Allison, *To Protect and Serve: A History of Police in America*, Upper Saddle River, NJ: Pearson, 2004.

31 Blake McKelvey, *American Prisons: A History of Good Intentions*, Montclair, NJ: Patterson Smith, 1977, p. 49.

32 Scott Christianson, *With Liberty for Some*, Boston: Northeastern University Press, 1998, p. 177.

33 Quoted in Ibid., p. 180.

34 Margaret Hope Bacon, *Abby Hopper Gibbons: Prison Reformer and Social Activist*, Albany: State University of New York Press, 2000, p. 52; Nicole H. Rafter, *Partial Justice: Women in State Prisons, 1800–1935*, Boston: Northeastern University Press, 1985.

35 Frankie Y. Bailey and Donna C. Hale, *Blood on Her Hands: Women Who Murder*, Belmont, CA: Wadsworth Cengage, 2004.

36 Friedman, 1993, p. 233.

37 Larry E. Sullivan, *The Prison Reform Movement*, Boston: Twayne Publishing, 1990, p. 14.

38 Nicole H. Rafter, *Partial Justice: Women in State Prisons, 1800–1935*, Boston: Northeastern University Press, 1985, p. xx.

39 Friedman, 1993, p. 233.

40 Quoted in Bacon, 2000, p. 54.

41 Lucia Zedner, "Wayward Sisters: The Prison for Women," in *The Oxford History of the Prison*, ed. Norval Morris and David Rothman, New York: Oxford University Press, 1998, p. 302.

42 Bacon, 2000.

43 Zedner, 1998, p. 316.

44 Harry Barnes and Negley Teeters, *New Horizons in Criminology*, New York: Prentice Hall, 1943, pp. 373–375.

45 Sullivan, 1990, p. 29.

46 Anthony M. Platt, *The Child Savers: The Invention of Delinquency*, Chicago: University of Chicago Press. 1969, p. 77.

47 Meaning the power of the state to act on behalf of the child and to provide care and protection as a surrogate parent would.

48 For a richly nuanced account of New York City's homicide rates during the nineteenth century, see Eric Monkkonen, *Murder in New York City*, Berkeley, CA: University of California Press, 2001.

49 Ben Macintyre, *The Napoleon of Crime: The Life and Times of Adam Worth*, New York: Farrar, Straus and Giroux, 1997, p. 31.

50 Jenna Weissman Joselit, *Our Gang: Jewish Crime and the New York Jewish Community, 1900–1940*, Bloomington, IN: Indiana University Press, 1983, p. 35; J. North Conway, *"Queen of Thieves" The True Story of "Marm" Mandelbaum and Her Gangs of New York*, New York: Skyhorse Publishing, 2014, p. xiii.

51 Gilfoyle, 2006, p. 151.

52 Quoted in Nicole Rafter, *The Criminal Brain: Understanding Biological Theories of Crime*, New York: New York University Press, 2007, p. 67.

53 Edwin H. Sutherland, *Principles of Criminology*, 4th ed, Philadelphia: Lippicott, 1947, p. 57.

54 Marvin E. Wolfgang, "Cesare Lombroso," *Journal of Criminal Law, Criminology and Police Science*, 52(4), November–December, 1961, p. 287, *Pioneers in Criminology*, ed. Hermann Mannheim, Montclair, NJ: Patterson Smith, pp. 232–294.

55 Cesare Lombroso and William Ferrero, *The Female Offender*, New York: D. Appleton and Company, 1909, p. 258.

56 Ibid., p. 162.

57 S.K. Mukerjee and Jocelynne A. Scutt, eds., *Women and Crime*, London: Routledge, 1981, p. 41.

58 Quoted in Ibid., p. 147.

59 Quoted in Lawrence M. Friedman, *Crime and Punishment in American History*, New York: Basic Books, 1993, p. 146. For a full account of the trial see Charles E. Rosenberg, *The Trial of Charles Guiteau: Psychiatry and the Law in the Gilded Age*, Chicago: University of Chicago Press, 1968.

60 Roger Lane, *Roots of Violence in Black Philadelphia, 1860–1900*, Cambridge, MA: Harvard University Press, 1986, pp. 105–107.

61 Ibid., p. 107.

62 J. S. Adler, "I Loved Joe, But I Had to Shoot Him: Homicide by Women in Turn of the Century Chicago," in *Journal of Criminal Law and Criminology*, 92, 2003, pp. 867–898.

63 Bailey and Hale, 2004, pp. 124–125.

64 Elaine S. Abelson, *When Ladies Go A-Thieving*, New York: Oxford University Press, 1989, p. 174.

65 Timothy J. Gilfoyle, *City of Eros: New York, Prostitution, and the Commercialization of Sex, 1820–1920*, New York: W.W. Norton and Company, p. 18.

66 Friedman, 1993, p. 225.

67 Mara L. Keire, "The Vice Trust: A Reinterpretation of the White Slavery Scare in the United States, 1907–1917," *Journal of Social History*, 35(1), 2001, p. 12; Charles Winick and Paul M. Kinsie, *The Lively Commerce: Prostitution in the United States*, Chicago: Quadrangle Books, 1971, p. 289.

68 William J. Bowers, *Executions in America*, Lexington, MA: Lexington Books, 1974.

69 Quoted in Bryan Vila and Cynthia Morris, *Capital Punishment in America*, Westport, CT: Greenwood Press. 1997, p. 68.

70 Michael A. Bellesiles, *Arming America: Origins of a National Gun Culture*, New York: Alfred A. Knopf, 2000, p. 433.

71 Ibid.

72 Rousey, 1991, p. 175.

73 Quoted in Leonard Beeghley, *Homicide: A Sociological Explanation*, Lanham, MD: Rowman and Littlefield, 2003, p. 66.

74 Quoted in Richard E. Nisbett and Dov Cohen, *Culture of Honor: The Psychology of Violence in the South*, New York: Westview Press, 1996, p. 1.

75 While Redfield's methodology is considered flawed by most historians, having based most of his research on newspaper accounts, he is still credited with making the most extensive examination of regional homicide rates in the nineteenth century.

76 Horace V. Redfield, *Homicide, North and South*, Philadelphia: JP Lippincott, 1880.

77 Horace V. Redfield, *Homicide, North and South*, Columbus: Ohio State University, 1880, 2000, p. 10.

78 Nisbett and Cohen, 1996, p. 4.

79 Roger Lane, *Murder in America*, Columbus: Ohio State University Press, 1997, p. 149.

80 For similar conclusions, see Eugene Hollon, *Frontier Violence: Another Look*, New York: Oxford University Press, 1974, and Frank Prassel, *Western Peace Officer*, Norman: University of Oklahoma Press, 1972. Roger McGrath, *Gunfighters, Highwaymen, and Vigilantes: Violence on the Frontier*, Berkeley, CA: University of California Press, 1984, incorporated more statistical rigor in his study of mining towns in Aurora, Nevada, and Bodie, California, where the author found high homicide rates. However, Clare V. McKanna, *Homicide, Race and Justice in the American West, 1880–1920*, Tucson: University of Arizona Press, 1997, p. 3, finds fault with this examination because it dealt with only a relatively short time period, and at the end of McGrath's study, the author states that "in most ways the towns were not violent or lawless places."

81 Gary Krist, *City of Scoundrels: The 12 Days of Disaster That Gave Birth to Modern Chicago*, New York: Crown Books, 2012, p. 75.

82 Lane, 1997, p. 4.

83 Jacqueline Jones Royster, ed., *Southern Horrors and Other Writings: The Anti-Lynching Campaign of Ida B. Wells, 1892–1900*, Boston: Bedford Books, 1997, p. 4.

84 For one of the best examinations of the Molly Maguires, their crimes, trials, and execution as well as the role played by private detectives in the investigation, see Kevin Kenny, *Making Sense of the Molly Maguires*, New York: Oxford University Press, 1998.

85 One of the best biographies of a Pinkerton agent see Beau Riffenburgh, *Pinkerton's Great Detective: The Amazing Life and Times of James McParland*, New York: Viking, 2013.

86 In 1979, one of the executed Mollies was given a full state pardon over a century too late, when it was determined that he was probably framed by detectives.

87 Michael A. Bellesiles, *1877: America's Year of Living Violently*, New York: New Press, 2010.

88 Robert V. Bruce, *1877: Year of Violence*, New York: Bobbs-Merrill, 1959.

89 Jeremy Brecher, *Strike!*, San Francisco: Straight Arrow Books, 1972, p. 47. See also James Green, *Death in the Haymarket: A Story of Chicago, the First Labor Movement and the Bombing Trial That Divided Gilded Age America*, New York: Anchor, 2007.

90 Janice Schuetz, *The Logic of Women on Trial: Case Studies of Popular American Trials*, Carbondale: Southern Illinois Press, 1994, p. 63.
91 Ann Jones, *Women Who Kill*, New York: Fawcett Columbine, 1981, p. 231.
92 Richardson, 1974, p. 53.

Sources

Abelson, Elaine S. 1989. *When Ladies Go A-Thieving: Middle-Class Shoplifters in the Victorian Department Store*. New York: Oxford University Press.

Ackerman, Kenneth D. 2007. *Young J. Edgar: Hoover, the Red Scare and the Assault on Civil Liberties*. New York: Carroll and Graf Publishers.

Adler, Jeffrey S. 2003. "I Loved Joe, But I Had to Shoot Him: Homicide by Women in Turn of the Century Chicago." *Journal of Criminal Law and Criminology*, 92:867–898.

Ayers, Edward L. 1986. *Vengeance and Justice: Crime and Punishment in the 19th-Century South*. New York: Oxford University Press.

Bacon, Margaret Hope. 2000. *Abby Hopper Gibbons: Prison Reformer and Social Activist*. Albany: State University of New York Press.

Bailey, Frankie Y. and Donna C. Hale. 2004. *Blood on Her Hands: Women Who Murder*. Belmont, CA: Wadsworth Cengage.

Barnes, Harry and Negley Teeters. 1943. *New Horizons in Criminology*. New York: Prentice Hall.

Barry, Dan. 2018. "Cheats, Swindlers and Ne'er-Do-Wells." *New York Times*, February 11, p. 24.

Beavan, Colin. 2001. *Fingerprints: The Origins of Crime Detection and the Murder Case That Launched Forensic Science*. New York: Hyperion.

Beisel, Nicola. 1997. *Imperiled Innocents: Anthony Comstock and Family Reproduction in Victorian America*. Princeton, NJ: Princeton University Press.

Bellesiles, Michael A. 2000. *Arming America: Origins of a National Gun Culture*. New York: Alfred A. Knopf.

———. 2010. *1877: America's Year of Living Violently*. New York: New Press.

Bodenhamer, David J. 1992. *Fair Trial: Rights of the Accused in American History*. New York: Oxford University Press.

Bowers, William J. 1974. *Executions in America*. Lexington, MA: Lexington Books.

Boyer, Paul S. 1968. *Purity in Print: Book Censorship in America*. New York: Charles Scribner's Sons.

Brecher, Jeremy. 1972. *Strike!* San Francisco: Straight Arrow Books.

Bridges, B. C. 1942. *Practical Fingerprinting*. New York: Funk and Wagnalls Co.

Bruce, Robert V. 1959. *1877: Year of Violence*. New York: Bobbs-Merrill.

Burleigh, Michael. 2009. *Blood & Rage: A Cultural History of Terrorism*. New York: Harper Collins.

Christianson, Scott. 1998. *With Liberty for Some: 500 Years of Imprisonment in America*. Boston: Northeastern University Press.

Cole, Simon A. 2001. *Suspect Identities: A History of Fingerprinting and Criminal Identification*. Cambridge, MA: Harvard University Press.

Conway, J. North. 2009. *King of Heists: The Sensational Bank Robbery of 1878 That Shocked America*. Guildford, CT: Lyons Press.

———. 2010. *The Big Policeman: The Rise and Fall of America's First, Most Ruthless and Greatest Detective*. Guildford, CT: Lyons Press.

———. 2014. *"Queen of Thieves": The True Story of "Marm" Mandelbaum and Her Gangs of New York*. New York: Skyhorse Publishing.

Cresswell, Stephen. 1991. *Mormons and Cowboys, Moonshiners and Klansmen: Federal Law Enforcement in the South and the West, 1870–1893*. Tuscaloosa: University of Alabama Press.

Friedman, Lawrence M. 1993. *Crime and Punishment in American History*. New York: Basic Books.

Galton, Francis. 1892. *Finger Prints*. London: Macmillan and Co.

Gilfoyle, Timothy J. 1992. *City of Eros: New York, Prostitution, and the Commercialization of Sex, 1820–1920*. New York: W.W. Norton and Company.

———. 2006. *A Pickpocket's Tale: The Underworld of Nineteenth Century New York*. New York: W.W. Norton and Company.

Green, James. 2007. *Death in the Haymarket: A Story of Chicago, the First Labor Movement and the Bombing That Divided Gilded Age America*. New York: Anchor.

Hollon, Eugene. 1974. *Frontier Violence: Another Look*. New York: Oxford University Press.

Jeffers, H. Paul. 1994. *Commissioner Roosevelt: The Story of Theodore Roosevelt and the New York City Police, 1895–1897*. New York: John Wiley and Sons.

Jones, Ann. 1981. *Women Who Kill*. New York: Fawcett Columbine.

Joselit, Jenna Weismann. 1983. *Our Gang: Jewish Crime and the New York Jewish Community, 1900–1940*. Bloomington, IN: Indiana University Press.

Keire, Mara L. 2001. "The Vice Trust: A Reinterpretation of the White Slavery Scare in the United States, 1907–1917." *Journal of Social History*, 35(1).

Kendall, John S. 1939. "Who Killa de Chief?" *Louisiana Historical Quarterly*, 22(2).

Kenny, Kevin. 1998. *Making Sense of the Molly Maguires*. New York: Oxford University Press.

Kinney, John J. 2005. *Captain Jack and the Dalton Gang: The Life and Times of a Railroad Detective*. Lawrence: University of Kansas Press.

Krist, Gary. 2012. *City of Scoundrels: The 12 Days of Disaster That Gave Birth to Modern Chicago*. New York: Crown Books.

Lane, Roger. 1986. *Roots of Violence in Black Philadelphia, 1860–1900*. Cambridge, MA: Harvard University Press.

———. 1997. *Murder in America*. Columbus: Ohio State University Press.

Lardner, James and Thomas Reppetto. 2000. *NYPD: A City and Its Police*. New York: Henry Holt.

Lombroso-Ferrero, Gina. [1911] 1972. *Criminal Man According to the Classification of Cesare Lombroso*. Reprint, Montclair, NJ: Patterson Smith.

MacIntyre, Ben. 1997. *The Napoleon of Crime: The Life and Time of Adam Worth*. New York: Farrar, Straus and Giroux.

McGrath, Roger. 1984. *Gunfighters, Highwaymen, and Vigilantes: Violence on the Frontier*. Berkeley, CA: University of California Press.

McKanna, Clare V. 1997. *Homicide, Race and Justice in the American West, 1880–1920*. Tucson: University of Arizona Press.

McKelvey, Blake. 1977. *American Prisons: A History of Good Intentions*. Montclair, NJ: Patterson Smith.

Monkkonen, Eric H. 2001. *Murder in New York City*. Berkeley, CA: University of California Press.

Morn, Frank. 1982. *"The Eye That Never Sleeps": A History of the Pinkerton National Detective Agency*. Bloomington, IN: Indiana University Press.

Nisbett, Richard E. and Dov Cohen. 1996. *Culture of Honor: The Psychology of Violence in the South*. New York: Westview Press.

Olsen, Robert D., Sr. 1987. "A Fingerprint Fable: The Will and William West Case." *Identification News*, 37(11). www.scafo.org/library/110105.html.

Platt, Anthony M. 1969. *The Child Savers: The Invention of Delinquency*. Chicago: University of Chicago Press.

Prassel, Frank. 1972. *Western Peace Officer*. Norman: University of Oklahoma Press.

Rafter, Nicole Hahn. 1985. *Partial Justice: Women in State Prisons, 1800–1935*. Boston: Northeastern University Press.

———. 1997. *Creating Born Criminals*. Chicago: University of Illinois Press.

———. 2000. *Homicide, North and South: Being a Comparative View of Crime against the Person in Several Parts of the United States*. Columbus: Ohio State University Press.

Reinders, Robert C. 1977. "Militia and Public Order in 19th Century America." *Journal of American Studies*, 11(1):81–101.

Rhodes, Henry T. 1956. *Alphonse Bertillon: Father of Scientific Detection*. London: George Harrap.

Richardson, James F. 1970. *The New York Police: Colonial Times to 1901*. New York: Oxford University Press.

———. 1974. *Urban Police in the United States*. Port Washington, NY: Kennikat Press.

Riffenburgh, Beau. 2013. *Pinkerton's Great Detective: The Amazing Life and Times of James McParland*. New York: Viking.

Roe, George M. [1890] 1976. *Our Police: A History of the Cincinnati Police Force, from the Earliest Period until the Present Day*. Reprint, New York: AMS Press.

Rousey, Dennis C. 1997. *Policing the Southern City: New Orleans, 1805–1889*. Baton Rouge: Louisiana State University Press.

Royster, Jacqueline Jones, ed. 1997. *Southern Horrors and Other Writings: The Anti-Lynching Campaign of Ida B. Wells, 1892–1900*. Boston: Bedford Books.

Sante, Luc. 1992. *Evidence*. New York: Farrar, Straus and Giroux.

Schuetz, Janice. 1994. *The Logic of Women on Trial: Case Studies of Popular American Trials*. Carbondale: Southern Illinois University Press.

Schwartz, Bernard. 1997. *A Book of Legal Lists: The Best and Worst in American Law*. New York: Oxford University Press.

Smith-Rosenberg, Carroll. 1985. *Disorderly Conduct: Visions of Gender in Victorian America*. New York: Oxford University Press.

Sullivan, Larry E. 1990. *The Prison Reform Movement*. Boston: Twayne Publishing.

Sutherland, Edwin. 1947. *Criminology*. 4th ed. Philadelphia: Lippincott.

Vandal, Gilles. 2000. *Rethinking Southern Violence: Homicides in Post: Civil War Louisiana, 1866–1884*. Columbus: Ohio State University Press.

Vila, Bryan and Cynthia Morris. 1997. *Capital Punishment in America*. Westport, CT: Greenwood Press.

Winick, Charles and Paul M. Kinsie. 1971. *The Lively Commerce: Prostitution in the United States*. Chicago: Quadrangle Books.

Wolfgang, Marvin E. 1961. "Cesare Lombroso." *Journal of Criminal Law, Criminology and Police Science*, 52(4), November–December: 232–291. *Pioneers in Criminology*, ed. Hermann Mannheim, pp. 232–294. Montclair, NJ: Patterson Smith.

Woloch, Nancy. 2000. *Women and the American Experience*. 3rd ed. Boston: McGraw-Hill.

Zedner, Lucia. 1998. "Wayward Sisters: The Prison for Women." In *The Oxford History of the Prison*, ed. Norval Morris and David Rothman, pp. 295–324. New York: Oxford University Press.

1900	1901	1905	1906	1907	1908	1909
Assassination of President William McKinley	Theodore Roosevelt makes Secret Service responsible for presidential protection	Lola Baldwin hired as "operative" by Portland Police Department	Passage of Pure Food and Drug Act	Indiana passes first involuntary sterilization statute	Creation of a permanent Justice Department investigative bureau	Justice special agent force renamed Bureau of Investigation

CHAPTER NINE

Crime and criminal justice in the Progressive era (1900–1919)

Learning objectives

After reading this chapter students should understand and be able to discuss:

- How the federal government expanded its role in law enforcement beginning a trend that would be continued over the following decades
- How congressional legislation criminalized certain unpopular political views during the era of the Russian Revolution and the World War I and its lessons for today
- The passage of federal legislation directed toward drug prohibition and prostitution
- Why the years surrounding World War I were marked by racial tensions and so much violent crime
- The mixed legacy of Progressive reformers on criminal justice reform
- How criminalizing once noncriminal offenses such as alcohol consumption and prostitution fostered widespread disrespect for law enforcement and overwhelmed the criminal justice system
- The emergence of state police forces in America in the early twentieth century
- The challenges faced by women and minorities seeking careers in law enforcement

The **Progressive era** (1900–1919) was a time of tumultuous change as urban America tried to accommodate waves of immigrants from eastern and southern Europe and African Americans fleeing the **Jim Crow**[1] South. Despite tremendous urban and industrial growth, unprecedented social problems created deep anxieties among many native-born Americans who lent their support to immigration restriction and other exclusionary policies.

DOI: 10.4324/9781315148342-9

1909	1909	1910	1910	1910	1911
August Vollmer begins twenty-four-year stint as Berkeley police chief	National Association for the Advancement of Colored People (NAACP) formed	Alice Stebbins Wells becomes first female police officer after being hired by the Los Angeles Police Department	*Weems v. United States,* the first interpretation of the Eighth Amendment's "cruel and unusual" punishment clause by the Supreme Court	Congress passes White Slave Traffic Act (Mann Act)	August Vollmer puts Berkeley police on bicycles

Between the 1890s and 1920, a variety of Progressive reform efforts were directed at a nation in political, social, and economic transformation. By the 1920s, women had won the right to vote, and electoral reforms were introduced that included the secret ballot, direct election of senators, and a system for recalling elected officials. Workers saw their lots improve with the passage of the first labor protection laws for women and children as well as the shortening of the workday from almost fourteen hours to only eight.

Progressive reformers worked on many fronts in an era when 1 percent of the country's families owned seven-eighths of the nation's wealth. Meanwhile, four-fifths of the nation's population lived a marginal existence, presenting a remarkable juxtaposition to the opulent lifestyles of the captains of industry, such as Andrew Carnegie, who earned $23 million per year when the average workingman brought home perhaps $500 per year.

For the middle classes, the increase in the cost of living surmounted any advantages that may have come their way as the country's monopolies and trusts flourished despite the passage of the Sherman Act in 1890. It is estimated that almost three-quarters of all trusts in 1904 were created since 1898, leading to decreased competition and a declining faith in America as a land of opportunity.

Most of the problems that came to the public's attention were rooted in the so-called *Gilded Age* of the late nineteenth century. Although reformers had addressed many of the nation's problems in the previous decades, by the first decades of the new century, reform became a national obsession as diverse interests lent their voices in a call for social change. Among the most vocal reformers were investigative journalists known as "**muckrakers**,"[2] who capitalized on the American fascination with evil in a series of exposés published serially in popular magazines. Among the most famous and far-reaching were Upton Sinclair's description of the appalling conditions in the meatpacking industry published as *The Jungle* and Lincoln Steffens' *The Shame of the Cities*, which examined the crass urban political scene.

Many of the reformers saw themselves as "progressives," as they endeavored to reform the nation's social problems. They believed that injustice and sin could be dispensed with merely through new legislation. At the same time, they rejected **Social Darwinist** individualism and competition in favor of social cooperation. In the process, a cornucopia of organizations were founded that reflected the diversity of reform activity, including efforts for safer working conditions, abolition of child labor, shorter workweeks and higher wages, old age pensions, and workmen's compensation.

Chief among the advocates for reform were middle-class women and church-related organizations. They found expression in the creation of the Women's Christian Temperance Union (1898) and the Anti-Saloon League (1893), which waged a war against alcohol abuse. In little more than twenty years, their crusade led to nationwide prohibition with

1911	1911	1912	1913	1913	1914	1914
Sullivan handgun law	Triangle Shirtwaist Company fire in New York City exposes unsafe workplace conditions	August Vollmer establishes motorcycle patrols	Vollmer establishes automobile patrols	Thomas Mott Osborne spends week in Auburn Prison as "Tom Brown"	Osborne appointed warden at Sing Sing Prison and establishes Mutual Welfare League	Passage of Harrison Narcotic Act

the passage of the **Volstead Act** in 1920. Urban reformers had long recognized the consequences of alcohol consumption, including social problems, such as accidents, pauperism, and domestic violence.

The legislation of morality grew to include the sexual sphere, as opponents of prostitution found expression in the red light abatement movement and the passage of the 1910 White Slavery Act, or Mann Act. While prostitution was seen as a social evil because of its association with the sexual exploitation of women and its links to venereal disease, others linked prostitution and alcohol abuse to rising immigration from eastern and southern Europe.

Progressivism was concerned largely with mounting urbanization and the modernization of America as small-town governments attempted to confront rapid population increases. Formerly reliant on political machines to provide the most needed services, by the turn of the century most of these were on their last legs – corrupt and inefficient. Progressive social reform aimed at control and justice, and the criminal justice system in particular would benefit from Progressive concerns over problems of political patronage. In the process of breaking up the political machines, the informal welfare systems that helped the poor were dismantled. It soon became apparent that the states would have to become more involved in solving the problems of the cities.

One of the major goals of the Progressives was workmen's compensation and better working conditions. No event symbolized this concern to America at large more than New York City's 1911 **Triangle Shirtwaist Company fire**, in which 147 women employees lost their lives. A subsequent investigation of the Manhattan fire discovered that the women were locked inside to prevent them from leaving early and that many of the fire escape ladders were missing. This tragedy only emphasized the escalating number of industrial accidents. Over the next five years, more than half the states would enact workmen's compensation laws.[3]

Further complicating the development of the criminal justice system in the early twentieth century was the immigration of more than 12 million people to America between 1890 and 1910. In 1910, fully one-seventh of the population was foreign-born. Of the Irish, German, Russian, Polish, Slavic, and Italians who thronged urban America, the Irish were the most politically significant, in part because of their literacy and English-speaking skills. Abandoned by the formal political system, immigrants rapidly fell into poverty and under the influence of corrupt political bosses and their city machines. Immigrants were quickly branded with stereotypes. Jews were scorned as anarchists, while Italians fell under the specter of the Mafia and the Black Hand. Mobs targeted European immigrants as well as African Americans, although the brunt of the violence fell on America's impoverished classes. According to sociologist Mark Colvin,

The Progressive movement, and much of what occurred in the arena of criminal justice between 1900 and 1920, must be understood within [the] context of rival

1914	1914	1915	1915	1917	1917	1917	1917	1917
Weeks v. United States	First public defender's office opens in Los Angeles	Resurgence of Ku Klux Klan	Organization of the International Association of Policewomen	Congress enacts Espionage Act	Beginning of the Russian Revolution	Camp Logan Riot	United States enters World War I	Espionage Act passed by Congress, limiting dissent against war

orientations and divergent interests of a native, white, Protestant, urban middle-class and an ethnic, non-Protestant, urban working-class.[4]

Resentment of the new immigrants translated into immigration restriction legislation, beginning with America's first federal law to check the immigration of a specific ethnic group in 1882, when the Chinese were excluded for ten years. Nativist and racist violence broke out over immigration, while the Ku Klux Klan reorganized and the Immigrant Restriction League emerged as a powerful voice of nativism. Not everyone who came to America would stay, with anywhere from a fourth to a third returning to their native lands.

The lawgivers

Following the assassination of President William McKinley in 1901, progressive reform moved to the national level with the ascendance of Vice President Theodore Roosevelt (1901–1908) to the nation's top office. From his experience as New York City police commissioner in the 1890s, Roosevelt became a supporter of centralized law enforcement. He chose the Treasury Department's Secret Service as the preferred agency for launching federal crime investigations. However, Congress balked at this and enacted legislation prohibiting Treasury detectives from being employed by other government departments, including the Department of Justice. In response, the president ordered the attorney general to "create an investigative service within the Department of Justice subject to no other department or bureau" and was only answerable to the attorney general. The creation of the Bureau of Investigation as an agency of the Treasury Department in 1908 led the federal government to expand its role in law enforcement, a trend that continued into the 1930s and 1940s. Joining in the spirit of Progressive reform, Congress passed the White Slave Traffic Act in 1910 and the Harrison Narcotic Act in 1914 to attack the "moral evils" of prostitution and narcotics addiction. Influenced by the publication of *The Jungle*, Congress passed the Pure Food and Drug Act and the Meat Inspection Act, both on the same day in 1906.

The passage of congressional legislation in October 1917 signaled the beginning of a new era of persecution in America, leading to the criminalization of certain unpopular political views. In June 1917, Congress passed the Espionage Act, which authorized postal officials to ban newspapers and magazines from the mail and threatened individuals convicted of obstructing the draft with $10,000 in fines and twenty years in jail. The **Sedition Act** of 1918 made it a federal offense to use "disloyal, profane, scurrilous, or abusive language" about the Constitution, the government, the American uniform, or the flag. More than 2,100 individuals were prosecuted under these acts as civil rights fell victim to the power of the state.

1918	1919	1919	1919	1919	1919
President Wilson passes Sedition Act	Boston police strike	Chicago race riots	*Webb et al. v. United States*	Passage of the Motor Vehicle Theft Act (Dyer Act)	Eighteenth Amendment ratified (Prohibition)

By 1915, the American divorce rate had become the highest in the world, with one out of seven marriages ending in divorce. In California, the rates were even higher, with one out of five in Los Angeles and one out four in San Francisco. In an attempt to stop this growing trend, a number of state legislatures stepped in, passing laws raising the marital age of consent, prohibiting common law and interracial marriages and polygamy, and imposing new physical and mental health requirements. Various states established separate family courts to handle cases dealing with desertion, child abuse, juvenile delinquency, and divorce. Some states went as far as to strengthen divorce legislation by requiring longer residence requirements before a divorce could be granted. There is little consensus as to why the American divorce rate increased during the Victorian era. Explanations ranged from a decline in family values and the liberation of women to the chauvinism of men and the pressures of urbanization.

The White Slave Traffic Act

The passage of the White Slave Traffic Act,[5] better known as the **Mann Act** (sponsored by the puritanical Republican congressman James Robert Mann), in 1910 was the culmination of Progressive reform efforts to legislate morality at a time when middle- and upper-class Americans felt threatened by waves of new immigrants who were rapidly changing the demographics of urban America. One historian suggests that it was the Progressive era reformers "who sent the country in a frenzy with lurid tales of 'white slavery'" that allegedly involved kidnapping young women and forcing them to work in brothels.[6]

Under the direction of the Department of Justice, between 1910 and 1920, 2,801 individuals were convicted of violating the Mann Act. The law specifically prohibited the transportation of women in interstate or foreign commerce "for the purpose of prostitution or debauchery, or any other immoral purpose."[7] Theoretically, it meant that any man who took a woman other than his wife across state lines and had sex were violating the law. However, one historian of the era suggests that it was actually "not so forbidding," but similar to other progressive era legislation, it was mostly expressing the fears of the upper and middle classes. The inauguration of the White Slave Traffic Act was in truth trading "on the exaggerated belief that large numbers of foreign women were being smuggled into the United States for prostitution," threatening "the moral fiber of American men."[8]

Historian Timothy Gilfoyle claims that the significance of the Mann Act was "more symbolic than real" in diminishing prostitution but in any case did "hurt organized syndicates" most.[9] Supporters of the Mann Act probably recognized that the law would not cripple commercialized prostitution, because the only people being prosecuted were low-level pimps and madams. As a result, supporters shifted their efforts from policing people to policing places and the best way to do this would be to begin closing down red light districts, the most visible reminders of the sex trade.[10]

Author Karen Abbott has posited that the white slavery controversy "shaped America's sexual culture and had repercussions all the way to the White House." She also makes a case for the Mann Act indirectly leading to the creation of the FBI after special investigators were hired in 1910 to go after violators of this federal legislation. The Bureau of Investigation, precursor to the FBI, opened its doors as a new branch of the Department of Justice with only twenty-three agents, but the Mann Act propelled it from a small office concerned with "miscellaneous crimes to the government's most recognizable and powerful legal arm."[11]

Jack Johnson v. the Mann Act

No case epitomized the Mann era more than the prosecution of the African American world heavyweight boxing champion Jack Johnson (1878–1946). Born into a large, poor family in Galveston, Texas, Johnson ran away from home at a young age and by his teens had gravitated to boxing. Blessed with natural athletic ability, Johnson honed his fighting skills leading to his entrée into the world of professional boxing. His lavish tastes and flaunting of the color barrier in an age of segregation did not deter his winning the world heavyweight title in 1908. Soon the boxing world was searching for a "great white hope" to dethrone the black champion.

Refusing to accept his place in segregated America, Johnson's unconventional behavior and his well-chronicled involvement with white women generated racial prejudice, and soon federal authorities targeted Johnson for violating the 1910 Mann Act, which prohibited the interstate transportation of women for immoral purposes. In 1912, Johnson was charged with sending money to a white girlfriend to meet him in another state. Apparently irked at Johnson's having married another woman, she claimed that he had taken her across state lines for prostitution and other immoral purposes. However, in this case, historian Lawrence M. Friedman suggested he was arrested for "crossing color lines, not state lines."[12] Nevertheless, in 1913, he was convicted of trafficking in white slavery and was sentenced to one year in prison. While out on bail, Johnson and his wife fled the country for Europe and did not return until 1920. On his return, he surrendered to the authorities and served eight months of a one-year sentence in federal prison.

The Raines Law

In 1896, New York City passed the Raines Law in in an attempt to "minimize the evils connected with saloons." In terms of organized prostitution, its passage led to "the immediate growth [of this] social evil." The law raised the established saloon tax from $200 to $800 and was designed to mobilize increased law enforcement because as a state law it would be "beyond the reach of local influences" in an effort to enforce Sunday blue laws.[13]

Saloon keepers managed to get around the law by adding hotels to their establishments with the requisite ten bedrooms, kitchen, and dining room. They were dubbed *Raines Law*

Hotels after the ordinance that forbade the sale of alcohol on Sundays except in hotels, a *hotel* being defined as having the aforementioned ten-bedroom accommodations. By 1905, there were 1,000 such places in Manhattan and the Bronx alone, adding 10,000 new bedrooms to the city's total.[14] The conundrum was that the city already had enough hotels rooms, and the only way owners could fill these extra rooms to make ends meet was by renting them out for prostitution. If investigators discovered this ruse, they could label the premises as a *disorderly hotel*. During the early twentieth century, these hotels became the scene of a number of crimes, from murder to theft.[15] More recent research describes Raines Law hotels as "threadbare establishments consisting of several rooms and a saloon, a favorite place for a relaxing evening."[16]

The Sullivan Law and handgun legislation

While firearms came to America with the first European settlers, it was not until the twentieth century that a concern over firearms entered the national consciousness. A new approach to gun ownership came into conflict with the traditional right to bear arms at the very moment that law enforcement adopted new methods of enforcement and gained new insights into police science and criminology. Legal journals soon were awash in articles examining the Second Amendment and its implications for criminal justice. The avalanche of articles such as "Is the Pistol Responsible for Crime?" coincided with a rising concern over new societal demographics as the complexion of urban America was altered by the influx of immigrants from southern and eastern Europe and African Americans from the Jim Crow South.

In 1910, Manhattan, Brooklyn, and Bronx reported a combined 177 murders by firearms, with less than half the perpetrators arrested.[17] That same year, 912 arrests were made for carrying concealed weapons in the same cities. The following year, handgun legislation was discussed by New York politicians, including Senator Timothy Sullivan. Opposition soon came from familiar opponents of gun control – arms manufacturers, hardware dealers, and pawnbrokers. Despite the opposition, criminal court judges and the city's leading newspapers publicly supported gun control measures. After Sullivan delivered a rousing speech to the state legislature, the senate passed a bill that was signed into law by the governor. Similar attempts were made to pass legislation in adjacent states, but all were unsuccessful.

Drug laws

In 1900, American officials estimated that there were between 250,000 and 1 million addicts of opium and its derivatives in the country, leading one authority to describe America as "a nation of drug takers."[18] With a total population of 75 million, this would be the equivalent of 1 person out of 400. Unlike today, opiates in this era were unadulterated and would probably kill the average heroin addict of today. Although public concern about drug addiction peaked in the first two decades of the twentieth century, these years were crucial in shaping future American drug policy. More recent studies by David Courtwright and Mike Gray suggest that the number of American "dope fiends" has been exaggerated and that the typical addict was "a middle aged southern white woman strung out on laudanum,"[19] a potion of opium and alcohol. By most accounts, addiction had actually peaked in the United States by 1900.

In 1906, the **Pure Food and Drug Act** imposed federal standards on the patent-medicine industry. Three years later, Congress restricted the importation of opium except for certified medical purposes. Progressive reformers remained unsatisfied, demanding a codified, nationally applied antidrug law. Their idealized society would not tolerate drug addiction, just like it would not tolerate alcohol abuse and political patronage. Reflecting the concerns of Progressive reformers, on December 17, 1914, President Woodrow Wilson signed into law the **Harrison Narcotic Act**. In contrast to alcohol prohibition, there was little political debate over the act. Primarily a tax law, the act made it unlawful for any "nonregistered" person to possess heroin, cocaine, opium, morphine, or any of their products. Drug enforcement began the following year, resulting in 106 convictions.

Between 1916 and 1928, the vaguely written Harrison Act was the subject of a number of important Supreme Court decisions. One of the most prominent was the 1919 *Webb et al. v. United States* case. This decision developed out of a case in which a Memphis doctor and a druggist were indicted for conspiring to violate the Harrison Act by prescribing morphine only to addicts so that they could maintain their addiction. The high court examined the question as to whether this was allowable under the act and decided against the complainants. This decision had the long-range effect of ruling that providing drugs to an addict "not as a 'cure' but to keep the user 'comfortable by maintaining his customary use' was a 'perversion' of the meaning of the [Harrison] act."[20]

The climax of a generation of concern about drug addiction, the Harrison Act did not stop drug addiction but did make it a more difficult habit to maintain. Once the new antidrug laws went into effect, drug addicts were forced into treatment. The focus would soon be shifted to alcohol in the 1920s.

The eugenics movement

Best known to criminalists for developing the modern science of fingerprinting, **Sir Francis Galton** is also responsible for founding the eugenics[21] movement in the early twentieth century. Galton's biographer claims that his support for eugenics was rooted in a sense of the superiority of his own family and social class.[22] Building on Cesare Lombroso's biological theories of criminality (see Chapter 8), by playing on the fears evoked by the "new dangerous classes," eugenicists were responsible for the forced sterilization of hundreds of thousands of people in America and elsewhere.

In her history of the social history of biological theories of crime, Nicole H. Rafter argued that, between 1875 and the 1920s, "**born-criminal theories** incorporated popular hereditarian explanations of social problems and significantly affected public policy."[23] Coming at a time of intense immigration from eastern and southern Europe, the goal of eugenics was to "improve" the human genetic stock. Many of the assumptions about the quality of the new immigrants were based on test scores that suggested that immigrants scored poorly on IQ tests (usually because their English was limited and they had a poor knowledge of American customs).

In 1907, Indiana became the first state to make sterilization policy official policy, noting that "heredity plays a most important part in the transmission of crime, idiocy, and imbecility."[24] Each Indiana institution that housed "unfit" inmates hired two surgeons to its staff. California implemented a law that would "asexualize" prisoners convicted twice for sexual offenses beginning in 1909.

Proponents of eugenics became less prominent in the 1920s, as the Progressive movement ebbed away. In 1921, the Indiana supreme court ruled that forced sterilization denied "due process."[25] Rafter suggested that with "middle-class authority once again secure," there was less reason to pursue the goals of eugenics. She further argued that the most important legacy of eugenic criminology "lies in the structuring of social values and assumptions about what is good or bad (for example, our society values intelligence)."[26]

Following Galton's death in 1911, his views about the desirability of eugenics flourished in the United States. By the 1930s, more than half the states had passed forced sterilization laws aimed at those regarded mentally, physically, or even morally and socially unfit.[27] In 1942, the Supreme Court finally ruled against sterilizing criminals in the case of **Skinner v. Oklahoma**. According to the Oklahoma Habitual Criminal Sterilization Act, if an individual was convicted three or more times for "felonies involving moral turpitude," the defendant could be sterilized. After Skinner was arrested for the third felony, he was sentenced by the state to undergo a vasectomy. However, the Supreme Court ruled against the statute, stating that it violated "the equal protection clause of the Fourteenth Amendment."[28] According to this line of reasoning, only certain crimes, such as robbery, were punishable by sterilization, while others, such as embezzlement, were not. Despite this ruling, sporadic sterilizations continued into the 1970s.

The First Red Scare

Prior to the so-called "First Red Scare," except for the Alien and Sedition laws of 1798, the U.S. Congress had never attempted to establish peacetime restriction of opinions. Between 1919 and 1920, a national hysteria over political radicalism led states to introduce laws that surpassed the federal government's actual suppression of nonconforming and perceived threatening behaviors. Prior to 1919, several states had some legislation on the statute books targeting criminal anarchy. As early as 1902, New York had passed a criminal anarchy law to deal with anarchist similar to the type that assassinated President William McKinley in Buffalo, New York, the previous year. It was not long before some Western and Midwestern states followed suit, with Idaho, Minnesota, Montana, and South Dakota enacting similar legislation to facilitate the prosecution of **International Workers of the World (IWW)** members.[29]

America's entrance into World War I in 1917 saw a backlash against the German American community. Teaching the German language was banned in schools. Beethoven and Bach disappeared from symphony programs, and temperance leaders used the fact that most brewers were of German nativity to help push through the **Eighteenth Amendment**. The passage in quick succession of the Espionage Act (1917), the Sedition Act (1918), and the Alien Deportation Act (1918) elevated pacifism and government criticism to acts of sedition. Beginning in 1917, **Bureau of Intelligence** agents raided the headquarters of the radical IWW in twenty-four cities, suspecting the union of supporting the enemy war effort. In just Chicago alone, 100 IWW members were put on trial for violating wartime statutes. The IWW would never recover from its attacks during World War I. According to one Justice Department official, its main goal was "to put the IWW out of business."[30]

Although many observers hoped the judicial system would protect dissenters, the court system came down hard on IWW members, better known as "**Wobblies**." Even Oliver Wendell Holmes, the Supreme Court's leading champion of civil rights, approved attacks on civil liberties as he upheld the **Espionage Act** in *Schenck v. United States* in 1919 by comparing the denial of free speech during the war to the prohibition against "a man falsely shouting fire in a theater and causing panic."[31] However, Holmes reversed himself by arguing against the Sedition Act later that year in *Abrams v. United States*, but he was outvoted seven to two. Enthusiasm for this legislation continued until 1920.

The Palmer raids

In the summer of 1919, federal, state, and local government agencies targeted a wide range of radical activists fearful of a Bolshevik-style revolution in the United States. The subsequent "Red Scare" was ignited by the successful Bolshevik Revolution in Russia and postwar labor unrest, which included the 1919 Boston police strike and several bombing campaigns. On the night of June 2, 1919, a bomb was detonated (apparently before the bomber meant to) in front of the residence of the new attorney general. Attorney General **A. Mitchell Palmer** and his assistant, future FBI Director **J. Edgar Hoover**, would lead the federal attack on radical activists.[32] Wartime legislation allowed the federal government to repress criticism of the war effort. Consequently, hundreds of foreign-born anarchists, socialists, and communists were deported in the summer of 1919.

In August 1919, Attorney General Palmer appointed Hoover to lead the recently organized General Intelligence Division. It was here that Hoover demonstrated his proficiency for collecting data and names of enemies. Setting up a card index system listing every radical leader, organization, and publication in the United States, by 1921, Hoover had amassed a file of 450,000 names.[33] It was during this period that Hoover discovered what he thought was a worldwide communist conspiracy as well as justification for the raids.

The following year witnessed nationwide raids on IWW halls and offices sympathetic to the communist cause. Palmer's raids led to thousands of arrests, but his star began to dim because of criticism of his unconstitutional methods, and with it went his presidential ambitions. According to Hoover historian Curt Gentry, "The antiradical crusade had been, from its inception, an anti-labor crusade" that played on nativist fears. In the end, Palmer lost the support of big business because the new restrictive immigration quotas threatened to end the supply of cheap foreign labor and the Red Scare "was no longer good for business."[34]

Weeks v. United States (1914)

In 1914, Fremont Weeks was convicted for illegally using the mail. His conviction for promoting an illegal lottery through the mail was based to a great extent on information found in his home by police officers who lacked a search warrant. These papers were turned over to the U.S. marshal, who made another search of his home and found more evidence, again without a warrant. Despite Weeks' petition to have the documents returned to him and his attorney's objections, he was convicted. The Supreme Court subsequently overturned the conviction on the grounds that their seizure violated the Fourth Amendment protection against illegal search and seizure. This ruling established what has become known as the "**exclusionary rule**," which disallows the use of illegally obtained evidence in a criminal trial.

The *Weeks v. United States* ruling had a profound impact on the admissibility of evidence seized by police in federal trials. Before 1914, violations of the Fourth Amendment's protection against unreasonable search and seizures were perceived as common law trespassing. In order to keep the seized evidence from being admitted at trial, the defendant only had to petition for the property to be returned and then sue the responsible police officer for damages. In 1914, the Supreme Court held for the first time that a violation of the Fourth Amendment in itself could justify excluding evidence from trial. One of the most vexing judicial obstacles for police officers today, after *Weeks v. United States*, only property that was legally owned by the defendant and that the defendant specifically requested to be returned could be excluded from the case.

Although this was a landmark case, its greatest limitation was that it did not apply to the states. However, in a practice known as the "**silver platter**," if state or local police conducted the search and turned over otherwise illegally obtained evidence to federal officials, the evidence was declared admissible. This exception to the exclusionary rule meant that local prosecutors could use illegally seized evidence in trials under state law (if state laws allowed it).[35]

Law enforcement

During the first decades of the twentieth century, the world of work began to change, thanks to the influence of radical politics and unionization. While police work had more responsibilities than most jobs, it shared many of the concerns of other wage-earning occupations. In the early 1900s, the typical patrolmen worked twelve-hour days and was remunerated with low wages. Between 1910 and 1920, policemen began to take an active role in creating labor unions and police organizations. In 1915, two veteran Pittsburgh police officers were inspired to create an organization for the social welfare of police known as the Fraternal Order of Police (FOP). In order to assure the mayor of their non-radical intentions, they promised that the word *strike* would be omitted from any references to the nascent organization since, as police officers, they were "obligated to protect life and property." With the support of the mayor, within months the FOP had 600 members in Pittsburgh. The growth of the FOP continued over the next several decades as it grew into a national organization. While other police organizations were subsequently created, efforts at unionization lagged behind.

The Boston police strike

The police crusade for better working conditions reached a crescendo of sorts in 1919, when the Boston police force went on strike. As part of one of the most underpaid and overworked urban police forces, the average Boston policeman worked between seventy-three and ninety-eight hours per week for a yearly salary of less than $1,300. With salaries averaging roughly twenty-five cents per hour, this amounted to half the wage earned by workers in war-related factories. Morale had plummeted to an all-time low by 1919. Precinct houses were in dismal condition, and political patronage ran supreme as politicians continued to promote political cronies over more qualified officers who had demonstrated their proficiency on promotional exams. In addition, police officers were still required to perform tasks unrelated to law enforcement.

In 1919, a Boston police fraternal organization known as the Boston Social Club petitioned the American Federation of Labor for a charter. This led Edwin Curtis, the commissioner of police, to issue a proclamation prohibiting union membership among his rank and file. When the union refused to disband, Curtis fired nineteen officers. In response, 1,117 of Boston's 1,544-member force went on strike. The resulting crime wave and civil disorder led to the creation of a volunteer civilian force that resorted to physical violence to suppress the outbreak of crime. The strike and subsequent disorder lost any public support that the police may have garnered. All the striking police were eventually fired, and a new force was recruited. If anything came of the strike, it was the setting back of the **police union movement** until the 1960s.[36] Police Commissioner Curtis was soon vindicated by the Boston media for standing up against the "Bolshevik" unionizers. By the time of death just three years later, Curtis was credited with having rebuilt the police force.

Civilian police reformers

Police professionalism developed along two fronts in the early 1900s. While reform-minded police chiefs such as August Vollmer and Richard Sylvester received much of the credit for police reform, civilian police reformers such as **Leonhard Fuld**, **Raymond Fosdick**, and **Bruce Smith** placed their stamps on law enforcement agencies as well. Although Fuld (1883–1965) lacked a police background, this Columbia University-trained lawyer wrote the one of the first comprehensive and readable studies of police administration. His prescient vision for policing forecast many of the Progressive reforms that would characterize policing in the coming years, including a better use of police discretion while performing daily duties, more stringent hiring requirements, and a recognition of the dangers of political patronage. Fuld also recommended better police training in the proper use of deadly force and better systems for scrutinizing police misconduct.

At the urging of John D. Rockefeller Jr., Raymond Fosdick (1883–1972) embarked on a study of European police systems that resulted in the 1915 publication of *European Police Systems*. His study of virtually every major European police force fostered an image of a professional brand of policing that outshone the decentralized and more amateurish American counterparts. Fosdick would publish a complementary volume titled *American Police Systems* in 1920. Following a study of seventy-two urban police forces, the author concluded that American policing was victimized by a lack of professionalism and rife with political corruption. The publication of his work created a backlash from the American police establishment but also led to reform efforts in many cities.

In 1916, Bruce Smith (1892–1955) began his career as a police consultant and criminologist when he was hired by the New York Bureau of Municipal Research and studied the

Harrisburg, Pennsylvania, police department. After stints with the National Crime Commission and several other criminal justice associations, Smith devoted the remainder of his life to surveying police departments. Following an extensive study of European police procedures, he was instrumental in creating the *Uniform Crime Reports* in 1930. Over the next twenty-five years, he would become the country's foremost expert on police operations as he helped improve many forces, including those in Chicago, Baltimore, San Francisco, Pittsburgh, and Philadelphia.

Police professionalism

At the outset of the twentieth century, urban governments increasingly came to grips with the partisan manipulation of police agencies. Following several police scandals and the sensational revelations gleaned from the Lexow hearings, New York City finally abolished the police board in 1901 in favor of a single commissioner, appointed by the mayor for a five-year term. According to the new system, the police commissioner could be removed from office at any time by the mayor or state governor. During the first two decades of the twentieth century, of the 52 cities with populations exceeding 100,000, only 14 still used police boards.[37] Boston followed the lead of New York in 1906, Cleveland and Cincinnati in 1908, and Buffalo in 1916.

Efforts to replace partisan police boards with professional chiefs of police was an important first step toward police professionalism. During the Progressive era, police reform advocates such as Fosdick and Fuld made a point of comparing the unprofessional early twentieth-century American police administrators with their European counterparts.

Among the new crop of professional police commissioners influenced by Progressive police reform efforts was **Arthur Woods** (1870–1942). The Harvard-educated Woods joined the New York City detective bureau in 1907. After studying European detective bureaus while pursuing postgraduate work, Woods returned to the United States and became a protégé of Theodore Roosevelt. Woods was appointed deputy police commissioner and then police commissioner of the 10,000-man New York City Police Department in 1914. During his tenure, he vigorously attacked the vice problem but made his greatest contributions in the realm of police training and professionalism. Influenced by Scotland Yard and other European police organizations, Woods introduced a homicide clinic and psychopathic laboratory to train homicide and sex crime investigators and established the first school for patrolmen, a precursor of the city's police academy.

August Vollmer: father of American policing[38]

Considered the father of the modern American police organization, August Vollmer was born in New Orleans in 1876. After a stint in the military, in which he distinguished himself in combat during the Philippines campaign of the Spanish–American War, he settled in Berkeley, California. In 1905, he was elected city marshal and four years later began a twenty-four-year career as the city's police chief. As police chief of Berkeley, California, he became one of the preeminent proponents of police professionalism during the Progressive era. Among his earliest achievements was establishing a department code of ethics that barred the acceptance of gratuities and favors under penalty of dismissal.

In 1907, Vollmer was elected president of the California Chiefs of Police and in 1922 accepted the presidency of the **International Association of Chiefs of Police (IACP)**. In between his teaching at the University of California and running his police department, Vollmer was called on to reorganize a number of police departments, including those in San Diego (1915); Los Angeles (1923–1925); Havana, Cuba (1926); Kansas City (1929); and Minneapolis, Minnesota (1930). The author and coauthor of numerous books and articles, his best-known work includes *The Police and Modern Society* (1936).

Vollmer rose to prominence for his requirement that prospective police officers pursue a college education in an era when a high school education was not even required by most departments. Vollmer set up the first formal training school for policemen in 1908, and over the following decade, departments in New York City, Detroit, and Philadelphia established similar training academies. In 1916, Vollmer was instrumental in creating the first university-level police training school at the University of California, Berkeley.

Vollmer's other innovations included rigorous in-service training and probation for first-time offenders. He was the first police executive to champion the lie detector as an investigative tool and in 1922 implemented a single fingerprint classification system. Vollmer was instrumental in inaugurating a series of innovations during his tenure as police chief, including the first modus operandi system (1906) and the first motorcycle patrol (1911) as well as many others. By 1914, Berkeley's police force was the first in the country to be completely mobile, with all officers patrolling in automobiles. Officers were expected to provide their own cars, but the city paid them for their use, thus saving the city budget a huge outlay at one time. Vollmer's emphasis on scientific policing, education, higher standards, and the centralization of police services influences the role of police in society to this day.

Cleveland police chief Fred Kohler

Following in the footsteps of other reform-minded police managers in the Progressive era, Fred Kohler (1869–1933) took over the Cleveland Police Department, a force with a reputation for corruption, in 1903 and placed his stamp of reform on the force. Among the reforms implemented by Kohler was a "sunrise court," which allowed minor offenders to get to work on time through quick processing following a minor violation and therefore keep their jobs.

In 1908, Kohler introduced his "**Golden Rule Policy**,"[39] which dealt more informally with juvenile offenders. Although he claimed it was his own innovation, this policy was probably the 1907 brainchild of Toledo, Ohio, Mayor Samuel "Golden Rule" Jones and his police chief.[40] By diverting minor offenders out of the formal criminal justice system, courts could concentrate on more serious matters, and the offender would avoid stigmatization. Kohler's strategies were viewed with skepticism from some quarters, but Theodore Roosevelt thought he was the best police chief in America. Kohler's career came to an abrupt ending in 1913, when he was forced to step down after an extramarital affair became public knowledge. His legacy was further tainted when it was revealed that he delivered a plagia-rized speech to the IACP in 1912 and when, after his death, his safe deposit box was found to contain half a million dollars in probably illegal payoffs.

Women and minorities

The first female police officers were hired in the early twentieth century. While most female participation in law enforcement was limited to serving as matrons in jails in earlier years (since 1845), in 1910, **Alice Stebbins Wells** became the first full-time paid policewoman in America (according to a recent biography of **Lola Baldwin**, this claim has been brought into question, but although Baldwin was sworn in as the "nation's first municipally paid policewoman"[41] in 1908, Wells is still widely considered the nation's first policewoman).[42]

A strong advocate for women in modern police work, Wells lobbied Los Angeles social and political leaders before obtaining her appointment. According to her job requirements, she was expected to

> enforce laws concerning dance halls, skating rinks, penny arcades, picture shows, and other similar places of recreation; the suppression of unwholesome billboard displays; and maintenance of a general bureau for women seeking advice on matters within the scope of the Police Department.[43]

Over the next five years, twenty-five cities appointed policewomen to the forces. Initially, police-women were expected to repress dance hall vice,[44] help children, and return runaway girls.

One of the early pioneers in female law enforcement, Lola Baldwin was working for the Portland, Oregon, National Traveler's Aid Association in 1905, when she was asked to per-form protective work on behalf of women attending the city's Lewis and Clark Exposition that year. She performed her duties with such distinction that, when the fair ended, she con-tinued to provide the same services for women visitors to Portland and was eventually given police powers by the Portland police. She focused much of her energies on closing down saloons and brothels. By 1913, she held the rank of captain, and she directed her officers to prohibit young women from working in sordid environments such as pool halls and bowl-ing alleys. During her long career with the organization, she outlasted six police chiefs and five mayors but was never officially referred to as a policewoman. However, her biographer considers her the "first female police agent hired under civil service in the United States." Author Gloria E. Myers claims that many firsts attributed to Alice Stebbins Wells are "easily discredited by Baldwin's ample records."[45]

In 1915, the **International Association of Policewomen (IAP)** was established, lead-ing the effort to include more women in policing. According to recent research, while this meeting in Baltimore "was the point at which the policewoman movement became self aware," its success was the result of Lola Baldwin's work with women's organizations and social service agencies.

By the end of World War I, 220 cities across the nation employed 300 policewomen, including Georgia Robinson of the Los Angeles Police Department in 1919, the first Afri-can American policewoman. In 1920, the IAP was encouraging women police candidates to pursue college educations in order to join police departments, but as late as 1950, according to the U.S. census, women made up only 1 percent of the nation's police force.

African Americans found many obstacles blocking attempts to enter law enforcement. In 1900, police forces were overwhelmingly white, with blacks making up only 3 percent of urban police forces. Those African Americans that were fortunate enough to find employment often faced hostility and were usually placed in black communities. The career of Samuel J. Battle (1883–1966) offers a glimpse at early twentieth-century policing. The son of former slaves, **Samuel Battle** moved north to escape segregation. Early on, he set his sights on becoming a police officer, a rare accomplishment for an African American in turn-of-the-century America. While working grueling twelve-hour days as a porter in New York City, Battle prepared for the civil service exams that were required to join the police force. He passed the exam in 1910; nonetheless, administrators vacillated on whether to hire him. Battle became the first African American on the New York City police force in 1910 but was given the silent treatment by officers for his first year. Accepting his initial rejection, he flourished as a police officer consigned to the African American community. It was not until he saved the life of a white officer during a race riot that he won acceptance from his peers.

Despite passing the sergeant's exam, he was forced to wait seven years before becoming the first black sergeant on the force. Battle would make headlines in 1943, when Mayor Fiorello La Guardia authorized now parole commissioner Battle to quell race riots in Harlem following a police shooting of a black youth. His influence in the black community helped end the disturbance in short order. Retiring in 1951, Battle was honored in a special ceremony in 1964 as "the father of all Negroes in the Police Department."[46] Battle eventually became the first black sergeant on the force and continued to march through the ranks, rising to parole commissioner in 1941. Despite Battle's inspiring story, few African Americans found success on American police forces until after World War II, with most relegated, like women, to secondary status.

Federal law enforcement

By the Progressive era, the Justice Department, inaugurated in 1870, would also be responsible for investigating antitrust violations, fraudulent land sales, crimes on Indian reservations, the shipment of stolen goods from one state to another, and violations of national banking laws. But without a federal police organization, the Justice Department had to borrow investigators and special agents from other departments, including Customs, the Department of the Interior, and the Treasury Department. With the ascendance of former New York City police commissioner Theodore Roosevelt to the presidency in 1901 after the assassination of President McKinley, America now had a chief executive familiar with criminal justice issues. In 1905, Roosevelt appointed fellow Progressive Charles Bonaparte (grandnephew of the French emperor Napoleon I) as his attorney general.

Among Roosevelt's earliest actions in this arena was requesting funds from Congress to hire a detective force for the Justice Department. Despite the opposition of those who feared that a bureau of investigation would be used for political reasons, the Bureau of Investigation (BOI) was officially inaugurated by the attorney general in 1908, when he appointed a small force of special agents on his own (in the 1930s, Congress would change its name to Federal Bureau of Investigation).

The early activities of the BOI were rather limited since the number of federal crimes was much smaller than in succeeding years. Most investigations focused on banking, naturalization, antitrust, and land fraud. The passage of the Mann Act in 1910 expanded the activities of the BOI when it was made a crime to transport women overstate lines for immoral purposes. In 1919, the passage of the National Motor Vehicle Act, better known as the **Dyer Act**, added the transportation of stolen automobiles overstate lines to the BOI's responsibilities.

America's entrance into World War I in 1917 led to an expansion of the BOI, which grew to 600 agents and support staff with field offices in major cities and along the Mexican border. During the war, the BOI assumed additional duties with the passage of the Espionage, Selective Service, and Sabotage Acts. Just three months after America entered the war, an ambitious young attorney named J. Edgar Hoover (1895–1972) began working for the Justice Department. Hoover's meteoric rise through the department would lead to a fifty-year career as head of the FBI, beginning in 1924. In the 1920s, the bureau was plagued by problems shared by most civil service agencies. Promotions were based on seniority instead of merit, and investigations were inefficient. When Hoover took over in 1924, he established rigorous rules of conduct and procedure for all agents and investigations and instituted a promotion system based on merit.

U.S. marshals became increasingly involved in law enforcement in the years surrounding World War I. The passage of the Espionage and Sedition Acts in 1917, which set limits on the right of free speech, required marshals to enforce measures aimed at public opposition to the war. Marshals were also expected to arrest violators of the Selective Service laws.

The passage of the Volstead Act in 1919 inaugurated the Prohibition era. Despite the availability of Prohibition agents to enforce the laws, the marshals of the Justice Department would be saddled with conducting arrests and investigations and seizing breweries and other bootlegging equipment.

State police

The first decades of the twentieth century saw the creation of numerous state police forces. Some, such as the short-lived New Mexico Mounted Police and the **Arizona Rangers**, were inspired by the Texas Rangers. The Arizona Rangers were inaugurated in 1901 after a consortium of Republican cattlemen, mine owners, and railroad officials convinced the territorial governor that a force modeled on the Texas Rangers was required to dispatch the growing lawlessness in Arizona. Shortly after its creation, Democrats complained to the governor that the Rangers were all Republicans. The patronage issue would creep into any discussion of the Rangers. The demise of the Rangers was the result of several developments. While opposition to the force revolved around its payroll and expenditures, it seemed that the force worked itself out of a job when only two dozen arrests were reported in just more than eight years of existence. In 1909, the Arizona Rangers were disbanded following an anti-Ranger campaign led by county sheriffs and district attorneys.

The Arizona Ranger legacy suggests that they had much better relations with the Mexican government than with their Texan counterparts. Unlike the relationship between the Texas Rangers and the Mexican Rurales, the Arizona Rangers cooperated with the Mexican government, which permitted them to launch manhunts and extradite criminals to the United States. Ultimately, in 1912, Arizona achieved statehood, and a highway patrol was created in 1931. As with past mounted police forces, the introduction of the automobile, rapid population growth, and political infighting signaled the end of the Arizona Rangers. The New Mexico Mounted Police was established in 1905 "for the protection of the frontier."[47] However, this organization would be dissolved after persistent friction with local law enforcement.

A new era of state policing was launched in 1905 with the creation of the **Pennsylvania State Police**. Following a half century of rural crime, industrial disorder, and ethnic conflict, widespread labor strikes continued to paralyze the Pennsylvania economy. In the late nineteenth-century, immigrants from eastern Europe and Italy were drawn to the mining country once dominated by Irish, English, and Welsh miners. In 1902, Pennsylvania took steps toward creating a state police force based on the Royal Irish Constabulary and Philippines Constabulary military models.

Under the command of Spanish–American War veteran John C. Groome, the 220-man force was selected from the ranks of the armed forces and required to be unmarried and live in barracks. While they were charged with policing the entire state, for the most part, the force patrolled the immigrant-dominated mining districts. Mounted on horses and equipped with carbines, pistols, and riot batons, opposition groups compared them to the nefarious Cossacks of Russia.

Supporters saw the force as protecting the country against foreigners, labor agitators, and people of color, as the state police often were embroiled in jurisdictional disputes with local police. As the labor strikes of the 1910s diminished, the state police became more involved in rural crime and traffic problems as well as enforcing Prohibition laws.

After reading about the "heroic" exploits of the Pennsylvania State Police, former New York City police commissioner Theodore Roosevelt lobbied the state legislature to contemplate a state police force on the Pennsylvania model, and in 1917, the New York State Police was established. The New York legislature had considered a state police force for years prior to 1917, in part because of the success of the neighboring state police force as well as the inadequacy of New York's rural police. America's entrance into World War I in 1916 apparently provided the impetus for the force. A large force of 232 men and officers, like its neighbor, it was commanded by a superintendent appointed by the governor. Unlike its neighbor, however, it developed a rapport with organized labor because it was not imbued with the powers to suppress riots in cities without the approval of the governor and was not used for strikebreaking. In addition, it had the power to arrest, without warrant, anyone violating state or federal laws throughout the state.

The emergence of the New Jersey State Police force in 1921 is considered a turning point in the history of American state policing. The impetus for its creation was the ineffectiveness of county law enforcement and a rash of violent industrial disorders between 1910 and 1915. Between 1915 and 1923, twenty-seven states would create some type of state police force. While some states created highway patrols in response to increasing popularity of the automobile, others adhered to the Pennsylvania paramilitary model of policing.

Burns National Detective Agency: private police

In the years before an effective federal police apparatus and the birth of the FBI, banks, railroads, and other enterprises often avoided local law enforcement by hiring private agents to cross jurisdictions to apprehend wide-ranging criminal gangs, such as the James Gang and the Younger brothers. A variety of private police services were established during the early twentieth century to compete with the Pinkertons and traditional law enforcement. Among the most prominent was the Burns National Detective Agency, the brainchild of William John Burns (1861–1932), who had served a stint with the U.S. Secret Service in 1889. He left government employ to co-found the Burns and Sheridan Detective Agency, which was operated like the Pinkertons as a quasi-private police force. After buying out his partner and shortening the agency's name to its more familiar title, regional offices were opened across the nation. However, the Burns agency came under heavy criticism for its unpopular support of big business interests against labor unions. Despite such controversy and Burns' heavy-handed investigation of the 1910 bombing of the *Los Angeles Times* building, the agency prospered, and Burns returned to government service in 1921 to head the fledgling Bureau of Investigation, the precursor to the FBI. Although he would win acclaim for successfully prosecuting the Ku Klux Klan in the 1920s, his mishandling of the Teapot Dome scandal, involving the sale of federal oil leases to private interests for profit, would force Burns to resign in 1924 and return to private life.

Technological innovations

Although the call box, telephone, and telegraph had made the transition to police stations prior to the 1900s, technological advances in the new century would transform American policing. In the years following the war, the **teletypewriter** evolved into a "police workhorse" as it was used for printing telegrams. By 1911, police could transmit a facsimile photo of a criminal from one city to another (telephotography). Transportation technology would see police officers make the transition from bicycle "**scorcher squads**" to the motorcycle and automobile. By the 1920s, many cars would be equipped radios, although the two-way radio would not be installed until the 1930s. The authentication of fake documents, fingerprint classification, and the modern polygraph would round out the new police technology.

Corrections

Chief among the criminal justice-oriented reform movements of the Progressive era were attempts to transform the prison system. According to historian Larry E. Sullivan, during this period "criminal justice was largely taken out of the hands of judges and prosecutors and given over to bureaucrats, psychiatrists, social workers, and professional penologists."[48] In this new climate, the important correctional innovations of probation, parole, and indeterminate sentencing flourished. Beginning in the 1840s, probation took years to gain widespread acceptance. Only six states had statutes offering this alternative in 1900, but within a decade, all the northern states outside New Hampshire had adopted it. Over the next five years, the majority of western states adopted probation as well.

Explanations for the popularity of probation in these years revolved around the Progressive predilection for community improvement, hence the use of supervised freedom over incarceration. Other explanations suggest that it was cheaper to use probation instead of incarceration.

The beginnings of parole can be traced back to Alexander Maconochie's mark system in the 1840s, in which prisoners had to work through various stages to win release. By 1900, more than half the states offered some form of parole or indeterminate sentencing alternative. Unfortunately, parole boards created to decide each case became increasingly politicized and inefficient. According to one estimate, in 1920s New York, the state board gave only five minutes to each case.[49]

Throughout the first decade of the twentieth century, yearly prison congresses gave rise to a number of new recommendations for prison reform. In 1908, the **American Prison Association** was created. Here was a forum for experts to debate the evils of the southern lease system and to discuss European developments that revolved around the causes of crime and the fate of discharged inmates. Occasionally, debate would degenerate into acrimony as European criminologists belittled the American efforts at reform that elucidated new theories of crime causation and criminal types. At the same time, England was developing the Borstal system for the care of offenders under twenty-one and applying Elmira-like control.

America's state prisons saw their inmate populations swell by 62 percent between 1870 and 1904. However, this would be only a precursor to the tremendous increase in population over the next three decades. According to the Bureau of the Census, state prisons experienced an unprecedented 162 percent population growth between 1904 and 1935. During this era, ten new prisons based on the Auburn design were built, and one following Jeremy Bentham's Panopticon model was constructed at Stateville, Illinois, in 1925.

The reformatory prison movement peaked in 1910. Although, several prisons were inspired by the Elmira pattern over the next twenty years, the reform movement had reached an impasse. During the first twenty-five years of the new century, American prison policy relied on total control, punishment, and hard labor. With less emphasis on classification, moral instruction, and education, prison practice seemed to have drifted back to a nineteenth-century policy that was custodial, punitive, and financially productive. This period has been referred to as the industrial period for its concentration on producing a wide range of products for government consumption in prison factories. The military, public, and state government sectors in regions outside the South provided a ready market for prison-made materials. Paralleling the growth of prison industry was a steady breakdown in the former silent system as some American correctional practices made a significant departure from the formerly punitive regime. Emphasis was shifted from strict discipline and negative sanctions, such as corporal punishment as well as religious instruction, education, and trade training, and refocused on promoting parole in return for good behavior.

One of the most prominent prison reformers of the era was **Katherine Bement Davis** (1860–1935). The Vassar-educated penologist and social worker earned a PhD in 1900 and the following year was selected as superintendent of the Reformatory for Women at Bedford Hills, New York, where she earned a reputation as an innovator in female penology. Over the next dozen years, Davis experimented with a medical model of incarceration and was instrumental in establishing a diagnostic laboratory of social hygiene that allowed sociologists, psychologists, and psychiatrists to study prisoners. An early example of the Progressive reformer, Davis emphasized the role of professionals in treating social problems, so after the classification of offenders, those who were considered incurable were given life sentences, while others entered treatment programs.[50]

Thomas Mott Osborne and the Mutual Welfare League

One of the most controversial prison reformers of the early twentieth century, Thomas Mott Osborne (1859–1926) was the Harvard-educated scion of a wealthy manufacturer. Following graduation from college, Osborne entered local politics in Auburn, New York, where he was elected mayor in 1903. It was natural that he would take an interest in prison reform in one of America's leading prison towns. By 1906, he had developed a keen interest in reform and addressed a meeting of the National Prison Association, where he expounded his notion that "prison must be an institution where every inmate must have the largest practical amount of individual freedom, because it is liberty alone that fits men for liberty."[51]

Osborne was given a chance to put his philosophy to the test in 1913, when he was appointed chairman of the New York State Commission for Prison Reform. To prepare himself for the task, he served as a convict under an alias for a week behind the walls of Auburn Prison. The following year, he published an account of his experience in his book *Within Prison Walls*, which he used to illustrate the weaknesses of a current prison regime that stamped out individuality and destroyed manhood. The erstwhile reformer claimed that while he was behind bars, an inmate offered him a plan for limited self-government. Osborne based his Mutual Welfare League experiment on this advice, and on his appointment as warden of Sing Sing Prison in 1914, he instituted a system of self-government that was fashioned to give inmates a sense of corporate responsibility that, it was hoped, would aid in their subsequent rehabilitation.

Osborne's penchant for criticizing political overseers of the prison system earned him a number of enemies who mounted a campaign against his administration. Although charges of perjury and neglect of duty were never proven, he resigned as warden in 1916. Over the next four years, he continued his efforts at prison reform, leading to the founding of the Welfare League Association, which helped recently discharged prisoners, and the creation of the National Society of Penal Information, a clearinghouse for data on prison conditions.[52]

Thomas Mott Osborne's Mutual Welfare League experiment

1 The League is a prison system not imposed arbitrarily by the prison authorities, but one, which is desired and requested by the prisoners themselves.

2 There must be no attempt on the part of the prison administration to control the result of the League elections.

---

3 Membership in the League must be common to all prisoners; any other basis is false and will not attain the desired object-universal responsibility.

4 Under the League better discipline is secured because the prisoners will cooperate with the authorities when precious privileges are granted through the League.

5 Under the League all privileges are utilized as means of obtaining responsibility for the good conduct of the prison community.

6 The open courts of the League mean better conduct and fewer punishments.

7 The League has proved to be the most effective agent of stopping the drug traffic and combating unnatural vice.

8 The League, when properly handled by prison authorities, can largely increase the output of work and improve its quality.[53]

The federal prison system

Prior to the late nineteenth century, prisoners convicted of federal crimes were housed in state prisons. Initially, state prisons were given boarding fees and were allowed to use federal prisoners in the prison labor system, including the leasing system. Between 1885 and 1895, the number of federal prisoners more than doubled. But by 1887, Congress was becoming disenchanted with convict leasing and subsequently outlawed the contracting of federal prisoners. In response, a number of state prisons refused to accept federal prisoners. In 1891, the federal government decided to construct a federal prison at **Leavenworth**, Kansas. (Construction began 1898.)

The federal prison system diverged from its state counterparts in the early 1900s. The construction of the **Atlanta Penitentiary** in 1902 introduced several new innovations. It would be among the first prisons to feed prisoners in a dining hall at eight-person tables as opposed to the one-way bench tables of state facilities. Atlanta also implemented an eight-hour workday for guards. In 1910, federal prisoners were afforded the opportunity to earn parole with the passage of the first Federal Parole Law. In less than two decades, problems caused by prison overcrowding and poor record keeping would lead to the creation of the Federal Bureau of Prisons in 1929.

Crime and punishment

The years before World War I saw Americans becoming increasingly concerned with the rising crime problem. By 1914, New York and Chicago were experiencing more murders than England, Scotland, and Wales combined, and smaller cities, such as Detroit and Cleveland, were witnessing more burglaries than London. Public confidence in American policing had fallen to an all-time low.

Before Italian Americans were linked to Mafia-related organized crime later in the twentieth century, the extortion activities of **Black Hand gangs** "came to define the perception of southern Italian immigrants in the mind of the public."[54] Despite the failure of Black Hand gangs to monopolize any criminal markets or territories, by the first decade of the twentieth century, most crimes associated with urban Italian immigrants were linked to the Black Hand's nefarious activities. Gangs were estimated to range in size from six to ten members under one leader. Members extorted money from fellow Italians by sending threatening letters promising death or injury if the targeted individual did not comply with their financial demands. One of the most famous targets of the Black Handers was the famous opera star Enrico Caruso, who reportedly paid a $2,000 extortion payment in the 1910s. Before the popularity of fingerprinting, in the 1880s and 1890s, the letters were typically signed only with a black-inked imprint of a hand. With the advent of fingerprinting, other methods were used to get their message across to prospective victims. Despite its reputation, the Black Hand was never a monolithic crime organization nor widespread. In fact was not uncommon for Italian immigrants to band together to face down the extortionists from time to time. Nonetheless, its outsized reputation, thanks to the complicity of reporters who sensationalized their exploits, forced the New York Police Department to respond by creating an Italian squad. Giuseppe "Joe" Petrosino, born in Padula, Italy in 1860, had arrived in the United States with his family when he was a teenager. In 1883, he joined the New York Police Department. His native background and Italian linguistic facility made him the perfect choice to head of the NYPD Italian Squad. In 1909, he acquired permission to gather information on Sicilian criminals in Palermo, Italy. But soon after landing on the island, he was ambushed and shot dead on March 12, 1909. He was the first NYPD member to be killed outside the United States. His biographer suggested than more than 200,000 mourners paid their last respects as his funeral procession wound through the streets of Manhattan on the day of his funeral.[55] One former member of the Italian Squad suggested that the onslaught of alcohol prohibition helped get rid of the Black Handers, by taking a bad thing and turning it into something much worse. According to Mike Fiaschetti, it offered various ethnic gangs opportunities, including the fledgling Mafia, opportunity to make more money than ever before.[56]

In the years leading up to World War I, New York City experienced a growing youth gang problem. Nurtured by poverty and discrimination, gangs became part of urban America as Jews and Italians replaced the Irish and German immigrants who preceded them. Future Jewish and Italian gangsters, such as Meyer Lansky, Lucky Luciano, and Bugsy Siegel, entered the criminal world after graduating from juvenile gang activity.

One of the worst calamities for police reform was the implementation of national alcohol prohibition with the passage of the Volstead Act in 1920. Although it was intended to end the social problems associated with alcohol abuse, it would have the opposite effect as wealthy crime syndicates emerged, energized by the enormous financial opportunity associated with illicit alcohol activities. Extensive corruption of politicians, police, and other officials in this era seriously undermined public respect for the law and government.

Race violence

By the twentieth century, African Americans faced disenfranchisement and discrimination throughout the country, as they found themselves excluded by employers and labor unions from white-collar jobs and many of the skilled trades. In the South, Jim Crow laws and tenancy characterized daily life, leading to a significant migration of blacks to the North. Unfortunately, they would be met by the very hostility they sought to flee from. Often, hostility led to violence and riots in cities ranging from New York (1900) and Springfield, Ohio (1904), to Springfield, Illinois (1908), and Greensburg, Indiana (1906).

The birth of the **National Association for the Advancement of Colored People (NAACP)** sought to eliminate class distinctions and end Jim Crow laws. But during the first quarter of the twentieth century, the federal government failed to pass new legislation to protect black civil rights, and by the 1910s, the nation's capital was as segregated as any of the southern states.

Violence continued to be directed at black communities in both the North and the South. In 1917, a riot in East St. Louis claimed the lives of thirty-nine blacks and nine whites. Although its cause is clouded in rumor and innuendo, the consensus was that it resulted from white fears that black migrants would take their jobs. During World War I, African Americans were drafted but were reserved for mostly menial duties. Race relations would continue to deteriorate as black veterans returned home. In 1919 alone, ten black veterans were lynched in the South and fourteen burned at the stake.

During the first two decades of the twentieth-century African Americans were not the lone victims of vigilante violence, with numerous incidents targeting Native American, Hispanic, Chinese, and Jewish individuals. Among the most famous of these tragic stories was the case of Leo Frank in 1915. Frank was the scion of Jewish parents, born in Paris, Texas (location of another famous lynching), in 1884 and educated at Cornell University. In 1908, he moved to Atlanta, Georgia, to help his uncle in his pencil business. He married a local woman in 1910. Three years later, he was accused of murdering a thirteen-year-old employee named Mary Phagan. Unfortunately for Frank, he was reportedly the last person to see her alive and almost came apart at his police interrogation. From April to August 1913, the case dominated the Atlanta news. At the end of August, Leo Frank was sentenced to hang for the murder. But there were numerous questions and concerns expressed over the circumstantial evidence, inept defense and zealous prosecution from the start. One early suspect was used as the main witness against Frank. An African American custodial worker at the factory named Jim Conley changed his testimony several times. Especially suspect was the fact that, when Conley was brought in for questioning, he had apparently washed blood off his shirt in the basement. He spent six weeks in custody and eventually testified he helped Frank get rid of the body. During his more than half day of testimony, he regaled jurors with tales of Frank molesting plant workers in his office. There were fears that, when Frank was convicted that a mob might lynch him, so he was kept in his cell when the verdict was announced. After three appeals to the Georgia Supreme Court and two to the U.S. Supreme Court, it was up to the governor, who after careful deliberation converted Frank's death sentence to life in prison, setting off four days of unrest that forced the governor to leave the state. In 1915, another inmate tried to cut Frank's throat, but Frank was patched up by the prison doctor. The following month, on August 15, 1915, a horde of citizens from Mary Phagan's hometown of Marietta stormed the prison farm where Frank was held and drove him back to Marietta before lynching him the following morning. A number of Georgians thought Frank was tried, convicted, and lynched because he was Jewish. But for many others Frank was a symbol of regional resentment over industrialization and an example of how rich Jewish outsiders could influence the state's criminal justice system. More than a century later, the case remains one of the most tragic reminders of anti-Semitism in American history. As a postscript, in 1982, a Nashville, Tennessee, newspaper examined the case after interviewing an octogenarian who claimed to have seen Jim Conley carrying the girl's body the day she was murdered. He appeared to have lived with the fact all of those years that, if he had come forward with the information at the outset, Leo Frank would still have been a stranger to the justice system.[57] In 1986, a second application for a state pardon from the Georgia Board of Pardon and Paroles was approved absolving Leo Frank of the crime for which he was lynched.

The Chicago race riots

The Chicago riots of 1919 were among the worst of this era. Sociologist Morris Janowitz draws a distinction between the riots prior to the 1960s and more recent unrest, describing the earlier riots as communal in nature, involving "a direct struggle between the residents of white and Negro areas."[58] The riots were rooted in several years of tension between the races in which twenty-seven black dwellings had been targeted by bombers. Other complex issues played a part in the riots. Chicago's black population had more than doubled by 1919, but no new housing or tenements were erected to absorb the new residents. Meanwhile, thousands of black soldiers had returned from World War I determined to find a voice in the "new" America. In Chicago, housing, the psychological effects of war, and the organization of jobs and labor would collide with the racial politics of the early twentieth century. This contributed to a new development in race rioting: African Americans were now fighting back with fists and weapons.

Chicago was one of the northern cities most impacted by black migration in the aftermath of the war. A riot began on a summer afternoon when a young black man swam past an invisible line of segregation at a Chicago public beach and was hit with rocks and drowned. This set off three days of rioting that led to the deaths of twenty African Americans and fourteen whites. More than 100 people were injured, and numerous black properties went up in smoke.

Following the Chicago riots, the Chicago Commission on Race Relations was created in 1922 to investigate the causes of the riots and to seek solutions for preventing future conflagrations. The formation of this commission signaled a new element in criminal justice: commissions to study the reasons for race riots. Such commissions would become familiar to Americans following riots in Los Angeles (1964 and 1992), Newark,

Detroit, and Chicago and in the aftermath of Martin Luther King Jr.'s assassination in 1968. The Chicago Commission was comprised of eighty-one leading citizens, both black and white. Members examined the role of the police in the riots, riot control problems, examples of racial discrimination, and the generally poor relations between the races in Chicago.

The Camp Logan riot

On August 23, 1917, the Houston Police Department (HPD) experienced the bloodiest day in its history. Five Houston police officers lost their lives in what became known as the Camp Logan riot. However, there was much more to this story. The years surrounding World War I found HPD officers enforcing the law at their own discretion. Local black residents coped with the rampant discrimination by assuming what various scholars have described as "dissembling." Historian Ronald L. Davis defined this as the "psychological ploy in which blacks assumed positions and the appearances of non-confrontation," sometimes feigning irresponsibility and accepting a "demeaning racial etiquette."[59]

As the United States prepared for World War I, the War Department selected Camp Logan just outside Houston city limits for National Guard training. When local officials found out that the segregated all-black 24th Infantry Division of the 3rd Battalion (better known as the "Buffalo Soldiers") would be housed there, not all were happy in this Jim Crow city. The soldiers had distinguished themselves in a number of previous conflicts and had been given their due respect in its previous duty stations and were unaccustomed to the Jim Crow laws so prevalent in the South. When the 24th arrived, their barracks were not ready. Making matters worse was that they could not even find room and board and had to be sheltered in nearby neighborhoods.

The riot began along a street car line where passengers were expected to sit in segregated seating arrangements. Moreover, segregation laws zealously barred the black soldiers from movie houses, lunch counters, restrooms, and white-owned businesses. Further contributing to the tension was routine racial taunting by local residents and white workers at the camp under construction.

The HPD's well-earned reputation for brutality and the racism of the local resident created a perfect storm of hostility when the riot was ignited that torpid August day. When the day was over, sixteen whites had been killed (including five HPD officers) and only four troopers from the 24th were killed. It remains the only American race riot in which more whites than blacks perished. Its aftermath resulted in what is still the largest mutiny and the largest domestic court martial in U.S. Army history. Of the 118 men put on trial for murder, rioting, and mutiny, 110 of them were found guilty of at least one charge; 82 were found guilty of all charges and 29 sentenced to hang. Justice was swift. On December 11, 1917, thirteen black soldiers were escorted to a remote area outside San Antonio to a specially prepared gallows. Not one word was spoken and the executions were over in less than one minute. Subsequently, six other were hanged and the rest sent to prison. The last rioter was freed on April 5, 1938. As a result of the riot, the Army introduced a policy that would prohibit black soldiers from being stationed in the rural South. Camp Logan was dismantled by the end of 1918.[60]

Labor violence

According to professors Philip Taft and Philip Ross, "The United States has had the bloodiest and most violent labor history of any industrial nation in the world."[61] Industrial violence reached its zenith between 1911 and 1916 with major confrontations occurring in Michigan, West Virginia, and Colorado. Two of the bloodiest episodes occurred in Washington State in 1916, when members of the IWW tried to organize lumber workers. Both incidents led to killings on both side of the picket lines and subsequent prison terms for IWW members.

Between 1916 and 1920, labor union membership almost doubled to close to 5 million members, heightening tensions between workers and management. In one of the worst episodes of labor violence, a fifteen-hour battle between strikers and militiamen at Ludlow, Colorado, in 1914 led to the suffocation deaths of two mothers and eleven children during a fire in the strikers' tent city. Over the next ten days, miners took part in a violent episode of "class warfare" in southern Colorado. The culmination of thirty years of sporadic conflict in the region, the events at Ludlow shocked the nation.

Capital punishment

The introduction of the electric chair in 1890 appealed to the efficiency-motivated reformers of the Progressive era. During the first decades of the new century, the technologically efficient electric chair replaced the noose in most states. Meanwhile, studies by social scientists demonstrating the lack of deterrence value of the death penalty convinced nine more states to abolish capital punishment. But this second crusade against the death penalty would end in the aftermath of the Progressive era as concerns shifted to race riots, the Red Scare, and rising crime rates. Four states would in fact reinstate the death penalty in the early 1920s, while others would add new capital offenses. Despite the machinations of death penalty foes during the Progressive era, there was no real diminution of executions, which continued at the rate of 2 per 100,000 as in the late nineteenth century.[62] Two of the most famous death penalty trials of the century would take place in the 1920s (Sacco and Vanzetti and Leopold and Loeb).

The twentieth century began with a recrudescence of abolitionist activity against the death penalty. Throughout the Progressive era, abolitionists, such as lawyer **Clarence Darrow** (1857–1938), eloquently attacked capital punishment.

Clarence Darrow was one of America's greatest criminal defense lawyers. With little in the way of a formal legal education, Darrow rose to national prominence while representing radical leaders Eugene V. Debs (1895) and William "Big Bill" Haywood (1907). Over time, Darrow became disenchanted with his labor clients but continued to represent publicly unpopular clients. His participation in the Leopold – Loeb murder case in 1924 marked perhaps his greatest victory. In this case, two wealthy and intellectually gifted young men kidnapped and murdered a small boy, hoping to get away with the perfect murder and demonstrate their intellectual superiority. Both men were caught, and the public clamored for the death penalty.

Hired by Leopold and Loeb's wealthy parents, Darrow decided to forgo a jury trial and plead his case directly to the judge, asking for life in prison. According to most sources, this case was the first one in legal history to introduce the concept of psychopathology as a mitigating circumstance. Arguing that the defendants were unable to comprehend moral right from wrong (not the insanity defense), the attorney was successful in persuading the judge to sentence them to life in prison. Darrow would capture the nation's attention again the following year, when he defended biology teacher John T. Scopes, who was arrested for violating state law by teaching Darwin's theory of evolution.

The years surrounding World War I were marked by increased racial tensions and violent crime. Following the war, the media began to sensationalize crimes such as bank robbery, while law enforcement began to concentrate on better firearms training to combat the era's well-armed desperadoes. During the late 1890s, New York City police commissioner Theodore Roosevelt had introduced firearms training after a spate of "firearms-related accidents." But it was not until the 1920s that police firearms training, with the help of the National Rifle Association, began in earnest.

Notable trials

Sacco and Vanzetti trial (1921)

Nicola Sacco and Bartolomeo Vanzetti were Italian-born anarchists who immigrated to America and became involved in the radical politics of the World War I era. They settled into an Italian community in eastern Massachusetts but in 1917 moved to Mexico for a brief time to avoid military conscription, an act that would further stigmatize them as "draft dodgers" during their subsequent murder trial.

On April 15, 1920, a paymaster and a guard were gunned down during a payroll robbery in South Braintree, Massachusetts. The two gunmen made away with more than $15,000 and were seen getting into a car with several others while making their getaway. Witnesses identified the suspects as Italian in appearance. Police were already investigating a similar holdup by Italians in a nearby town and were soon focusing on a suspect's car waiting for repairs at a garage.

On May 5, Sacco and Vanzetti, along with two friends, went to pick up the car at the garage and were arrested as they returned home on a street car. At the time of their arrest, both were carrying handguns. During questioning at the police station, both gave evasive answers and reportedly acted "suspiciously." While the prosecution would use this to suggest guilt, defense attorneys emphasized that they did not even know what the charges were at this point (they were not told the charges until four months later, when they were arraigned by the grand jury) and thought they were being held because of their radical views. Nonetheless, both were charged in the earlier holdup attempt and the double murder during the payroll robbery.

Despite other possible suspects, police concentrated solely on gathering evidence on the two anarchists. This should not be surprising when gauging the current political climate. It is impossible to separate the Sacco–Vanzetti case from the events of 1918 and 1919, when the U.S. government in effect waged war against subversive political groups.

During the trial for the earlier robbery, Sacco had a solid alibi since he could prove he was at work at a shoe-making factory at the time. However, Vanzetti, who worked as a fish peddler, claimed he was selling fish that evening. But witnesses identified him as one of the robbers, and he was sentenced to twelve to fifteen years in prison. Both men would be forced to face trial for the Braintree murders when it was found that Sacco had taken the day off from work.

Anarchist supporters organized a fund drive and hired radical labor lawyer Fred H. Moore to defend the two men. In the opening proceedings of the trial, it was found that both anarchists lied about their guns and that Vanzetti's weapon was identical to that of the murdered guard's, which happened to be missing at the scene of the crime. Next, the prosecution made Sacco try on a cap found at the scene that was similar to one he regularly wore. Foreshadowing the famous O. J. Simpson trial faux pas when the prosecution had him try on gloves that did not fit, the prosecution had Sacco try on the cap, which was much too big, and as the defendant drew it down over his ears for effect, the courtroom burst into laughter, a rare instance of levity in the proceedings. Lawyers for the state then introduced a cap that was the same size as that found in Sacco's home. When it proved to be oversized as well, it seemed that the joke was on the defense.

During the ensuing proceedings, both Sacco and Vanzetti admitted lying about their reasons for visiting the garage because they feared deportation for radical charges if they told authorities they went to get the car to deliver radical literature. On July 14, 1920, the jury returned a guilty verdict on both murder charges, unleashing a wave of violent protest around the world. Embassies from Europe to South America were bombarded by letters of protest. Ten thousand police protected the American embassy in Paris against thousands of protesters.

During the next six years, numerous motions for a new trial were denied. In 1927, the Massachusetts governor reviewed the entire case while considering an appeal for clemency. Despite a whirlwind of protest, the governor concluded that the initial findings were fair and that Sacco and Vanzetti were guilty. On August 23, 1927, both men were executed in the electric chair. Concluding that much of the evidence was questionable and that the judge and jury were prejudiced against the defendants because they were aliens and anarchists, fifty years later, Massachusetts Governor Michael Dukakis signed a special proclamation admitting the unfairness of the trial.

To many critics, this case symbolized the failure of the criminal justice system as well as the inequity of capitalism. Over the past seventy years, debate over the case has continued as revisionists examined court transcripts and interviewed surviving participants. In the 1960s and 1980s, ballistics tests on Sacco's rusting forty-year-old gun seemed to determine that it did indeed fire a fatal round during the payroll robbery, calling into question the innocence of at least one of the "martyrs."

Summing up the impact of the case on American criminal justice, historian Vincenza Scarpaci stated,

> Perhaps the greatest legacy of the Sacco-Vanzetti case concerns state authorized violence: the methods used to bring criminals and terrorists to justice and efforts to ensure fair trial continue to place the political and judicial system in a delicate balancing act, attempting to protect the rights of the accused while also ensuring the public right to safety.[63]

To this day, there are still more questions than answers about the case: who were the other three bandits in the car? What happened to the $15,000? How and when did Sacco and Vanzetti plan the perfectly executed robbery? Even noted Harvard law professor Felix Frankfurter penned a critique of the American justice system in the 1920s in which he noted the prejudices, errors, and absurdities of the prosecution's case. Perhaps the most enduring legacy of this "crime of the century" are the twenty-three gouaches by artist Ben Shahn and a number of poems, plays short stories, and novels that commemorate the case for posterity. Although opinion is still split as to whether Sacco and Vanzetti were guilty, we can never know with certainty whether they took part in the murders. However, a survey of the physical evidence suggests that Sacco was probably guilty (he shouted "Long live anarchy" as he was put to death) and that Vanzetti was innocent (declaring his innocence to his death).

Conclusions

According to criminal justice historian Samuel Walker, during the Progressive era, "virtually every state completed the modern criminal justice system, establishing probation, parole, and the juvenile court."[64] But the Progressive reformers left behind a mixed legacy. An era in which it was believed that progress could be legislated saw a plethora of reform legislation, most of which was disappointing and rarely worked. Some urban reforms led to more efficient and non-corrupt civic government; however, the criminal opportunities of the Prohibition era that followed would nullify many of the Progressive reforms. In the end, most attempts to legislate morality led to profitability at the hands of organized crime groups. Most important, the criminalizing of once-noncriminal offenses, such as alcohol consumption and prostitution, fostered a widespread disrespect for law and its enforcement that would last for decades.

In the years following World War I, the abolition of the death penalty became a low priority, as tremendous changes in demographics focused the attention of reformers on poverty, civil rights, and political reform. In contrast to the idealistic prognostications of the reformers, the era actually deepened ethnic tensions and threatened civil liberties, dashing the hopes of the Progressive reformers. The war years intensified the old fears of nativist Americans who saw their vision of a strong, isolated country inhabited by white middle-class Protestants changing before their eyes. In response, they lashed out at those who had contributed to the transformation: immigrants, socialists, anarchists, communists, and radical labor organizers.

However, prison reformers are credited with breaking down the former punitive penal regime and by the 1930s could cite such victories as the end of striped uniforms, lockstep marching, silence, and draconian punishments outside the southern states. The onset of Prohibition in 1920 began the most disastrous period in twentieth-century law enforcement. Prohibition not only required the police to enforce laws that were almost impossible to enforce but also triggered widespread corruption in police departments throughout the nation.

As criminal justice historian Roger Lane has noted in his history of murder in America, "Progressive reforms had begun, and were always strongest at the local level, with attacks on municipal waste and corruption."[65] Local attempts at crime control and regulating morality stimulated the federal response to Progressive era social problems that found expression in broadly worded federal laws against drugs and prostitution as well as the creation of the Bureau of Investigation.

Point – counterpoint

Cossacks or Constabulary: The Pennsylvania State Police (1911)

The state of Pennsylvania had been beset by widespread rural crime, industrial disorder, and ethnic conflict since the 1850s. In 1905, the Pennsylvania State Police was created and charged with policing the entire state. However, for the most part, they patrolled the immigrant dominated mining districts, to their opposition they were the Cossacks and top their supporters the Black Hussars. In the following passages, state police advocate Katherine Mayo (1867–1940) describes a 100 percent American state police protecting the nation from foreigners, labor agitators, and people of color. In grim contrast, the Pennsylvania State Federation of Labor collected a number of letters and abstracts testifying to the brutality and xenophobia of the new force.

Source: Katherine Mayo, *Justice to All: The Story of the Pennsylvania State Police*, Boston, 1929, pp. 24–25, 31–34; Pennsylvania State Federation of Labor, *The American Cossack*, pp. 17, 18, 20–22

The period immediately following the enlistment of the command, laconically as it was summarized by Captain Groome, was a period long to be remembered by the men of the four Troops. Assembled in their four quarters of the State they now faced each other practically for the first time. A few of them had served in the regular army together, here and there about the world, but for the most part they were as strange one to another as to the questions that they had to solve.

"Now, you are the State Police Force," they heard. And the Superintendent, interviewing them severally and apart, had said, in a way that none of them will ever forget:

Your duty is to make the Pennsylvania State Police Force the finest thing in the world.

The Superintendent, in those memorable private interviews, had probed their minds as to their own conception of the work, giving them therewith certain illuminating flashes of his own purpose. He had indicated, also, a cardinal point or two, as:

It is possible for a man to be a gentleman as well as a policeman.

I expect you to treat elderly persons, women, and children at all times with the greatest consideration.

CRIMINAL JUSTICE IN THE PROGRESSIVE ERA

When once you start after a man *you must get him*.
In making an arrest you may use no force beyond the minimum necessary.
One State Policeman should be able to handle one hundred foreigners.

The general locations of the four Troop stations had been determined by two consider-ations: First, that the entire command should be so distributed as to reach as far as might be over the State; and, second but not less, that the regions of greatest criminality should be under the closest observation. A glance at the map shows that the posts are placed in the northern and southern halves of the eastern and western sections. These sections, by year-round criminal record, produced more murder, more manslaughter, more robbery, more rape, more burglary and thieving, more lawlessness and disorder of every sort, by far, than were shown by the records of the other parts of the Commonwealth. The central section of the State was and is mainly a farming region, with an old, homogeneous popu-lation, by no means free from trouble but not yet as ceaselessly troubled as the regions to the east and west.

The reason of this condition was obvious. In the eastern and western sections lie the great coal fields, with other allied industries. The coal fields, ever since their opening, have attracted an unending stream of foreign immigration. This immigration, at first largely tainted with lawlessness and turbulence, constantly undergoes a process of assimilation and improvement and is as constantly reflooded below by crude material of the roughest type.

In the beginning the major part of the mine laborers came from Ireland and from the Scandinavian peninsula. Out of the former of these two elements sprang that unspeakable society of murderers, the "Molly McGuires." After successfully maintaining a reign of night-mare for some years, these monstrosities were wiped out of existence by heroic methods, while the Irish in general, like the Scandinavians, are now but little found in their earlier walks, having graduated to more desirable employ. The Welsh passed quickly through the transition stage and beyond it. Then came the Slavs and the Italians, who practically filled the field at the period in hand.

Peoples totally unused in their countries of origin to any form of self-government, but accustomed on the contrary to see the sword of the king always bared before their eyes, Slavs and Italians alike here looked in vain for outward evidence of authority and law. Peoples used to the narrowest means, they here found themselves suddenly possessed of greater earnings than they had ever dreamed of before. Peoples used to free drinking, in climates where the effect of alcohol is less marked than here, they still continued that free drinking, and in strange raw mixtures of peculiar virulence. Liberty that they knew not how to use, money that they knew neither how to spend nor how to save, meant license, greed, drunk-enness – and through drunkenness all brutalities let loose.

The State Police has no purpose save to execute the laws of the State.

The State Police, therefore, was properly placed in the centers of greatest offense to the people. Its sole concern was to protect the people in their peace. At no time could it check in the slightest degree the movements of any person not breaking the law. A "strike" is a perfectly lawful proceeding, and the State's Police could have no cognizance of a "strike" other than of a picnic or a county fair. Called in by the proper authorities with convincing proof of need, the State Police would see to it, at picnic, strike, or country fair, alike, that general order was maintained by all present without fear, favor, or respect to persons. And therein lies the whole story.

The first activities of the four Troops now entering the field were of a general and various nature. Here they picked up a country store robber; there a stabber of a night watchman; again, a molester of women; a carrier of concealed weapons; a farm thief; a setter of forest fires; and always a little harvest of killers of song-birds, greatly to the derision of the imperfectly endowed. Meantime they were dealing constantly with the unassimilated foreign element, teaching it by small but repeated object-lessons that a new gospel was abroad in the land.

At feasts, christenings, balls, and the like, these alien people were given to heavy and prolonged drinking bouts, which ended often in wild and murderous disorder.

New Alexandria, Pa., Feb. 21, 1911.

Gentlemen:

State Police came to New Alexandria July 31, 1910, Sunday.

The State Constabulary are of no use in this country to farmers and workingmen. They make all efforts to oppress labor.

Six of them were stationed at this town for a period of two months for the benefit of the coal company. Their duty was in and around the works.

At the time they were here there was trouble between them and the miners. There was a camp located within two hundred feet of my house. There were three State Constabulary and two deputy sheriffs went into camp. They rode their horses over men, women, and children. They used their riot clubs freely on the miners without cause or provocation.

One of the men had to be sent to the hospital, one received a broken arm, one woman was clubbed until she was laid up for two weeks. At that time she gave birth to a child and remained in bed for four weeks after the birth of her child. They used their clubs on everyone that protested against their conduct and I was an eyewitness to the affair.

There were no lives lost and no one hurt before their arrival.

The majority of citizens are not in favor of the Constabulary.

I cannot see that anyone but the coal company is benefitted by the Constabulary.

Yours truly,
S. P. Bridge,
New Alexandria, Westmoreland County, Pa.
Latrobe, Pa., Feb. 13, 1911.

Report of Investigating Committee, Local No. 405, U. M. W. of A., as follows:

Question No. 1. The first arrival of the State Constabulary was at Bradenville, morning of April 22, 1910. On their arrival at Bradenville on said morning, they acted more like heathens than human beings. They drove their horses up on the sidewalks and knocked people in all directions, ordering people away from their own homes. They arrested one man for hollering "bah," drove others from the public highway and away from the street car station, regardless of who they were.

Question No. 2. The conditions before their arrival were good, no trouble having occurred whatever.

Question No. 3. No lives were lost prior to their arrival, and no property had been destroyed.

Question No. 4. There were four lives taken, namely: Mike Cheken, Mike Mizrak, one colored man and one deputy sheriff. After the arrival of the Constabulary the property loss was – three double houses at Superior No. 2, private property damaged by explosion, one small child lost its life, which occurred at 12 P. M. There was also damage done to the property of Mike Godula at Peanut Works, blowing down his bake-oven and fence, on the morning of July 4, 1910. There was dynamite found in the yard next morning.

Mary Riech lost her life at Superior No. 2, in an explosion which occurred on Jan, 27, 1911.

Two were blown up in Superior No. 2, between the 27th and 28th. The explosion damaged the houses and all the things in them. About ten minutes after there was about eighteen to thirty rifle shots fired at the house. Some went into the bed but no one was hit. After the explosion, the man came out on his porch and all of the company employees told him to go into the house.

There were people who saw them placing some dynamite against the house.

Signed by the citizens of Superior No. 2.

Noah Panizza,

Emrico Balarmene,

Tonie Debaco,

Mary Perodi.

Irwin, Pa., Feb. 21, 1911.

To the Legislature of Pennsylvania:

This is to certify that the following evidence is true, as given by different members of our Local Union, No. 2088:

1 The State Police came to Irwin about the 15th of June.
2 The condition of the town of Irwin was peaceable before the arrival of the police, no lives being lost or property damaged before they arrived, and the town being quiet until the arrival of the State Police.
3 I, Frank Nameska, was going home peaceably from the election board at the hour of 5.30 and was stopped by two State Police and compelled to be searched.

   The second time I was going to Irwin, with three other men and was stopped and asked where we were going. We said, "None of your business." One man jumped from his horse and said, you better go back. Then they pushed us about, trying to start a fight because we were out on strike, but we managed to get to Irwin after them pushing us about, during which I received a crack on the jaw.
4 I, Frank Fletcher, was going to Irwin and was arrested by two State Police, taken to burgess' office after being taken from jail for being drunk and disorderly, and forced to pay the sum of $6.75.
5 I, William Colliner, was at Rilton; when I came back to Irwin, I was arrested by the State Police and taken to Greensburg. After I was put in jail, I was released the next day.
6 I, David Thomas, was arrested and abused by the State Police on the 16th day of December. The State Police were taking a few men to the mines. I just asked the men if they knew that there was a strike going on. One of the State Police turned and hit me with a black-jack, bursting my head and I was taken to jail, then to 'Squire Davis. He put the case to Greensburg, where I was fined $14.14 for witness fees and $41.32 costs,

for assault and battery and resisting an officer. The State Police were dressed in citizens' clothes, not having any badge.

7   I, David Thomas, Jr., was coming down street and saw my father all over blood. I asked him what was the matter. He then told me of being hit by a man. I asked where the man was then. I was shown. I asked the man why he hit my father. I, not knowing that he was a State Police, asked him again what was the matter. The State Police said, "He is under arrest." Then I said, "Well, if he is under arrest, don't knock his brains out." Then the other State Police yelled out, "You are under arrest." I was then taken with my father to jail, but was let free.

The State Police acknowledged, at court, that they arrested the men without showing any badge or having on their uniforms.

8   The conduct of the State Police toward citizens not interested in the strike was favorable.

9   The names of the men abused are Mike Klemans, Frank Fletcher, Tony Fletcher, Frank Nameska, David Thomas, Jr., David Thomas, Sr., William Colliner, John Clark.

10   The conduct towards the strikers is very severe and on all occasions they tried to raise trouble on the slightest provocation, beating men, women, and even children.

11   About 85 percent, of the people of Irwin signed petition against the State Police.

12   Their conduct is very bad. Known to sit back of Brunswick Hotel and drink.

13   The presence of the State Police is favorable to the coal companies.

14   The farmers are not being benefitted at all by the State Police.

Key terms

Progressive era
Mann Act
Sullivan Law
Webb et al. v. U.S.
Sir Francis Galton
Red Scare
Espionage Act
Sedition Act
"silver platter"
Leonhard Fuld
Arthur Woods
Fred Kohler
Lola Baldwin
Samuel Battle
Black Hand gangs
Atlanta Penitentiary
Clarence Darrow
Chicago race riots
Triangle Shirtwaist
   Company fire

Harrison Narcotic Act
muckrakers
Pure Food and Drug Act
born-criminal theories
International Workers of the
   World (IWW)
A. Mitchell Palmer
Weeks v. U.S.
Boston police strike
Bruce Smith
August Vollmer
Bureau of Intelligence
Alice Stebbins Wells
teletypewriter
Thomas Mott Osborne
Leavenworth Penitentiary
Wall Street bombing
KKK reorganization
White Slave Traffic Act
Jack Johnson

Jim Crow
eugenics
Skinner v. Oklahoma
Wobblies
J. Edgar Hoover
exclusionary rule
police union movement
Raymond Fosdick
police professionalism
Arizona Rangers
Pennsylvania State Police
Burns National Detective Agency
American Prison Association
Mutual Welfare League
National Association for the
   Advancement of Colored
   People (NAACP)
Sacco–Vanzetti trial

Critical thinking questions

1 What criminal justice issues were Progressive reformers most concerned with?
2 Why were laws passed controlling so-called victimless crimes, such as prostitution and narcotics addiction? Discuss the transition from legality to prohibition of these vices.
3 Who were the "new dangerous classes?" What was their impact on the development of the "science" of eugenics?
4 Discuss the impact of the years 1919 and 1920 on the criminal justice system.
5 How did civilian police reformers such as Leonhard Fuld, Bruce Smith, and Raymond Fosdick impact police professionalism? Contrast their contributions with traditional police reformers such as August Vollmer and Fred Kohler.
6 Trace the development of state police forces in the early twentieth century.
7 Discuss the evolution of parole from indeterminate sentencing.
8 Discuss the following statement: Progressive reformers left behind a mixed legacy.
9 How did the criminal justice system change between 1895 and 1925?

Notes

1 "Jim Crow" referred to the de facto segregation that characterized the South. The name of Jim Crow was tied to a white actor in blackface who worked as a song-and-dance man in the 1830s. According to historian Lerone Bennet Jr., by 1838, the term was being used as a "synonym for Negro," enforcing the image of the African American as a "comic, jumping, stupid rag doll of a man."
2 Some of the critics of the journalists compared them to a character in John Bunyan's, *The Pilgrim's Progress*, who was too engrossed in raking muck to look up and accept a celestial crown, hence the moniker "muckraker."
3 For an excellent account of this tragedy, see Leon Stein, *The Triangle Fire*, New York: Carroll & Graf Publishers, 1962.
4 Mark Colvin, *Penitentiaries, Reformatories, and Chain Gangs: Social Theory and the History of Punishment in Nineteenth-Century America*, New York: St. Martin's Press, 1997, p. 174.
5 Although the term "white slavery" was often equated with "compulsory prostitution," beginning in the late nineteenth century, the origins of the term can be traced back to labor movements in the 1830s, when English and American laborers adopted the expression "to describe their low wages and intolerable conditions" in an era when criticism of the capitalist system was not uncommon. Mara L. Keire, "The Vice Trust: A Reinterpretation of the White Slavery Scare in the United States, 1907–1919," *Journal of Social History*, 35(1), Autumn 2001, p. 7.
6 Karen Abbott, *Sin in the Second City: Madams, Ministers, Playboys, and the Battle for America's Soul*, New York: Random House, 2007, p. 207.
7 Randy Roberts, *Papa Jack: Jack Johnson and the Era of White Hopes*, New York: Free Press, 1983, p. 144.
8 Ibid.
9 Timothy J. Gilfoyle, *City of Eros: New York, Prostitution, and the Commercialization of Sex, 1820–1920*, New York: W.W. Norton and Company, 1992, pp. 308–309.
10 Keire, 2001.
11 Abbott, 2007, p. 207.
12 Lawrence M. Friedman, *Crime and Punishment in American History*, New York: Basic Books, 1993, p. 328.

13 George J. Kneeland, *Commercialized Prostitution in New York City*, New York: Century, 1913, p. 34.

14 Albert Fried, *The Rise and Fall of the Jewish Gangster in America*, New York: Holt, Rinehart and Winston, 1980, p. 13.

15 Kneeland, 1913, pp. 34–35.

16 Fried, 1980, p. 13.

17 George P. LeBrun, (as told to Edwin D. Radin), *It's Time to Tell*, New York: William and Morrow, 1962, p. 105.

18 H. Wayne Morgan, *Yesterday's Addicts: American Society and Drug Abuse, 1865–1920*, Norman: University of Oklahoma Press, 1974, p. 8.

19 Mike Gray, *Drug Crazy*, New York: Routledge, 2010, p. 43.

20 Quoted in Friedman, 1993, p. 355. See also *Webb et al. v. United States, U.S. Reports 96*, March 3, 1919.

21 The term *eugenics* was first coined in 1883 by Galton but did not enter the American lexicon until the turn of the century.

22 Nicholas Wright Gillham, *A Life of Sir Francis Galton: From African Exploration to the Birth of Eugenics*, New York: Oxford University Press, 2001.

23 Nicole H. Rafter, *Creating Born Criminals*, Urbana: University of Illinois Press, 1997, p. 6.

24 Quoted in Friedman, 1993, p. 335.

25 Indiana passed new laws that incorporated new sterilization procedures in 1927 and 1931.

26 Rafter, 1997, p. 12.

27 Galton biographer Gillham, 2001 noted that eugenic experiments in America "were followed with interest by German race hygienists" (p. 355).

28 Friedman, 1993, pp. 338–339.

29 Robert K. Murray, *Red Scare: A Study in National Hysteria, 1919–1920*, New York: McGraw Hill, 1955, p. 233.

30 Charles H. McCormick, *Seeing Reds*, Pittsburgh: University of Pittsburgh Press, 1997, p. 54.

31 Ralph Keyes, *I Love it When You Talk Retro*, New York: St. Martin's Press, 2008, p. 242.

32 Kenneth D. Ackerman, *Young J. Edgar: Hoover, the Red Scare and the Assault on Civil Liberties*, New York: Carroll & Graf Publishers, 2007.

33 Curt Gentry, *J. Edgar Hoover: The Man and His Secrets*, New York: W.W. Norton and Company, 1991, p. 79.

34 Ibid., p. 103.

35 In 1961, *Mapp v. Ohio* would apply the exclusionary principle to all federal and state criminal trials.

36 Francis Russell, *A City in Terror: 1919, the Boston Police Strike*, New York: Viking, 1975.

37 James F. Richardson, *Urban Police in the United States*, Port Washington, WA: Kennikat Press, 1974, p. 69.

38 The most comprehensive and scholarly biography of Vollmer is Willard M. Oliver, *August Vollmer: The Father of American Policing*, Durham, NC: Carolina Press, 2017.

39 According to police historian Richardson, 1974, p. 79, Kohler borrowed this idea from the mayor and police chief of Toledo, Ohio, but "characteristically claimed it was his original idea."

40 Richardson, 1974, p. 79.

41 Gloria E. Myers, *A Municipal Mother: Portland's Lola Greene Baldwin, America's First Patrolwoman*, Corvallis: Oregon State University Press, 1995, p. 22.

42 Although Wells is generally regarded as the first woman given the title of police officer as well as the powers of arrest, in 1893, the Chicago Police Department gave police widow Marie Owens the title of police officer, albeit without any arrest powers.

43 Quoted in Arthur W. Sjoquist, *Los Angeles Police Department Commemorative Book: 1869–1984*, Los Angeles: Los Angeles Police Revolver and Athletic Club, 1984, p. 148.

44 The dance halls were one of the most popular entertainment spots for young men and women at the turn of the century. Here, for as little as a nickel, men and women could come and escape the

tedium of the twelve-hour workday. According to historian Albert Fried, by 1900, New York City had one or two on every block. Reformers would naturally target the immorality of the dance halls during the Progressive era.

45 Myers, 1995, p. 171.
46 W. Marvin Dulaney, *Black Police in America*, Bloomington, IN: Indiana University Press, 1996.
47 *1905 Acts of the Legislative Assembly of the Territory of New Mexico, 36th session*, Santa Fe: The New Mexico Printing Co., 1905, p. 31.
48 Larry E. Sullivan, *The Prison Reform Movement*, Boston: Twayne, 1990, p. 27.
49 Ibid., p. 31.
50 Sullivan, 1990; Marilyn D. McShane and Frank P. Williams, eds., *Encyclopedia of American Prisons*, New York: Garland Publishing, 1996, pp. 141–142.
51 Proceedings of the Annual Congress of the National Prison Association of the U.S., Albany, NY: Wm. B. Burford, 1906, p. 38
52 Miriam Allen DeFord, *Stone Walls: Prisons from Fetters to Furloughs*, Philadelphia: Chilton, 1962; Blake McKelvey, *American Prisons: A History of Good Intentions*, Montclair, NJ: Patterson Smith, 1977.
53 Thomas Mott Osborne, *Prisons and Common Sense*, New York: Lippincott, 1924.
54 Federico Varese, *Mafias on the Move*, Princeton, NJ: Princeton University Press, 2011, p. 112.
55 Arrigo Petacco, *Joe Petrosino: The True Story of a Tough, Turn of the Century New York Cop*, New York: Palgrave and Macmillan, 1974.
56 Michael Fiaschetti, *You Gotta Be Rough: The Adventures of Detective Fiaschetti of the Italian Squad*, New York: Doubleday and Doran, 1930, pp. 14–15.
57 Leonard Dinnerstein, *The Leo Frank Case*, New York: Columbia University Press, 1968; Steve Oney, *The Dead Shall Rise: The Murder of Mary Phagan and the Lynching of Leo Frank*, New York: Pantheon, 2003.
58 Quoted in Richard Maxwell Brown, ed., *American Violence*, Englewood Cliffs, NJ: Prentice Hall, 1970, p. 126.
59 Ronald L. Davis, "Creating Jim Crow: From Terror to Triumph, Historical Overview," www.africanamerica.org/topic/creating-jim-crow
60 Robert V. Haynes, *A Night of Violence: The Houston Riot of 1917*, Baton Rouge: Louisiana State University Press, 1976, p. 18; C. Calvin Smith, "The Houston Riot of 1917, Revisited," *The Houston Review*, 13(2), 1992, pp. 85–102; Mitchel P. Roth and Tom Kennedy, *Houston Blue: The Story of the Houston Police Department*, Denton: University of North Texas Press, 2012, pp. 68–76.
61 Philip Taft and Philip Ross, "American Labor Violence: Its Causes, Character, and Outcome," in *The History of Violence*, ed. Hugh Davis Graham and Ted Robert Gurr, New York: Bantam Books, 1969, p. 281.
62 Roger Lane, "Capital Punishment," in *Violence in America*, Vol. 1, ed. Ronald Gottesman, New York: Scribner, 1999, p. 201.
63 Vincenza Scarpaci, "Sacco and Vanzetti," in *Violence in America*, Vol. 1, ed. Ronald Gottesman, New York: Scribner, 1999, p. 77. For most comprehensive account of the crime and trial see Bruce Watson, *Sacco and Vanzetti: The Men, the Murders, and the Judgment of Mankind*, New York: Penguin Books, 2008.
64 Samuel Walker, *Popular Justice*, New York: Oxford University Press, 1998, p. 112.
65 Roger Lane, *Murder in America*, Columbus: Ohio State University Press, 1997, p. 211.

Sources

Abbott, Karen. 2007. *Sin in the Second City: Madams, Ministers, Playboys, and the Battle for America's Soul*. New York: Random House.

Ackerman, Kenneth D. 2007. *Young J. Edgar: Hoover, the Red Scare and the Assault on Civil Liberties.* New York: Carroll and Graf Publishers.

Appier, Janis. 1998. *Policing Women: The Sexual Politics of Law Enforcement and the LAPD.* Philadelphia: Temple University Press.

Asinof, Eliot. 1990. *1919: America's Loss of Innocence.* New York: Donald I. Fine.

Avrich, Paul. 1991. *Sacco and Vanzetti: The Anarchist Background.* Princeton, NJ: Princeton University Press.

Bennet, Lerone, Jr. 1984. *Before the Mayflower: A History of Black America.* New York: Penguin Books.

Brown, Richard Maxwell, ed. 1970. *American Violence.* Englewood Cliffs, NJ: Prentice Hall.

Caesar, Gene. 1968. *Incredible Detective: The Biography of William J. Burns.* Englewood Cliffs, NJ: Prentice Hall.

Carte, Gene E. and Elaine H. Carte. 1975. *Police Reform in the United States: The Era of August Vollmer.* Berkeley, CA: University of California Press.

Colvin, Mark. 1997. *Penitentiaries, Reformatories, and Chain Gangs: Social Theory and the History of Punishment in Nineteenth-Century America.* New York: St. Martin's Press.

Courtwright, David, Herman Joseph, and Don Des Jarlais. 1989. *Addicts Who Survived: An Oral History of Narcotic Use in America, 1923–1965.* Knoxville: University of Tennessee Press.

Davis, Ronald L. "Creating Jim Crow: From Terror to Triumph, Historical Overview." www.africanamerica.org/topic/creating-jim-crow.

Ellis, Edward Robb. 1975. *Echoes of Distant Thunder: Life in the United States 1914–1918.* New York: Coward, McCann and Geoghegan.

Fried, Albert. 1980. *The Rise and Fall of the Jewish Gangster in America.* New York: Holt, Rinehart and Winston.

Friedman, Lawrence M. 1993. *Crime and Punishment in American History.* New York: Basic Books.

Gentry, Curt. 1991. *J. Edgar Hoover: The Man and His Secrets.* New York: W.W. Norton and Company.

Gilfoyle, Timothy J. 1992. *City of Eros: New York, Prostitution, and the Commercialization of Sex, 1820–1920.* New York: W.W. Norton and Company.

Gillham, Nicholas Wright. 2001. *A Life of Sir Francis Galton: From African Exploration to the Birth of Eugenics.* New York: Oxford University Press.

Graham, Hugh Davis and Ted Robert Gurr. 1969. *The History of Violence in America.* New York: Bantam Books.

Grant, Robert and Joseph Katz. 1998. *The Great Trials of the Twenties: The Watershed Decade in America's Courtrooms.* Rockville Centre, NY: Sarpedon.

Gray, Mike. 1998. *Drug Crazy: How We Got into This Mess and How We Can Get Out.* New York: Random House.

Haynes, Robert V. 1976. *A Night of Violence: The Houston Riot of 1917.* Baton Rouge: Louisiana State University Press.

Keire, Mara L. 2001. "The Vice Trust: A Reinterpretation of the White Slavery Scare in the United States, 1907–1919." *Journal of Social History*, 35(1), Autumn.

Kennett, Lee and James LaVerne Anderson. 1975. *The Gun in America: The Origins of a National Dilemma.* Westport, CT: Greenwood Press.

Keve, Paul W. 1991. *Prisons and the American Conscience: A History of U.S. Federal Corrections.* Carbondale: Southern Illinois University Press.

King, Joseph. 1999. "Police Strikes of 1918 and 1919 in the United Kingdom and Boston and Their Effects." Doctoral diss., City University of New York.

Kneeland, George. 1913. *Commercialized Prostitution in New York City.* New York: Century.

Lane, Roger. 1997. *Murder in America.* Columbus: Ohio State University Press.

———. 1999. "Capital Punishment." In *Violence in America*, Vol. 1, ed. Ronald Gottesman, pp. 198–203. New York: Charles Scribner's Sons.

LeBrun, George P. (as told to Edward D. Radin). 1962. *It's Time to Tell.* New York: William Morrow.

Morgan, H. Wayne. 1974. *Yesterday's Addicts: American Society and Drug Abuse, 1865–1920.* Norman: University of Oklahoma Press.

Morris, Norval and David J. Rothman, eds. 1995. *The Oxford History of the Prison: The Practice of Punishment in Western Society*. New York: Oxford University Press.

Murray, Robert K. 1955. *Red Scare: A Study in National Hysteria, 1919–1920*. New York: McGraw Hill.

Myers, Gloria E. 1995. *A Municipal Mother: Portland's Lola Greene Baldwin, America's First Police-woman*. Corvallis: Oregon State University Press.

Oliver, Willard M. 2017. *August Vollmer: Father of American Policing*. Durham, NC: Carolina Academic Press.

Rafter, Nicole H. 1997. *Creating Born Criminals*. Urbana: University of Illinois Press.

Richardson, James F. 1974. *Urban Police in the United States*. Port Washington, NY: Kennikat Press.

Roberts, Randy. 1983. *Papa Jack: Jack Johnson and the Era of White Hopes*. New York: Free Press.

Rosen, Ruth. 1982. *The Lost Sisterhood: Prostitution in America, 1900–1918*. Baltimore: Johns Hopkins University Press.

Roth, Mitchel P. and Tom Kennedy. 2012. *Houston Blue: The Story of the Houston Police Department*. Denton: University of North Texas Press.

Russell, Francis. 1975. *A City in Terror: 1919, The Boston Police Strike*. New York: Viking.

———. 1986. *Sacco and Vanzetti: The Case Resolved*. New York: Harper and Row.

Sandburg, Carl. [1919] 1969. *The Chicago Race Riots, July, 1919*. Reprint, New York: Harcourt, Brace and World.

Scarpaci, Vincenza. 1999. "Sacco-Vanzetti." In *Violence in America: An Encyclopedia*, Vol. 3, ed. Ronald Gottesman, pp. 75–78. New York: Charles Scribner's Sons.

Schelzig, Erik. 2009. "Tennessee at Front of a Trend toward Looser Gun Laws." *Houston Chronicle*, December 12, p. A12.

Sjoquist, Arthur W. 1984. *Los Angeles Police Department Commemorative Book: 1869–1984*. Los Angeles: Los Angeles Police Revolver and Athletic Club.

Smith, C. Calvin. 1992. "The Houston Riot of 1917, Revisited." *The Houston Review*, 13(2).

Stein, Leon. 1962. *The Triangle Fire*. New York: Carroll and Graf Publishers.

Sullivan, Larry E. 1990. *The Prison Reform Movement: Forlorn Hope*. Boston: Twayne Publishing.

Taft, Philip and Philip Ross. 1969. "American Labor Violence: Its Causes, Character, and Outcome." In *The History of Violence in America*, ed. Hugh Davis Graham and Ted Robert Gurr, pp. 281–395. New York: Bantam Books.

Tuttle, William M. 1980. *Race Riot: Chicago in the Red Summer of 1919*. New York: Atheneum.

Walker, Samuel. 1998. *Popular Justice*. New York: Oxford University Press.

Ward, Nathan. 2001. "The First Last Time: When Terrorists First Struck New York's Financial District." *American Heritage*, December, pp. 46–49.

Watson, Bruce. 2008. *Sacco and Vanzetti: The Men, the Murders, and the Judgment of Mankind*. New York: Penguin Books.

Weiner, Tim. 2012. *Enemies: A History of the FBI*. New York: Random House.

Wilder, Harris Hawthorne and Bert Wentworth. 1918. *Personal Identification*. Boston: Richard G. Badger.

1920	1920	1921	1924	1924	1927	1928	1921
Nineteenth Amendment grants women right to vote	Wall Street bombing	Sacco and Vanzetti trial	*Leopold and Loeb* trial	Immigration legislation limits immigration to 2 percent of 1890 census; sets maximum quota at 150,000	Execution of Sacco and Vanzetti	Supreme Court approves Virginia statute authorizing sterilization of imbeciles	Tulsa race riot

TIMELINE

CHAPTER TEN

Crime and criminal justice in the crisis decades (1920–1940)

Learning objectives

After reading this chapter students should understand and be able to discuss:

- Why this era was branded the 1920s the "lawless decade" and the "Roaring Twenties"
- The expansion of federal law enforcement, particularly the FBI, during the 1930s
- The impact of the news media on perceptions of crime and violence
- The roots of America's "war on drugs"
- The impact of alcohol prohibition on the development of modern organized crime
- Why prison populations increased and how this stimulated the development of the federal prison system
- The rash of "crimes of the century" cases during this period
- The rise of police professionalism and new training programs for officers
- The impact of prison anti-labor legislation and the rise of the state-use system

The passage of the Eighteenth Amendment and the onset of **Prohibition** in 1920 led to what many observers have referred to as the "**lawless decade**." Others have described the 1920s and 1930s as "the crime control decades."[1] Prohibition would cast a pall over the presidencies of Woodrow Wilson, Warren G. Harding, Calvin Coolidge, and Herbert Hoover before being brought to an end in 1933 under the Roosevelt administration.

Following the Wall Street crash in 1929, America and the Western world seemed to be standing on the brink of an abyss. As America's farmers saw their dreams turn to dust, by

DOI: 10.4324/9781315148342-10

1921	1921–1941	1924	1924	1924	1924	1924	1925
J. Edgar Hoover transferred to the Bureau of Investigation	Fifteen state police forces created	Congress approves transfer of fingerprint records to FBI	Nevada introduces nation's first gas chamber	Teapot Dome scandal	J. Edgar Hoover appointed director of Bureau of Investigation	Publication of Edwin Sutherland's *Criminology*	*Carroll et al. v. United States* establishes right of the police to search a vehicle without a warrant if sufficient probable cause of illegal activity exists

1932, between one-quarter and one-third of America's workers stood in unemployment lines as the country's national output was pared in half.

During the 1920s and 1930s, crime emerged as one of the nation's greatest political and social issues as popular attention was focused on the exploits of bootleggers, gangsters, public enemies, and crime waves, both real and imaginary. One historian of the social bandit tradition noted that although the 1930s saw a sustained drop in serious crimes, the "concentration of famous fugitives and their infamous crimes [between 1933 and 1935] has no equal in the nation's history."[2] By the 1930s, law enforcement became a national obsession thanks to the publicity-minded genius of FBI director J. Edgar Hoover, who consciously projected the onset of a fearful crime wave. In response, Congress would broaden the mandate of federal law enforcement to include policing prostitution, drugs, and the sale of alcohol.

Until recently, many chroniclers of the 1920s and 1930s have persuasively perpetuated an image of a lawless land of tommy-gun-toting killers, when in actuality the 1930s was a safer era than the 1980s. The numbers spewed out by the publicity machine have long overshadowed a reality that would suggest that the numbers of violent and serious property offenses actually fell in the 1930s. America's homicide rate had doubled between 1900 and 1919, but in the 1920s, there was little increase and perhaps a slight decline. What had increased by the 1920s and 1930s was an awareness and fear of crime thanks in part to the omnipresent news media. Highly publicized "crimes of the century," such as the Lindbergh kidnapping, the St. Valentine's Day Massacre, and the Leopold and Loeb case, transfixed the country. Forecasting the modern era, newspaper and radio station owners had figured out that crime news sells. As Prohibition criminalized once-acceptable behavior, it just added to America's fixation on rising crime rates.

The years between World War I and World War II saw the federal government become increasingly involved in crime fighting. In 1929, President Herbert Hoover authorized the Wickersham Commission to direct the first "comprehensive survey of American criminal justice at the national level."[3] That same year, Hoover appointed Sanford Bates to lead the new U.S. Bureau of Prisons. During the next five decades, the federal correctional system would set the standards for state prisons.

On the national level, President Franklin D. Roosevelt exploited political and economic crises to maneuver through Congress a series of laws to promote economic recovery and reduce social and economic misery. The creation of the New Deal ran counter to the prevailing policy of laissez-faire, which placed limits on the federal government's power to set standards governing prices, pensions, wages, and labor relations. The New Deal empowered the federal government to assume more social welfare responsibilities at the expense of states' rights. Coinciding with the sharp rise in crime, New Deal principles would be

TIMELINE

1928	1929	1929	1929	1930	1930	1930	1931
O. W. Wilson professionalizes the Wichita, Kansas, police	Stock market crash and beginning of the Great Depression	St. Valentine's Day Massacre	Passage of the Hawes-Cooper Act	*Uniform Crime Reports* comes under management of Justice Department's Bureau of Identification	Seabury Investigation	Bureau of Narcotics created	Arrest of Scottsboro Boys

applied to criminal justice as well, leading to a revolution in law enforcement. Paralleling the growth of most federal agencies during this era was the expansion of the FBI in the 1930s and a burgeoning federal war against crime. During the early New Deal years, federal control over crime was expanded to include kidnapping (1932), crossing state lines to avoid prosecution (1933), interstate transportation of stolen goods (1934), and marijuana prohibition (1937).

The lawgivers

In the first half of the twentieth century, the court system saw a major shift in emphasis from property to personal rights. The Bill of Rights had little practical impact on government powers until the 1920s and 1930s, when the first amendments were given practical meaning by the law. It should not be surprising that this was the case since the Bill of Rights was aimed at the federal government and its policies. The federal government had little concern for individual rights until the Progressive era. Even the interpretation of the post-Civil War amendments was usually confined to economic issues (e.g., the Fourteenth Amendment and the *Slaughterhouse* cases). Historian David Bodenhamer, one of the foremost authorities on the rights of the accused, suggested that "the nationalization of the Bill of Rights traveled an uncertain course because the justices lacked a sure theoretical foundation for their decisions." He concluded that "there was no consensus on principles to guide interpretation of the amendments, in part because of the novelty of the idea that defendants' rights needed protection against state misconduct."[4]

Beginning in the 1920s, the Supreme Court held that states were bound by certain guaranties of the Bill of Rights. In 1923, the Court for the first time reversed a state criminal conviction on the grounds that the trial had departed from due process. Two years later, the Court issued two decisions that held that certain guarantees of the Bill of Rights were so fundamental as to be included in due process. Both decisions involved rights protected by the First Amendment.

Among the most significant challenges to search-and-seizure laws during the 1920s was the 1925 **Carroll et al. v. United States** Supreme Court ruling. In this case, a bootlegger by the name of George Carroll and some of his associates were arrested and convicted of violating Prohibition statutes after law enforcement officers seized sixty-eight bottles of whiskey and gin from his car during a search of his car without a warrant. The defendants charged that this search violated their Fourth Amendment rights and that the liquor found in the car should have been inadmissible as evidence in court. However, the Supreme Court upheld

1931	1931	1931	1931	1932	1932	1933	1933
Al Capone convicted of tax evasion after IRS investigation	Wickersham Commission issues *Report on Police*	San Jose State College opens first complete police major program	282 reported kidnappings	In wake of Lindbergh case, Congress makes kidnapping a federal crime when victim is transported across state lines	*Powell v. Alabama*	Kansas City Massacre	Prohibition ends

the convictions despite the absence of a warrant, citing the fact that the search of a moving vehicle is not the same as searching a home because crucial evidence can be moved quickly in moving vehicles and thus lost forever. Therefore, if there is probable cause of illegal activity, under what has become known as the "**Carroll Doctrine**," police can conduct a search of a vehicle, such as a car or a boat, without a warrant.

The campaigns against narcotics and alcohol shared many similarities in part because "both were first directed against the evils of large-scale use and only later against all use."[5] However, where the two efforts differed was in the realm of public opinion. Few Americans argued with the antinarcotics crusade, while temperance was a matter of vitriolic public debate for decades.

Drug prohibition

Individuals have used narcotics for medicinal, recreational, and religious purposes for millennia. As early as the eighteenth century, Spanish colonial officials were taxing and selling the coca leaf to pay for New World expansion.[6] During the nineteenth century, a number of new drugs were heralded as "miracle cures" and used to treat a wide assortment of maladies. It was not until the late-nineteenth century that Americans acknowledged that these opiate-laden drugs could be addictive.

Few states had any drug control statutes by 1930, but with the establishment of the new federal bureau, the states were encouraged to enact their own antidrug legislation. The following year, every state had introduced laws to restrict the sale of cocaine, and most also restricted the sales of opiates. However, drug enforcement was hampered by the lack of uniformity in state statutes and the weakness of enforcement strategies. By the late 1930s, thirty-five states had embraced the Uniform Narcotic Act, which regulated or prohibited cocaine and opium and their derivatives. Despite opposition to including marijuana on the list, most of the states had already enacted marijuana statutes.

There was little fear over marijuana use throughout the 1920s, although the federal government was expressing increased concern. By the 1930s, sixteen states, most with relatively large Mexican populations, enacted anti-marijuana legislation. Thanks in part to hysterical films such as *Reefer Madness* (1936) and recommendations by drug commissioner Harry Anslinger, a growing concern among the public and legislators led Congress to pass the **Marijuana Tax Act** in 1937. Although it made the recreational use of marijuana illegal, it did not become much of an issue until the 1960s. In fact, the **Bureau of Narcotics** opposed publicity campaigns by private organizations that portrayed the marijuana problem as out

1934	1934	1934	1935	1935
Congress empowers Bureau of Investigation agents to make arrests and carry firearms	Bank robber John Dillinger killed in Chicago	Bonnie and Clyde ambushed and killed in rural Louisiana	Bureau of Investigation renamed Federal Bureau of Investigation	FBI establishes National Police Academy

of hand and discouraged the creators of the "killer drug marijuana" posters from selling their materials.[7]

The chronicle of tobacco and its road to societal acceptance offers an instructive lesson as cultures around the world continue to regulate popular substances through prohibition and criminalization. Among the most widely used drugs in the contemporary world, tobacco and its related products have been targeted for centuries, with smokers sometimes facing severe sanctions for indulging. By the time Christopher Columbus reached the New World in 1492, tobacco was being smoked throughout the richly populated Americas. Its eventual spread to Spain led to what was probably the world's first recorded tobacco prohibition. In 1588, a Church decree was issued in Lima that prohibited

> under penalty of eternal damnation for priests, about to administer sacraments, either to take the smoke of . . . tobacco into the mouth, or the powder (snuff) into the nose, even under the guise of medicine, before the service or the mass.[8]

By the end of the sixteenth century, tobacco use was somewhat widespread in England, thanks to the peregrinations of English mariners and privateers. Its ubiquity would be instantly recognizable to anyone who has studied how the initial use of new drugs and stimulants makes the transition from a novelty to a craze. However, King James I made clear his objections to the "stinking weed," as he launched into screeds against its smell and the expectoration of smokers. The noted scientist Francis Bacon, in a time before addiction was understood, was among the first to comment on its habit-forming properties.

Other countries took tobacco use much more seriously. In 1643, Russian Tsar Michael prohibited its sale, ordering nose amputation for snuff takers and execution for persistent smokers.[9] A Chinese law from 1638 ruled that using or distributing tobacco was punishable by decapitation. Like marijuana today, prohibitions are constantly evolving, waxing, and waning. When the Manchu arrived from northeastern China in 1644, their affinity for tobacco, which had been well documented in their native Manchuria, ensured that their familiarity with the product would lead to its acceptance under Manchu rule. This turnabout contrasted sharply with the Russians in the first half of the seventeenth century, a time when smokers were faced with draconian punishments, ranging from splitting the lips of smokers to flogging them with a corded lash, known as the knout. Some were even castrated. Between 1865 and 1921, fourteen American states prohibited tobacco sales due to health concerns related to smoking by women and children.

1935	1936	1936	1937	1937	1937	1937	1938
Ashurst-Summers Act	Bruno Hauptmann executed	Movie *Reefer Madness* released	First Gallup Poll on death penalty finds overwhelming support	Marijuana Tax Act	*Norris v. Alabama*		*Johnson v. Zerbst*

Harry Anslinger and the Federal Bureau of Narcotics

Harry Anslinger (1892–1975) rose to national prominence as the first commissioner of the Bureau of Narcotics of the U.S. Treasury Department in the 1930s. Born in Altoona, Pennsylvania, after graduating from law school, Anslinger entered public service with the War Department before moving to the Treasury Department in 1926. In the 1920s, the association of the Narcotics Division with the Prohibition Bureau led to public disenchantment with the bureau in part because of the unpopularity of Prohibition as well as the ineptitude of its enforcement. During the early Prohibition years, Anslinger attended seminars on international drug and alcohol smuggling, which would lead to his appointment as commissioner of Prohibition in 1929. In 1930, Congress removed drug enforcement from the Prohibition Bureau and created a separate agency in the Treasury Department. Initially, the powers of the Bureau of Narcotics were limited to the enforcement of registration and record keeping laws. Following his appointment as commissioner of the Bureau of Narcotics, he embarked on a get-tough policy against drug abusers. During the 1930s, he led the crusade against marijuana, which culminated in the passage of the Marijuana Tax Act of 1937. During World War II, Anslinger made the unsubstantiated claim that the Japanese were using an "opium offensive" as part of a strategy to enslave conquered countries through drug trafficking. The U.S. government was sufficiently alarmed to grant him access to the Coast Guard, the U.S. Customs Service, and the Internal Revenue Service in his battle against the narcotics trade.

Alcohol prohibition

Deeply rooted in European social custom, alcohol prohibition was a subject of much contention, in stark contrast with anti-opiate legislation, which had only a brief history in Western culture. But the crusade for national prohibition was decades in the making. Recent research asserts that alcohol prohibition had many supporters and "inspired more fervor than any reform movement except the abolition of slavery."[10] The Prohibition movement saw its first national victory in 1913 with the passage of the Webb-Kenyon Act, which allowed dry states to interfere with the transportation of alcohol across their state lines. The following year, those concerned with the large amounts of narcotics in patent medicines celebrated the passage of the Harrison Narcotic Act, which required a doctor's prescription for the sale of controlled dangerous substances. In addition, Congress demanded drug manufacturers to register with the government and maintain sales records.

In December 1919, Congress approved the Eighteenth Amendment, which was ratified by the states the following year. Under the new law, in 1920, it became illegal to manufacture, import, distribute, or sell alcoholic beverages in the United States. However, it created a major paradox in that the amendment did not prohibit the purchase and consumption of alcoholic beverages. What is often lost on Americans as the 1920s fades into distant history is that private drinking was not against the law during the Prohibition years 1920–1933. According to the Eighteenth Amendment, what was prohibited was the manufacture, sale, or transportation of "intoxicating liquors," defined as any beverage with more than 0.5 percent alcohol. Beer had anywhere from 3 to 8 percent, wine 10 to 20 percent, and spirits 40 percent. Courts typically threw out attempts to make social drinkers guilty of conspiracy, concentrating instead on the suppliers. By 1916, saloons were banned in twenty-one states, but the enforcement of Prohibition was never fully financed and supported by the government, and the large breweries continued to make beer unimpeded. According to one Prohibition agent, it was easy to find alcoholic beverages in most cities in only half an hour.

Although Prohibition has been branded an unmitigated disaster for providing the opportunity for **organized crime** to thrive, it was not the total failure as popularly depicted. During Prohibition, public drunkenness all but vanished, and deaths and diseases from alcohol, such as cirrhosis of the liver, declined. Looming large in the face of historians who would suggest that Prohibition had more beneficial effects than negative ones, the increased fatalities from the deadly concoction of rubbing alcohol-based consumption of "bathtub gin" and the hundreds of killings associated with the rise of organized crime must be taken into consideration. One tabulation of Prohibition killings surpassed 1,100 civilians and 512 **Prohibition agents** between 1920 and 1932.[11]

The consumption of alcohol would not return to pre-Prohibition levels until the 1970s. In the early 1920s, public sentiment favored enforcement, but with the growing corruption and crime, public opinion changed, and in 1930, a poll of 5 million people found only 10.5 percent in favor of enforcement.

Impact of Prohibition on American society

Prohibition went far beyond simply transforming American crime and the criminal justice system. It had a great impact on the social interaction of men and women in mostly urban public spaces. Not only were the genders mingling in new social settings, but they were doing it often in the big cities. Even novelist Willa Cather observed that "Nobody stays home anymore."[12] Prohibition chronicler Daniel Okrent suggests "social life changed forever . . . the first time men and women were drinking together outside the home, at events where dinner wasn't served."[13] The same was true with the mixing of whites and African Americans. According to one New York City, the city's nightlife and jazz clubs did "more to improve race relations in the years than the churches, white and black, have done in ten decades."[14] At the so-called "black and tans," African American jazz musicians "integrated cabarets and nightclubs" in black neighborhoods and, like so many aspects of city living, rearranged the proprieties of urban living.

No business was associated with Prohibition drinking habits more than the "**speakeasy**," which became "ubiquitous" and "so indelibly part of American culture." For many Americans intent on going out for a good time, the speakeasy did more than just replace the traditional local saloon. One well-known critic described what went on in the speakeasy as the invention of "the party," a place where men and women congregated to "drink gin cocktails, flirt, dance to the phonograph or radio and gossip about absent friends."[15] According to the American social commentator H.L Mencken, the term "speakeasy" came from the nineteenth-century Irish expression, "speak softly shop." During Prohibition, it was used to describe any illegal drinking place where guests were expected to keep their voices down to avoid attention.[16]

The Wickersham Commission (1929–1931)

In 1929, former U.S. Attorney General George Wickersham (1858–1936) was selected to chair the National Commission on Law Observance and Enforcement. His dominant presence ensured that his name would become synonymous with police reform after the commission became better known as the Wickersham Commission. Although derided by some as "a monument to equivocation"[17] for its failure to reach any conclusions about crime and Prohibition, it is considered the first national commission to consider issues of crime and law enforcement in a serious manner as well as to make recommendations. Under President Herbert Hoover, the commission was given the task of proposing methods for the enforcement of the Eighteenth Amendment. In addition, the commission was charged with surveying the entire federal criminal justice system and examining the administration of justice in relation to the amendment. The Wickersham Commission recommended not repealing the Eighteenth Amendment but urged better methods of enforcing it.

Between 1929 and 1931, the commission produced a fourteen-volume report. Its most important findings related to policing were published in two volumes, *Report on Lawlessness in Law Enforcement* (No. 11) and *Report on Police* (No. 14). According to No. 11, the use of the third degree[18] was a violation of constitutional privileges. The commission recommended eleven solutions for eradicating procedures that often denied fundamental rights to suspects and defendants.

Report No. 14 was a critique of police administration and bore the stamp of August Vollmer, who was credited with directing the report and writing several of the chapters himself. The conclusions of this survey inveighed against the corrupting influence of politics on police organizations. Despite the noble intentions of the Wickersham Commission, most of its suggestions went unheeded. Its main legacy was informing the public that the criminal justice system needed to be reevaluated and improved. Among its harshest critics were police executives who found that many of the conclusions were hastily drawn.

The Seabury Investigation (1930)

The 1930 Seabury Investigation began as a probe of the New York Magistrate's Court after several judges were linked to mobster Arnold Rothstein and other organized crime figures. Judge Samuel Seabury concluded that not much had changed since the Lexow Committee investigation of the 1890s and that the New York City Police Department was riddled with corruption. Seabury had started his legal career as a champion of the poor and the labor unions before serving terms on the state supreme court and the court of pleas. His findings led to the dismissal of twenty members of the vice squad and the exposure of rampant political bribery and corruption among city leaders, including police commissioners and the mayor.[19]

Other scandals involving corrupt judges led to the adoption of a plan for selecting judges that had been proposed almost twenty years earlier. According to the plan endorsed by the American Bar Association and the American Judicature Society, judges would be selected by a merit plan that allowed voters some choice in the selection of judges through nonpartisan elections. Judges would in this way run on their records. In 1940, several cities in Missouri adopted a plan that allowed an impartial committee of lawyers and laypeople to compile a list of qualified candidates when there was a vacancy and submit the list to the governor for selection.

Law enforcement

Perhaps the greatest development in policing in the 1920s and 1930s was the growing involvement of the federal government in law enforcement. While the expansion of the FBI is well documented, other federal agencies saw their duties change because of the exigencies of Prohibition- and Depression-related crime. Between 1920 and 1933, the Bureau of Alcohol, Tobacco, and Firearms, which traces its origins back to 1862 (Alcohol, Tobacco, and Tax Unit), saw considerable action disposing of illegal whiskey and arresting bootleggers. Meanwhile, the Customs Service was kept busy trying to stem the flow of illegal liquor into America by boat. The Internal Revenue Service (IRS) enjoyed one of its brightest moments in the 1930s with the conviction of Al Capone on income tax evasion. And in 1940, the Immigration and Naturalization Service became part of the Department of Justice.

Also reflecting the influence of the police professionalism movement was the emphasis placed on professional police training programs at various levels of government. State police forces led the way in implementing professional training programs in the 1930s. As early as 1931, San Jose State College boasted the first complete police major program, and in 1935, the FBI introduced an academy for training local police officers.

J. Edgar Hoover and the FBI

The Bureau of Investigation grew gradually during its first decades. The Mann Act (1910), World War I, and the Russian Revolution saw the expansion of the bureau's role in federal law enforcement. In these years, the bureau investigated white slavery, espionage, sabotage, and draft violations. In 1919, the force was empowered to investigate interstate motor vehicle theft with the passage of the National Motor Vehicle Theft Act.

The bureau underwent growing pains in the 1920s, and to lead the organization into the new era, J. Edgar Hoover was selected as director in 1924. Hoover brought professionalism to the agency, establishing rigid codes of conduct and replacing the seniority-based system of promotion with one based on merit. Under his direction, special agents were required to be college educated, with degrees in law or accounting. Born in Washington, DC, J. Edgar Hoover (1895–1972) graduated from law school in 1917 and joined the U.S. Department of Justice, where he would devote the next fifty-five years of his life, forty-eight of them as head of the FBI. Hoover rose to prominence as head of the Justice Department's Intelligence Division under Attorney General A. Mitchell Palmer. During his first years under Palmer, Hoover oversaw a campaign of persecution of foreigners who had been identified as communist sympathizers. Mass arrests and the trampling of constitutional protections resulted in hundreds of deportations and illegal searches and seizures. It was in this period that Hoover developed a predilection for maintaining secret files on individuals under investigation, a practice that would haunt civil libertarians for the next half century. In 1921, he was transferred to the Bureau of Investigation, where he served as assistant director. Following a series of scandals, Bureau director William Burns retired in 1924, and Hoover took the reins, inaugurating a new era in professionalism that introduced the latest scientific methods of detection, expanded the fingerprinting bureau, and began the hiring of better educated agents. In 1924, Congress approved the transfer of fingerprint records at Leavenworth Federal Prison and the criminal records maintained by the International Association of Chiefs of Police to the FBI. The collection of over 810,000 records became the nucleus of the FBI Identification Division, created in 1924. In 1932, an FBI laboratory was established to aid federal and local investigations through the scientific analysis of blood, hair, firearms, handwriting, and other types of evidence.

In 1930, the power of the FBI was enhanced by a congressional act that required police agencies to compile crime statistics that would be disseminated through the FBI *Uniform Crime Reports*. This proved a major coup for Hoover's FBI. Although these reports have come under fire as being flawed because of their reliance on only crimes known to police, these yearly reports represent America's first national crime records system.

Throughout the 1930s, Hoover concentrated his war on crime on bank robbers and high profile crimes, targeting such "public enemies" as Pretty Boy Floyd, Machine Gun Kelly, and Baby Face Nelson. One historian commented that John Dillinger "became the poster boy for new anticrime legislation."[20] According to Elliot Gorn, "Hoover won the publicity war, at least in the short-term, and bringing down Dillinger became the FBI's founding myth."[21] A genius at public relations, Hoover convinced Hollywood to produce a series of films promoting the traditional image of the FBI agent as incorruptible and professional. In 1935 alone, more than sixty films fostered this portrait, including the James Cagney vehicle *G-Men*.

Hoover proved a master at promoting the FBI by enhancing the federal role in law enforcement. Rising crime and repercussions from the 1933 **Kansas City Massacre** (covered later in this chapter) led Congress to enact a wave of legislation in 1934 that increased the power and prestige of the FBI. Agents were henceforth given full arrest powers and the authority to carry firearms, and new laws significantly expanded the number of federal crimes as well as the FBI's jurisdiction. Subsequently, it became a federal crime to cross state lines to avoid prosecution, to extort money with telephones or other federally regulated methods, to rob a federal bank, or to transport stolen property valued at over $5,000 across state lines.

During the Prohibition and Depression years, the FBI focused much of its attention and energies on the pursuit of "public enemies," such as John Dillinger, the Barker gang, Pretty

Boy Floyd, Machine Gun Kelly, and other media sensations. Although Kelly was credited with introducing the **G-men** (government-men) moniker in reference to the FBI, its origins can be traced to earlier sources. All the bureau's functions were consolidated and transferred to the Division of Investigation in 1933, and on March 22, 1935, it was renamed the Federal Bureau of Investigation.[22]

One of the unanticipated results of the growth of the FBI was the diminution in importance of the U.S. marshals, America's first federal crime fighters. As Prohibition ended in 1933, the bureau had reached national prominence. Under Hoover's direction, the FBI became increasingly specialized and professionalized. Unable to keep pace with these developments, the U.S. marshals were forced to make the transition to little more than process servers and court policemen.

Prior to America's entry into World War II, the FBI was authorized to gather information regarding potential **espionage** activity. With more than 1 million aliens from Axis countries residing in America, the FBI soon focused its attentions once more on spying on American residents. Between 1933 and 1937, the FBI investigated an average of thirty-five espionage cases per year. But as the war heated up, so did FBI investigations, reporting almost 20,000 cases of suspected espionage during the war years.

Hoover took one of his most controversial steps when President Roosevelt removed the information gathering limitation on the FBI, allowing the bureau to investigate individuals for their beliefs rather than actual deeds. However, their pursuit of Nazi agents during the war would lead to some spectacular successes, including the 1941 destruction of one of the largest spy rings to operate in the United States.

Frank Wilson: Internal Revenue Service agent

Despite the best efforts of the FBI and the Chicago Police Department, Al Capone (1899–1947), America's public enemy number one and the architect of perhaps 300 unsolved murders, was finally brought to justice by agents of the **IRS** in 1931. Long pursued by Prohibition agent Eliot Ness and his "**Untouchables**," it was not until IRS agent **Frank J. Wilson** (1887–1970) convinced a Capone employee to testify to Capone's illicit income that the crime boss was brought to justice. Thanks to a 1927 Supreme Court case that ruled that income from illegal transactions was taxable, the IRS used its agents to demonstrate that Capone had cheated the IRS, and on October 24, 1931, he was sentenced to eleven years in prison, effectively ending his reign as Chicago crime boss. Best remembered as the IRS agent that nabbed Al Capone, Frank Wilson joined the U.S. Treasury Department's Intelligence Unit in 1920. Ten years later, he was given the task prosecuting Capone using a 1927 Supreme Court decision that made illegal income subject to income tax. Since Capone had not filed income tax returns for several years, did not have any property or bank accounts in his own name, and had no endorsed checks, Wilson had quite a challenge ahead of him. Without a paper trail, he based his investigation on his estimate of net worth and net expenditures. Capone got wind of the investigation and hired a hit team to kill Wilson. However, he was pressured by associates to withdraw the contract. Wilson soon got his man, and Capone was off to prison in 1931. Wilson also played a prominent but unheralded role in the Lindbergh kidnapping investigation by insisting that the serial numbers of the ransom money be recorded. In 1936, he was selected to head the U.S. Secret Service and, during his eleven years on the job, reduced counterfeiting to an all-time low. He retired in 1947.[23]

State policing

The proliferation of the automobile in the 1920s led many states to establish police agencies to handle traffic problems. Maryland created the first of these in 1916 and was followed by six more states in 1921. These highway patrol units were typically small, unarmed, and restricted to enforcing state highway laws.[24] The state police movement lost momentum between 1923 and 1928, with only seven states establishing such units, most of which were of the highway patrol variety.

The onset of the Depression stimulated the state police movement, leading to the creation of fifteen state forces between 1929 and 1941. Of these, twelve were along the highway patrol model. A new pattern also developed in which earlier state forces were reorganized into larger forces. Some states formed highway patrols or state police forces to replace more specialized units, while other opted to increase existing manpower or to ease limits on police powers.

The evolution of the Texas Rangers offers an excellent example of the need for police departments to reorganize to meet a changing social climate. Between 1919 and 1935, the Rangers were faced with new social problems, including labor strikes, Mexican border raids, Prohibition violations, and surging Ku Klux Klan activities, as Texas made the transition from the frontier era. By the 1930s, the Texas Ranger tradition was in dire need of updating. Traditionally undermanned, their numbers were cut back and were in danger of obsolescence because of urbanization and modern science. With the introduction of the automobile and the train, the Rangers' days as an effective mounted police unit became a nostalgic memory, and in 1935, they were consolidated into the Texas Department of Public Safety.

As 1941 came to an end, each state had developed some type of police force based on either the state police or the highway patrol model. Managing to stay above the political fray and maintaining good relations with the public, according to historian David R. Johnson, "until the 1940s, at least, the state police were America's elite lawmen."[25]

Drug enforcement

The forerunner of today's Drug Enforcement Administration (1973), the Federal Bureau of Narcotics (FBN) was established in 1930 under the direct control of the Treasury Department. Most studies trace the inception of federal drug enforcement to the 1914 Harrison Narcotic Act. Drug enforcement began the following year, and by the 1920s, federal agents were homing in on Chinese opium smugglers. At the time of the **Volstead Act** and the inauguration of Prohibition in 1920, the Narcotics Division of the Prohibition Unit of the Revenue Bureau consisted of 170 agents and 17 offices. In 1922, the drug agents saw their power expanded with the passage of the Narcotic Drugs Import and Export Act. Following a scandal in which drug agents were arrested for accepting payoffs from drug dealers, Congress established the Bureau of Narcotics in 1930 and removed drug enforcement from the Bureau of Prohibition.

Prohibition enforcement

Once Prohibition was legislated into reality, it dawned on most observers that it was virtually unenforceable. Unpopular with both the public and organized crime, Prohibition agents were drawn from a relatively weak pool of applicants. The qualifications and pay were so lackluster that many agents accepted bribes and kickbacks. One agent was reportedly offered $300,000 per week. In an era characterized by corruption, it should not be surprising that many agents were attracted by the lucrative prospects for graft. The Treasury Department fired more than 700 agents for corruption between 1920 and 1928. The following year, the Department of Justice took over the enforcement of Prohibition.

Eliot Ness and the "Untouchables"

No crime fighter captured the public's imagination during the Prohibition years more than Eliot Ness (1902–1957), who rose to prominence as head of Chicago's "Untouchables" during the heyday of nemesis Al Capone. After being selected to lead a special Prohibition unit, Ness personally selected members of his unit. In Chicago, Eliot Ness reportedly had to go outside the Windy City to find enough suitable agents to fill the ranks of the Untouchables. The Untouchables received its moniker in 1930 following an incident when mobsters tossed a bomb into a vehicle containing two members of the team. Tossing the bundle back into the gangster's car, the Prohibition agents rushed back and reported the incident to Ness. He wasted no time in relating the story to local newspapers that the dubbed the crime unit with its famous name.

Despite the recognition accorded the Ness legend, the Untouchables, as with most Prohibition-oriented law enforcement units, was rather ineffective in its war against Capone's bootleg empire. Nonetheless, his crew did achieve several victories, such as causing Capone's alcohol production to drop by 80 percent, forcing him to buy overpriced liquor elsewhere. Following Capone's conviction by the IRS, Ness turned to Capone subordinates such as Frank Nitti and later to moonshine operations in America's heartland.

Ness and his Untouchables made great newspaper copy but were rather underwhelming in the war against alcohol. Ness claimed to have survived three assassination attempts by Capone's henchmen, including a drive-by, a car bomb, and a run over. However, recent research suggests these are rather spurious claims since Capone had ordered his men not to resist federal agents. Moreover, the Chicago mob had numerous professional killers, "and while Ness's car was vandalized and other attempts were made to scare him, the fact that he and his men lived to tell about it indicates that there were no serious efforts to kill" him or his team.[26]

He would have more success as public safety director in Cleveland, Ohio. Following the repeal of Prohibition, he moved to Cleveland in 1935 and made short work of a police department riddled with corruption, forcing several hundred policemen to resign and sending at least a dozen officers to state prison. By the 1940s, his squeaky-clean image had been tarnished by divorce and a drunk driving case, and he left law enforcement in 1942.

Izzy and Moe: Prohibition agents

Two of the most famous Prohibition agents were New Yorkers Izzy Einstein and Moe Smith, better known as Izzy and Moe. The pair were credited with making a total of 5,000 arrests. Isadore "Izzy" Einstein and Moe Smith were two of the most successful and honest Prohibition agents at a time when 706 agents were dismissed for corruption and incompetence. Both weighed well over 200 pounds, leading to their monikers "Tweedledum" and "Tweedledee." They made great newspaper copy during a time when there was little good news to report. Disguised as rabbis, bootleggers, or football players, they were credited with confiscating 5 million bottles of contraband liquor and making thousands of arrests. In order to successfully prosecute liquor scofflaws, it was necessary to produce samples of evidence in court. The pair's modus operandi began with gaining entry to a speakeasy. After ordering a drink, they would pour the illegal beverage into a funnel connected by a tube to a flask hidden in one of the agent's back pockets. They were so successful that other cities soon coveted the duo. They set the record for the quickest bust in New Orleans, where they made their first arrest thirty-five seconds after arriving. In the end, their careers were short-circuited because of their penchant for publicity, and they resigned in 1925.

Criminology and police professionalism

Shortly after the turn of the twentieth century, the more theoretical field of criminology emerged, with its emphasis on the behavioral and social aspects of criminal activity and the accompanying explanations for its causes. In the 1920s, the earliest criminology textbooks were written by sociologists such as Edwin H. Sutherland (1924), John Lewis Gillin (1926), and Talcott Parsons (1926). Between 1930 and 1950, criminology continued to develop as an academic discipline but was confined to university sociology programs.

During the early 1900s, the first hesitant steps were taken toward developing schools for training law enforcement officers. As previously mentioned, August Vollmer initiated the first college-level training programs for police in 1908, when he established America's first formal training for police officers with his **Berkeley Police School**, a forerunner of in-service and academic programs in California. The **Great Depression**, however, halted the further development of police and criminological studies program at the University of California at Berkeley.

As Vollmer became increasingly identified with academe in the 1930s, he began to lose some of his credibility among leading police figures. His efforts to establish a professional school of criminology at Berkeley were obstructed both by economic hard times and by the intransigence of police leaders who felt that he was concerned more with publicity than with police training. His goal of creating a professional police school where police personnel could be trained at the higher administrative levels eluded him at Berkeley throughout the 1930s. However, his former students carried his work into the 1940s. In 1939, Vollmer's position at Berkeley was filled by his protégé **Orlando Wilson**. Formerly a police officer in Berkeley, Wilson studied engineering before returning to policing in 1928. Following Vollmer's example, he advocated the use of higher education facilities for police training whenever possible. Between 1928 and 1939, Wilson professionalized the Wichita, Kansas, Police Department and then returned to academic work. In 1936, during his tenure at Wichita, he persuaded the political science department at the Municipal University of Wichita to integrate courses such as criminal law, patrol practices, traffic control, police administration, and identification procedures into the existing curriculum.

In 1939, a Bureau of Criminology was organized within the Department of Political Science at the University of California at Berkeley, although eleven years would pass before a separate School of Criminology offered degrees. Wilson was appointed a professor of police administration in 1939 and in 1950 was promoted to dean of the School of Criminology. The Berkeley Police Program spurred other schools into action. By the end of the 1930s, the University of Chicago, Indiana University, Michigan State University, San Jose State University, and the University of Washington had established criminal justice programs. Although they adhered in part to Vollmer's program, they emphasized the practitioner and training components of the curriculum.

Corrections

Throughout American history, African Americans have been disproportionately represented in the prison system. As more blacks left the South, northern prison statistics reported that blacks were imprisoned at a higher rate than whites for the same crimes. One historian suggests that because World War I drastically reduced immigration, northern industrialists turned to the South for unskilled labor, leading to a new migration of blacks to the North.[27] Trading one region's racism for another, many of the migrants were victimized by the discrimination practiced by social and legal agencies in the North. This in turn would be reflected by the increase of blacks in northern prisons in the postwar years. According to the U.S. Bureau of the Census, in 1926, African Americans made up 9.3 percent of the adult population but 31.3 percent of the prison population.[28] Meanwhile, the South persisted with the highest rates of execution and overall imprisonment. Conversely, the South had the highest regional rate of crime and violence.

As the nation's economy plunged into the depths of depression, the country's rate of imprisonment rose from 79 to 137 per 100,000 in the years between 1925 and 1939. According to national surveys, the United States contained almost 4,300 penal institutions by 1933. Out of a total prison population of 233,632, there were 137,721 housed in state penal institutions.[29]

While prison camps and leasing continued to dominate southern penology in the 1920s, the 1920s and 1930s saw the introduction of the "**new penology**" in many northern states with the implementation of the concepts of diagnosis and classification. Specialized personnel, such as psychologists and psychiatrists, were introduced to the prison environment as well. By 1926, 112 prisons employed either a psychologist or a psychiatrist. The dark side of these figures is that the professional-to-inmate ratio was too small to make much of an impact. The same was true with classification. Although the intention of classifying prisoners by psychological types was commendable, again, because of the dearth of qualified therapists on prison staffs, there was little hope of effective treatment.

Reform efforts directed at classification, education, vocational training, and discipline made little headway in the interwar years, leading noted prison educator Austin McCormick to report in 1929 "that prison education was a failure."[30] While most of the vestiges of the Auburn system, including lockstep marching, striped uniforms, and silence, were eliminated, many prisons continued to use solitary confinement in the "pit" or "hole" during the 1920s and 1930s. Although new prison routine allowed for more freedom, including communication between inmates, athletics, and exercise, as late as 1926, prisoners in Ohio and Illinois were punished in solitary confinement in small cages, nourished on a starvation diet of bread and water.

The Big House

Between 1910 (when the expression "Big House" had become part of the underworld lexicon) and 1930, America's prison population had more than doubled. By 1930, in fact, there were as many Americans behind bars as there were in the military,[31] the majority in Big Houses. More than one-third of the nation's convicts were housed in 12 state facilities that could hold more than 2,000 inmates each, scattered across the country. Columbus, Ohio was home to the biggest of the Big Houses, with more than 4,300 inmates crammed into cells designed for one-third that number. The huge capacity of prisons, many in Midwestern states such as Indiana, Missouri, and Illinois, as well as California and Oklahoma saw the development of more diverse populations, often leading to complicated social divisions among the inmates. Managed by a new generation of penal professionals instead of political appointees, prisons such as San Quentin and Sing Sing went to great lengths to root out abusive punishment and prison labor. At the same time, these institutions attempted to integrate mass production into the practice of incarceration.

Prison overcrowding and the rise of minimum sentencing

During the 1920s, most of the nation's prison populations rose sharply. New York's prisons increased from 1.598 to 6,618 in just 7 years, a 44 percent increase. Illinois's inmate population nearly doubled and Ohio's rose 120 percent. In 1929 and 1930, America's Big Houses experienced some of their worst uprisings. During a ten-month span between July 22, 1929, and April 21, 1930, prison violence broke out in New York's Auburn and Clinton (Dannemora) prisons; Leavenworth, Kansas; Canon City, Colorado; and elsewhere. These were topped off by an arson at the Ohio State Penitentiary on Easter Monday 1930 that took the lives of 322 inmates, the worst prison disaster in American history. At the time of the Columbus, Ohio, conflagration there were nearly three times as many inmates as the institution was meant to hold. By most accounts, prison overcrowding was at the root of these disorders.

It was no coincidence that some of the worst riots took place in New York State, where, due to new legislation, more inmates were doing time as four-time losers than ever before. In 1926, the New York State Crime Commission, better known as the "Baumes Commission" after its eponymous chairman, State Senator Caleb H. Baumes, introduced stringent sentencing provisions, including the particularly punitive "fourth offender act," which mandated that whenever and individual was convicted for the fourth time it automatically resulted in a life sentence, thus taking all sentencing discretion out of the judges' hands. Another punitive Baumes Law was the "second offender act," which kicked in when an individual was convicted for a second felony. Making matters worse in New York was the fact that the Commission had reduced a number of rules that greatly reduced good conduct time.

At the time of the 60th Annual Meeting of the American Correctional Association, six months after the Ohio prison fire, speakers castigated the Big Houses and the systems that created them. It was not difficult to pinpoint the underlying causes for the riots, which included inadequate and inedible food, lack of work, abolition of good time and the merit system, denial of parole, and long and hopeless sentences.[32]

Prison industries

Further augmenting the serious overcrowding issues was the number of inmates sitting idle. At the Ohio State Penitentiary, for example, at the time of the fire, there were 1,200 to 2,000 non-working prisoners at any given time.[33] Since the early nineteenth century, prison industries flourished in America, with many prisons showing a healthy profit. Perhaps the biggest change in prisons during the interwar era was the rapid decline in the number of inmates employed in prison industries. According to prison historian Blake McKelvey, between 1895 and 1923, anti-labor legislation saw a drop in employment from 72 to 62 percent. Leading the opposition against prison labor was organized labor, which recognized the unfair business competition that prisoners posed to free paid workers.[34] Between 1932 and 1940, the proportion of productively employed prisoners in state and federal institutions fell from 52 to 44 percent. Paralleling this development was the value of goods produced, which dropped by 25 percent.

In 1929, Congress passed the **Hawes-Cooper Act**, which allowed any state to ban the sale of any goods made in another state's prison within its borders. Although it did not become effective until 1934, most states had already passed legislation placing limits on the sale and shipping of prison products. The passage of the **Ashurst-Summers Act** in 1935 would strengthen Hawes-Cooper by prohibiting transportation companies from accepting prison products for transportation into any state in violation of the laws of the state and provided for the labeling of all prison products shipped in interstate commerce. Despite the intentions of these statutes, the death knell of prison industries would sound with the 1929–1933 Depression, when state legislatures responded to the needs of unemployed free workers. Twenty-nine states passed laws restricting the sale of prison goods to government use only. The passage of these laws in effect eliminated the "industrial prison" as it made the transition back to its original functions as a custodial and punishment facility.

One of the unforeseen results in the decline of prison contracting and leasing and the victory of free labor was that prisons saw their budgets precipitously decline. Without any feasible alternatives to profitable labor, by the 1930s, convicts languished in interminable idleness.

The only form of labor supported by labor was the **state-use system**, which saw labor involvement rise from 33 to 65 percent between 1915 and 1930. Support for the state-use system led to the diminished influence of independent industrial managers and contractors on prison administrators. According to the state-use system, prison-manufactured goods could be produced if they did not compete with free manufacturers. By 1940, state purchase of furniture, stationary, and other state-used goods had become mandatory in twenty-two states. Despite the best intentions to constructively occupy the prisoners with work, one estimate in the mid-1930s suggests that 60 percent of the prisoners nationwide remained idle.[35] Steps were slowly taken to introduce a modicum of vocational and educational training programs. Perhaps, one prison historian, commenting on the decline in prison labor, put it best when he noted that "Labor was one of the few features of prison life that changed considerably from the nineteenth to the twentieth century."[36]

The federal prison system

As Congress became increasingly uncomfortable with the prisoner leasing systems and state prisons began refusing federal prisoners, the federal government decided to join the prison business in the 1890s. One of the most important developments in prison reform was the organization of the United States Bureau of Prisons in the late 1920s. With an increase in the number of federal offenses, including violations of prohibition laws, the three existing federal prisons were overcrowded, prompting the federal government to step in and assume some of the responsibilities.

To deal with the burgeoning number of federal prisoners during Prohibition, the Bureau of Prisons converted **Alcatraz** Island to "a prison of last resort." Prisoners who ended up here were considered the worst of the worst with little hope for rehabilitation. With no privileges and little opportunity for contact with the outside world, prisoners were not even allowed to receive original copies of their mail. To prevent secret messages, prison employees transcribed the letters before passing them on to the prisoner. To counter the punitive nature of confinement at Alcatraz, inmates were afforded better food and library facilities than most prisons.

Home to America's first fortification on the Pacific Coast in the 1850s, Alcatraz Island received its name from Spanish explorers in the 1770s when the island's only inhabitants were pelicans, hence the name Isla de Alcatraces, or Island of Pelicans. Never sufficiently utilized by the U.S. Army, the site was turned over to the Department of Justice in the 1930s. Envisioning it as maximum security facility for housing escape-prone inmates, the Justice Department also hoped to use "the Rock" to punish the worst denizens of America's prison system. It opened as a maximum security prison in June 1934. During its short history, it earned a reputation as "America's Devil's Island." Alcatraz's thirty years of serving federal prison castoffs came to a tumultuous end in 1963, when the federal penitentiary at **Marion** took its place. Belying its reputation, few inmates actually served time at Alcatraz, with its highest population at 302 in 1937.[37]

Despite its physical isolation and prison security, there were a number of unsuccessful and controversial prison escapes. Prisoners had twenty minutes to eat each meal and were counted as many as twelve times a day. The prison consisted of four three-tiered cellblocks that were never fully utilized, with the average inmate population at never more than 275 prisoners. Under the reign of James A. Johnston, its first warden, there was a ratio of one guard for every three prisoners. Contrary to popular belief, no one was sentenced to Alcatraz; all earned their way through disruptive behavior at other federal pens. Al Capone, George "Machine Gun" Kelly, atomic spy Martin Sobell, and Robert "the Birdman" Stroud (who only raised birds at his previous prison at Leavenworth) were among its most famous inmates.

Six years after its closure, American Indian activists took over the island hoping to make it into a Native American cultural and educational center. In June 1971, U.S. marshals removed the protestors from the island, but not before they had destroyed a number of the island's prison buildings. In 1972, Alcatraz became part of the National Park Service and is one of San Francisco's most popular tourist destinations.

Taking the lead in prison reform in the 1930s, the Federal Bureau of Prisons under Sanford Bates not only improved training for corrections officers but also enhanced a number of educational and vocational programs within the prisons. Other innovations followed, including a new type of prison design known as the "telephone pattern," which is credited with placing cellblocks and buildings in order to maximize the segregation of offenders by type. Bates also supported a classification program to place inmates in maximum-, medium-, and minimum-security prisons. The federal government has also been acknowledged for reorganizing the parole system by centralizing its administration in 1930.

While Alcatraz was America's most famous island prison, no island prison has captured the world's attention more than Devil's Island off the coast of French Guiana. Immortalized in film and literature, the storied *Ile du Diable* has passed through the colonial control of several European powers before coming under French control first in 1663. Between 1852 and 1946, more than 80,000 prisoners served time in the fetid penal colony. In the early 1850s, at the same time that Great Britain was abandoning penal transportation, France began sending convicts to Guiana. There was opposition to the penal colony from the very beginning. Despite full-throated critics, for almost ninety years, proponents of the penal regime sent twice yearly convoys of new prisoners to Devil's Island. The island prison was not shut down until 1946, although a number of prisoners decided to remain behind. Several books have been instrumental in bringing the horrors of the island to public attention including Rene Belbenoit's 1938 autobiography *Dry Guillotine*. The most prominent modern chronicle of the penal colony, *Papillon* (1969) was from the pen of former prisoner Henri Charrière. It was translated into an epic film in 1973 starring Steve McQueen and Dustin Hoffman.

Prisoner classification

Prisons had dabbled in inmate classification since the Progressive era. However, without effective rehabilitation programs, there was little to do with prisoners once they were classified other than to let them mix with other convicts. The movement for prisoner classification began in earnest in the years leading up to World War I. At that moment, prison administrators began to apply some of the findings of the rapidly developing field of the social sciences. In the process of putting theory into practice, prison administrators set up clinics to screen and separate certain types of prisoners, including the mentally ill and the developmentally disabled.

In the aftermath of the 1930 Ohio State Prison fire, in which 322 prisoners died, efforts were directed toward finding better ways to house and employ inmates as well as better systems of classifying inmates. In the 1930s, classification "advocated greater institutionalization diversification for reform goals, along with segregation of types of prisoners."[38] Using various methods, institutions classified prisoners on the basis of their medical, psychiatric, psychological, educational, religious, and disciplinary backgrounds. In addition, attention was paid toward classifying inmates for treatment according to their crimes, personalities, and special needs. It was hoped that classification would lead to attempts to separate hard-core offenders from those who could be rehabilitated, that narcotics addicts would be placed on penal farms, and that minor offenders could be directed to minimum-security settings.

I Am a Fugitive from a Georgia Chain Gang

Dramatizing the deplorable conditions of southern prisons was the 1930s release of the book and motion picture *I Am a Fugitive from a Georgia Chain Gang*. (Georgia was deleted from the movie title due to legal pressure from that state.) The true story of **Robert Elliott Burns**, a World War I veteran who was sentenced to six to ten years on a Georgia chain gang for a $5.80 grocery store robbery, touched a chord with many Americans and was in part responsible for the exposure (and eventually the end) of the punitive Georgia chain gangs. Burns escaped from the prison gang in 1922 and remained free until 1930. By that time, he had worked his way up the management ladder at a Chicago newspaper. On his own volition, he returned to Georgia on the condition that he would be given a pardon. However, he was sent back to the chain gang. He then became the first person to escape a chain gang for the second time. Assuming a new identity in New Jersey, he began publicizing the barbaric conditions in Georgia in a series of magazine articles. These became the basis for a book and then a movie starring Paul Muni.

Georgia officials were offended and demanded his extradition. Hearings over this matter turned into an examination of the Georgia penal system. Through his attorney, Clarence Darrow, Burns described the "**sweat box**" and other punishments endured by chain gang prisoners, and ultimately the New Jersey governor refused the request for extradition. In 1945, Georgia repealed the chain gang system and soon after commuted Burns' sentence to time served.

As early as the late eighteenth century, Pennsylvania prisons employed prison labor outside the walls. Clothed in gaudily colorful uniforms and chained together, prisoners were subject of humiliation and scorn, something strongly objected to by Quaker reformers. At least one observer reported that some convicts were so embarrassed they would have selected the gallows instead. Other states would pass statutes requiring convicts to work hard at labor before the era of the penitentiary. In 1825, Kentucky became the first state to lease out convicts to private employers. Michigan, Missouri, Alabama, Indiana, Illinois, California, Nebraska, Montana, Wyoming, Oregon, Texas, and Louisiana leased out inmates as well. Chain gangs were used sporadically by various American states during the late nineteenth and early twentieth centuries as an alternative to the physical prison. More a cost-saving venture for poor states with inadequate budgets and infrastructures than a humanitarian alternative, the chain gang was a staple of southern penology after the Civil War. In one 1886 study of convict labor by the federal commissioner of labor, outside the South, eighteen states and territories had laws for working prisoners sentenced to jail on streets and public roads. Some explanations for the wider popularity and adoption of chain gangs in the south were budgetary issues and the more temperate weather in winter and fall. By 1912, the National Committee on Prison Labor vilified chain gangs as "the last surviving vestige of the slave system,"[39] referring to the overwhelmingly black chain gangs. There are no formal statistics, but according to most estimates, hundreds, if not thousands, perished from malnutrition, physical abuse, or being shot while escaping. Rules governing chain gangs varied from state to state. In Texas, for example, a prisoner could avoid labor by paying $1 per day. Alabama prisoners were expected by law to be shackled or chained and guarded while on work details. Sleeping arrangements were as fraught as working conditions. In many inmate camps, chain gang members were confined together in cages measuring 8 feet by 18 feet. According to one early study,[40] by 1923, every state except for Rhode Island had experimented with using chain gangs to improve or build roads. In the early twentieth century, it was not uncommon to see chain gangs of striped uniformed prisoners alongside armed guards along southern roadsides. As the automobile rose in popularity in the 1920s, there was an increased emphasis on using free labor to build new roads. In the 1940s, Georgia became the last state to abandon chain gangs, due in no small part to the furor caused by Robert Burns' escape form the Georgia chain gang, chronicled in his popular book and its motion picture version, *I Am a Fugitive from a Georgia Chain Gang*. In 1995, Alabama became the first state to bring back the chain gang. Arizona, Florida, and Iowa followed suit, and six other states prepared legislation for its return. Amnesty International and other human rights groups were quick to claim its use violated the United Nations Standard Minimum Rules for the Treatment of Prisoners, calling its revival "a retrograde step in human rights."[41]

Crime and punishment

The 1920s and 1930s were marked by rampant lawlessness. Exacerbating rising crime fears were a combination of factors, including the onset of Prohibition and the beginning of the Great Depression. As crime seemed to be spiraling out of control throughout the country in the spring of 1919, one police chief blamed it on "too many soldiers returning from the war and failing to find jobs." In Chicago, according to some observers, these problems were exacerbated by the legions of unemployed black migrants newly arrived from the South.[42]

This era proved one of the deadliest for peace officers, with an average of 169 killed in the 1920s and 165 per year in the 1930s. Police deaths on duty would not surpass these figures until the 1970s. The lawlessness and sporadic violence that gripped the nation during the crisis years led Baltimore journalist H. L. Mencken to conclude that it was safer to kill a man in America "than in any other civilized society." According to one 1932 crime survey of 130 cities in the United States, the total homicide rate had reached 1 per 10,000. During the same period, the combined murder rate for Wales, England, and Scotland was 1 per 200,000.

Although studies of individual cities exist demonstrating the characteristic waxing and waning of crime rates, prior to the 1930s, there are no comprehensive crime figures for the entire nation. Most evidence suggests that the crime rate rose after World War I and the 1920s and that crime rates dropped as the nation sank into the Depression and continued to decline into the 1940s.

Despite the run on the banks that inaugurated the Depression, between 1929 and 1934, two banks were robbed every day (twenty-five per day are robbed today). Faced with growing demands from the government to crackdown on bank robbers and public enemies, J. Edgar Hoover began a crusade to change public attitudes about criminals – attitudes that had formerly elevated desperadoes such as John Dillinger to hero status.

The **Roaring Twenties** began with a peculiar tolerance of crime due in part to Prohibition, which is credited with criminalizing the behavior of otherwise law-abiding citizens. Stigmatized for breaking Prohibition laws, many of these citizens developed sympathy for other lawbreakers. However, the Kansas City Massacre in 1933 (see sidebar) and the murderous crime sprees of Bonnie and Clyde and other Depression era bandit gangs led to a public backlash against lawbreakers. Concern with the random brutality led to support for expanding the role of the federal government in law enforcement. The deaths of Bonnie and Clyde, John Dillinger, Pretty Boy Floyd, and others during the 1930s ended the American tradition of the social bandit that began with the James brothers and Billy the Kid in the years following the Civil War.

The 1920 Wall Street bombing

While many Americans assume that the World Trade Center bombing of 1993 was the first attack on the nation's financial district, in reality the Wall Street bombing on September 16, 1920, was the first and, until the Oklahoma City bombing, the "most deadly terrorist attack in American history."[43] Today, scars can still be seen if you look closely enough at the old J. P. Morgan offices on the corner of Wall and Broad streets. At least 38 were killed and scores more injured by the bombing. Although no one was ever brought to justice for the crime, investigators figured that the explosion was the result of a horse-drawn cart carrying dynamite and sash weights that acted as shrapnel. The blast was so strong that an automobile was thrust twenty feet into the air.

William J. Flynn, chief of the Secret Service, concluded that the bomb was not directed at J. P. Morgan, although one of his firm's clerks was beheaded by the blast; rather, it was directed at the financial heart of American society. Others thought that it was either an accident or the result of a botched robbery or attack on the U.S. Treasury (on that particular day, $900 million in gold bars was being moved next door, which was the epicenter of the blast). A. Mitchell Palmer, the attorney general, suspected that the attack was the work of anarchists or communist workers and as "a precaution" arrested IWW leader William "Big Bill" Haywood. Still others were convinced that it was payback for the arrests of anarchists Nicola Sacco and Bartolomeo Vanzetti. Considering the tensions of the day, there was no lack of potential suspects.

According to several sources, the bomber was probably a veteran Italian immigrant anarchist named Mario Buda, who was responsible for parking his horse-drawn wagon across from J.P. Morgan and Company.[44] However, the most recent and comprehensive account of the bombing suggests it will never be substantiated for certain which individual parked the wagon.[45] Nonetheless, if Buda was not actually the detonator, he was probably involved with the anarchist group that did. As a harbinger of future car bombs, one historian put the heinous act into its proper context, noting "a poor immigrant with some stolen dynamite, a pile of scrap metal, and an old horse had managed to bring unprecedented terror to the inner sanctum of American capitalism."[46]

The Teapot Dome scandal (1924)

No scandal overshadowed the 1920s as much as the Teapot Dome scandal, which, according to one source, "proved to be a major watershed in U.S. political history."[47] Named after an oddly shaped geological feature near its location in Wyoming, Teapot Dome was a naval oil reserve that had been set aside by the government for emergency use in 1915. But in 1920, Congress passed legislation to establish private leasing of public mineral lands. Soon contracts for Teapot Dome and other oil reserves were given to various bidders with the support of Secretary of the Interior Albert Fall (1861–1944). Ironically, in the months before his death (1923) and the Teapot Dome scandal, President Warren G. Harding had remarked that "if Albert Fall isn't an honest man, I'm not fit to be president of the United States."[48]

By 1922, the Interior Department was leasing the emergency oil reserves. As it turned out, Fall had begun leasing the oil reserves to close friends without allowing competitive bidding on the property. In return, they secretly compensated Fall with almost $400,000. A subsequent senatorial inquiry uncovered the scandal, and the government canceled the leases with the support of a Supreme Court decision. In 1929, Fall was found guilty of bribery and sentenced to one year in prison. It was the first time a cabinet officer had been jailed for crimes committed in office. Teapot Dome entered the American lexicon as a synonym for government graft and a lingering reminder of the corruption-plagued Harding administration.

Prohibition and organized crime

One of the greatest ironies of the Prohibition era is that, while it was intended to impose virtue on ethnic Americans through repression, it actually made them the beneficiaries of the very laws intended to limit their cultural influence. In a short time, second-generation

Italians, Jews, and Poles would control a $2 billion-per-year illegal industry. No criminal enterprise is more shrouded in myth than the development of organized crime and the growth of "Mafia"-inspired crime syndicates in the United States. As historian David Johnson succinctly noted, while some Italian gangsters "borrowed some terms and concepts from the Sicilian Mafia," their "basic rationale and structure were purely American."[49]

Envisioned by its supporters as a cure for America's social ills, Prohibition instead created new ills and in the process gave birth to modern organized crime. Seduced by the lure of beer money, peace officers were bribed like never before. While organized gangs had operated in urban America since the 1830s, they functioned with the support of political machines. With the onset of various Progressive reform efforts and the changing face of urban America, by 1914, most of the gangs were in disarray. With red light abatement in full sway, vice centers from New Orleans' *Storyville* to San Diego's *Stingaree* were closed down. It seemed that the era of the gangs had ended by the end of World War I.

However, the birth of Prohibition resuscitated organized gangs. With tens of thousands of speakeasies flourishing throughout the country, bootleggers had to replenish the illegal liquor supply either by smuggling across borders or by making their own illegal potions. It was not long before alcohol became an underground cottage industry with entire neighborhoods besieged by the foul odors of bootleg brew.

In New York, Bugsy Siegel, Frank Costello, Lucky Luciano, Meyer Lansky, and other future mob luminaries collaborated to make $12 million a year from booze alone. In Chicago, Al Capone and his mentor John Torrio made tens of millions of dollars. Capone was the best-known American of his era, and although his career as Chicago crime boss was rather ephemeral, in 1930 alone, he made $100 million.

One of the more perplexing questions left unanswered from this era is why J. Edgar Hoover refused to recognize the rise of criminal syndicates in big cities from coast to coast. While the Bureau of Narcotics, big-city police forces, and crusading journalists recognized the growth of organized crime, the FBI seemed to ignore this phenomenon until the 1950s. As late as 1959, Hoover employed 400 agents in the New York City office investigating communists and only four concentrating on organized crime. Although several unsubstantiated reasons for Hoover's inaction have been cited, including the blackmail of his personal life and horse-betting debts to the mob, others have offered more convincing explanations. Obsessed with maintaining the bureau's reputation for high conviction rates, Hoover set his sights on kidnappers and bank robbers, who were much easier to catch than complicated cases of organized criminal activity. With access to the best lawyers that money could buy, mob figures often were acquitted. Hoover also feared that his agents could be corrupted in the process of taking on the mob.

Thomas Dewey: racket buster

Prohibition introduced modern organized crime to urban America. In response, cities such as New York responded with special prosecutors such as Thomas Dewey to round up the denizens of organized crime ranging from bookmakers and loan sharks to mob leaders. Born in Michigan, Thomas Dewey (1902–1971) practiced law after earning his law degree from Columbia Law School in just two years. In 1935, he was appointed by the New York governor to investigate statewide organized crime. Over the next two years, he successfully attacked police corruption and organized crime figures. Not only was he credited with restoring integrity to the New York Police Department, but he engineered the demise of criminals Lucky Luciano and Dutch Schultz. Dewey became a national hero and revered racket buster in his time, survived death threats from Dutch Schultz, and served as New York governor three times. As New York's crusading district attorney, Dewey is considered the quintessential law-and-order prosecutor.

Social bandits in the twentieth century

Continuing an American tradition dating back to the years following the Civil War, the rural admiration for a certain breed of bandit would carry well into the twentieth century in a number of Southern and Midwestern border states in the wake of economic downturns and social upheaval. One chronicler of the era asserts that icons such as John Dillinger "fit the social bandit mold, but only imperfectly." Rather, according to Elliott Gorn, Dillinger and his men could not be more American than in their desire to seize the good life for themselves.[50]

The crisis years were rife with outlaw bands. As the frontier continued to diminish in the early 1900s, the number of bank and armed robberies plummeted until the 1920s and 1930s, when bad economic times left a generation of desperate, unemployed young men. However, the publicity given to the so-called Kansas City massacre (see below) and a wave of other widely publicized crime sprees caused a public backlash against these malefactors, even among their agrarian supporters.

Until the 1930s, American bandits were able to take advantage of the lack of federal policing, due to the fact that there were few federal crimes to be policed. With added technological benefits of the Thompson submachine gun and the automobile, gangsters gave up their horses for the relative comfort of the sedan, taking advantage of the lack of state police forces and coordination between different police jurisdictions. Apparently the 1930s was a "good time for robbing banks in the Midwest," made easier by the inability of "heartland constabularies" to keep up with their new mobility. Compared to their counterparts in the eastern states, who were better equipped with speedy vehicles, automatic weapons, and two-way radios, Midwestern police forces were especially underfunded.[51]

One unintended consequences of this rural crime wave was that the majority of Americans were soon supporting new federal crime statutes that would erase many of these advantages. The FBI would "gain relevance overnight" as it was empowered to chase kidnappers and other miscreants across state lines. After a new crime bill was passed that gave the FBI greater powers and more federal laws to enforce, its first major targets were in the "drought plagued and Dust Bowl afflicted states" where gangsters operated with impunity.[52] In quick succession, a variety of law enforcement efforts led to the demise of John Dillinger, Pretty Boy Floyd, Bonnie Parker and Clyde Barrow, Baby Face Nelson, and others.[53]

The Kansas City Massacre

On June 17, 1933, four law enforcement officers, including an FBI agent, were reportedly ambushed and killed by machine gun fire in what has become known as the Kansas City

Massacre. Three other FBI agents were wounded. This being 1933, the agents were not yet authorized to carry weapons, but all this would change following the carnage. Although recent research conflicts with the accepted account of events,[54] FBI director J. Edgar Hoover used its tragic consequences to launch a high profile campaign to hunt down public enemies in the nation's heartland. In 1934, President Franklin Roosevelt signed into law nine anti-crime bills that enlarged the crime fighting powers and jurisdiction of the FBI. Following the passage of these measures, FBI agents would be responsible for suppressing federal bank robberies, the transportation of stolen property across state lines, and other crimes and would be allowed to carry and use firearms.

Kidnapping

Most historians trace the first kidnapping for ransom in America back to the 1874 abduction of "little Charles Ross." This case was never solved and his body never found. No era saw more kidnappings than the 1920s and 1930s. In 1931 alone, there were 282 reported kidnappings. According to ransom expert Ernest Kahlar Alix, two types of ransom cases predominated: the ransom of wealthy (unharmed) businessmen and the ransom slayings of children. The most prominent ransom cases of this era involved the deaths of Bobby Franks by Richard Loeb and Nathan Leopold (1924) and Charles A. Lindbergh Jr. by Bruno Hauptmann (1932).

Organized criminals were often kidnapped by other members of the underworld and Black Hand members targeted fellow Italian immigrants. In the 1930s, organized kidnap rings began to victimize private citizens as well. One estimate suggests there had been 2,000 ransom abductions between 1930 and 1931. By 1933, the so-called "Snatch Racket" was in full swing. The increasing number of abductions of prominent citizens inspired a number of companies to begin offering kidnapping insurance.[55] The 1933 kidnappings of William A. Hamm Jr. by Alvin "Kreepy" Karpis and that of Charles F. Urschel by the George "Machine Gun" Kelly gang ended with the payments of ransoms of $100,000 and $200,000, respectively, and the safe release of both victims. By this time, the public was clamoring for the suppression of this crime.

The Lindbergh case

No criminal case of this era garnered more publicity than the kidnapping of the twenty-month-old son of America's aviation hero Charles Lindbergh, the first person to fly solo across the Atlantic Ocean. At this time, kidnapping was not a federal offense, and the FBI had no jurisdiction in the case. However, once the baby's body was discovered in 1932, President Herbert Hoover ordered all federal agencies to participate in the subsequent investigation. The arrest and trial of Bruno Hauptmann became one of the most sensational murder trials of the century. Although the evidence seemed overwhelming – Hauptmann had the ransom money, and experts testified that he made the ladder from wood in his attic and that he had written the ransom note – questions linger to this day as to Hauptmann's culpability. Nonetheless, he was electrocuted in 1936.

The Lindbergh case foreshadowed the sensationalism that would plague news reporting over the next century. What made this possible was the "emergence of modern media technology," which made this trial an even "more compelling national drama than the Lizzie Borden case" four decades earlier.[56] As Walter L. Hixson makes clear in his examination of sensational crime trials, with the emergence of the radio and movie newsreels in the 1920s, America became linked in a "single media culture."[57]

By most accounts, the Lindbergh kidnapping case had major ramifications for law enforcement when Congress passed the Federal Kidnapping Act, or "Lindbergh Law," in June 1932 after the baby's body was discovered, giving the FBI jurisdiction in kidnapping cases where the victim had been taken across state lines. However, less well known is the fact that, besides making it a felony, the new law allowed federal judges upon conviction to impose any penalty up to life in prison, "the only federal statute to allow such discretion."[58] But at least one authority argued that it is historically false to attribute the passage of this legislation to the Lindbergh kidnapping. Sociologist Ernest Kahlar Alix suggests that "the Lindbergh case initiated neither the noncapital nor the capital federal legislation, despite the fact that the legislation came to be known as the Lindbergh Law." To support his case, Alix notes that the 1932 federal ransom legislation was introduced four months earlier than the Lindbergh kidnapping and had nothing to do with the "ransoming or ransom slaying of any child."[59]

The Ku Klux Klan

The Ku Klux Klan reorganized in 1915 and within four years was flourishing once again. The second and largest incarnation of the Klan began in Atlanta, Georgia, in 1915. Initially concentrating its animosity against blacks, in 1920, it launched a nationwide membership drive under the slogan "native, white, and Protestant." Taking advantage of the temper and fears of the time, the Klan used the nation's anticommunism and rampant xenophobia as a device for rallying members to their repugnant banner. In 1925, Klan membership crested at between 4 and 5 million. Not just a southern phenomenon, crosses would burn from coast to coast as the Klan used the whip and the noose to terrorize Jews, Catholics, blacks, evolutionists, bootleggers, Bolshevists, and any others who crossed the moral divide. The second coming of the Klan was more national in scope than its predecessor and had a smaller "footprint in the South." Moreover, its highest per capita membership was in states like Indiana, Oregon, and Southern California.[60] Between 1921 and 1926, the Klan controlled the election of governors and senators in Alabama, Georgia, Arkansas, Texas, Oklahoma, California, Oregon, Indiana, and Ohio. Although a number of politicians launched their administrations under the Klan aegis, by the late 1920s, the second resurgence of the organization was in decline after several well-publicized scandals and corruption discredited Klan leaders.

Perhaps, no event signaled the acceptance of the KKK in 1920s America than when 30,000 Klan members boldly paraded down Pennsylvania Avenue in 1925. As one historian recently put it, the Klan of this era was "well-integrated into American life." According to Linda Gordon, "The KKK may actually have enunciated values with which a majority of 1920s Americans believed."[61] Contrary to the popular images of this era that portrayed America as a nation of flappers, speakeasies, and gangland killing, these actually represented "an urban bubble." By contrast, "xenophobia, white nationalism and patriarchy" were the norm. Nonetheless, its fall was almost as meteoric as its rise, from its zenith of several million members in the mid-1920s to roughly 350,000 towards the end of the decade.

Capital punishment

Between 1918 and 1959, more than 5,000 Americans were executed, with few generating much publicity. Except for high profile capital cases, such as those of Sacco and Vanzetti and Bruno Hauptmann, most executions were followed with little fanfare. In 1937, the first Gallup Poll on the death penalty found that a vast majority of Americans supported the death penalty. For the next twenty years, support would remain strong for capital punishment.

During the 1930s, America used the death penalty more than any previous decade in American history. According to one study, 1,676 executions took place in this decade, compared to an average of 1,148 per decade between 1880 and 1920. However, this spate of executions coincided with a rising population and murder rate.[62] Death penalty scholar Stuart Banner suggests that the American use of the death penalty crested at 199 in 1935 and subsequently dropped "sharply" over the ensuing decades.[63]

The gas chamber

In the never-ending quest for more humane methods of execution, death by lethal gas was introduced by Nevada in 1924 after the state's deputy attorney general persuaded the state assembly (in 1921) that using lethal gas was more humane than the firing squad and hanging, its current method of execution. As originally conceived, the prisoner was supposed to be put to death while sleeping in his cell. However, this would prove to be impractical. Ultimately, it was decided to use a "small airtight chamber" with a window that spectators could see through. It also had to be big enough to fit a chair for the condemned to sit on. After discussing various types of lethal gas, it was decided to use hydrocyanic acid, a chemical that proved effective killing parasites on Southern California orange trees.[64]

First used in 1924, for the next ten years, Nevada was the only state to use it. Eventually eleven states (western and southern ones) would use lethal gas. Eight of these states had not adopted the electric chair at this point. The gas chamber remained an "entirely western and southern phenomenon."[65] One of the riskiest facets of using gas was the potential for participants in the execution process to be injured or killed by the gas. The gas chamber was used for the last time in Arizona in March 1999.

Mob violence

America witnessed every variety of violence in the crisis decades, much of it collective in nature. Labor violence, race riots, mob warfare over the liquor trade, and police brutality contributed to a climate of fear and social disorder as the country entered the 1920s.

In the 1930s, industrial violence resulted in dozens of killings as police and army troops battled strikers during a national cotton textile strike and several steel strikes. One of the last memorable labor confrontations resulted in the Memorial Day massacre of ten strikers during the 1937 Republic Steel strike. Killings also resulted from assaults by strikers against strikebreakers, as was the case in 1922, when union workers savagely murdered nineteen scabs at the Herrin massacre in Illinois.

The Tulsa, Oklahoma, race riot (1921)

Perhaps the worst race riot of the interwar years, the 1921 Tulsa, Oklahoma, riot was ignited after a black resident was accused of rape and arrested. When rumors of a lynching reached the black community, a group of armed blacks hurried to the jail to protect the potential victim. After gunfire broke out, the overwhelming force of whites chased the blacks back into their neighborhood. In the ensuing violence, at least sixty blacks were killed, although the director of gravediggers later reported burying 150 victims. By the time martial law was declared, virtually the entire one-mile-square black district had been burned to the ground. In February 2001, nearly eighty years after whites laid waste to Tulsa's black community, a state panel investigating the violence agreed that reparations should be paid to survivors. The result of a four-year effort to uncover the truth of one of the nation's deadliest race riots, the Tulsa Race Riot Commission recommended that the 118 survivors and descendants be compensated for their losses, adding that the death toll was probably as high as 300.[66]

One of the turning points in racial violence came in 1935 during the Harlem riot. Here the racial pattern of rioting diverged from tradition. Formerly, whites initiated race riots, leading to violence between the races. But the Harlem riot featured not fighting between the races but rather mostly black rioters attacking white property and the police. While few deaths resulted, property damage reached more than $2 million. The subsequent commission impaneled to look into the causes, following an example set by the 1919 Chicago riot, blamed the outbreak of violence on police brutality, discrimination, and unemployment.

If there was one positive development in race relations during the crisis years, it was the decline in lynchings. According to the National Association for the Advancement of Colored People, between 1882 and 1927, almost 5,000 mostly African American victims perished at the hands of lynch mobs. Lynchings substantially declined in the early 1900s, with an average of sixty-two a year between 1910 and 1919. By the late 1930s and 1940s, lynchings became a much rarer event.

The St. Valentine's Day Massacre (1929)

No event signified the brutality of the bootlegging wars and the brazenness of the 1920s more than the St. Valentine's Day Massacre, the biggest gangland murder of the era. This event was the culmination of a long-term war in Chicago between the Capone gang and the North Side gang led by Dion O'Banion. By 1929, O'Banion and numerous allies had been killed, leaving George "Bugs" Moran as Capone's last obstacle to taking over the bootlegging empire.

In an attempt to lure Moran into his own demise, Capone arranged for a gangster to offer Moran a load of hijacked liquor that would be delivered to the gang's garage headquarters. Several Capone henchmen, dressed in police uniforms, drove up to the garage and lined up the seven occupants against the wall, a group that included a gang groupie and local optometrist. Figuring that it was just a routine police roust, the gangsters offered no resistance and meekly stood face first against a wall. All seven were cut to ribbons with submachine fire. However, Bugs Moran was not among them, having overslept that day. Moran arrived shortly after the massacre, and when he was queried as to the perpetrators, he responded, "Only Capone kills like that."[67] Initially, there was a split opinion as to the killers. The police were held in such low esteem to many that it seemed altogether possible that they were the perpetrators. But public opinion soon turned against Capone.

Any question as to the killers was put to rest when ballistics expert **Calvin H. Goddard** (1891–1955) tested the bullets and reported that they did not come from any machine gun owned by the Chicago Police Department. In 1930, machine guns and bullets found in the home of Fred Burke, a known killer for hire, matched the St. Valentine's Day bullets. Chicago authorities were so impressed with his acumen that they decided to establish a special institute under the leadership of Goddard. The forensic expert would spend three months in Europe visiting police laboratories before returning to set up the Scientific Crime Detection Laboratory in Evanston, Illinois. The facility would eventually become part of Northwestern University Law School, and as a professor, Goddard would teach the world's first courses in police science.

The massacre not only led more quickly to the demise of Al Capone, but also helped revive the Chicago Crime Commission, whose members personally financed the country's first crime lab and also advanced the movement for Prohibition repeal.

In 1822, prior to the advent ballistic science, the pioneering French detective Eugene Vidocq was said to have solved a murder case by removing a bullet from the head of a female victim and proving it was too large to have come from her husband's gun, but the correct size to have come from her lover's gun.[68] One true crime expert has cited a 1794 case as the birth of ballistics. In this incident, an English resident was shot dead, and the examining physician found a wad of paper used to pack the shot inside a body wound. The paper was dutifully unfolded, "and in its flattened state found to be an exact match with the ton corner of a ballad sheet still in the suspect's pocket."[69] As in most cases of tracking down origins of various investigative methods, the jury is still out on the first use of this important forensic tool. Other evidence of early uses of ballistics include an 1835 case in which Bow Street Runner, Henry Goddard, solved a burglary case, the 1869 French case, when Professor Alexandre Lacassagne, the so-called "father of forensic science," matched the seven rifling grooves on in a gun to a particular projectile with seven grooves.[70] While it would take until the next century and the development of the comparison microscope to bring the science into the modern era, by most accounts, the aforementioned case suggests this was an important first step on the way to making ballistics an exact science. In famous twentieth-century American homicide cases such as the St. Valentine's Day Massacre and the Sacco and Vanzetti murder case, ballistics played prominent roles in their subsequent investigations.

Murder Incorporated

For most of its existence, Murder Incorporated, a group of hired killers composed of a combination of second-generation Jews and Italians, worked behind the scenes in anonymity. During Prohibition, ethnic mobs had discovered the advantages of working together, and by 1930, rules of cooperative behavior had been laid down and territories mapped out by a national board of directors, which reportedly included Lucky Luciano, Frank Costello, Meyer Lansky, and other notables. As the days of Prohibition came to a close, organized crime diverted its attention to other lucrative businesses, ranging from loan-sharking, gambling, and narcotics to prostitution and labor racketeering.

Organized crime turned to Brooklyn-based Murder Incorporated for "muscle" and for the hiring of hit men. The group was led by Albert "Lord High Executioner" Anastasia and Louis "Lepke" Buchalter as the enforcement arm of the mob. Each contract murder had to be approved by the national board. The killing of peace officers and journalists was prohibited, and the killers were not available to civilians. During the 1930s, the killers are suspected of at least 300 murders in New York alone. They also introduced the terms *contracts* and *hits* into the popular underworld lexicon.

One enduring slogan and principle credited to the gang was the notion that "we only kill each other." In 1935, this ethic was tested when crime lord Dutch Schultz demanded that Murder Incorporated kill Thomas Dewey in violation of organization protocol. When his request was voted down, Schultz vowed to do the job himself. In response, Schultz was given the death penalty by his mob associates, and a contract on his life was approved. Arthur Flegenheimer (a.k.a. Dutch Schultz) was killed shortly thereafter as he ate dinner at a Newark chophouse.

In 1940, Murder Incorporated came to the attention of law enforcement when killer Abe Reles turned state's evidence following his implication in several murders. His testimony stunned the New York district attorney as Reles laid out the existence of a national crime syndicate that had probably committed more than 1,000 murders across the country. As to the moniker Murder Incorporated, most sources credit it to a New York police reporter named Harry Feeney. Reles' testimony would lead to the end of the gang and would send several killers to the electric chair, including Louis "Lepke" Buchalter (1897–1944), the highest-ranking mob boss to ever be executed. Stool pigeon Abe Reles met his ignominious end when he either committed suicide or was pushed out of a hotel window.

Notable trials

The Scottsboro trials (1931 – 1937)

On March 25, 1931, nine black youths aged thirteen to twenty were arrested at Paint Rock, Alabama, accused of raping two white girls as they traveled as hoboes on a freight train headed south from Chattanooga through Alabama. The subsequent trial and sentencing of the so-called Scottsboro Boys focused international attention on the segregated Jim Crow

South and "exercised a profound influence on the way that criminal justice came to be administered in the United States forever after."[71]

Rape was still a capital crime in Alabama, and the rape of two white women at the hands of African Americans in this era was considered acceptable grounds for lynching. Despite the suspects' claims that they did not rape the girls or ever see them prior to their arrests, armed farmers waited for the delivery of the prisoners at the Jackson County seat. It was not long before the nine men were confined in a cage in a small Jim Crow jail fearing for their lives. The National Guard was called out for protection, and the prisoners were moved to another jail for safekeeping.

The nine men were indicted by an all-white jury in Scottsboro, and the following week the capital case began. The accused were not offered lawyers or any contact with each other, typical of such trials in the Deep South in this era. Although physicians testified that after examining the two women they could find no evidence of a rape, this had little influence on the racially charged atmosphere. In the words of Haywood Patterson, who later published his own account of the trial, "Color [was] more important than evidence down there."[72]

The subsequent evidence presented against the accused consisted primarily of the allegations presented by the two women. Since the defendants could not afford counsel, the local judge appointed the entire bar of Scottsboro, which included six men, to defend the Scottsboro boys. Of these, only one agreed to comply, and then only on the morning of the trial. With little preparation or time to investigate, the final reckoning was a forgone conclusion, and all eight defendants were sentenced to death by the all-white jury. Less than four months after the trial began, eight of the nine men were sentenced to the electric chair. The ninth was a fourteen-year-old who was given life imprisonment because of his small stature and youthful appearance. Haywood Patterson proved one of the most visible of the nine and soon began to learn to read and write while he awaited his death. The widespread publicity accorded the case won the young men support from around the world, including contributions from Albert Einstein and writers Thomas Mann and Maxim Gorky.

On November 8, 1932, the Supreme Court reversed its convictions in *Powell v. Alabama*, citing the fact that the defendants had been denied their right to adequate counsel. This was a landmark decision in that, for the first time, the Supreme Court took steps to guarantee that almost all criminal defendants would actually have counsel. It did this by requiring the government to appoint and pay for a lawyer if a defendant could not do so. The Court based its decision to reverse the original convictions on the protection guaranteed by the Fourteenth Amendment, which prohibits states from depriving any person of life, liberty, or property without due process of law. However, many issues were still unsettled, and the case left unresolved "whether appointed counsel would be required in noncapital cases."[73] Although the Court's decision was based on the specifics of the Scottsboro case, the ruling came to be viewed as requiring appointment of counsel for young, inexperienced, illiterate, and indigent defendants in capital cases.

In 1935, the Supreme Court ruled unanimously in *Norris v. Alabama*, after the retrial of defendant Clarence Norris, that his conviction violated his right to equal protection of the laws under the Fourteenth Amendment. Chief Justice Charles Evans Hughes noted in the ruling that no black had served on a county jury within the memory of any living person and found the evidence sufficient to reverse Norris' conviction. *Powell v. Alabama* (1932) and *Norris v. Alabama* (1935) became collectively known as the Scottsboro cases.

In their subsequent, second trial, four of the nine were convicted. One was sentenced to death and the other three to seventy-five to ninety-nine years in prison. The rape indictments were dismissed against the other five defendants. Despite the severity of the sentences, in some quarters, the result was seen as a victory during this era of rising racial violence and lynchings.

Lawyers continued the appeals process until 1937 as Patterson and his fellow defendants languished in jail. Tired of waiting in jail for a crime he did not commit, Patterson made an escape attempt in 1948 and was arrested two years later in Detroit, but the Michigan governor refused to sign extradition papers. The three other defendants were released on parole between 1943 and 1950.

In 1938, the Supreme Court ruled in *Johnson v. Zerbst* that, according to the Sixth Amendment, the government is required to pay for a lawyer if a defendant could not afford one. But this applied only to federal criminal trials. Since almost 90 percent of criminal prosecutions were tried in state courts, this ruling had little impact. In 1942, the Court refused to extend the *Johnson* decision to state trials. Until *Gideon v. Wainwright* in 1963 (see Chapter 12), "states remained free" to "prosecute and convict indigent defendants in one-sided proceedings in which the state was represented by a lawyer and the defendant was left to fend for himself."

The Scottsboro case captured international attention at a time when African American defendants rarely made it so far through the court and appeals process. For police historian Samuel Walker, the legacy of this case and the subsequent *Powell* decision was that it was the "first organized attack on race discrimination in the southern criminal justice system."[74]

In 2013, more than eighty years after the false accusations of the "Scottsboro Boys," the Alabama Board of Pardons and Paroles voted unanimously during a hearing in the state capitol to issue pardons to three of the men (Haywood Patterson, Charles Weems, and Andy Wright). This step, according to one reporter, "brought to an end a case that yielded two landmark Supreme Court opinions," including one focused on the inclusion of blacks on juries and another about the need for adequate representation at trial.[75]

Conclusions

For better or worse the crisis decades and Prohibition changed America forever. It newly demonstrated the growing power of the woman suffrage movement, which joined ranks with the crusade against "demon rum." Conversely, women came into contact more and more with the criminal justice system as they ventured into criminogenic social spaces. In New York City, the arrest rate of women remained at elevated levels throughout the 1920s and into the next decade. By the 1920s, prison reformers were once again grappling with the horrendous state of prison affairs. In the wake of a series of prison riots in Illinois, Colorado, Kansas, and New York, the National Commission on Law Observance and Enforcement issued a report detailing the deplorable state of the nation's prisons. Following in the footsteps of Progressive reformers, the authors of what became known as the *Wickersham Report* linked the current climate of lawlessness in America with the failure of the prisons to rehabilitate inmates. Noting the impact of immigration and unemployment on crime rates as well as the concomitant costs of crime, the report placed the blame for failure of the prison system squarely on the backs of prison administrators who promulgated arbitrary rules and punishments.

Prison populations dramatically increased, as did some crime rates, in the 1920s. With the growth in interstate regulatory laws and Prohibition, the number of state and federal prisoners increased as well. In response, the federal government created the Federal Bureau of Prisons. With the jobless rate spiraling out of control, thirty-three states passed laws in the 1930s that prohibited the sale of prison-made commodities on the free market.

After 100 years of success, with the impetus of the Depression and rising unemployment, the 1930s saw federal and state legislation eliminate the sale of prison products on the open market as prisons returned to the more punitive and custodial roots of an earlier era. Despite advances in classification and efforts at reform, America's prisons became overcrowded, leading to tension and prison riots.

The 1920s and 1930s had fanned the flames of a burgeoning civil rights struggle that would culminate with the civil rights crusade of the 1960s. Changes in national attitudes and public opinion toward race indicated that Jim Crow and *Plessy v. Ferguson* were losing support. No juxtaposition of images makes this clearer than the 1925 Ku Klux Klan march through the streets of Washington, DC, and the 1939 concert honoring black singer Marian Anderson in front of the Lincoln Memorial. The concert drew more than 75,000 people after Anderson was barred from singing in Constitutional Hall by the Daughters of the American Revolution.

Prohibition and the Depression, like other pivotal events of this era, ultimately contributed to making the federal government even stronger. No single episode in the early twentieth century conspired to increase the mandate of the criminal justice system than did Prohibition. According to criminal justice historian Lawrence M. Friedman, "Prohibition filled the federal jails; it jammed the federal courts," and "under prohibition, the idea of a national police force became no longer unthinkable."[76] Not the final word but a warning of what was to come, historian Claire Bond Potter noted that "the legacy of the transformation of federal policing during the New Deal has been a continuing war on crime, one that is fully integrated into daily political and civic life in the United States."[77]

In 1933, following the repeal of Prohibition, a news publication revealed that the final cost of Prohibition was more than one-third greater than the national debt of $22 billion and $10 billion more than the cost of America's participation in World War I, which was $26.361 trillion. A tabulation of Prohibition killings totaled 1,170 citizen and 512 agent deaths between 1920 and 1932.[78]

On the other hand, with criminal syndicates deeply embedded in American society by the end of Prohibition, they were organized well enough to successfully turn their attention to traditional vices, such as gambling, drugs, labor racketeering and prostitution. By the 1930s, American policing was dismal if not ineffective. While the hiring of more police officers has proved a panacea for contemporary policing, a 1926 report noted that the New York City police hired 3,522 officers in 1926 and 1927 but saw only a 4 percent drop in crime. Even the 1931 Wickersham Commission concluded that many police departments were corrupt, untrained, and poorly administered. Police professionals such as J. Edgar Hoover, August Vollmer, O. W. Wilson, and others would help guide the transformation and professionalization movement that would lead to tremendous improvements in American policing by the 1950s. The end of Prohibition and the Depression would usher in an era of police professionalism. With the diminished influence of political machines on police departments, efforts at reform could be directed at raising salaries and improving hiring practices, training, technology, and investigative procedures.

Point – counterpoint

National prohibition: legislating morals (1930)

Between 1920 and 1933 the government of the United States prohibited the manufacture and sale of alcoholic beverages. Following his election to the presidency in 1928, Herbert Hoover felt that more knowledge of prohibition enforcement was needed. In 1929 he created the National Commission on Law Observance and Enforcement, chaired by former Attorney General George Wickersham. There was little consensus among commission members about prohibition enforcement practices. When the Commission's final report was released in 1931, its pessimistic approach to Prohibition added morn ammunition to the wets who supported repeal. In the following passage from the report the authors assess the difficulties of enforcing Prohibition. The second excerpt is from an address given at Harvard University in support of Prohibition. The author, Charles W. Eliot, president of Harvard University from 1869 to 1909, notes an association between alcoholism, venereal disease, and threats to "white civilization."

Source: *National Commission on Law Observance and Enforcement,*
Report on the Enforcement of the Prohibition Laws of the
United States, 71st Congress, third session, House Document 722, 1931,
pp. 44–56; Charles W. Eliot, *A Late Harvest,* Boston, 1924, pp, 261–267

A number of causes of resentment or irritation at the law or at features of its enforcement raise difficulties for national prohibition. A considerable part of the public were irritated at a constitutional "don't" in a matter where they saw no moral question. The statutory definition of "intoxicating" at a point clearly much below what is intoxicating in truth and fact, even if maintainable as a matter of legal power, was widely felt to be arbitrary and unnecessary. While there was general agreement that saloons were wisely eliminated, there was no general agreement on the universal regime of enforced total abstinence. In consequence many of the best citizens in every community, on whom we rely habitually for the upholding of law and order, are at most lukewarm as to the National Prohibition Act. Many who are normally law-abiding are led to an attitude hostile to the statute by a feeling that repression and interference with private conduct are carried too far. This is aggravated in many of the larger cities by a feeling that other parts of the land are seeking to impose ideas of conduct upon them and to mold city life to what are considered to be their provincial conceptions.

Other sources of resentment and irritation grow out of incidents of enforcement. In the nature of things it is easier to shut up the open drinking places and stop the sale of beer, which was drunk chiefly by workingmen, than to prevent the wealthy from having and using liquor in their homes and in their clubs. Naturally when the industrial benefits of prohibition are pointed out, laboring men resent the insistence of employers who drink that their employees be kept from temptation. It is easier to detect and apprehend small offenders than to reach the well organized larger operators. It is much easier to padlock a speakeasy than to close up a large hotel where important and influential and financial interests are involved. Thus the law may be made to appear as aimed at and enforced against the insignificant while the wealthy enjoy immunity. This feeling is reinforced when it is seen that the wealthy are generally able to procure pure liquors, where those with less means may run the risk of poisoning through the working over of denatured alcohol, or, at best, must put up with cheap, crude, and even deleterious products. Moreover, searches of homes, especially under state laws, have necessarily seemed to bear more upon people of moderate means than upon those of wealth or influence. Resentment at crude methods of enforcement, unavoidable with the class of persons employed in the past and still often employed in state enforcement, disgust with informers, snoopers, and under-cover men unavoidably made use of if a universal total abstinence' is to be brought about by law, and irritation at the inequalities of penalties, even in adjoining districts in the same locality and as between state and federal tribunals – something to be expected with respect to a law as to which opinions differ so widely – add to the burden under which enforcement must be conducted.

Resentment is aroused also by the government's collecting income tax from bootleggers and illicit manufacturers and distributors upon the proceeds of their unlawful business. This has been a convenient and effective way of striking at large operators who have not returned their true incomes. But it impresses many citizens as a legal recognition and even licensing of the business, and many who pay income taxes upon the proceeds of their legitimate activities feel strongly that illegitimate activities should be treated by the government as upon a different basis.

Lawyers everywhere deplore, as one of the most serious effects of prohibition, the change in the general attitude toward the federal courts. Formerly these tribunals were of exceptional dignity, and the efficiency and dispatch of their criminal business commanded wholesome fear and respect. The professional criminal, who sometimes had scanty respect for the state tribunals, was careful so to conduct himself as not to come within the jurisdiction of the federal courts. The effect of the huge volume of liquor prosecutions, which has come to these courts under prohibition, has injured their dignity, impaired their efficiency, and endangered the wholesome respect for them which once obtained. Instead of being impressive tribunals of superior jurisdiction, they have had to do the work of police courts and that work has been chiefly in the public eye. These deplorable conditions have been aggravated by the constant presence in and about these courts of professional criminal lawyers and bail-bond agents, whose unethical and mercenary practices have detracted from these valued institutions. . . .

I remember well that, twenty years ago or thereabouts, I was entertained by the Harvard Club of Louisiana at a large dinner in the city of New Orleans, where I sat next to a gentleman who was generally recognized in New Orleans as the leader of their Bar. I noticed the moment we sat down that there was an extraordinary variety of things to drink on the table; and I also noticed that my neighbor took everything that was passed and in large quantity, so much so that I began to be a little anxious about his condition later. But suddenly he turned to me and said, "Mr. President, do you know that the New Orleans Bar, and I as its leader, are going in for complete prohibition in the State of Louisiana?" I could not help expressing surprise that *he* was going in for that. Whereupon he said, "Well, you don't suppose that we, the members of the Bar, expect to have the law applied to us, do you?" *(Laughter)* He was positively a vigorous advocate of complete prohibition for Louisiana, but all the time had not the slightest notion that a prohibitory law could be applied to him or any of his friends, or would be.

That opened my eyes somewhat in regard to the expectation with which the sudden, unanimous support of prohibition came to pass in the Southern States. It was nearly unanimous, you remember, and remains so to this day. The Southern States are the strongest supporters in this country of prohibitory legislation.

Then, some time later, I found myself attending a Harvard Club dinner in the State of Missouri. There were many things to drink at that dinner also. I was informed that some of the leading citizens of Missouri, engaged in manufacturing operations, were going to move their plants over into the State of Kansas. I observed later that a large number of Missouri manufacturers did move their plants over into the State of Kansas, and learned, on inquiry, that those manufacturers had made up their minds that they could conduct their businesses much better in a State where a prohibitory law existed than they could in a State where the law did not exist.

I have had the delight of passing my summers for more than forty years – yes, it is fifty-two years since I first began to go to Mount Desert in summer – in the State of Maine. There I observed that the prohibitory law in Maine was not observed at all excepting in communities where, as one guest has said to-night, the great majority of the population was in favor of prohibition. There alone was the distribution of alcoholic drinks restrained. I lived there fifty summers, observing the fact that the prohibitory law in Maine was not generally enforced; observing that the summer residents of the State of Maine, who, as you know, live all along the shore and in several of the beautiful lake regions, paid no attention to the prohibitory law.

What inference did I draw from that experience? Simply that unless the strong majority of any government unit in the States where prohibitory laws exist was in favor of prohibition, the law would, as a matter of fact, not be enforced.

But further: It was obvious that no single State could possibly enforce prohibition, because it had no power to prevent the manufacture of alcoholic drinks outside the State or their importation into it. You must have national prohibition to make prohibition effective. It must be nationwide, or it simply cannot be enforced.

So I supported for many years in Massachusetts, not prohibition, but local option; but then I learned that the sale of distilled liquors in saloons licensed to sell light wines and beer cannot be prevented. Nobody should advocate the repeal of the Volstead Act except those who believe in the unrestricted sale of alcoholic beverages. I ought perhaps to say that I took wine or beer when I was in the society of people who were using them. I never had any habit of drinking them at home; but I always took them when I was in the company of men or women who were using them. I had no feeling that alcohol was bad for everybody, or bad for me. I never knew alcohol to do me any harm; but then I never drank distilled liquors at all. When the United States in the spring of 1917 went to war, you remember that with the support of all the best civilian authorities and of the officers in the Army and Navy, our Government enacted a prohibitory law for the regions surrounding the camps and barracks where the National Army was being assembled. The Act proved to be effective and highly beneficent.

Then I said to myself, "If that is the action of my Government to protect our soldiers and sailors preparing to go to war, I think it is time for me to abstain from alcoholic drinks altogether." It is only since 1917 that I have been a total abstainer; but that is now six years ago, and I want to testify here, now, that by adopting total abstinence, after having had the opposite habit for over seventy years, one loses no joys that are worth having, and there is no joy-killing about it. On the contrary, I enjoy social life and working life more since I ceased to take any alcohol than I did before.

That talk, gentlemen, about joy-killing and pleasure-losing, and so forth, is absolute nonsense for a man who has any sense himself. . . .

We all know that our Puritan ancestors and our Pilgrim ancestors were not persons who cultivated the finer joys of life. They left behind them the great architecture of England, and its parks and its music. The Pilgrims came over from Holland, having lived there for ten or fifteen years in sight of all the glorious Dutch paintings, sculpture, and architecture. They abandoned all those things, and settled in the wilderness, where there was little possibility of cultivating the love of beauty and little power, too, of resisting the theological dogmas they had imbibed, which taught that human nature was utterly depraved, and that most of the human race were bound for a fiery hell.

Those are the people from whom the leading thinkers and doers of America sprang; and it is naturally inevitable that we, their descendants, should lack the love of beauty in nature and in art, and even in music. We do lack it. The Pilgrims and the Puritans lacked it to an extraordinary degree.

Where did they find their pleasures? Largely in drink. They drank hard at weddings, funerals, and all public festivals. We have that inheritance, but can we not resist and overcome it? Can we not grow up into a love of beauty in nature and in art? Can we not cultivate in ourselves the delight in music – in singing and in playing instruments? We are not hopeless in those respects; and those are the things we have got to learn to love, in order to escape from this wretched evil of alcoholism.

But how shall we do it? We must cultivate in ourselves the finer inspirations, the purer delights, and the greater joys in art and in work. But, more than that, we have got to practice resistance to acknowledged manifest evils in our common life.

That has always been my way of living, from day to day, in the practice of my profession. From the beginning, that was the way I lived. I attacked what seemed to me a plain, acknowledged, manifest evil, and advocated the best remedy I knew for that evil. That is just what we have got to do today, gentlemen, about this abominable evil of alcoholism associated with venereal disease; because that evil will kill us unless we kill it. By "us" I mean the white race, and particularly the American stock. Must we not accept the proposition that we must either destroy alcoholism and venereal disease, or those evils will destroy us? I believe that to be the plain truth; and I want to call on every lover of his kindred and of his country, hourly, daily, year after year, to contend against these evils, alcoholism, and venereal disease, until they are obliterated from the world. Finally, may we not reasonably distrust the legal view that has been repeatedly presented here this evening, namely, that the rights and privileges of decent and vigorous people should not be abridged for the sake of indecent or weak people who abuse their privileges?

Key terms

lawless decade	*Carroll et al. v. U.S.*	Harry Anslinger
Marijuana Tax Act	Bureau of Narcotics	*Reefer Madness*
Eighteenth Amendment	Prohibition	Wickersham Commission
Seabury Investigations	J. Edgar Hoover	Kansas City Massacre
G-men	*Uniform Crime Reports*	Eliot Ness
Untouchables	Frank J. Wilson	IRS

Espionage	Prohibition agents	Volstead Act
Berkeley Police School	Orlando W. Wilson	"new penology"
Big House prisons	prison industries	state-use system
Hawes-Cooper Act	Ashurst-Summers Act	prisoner classification
Robert Elliott Burns	sweat box	*I Am a Fugitive from a*
Teapot Dome scandal	organized crime	*Georgia Chain Gang*
kidnapping	Lindbergh kidnapping	Thomas Dewey
Calvin H. Goddard	St. Valentine's Day Massacre	Tulsa race riot
Scottsboro trials	*Johnson v. Zerbst*	Murder Incorporated

Critical thinking questions

1 How did the passage of the Eighteenth Amendment affect patterns of criminality and the American criminal justice system?
2 What is meant by the phrase "police professionalism?"
3 How did the nation's prison systems respond to the 1920s and 1930s?
4 What role did the media play in creating an image of lawlessness during this era? How did law enforcement exploit the rise of sensationalism in the press?
5 How did the crisis decades affect American opinion on the death penalty?
6 Discuss the growth of organized criminal activity in this era.
7 What impact did the civil rights movement have on the criminal justice system?
8 Compare and contrast regional differences in crime and criminal justice in the crisis era.
9 What was J. Edgar Hoover's impact on federal law enforcement?
10 How did the New Deal years affect the growth and development of the criminal justice system?

Notes

1 Kermit L. Hall, *The Magic Mirror: Law in American History*, New York: Oxford University Press, 1989, p. 253.
2 Frank Richard Prassel, *The Great American Outlaw: A Legacy of Fact and Fiction*, Norman: University of Oklahoma Press, 1993, p. 271.
3 Samuel Walker, *Popular Justice*, New York: Oxford University Press, 1998, p. 173.
4 David Bodenhamer, *Fair Trial: Rights of the Accused in American History*, New York: Oxford University Press, 1992, p. 94.
5 Richard J. Bonnie and Charles H. Whitebread, "The Forbidden Fruit and the Tree of Knowledge: An Inquiry into the Legal History of American Marijuana Prohibition," *Virginia Law Review*, 56(6), 1970, p. 976.
6 Steven B. Karch, *A Brief History of Cocaine*, Boca Raton, FL: CRC, 1998, p. 1.
7 David F. Musto, *The American Disease: Origins of Narcotic Control*, New York: Oxford University Press, 1987, p. 228.
8 Iain Gately, *Tobacco: A Cultural History of How an Exotic Plant Seduced Civilization*, New York: Grove Press, 2001, p. 36.
9 Ibid.

10 Lisa McGirr, *The War on Alcohol: Prohibition and the Rise of the American State*, New York: W.W. Norton and Company, 2016.

11 William Helmer and Rick Mattix, *Public Enemies: America's Criminal Past, 1919–1940*, New York: Checkmark Books, 1998, p. 65.

12 David Oshinsky, "Temperance to Excess," *New York Times Book Review*, May 21, 2010, https://www.nytimes.com/2010/05/23/books/review/Oshinsky-t.html

13 Daniel Okrent, *Last Call: The Rise and Fall of Prohibition*, New York: Scribner, 2010, pp. 207, 211.

14 Quoted in Ibid., p. 272.

15 Ibid., p. 207.

16 Ibid., p. 212.

17 Helmer and Mattix, 1998, p. 61.

18 The phrase "third degree" refers to police-sanctioned brutality, which was more prevalent during the pre-Miranda rights era. In the 1930s, parlance ranging from "shallacking" and "massaging" to "breaking the news" and "giving him the works" was synonymous with giving a criminal suspect the third degree. Many police departments condoned the beating of suspects to extract confessions. Methods of third degree interrogation included the water cure (which involved forcing water down the nostrils of supine victims), beatings with a rubber hose, and drilling into the nerves of the teeth.

19 For detailed account of Seabury and his crusade against corruption, see Herbert Mitgang, *Once Upon a Time in New York: Jimmy Walker, Franklin Roosevelt, and the Last Great Battle of the Jazz Age*, New York: Free Press, 2000.

20 Elliott Gorn, *Dillinger's Wild Ride: The Year That Made America's Public Enemy Number One*, New York: Oxford University Press, 2009, p. 168.

21 Elliott J. Gorn, *Dillinger's Wild Ride: The Year That Made America's Public Enemy Number One*, New York: Oxford University Press, 2009, p. 168.

22 The bureau had actually been renamed the United States Bureau of Investigation in 1932. However, confusion ran supreme when the Department of Justice began a two-year experiment with a Division of Investigation that also included a Bureau of Prohibition. The public soon could not differentiate between Bureau of Investigation special agents and Bureau of Prohibition agents, leading to the permanent name change to Federal Bureau of Investigation in 1935.

23 Frank Spiering, *The Man Who Got Capone*, New York: Bobbs-Merrill, 1976.

24 H. Kenneth Bechtel, *State Police in the United States: A Socio-Historical Analysis*, Westport, CT: Greenwood Press, 1995, pp. 40–41.

25 David R. Johnson, *American Law Enforcement: A History*, Wheeling, IL: Forum Press, 1981, p. 164.

26 John J. Binder, *Al Capone's Beer Wars: A Complete History of Organized Crime in Chicago during Prohibition*, New York: Prometheus Books, 2017, pp. 24–242. See also Douglas Perry, *Eliot Ness: The Rise and Fall of an American Hero*, New York: Viking, 2014.

27 Blake McKelvey, *American Prisons: A History of Good Intentions*, Montclair, NJ: Patterson Smith, 1977, p. 293.

28 Quoted in Scott Christianson, *With Liberty for Some: 500 Years of Imprisonment in America*, Boston: Northeastern University Press, p. 228.

29 Ibid., p. 238.

30 Edgardo Rotman, "The Failure of Reform: United States, 1865–1965," in *Oxford History of the Prison*, ed. Morris and Rothman, New York: Oxford University Press, 1998, p. 164.

31 Lewis E. Lawes, *Life and Death at Sing Sing*, New York: Doubleday, Doran and Company, 1928; Stephen Cox, *The Big House: Image and Reality of the American Prison*, New Haven, CT: Yale University Press, 2009.

32 *Proceedings of the 60th Annual Congress of the American Prison Association*, New York: American Correctional Association, 1930, pp. 111–113.

33 George W. Kirchway, "The Prison's Place in the Penal System," in *The Annals*, ed. Edwin H. Sutherland and Thorsten Sellin, Philadelphia: The American Academy of Political and Social Science, 1931, p. 13.

34 Convict wages had little if any impact on the popularity of prison labor since only a small percentage of prisons paid any wages. In 1940, Auburn was paying its agricultural workers five cents per day and shop employees twenty cents per day.

35 Lawrence E. Sullivan, *The Prison Reform Movement: Forlorn Hope*, Boston: Twayne Publishers, 1990, p. 40.

36 Blake McKelvey, *American Prisons: A Study in American Prisons*, New York: Putnam, Montclair: Patterson Smith, 1977.

37 Rotman, 1998, p. 168.

38 Sullivan, 1990, p. 40.

39 Scott Christianson, *With Liberty for Some*, Boston: Northeastern University Press, 2000, p. 182.

40 Jesse Steiner and Roy M. Brown, *The North Carolina Chain Gang: A Study of Convict Road Work*, Chapel Hill: University of North Carolina Press, 1927.

41 Scott Christianson, *With Liberty for Some: 500 Years of Imprisonment in America*, Boston: Northeastern University Press, 1998; Marilyn McShane, "Chain Gangs," in *Encyclopedia of American Prisons*, ed. Marilyn D. McShane and Frank Williams, III, New York: Garland Publishing, 1996, pp. 71–73.

42 Gary Krist, *City of Scoundrels: The 12 Days of Disaster That Gave Birth to Modern Chicago*, New York: Crown Books, 2012.

43 Nathan Ward, "The Fire Last Time: When Terrorists First Struck New York's Financial Distract," *American Heritage*, December 2001, p. 46.

44 Paul Avrich, *Sacco and Vanzetti: The Anarchist Background*, Princeton, NJ: Princeton University Press, 1991, p. 137; Mike Davis, *Buda's Wagon: A Brief History of the Car Bomb*, London: Verso, 2007.

45 Beverly Gage, *The Day Wall Street Exploded: A Story of America in Its First Age of Terror*, New York: Oxford University Press, 2009, pp. 32–326.

46 Davis, 2007, p. 3.

47 Laton McCartney, *The Teapot Dome Scandal: How Big Oil Bought the Harding White House and Tried to Steal the Country*, New York: Random House, 2009; Shelley Ross, *Fall from Grace: Sex, Scandal, and Corruption in American Politics from 1702 to the Present*, New York: Ballantine Books, 1988, p. 159.

48 Quoted in Don Cusic, *The Trials of Henry Flipper, First Black Graduate of West Point*, Jefferson: McFarland, 2009, p. 163.

49 Johnson, 1981, p. 147.

50 Gorn, 2009, pp. 170–171.

51 Ibid., p. 33.

52 Joe Urschel, *The Year of Fear: Machine Gun Kelly and the Manhunt That Changed the Nation*, New York: Minotaur Books, 2015, p. 38.

53 One of the best accounts of the Depression era bandits can be found in Bryan Burroughs, *Public Enemies: America's Greatest Crime Wave and the Birth of the FBI, 1933–1934*, New York: Penguin, 2004.

54 Unger (1997) claims that none of the official accounts was true. After an exhaustive search through the eighty-nine-volume FBI case file, he concluded that most of the victims were killed by friendly fire because of the proximity of the individuals to one another and one agent's unfamiliarity with his shotgun.

55 Urschel, 2015, p. 51.

56 Walter L. Hixson, *Murder, Culture, and Injustice: Four Sensational Cases in American History*, Akron, OH: Akron University Press, 2001, p. 75.

57 Ibid.

58 Urschel, 2015, pp. 51–52.

59 Ernest Kahlar Alix, *Ransom Kidnapping in America, 1874–1974: The Creation of a Capital Crime*, Carbondale: Southern Illinois University Press, 1978, p. 186.

60 Linda Gordon, *The Second Coming of the KKK: The Ku Klux Klan and the American Political Tradition*, New York: Liveright Publishing, 2017.

61 Ibid.

62 Victoria Schneider and John Ortiz Smylka, "A Summary Analysis of Executions in the United States, 1608–1987: The Espy File," in *The Death Penalty in America: Current Research*, ed. Robert Bohm, Cincinnati: Anderson Publishing, pp. 6–7.

63 Stuart Banner, *The Death Penalty: An American History*, Cambridge, MA: Harvard University Press, 2003, p. 209.

64 Ibid., p. 197; Scott Christianson, *The Last Gasp: The Rise and Fall of the American Gas Chamber*, Berkeley, CA: University of California Press, 2010.

65 Ibid.

66 See, for example, Tim Madigan, *The Burning: Massacre, Destruction, and the Tulsa Race Riot of 1921*, New York: St. Martin's Press, 2003; Alfred L. Brophy, *Reconstructing the Dreamland: The Tulsa Race Riot of 1921: Race, Reparations, and Reconciliation*, New York: Oxford University Press, 2003.

67 Laurence Bergreen, *Capone: The Man and the Era*, New York: Simon and Schuster, 1994, p. 315.

68 Colin Beavan, *Fingerprints: The Origins of Crime Detection and the Murder Case That Launched Forensic Science*, New York: Hyperion, 2001, p. 30.

69 Brian Lane, *The Encyclopedia of Forensic Science*, London: Headline Publishing, 1992, p. 53.

70 Ibid.

71 Gilbert Geis and Leigh B. Beinen, *Crimes of the Century: From Leopold and Loeb to O. J. Simpson*, Boston: Northeastern University Press, 1998, p. 75.

72 Haywood Patterson and Earl Conrad, *Scottsboro Boy*, Garden City, NY: Doubleday, 1951, p. 299.

73 David Cole, *No Equal Justice: Race and Crime in the American Criminal Justice System*, New York: New Press, 1999, p. 68.

74 Samuel Walker, *Popular Justice*, New York: Oxford University Press, 1998, p. 156.

75 Alan Blinder, "Clear Names for the Last 'Scottsboro Boys'," *New York Times*, November 22, 2013, p. A12.

76 Lawrence M. Friedman, *A History of American Law*, New York: Oxford University Press, p. 568.

77 Claire Bond Potter, *War on Crime: Bandits, G-Men, and the Politics of Mass Culture*, New Brunswick, NJ: Rutgers University Press, 1998, p. 196.

78 Quoted in Helmer and Mattix, 1998, p. 65.

Sources

Alix, Ernest Kahlar. 1978. *Ransom Kidnapping in America, 1874–1974: The Creation of a Capital Crime*. Carbondale: Southern Illinois University Press.

Avrich, Paul. 1991. *Sacco and Vanzetti: The Anarchist Background*. Princeton, NJ: Princeton University Press.

Banner, Stuart. 2003. *The Death Penalty: An American History*. Cambridge, MA: Harvard University Press.

Bechtel, H. Kenneth. 1995. *State Police in the United States: A Socio-Historical Analysis*. Westport, CT: Greenwood Press.

Binder, John J. 2017. *Al Capone's Beer Wars: A Completer History of Organized Crime in Chicago during Prohibition*. New York: Prometheus Books.

Blinder, Alan. 2013. "Clear Names for the Last 'Scottsboro Boys'." *New York Times*, November 22, p. A12.

Bodenhamer, David. 1992. *Fair Trial: The Rights of the Accused in American History*. New York: Oxford University Press.

Bonnie, Richard J. and Charles H. Whitebread. 1970. "The Forbidden Fruit and the Tree of Knowledge: An Inquiry into the Legal History of American Marijuana Prohibition." *Virginia Law Review*, 56(6):971–1970.

Brophy, Alfred L. 2003. *Reconstructing the Dreamland: The Tulsa Race Riot of 1921, Race: Reparations, and Reconciliation*. New York: Oxford University Press.

Burroughs, Bryan. 2004. *Public Enemies: America's Greatest Crime Wave and the Birth of the FBI, 1933–34*. New York: Penguin.

Carter, Dan T. 1969. *Scottsboro: A Tragedy of the American South*. Baton Rouge: Louisiana State University Press.

Cashman, Sean David. 1981. *Prohibition: The Lie of the Land*. New York: Free Press.

Christianson, Scott. 1998. *With Liberty for Some: 500 Years of Imprisonment in America*. Boston: Northeastern University Press.

Cole, David. 1999. *No Equal Justice: Race and Crime in the American Criminal Justice System*. New York: New Press.

Davis, Mike. 2007. *Buda's Wagon: A Brief History of the Car Bomb*. London: Verso.

Friedman, Lawrence. 1973. *A History of American Law*. New York: Simon and Schuster.

Gage, Beverly. 2009. *The Day Wall Street Exploded: A Story of America in the First Age of Terror*. New York: Oxford University Press.

Geis, Gilbert and Leigh B. Beinen. 1998. *Crimes of the Century: From Leopold and Loeb to O. J. Simpson*. Boston: Northeastern University Press.

Gordon, Linda. 2017. *The Second Coming of the KKK: The Ku Klux Klan and the American Political Tradition*. New York, NY: Liveright Publishing.

Gorn, Elliott J. 2009. *Dillinger's Wild Ride: The Year That Made America's Public Enemy Number One*. New York: Oxford University Press.

Hall, Kermit L. 1989. *The Magic Mirror: Law in American History*. New York: Oxford University Press.

Helmer, William and Rick Mattix. 1998. *Public Enemies: America's Criminal Past, 1919–1940*. New York: Checkmark Books.

Hixson, Walter L. 2001. *Murder, Culture, and Injustice: Four Sensational Cases in American History*. Akron, OH: University of Akron Press.

Johnson, David R. 1981. *American Law Enforcement: A History*. Wheeling, IL: Forum Press.

Karch, Steven B. 1998. *A Brief History of Cocaine*. Boca Raton, FL: CRC.

Kennedy, Randall. 1997. *Race, Crime, and the Law*. New York: Pantheon Books.

Kirchway, George W. 1931. "The Prison's Place in the Penal System." In *The Annals*, ed. Edwin Sutherland and Thorsten Sellin. Philadelphia: The American Academy of Political and Social Science.

Kobler, John. 1974. *Ardent Spirits: The Rise and Fall of Prohibition*. London: Michael Joseph.

Krist, Gary. 2012. *City of Scoundrels: The 12 Days of Disaster That Gave Birth to Modern Chicago*. New York: Crown Books.

Lane, Roger. 1997. *Murder in America: A History*. Columbus: Ohio State University Press.

Lender, Mark Edward and James Kirby Martin. 1987. *Drinking in America: A History*. New York: Free Press.

Madigan, Tim. 2003. *The Burning: Massacre, Destruction, and the Tulsa Race Riot of 1921*. New York: St. Martin's Press.

McCartney, Laton. 2009. *The Teapot Dome Scandal: How Big Oil Bought the Harding White House and Tried to Steal the Country*. New York: Random House.

McGirr, Lisa. 2016. *The War on Alcohol: Prohibition and the Rise of the American State*. New York: W.W. Norton and Company.

McKelvey, Blake. 1977. *American Prisons: A History of Good Intentions*. Montclair, NJ: Patterson Smith.

Mitgang, Herbert. 2000. *Once upon a Time in New York: Jimmy Walker, Franklin Roosevelt, and the Last Great Battle of the Jazz Age*. New York: Free Press.

Musto, David F. 1987. *The American Disease: Origins of Narcotic Control*. New York: Oxford University Press.

Okrent, Daniel. 2010. *Last Call: The Rise and Fall of Prohibition*. New York: Scribner.

Patterson, Haywood and Earl Conrad. 1951. *Scottsboro Boy*. Garden City, NY: Doubleday.

Perry, Douglas. 2014. *Elliot Ness: The Rise and Fall of an American Hero*. New York: Viking.

Potter, Claire Bond. 1998. *War on Crime: Bandits, G-Men, and the Politics of Mass Culture*. New Brunswick, NJ: Rutgers University Press.

Powers, Richard Gid. 1983. *G-Men: Hoover's FBI in American Popular Culture*. Carbondale: Southern Illinois University Press.

Prassel, Frank Richard. 1993. *The Great American Outlaw: A Legacy of Fact and Fiction*. Norman: University of Oklahoma Press.

Proceedings of the 60th Annual Congress of the American Prison Association. 1930. New York: American Correctional Association.

Ross, Shelley. 1988. *Fall from Grace: Sex, Scandal, and Corruption in American Politics from 1702 to the Present*. New York: Ballantine Books.

Rotman, Edgardo. 1998. "The Failure of Reform: United States, 1865–1965." In *The Oxford History of the Prison*, ed. Norval Morris and David J. Rothman, pp. 151–177. New York: Oxford University Press.

Ruth, David E. 1996. *Inventing the Public Enemy: The Gangster in American Culture, 1918–1934*. Chicago: University of Chicago Press.

Schneider, Victoria and John Ortiz Smykla. 1991. "A Summary Analysis of Executions in the United States, 1608–1987: The Espy File." In *The Death Penalty in America: Current Research*, ed. Robert M. Bohm, pp. 1–19. Cincinnati: Anderson Publishing.

Sloman, Larry. 1979. *Reefer Madness: The History of Marijuana in America*. New York: Bobbs-Merrill.

Spiering, Frank. 1976. *The Man Who Got Capone*. New York: Bobbs-Merrill.

Sullivan, Lawrence E. 1990. *The Prison Reform Movement: Forlorn Hope*. Boston: Twayne Publishers.

Unger, Robert. 1997. *The Union Station Massacre: The Original Sin of J. Edgar Hoover's FBI*. Kansas City: Andrews McMeel Publishers.

Urschel, Joe. 2015. *The Year of Fear: Machine Gun Kelly and the Manhunt That Changed the Nation*. New York: Minotaur Books.

Walker, Samuel. 1998. *Popular Justice: A History of American Criminal Justice*. New York: Oxford University Press.

Ward, Nathan. 2001. "The First Last Time: When Terrorists First Struck New York's Financial District." *American Heritage*, December, pp. 46–49.

1941	1942	1942	1943	1943	1944	1946	1947
America enters World War II after attack on Pearl Harbor	Internment of Japanese Americans	Nazi saboteurs arrested along coasts of Florida and Long Island	Zoot-Suit Riot	Race riots in Detroit and Harlem	IACP argues against police unionism	Sodium pentothal used for first time in William Heirens case	House Un-American Activities Committee hearings

CHAPTER ELEVEN

Crime and criminal justice at midcentury (1940 – 1959)

Learning objectives

After reading this chapter students should understand and be able to discuss:

- The impact of World War II on the American criminal justice system
- The strain of paranoia that drove McCarthyism and the communist hysteria and its roots in early American criminal justice
- The decisions of the Warren Court and their ramifications for criminal justice in the following decades
- How the FBI made the transition from chasing gangsters to communists
- Prison conditions before and after World War II
- The rising specter of organized crime and the response of federal law enforcement to it
- The diminished use of the death penalty
- Changing patterns of American violence and the hysteria over rising juvenile crime

World War II transformed American society more than any other conflict in its history. During the 1940s, the federal government became much more centralized and united the population as never before. Wartime industry not only ended the Great Depression but also began several decades of unrivaled prosperity. But old fears still lingered. Fear of communist subversion at home and rising juvenile crime and the battle for civil rights presented the criminal justice system with new challenges in the 1940s and 1950s.

Fortunately, the end of World War II did not end on a somber note like World War I, which saw America reeling from race riots, labor strife, police strikes and attacks on civil

DOI: 10.4324/9781315148342-11

1947	1947	1947	1948	1949	1949	1950	1950
Patton v. Mississippi	The Flamingo Hotel and Casino opens in Las Vegas	Bugsy Siegel murdered in Los Angeles	Caryl Chessman trial	Psychologist William H. Sheldon inaugurates discipline of "constitutional psychology"	Howard Unruh commits first rampage killing of modern era	Beginning of Korean War	Publication of O. W. Wilson's *Police Administration*

liberties. In sharp contrast, the postwar years were marked by great advances in civility, with race relations improving in different regions and murder rates declining. Rather than slipping into the post-World War I violent chaos surrounding Prohibition, the 1940s and 1950s seemed mighty tame in comparison.

However, there was a darker side, a harbinger of sorts that would find resonance in the 1990s and beyond, such as a sensational rampage killing that dominated the headlines in the 1940s and 1950s. When **Howard Unruh** stepped out on a busy Camden, New Jersey street in 1949, mowing down twelve of his neighbors in thirteen minutes, few could have imagined the school-yard and workplace shootings that would punctuate the 1990s and 2000s.

Returning home from the world war, servicemen were confronted with a changing home front. Many returned with different cultural values than the ones they went off to war with. In the years following the war, **outlaw motorcycle gangs** were organized by "groups of young men, many newly-returned soldiers, who formed motorcycle clubs and rejected normal civilian lifestyles. In the next several years their behavior became not so boisterous as surly, less rebellious than openly criminal."[1] In the aftermath of a motorcycle riot in Hollister, California, in 1946, the phrase "outlaw motorcycle" was reportedly used for the first time, referring to the actions of a gang that evolved into the notorious Hell's Angels.

Others challenged the status quo on a less bellicose level but would still disrupt the social fabric and arouse fear among conservatives. On May 21, 1957, a San Francisco police officer arrested bookstore owner Lawrence Ferlinghetti for selling "obscene literature" shortly after purchasing a copy of poet Allen Ginsberg's *Howl and Other Poems* from his establishment. In the 1950s, "beats" or "**beatniks**," such as Allen Ginsberg and Jack Kerouac, captured media attention with their writings as they tapped into a reservoir of discontent among the younger generation.

While informal networks of gambling halls operated in various parts of the country prior to the war, no one could have imagined the development of the American gambling scene beginning in the 1940s nor how widespread gambling would become by the end of the twentieth century. In the months before Pearl Harbor, several gambling clubs and fledgling casinos were operating in Las Vegas, where gambling was legalized in 1931. However, most visitors still came to marvel at Hoover Dam or perhaps to take advantage of the easy divorce laws.

The lawgivers

While cultural tensions seemed to have diminished in America since the 1920s, they were still a source of social conflict. In December 1941, just weeks after the attack on Pearl Harbor, President Franklin D. Roosevelt issued an executive order suspending naturalization

1950	1950	1950	1950	1950	1952	1953	1953	1954
William Henry Parker appointed Los Angeles police chief	National execution statistics to National Prisoner Statistics Series	Beginning of the Kefauver hearings	FBI introduces "Ten Most Wanted" program	Brink's robbery	Riot at State Prison of Southern Michigan	Execution of the Rosenbergs	Earl Warren appointed chief justice of U.S. Supreme Court	Sam Sheppard convicted of wife's murder

proceedings for immigrants from enemy nations (Italy, Germany, and Japan). The new legislation required these immigrants to register, restricted their movements, and prohibited them from owning items that could be utilized for sabotage, such as cameras and shortwave radios. In reality, not all enemy aliens were treated the same. German and Italian aliens would receive more compassionate treatment compared to the Japanese.

The Japanese had been barred from immigrating to the United States by the **Immigration Act of 1924**, when only 110,000 lived on the mainland, mostly in California (another 150,000 lived in Hawaii). The outbreak of World War II ignited simmering racial tensions on the West Coast, where many Japanese Americans had lived for generations. An amalgamation of factors, including racism, nativism, and wartime security concerns, led President Roosevelt to issue **Executive Order 9066** on February 19, 1942. Less than six months after America's entry into the war, the president signed into law the order that relocated more than 100,000 Japanese Americans, most of whom were American citizens, from the West Coast to ten relocation camps in remote locations, including Jerome, Arkansas, and Heart Mountain, Wyoming. There, American citizens who had committed no crimes were locked behind barbed wire and crowded into accommodations resembling minimum-security prisons.

Most constitutional historians consider this one of the greatest violations of individual rights in the history of the country. Almost overnight, thousands of Japanese Americans, without trial or hearings, were forced to dispose of their homes, personal property, and businesses, leading to tragic consequences for many families. However, almost 18,000 Japanese American men effected their release from the camps and served gallantly in combat.

Throughout the war years, Japanese Americans protested their treatment, claiming that their civil rights had been violated. However, in 1944, the Supreme Court supported the federal government by a vote of six to three in **Korematsu v. United States**, citing current national security concerns. It was not until the waning months of the war that the federal government ended a shameful chapter in American legal history by taking steps to close down the camps. However, many were still held prisoner until mid-1946, almost one year after the ending of hostilities.

Ex parte Quirin: landmark secret tribunal case

The capture of eight Nazi saboteurs by the FBI allowed J. Edgar Hoover to convince President Franklin D. Roosevelt to convene secret tribunals to try the men as "unlawful combatants." This U.S. Supreme Court case would be cited during the "war on terrorism"

1954	1954	1955	1957	1957	1957	1958	1959
Brown v. Board of Education	Army-McCarthy hearings	Murder of Emmett Till	Publication of *Parker on Police*	Apalachin Conference alerts nation to existence of organized crime	Publication of Marvin Wolfgang's *Patterns of Criminal Homicide*	J. Edgar Hoover details his strategy for defeating communism at home in *Masters of Deceit: The Story of Communism in America and How to Fight It*	Murder of Clutter family inspires Truman Capote to write *In Cold Blood*

in the 1990s and 2000s during the administration of President George W. Bush. Following the post-9/11 anti-terrorism campaign, it was cited as precedent for the detention and secret trials of al-Qaeda terrorist suspects. The challenge of how to try foreign terrorists in the United States has been a subject of much debate: should they be tried in a civil court or a military tribunal?

The Operation Pastorius trial (named after one of the saboteurs) was tried by a military commission. Like his future counterpart, Roosevelt ordered this form of trial because it could be held in secret and a death sentence was available and likely. These types of trials were noteworthy for their relative speed and less stringent court rules. Perhaps one government official put it best when he commented, "You didn't need to prove anything beyond a reasonable doubt."[2] The proceedings went along as expected, with six defendants sentenced to death and two others to prison. Their convictions were challenged by the defense, who argued they were not "lawful combatants" and therefore should not be judged by a military trial. However, the U.S. Supreme Court would have the final say on July 31, 1942. In the ruling *Ex parte Quirin* (also named after one of the saboteurs), the court agreed the defendants were not "lawful combatants." However,

> our government has likewise recognized that those who during the war surreptitiously enter from enemy territory, discard uniforms on entry for commission of hostile acts involving the destruction of life and property have status of unlawful combatants punishable as such by a military commission.[3]

After having their petitions for habeas corpus denied on August 3, they were found guilty and electrocuted five days later.

In his continuing quest for publicity, FBI Director Hoover used the capture and execution of the saboteurs to further burnish his credentials and those of his G-Men. It would later come out that the FBI actually had very little to do with their capture and the break-up of the Nazi sabotage ring. Rather, saboteur George Dasch voluntarily telephoned authorities and revealed the Operation Pastorius plot. His actions would ultimately save his life. But for the time being, the FBI director was an American hero.[4]

In the 1944 case of *Rex v. Duncan*, Helen Duncan was sentenced to nine months in prison (later reduced to six months), for violating the Witchcraft Act of 1735. According to the Act, if any person shall pretend to exercise or use any kind of witchcraft, sorcery, enchantment, or conjuration, or undertake to tell fortunes, every person so offending shall suffer imprisonment by the space of one whole year without bail. "Yes, this was 1944!" Dubbed the trial of "Hellish Nell," the case seemed so ludicrous that even the defendant could not suppress a grin during the proceedings. In the end, she was charged with using her spiritualistic claims to "manifest spirits of the dead" for a fee. As a result, in 1951, the British Parliament revoked and replaced the Witchcraft Act of 1735 with the 1951 Fraudulent Mediums Act, which targeted individuals who connived to cheat and commit defraud.[5]

Joseph McCarthy and communist hysteria

Fear of communism in America had existed since the Bolshevik Revolution in 1917. However, with the birth of the atomic age and Russian nuclear power, tensions over the Soviet threat were heightened. Soon, politicians such as Richard M. Nixon and Joseph McCarthy would use communist bashing as a strategy for political advancement. As early as 1947, President Harry S. Truman was pressured to inaugurate the communist "witch hunts" by creating loyalty boards to check on reports of communist sympathizers in the federal government. Thousands were investigated as innuendo superseded evidence in the hunt for communist spies. Out of this venomous cloud of hysteria emerged Wisconsin Senator Joseph McCarthy. During the 1950s, paranoia over communist subversion swept America. No politician is more associated with the excesses of this era than McCarthy, who took advantage of the political climate of the time to further his own career by destroying the working lives of hundreds of individuals.

Beginning with the 1798 Alien and Sedition Acts, there have been several attempts to limit civil liberties at the expense of the Constitution. One of the more notable twentieth-century examples involved the 1947 **House Un-American Activities Committee (HUAC)**, which attempted to outlaw the Communist Party. The HUAC had been created in the 1930s and had become increasingly oppressive in its dedication to stifling dissent and liberty of thought. In 1947, the HUAC targeted Hollywood and in the process destroyed the livelihoods of the "Hollywood Ten" (writers, directors, and producers). Their hearings proved a travesty of justice. The committee refused to allow nine of the witnesses to make prefatory statements on their civil rights privileges. When the ten refused to give yes-or-no answers to the questions "Are you now or have you ever been a member of the Communist Party of the United States?" and "Are you a member of the Screenwriters' Guild?" they were found guilty of contempt, jailed for a year, and illegally blacklisted by Hollywood. The so-called American Inquisition contributed to the climate of fear that would allow Senator McCarthy to ride roughshod over the Constitution and the Fifth Amendment in the 1950s.

As chair of the Senate Committee on Government Operations, McCarthy accused the military of harboring communist infiltrators. In response, the army demanded that he support his allegations, and on April 22, 1954, an estimated 20 million viewers watched the televised Army–McCarthy hearings.

Deviating little from his aggressive no-holds-barred style of examining witnesses, McCarthy seemed at the outset of the hearings to overmatch his sixty-three-year-old opponent and attorney for the army, Joseph Welch. But he had taken up a battle that would turn against him when he challenged the U.S. Army to purge supposed communists from the

Pentagon. Welch proved more than a match for his antagonist. After McCarthy launched into his usual relentless attacks, Welch asked the senator to support his accusations. After a withering barrage of cross-examination, McCarthy accused Welch's own Boston firm of harboring a communist. Welch responded in a calm dignified manner. His response is considered a high point of civility in an era dominated by baseless attacks on persons and civil liberties. Welch ended his rebuke of McCarthy with the familiar "Have you no decency left at all?" – a question that by that point must have resonated with many of the millions of viewers. Although the hearings continued for five more days, McCarthy's inquisition had been brought to a stunning climax, and two months later, he was censured by the Senate. "Tail-gunner Joe" would die in 1957 from the effects of alcoholism. (Welch would enjoy a scintilla of celebrity as a lecturer and as an actor, playing a judge in the 1959 James Stewart vehicle *Anatomy of a Murder*.)

During the 1920s and 1930s, several decades before the HUAC Hearings, "witch hunt" became synonymous with government repression after American journalists covering the Soviet beat applied the label to the ongoing Stalinist purges of dissenters. The term was later adopted back in the United States as "hyperbole for unreasonable government regulation" of just about anything. In the decade leading up to the 1950s McCarthy hearings, the *New York Times* contained references to witch hunts against bathing suit wearers, horse racing bookies, and a group of New England egg dealers accused of price fixing. As the communist hearings died out in the mid-1950s, the hysteria over "Reds" lingered in the American consciousness. In the 1970s, President Nixon referred to the Watergate scandal as a witch hunt to intimates. According to one journalist, "Nixon helped introduce a new way of thinking about the witch hunt – a persecution not by, but of, the powerful." More recently, "witch hunt" has entered the political lexicon during the presidential administration of Donald Trump. Caught in the crosshairs of investigators, President Trump tweeted that the special prosecutor appointed to investigate collusion between his campaign and Russian operatives was "the single greatest witch hunt of a politician in American history!"[6]

Brown v. Board of Education of Topeka

Since the Supreme Court's *Plessy v. Ferguson* (1896) ruling, everything from maternity wards to morgues, even prisons and polling places, were either segregated or for whites only. While white schools were well staffed and maintained, black schools, particularly in the South, were typically single-room shacks without toilets or heat. It should be little wonder, then, that illiteracy among America's largest racial minority was commonplace. Among the most important spokesmen in the battle to end the injustice of "separate but equal" educational systems was **Thurgood Marshall**. As the head of the Legal Defense and Educational Fund of the National Association for the Advancement of Colored People (NAACP), Marshall represented the plaintiffs in what would become known as *Brown v. Board of Education*.[7] When eleven-year-old Linda Brown decided that she did not want to make the long ride to school from her home in Topeka, Kansas, when there was a school just blocks away, she sued the Board of Education. The board ruled that since she was African American, she must attend an African American school despite its distance from her home. The Topeka court responded that the "buildings, transportation, curricula, and educational qualifications of the teachers" at her black school were equal to those provided to white students as mandated in the *Plessy v. Ferguson* decision.

When several other African American children in other parts of the country sued to switch from segregated schools as well, the Supreme Court agreed to hear the case. Represented by a legal team headed by Thurgood Marshall, between 1952 and 1954, the nation's highest court listened to testimony before taking six months to conclude by a unanimous vote that separate educational facilities were not equal in the arena of public education.

In 1954, the Supreme Court struck down the principle of "separate but equal," which had buttressed legally sanctioned segregation as unconstitutional. The Court's decision called on states to move "with all deliberate speed" to desegregate, but most ignored the order. During a painfully slow process, the NAACP would lead the civil rights struggle by challenging specific segregationist systems through a series of individual lawsuits.

In 1957, the NAACP won a court order that allowed nine black students to enroll in an all-white Little Rock, Arkansas, high school. In response, the segregationist governor ordered the Arkansas National Guard to surround the school to prevent the students from entering. Following a riot by white citizens, President Dwight D. Eisenhower federalized the National Guard and sent in 1,000 members of the 101st Airborne to protect the nine teenagers, the first time since Reconstruction that U.S. troops were ordered to the South to protect the rights of black citizens. While some question Eisenhower's intentions, to many, it was clear that he was concerned more with enforcing federal law than with protecting the students.

The U.S. Supreme Court

President Roosevelt placed his stamp on the Supreme Court with his nomination of former law professor **William O. Douglas** (1898–1980) in 1936. During a thirty-six-year tenure, longer than any other justice in history, Douglas often shocked America with his opinions. His best-known work was associated with civil liberties, opposing censorship and the death penalty, and even granting the Rosenbergs a stay of execution in 1953 (leading to a call for his impeachment). A staunch supporter of the Bill of Rights, this steadfast support of the First Amendment angered many, particularly in the 1960s, because he refused to impose any restrictions on the publication of "obscene" material.

One of the most influential chief justices in American history, **Earl Warren** (1891–1974) was nominated to the Supreme Court by President Eisenhower in 1953 after becoming the first three-time elected governor of California. Over the next two decades, Warren placed his indelible liberal stamp on the Court, leading Eisenhower to declare that his nomination was one of the worst mistakes of his presidential administration. It is often deceptive to identify the Supreme Court by the name of its chief justice, but in rare instances (in the nineteenth century, John Marshall and Roger B. Taney had similar influence), the chief justice can influence the direction of the court in such a way that the court is overshadowed by the chief justice. A testament to Earl Warren, his court is one of the few in American history to be so identified (as in "Warren Court"). According to one study of the legal profession, "Chief Justice Earl Warren changed the legal landscape of America more than any other judge except Chief Justice John Marshall."[8] His tenure was marked by a judicial activism that made the Court an active participant in the campaign for social change and civil rights.

Among the Warren Court's most significant rulings was *Brown v. Board of Education of Topeka, Kansas* (1954), which overturned the earlier decision of *Plessy v. Ferguson*, which established the doctrine of "separate but equal" public facilities for whites and African Americans. Warren's court held that separate but equal facilities were intrinsically unequal, taking the first major strides toward ending segregation not only in education but also in all other facets of American life as well. In 1966, the Court profoundly altered law enforcement with the *Miranda v. Arizona* decision, which ruled that defendants must be made aware of their rights to counsel and that anything they say can be used against them in a trial (see Chapter 12 for more on this decision).

Thurgood Marshall

The grandson of slaves, Thurgood Marshall (1908–1993) was born in Baltimore, Maryland, and educated at several universities before graduating first in his class at the Howard University Law School in 1933. Shortly after graduation, Marshall was hired by the National Association for the Advancement of Colored People. Between 1940 and 1960, he served as the director of the organization's Legal Defense and Education Fund.

Marshall rose to national prominence in the civil rights struggle of the 1950s. In 1954, he helped convince the Supreme Court to declare segregation unconstitutional in the *Brown v. Board of Education* decision. President John F. Kennedy appointed Marshall as a federal district judge in 1961, and four years later, President Lyndon Johnson made him the nation's first black solicitor general. In 1967, Marshall became the first African American Supreme Court justice. Over the next twenty-four years, Marshall would stamp his enduring imprint on civil rights law in the United States.

Law enforcement

The 1940s and 1950s witnessed police departments across the nation continue the trend toward professionalization. Following trails blazed by Bruce Smith and Raymond Fosdick, police administrators began to upgrade standards for new officers while casting off the yoke of political interference and manipulation of police forces by political bosses and ward leaders. By the 1930s, it had become clear that the only way to gain the public's trust and respect was to reduce the influence of politicians, train and educate police officers, and promote an image of professionalism in the eyes of the public.

Police reformers such as William H. Parker and Orlando W. Wilson personified the model of professional, impartial law enforcement. Both eschewed political involvement in professional decision making, and both would write new chapters in their careers as they took office in Los Angeles and Chicago, respectively, in the wake of police scandals.

It had been more than twenty years since the Boston Police Department's unsuccessful attempt to unionize. Similar to the union movement of the post-World War I era, police union activities in the 1940s were stimulated by wartime inflation. Despite the support of AFL-CIO affiliates, the International Association of Chiefs of Police (IACP) vehemently opposed unionization, arguing in 1944 that police unions were "contrary to the basic nature of police duties." Ultimately, the police union movement was stopped dead in its tracks by a combination of IACP opposition and the banning of police unions by police authorities in Los Angeles, St. Louis, Detroit, Chicago, and other cities. Those officers who refused to cooperate were fired.[9]

Orlando W. Wilson

Orlando "O. W." Wilson (1900–1972) succeeded his mentor August Vollmer on the faculty at the University of California after winning a national reputation for cleaning up the Wichita, Kansas, police department. When the IACP adopted a "Law Enforcement Code of Ethics" in 1957 as a standard for ethical police conduct, it borrowed in part from Wilson's "Square Deal Code," which he developed in 1928 as chief of police in Wichita. Wilson taught police administration at Berkeley for several years before leaving to fight in World War II. He returned to the university in 1950 as dean of the School of Criminology, and despite attempts to diminish the academic standing of the criminology program, over the next decade, he elevated the program to one of the best in the country. Sensitive to criticism that he lacked a PhD and was a poor lecturer, Wilson was most comfortable when visiting police departments, where his real acumen was appreciated. Wilson resigned his position at Berkeley to become commissioner of the Chicago Police Department in 1960 after Mayor Daley promised him there would not be any political meddling. Wilson reorganized the number of police districts to eradicate remnants of the patronage system and established the Internal Investigative Division to root out police corruption. By hiring hundreds of new employees, 1,000 police officers were released from clerical duties to pursue criminals on the streets.

Wilson watchers had learned to expect the unexpected. In 1966, he invited police critic and civil rights leader Martin Luther King Jr. to police headquarters to discuss how to improve interactions between the police and African Americans. King was quick to draw comparisons between his treatment by southern police officers and Wilson's respectful approach. Wilson retired from the force in 1967. Of his books and articles, his most influential was *Police Administration* (1963).

William H. Parker and the Los Angeles Police Department

The Los Angeles Police Department (LAPD) is one of the most storied and controversial police agencies in American history. During the Prohibition era, corruption reached into the highest levels of the department, and despite attempts by its chief, August Vollmer (1923–1924), to reform the force, Depression- and Prohibition-related corruption pervaded city politics unabated. To Vollmer's credit, he reorganized the department and implemented drastic changes that led to more efficient administration and scientific investigation.

Although the 1930s saw the introduction of police radios, improved communications, a border patrol, and a new police academy, the tumultuous years following Vollmer's stint as police chief continued to be characterized by political patronage and corruption. In the late 1920s, Police Chief James Edgar Davis resigned after a major bootlegger testified that he had paid the chief $100,000 per year for police protection. In 1939, many corrupt high-ranking officers were purged from the ranks, ushering in an era of reform and professionalism.

In 1950, William Henry Parker (1902–1966) was appointed police chief, a position he would hold until his death sixteen years later. Born in Lead, South Dakota, Parker moved to California in the 1920s and joined the Los Angeles Police Department (LAPD) in 1927. At night, he studied law, earning his degree in three years. His rise through the ranks was meteoric before leaving the force to fight in World War II. Following the war, he helped organize new police systems in Munich and Frankfurt, Germany. Returning to the LAPD, he was tabbed as police chief in 1950.

As police chief, Parker implemented higher standards for police officers and encouraged his recruits to pursue additional academic training. An advocate of professionalism, Parker introduced the Internal Affairs Division; coauthored the board of rights procedure, which guaranteed the separation of police discipline from municipal politics; and founded the Bureau of Administration.

Almost as skilled as FBI director J. Edgar Hoover in the arena of public relations, the radio and then television show *Dragnet* promoted Parker and the LAPD, which became a nationally recognized police department in the 1950s. The 1952 Kefauver crime investigation commended Parker's department for its crime fighting prowess. The 1957 publication of *Parker on Police*, edited by O. W. Wilson, did much to enhance Parker's impact on the professionalization of American policing. Parker's tenure as police chief was tarnished by racial conflict in Los Angeles, culminating in the 1965 Watts riots. Parker regarded the growing liberal shift of the 1960s with some suspicion, and in 1962, he was accused of racial bigotry and discrimination by a group of Los Angeles religious leaders. Despite a public outcry for his resignation, he refused to step down. Parker died of heart failure in 1966.

Federal law enforcement

The outbreak of World War II saw the mandate of the FBI change course from chasing gangsters to more sophisticated cases involving spies, espionage, and intelligence gathering. During the war, Hoover shifted the focus of the FBI toward fighting the activities of the communists and fascists, and in 1939, President Roosevelt placed Hoover in charge of domestic counterintelligence, a role that suited him well. The years surrounding World War II saw the rapid expansion of the FBI, with the number of agents increasing from 896 in 1940 to 4,370 in 1945 and appropriations rising from $8.8 million to $44.2 million.[10]

Hoover solidified public support by collaborating on books and films such as *The FBI in Peace and War* (1943) and *The House on 92nd Street* (1945) and took credit for the capture of German saboteurs off Long Island in 1942, although recent research indicates that one of the Germans gave up his comrades in order to save his own life.

In the 1950s, FBI director Hoover continued his hunt for subversives, making the transition from hunting "Hot War" Nazi saboteurs to Cold War communists and spies. Although Hoover's FBI performed admirably in the war years, during the post-1945 Cold War years, Hoover once again reverted to red-baiting tactics as the FBI's war against the Communist Party led to his veneration among conservatives and loathing and fear among liberals. During the 1950s, the FBI gathered evidence that uncovered the Klaus Fuchs atomic spy ring and led to the execution of Julius and Ethel Rosenberg for espionage activities. Hoover allied his organization with his close friend Senator Joseph McCarthy during the communist "witch hunt" of the 1950s and wrote the book *Masters of Deceit: The Story of Communism in American and How to Fight It* (1958), which detailed his strategies for defeating communism and contributed to the growing hysteria over Soviet expansion. Hoover continued his masterful manipulation of popular entertainment with the release of the hagiographic *The FBI Story* (1959). Also published was Don Whitehead's best-selling book by the same name.

In 1950, the FBI introduced its list of "**Ten Most Wanted**" fugitives. The first number one on the list was a convicted train robber and murderer named Thomas J. Holden. Director Hoover loved publicity, and with this new strategy, he found a perfect tool for trumpeting the FBI's war against the underworld. What is less known is that Hoover probably borrowed the "Ten Most Wanted" concept from a newspaper reporter who wrote a popular story based on names and descriptions of the ten fugitives the FBI would most like to apprehend. According to the bureau, the list was created to publicize certain fugitives. As testimony to its success rate, more than one-quarter of those captured since its inception were located through the assistance of citizens familiar with the list.

The names of fugitives placed on the list are submitted by the fifty-six FBI field offices and then reviewed by the agency's Criminal Investigative Division and the Office of Public and Congressional Affairs. Criminals who are selected for the list must either have lengthy records or pose a serious threat to the public. If a criminal is already notorious, it is doubtful he or she will make the list. The changing nature of America's crime problem can be documented by each decade's most wanted lists. In the 1950s, it was dominated by bank robbers, car thieves, and burglars, whereas in the 1960s, it was dominated by radicals wanted for the destruction of government property and kidnapping. Most recently, terrorists and organized crime figures have predominated, along with serial killers and drug kingpins.

Corrections

The American declaration of war on Japan, following on the heels of the attack on Pearl Harbor, brought out strong expressions of patriotism from the most unlikely of places: America's prisons. Prisoners not only volunteered blood to the Red Cross but also purchased war bonds. According to a new Selective Service Act, all convicts were required to register for the draft. Many who were allowed to enlist did so. As prisons and prisoners lent their hand to the war effort, the number of inmates declined for the first time in more than a decade, dipping from 190,000 in 1940 to less than 120,000 in 1943.[11]

America's entry into World War II led to a temporary correctional philosophy that found expression in vocational training in support of the war effort. Soon prison assembly lines were turning out twine, model planes for pilot training schools, army mattresses, shoes, assault boats, and even aircraft engines. Institutions made the transformation to factories, churning out a wide range of products, with perhaps 98 percent of all convicts engaged in the work.[12]

Paralleling the war effort was the willingness of qualified teachers, counselors, and psychologists to help staff prison administrations. By the time the war ended in 1945, the American prison system had made the transition from a warden-dominated authoritarian system to one that embraced the developing social sciences and that increasingly relied on professional treatment in dealing with criminals.

While the prison population increased slightly between 1930 and 1940 from 121 to 132 per 100,000, by 1950, America's inmate population had declined to 110 per 100,000. As the soldiers returned from the war, prison populations began to increase once more. By 1950, African Americans represented 7 percent of the population of Michigan but made up 40 percent of the prison population. As foreign-born white immigrants became a rare presence in correctional facilities (in 1946 only 3.2 percent of American prisoners), their places were filled by Hispanics, blacks, and Native Americans. One explanation for the rising number of inmates was the increasingly punitive nature of drug penalties in the postwar years.[13] By the mid-1950s, Louisiana enacted mandatory prison sentences from between five and ninety-nine years for minor narcotics violations.

Introduced in 1932, by the 1950s, the "**telephone pole**" plan of penitentiary flourished from California (Soledad, Tracy, and Vacaville) and Texas (Eastham and Ferguson units) to Massachusetts and Connecticut. In this plan, cellblocks, dining halls, chapels, shops, and administrative offices diverged from a central corridor. This design better accommodated new treatment programs, maintained security, and offered inmates a new openness with the introduction of floor-to-ceiling security windows.

Despite advances in treatment and the decreasing emphasis on punitive methods, the 1950s were plagued by numerous **prison riots**, with one of the largest occurring in 1952 at the State Prison of Southern Michigan (resulting in the death of only one inmate). A subsequent investigation by the American Correctional Association concluded that the riot was caused by poor sentencing and parole practices, overcrowding, lack of professionalism at all levels, enforced idleness, inadequate funding, and the political domination of management. Between 1950 and 1955, more than forty-seven riots broke out in American prisons.

Although several outbreaks of prison violence took place in the South, the major prison riots occurred in northern and western prisons. One of the explanations for the dearth of southern prison riots was the fact that large penal farms were the dominant form of incarceration in the South. Therefore, it was more difficult to foment a riot in these conditions than in the fortress-like settings of the northern penitentiaries.

While most southern states had at least a centrally located penitentiary, the majority of prisoners languished in the plantation-like settings of the immense prison farms. With little opportunity for rioting or other mass expressions of resistance, to express their contempt for the punitive system, prisoners resorted to self-mutilation or escape. One of the more shocking examples of protest took place on the Louisiana prison farm at Angola, when thirty-seven prisoners slashed their heel tendons with razor blades in 1951 to remonstrate against the intolerable conditions at what was characterized as "America's worst prison."[14]

Several commissions were convened to study prison conditions in the 1950s. In 1953, the American Prison Association identified the causes of riots as relating to official indifference, substandard personnel, lack of professional leadership and professional programs, excessive size and overcrowding of institutions, and unwise sentencing and parole practices. Much of the criticism was leveled at the "Big House" design of the 1940s, but few if any remedies to the situation were offered.

The prosperity and declining crime rates of the 1950s gave rise to a rehabilitative optimism and led to more input by behavioral scientists. Working on the assumption that most inmates were psychologically disturbed, a therapeutic orientation gained increased support among correctional administrators. Borrowing a page from the inmate classification systems of the earlier twentieth century, in the years following the war, teams of professional psychologists, sociologists, vocational counselors, caseworkers, and other specialists worked together to create a case history for each inmate. Prisoners could then be assigned to the appropriate prison for treatment and rehabilitation.

Joseph Edward Ragen: penologist

One of the foremost American penologists of his era, Joseph Edward Ragen (1896–1971) rose to prominence as the reform-minded warden of the Illinois State Penitentiary at Joliet in the 1940s and 1950s. During his tenure at Joliet, Ragen eliminated the barn-boss system, which created a hierarchy of power among the inmates, worked on beautifying the prison grounds, and introduced a policy for allowing prisoners to volunteer for medical research experiments. He would receive a special award for his prison's contribution to research on hepatitis and malaria. As a penologist reformer, he was credited with introducing progressive programs of rehabilitation, vocational training, and educational programs, including college-accredited courses, while at the same time maintaining strict discipline among his charges. During his twenty-five years at Joliet-Stateville, his strict control transformed the institution into a "paramilitary institution." However, in an era when many facilities were plagued by escape and riots, Joliet-Stateville did not report any riots or escapes.[15]

Crime and punishment

The 1940s and 1950s were punctuated by a number of sensational crimes. The 1950s were inaugurated on January 17, 1950, with the **Brinks robbery**, the biggest heist in American history up to that time. While the FBI would unravel the case, none of the more than $1.2 million was ever recovered. In an event that eerily resembles the rampage killings of the 1990s, war veteran Howard Unruh stepped out on a Camden, New Jersey, street in 1949 and for no apparent reason killed twelve of his neighbors in less than fifteen minutes. In 1957, James Dean wannabe **Charles Starkweather**, with girlfriend in tow, embarked on a murderous spree in rural Nebraska. On the surface, they seemed like typical teenagers except for one important difference: their youthful rebellion included murdering eleven persons during an eight-day rampage through two states. Further demonstrating that crime was no longer the bailiwick of the big city, novelist Truman Capote would chronicle the 1959 murder of a close-knit farm family in rural Kansas in his groundbreaking book *In Cold Blood* (1965).

The Sam Sheppard murder case

Providing the inspiration for the television series *The Fugitive*, on July 4, 1954, Dr. Sam Sheppard described a "bushy-haired intruder" who bludgeoned to death his pregnant wife and knocked him out. The public was fascinated by the case, which became one of the most notorious murder trials of the 1950s. In the moralistic atmosphere of the mid-1950s, the case featured a well-to-do handsome doctor, a pregnant wife, a secret lover, and a mysterious killer, all feeding the public's curiosity and creating a media sensation. Sheppard was found guilty of second degree murder in 1954, and his conviction would be overturned twelve years into a life sentence because the judge in the original case "did not fulfill his duty to protect Sheppard from inherently prejudicial publicity which saturated the country."[16]

During the 1990s, an ongoing investigation by Sam Sheppard's son, Sam Reese Sheppard, and private investigators uncovered evidence that has led some authorities to link the murder of Marilyn Sheppard to the family window washer, who was currently serving time for another homicide. Sam Sheppard Jr. believed that there was sufficient evidence to warrant a civil suit, charging the State of Ohio with wrongful imprisonment. The subsequent three civil trials proved to be three more media sensations. Facing a judgment that could have cost the state millions of dollars, the state mounted a spirited defense. After a brief deliberation, a jury on April 12, 2000, ruled unanimously in favor of the state. This case, like other controversial cases that seem to linger in the American consciousness, demonstrates the continuing advances in DNA and other investigative technologies. It also demonstrates how history is an ongoing process, particularly in the arena of modern crime and punishment.[17]

The specter of organized crime

Explanations for Hoover's reluctance to go after organized crime have run the gamut from mob blackmail over his rumored sexual preferences to his fondness for horse racing and an unwritten agreement that protected him from paying his losses. However, these rumors have never been substantiated and are highly unlikely. One, more convincing explanation, was proposed by one of his biographers, who suggested that, if Hoover had admitted that organized crime was a national problem, he might have to concede some of his powers to others since it would require a multi-task force strategy using other law enforcement agencies to counter such a widespread crime problem. Still others would argue that Hoover suspected his agency would never defeat well-entrenched crime syndicates and that agents might possibly be compromised by bribes.

The Kefauver Committee

During the 1930s and 1940s, Hoover's FBI had carte blanche to chase Nazi saboteurs, Russian spies, and black marketeers, ignoring the more threatening criminal threat of organized crime syndicates. By the 1950s, it was impossible to deny the existence of organized crime on the national level. In 1950, Senator Estes Kefauver convened a committee to investigate racketeering. The Senate Special Committee to Investigate Crime in Interstate Commerce, better known as the Kefauver Committee, would subsequently hold hearings in 14 cities and listen to testimony from over 600 witnesses, many of whom testified to the existence of a sinister nationwide criminal conspiracy known as the "Mafia."

The Kefauver Committee hearings were a landmark television event. Thanks to the introduction of the television, Americans were treated to the Kefauver Committee hearings, the longest-running television series of 1950–1951 and the first significant investigation of organized crime in America. Numerous crime figures and politicians were introduced to a national audience as the hearings were convened in city after city. The hearings reintroduced the public to the Bill of Rights as the phrase "taking the Fifth" became part of the American lexicon. Following the denouement of the hearings, the committee recommended tightening up the law against the Mafia, corrupt politicians, and other racketeers.

These were the first Congressional Hearings to be broadcast to a national audience. They were not even supposed to have been televised until a last minute decision. Television was still a new medium in 1951, and there were few choices for television viewers, which ensured a large audience. Television ownership in New York City alone (where the hearings were being taped) had increased from 29 percent to 51 percent over the previous year. In his 1993 book on the 1950s, David Halberstam noted this "meant that for the first time in any metropolitan area in any city of the world there were more homes with televisions than without." The hearings were filmed in black and white and featured a cast of characters that included mob boss Frank Costello, "the Prime Minster" of organized crime. He objected to having his face filmed so one of the technicians suggested just focusing on his hands. Viewers were captivated by his hands as he drummed the table, gripped a water cup, tore paper to small bits, as his hands glistened with sweat. In the end, the findings of the committee chronicling the existence of an Italian American Mafia was accepted by most viewers (although modern scholarship debunks most of its findings). Kefauver won an Emmy Award from the Academy of Television Arts and Sciences for special achievement for offering the American people the chance to observe the workings of the national government on television.

Apalachin Conference

On November 14, 1957, acting on a tip he received the previous day, New York State Police Sergeant Edgar D. Croswell along with another state trooper and two Alcohol Tax Bureau agents decided to check in on a Mr. Joseph Barbara. Except for several arrests on suspicion of murder in the 1930s, the Sicilian immigrant's record was clean. However, his palatial eighteen-room house was regarded as one of the more lavish residences on the edge of the hamlet of Apalachin, New York. His local business reputation was so solid that a local police chief recommended him for a gun permit. However, others were not so sure. State authorities long suspected that, as owner of the local Canada Dry Bottling Company, he was using it as a front for illicit bootlegging.

When Croswell pulled up to the house, he observed numerous cars with out-of-state plates parked next to his house and several dozen more in a field behind his horse barn. Croswell began jotting down license plates before setting up a roadblock on the only passable road to check out the guests on their way out. Meanwhile he sent for backup. Gangland luminaries such as Vito Genovese, Carlo Gambino, and Joe Bonanno were among the sixty-five suspects questioned down at a police sub-station (Barbara's house was never searched). None carried any contraband, not even a gun. When it came to explaining to law enforcement why they were all there at one time, most politely explained that they were there to pay respects to their sick friend Joe Barbara, and it was a coincidence they all arrived at the same time. More likely, the Apalachin meeting was a meeting of Mafia bosses to discuss a long-simmering dispute over the heroin trade and other crime family business.[18]

The 1957 Apalachin Conference of organized crime kingpins in rural upstate New York is generally considered a turning point in the war on organized crime. Prior to this episode, J. Edgar Hoover had denied the existence of organized crime syndicates for almost thirty years. However, once a New York State police officer stumbled on the clandestine meeting of some sixty mobsters at the home of Joseph Barbara Sr., Hoover could demur no longer. Soon the FBI was forced into the fray, beginning a campaign of wiretapping and electronic eavesdropping that would see few triumphs before the 1980s.[19]

Part of the problem was that having denied the existence of the Mafia or any monolithic crime organizations for decades, the FBI was forced into a game of catch-up. This was most noticeable in the agency's early attempts to interpret surveillance, when they could not recognize much of the wise-guy vernacular. Hearing the Mafia phrase "**cosa nostra**," meaning "our thing," agents concluded that this "new" criminal organization they had uncovered was called "La Cosa Nostra," hence another chapter in the Mafia legend.

When authorities rounded up the underworld leaders, they discovered that nineteen were from upstate New York, twenty-three from New York City, three from the mountain West, two from the South, eight from the Midwest, two from Cuba, and one from Italy. These demographics were used by the media to pressure Hoover to admit the existence of a national organized crime syndicate. In the process, not only was Hoover embarrassed, but the revelations had a damaging effect on the FBI's image and reputation for professionalism.[20]

While Hoover would only privately concede the existence of an organized crime syndicate, publicly he established the **Top Hoodlum program**, an initiative against organized crime by which each FBI field office was required to identify ten major mob members in its geographic area and then closely watch their activities.

The death penalty

American executions substantially decreased between the late 1940s and early 1950s. In fact, the number of capital crimes had been steadily reduced since the eighteenth century. By the beginning of the 1950s, there were capital crimes for which no one had been executed in years, including kidnapping, treason, and bombing. Since the 1930s, the only capital crime that had regularly received the death penalty was murder. Although public opinion continued to support the death penalty, fewer executions were taking place. Between 1950 and 1954, an average of eighty-three executions were conducted, compared to 155 per year between 1930 and 1934.[21]

A watershed of sorts for the study of American executions was the commencement of collecting and publishing national statistics on executions. Before the 1930s, most figures concerning execution were unofficial, but beginning in 1930, the Bureau of the Census began including execution as one of the causes of death in the *Vital Statistics of the United States*.

National execution statistics were disseminated to a wider audience beginning in 1950, thanks to the inclusion of these figures in the Federal Bureau of Prisons' *National Prisoner Statistics Series*. A survey of the execution data "unequivocally documented the fact that for the preceding twenty years, the black man had been the principal victim of the death penalty in America, and almost the exclusive victim of executions for rape."[22] Further research demonstrated that blacks on death row were less likely to receive commutations than their white counterparts.

In the postwar years, several Supreme Court decisions addressed the unequal application of the death penalty. In 1947, an African American man named Eddie Patton was sentenced to death by an all-white jury for killing a white man. Citing the exclusion of blacks from the juries that indicted him and then convicted him, Patton argued that he had been denied equal protection under the law as guaranteed by the Fourteenth Amendment. Patton claimed that it had been a long-established tradition in his county to exclude blacks from jury lists, jury boxes, and jury service. In the 1947 decision *Patton v. Mississippi*, the Supreme Court reversed the decision of the state court. By ordering a new trial, the Court established a new precedent for the prohibition of racial discrimination in jury selection.

Caryl Chessman: the Red Light Bandit

Among the capital murder cases that led many to begin questioning the wisdom of the death penalty was the case of Caryl Chessman (1921–1960), California's infamous "Red Light Bandit." By the time he was sixteen, Chessman, a veteran of California's juvenile criminal system, had learned how to expertly manipulate the legal system. Beginning in early 1948, however, he made the transition from committing petty crimes to capital ones. He was suspected of using a flashing red light to stop cars by creating the impression that he was somehow connected to law enforcement. He robbed several victims at gunpoint in two cases and in a third incident ordered a woman to undress and perform oral sex on him. Two more robberies followed, including one in which he forced a woman into his car and attempted to rape her.

It was not long before Chessman was arrested on suspicion of armed robbery. When police found tools that seemed to connect him with the Red Light Bandit case, he was arraigned on eighteen charges. In the subsequent trial, Chessman was convicted of kidnapping (for moving a woman from her car into his) and committing "unnatural sexual acts." Sentenced to death for violating the so-called **Little Lindbergh Law** by kidnapping with intent to commit robbery, the Chessman case was the harshest sentence handed down in California to a criminal who had not actually killed anyone. Between 1948 and 1960, his execution was repeatedly postponed as it went through the appellate process. During those twelve years, he became a well-known, articulate opponent of the death penalty. He wrote three books, including *Cell 2455, Death Row*, selling hundreds of thousands of copies. But after eight stays of execution, he was finally confronted with the gas chamber on May 2, 1960.

Like many controversial American executions, this one resonated throughout the world, leading to demonstrations and attacks on U.S. embassies in Europe and South America. Governor Edmund "Pat" Brown of California, who had been widely criticized for his vacillation over the fate of Chessman, would later write that he believed he "should have found a way to spare Chessman's life."[23] Over the next few years, unfavorable public opinion would lead to an informal moratorium on the death penalty beginning in 1965.

The 1950s and 1960s saw the NAACP and the American Civil Liberties Union come to the aid of a number of individuals sentenced to death, leading to the reversal of several convictions. During the 1960s, five states abolished the death penalty, and still more demonstrated a reluctance to schedule and perform executions. Judges and juries also became increasingly disinclined to impose death sentences.

The definition of rape varies widely throughout the world in the twenty-first century. There is an average of 232 rapes reported to police in the United States every day, where there is still no nationwide definition of rape. According to the federal penal code, rape refers to aggravated sexual abuse, but it is defined state by state, according to such distinctions as to whether force was used or not. English common law defines rape as "non-consensual penetration of any of three orifices by a penis."[24] According to Islamic Sharia law, rape is especially hard to prove since it cannot be proven without a confession from the actual rapist or four witnesses. In countries such as Somalia and Bangladesh, there have been a number of cases where rape victims have been punished by either lashing or stoning for engaging in illegal sex. In recent years, some cases in majority Muslim countries have demonstrated a certain amount of flexibility when it came to the adjudication of rape. While the cases usually favor the perpetrator, one ruling went against this this trend. In 2014, Morocco's parliament voted to unanimously amend the rape law that had previously permitted men convicted of statutory rape to evade punishment if they agreed to marry underage victims. The Justice Ministry followed the ruling by promising to seek harsher penalties for rape, while others sought to criminalize a variety of behaviors toward women, as well as to move away from the stigmatization of giving birth out of wedlock.[25]

The William Heirens murder case: first use of truth serum

There were a number of high profile crimes that accented the war years. None was stranger than that of the teenage killer and burglar William Heirens. An alarming case that presaged the sex criminals and serial killers of the modern era, Heirens was arrested for burglary in 1946. A subsequent fingerprint check connected him to a number of unsolved crimes, including the murders of two women and of a six-year-old child who had been dismembered. Heirens was then questioned under the influence of the highly promoted truth serum **sodium pentothal**. Originally used to treat shell-shock victims during the war, its use in the Heirens case was its first in a criminal case. Despite warnings from a director of a psychiatric institute that the drug was not reliable and that any revelations uncovered could not be used in court, the state's attorney went ahead with the procedure.

Under the influence of the drug, Heirens revealed the existence of what proved an imaginary companion whom he blamed for the murders. The American Civil Liberties Union soon protested the use of sodium pentothal, citing it as a violation of the defendant's civil rights. In later years, Heirens claimed to have been taking the drug for months prior to the questioning so that he could manipulate his inquisitors. The seventeen-year-old Heirens eventually reached a plea agreement and confessed to three murders. In one of the murders, Heirens wrote with lipstick on a living room wall "For Heaven's sake catch me before I kill more. I cannot control myself," probably one of the most memorable quotes in the annals of American homicide. Despite the potential of sodium pentothal as a truth serum, the business of lie detecting would remain the bailiwick of the polygraph machine, pioneered by the Berkeley Police Department years earlier.

Juvenile delinquency

In the 1950s, America was confronted with a new wave of hysteria: rising juvenile delinquency. During hearings on the problem chaired by Estes Kefauver, a now familiar refrain was heard: "blame it on the mass media." However, one needs to go back only to the 1920s and 1930s to discover similar concerns about the impact of mass culture on America's youth. Historian James Gilbert suggests that "the 1950s' dispute over mass culture was protracted and perhaps more universal and intense than at earlier periods."[26] Gilbert explained that while the 1950s was a decade of "declining civil liberties," it was also an era of "remarkable liberalization," citing the civil rights movement and class mobility stimulated by the GI Bill of Rights, which offered educational opportunities to more people.

As America reaped the economic benefits of the postwar boom, the mass media industry enjoyed greater independence from censorship and control. As juvenile delinquency rose, so did the furor over violent comic books, rock-and-roll music, clothing styles, and hot-rodders. However, what escaped many of the era's critics was that delinquency had been on the rise since 1940. Criminal justice authorities cited a variety of explanations, including broken families, mothers away from home working for the war effort in factories, and family mobility, all of which were slowly creating a nation of strangers.

In 1949, following in the discredited steps of Lombroso, who had concluded that one could recognize "born criminals" by studying body measurements and physical traits, William Sheldon collected the physical measurements of 200 boys at a Boston reform school. Whereas Lombroso argued for atavism – that born criminals were biological throwbacks to an earlier stage of evolution – Sheldon determined that basic body structures were linked to delinquency. He found that the more athletic and aggressive mesomorphs were more inclined to delinquency over the more lethargic endomorphs and taller and intellectually inclined ectomorphs. However, unlike Lombroso, Sheldon argued that mesomorphy did not result in delinquency but rather predisposed delinquents to delinquency.

In subsequent years, Sheldon's findings came under increasing scrutiny and have been roundly criticized for lacking empirical rigor. In 1956, **Sheldon and Eleanor Glueck** tested Sheldon's hypothesis by comparing 500 identified delinquents with 500 non-delinquents in a controlled experiment. What they found was that body type in itself did not incline individuals to delinquent behavior but was one of many factors that led to delinquency.

In feudal China, execution by beheading or involving bodily mutilations was considered the ultimate form of punishment since it was believed that that the body of the deceased needed to be whole before the soul of the body could make a proper passage to the hereafter. The "loss of somatic integrity" was the outcome most feared under China's imperial rulers. To dismember the body in any way, particularly through decapitation, meant extending punishment beyond the grave. To add even more humiliation to the sanction in China's earliest era, the bodies and heads were often buried separately. Compared to beheading, another form of execution, strangling, while more painful, was less feared because it left the body complete.

Homicide

The nation's prospects for peace and order following World War II stood out in sharp contrast to the denouement of World War I, which was followed by racial and economic turmoil. Thanks in part to a long duration of full industrial employment in the war years, the late 1940s and 1950s saw homicide rates plummet to an all-time low of less than five per 100,000. According to historian Roger Lane, a new pattern of homicide emerged in which murders were "domesticated," explaining that "compared to earlier eras, proportionately more of them [murders] involved fights with family, friends, and acquaintances, rather than strangers or robbers."[27]

As Lane and others have demonstrated, America's urban homicide rate declined in the 1940s and 1950s. A pioneering study by criminologist Marvin Wolfgang, *Patterns of Criminal Homicide* (1957), analyzed homicides in Philadelphia between 1948 and 1952. His findings are considered the era's most accurate academic study of homicide and demonstrate the long-term impact of the "ongoing urban industrial revolution."[28]

However, while homicide rates had declined, racial tensions and violence persisted throughout the country. The war years saw an African American migration to cities in the Northeast (New York and Philadelphia), the Midwest (Chicago and Detroit), and the West (Los Angeles and Portland), particularly as barriers to black employment were lifted in industrial centers. While most tensions were held in check by the ongoing war and patriotic fervor on the home front, the end of the war brought lingering animosities to the surface.

Homicide historian Randolph Roth found that except for several years in the 1950s, America's cumulative homicide rate "was remarkably stable since World War I."[29] It has typically fluctuated between 6 and 9 per 100,000 per year. During the twentieth century it typically fluctuated between 6 and 9 per 100,000. During the zenith of the Cold War, 1957–1958, he found a homicide rate of 4.5 per 100,000 persons per year. Roth chalks up these lower numbers to the relative stability and patriotic zeal that united the country against challenges posed by communism.[30]

Race riots and hate crimes

An unforeseen result of the war years was the labor shortage that imperiled America's war industries as the country slowly rebounded from the Great Depression. Both Puerto Rican and Mexican immigration flourished. Most Puerto Ricans ended up in the New York City area, while Mexicans recruited for agricultural labor settled in the Southwest. Although racial tensions were exacerbated by these migrations, with the most serious riots breaking out in Detroit in 1942 and 1943, it was not until the end of the war that a wave of violence engulfed cities in every region of the country.

An examination of the 1943 Detroit riot offers an excellent microcosm from which to view similar race riots in the 1940s. While the armed forces were still segregated as America went to war, steps were taken against segregation and discrimination on other fronts. In one campaign, black organizations promoted the "double V" as a symbol for victory at home and overseas. Blacks had traditionally been barred from the automobile unions, and the United Automobile Workers-Congress of Industrial Organizations (UAW-CIO) sought to remedy the situation at Ford plants in 1941. Subsequently, the strike succeeded, and they were accepted into the union by the thousands.

Whites, however, felt threatened by such advances. Egged on by right-wing demagogues such as Father Charles Coughlin and the almost-fascist Black Legion, a violent campaign of terror was initiated against Detroit's black population, culminating in a June riot. According to one study by Dominic Capeci, white rioters in Detroit were often young, single, and unemployed men who went to great lengths to reach the riot, where they could confront black rioters, who were typically "older, married, and employed" but had a stake in a community that seemed to unfairly deny them advancement in the building trades.[31] Fueled by racism and rumor, Detroit's blacks fought back against white agitators, looting and burning stores. Whites responded with iron pipes, knives, and clubs. Police gunfire raked the rioters as well. When the riot finally ended, thirty-four people were dead, including twenty-five blacks.

In Birmingham, Alabama, a city that was 43 percent black, several homes were dynamited in 1949 as the resurgent southern Klan returned to threatening black citizens. Far from an isolated incident, between 1950 and 1951 racially motivated bombings were reported in Nashville, Miami, Dallas, and other cities. As segregation came under attack throughout the 1950s, individual instances of bombings, arson, and violence were directed at black communities from California to Florida.

The *Brown v. Board of Education* decision led to racial violence in most southern states. With little opposition from state law enforcement, more than 500 reprisals against African Americans were reported between 1955 and 1958. As the leader of the school integration movement, the NAACP was often targeted by segregationists. In an attempt to block the integrationists, Virginia passed sedition laws, South Carolina barred public employment of NAACP members, and Texas and Alabama initiated injunctions against association branches.

The murder of Emmet Till

The notorious murder of fifteen-year-old Emmett Till further reinforced black fears of racially motivated violence in the South. In August 1955, Till, who was raised in Chicago, was spending a summer vacation with relatives in rural Tallahatchie County, Mississippi, when he mistakenly broke the conventions of southern etiquette. Unfamiliar with a culture that expected black men to answer whites with "yes sir" or "no sir," Till responded in several confrontations with the less conventional "yeah" and "naw." Compounding his "flaunting" of southern racial etiquette, Till kept a photograph of his white girlfriend back home in his wallet. Till sealed his fate when, on a dare by local friends, he whistled at a young, married white woman and even went so far as asking her for a date. It was not long before he disappeared. Till's badly decomposed body was soon found in the Tallahatchie River. Initially, the state of Mississippi ordered the immediate burial of the badly beaten body. His mother resisted, insisting that his body be returned home to Chicago. His remains were boxed up and sent to Chicago. His mother decided to open the box and let *Jet Magazine* publish a photo of Emmett's disfigured face. In his recent book, *Writing to Save a Life*, author John Edgar Wideman described in stark detail Emmett's missing eye and crushed in head – he had "all the human being battered out of it."[32] Suspicion focused on the white woman's husband and another man, who were identified as having visited the cabin where Till had been staying to inquire about his whereabouts. Both men were arrested and indicted for the murder. After a trial in front of an all-white jury (despite blacks making up 63 percent of county residents) and deliberating for little more than one hour, both defendants were acquitted. According to one of the jurors, "If we hadn't stopped to drink pop, it wouldn't have taken that long." Despite an international uproar, the case had little impact on race relations and the criminal justice system in the South.[33]

The Zoot-Suit Riot

By 1943, the racial demographics of Los Angeles were clearly changing. In 1940, its African American population stood at 62,000. However, more than 200,000 blacks would arrive in the city in the mid-1940s to fill the demand for workers in the aviation, shipbuilding, and other wartime industries. Although the LAPD employed black officers as early as the nineteenth century, segregation became the hallmark of the early LAPD. Black and white officers were forbidden to work together. If blacks were promoted, it was only to the plain-clothes division. There was an unspoken rule against blacks wearing stripes, which would allow them to supervise white officers. With the introduction of the police car in the 1920s and 1930s, black officers were consigned to the midnight shift (apparently so that whites would not see them in a patrol car) and were still segregated and restricted to black neighborhoods. Reflecting the rampant discrimination of the era, similar conditions existed for Mexican Americans on the force, with little opportunity for advancement, except as detectives, in which case bilingualism was necessary.

The racial tensions that exploded in Los Angeles in the 1940s "were a precursor of the searing racial turbulence that would mark America's cities in the decades to follow."[34]

During the war years, Los Angeles was teeming with young men – black, Mexican American, and white. In the racially charged atmosphere of the period, there was little interference from the Los Angeles Police Department (LAPD) if whites sometimes lashed out at defiant African Americans seeking jobs in wartime industries or stylish Mexican "zoot suiters," recognizable for their broad-shouldered fashion popular at the time in the burgeoning jazz culture. According to Eduardo Obregon Pagan, while the origins of the zoot-suit are still debated, "its stylistic antecedents" can be traced back to the sometime in the late 1930s.[35]

In the same summer that witnessed the Detroit race riot, tension resulting from the assault of several sailors by a group of Mexican youths resulted in violence between Mexicans and whites on the streets of Los Angeles. Between June 3 and June 13, 1943, mobs attacked Mexican and black youths in Los Angeles. Those attired in zoot-suit garb were most often singled out. One historian suggests that the zoot suiters were targeted by servicemen because they were enraged by its "ethnic and cultural symbolism," and "it was a cultural badge sported by Mexican-Americans and by blacks."[36] In the course of one week, anyone who was spotted wearing one was attacked by groups of servicemen. On June 7 alone, over 1,000 soldiers, sailors, and civilians dragged mostly Mexican youths from movie theaters, street cars, and homes and into the streets, where they were summarily stripped and beaten. Police stood by, either helpless or reluctant to intervene. What was probably most remarkable about this riot was that no one was killed or seriously injured, and there was little property damage.

Following the Zoot-Suit Riot, Governor and future Supreme Court Justice Earl Warren ordered an investigation into its causes. The resulting Citizen's Committee Report was a classic in understatement, concluding that racial prejudice was a factor in the outbreak. Demonstrating the long-standing animosity between Mexicans and Anglos in southern California, the Hearst papers headlined every episode that reflected negatively on Mexicans. Despite attempts by the Office of War Information to end this practice, following the riot, one Los Angeles County supervisor proclaimed to the media that "all that is needed to end lawlessness is more of the same action as is being exercised by the servicemen."[37]

After the June riots, the Los Angeles City Council made wearing this form of attire a misdemeanor, foreshadowing the uproar over gang paraphernalia in schools today. According to James Gilbert, the Zoot-Suit Riot more importantly also "pushed delinquency to the forefront of national concern."[38]

Notable trials

The trial of Julius and Ethel Rosenberg (1951)

Julius and Ethel Rosenberg were arrested in 1950 for what J. Edgar Hoover labeled the "crime of the century": allegedly passing the secret of the atomic bomb to the Soviets five years earlier, only three months before America dropped the atomic bomb on Hiroshima. The Rosenbergs were taken into custody after a Russian espionage ring in the United States began to unravel. Along with associate Morton Sobell, the three were charged and tried in 1951 for "conspiracy to commit espionage." What makes this case stand out was that, while it was probably the most publicized capital case of its era, it concerned espionage rather than homicide.

The Rosenbergs pleaded innocence at their trial and took the Fifth Amendment when queried as to whether they were communists. Their trial was conducted in a climate of fear and conspiracy while American forces were in the midst of the Korean conflict. Following the trial, the Rosenbergs were found guilty and sentenced to death, and Sobell was sentenced to thirty years in prison. Julius and Ethel Rosenberg spent the next two years at New York's Sing Sing Prison as their lawyer filed numerous appeals on their behalf. Despite international pressure to spare the parents of two children and the persistent claims of innocence by the Rosenbergs, both went to the electric chair in June 1953.

Harking back to past history when treason was always treated as the worst secular offense, the Rosenbergs were the first and last Americans executed for treason against the United States (John Brown had been executed for treason against the State of Virginia). What is most noteworthy about the case, which was the endgame of a complicated series of Cold War spy cases, was that the Rosenbergs had not given information to an enemy during wartime but rather to America's wartime ally, an act that technically would not be considered an act of treason. Gripped in the postwar anticommunist hysteria of the McCarthy era, America no longer held a monopoly on the atomic bomb. Prosecutors and the public alike were eager to find a scapegoat. The testimony of fellow spies Harry Gold and Ethel Rosenberg's brother David Greenglass, both of whom cooperated with the authorities, made a compelling case for their guilt. In 1995, decoded wartime cables from the Soviet consulate in New York to the KGB in Moscow were made public, revealing the complicity of Julius Rosenberg beyond a reasonable doubt (but there was little evidence against Ethel). None of these intercepts were made public in the 1951 trial because the United States did not want the Soviets to know that their "unbreakable code" had been broken.

Conclusions

The Cold War and "Hot War" tensions of the 1940s and 1950s transformed criminal justice institutions, but many American tensions remained unchanged. The 1955 murders of Emmett Till and Reverend George Lee[39] demonstrated that white murderers who killed blacks in southern white communities had little to fear from the criminal justice system.

In the climate of the postwar era, security at home and abroad dominated American concerns. Many civil libertarians were alarmed by the government's attempt to protect national security at the expense of certain constitutional liberties. For the first time since the Alien and Sedition Acts of 1798, people were imprisoned for peacetime sedition, beginning with the Smith Act of 1940. By the late 1940s, leaders of the American Communist Party were prosecuted because of the postwar standoff with the Soviet Union. The Cold War concern for national security would give rise to another series of *witch hunts* against dissenters, this time finding expression in the House Un-American Activities Committee hearings and the McCarthy hearings.

While the trial of the Rosenbergs and Caryl Chessman garnered domestic headlines, trials in Nuremberg and Tokyo unveiled an underworld of criminal excess unsurpassed in criminal justice history. More than 12 million Jews, Gypsies, Russians, and homosexuals were murdered in the Nazi holocaust. Millions more perished in Russia during Stalin's reign. Forty percent of Americans held by the Japanese perished in death marches and from disease. Sixty percent of Soviet prisoners held by the Germans died in captivity.

As America's crime rates declined into the 1950s, so too did the nation begin to abandon capital punishment. According to death penalty authority William J. Bowers, the decline initially coincided with the decline in the homicide rate, but by 1950, "there were definite indications that the nation was becoming more reluctant to execute."[40] As the 1960s approached, research by the social scientist Thorsten Sellin (1896–1982) suggested that capital punishment was not an effective deterrent and that it had little impact on homicide rates.

The impact of the 1940s and 1950s on Americans varied from group to group. The war had a great impact on population demographics, as people flocked from the countryside to the cities. New opportunities opened for women and minorities, yet sexual and racial barriers persisted. With the birth of the civil rights movement in the late 1950s, remnants of the Ku Klux Klan that had remained active in the South through the war years returned with a fury in the early 1960s.

Point – counterpoint

Separate but equal? (Mississippi 1948–1954)

By the 1890s, Jim Crow laws had spread through the South, leading some African Americans to turn to the courts to defend the rights they felt had been granted them under the Fourteenth Amendment. In Plessy v. Ferguson *(1896), the Court ruled that "separate but equal" accommodations did not violate the equal protection clause. Midway through the next century not much had changed with most southern states enforcing the separation of blacks and whites at schools, train stations, and even having separate schools for blind children of both races. In 1948, Southern whites launched a third-party presidential campaign with a platform based on segregation. The first reading is a set of passages from Mississippi's legal code in the late 1940s. In 1954,* Plessy *was overturned when the Supreme Court concluded that "separate educational facilities are inherently unequal." The second passage is an excerpt from Brown* v. Board of Education of Topeka *(1954). The struggle against segregation still had a long way to go.*
Source: Mississippi State Criminal Code, 6927, 6973, 6974, 2339, 7848, 2351, 7784, 7785, 7786, 7787; *Brown v. Education*, 347 U.S. 483 (1954)

In the first cases in this Court construing the Fourteenth Amendment, decided shortly after its adoption, the Court interpreted it as proscribing all state-imposed discriminations against the Negro race. The doctrine of "separate but equal" did not make its appearance in this Court until 1896 in the case of Plessy v. Ferguson . . . involving not education but transportation. American courts have since labored with the doctrine for over half a century. In this Court, there have been six cases involving the "separate but equal" doctrine in the field of public education. . . . In more recent cases, all on the graduate school level, inequality was found in that specific benefits enjoyed by white students were denied to Negro students of the same educational qualifications. . . . In none of these cases was it necessary to reexamine the doctrine to grant relief to the Negro plaintiff. . . .

In the instant cases, the question is directly presented. Here . . . there are findings below that the Negro and white schools involved have been equalized, or are being equalized, with respect to buildings, curricula, qualifications, and salaries of teachers. . . . Our decision, therefore, cannot turn on merely the comparison of these tangible factors in the Negro and white schools involved in each of the cases. We must look instead to the effect of segregation itself on public education.

In approaching this problem, we cannot turn the clock back to 1868 when the Amendment was adopted, or even to 1896 when *Plessy v. Ferguson* was written. We must consider public education in the light of its full development and its present place in American life throughout the Nation. Only in this way can it be determined if segregation in public schools deprives these plaintiffs of the equal protection of the laws.

Today, education is perhaps the most important function of state and local governments. Compulsory school attendance laws and the great expenditures for education both demonstrate our recognition of the importance of education to our democratic society. It is required in the performance of our most basic public responsibilities, even service in the armed forces. It is the very foundation of good citizenship. Today it is a principal instrument in awakening the child to cultural values, in preparing him for later professional training, and in helping him to adjust normally to his environment. . . .

We come then to the question presented: Does segregation of children in public schools solely on the basis of race, even though the physical facilities and other "tangible" factors may be equal, deprive the children of the minority group of equal educational opportunities? We believe that it does. . . .

To separate them from others of similar age and qualifications solely because of their race generates a feeling of inferiority as to their status in the community that may affect their hearts and minds in a way unlikely ever to be undone. The effect of this separation on their educational opportunities was well stated by a finding in the Kansas case by a court which nevertheless felt compelled to rule against the Negro plaintiffs:

"Segregation of white and colored children in public schools has a detrimental effect upon the colored children. The impact is greater when it has the sanction of the law; for the policy of separating the races is usually interpreted as denoting the inferiority of the Negro group. A sense of inferiority affects the motivation of a child to learn. Segregation with the sanction of law, therefore, has a tendency to retard the education and mental development of Negro children and to deprive them of some of the benefits they would receive in a racially integrated school system." Whatever may have been the extent of psychological knowledge at the time of *Plessy v. Ferguson*, this finding is amply supported by modern authority. Any language in *Plessy v. Ferguson* contrary to this finding is rejected.

We conclude that in the field of public education the doctrine of "separate but equal" has no place. Separate educational facilities are inherently unequal. Therefore, we hold that the plaintiffs and others similarly situated for whom the actions have been brought are, by reason of the segregation complained of, deprived of the equal protection of the laws guaranteed by the Fourteenth Amendment. . . .

State charity hospitals

Mississippi state charity hospital

§6927. Races to be separated. – The white and colored races shall be kept separately in said hospital and suitable provisions made for their care and comfort by the board of trustees. [Codes, Hemingway's 1917, §3949; 1930, §4594; Laws, 1910, ch. 115.]

§6973. Separate entrances for races. – There shall be maintained by the governing authorities of every hospital maintained by the state for treatment of white and colored patients separate entrances for white and colored patients and visitors, and such entrances shall be used by the races only for which they are prepared. [Codes, 1930, §4618; Laws, 1928, Ex. Ch. 95.]

Source: 347 U.S. 483 (1954)

§6974. Separate nurses for different races. – In all such institutions it shall be the duty of the superintendent and others in authority to furnish a sufficient number of colored nurses to attend colored patients, such colored nurses to be under the supervision of such white supervisors as the head of the institution may determine. A failure to comply with this and the next preceding section shall authorize the governor to remove the person in authority responsible for such violation. [Codes, 1930, §4619; Laws, 1928, Ex. ch. 95.]

Social equality

§2339. Races – social equality, marriages between – advocacy of punished. – Any person, firm or corporation who shall be guilty of printing, publishing or circulating printed, typewritten or written matter urging or presenting for public acceptance or general information, arguments or suggestions in favor of social equality or of intermarriage between whites and negroes, shall be guilty of a misdemeanor and subject to a fine not exceeding five hundred [$500.00] dollars or imprisonment not exceeding six [6] months or both fine and imprisonment in the discretion of the court. [Codes, Hemingway's 1921 Supp.§ 1142e; 1930, §1103; Laws, 1920, ch. 214.]

Transportation

Depots

§7848. Regulations for passenger depots. – [Requires passenger depots in cities of 3,000 or more inhabitants to maintain in connection with reception room for whites, two closets labeled respectively "Closet, white; females only," "Closet, white; males only," and similarly in the waiting room for Negroes, closets labeled respectively substituting the word "colored" for "white."] [Codes, 1892, §4303; 1906, §4855; Hemingway's 1917, §7640; 1930, §7072.]

Railroads

§2351. Railroads – not providing separate cars. – If any person or corporation operating a railroad shall fail to provide two or more passenger cars for each passenger train, or to divide the passenger cars by a partition, to secure separate accommodations for the white and colored races, as provided by law, or if any railroad passenger conductor shall fail to assign each passenger to the car or compartment of the car used for the race to which the passenger belongs, he or it shall be guilty of a misdemeanor, and, on conviction shall be fined not less than twenty [$20.00] dollars nor more than five hundred [$500.00] dollars. [Codes, 1892, §1276; 1906, §1351; Hemingway's 1917, §1085; 1930, §1115.]

> [Note: This provision applies to sleeping cars. See *Alabama & V. R. Co. v. Morris*, (1912) 103 Miss. 511, 60 So. 11, Ann. Cas. 1915B 613.]

§7784. Equal but separate accommodations for the races. – Every railroad carrying passengers in this state shall provide equal but separate accommodations for the white and colored races by providing two or more passenger cars for each passenger train, or by dividing the passenger cars by a partition to secure separate accommodations; and the conductor of such passenger train shall have power, and is required, to assign each passenger to the car, or the compartment of a car, used for the race to which such passenger belongs; and should any passenger refuse to occupy the car to which he or she is assigned by the conductor, the conductor shall have power to refuse to carry such passenger on the train, and for such refusal neither he nor the railroad company shall be liable for damages in any court. [Codes, 1892, §3562; 1906, §4059; Hemingway's 1917, §6687; 1930, §6132; Laws, 1904, ch. 99.]

Street railways and buses

§7785. [1948 Cum. Supp.] – Separate accommodaitons for races in street cars and buses – common carriers by motor vehicle. – All persons or corporations operating street railways and street or municipal buses, carrying passengers in this state, and every common carrier by motor vehicle of passengers in this state as defined by section 3 (e) of Chapter 142 of the laws of 1938 [§7634, Code of 1942] shall provide equal, but separate, accommodations for the white and colored races.

Every common carrier by motor vehicle of passengers in this state, as defined by section 3 (e) of Chapter 142 of the laws of 1938 [§7634, Code of 1942], by buses or street cars operated entirely within the corporate limits of a municipality, or within a radius of 5 miles thereof, shall divide its passengers by the use of an appropriate sign 4 × 9 inches, for the purpose of, and in a manner that will suitably provide for, a separation of the races, and all other buses and motor vehicles carrying passengers for hire in the state of Mississippi shall use a latticed movable partition extending from the top of the seat to the ceiling of the vehicle, said partition not to obstruct the view of the driver of the vehicle to secure such separate accommodations; provided, however, that this act shall not apply to buses operated exclusively for the carrying of military personnel, and the operators of such passenger buses shall have power, and are required, to assign each passenger to the compartment of the bus used for the race to which such passenger belongs; and in no case shall any passenger be permitted to stand in the aisle of the compartment in which he does not belong and is not so assigned; and should any passenger refuse to occupy the compartment to which he or she belongs and is assigned, the operator shall have power to refuse to carry such passenger on the bus; or should either compartment become so loaded in transit as not to permit the taking on of any further passengers for that compartment, then the bus operator shall not be required and shall refuse to take on any further passengers in violation of this act. Even though such additional passengers may have purchased and may hold tickets for transportation on the said bus, the only remedy said passengers shall have for failure or refusal to carry them under such circumstances is the right to a refund of the cost of his ticket, and for said refusal in either case neither the operator nor the common carrier shall be liable for damages in any court. Such partition may be made movable so as to allow adjustment of the space in the bus to suit the requirements of traffic. [Amends §7785, Code of 1942.] [Codes, 1906, §4060; Hemingway's, 1917, §7558; 1930, §6133; 1942, §7785; Laws 1904; ch. 99; 1940, ch. 169; 1944, ch. 267, 1.]

[Note: §7634, Code of 1942, Subsection (e): The term "common carrier by motor vehicle" means any person who or which undertakes, whether directly or by a lease or by any other arrangement, to transport passengers or property for the general public by motor vehicle for compensation, over regular routes, including such motor vehicle operation of carriers by rail or water, and of express or forwarding companies under this Act. [Laws 1938, ch. 142]

§7786. [1948 Cum. Supp.] – Passengers required to occupy compartments to which they are assigned. – The operators of such street cars and street buses and motor vehicles, as defined by Chapter 142 of the laws of 1938 [§7632–7687, Code of 1942] shall have the power and are required to assign each passenger to the space or compartment used for the race to which such passenger belongs. Any passenger undertaking or attempting to go into the space or compartment to which by race he or she does not belong shall be guilty of a misdemeanor, and, upon conviction, shall be liable to a fine of twenty-five dollars ($25.00) or, in lieu thereof, by imprisonment for a period of not more than thirty (30) days in the county jail; and any operator of any street car or street bus or motor vehicle as herein defined, assigning or placing a passenger to the space or compartment other than the one set aside for the race to which said passenger belongs shall be guilty of a misdemeanor and, upon conviction, shall be liable to a fine of twenty-five dollars ($25.00) or, in lieu thereof, to imprisonment for a period of not more than thirty (30) days in the county jail. [Amends §7786, Code of 1942.] [Codes 1906, §4061; Hemingway's 1917, §7559; 1930, §6134; 1942, §7786; Laws, 1904, ch. 99; 1940, ch. 169; 1944, ch. 267, §1.]

§7786–01. [1948 Cum. Supp.] – Penalty for Violation. – Every person or corporation operating street railways and street or municipal buses carrying passengers in this state, and every common carrier of passengers in this state by motor vehicle, as defined by section 3 (e) of Chapter 142 of the laws of 1938 [§7634, Code of 1942], guilty of wilful and continued failure to observe or comply with the provisions of this act shall be liable to a fine of twenty-five dollars ($25.00) for each offense, and each day's violation of the provision hereof shall constitute a separate violation of this act; provided, however, that in the case of persons or corporations operating street railways and street or municipal buses, the fine shall be ten dollars ($10.00) instead of twenty-five dollars ($25.00). [Laws 1944, ch. 267, §2.]

§7787. Penalty for refusal of street railway officers and employees to comply with this provision. – [Officers and directors who neglect or refuse to comply with §§7785, 7786, 7787, Code of 1942 are punishable by fine of not less than $100 or 60 days to 6 months in prison in the county jail. Conductors and other employees who have charge of vehicles to which this section applies are punishable by fine of not less than $25.00 or imprisonment of 10 to 30 days for each and every offense; *provided*, however, chapter is not to apply to nurses attending children of the other race.] [Codes, 1906, §4062; Hemingway's 1917, §7560; 1930, §w6135; Laws 1904, ch. 99.]

Key terms

beatniks	Joseph McCarthy	*Brown v. Board of Education*
Korematsu v. U.S.	House Un-American Activities	*of Topeka*
McCarthyism	Committee (HUAC)	Earl Warren
Thurgood Marshall	William O. Douglas	Los Angeles Police Department
O. W. Wilson	William H. Parker	(LAPD)
Ten Most Wanted	Joseph E. Ragen	telephone pole penitentiary
prison riots	Brinks robbery	plan
In Cold Blood	Howard Unruh	Sam Sheppard murder case
Apalachin Conference	Kefauver hearings	Charles Starkweather
Top Hoodlum program	Caryl Chessman	cosa nostra
William Heirens	sodium pentothal	Little Lindbergh Law
The Gluecks	Zoot-Suit Riot	juvenile delinquency hysteria
Trial of the Rosenbergs	Immigration Act of 1924	Emmett Till murder case
outlaw motorcycle gangs	Executive Order 9066	

Critical thinking questions

1 Discuss the postwar impact of World War II on the American criminal justice system.
2 What impact did the McCarthy "witch hunts" have on civil liberties?
3 How did the growth of the civil rights movement impact criminal justice institutions and the legal system?
4 How did police reformers William H. Parker and Orlando W. Wilson personify police professionalism? What innovations can be attributed to them? What did their critics think?
5 How did the war years affect the mandate and role of law enforcement? The corrections system?
6 What were some of the explanations for prison violence in this era?
7 What was the impact of the Apalachin Conference on American perceptions of organized crime?
8 Discuss race relations, riots, and the criminal justice system in the war years.
9 What lessons do the Zoot-Suit Riot offer the student of justice in America?
10 Why were the Rosenbergs executed? Should they have been? Why are similar crimes not punished the same way today?

Notes

1 President's Commission on Organized Crime, *The Impact: Organized Crime Today*, Washington, DC: U.S. Government Printing Office, 1986, p. 58.
2 David Alan Johnson, *Betrayal: The True Story of J. Edgar Hoover and the Nazi Saboteurs Captured During WWII*, New York: Hippocrene Books, 2007, p. 260.
3 Ibid., p. 261.

4 Ibid.

5 Nina Shandler, *The Strange Case of Hellish Nell: The Story of Helen Duncan and the Witch Trial of World War II*, Cambridge: Da Capo Press, 2006, p. 101.

6 Annalisa Quinn, "Fever Dreams," *New York Times Magazine*, June 11, 2017, pp. 13–15.

7 Although this case included suits from four different states, the Supreme Court's majority opinions in all four became known as the *Brown* decision because the name was first alphabetically among the plaintiffs.

8 Darien A. McWhirter, *The Legal 100: A Ranking of the Individuals Who Have Influenced the Law*, Secaucus, NJ: Charles Scribner's Sons, 1998, p. 69.

9 Robert M. Fogelson, *Big City Police*, Cambridge, MA: Harvard University Press, 1977, pp. 195–196.

10 Athan G. Theoharis, ed., *The FBI: A Comprehensive Reference Guide*, New York: Checkmark Books, 2000, p. 58.

11 Scott Christianson, *With Liberty for Some: 500 Years of Imprisonment in America*, Boston: Northeastern University Press, 1998, p. 244.

12 Ibid.

13 Ibid., p. 250.

14 Larry E. Sullivan, *The Prison Reform Movement*, Boston: Twayne, 1990, p. 48.

15 Ibid., pp. 58–59.

16 Quoted in Edward W. Knappman, *American Trials of the 20th Century*, Detroit: Visible Ink Press, 1995, p. 250.

17 For more on this case, see Cynthia C. Cooper and Sam Reese Sheppard, *Mockery and Justice: The True Story of the Sheppard Murder Case*, Boston: Northeastern University Press, 1995; Walter Hixson, *Murder, Culture, and Injustice: Four Sensational Cases in American History*, Akron, OH: University of Akron Press, 2001.

18 So much emphasis has been placed on the Apalachin Conference that it obscures the fact that previous meetings in other cities were much more influential in the creation of the modern mob.

19 For best recent accounts of the Apalachin meeting see Gil Reavill, *Mafia Summit: J. Edgar Hoover, the Kennedy Brothers, and the Meeting That Unmasked the Mob*, New York: St. Martin's Press, 2013; Michael Newton, *The Mafia at Apalachin*, Jefferson, NC: McFarland, 2012.

20 William Howard Moore, *The Kefauver Committee and the Politics of Crime, 1950–1952*, Columbia: University of Missouri Press, 1974; Lee Bernstein, *The Greatest Menace: Organized Crime in Cold War America*, Amherst: University of Massachusetts Press, 2002.

21 William Bowers, et al., *Legal Homicide: Death as Punishment in America, 1864–1982*, Boston: Northeastern University Press, 1984, pp. 25–26.

22 Ibid., p. 18.

23 Edmund Brown, *Public Justice, Private Mercy: A Governor's Education on Death Row*, New York: Weidenfeld and Nicolson, 1989, p. 52.

24 "Rape Laws: Crime and Clarity," *The Economist*, Sept 1, 2012.

25 Aida Alami, "A Loophole for Rapists is Eliminated in Morocco," *New York Times*, January 24, 2014, p. A10.

26 James Gilbert, *A Cycle of Outrage: America's Reaction to the Juvenile Delinquent in the 1950s*, New York: Oxford University Press, 1986, p. 5.

27 Roger Lane, "Capital Punishment," in *Violence in America*, Vol. 1, ed. Ronald Gottesman, New York: Charles Scribner's Sons, 1999, p. 201.

28 Roger Lane, *Murder in America: A History*, Columbus: Ohio State University Press, 1997, p. 255.

29 Randolph Roth, *American Homicide*, Cambridge, MA: Harvard University Press, 2009, p. 436.

30 Ibid., p. 448. In his study of American homicide, Roth explores what circumstances has driven homicide rates from the colonial era to the present. Chief among his conclusions is that the waxing and waning of murders among adults might be correlated with how Americans feel about their government at any particular time.

31 Dominic J. Capeci and Martha Wilkerson, *Layered Violence: The Detroit Rioters of 1943*, Jackson: University of Mississippi Press, 1991.

32 John Edgar Wideman, *Writing to Save a Life*, New York: Scribner, 2016. Wideman's critically acclaimed book adds a postscript to the murder, focusing instead on the execution of his twenty-three-year-old father, Louis Till, just ten years earlier for murder and rape while serving in Italy during the last days of World War II. According to Wideman, the charges were more than spurious and fit in with the pattern of a disproportionate number of black soldiers being executed for rape during the war. Wideman states that they were convicted and executed for "being the wrong color in the wrong place at the wrong time."
33 For a comprehensive examination of this case, see Stephen J. Whitfield, *A Death in the Delta: The Story of Emmett Till*, Baltimore: Johns Hopkins University Press, 1988.
34 Joe Dominick, *To Protect and Serve: The LAPD's Century of War in the City of Dreams*, New York: Pocket Books, 1994, p. 137.
35 Eduardo Obregon Pagan, *Murder at Sleepy Lagoon: Zoot Suits, Race, & Riot in Wartime L.A.*, Chapel Hill: University of North Carolina Press, 2003.
36 Gilbert, 1986, pp. 30–31.
37 Richard Hofstadter and Michael Wallace, eds., *American Violence: A Documentary History*, New York: Vintage Books, 1971, p. 336.
38 Gilbert, 1986, p. 32.
39 Lee was shot to death while driving his car, although the coroner reported that he died from a heart attack and that the buckshot that riddled his face was probably just "dental fillings."
40 Bowers, 1984, 29.

Sources

Allen, William. 1976. *Starkweather: The Story of a Mass Murderer*. Boston: Houghton Mifflin.
Appier, Janis. 1998. *Policing Women: The Sexual Politics of Law Enforcement and the LAPD*. Philadelphia: Temple University Press.
Bernstein, Lee. 2002. *The Greatest Menace: Organized Crime in Cold War America*. Amherst: University of Massachusetts Press.
Bopp, William J. 1977. *O. W. Wilson and the Search for a Police Profession*. Port Washington, NY: Kennikat Press.
Bowers, William J., Glenn L. Pierce, and John F. McDevitt. 1984. *Legal Homicide: Death as Punishment in America, 1864–1982*. Boston: Northeastern University Press.
Brown, Edmund. 1989. *Public Justice, Private Mercy: A Governor's Education on Death Row*. New York: Weidenfeld and Nicolson, 1989.
Capeci, Dominic J., Jr. and Martha Wilkerson. 1991. *Layered Violence: The Detroit Rioters of 1943*. Jackson: University Press of Mississippi.
Christianson, Scott. 1998. *With Liberty for Some*. Boston: Northeastern University Press.
Cooper, Cynthia L. and Sam Reese Sheppard. 1995. *Mockery and Justice: The True Story of the Sheppard Murder Case*. Boston: Northeastern University Press.
Domanick, Joe. 1994. *To Protect and to Serve: The LAPD's Century of War in the City of Dreams*. New York: Pocket Books.
Fogelson, Robert M. 1977. *Big-City Police*. Cambridge, MA: Harvard University Press.
Gilbert, James. 1986. *A Cycle of Outrage: America's Reaction to the Juvenile Delinquent in the 1950s*. New York: Oxford University Press.
Halberstam, David. 1993. *The Fifties*. New York: Villard Books.
Hixson, Walter. 2001. *Murder, Culture, and Injustice: Four Sensational Cases in American History*. Akron, OH: University of Akron Press.
Hofstadter, Richard and Michael Wallace, eds. 1971. *American Violence: A Documentary History*. New York: Vintage Books.

Johnson, David Alan. 2007. *Betrayal: The True Story of J. Edgar Hoover and the Nazi Saboteurs Captured during WWII*. New York: Hippocrene Books.

Kennedy, Randall. 1997. *Race, Crime, and the Law*. New York: Pantheon Books.

Kluger, Richard. 1976. *Simple Justice: The History of Brown v. Board of Education and Black America's Struggle for Equality*. New York: Alfred A. Knopf.

Knappman, Edward W. 1995. *American Trials of the 20th Century*. Detroit: Visible Ink Press.

Lane, Roger. 1997. *Murder in America: A History*. Columbus: Ohio State University Press.

———. 1999. "Capital Punishment." In *Violence in America*, ed. V. I. Ronald Gottesman, pp. 198–203. New York: Charles Scribner's Sons.

McWhirter, Darien A. 1998. *The Legal 100: A Ranking of the Individuals Who Have Influenced the Law*. Secaucus, NJ: Citadel Press.

Moore, William Howard. 1974. *The Kefauver Committee and the Politics of Crime, 1950–1952*. Columbia: University of Missouri Press.

Newton, Michael. 2012. *The Mafia at Apalachin*. Jefferson, NC: McFarland.

Pagan, Eduardo Obregon. 2003. *Murder at the Sleepy Lagoon: Zoot Suits, Race, & Riot in Wartime L.A.* Chapel Hill: University of North Carolina Press.

President's Commission on Organized Crime. 1986. *The Impact: Organized Crime Today*. Washington, DC: U.S. Government Printing Office.

Reavill. 2013. *Mafia Summit: J. Edgar Hoover, the Kennedy Brothers, and the Meeting That Unmasked the Mob*. New York: St. Martin's Press.

Richardson, James F. 1974. *Urban Police in the United States*. Port Washington, NY: Kennikat Press.

Roth, Randolph. 2009. *American Homicide*. Cambridge, MA: Harvard University Press.

Sabljak, Mark and Martin H. Greenberg. 1990. *Most Wanted: A History of the FBI's Most Wanted List*. New York: Bonanza Books.

Schrecker, Ellen. 1994. *The Age of McCarthyism: A Brief History with Documents*. New York: St. Martin's Press.

Shandler, Nine. 2006. *The Strange Case of Hellish Nell: The Story of Helen Duncan and the Witch Trial of World War II*. Cambridge: Da Capo Press.

Sullivan, Larry E. 1990. *The Prison Reform Movement*. Boston: Twayne Publishers.

Theoharis, Athan G., ed. 2000. *The FBI: A Comprehensive Reference Guide*. New York: Checkmark Books.

Whitfield, Stephen J. 1988. *A Death in the Delta: The Story of Emmett Till*. Baltimore: Johns Hopkins University Press.

Wideman, John Edgar. 2016. *Writing to Save a Life*. New York: Scribner.

1960	1961	1963	1963	1964	1964	1965	1966
National murder rate stands at 4.7 per 100,000	*Mapp v. Ohio*	President John F. Kennedy assassinated	*Gideon v. Wainwright*	*Escobedo v. Illinois*	*Cooper v. Pate*	Los Angeles Watts riots leave thirty-four dead	*Miranda v. Arizona*

TIMELINE

CHAPTER TWELVE

Crime and the nationalization of criminal justice (1960 – 1979)

Learning objectives

After reading this chapter students should understand and be able to discuss:

- American's increasing fear of crime during the 1960s and 1970s
- The widespread riots of the era and the findings of the commissions set up to investigate them
- The various explanations for the rising crime problem
- How and why politicians used civil order and rising crime as a platform for winning office
- The numerous crime fighting strategies launched by the federal government
- The impact of civil rights legislation on various regions of the country
- The transition from the Warren-led to the Burger-led Supreme Court and its ramifications for criminal justice policy
- How the woman's movement and equal opportunity legislation effected the employment of women in policing

In 1960, the national murder rate stood at 4.7 per 100,000, the lowest for any census year. As America made the transition from the 1950s to the decade of **President John F. Kennedy's** "New Frontier," the crime rate was so low that sociologist Daniel Bell commented that "there is probably less crime today in the United States than existed a hundred, or fifty, or even twenty-five years ago."[1] He had reasons for such optimism, as America enjoyed a decrease in murder from 6.9 per 100,000 in 1946 to 4.5 per 100,000 by 1962[2]; other crimes fell as well.

DOI: 10.4324/9781315148342-12

1966	1966	1967	1967	1967	1967	1968
Richard Speck murders eight nurses in Chicago	Charles Whitman's mass murder at the University of Texas	Publication of *The Challenge of Crime in a Free Society*	*In re Gault*	Riots take place in 127 cities	*Katz v. United States*	*Terry v. Ohio*

But the assassination of John F. Kennedy in 1963 and America's participation in the Vietnam War would touch off a decade of national turmoil that did not diminish until well into the 1970s. One of the most tumultuous eras in American history, the 1960s and 1970s were marked by civil rights and war protests, boycotts and sit-ins, race rioting, and domestic terrorism. Criminal justice historian Samuel Walker has described this period as "the most turbulent in all of American criminal justice history."[3]

The criminal justice system was challenged on many fronts in this era. In an attempt to understand rising crime rates and to create strategies for suppressing crime in the 1960s, the federal government launched a variety of official inquiries. Among the most significant was the 1965 President's Commission on Law Enforcement and Administration of Justice (LEAA), which concluded that police officers had become increasingly isolated from the communities they served. Its report, *The Challenge of Crime in a Free Society*, published in 1967, found that city officials had given police chiefs too much latitude in running their departments. In an era of rising concerns over the role of police in contemporary society, the extensive report suggested more than 200 recommendations concerning criminal justice reform, including raising educational requirements and improving training programs for police officers.[4] A number of other crime commissions were created to study a criminal justice system in crisis during the 1970s, most focusing on the changing nature of policing. Many of these investigations were not limited to policing, focusing attention on organized crime, corrections, drug abuse, and juvenile delinquency.

Politicians saw the potential of using the civil disorder to their advantage. Senator Barry Goldwater in 1964 and presidential candidate Richard Nixon in 1968 began to link street crime to the civil disobedience that accompanied the civil rights movement. In the process, law and order emerged as an important campaign issue that found an audience with conservative and mostly white Americans.

The lawgivers

The social unrest of the 1960s prodded the federal government to establish a number of inquiries into the causes and prevention of crime. In 1968, Congress passed the **Omnibus Crime Control and Safe Streets Act**, creating the **Law Enforcement Assistance Administration (LEAA)** as its centerpiece in a "national war on crime." By design, the LEAA was supposed to support state and local crime control efforts by carrying out a broad program of aid to state and local authorities for crime control, targeting street crime, riots, and organized crime. Starting with $60 million in seed money in 1968, by 1982, the agency had spent more than $7 billion on updating law enforcement departments around the country.[5]

1968	1968	1968	1968	1968
Congress passes Omnibus Crime Control and Safe Streets Act	LEAA established	Kerner Commission on civil disorder issues report	Assassination of Martin Luther King Jr. in Memphis, Tennessee, is followed by rioting in 168 cities	Robert F. Kennedy assassinated

The Omnibus Crime Control and Safe Streets Act impacted the criminal justice system in a number of ways. Building on *Katz v. United States*, the 1967 Supreme Court decision that limited the use of electronic eavesdropping because of concerns about invasions of privacy, the Omnibus Crime Control Act in 1968 prohibited lawful interceptions except by warrant or with consent. Other features of the crime control legislation focused on the regulation of firearms sales, the establishment of the Bureau of Justice Statistics, and the awarding of grants for the construction and renovation of courtrooms, correctional facilities, treatment centers, and other criminal justice related structures.

No region in the nation's criminal justice system was transformed more than the southern states. The onset of the civil rights movement of the 1950s and 1960s has sometimes been referred to as a "Second Reconstruction," particularly in the South.[6] Beginning with the civil rights laws of 1957 and subsequent legislation, such as the Voting Rights Act of 1964, millions of black voters regained the franchise after several generations of racial confrontation over the ballot box.

The South proved one of the most challenging fronts for law enforcement during this period as white segregationists brutally attacked nonviolent civil rights protesters, while police officers targeted peaceful black marchers with high-pressure hoses and attack dogs. The early 1960s witnessed a number of well-publicized murder cases in the South, including the murder of Medgar Evers, organizer of the National Association for the Advancement of Colored People (NAACP) and the bombing deaths of four young black girls in a Birmingham, Alabama, church.

In order to win southern congressional support, President John F. Kennedy did little to placate civil rights activists in his first two years in office. Influenced by daily television coverage demonstrating the repugnant brutality in the South and partly at the behest of his brother, Attorney General **Robert F. Kennedy**, in 1963, Kennedy changed his position on civil rights. During the Kennedy administration of the early 1960s, Attorney General Kennedy pursued an aggressive agenda of crime control, shifting the federal government's attention to civil rights and suppressing organized crime. Publicly proclaiming that the time for "the nation to fulfill its promise" had arrived, President Kennedy did not live to fulfill his pledge, gunned down by an assassin's bullet in November 1963.

Lyndon Johnson's ascendance to the presidency in 1963 coincided with some of the most significant civil rights legislation since the post-Civil War period. Events in Birmingham, Alabama, roused the national conscience and stimulated a formerly reluctant administration into becoming a stalwart supporter of potent civil rights legislation. Intended to protect the right to equality in public accommodations, the right to have federal funds spent in a nondiscriminatory manner, and the right to racial and sexual equality in employment, the passage of the 1964 **Civil Rights Act** enacted the strongest civil rights measures since the

1970	1970	1970	1970	1971	1972
Organized Crime Control Act	National Guardsmen kill four Kent State University students	Police shooting at Jackson State College	*Holt v. Sarver*	Attica Prison riot	*Furman v. Georgia* leads to commutation of all death row prisoners' sentences

Reconstruction era. Considered the most far-reaching statute enacted by Congress, the Voting Rights Act of 1965 provided for the replacement of state election machinery by federal law and ad hoc federal officials when it was found necessary to eliminate a pattern of Fifteenth Amendment violations of voting rights.

American Indian Movement

For many other Americans, the 1964 civil rights legislation had little if any impact. Generations of government neglect had left the country's Native American population demoralized with attendant high rates of disease and infant mortality rates, unemployment, illiteracy, malnutrition, and alcoholism. In response to these conditions and the continued plight of the first Americans, Native American activists Dennis Banks and Clyde Bellecourt organized the American Indian Movement (AIM) in 1968. Although they championed earlier reform efforts, their goals and tactics were guided by a more militant approach than past efforts. Borrowing a page from the black militants of the era, they used guns in their takeovers and effected a sinister image to threaten those who opposed them. AIM members used these new tactics to occupy the abandoned prison island of Alcatraz in 1969 and take over the main offices of the Indian Bureau in Washington, DC, in 1972. Their most significant protest took place at Wounded Knee, South Dakota, in 1973, where several hundred Sioux had been massacred by the army in 1890.

During the subsequent seventy-one-day protest, AIM leaders held firm to their demands for the restoration of treaty lands. Several gunfights ensued between Indians and FBI agents and National Guardsmen, leaving two dead. While 300 protesters were eventually arrested, most were acquitted on legal technicalities. Over the rest of the 1970s, Native Americans across the nation launched lawsuits to recover their treaty lands and rights.

The Supreme Court

In the 1960s, the Supreme Court played a crucial role in promoting a climate of political liberalism during the Kennedy and Johnson presidencies. Beginning with the *Brown v. Board of Education* decision in 1954, the Court demonstrated remarkable courage in erasing the distinctions that had supported a racially segregated society and, through a series of decisions, diminished Jim Crowism. While discrimination and poverty persisted in black communities, so too did the goals for equality set forth by the chief justices. In their crusade for equal rights, African Americans became increasingly politicized during the 1960s.

1972	1972	1973	1973	1976	1977
Death of J. Edgar Hoover	Watergate break-in	*Roe et al. v. Wade* decision makes abortion widely available	Creation of the Drug Enforcement Administration	*Gregg v. Georgia* upholds new death penalty statutes	Execution of Gary Gilmore by firing squad

Sweeping decisions on the electoral process, political representation, school desegregation, public support of religion, obscenity, and free speech were accompanied by widespread debate and vitriol. But according to legal historian David Bodenhamer, "No judicial reforms were as bold or ignited more protest as the landmark cases involving criminal process."[7] Diverging from preceding courts, the Warren Court applied the federal procedural guarantees of the Bill of Rights to the application of state criminal justice. In the process of "nationalizing" the Bill of Rights, the Supreme Court reshaped the nature of federalism by applying the same standards to both state and federal criminal proceedings. The high court rejected the application of the entire Bill of Rights, rather emphasizing those amendments that apply to "due process" as defined by the Fourteenth Amendment.

The 1960s and 1970s provided a stage for some of the Supreme Court's most important decisions, leading some commentators to suggest that the Court "made more changes in criminal procedure" during this period "than had been made by the Court in the previous 175 years of its existence."[8]

Although "stop and frisk" police tactics gained prominence in the 1990s in New York City, the issue of its constitutionality had been addressed as early as 1968, when the U.S. Supreme Court took up the question of stop and frisk in the case of **Terry v. Ohio**. In this case, a man was stopped because he appeared to be casing a jewelry store. The state argued that since it was only a short-term stop with no formal arrest and since pat downs of outer clothing were not full-scale searches, this sort of stop should not be limited by the Fourth Amendment. Conversely, civil right attorneys argued that a short-term encounter should require the same probable cause that formal arrests and searches do.[9] Ultimately, the Earl Warren-led court took the middle ground, ruling that a stop was permissible when "a police officer observes unusual conduct which leads him to reasonably conclude in light of his experience that criminal activity" was taking place. In such cases, the stops and pat downs of external clothing had to be temporary, and solely for the purpose of confirming whether or not the police officer's suspicion that an individual was armed was warranted. Statistics in New York City have confirmed what critics have asserted. In 2011, NYPD officers recovered weapons in 0.15 percent in 685,000 stops. In 2015, stops plummeted to 25,000 as New York's homicide rate witnessed historic declines.[10] Nonetheless, the evidence is overwhelming that the vast majority of those affected by stop and frisk were black and Hispanic. The *Terry v. Ohio* case lives on in the police lexicon, where stops and frisks are sometimes referred to as "terry stops."[11]

Mapp v. Ohio

In 1961, the Supreme Court greatly increased the ability of criminal defendants to defend themselves in the landmark case of *Mapp v. Ohio* by ruling that evidence secured by the police through unreasonable searches must be excluded from trial. This decision was shortly followed by the **Escobedo v. Illinois** (1964) and the **Miranda v. Arizona** (1966) decisions by the Warren Court, both of which are credited with significantly changing the way law enforcement officers carried out interrogations and at the same time guaranteed the rights of the accused.

In the *Mapp* case, Cleveland police officers arrived at the home of Ms. Dollree Mapp to search for a suspect in a recent bombing case. After forcing their way into the residence, the officers searched the house without a warrant and found obscene material unrelated to their initial search. Mapp was subsequently convicted for possessing the obscene materials. Building an appeal based on the 1914 *Weeks* decision, which held that the Fourteenth Amendment barred the use of evidence secured through an illegal search and seizure, Mapp's conviction was overturned by the Supreme Court in 1961. In the process, the exclusionary rule was extended to the states.

Miranda v. Arizona

Two years before *Miranda*, Daniel Escobedo was arrested for killing his brother-in-law in Chicago. After two rounds of intense police interrogation, Escobedo confessed and was then convicted in court. According to the narrow five-to-four Supreme Court decision, without an attorney present during his police interrogation, it was ruled that his confession had been illegally obtained under the Sixth Amendment, which guarantees the right to legal counsel during police questioning.

The landmark *Miranda* decision stemmed from the arrest of Ernest Miranda (1940–1976) for rape and kidnapping on March 12, 1963. Miranda would claim that police officers coerced him into confessing to the crime during a grueling two-hour interrogation and was not allowed to consult an attorney. Despite objections from his attorney, who protested that Miranda had not been informed of his rights or given legal counsel to apprise him of his protection against self-incrimination under the Fifth Amendment, Miranda was convicted.

In 1966, *Miranda v. Arizona* reached the Supreme Court, where Miranda's conviction was overturned. The landmark case substantially altered American police practices in the interviewing of suspects. According to the Warren Court's majority decision, all individuals must be notified of their constitutional rights, including the right to have an attorney present during questioning. Lauded by civil libertarians, the "Miranda decision" has been roundly criticized by law enforcement and was later modified under the more police-friendly Warren Burger Court in the 1980s. Miranda was retried and reconvicted. Released from prison in 1972, Miranda was stabbed to death in a barroom fight four years later. Not lost on most historians was the irony of Miranda's killer being read his Miranda rights in Spanish while Ernest Miranda was succumbing to his stab wounds.

These Supreme Court rulings have come under fire in recent years, with peace officers arguing that the decisions have placed unreasonable burdens on them. What is often forgotten is that the decisions regarding Miranda, Escobedo, and Mapp had little effect on their ultimate fates since all were eventually sentenced to prison on various other charges. Although the fundamental rights guaranteed by these decisions will never be taken away from defendants, many legal experts believe that the decisions will be modified. One major Supreme Court decision from the late 1960s did just that. In the 1968 *Terry v. Ohio* ruling, the Court validated an officer's right to stop, question, and even search a person who acted suspiciously as long as the officer had reasonable grounds for doing so. During a decade that was notable for placing restrictions on police powers, *Terry v. Ohio* clearly augured a new climate that was more favorable for enhancing them.

In re Gault

Following on the heels of the 1963 Supreme Court decision *Gideon v. Wainwright* (see the "Notable Trials" section later in this chapter), in 1967, the Court extended the *Gideon* ruling to juvenile delinquency proceedings in *In re Gault*, giving children many of procedural rights guaranteed to adults. Five years later, the decision was extended to adult misdemeanor cases if imprisonment was sanctioned in the *Argersinger v. Hamlin* decision.

The due process clause contained in the Fourteenth Amendment guaranteed certain protections to "persons." But until 1967, the word *person* did not apply to the nation's children, which made up one-third of the population. In that year, the Supreme Court ruled for the first time that many of the procedural protections extended to adults charged with crimes should also apply to juveniles.

The events leading up to this landmark decision began in June 1964, when fifteen-year-old Gerald F. Gault and a friend were picked up by the Gila County, Arizona, sheriff. According to a neighbor, the boys had made an obscene phone call to her. The boys were then picked up and held for several days at a detention center. Gault was already on probation for petty theft when he was picked up, and the juvenile officer had enough reason to hold him.

Gault appeared before the juvenile court judge and, when questioned, admitted to placing the obscene call. The judge then gave Gault's family the impression that there would be little repercussions despite his probationary status. However, they were soon asked to appear before the judge for a second hearing. Following the usual juvenile court practices of the time, no records of the previous hearing had been kept. Disagreement over what Gerald admitted in the first hearing suddenly became important after finding out that a report had been made charging him for having made lewd and obscene remarks in the presence of a woman. Following the usual protocol, no copy of this report had been made available to the youth's family, nor were they allowed to confront their accusers. After another period of questioning and some discussion over what took place during the first hearing, the judge sentenced the teenager to the state reform school until he reached the age of twenty-one.

If Gault had been an adult and was convicted of similar charges, he would have been fined between $5 and $50 or faced a prison term of not more than two months. As a youth, he faced six years in prison. At the time, the Gaults had little recourse since the state did not provide for appealing juvenile cases to a higher court.

While Gerald was in the state reformatory, his parents filed a writ of habeas corpus (a petition for a hearing on the legality of confinement). The writ asserted that Gerald was being confined illegally. This was the only way they could appeal the case. The family argued for the writ on the grounds that he had been denied due process of law, claiming the son had been denied his basic constitutional rights during the juvenile court proceedings. After being denied by the state supreme court, the ruling was appealed to the U.S. Supreme Court, making it only the second time in American history that the court reviewed a juvenile proceeding. After listening to arguments from both sides, almost three years after the initial obscene phone call, the Court ruled that due process of law as guaranteed by the Fourteenth Amendment applies to juvenile proceedings when a child is charged with being delinquent. As a result, the juvenile court hearings became more equitable by granting standards of due process to juveniles.

Roe v. Wade

When Richard M. Nixon was elected president in 1968, he promised to alter the balance between the rights of criminal defendants and society's rights, choosing **Warren Burger** (1907–1995), a moderate conservative, to replace the retiring Earl Warren as chief justice. Considered a "law and order" judge with little approval for the recent due process revolution, the Burger Court disappointed many conservatives by continuing to support laws governing the rights of defendants while attempting to limit the role of the Court.

Roe v. Wade (1973), which gave women a qualified constitutional right to abortion, was one of the most controversial Supreme Court decisions of the twentieth century, setting off a legal debate that continues to resonate today. This highly charged case reached the high court in two cases brought by women under pseudonyms. In *Roe v. Wade*, a Texas woman challenged the state law that forbade abortion except to save a pregnant woman's life. Georgia's *Doe v. Bolton* case confronted provisions in the state's law that dictated that abortions could be performed only in an accredited hospital and required several other points of procedure, including an examination of the woman by two other doctors besides her own physician. By a vote of seven to two, the Supreme Court upheld the challenges, citing an individual's constitutional right to privacy. However, the right to abortion was limited to include government regulation "at some point in the pregnancy" to ensure the state's "important interests in safeguarding health, maintaining medical standards, and protecting potential life."[12] This landmark court case was the first to confirm that a woman, rather than her physician, might be the party harmed by a state's criminalization of abortion.

In February 2018, a Salvadoran woman who had spent almost eleven years in prison under El Salvador's draconian ban on abortion was freed after nation's supreme court commuted her sentence. This case, for many observers, highlighted the punishment faced by Salvadoran women convicted of homicide after losing a pregnancy. El Salvador forbids abortions under any circumstances, even to save the life of the mother. The thirty-four-year-old woman was working at a school dining hall in 2007 when she began bleeding and suffered a stillbirth in the last month of her pregnancy. She was convicted of aggravated homicide and sentenced to thirty years behind bars. This small Central American country is one six countries (Nicaragua, Honduras, Dominican Republic, Haiti, and Suriname are the others) in the Americas that ban abortion, thanks to the complicity of its courts which enforce the law with harsh penalties directed at women and the physicians that help them. In the case above, the supreme court ruled that there had been insufficient evidence to support the contention that she had ended the pregnancy on purpose and that for "powerful reasons for justice" and "equity" should be released after serving ten years and seven months.[13]

Law enforcement

The turbulence and social conflict that shook America in the 1960s had important consequences for law enforcement. Police organizations were tested on a number of fronts. The 1960s saw a convergence of a variety of large-scale protests involving civil rights and antiwar demonstrators. Meanwhile, a revolution in U.S. civil rights law championed by the Supreme Court placed limitations on police work. Supreme Court decisions challenged long-standing police customs and practices, including search and seizure, brutality, and in-custody investigations.

In 1967, the LEAA reported that "the quality of police service will not significantly improve until higher educational requirements are established for its personnel."[14] August Vollmer had created a police school at Berkeley as early as 1916, and by the 1960s, criminal justice programs flourished. In 1968, a survey by the International Association of Chiefs of Police found that sixty-four colleges and universities offered classes in criminal justice education. Many of the programs had been established in response to the large numbers of Korean War veterans taking advantage of the GI Bill and returning to school to follow programs related to criminal justice in the 1950s and 1960s. Within thirty years, more than 1,000 programs were offered throughout the country.

SWAT

In 1964, the Philadelphia Police Department established its 100-member Special Weapons and Tactics Squad, considered by many to be the precursor to modern SWAT teams. Designed to respond quickly and decisively to bank robberies in progress, it was soon also used to resolve other types of incidents involving heavily armed criminals. Its media popularity and successful field implementation led other police forces to develop similar units, most notably the Los Angeles Police Department (LAPD). During the late 1960s, the LAPD created Special Weapons and Tactics (SWAT) teams in response to new trends in criminal violence that included skyjackings, shoot-outs, and hostage taking.

Following the **Watts Riot** in 1965, LAPD Chief Daryl Gates made a case for a unit trained in military-style tactics, an elite team of officers armed with rifle, shotguns, and armored cars. Gates told the Los Angeles Time in 1968 that during recent civil disorders, "suddenly we found ourselves with almost a guerrilla warfare without weaponry. . . . I felt the frustration of being almost helpless."[15] While many worried about how such a unit might damage already tenuous community relations, "lax gun regulations and strict national drug laws encouraged cities and towns to invest in bigger weaponry."[16] Incidents like the televised 1974 gun battle between the LAPD and the Symbionese Liberation Army catapulted SWAT teams to national prominence. The drug war would place even more pressure on police to adopt "militarized drug enforcement," a policy that would be heavily debated well into the second decade of the twenty-first century.

Kansas City Preventive Patrol Experiment

Beginning in the early 1970s, research in several cities, including Kansas City, demonstrated that increasing neither the number of police officers on random motor patrol nor the speed of their response had little effect on crime reduction. The 1973 Kansas City study was one of the best-known and most controversial studies of police patrol efficiency in this era. Since the inception of the London "bobbies" and New York City "cops" in the first half of the nineteenth century, routine police patrol has been considered a hallmark of modern preventive policing. The notion that crime could be prevented or at least suppressed by a highly regular and visible police presence has been a long held belief. Beginning in 1972, a one-year study was conducted in Kansas City to test this conviction. The release of *The Kansas City Preventive Patrol Experiment* report in 1974 found that police patrols, whether stepped up or diminished, had no significant impact on crime, police response time, public fears of crime, or their attitudes toward police in the area. Led by George L. Kelling and supported by the Police Foundation, Kelling described this experiment as "unique in that never before had there been such an attempt to determine through such extensive scientific evaluation the value of visible police patrol."[17] With traditional methods of policing under scrutiny, new concerns about the role of police in American society sent police experts back to the drawing board for answers.

Policewomen

The 2,610 total policewomen in the United States in 1950 represented just 1 percent of the nation's total number of police officers. But as the women's movement gathered steam in the 1960s, these numbers multiplied. It was not until 1968 that women were assigned to official police cars for the first time, when two women on the Indianapolis Police Department achieved this level of responsibility. The following year, the Washington, DC, police chief tore down another barrier when he eliminated separate police force applications for men and women.

Although the first documented employment of women with police powers can be traced back to 1910, women made few inroads as crime fighters in the male-dominated profession until the 1960s and 1970s. According to one of the foremost authorities on policewomen, women made significant progress in this direction in the 1950s but did not make the transition "from social workers to crime fighters" until 1968.[18]

The federal government led the way in removing impediments blocking women from the police ranks. The creation of the Equal Opportunity Commission in 1968 provided the impetus for bringing women into policing in more meaningful roles. Another barrier fell when the federal government amended the 1964 Civil Rights Act in 1972. The passage of the **Equal Employment Opportunity Act** prohibited discrimination by public and private employers.

A number of court decisions removed many administrative and social barriers, further opening law enforcement to women. But the reality was that while women were joining the "thin blue line" of policing, they were being utilized in a secondary capacity, consigned to gender-based roles from another era. In Catherine Milton's 1972 report on policewomen, she found that women were being used mainly in clerical and juvenile functions, much like their counterparts a half century earlier. Milton also found that women were required to conform to higher educational standards, regulated by hiring quotas based on gender, and were allowed to compete for positions only in the women's bureau.[19] By 1974, women made up only 2 percent of the country's 166,000 police officers, with few assigned to street duty.[20]

The social ferment of the 1960s led many women to question the limitations imposed on them based on gender. However, in 1968, when Indianapolis policewomen Betty Blankenship and Elizabeth Coffal "donned uniforms, strapped gunbelts to their waists, and got into their marked police car," they left "behind their history as police social workers to assume the role of crime fighters along with their male colleagues."[21]

While women had indeed made the transition to crime fighters, by the 1970s, they still represented only a small percentage of the total number of police officers nationwide. According to one authority, female police officers only represented 2.1 percent of sworn officers in 1975. This number grew to 9,000, or 3 percent of all law enforcement personnel, three years later, and by 1980, the number of women in policing had doubled since 1960.[22] However, a trend developed in which larger cities lagged behind smaller cities in the hiring of policewomen.

The Knapp Commission: Frank Serpico vs. corruption on the NYPD

Born Francisco Vincent Serpico in New York City in 1936, Frank joined the NYPD in 1959. He came to national attention in the 1970s after he broke the "blue wall of silence" and reported his corrupt colleagues, first to his superiors (who ignored him) and then the *New York Times*. Soon after testifying against one of his fellow cops, Serpico was shot in the face by a drug suspect while making arrest after the other officers failed to back him up. Most beat officers considered him a "rat" and ignored timeworn police tradition of visiting their fellow wounded officers. One even sent him a card with the message, "With sincere sympathy . . . that you didn't get your brains blown out rat bastard."[23] After the *New York Times* published an investigative series on police corruption, an investigation known as the Knapp Commission was convened and led to mass resignations in the NYPD. Led by Wall Street Lawyer Whitman Knapp, the commission investigated the force for two years before releasing its final report in 1973. According to its conclusions more than half of the city's 29,600 police officers had participated in some type of corrupt activity. The Knapp Commission uncovered two types of corrupt officers. "Meat-eaters" were the relatively small contingent of officers who spent most of their working hours looking for opportunities that they could exploit for financial gain (including gambling and illegal drugs). "Grass-eaters," on the other hand, were the vast majority of patrolmen who did not necessarily accept payoffs but occasionally received gratuities from various entrepreneurs (such as free meals and coffee and donuts). Frank Serpico retired in 1974 and left the U.S. to live in Europe.

Federal law enforcement

Few critics had dared to publicly challenge J. Edgar Hoover and the FBI prior to the 1960s. But the new era witnessed an increasing chorus of Hoover critics, including journalists, college professors, congressmen, and even ex-FBI agents. In 1969, the *New York Times Magazine* published what became a much-quoted article by the respected journalist Tom Wicker titled "What Have They Done since They Shot Dillinger?"

Disapproval of Hoover and the FBI had been building since the 1950s, when the FBI supplied Senator Joseph McCarthy and the House Committee on Un-American Activities with information on "suspected" communists. With the election of John F. Kennedy as president and the ascendance of his brother Robert to attorney general, it seemed that Hoover's days were numbered as FBI director. It has been speculated that despite rancor between Hoover and the Kennedys, he kept his job because he had secret files on the two brothers. Waiving the mandatory retirement age of seventy, Hoover was reappointed by Presidents Lyndon Johnson and Richard Nixon.

COINTELPRO

In the Johnson years, Hoover expanded his COINTELPRO (counterintelligence) program from investigating the Communist Party to the Ku Klux Klan, antiwar radical groups, and black activists. Hoover reserved his harshest words for **Martin Luther King Jr.**, whom he once referred to as a "tom cat with obsessive degenerate urges."[24] COINTELPRO was a secret FBI program established along the lines of what FBI historian Athan Theoharis referred to as a "department of misinformation." In 1956, FBI Director J. Edgar Hoover authorized a project which was called COINTELPRO-Communist Party with the goal of countering communist influence in America. Its anticommunist campaign become even more aggressive than the one it had begun after World War II. By the 1960s, its goal was to create a climate of confusion and distrust among America's numerous radical left-wing organizations in the 1960s. The Black Panthers organization was one of its main targets. (It also targeted hate groups such as the KKK in the South and black nationalists elsewhere.) Under the administration of FBI director William H. Webster in the 1980s, these type of secret police tactics were diminished, if nor discarded, as leftist groups faded into obscurity and civil right activism declined.

While Martin Luther King Jr. and other civil rights leaders held to a path of peaceful nonviolence, others, such as the Black Panthers and black Muslims, stressed black separatism and militancy. Both Presidents Johnson and Nixon were outraged by the activities and success of the Black Panthers. Johnson was convinced they had a subversive agenda and directed the FBI to begin collecting information on them. Under Nixon, the FBI used surveillance to infiltrate and suppress the organization. In a short span of time, twenty-eight Panthers were killed and many imprisoned on debatable charges.

In March 1981, Henry Hays and James Knowles, two Alabama members of the United Klan of America (UKA), picked up an unsuspected nineteen-year-old African American man named Michael Donald on the streets of Mobile. They would later explain that their actions that evening were in retaliation for the murder of a white policemen by a black man. The two Klan members cut the young man's throat and left his body hanging from a tree limb in a "racially mixed residential neighborhood." Both men were arrested, charged, and convicted of murder. Hays became the first white man in Alabama in more than fifty years to be given the death penalty for killing a black man. This case proved a turning point of sorts for the Klan after Morris Dees, cofounder of the Southern Poverty Law Center (SPLC), filed a lawsuit on behalf of Michael's mother, Beulah Donald, against the entire UKA, the first time a civil lawsuit targeted the Klan organization and its leaders with conspiracy. The trial ended up in a stunning "precedent-setting" victory, bringing down the UKA in the process. This strategy would be used a number of times by the SPLC as it challenged other racist organizations. Mrs. Donald was awarded a $7 million victory against the Klan but had to settle for much less in the end, but enough for her to purchase her very first house. She died in 1988, not even a year after moving in.[25]

MIBURN: Mississippi Burning

Although the popular media has tended to promote FBI agents as heroes in the civil rights movement, it was not until Attorney General Robert Kennedy pressured FBI director Hoover to send a large contingent of agents to investigate the killing of three civil rights workers in 1964 that the FBI became actively involved in the murder case.

As testament to the concern that Hoover had for the civil rights movement and the return of the **Ku Klux Klan**, the FBI did not even have a field office in Mississippi. The thirteen FBI agents who were responsible for federal law enforcement in the state either worked out of their homes or were housed in federal buildings. Most of their attention was focused on tracking down stolen cars and fugitives. Despite a mounting terror campaign that included the bombing of twenty black churches in Mississippi, at the time of the disappearance of the three civil rights workers, FBI agents claimed they had no authority to act. It was not until Attorney General Kennedy ordered the case to be treated under the Lindbergh kidnapping law that the FBI was called into the case, which became known as MIBURN, or "Mississippi Burning."

An informant's tip would lead agents to the missing workers' burned-out car and eventually their bodies, buried in an earthen dam. However, murder was not a federal crime, so charges against the suspected nineteen Klan perpetrators would have to come from the state.

In order to arrest and convict the Klansmen, the FBI turned to federal legislation from the late 1860s. By falling back on Reconstruction-era statutes, the Justice Department brought charges that the Klan members had participated in a conspiracy to deprive the three civil rights workers of their constitutional right to register voters in the state of Mississippi. After several false starts, seven of the nineteen defendants were convicted by an all-white jury, the first time in the state's history that an all-white jury convicted white officials or Klan members for crimes against civil rights workers and African Americans. However, the maximum sentence received by the seven was for ten years. None would serve a full term in prison, and by the mid-1970s, most had returned to their homes.

Resurgence of the U.S. marshals

Having receded into the background as federal peace officers, the social unrest and protests of the 1960s led to a resurgence of the U.S. marshals. Beginning in the early days of the civil rights movement in the mid-1950s, the Justice Department recommended the creation of the Executive Office for U.S. Marshals to supervise the marshals in their new duties. In 1962, U.S. marshals protected black student James Meredith from violent protesters as he broke the color barrier at the all-white University of Mississippi. U.S. marshals were called on during the 1960s to protect government buildings from antiwar demonstrators and to assist peace officers whenever federal laws were violated. In 1969, the Executive Office for U.S. Marshals made the transition into the U.S. Marshals Service. For the first time, the marshals, America's oldest federal law enforcement organization, had a headquarters and a bureaucracy directly under the executive branch of government.

Under President Nixon, marshals' duties were expanded to include suppressing air piracy and civil disturbances, prisoner transportation, and court, personal, and witness security. Early in 1971, following the passage of the **Organized Crime Control Act** (1970), marshals became responsible for protecting witnesses in the Witness Protection Program. In 1970, Congress passed the Racketeer Influenced and Corrupt Organizations (RICO) Act, as Title 9 of the Organized Crime Control Act of 1970. It would revolutionize the war against organized crime syndicates. RICO was the brainchild of Special Attorney with the Justice Department G. Robert Blakey. It has been speculated by many that the acronym RICO was actually homage to the movie *Little Caesar*, where Edward G. Robinson played a character modeled after Al Capone named "Rico." Blakey has never confirmed or denied this claim. The RICO statute is distinct for taking a number of state and federal crimes and mandating that, if an individual or individuals commit two of these offenses, the person is guilty of a pattern of racketeering and subject to harsh penalties. The crimes range from bribery, counterfeiting, drug violations, and loan-sharking to selling contraband cigarettes, mail and wire fraud, and acts of terrorism.

Creation of the Drug Enforcement Administration (DEA)

The origins of the U.S. Drug Enforcement Administration (DEA) can be traced back to the early twentieth century, when the federal government began to institute gradual restrictions on dangerous drugs such as heroin and cocaine. In 1915 (a year after the Harrison Narcotics Act), drug enforcement was placed in the hands of the Bureau of Internal Revenue. During the 1920s, the association of the Narcotics Division with the Prohibition Bureau led to public disenchantment with the bureau, in part because of the unpopularity of Prohibition, as well as the ineptitude of its enforcement. At the inauguration of Prohibition in 1920, the Narcotics Division of the Prohibition Unit of the Revenue Bureau consisted of 170 agents and 17 offices. In 1922, the drug agents saw their power expanded with the passage of the Narcotics Drug Import and Export Act. Following a scandal in which drug agents were arrested for taking payoffs from drug dealers, Congress established the Bureau of Narcotics in 1930, removing drug enforcement from the Prohibition Bureau and creating a separate agency in the Treasury Department – the forerunner of the DEA, the Federal Bureau of Narcotics (FBN).

There were some similarities between the Federal Bureau of Narcotics and the much larger and powerful FBI, but they were mostly superficial. Particularly distinctive were the agents themselves. Although FBI agents were typically products of white Anglo-Saxon America, with many coming from "middle American" backgrounds, the FBN agents were just as likely to be drawn from urban ethnic communities, boasting black and Asian agents long before the FBI. Tactics distinguished the two as well, with the FBI more likely to pursue traditional criminals with traditional tactics. Conversely, FBN agents, often referred to as narcs, were often assigned undercover investigations, something Hoover particularly disdained, fearing the corruptive influence of consorting with known criminals.[26] It should not be surprising that the FBN was chasing organized crime syndicates years before they registered on Hoover's radar screen following the 1957 Apalachin debacle (see Chapter 11).

A growing drug problem led to the creation of the Drug Enforcement Administration (DEA) in 1973, resulting in the merger of several agencies. A branch of the Department of Justice, the DEA was given the single mission of enforcing federal drug statutes and investigating major drug traffickers. While illegal drugs were nothing new to American culture, the explosion of the counterculture in the 1960s led to a vociferous antidrug lobby. The growing drug culture had several dimensions that made it increasingly incomprehensible to the non-drug-taking public in the 1960s and 1970s. As the following chapters demonstrate, the so-called "war on drugs" was a conflict that the criminal justice had few answers for.

Corrections

During the early 1960s, correctional facilities began to experiment with less formal arrangements. New prison architectural designs were created to accommodate treatment programs while maintaining security. In March 1963, Alcatraz closed after nearly thirty years as America's foremost maximum "prison of last resort." After several highly publicized but unsuccessful escape attempts, the Bureau of Prisons was convinced that the structure had outlived its usefulness. Increasingly seen as unsafe and too expensive to run, its proximity to San Francisco led to its demise. Officials soon sought a replacement somewhere in America's heartland, settling on the Illinois town of Marion.

Although America's prison population enjoyed a short decline in the early 1960s, by 1968, it was on the increase once more, and by 1971, new commitments had risen 35 percent over 1968. The following year saw a trend develop toward longer sentences that would contribute to swelling prison populations. By the end of 1976, the prison population was 42 percent higher than the 1968 low. With 196,000 prisoners by 1970, rising crime rates and longer sentences led to widespread overcrowding. Despite new prison construction, the number of inmates continued to outstrip the number of cells into the 1980s.

The burgeoning civil rights movement also impacted the history of the prison system as inmates familiarized themselves with their constitutional rights. Among the most popular mainstays of the so-called prison lawyer were the writ of habeas corpus and the Civil Rights Act.[27] By means of the writ of habeas corpus, inmates can challenge the legality of their confinement. Other prisoners fastened their hopes to the Reconstruction-era Civil Rights Act, which protected freed slaves from having their new civil rights violated. In any case, some prisoners began to accept litigation as a better alternative to violence.

In 1961, the Supreme Court (inspired by the Civil Rights Act of 1871) ruled in *Monroe v. Pape* that blacks could avoid biased local courts and sue directly in federal court on constitutional matters. This decision laid the foundation for the Court to allow prison inmates to sue state officials in federal court for the first time in *Cooper v. Pate* (1964).[28] These edicts laid the groundwork for the avalanche of litigation that transformed prison conditions in the 1970s. Prior to the 1960s, American courts allowed prisons and their wardens to operate with little outside interference or oversight. But, in 1964, the U.S. Supreme Court decision *Cooper v. Pate* established the precedent that allowed inmates to sue state officials in federal court. This and other rulings laid the foundation for the avalanche of litigation that transformed prison conditions in the following decades.

Cooper v. Pate

In 1962, twenty-two-year-old Thomas Cooper was serving a life sentence for murder. A recent convert to Islam, he had changed his name to Thomas X. Cooper. He had been housed in solitary confinement for almost ten years at Illinois's Stateville Prison for attacking a corrections officer. He sued Stateville Prison Warden Frank Pate. In 1964, the suit appeared before the U.S. Supreme Court, and against the odds, the next year the Court issued its landmark decision *Cooper v. Pate* setting into motion a series of prisoner lawsuits protesting the often brutal conditions of the nation's prisons. This led to an unprecedented "liberalization" of American prisons. A number of authorities have suggested that it is no coincidence that a number of powerful prison gangs were able to form due to their enhanced liberties and ability to meet as groups (as long as they demonstrated some type of religious affiliation) following this decision. Gangs quickly spread in the new liberal prison environment that prevailed, as African Americans, Latinos, and white supremacists fought for dominance behind prison walls. Prior to *Cooper v. Pate*, only Washington and California reported the presence of gangs. By 1984, more than 60 percent of the country's state and federal prisons reported gang activity. One must also take into account tougher sentencing laws in the 1970s and 1980s ensured that an unprecedented number of street gang members ended up behind bars due to the draconian laws targeting street gang crack cocaine sales activities on the outside. So in effect, street gang members transferred their solidarity and cohesion from the outside to the inside.

Prison reform

Until the 1960s, U.S. courts allowed prisons to operate unimpeded by the courts. This "hands-off" policy was dramatically altered, with virtually every aspect of correctional operation coming under court scrutiny by the 1970s as inmates played a vital role in prompting the courts to define the scope of their constitutional rights. Housing, health care, recreation, mail privileges, classification, and diet were targeted by the increasingly litigious prisoners, leading the federal courts to declare nine state correctional systems to be unconstitutional in the 1970s.

During the 1960s, prisoners in several states filed complaints with the federal court, complaining that they were being brutally disciplined. In many prisons, particularly in the South, a "trustee" system had been institutionalized to make up for the shortage of prison guards and to save money. So-called trusties were empowered to help control the other inmates with an iron fist, leading to a number of lawsuits. In one of its more high profile decisions, the federal district court ruled in **Holt v. Sarver** (1970) that the practices at the Arkansas prison farms at Cummins and Tucker were so atrocious that the entire correctional system was censured. In its condemnation of the Arkansas prison system, the federal court noted that its management was "so bad as to be shocking to the conscience of reasonably civilized people."[29] This case led to the hiring of a more professional corrections staff and the dismantlement of the trustee system.

Thomas O. Murton was teaching penology at Southern Illinois University in 1968 when Arkansas governor Winthrop Rockefeller recruited him to be the state's first professional penologist. He was named the superintendent of the Cummins Prison Farm and the administrator of the Tucker Prison Farm. Before his arrival, Tucker Prison Farm harkened back to the dark ages of confinement. Punishments for certain infractions included inserting needles under fingernails, crushing knuckles and testicles with pliers, beating inmates with a five-foot leather strap up to ten times a day, and the so-called "Tucker Telephone," which involved stripping the inmate and strapping him to a table and then attaching electrodes to the big toe and penis until he passed out. Initially state officials supported Murton's reform efforts, including the abolition of flogging and physical torture. But he ran into a brick wall when he attempted to eliminate the Cummins trustee system, which allowed certain inmates to run roughshod over the rest of the inmates. The Arkansas Prison System had little public funding. While most prisons operate with a ratio of 1 officer for 7 inmates, in Arkansas, it was closer to 1 to 65. The prison system filled the void by using trustees and mounted inmates to guard convicts in the fields of the 4,500-acre Tucker and 16,227-acre Cummins prison farms. Typically, prisoners worked fourteen-hour days, six days a week, with no remuneration. What set the Cummins

Prison scandal into motion was Murton's discovery that more than 200 prisoners had been listed as escapees. The story received international prominence and inspired the fictional film *Brubaker* starring Robert Redford in 1980. However, Murton's penchant for publicity and his reforming zeal led to his dismissal soon after excavations began on the farm to look for bodies. Although only three unmarked graves were found, Murton felt vindicated two years later when a federal court cited conditions at Cummins as a violation of the Eighth Amendment against cruel and unusual punishment. Following his stint in Arkansas, Murton found it impossible to find a job in corrections and instead pursued a PhD in criminology at UC Berkeley. He would go on to teach criminal justice at the University of Minnesota before retiring in 1980.

One of the earliest forays by the Supreme Court into correctional reform in the 1960s took place in 1962, when it used the Eighth Amendment for the first time to invalidate a state law. By a vote of six to two, the Court held in *Robinson v. California* that it was cruel and unusual punishment to sentence individuals whose only crime was habitual drug use to prison terms.

The prisoner rights movement applied standards of due process to a number of correctional issues that were ultimately arbitrated by the Supreme Court, including prisoner disciplinary hearings. In *Wolff v. McDonnell*, the Court ruled in 1974 that due process rights did apply to inmates since "the state did give some valued things to prisoners that could later be taken away."[30] Due process in front of a prison disciplinary board gave prisoners a chance to hear the charges against them twenty-four hours before the hearing and permitted inmates to call witnesses and present evidence that favored their defense. In addition, substitute counsel would be provided for illiterate prisoners.

Although a series of court decisions ruled the racial segregation of prisoners unconstitutional in the 1960s, as late as the 1970s, the practice continued in many prisons, especially in the South, leading one convict to observe, "I thought segregation was dead, but there it was, as vivid as an Alabama lunch counter in the 1950s."[31] Although this policy has been outlawed, research indicates inmates often self-segregate along racial and ethnic lines by choice. The rise and expansion of prison gangs has perpetuated the **de jure** (or officially sanctioned) segregation that characterized prisons until the 1960s.[32]

One of the consequences of the war on crime was the growing racial disparity among prison populations beginning in the 1960s. In 1960, close to 40 percent of prison inmates were classified as "nonwhite." Less than fifteen years later, this figure grew to 49 percent. Nationwide black incarceration rose from 46.3 to 65.1 per 100,000 between 1973 and 1979, a figure more than nine times higher than for whites.[33]

Mandatory sentencing

Further exacerbating the prison overcrowding dilemma was the introduction of mandatory sentencing laws beginning in 1973, when New York State experimented with the Second Felony Offender Law, which required those convicted of selling illegal drugs to serve a minimum prison sentence. Subsequent studies indicated that the law had no impact on recidivism, but this did little to stop the clamor for sentencing reform as conservatives continued to push for stricter punishments.

In 1974, Florida followed New York's example, stipulating three-year minimum prison sentences without parole for any felony involving a firearm. By the mid-1970s, other states implemented mandatory sentencing guidelines, all resulting in prison overcrowding. The trend toward mandatory sentencing filled American prisons beyond capacity by the end of the 1990s, facilitating a prison building boom and a growing opposition to this type of fixed sentence in the following years.

Prison construction

In 1972, the LEAA required a survey of American prisons in order to decide how to utilize funds granted by the federal government for the construction of state and local prisons. After visiting more than 100 facilities in 26 states, a team that included an architect and a psychologist reported they were shocked by the oppressive regimes they found at various prisons, reformatories, jails, and correctional institutions.[34] Instead of recommending any precise reforms, they advocated halting any new prison construction until the existing institutions were better managed. The moratorium on prison construction eventually contributed to more prison overcrowding as the decade wore on.

At the beginning of the 1970s, of the 113 maximum security state prisons in operation, only 6 had been built in the previous century. One of the solutions to the traditional overcrowding of prisons in the 1970s was to start building more prisons, a trend that continues into the twenty-first century. Between 1971 and 1978, America's prison population swelled by 64 percent, in part because of the return to a punishment model of corrections that saw prisoners serving longer periods of time behind bars. Almost 100 riots convulsed prisons between 1969 and 1970, convincing even the most die-hard progressive reformers that the correctional system was a failure. Confidence in most rehabilitation programs was waning and support for the treatment model of corrections rapidly eroding.

Attica uprising

Reflecting the increasingly tense social relations in the free world, America's prisons seethed with racial tension beginning in the 1960s. Racial segregation and the continuing inequities of the prison system may "explain why more than 90 percent of all recorded prison riots, strikes, protests, rebellions, and other disturbances in the United States have occurred since 1960."[35]

New York's Attica uprising in 1971 saw the worst fears of prison administrators come to reality when, on September 9, more than half the prison inmate population of 2,200 went on the rampage, taking guards hostage, destroying property, and preparing for a showdown with the rapidly assembling force of correctional and police officers and National Guardsmen gathering outside the prison walls.

The riot was *not* actually planned. Attica inmates had endured years of awful conditions, poor food, a shower once a week, and only one piece of soap and one toilet roll per month. Prisoners lacked basic dental care, broken bones were left untreated, and Islam was not recognized as a religion. Any letter written in a foreign language was consigned to the dust-bin.[36] According to its most recent chronicler, the riot was sparked by a "misunderstanding more than anything."[37] Apparently, an inmate had been accused of assaulting a guard on September 8. The next morning, fearing reprisals, the inmates attacked the guards. From September 9 to 13, the inmates assembled selected leaders and made rules as the eyes of America focused on the New York penitentiary.

Following on the heels of the assassinations, urban riots, and war coverage that rocked the 1960s, televised images of the Attica uprising were seared into the national conscious-ness. Several days of negotiations followed the outbreak, involving a stellar cast of characters, including radical attorney William Kunstler, Black Panther Bobby Seale, and *New York Times* writer Tom Wicker. But fearing for the safety of the numerous hostages, New York Governor Nelson Rockefeller, who had refused to come to the prison in person to negotiate, ordered prison officials to retake the prison.

On September 13, eight blindfolded hostages were brought to Attica's catwalks, each with an inmate holding a knife to his throat. Rejecting an ultimatum to surrender, the assault team fired tear gas and bullets into the hundreds of inmates huddled in the make-shift village in the yard. In the ensuing confusion, forty-three individuals were killed (one of them died after incident), including ten hostages. It turned out that nine had been killed by friendly fire. Initially, officials claimed that the hostages had their throats slashed by the inmates. However, a medical examiner's report the next day announced that all had been killed by gunfire. According to the New York State Commission Report on Attica, "With the exception of the Indians massacred in the late nineteenth century, the State Police assault which ended the four-day prison uprising was the bloodiest one day encoun-ter between Americans since the Civil War."[38]

After many years of litigation, New York State reached a settlement with the survivors of Attica that would award them $8 million. But by the time the case went through the appeals process and was finally settled in 2000, more than 400 of the prisoners had died, but those that did survive shared the settlement.

The Attica riot spurred a number of important reform efforts, yet many of those prom-ised in 1971 are still on the drawing board. But some good did come out of the carnage. Prisoners for a time would receive true religious freedom, better medical care and food, censorship of mail and newspapers would halt, and there would be more counseling and rehabilitation services provided. As a result of the riot, most state prisons today have Mus-lim chaplains available, inmates can take their high school equivalency tests in Spanish, and prisoners are guaranteed access to the law library.[39] In the long run, the immediate impact of Attica was providing impetus for serious reforms of the American correctional system.

Governor Rockefeller and the backlash to Attica-driven prison reform

Pulitzer Prize-winning historian Heather Ann Thompson suggests there is direct connec-tion between the 1971 insurrection and the subsequent drug legislation championed by New York Governor Nelson J. Rockefeller. The governor had widespread support for a more punitive campaign against recreational drug use. The rising popularity in manda-tory-minimum sentences that took sentencing discretion out of the hands of judges would plague America overcrowded prison system over the next fifty years. Thompson asserts that Rockefeller's new drug laws were "more draconian than anything that had ever before been on the books."[40]

Rockefeller and other American hard-liners were primed by the growing public support for tougher laws. More importantly, the impact of Attica and its aftermath not only "fueled an unprecedented backlash against all efforts to humanize prison conditions in the United States" but had also "unwittingly helped fuel an anti-civil rights and anti-rehabilitation ethos in the United States."[41] The so-called "Rockefeller laws" created a mandatory-minimum sentence of fifteen years to life for possession of four ounces of narcotics (the same as second degree murder). Other states duplicated these laws over the next twenty years in one iteration or another. For example, in 1978, Michigan passed what became known as the "65-lifer law," which gave life automatically to anyone caught with 650 grams of cocaine.

Crime and punishment

In a poll taken in February 1968, Americans rated crime as the nation's leading domestic problem for the first time since scientific public opinion polls were introduced in the 1930s.[42] The 1968 **assassinations** of Robert F. Kennedy and Martin Luther King Jr. exacerbated these crime concerns. By 1970, murder rates were double those of the previous decade, and violent crime rose from 190 to 298 per 100,000 people between 1963 and 1968. A reflection of public opinion and the social ferment of the 1960s, state authorities became more reluctant to utilize capital punishment in these years, although the number of death row prisoners grew from 219 in the 1960s to 608 a decade later.[43]

Juvenile crime continued to be a serious national problem. Between 1960 and 1973, juvenile arrests for violent crimes rose by 144 percent. Richard Nixon exploited the crime issue to win the presidency in 1968, but in 1974, during his second term in office, he was forced to resign from office after he was implicated in a "third-rate" burglary at the Democratic headquarters in the Watergate Hotel.

There is no consensus as to why crime became such a problem in the early 1960s. Law-and-order advocates argued that the upsurge in lawlessness was a result of growing social tolerance. However, criminologists have persuasively argued that it was probably more due to changing demographics and social mores, as postwar baby boomers reached their crime-prone years at the same time.

The federal campaign against organized crime

Finally forced to publicly acknowledge the existence of organized crime after the 1957 Apalachin meeting in upstate New York, the FBI intensified efforts in its war against organized crime through its so-called Top Hoodlum program. But few if any convictions followed. In response, the government, under Attorney General Robert F. Kennedy in 1961, proposed new legislation to intensify the war against the mob, including the use of wiretapping.

During the 1960s and 1970s, a number of government commissions and hearings were convened to investigate organized crime, including investigations by the **Task Force on Organized Crime** in 1967 and 1976. The 1967 task force was most influenced by the hearings of the 1950s Kefauver Committee and the 1963 **McClellan hearings** led by Senator John McClellan. During the 1963 hearing, small-time mobster Joseph Valachi testified to the existence of a nationwide, organized conspiracy that he called "La Cosa Nostra." Although his testimony did not directly lead to any arrests, the barely literate mobster became one of the first Mafia members to break the vow of silence. His conspirational description of a monolithic organized crime presence in America became the accepted portrait of organized crime during the 1960s. While Congress did not immediately pass the new legislation promulgated by Attorney General Kennedy, federal efforts against organized crime did intensify. Legislation legalizing wiretapping was enacted in 1968, and two years later, new legislation to facilitate the prosecution of racketeering was signed into law.

Following on the heels of the Omnibus Crime Control and Safe Streets Act, the 1970 Organized Crime Control Act (OCCA) was created

> to seek the eradication of organized crime in the United States by strengthening the legal tools in the evidence gathering process, by establishing new penal prohibitions, and by providing enhanced sanctions and new remedies to deal with the unlawful activities of those engaged in organized crime.[44]

Chief among the crime control provisions of the OCCA was the creation of the **Racketeer Influenced Corrupt Organizations (RICO) statute**. RICO is considered by many to be the most significant piece of legislation ever enacted against organized crime. Originally designed to keep organized crime from infiltrating legitimate business, it has been used to combat all manner of criminal enterprises.

Despite its success, the RICO Act is not without its critics, who claim that it is too vague and broadly worded and violates many due process standards. Although RICO was enacted in 1970, it was not used until almost ten years later. Since then, it has been used in more than 100 cases each year, mostly against white-collar crime, violent groups, organized crime, and political corruption.

Capital punishment

Beginning in the 1950s, the NAACP and the American Civil Liberties Union became increasingly involved in the defense of death row inmates, leading to the reversal of numerous sentences. As state court systems paid more attention to death row appeals, some became more reluctant to schedule executions. Together with growing death row populations and the declining number of executions, the Supreme Court focused its attention on the constitutionality of the death penalty.

American public opinion had turned against the death penalty by the mid-1960s, leading states to informally stop executions in 1967, with the last ones occurring in Colorado and California. For the next five years, an informal moratorium on the death penalty existed while the Supreme Court evaluated its constitutionality. But executions had been declining since the height of capital punishment in the 1930s, when 218 were executed. In the first half of the 1950s, forty-two inmates were executed. However, only sixteen were put to death between 1955 and 1959 and again between 1960 and 1964.[45]

Furman v. Georgia

On September 20, 1968, twenty-six-year-old William Henry Furman was charged in the superior court of Chatham County, Georgia, with murdering a white man while fleeing a burglary. Furman, who was African American, was caught shortly after the crime still holding the murder weapon. As a poor man, he was given the typical poor-man's trial, defended by a court-appointed lawyer. During a one-day trial, a jury was selected in the morning, the trial heard by 3:30 P.M., and the judge's guilty verdict delivered at 5:00 P.M. Despite a psychological examination prior to the trial in which Furman was diagnosed as mentally deficient and prone to psychotic episodes, the court denied his insanity plea.

Furman had testified that he accidentally fired the weapon as he was fleeing the crime scene and had not intended to hurt anyone. But according to Georgia's death penalty statute, capital punishment stood for accidental killings as well as intentional ones. In April 1969, Furman's death sentence was affirmed, but his execution was stayed the following month so that he could file a petition with the Supreme Court. Three years later, in 1972, his case reached the high court, where it was argued in the context as to whether the death penalty violated the Eight Amendment. His attorney made a case that the death penalty was disproportionately used against minorities. Moreover, since the death penalty was being used with less frequency, its imposition on Furman violated the Eighth and Fourteenth Amendments (guarantee of equal protection).[46]

Despite deep divisions among the justices, Furman's conviction was overturned by a five-to-four margin, with the judges voting that the death penalty did indeed constitute cruel and unusual punishment. In one fell swoop, the Supreme Court gave some 600 death row prisoners new life, including Robert F. Kennedy's assassin Sirhan Sirhan and murder cult leader Charles Manson.

Speaking for the majority, after reviewing the history of capital punishment under common law, Justice William O. Douglas (1898–1980) concluded that the death penalty was disproportionately applied to blacks, the poor, and other disadvantaged groups. *Furman v. Georgia* is regarded as a landmark decision protecting marginalized Americans from the death penalty. The decision did not abolish the death penalty but merely placed stricter requirements on death penalty statutes at both the state and the federal level. According to the Court, the death penalty had become "cruel and unusual" punishment because it was being invoked in a capricious and arbitrary manner, violating the constitutional protections guaranteed by the Eighth Amendment.

Gregg v. Georgia

In 1976, the Supreme Court upheld the death penalty in the case of *Gregg v. Georgia*, and in 1977, the states, under public and political pressure, began revising their capital punishment statutes to fall under the new Supreme Court guidelines. As directed, the death penalty should be the ultimate sanction for the worst offenders and "must be imposed in a more consistent and rational manner." More than two-thirds of the states began rewriting their death penalty laws making sure to include the discretion mandated by the Supreme Court. As a result, new death penalty laws identified crimes with specific aggravating circumstances such as murder of a peace officer in the line of duty, murder while in prison, and murder in the course of a violent crime such as kidnapping.[47] In the *Gregg* decision, the Court ruled that convicted killers in Georgia were protected by a revised statute that required sentencing hearings and other protective procedures. The majority of other death penalty states have revamped their statutes in a similar manner. In addition to making strides to protect the poor, the mentally ill, and minorities, most states have repealed the death penalty for accidental killings and other homicides less serious than premeditated murder.

Ten years after America's last execution, the death penalty returned to American criminal justice. Despite a crescendo of protest from opposition groups, **Gary Gilmore** was determined to die for his crimes. There was little that could be done when a convicted prisoner was determined not to miss his own execution. Sentenced to die for two robbery/murders in 1976, Gilmore was steadfast in his resolution to see the state execute him. This rather ordinary murder case eventually led to an extraordinary conclusion, as Gilmore would become the first person to be executed in ten years. The case received worldwide attention and inspired famed author Norman Mailer to chronicle Gilmore's plight in the Pulitzer Prize-winning account of his life and death in ***The Executioner's Song***. On January 17, 1977, Gilmore's lawyers managed to overturn a restraining order halting the execution, and Gilmore had his final wish granted when he was shot to death by a firing squad at the Utah State Prison.

Violent crime

The civil rights movement of the late 1950s and early 1960s led the dormant Ku Klux Klan to once more raise its pestilent head. Not as large or powerful as the Reconstruction-era Klan, the 1960s incarnation was no less violent. Of the numerous Klan factions, the most violent was in Alabama, where it was responsible for a number of murders, including the 1963 Birmingham church bombing in which four black schoolgirls were killed.

No era in American history was marked by the murder of as many leading public figures as the 1960s. Leaders as diverse as Martin Luther King Jr., John F. Kennedy, Medgar Evers, Robert F. Kennedy, and Malcolm X were silenced by assassin's bullets. In the 1970s, President Gerald Ford narrowly escaped death on two separate occasions at the hands of female assassins. And in 1972, presidential candidate George Wallace was permanently crippled by gunfire while campaigning.

The assassination of President John F. Kennedy (1917–1963) on November 22, 1963, is one of the most chronicled murders in American history. Sworn in as the thirty-fifth president on January 20, 1961, his term was cut short when he was shot and killed by a sniper's bullet while traveling in a motorcade in Dallas, Texas. Lee Harvey Oswald was arrested for the murder, but only two days after his arrest, Oswald was shot and killed by Dallas nightclub owner Jack Ruby.

Assuming the presidency, Vice President Lyndon B. Johnson appointed a commission to investigate the killing. Led by Chief Justice Earl Warren, the **Warren Commission** ruled in 1964 that Oswald acted alone, firing the fatal shots from a window of the sixth floor of the Texas Book Depository. The assassination has been shrouded ever since in mystery and rumors of conspiracy plots. A number of commissions have investigated myriad conspiracy theories, but despite many unanswered questions, no evidence of conspiracy has been substantiated.

In 1965, American black-nationalist leader Malcolm X was shot to death while addressing a crowd in New York City. In April 1968, the Reverend Martin Luther King Jr. (1929–1968), America's leading civil rights figure, was murdered in Memphis, Tennessee. The recipient of the Nobel Peace Prize in 1964, King had become nationally identified with the civil rights movement in the 1950s while leading boycotts and protests in the segregated South. Murdered by a sniper while standing on the balcony of his hotel, King was in Memphis in support of striking sanitation workers. Black urban neighborhoods erupted in violence following the assassination. James Earl Ray was eventually arrested for murder. Although Ray pleaded guilty and was sentenced to life imprisonment, questions still persist as to how the uneducated, provincial, and indigent Ray was able to escape to London (unassisted), where he was apprehended.

Robert F. Kennedy: organized crime nemesis, attorney general, and assassination victim

On the election of his brother as president in 1960, Robert F. Kennedy became the youngest attorney general in U.S. history. Although his earlier career was tarnished by his association with communist hunter Joseph McCarthy in the 1950s, by the 1960s, Kennedy had become a leading supporter of the civil rights movement and an implacable foe of organized crime. Three months after announcing his own candidacy for president, on June 5, 1968, Robert Kennedy was slain by Sirhan Sirhan the very night he celebrated his victory in the California primary.

Best remembered as a presidential candidate and assassination victim in 1968, Robert F. Kennedy (1925–1968) emerged on the American criminal justice scene in the 1950s, first as an attorney in the criminal division of the Justice Department and then while serving on the legal staff of Senator Joseph McCarthy and the House Un-American Activities Committee. He had his first run-in with future nemesis and labor leader Jimmy Hoffa in 1957, when he was the chief counsel to the Select Committee on Improper Activities in the Labor or Management Field. However, the committee failed to indict Hoffa and only solidified Kennedy's resolve to bring the mobbed-up labor boss to justice. He got his chance in 1961 when he was appointed U.S. attorney general by his brother President John F. Kennedy in 1961.

As one of his first points of business, he launched a campaign against organized crime. Under his watch, federal prosecution of organized crime cases increased from 19 in 1960 to 687 in 1964. However, due to weak federal anti-racketeering laws in the pre-RICO era, his office had only limited authority in this arena. His crusade to convict prominent crime bosses and mobbed-up labor leaders such as Jimmy Hoffa was an uphill battle. Hoffa was ultimately sentenced to prison for jury tampering rather than racketeering. His zealousness in the pursuit of organized crime and Hoffa led some to describe the labor and racketeering subdivision of the Organized Crime Section as the "Get Hoffa Squad," while others evoked comparisons to the inquisitors of the "Spanish Inquisition." Perhaps his greatest achievement was bringing together for the first time in American history so many (more than two dozen) federal agencies in the campaign against organized crime. Critics aside, those that worked under him testified they never worked under a more dedicated highly ranked official.

Rioting and civil disobedience

During the 1960s, the law enforcement establishment was increasingly tested by a wide variety of mass confrontations. Violent riots have sporadically punctuated urban American life since the colonial era. Despite the deaths of thirty-eight individuals in the 1943 Detroit riot, race riots began to follow a new pattern in which rioters targeted buildings and commercial goods more than people. The race riots of the 1960s were marked by the destruction of property and communities, shocking citizens of all races.

The best-known race riot of the 1960s occurred in the Watts area of Los Angeles in 1965. On the evening of August 11, two young African American men were stopped by the California Highway Patrol for reckless driving in the inner-city neighborhood of Watts. Soon after the arrival of members of the Los Angeles Police Department, the scene deteriorated into chaos. The department had a reputation for brutality and bad relations with the city's black community. A rumor spread through the area that police had roughed up a pregnant black woman. Although it proved false, it was enough to ignite one of the nation's worst episodes of civil unrest. Over the following week, more than thirty mostly black residents were killed. Looting and arson damage estimates reached $200 million. President Johnson appointed a commission led by former CIA director John McCone to investigate the riots.

According to the findings of the **McCone Commission**, black Los Angeles was like a powder keg ready to explode. Black migrants had been drawn to the city during the 1940s to take advantage of wartime employment. However, they were confronted with limited housing opportunities and racial discrimination. Since mass transportation was limited in the city, blacks had to shop locally, where stores were notorious for selling poor goods at high prices. The retail community bore the brunt of most of the property damage during the riot.[48]

The urban riots of 1966 and 1967 proved particularly destructive. Of the thirty-eight riots that took place in 1967, some of the most serious took place in Chicago, Cleveland, and San Francisco, resulting in 7 deaths, more than 400 injuries, 3,000 arrests, and property damage exceeding $5 million. The following year would be even worse. By the end of October, there had been more than 150 outbreaks of civil unrest. Of these, thirty-three necessitated the intervention of the state police and eight the National Guard. Observing the aftermath of the Detroit riot that left thousands of buildings in ruins, Mayor Jerome Cavanaugh remarked that the city "looks like Berlin in 1945."[49] The forty-three deaths during the Detroit riot surpassed those during the Watts uprising.

In the wake of the assassination of Martin Luther King Jr. in 1968, looting and burning erupted in more than 150 cities, with some of the worst damage occurring in the nation's capital. Of the forty-six deaths during the riots, all but five were black. While this ratio of black to white deaths was a familiar refrain from past rioting, what was new was the amount of power summoned to end the disturbances. In what was probably the largest single deployment of military and paramilitary forces for a civilian purpose since the Civil War, 34,000 National Guardsmen, 21,000 federal troops, and thousands of local police were brought in to quell the "disturbances."

Many black and white residents of the nation's capital had considered the city "riot-proof" in 1968. Unlike other urban centers with large black populations, many blacks were well entrenched in good-paying government jobs. According to one study[50] of the Washington riot, one out of every four federal employees in the area was African American. A black sat on the Supreme Court (Thurgood Marshall) and in the president's cabinet (Housing Secretary Robert C. Weaver). Federal troops had been called to Washington, DC, on three previous occasions during the past fifty years but only once for racial strife.

However, like most other cities, there was a darker side that tourists and visitors rarely saw. By the 1960s, Washington, DC, had foundering hospital and school systems and was surpassed only by Mississippi in infant mortality. More than one out of every four families lived below the poverty line. In addition, the city had some of the highest rates of tuberculosis and syphilis in the nation. Large sections of the city were bereft of public transportation, limiting job prospects in the suburbs. Civic leaders began warning of unrest, which was narrowly averted on several occasions. Particular disdain in the black community was reserved for the Washington police force, which they regarded as racist. With blacks representing 67 percent of the population, the highest percentage in any major city, four out of every five police officers were white. Despite urgings from the White House to modernize and become more responsive to the community, the department dragged its feet.[51]

In 1967, President Johnson appointed the National Advisory Commission on Civil Disorders, chaired by Otto Kerner, former Illinois governor. Kerner's committee queried social scientists, police officers, politicians, and civic leaders for solutions to the civil unrest plaguing the nation. According to the commission's findings, better known as the **Kerner Commission** Report, the torpid initial police response to many riots allowed civil unrest to often flare out of control. The Kerner Commission was reminiscent of the commission created in the wake of the 1919 Chicago riot. Whereas earlier commissions convened to study civil disorder, the Kerner Commission was the "first federally funded, national and Presidential-level examination of race relations in the United States."[52] The ***Kerner Report*** was published in 1969, selling 2 million copies.

A survey of the black residents in Detroit following the 1967 riot revealed that three-quarters of them believed that the police acted too slowly to control the disorder.[53] Henceforth, departments would need to adhere to new requirements if they were to be effective in controlling disorder, which meant being able to deploy manpower quickly and efficiently. This would take some doing since the Kerner Commission noted that the average police department had only 13 percent of its patrol force available between the hours of 4:00 P.M. and midnight, the hours when most riots began. There were other concerns that needed to be addressed as well. Few if any departments had any contingency plans for controlling disorder once it began, and most were likely to be short of essential equipment. During one major eruption of civil disorder, the commission found that out of a police force of 5,000, only 192 were on duty for a city of 1 million.[54] However, the commission reserved its greatest criticism for the lack of police training for riot control, finding that the only riot training was provided in recruit school.[55]

Running on a law-and-order platform in the 1968 presidential campaign, Richard Nixon castigated the Kerner Commission for blaming "everybody for the riots except the perpetrators."[56] After taking office in early 1969, Nixon recommended more funding for the LEAA in order to supply police departments with tanks, armored cars, helicopters, riot control equipment, and a national computerized identification system for fighting crime. A reflection of the new administration's support for law enforcement was its increased funding for LEAA, from $63 million in 1969 to $268 million in 1970 and $700 million just two years later. In order to seem tough on crime, Congress was coerced by the White House to pass questionable bills, such as the "no-knock" provision, which allowed police to break into a house without a search warrant, and preventative detention, which would allow judges to jail suspects for sixty days before trial. In response, Senator Sam Ervin Jr., who would later receive prominence for his performance at the Watergate trial, referred to these provisions as "A Bill to Repeal the Fourth, Fifth, Sixth, and Eighth Amendments to the Constitution."[57]

In the early 1960s, leftist groups, such as Students for a Democratic Society (SDS), participated in freedom rides and voter registration drives in the still segregated South. By the mid-1960s, their attention was diverted to the antiwar crusade, and in 1968, the organization counted more than 100,000 members. Still, thousands more belonged to the Yippies and other radical groups.

One of the most memorable images of 1968 was of thousands of antiwar protesters being beaten by Chicago police during the Chicago Democratic Convention. A subsequent investigative commission later described police tactics as a "police riot."[58] In reality, much of the blame rested with the administration of Chicago Mayor Richard Daley.[59] In the riots following the assassination of Martin Luther King Jr. earlier in the year, the Chicago police had reacted with remarkable leniency. Afterward, the mayor had admonished the force for its timidity in putting down the riot, having ordered them "to shoot to kill arsonists and maim looters."[60]

One of the most egregious episodes of the Vietnam War era, the **Kent State shootings** on May 4, 1970, demonstrated the growing antipathy between pro-war and antiwar factions. President Nixon's order for an American incursion into Cambodia on May 1 ignited strident student protests on many campuses across the country. Protests at Kent State University in Ohio led the mayor to declare a state of civil emergency and to request the National Guard to keep order. With the arrival of the Guard, tensions mounted. As students launched projectiles and profanities at the National Guard, the armed guardsmen directed tear gas canisters at their adversaries. Shortly after noon, the Guardsmen opened fire on the protesters, wounding nine students and killing four in just thirteen seconds. Following an investigation by the FBI, the Justice Department declared the shootings unwarranted. Following several other investigations, the National Guardsmen were exonerated, leading to many years of civil and criminal suits.

Equally controversial but less well-known were the shooting deaths of two black students and the wounding of twelve others by state troopers and city police at **Jackson State** University (formerly Jackson State College) in Jackson, Mississippi, ten days after the shootings at Kent State. The shootings followed anti-Vietnam War draft protests targeting Mississippi's all-white draft boards. This, combined with the ongoing legacy of racial discrimination, led to the fatal encounter on May 14, 1970. Tensions escalated after a series of confrontations between African American students and white police officers. After one student threw a bottle in their direction, the police unleashed a barrage of gunfire in front of one of the dormitories. As at Kent State, no one was ever indicted for the homicides, adding to the political divide that cleaved the nation. Many attributed the Jackson State shootings to tensions lingering from the "**Freedom Summer**" of the late 1960s, when civil rights activists targeting the state to register black voters antagonized white police officers.[61] Although this incident provoked nationwide indignation for several days, it soon faded from memory. Many observers suggested that national outrage at the shooting of the African American students would have been greater if they had been white.

Domestic terrorism

America's domestic terrorism threats in the 1960s and 1970s seem rather quaint compared to the mass killings that took place in the 1990s and over the next two decades. However, there was probably no era in American history with more bombings than the 1970s. Bombings by leftist groups such as the Black Liberation Army, the Weathermen, the Symbionese Liberation Army, the Puerto Rican nationalist group, the Puerto Rican Nationalist Party, and others took place on almost a daily basis. Indeed, "Because radical violence was so deeply woven into the fabric of 1970s America," according to a recent chronicler of the era, "many citizens, especially in New York and other hard hit cities, accepted it as a fact of daily life." In 1972 alone, there were more than 1,900 domestic bombings in the U.S.[62] What set this era apart from the coming age of terrorism was the fact that the bombings were rarely lethal. In fact, the deadliest bombing by the "radical underground" killed *only* four people.[63]

Following the demise of most of these left-wing–oriented extremist groups by the end of the 1970s, a new phenomenon captured the attention of the nation and law enforcement. During the 1980s, in the midst of America's "get-tough" war on crime, white supremacist extremists launched a terrorist campaign and a crime spree to financially support it. None was more prominent or criminally inclined than the Silent Brotherhood, better known as the Order. By the time it went into action, it had almost 50 members. By most accounts, they followed a script provided by William Pierce's *Turner Diaries*. Considered a primer for urban warfare, the book featured the violent overthrow of the government and subsequent race war to establish an Aryan nation. In 1983, the Order put its theories into practice and began a campaign of bombings, robberies, and a counterfeiting operation. In little more than one year, the gang had banked a war chest of almost $4 million and had assassinated the prominent Jewish radio talk show host Alan Berg in Denver, Colorado. By some accounts, "The Order was the most organized group of terrorist-type people ever to have operated in the United States."[64] After a string of armored car heists and other crimes the group was brought to bay by the FBI and its leader, Robert Jay Mathews died in a shoot-out at his compound on Puget Island, Washington. The terrorist/criminal group was tried under the RICO Act in the mid-1980s. This was the first case that the statute was used in a political case (earlier cases were against Mafia-type organizations).[65]

Homicide

Seemingly new types of homicides captured the nation's and the law enforcement community's attention beginning in the 1960s. The omnipresence of television, together with the newsprint media, would bring the horrors of Vietnam and mass murder to the evening dinner table. There were ample crimes to capture their attention. During the early 1960s, Albert DeSalvo captured the media's attention, claiming that he was the serial killer and rapist, "the Boston Strangler," responsible for hundreds of rapes and the murders of at least thirteen women (although there was no evidence to link him to the murders and recent research suggests that he was probably not responsible for most, if not all of the murders). As the decade moved to a conclusion, the "Zodiac" killer targeted couples in the hills outside San Francisco, and serial killer Edmund Kemper began a killing spree in Santa Cruz, California, that would conclude with the murder of his mother in 1973. According to one expert, "serial murder" became much "more frequent since the late 1960s and offenders tend to kill larger number of victims."[66]

James Alan Fox, one of the country's leading authorities on homicide, suggested that "the onset of the age of mass murder" began in 1966. The summer of 1966 would introduce Americans to the horrors of mass murder as **Charles Whitman** gunned down sixteen people with devastating accuracy from the top of a tower at the University of Texas (like Kennedy assassin Lee Harvey Oswald, Whitman was also a former Marine) and Richard Speck stabbed to death eight student nurses in Chicago.

The rising incidence of mass murder in the 1970s led several states to recognize this crime as a distinct type of homicide. California, for instance, had previously made first degree murder punishable by seven years' imprisonment followed by parole eligibility. In the aftermath of highly publicized mass shootings in the 1970s, the law was amended to allow the jury to add the additional charge of multiple murder. In these cases, the only applicable sentence was the death penalty or life in prison.

Meanwhile, older, more traditional regional patterns of homicide continued to prevail. In the summer of 1964, three civil rights activists, two of them white, were arrested for speeding in Philadelphia, Mississippi. After their arrests, they were then conveniently released into the waiting hands of local white supremacists who brutally murdered them and then hid their bodies in an earthen dam. At the time of the crime, Mississippi was considered the nation's most segregated state. It had the highest percentage of blacks and the lowest percentage of registered black voters, with only 6 percent of its black population of almost 1 million eligible to vote.

In the summer of 1964, national civil rights leaders called on student volunteers to use their vacation to help register Mississippi's black citizens to vote in what became known as "Freedom Summer." While students were given a "survival course" before leaving for Mississippi, it would do little to prevent the murder of three civil rights workers and the beating of dozens more. More than 150 FBI agents ultimately investigated the murder of the civil rights workers, and an investigation led to the arrest and conviction of seven members of the newly revived Ku Klux Klan.

Klan membership had peaked in the 1920s. However, membership surged upward in response to the growing civil rights movement and then after the election of a Catholic president (Kennedy) in 1960. The Klan was far from monolithic. There was no central headquarters, but regional offices flourished throughout the South. By 1965, the Mississippi Klan boasted 5,000 members.

No murders or crimes symbolized the 1960s more than those committed by the **Manson family** in California in the late 1960s. After Charles Manson left prison in 1967, he moved to San Francisco, which was in the last stages of the so-called Summer of Love. Manson used his magnetic personality to great advantage, drawing a number of runaways and homeless young girls to his paranoid banner, forming the nucleus of what became known as the "Manson Family." Their many crimes have been well chronicled and reached a crescendo of sorts with the massacre of movie starlet Sharon Tate and four others on the evening of August 9, 1969. The subsequent nine-and-a-half-month trial led to the conviction of four defendants for murder, but their lives would be spared in 1972 when the Supreme Court declared the death penalty unconstitutional, converting all death sentences to life in prison.

Notable trials

Gideon v. Wainwright

Early on a June morning in 1961, a Panama City, Florida, police officer on patrol noticed an open door at a local pool hall well after closing time. On further examination, the officer noted that someone had burglarized a jukebox and a cigarette machine. This was hardly the crime of the century, but nevertheless, suspicion quickly settled on an indigent drifter named Clarence Gideon. Few could have imagined the consequences of such a seemingly inconsequential crime.

While federal law had guaranteed the right to counsel at the federal level since the inception of the Republic, as the law stood on the state level, courts did not have to offer court-appointed attorneys to defendants in noncapital trials. Most penniless defendants had no recourse but to defend themselves without the benefit of a court-appointed attorney.[67] Although several states provided felony defendants with counsel, Florida was not among them. Chronicling Gideon's case in *Gideon's Trumpet*, author Anthony Lewis wrote, "Judging from the externals it would be hard to imagine a figure less likely to be the subject of a great case in the Supreme Court"[68] than Clarence Gideon. With little education, Gideon was no match for the prosecuting attorney, particularly after the jury heard the testimony of an individual who claimed to have observed Gideon pilfering the poolroom vending machines. In a trial that lasted less than one day, Gideon was found guilty of breaking into a poolroom in order to commit a felony and was sentenced to five years in prison.

But the Supreme Court had not counted on the resourcefulness of the intrepid Gideon. After having a writ of habeas corpus denied by the Florida Supreme Court, in which he claimed to have been illegally imprisoned, Gideon wrote a five-page penciled document to the U.S. Supreme Court asking the court to hear his case. With thousands of similar petitions filed each year, the odds were stacked against the Court's considering his case. However, for once in his life, the odds were in his favor, and the Court agreed to hear his case in January 1963.

Shortly before the case was heard, the director of Florida's Division of Corrections was replaced by Louie L. Wainwright, ensuring the new director of his place in legal history. In the initial hearing of *Gideon v. Wainwright*, there was harsh debate among the justices over the need to change the law. But the 1960s had inaugurated a new vantage point from which to discuss the rights of defendants, and on March 18, 1963, the Supreme Court unanimously ruled that all felony defendants were entitled to legal representation no matter what crime had been committed. Overturning Gideon's conviction, Justice Hugo L. Black wrote, "Reason and reflection requires us to recognize that in our adversary system of criminal justice, any person hauled into court, who is too poor to hire a lawyer, cannot be assured a fair trial unless counsel is provided for him."[69]

In August 1963, Gideon returned to court, this time accompanied by an experienced trial lawyer. But angered by adverse publicity, the prosecution made sure a "dream team" of lawyers were on hand to see that the charges stuck this time. However, with the aid of his defense attorney, the witness from the first trial was shown under questioning to have withheld his criminal record from the earlier jury. Subsequently, Gideon was acquitted of all charges. Clarence Gideon died at the age of sixty-one in 1972 but not until he had ensured that the right to counsel under the Sixth Amendment had become absolute and applicable everywhere in all courts of the land.

Conclusions

As the 1960s spiraled to an end, Americans had become increasingly concerned about the high levels of disorder and violence in the culture. Between 1963 and 1970, the national homicide rate had doubled from 4.6 to 9.2 per 100,000.[70] No place was more deadly than America's urban centers. Americans increasingly feared crime during the 1960s and 1970s. By 1978, 85 percent of Americans believed that the criminal justice system should be more punitive.[71] Public opinion that once favored a moratorium on the death penalty was shifting as well. The 1960s began with a decline in executions and then an informal moratorium that existed from 1967 to 1972. By the 1980s, two out of every three Americans favored the death penalty.[72]

The National Commission on the Causes of and Prevention of Violence recorded 239 urban riots in America between 1963 and 1968. Historian Paul Gilje suggested that there was "a contagion of disorder, just as in the 1760s and 1770s and the 1830s and 1840s spreading across the land."[73] Subsequent commissions blamed the riots on insufficient police response, while others saw the conflagrations as an outgrowth of police and civilian confrontations. Whatever the cause, extensive television coverage reminded Americans that while there was progress in breaking down southern segregation, de facto segregation persisted in much of urban America. Among the commissions to investigate the rioting was the Kerner Commission, which concluded that urban disorder resulted from the unequal treatment of blacks that created two separate societies.

Building on a tradition begun by the 1930 Wickersham Commission Report, communities convened committees to investigate various facets of the criminal justice system during the 1960s and 1970s. According to John Conley, "The establishment of blue ribbon commissions to study complex social problems has been a common element of

American political history . . . to study problems related to crime and the administration of justice."[74]

Although the Wickersham Commission was the first national commission on crime, some of the best-known commissions of the 1960s and 1970s were more local in scope. While the Kerner Commission investigated civil disorders nationwide, the Knapp Commission examined corruption in New York City only. There were a number of lesser-known investigations conducted at almost every level of government. Cities, including Philadelphia, Chicago, and Washington, DC, were examined in great detail. In 1965, President Johnson oversaw the creation of the President's Commission on Crime in the District of Columbia. Assisted by a staff of criminologists, psychologists, social workers, and correctional experts, the commission investigated the causes of crime and delinquency, the adequacy of existing criminal laws, the relationships between the police and the community, and many other related issues. Its mammoth 1,041-page report was published in 1966.[75] Despite many well thought-out conclusions and recommendations, most went unheeded, and these cities continued to be characterized by criminal activity and economic despair as the 1980s loomed on the horizon.

Police work changed dramatically in the 1960s and 1970s. The publication of *The Challenge of Crime in a Free Society* in 1968 devoted considerable attention to the changing nature of police work. Among its most controversial conclusions was that it had been unable to discover "the relationship between police patrol and deterrence."[76] Rising crime rates, urban riots, and antiwar violence led police executives and political leaders to examine the role of police as crime fighters. Although a number of police authorities blamed the rising crime problem on the limitations imposed on them by *Miranda*, *Mapp*, and *Escobedo*, a more convincing explanation perhaps could be found in the number of young males fifteen to twenty-four coming of age in the 1960s and 1970s, an age group that has traditionally been responsible for most violations of the law.

In its final report on the riots following the killing of Martin Luther King Jr., the Kerner Commission noted, "Our nation is moving toward two societies, one black and one white – separate and unequal." However, the commission's report was not all doom and gloom, suggesting that the "deepening racial division is not inevitable" and could "be reversed."[77]

The death of J. Edgar Hoover in 1972 ended an era in American criminal justice history. His last years as FBI director became increasingly bizarre, and although he is credited with creating the professional FBI, suppressing kidnapping and bank robbery in the 1930s, and containing the espionage menace during World War II, Hoover will probably be remembered for violating constitutional protections and keeping secret files. Unfortunately, future historians will be able to only presume what was in his personal files since his secretary apparently had them destroyed following Hoover's death.

Congressional investigations during the 1970s uncovered numerous flagrant violations of civil liberties by the FBI. Defying federal laws, FBI agents broke into the homes, tapped the phones, and opened up the mail of American citizens; illegally infiltrated antiwar groups and black radical organizations; and compiled dossiers on thousands of dissidents. Following these investigations, Congress laid down strict guidelines for FBI activities.

The correctional system was rent by political activism and large-scale violence in the 1970s, leading by the end of the decade to the "demise of the treatment model . . . a breakdown in prisoners' unity, and a return to classical notions of punishment."[78] The extensive media coverage of the Attica riot in 1971, still the bloodiest prison riot in American history, "crystallized doubts about the purposes of imprisonment in America" at a time when the criminal justice system was becoming increasingly punitive.[79] Rising prison populations in the next two decades would only intensify doubts about these institutions.

While law enforcement and the machinery of crime fighting were bolstered by hundreds of millions of dollars through the LEAA, little attention was paid to the underlying social and economic problems that led to crime and incarceration. Despite the concerted get-tough war on crime, serious crimes continued to skyrocket into the 1980s.

Point – counterpoint

On the pad: the criminal justice system and police corruption

Corruption is nothing new to metropolitan America. Cities big and small have been plagued by this problem since the inception of modern policing. In 1967, the President's Commission on Law Enforcement and Administration of Justice released its Task Force Report on the Police. The main charge of the task force was to examine the role of the police in modern America. Among its many conclusions was that there was a need to emphasize police integrity and ethical conduct. According to the authors of the report, police leaders were currently making inroads on stemming police corruption. However, within five years, the nation's best-known city force was rocked by scandal. The first passage is from the task force report chapter on police integrity. The Knapp Commission investigated police corruption in New York City for more than two years before releasing its report in late 1972. According to the report, more than half of the city's 29,600 police officers had participated in some type of corrupt activity. The Knapp Commission uncovered two types of corrupt officers – "grass-eaters" and meat-eaters. The passage from the Knapp report describing these types follows.

Source: Task Force on the Police: *The Police*, Washington, 1967, pp. 212–213;
Knapp Commission, *Commission to Investigate Allegations of Police Corruption and the City's Anti-Corruption Procedures*, Dec. 26, 1972, pp. 65–66

Grass-eaters and meat-eaters

Corrupt policemen have been informally described as being either "grass-eaters" or "meat-eaters." The overwhelming majority of those who do take payoffs are grass-eaters, who accept gratuities and solicit five- and ten- and twenty-dollar payments from contractors, tow-truck operators, gamblers, and the like, but do not aggressively pursue corruption payments. "Meat-eaters," probably only a small percentage of the force, spend a good deal of their working hours aggressively seeking out situations they can exploit for financial gain, including gambling, narcotics, and other serious offenses which can yield payments of thousands of dollars. Patrolman William Phillips was certainly an example of this latter category.

One strong impetus encouraging grass-eaters to continue to accept relatively petty graft is, ironically, their feeling of loyalty to their fellow officers. Accepting payoff money is one way for an officer to prove that he is one of the boys and that he can be trusted. In the climate which existed in the Department during the Commission's investigation, at least at the precinct level, these numerous but relatively small payoffs were a fact of life, and those officers who made a point of refusing them were not accepted closely into the fellowship of policemen. Corruption among grass-eaters obviously cannot be met by attempting to arrest them all and will probably diminish only if Commissioner Murphy is successful in his efforts to change the rank and file attitude toward corruption.

No change in attitude, however, is likely to affect a meat-eater, whose yearly income in graft amounts to many thousands of dollars and who may take payoffs of $5,000 or even $50,000 in one fell swoop (former Assistant Chief Inspector Sydney Cooper, who had been active in anti-corruption work for years, recently stated that the largest score of which he had heard – although he was unable to verify it – was a narcotics payoff involving $250,000). Such men are willing to take considerable risks as long as the potential profit remains so large. Probably the only way to deal with them will be to ferret them out individually and get them off the force, and, hopefully, into prisons.

It is the police themselves, in the vast majority of cases, who are ridding their profession of the unethical and the corrupt. An ever-increasing number of law enforcement leaders are realizing that vigilance against such practices is a continuing part of their responsibilities. For over forty years, Director J. Edgar Hoover and his associates throughout the FBI organization have set an outstanding example of integrity within a law enforcement agency. Through the influence of its special agents throughout the country, working in close contact with local police officers, and through its training programs at the FBI National Academy and local training schools, the FBI has encouraged thousands of police officers to emulate its standards.

National, State, and local police associations have also done a great deal to encourage police integrity. The Law Enforcement Code of Ethics has been adopted by all major police associations and agencies throughout the Nation. In California, for example, State law requires that police ethics be taught and that the code be administered as an oath to all police recruits training in the 45 police academies certified by the State Commission on Peace Officers Standards. In 1955, the International Conference of Police Associations developed a lesson plan for the teaching of ethics within police organizations. The California Peace Officers Association and the Peace Officers Research Association maintain highly active committees on police standards and ethics and are responsible for most of the high ethical standards established throughout the State. And the International Association of Chiefs of Police constantly strives to establish and maintain honest police leadership. Other police consulting firms have made similar recommendations. Through numerous surveys of police departments, it has pointed up the need for maintaining police integrity through the establishment of internal investigation units. The Fraternal Order of Police has stressed the need for attracting high caliber police recruits through adequate salaries, sound retirement systems and other benefits.

Such groups should increase their activity in this field. Local police associations especially must be alert to the problem, recognizing the relationship between maintaining integrity and good conduct and improving the public image of the police. This can lead to more adequate pay and equipment, along with improved working conditions. Associations that come to the aid of dishonest officers render an obvious disservice, not only to themselves, but to the entire police profession.

Key terms

Law Enforcement and
  Administration of
  Justice (LEAA)
American Indian Movement
Terry v. Ohio
Warren Burger
COINTELPRO
Organized Crime Control
  Act
Knapp Commission
Marion
mandatory sentencing
John F. Kennedy
McClellan Hearings
Gregg v. Georgia
Warren Commission
assassinations
Jackson State shootings
Freedom Summer

Omnibus Crime Control and
  Safe Streets Act
Escobedo v. Illinois
In re Gault
SWAT
MIBURN
Drug Enforcement
  Administration (DEA)
meat-eaters
Cooper v. Pate
Attica prison riot
Martin Luther King Jr.
Racketeer Influenced Corrupt
  Organizations (RICO) statute
Gary Gilmore
Watts Riot
Kerner Commission
Charles Whitman
Manson Family

Civil Rights Act
Miranda v. Arizona
Roe v. Wade
Kansas City Preventive
  Patrol Experiment
Equal Employment
  Opportunity Act
Frank Serpico
grass-eaters
Holt v. Sarver
Robert F. Kennedy
Task Force on Organized
  Crime
Furman v. Georgia
The Executioner's Song
McCone Commission
Kent State shootings
Ku Klux Klan
Gideon v. Wainwright

Critical thinking questions

1 What does the "nationalization of criminal justice" refer to?
2 Explain why there was so much friction between different segments of the public and law enforcement during the 1960s.
3 Discuss the transition from the 1967 "Summer of Love" to the bloodshed and civil disruptions that marked the 1960s and 1970s.
4 According to Samuel Walker, this era was "the most turbulent in all of American criminal justice history." Do you agree or disagree? Explain your reasons.
5 Discuss the changing nature of policing and corrections during this period.
6 Examine American popular opinion concerning the death penalty during the 1970s. How did it impact the legal system?

Notes

1 Daniel Bell, *The End of Ideology*, New York: Free Press, 1960, p. 151.
2 James Q. Wilson, *Thinking about Crime*, New York: Basic Books, 1983, p. 15.
3 Samuel Walker, *Popular Justice*, New York: Oxford University Press, 1998, p. 180.
4 President's Commission on Law Enforcement and Administration of Justice, *The Challenge of Crime in a Free Society*, Washington, DC: U.S. Government Printing Office, 1967.

5 Sue Titus Reid, *Criminal Justice Procedures and Issues*, New York: West Publishing, 1987, p. 130.

6 See for example, Carl M. Brauer, *John F. Kennedy and the Second Reconstruction*, New York: Columbia University Press, 1977.

7 David Bodenhamer, *Fair Trial: Rights of the Accused in American History*, New York: Oxford University Press, 1992, p. 113.

8 Alexander B. Smith and Pollack Harriet, *Criminal Justice: An Overview*, New York: Holt, Rinehart and Winston, Pollack, 1980, p. 199.

9 Michael D. White and Henry F. Fradella, *Stop and Frisk: The Use and Abuse of a Controversial Policing Tactic*, New York: New York University Press, 2016.

10 Ibid.

11 Jeffrey Toobin, "Rights and Wrongs," *The New Yorker*, May 27, 2013, pp. 36–43.

12 David W. Neubauer and Stephen S. Meinhold, *Judicial Process: Law, Courts. And Politics in the United States*, Boston: Wadsworth, 2012, 6th ed, p. 425.

13 Elisabeth Malkin, "Long Jailed for Stillbirth, But Now Free," *New York Times*, February 16, 2016, p. A10.

14 President's Commission on Law Enforcement and Administration of Justice, 1967, p. 126.

15 Quoted in Jason Fagone, "Swatted," *New York Times Magazine*, November 29, 2015, p. 36.

16 Jason Fagone, "The Serial Swatter," *The New York Times Magazine*, Nov 24, 2015.

17 George Kelling, et al., *The Kansas City Preventive Patrol Experiment*, Washington, DC: Police Foundation, 1974.

18 Dorothy Moses Schulz, *From Social Worker to Crimefighter: Women in United States Municipal Policing*, Westport, CT: Praeger, 1995, p. 115.

19 Catherine Milton, *Women in Policing*, Washington, DC: Police Foundation, 1972.

20 Leslie Kay Lord, "Policewomen," in *The Encyclopedia of Police Science*, ed. William G. Bailey, New York: Garland, 1995, p. 629.

21 Schulz, 1995, p. 131.

22 Ibid., p. 135.

23 Doug Poppa, "Frank Serpico: NYPD Corruption Buster," *Baltimore Post Examiner*, June 2, 2017.

24 Richard Gid Powers, *Secrecy and Power: The Life of J. Edgar Hoover*, New York: Free Press, 1987, p. 417.

25 The best account of this case is Laurence Leamer, *The Lynching: The Epic Courtroom Battle That Brought Down the Klan*, New York: William and Morrow, 2016.

26 Douglas Valentine, *The Strength of the Wolf: The Secret History of America's War on Drugs*, London: Verso, 2004; Thomas Reppetto, *American Mafia: A History of Its Rise to Power*, New York: Henry Holt, 2004.

27 Edgardo Rotman, "The Failure of Reform: United States, 1865–1965," in *Oxford History of the Prison*, ed. Norval Morris and David Rothman, New York: Oxford University Press, 1995, p. 172.

28 Larry E. Sullivan, *The Prison Reform Movement*, Boston: Twayne Publishing, 1990, p. 92.

29 Quoted in Lawrence M. Friedman, *Crime and Punishment in American History*, New York: Basic Books, 1993, p. 313.

30 Thomas G. Blomberg and Karol Lucken, *American Penology: A History of Control*, New York: Aldine de Gruyter, Lucken, 2000, p. 195.

31 Quoted in Christian Parenti, *Lockdown America: Police and Prisons in the Age of Crisis*, London: Verso, 2001, p. 195.

32 Eric Cummins, *The Rise and Fall of California's Radical Prison Movement*, Stanford: Stanford University Press, 1994.

33 Scott Christianson, *With Liberty for Some*, Boston: Northeastern University Press, 1998, p. 280.

34 McKelvey, 1977, p. 380.

35 Christianson, 1998, p. 268.

36 Heather Ann Thompson, *Blood in the Water: The Attica Prison Uprising in 1971 and Its Legacy*, New York: Pantheon Books, 2016.

37 Ibid.
38 New York State Special Commission on Attica, *Attica*, New York: Praeger, 1972, p. xi.
39 Thompson, 2016.
40 Ibid., p. 563.
41 Ibid., p. 561.
42 Christianson, 1998, p. 276.
43 William J. Bowers, *Executions in America*, Lexington, MA: D.C. Heath and Co, 1974, p. 12.
44 United States Code, 2012 Edition, Vol. 12, Title 18, p. 452, Washington DC: Government Printing Office, 2013.
45 *National Prisoner Statistics*, Number 46, Capital Punishment, 1930–1971, U.S. Bureau of Prisons, August 1971. https://babel.hathitrust.org/cgi/pt?id=ucl.31210014397960;view=1up;seq=1, table 3.
46 Martin Clancy and Tim O'Brien, *Murder at the Supreme Court: Lethal Crimes and Landmark Cases*, New York: Prometheus Books, 2013, p. 42.
47 Ibid.
48 Gerald Horne, *The Fire This Time: The Watts Uprising and the 1960s*, Charlottesville: University of Virginia Press, 1995.
49 B.J. Widick, *Detroit: City of Race and Class Violence*, Detroit: Wayne State University Press, 1989, p. 166
50 Ben W. Gilbert, *Ten Blocks from the White House: Anatomy of the Washington Riots of 1968*, New York: Praeger, 1968, p. 1.
51 Ibid., pp. 1–12.
52 Anthony M. Platt, ed., *The Politics of Riot Commissions, 1917–1970*, New York: Palgrave and Macmillan, 1971, p. 341.
53 James F. Richardson, *Urban Police in the United States*, Port Washington, NY: Kennikat Press, 1974, pp. 190–191.
54 Kerner Commission, *Report of the National Advisory Commission on Civil Disorders*, New York: Bantam Books, 1968, p. 485.
55 Ibid., pp. 484–493.
56 Tom Schachtman, *Decade of Shocks: Dallas to Watergate, 1963–1974*, New York: Poseidon Press, 1983, p. 79.
57 Ibid., p. 267.
58 Daniel Walker, *Rights in Conflict: The Walker Report*, New York: Bantam Books, 1968, 1968, pp. 255–265.
59 In Melvin G. Holli, *The American Mayor: The Best and Worst Big-City Leaders*, University Park, Pennsylvania State University Press, 1999, Daley is ranked as one of the best mayors in American history between 1820 and 1993.
60 Peter B. Levy, *The Great Uprising: Race Riots in Urban America During the 1960s*, Cambridge: Cambridge University Press, 2018, p. 200.
61 Tim Spofford, *Lynch Street: The May 1970 Slayings at Jackson State College*, Kent, OH: Kent State University, 1988.
62 Bryan Burrough, *Days of Rage*, New York: Penguin Books, 2015, p. 4.
63 Ibid.
64 Quoted in Mark S. Hamm and Cecile Van de Voorde, "Crimes Committed by Terrorist Groups: Theory, Research, and Prevention," in *Trends in Organized Crime*, Winter 2005, pp. 18–51.
65 Kevin Flynn and Gary Gerhardt, *The Silent Brotherhood: The Chilling Inside Story of America's Violent, Anti-Government Militia Movement*, New York: Signet Books, 1995; Hamm and de Voorde, 2005.
66 Philip Jenkins, *Using Murder: The Social Construction of Serial Homicide*, New York: Aldine de Gruyter, 1994, p. 41.
67 Under the 1942 Supreme Court decision *Betts v. Brady*, only defendants facing capital charges were entitled to a court-appointed attorney at the state level.
68 Anthony Lewis, *Gideon's Trumpet*, New York: Vintage Books, 1989, p. 101.

69 Saul K. Padover, *The Living U.S. Constitution: Including the Complete Text of the Constitution and 35 Historical Supreme Court Decisions*, New York: World Publishing, 1969, p. 345.
70 Fox Butterfield, "Historical Study of Homicide and Cities Surprise the Experts," *New York Times*, October 23, 1994. https://www.nytimes.com/1994/10/23/us/historical-study-of-homicide-and-cities-surprises-the-experts.html
71 Michael Hindelang, et al., eds., *Sourcebook of Criminal Justice Statistics, 1980*, Washington, DC: Government Printing Office, 1981, pp. 196–197.
72 Ibid., pp. 200–201.
73 Paul A. Gilje, *Rioting in America*, Bloomington, IN: Indiana University Press, 1996, p. 158.
74 John Conley, ed., *The 1967 President's Crime Commission Report: Its Impact 25 Years Later*, Cincinnati: Anderson Publishing, 1994, p. ix.
75 Originally published in 2 volumes, I used Report of the President's Commission on Crime in the District of Columbia on Metropolitan Police Department, Washington, DC: Government Printing Office, 1966.
76 President's Commission on Law Enforcement and Administration of Justice, 1967, p. xxx.
77 Kerner Commission, , 1968, p. 1.
78 Sullivan, 1990, p. 114.
79 Bert Useem and Peter Kimball, *States of Siege: U.S. Prison Riots, 1971–1986*, New York: Oxford University Press, 1989, p. 11.

Sources

Bell, Daniel. 1960. *The End of Ideology*. New York: Free Press.
Blomberg, Thomas G. and Karol Lucken. 2000. *American Penology: A History of Control*. New York: Aldine de Gruyter.
Bodenhamer, David J. 1992. *Fair Trial: Rights of the Accused in American History*. New York: Oxford University Press.
Brauer, Carl M. 1977. *John F. Kennedy and the Second Reconstruction*. New York: Columbia University Press.
Burrough, Bryan. 2015. *Days of Rage: America's Radical Underground, the FBI, and the Forgotten Age of Revolutionary Violence*. New York: Penguin Books.
Clancy, Martin and Tim O'Brien. 2013. *Murder at the Supreme Court: Lethal Crimes and Landmark Cases*. New York: Prometheus Books.
Cohen, Jerry and William S. Murphy. 1966. *Burn, Baby, Burn!: The Los Angeles Race Riot, 1965*. New York: E. P. Dutton.
Congressional Record. 1970. 116th Congress. https://www.gpo.gov/fdsys/granule/GPO-CRECB-1970-pt34/GPO-CRECB-1970-pt34-2
Conley, John, ed. 1994. *The 1967 President's Crime Commission Report: Its Impact 25 Years Later*. Cincinnati: Anderson Publishing.
Cummins, Eric. 1994. *The Rise and Fall of California's Radical Prison Movement*. Stanford, CA: Stanford University Press.
Fagone, Jason. 2015. "Swatted." *New York Times Magazine*, November 29.
Friedman, Lawrence M. 1993. *Crime and Punishment in American History*. New York: Basic Books.
Garrow, David J. 1983. *The FBI and Martin Luther King, Jr.* New York: Penguin Books.
Gilbert, Ben W. 1968. *Ten Blocks from the White House: Anatomy of the Washington Riots of 1968*. New York: Praeger.
Gilje, Paul A. 1996. *Rioting in America*. Bloomington, IN: Indiana University Press.
Hindelang, Michael J., Michael R. Gottfredson, and Timothy J. Flanagan, eds. 1981. *Sourcebook of Criminal Justice Statistics-1980*. Washington, DC: U.S. Government Printing Office.

Holli, Melvin G. 1999. *The American Mayor: The Best and the Worst Big-City Leaders*. University Park: Pennsylvania State University Press.

Horne, Gerald. 1995. *Fire This Time: The Watts Uprising and the 1960s*. Charlottesville: University of Virginia Press.

Jenkins, Philip. 1994. *Using Murder: The Social Construction of Serial Homicide*. New York: Aldine de Gruyter.

Jonnes, Jill. 1996. *Hep-Cats, Narcs, and Pipe Dreams: A History of America's Romance with Illegal Drugs*. New York: Scribner.

Kerner Commission. 1968. *Report of the National Advisory Commission on Civil Disorders*. New York: Bantam Books.

Levin, Jack and James Alan Fox. 1985. *Mass Murder: America's Growing Menace*. New York: Plenum Press.

Lewis, Anthony. 1964. *Gideon's Trumpet*. New York: Random House.

Lord, Leslie Kay. 1995. "Policewomen." In *The Encyclopedia of Police Science*, ed. William G. Bailey, pp. 627–636. New York: Garland.

McKelvey, Blake. 1977. *American Prison: A History of Good Intentions*. Montclair, NJ: Patterson Smith.

Meltsner, Michael. 1974. *Cruel and Unusual: The Supreme Court and Capital Punishment*. New York: William Morrow.

Milton, Catherine. 1972. *Women in Policing*. Washington, DC: Police Foundation.

New York State Special Commission on Attica. 1972. *Attica*. New York: Praeger.

Padover, Saul K. 1969. *The Living U.S. Constitution: Including the Complete Text of the Constitution and 35 Historical Supreme Court Decisions*. New York: World Publishing.

Parenti, Christian. 2001. *Lockdown America: Police and Prisons in the Age of Crisis*. London: Verso.

Platt, Anthony M., ed. 1971. *The Politics of Riot Commissions, 1917–1970*. New York: Palgrave and Macmillan.

Powers, Richard Gid. 1987. *Secrecy and Power: The Life of J. Edgar Hoover*. New York: Free Press.

President's Commission on Law Enforcement and Administration of Justice. 1967. *The Challenge of Crime in a Free Society*. Washington, DC: U.S. Government Printing Office.

Reid, Sue Titus. 1987. *Criminal Justice Procedures and Issues*. New York: West Publishing Company.

Reinert, Patty. 2001. "Court to Revisit Execution of Retarded." *Houston Chronicle*, March 27, pp. 1A, 6A.

Schulz, Dorothy Moses. 1995. *From Social Worker to Crimefighter: Women in United States Municipal Policing*. Westport, CT: Praeger.

Shachtman, Tom. 1983. *Decade of Shocks: Dallas to Watergate, 1963–1974*. New York: Poseidon Press.

Smith, Alexander B. and Harriet Pollack. 1980. *Criminal Justice: An Overview*. New York: Holt, Rinehart and Winston.

Spofford, Tim. 1988. *Lynch Street: The May 1970 Slayings at Jackson State College*. Kent, OH: Kent State University Press.

Stolberg, Mary M. 1998. *Bridging the River of Hatred: The Pioneering Efforts of Detroit Police Commissioner George Edwards*. Detroit: Wayne State University Press.

Sullivan, Larry E. 1990. *The Prison Reform Movement*. Boston: Twayne Publishing.

Thompson, Heather Ann. 2016. *Blood in the Water: The Attica Prison Uprising in 1971 and Its Legacy*. New York: Pantheon Books.

Useem, Bert and Peter Kimball. 1989. *States of Siege: U.S. Prison Riots, 1971–1986*. New York: Oxford University Press.

Wilson, James Q. 1983. *Thinking about Crime*. New York: Basic Books.

Wright, Kevin N. 1985. *The Great American Crime Myth*. Westport, CT: Greenwood Press.

TIMELINE	1980	1981	1982	1982	1982
	New Mexico State Prison riot	Sandra Day O'Connor becomes first woman Supreme Court justice	Lethal injection used for first time	Publication of Kelling and Wilson article "Broken-Windows"	*Eddings v. Oklahoma* rules that courts must take into account youthfulness of juvenile offenders during capital sentencing

CHAPTER THIRTEEN

Crime and criminal justice at the end of the twentieth century (1980 – 1999)

Learning objectives

After reading this chapter students should understand and be able to discuss:

- How the "get-tough" sentencing policies and the "crack cocaine epidemic" of the 1980s impacted the criminal justice system
- How the death of college basketball star Len Bias in 1986 influenced America's war on drugs
- The evolution of mandatory-minimum sentencing, three strikes legislation, and truth-in-sentencing and its impact on the criminal justice system
- The debate over gun control after the assassination attempt on President Reagan and the passage of the Brady Bill
- The myths surrounding the "Twinkie defense"
- The debate over the "broken-windows thesis"
- The introduction of community-based policing and other new crime fighting philosophies
- Why most forms of violent crime decreased in the 1990s
- The debate over the federal abuse of power after several prominent standoffs were mishandled by the FBI in the 1990s
- America's love affair with incarceration
- The influence of faith-based initiatives and restorative justice strategies on the criminal justice process
- Public opinion concerning the death penalty when life without parole is an alternative
- What the Rodney King case and the trial of O. J. Simpson say about racism and the criminal justice system
- Why rampage killings became more common in the 1990s

DOI: 10.4324/9781315148342-13

TIMELINE

1982	1983	1984	1984	1986	1986
LEAA abolished	President Reagan survives assassination attempt	Comprehensive Crime Control Act	Washington State first state to adopt truth-in-sentencing statutes	Number 2 pick of 1986 basketball draft Boston Celtic Len Bias dies from cocaine-induced cardiac arrhythmia	Anti-Drug Abuse Act becomes country's first mandatory-minimum sentence for drug offenders

By the time the federal Law Enforcement Assistance Administration was abolished in 1982 (it became the National Institute of Justice, which still sponsors criminal research projects), hundreds of millions of dollars had been directed at improving the criminal justice system. So much focus on crime and criminal justice (and so much federal money available) led many colleges and universities to establish criminal justice programs. Additional funding for more police officers, prosecutors, courts, and prisons led to more reported crimes and arrests and convictions, leading to more prisoners for an overcrowded prison system. Not surprisingly, between 1970 and 1983, the number of criminal justice employees rose from 701,767 to 1,270,342.[1] But despite better trained and better equipped law enforcement personnel, crime rates and prison populations continued to escalate.

The ascendance of Ronald Reagan to the presidency in 1980 signaled a new era in criminal justice policy. With the support of the New Right, fundamentalist Christians, and a loose coalition of conservative idealists, the 1980s would witness the reversal of many liberal social, political, and economic forces, as a conservative backlash targeted the increasing availability of abortion, the spread of pornography, and illegal drug use.

The economy was deep in recession in the late 1970s and early 1980s. Since the 1960s, wages had been consistently on the rise, and union wages remained high. But beginning in 1980, union workers faced pay freezes and cuts for the first time in the modern era, and unemployment reached 10 percent. "**Reaganomics**" was blamed by many critics for exacerbating class and race tensions, the deterioration of the inner cities, declining public education, and increased homelessness. By 1987, several million desperate and poor Americans were homeless.

The Reagan and Bush administrations of the 1980s and early 1990s responded to the drug crisis by boosting spending for law enforcement. Preparing for a new blitzkrieg in the so-called drug war, the Reagan administration doubled the FBI's funding, and the U.S. Bureau of Prisons was the benefactor of a 30 percent increase in spending. Legal restraints were loosened on police investigators as well, with federal wiretaps increasing by more than 20 percent between 1981 and 1982.

The get-tough policies of the 1980s led to the hiring of more than 1,000 new DEA agents; 200 more district attorneys; and an unprecedented reallocation of funds from drug treatment, research, and prevention to law enforcement. By the late 1980s, the Reagan administration had announced a **"zero tolerance" policy**, leading to a record number of drug seizures, indictments, arrests, convictions, and asset forfeitures.

Spurred on by fears of a **crack cocaine** epidemic in the 1980s, the criminal justice system became increasingly more punitive. During the late 1990s, construction of a new jail or prison was completed almost every week. Crack cocaine poisoned many communities as dealers waged war against each other over markets, leading to an upsurge in homicides. However, by the end of the 1980s, the worst fears of urban America had failed to materialize as the crack trade began to diminish. But the so-called "crack wars" made a lasting imprint

1987	1987	1988	1988	1990	1991
McCleskey v. Kemp	DNA first used in a criminal case	Omnibus Drug Law	*Thompson v. Oklahoma*	Congress passes Omnibus Crime Control Act	Beating of black motorist Rodney King by LAPD officers captured on videotape

on American criminal justice, prompting the country to rewrite its drug laws, shift money from schools to prisons, and lock up a record number of people. Yet the new harsh laws did not reduce overall drug use in America.

According to a National Household Survey on Drug Abuse conducted by the Department of Health and Human Services, despite the limited appeal of crack cocaine, a high percentage of prisoners serving time for drug offenses were incarcerated for crack cocaine. Yet it is estimated that in 1997, 11 million Americans smoked marijuana, 1.5 million used powder cocaine, and 0.6 million used crack. However, incarceration rates tell another story. More than 40 percent of drug offenders were in state prisons for crack cocaine (26.6 in federal prisons), 33.4 for powder cocaine (42.1 in federal prisons), and 12.9 for marijuana violations (18.9 in federal prisons).[2]

The rising crime concerns of the 1980s led to a change in sentencing laws throughout the country. In 1984, Congress passed the **Comprehensive Crime Control Act**, which created the United States Sentencing Commission. Two years later, the commission announced that "the rehabilitation of a criminal was of secondary importance to protecting the public and that sentences should reflect the seriousness of the crime committed."[3] This reflected a major transition from a rehabilitative model to a punitive one, where there was little to confuse the purpose of prison: punishment not rehabilitation.

Public concern over crime and criminal justice issues continues to dominate the national agendas of politicians and pundits. Some observers suggest that "media coverage of crime stories explains much of the public's interest in criminal justice, as well as the limited extent of their knowledge of the criminal justice system."[4] For most Americans, the perception of crime often conflicts with the reality of crime statistics.

During the past thirty years, crime has surfaced as a concern of the public, but not until the mid-1990s did it register as the major concern of the public. With the concomitant merging of news and entertainment in the 1990s, an excellent opportunity was created to manipulate and sensationalize crime concerns as witnessed by a number of sensational trials of the rich and famous.

The lawgivers

During the 1980s, President Reagan took advantage of his opportunity as chief executive to appoint conservative-minded justices to the Supreme Court. While the new court leadership did not abandon the advances of the due process revolution, the Court became "more tolerant of police behavior and less receptive to further expansion of rights for criminal defendants."[5] Compared to the 1960s, subsequent rulings would lean toward the prosecution.

TIMELINE

1991	1991	1991	1992	1992
Christopher Commission recommends that LAPD abandon professional model of policing in favor of community policing approach	George Hennard murders twenty-three in Killeen, Texas, coffee shop	Arrest of serial killer Jeffrey Dahmer in Milwaukee	Riots break out in Los Angeles after officers cleared in Rodney King beating	Ruby Ridge–FBI confrontation

Crime control measures had entered the political debate in presidential elections during the 1960s when Republican presidential candidate Barry Goldwater ran on a platform that claimed that rising crime rates were the product of misguided Democratic policies and that, by electing Republican candidates, voters could reduce the rising tide of violence and lawlessness. Republican candidates for president continued to exploit the crime problem through the candidacies of Richard Nixon, Ronald Reagan, George H. W. Bush, and George W. Bush. During George H. W. Bush's successful run for president in 1988, many observers credited this campaign issue with helping then-Vice President Bush defeat Massachusetts Governor Michael Dukakis after convicted felon Willie Horton, out on a weekend furlough from a Massachusetts prison, raped a woman and stabbed her fiancé.

In 1983, the Supreme Court ruled in *Gates v. Illinois* that police could obtain a search warrant on the basis of an anonymous tip rather than going through an extensive investigation to corroborate by independent sources the reliability of the tip (as in *Aguilar v. Texas*, 1964). Another important decision reflecting the new conservative bias of the Court was *United States v. Leon*, which held that the exclusionary rule did not apply to evidence obtained by law enforcement who seized the evidence using a warrant that was unsupported by probable cause. In effect, this allowed the police to use warrants that contained factual errors and inadequate probable cause. According to one critic, this decision "gave police a 'good faith' exception to the 'exclusionary rule' which requires that courts suppress or disregard illegally obtained evidence."[6]

Sandra Day O'Connor: first woman Supreme Court justice

In 1981, Sandra Day O'Connor became the first woman to be appointed to the Supreme Court. Born in El Paso, Texas, in 1930, Sandra Day graduated from the Stanford University Law School in 1950 (along with William H. Rehnquist). Rebuffed in her attempts to join major law firms in San Francisco, Day married and raised three sons before opening her own law office in Arizona. She would serve in the Arizona state senate between 1969 and 1974, when she was elected Superior Court judge. Appointed by President Ronald Reagan to the Supreme Court in 1981, during the 1980s and 1990s, O'Connor is credited with writing some of the most significant decisions in the area of constitutional law. Among her most important decisions was the case of *Planned Parenthood v. Casey*, in which she upheld *Roe v. Wade*, which made a woman's right to have an abortion a constitutionally protected right in 1973. Resisting pressure from her more conservative colleagues, she convinced two of her more moderate colleagues to join her in upholding the right to choose abortion. In

1993	1993	1993	1993	1993	1994
Four federal agents killed at Koresh compound in Waco, Texas	Bombing of World Trade Center in Manhattan	Washington State hangs child killer Westley Allan Dodd, the first hanging since the 1960s	Passage of Brady Handgun Violence Prevention Act	*Daubert v. Merrell Dow*	New Jersey passes "Megan's Law"

July 2005, she announced she would retire as soon as her replacement could be confirmed. O'Connor stepped down effective January 31, 2006, giving way to incoming justice Samuel Alito. On August 12, 2009, she was awarded the Presidential Medal of Freedom, the highest civilian honor of the United States, by President Barack Obama.

The death of Len Bias and the Anti-Drug Abuse Act of 1986

What often gets overlooked in the war on drugs of the 1980s was the impact of the death of star University of Maryland basketball player Len Bias in 1986. Chosen as the number two NBA draft pick that season by the Boston Celtics on June 17, two days later, he was dead. The subsequent autopsy revealed he had cocaine in his system and that it triggered fatal cardiac arrhythmia. His death launched a nationwide debate as to whether top college athletes were coddled with special treatment. It also brought the discussion of drug abuse once more to the top of the agenda for lawmakers. Speaker of the House Tip O'Neill seized the incident to successfully lobby for and win backing for the country's first mandatory-minimum sentence for drug offenders, the Anti-Drug Abuse Act of 1986. The law mandated 5 years in prison with no parole for the sale of 100 grams of heroin, 100 kilos of pot, or 10 grams of methamphetamine. Its most controversial clause was the 5-year minimum for selling 5 grams of crack cocaine or 500 grams of powder cocaine. Two years later, Congress designated crack cocaine as the only drug requiring a mandatory-minimum sentence on the first offense.[7] It would take almost thirty years for the cocaine sentencing disparity to be addressed.

The get-tough sentencing of the 1980s and the criminal justice system's special treatment of crack cocaine dramatically altered the balance in the prison population. America, unlike any other country at the time, made no distinction between the properties of crack and powder cocaine. Under federal law, 5 grams of crack (which is cocaine processed to be smoked) was recognized as the equal to 500 grams of cocaine, a 1-to-100 ratio. The possession of five grams of crack by statute was a felony, while five grams of the drug in powder form was a misdemeanor, with rarely any jail time required. The disparity was glaring as the century ended.

Mandatory sentencing

Congress implemented more than twenty new mandatory sentencing laws between 1985 and 1991. By 1994, virtually every state had adopted at least some form of mandatory

1994	1995	1995	1995	1996
1994 Crime Bill (Violent Crime Control and Law Enforcement Act)	O. J. Simpson murder trial ends in acquittal	Bombing of Alfred P. Murrah Federal Building in Oklahoma City	Alabama reintroduces the chain gang	Terrorist attack at Centennial Park during Atlanta Olympics

TIMELINE

sentencing legislation. These laws typically applied to serious offenses, such as murder, rape, and handgun crimes, but also applied to drunk driving and drug offenses.[8] Mandatory-minimum drug sentences came under increasing scrutiny by critics because they take sentencing discretion away from the hands of the judges who in times past could consider an offender's life history, potential for rehabilitation, job status, and family responsibilities before delivering sentence. As a result of this facet of the war on drugs, the proportion of incarcerated drug offenders increased, while that of violent offenders decreased. Most alarming was the overrepresentation of minorities due to disparities in drug sentencing.

Three strikes laws

In 1993, the refrain "**Three strikes and you're out**" became the rallying cry for get-tough politicians. This phrase was coined in Washington State after voters approved a ballot measure requiring life sentences without the possibility of parole for third time serious felony offenders. Over the next few years, more than a dozen states introduced similar provisions. California introduced three strikes legislation that sentenced any adult convicted of a third serious felony to prison from twenty-five years to life. Although the intent of this legislation was to remove vicious predators from the streets, these laws proved somewhat misleading to a public enamored by get-tough legislation. Initially the federal three strikes law did not even distinguish between violent and nonviolent felons.

The three strikes sentencing policy originated in California after the abduction and murder of **Polly Klaas** in the early 1980s by a career criminal who had been in and out of prison for most of his life. This high profile case led to harsher sentences for violent offenders for their second offense and life without parole for their third offense. The murder of Polly Klaas resonated throughout the country. A young girl was snatched from her own bedroom and brutally killed. This crime, according to legal historian Lawrence M. Friedman, "was a powerful stimulus to some draconian pieces of legislation."[9] Unfortunately, as Friedman and others have noted, never have television and the news media influenced criminal justice policy as they do today.

Although California's statute remained the most austere, other states followed its example in subsequent years. In 1994, New Jersey passed "**Megan's Law**" after young Megan Kanka was raped and murdered by a neighbor. Area residents had no idea that the perpetrator who lived among them had two prior convictions for sex offenses. Under the new law, on release from prison, sex offenders were required to register with the police. By 2000, twenty-two states even listed sex offender registries on the Internet.

1996	1999	1999	1999	2000	2000
U.S. passes its first comprehensive counterterrorism legislation, the Anti-Terrorism and Effective Death Penalty Act	New York City police shoot an unarmed Amadou Diallo	First challenges to Daubert guidelines for fingerprinting	Columbine school-yard shootings	Supreme Court reviews electrocution for the first time since its inception in 1999	Illinois announces moratorium on death penalty

Despite the good intentions of three strikes legislation, defendants were less likely to plea bargain (plead guilty) if they already had two felonies. One of the unforeseen results has been an increase in the amount of defendants going to trial. As a result, an already overburdened criminal justice system is faced with a growing number of nonviolent criminals facing their third strike in court. In previous years, close to 90 percent of similar cases were handled with plea bargains, saving the expense and time of a trial. Unwilling to plead guilty, these defendants wait in jail pending trials, further contributing to overcrowded correctional facilities.

The Brady Handgun Bill and guns in America

As America approached the twenty-first century, it continued to exhibit certain tendencies that distinguished it from other industrialized nations, such as Germany, Japan, France, and the United Kingdom. None was more glaring than the numbers of firearms in America. Despite a decline in murder over the past decade, America continued to lead the industrialized world in this category. An examination of American violence suggests that national violence patterns are rooted in the past. Nowhere is this truer than in America's love affair with guns. In the 1980s and 1990s, more than half the country's murders were committed with handguns.

The reported decline of the American handgun industry in the 1990s offered perhaps a glimmer of hope to gun control advocates for the reduction of future handgun violence. The decline followed a thirty-year period of growth fueled in part by the threat of crime, civil unrest, and the violence associated with the various dimensions of the illegal drug trade, particularly crack cocaine epidemic of the 1980s. In 1998, handgun production plummeted to its lowest level in more than three decades. According to a 2001 report (that would probe illusory), "The American handgun market has dropped off so steeply that some industry experts worry it may never recover."[10] Among the reasons cited for the decline were tougher rules for purchasing them, an already saturated market, and a backlash from recent highly publicized school-yard and workplace murders.

Gun control was a hot topic between 1987 and 1993, as gun control advocates campaigned for an enactment of a waiting period for handgun purchases and the passage of what would become the Brady Bill. The bill was named after James Brady, Reagan's former press secretary, who was seriously injured in the assassination attempt on the president in 1981. The bill was first introduced in Congress in 1987 but was quickly challenged by the National Rifle Association (NRA), which argued that any handgun legislation would lead only to stricter gun control. NRA spokespersons claimed that the proposed law would not prevent criminals from getting guns but merely inconvenience legitimate purchasers. After several unsuccessful attempts, the Brady Bill, imposing a seven-day waiting period, was finally approved by Congress in 1991. Although then President George H. W. Bush opposed the bill, he agreed to sign the measure if it included a five-business-day waiting period in 1993. The Brady Handgun Violence Prevention Act of 1993 emerged after a lengthy debate in Congress.

The notion of having a waiting period for gun buyers can be traced back to at least the 1930s, when the District of Columbia enacted a forty-eight-hour waiting period for gun buyers. Gun control proponents argued that a waiting period for gun purchases was necessary to provide authorities time to conduct a background check on the purchaser and to void gun purchases by felons and the mentally incompetent. Although the idea of a waiting period seems moderate, it touched off a rancorous debate between supporters and opponents.

According to the Brady Bill, handgun purchases were to be rejected if the applicant had been convicted of a felony that carried a sentence of at least one year. Others prohibited included anyone with a violence-based restraining order pending, persons convicted of domestic abuse, those arrested for using or selling drugs, fugitives from justice, anyone certified as mentally unstable, and illegal aliens. In 1998, the five-day waiting period was replaced by instant background checks conducted by the FBI's National Instant Criminal Background Check System (NICS). While it is difficult to measure whether the bill had had much impact on gun crime, between 1994 and 2008, almost 1.8 million handgun sales were blocked by Brady background checks by the FBI. In 2008 alone, felons accounted for 56 percent of denied applications and fugitives from justice with 13 percent of denials. Some advocates claim the legislation dissuaded some potential gun buyers from purchasing weapons because of its requirement of background checks. Others point out that many people buy guns for security reasons and that, with the recent drop in crime to a thirty-three-year low, they are less inclined to go gun shopping.

Another explanation for the drop in handgun sales is the changing strategy of the gun control lobby. Formerly, advocates of gun control focused on lobbying politicians to pass stricter legislation. A hot potato in any election, most politicians were reluctant to join the fray. Thus, in the late 1990s, champions of gun control set their sights on a new target by suing various gun manufacturers. During one three-year period, more than thirty suits were filed against gun makers and sellers by cities and government committees nationwide. The lawsuits charged gun makers with negligence for producing dangerous weapons that resulted in serious consequences in the hands of children and criminals. As part of their strategy, gun control proponents sought to hit the gun manufacturers where it hurt most, in the pocket, by seeking reimbursement for the high cost of preventing gun violence and the enormous costs of treating gunshot casualties in local trauma wards. While some lawsuits were dismissed, the potential for financial ruin still threatens the future of most manufacturers. Focusing its historic trade on a military and police market, the venerable Colt Manufacturing chose to end its retail handgun sales in 1999, largely because of potential lawsuits. In 2000, Smith & Wesson agreed to include safety locks on all guns and to make significant changes in its marketing campaign.[11] Nonetheless, in April 2009, the FBI announced that it had completed its 100 millionth NICS approval since the advent of the system almost a decade ago (coinciding with a 27.1 increase in firearms sales in the first quarter of 2009 over the previous year).[12]

The insanity defense and the myth of the "Twinkie defense"

The insanity defense was prominent in several high profile murder cases in the late 1970s and early 1980s. None earned more publicity than that of former policeman Dan White's killings of San Francisco Mayor George Moscone and city supervisor and gay rights activist Harvey Milk in 1978. This case became part of popular culture by introducing the so-called "Twinkie defense" to the modern legal lexicon. In this case, it implied that White's mental capacity was diminished by his fondness for "junk food." White's trial attracted wide media attention not only for the novelty of the defense but also for its volatile mix of politics, revenge, and homosexual intolerance. White's insanity defense led to two verdicts of voluntary manslaughter, and after only five years in prison, White was released in 1984. The following year, he committed suicide. For homosexuals, the trial became a battle cry in that it seemed to them that the jury sanctioned gay murder. Most felt that, if White had killed only the mayor, he would still be in jail.

Despite its association with the "Twinkie defense," few people are aware that its centrality to the trial is actually a myth. As journalist Carol Pogash and others have demonstrated, Twinkies were only mentioned in passing during the trial and "Junk food was an insignificant part of the defense."[13] In fact the chief defense attorney for White admitted it was "a throwaway witness . . . with a throwaway line"[14] and the case of the defense at the 1979 trial mainly rested on claims of "diminished capacity" and bouts of "mental illness" in which White's consumption of junk food was a symptom of his depression and not a cause. Most of those familiar with the trial either as observers or participants blamed the news media for inventing the "Twinkie defense." Perhaps UC Berkeley professor of anthropology and folklore Dr. Alan Dundes said it best when he noted that "America loves labels."[15]

In 1982, another celebrated crime once more challenged the foundations of the insanity defense. On March 30, 1981, John Hinckley Jr. fired six shots at President Ronald Reagan and members of his staff as they entered the Washington Hilton Hotel. Several people were hit, including the president, Press Secretary James Brady, a police officer, and a Secret Service agent. Hinckley was quickly arrested and charged with attempted murder.

Testimony during the 1982 trial escalated into a battle between medical opinions. Almost immediately, the defense team entered a plea of not guilty by reason of insanity. What would soon shift the outcome of the trial toward the defendant was the judge's decision to hear the case under federal procedural rules, which meant that the prosecution would bear the burden of proving Hinckley's sanity beyond a reasonable doubt. If the case had been tried under local rule, the defense attorneys would have borne the pressure of having to prove their client insane. In June 1982, after listening to hours of confusing and contradictory testimony, the jurors brought back a verdict of not guilty by reason of insanity. Although Hinckley was committed to a mental institution, the verdict stimulated a vociferous debate over the insanity defense.

Violent Crime Control and Law Enforcement Act of 1994

The $30 billion package that made up the Violent Crime Control and Law Enforcement Act was "the largest crime control bill in U.S. history." Supporters of the bill argued that the bill led to a large decline in violent crime beginning in the mid-1990s, while critics countered that it actually "decimated communities of color and accelerated mass incarceration."[16] Nonetheless, the bill was hailed in some corners as "an unprecedented federal venture into crime fighting."[17]

During his run for president, Clinton promised to add 100,000 more police officers to the nation's police departments. When President Bill Clinton's administration took office in 1993, violent crime had more than tripled over the previous thirty years, leaving police forces and officials grasping for solutions. Almost 11 million Americans had been victimized by violent crime, and another 32 million were victims of thefts and burglaries. Millions of American lived in fear. Clinton worked with Democratic allies to devise a bill that "reduced sentences for federal drug crimes by exempting first time, nonviolent drug offenders from the onerous 'mandatory-minimum' penalties created by previous administrations."[18] It also funded boot camps, drug treatment programs, and other rehabilitation efforts as alternatives to incarceration. The bill also banned semiautomatic weapons and built on the Brady Law background checks passed a year earlier. However, at the same time it left in place many Reagan era sentences and expanded the federal death penalty. One supporter went as far as asserting that "it was indisputably a de-escalation of the so-called war on drugs, a first step toward the more wholesale decriminalization under way"[19] during the last years of the Obama presidency.

The Violent Crime Control and Law Enforcement Act crime bill targeted nonviolent drug offenses with tougher laws.

The strategy of adding 100,000 more police officers to the ranks of urban police forces, was a major component of Clinton's solution to bring down violent crime. The jury is still out as to whether added police reduced the crime rate. According to a review of twenty-seven different case studies focused on the size of police forces, it could not find "consistent evidence that increase in police strength produce decreases in violent crime."[20] What's more, a 2005 report by the Government Accounting Office (GAO) estimated that 88,000 police were added between 1994 and 2001, leading to only a "modest" drop in crime. Before attributing too much of the **crime drop** in the 1990s to the 1994 bill, other factors should be examined, including increased employment, better policing, an aging population, growth in incomes, and other demographics.[21]

While crime had dropped substantially after Clinton left office, crime had fallen to a twenty-five-year low and homicide rates had declined by more than 40 percent, "experts suggest that forces independent of the law were mostly responsible for the crime drop."[22] However, it can also be said that the crime bill also ended up leading to higher incarceration rates and increasing tensions between police officers and black communities.

During the 2016 presidential campaign, former President Clinton came under fire for his 1994 crime bill during his wife Hillary's campaign run. Supporters from the Black Lives Matter campaign targeted the bill as one of the drivers for the mass incarceration of African American men during the years surrounding the crack cocaine hysteria. By most accounts, the 1994 legislation "only intensified the tough on crime climate of the Democratic administration," leading to a massive rise in incarceration.[23] The number of incarcerated Americans increased from 1.3 million at the time President Clinton took office in January 1993 to 1.95 million when he left office in January of 2001. Recent research asserts that the extra 650,000 prisoners during the two terms of the Clinton era "represents an even greater increase in raw numbers than the additional 447,000 people who were incarcerated over the 1980–1988 Reagan years."[24] From an historical perspective, the increasing mass incarceration blamed on the three strikes provision of the crime bill exaggerated the effect of the bill. By most accounts, the trend toward mass incarceration had actually begun in the 1970s and quadrupled over the next forty years. According to a 2014 report by the National Research Council (NRC), the increase was unparalleled and outpaced incarceration rates around the world.[25] It was during the 1970s that a vast rise in arrests and court caseloads was paralleled by increasingly harsher sentences and charging. During the following decade, defendants were much more likely to do prison time than in the past, a trend that continued in the 1990s as the trend in tougher sentencing continued. So, while the 1994 crime bill did impact incarceration rates – the prison population had actually doubled in the previous two decades – the rise in prisoners was more a case of the bill exacerbating a trend that had begun as far back the administrations of Presidents Lyndon B. Johnson and Ronald Reagan. According to a number of scholars, giving so much credit to a single piece of legislation was "a stretch."[26]

The 1994 crime bill has increasingly come under fire in recent years as America continues to lock up more people than any other industrialized country. The narrative surrounding mass incarceration has been shrouded in a number of myths. One of the most widely accepted myths was that most prison inmates are actually non-violent drug offenders who pose little threat to public safety. However, since the 1990s, only an estimated one-fifth of the prisoners fit into this category.[27] In actuality, most prisoners are behind bars for "relatively low-level crimes" of violence and theft. "If prisons in the United States released every drug offender tomorrow, we would still have the highest incarceration rates in the world."[28]

Assault Weapons Ban

Following a number of high profile mass shootings, Congress passed and President Bill Clinton signed the Public safety and Recreational Firearms Use Protection Act of 1994, better known as the Assault Weapons Ban. This law prohibited the manufacture for civilian use of certain semiautomatic firearms that it defined as assault weapons. Likewise, it prohibited large capacity magazines. This bill was not intended to be perpetual and included a sunset provision that allowed the ban to expire ten years later if it was not extended by Congress.

The Anti-Terrorism and Effective Death Penalty Act

In the aftermath of the Centennial Park bombing during the Atlanta Olympics and the suspicious explosion of TWA Flight 800 (which later proved to be an accident) off the coast of Long Island, New York, the U.S. Congress passed the 1996 Anti-Terrorism and Effective Death Penalty Act, which one leading expert noted was the country's "first comprehensive counterterrorism legislation."[29] The goal of the legislation was "to regulate activity that could be used to mount a terrorist attack, provide resources for counterterrorist programs and punish terrorism."[30] Its provisions included a federal death penalty for deaths that resulted from acts of terrorism, added funding for terrorism prevention and counterterrorism, prohibitions against the government or business transactions with terrorist states, as well as granting the secretary of state the power to designate private groups as terrorist organizations, which would forbid them from raising funds in America.

Law enforcement

Women and minorities continued to make inroads on police forces in ever-increasing numbers. By the early 1980s, women would make up more than 5.5 percent of sworn officers nationwide.[31] Over the next decade, the portrait of the typical police officer had changed substantially. Most studies credit "the women's movement and laws barring employment discrimination based on sex" for a quadrupling of the number of female sworn officers between 1972 and 1986.[32] The number of racial minority peace officers increased as well. By the end of the 1980s, major American cities boasted African American police chiefs, including New York City, Atlanta, Chicago, and Houston. During the 1980s, police forces made concerted efforts to improve their tarnished image and relations with the communities they served. Among the public relations strategies toward this end were crime prevention programs that instructed communities on how to protect themselves and initiating identification pro0grams so that residents could mark their possessions for future identification. Many communities also established "neighborhood watch" programs that encouraged citizen cooperation with the police.

Attempts at improving the often rancorous relationships between police departments and the communities they served were widely heralded in the 1980s. Better police–community relations were given a high priority by most departments, particularly after the publication of George Kelling and James Q. Wilson's widely read *Atlantic Monthly* article in 1982, "Broken-Windows: The Police and Neighborhood Safety," in which the authors articulated a vision for improving police relations in the community, using what the two justice policy experts called the "broken-windows model."

According to the broken-windows model of policing, neighborhood disorder creates fear, and neighborhoods give out crime-promoting signals, such as broken windows and deteriorated housing. An increase in the physical deterioration of a neighborhood then leads to increased concern for personal safety among local residents. Offenders often target these neighborhoods because they see certain signs that translate to vulnerability. Police, then, need the cooperation of citizens if they intend to reduce fear and successfully fight crime in these environments.

The endorsement of "broken-windows" by many police administrators represented a major step toward enlisting communities in the war against crime by theoretically reverting back to an earlier historical model of policing. Since the Progressive era, August Vollmer, and the introduction of the police car, proponents of "broken-windows" claim that the patrol officer has been increasingly removed from the mainstream of the community. Rather than encouraging citizen confidence and cooperation, generally the reverse was occurring. While police cars maintained a presence, ensured rapid response to a crime scene, and covered a wider area, they also alienated many community members who might otherwise help the police.

In the 1980s, some urban police departments returned to an earlier style when police walked a beat or foot patrol and maintained intimate contact with the area they served. The implementation of **community policing** took officers out of patrol cars and put them on a walking beat to strengthen ties to the community. Although early studies indicated that foot patrols did not decrease the crime rate, residents who lived in these areas reported they were less afraid of crime and felt safer.

However, some observers believed that community policing was anything but new. Police and criminal justice historian Samuel Walker has suggested that the authors of the "broken-windows" thesis "have misinterpreted police history in several important respects," while former San Jose Police Chief Joseph McNamara added that "the good old days [of policing] weren't all that good."[33] Walker, McNamara, and others argued that, although modern police departments and officials claimed to be returning to an earlier "watchman style of policing," this style was "inefficient and corrupt" and did "not involve any conscious purpose to serve neighborhood needs." According to Walker, "There is no older tradition worthy of restoration."[34] Reaching back in time using a historical analysis, historians such as Walker have been able to demonstrate that "depersonalization" of policing has been "greatly exaggerated." The introduction of the squad car may have isolated police to a certain extent, but other technological advances, such as the telephone, allowed more private contact between residents and police who were called in to mediate personal disputes more than ever.

Flood and frisk

A reflection of the conservative mood of the country, the New York City Police Department, under Mayor Rudolph Giuliani, embarked on a campaign to take illegal handguns off the streets in the mid-1990s. Although civil liberties groups claimed that the police targeted minority group members with "street justice tactics," new police strategies were credited with helping to reduce violent crime in New York City in the 1990s. Targeting certain precincts where gun violence was high, the police department saturated the area with plainclothes officers and detectives using what was referred to as "flood and frisk tactics" and followed by uniformed officers flooded into the anointed "hot zone." Looking for any legal excuse to stop and question suspected drug dealers or suspicious drivers, officers frisked individuals, hoping to find illegal guns or contraband. While only a few guns were taken off the streets, the aggressive police presence convinced many to keep their guns at home and off the streets. Many police departments retooled for the 1990s, including New York City, which added thousands of police officers to the force. At the end of 1996, 37,871 police officers served New York City's 7.3 million residents, a ratio of 1 for every 193 citizens.[35]

Residency requirements

Although there is little evidence that having officers live where they work makes any difference in the quality of policing, in the late 1990s, police residency requirements became an issue. According to figures released in early 1999, only 54 percent of New York City's police force lived in the city (down from 60 percent the previous decade). Following the botched shooting of unarmed West African street vendor named Amadou Diallo, community advocates intensified calls for a residency requirement after it was revealed that two of the four officers did not live in the city. Mr. Diallo was the target of forty-one bullets as he stood in the vestibule of his Bronx apartment. While community leaders and civil libertarians are quick to suggest that residency requirements would familiarize officers with the environment they serve, others argue there is no empirical evidence to back up this contention. Nevertheless, police and city officials quickly embarked on a hiring campaign to lure more New Yorkers to the force in hopes that it would lead to more racial diversity.

Residency requirements for city workers originated in the nineteenth century. According to the Justice Department, close to 25 percent of America's municipal police departments with more than 100 officers require them to live within city limits. Forty percent of departments require officers to live within a certain radius of the city they serve. In New York City, where police are currently exempt from residency restrictions, less than 43 percent of the white officers lived in the city, while more than 70 percent of black, Hispanic, and Asian American officers lived in the city's five boroughs. Compared to New York City, in 1994, more than 80 percent of the Los Angeles Police Department lived outside the city.

Community policing at the end of the twentieth century

By 2001, most major police departments had adopted the "community-based" policing philosophy, demonstrating "a fundamental shift from traditional reactive policing" to a more proactive approach. Between 1997 and 1999, the percentage of police departments using routine foot patrols increased from twenty-eight to thirty-four, according to a 2000 Department of Justice report. In 1999, more than two-thirds of departments across the country had some type of community-based police program compared to just 34 percent in 1997. The number of officers designated as community police climbed from more than 20,000 in 1997 to 113,000 in 1999. This crime fighting philosophy, which came to prominence in the 1980s, typically utilizes foot and bicycle patrols as it attempts to involve local communities in making their neighborhoods more secure.

Except for anecdotal evidence, experts caution that it is difficult to measure how effective **community-based policing** has been. By the beginning of 2001, almost 12,000 law enforcement agencies across the nation had applied for federal grants to implement some form of community-oriented policing.

According to Katherine Beckett and Theodore Sasson, several new developments in policing, including proactive problem-oriented policing and zero tolerance strategies, may "further reduce the potential democratizing impact of community policing."[36] Despite a movement from reactive to proactive policing, there is little evidence that the new policy is responsible for suppressing criminal activity.

Civil libertarians and police critics cite the emergence of paramilitary SWAT teams in police departments across the nation as an alarming departure from the community policing model. Supported by federal grants and asset forfeiture laws, these units were initially aimed at the drug trade.

The NYPD, Bratton, Maple, and Compstat: challenging "broken-windows"

No police strategy was more influential in the 1980s and 1990s than the previously mentioned "broken-windows" thesis espoused by **James Q. Wilson** and **George L. Kelling**. Following a significant drop in serious crimes in many American cities during the 1990s, a number of scholars began to reexamine and challenge the crime reduction phenomenon in cities such as New York as a result of the broken-windows thesis.

New York City has been used as the "poster child" by broken-windows advocates. Few could argue that the crime decline in the city was almost unprecedented over the past twenty years; however, there is little consensus as to why it occurred. Under the leadership of New York City Police Chief **William Bratton**, police activities were directed at "order maintenance," an often aggressive crusade against a legion of minor offenders such as panhandlers, squeegee men, and jaywalkers. But skeptics argue that the crime drop was the result of a more complicated set of circumstances.

In the early 1990s, criminologist George Kelling convinced Bratton to apply the broken-windows concept to New York's massive transit system. Following the high profile murder of a Utah tourist in the New York subway, the Transit Police was given $40 million to improve its performance. In his autobiography, Bratton credited this killing with providing the catalyst for causing a turnaround in the crime rate in New York City. While chief of the transit police, Bratton applied the thesis to fighting crime in the subways. Bratton redesigned transit uniforms, renovated and upgraded the Transit Police Academy, introduced better weapons and communications equipment, and improved morale on the force. After identifying fare evasion as the most widespread problem, Bratton stationed police at strategic points to capture turnstile jumpers. Many of those arrested carried concealed illegal weapons, so in the process of arresting minor offenders, they might have been preventing more serious offenses by confiscating weapons. Many erstwhile criminals probably began leaving their weapons at home. In any case, subway crime plummeted.

Selected as police commissioner in 1993, Bratton took credit for reducing felonies by almost 30 percent by combining the computerized tracking of **crime hot spots** with a "quality-of-life initiative" that targeted disorderly behavior, street prostitution, panhandling, and other unsolicited behaviors. Another crime control initiative involved determining the origin of every gun used in a crime, whereby every handgun suspect was interviewed by a detective. Teaming with his executive assistant, **Jack Maple**, Bratton took the handcuffs off police officers and used civil law and the broken-windows strategy to enforce regulations against harassment, assault, disorderly conduct, and vandalism.

Bratton, Maple, and his dream team created the Compstat system, a combination of computer statistics analysis and an unrelenting demand for accountability. As Bratton's chief strategist, Jack Maple introduced a groundbreaking computerized map system that was given the moniker Compstat, short for "computer statistics." Maple demanded that every precinct map out shootings, gun arrests, and narcotics violations in order to more accurately deploy police officers. As New York City enjoyed its historic crime drop, other large cities adopted Maple's strategies, which hinged on accurate and timely intelligence, rapid deployment, effective tactics, and relentless follow-up and assessment.

As academics reconsider "broken-windows," a growing number of authorities are questioning its most crucial assumptions. One political scientist even argues that the "zero tolerance" panacea in New York City "clogged up municipal courts and sapped judicial resources." Still others would suggest that it is too simple to blame all crime on urban decay when there is "rather a constellation of only loosely connected, somewhat separate problems that may require somewhat unique policy responses."[37]

At the same time that New York was enjoying its success, other cities enjoyed similar crime drops using alternative strategies. According to Eli B. Silverman, in cities such as San Diego, the real turnaround is credited to "more intelligent policing."[38] Although there are still critics of "broken-windows policing," most polls indicate that New Yorkers strongly supported the enforcement of quality-of-life laws. According to a July 2001 poll by the Citizens Crime Commission, a nonprofit research organization, support varied little between African Americans, Hispanics, Asian Americans, and whites.

Federal law enforcement

During the 1980s and 1990s, the FBI turned its focus to a number of new militant anti-government groups. Domestic in origin, **militia groups** popped up throughout America's heartland. It was not until 1985 that the FBI targeted specific groups, when the white supremacist group known as The Order committed a string of violent bank robberies to finance future activities. During the early 1990s, the FBI came under heavy criticism for its mishandling of several high profile standoffs. The following two incidents in particular, "would bedevil the Bureau for years to come."[39]

The confrontation between federal agents and the Randy Weaver family in **Ruby Ridge**, Idaho, in 1992 led to public condemnation and debate over the abuse of federal power. What is lost in much of the controversy was the connection between this incident and the ongoing federal campaign against The Order in its stronghold in the Northwest. Randy Weaver came to the attention of federal agents of the Bureau of Alcohol, Tobacco, and Firearms (ATF) when he sold illegal sawed-off shotguns to an ATF informant. In January 1991, Weaver was arrested on gun charges in Idaho. Posting bond, Weaver retreated to his mountain cabin, where he held out with his wife and three children, ignoring a failure to appear warrant.

Fearing impending arrest and the possibility of losing their home, the Weavers became increasingly militant during the eighteen-month standoff. In August 1992, a U.S. marshal was killed during an exchange of gunfire, signaling an escalation of the tension. The following day, an FBI sniper killed Weaver's wife and wounded a houseguest. Soon after, Randy Weaver was persuaded to surrender. The siege at Ruby Ridge had major ramifications for federal law enforcement fighting domestic terrorism in the twentieth century. According to one writer, "The distinguishable features of the American right were becoming blurred," and "in time it would allow anti-government sentiment to become nationalized, thus gaining a larger and more moderate constituency."[40]

A young cult leader named David Koresh tested federal agents in **Waco**, Texas, the following year. The handling of the initial raid on the Branch Davidian compound by the FBI led once more to questions about the judgment of the FBI. The FBI took over after the efforts by the ATF failed, leading to one of the longest standoffs in law enforcement history. After trying for fifty-one days to convince Branch Davidian members to peacefully withdraw from their sanctuary, the FBI stormed the compound with the aid of tanks and tear gas. The entire facility was almost immediately consumed by fire, leading to the deaths of eighty-five men, women, and children.

Subsequent congressional hearings in 1995 witnessed FBI Director Louis J. Freeh admitting to "serious deficiencies in the FBI's performance during the crisis."[41] Further investigation found the operation to be flawed and a violation of FBI policy and the Constitution. Following this episode, the FBI director promised to revise the agency's deadly force policy and to limit the use of the rules of engagement. With the lessons gleaned from Ruby Ridge and Waco, the FBI peacefully negotiated a lengthy standoff with a "patriot group" called the Freemen in 1996.

Fifty years ago, the FBI introduced its Ten Most Wanted list. Long considered a publicity gimmick rather than a measure of criminal menace, the list does chronicle the changing nature of American crime over the past half century. In the past, bank robbers, serial killers, and campus radicals dominated the list in various time periods. The current list reflects contemporary concerns over the globalization of crime, the drug wars, and domestic terrorism. In 1999, Osama bin Laden, suspected of masterminding two deadly embassy bombings the previous year, was added to the list, where he joined Eric Rudolph, who was and implicated in several bombings that included an Alabama abortion clinic and the 1996 Atlanta Olympics. Of the 458 men and women who have graced the FBI's most wanted lists over the past 50 years, 429 have been apprehended, 134 of them with the help of private citizens. Where formerly the radio and newspapers primed the FBI's publicity machine, citizens can now find twenty-four-hour descriptions of wanted fugitives on the Internet, which sometimes includes home movies of the fugitives showing undisguisable mannerisms, accents, and idiosyncrasies.

The brave new world of forensic science

Forensic science technology became increasingly reliable between the 1980s and the end of the 1990s. While the best-known identification techniques include DNA and fingerprint analysis, new methods were developed that allowed investigators to use retinal scanning, voiceprinting, and chromatography (the analysis of certain chemicals contained an individual's saliva). The use of computers and digital technology greatly enhanced the ability of investigators to sort and process reams of evidence that would be inaccessible without computer databases.

A number of other suggestions for improving criminal identification systems were recommended, including requiring individuals accused of telephonic offenses involving threats, ransom demands, and nuisance calls to have their voiceprints recorded at the same time they are fingerprinted. As part of standard post-trial processing, some states were already requiring criminals to give blood or saliva samples for possible **DNA profiling**. No matter what identification innovations crime investigators introduce to crime fighting, there is a strong public fear that these techniques could threaten civil liberties or implicate innocent individuals because of errors in taking samples or record keeping.

In April 2000, Texas, with perhaps 3,500 unsolved cases of serial murder, began experimenting with new computer software that targeted serial killers. Similar to psychological profiling in which details of crime scenes are used by experts to make predictions about the emotional and intellectual characteristics of offenders, the new geographic profiling used computer software programs to disseminate the particulars of crimes and pinpoint the most likely residence or workplace of perpetrators.[42]

Brain "fingerprinting" was another new tool being tested by law enforcement. One of the latest advances in computer-based technology, it allowed investigators to identify or acquit subjects on the basis of measuring brain-wave responses to crime-related pictures or words presented on a computer screen. Invented by Dr. Larry Farwell, this innovation is grounded in the pretext that the brain permanently records information, including information related to criminal activity. Through accurate training and technology, brain fingerprinting can retrieve memories stored in the brain. Unlike a polygraph, brain fingerprinting does not look for the distinction between truth and lies but only indicates whether an individual has information related to a specific crime. In one of the first tests of this technology, the FBI and then the U.S. Navy found a 100 percent accuracy rate in its employment.[43]

Fingerprinting evidence under fire

In the summer of 2001, more than 400 delegates from twenty-six countries gathered in London to celebrate the centennial of Scotland Yard's fingerprint bureau. Officials claimed that they solved 10,000 cases the previous year using fingerprint evidence. Although Argentina opened the first such branch in 1892, Scotland Yard was more influential in sparking the adoption of fingerprinting in English-speaking countries.

Beginning in 1911, when American courts first allowed fingerprint evidence, for most of the twentieth-century, fingerprinting remained one of the standard methods of criminal identification. At the turn of the century, some authorities were speculating that, in the next few decades, its use will be superseded by DNA identification.

Fingerprint evidence faced a number of court challenges during the 1990s. Beginning with the 1993 Supreme Court decision of *Daubert v. Merrell Dow*, judges were required to take a more active role in determining what scientific evidence is admissible in court. According to the **"Daubert" guidelines**, new questions would be answered before fingerprints could be entered into evidence. By this decision, the Court introduced five criteria that had to be met before evidence could be considered scientific: (1) peer review and sound methodology, (2) a known error rate, (3) testable hypotheses, (4) application outside of legal proceedings, and (5) general acceptance.[44]

As one forensic scientist noted, "Twins have the same DNA, but different fingerprints."[45] But one of the main challenges to fingerprinting lies in the fact that there is a lack of universal standards for comparing prints. This has led to several mismatches of partial fingerprints. Regardless of the continuing controversy, the science of fingerprinting has held up to scrutiny. But as one expert has suggested, "The relevant question isn't whether fingerprints could ever be exactly alike – it's whether they are ever similar enough to fool a fingerprint examiner. And the answer is yes."[46] Naturally, police and prosecutors were concerned that recent challenges to fingerprinting could also undermine ballistics and handwriting tests and other evidence. Law professor Michael Saks of Arizona State University probably summed up the dilemma of forensic scientists best, commenting that "courts are forcing forensic science to become science – to actually test its claims, determine its error rates, and not overstate conclusions."[47]

Corrections

Between 1970 and 1980, the population of America's prisons doubled. By the time they doubled once more between 1981 and 1995, American prisons and jails held 1.75 million inmates. With a rate of imprisonment of 426 per 100,000 in 1991, America had one of the highest rates of incarceration in the world and the highest in its brief history.[48] However, prison overcrowding would only get worse over the following years. Unlike the 1970s, which saw a marked increase in crime rates, the 1980s and 1990s saw only periodic increases in crime (1985–1990), never reaching the heights of the previous decade. But prison populations continued to soar at record levels. Rates of incarceration continued to vary by region, with the South imprisoning more people per capita than any other region.

While blacks made up only 12 percent of the nation's population, they represented more than 44 percent of the total local, state, and federal prison population. According to one authority, America's black incarceration rate was "more than 4.2 [times] higher than South Africa's before the fall of Apartheid."[49] By the middle of 1994, the number of black inmates exceeded whites for the first time, with almost 7 percent of all black men in prison or jail compared to less than 1 percent of the white male population.[50]

When considering the racial disparity of America's prisons, there are other implications to consider. A substantial number of African Americans are disenfranchised since many states prohibit convicted felons from voting. Together with the fact that the imprisoned are universally prevented from voting, this is a large voting bloc that has effectively lost its political voice.

By the 1990s, the federal prison system had kept pace with rising crime rates and the expanding state prison systems. In previous eras, federal criminal law targeted violators of the Mann Act, bootleggers, and the interstate transportation of stolen motor vehicles. In the 1990s, more than 60 percent of federal prisoners were convicted for drug offenses.

Except for the "dot-com" explosion at the end of the twentieth century, no business flourished to the extent of the prison business. In former days, prison construction was a tough sell to communities. With a downward turn in the economy in the 1980s, communities were less reluctant to host such enterprises. By the middle of the 1990s, more than 5,000 correctional facilities dotted the landscape, including more than 3,000 local jails. In rural America, towns even competed for prison construction. There was no greater job security than working for a prison. Unlike General Motors or a military base, there was no threat of closure or moving south of the border.

Since the 1970s, correction officers have followed their police counterparts who in the 1960s formed labor unions. The unionization of corrections coincided with the unprecedented expansion of the prison system. Other segments of the working force benefited from prison expansion, including legions of building contractors, architects, hardware and electronics companies, and security firms.

By the end of the 1990s, California was operating the nation's largest prison system with a budget of almost $4 billion a year. The state added twenty-one prisons between 1984 and 1999. Many politicians feared that this building boom was taking place at the expense of other budget items, such as higher education. While salaries remained stagnant in the state's university system (average pay for a first year professor was $41,000), prison guards were making $51,000 per year.

By the 1980s, it became clear to most correctional authorities that the rehabilitative model of corrections was a failure, citing high rates of recidivism. Thus, a new policy of warehousing serious offenders to protect society gained increasing popularity as deinstitutionalization initiatives soon fell by the wayside. As a consequence of the new "lock-'em-up" strategy, American prisons became seriously overcrowded. Beginning in 1990, a major program of prison expansion was implemented that helped reduce some of the overcrowding by the end of the decade. Among the biggest administrative difficulties caused by warehousing of prisoners were the extreme expense and the unmanageability of prison populations.

At the close of the twentieth century, the number of adults either incarcerated, on parole, or on probation reached a record high of 6.49 million, or one in thirty-two American adults. While this was the bad news, the good news was that the percentage increase from 1999 to 2000 was only half the annual average rate since 1990.

Following on the heels of three decades of prison building and tougher sentencing laws, at the beginning of 2002, a number of states were forced by budget deficits to close some prisons, lay off guards, or even shorten prison sentences. In January alone, the states of Ohio, Michigan, and Illinois closed prisons. Washington was among the states experimenting with shortening sentences for nonviolent crimes in order to relieve the overburdened correctional system.

One of the leaders of the prison building boom was California. However, the state was a victim of its own policies and was forced to shut down five small, privately operated minimum-security prisons and to consider amending the state's three strikes sentencing law in order to relieve congestion.

Close to 2.5 million people were released on probation or parole in 2000. In 1990, half of all parolees successfully completed the terms of their release. Ten years later, only 43 percent completed parole and stayed out through the end of the year. By 2001, Georgia (6.8 percent) and Texas (5 percent) had the largest percentage of their adult population in the corrections system.[51]

Truth-in-sentencing and the prison building boom

The passage of the 1994 Crime Bill was heralded by the Clinton administration for funding 100,000 new police officers. However, in order to get the bill passed, the White House and Congressional Democrats had to accept the Republican proposal for the federal government to provide $10 billion to states for prison construction between 1995 and 2000. The catch was that the funding would only be made available to states that passed "truth-in-sentencing laws that eliminated most 'good time' provisions and required convicted offenders to serve 85% of their prison sentence."[52] According to one criminologist, the effects were felt almost immediately as the number of states with truth-in-sentencing laws increased from 4 in 1992 to 17 in 1995 and 27 in 1998. The crime bill thus increased prison populations, making it cheaper for states to build prisons. Between 1994 and 2005 state prison populations increased by 372,000 (if not for the truth-in-sentencing proviso, it would only have increased by 305,000).[53]

Prison privatization

During the 1980s, in order to reduce some of the costs of warehousing inmates, prisons increasingly turned to the private sector in order to handle the increase in both prison populations and prison labor. Between 1985 and 1995, private prisons increased at a 500 percent clip. By the mid-1990s, at least thirty states were contracting out prison labor to private companies. Returning to developments of a previous century, there was a movement to deregulate prison industry so that prison-made items could be sold on the free market.

With "the growth of privatization and anti-government and anti-union sentiments" in the 1990s, "the appeal of prison as a source of cheap labor"[54] led to a variety of privatization models. In some cases, private companies built and operated prisons and jails on behalf of various branches of the government, while others leased prisons to the government to be run by the department of corrections. Often paid less than the minimum wage, inmates performed a multitude of tasks, including packing golf balls for Spalding, sorting inventory for Toys R Us, and manufacturing uniforms for McDonald's. While unions and civil rights organizations have lobbied against the privatization of prisons, few critics of human rights violations overseas have made the connection with the use of American prison labor at home.[55]

At the conclusion of the 1990s, the debate over prison labor became a topic of conversation once more. Recalling the prison labor movement of the late nineteenth century, when prisoners worked for private employers without pay, prison laborers now worked under better conditions. In 1979, Congress authorized the hiring of prisoners by private employers after years of prohibiting this arrangement.

In sharp contrast with traditional prison labor, such as making license plates and painting school buses, the 1990s saw prisoners working in telemarketing and the computer industry. By the end of the first quarter of 2000, more than 80,000 inmates were employed at traditional jobs, working for companies and government at anywhere from 25 cents to $7 per hour.[56]

While criminal justice officials saw these programs as a path to reform and employers appreciated the cheap labor, others insisted that prison labor was a human rights abuse and a potential economic threat to free world workers. According to one California lawsuit, since prisoners have no bargaining power, they can be easily exploited. By 2000, the verdict was still out on the viability of prison labor programs. Nonetheless, most law enforcement authorities and small businessmen regarded it as a panacea for the current labor shortage and the swelling prison populations, which reached 2 million in 2000.

Supermax prisons

One trend that continued to draw support was the construction of super-maximum security, or "supermax," prisons in the 1990s. Although the federal government opened its first maximum-security prison at Alcatraz in 1934, it was not until 1994 that the Federal Bureau of Prisons opened its first supermax prison at Florence, Colorado. It has housed criminal luminaries ranging from Oklahoma City bomber Timothy McVeigh and "Unabomber" Theodore Kaczynski to World Trade Center bomber Ramzi Yousef (all in the same wing). It is estimated that one-fourth of the 387 inmates in Florence have killed or attempted to kill another prisoner.

Prison rights advocates have criticized these solitary confinement prisons as inhumane, much in the way Charles Dickens attacked Eastern State Penitentiary in the 1840s. At supermax prisons, inmates spend almost twenty-three hours per day confined in seven-by-twelve-foot cells. One critic suggests that there was barely room to hold a sports-utility vehicle in one of these cells. Every cell contained a stool, a writing desk, and a mattress pedestal made of concrete (to prevent weapon making). At least thirty-six states operate such institutions, where prisoners can squint through a four-foot-by-four-inch vertical window at the exercise yard below or at a sky crisscrossed by steel beams and helicopter-resistant wires. Some prisons prohibit cigarettes and television.

The United States is not the only country to use supermax-style prisons in the twenty-first century. Argentina's Ezeiza Penitentiary Complex is protected by underground movement detection cables, remotely controlled doors, and extensive video surveillance. Demonstrating that no prison is 100 percent escape proof, in 2013, thirteen inmates managed to escape by tunneling under the facility. The Al-Ha'ir Prison is Saudi Arabia's version of the high security prison. It mostly houses prisoners charged with terrorist activities. However, it is known for its apparent "high level of comfort." By most accounts, the institutional service offers welfare payments for families and a hotel for extended family visits, all intended to entice dissenters and insurgents to "recommit" to Islamic society. India's Tihar Jail is considered the largest prison complex in Southeast Asia. The complex comprises nine high security facilities and, despite an official capacity of 5,200 inmates, is now home to more than 11,000 inmates. Inmates here are offered rehabilitation programs including art and music therapy, meditation, carpentry workshops, and training in baking and textiles. Long known for its expansive Gulag prison system, Russia is also home to the Petak Island Prison. Russia's version of Alcatraz, the institution offers total isolation on an island in Novozero Lake. Its almost 200 inmates are all doing life. The island is connected to the mainland by two small bridges. Prisoners spend an average of 22.5 hours a day in either a small group or single cell. Another hour and a half is spent in an outdoor cage. China's Qincheng Prison is a maximum-security prison holding mostly political prisoners accused of crimes against the state. They are typically isolated from each other and identified only by numbers.[57]

Juvenile corrections

By the end of the 1990s, the treatment of juvenile offenders by the correctional system signaled a backlash against the century-old notion of viewing children and adolescents as less censurable and more redeemable through rehabilitation than adults. A harsher view of child criminals emerged in which they juveniles were barely distinguishable from their more adult counterparts. During the 1990s, forty-five states passed legislation making it easier to prosecute juveniles as adults. Motivated by high profile crimes committed by juvenile offenders, such as recent school-yard massacres, fifteen states allowed prosecutors to transfer juveniles from the juvenile system into adult courts for certain categories of crime, most often violent offenses. There was still no consensus as to what constituted adulthood at the end of the twentieth century. Children as young as ten were prosecuted as adults in Vermont and Kansas, while most other states set the bar at fourteen and older. Between 1985 and 1997, the number of youths under the age of eighteen in adult prisons more than doubled.

Female juvenile offenders

According to a 2001 American Bar Association (ABA) study, young girls were being arrested and jailed in record numbers, and the current juvenile justice system was unable to handle the special needs of young girls. While juvenile crime had fallen overall, the fastest growing segment of the juvenile justice population was girls under the age of eighteen. Between 1988 and 1997, delinquency cases involving white girls rose 74 percent compared to a 106 percent increase for African American girls. In the wake of its findings, the ABA has recommended that communities develop alternatives to detention and incarceration for minor offenses. The ABA report suggested that girls were detained for less serious offenses than boys and were more likely to be detained for minor offenses, such as public disorder, traffic offenses, and probation violations. Other explanations for this trend target get-tough mandatory sentencing, changes in police practice for domestic violence, and relabeling family conflicts as violent offenses.

Faith-based initiatives

Almost two years before the 2000 presidential election, several prominent conservatives that included "Reagan-era" criminologist James Q. Wilson, former drug czar William Bennett, and future director of faith-based (FB) initiatives John DiIulio (he resigned due to political use of the program and related interference) met privately with the prospective candidate George W. Bush to develop a "faith-based agenda." Several weeks after taking office in January 2001, President Bush led the creation of a special White House Office of Faith-Based and Community Initiatives (OFBCI), directing five Cabinet departments to inaugurate Centers for Faith-Based and Community Initiatives. (President Barack Obama would change the name to the White House Office of Faith-Based and Neighborhood Partnerships in 2009.)

One major stumbling block was the fact that there was no consensus as to what exactly constituted a faith-based program initiative. In fact, the White House was not even able to offer a "precise definition or what criteria must be met to be one."[58] The main claim of its supporters was that poverty and crime were the result of a person's "lack of morality." Therefore, while neighborhood and family cohesion in poor communities could go a long way toward addressing the problem, supporters of faith-based initiatives took an approach focused primarily on religious programming. Initially faith-based legislation augured toward scaling back spending on rehabilitation and treatment with the intention of channeling resources instead to private faith-based groups.

From a criminal justice perspective, the Bush-era initiatives can be viewed as a number of crime prevention efforts linking various religious communities with the goal of preventing and reducing crime, ensuring public safety, and improving education and employment opportunities for ex-prisoners in an attempt to reduce recidivism rates as they reenter society. A number of faith-based programs were located in neighborhoods where a high proportion of the residents were from minority groups. By the end of the 1990s, the jury was still out as to whether these organizations were any more effective than public or nonsectarian organizations.

Faith-based organizations have provided funding and services to individuals and communities in the U.S. for many years. Prominent faith-based charities have included such organizations as the Salvation Army, the Catholic Charities, and the Jewish Federations. But, the concept of "faith-based initiatives" dates back to the prison reform efforts of Pennsylvania Quakers at the end of the eighteenth century, when prisoners were expected to read the Bible in hopes of penitence for past sinful behavior (see Chapter 4). For more than 200 years, these religious programs have been a staple of the American prison system. What distinguished the current crop of programs was their affiliation with federally based legislation. Some critics suggested that faith-based programming was conceived by supporters in an attempt to gain religious service providers access to federal funding previously reserved for mostly non-faith based groups. Nonetheless, faith-based programs have been increasingly promoted as an effective strategy for problems of prisoner-reentry into society.

Embarking on a platform of what Bush called "compassionate conservatism," he went even further to give his evangelical followers "faith-based war, faith-based law enforcement, faith-based education, faith-based-medicine, and faith-based science."[59] In the president's pursuit of "faith-based justice," one of his first hires was the Pentecostal Christian **John Ashcroft** as his new attorney general. Ashcroft staunchly believed that the separation of church and state resulted in a "wall of religious oppression." As if seeking to bolster his bonafides, shortly before his confirmation, Ashcroft promised to put an end to the task force set up by his predecessor Janet Reno to combat violence against abortion clinics. A number of domestic terrorism experts suggested that the 2001 spike in violence against these clinics (from 215 to 795) might have been the result of Ashcroft's announcement and his refusal to send U.S. marshals to stem the violence.

Crime and punishment

The 1980s and early 1990s were characterized by an overwhelming fear of crime. While serial killers, mass murderers, and drug crime continued to dominate the nightly television news blitz, new crime fears beckoned on the horizon featuring school-yard shootings and domestic terrorism. In 1999, the "deadly tower" on Austin's University of Texas campus was reopened. It had been closed following the murderous sniper shootings by Charles Whitman in 1966. Demonstrating the continuing threat of mass murder in American society, Whitman's body count of sixteen dead and thirty-one wounded would be exceeded several times in the 1980s and 1990s, most notably by George Hennard, who killed twenty-three and wounded twenty-three at a Killeen, Texas, restaurant in 1991. In 1984, James O. Huberty murdered twenty-one and wounded nineteen at a California McDonald's restaurant. Two years later, a disgruntled postal worker killed fourteen and wounded six, giving credence to the expression of "going postal."[60]

The increased concerns over crime victimization in the 1980s led many Americans to carry concealed weapons. No case illustrated the potential ramifications of carrying concealed weapons better than the Bernard Goetz trial. In December 1984, a thirty-six-year-old electrical engineer named Bernard Goetz was approached by four black youths while riding a New York City subway. Having been injured in an assault just three years earlier, Goetz took to carrying a concealed handgun whenever he went out. When one of the youths asked him for $5, Goetz went for his revolver and shot at the men. Two were critically wounded, including one that Goetz shot in the spinal cord after he fell down while trying to escape. Goetz turned himself in to the police nine days later and was charged with a number of offenses, including attempted murder and criminal possession of a gun.

During the subsequent trial two years later, Goetz was turned into the victim of the case by his defense team, noting the criminal backgrounds of the actual victims. The trial would challenge the criminal justice system on several fronts, addressing the question of a citizen's right to defend oneself. In June 1987, the jury returned a verdict of not guilty on twelve counts and guilty on one charge of criminal possession of a weapon in the third degree. Three months later, Goetz was sentenced to six months in prison (two years later, on review, his sentence was doubled to one year).

The crime decline of the 1990s

There is no consensus as to why violent crime dropped in the 1990s. Surely, there were many factors at work. In urban America, the decline of the crack market and police efforts to seize handguns from criminals and juveniles get much of the credit.[61] Crime dropped precipitously throughout the country in the 1990s. There was no one explanation for this development at the time that was generalizable to all cities.

Between 1991 and 1998, homicide and robbery rates declined more sharply than any other serious crimes. According to criminologists, these two offenses were most often linked to the crack epidemic and were most associated with handguns. In 1995, the 30 percent drop in murders and shootings in New York City was considered the result of police frisking efforts that drove illegal guns off the street. Gang members and drug dealers reportedly began to leave their guns at home rather than risk losing them to a police search. Despite criticism from civil libertarians, few would argue that police assertiveness in this arena did not at least contribute to the crime decline.[62]

Others suggest that the decline in violent crime was attributable to the aging of the population and the growing number of police officers on the street. Still others pointed to a growing prison population and longer sentences. However, this correlation was brought into question due to the fact that incarceration also increased during the crime rise of the 1980s.[63]

Other explanations focused on the demographics of age. During the late 1980s and early 1990s, the explosion of homicides coincided with the rise in killings perpetrated by persons under twenty-four years of age. The drop in such crimes in the 1990s might have been associated with a downturn in youthful involvement in the crack trade.

Not every region experienced a dramatic decrease in violent crime in the 1990s. There were few places more violent in America than the Indian reservations of the American West. In 1995, New Orleans had one of the highest murder rates in the country, at one per 1,259 residents. The Fort Peck Reservation in sparsely populated Montana had a murder rate of one per 675 residents, twice as high as New Orleans. The results were similar on other Indian reservations. While residents remained frustrated over the ongoing crime wave, it has proven almost impossible to stem the violence because of the lack of police officers and lack of equipment.[64]

Between 1980 and 1997, property crimes in the United States declined by almost 50 percent. The drop in property crimes, such as burglary, larceny, and auto thefts, did not receive the same attention as more dramatic crimes of violence. However, explanations for the decline of both types of crimes received similar explanations. Many law enforcement administrators and criminologists suggested that the drop in property crime was the result of improved police tactics, a decline in the teenage population, and greater community involvement and that longer prison sentences were responsible for the drop in violence in crime. Others explained that the drop in property crime was the result of the enhanced use of alarm systems. However, criminologist Scott Decker dissented, noting that most burglaries take place in poor neighborhoods that lack alarm systems, not the more affluent suburbs. Decker argued that the decline had more to do with crack addicts giving up "burglary because it required too much planning and involved the uncertainty of whether a resident might be home, perhaps with a gun." In need of a quick high, crack addicts made the transition to robbery, which was considered a faster and safer strategy for providing quick cash.[65]

Although the drop in property crime was felt in most major cities, none saw the numbers drop as great as San Diego, California. As of 1997, San Diego witnessed a 68 percent drop in burglary between 1980 and 1996. Police also claimed that larceny crimes, such as petty theft, shoplifting, pickpocketing, and motor vehicle break-ins, declined by 37 percent. In addition, auto thefts plummeted 61 percent.[66] Unlike New York City's former police commissioner William Bratton, who credited his city's crime decline to an increased police presence, San Diego Police Chief Jerry Sanders gave credit to new types of community-oriented policing.

In the late 1990s, San Diego had a 2,036-member police force that was augmented by 8,000 volunteers. Many of these volunteers patrolled their neighborhoods during the weekends or helped fill out excess paperwork at the police stations. With only 1.7 police officers per 1,000 residents (compared to New York's 5.2 and Washington, DC's, 6.84), community-oriented policing proved crucial to San Diego, which had the lowest ratio of officers per capita in the country.[67]

Although American crime rates continued to drop in the early 1990s, homicides by juveniles increased. According to criminologist James Alan Fox, the rate of homicide by juveniles fourteen to seventeen years old rose from 8.5 per 100,000 in 1984 to 30.2 per 100,000 in 1993 before declining to 16.5 per 100,000 in 1997, still almost double that of 1984 levels.[68] Several high profile juvenile slayings led prosecutors and legislators to try more juveniles as adults. Traditionally, eighteen had been the age most commonly used to define adulthood in the United States. However, state, federal, and local laws responded by setting a variety of thresholds for young people's responsibilities. While in times past lawbreakers under eighteen were consigned to the juvenile courts where their names were kept private and sentence structured to maximize the chance for rehabilitation, during the 1990s, more and more juveniles were ending up in adult courts.

In 1998, a series of school shootings in Pennsylvania, Arkansas, and Oregon raised more concerns about juvenile access to firearms. In 1999, the worst of these shootings took place at Columbine High School in Littleton, Colorado, where two teenage students killed thirteen before committing suicide.

Sunset for traditional organized crime?

The 1980s finally saw law enforcement make inroads on organized crime. Mob expert James B. Jacobs credits the Racketeer Influenced and Corrupt Organizations (RICO) statutes and the government's campaign with winning convictions against twenty-three major mob bosses and their associates since 1981. While Jacobs suggests that it was too early to write the obituary for America's mob families, new crime fighting strategies demonstrated the sudden vulnerability of mobsters confronted by effective law enforcement.[69]

Since the 1920s and 1930s, the federal government has attempted a variety of methods to destroy if not cripple America's entrenched Mafia groups. However, until 1970 these groups were virtually immune from prosecution. The FBI was indifferent to organized crime for much of this period, and local policing was often inept or corrupt. The turning point in the war against organized crime was 1970, when Congress passed the Organized Crime Control Act, the first legislation designed specifically to strike at organized crime activity. This act created a witness protection program and established a formal system to encourage informers to testify by giving them new identities and financial aid and relocating them and their families far from the danger of reprisals. The most significant part of the new legislation was the RICO sections, under which mob bosses and their subordinates could be implicated if prosecutors proved they were linked to a criminal group or enterprise. Except for New York and Chicago, the American Mafia's major families have been largely destroyed or diminished in power.

Besides the utilization of RICO, generational changes have also conspired against the Mafia and have undermined mob discipline and weakened the code of silence. By the end of the 1980s, organized crime leaders were agreeing to cooperate with the government in return for leniency and admission into the Witness Security Program. In the 1992 trial of Gambino family crime boss John Gotti, the government used the testimony of his underboss Sammy "the Bull" Gravano (Gotti's second in command) to strengthen its case. It would be unthinkable in years past that someone of Gravano's stature would break the code of silence. But times had changed. Gotti had been acquitted in three previous trials, but this time, he was found guilty on all counts and was sentenced to life in prison without parole.

The changing face of organized crime in America

The changing immigration patterns of the late twentieth century transformed the face of organized crime in the United States. Not since the turn of the century, have so many immigrants flooded into the country. Between 1982 and 1989, some 685,000 legal immigrants settled in New York City alone. While there has been a backlash in some parts of the country, immigration has revitalized many older cities, such as Boston, Chicago, and New York, all of which had been losing residents for years.

The incredible diversity of America has always been reflected in the tapestry of organized crime. Jewish, Irish, and Italian immigrants predominated during the peak years of their respective migrations. However, the diversity and violence of this earlier era pales in comparison to the current-day version. Gangland violence has sporadically marked the assimilation of some Dominicans, Russians, Colombians, Jamaicans, Vietnamese, Laotians, and Chinese immigrants who have been drawn to certain criminal enterprises as they pursue their version of the American dream.

According to journalist William Kleinknecht, "As long as there is an underclass" and "as long as there are American cities," there will be opportunities for organized criminal activities.[70] Whatever the future of organized crime, drugs will surely continue to be a staple commodity as crime groups form stronger international links. International criminal conspiracies, such as the Sicilian and Russian Mafias, Colombian cartels, and Chinese triads, increasingly cooperate in a variety of illegal drug enterprises. In response, international law enforcement agencies have been forced to overcome their traditional reluctance to cooperate and have made strides toward collaborating to fight organized crime on a number of fronts. However, since 9/11, the crusade against organized crime has taken a back seat to the "war on terrorism."

Capital punishment (1976–2001)

In 1999, 3,555 men and women languished on death rows across the nation. Although most Americans continued to support the death penalty, only about 2 percent of death row inmates were actually executed. Never of one mind about the death penalty in America, twelve states and the District of Columbia did not use the death penalty, while several others imposed moratoriums on its use (Illinois and Maryland). Having legally shelved the death penalty in 1972, in 1977, following a nine-year moratorium (there were none between 1968 and 1972), it returned with a vengeance, beginning with the firing squad execution of Gary Gilmore in Utah in 1978.

Between the return of the death penalty in 1976 and May 2001, 705 men and 6 women were executed. An analysis of this group would find that most of them were poor, usually white (56 percent), and typically high school dropouts. Most were from the South, and most had never killed before. Of the 711 executions, 579 were carried out in the South, with Texas leading the way with 246.[71]

Between 1977 and 1989, the number of death row prisoners increased from 423 to 2,250. Death row stays of execution continued to keep pace as well, thanks in part to the frequency of habeas challenges and abolitionist strategies ranging from petitions for grants of clemency and public demonstrations to legislative lobbying. Between 1977 and 1989, average time between sentencing and execution increased from fifty-one months to ninety-five months.[72]

Rising public support for capital punishment in the 1970s and 1980s accompanied America's growing crime rates. A 1985 Gallup Poll study found that seven out of ten Americans favored the death penalty, the highest level of support since the poll began querying support for the death penalty in 1936. Often lost in any discussion of the death penalty was the drop in support for it when the alternative of life without parole was offered as well.

In 1987, the death penalty was once more called into question in the case of **McCleskey v. Kemp**. Charged with armed robbery and the murder of a white police officer during a robbery in Georgia, Warren McCleskey, who was black, was quickly arrested, convicted, and sentenced to death. McCleskey appealed his sentence on the grounds that it had been imposed in a racially discriminatory manner. His attorneys presented evidence from the results of a statistical study profiling 2,000 Georgia murder cases from the 1970s that demonstrated that black defendants were more likely than other defendants to be sentenced to death. Investigators concluded that black defendants who killed white victims were much more likely to receive the death sentence than any other racial combination. Ultimately, the Supreme Court denied McCleskey's appeal on the grounds that the statistical study presented as evidence was insufficient to prove racial discrimination in his case. The Court also held that his treatment did not violate the Eighth Amendment's prohibition of cruel and unusual punishment.

There are a number of observers that like to tout the high crime rates of non-Sharia (Islamic legal tradition) countries compared to the low crime rates that supposedly prevail in regions where Islamic law is prominent. However, this notion is strongly debated since crime data from these countries is rarely shared with the world at large. However, there are countries and regions where anecdotal evidence suggests that sharia law can bring order where there was none. For example, in 1999, Mogadishu, Somalia, was rife with clan warfare, rape, robbery, and what one *New York Times* reporter described as "almost post-apocalyptic" random killings. With few alternatives responses on the horizon, a sharia court was created and tasked with rescuing the Somalian capital from "a state of anarchy into a relatively safe and civilized area."[73] Few witnesses or potential criminals could fail to see the aftermath of brutal punishments, particularly the amputated hands and feet of local thieves left in public places as a warning to future malefactors. During the 1990s and its revival in the 2010s, the Taliban defined itself with its version of sharia law. As it rose to prominence in Afghanistan, it introduced such punishments as stoning, which was not commonly practiced before they took over. Whenever sharia law was used, it was done under strict religious supervision, after a fair trial and with sanctions limited by religious scholars. For example, when stoning was mandated, the stones had to be small and anyone who took part in the community punishment could lift their arms above their heads to throw. Taliban members took the sharia literally. In 1999, for instance, a man was sentenced to death for homosexuality. The court ordered that he be crushed by a fifteen-foot high wall that was supposed to be knocked down on top of him. The sixty-year-old victim somehow survived, albeit with serious head injuries. Under Taliban law, since he survived execution, his sentence was commuted. Happy to be alive, despite the aches and pains, he told a journalist, "I was wrongfully convicted for sodomy. And God proved my innocence."[74]

Executing juveniles

Although most nations in the world that used the death penalty in the last decades of the twentieth century prohibited the execution of juvenile offenders, seventeen of those executed between 1976 and 1999 committed their crimes before they turned eighteen. By 2001, of the thirty-eight states that authorized the death penalty, eighteen had established sixteen as the minimum age at the time of the crime, five had set it at seventeen, and fifteen had set it at eighteen.

In the 1980s, several Supreme Court cases took up the constitutionality of executing juveniles. In *Thompson v. Oklahoma*, the Court overturned the death sentence of Monty Lee Edwards, who was fifteen when he participated in a murder in 1982. The defense argued that the sentencing judge failed to consider the defendant's age and abusive child-hood. In 1988, the Court ruled that executing an individual who committed a crime before the age of sixteen violated the Eighth Amendment's prohibition against cruel and unusual punishment, thereby establishing sixteen as the minimum age for the death penalty at the time of offense (eighteen states had already set this age as minimum for death penalty).

From hangings, firing squads, and electrocutions to lethal injection

In January 1993, Washington State conducted the nation's first hanging in twenty-eight years when Westley Allan Dodd was hanged for raping and murdering several children. Although by law Dodd was allowed to choose between hanging and lethal injection, he selected hanging since, as he explained, that was the method he used to dispatch his young victims.

Since the eighteenth-century Enlightenment, criminal justice reformers have continued to seek more humane methods of execution. For many, 1982 would represent a watershed of sorts when Texas inmate Charles Brooks became the first person to be executed by lethal injection. With no sparks, blood, or the wafting odor of burning flesh, reformers were convinced that they had hit on a scientific method of execution that would be amenable to the modern era. However, law-and-order advocates opposed it on the basis that the criminal should suffer like the victim.

In May 2000, the Supreme Court reviewed electrocution for the first time since its inception in 1890. By 2001, most states had abandoned electrocution in favor of lethal injection. Since its inception in 1890, more than 4,300 people in 26 states were executed in the electric chair. In 2000, only Nebraska and Alabama used this method as its primary mode of execution. According to this case, the court was to consider whether Nebraska's particular method constituted cruel and unusual punishment since it entailed four separate jolts of electricity. In November of the same year, the Georgia Supreme Court rejected a similar challenge to the electric chair, claiming that the condemned prisoner raised his electrocution challenge too late in his appeal, barring it on procedural grounds.

Execution versus life without parole

By 1990, thirty states had adopted life without parole as an alternative to the death penalty while 2,400 prisoners awaited execution on death rows from coast to coast. In 1994, the Gallup Poll continued to demonstrate overwhelming support for the death penalty, registering an all-time high of 80 percent. However, by 2001, support for the death penalty was eroding, although the majority of Americans still favored it. In an October 2001 Gallup Poll, 68 percent of the American public favored the death penalty. Reasons cited for opposition included that it was administered unfairly and that it disproportionately targeted minorities. Others changed their minds after thirteen prisoners on death row in Illinois were discovered to be innocent, an admission that led Governor George Ryan of Illinois to declare a statewide moratorium on the death penalty in 2000. According to Austin Sarat, author of the book *When the State Kills*, the moratorium should be considered the turning point in the national dialogue about the death penalty.[75]

At the end of the twentieth century, America was the only country in the world that still used the electric chair and the gas chamber for executions, while Utah, Oklahoma, and Idaho continued to offer firing squads (and every few years Delaware, Washington, or New Hampshire resorted to hanging). In 1999, the last execution in a gas chamber took place in Florence, Arizona. Brothers and German nationals, Walter and Karl LaGrand had been sentenced to death for stabbing a bank robbery during a robbery gone wrong. The appeals process took their case to the U.S. Supreme Court, which denied a review of the case. They then filed petitions for writs of habeas corpus. According to Arizona law, they had the choice of lethal injection or gas. They decided to choose gas, hoping the courts would find this form of execution unconstitutional. Their strategy failed. At the last minute, Karl decided to opt for lethal injection, while his brother stuck to his first choice, hoping to make a statement. He would be the last person to die in the gas chamber in the twentieth century.[76]

An ABC News Poll in early 2000 found that support for the death penalty decreased from 64 to 48 percent when there was an option of life without parole. Other surveys captured similar sentiments. With recent accounts of wrongfully convicted death row inmates having their sentences overturned because of DNA evidence, a growing number of citizens favored alternatives to capital punishment. A 2000 Gallup Poll examined why Americans support state-sanctioned killings, or executions. According to the survey, the most frequently cited reason was "a life for a life," retribution so reminiscent of earlier and less sophisticated civilizations.[77]

In 1992, two professors at the Benjamin N. Cardoza School of Law at Yeshiva University founded the **Innocence Project. Barry C. Scheck** and Peter J. Neufeld have earned international acclaim for creating the Innocence Project and helping in the exoneration of the wrongly accused with the help of modern forensic technology. The Innocence Project only accepts cases "where postconviction DNA testing can yield conclusive proof of innocence." Since DNA was introduced to the courtroom more than a decade ago, 249 individuals have been exonerated in the United States through DNA testing (as of 2010). The majority had been previously convicted of sex crimes, and about one-quarter of them involved murder. Meanwhile, a number of states have passed laws addressing the causes of wrongful of convictions. The most frequent contributing causes of wrongful convictions include eyewitness misidentification (almost 70 percent), faulty forensic science, false confessions and admissions, government misconduct, informants, and bad lawyering.

Restorative justice

The search for alternatives to incarceration has a long history in the United States. Almost 170 years ago, John Augustus played an important role in the establishment of the probation sentence in 1841, which today is the most common sentence in the United States.[78] Until the 1980s, judges relied mostly on the standard options of probation or incarceration. Although community-based alternatives such as restitution and halfway houses had been around since the 1960s, "they lost credibility and support because they were shown to be ineffective."[79] In the early 1980s and the era of the "get-tough war on crime," prison overcrowding became such a serious problem other alternatives (intermediate sanctions) were adopted such as boot camps, home confinement, intensive supervision probation and parole, and others. However, these options did little to reduce the overcrowding, reduce rising recidivism rates, or provide adequate sentencing choices.[80]

Criminal justice researchers and officials have explored a number of alternatives to modern criminal sanctions. In most cases, they have revisited earlier eras in the history of criminal justice for inspiration. Although restorative justice is considered a recent trend, it has a timeworn legacy dating back in the United States to Native American cultures and colonial Americans; others assert its roots date back to the customs and religions of the ancient world, where the community played a pivotal role in the healing and retributive processes after a crime had been committed. In traditional cultures, new ways of managing conflict were met by offering "a ritualized process" involving members of the community and families from both sides of the conflict. According to one expert, the process that now dominates criminal proceedings dates back to the trials by battle of the Middle Ages, when "hired combatants" fought duels on behalf of the accused. Over time, this was replaced by the common law trial setting in which clients hired the modern incarnation of the "hired guns" – lawyers, who took part in determining guilt or innocence. Today this usually results in a plea bargain in which the victim has virtually no input. What's more, the malefactor's accountability to the victim or the community is rarely addressed.[81] One researcher has suggested that the implementation of restorative justice programs "Offers a new paradigm for structuring relationships among crime, offenders, and communities" and hopefully some type of "victim-offender reconciliation."[82]

By most accounts, the theory and expression "restorative justice" came into use in the 1970s as a reaction to the seeming excesses of a callous retribution process as well as inattention to the concerns of crime victims.[83] Canada has been given credit for introducing the first modern restorative justice project in Ontario in 1975. Albert Eglash has received the credit for coming up with the term, making a distinction between three types of criminal justice, which he argued were retributive, distributive, and restorative.[84] For Eglash, the retributive and distributive processes focused on the crime, barring "victim participation in the justice process" with only submissive participation by the offender. Contrasting with these two was the restorative process, which was intended to restore the harmful effects of the criminal act and actively involved the participation of both victim and offender in the criminal process.[85]

What started out as just a handful of "**victim-offender mediation (VOM)**" programs in the late 1970s had expanded by the 1980s and 1990s to more than a thousand restorative justice programs across North America. These new programs were an outgrowth and a response to the backlash against the medical model of criminal justice that persisted between the 1930s and 1970s, which insisted that the commission of crimes was often influenced by psychological, social, and economic forces beyond the control of the offenders. Its goal was rehabilitation. However, as crime rates skyrocketed in the mid-1970s, the public demanded harsher responses to the crime problem – anything that would reduce crime and high recidivism rates. By the end of the 1970s, the medical model had been sublimated by a justice model predicated on the notion that crime was a rational choice. Sentencing became more determinate and fixed, and it was left to offenders whether or not they wanted to take part in the rehabilitation process.[86] The goal of the justice model was to punish offenders, protect the community from the offender, and give society solace by punishing the criminal actor. As a result, the prison systems were soon overcrowded and prison budgets straining for resources.

There is little consensus as to the specific definition of restorative justice today. More than a decade ago, one survey found that it "emerged in varied guises with different names" including an alternative process for resolving disputes, alternative sanctioning options, or a "distinctly different, new model of criminal justice organized around principles of restoration to victims, offenders, and the communities in which they live." Other incarnations might include diversion from formal court processes, actions taken parallel with court decisions, and the meeting between offenders and victims at any stage of criminal process.[87] Supporters of restorative justice initiatives objected to the fact that prisoners were no longer required to take part in the rehabilitative process. By the end of the twentieth century, the concept of restorative justice became more prominent in Europe, stressing a maximum involvement in the justice process on the part of the offender, the victims, and the community. Several principles were at the heart of the process and operationalized under the direction of a specific court system and staff. The core principles assert that justice required society and its institutions to work and restore those who have been injured and those victims and their family members (those most directly affected by the crime) should have a chance to participate in the response to the crime.

Restorative justice at its root features an active role for crime victims. However, critics insist that the casual setting in which mediation between offender and victim takes place is likely to enforce existing relations of inequality between both parties. Detractors argue that, if an offender does not want to cooperate or be part of the process or if the community is not supportive of the programs, it stands little chance of success. Others suggest that there are inherent dangers in giving priority to this type of process over the time-tested ones of deterrence and incapacitation. By the twenty-first century, victim-offender mediation programs, restitution, and community service were the most common types of restorative justice programs in use in the United States.

Chain gangs and shaming: cruel and unusual or legitimate alternatives?

Originally used as a form of punishment in the South, the rattle of the chain gang returned to America in 1995, when Alabama reintroduced this measure as a cheaper and more effective way to manage exploding prison populations. Chained in five-man groups eight feet apart, prisoners worked twelve-hour days cutting and trimming roadsides and cleaning up litter. (The following year Alabama ceased using chain gangs arguing that chaining the prisoners individually was more effective than all together.) In the 1960s, Georgia became the last state to abolish the chain gang. According to one prison commissioner, the return of chain gangs should be considered a deterrence measure "that would leave a lasting impression on young people."[88]

Not confined to the South, the chain gang was revived in Arizona and Wisconsin as well. Reverting to criminal justice strategies of a previous era, the Wisconsin chain gang also borrowed a page from the future when it became the first state to equip its prisoners with stun belts. Capable of delivering an 8-second burst of 50,000 volts of electricity, the belt would be triggered by a guard at a control panel in the event of an escape attempt. Despite the concerns of Amnesty International, according to Wisconsin prison officials, prisoners were eager for any outside activity.[89]

For a country searching for alternative criminal justice strategies, it is surprising how rare it is for policy makers to draw lessons from the past. However, during the 1990s, several judges have experimented with forms of exhibitory punishment that are reminiscent of the Puritan New England colonies. Several cases in Texas made national news. In Houston, Judge Ted Poe wrote legislation in 1999 that allowed state judges in probation cases to order public notice of the crime where it was committed. Poe himself has issued close to 300 "public notice" sentences. In one case, a man who was convicted of domestic violence was required to publicly apologize to his wife on the steps of city hall. In another, a drunken driver was ordered to pace in front of a bar with the sign reading "I killed two people while driving drunk." Inspired by Nathaniel Hawthorne's *The Scarlet Letter*, the judge explained that "if we are held up to public ridicule, we don't like it and things will happen. We will change our conduct and our attitudes."[90]

The recrudescence of shaming led to opposition from critics who viewed it as an attempt to preach morality through the courts. Many of the concerns were based on the separation between church and state. Citing cases where judges ordered offenders to attend church in Texas and Louisiana in lieu of serving jail time or paying fines, the American Civil Liberties Union and other groups were worried that the move to shame-based punishment reflected a broader attempt by religious conservatives to impose their values on the political and legal systems.

Although there is no empirical evidence that shaming affects criminal behavior, it has become a popular alternative of justice. In one New Mexico town, bad-check writers were advertised on a large marquee; in Arizona, prisoners have been taped at bookings at the Maricopa County Jail and posted for viewing on the Internet; and one of the more popular programs in Kansas City, Missouri, was shame-based *John TV*, which offered photographs of individuals arrested for crimes involving prostitution.

Despite occasional criticisms, there have been few challenges to shame-based sentences. In many instances, shaming is directed at sexual offenders, with some judges requiring offenders to identify themselves. Because shame-based sentences are usually alternatives to prison sentences, there is little objection from the public since these sentences save the tax-payer money while publicizing the local threat of certain sex offenders. According to Marc Klaas, whose daughter Polly's murder in 1993 inspired the so-called Megan's Law (after a seven-year-old New Jersey girl was killed in her own neighborhood), "We all came to realize it is anonymity that breeds crime."

Homicide

Historian Roger Lane chronicled the history of American murder patterns in *Murder in America*. Published in 1997, his work came at a curious moment in American history, at a time when the nation was transfixed by the O. J. Simpson murder trial, several high profile acts of domestic terrorism, and a series of school-yard shootings and rampage killings, leaving most Americans under the impression that the nation was under siege by violent crime. Lane, however, concluded that, if one were to compare 1990s homicide rates with times past, except for intermittent ups and downs, "not much had changed."[91]

School-yard shootings and selective homicide reporting by media

No type of shooting received more news coverage than school shootings, particularly when the victims were white. But school-yard killings represented only a fraction of American homicides. Of the almost 150,000 Americans murdered during the 1990s, no more than 150 were killed in or around a school. Critics of selective media reporting of such events cite the discriminatory coverage that all but ignores shootings involving African Americans and other minority victims, the most likely target of school-yard violence. According to Mike Males of the Justice Policy Institute in Washington, DC, "White and black youths [are] less menaced by school violence now than a quarter century ago."[92] Less publicized than the school-yard shootings and mass murders that sporadically inundated the nightly news was the news in April 2002 that the rate of violent crime against Hispanics fell 56 percent over a seven-year period in the 1990s and was now similar to that against whites. This decrease coincided with drops in violence against other minority groups as well. Except for robbery, rates of victimization for Native Americans were the highest in every category. A spokeswoman for the National Council of La Raza credited the efforts of the nation's police departments to improve relations with Hispanics.

What gave Americans their bleak impression of current murder rates in this era was the saturation coverage given to certain high profile crimes. Some of these crimes were unprecedented in scope. Among the most notorious crimes of the era was the eighteen-year murderous bombing spree of "Unabomber" Theodore Kaczynski between 1978 and 1996. The math professor turned Luddite targeted university professors and a cornucopia of other representatives of what Kaczynski saw as the "Industrial Society." After killing three and wounding more than a dozen with carefully constructed mail bombs, Kaczynski blackmailed several newspapers to publish his manifesto "Industrial Society and Its Future." Despite the intense manhunt, it was his own brother who identified him after recognizing the jargon of the Unabomber as phrases and philosophy often espoused by his brother.

Antiabortion murders

In the 1990s, antiabortion violence escalated from picketing, verbal harassment, arson, and bombings to the outright assassination of physicians and clinic employees. By the late 1990s, antiabortion snipers began targeting doctors in their very homes, using high-powered rifles. One of the most prominent of these killings was the murder of Dr. Barnett Slepian near Buffalo, New York, killed by a gunshot through the window as he stood in his kitchen. His assailant was identified as James Kopp. In March 2001, Kopp was apprehended in France following an international manhunt. Aided by e-mail traffic and wiretapped conversations with friends, French police aided the FBI in the arrest. Kopp had been on the FBI's Ten Most Wanted Fugitives List since June 1999, and throughout his escape, he was helped along the way by antiabortion supporters.

Race riots at the end of the twentieth century

It would seem that, as the twenty-first century approached, America's increasing racial and ethnic diversity would have paved a more peaceful path to the future. But many of the country's old problems that had lain dormant for the past decades were rekindled for famil-iar reasons. Historian Paul Gilje suggested that one of the legacies of the 1960s was "the ghetto riot."[93] However, unlike the 1960s, which saw each hot summer explode into urban orgies of looting and arson after seemingly ordinary confrontations with police officers, race riots occurred only sporadically in the 1980s and 1990s but could be just as combustible and violent as in previous years. In May 1980, the Miami area was hit hard by rioting after an all-white Tampa jury acquitted four policemen charged with shooting a young black man. This disturbance, even by earlier standards of ferocity, was particularly violent. Three whites were beaten to death by blacks, but police officers would kill eleven blacks, and the riot would not conclude until the National Guard was called in.

Rioting was not to be confined to traditional patterns of black–white conflict as the century moved to a conclusion. Rioting would occur in Overtown, Florida, after a His-panic police officer was acquitted after shooting a black youth in 1984 and again in 1989. Dominican Americans rioted in New York City after a similar incident, and in 1991, Hasidic Jews were targeted by blacks in New York City after a Jewish man ran over and killed a young black girl. Reaching back to the patterns of race riots past, in 1986, whites in Howard Beach, Queens, chased a black youth onto a highway where he was struck and killed by an automobile. As America's racial and ethnic makeup became more diverse during the 1990s, so too did the characteristics of its rioters. Whether involving Vietnamese or Korean American, black or white, virtually all riots took place in urban America, where opportunities were scarce for America's newest underclasses.

In April 2001, the Cincinnati police faced three nights of rioting over the killing of an unarmed black man by police, the fifteenth such episode in the past six years. Pulling a page from criminal justice past, the city mayor implemented a dusk-to-dawn curfew. Police finally brought the riot under control with help from local residents and religious leaders. Several factors as old as policing help explain this outbreak of race rioting in Cincinnati, including the economic decline of inner-city communities, police harassment and brutality, racial profiling, and a disproportionate number of white police on the force, a force that did not reflect the demographics of the community it serves. Considering complaints by citizen board members who lament that police do not communicate with them and that they are not given the authority to properly investigate complaints against the police, from a historical vantage point, the imperious styles of the Los Angeles Police Department under William Parker and the pre-Roosevelt New York Police Department instantly come to mind. A number of scholars point to urban rioting as one of the stimuli that led to the creation of modern policing both in London and New York City. With the first police riot training occurring in the aftermath of the 1849 Astor police riot in New York City, riot training has been given short shrift on departments except for the civil rights and antiwar years of the 1960s and 1970s.

The Los Angeles riots

The **Los Angeles riot of 1993** proved once again how unprepared city police are for dealing with widespread civil unrest. Following a three-mile high-speed car chase in the early hours of March 3, 1991, **Rodney King** was ordered to get out of his car by several Los Angeles police officers. According to officers, King was noncompliant and scuffled with the officers, who were forced to resort to batons and stun guns to subdue the hulking King.[94] Unknown to the police was the fact that someone had tape-recorded much of the incident. The eighty-one second tape of police officers beating and kicking a supine King while other officers stood and watched resonated in African American and other minority neighborhoods of Los Angeles, where tension with police continued to fester since the 1960s Watts riot. According to a *Los Angeles Times* poll taken two weeks after the beating, 87 percent of the African American and 80 percent of the Hispanic respondents reported incidents of brutality at the hands of the Los Angeles Police Department (LAPD) as either "very common" or "fairly common."[95]

Following the beating of King, a commission was convened by Mayor Tom Bradley to investigate the LAPD. The so-called **Christopher Commission**, chaired by future U.S. Secretary of State Warren Christopher, published its findings and recommendations in July 1991. The ten-member commission was comprised of six lawyers, two professors, a college president, and a corporation chairman. The findings of the Christopher Commission report called for reform in the department, demanding the end of excessive force and racism by the police force. Its report would ultimately lead to the resignation of LAPD chief Daryl Gates.

Widespread anger over the taped beating led to grand jury indictments against four of the officers for assault (twenty-three were actually present at the assault) and the use of excessive force. The defense would successfully have the trial moved to the mostly white community of Simi Valley on the grounds that it would be impossible to get a fair verdict in the city of Los Angeles. With the eyewitness testimony of the videotape, conviction of the officers seemed a forgone conclusion. But on April 29, 1992, the jurors acquitted the four officers, sparking some of the worst race riots in American history.

Within minutes of the verdict, black and Hispanic Los Angeles exploded in violence. Whites were dragged from their cars and beaten as Korean merchants engaged in gunfights with gangs of looters. Fifty-eight deaths were reported during the riots. After several days of violence, the National Guard, together with federal troops, helped quell the riots. Their trial, acquittal, and the subsequent riots in 1992 made the second trial of the officers in 1993 one of the highest-profile cases in American legal history.

Rampage killings

Although rampage killing is not a new phenomenon, the 1990s witnessed a dramatic rise in such killings, in which one or two individuals went on killing sprees that would not end until they ran out of bullets or were killed or taken prisoner. One *New York Times* study identified 100 rampage killings between 1950 and 2000. Of these, only ten occurred before 1980, with seventy-three taking place in the 1990s. This phenomenon took 425 lives and injured 510 in half a century. Rampage killings occur in all cultures; in fact, the phrase "running amok," meaning "frenzied or indiscriminate killing," was first introduced in Malaysia.

Among the most overlooked issues concerning the perpetrators is that at least half had shown serious mental health problems prior to their crime sprees. While politicians have targeted a violent popular culture that includes video games, movies, and television, there is little evidence that these forms of entertainment predispose individuals to mass murder. The 1990s saw a drop in most types of murder but an increase in rampage killings. Although rampage killings represented less than 1 percent of all homicides, the sheer number of deaths often leads to rash judgments on behalf of legislators and the mass media and its poorly informed constituency.

In the wake of heavily publicized school-yard shootings that culminated but did not end with the 1999 **Columbine** shootings, there was an increased call for better law enforcement and greater security at American schools and workplaces. But according to the *New York Times*, closer scrutiny of each offender suggests that "these cases have more to do with society's lack of knowledge of mental health issues, rather than lack of security."[96] In virtually every case, teachers, family members, and mental health professionals overlooked signs of mental instability. However, as the final chapters in this book make clear, as late as 2018, schools and other public places in America continue to be targeted by well-armed shooters, while lawmakers continue to dither.

An examination of rampage killers indicates that these were "anything but random or sudden,"[97] with perpetrators often giving either verbal or behavioral warning signs. The most common precipitator for rampage killings was the loss of a job or romantic problems. What sets these crimes apart from typical murders is that the average murderer tries to get away with the crime. Of the more than 100 rampage killers in the *New York Times* survey, not one escaped apprehension. In fact, 89 never even left the scene of the crime.

Rampage killers differed from the typical profile of a murderer in that they were usually older, better educated, mostly white, and more likely to kill a stranger. Moreover, few of the demographic patterns of race and poverty usually associated with crime applied to rampage killers. As the *New York Times* report made clear, mental illness played a huge role in these killings, and since mental illness does not vary from race to race, a racial profile of the perpetrators reflects the actual diversity of America – the killers were mostly white, almost 18 percent black, and 7 percent Asian.

Explanations for the surge in this type of killing in the 1990s included the increasing availability of more lethal weapons with larger ammunition magazines and faster reloading. Although rampage killings increased in the 1990s, other types of multiple killings declined or remained static. Multiple killings of relatives and killings of three or more persons to cover up a felony declined in the 1990s. As the domestication of murder continued to decline, the workplace and school-yard become more dangerous than the home when it came to these types of killings. Some experts blame the news media for the saturation of crime coverage leading perhaps to "copycat" killings. At least fourteen of the rampage killers in the survey expressed knowledge of earlier killing sprees.

The expression "to run amok" comes from the Malay word, *amuk*, referring to someone who is "mad with uncontrollable rage." As noted previously, this form of multicide has become more common in America in recent years. By most accounts, the famous seafarer Captain James Cook was probably the first to observe this behavior. In 1770, during his first circumnavigation of the world, he witnessed it among Malay tribesmen. In the modern era, spree or rampage killers have been extensively studied. Criminologists and law enforcement are well aware that rampage killers often take their own lives after their killing sprees. Captain Cook offers a different vantage point from which to view this pathology. He described how one person could seemingly without cause, could go on a frenzied killing spree, indiscriminately killing people and animals during the rampage. Cook asserted that amok attacks averaged ten victims and only ended when the killer was stopped by fellow tribesmen, often by being killed. Later investigations have noted this behavior in the Philippines, Papua New Guinea, Puerto Rico, and other locales.[98]

Notable trials

People v. O. J. Simpson (1995)

Few "trials of the century" could top the public spectacle and intrigue of the 1995 trial of former football hero and movie star turned car rental pitchman O. J Simpson for the murder of his ex-wife Nicole Brown Simpson and Ron Goldman, a male friend. The Simpsons had divorced in 1992 but had continued to keep in contact and had even considered reuniting at one point even though Nicole reported to police dispatchers that O. J. had threatened to kill her during an assault as early as 1985.

According to the most irrefutable facts of the case, during the early morning hours of June 13, 1994, a lone intruder knifed to death Simpson and Goldman in the narrow entrance to Nicole's apartment. Forensic evidence indicates that the woman was attacked first. Twenty-five-year-old Ron Goldman apparently had the misfortune of stopping by to drop off a pair of sunglasses that Nicole had left at the restaurant where he worked earlier that evening. More than three hours after the murders, their savagely mutilated bodies were found.

Almost immediately, attention was focused on Nicole's former husband, Orenthal James (O. J.) Simpson. Reports filtered out of the Los Angeles Police Department that blood had been found matching that of O. J. outside his wife's residence. The news media would quickly report that a bloody glove was found behind Simpson's house that supposedly matched one at the crime scene. O. J.'s hastily assembled attorneys proclaimed his innocence.

After reneging on his promise to turn himself in on June 17, Simpson was spotted on Interstate 5 in the back of a Ford Bronco driven by his friend A. C. Cowlings. What ensued was perhaps one of the most bizarre live television events of all time. Before 95 million viewers, a legion of law enforcement officers slowly followed the white Bronco on the interstate past hundreds of cheering spectators who lined the roads leading to Simpson's upscale Brentwood home. Arriving home, Simpson was arrested, and the following month, he pleaded "100 percent not guilty."[99] In the process, he became one of the most famous murder defendants in the annals of American criminal justice. Simpson was denied bail and would languish in the Los Angeles County Jail during his almost two-year trial.

Without such unprecedented media coverage, the Simpson trial would have been rather mundane. The trial itself is well chronicled by now. Dozens of books were published after and during the trial. Friends and family of the victims, a houseguest of O. J.'s, O. J.'s friends, prosecutors, and defense members all published quickly forgotten books. While there were several that stood out, most were eminently forgettable and quickly were consigned to remainder tables.

The particulars of the case are all too familiar by now. The night of the murder, O. J. flew to Chicago for a business appointment. Returning to Los Angeles the next day, he was interrogated by the police, who focused attention on a deep cut on his right hand. Stating that he did not remember the cut, Simpson offered a number of explanations for the cut – then the sixty-mile car chase on the Los Angeles freeway, which, according to the media, was "the most famous ride on American shores since Paul Revere."[100]

The escape attempt and other crucial evidence should have made the case a slam dunk for the prosecution. But from the start, the prosecution was characterized by ineptitude and miscalculation. First of all, the district attorney's office allowed the trial to be held in downtown Los Angeles instead of Santa Monica, where the crime occurred. Having the trial in Santa Monica would have conformed to protocol since its court would have jurisdiction over crimes committed in the vicinity. Various explanations were given for the change of venue. Most convincing was the explanation that it was an attempt to avoid the sort of rioting and unrest that accompanied the initial acquittal of the police officers in the Rodney King case. What was clear was that the district attorney's office wished to avoid the implication that the jury would be stacked against Simpson.

The prosecution also gave up another strategic advantage by not seeking the death penalty. It is common knowledge in the legal field that "death-case-qualified" jurors tend to convict a defendant more readily than panels that are more reticent to inflict the death penalty.

Public opinion concerning Simpson's guilt became a national litmus test regarding race relations in America. According to attorney David Cole, the division in public opinion in this case reflected "an even deeper divide on the fairness and legitimacy of American criminal justice."[101] One finding that the news media focused on during the trial was the existence of a racial divide concerning the ex-football star's guilt or innocence. In poll after poll, it was reported that most white Americans believed the prosecution, while almost "three-quarters of black citizens" were inclined to side with the defense.[102] Some observers saw these polls as a statement on the racial inequities of the criminal justice system.

Joining civil rights activists and others in the growing media circus were women activists who used the case to campaign against domestic violence. Pointing out that the death of Nicole Brown Simpson was the result of systematic domestic abuse that led to murder, activists noted that almost one-third of all female homicide victims were killed by a husband or boyfriend. While O. J. would be acquitted, the activists were successful in drawing attention to the problem of domestic violence. Following their campaign during the trial, battered-women's shelters reported more calls, and judges began to hand down stiffer sentences in domestic violence cases. In Los Angeles alone, reports of domestic abuse to police increased by 60 percent.

As Gilbert Geis and Leigh Bienen make clear in their book *Crimes of the Century*, for the student of criminal justice, the Simpson case was remarkable for the number of challenges it posed to the criminal justice system. Should television be permitted in the courtroom? Should juries be sequestered?[103] Should unanimous verdicts be required in order to convict in a criminal trial? While the trial contributed little to the development of constitutional principle, it did demonstrate a number of interesting applications of existing legal principles. Among these was the right to confront accusers, which in California meant extending the right to the pretrial stages of a case. According to one legal authority, "The constitutional right most visibly on display was Simpson's Fifth Amendment privilege against self-incrimination."[104]

For almost two years, the world was transfixed by the O. J. Simpson trial played live on television. One could only wonder what Chief Justice Earl Warren would have thought about such a high profile trial televised in the courtroom, having stated in 1965 that, if television was allowed in the courtroom, "we can turn back the clock and make everyone in the courtroom an actor before untold millions of people." In the process, it would "make the determination of guilt or innocence a public spectacle and a source of entertainment for the idle and curious."[105]

The O. J. Simpson trial was one of the most expensive in America history. It is estimated that the defense team cost their client some $6 million, while the state spent $9 million on the prosecution, one-third of it going toward housing, feeding, and sequestering the jury.

Simpson was an atypical black defendant – famous, wealthy, and well represented. While in times past he would have faced an all-white jury, Simpson was judged by nine blacks, two whites, and one Hispanic. Attempting to place the case in a historical perspective, author David Cole, an African American attorney, suggested that, for a brief moment, "for many black citizens, the acquittal was a sign of hope," noting that

for much of our history, the mere allegation that a black man had murdered two white people would have been sufficient grounds for lynching. . . . To many blacks, the jury's not guilty verdict demonstrated that the system is not always rigged against the black defendant, and that was worth cheering.[106]

Ultimately, Simpson's acquittal, similarly to Lizzie Borden's a century earlier, hinged on one of the most prominent aspects of common law, namely, that a conviction requires proof beyond a reasonable doubt.

Conclusions

No matter what technological advances appear in the twenty-first century, the criminal justice system remains adamantly reliant on the time-tested traditions of the past. Witness the return of horse-mounted patrols in shopping mall parking lots and in urban centers and the return of shaming in the courtroom. Since the advent of law enforcement, it has been obvious that an officer on horseback has advantages over a purely bipedal counterpart, particularly when it came to controlling crowds. First introduced by King Charles in 1629, horse-mounted police branches are clearly on the increase. Almost forced out of existence by the automobile, over the past twenty years, mounted patrols have once again become a familiar presence in most large cities and are considered advantageous for riot control, community relations, and their high visibility. Also demonstrating the cyclical nature of innovation in criminal justice is the reinvigorated emphasis on community-oriented policing, which has taken the police officer from behind the wheel of an automobile and back to foot patrol in American communities.

Contemporary polls indicated shrinking support for capital punishment after a decade of almost unshakable support. The debate over the death penalty came into sharp focus after a confluence of several events in 2001, including the execution of Oklahoma City bomber Timothy McVeigh, protests during President Bush's European visit that focused on America's death penalty policy as a violation of human rights, the decision by a New York jury not to sentence one of the African embassy bombers to death, and the execution of a murderer in Ohio who claimed he was schizophrenic. Although a majority of Americans still were in favor of the death penalty, the size of that majority had diminished.

At the conclusion of 2001, a dramatic decline in the use of the death penalty in America saw sixty-six people put to death that year compared to eighty-five the year before. Texas, which executed forty in 2000, witnessed seventeen in 2001 and lost the lead to Oklahoma, which executed eighteen convicts in 2001. In addition to a combination of declining crime rates, a wave of DNA exonerations have made the courts and the public more skeptical about death sentences. While the decline in executions has encouraged the opponents of capital punishment, many are disturbed as the federal government began executing people again for the first time in decades.

America's state prison population increased by 500 percent between 1970 and 2000. Even while crime rates dropped in the 1990s, prisons remained the fastest growing item in state budgets. By 2002, more than 2 million inmates were incarcerated in state, federal, and local correctional facilities at a cost of more than $30 billion a year. Nationwide, guards accounted for 80 percent of prison costs. In order to slash budgets, some states began laying off guards and supervisory positions. Others are cutting back on educational programs and food services to save money.

In April 2002, the Justice Department announced that the number of people in prison grew by only 1 percent over the previous year, the slowest rate in thirty years (as June 30, 2001, 1 of every 145 residents was behind bars). Most U.S. prisoners were held in state prisons, where the population rose 0.4 percent. The federal prison population showed the most growth at 7.2 percent. However, this was due in part to the U.S. government's continuing to assume responsibility for District of Columbia prisoners (this transfer ended in 2001). Racial disparities in prison populations continued to haunt critics of the criminal justice system. The Justice Department released figures that showed that 13.4 percent of black males ages twenty-five to twenty-nine were incarcerated, compared with 4.1 percent of Hispanic men and 1.8 percent of white males.

A harbinger of the intelligence failure leading up to the terrorist attacks of 9/11, 2001, in December 1997, criminologists began focusing on one of the least discussed problems of the criminal justice system: the archaic state of record keeping in the criminal justice system. As late as May 2002, columnist Robert D. Novak claimed that, when the new FBI director Robert Mueller, took over on September 4, 2001, "the Bureau's computer system was so obsolete that he asked the CIA for help."[107] According to one 1994 Justice Department report, only 18 percent of the nation's felony records were complete and computerized. Without adequate records, police and prosecutors face obstacles in recognizing the dangerous offender from the non-dangerous, judges face obstacles hampering the recognition of multiple and repeat offenders, and prison officials cannot determine whether an inmate merits maximum security.

Although the FBI collects names of people who have been arrested, it does not reveal whether individuals have been convicted or acquitted (as of 1997). In its own defense, FBI officials explain that it is difficult to gather this information from the thousands of local agencies that vary in record keeping practices.

Throughout much of the Western world, countries have adopted a "harm-reduction" approach to illegal drug use. Proponents of the continuing drug war have learned little since the fourteen-year experiment with alcohol prohibition. According to Ethan Nadleman, director of a New York drug policy research institute, "Drugs are here to stay . . . we have no choice but to learn how to live with them so that they cause the least possible harm."

The United States spent $4 billion on drug control in 1980. Twenty years later, this figure stood at more than $32 billion per year. The number of people incarcerated on drug charges also increased by eight times, from 50,000 to more than 400,000. Because of mandatory sentencing, many thousands of otherwise law-abiding citizens were serving long sentences for first-time nonviolent offenses. Some critics of the drug war would argue that it has damaged our constitutional protections against abusive law enforcement without an appreciable impact in ending the drug trade.

The law enforcement community has been quick to take credit for the reduction of violent crime in the 1990s. New police strategies and the increase of police officers on the streets certainly share some of the credit for the decline in crime in this time period, but other factors have also contributed to this phenomenon, including declining unemployment rates, demographic changes, and the decline in the crack cocaine market.

Between 1977 and 1994, Americans were executed by firing squad, hanging, electrocution, the gas chamber, and lethal injection.[108] Twenty-six states used the electric chair at its peak, but over the past half a century, most of the thirty-eight death penalty states have switched to lethal injection. In 2000, only Nebraska and Alabama continued to use electrocution as the primary form of execution after Georgia and Florida agreed to switch to lethal injection. Florida switched only after a series of grisly executions led state legislators to brand electrocutions as unconstitutional as "cruel and unusual" punishment.

With close to 2 million prison inmates by the end of the 1990s, America incarcerates a greater percentage of its people than any industrialized country except Russia (which it would surpass in the next decade). Nationally, 1 of every 113 adult males was behind bars. Since 1990, the nation's state prison population increased 65 percent compared to 106 percent in the federal prisons. While there had indeed been a decline in serious crime, more people are going to prison under harsher sentencing laws. Critics of drug enforcement policies blamed the growing racial disparities of American prisons on sentencing disparities that saw crack cocaine (minorities were more likely to be convicted for crack-related offenses) offenses carry penalties that were 100 times greater than powdered cocaine (favored by middle-class white consumers).

The backlash against violent youth crime that saw zero tolerance strategies applied to public schools began to soften in 2001. These strategies came to prominence when the federal government mandated that any school that received federal funds was required to expel any student who brought a firearm onto campus. California widened the net to require expulsion for any student caught selling drugs. The spate of highly publicized school-yard shootings in the late 1990s led school boards to take these policies further, calling for expulsion of students who possessed any item that could be construed as a weapon, including toy guns and nail files. Others added home remedies, such as aspirin and Tylenol, to the list of banned substances.

Leading the resistance against the draconian policies were educators and other teachers who felt that suspensions for relatively minor alcohol and weapons infractions were too punitive a response. The rush to judgment that had been zero tolerance led to expulsions of Boy Scouts for mistakenly bringing scout knives to school as well as a ten-year-old girl who turned over her mother's kitchen knife to authorities when she realized she had brought it with her to school by mistake. But despite well-publicized exceptions, many school administrators credit these policies with reducing campus violence and deterring substance abuse. In the spirit of compromise, some campuses are implementing lighter sentences, attempting to make the punishment fit the offense.[109]

Point – counterpoint

The aftermath of Waco: changes in federal law enforcement

In July of 1995, hearings were held to examine the activities of federal law enforcement agencies during the siege of the Branch Davidian compound in Waco, Texas, in 1993. The sequence of events began with the killing of four law enforcement officers on February 28, 1993, and concluded with the deaths of more than eighty at the Branch Davidian compound, including twenty-two children. Subsequent Congressional hearings investigated the facts surrounding the entire operation and fifty-one-day standoff between the two incidents. In the first passage, Larry Potts, former Assistant Director for the FBI's Criminal Investigation Division, explains the FBI's strategy for resolving the Waco standoff. The second excerpt contains some conclusions by the committee chairman on how these types of episodes can be better handled.

Source: Committee on the Judiciary, U.S. Senate, 104th Cong., *Activities of Federal Law Enforcement Agencies Toward the Branch Davidians*, Part 2, July 25–27, 1995, pp. 591–593, 604–605; *The Aftermath of Waco: Changes in Federal Law Enforcement*, Oct. 31 and Nov. 1, 1995, pp. 216–217

The FBI's strategy for resolving the situation in Waco was twofold: (1) to verbally negotiate a peaceful surrender of Koresh and his followers; and, (2) to gradually increase the pressure on those inside the compound by tightening the perimeter around the compound and denying the Davidians certain comforts. In formulating this strategy and throughout the events in Waco, the FBI utilized its Behavioral Science Unit, the National Center for the Analysis of Violent Crime, and a host of outside experts in such specialties as religion and theology, psycholinguistics, cults, medicine, threat assessment, negotiation techniques, psychology, and psychiatry. The experts provided a wide range of information on Koresh's state of mind and behavior, as well as information on an array of issues the FBI faced. The FBI also received hundreds of unsolicited telephone calls from individuals offering advice on how best to resolve the standoff with the **Branch Davidians**. As part of its exhaustive efforts to gather as much information as possible, the FBI followed up on most of these telephone calls which appeared legitimate. Not all of the expert opinions were consistent on all issues but the FBI considered the information it received and made the best judgment it could towards achieving a peaceful resolution to the standoff.

Despite these efforts and all of the outside expert advice, the FBI was unable to convince the compound's occupants either as a group or individually to surrender peacefully. The response of Koresh was always to consistently promise to come out at certain times and to consistently break his promise and fail to do so. Eventually, he advised that the Davidians would emerge only when God gave such an instruction to him.

Based on the developments on-site and the advice of experts, the FBI concluded that permitting the standoff to continue would never lead to the peaceful surrender of Koresh, but instead would continue to elevate the risk to the innocent children inside the compound, as well as to the law enforcement officers at the scene. As a result, a strategic plan was then developed to deliver non-lethal tear gas into the compound in hopes of causing the evacuation of the occupants. For nearly two weeks, the FBI wrestled internally with the details of the plan, before presenting it to the attorney general for approval, to best ensure a safe and satisfactory end to the standoff. In developing its plan to release tear gas into the compound, the FBI thoroughly considered and examined numerous strategic and tactical issues, including the possibility of a hostile reaction from the Davidians; the night vision capability of the Davidians; the strategic firing point that the compound's tower provided the Davidians; the risk of harm to the children inside the compound; the possible harmful effects, if any, of tear gas; and, of course, the massive amount of weapons and ammunition in the compound and the dangerous people who had already killed four federal agents.

As a result of its extensive analyses of these issues, the FBI developed a non-combative plan to release tear gas incrementally into the compound over a two-day period, gradually causing certain portions of the compound to become uninhabitable. The plan provided for increasing the release of gas only to the degree needed to accomplish evacuation of the compound. The plan also included notifying the Davidians that the gas was going to be inserted into specific portions of the compound and providing them the time and means to exit the building safely. Extensive medical support, to include 12 physicians and 13 paramedics, would be standing by and loudspeakers and signs would be used to guide the people out of the compound. In the event that the Davidians opened fire on the FBI agents, the plan provided for the agents to return fire and to escalate the delivery of the tear gas into the entire compound to suppress the gunfire.

Since 1986, the FBI has been involved in the DOJ's quest for alternatives to the use of deadly force. This technology search has evolved into the current "Less Than Lethal Weapons"

(LTLW) Program. The SWAT Training Unit, now a component of CIRG, has participated in a number of research efforts during the past two years and has created a working LTLW Committee to review various avenues of research and development of LTLW technology. The LTLW Committee is keeping abreast of both classified and unclassified research and development in this area through liaison with the military, national laboratories, federal law enforcement, private industry, and other involved entities. Research encompasses the full spectrum of relevant technologies including mechanical/impact, electrical, chemical, and biomedical, all designed to safely subdue dangerous subjects without resorting to the application of traditional weapons.

In addition to the above changes in jurisdiction, operations, and research, the Attorney General, the FBI Director, a large number of SACs, all FBI profilers, and an FBI Agent from every field office are all receiving or have received crisis management training, including behavioral science expert training, to become familiar with CIRG, its components, capabilities, and procedures.

These and other changes have improved our crisis response capabilities and have maximized the likelihood that the FBI will be better prepared to resolve future crisis situations successfully.

The Chairman. Let me just thank all of our witnesses and the public at large for their close attention during these hearings. In conclusion, I want to reiterate the message that I began with yesterday. Throughout my years of service in Washington, I have been a very strong supporter of Federal law enforcement. I have the utmost respect for both agencies and the individual agents who put their lives on the line every day for us. It is the quality and heroism of these people that guarantees that, as a whole, Federal law enforcement is a success across the Nation.

As a result, none of us should overlook the fact that for every Waco or Ruby Ridge, there are thousands of safe, successful, and uneventful law enforcement actions carried out each year. It is because of my interest in and respect for law enforcement, though, that these hearings have become necessary.

During the past 3 years, I have become particularly aware of a number of growing problems in law enforcement. These problems include the increased militarization of law enforcement agencies, the inability of agencies to gather and assimilate gathered intelligence and act on it, the public's loss of confidence in law enforcement, the lack of organization between negotiations and tactical wings of law enforcement, and the reckless and overly aggressive attacks of field commanders. Both in Ruby Ridge and Waco, law enforcement actions failed as a direct result of these problems, and I therefore decided to convene these hearings with the intention of correcting these problems.

I am encouraged by the progress we have made during the past few days. We have learned that ATF and FBI have recognized the problems that exist in law enforcement. We have also learned of the various steps that both ATF and FBI are taking to correct the errors that occurred at both Ruby Ridge and Waco. Some of these steps include the placement of a greater emphasis on negotiations, the creation of the Critical Incident Response Group, the CIRG, and the development of better lines of communication between the various law enforcement teams.

Unfortunately, not all of the problems discussed have been addressed. More needs to be done to bolster the role of behavioralists and negotiations generally in barricade and hostage situations. We need to have greater data processing and computerization in our behavioral group of people down there at Quantico. That costs money, and it is Congress' fault that we are not putting enough money into these matters so that we are more skilled and better than we currently are.

But more needs to be done to rid law enforcement of its current militaristic mentality. We have got to bolster the role of behavioralists and negotiations generally, especially in these barricade and hostage situations.

Finally, more needs to be done to restore the confidence of the American people in law enforcement. This last issue becomes especially poignant in light of the tragedy at Oklahoma City. If law enforcement can work to accomplish these goals, my aims in convening these hearings and those of the other members of this committee, of course, are realized. If law enforcement fails, our Nation is going to suffer.

One thing is certain: In the future, this committee is going to redouble its efforts in diligently overseeing the use of force by law enforcement agencies. Misuses of power by law enforcement will be carefully investigated. As long as I am chairman of this committee, I will see to it that law enforcement in this country is held to the highest standards. I don't think you gentlemen mind that. I think you want to be held to the highest standards because that is what has always characterized the FBI and ATF through the years.

So, in summary, I believe that the best way to restore the public's confidence in law enforcement is for us to put Waco and Ruby Ridge behind us. Law enforcement has to move away from paramilitary operations and recommit itself to high-quality crime prevention. Additionally, I look forward to hearing from the administration as to how they further intend to ensure that tragedies like those at Ruby Ridge and Waco are never repeated.

Key terms

Reaganomics
Sandra Day O'Connor
mandatory sentencing
Brady Handgun Bill
Anti-Terrorism and Effective Death Penalty Act
Amadou Diallo
William Bratton
Jack Maple
DNA profiling
truth-in-sentencing
faith-based initiatives
McCleskey v. Kemp
restorative justice
antiabortion violence
Christopher Commission
crack cocaine

Len Bias
Polly Klaas
"Twinkie defense"
"flood and frisk"
Compstat
Ruby Ridge
Daubert guidelines
prison privatization
John Ashcroft
Innocence Project
victim-offender mediation (VOM)
Rodney King
rampage killings
Comprehensive Crime Control Act
Anti-Drug Abuse Act of 1986

"Three strikes and you're out"
broken-windows
James Q. Wilson and George Kelling
community-based policing
crime hot spots
Waco and the Branch Davidians
"lock-em up strategy"
supermax prisons
crime drop
Barry C. Scheck
Columbine
Los Angeles riot of 1993
O. J. Simpson trial

Critical thinking questions

1 What events led to the decreased prestige of the FBI in the 1980s and 1990s?
2 Contrast the tenor of criminal justice in America during the 1980s to that of the 1960s. What changes in law enforcement, court rulings, and corrections come to mind?
3 What led to the introduction of lethal injection? Contrast this innovation with the general pattern execution in American history.
4 Discuss how mandatory sentencing impacted the corrections and the court systems.
5 Since 1919, riot commissions have convened in the aftermath to discuss the reasons for the violence. What did the Christopher Commission's findings have in common with earlier reports?
6 What impact did the article "Broken-Windows" have on policing. Discuss the various opinions regarding the efficacy of this philosophy.
7 What are the various explanation for the decline in homicide during the 1990s?

Notes

1 *Sourcebook of Criminal Justice Statistics, 1973*, Washington, DC: U.S. GPO, 1973, 1974, pp. 58–59. In 1970, 146,273 of the employees were in corrections and 507,877 in policing. By 1980, corrections employed 298,722 and another 723,923 were in policing.
2 Allen J. Beck and Christopher J. Mumola, Prisoners in 1998, August 15, 1999. https://www.bjs.gov/content/pub/pdf/p98.pdf.
3 Larry E. Sullivan, *The Prison Reform Movement*, Boston: Twayne, 1990, p. 125.
4 Julian Roberts and Loretta J. Stalans, *Public Opinion, Crime, and Criminal Justice*, Boulder, CO: Westview Press, 1997, p. 3.
5 David Bodenhamer, *Fair Trial: Rights of the Accused in American History*, New York: Oxford University Press, 1992, p. 130.
6 Christian Parenti, *Lockdown America: Police and Prisons in the Age of Crisis*, London: Verso, 2001, p. 48.
7 Alan Elsner, *Gates of Injustice: The Crisis of America's Prisons*, Upper Saddle River, NJ: Prentice Hall, 2004.
8 Katherine Beckett and Theodore Sasson, *The Politics of Injustice: Crime and Punishment in America*, Thousand Oaks, CA: Pine Forge Press, 2000, p. 176.
9 Lawrence M. Friedman, *American Law in the 20th Century*, New Haven, CT: Yale University Press, 2002, p. 591.
10 Jeff Donn, "Plunging U.S. Handgun Market Unlikely to Recover, Experts Say," *Houston Chronicle*, April 14, 2001, p. A15.
11 Founded in 1852, Smith & Wesson began manufacturing a wide range of products to supplement its ailing gun business. In Smith & Wesson Outlet Stores, shoppers can purchase gym bags, Western-style leatherware, and jewelry, all with the familiar company logo.
12 National Shooting Sports Foundation, "FBI Firearm Background Checks Hit 100 Million Mark," April 9, 2009, www.opposingviews.com/articles/news-fbi-firearm-bakground-checks-hits-100-m
13 Carol Pogash, "Myth of the 'Twinkie Defense': The Verdict in the Dan White Case Wasn't Based on his Ingestion of Junk Food," *San Francisco Chronicle*, November 23, 2003, p. D1.
14 Quoted in Ibid., 2003.
15 Ibid.

16 Jessica Lussenhop, "Clinton Crime Bill: Why Is It So Controversial," April 18, 2016, www.bbc.com/news/world-us-canada-36020717

17 Quoted in Parenti, 2001, p. 65.

18 David Yassky, "Unlocking the Truth About the Clinton Crime Bill," *New York Times*, April 9, 2016. https://www.nytimes.com/2016/04/10/opinion/campaign-stops/unlocking-the-truth-about-the-clinton-crime-bill.html

19 Ibid. Yassky article.

20 John E. Eck and Edward R. Maguire, "Have Changes in Policing Reduced Violent Crime? An Assessment of the Evidence," in *The Crime Drop in America*, ed. Alfred Blumstein and Joel Wallman, Cambridge: Cambridge University Press, 2000, p. 217.

21 Robert Farley, "Bill Clinton and the 1994 Crime Bill," April 12, 2016, www.factcheck.oreg/2016/04/bill-clinton-and-the-1994-crime-bill/

22 Amy Chozick, "Bill Clinton Says He Regrets Protest Showdown," *New York Times*, April 9, 2016, pp. A1, 12; David Yassky, "Unlocking the Truth about the Clinton Crime Bill," *New York Times*, April 9, 2016.

23 Marc Morje Howard, *Unusually Cruel: Prisons, Punishment, and the Real American Exceptionalism*, New York: Oxford University Press, 2017, p. 166.

24 Ibid., p. 167.

25 National Research Council, *The Growth of Incarceration in the United States: Exploring Causes and Consequences*, Washington, DC: The National Academies Press, 2014.

26 Ibid.

27 Quoted in Yassky, , April 9, 2016.

28 Ibid.

29 Gus Martin, *Understanding Terrorism: Challenges, Perspectives, and Issues*, Los Angeles: Sage, 2010, p. 497.

30 Gus Martin, *Terrorism and Homeland Security*, Thousand Oaks, CA: Sage, p. 280

31 Dorothy Moses Schulz, *From Social Worker to Crimefighter*, Westport, CT: Praeger, 1995, p. 145.

32 Samuel Walker, *The Police in America: An Introduction*, New York: McGraw-Hill, 1992, p. 26.

33 Samuel Walker, "Broken Windows and Fractured History: The Use and Misuse of History in Recent Police Patrol Analysis," *Justice Quarterly*, March 1984, p. 76.

34 Ibid., p. 88.

35 Kristen Hays, "New York Celebrating Murder Toll for 1986," *Houston Chronicle*, January 1, 1997.

36 Beckett and Sasson, 2000, p. 208.

37 Quoted in D. W. Miller, "Poking Holes in the Theory of 'Broken Windows'," *Chronicle of Higher Education*, February 9, 2001, p. A15.

38 Eli B. Silverman, *NYPD Battles Crime: Innovative Strategies in Policing*, Boston: Northeastern University Press, 1999.

39 Garrett M. Graff, *The Threat Matrix: The FBI at War in the Age of Global Terror*, New York: Little, Brown and Company, 2011, pp. 175–176.

40 Mark Hamm, "Ruby Ridge," in *Violence in America*, Vol. 3, ed. Ronald Gottesman, New York: Scribner, 1999, p. 71; Graff, 2011.

41 Ruby Ridge Hearing, https://fas.org/irp/congress/1995_hr/s951019f.htm

42 S. K. Bardwell, "Police to Look at Software That Targets Serial Killers," *Houston Chronicle*, April 21, 1999, p. A36.

43 Tod W. Burke, "Brain 'Fingerprinting'," *Law and Order*, June 1999, p. 29.

44 Simon A. Cole, *Suspect Identities: A History of Fingerprinting and Identification*, Cambridge, MA: Harvard University Press, 2001b, p. 284

45 "Scotland Yard Marks 100 Years of Fingerprints," June 27, 2001, https://www.iol.co.za/business-report/technology/scotland-yard-marks-100-years-of-fingerprints-68739

46 Simon A. Cole, "The Myth of Fingerprints," *New York Times Magazine*, May 13, 2001a, pp. 13–14. Cole cites a proficiency test from the era that found that as many as one out of five fingerprint examiners misidentified fingerprint samples.

47 Quoted in Seth Stern, "A Harder Day in Court for Fingerprinting, Writing Experts," January 31, 2002, http://csmonitorr.com

48 Scott Christianson, *With Liberty for Some: 500 Years of Imprisonment in America*, Boston: Northeastern University Press, 1998, p. 283.

49 Ibid.

50 Department of Justice annual survey, quoted in Christianson, 1998, p. 281.

51 "Corrections Population Tops Record," *Houston Chronicle*, August 27, 2001, p. A3.

52 Paula Ditton and Doris James Wilson, "Truth in Sentencing in State Prisons," *Bureau of Justice Statistics*, January 1999, https://bjs.gov/content/pub/pdf/tssp.pdf

53 William Spelman, "Crime, Cash, and Limited Options: Explaining the Prison Boom," *Criminology and Public Policy*, 8(1), 2009, p. 69.

54 Christianson, 1998, p. 291.

55 Ibid.

56 David Leonhardt, "As Prison Labor Grows, So Does the Debate," *New York Times*, March 19, 2000, p. 22.

57 Jessica Benko, "Judgment Calls," *New York Times Magazine*, March 29, 2015, pp. 42–43.

58 David Mears, et al., "Faith Based Efforts to Improve Prisoner Re-Entry: Assessing the Logic and the Evidence," *Journal of Criminal Justice*, 34, 2006.

59 Gary Wills, "A Country Ruled by Faith," *The New York Review of Books*, November 16, 2006, p. 8.

60 James Alan Fox and Jack Levin, *Extreme Killing*, Los Angeles: Sage, 2015.

61 Fox Butterfield, "Drop in Crack Use, Crackdown on Guns Might Be behind Plunge in Violent Crime," *Houston Chronicle*, December 28, 1998.

62 Clifford Krauss, "Shootings Plummet in New York as Police Frisking Drives Illegal Guns Off the Streets," *New York Times*, July 30, 1995.

63 Joel Wallman and Alfred Blumstein, "After the Crime Drop," in *The Crime Drop in America*, ed. Wallman and Blumstein, New York: Cambridge University Press, 2006.

64 "On Indian Reservations in the West, Violent Crime Soars," *New York Times*, August 16, 1998.

65 Leonhardt, 2000, p. 22; Richard Wright and Scott Decker, *Armed Robbers in Action: Stickups and Street Culture*, Boston: Northeastern University Press, 1997.

66 Fox Butterfield, "Plunge in Rate of Property Crimes Catches Cities' Officials by Surprise," *New York Times*, October 12, 1997.

67 Ibid.

68 Butterfield, 1998.

69 James B. Jacobs, *Busting the Mob*, New York: New York University Press, 1994.

70 William Kleinknecht, *The New Ethnic Mobs: The Changing Face of Organized Crime in America*, New York: Free Press, 1996, p. 294.

71 Of the remaining 132 executions, 56 took place in the West, 73 in the Midwest and three in the Northeast.

72 Bryan Vila and Cynthia Morris, *Capital Punishment in the United States: A Documentary History*, Westport, CT: Greenwood Press, 1997, p. 294.

73 James C. McKinley, "Islamic Movement's Niche: Bringing Order to Somali's Chaos," *New York Times*, August 23, 1996; "Execution by Taliban: Crushed under Wall," *New York Times*, January 16, 1999.

74 James C. McKinley, 1999.

75 Austin Sarat, *When the State Kills: Capital Punishment and the American Condition*, Princeton, NJ: Princeton University Press, 2001.

76 Scott Christianson, *The Last Gasp: The Rise and Fall of the American Gas Chamber*, Berkeley, CA: University of California Press, 2010.

77 Robert J. Lifton and Gregg Mitchell, *Who Owns Death? Capital Punishment, the American Conscience, and the End of Executions*, New York: Harper Collins, 2000, pp. 218–219.

78 Edward J. Gumz, "American Social Work, Corrections and Restorative Justice: An Appraisal," *International Journal of Offender Therapy and Comparative Criminology*, 49(4), 2004.

79 Gail Caputo, *Intermediate Sanctions in Corrections*, Denton: University of North Texas Press, 2004, p. 22.

80 Ibid.

81 Katherine Van Wormer, "Restorative Justice: A Model for Social Work Practice with Families," *Families in Society: The Journal of Contemporary Human Services*, 84(3), 2003.

82 Richard Delgado, "Goodbye to Hammurabi: Analyzing the Atavistic Appeal of Restorative Justice," *Stanford Law Review*, 54(4), 2000, p. 755.

83 Ibid.

84 Albert Eglash, "Beyond Restitution: Creative Restitution," in *Restitution in Criminal Justice*, ed. J. Hudson and B. Galaway, Lexington, MA: DC Heath and Company, 1977.

85 Theo Gavrielides, "Restorative Justice-Perplexing Concept: Perpetual Fault lines and Power Battles within the Restorative Justice Movement," *Criminology & Criminal Justice*, 8(2), 2008, p. 167.

86 Gumz, 2004.

87 Gavrielides, 2008, p. 166.

88 Rick Bragg, "Chain Gangs Return to Roads of Alabama," *New York Times*, March 26, 1995, p. 9.

89 Richard P. Jones, "Stun Belts for Prisoners Controversial," *Houston Chronicle*, June 15, 1997.

90 Dean E. Murphy, "Justice as a Morality Play Ends with Shame," *New York Times*, June 3, 2001, p. 5.

91 Roger Lane, *Murder in America: A History*, Columbus: Ohio State University Press, 1997, p. 306.

92 Mike Males, "Real Story Behind School Shootings Going Untold," *Houston Chronicle*, March 13, 2001, p. A27.

93 Paul A. Gilje, *Rioting in America*, Bloomington, IN: Indiana University Press, 1996, p. 172.

94 Besides a number of stitches, King sustained fractures to the skull, cheekbone, and ankle from the beating. Blood and urine tests taken five hours after the incident indicated that he was legally drunk under California law and had recently smoked marijuana.

95 Willie L. Williams, *Taking Back Our Streets: Fighting Crime in America*, New York: Scribner, 1996, p. 17.

96 Ford Fessenden, "They Threaten, Seethe and Unhinge, They Kill in Quantity," *New York Times*, April 9, 2000, https://www.nytimes.com/2000/04/09/us/they-threaten-seethe-and-unhinge-then-kill-in-quantity.html?auth=login-email

97 Ibid.

98 See A. A. Hempel, et al., "Cross-Cultural Review of Sudden Mass Assault by a Single Individual in the Oriental and Occidental Cultures," *Journal of Forensic Sciences*, 45, 2000, pp. 582–588; Manuel L. Saint Martin, "Running Amok: A Modern Perspective on a Culture-Bound Syndrome," in *Primary Care Companion Journal of Clinical Psychiatry*, 1, 1999, pp. 66–70, www/ncbi.nlm.nih.gov

99 B. Drummond Ayres, Jr., "'Absolutely' Not Guilty A confident Simpson Says," NYT, July 23, 1994. https://www.nytimes.com/1994/07/23/us/absolutely-not-guilty-a-confident-simpson-says.html

100 Gilbert Geis and Leigh B. Beinen, *Crimes of the Century: From Leopold and Loeb to O. J. Simpson*, Boston: Northeastern University Press, 1998, p. 174.

101 David Cole, *No Justice: Race and Class in the American Criminal Justice System*, NY: New Press, 1999, p. 1.

102 David Cole, *No Justice: Race and Class in the American Criminal Justice System*, New York: New Press, 1999, p. 1.

103 Geis and Beinen, 1998, 171.

104 Alfred H. Knight, *The Life of the Law: The People and Cases That Have Shaped Our Society from King Alfred to Rodney King*, NY: Crown Pub, 1996, p. 263.

105 Alfred H. Knight, *The Life of the Law: The People and Cases That Have Shaped Our Society from King Alfred to Rodney King*, New York: Crown Publishers, 1996, p. 263.

106 Quoted in Bernard Schwartz, *A Book of Legal Lists*, New York: Oxford University Press, 1997, p. 257.

107 Robert D. Novak, "But FBI Intelligence Also Lets Us Down," *Houston Chronicle*, May 21, 2002, p. A22.

108 Bonnie Bobit, *Death Row: Meet the Men and Women of Death Row*, 9th ed., Torrance, CA: Bobit Publishing, 1999. Between 1978 and January 1, 1999, of the 500 inmates executed, 142 were executed by electrocution, 2 by firing squad, 10 by gas chamber, 3 by hanging, and 343 by lethal injection.

109 Jessica Garrison, "Some Public Schools Drop Zero Tolerance," *Houston Chronicle*, February 25, 2001, p. A2.

Sources

Bardwell, S. K. 2000. "Police to Look at Software That Targets Serial Killers." *Houston Chronicle*, April 21.

Barker, Jeff. 2000. "Tiny Delaware Boasts Highest Per-Capita Execution Rate in U.S." *Houston Chronicle*, December 25.

Beck, Allen J. and Christopher J. Mumola. 1999. *Prisoners in 1998*. Washington, DC: Bureau of Justice Statistics.

Beckett, Katherine and Theodore Sasson. 2000. *The Politics of Injustice: Crime and Punishment in America*. Thousand Oaks, CA: Pine Forge Press.

Berrien, Jenny and Christopher Winship. 2003. "Should We Have Faith in the Churches?: The Ten-Point Coalition's Effect on Boston's Youth Violence." In *Guns, Crime, and Punishment in America*, ed. Bernard E. Harcourt, pp. 222–248. New York: New York University Press.

Bessler, John D. 1997. *Death in the Dark: Midnight Executions in America*. Boston: Northeastern University Press.

Blomberg, Thomas G. and Karen Lucken. 2000. *American Penology: A History of Control*. New York: Aldine de Gruyter.

Blumstein, Alfred and Joel Wallman, eds. 2000. *The Crime Drop in America*. Cambridge: Cambridge University Press.

Bobit, Bonnie. 1999. *Death Row: Meet the Men and Women of Death Row*. 9th ed. Torrance, CA: Bobit Publishing.

Bodenhamer, David. 1992. *Fair Trial*. New York: Oxford University Press.

Bragg, Rick. 1995. "Chain Gangs to Return to Roads of Alabama." *New York Times*, March 26.

Bratton, William J. and Peter Knobler. 1998. *Turnaround: How America's Top Cop Reversed the Crime Epidemic*. New York: Random House.

Burke, Tod W. 1999. "Brain 'Fingerprinting'." *Law and Order*, June, pp. 28–31.

Butterfield, Fox. 1994. "Homicide Data Defy a Basic Crime Tenet." *Houston Chronicle*, October 23.

———. 1997. "Plunge in Rate of Property Crimes Catches Cities' Officials by Surprise." *New York Times*, October 12.

———. 1998. "Drop in Crack Use, Crackdown on Guns May Be behind Plunge in Violent Crime." *Houston Chronicle*, December 28.

Caputo, Gail A. 2004. *Intermediate Sanctions in Corrections*. Denton: University of North Texas Press.

Christianson, Scott. 1998. *With Liberty for Some*. Boston: Northeastern University Press.

———. 2010. *The Last Gasp: The Rise and Fall of the American Gas Chamber*. Berkeley, CA: University of California Press.

Cole, David. 1999. *No Justice: Race and Class in the American Criminal Justice System*. New York: New Press.

Cole, Simon A. 2001a. "The Myth of Fingerprints." *New York Times Magazine*, May 13, pp. 13–14.

———. 2001b. *Suspect Identities: A History of Fingerprinting and Criminal Identification*. Cambridge, MA: Harvard University Press.

Conley, John A. 1994. *The 1967 President's Crime Commission Report: Its Impact 25 Years Later*. Cincinnati: Anderson Publishing.

"Corrections Population Tops Record." 2001. *Houston Chronicle*, August 27.

Currie, Elliott. 1998. *Crime and Punishment in America*. New York: Metropolitan Books.

Daly Kathleen and Russ Immarigeon. 1998. "The Past, Present, and Future of Restorative Justice." *Contemporary Justice Review*, 1(1):21–45.

Delgado, Richard. 2000. "Goodbye to Hammurabi: Analyzing the Atavistic Appeal of Restorative Justice." *Stanford Law Review*, 52(4):751–775.

Dershowitz, Alan M. 1997. *Reasonable Doubts: The Criminal Justice System and the O. J. Simpson Case*. New York: Simon and Schuster.

Donn, Jeff. 2001. "Plunging U.S. Handgun Market Unlikely to Recover, Experts Say." *Houston Chronicle*, April 14.

Eck, John E. and Edward R. Maguire. 2000. "Have Changes in Policing Reduced Violent Crime? An Assessment of the Evidence." In *The Crime Drop in America*, ed. Alfred Blumstein and Joel Wallman. Cambridge: Cambridge University Press.

Eglash, Albert. 1977. "Beyond Restitution: Creative Restitution." In *Restitution in Criminal Justice*, ed. J. Hudson and B. Galaway. Lexington, MA: DC Heath and Company.

Eldredge, Dirk Chase. 1998. *Ending the War on Drugs: A Solution for America*. Bridgehampton, NY: Bridge Works Publishing.

Elsner, Alan. 2004. *Gates of Injustice: The Crisis of America's Prisons*. Upper Saddle River, NJ: Prentice Hall.

Friedman, Lawrence M. 2002. *American Law in the 20th Century*. New Haven, CT: Yale University Press.

Garrison, Jessica. 2001. "Some Public Schools Drop Zero Tolerance." *Houston Chronicle*, February 25.

Gavrielides, Theo. 2008. "Restorative Justice: The Perplexing Concept: Conceptual Fault-Lines and Power Battles within the Restorative Justice Movement." *Criminology & Criminal Justice*, 8(2):165–183.

Geis, Gilbert and Leigh B. Bienen. 1998. *Crimes of the Century: From Leopold and Loeb to O. J. Simpson*. Boston: Northeastern University Press.

Gilje, Paul A. 1996. *Rioting in America*. Bloomington, IN: Indiana University Press.

Grudowski, Mike. 1995. "Not-So-Lethal-Weapons." *New York Times Magazine*, August 13, pp. 40–41.

Gumz, Edward J. 2004. "American Social Work, Corrections and Restorative Justice: An Appraisal." *International Journal of Offender Therapy and Comparative Criminology*, 49(4):449–460.

Hallinan, Joseph T. 2001. *Going Up the River: Travels in a Prison Nation*. New York: Random House.

Hamm, Mark. 1999. "Ruby Ridge." In *Violence in America*, vol. 3, ed. Ronald Gottesman, pp. 69–71. New York: Scribner.

Harcourt, Bernard E. 2001. *Illusion of Order: The False Promise of Broken Windows Policing*. Cambridge, MA: Harvard University Press.

Hays, Kristen. 1997. "New York Celebrating Murder Toll for 1996." *Houston Chronicle*, January 1.

Hixson, Walter L. 2001. *Murder, Culture, and Injustice: Four Sensational Cases in American History*. Akron, OH: University of Akron Press.

Howard, Marc Morje. 2017. *Unusually Cruel: Prisons, Punishment, and the Real American Exceptionalism*. New York: Oxford University Press.

Jacobs, James B. Coleen Friel, and Robert Radick. 1999. *Gotham Unbound: How New York City Was Liberated from the Grip of Organized Crime*. New York: New York University Press.

Jacobs, James B., Christopher Panarella, and Jay Worthington. 1994. *Busting the Mob: United States v. Costa Nostra*. New York: New York University Press.

Jones, Richard P. 1997. "Stun Belts for Prisoners Controversial." *Houston Chronicle*, June 15.

Jonnes, Jill. 1996. *Hep-Cats, Narcs, and Pipe Dreams: A History of America's Romance with Illegal Drugs*. New York: Scribner.

Karmen, Andrew. 2000. *New York Murder Mystery: The True Story behind the Crime Crash of the 1990s*. New York: New York University Press.

Kelling, George and Catherine M. Coles. 1996. *Fixing Broken Windows: Restoring Order and Reducing Crime in Our Communities*. New York: Free Press.

Kleinknecht, William. 1996. *The New Ethnic Mobs: The Changing Face of Organized Crime in America*. New York: Free Press.

Knight, Alfred H. 1996. *The Life of the Law: The People and Cases That Have Shaped Our Society from King Alfred to Rodney King*. New York: Crown Publishers.

Krauss, Clifford. 1995. "Shootings Plummet in New York as Police Frisking Drives Illegal Guns off the Streets." *New York Times*, July 30.

Lane, Roger. 1997. *Murder in America: A History*. Columbus: Ohio State University Press.

Leonhardt, David. 2000. "As Prison Labor Grows, So Does the Debate." *New York Times*, March 19.

Levy, Harlan. 1996. *And the Blood Cried Out: A Prosecutor's Account of the Power of DNA*. New York: Basic Books.

Lifton, Robert J. and Greg Mitchell. 2000. *Who Owns Death?: Capital Punishment, the American Conscience, and the End of Executions*. New York: Harper Collins.

Males, Mike. 2001. "Real Story behind School Shootings Going Untold." *Houston Chronicle*, March 13. www.houstonchronicle.com.

Maple, Jack and Chris Mitchell. 1999. *The Crime Fighter: Putting the Bad Guys Out of Business*. New York: Doubleday.

Marion, Nancy E. 1994. *A History of Federal Crime Control Initiatives, 1960–1993*. Westport, CT: Praeger.

Martin, Gus. 2010. *Understanding Terrorism: Challenges, Perspectives, and Issues*. 3rd ed. Los Angeles: Sage Publications.

Martin, Keith. 2002. "Utilizing Identification Technology in Corrections." *Corrections Connection News Center*, March 19. database.corrections.co,/news/results2.asp?ID=1944.

McArdle, Andrea and Tanya Erzen, eds. 2001. *Zero Tolerance: Quality of Life and the New Police Brutality in New York City*. New York: New York University Press.

Mears, Daniel P., Caterina G. Roman, Ashley Wolff, and Janeen Buck. 2006. "Faith-Based Efforts to Improve Prisoner Re-Entry: Assessing the Logic and Evidence." *Journal of Criminal Justice*, 34:351–367.

Miller, D. W. 2001. "Poking Holes in the Theory of 'Broken Windows'." *Chronicle of Higher Education*, February 9, pp. A14–A16.

Miller, Jerome G. 1996. *Search and Destroy: African-American Males in the Criminal Justice System*. Cambridge: Cambridge University Press.

Monkkonen, Eric H. 2001. *Murder in New York City*. Berkeley, CA: University of California Press.

Murphy, Dean E. 2001. "Justice as a Morality Play That Ends with Shame." *New York Times*, June 3.

National Shooting Sports Foundation. 2009. "FBI Firearm Background Checks Hit 100 Million Mark." April 9. www.opposingviews.com/articles/news-fbi-firearm-bakground-checks-hits-100-m.

Novak, Robert D. 2002. "But FBI Intelligence Also Let Us Down." *Houston Chronicle*, May 21.

Olasky, Marvin. 2000. *Compassionate Conservatism: What It Is, What It Does, and How It Can Transform America*. New York: Free Press.

"On Indian Reservations in the West, Violent Crime Soars." 1998. *New York Times*, August 16.

Parenti, Christian. 2001. *Lockdown America: Police and Prisons in the Age of Crisis*. London: Verso.

Pierce, Neal. 2000. "Civil Death of Felons Is a New Civil Rights Issue." *Houston Chronicle*, December 24.

Pogash, Carol. 2003. "Myth of the 'Twinkie Defense': The Verdict in the Dan White Case Wasn't Based on His Ingestion of Junk Food." *San Francisco Chronicle*, November 23, p. D1.

Reinert, Patty. 2001a. "Supreme Court Weighs Drug Law." *Houston Chronicle*, March 25.

———. 2001b. "Court to Revisit Execution of Retarded." *Houston Chronicle*, March 27.

Remnick, David. 1997. "The Crime Buster." *The New Yorker*, February 24 and March 3, pp. 94–109.

Roberts, Julian and Loretta J. Stalans. 1997. *Public Opinion, Crime, and Criminal Justice*. Boulder, CO: Westview Press.

Sarat, Austin. 2001. *When the State Kills: Capital Punishment and the American Condition*. Princeton, NJ: Princeton University Press.

Schulz, Dorothy Moses. 1995. *From Social Worker to Crimefighter: Women in United States Municipal Policing*. Westport, CT: Praeger.

Schwartz, Bernard. 1997. *A Book of Legal Lists*. New York: Oxford University Press.

Silverman, Eli B. 1999. *NYPD Battles Crime: Innovative Strategies in Policing*. Boston: Northeastern University Press.

Sourcebook of Criminal Justice Statistics, 1973. 1974. Washington, DC: U.S. Government Printing Office.

Spelman, William. 2009. "Crime, Cash, and Limited Options: Explaining the Prison Boom." *Criminology and Public Policy*, 8(1):29–77.

Stern, Seth. 2002. "A Harder Day in Court for Fingerprint, Writing Experts." January 31. http://csmonitor.com.

Sullivan, Larry E. 1990. *The Prison Reform Movement*. Boston: Twayne Publishers.

Taylor, Ralph. 2001. *Breaking Away from Broken Windows*. Boulder, CO: Westview Press.

"Trial Will Revisit '63 Bombing." 2001. *Houston Chronicle*, April 16.

Umbreit, Mark S. and Jean Greenwood. 1999. "National Survey of Victim-Offender Mediation Programs in the United States." *Mediation Quarterly*, 16(3), Spring:235–251.

Van Wormer, Katherine. 2003. "Restorative Justice: A Model for Social Work Practice with Families." *Families in Society: The Journal of Contemporary Human Services*, 84(3):441–448.

Vila, Bryan and Cynthia Morris. 1997. *Capital Punishment in the United States: A Documentary History*. Westport, CT: Greenwood Press.

Walker, Samuel. 1984. "Broken Windows and Fractured History: The Use and Misuse of History in Recent Police Patrol Analysis." *Justice Quarterly*, 1(March):77–90.

———. 1992. *The Police in America: An Introduction*. New York: McGraw-Hill.

Wallman, Joel and Alfred Blumstein. 2006. "After the Crime Drop." In *The Crime Drop in America*. Revised ed., ed. Alfred Blumstein and Joel Wallman, pp. 319–347. New York: Cambridge University Press.

Williams, Willie L. and Bruce B. Henderson. 1996. *Taking Back our Streets: Fighting Crime in America*. New York: Scribner.

Wills, Garry. 2006. "A Country Ruled by Faith." *The New York Review of Books*, November 16., pp. 8–12.

Wright, Richard and Scott Decker. 1997. *Armed Robbers in Action: Stickups and Street Culture*. Boston: Northeastern University Press.

2001	2001	2001	2001	2001	2001
Supreme Court considers execution of the developmentally disabled	Mississippi votes to retain Confederate symbol on state flag	Suspects go on trial for 1963 Birmingham bombing that left four young girls dead	*Shafer v. South Carolina*	Arrest of suspected antiabortion sniper James Charles Kopp in France	Delegates from twenty-six countries celebrate centennial of Scotland Yard's fingerprint bureau

TIMELINE

CHAPTER FOURTEEN

Crime and criminal justice in the age of terrorism (2000 – 2010)

Learning objectives

After reading this chapter students should understand and be able to discuss:

- The reorganization of federal criminal justice after the 9/11 attacks
- The recent decline in death sentences and the growing disenchantment with capital punishment in America
- The impact of 9/11 on American civil liberties and the criminal justice system
- The increase in automatic weapons on the street and a surge in police officers killed in the line of duty by these weapons
- The reordering of the FBI's priorities since the so-called war on terrorism began
- Court challenges to lethal injection as a cruel and unusual punishment
- The prominence of white-collar crime in the new century
- Reasons why compassionate release programs are gaining more support
- The surprising continuity between the Bush and Obama presidencies in regards to the war on terror
- The debate over the legality of medical marijuana
- Why high profile crimes such as 9/11 often lead to the passage of "bad laws"

On 9/11, 2001, the United States and the world changed. No part of America's social, economic, and legal fabric faced more challenges than its criminal justice system. On 9/11, 2001, a concerted attack on America by 19 Arab airplane hijackers on 4 planes left almost 3,000 dead.[1] It was the second-bloodiest day in American history (next to the Civil War battle of Antietam

DOI: 10.4324/9781315148342-14

2001	2001	2001	2001	2001	2001
Timothy McVeigh executed for bombing of Alfred P. Murrah Federal Building in Oklahoma City	President Bush establishes White House Office of Faith-Based and Community Initiatives	FBI director Louis Freeh steps down in June	9/11 terrorist attacks on America leave almost 3,000 dead	FBI puts counterterrorism at top of Most Wanted List	New York City settles $8.75 million suit with police torture victim Abner Louima

in 1862). In the aftermath of the attacks, the criminal justice system faced reorganization and challenges unparalleled in its 200-plus-year history. Then Attorney General **John Ashcroft** said that he expected the Justice Department and federal law enforcement to undergo a "wartime reorganization" to prevent future terrorist attacks. Ashcroft recommended shifting many law enforcement responsibilities from the FBI to state and local authorities. In effect, local law enforcement was expected to be ready to act as first responders to future terrorist attacks, while the FBI was expected to make the dramatic and historic conversion from apprehending bank robbers and drug dealers to placing more emphasis on anti-terrorism efforts.

The impact of 9/11 on the American criminal justice system

9/11 demonstrated some of the shortcomings of the nation's crime prevention and security systems, leading many Americans to question the abilities of the government to protect them at any level. But research has suggested that much of the public's fear over the past decade is a response to the saturation of hysterical media reporting and the manipulation of public fear. A virtual panic has ensued over domestic terrorist threats much in the way the fears of child molesters, juvenile predators, and serial killers were blown out of proportion in the 1980s and 1990s.[2]

The most drastic anti-terrorism measures were implemented at the federal level. Among the most controversial was the most aggressive national campaign of ethnic profiling since the 1940s, resulting in the detention of hundreds of mostly Middle Eastern men. Very few were convicted of any crime at all. Other contentious measures adopted or considered to fight terrorism included convening military tribunals to try foreign suspects, expanded wiretapping, and the monitoring of conversations between lawyers and detainees. Despite the controversy over the new tactics, initially the majority of Americans in a survey conducted by the *National Law Journal* in October 2001 favored the increased wiretap and surveillance powers and pointed to a general pro–law enforcement shift among potential jurors in criminal matters. This was a dramatic shift in opinion from earlier polls that reflected an antipolice bias after highly charged police brutality cases in New York City and corruption cases in Los Angeles. More than half the respondents also indicated that racial profiling was acceptable under certain circumstances. Nonetheless, the polls indicated that the public was rather inconsistent on its opinions in criminal justice matters, as 9/11 caused many to reverse course in their thinking about racial profiling, the death penalty, and civil liberties protections.

Although polls suggested that Americans initially supported these measures, civil liberties groups and some lawmakers complained that the new tactics undermined a number

2001	2001	2001	2001	2001	2002
Enron Corporation files for Chapter 11 bankruptcy protection	President Bush signs USA PATRIOT Act into law	Department of Homeland Security created	Anthrax attacks kill five	Andrea Yates drowns her five children places the insanity defense on trial	Snipers John Lee Malvo and John Allen Muhammed terrorize I-95 corridor killing ten and wounding six between September 2 and Oct 20

of civil rights principles, comparing the roundup of terrorist suspects under the aegis of Attorney General John Ashcroft to the Justice Department's Palmer raids against communist subversives in 1919. What's more, these tactics only contributed to a growing prejudice against foreign-born Americans, immigrants, and visitors, especially those with Muslim, Arabic, or Middle Eastern heritage. It should not be surprising that hate crimes against these groups rose during the first decade of the twenty-first century.

Some researchers suggested that current counterterrorism efforts were "similar ideologically" to the crime-oriented model of justice, which were heavily focused on deterrence and reliance on speedy and efficient court proceedings. What's more, those arrested were presumed *guilty*, compared to the traditional due process model that presumed *innocence*. In the crime control model, interrogation rather than courtroom procedures produce efficient crime control. In other words, "In the war on terror the relationship between due process and crime control is sharply tilted in the direction of crime control."[3]

In many aspects of crime control, the legislation produced during President George W. Bush's first term did not differ noticeable from that of his predecessor President Bill Clinton. Although the **USA PATRIOT Act** has come under attack for its violations of due process, it was "not as far-reaching in the invasion of citizen privacy as was the **1996 Antiterrorism Act** signed into law by Clinton." Both presidents in fact have been accused at one time or another of expanding the role of government in counterterrorism in ways consistent with the conservative crime model.[4]

During the Bush Administration, "**enhanced interrogation** techniques," better known as torture, were approved by the Justice Department, a clear sign that times had changed because of 9/11. Lawyers for the president reportedly provided legal justifications for the torture of suspected terrorists. The Bush approach to national security led to a number of controversial policies that were adopted in secret including the disappearances of detainees into secret CIA prisons, use of torture to gather evidence, rendition of suspects to countries known to torture and the warrantless wiretapping of Americans.

The following are some major provisions from the 1996 Anti-terrorism Act inaugurated during the Clinton administration:

- A federal death penalty for deaths resulting from acts of terrorism
- Secretary of state authorized to designate private groups as terrorist organizations, to prohibit them from fund-raising in the U.S., and to freeze their assets

2002	2002	2002	2003	2004
100th prisoner freed because of DNA testing	More than $1 billion authorized to fight bioterrorism	Justice Department challenges reliability of fingerprint evidence	Illinois Governor George Ryan commutes sentences of 167 death row inmates, in part due to coerced confessions	The Intelligence Reform and Terrorism Prevention Act creates the National Counterterrorism Center

- Penalties up to ten years in prison provided for anyone supplying "material support or resources" to a foreign terrorist group
- The ability to prosecute crimes against federal employees while on duty as federal rather than state offenses
- Stronger procedural controls on asylum, deportation, and entry into the U.S.
- Private citizens who were victims of terrorism could sue for damages against state sponsors

Once terrorists were arrested, the next important decision was where to keep them. But, when it came to putting them on trial there were few acceptable choices. The Obama administration made plans in 2009 to try 9/11 mastermind Khalid Sheik Mohammed and four other suspects in New York City, not far from where the attacks took place. New Yorkers initially looked forward to hosting the trial as a symbolic show of the city's resilience and to showcase "the strength of the nation's criminal justice system."[5] Many survivors wanted to hold the trial in a civilian court rather than in a military tribunal. Families looked forward to attending. However, once the specter of Manhattan in virtual lockdown dawned on most New Yorkers, support dwindled. Especially when the Police Commissioner **Raymond W. Kelly** and Mayor Michael Bloomberg described plans to set up road blocks and checkpoints throughout the financial district at a cost of more than $200 million annually in order to address security concerns. Just seventy-seven days later, the Obama administration reversed its decision citing the dangers and challenges implicit in holding the trial in New York City.

The early and quick passage of the USA PATRIOT Act had a tremendous impact on American life, increasing government secrecy on a number of levels. Many critics saw the Department of Homeland Security tactic of using color codes to indicate the level of probability of terrorist attack as a government strategy to ramp up fear among the population in order to grant increased power to the FBI or as a way of ameliorating protests against civil liberty transgressions. However, the Bush strategy against terrorism developed over a period of years. Under pressure from Supreme Court rulings, Congressional legislation, and disclosures in the news media, Bush in his second term trimmed back some of his most expansive programs and claims to executive power, and by the time Obama took office in 2010, waterboarding had been halted for years, secret **black site prisons** purportedly emptied, and the warrantless surveillance program and military commission system had been restructured and approved by Congress. What was most unforeseen after all the campaign rhetoric directed against the current administration was that President Obama would leave the surveillance program intact, embrace the Patriot Act, retain the authority to use

TIMELINE	2004	2004	2005	2005	2005	2006
	Abu Ghraib Prison scandal breaks	Massachusetts legalizes gay marriage	Alberto Gonzalez replaces John Ashcroft as attorney general in February	John Roberts becomes Supreme Court's new chief justice	*Roper v. Simmons* Supreme Court decision rules that executing minors was "cruel and unusual" punishment	President Bush signs the USA PATRIOT Improvement and Reauthorization Act of 2005

rendition, and embrace some of Bush's claims to state secrets. He even preserved the military commissions and the national security letters he criticized during his campaign (albeit with more due process safeguards).[6]

The lawgivers

The U.S. Supreme Court saw 2009 finish with 76,655 criminal case filings, the largest number since 1932 (92,174 cases), the year before the end of Prohibition, and a time when most of the cases were federal alcohol-related offenses. Several patterns emerged. For example, the number of drug cases fell for all drugs except marijuana as did gun-related cases. However, the largest increase was in immigrant crimes (+19 percent), mostly related to illegal reentry by immigrants or the abuse of visas and entry permits. The Supreme Court also reported a drop in appeals from 8,241 to 7,738. By most accounts this is related to the huge odds against having a case heard, which typically amounts to about a 1-in-100 chance of making it.

The terrorist attacks of 9/11 had a tremendous impact on America's criminal justice system. Taking a page from the historical record (such as martial law and the suspension of habeas corpus during the Civil War and the internment of Japanese Americans during World War II), following 9/11, many civil liberties long taken for granted took "a back seat to safety." Some scholars suggested that American civil liberties had already "grown to an extent that the Founding Fathers probably never imagined."[7] Historian Eric Foner argued that the acceptance of civil liberties as being "very ingrained in our culture" was a fairly recent phenomenon. Foner asserted that "for most of our history, the Bill of Rights was pretty irrelevant," citing examples of violations during the Red Scare of the 1920s and the detention of Japanese Americans during World War II.[8]

An examination of the development of civil liberties in America suggests that rather than being "fixed and immutable," civil liberties have often "expanded and contracted" throughout American history, particularly during periods of social upheaval and war. In the months following 9/11, the federal government gave law enforcement permission to tap telephones and read electronic mail and created an environment that endorsed self-censorship of free speech. On October 26, 2001, President George W. Bush signed the USA PATRIOT Act into law, which expanded the government's power to monitor private conversations and e-mail and allowed police to obtain search warrants and enter a citizen's home without their knowledge. The new law also made it easier to deport noncitizens suspected of being security threats. Foreigners, in most cases of Middle Eastern background, were targeted

2007	2007	2007	2007	2008	2008
New Jersey bans executions	Moratorium begins on lethal injection executions	Deadliest shooting rampage in U.S. history ends when gunman Seung-Hui Cho commits suicide after killing thirty-two on Virginia Tech campus	Federal District Court in Nashville finds Tennessee's lethal injection procedure unconstitutional	President Bush signs the Second Chance Act of 2007	Supreme Court decision *Baze v. Rees* ends moratorium on lethal injection executions

by investigators and suspicious citizens, following an era in which noncitizens had been enjoying their greatest freedom in American history thanks to a number of Supreme Court decisions.

President Barack Obama led the way in building a more diverse federal bench. Besides appointing Sonia Sotomayor as the first Latina woman on the U.S. Supreme Court, he also nominated sixteen judges to lifetime seats (only six were white men). Although Obama is behind his predecessor in the pace of selection, only sixteen to Bush's forty-eight at the same time in his presidency, Bush's appointments were 78 percent men and 82 percent white. In 2010, the United States employed 1,700 full-time federal judges, "a caste of elite jurists handpicked for the difficult and sometimes dangerous job of enforcing our nation's laws and protecting our rights."[9]

USA PATRIOT Act (2001)

On October 26, 2001, President George W. Bush signed into law the Uniting and Strengthening America by Providing Appropriate Tools Required to Intercept and Obstruct Terrorism Act, better known by its acronym USA PATRIOT Act. Many of its critics charged it was rushed into law too quickly by a nervous Congress in the aftermath of 9/11. The USA PATRIOT Act revised the standards for government surveillance, including federal access to private records. It enhanced electronic surveillance authority, such as tapping into e-mail, electronic address books, and computers, and permitted the use of **roving wiretaps** that allowed the surveillance of individual telephone conversations on any telephone anywhere in America. It also required banks to become more transparent, identifying sources of money deposited in some private accounts while requiring foreign banks to report suspicious transactions. Any immigrants who were associated with raising money for terrorist organizations faced deportation. One of its most controversial passages permitted detaining immigrants without charges for up to one week on suspicion of supplying terrorists.

The Patriot Act established several new laws that were equally applicable to the campaign against organized crime, such as anti-money laundering laws and granting extensive powers to the U.S. attorney general. These rules have been highly controversial, especially when it came to detaining foreign citizens and other non-residents, as well as for simplifying wiretaps and other surveillance measures. Other criticisms targeted the detention of terrorist suspects indefinitely without filing formal charges, roving warrants (Section 206) that allowed law enforcement to potentially gain access to electronic surveillance of innocent citizens, and "sneak and peak" warrants (Section 2130), that permitted law enforcement

	2008	2009	2009	2009
TIMELINE	Barack Obama elected America's first African American president	Ohio becomes first state to switch from three-drug cocktail to a single-drug one	Sonia Sotomayor becomes first Hispanic woman nominated to the Supreme Court	Supreme Court overturns Washington, D. C. handgun ban

to secretly search a private residence; if showing good cause, they could deliberately delay notifying the property owner of the warrant.

Supporters of the legislation on the other hand claimed critics overreacted to its "Orwellian name (as in George Orwell's *1984*)." Others would argue it had not really created any great revolution in government powers and merely contained "a series of evolutionary changes in law enforcement that improve upon, and expand, existing powers already exercised by the government."[10] Still there were those from the Justice Department that asserted, delayed notification search warrants were a "long-existing crime fighting tool upheld by courts nationwide for decades in organized crime, drug cases, and child pornography."[11] At its inception, the Patriot Act enjoyed widespread support. But over the years, it has lost much of its luster as various constituencies' targeted controversial provisions. In fact, as soon as it went into effect, critics began comparing it to the controversial RICO statute. One critic castigated it as a "knee-jerk reaction to a seemingly insurmountable problem" while another suggested it modified existing laws to expand the powers of the federal government in areas such as surveillance and information gathering, making the United States "a nation of potential suspects."[12]

From a purely criminal justice perspective, its passage eliminated some of the barriers that formerly prevented law enforcement agencies from collaborating, created new money laundering crimes, while increasing penalties for existing money laundering violations. Although the act was intended to confront the challenges of terrorism, law enforcement found it also was applicable to other crimes, such as money laundering, political corruption, and **cybercrime**.

The debate over the provisions of the Patriot Act crossed the ideological divide. In order to address some of the concerns of lawmakers when it was constructed, the Patriot Act included a "sunset provision," mandating that its major provisions will automatically expire unless periodically extended. When it was renewed in 2006, it incorporated compromise provisions that included restrictions on federal agents' access to library records. In March 2007, FBI Director **Robert Mueller** admitted that "his agency had improperly, and sometimes illegally, used the USA PATRIOT Act to obtain information about people and businesses."[13]

Patriot Act Reauthorization (2005)

Nearly four years after the 9/11 attacks and the subsequent passage of the USA PATRIOT Act, then president George W. Bush signed the USA PATRIOT Act Improvement and Reauthorization Act of 2005. This legislation allowed law enforcement and intelligence officials to continue sharing information and using the same tools used against drug dealers

2009	2009	2010
Federal appeals court overturns court decision that made Tennessee's execution protocol unconstitutional	Ohio becomes first state to switch to single-drug from three-drug cocktail in lethal injection procedure	New Jersey becomes 14th state to legalize medical marijuana

and other criminals against terrorists, while giving them the necessary tools required for the task. The Bush administration claimed the reauthorization was intended "to safeguard civil liberties while strengthening the U.S. Department of Justice so it can better detect and disrupt terrorist threats." The Patriot Act Reauthorization created the new assistant attorney general for national security, allowing the Department of Justice to bring national security, counterterrorism, counterintelligence, and foreign intelligence surveillance operations under the mantle of a single authority. What's more, the bill enhanced penalties for terrorism financing and closed a loophole concerning terrorist financing through "**hawalas**" (informal money transfer systems) rather than traditional financial institutions.[14]

The reauthorization bill also included the Combat Methamphetamine Act of 2005, which introduced safeguards that would make it more difficult to obtain precursor chemicals for methamphetamine manufacturing by placing limits on large-scale purchases of over-the-counter drugs used in the manufacture of meth. It also increased penalties for trafficking in methamphetamine and required stores to keep these ingredients behind the counter or in locked display cases.

USA PATRIOT Act Sunset Extension Act of 2009

In October 2009, despite expectations to the contrary, President Obama and his Attorney General **Eric Holder** expressed support for the congressional reauthorization of three controversial provisions scheduled to "sunset" at the end of 2009. Both the House and the Senate Judiciary Committees agreed on separate bills that would address the expiring provisions and make other amendments to national security laws. On December 19, 2009, all three provisions were "temporarily" extended until February 28, 2010, citing concerns about the "legislation's potential detrimental effects to national security."[15] The controversial provisions included the **"National Security Letter" (NSL) provision**, which lowers the evidentiary requirements for NSLs, allowing the FBI to require Internet service providers, banks, and credit card reporting companies to turn over sensitive information about their customers and patrons. Most troubling to its critics was the so-called "blanket gag order" that prohibited recipients of NSLs from discussing FBI record demands. Most challenges to this provision have been based on violations of the First and Fourteenth Amendments. Another provision set to expire permitted the government to use roving wiretaps to monitor phone lines or Internet accounts that a terrorist suspect might be using, "whether or not others who are not suspects also regularly use them." Once authorities get a "roving wiretaps" court orders (basically wiretaps on people *not* phones), they were authorized to follow a target who switched phone numbers or phone companies, rather than having to apply for a new warrant each time. By 2009, the FBI had used it 140 times. Another provision, referred to as the **lone wolf provision**, allowed the FBI to get a court order to wiretap a terrorism suspect who was not connected to any foreign terrorist group or government. However, it only applied to non-U.S. persons and as of the end of 2009 had not even been used yet. Finally, the "Material Support Statute" was targeted for criminalizing the "providing of support" to terrorists. This is defined as "any tangible or intangible good," service or advice to a terrorist or designated group. Tangible things can include business and customer records, diaries, and computers. It criminalizes a wide variety of activities, whether or not they actually of intentionally further terrorist goals or organizations. FBI used this authority more than 250 times between 2004–2009.[16]

Extraordinary rendition

One of the most controversial tactics used by the federal government against terrorists was the use of "extraordinary rendition" better known as just "rendition." Rendition is a rather simple process that entails apprehending suspects in any part of the world and then transporting them back to the United States where they will be forced to appear before state or federal court.[17] Although its inception was typically credited back to the late 1980s of the Reagan administration (others suggest the Clinton White House began it in 1995) when it was authorized as a method for capturing drug traffickers, terrorists, and others, its roots date back more than a century.

Sometimes referred to as the **Ker-Frisbie Doctrine**, modern rendition is based on two U.S. Supreme Court decisions in 1886 and 1952. In 1886, a federal agent forcibly kidnapped Frederick Ker from Lima, Peru, and transported him back to Cook County, Illinois, to stand trial for larceny and embezzlement. His subsequent challenge based on the due process clause of the Fourteenth Amendment led the U.S. Supreme Court decision to rule in *Ker v. Illinois* (119 U.S. 436) that American courts were not interested in the manner in which a defendant comes to stand before them, and he was duly convicted and sentenced under proper procedures. This was followed in 1952 by the *Frisbie v. Collins* Supreme Court ruling (342 U.S. 519), in which the defendant Shirley Collins was abducted in Chicago and brought to Michigan to stand trial for murder. Following his conviction, he appealed his sentence citing the federal Kidnapping Act and argued he should be freed due to the manner he was "forcibly seized, handcuffed, blackjacked" and taken to Michigan.[18] The doctrine once more was a target of a U.S. Supreme Court case in 1992, after a Mexican doctor and citizen named Alvarez Machain, indicted for participating in the kidnapping and murder of DEA agent Enrique Camarena (*U.S. v. Machain*, 504 U.S. 655) was abducted from Mexico and brought to the United States in a covert DEA operation. During the high court proceedings, the Supreme Court rejected the argument that this type of abduction undermined the purpose of extradition treaties and upheld the notion that U.S. courts have jurisdiction over a criminal defendant regardless how the defendant is brought to court.

There were a number of observers who would suggest that what was once a tool that served its purpose "in a more carefully monitored form" was transformed under the Bush administration into "an abomination."[19] Rendition has received its harshest criticism for its affiliation with black sites (secret detention centers), operated by the CIA outside U.S. territory and jurisdiction, and where many allegations of abuse and mistaken identities and abductions of "alleged unlawful enemy combatants" took place. President Bush first acknowledged the existence of black sites in the autumn of 2006. They were closed by Obama in January 2009. However, as late as June 2009, President Obama still supported rendition. Around that time, there were several legal challenges to the CIA interrogation program working their way through the court system. One of the chief barriers to any litigation surrounding this process has been the official stance that the existence of rendition is a state secret; therefore, a victim cannot sue the government or ask for an apology. More recently, a judge in California rejected claims of "blanket state secrecy" by the Justice Department in the cases of five rendition victims.[20]

Military tribunals

In November 2001, President George W. Bush issued an executive order authorizing the creation of military tribunals to try noncitizens on charges of terrorism. While many supporters of the new security proposals claimed that "extraordinary times call for extraordinary measures," civil libertarians expressed outrage at some of the post-9/11 measures, particularly plans to permit suspected foreign terrorists to be tried by military tribunals. Military tribunals have rarely been used outside military circles and are regarded as rather sinister by liberals and civil libertarians.

Recalling the sessions of the Star Chamber that began in fifteenth-century Tudor England, military tribunals are held in secret and afford defendants less rights than regular courts do. In these trials, a panel of military judges has the latitude to decide guilt or innocence without a unanimous vote and can even impose the death penalty. Once defendants are sentenced, they have little recourse, being barred from appealing to a higher court. A verdict of a military tribunal can be overturned only by the president or the secretary of defense.

The United States has used military tribunals as far back as the Mexican–American War (1846–1848) and the Civil War (1861–1865), when by some accounts almost 4,000 military tribunals might have been carried out.[21] Most prominently was the one used to try the Lincoln assassins in 1865 (see Chapter 7). The United States has not tried foreigners accused of violating the rules of law in a military tribunal since Nazi saboteurs were tried, convicted, and executed during World War II. However, this process was allowed to go forward only because Congress had declared war against Germany already. Only Congress can declare war. After 9/11, President Bush did not ask Congress to declare war. However, Congress enacted an Authorization for the Use of Military Force. The administration treated this as if it gave it the same *carte blanche* that a declaration of war would have given them – to treat the hunt for terrorists as the "war on terror." Among the powers that come with an actual declaration of war is the ability to use military tribunals to try those who violated the rules of war. In 2003, the Second Circuit Court of Appeals rejected the president's claim that he had constitutional authority as commander in chief to decide who is an enemy of the U.S. Following the appeals process the U.S. Supreme Court ruled in June 2004 that the president did not have the power to order individuals locked up for an indefinite period those considered enemy combatants. In ***Hamdi v. Rumsfeld***, the Court "reaffirmed the principle of habeas corpus" noting "the practice of arbitrary imprisonment . . . in all ages is one of the favorite and most formidable instruments of tyranny."[22] What this meant was that non-U.S. citizens detained at **Guantanamo Bay** could now contest their captivity in U.S. courts (but did not apply to foreign detainees held elsewhere). Furthermore, anyone in U.S. custody, whether they were citizens or foreigners, had the right to challenge the basis for their incarceration. In the end, the U.S. Constitution protects all prisoners from military courts when there is no declaration of war. It has thus been established that all of those detained on terrorism charges since 9/11 have the right to be tried in federal courts.

Torture and the law

Brutal forms of interrogation are nothing new to the criminal justice system. Criminal justice officials have used torture for interrogations for centuries. One needs look no further than the medieval inquisition in Spain and America's own Salem witch trials. In the modern era, the Wickersham Commission reported in 1931 that it found a pattern of brutality across the U.S. and that police all over country used torture (twenty-nine major cities). In 1944's *Ashcraft v. Tennessee*, the Supreme Court struck down confessions secured by relay interrogations under bright lights. Ashcraft had been interrogated continuously for thirty-six hours until he admitted killing his wife.[23]

After 9/11, "the White House made torture its secret weapon in the war on terror."[24] Authorized in the wake of 9/11, evidence suggest that torture and degrading punishments were first documented at Guantanamo Bay, Cuba, then Afghanistan, and finally in Iraq with the most notorious and best documented cases of abuse.[25] The public supported "enhanced interrogation" until confronted by photos of prisoner abuse at **Abu Ghraib Prison** and first shown on CBS 60 Minutes in April 2004. The scandal involved Iraqi detainees held at the Abu Ghraib Prison near Baghdad between October and December 2003. Ultimately, several guards were convicted and went to prison after the release of the pictures. Nonetheless, it tarnished the U.S.'s image and its claims of owning the moral high ground.

From the law enforcement perspective, torture often produces false confessions or leads the wrong people to be punished while the actual perpetrators go free, leaving the public with doubts about whether duress figured in even legitimate confessions. In the month after 9/11, the use of torture to foil potential attacks had a 45 percent approval rating; by 2005, it had fallen to 39 percent.

Torture not only violated the **Geneva Conventions**, but it violated a number of constitutional protections against torture, although "somewhat indirectly."[26] From a purely criminal justice perspective, torture can be interpreted to violate the Fourth Amendment restrictions on search and seizure and protections against arbitrary arrests and "outrages of the body." What's more, torture some have argued, violated the Fifth Amendment protection against self-incrimination, "guarding against compelled testimony and coerced confessions." It can also be construed that it violates the Sixth Amendment guarantee of legal representation, the Fifth and Fourteenth Amendments requiring "due process of law," and the Eighth Amendment's prohibition against "cruel and unusual punishment." Even the the U.S. State Department was prohibited from using torture by law in America as well as its use as a matter of policy and as a tool of state authority. In 1996, more bite was put into the laws against torture with the passage of the 1996 War Crime Act (18 USC 2441), which established in law the standards upheld by the 1949 Geneva Conventions. Therefore, by federal law, U.S. criminal jurisdiction is over any act of torture "committed by a U.S. national, no matter where the act occurs."[27]

President Obama fulfilled one of his campaign promises in January 2009 when he announced a ban on "enhanced interrogation" techniques that been acceptable tactics in the previous administration, including prohibition against waterboarding, sleep deprivation (up to eleven days in some cases), and most other aspects of the former interrogations policy. But to be fair, many of the most egregious practices of the Bush era had already been corrected by the end of his presidency. Obama would expand the ban to include prohibiting inhumane treatment of prisoners by government officials and the closing of the CIA's network of "black site" prisons, which reached from Poland to Thailand.[28]

In the aftermath of 9/11 and the USA PATRIOT Act, the United States came under fire for violating the Geneva Conventions. The Third and Fourth Geneva Conventions were written and ratified following the civilian carnage that accompanied World War II. The U.S. ratified them in 1955. Their stated purpose was to codify international norms and offers special protections to captured soldiers and civilians living under military occupation. Both identify specific forms of treatment that are prohibited and affirm the responsibility of military authorities to actively protect enemy prisoners and those civilians under their control. Article 31 of the Fourth Geneva Convention notes, "No physical or moral coercion shall be exercised against protected persons, in part to obtain information from them or their parties."[29] The Conventions directly and indirectly prohibit many of the practices that featured prominently in the prison scandal at Abu Ghraib, including prohibitions against the use of violence to control inmates, coercive interrogations, prolonged solitary confinement, dark cells, and the use of photographs to humiliate prisoners. Although these actions occurred far from American shores, Article VI of the U.S. Constitution asserts that when the U.S. government ratifies such treaties they become part of the "supreme law of the land."[30]

Department of Homeland Security

Just one month after the 9/11 attacks, President George W. Bush signed Executive Order 13688, creating the Office of Homeland Security and Homeland Security Council. The creation of the new cabinet position – the Department of Homeland Security – was supposed to reorganize the American security community. However, the CIA and the FBI, the agencies that "arguably precipitated the organizational crisis managed to maintain their independence from the DHS juggernaut"[31] By the beginning of the second decade of the twenty-first century, DHS was the third largest federal agency just behind the Department of Veteran Affairs and the Department of Defense in size. Former Pennsylvania Governor Tom Ridge (1995–2001) was selected as its first director with the mandate to develop and coordinate a comprehensive national strategy to protect the United States against terror threats or attacks. The passage of the Homeland Security Act of 2002 abolished the Office of Homeland Security and the Department of Homeland Security (DHS) was established in its stead. Ridge continued as the first secretary of the DHS (he resigned at end of 2004). By 2003, the department had some 180,000 employees. But critics argued that the existence of the DHS was only the "the first step toward the erasure of the principle of keeping domestic and foreign intelligence separate."[32]

By 2004, the DHS claimed that it had established "connectivity" in every state as well as with National Guard units, police forces, local emergency services, and private security operators in all major cities.[33] In 2005, Ridge was succeeded by Michael Chertoff. The DHS consists mainly of components transferred from other cabinet departments because of their role in homeland security, including the U.S. Secret Service, the Coast Guard, Immigration and Customs Enforcement (ICE), Federal Emergency Management Agency (FEMA), and others. ICE is the largest investigative arm of the DHS and is responsible for the enforcement of immigration policy and identifying criminals and organizations involved in human smuggling and trafficking. More than half of the agencies under the DHS have police powers. However, the organizational status of the FBI and the CIA were not changed, allowing them to keep their cherished autonomy. Meanwhile, state and local governments were expected to rely on their law enforcement agencies as first responders (rather than federal agencies) in case of terrorist attacks as well as protecting against them. With the Obama administration taking office in 2009, Chertoff passed the reins of directorship to former Arizona Governor Janet Napolitano on January 21.

Reorganization of Federal Justice Agencies

Agency	Parent Organization pre-9/11	New Parent Organization
CIA	Independent	Independent
Coast Guard	Department of Transportation	Department of Homeland Security
Customs	Treasury Department	Department of Homeland Security
FBI	Justice Department	Justice Department
FEMA	Independent	Department of Homeland Security
INS	Justice Department	Department of Homeland Security
U.S. Secret Service	Treasury Department	Department of Homeland Security

Criminal terrorism enforcement in America since 9/11: success or failure?

In 2001, Attorney General John Ashcroft reportedly told the FBI Director Robert Mueller that "The chief mission of U.S. law enforcement . . . is to stop another attack and apprehend any accomplices to terrorists before they hit us again."[34] In the years following 9/11, the Bush administration asserted that its counterterrorism strategy in the U.S. was responsible for preventing any further attacks on American soil. Gauging from the number of successful foreign terrorist attacks on American soil since 9/11 (zero), the country's criminal terrorism enforcement apparatus has either been doing something right or has just been lucky.

However, this claim needs closer scrutiny beginning with the roundup of Arab and Muslim nationals who were required to register in the days following the attacks. More than 8,000 were interviewed by the FBI and over 5,000 were incarcerated in "**preventive detention**." Of these 13,000, not one of them was convicted of a terrorist crime.[35] One indeed must consider the overwhelming political pressure that was on politicians of all suasions to stop another attack on America. There was little doubt that the government overreacted in a number of instances and that evidence shows that the Bush administration was responsible for a number of abuses in the poorly defined war on terror; nonetheless, during the next election "no serious Democrat presidential candidate in 2004 had the courage to speak out against their illegal practices."[36]

The year 2009 produced the highest number of terror charges since 9/11. According to one Associated Press (AP) survey, fifty-four defendants were charged with federal-terrorism related charges. By all accounts, the number of arrests surged after September 2009, ending the year with the attempted Christmas day bombing by the "underpants bomber" on a Detroit-bound jet. On September 24 alone, charges were announced in five separate terrorism cases in Illinois, New York, North Carolina, and Texas. There is, however, a lack of consensus as to what constitutes a terrorism case. The AP study claimed to have used a "rigorous standard that produced a conservative count."[37] Charges that made the list included conspiring to provide material support to terrorists, conspiring to murder people abroad, and conspiring to use a weapon of mass destruction. However, what is curious are the cases left out, including the Army psychiatrist suspected in the Fort Hood military base shootings, who initially faced non-terrorism related murder charges by military prosecutors (and treated as a workplace crime). Also missing were five youths from the Washington, DC, area charged in Pakistan. More recently, the Justice Department was asked to provide a figure of its own. However, its only response was that more defendants were charged that year than any since the attacks.[38]

Medical marijuana and drug laws

With marijuana arrests reaching a record high in 2007 (43,000 more than the year before) and constituting 47.5 percent of national drug arrests, a number of law enforcement agencies were taking the drug more seriously. According to NORML, the group supporting the legalization of marijuana, the rise could be attributed to a combination of factors including the result of federal justice assistance grant systems, which tended to push local police toward meeting certain performance levels, rather than "on the harder drug offenses they would prefer to pursue."[39] Nonetheless, the expansion of medical marijuana became one of the more contentious debates over the last decade. Few could have forecast that in the following decade medical and recreational marijuana would be available in a number of states. Nonetheless, it remains the subject of the long-simmering controversy over the legality of state laws permitting medical marijuana use, although it is still classified under the 1970 Federal Controlled Substances Act as a drug in the highest category for potential abuse. Despite numerous studies testifying to its therapeutic qualities by patients and doctors, federal prosecutors refused to budge from their prohibition approach until the end of the Bush administration in 2008.

The election of President Barack Obama to the White House brought a more pragmatic leader into the drug debate. In 2009, a reversal of the previous policy was announced by the new Attorney General Eric H. Holder, asserting that the U.S. Justice Department would not enforce federal laws that conflicted with state laws on the possession of marijuana, nor what they prosecute medical marijuana distributors who complied with state laws. This was in sharp contrast to the previous administration's stated policy of zero tolerance for marijuana, regardless of state laws.[40]

A Zogby poll in 2009 revealed that 52 percent of voters would support the legalizing, taxing, and regulating the growth and sale of marijuana.[41] In May 2009, President Obama's new drug czar, former Seattle Police Chief R. Gil Kerlikowske took office, vowing that the new administration would desist using the expression "war on drugs" due in part because it implied that the government was at war with American citizens over this issue.[42] The goal of President Obama and his new czar was to change the country's drug control strategy by "redirecting some of its resources into prevention and treatment and away from law enforcement and anti-trafficking efforts, which had consumed 75 percent to 90 percent of the budget during the Bush administration."[43] President Obama also announced that the position of drug czar would no longer be a cabinet-level position. Although the president's new drug policy strategy would be released with his budget in February 2010, insiders offer that, of America's estimated 25 million substance abusers, only 2 million were in treatment and that the new administration wants to triple that, partly by devoting more money and through other tactics such as integrating addiction treatment into the primary health care system.

According to critics, regulations and protocol for this shift in marijuana policy have not been fully developed as well as who could grow it or buy it. In California, with the country's oldest medical marijuana program (1996), 56 percent of the voters support it, and in 2010, Los Angeles alone had close to 600 dispensaries, which some claim was more than the number of the city's Starbucks coffeehouses. America was not the only country revisiting its marijuana laws. In June 2009, the Mexican legislature voted to decriminalize possession of small amounts of marijuana, cocaine, methamphetamine, and other drugs for personal use, and just two months later, Argentina's Supreme Court prohibited the incarceration of individuals for marijuana possession. Officials have agreed that major traffickers should be targeted and that more drug treatment programs should be provided to keep addicts out of the criminal justice system.[44]

Once home to the country's toughest drug laws, New York jumped on the bandwagon to ease drug laws away from mandatory-minimum sentences. Although the strictest provisions of the state's famously draconian drug laws had been removed in 2004, in March 2009, New York Governor David Paterson and legislative leaders announced a movement to reduce the state's drug laws, reversing the trend that began in 1973 when Governor Nelson Rockefeller lobbied for strict laws as part of a Republican effort to fight the rising popularity of recreational drugs in America. This and similar steps in other states were part of a trend across the country that saw a movement toward alternatives to imprisonment as a way of cutting the enormous budgets required to incarcerate tens of thousands of individuals for minor drug-related crimes. It was also part of a trend that gave judges more discretion in sentencing some nonviolent offenders and in sending felony offenders to alternatives such as local jail, probation, parole, or military-style shock camps. In New York alone, it was estimated that this move would reduce the prison population by more than 10,000 additional inmates (at costs of $45,000 per year per inmate) and save millions of dollars by offering residential drug treatment ($15,000) at one-third the amount it costs to house an inmate.[45]

The Second Amendment and gun control

The last time the U.S. Supreme Court examined the Second Amendment was the case of *United States v. Miller* in 1939, which ruled that a bootlegger who was arrested for transporting a sawed-off shotgun across state lines violated the intentions of the amendment. In the summer of 2008, the Supreme Court ruled in a 5–4 vote that the Washington, DC, handgun possession ban was unconstitutional. What made this reversal of the 1976 law (one of the nation's toughest, which prohibited residents from registering and purchasing handguns in almost all circumstances) so unique was that it was the first time American history that the court ruled that the Second Amendment guarantees an individual's right to own a gun for self-defense. On one hand, Justice Antonin Scalia noted that the Second Amendment "surely elevates above all other interests the rights of law-abiding, responsible citizens to use arms in defense of hearth and home," while dissenting Justice Stephen G. Breyer warned that the decision "threatens to throw into doubt the constitutionality of gun laws throughout the United States." President Bush applauded the decision, while presidential candidate and eventual nominee Senator Barack Obama feared the rise in gun-related violence in "crime-ravaged" neighborhoods. The fallout from this decision was still unclear as of 2010.[46]

Law enforcement

One police historian recently noted that, on 9/11, "policing in America moved out of the community policing era and into the era of homeland security," leading to the "largest reorganization of the federal bureaucracy since World War Two."[47] What has become clear is that the most successful method for detecting and prosecuting terrorism cases was through the use of traditional crime fighting strategies.[48] Police historian Samuel Walker has suggested the current era is "'a critical time in local policing,' noting such new challenges as taking a larger role in national counterterrorism strategy, working with less financial resources and lower budgets, and reintegrating veterans returning from war in Afghanistan and Iraq."[49]

The International Association of Chiefs of Police (IACP) issued a "white paper" in 2004 that was critical of the National Strategy for Homeland Security, charging that the national strategy released in 2002 was developed by mostly federal departments and despite assertions to the contrary that it was a "national strategy" without the feedback of local, state, and tribal police agencies it remained a federal strategy and not a national one.[50]

At the federal level, the passage of the Intelligence Reform and Terrorism Prevention Act in 2005 required the FBI to create a National Intelligence Workforce requiring every new agent hired in the future have intelligence as well as police training.[51] In the years since 9/11, police forces at the federal and state levels have been expanding their databases at an unprecedented rate. In April 2009, the FBI joined fifteen states in collecting DNA samples from detained immigrants and those awaiting trial. The FBI database of 6.7 million profiles was expected to increase by from 80,000 new entries a year to 1.2 million by 2012.[52] Police officials expect these to solve more violent crimes, pointing to the fact that the database had already helped convict thousands (and exonerated several hundred others).[53] However, there is still a debate about whether having such a large database poses potential privacy concerns. On one hand, police and prosecutors enjoy having a larger pool of suspects, while on the other, civil libertarians and other activists have point to Fourth Amendment privacy concerns and fears that we are becoming a "genetic surveillance society."[54] In recent years, DNA has become an even more integral part of the evidence gathering process. For example, in 2010, at least sixteen states collected DNA from guilty misdemeanants, and in thirty-five states, minors were required to provide samples on convictions (and in some states upon arrest).[55]

Assault weapons and line of duty deaths in the twenty-first century

In most states, gun dealers were monitored by federal firearms inspectors instead of state or local police. That means there were 600 monitors for roughly 115,000 gun dealers. In most cases, they can only make one visit per year. In November 2009, police chiefs attending a meeting of the Police Executive Research Forum took up the issue of guns and crime. What was most troubling for the chiefs was the number of high-powered assault rifles on the streets. With the expiration of the ten-year assault weapon ban in 2004, police chiefs noticed an increase of these weapons on the streets. More than 130 police chiefs and officials answered a survey that found a 37 percent increase in assault weapons in street crime.[56] Many of these weapons end up pointing in the direction of police officers.

The end of the first decade of the twenty-first century was accompanied by an increase in the number of police officers killed in the line of duty by gunfire, increasing 24 percent over the previous year. As of the middle of December 2009, forty-seven officers had died from gunshots across the country. The year before saw "only" thirty-eight killed, which was the lowest number of gunfire deaths since 1956. What has most surprised experts has been the numbers of police officers that have been specifically targeted by shooters. This rising problem was highlighted by the ambush murder of four police officers in a Seattle coffee shop in November. This was preceded by the murder of four Oakland police officers in March; three in Pittsburgh; and two in Okaloosa County, Florida, that April.[57]

A number of researchers have argued that, with more guns, there are more gun crimes, making it more likely police officers will be shot in the line of duty. But, this is not true across the board. Pennsylvania, for example, led the nation in gun-related officer deaths in 2009, yet had some of the nation's strictest gun laws. On the other hand, the states of Louisiana, Oklahoma, and Kentucky have had few if any gun-related deaths of police that year, yet have some of the most lenient laws. Nonetheless, the spokesman for the Officers Memorial Fund optimistically reported that, "The chances of being killed in the line of duty are lower" than many previous years of the modern era. This is especially true of gun-related deaths. In 1973, there were 600,000 police officers and 156 gun-related deaths. In 2009, there were 900,000 officers and 47 deaths. Much of the decline is attributed to better police protective equipment and better and faster medical treatment.

Policing in the age of terrorism: getting by with less

In the course of his first two terms as mayor of New York City, Michael R. Bloomberg has supervised the "greatest expansion of police surveillance of political activity in at least half a century."[58] The mayor's response to this claim was that the federal government was not doing enough to protect the city from possible terrorist attacks so it was necessary to mount internal intelligence operations. As 2009 came to a close, the NYPD was contemplating how to adjust to the pending decline from 41,000 at its peak a decade ago to 34,304 officers (–16 percent). What's more, almost 1,000 officers are tasked to counterterrorism-related duties. On the bright side, New York City's crime rate continues to decline. During the first half of 2009, there were only 200 murders, compared to 2,200 in the year 1990, a peak year for homicide. Observers have marveled how this storied force has been able to improve upon critical aspects of crime fighting of late, especially considering the reduction in officers and its new responsibilities in the terrorism arena. Among the tactics that worked well has been "**predictive policing**," which relies on utilizing crime statistics and other data to predict where crime will take place next. Police Chief Raymond W. Kelly claims some inspiration from the noted nineteenth-century military tactician Carl von Clausewitz, "who advised massing forces at certain important points, instead of deploying scare personnel thinly along an entire enemy line."[59]

NYPD is not alone among police departments having to do more with less. Many police forces are suffering from soaring budget demands unrelated to hiring new officers. Much of the increase is due to the spiraling costs of salaries and skyrocketing increase in pension and health care benefits built into recent police contracts. For example, the Houston Police Department, one of the nation's largest police forces, has fewer officers per square mile and the number of officers has remained the same from 2004 to 2009, yet its budget increased 40 percent due to the aforementioned issues. Houston is caught in a no-win situation. Despite a violent crime rate that was among the highest in the nation, the federal government recently denied it stimulus funding for more police academy classes due to the city's fiscal health and its decline in crime over the past several years.[60] In late December 2009, the Colorado Springs Police Department was forced to reassign three full-time helicopter pilots and auction off its two Bell helicopters. Similar budget cuts led the Tulsa, Oklahoma, and Oakland, California, police departments to ground their helicopters as well. Smaller departments eliminated their helicopter units altogether. It costs a city almost $500 per hour to man and fuel a helicopter. Helicopters have longed served as the eye in the sky for urban police tracking suspects through labyrinthine streets, and as one law enforcement lamented, "There is no replacement for a helicopter overhead, particularly when violent and felony crimes are unfolding."[61]

Police tactics

Civil libertarians continue to rail against law enforcement tactics such "stop-and-frisk," calling it racist and unacceptable while claiming it fails to deter crime. Supporters of this strategy, cite the success rate of the NYPD in reducing crime when it implemented the strategy in the 1990s during the administration of Mayor Rudy Giuliani. More recently, current commissioner Raymond W. Kelly estimated that his officers stopped as many as 600,000 people in 2009 alone, with only 10 percent being arrested.[62] By most accounts, more people were being stopped and questioned than in previous years. According to Commissioner Kelly, "This is a proven law enforcement tactic to fight and deter crime, one that is authorized by criminal procedure."[63] Police in Philadelphia adopted the tactic in 2007–2008, nearly doubling the amount of stops over the previous year; supporters cited it for a drop in crime. Proponents of "**stop and frisk**" refer to a 1968 Supreme Court decision that "established the benchmark of 'reasonable suspicion' – a standard that is lower than the 'probable cause' needed to justify the arrest."[64] Nonetheless, some major police departments either do not release or keep records of police stops, a barrier to making any conclusive comparisons.

The FBI and 9/11: a prisoner of history?

Even before the two jets hit the twin towers of the World Trade Center, the FBI had been elevated by law and presidential directives to America's lead agency against terrorism. Under the Clinton administration, law enforcement had emerged as the nation's preferred weapon against terror. FBI historian Richard Gid Powers suggested, that where in the past the Marines would have been sent in, the Reagan, H. W. Bush, and Clinton administrations "had ordered the FBI to investigate embassy bombings, barracks explosions, and assaults on American warships" in the 1980s and 1990s.[65] In 2001, the agency had 27,000 agents and support workers with a budget of $3.4 billion. By the time FBI chief Louis Freeh retired in 2001, he had persuaded Congress to raise the FBI counterterrorism budget from $79 million to $372 million (an increase of 471 percent).[66]

The 9/11 attacks sounded a clarion call for change at every level of law enforcement, particularly at the federal level. On that September day, the FBI had only one analyst working on al Qaeda.[67] By 2003, not much had changed, when out of 11,500 field agents only 6 were Muslims.[68] In the fall of 2002, demands were made for a new government enquiry into 9/11, resulting in the U.S. **9/11 Commission** chaired by former New Jersey Governor Thomas H. Kean (1982–1990). The commission conducted one of the largest government investigations in American history. After all was said and done, the chairman delivered his verdict that the "FBI failed," lamenting "This is an agency that does not work."[69] Since then, much of the blame for what turned out to be a colossal intelligence failure has been directed at the FBI. What made matters worse were revelations that several FBI agents had prior knowledge of possible attacks; while others claimed they were restricted in their efforts to detect the hijackers due to the dismantlement of much of the intelligence gathering system following the Watergate scandal of the 1970s. If there was a smoking gun on 9/11 that could have averted this tragedy, "it went off back in the 1970s" during the Carter administration, said one FBI scholar, a period when its approval rating dropped from 84 percent in 1965 to 37 percent in 1975.[70]

During the 1970s, the investigations of the FBI and CIA exposed some of FBI Director J. Edgar Hoover's most nefarious efforts to repress political dissent and in the process "convinced many in the FBI that investigations of domestic groups were unconstitutional and illegitimate and unconstitutional."[71] As a result the FBI refocused itself toward criminal cases under the Ford and Carter administrations rather than the political ones that so dominated the Nixon years. In 2002, FBI Director Robert Mueller told a Senate Judiciary Committee "that fear of political punishment over concerns about profiling may have hindered the FBI's investigation of terrorists."[72] The events of the previous decades had made the FBI "a prisoner of its history"[73] Under FBI Director Louis Freeh, the bureau wanted to prove it was most concerned with protecting civil liberties and was a counterpoint to the Hoover FBI. But probably more important was the fact that the agency had made so many poor decisions and errors in judgment in such high profile cases as Ruby Ridge and Waco, which ruined the careers of several top ranking agents. By most accounts, this led to a "risk aversion" culture in which FBI managers found that the safest career choice was an avoidance of unnecessary decisions.[74]

The retirement of FBI director Louis Freeh in June 2001 (his term would have expired in 2003), shortly before the 9/11 attacks, concluded one of the most controversial administrations in the history of the agency. Despite the number of controversies and missteps during his eight years at the helm, Freeh could also point to some accomplishments during his administration. Under his leadership, the FBI hired thousands of new agents, enjoyed better cooperation with the Central Intelligence Agency, more than doubled the FBI's presence in other countries, and secured a $3.44 billion crime fighting budget, a 58 percent increase over his first year in office. Freeh left a mixed legacy as head of the FBI. While the FBI did make great strides in increasing the diversity of the bureau, adding more women and minorities, his tenure as chief was mired in controversy. High profile embarrassments that marred his administration included the botched interview with falsely accused Olympic bombing suspect Richard Jewell; the investigation of a Pan-Am plane crash; a series of domestic bombing cases; inefficiency in the FBI crime lab; the Waco, Texas, and Ruby Ridge, Idaho, shoot-outs; and security lapses in the atomic weapons labs.

Changes for the FBI had been in the works even before the departure of Louis Freeh. The FBI implemented some of these modifications beginning in July 2001, when the Justice Department's inspector general was given permission to begin investigations of the bureau without needing the previously required permission of the attorney general. In addition, a program was set up to give periodic polygraphs to agents with access to sensitive materials. These changes followed a number of high profile embarrassments for the FBI, including the loss of weapons and computers, the discovery of the FBI-spy Robert Hanssen, and the bungled investigation of former nuclear scientist Wen Ho Lee. However, the new legislation went even further. Besides making it clear that the Justice Department's inspector general had jurisdiction over the FBI, their bill included provisions for the inclusion of FBI employees under the Federal Whistleblower Act, the creation of an FBI internal security division, and other reporting requirements to Congress (see FBI priorities sidebar).

FBI priorities after 9/11

1 Protect the United States from terrorist attack.
2 Protect the United States against foreign intelligence operations and espionage.
3 Protect the United States against cyber-based attacks and high technology crimes.
4 Combat public corruption at all levels.

> 5 Protect civil rights.
>
> 6 Combat transnational and national criminal organizations and enterprises.
>
> 7 Combat major white-collar crime.
>
> 8 Combat significant violent crime.
>
> 9 Support federal, state, county, municipal, and international partners.
>
> 10 Upgrade technology to successfully perform the FBI's mission.[75]

U.S. Air Marshals

The U.S. Air Marshals was "a nearly forgotten force of 33 agents" until 9/11.[76] While their official number was classified, there were an estimated 3,000 to 4,000 agents operating out of the Transportation Security Administration with a budget of more than $780 million. However, the program has been less than a rousing success and has been stung by Congressional criticism that, because of enforcing a dress code that blows their covers, it has had three leaders and had been moved to four different parent agencies. After the 9/11 attacks, there was a rush to hire new marshals, and almost 200,000 applied. But perhaps only one in forty was accepted, making it tougher than getting into Harvard.[77] Prospective air marshals were expected to pass top security clearance background checks, which included ten years of criminal history; credit reports; and interviews with employers, neighbors, and relatives. This was no guarantee that they would hire the best employees. A 2004 inspector's report found 753 misconduct cases over a 20-month period, with infractions that included failed drug tests and sleeping on duty.

Corrections

Much attention was devoted to a 2007 revelation, based on a Census Bureau report for 2006 that more than three times as many African Americans lived in prison cells as in college dormitories (not including those living off-campus). The ratio was only slightly better for Hispanics. That same year, one in fifteen adult black men were incarcerated. On average, states spend 7 percent on corrections budgets, which is just behind health care, education, and transportation. With costs for medical care skyrocketing by 10 percent each year, states and the federal government were grappling with cheaper alternatives to incarceration. Nonetheless, as 2010 dawned, the United States had the world's highest incarceration rate. With only 5 percent of the world's population the U.S. housed almost 25 percent of the world's reported prisoners; an imprisonment rate of 756 per 100,000, almost five times the world's average (125 per 100,000). If one were to include all adults in jail or on supervised releases, the rate would be closer to 1 in every 31 adults.[78]

One of the more curious aspects of the "war on crime" and the use of prisons was that, as America's crime rate declined, the total prison population continued to increase over the past two decades. Criminologists and legal experts for the most part agree that the high incarceration rate helped diminish crime, but many assert that there were other factors that should be considered including harsher sentencing laws, the zealous commitment to combating illegal drugs, the lack of social safety nets, and a legacy of racial tumult.[79]

There were a number of reasons why prisoners are locked up in such numbers. Obviously, their criminal behavior is foremost. One must also consider that, over the past thirty years, policy choices driven by the electorate, elected officials, and representatives of the criminal justice system have offered few other alternatives for most crimes. Parole was once viewed as the lever for reducing prison populations through good time programs and the like. However, in recent years, get-tough policies were sending parolees back to jail at an unprecedented rate. As a result, parole became the "key source behind the policy" as various pieces of legislation were passed to make it easier to send parolees back to jail. Between 1983 and 2003, the proportion of parolees returned to custody rose from 13 percent to 29 percent.[80]

There were some signs at the end of 2009 that some type of threshold had been reached, as several states with tight budgets were forced to rethink sentencing policies. While Florida continued to adhere to strict sentencing polices and continued to require all inmates to serve a large percentage of the sentences, despite its toll on the state's resources, other states were moving in another direction.[81] Mississippi's truth-in-sentencing laws, for example, that once required drug offenders to serve 85 percent of their time were reduced to 25 percent. Texas once had one of the lowest parole rates in the country (as little as 15 percent just five years ago). By 2010, the rate was more than 30 percent, in part due to a new strategy that had Texas vetting the prison population for low-risk candidates that could be paroled. In fact, Texas, once home to one of the country's largest prison populations, was actually experiencing a decline in its prison population. This was unexpected to say the least, and three new prisons that had been scheduled for construction were been taken off the drawing board. By 2005, Texas had reached an impasse – either spend half a billion dollars to house a projected 17,000 new prisoners each year or spend less than half of that and reduce the prison population through treatment programs. According to one journalist, Texas "is becoming the unlikely new role model for a prison reform movement spreading across the country."[82] By most accounts, this trend began in 2007 with what has been called the "**reinvestment movement**." The program had the benefit of support across the board and allowed state funds to be invested in alcohol, drug, and mental health programs to treat offenders rather than warehouse them. As one observer put it, "States are learning they just can't build their way out of crime."[83]

Now that so many states were facing major budgetary problems, states began looking to alternatives to imprisonment. New York State, on the cusp of repealing its draconian mandatory sentences, and California, with a prison system so overcrowded and underfunded that a federal judge recently ordered the state to release almost one-third of its 158,00 prisoners by 2012, were just two of the states looking for solutions. Michigan, New Jersey, and North Carolina were either releasing prisoners who had served minimum time or putting drug offenders in treatment programs instead of in stir.[84]

A Bureau of Justice Statistics report for 1999–2005 broke down state prison populations by race and drug offense. Its most interesting revelation was the decrease in the number of black Americans (–21 percent) in state prisons for drug offenses; at the same time, there has been an increase in number of whites (+42 percent) convicted of drug crimes, while Latino numbers stayed flat. With drug offenders making up more than a quarter of the prison population, some observers are hoping that this is signaling a gradual change in demographics. Explanations have varied. Some attribute the new numbers to an increased emphasis on prison alternatives by judges and prosecutors; others suggest a shift from police focus from crack cocaine to methamphetamines (most popular with whites). Drug courts have become one popular alternative, offering nonviolent offenders the option of a strict substance abuse program and criminal rehabilitation or incarceration behind prison bars. Drug courts reportedly cost 10 percent to 30 percent less than it costs to send someone to prison.[85]

Drug courts

The first drug court in the United States was introduced in Dade County, Florida, in 1989. The concept was a response to a federal mandate to reduce the state's inmate population or suffer the loss of federal funding. The state's Supreme Court directed a research program to look for solutions. It turned out that a large proportion of inmates had been imprisoned due to drug violations and often found themselves in a revolving door of recidivism that ultimately always led back to jail without addressing the underlying causes of drug addiction Thus, it was determined that a program was necessary that would bring drug treatment services and the criminal justice system together. Typically, a participant takes part in a demanding routine of substance abuse treatment, case management, drug testing, and probation supervision while reporting on a regular basis to scheduled hearings held before a judge with expertise in the drug court model. The drug treatment is supplemented by additional services offering mental health treatment, trauma and family therapy, job skills training, and other "life-skill enhancement" services. All of this is accomplished with a minimal use of incarceration. Since the 1990s, a number of studies support the contention that "no other justice intervention can rival the results produced by drug courts." A substantial body of research demonstrates that drug courts "improve substance abuse outcomes, substantially reduce crime, and produce greater cost benefits than any other justice strategy."[86] By 2008, there were more than 2,147 drug courts in the country. Former Director of the Office of U.S. National Drug Control Policy General Barry McCaffrey is among the growing number of supporters who highly endorse the program, suggesting that, "If you don't like paying for jails, if you don't like a waste of tax dollars, then you'll like the concept of drug courts. This is an initiative that's been working."[87]

The Second Chance Act

One looming challenge for society if new programs focusing on alternatives to prison become de rigueur will be the impact of the hundreds of thousands of ex-convicts reentering society. Traditionally prisoners upon release were given $50 dollars and a bus ticket and were sent on their way without preparation for what came next. Typically a good percentage (more than two-thirds) would end up back in prison within three years, through what some have termed the "revolving door of recidivism"[88] What often goes unstated is that almost half are returned for "technical violations" of parole that include not reporting to parole officers on time or failing drug tests.

In 2008, President Bush signed the Second Chance Act 2007 (H.R. 1593) amending the Omnibus Crime Control and Safe Streets Act of 1968 and designed to address the reintegration of legions of ex-convicts back into society and lower recidivism rates. Its goal was to improve reentry programs for adult and juvenile offenders and developing new and better ones. The Act was intended to authorize essential parts of the administration's Prison Reentry Initiative to help prisoners by expanding job training and placement services, improving their ability to find transitional housing, and helping newly released prisoners get mentoring (including from faith-based groups). President Bush hoped the act would "give prisoners across America the second chance for a better life."[89] One expert observed that this was "an unexpected return to his original rhetoric of 'compassionate conservatism' that has so swiftly dissipated upon his acquiring office."[90]

The aging prison population

One of the unintended consequences of get-tough sentencing policies has been the rising number of aging inmates. Older offenders who commit violent crimes have been serving longer sentences since the 1990s and represent the fastest growing segment of the federal and state prison systems. This is the first time in American history that the prison system as had to face the challenges of a graying prison population. With an aging population comes a range of new treatment issues ranging from dementia and cancer to incontinence and hypertension.[91] A report by the National Institute of Corrections in 2004 noted that the number of prisoners aged fifty and over had increased 172.6 percent between 1992 and 2001 (41,000 to 113,000). According to the most recent report by the Federal Bureau of Justice Statistics, 4.3 percent of all inmates in state, federal, and local jails were over 55 as of mid-2008, a 23 percent increase since 2004. This trend would continue throughout the next decade, in part reflecting the general aging of the American population. What's more, this increase is more than three times the increase in the overall number of inmates (at only 7 percent). Other contributing factors have included the get-tough reforms of the 1980s and 1990s, three strikes and truth-in-sentencing laws – all contributing to more offenders locked up behind bars for longer periods of times. As inmates serve longer sentences, it should not be surprising that there is a surge in aging and sick inmates. What often goes unstated is that prisoners are also probably living longer due to better medical care, a reflection of longer living Americans on the outside.

Between 1999 and 2008, there was a 79 percent increase in inmates 55 and older. It is expected that this problem will only get worse, putting more burdens on already underfunded prison systems. Among the barriers to research in this arena is the fact that every state defines geriatric prisoners differently (it is generally regarded as 65 and older on the outside). Furthermore, it has been documented that the prison experience contributes to the aging process. Ultimately, older prisoners contract chronic illnesses and experience disabilities at younger ages making any definition irrelevant. Others point to the fact that, besides normal aging problems, elderly inmates have more chronic illnesses due to lifestyle choices including poor diets, risky behavior, drugs, smoking, and alcohol consumption.

These conditions are probably exacerbated by lives spent in poverty and poor health care. In addition, elderly inmates face a number of individual and environmental stressors than can aggravate existing health problems.[92]

Elderly inmates are at high risk in some facilities for self-harm, suicide, and victimization by younger inmates. One contemporary study indicated that it costs $70,000 to house an older inmate, almost two to three times what it costs for younger ones. According to one interesting perspective, the rise in elderly is a reflection of the first wave of baby boomers born in 1946 moving into their sixties. "Just as this demographic group challenged schools and public services decades ago, the presence of the baby boom is felt in jails and prison today."[93]

Demonstrating that elderly citizens are just as capable of murder as younger ones, on January 6, 2010, the Associated Press announced that an eight-nine-year-old white supremacist, who had been charged in a fatal shooting at the Washington Holocaust Museum, had died while awaiting trial. His medical records indicated that he had been suffering from a range of health problems including sepsis and chronic congestive heart failure. His death and health problems confirm recent research on America's aging prison population demonstrating the numerous health problems facing elderly prisoners as well as the budgetary problems with caring for them in prison.

HIV, AIDS, and other health issues in prison

In 2004, the three leading causes of death in prison were natural causes, AIDs, and suicide, (double the suicide rate of the general population). Of course, prisoners entered incarceration suffering a variety of maladies, both physically and mentally. This is not a new phenomenon. One merely needs to step back in time to the eighteenth century when prison reformers lobbied for more hygienic conditions as they battled "gaol fever." Prisons continue to be incubators for deadly diseases including tuberculosis, Hepatitis C, and AIDs – what one expert has referred to as a "perfect storm" for disease transmission, noting the proliferation of overcrowding, unprotected sex, and needle sharing.[94] It has been almost thirty years since the beginning of the AIDS epidemic, yet as of 2008, only twenty-four states required testing all inmates for HIV at admission or during custody.[95] Nonetheless, once behind bars, there are many opportunities to contract AIDs through sex or by sharing needles for drug use and tattooing. More than a decade ago. one health study commissioned by Congress found 17 percent of all Americans living with AIDs had passed through correctional institutions in 1996. Although the rate of HIV and AIDs among state prisoners fell from 100 to 25 per 100,000 between 1995 and 2001, the same period saw the rate among the U.S. population drop from 29 to 9 per 100,000.[96]

In April 2009, New York passed legislation as part of the state budget that would make chronically and terminally ill patients eligible for early release beginning in 2010. Many of them are part of an increasingly aging prison population. In order to be considered, inmates had to be vetted to determine that they were unable to pose a threat to society, "physically or cognitively."[97] The law expanded the list of eligible inmates to include inmates convicted of violent crimes that included second degree murder, first degree manslaughter, and sex offenses. However, they must have already served half their sentences. New York is among about a dozen states to have enacted these programs between 2008 and 2010.

By the end of the decade, 39 states offered so-called **"compassionate release" programs**. When prisoners were released, they were expected to be cared for by family members or placed in nursing homes or hospices, with expenses mostly covered by Medicare and Medicaid. However, by most accounts, compassionate release programs have had minimal impact up to now. For example, New York only released seven in 2009; California, three; and Alabama, four, despite an increase in applications. Many die waiting for parole. New York adopted **medical parole** in 1992 at height of AIDs crisis (364 released since then). New York officials estimate it costs $150,809 a year to care for a seriously ill inmate.

Prisoners and mental health

By most accounts, the origins of how U.S. prisons and jails were turned into "de facto insane asylums" can be found in the early 1960s during an era when the **"deinstitutionalization movement"** was in vogue.[98] It was during this period that the first psychotropic drugs for treating the mentally ill were widely available. This led observers to believe that, instead of being warehoused in large state mental hospitals such as the one that was portrayed in Ken Kesey's *One Flew Over the Cuckoo's Nest* (1962), those with mental issues could live and receive treatment in the community. The main barrier to this way of thinking was the utter lack of funding for clinics and treatment. Many states closed mental hospitals to save money without making provisions for patients (in 1955, there were 559,000 patients in state mental hospitals; in 2004, 72,000, even though population had grown by two-thirds).[99] As a result, many ended up on the streets and quickly found their selves homeless and destitute. Not surprisingly, many found themselves in the criminal justice system, especially as cities cracked down on "quality of life offenses" such as drinking in public, urinating in public, and panhandling. Many become substance abusers. A 2002 study called the Sentencing Project estimated that 700,000 of the 10 million adults booked into local jails each year had symptoms of mental illness. A typical pattern is for someone to cycle in out of jail dozens of times (referred to as "frequent fliers") without treatment until he/she commits a serious offense and lands in prison. For example, by 2010, Florida had five times as many mentally ill people in jails and prisons as in mental hospitals. As one journalist noted, "It is hard to write this without suspending disbelief; nevertheless it is a fact that the three largest mental institutions in the world are the Los Angeles County Jail, Rikers Island in New York and Cook County Jail in Chicago."[100]

Race, ethnicity, and prison gangs in the twenty-first century

American correctional facilities have been accorded the distinction as the "most racially segregated" places in America. Much of the segregation is the result of prison policies seeking to prevent bloodshed by separating various ethnic and racial groups, to avoid a gang-based subculture that pits white gangs (Aryan Brotherhood) against blacks (Black Guerrilla Family);

northern California Mexicans (*nortenos* such as La Nuestra Familia) against southern California Mexicans (*surenos* such as the Mexican Mafia); and so forth. With little chance of breaking up prison gangs, prison officials have opted to cluster the various groups for protection. Since 9/11, illegal immigrants and other noncitizens have become one of the fastest growing segments of the prison populations. What makes prison so daunting for noncitizens is the fact that, unlike their American counterparts, non-residents do not automatically have the right to legal representation and due to poverty and other factors are often left powerless.

Desegregation and the political awakening among inmates in the 1960s and 1970s made these transitional years for the development of prison gangs. With politicization came polarization between various racial and ethnic groups, diminishing what had been a more tradition bound and stable prison culture. As mentioned previously (Chapter 12), the new liberal prison environments that prevailed after *Cooper v. Pate* in 1964 allowed gangs to spread quickly. Before this ruling, only several states reported the presence of gangs; by 1984, more than 60 percent of the state and federal prisons reported gang activity. With the expansion of the free world crack cocaine trade in the 1980s and the concomitant tougher sentencing laws, an unprecedented number of street gang members ended up in the various prison systems, in the process often transferring street gangs from the outside to the inside. By the late 1990s, a number of these prison gangs have made the transformation to extremely organized gangs, causing alarm for law enforcement on both sides of the prison walls. Some modern gangs are quite distinct from earlier ones. A number of them demand obedience based on a "death oath," better known as "Blood In, Blood Out." In other words, you shed blood to get in and die to get out. Others have adopted paramilitary structures.

A number of prison officials and police organizations refer to more sophisticated prison gangs as **Security Threat Groups** (STGs). More recently, the Gangs and Security Threat Group Awareness organization asserted that there were six prison gangs nationally recognized "for their participation in organized crime and violence."[101] These included Neta (Puerto Rican), the Aryan Brotherhood, the Black Guerrilla Family, the Mexican Mafia, La Nuestra Familia, and the Texas Syndicate. Besides these groups are ever-growing populations of apolitical street gangs. Prison gangs eluded the scrutiny of law enforcement for many years by using racially charged language to obscure the true nature of their criminal activities, which include drug trafficking, extortion, and assaults. The best evidence of the profit motive now trumping the racist one is the willingness of white supremacist gangs to form alliances with black or Hispanic prison gangs to increase profits.

Giving credence to the notion that some prison gangs are equivalent to organized crime groups, in 1982, twenty-five members of La Nuestra Familia, a prison gang created in the California state prison system in 1968, were indicted for criminal acts that included extortion, robbery, drug trafficking, murders, and witness intimidation. This was the first time a prison gang was federally indicted for violating the RICO Act.

Crime and punishment

Mired in high unemployment (10 percent) and economic recession that brought to mind for many people images of the Great Depression and the "crisis years" of criminal justice (see Chapter 10), researchers and officials have had a difficult time explaining the crime rate at the end of the first decade of the twenty-first century which had not been so low since the 1960s. Indeed, most previous recessions were accompanied by a rise in crime. But during the first six months of 2009, the FBI reported a crime decline throughout the country, including murder and manslaughter, which had dropped 10 percent over the same period the previous year. Property crimes fell by 6.1 percent and violent ones by 4.4 percent; violent crime dropped nearly 7 percent in cities with more than 1 million or more.[102]

Most criminologists opine that these crime drops cannot be sustained over time. Criminologists have suggested various explanations for the recent crime drop, suggesting that as the population ages and with fewer individuals in the crime-prone years, this decrease should not be unexpected. Others surmise that the availability of unemployment benefits, food stamps, and "other government-driven economic stimulus have cushioned and delayed for many people the big blows that come from a recession."[103] Police officials point to better law enforcement strategies that are often driven by technology. For example, car theft has dropped due in large part to modern security locking systems on most cars and high-tech deterrents such as car-recovery devices such as global positioning systems.

For a nation seemingly inured to serial killers, bank robbers, and deadly drug traffickers, the face of crime in the twenty-first century would have a new cast – peopled by terrorists and white-collar corporate and banking scoundrels. Both types would have a hand at bringing the country to the depths of despair during the first decade of the new century.

The FBI stepped up its investigations in 2009 during the recent recession, launching more than 2,100 probes into securities fraud (compared to 1,750 in 2008). The FBI increased the amount of agents devoted to this crime by one-third. In addition, the Securities and Exchange Commission (SEC) issued 82 percent more restraining orders and devoted more time to potential financial scams in 2009 over the prior year.

America's greatest strength is its freedom and openness. For the domestic terrorist, it is also America's greatest weakness. With loosely controlled borders, people, and goods legally and illegally flow back and forth across these borders every hour, every day. Every year, more than 400 million people enter the United States. Every year, there are 800,000 aircraft arrivals, and every year, some 9 million cargo containers arrive at U.S. ports. Customs officials report that they can inspect only 2 to 3 percent of these.

Modern criminal threats to American security have new generations of law enforcement officials preparing for unprecedented criminal acts. Among the most feared are chemical, biological, and computer-based instruments of mass destruction. What is so threatening is that some weapons of mass destruction are often cheap to build and can be easily constructed and transported. One need look no further than the bombing of the Alfred P. Murrah Federal Building in Oklahoma City (1995) and the first World Trade Center bombing (1993), each accomplished with one motor vehicle and one bomb. However, few could have predicted that the worst fears of criminal justice and security experts would become reality on 9/11, 2001.

White-collar crime

White-collar crime has become one of the most prominent crimes of the twenty-first century, especially in the developed world. Financial crimes such as fraud have been reported as far back as the fourth-century B.C. Egyptians of antiquity counted fraud and tax evasion as serious offenses.[104] In 2001, **Enron** became synonymous with white-collar fraud. Once one of the world's leading energy companies, by this time, Enron executives had hidden millions of dollars in "offshore entities" to avoid taxes, hide losses, and boost the perceptions of profitability. Although share prices had continued to rise, only company bigwigs knew Enron was running at a loss. When shares reached their peak in 2000, executives sold their shares using inside information.

Once the country's seventh largest corporation, by the end of 2001, the former energy trading giant Enron had filed for Chapter 11 bankruptcy protection. This was the largest bankruptcy in American history up to that time. Enron's demise was followed closely by that of the Arthur Anderson accounting firm (one of the largest accounting firms in the world) and trials that sent Enron's top executives to prison. However, justice was probably cheated when its leader Ken Lay succumbed to a heart attack before sentencing. The Enron scandal and other similar scandals led Congress to enact the **Sarbanes-Oxley Law**, which brought a sweeping overhaul of security regulations not seen since the 1930s. The legislation was significant not just for holding auditing firms to increased accountability, but also for expanding the sanctions for those found guilty of destroying, altering, or fabricating records in federal investigations or attempting to defraud shareholders.

Bernard Madoff and the return of the Ponzi scheme

Between 2008 and 2009, several enormous Ponzi schemes unraveled as Securities and Exchange Commission (SEC) regulators haplessly stood by. Despite numerous warnings, SEC regulators stood pat as such luminaries as Bernard L. Madoff and R. Allen Stanford shattered the dreams and retirements of thousands of investors. The fraud was estimated to be in the tens of billions of dollars. The Madoff scandal that broke in 2008 was the "biggest financial scam in history." The allegations against Stanford that claimed he cost investors $7 billion, in which he was sentenced to 110 years in prison in 2012, made him a piker compared to the losses incurred by Madoff investors.

On March 12, 2009, Madoff pleaded guilty to eleven counts in relation to a Ponzi scheme, which the government claimed involved more than $60 billion. He was sentenced to 150 years in jail. What distinguished Madoff from other white-collar criminals was not just the size and longevity of his scam, but the fact that he was so trusted, as a former chairman of the Nasdaq stock company, and the high regard with which he was held in New York City's management circles. In an ironic postscript, Madoff was transferred to the Atlanta Federal penitentiary in July 2009, a jail where Charles Ponzi did time.

The father of the Ponzi scheme

Charles Ponzi (1877–1949) orchestrated one of the most famous swindles in American history, and his name has been forever linked with his 1919 scheme that brought in millions of dollars, although no one knows for sure how much was lost by investors. The

Italian immigrant had a checkered career as a dishwasher, forger, and alien smuggler after coming to America in 1899. He came upon the scheme rather serendipitously when he discovered he could buy up international postal union reply coupons at low prices in various countries and then mark them up and sell at a 50 percent profit in the United States. Through an astute advertising campaign claiming that investors could expect large returns, investors flooded him with requests to get in on the bargain. As word spread, millions of dollars poured into Ponzi's coffers. In one day alone in 1920, he reportedly reaped at least $2 million. On the face of it, the scheme was rather simple, as twenty-first-century practitioners have found out. He would pay the high returns to early investors as new money came in from others. As long as the funds mounted, he could continue to pay interest on old accounts, whose owners could vouch for his sincerity. Ponzi never had to actually invest any of his own money, and he spent most of the money on his dandified lifestyle while paying off early investors. But after about six months, newspapers began to investigate this unlikely "rags-to-riches" story. However, Ponzi was able to buy time by filing lawsuits against the newspapers. Ponzi sued one newspaper for libel and won a $500,000 judgment, which effectively tabled the investigation for the moment. Subsequently, another newspaper revealed that his past included a stint in prison for forgery and alien smuggling. He would eventually be convicted and sentenced to prison for his fraud, and in 1934, he was deported back to Italy upon his release. During the investigation of Ponzi, it was discovered that, out of the millions of dollars he took in, he had only purchased $30 in international mail coupons. He died in Brazil in 1949.[105]

Subprime mortgage crisis

One of the tragedies of the 9/11 terrorist attacks was that warning signs were missed early on, even though several agents from the FBI reported suspicious activities that would eventually be linked to the tragedy to their superiors. Likewise, at least two years before the subprime mortgage scandal, one top FBI official had warned of a widening mortgage fraud crisis up the road, but no one within the agency responded. In this case, the agent seems omniscient having predicted in 2004, "The booming mortgage business, fueled by low interest rates and soaring home values, was starting to attract shady operators and billions in losses were possible."[106]

In many respects, the mortgage-fraud debacle was another by-product of the massive reassignment of agents to counterterrorism duties after 9/11. One high-ranking FBI official admitted in 2009 that the agency knew of the fraud as far back as 2002 while other officials concede that they were stretched too thin due to their new duties in the war on terrorism. But there was enough blame to go around. The FBI also blamed the SEC for failing to detect the mortgage fraud schemes in a timely fashion.[107] Despite the mea culpas, the early twenty-first century was no ordinary era. The FBI, like its "parent agency" the Justice Department, directed its attention toward other national priorities, particularly national security, and paid scant attention to "bloodless" white-collar crimes and fraudulent banking practices.

The financial crisis was widely considered the country's worst since the Great Depression. Most observers asserted its roots were firmly planted in the subprime mortgage crisis, which began in 2006. The mortgage crisis was caused by several factors including unprincipled lending practices in the mortgage industry, deceptive credit ratings, and years of deregulation and loose mortgage standards.

Less than a decade ago, banks assiduously examined a borrower's credit history and income, and if they did not the meet the qualification criteria for the loan, it was refused. But the lending fraud at the root of the recent scandal involved mortgage lenders who issued loans based on information that lenders knew mischaracterized the customer's actual financial status, such as exaggerating income or assets, perhaps using false employment information or even overstating property values.[108] Industry insiders began referring to subprime loans as "ninja loans" – in other words "no income, no job, no questions asked." Many of the victims tended to be "lower income borrowers" who in many cases were "duped" into taking loans they did not understand and could ill afford. Victims of naiveté, the proud new homeowners eventually found themselves weighted down with escalating interest payments, prepayment penalties, and dubious fees. Facing the fact they were on the cusp of not only losing their homes but any equity as well, many just walked away, leaving in some cases parts of entire new subdivisions deserted.

Eventually the subprime mortgage crisis cost investors billions of dollars and left taxpayers with a bill in the hundreds of billions of dollars. Few segments of the real estate market escaped this calamity. Victims included borrowers who had their homes foreclosed; neighborhoods with a number of foreclosed homes watched home values plummet; employees of failed investment banks and investors who purchased mortgage-based securities. In addition, anyone trying to finance a home faced the barrier of much tighter credit standards.[109]

In every major white-collar scam, there are always those who walked away with a fortune. The chief beneficiaries this time around were CEOs and the top executives of major mortgage lending companies and investment banks who earned tens of billions of dollars in salaries, bonuses, and stock options.

As far back as March 2008, the FBI Criminal Investigative Division had 1,253 mortgage fraud investigations ranging the gamut from "illegal property flipping" and home equity scams to check fraud cases.[110] A year later, the number of pending cases had almost doubled to 2,440. Estimated annual losses were in the billions of dollars. In 2008, the Department of Justice launched "Operation Malicious Mortgage," which involved a joint task force of federal agencies including the FBI, IRS, and Postal Inspection Service. During the three-and-a-half-month operation between March and June, 406 defendants were charged in 144 mortgage fraud cases. The FBI has also responded to the crisis by ordering twenty-six of its fifty-six field offices to focus on the subprime-mortgage crisis and drop other financial crimes investigations for the time being.

Contemporary China has some of the most punitive white-collar crime laws. Taking a hard-line approach towards financial crimes as the country become increasingly globalized in the market economy, in recent years, real estate investors, small business owners, political figures, and CEOs of large companies have landed on death rows, and many of them have been executed, unless they are politically well protected. Ii is not uncommon for those capitally convicted to be given two-year reprieves. In the event one maintains a record of good behavior during these two years, they have a chance of having their sentences converted to life in prison. In late 2009, two businessmen were put to death for selling more than 3 million gallons of contaminated milk powder, killing 6 children and sickening 300,000. Their crime involved adding a toxic industrial product to milk in order to give it the illusion of having a higher protein content than it actually did. In another case that same year, a beauty parlor operator was executed for illegally raising $100 million from investors, which she diverted to supporting her lavish lifestyle. Despite ending the death penalty for thirteen economic crimes in 2011, including tax fraud and forms of smuggling, an unknown number of white-collar criminals are no doubt still put to death each year.[111]

Capital punishment

Having set a one-year record of forty executions in 2000, Texas joined other states by considering the alternative of life without parole as a sentencing option to the death penalty in 2001.[112] As the nation's leading executioner, Texas offered juries the choice of sentencing a capital murderer to either death or life in prison, which carried the potential for parole after forty years. Most opinion polls suggest that, if life without parole was an option, few juries would recommend the death penalty. If Texas chose to offer this option, it would join forty-five states that provided the alternative at the end of the century. Opponents of this option in Texas argue that, if this passes, it would be one more step toward abolition of the death penalty and would necessitate the construction of more prisons.

For death penalty opponents, it is difficult to fathom that, almost thirty years after the *Furman* decision, the Supreme Court was still considering whether to execute the developmentally disabled killers. In March 2001, justices heard the appeal of a North Carolina death row inmate whose execution was interrupted earlier in the month. It had been twelve years since the Court upheld the constitutionality of executing the developmentally disabled in the case of Texas killer Johnny Paul Penry. Justice had initially overturned Penry's conviction in 1989 on the grounds that his trial failed to consider his mental retardation as a possible mitigating factor. Penry was later retried, convicted, and sentenced to death for his crime.[113]

At the time of the *Penry* decision, only Maryland and Georgia barred executing the developmentally disabled murderers. But this practice has become increasingly viewed as a human rights violation. By the twenty-first century, eighteen of the thirty-eight death penalty states and the federal government banned the execution of the developmentally disabled.[114]

In March 2001, the Supreme Court ruled that jurors must be told the full truth when they are deciding whether to sentence a killer to death or life in prison. In the case of ***Shafer v. South Carolina***, the Court reversed the death penalty for a South Carolina man who was condemned by jurors who were confused about the meaning of the phrase "life imprisonment." In this particular case, eighteen-year-old Wesley Aarin Shafer went to trial for the killing of a convenience store clerk during a robbery. Recent state law offered the possibility of either death or life in prison without the possibility of parole. The judge advised the jurors that they could decide on either "life imprisonment or death." When asked for clarification, the judge refused to respond to the jurors, leading to the death sentence. During the 1990s, all but five states approved laws that imprison convicted murderers for the rest of their natural lives with no parole option. Of the thirty-eight states with capital punishment, only four did not adopt no-parole laws.

David Fathi, director of the U.S. program at Human Rights Watch, suggested in 2008 that the U.S. has become "a global pariah" for its continued support for the death penalty, claiming that it was the world's fourth leading executioner behind China, Iran, and Saudi Arabia. Since the return of the death penalty in 1977, more than 1,160 American prisoners have been hanged, shot gassed, or lethally injected. Of these, only three executions carried out since 1997 have been by the federal government, with the rest carried out by mostly a handful of states – Texas, Virginia, and Oklahoma accounted for more than half of the executions in the modern era. And of the thirty-five states whose laws allow it, two have carried out none since 1977, and five only one each.

One of the unexpected trends in American criminal justice in 2009 was a decline in the amount of death sentences being doled out by juries. In 2008, 111 people were sentenced to death in America, the lowest number of any year since the reinstatement of the death penalty in 1976. There are several explanations for this turn of events. This reversal in course did not happen overnight. With the option of life without parole in all death penalty states, jurors, and judges were more willing to avoid the death penalty (ruling in costs and suspect convictions). Some suggest it lies on a question of innocence and greater scrutiny of capital cases. More than 130 individuals have been released from death rows between 1973 and 2009 after they were exonerated for the crimes. With the addition of DNA evidence beginning around 1999, the question of evidence resonated even stronger. Some authorities have suggested that the decline in death sentences mirrored the decline in murder rates. Still others point to the increased awareness of the racial disparities, especially that a white person that kills a black person is much less likely to be sentenced to death than a black person who kills a white person. State budgets have also played a role. Studies have demonstrated that states that seek the death penalty increase the cost of a murder prosecution from 38 percent to 70 percent. These concerns came at an inopportune moment, when states were already slashing budgets for education, health, and other vital services.

In 2007, New Jersey became the first state to ban executions since it was reinstated in 1976, and in 2009, New Mexico followed suit, becoming the 15th state to repeal the death penalty. Officials cite less than humanitarian reasons for the decision, citing time and money as the main reasons, but also conceding the potential for error as well. One observer noted "This is the first time in which cost has been the prevalent issue in discussing the death penalty."[115] What's more, death penalty trials are more expensive because they often require extra lawyers, strict experience requirements for attorneys, leading to lengthy appellate waits while competent counsel is sought for the accused; security costs are higher as well, as costs for processing evidence DNA testing, for example, is much more expensive than blood analysis. After sentencing costs continue to rise – it costs more to house death row inmates held in segregated sections of prisons in separate cells with guards expected to deliver everything required for the feeding and housing of inmates.[116]

Executions increased in 2009 over the previous year from thirty-seven to fifty-two. Although this was a period in which juries and judges had become less likely to sentence someone to death, the rise was likely due to the previous year's low number of executions as state's dealt with the backlog of forty canceled executions before the 2008 Supreme Court decision on lethal injection.

Cruel and unusual? The debate over lethal injection

Between 2007 and 2009, the legitimacy of lethal injection as a humane form of capital punishment was at the center of several court appeals that brought a seven-month de facto nationwide moratorium on the process. However, on April 16, 2008, in a 7–2 ruling, the Supreme Court in **Baze v. Reese**, upheld the use of lethal injection for capital punishment giving the go-ahead for the forty executions that had been put on hold until this issue was decided. In this case, two Kentucky inmates, Ralph Baze and another inmate, challenged the state's administration of the four-drug cocktail process as a violation against the Eighth Amendment against cruel and unusual punishment.[117] The Court ruled that the procedure used in Kentucky and other states with similar methods did not violate the constitutional prohibition against cruel and unusual punishments (as long as it was performed correctly). However, this was not the end of the story, at least as far as Kentucky was concerned. In November 2009, executions were suspended in Kentucky after the state's Supreme Court ruled that the state did not follow proper administrative procedures, including offering a public hearing, when it adopted the lethal injection method.[118] As of 2018, no new execution date had been set for Baze, the convicted killer of two peace officers.

Supreme Court challenges to the death penalty as a violation of the Eighth Amendment have a long sordid history in America. In the 7–2 decision, the Court noted its principle that defined cruelty as limited to punishments that "involve torture or a lingering death." This became especially clear after the 2008 decision to continue on with lethal injections. Two decisions illustrate the disparity between theory and practice on such occasions. In the 1879 decision *Wilkerson v. Utah*, Wallace Wilkerson's execution by firing squad was upheld after the Court found the method did not constitute cruel and unusual punishment. When it was his time to face the firing squad, Wilkerson declined the offer of a blindfold. As soon as he heard the command to fire he braced his body for death but happened to budge just enough for the bullets to miss his vital organs and hit his arm and torso instead. He reportedly cried out, "My God! They have missed." It took him almost a half hour to bleed to death in full viewing of a physician and witnesses. In 1890, the court ruled that the state of New York could carry on with the country's first execution by the electric chair, arguing William Kemmler could be executed in this manner because the method reduced substantial risks of a "lingering death" if compared to hanging. However, when Kemmler was executed, it took several surges of electricity to kill him and enough voltage to light his coat on fire.[119]

The next major challenge to lethal injection came out of Ohio after a botched execution under the state's traditional three-drug method. In this case, Romell Broom had been sentenced to die for the rape and murder of a fourteen-year-old girl in 1984. On September 15,

2008, he was placed on the gurney for his lethal injection. A lifetime intravenous drug user, prison officials spent almost two hours searching for a usable vein leading the convict to burst into tears. It was then decided to reschedule the execution for another date – the *first* time in U.S. history that an execution by lethal injection was rescheduled after a failed attempt. Broom later claimed he was stuck at least eighteen times. His attorneys challenged the process as cruel and unusual punishment while the state's assistant attorney general responded, "there is no evidence that Broom suffered pain of such severity as to rise to the level of severe pain prohibited by the Eight Amendment."[120] His new scheduled execution date is in 2020.

In 2009, Ohio became the first of the thirty-six states that used lethal injections to switch to a single powerful anesthetic, one dose of thiopental sodium (with a backup method using two intramuscular injections). Experts compared this method to the way pets were euthanized by veterinarians. While other states such as California have considered the one-drug method, fears about "unpredictable consequences" have so far prevented it. Even Chief Justice John Roberts weighed in suggesting that this method "has problems of its own" before it was used for the first time.[121] Nonetheless, it was used for the first time on December 8, 2009, in the execution of killer Kenneth Biros the same day his appeal was rejected by the U.S. Supreme Court.

Juvenile criminal justice: life without parole?

As of late 2009, 109 people were serving sentences of life without parole for non-homicide crimes committed while under the age of 18 (at least 2,500 were serving life without parole for murder or participating in a crime that led to murder). All of these prisoners were in the United States, and almost three-quarters of them were in Florida prisons.[122] By 2010, eight states had juvenile offenders serving life without parole for non-homicide crimes, including Louisiana, California, Delaware, Iowa, Mississippi, Nebraska, South Carolina, and Florida. In stark comparison, the maximum juvenile sentence for any crime in Germany was ten years and twenty-four years in Italy.

The controversy over how to sentence juvenile offenders for serious felonies had been brewing for many years and would continue well into the second decade of the twenty-first century. During the 1990s, Florida was at the epicenter of the debate at a time when the state was rocked by a rising juvenile crime rate and a number of high profile crimes by juveniles that tarnished the image of this vacation haven and threatening the state tourism industry. In 1992–1993 alone, nine foreign tourists were killed during a single eleven-month period, including one committed by a fourteen-year-old. One state legislator opined that Florida should be called the "Gunshine State" instead of the "Sunshine State."[123] This moniker would still be applied more than twenty years later after several of America's worst mass murders took place here.

In its rush to judgment, the state of Florida began moving more juveniles into adult courts, lengthening sentences and doing away with parole for capital crimes. In the 1990s, these actions were heavily supported by "law and order" advocates. However, as juvenile crime declined in the state by 30 percent between 1994 and 2004, critics charged that the continued draconian legislation was a hysterical response to a looming juvenile crime wave promised by criminologists, but that never materialized.

In 1989, a thirteen-year-old Floridian was sentenced to life in prison without parole for robbing and raping an elderly woman. In 2005, a sixteen-year-old in Florida was deemed "incorrigible" by a judge and given the same punishment as above after several arrests for robbery. Both these cases were at the center of a court debate to determine whether it was cruel and unusual to send a teenage to prison with no chance of parole. These are just 2 of the 109 inmates serving life sentences for non-homicide crimes committed when they were younger than 18. In November 2009, the U.S. Supreme Court heard arguments about whether children should ever be sentenced to life without parole for crimes that don't involve murder. The Court had already ruled (5–4) in 2005 in **Roper v. Simmons** that executing convicts for offenses committed before the age of eighteen was unconstitutional. The jurists cited such factors as immaturity, irresponsibility, and susceptibility to peer pressure and potential for turning lives around.[124]

The distinction between childhood and adulthood remains a point of contention for the American criminal justice system. Research has shown that different people mature at different ages. Behavioral and neurological research by Professor Laurence Steinberg at Temple University revealed that "young teenagers seek out risk and have trouble controlling their impulses" which by all accounts is "a very bad combination when it comes to crime." These studies were used as mitigating factors in considering the execution of convicts for crimes committed under the age of eighteen in 2005 and are now a "centerpiece in the current Supreme Court cases about life without parole."[125]

The continuing war on drugs

The 2009 National Drug Threat Assessment stated that "Mexican drug trafficking organizations represent the greatest organized crime threat to the United States."[126] According to its findings, the number one drug threat was cocaine followed by methamphetamine and then, in descending order, marijuana, heroin, pharmaceutical drugs, and ecstasy (MDMA). One of the more troubling findings was that numerous urban street gangs were becoming increasingly involved in "wholesale drug distribution aided by their connections with Mexican and Asian drug trafficking organizations."[127]

Historically poor relations between the United States and Mexico dating back to the Mexican–American War of 1846 have hampered cooperation between the two countries' police agencies. Cooperation began to improve during the administrations of Vicente Fox (2000–2006) and current president Felipe Calderon. As a result, Mexico for the first time is allowing U.S. military personnel to offer training. In 2010, the most powerful drug gangs in the Americas were headquartered in Mexico, but flourished on both sides of the border. Their criminal activities included money laundering, armed robbery, kidnapping for ransom, extortion, and illegal weapons trafficking. These operations have become much more lucrative since the passage of the North American Free Trade Agreement (NAFTA) between Canada, the U.S., and Mexico in 1994. Being strategically located on the American border allowed Mexican drug trafficking organizations to respond quickly to changing drug trends in the U.S., where most drug users live. During this period, the violent war between the drug gangs has often spilled across the border into the United States. American officials identified 230 cities where these gangs operated including Boston, Atlanta, and Anchorage.

In 2009, the U.S. Center for Disease Control (CDC) announced that drug-related deaths outnumbered those from car accidents in many states. According to their calculations, the rate of drug-induced deaths outpaced car wrecks in sixteen states in 2006, double the number since 2003. The overwhelming majority of drug-related deaths were the results of overdoses. One explanation for this is that the number of car crash victims spiraled downward between 1999 and 2006 at the same time drug deaths were increasing due to the rising popularity of opioid analgesics such as methadone and fentanyl, sedatives, and painkillers such as Vicodin and OxyContin, and the old standby, cocaine. Few could have forecast the precipitous rise in drug overdoses in the 2010s.

Restitution

In 2004, almost one-fifth of all felons convicted in the United States were given an additional penalty of restitution. Nationwide unpaid court-ordered restitution was estimated in the billions of dollars.[128] When convicted offenders are sentenced, their punishment might include incarceration, fines, restitution, and other penalties. But when it comes to restitution, there is more bark than bite in the law. Often the punishment is regarded as symbolic, since the offender is rarely in the financial position to pay what is owed or is incarcerated. For example, almost two decades earlier, a young burglar was found guilty of burning down a church and was ordered to pay $2.4 million. By the time the church was completed, he had contributed less than $400.[129] However, states began to back up these judgments, even turning to outside collection agencies to supplement their own in-house efforts. In 2003, Arizona reported $831 million in unpaid court costs, fines, fees, and restitution. After contracting with a major collection company, it brought in $90 million over the next four years. Arizona is even going after tax refunds and preventing individuals from registering cars if they don't pay up. A variety of strategies are used in other states for collecting these funds. Pennsylvania used a computer system that allows counties to customize payment plans, track overdue payments, and create delinquency papers. Florida enforces an income deduction order as part of a restitution agreement, while Colorado employs 100 collection investigators who collaborate with offenders to come up with a repayment scheme.

The decline in violent crime

At the end of the first decade of the new century, America's crime rates were noticeably lower than in the past. In fact, there were declines in all serious crimes and pronounced decreases in violent crime. Nowhere has the decline been felt more than among lower income households and minorities.[130] A number of studies asserted that the spike in violence in mostly poor minority communities in the mid-1980s and early 1990s was instigated by the nature of the crack trade. Crack, it has been noted, "has unique psychopharmacological effects on users" that includes high sense of paranoia and a predisposition to violence when compared to other drugs. What's more, compared to other drugs, the number of purchases per user, due to its small and inexpensive quantities, makes higher frequency of contact between dealers and users unavoidable and increases potential for violence. Raphael and Stoll made an interesting case for the coterminous relationship between the rise and fall of the crack cocaine and the rise and fall of inner-city violence during this era.[131]

For Americans at home and abroad, the first decade of the twenty-first century was an era punctuated by violence. Book-ended by two high profile domestic terrorist attacks, first on 9/11, 2001, and then ending with the Ft. Hood shootings (and the failed Christmas Day attack by the "underpants bomber") at the end of 2009. These attacks revealed the continuing futility and failures of American anti-terrorism strategies, what President Obama has alluded to as "human and systemic failures."[132]

The relationship between mental health issues and violence was brought home with several high profile cases involving child homicide and mass murder. This decade witnessed the case of Andrea Yates, who drowned her five children in a bathtub, and further debate about the insanity defense and increased awareness about postpartum depression and psychoses. Yates was quickly convicted of capital murder and sentenced to life only to have it overturned and found not guilty by reason of insanity. She was transferred from prison to Kerrville State Hospital. And on April 16, 2007, a senior at Virginia Polytechnic Institute and State University (Virginia Tech), went on a campus rampage that left thirty-two students and faculty dead and twenty-five wounded, in what became known as the **Virginia Tech Massacre.** It was the nation's worst mass murder until the following decade, when it was surpassed several more times. According to the subsequent report of the Virginia Tech Review Panel, a 260-page report issued in August 2007, mental health staff at the school had failed to "connect the dots" after missing numerous warning signs of mental instability of the shooter Seung-Hui Cho. What perhaps was most troubling was that he had been able to purchase two guns in violation of federal law because the state of Virginia had inadequate background check requirements.

Part serial killers and terrorists, domestic terrorism struck urban America in 2002 when traveling snipers Lee Boyd Malvo John Allen Muhammed, known as the **DC Snipers**," shot sixteen individuals, killing ten in a shooting spree that lasted from September to October, paralyzing holiday shoppers in the Washington, DC, corridor. Muhammed was executed in November 2009. His accomplice, who was seventeen at the time of the shooting spree, was sentenced to life in prison without parole in Virginia.

In 2006, the FBI *Uniform Crime Reports* showed a rise in violent crime for the second year in a row. What was most troubling was this was the first sustained increase in homicides, robberies, and other serious offenses since the early 1990s, almost fifteen years earlier. Much of the increase was accounted for in medium-sized cities such as Washington, DC. Researchers and law enforcement officials offered varying explanations for the increase, including the usual culprits – an increase in juvenile population, growing numbers of released prison inmates, and the rise of serious gang problems in smaller jurisdictions. Democratic lawmakers blamed the Bush administration for a lack of federal assistance to local police forces. Then Senator Joseph Biden, as chairman of a Senate Subcommittee on Crime and Terrorism, asserted "It's time to get back to crime fighting basics – that means more cops on the streets, equipped with the tools and resources they need to keep neighborhoods safe."[133] Former Attorney General Alberto Gonzalez bristled at this criticism, claiming, "it doesn't appear that the current data reveal nationwide trends" but "show local increases in certain communities," and in many places, he noted "violent crime continues to decrease."[134] In some respects, the attorney general was correct, for indeed crime patterns often vary according to region and demographics.

In 2009, the FBI released the previous year's crime data, which indicated a 4 percent drop in murder and manslaughter compared to the prior year, part of a nationwide drop in violent crime. Violent crime is a metric kept by the FBI and police departments across country as a gauge of an area's safety, includes murder, rape, robbery, and aggravated assault. Rapes declined to the lowest national average in 20 years (14,180 murders in 2008). In 2009, Houston Police Chief Harold Hurtt suggested that a better measure of crime rates is to compare crime rates to previous years "since different places present different crime fighting scenarios, such as the geographic area of a city or its number of high crime apartment complexes." The FBI warns against comparisons for these same reasons.[135]

Hate crimes

A number of experts and other observers who monitor hate groups were worried that the election of an African American president would spur the activities of hate groups and reinvigorate the white power movement. In 2009, the Southern Poverty Law Center (SPLC) noted that, in 2008, there were 929 hate groups nationally compared to 602 in 2007. While it is not clear how many are active, the number of reported hate crime remained steady at almost 7,500 each year over the past ten years.[136] According to 2008 hate crime statistics, 7,783 hate crime incidents involving 9,168 offenses were reported through Uniform Crime Reporting. More than half were racially biased, followed those based on sexual orientation (17.7 percent), religious bias (17.5 percent), and ethnicity/national origin bias (12.5 percent).[137]

The immigrant factor in homicide rates

Between 2002 and 2007, homicide increases were reported in Philadelphia, Baltimore, Newark, and other East Coast cities (New York remained steady).[138] There were some interesting anomalies in the murder rates as the decade moved to conclusion. One explanation that has been bandied about by criminal justice experts was that this is because there is "not enough new immigrants." Supporters of this theory suggest that "waves of hardworking, ambitious immigrants reinvigorate desperately poor black and Hispanic neighborhoods and help keep crime down."[139] This runs counter to the propagated notion that immigrants were more a source of crime and disorder. One researcher pointed out that, in many cities, immigrants "tend to be crime victims rather than perpetrators."[140]

Sociologists such as Harvard's Robert Sampson countered that cities experiencing waves of immigration such as Los Angeles and New York were actually being transformed and revitalized by waves of new immigrants who had gone to great trouble to reach America where they could work hard and avoid trouble. Nonetheless, the immigration factor was only one explanation. Others offer that cities that do not integrate innovative practices that have lowered violence in larger cities, such as limiting gun purchases, suing rogue dealers, and deploying officers strategically based on crime data analysis are missing the boat. Still others blame the availability of high-powered weapons, the ongoing shift in resources from fighting street crime to homeland security and terrorism prevention, and the resigned acceptance of "quality-of-life crimes" such as vandalism and traffic infractions – actions that breed disrespect for law and order.

Newark experiment

Between 2002 and 2006, Newark, New Jersey, the state's largest city, saw a 50 percent rise in homicides, continuing a trend that existed for almost forty years. However, in January 2008, a new strategy resulted in no homicides in thirty-three days, something that had not occurred since 1963. According to the Newark Police Chief and former chief crime strategist for the NYPD Garry J. McCarthy, this could be chalked up to several factors that were part of a larger crime fighting strategy that included prosecuting petty crimes such as loitering and public drunkenness along with more serious crime, as well as better sharing of information and resources with other police departments, including the FBI, the DEA, and the state police. The city has supplemented this program by installing 120 surveillance cameras in high crime areas of the city.[141]

Notable trials

The trial of George Zimmerman

On February 26, 2012, a seventeen-year-old African American man named **Trayvon Martin** was walking home from a store in central Florida. The young man was actually visiting his father who lived in the neighborhood and was returning home after a short walk to a convenience store.

He had a box of Skittles and a bottle of iced tea and was talking on his cellphone to a girlfriend when he was confronted by a gun-wielding neighborhood watchman named George Zimmerman. The twenty-eight-year-old man of mixed Hispanic ethnicity, was acting as a so-called "block watch coordinator" for his gated community when he noticed a young black male sporting a hooded sweatshirt who appeared to be aimlessly walking down the sidewalk. He called 911 to report a suspicious person walking in the neighborhood. Zimmerman concealed his handgun and followed Martin, ignoring the admonitions of the 911 dispatcher not to. After this call, the consensus on the events that followed are still clouded in suspicion, innuendo, and doubt. Disregarding the 911 operator's instructions, the two men had a brief altercation, leaving Martin dead from one gunshot wound.

Zimmerman and Martin were the only direct witnesses to what happened, and one was dead. The only fact that most agreed on was that there *was* some type of physical confrontation and Zimmerman fired as he was losing a fight with Trayvon. Initially, Zimmerman was taken into custody but was released after five hours of questioning. No charges were filed after Zimmerman convinced the police he fired in self-defense.

Martin's parents were outraged, and in order to spur an investigation and arrest, they launched an online petition that eventually tallied more than a million signatures. Subsequent rallies ignited a social media firestorm as protesters sought Zimmerman's arrest. One indelible image was of rally participants wearing hoodies as Trayvon did the night he died, with many carrying signs with the phrase, "I am Trayvon Martin." Even President Obama famously weighed in, commenting, "If I had a son, he'd look like Trayvon."[142] Just several days later, the Justice Department and the FBI announced an investigation. Concomitantly, the Sanford, Florida, police chief stepped down amid the controversy over his handling the case. A special prosecutor was appointed and on April 11, 2012, forty-three days after the killing, Zimmerman was charged with second degree murder, subsequently turning himself in. He was released on bail after a new bond of $1 million was set.

The delay between the shooting and the arrest of Zimmerman was, according to police, attributable to Florida's "Stand Your Ground" law.[143] According to this statute, one does not need to retreat from a violent attack by another person; moreover, the law can be used to justify using deadly force to protect oneself.[144] In Florida, the "Stand Your Ground" law provided that a person attacked "in any other place whether he or she has the right to be" has *no* **duty to retreat** before killing in self-defense.

As he raised money for his trial and made the rounds of the news circuit offering his version of events and admitting he would not have done anything differently, his defense attorney Mark O'Mara decided to eschew the "**stand your ground defense**" in favor of the more traditional self-defense strategy in the subsequent criminal trial. Some observers have opined that the prosecution erred from the start by filing a second degree murder charge against Zimmerman instead of manslaughter, essentially "overcharging" the case. Florida State Attorney Angela Corey disagreed, arguing that the allegations against the defendant "fit the bill" for the second degree murder charge, which in Florida is defined as "a killing carried out with hatred, ill will or spite, but is not premeditated."[145] Thus, in order to convict him, the jury would have to accept that Zimmerman "intentionally committed an act or acts" that caused the death of Trayvon Martin. With little evidence, the case was a tough sell for both sides.

Judge Debra Nelson ruled in a number of pretrial issues, excluding testimony about previous altercations Martin might have been involved in and also denying a jury request to visit the crime scene. Once an all-female jury of six white women was empaneled, on June 24, 2013, opening arguments were presented and on July 5, Zimmerman's defense team began presenting its case to the jury.

As the only survivor of the confrontation, the trial hinged on the testimony of Zimmerman. The case was a challenge for the prosecution. One law enforcement analyst noted that the "various adverse conditions played into the initial investigation that night: A dark rainy scene isn't ideal for homicide investigation."[146] One important inconsistency was the fact that there was little blood or evidence of a fight before the shooting, although Zimmerman claimed he feared for his life after he was "attacked" by Martin. Likewise, a medical examiner and expert on gunshot wounds testified that "the rain could have washed away and affected evidence collected from Martin's hands."[147]

Trials come down to what you can prove in court. There was so little evidence that the defense put together an animated video reconstruction of the events based on witness accounts, police reports, and Zimmerman's statements. The judge ruled against introducing the video.

Among the highlights of the trial was the testimony of nineteen-year-old Rachel Jeantel. Trayvon had been speaking with her on his cellphone when he was confronted by Zimmerman. Expected to be the prosecution's star witness, her performance on the witness stand was, according to one TV news commentator, a "train wreck." Initially reluctant to testify, she did the prosecution no favors, exhibiting what many described as a combative personality over her two days of testimony (about seven hours in all). For some viewers, her mumbling and impudence just reinforced negative racial stereotypes that played an increasingly important role in the trial. Others, however, suggested that the reaction to her testimony "steered the trial into a new phase, reflecting more on America's privileged classes, including blacks, then Jeantel's trustworthiness as a star witness."[148]

According to one Drexel University professor, the reaction to the witness was more a case of "aesthetics . . . of disregarding a witness on the basis of how she talks, how good she is at reading and writing." Professor George Ciccariello-Maher asserted that

> These are subtle things that echo literacy testing at the polls, echo the question of whether black Americans can testify against white people, of being always suspect in their testimony. It's the same old dynamics emerging in a very different disguise.[149]

Put another way by a Florida reporter,

> What so much of this really revealed was the gulf between middle-age, middle-class, mainstream codes of behavior and life among youth from poorer, nonwhite neighborhoods . . . they couldn't have been further apart if Jeantel were born on the moon.[150]

Later, after her intelligence was being mocked in the media, the prosecution revealed she was multi-lingual, conversant in Spanish and Haitian Creole as well as English. However, by this time, it was probably too late to change anyone's first impressions.

For many trial observers, according to Jelani Cobb, the social media response to Jeantel's testimony brought "out the worst in all of us." He described her almost two days on the stand as often "hard to watch." Not just because of the details she offered on the final moments of Martin's life, but also due to her "appearance, diction, size, and intelligence," all of which were an unspoken ingredient of the "all-encompassing part of the proceedings."[151]

Although she had known had known Trayvon since second grade, she admitted lying about why she didn't attend his wake. Telling some people she had to go to the hospital and others that she couldn't bear to see his body, commenting "You got to understand I was the last one to see him alive."[152]

Jeantel's almost seven hours on the stand were riveting. Attorneys for both sides attempted to prove that prejudicial views and tendencies were attributed to both sides of the deadly incident, both on the part of Martin and Zimmerman. Jeantel famously testified that she heard a "heavy-breathing man" ask Martin, "What are you doing around here?" This was just after Trayvon had told her a "creepy-ass cracker" was trailing him. To counter this, the defense followed with several murky accounts of purported witnesses describing Martin beating up Zimmerman before the fatal shot was fired.

The state alleged that Zimmerman had racially profiled Trayvon, when he chased and confronted him and then shot Martin after he found himself losing a fight. The question that loomed largest over the trial had the right to self-defense against the armed adult stranger following him the dark and whether Zimmerman waived his self-defense rights when he made the decision to pursue Trayvon after he told a 911 dispatcher that "these [guys] always get away."

On July 13, 2013, the jury found Zimmerman not guilty. One commentator described the killing of Mr. Martin as a double homicide, asserting that the first homicide took place when Trayvon was shot and the second involved "a series of escalating failures of a legal system and process that resulted in the acquittal of Zimmerman."[153] The trial and acquittal of George

Zimmerman for the murder of Trayvon Martin sparked an intense national debate about race and criminal justice. The debate would reach a crescendo in the years to come as more and more cases involving the killing of unarmed black men by white police officers became part of a national conversation over race. The killing of Martin and the acquittal of Zimmerman and the subsequent demonstrations and rallies protesting what many Americans saw as another example of racial profiling anticipated the Black Lives Matter movement several years later. In the years following this case, verdicts have played out in courtrooms around the country. In the killing of Michael Brown in Ferguson, Missouri, for example, a grand jury found no probable cause in the shooting of the unarmed teenager, while holding arms up and only yards away from police. Likewise, the stunning failure to bring charges against officers in the death of Eric Garner in New York City. The final word on the Zimmerman case came down from the Justice Department on February 14, 2015, when it closed the federal investigation into the death of Trayvon Martin. High profile cases, such as the one just chronicled, have proven to be capable of shaping and reflecting public attitudes about offenders and the criminal justice process in America. Examining criminal cases in their historical contexts offers readers a portal into the how the American criminal justice system operates, while raising important questions about whether justice administered impartially and efficiently.

Conclusions

No decade in modern American history was defined by terrorism as much as the first ten years of the twenty-first century. It began with the 9/11 attacks that led to two foreign wars and big changes in the way Americans lived and traveled. As the first decade of the new century came to an end, the country was beginning to come out of its deepest recession since the 1930s. The unemployed stood at 15.4 million and the jobless rate at 10 percent (historically normal 5.5 percent) at the end of 2009. It dropped just below 10 percent in the first month of 2010. Nonetheless, millions of jobs had disappeared, leading some economists to label the next decade as the "New Abnormal," fearing that high unemployment will average at 8 percent.

A number of hopeful new criminal justice trends began during the 2000s, including the diminished reliance on mandatory-minimum sentences. Perhaps, none had more impact than the movement in some states to soften laws on harsh drug sentences. The movement toward lessening sentences made its greatest strides in 2004. One of the more encouraging developments has been the decrease in black imprisonment rates, which paralleled the decline in the number of black offenders between 2000 and 2008. However, black males were still incarcerated at a rate six and a half times that of whites. The decline in the black imprisonment rate overall is probably due to fewer blacks being imprisoned for drug offenses.[154] Nonetheless, about 1 in every 198 United States residents was incarcerated in state or federal prisons at the end of 2008.

One of the more unforeseen results of the age of terrorism has been the increasing role played by federal corrections in the criminal justice process – albeit in crimes revolving around terrorist criminal acts. President Obama called for an additional $527.5 million dollars for the federal prison service (and judicial security) in the 2011 budget proposal, increasing the Bureau of Prisons budget to $6.8 billion. This is in stark contrast to state prisons, which were cutting budgets and adopting a wide range of alternatives and even closing some prisons. Almost half of the federal funding was directed at plans to close the military detention unit at Guantanamo

Bay, Cuba, and the transferal of a number of terrorist suspects to a prison in Illinois. Other provisions in the budget related to criminal justice include increased expenditures for hiring new prison guards and adding agents to the FBI, DEA, ATF, and U.S. Marshals Service.[155]

Americans never have been of one mind about the death penalty. At the turn of the decade, a number of states facing budget shortfalls were reconsidering the high cost of executions. At least ten states were considering ending it altogether. New Jersey jumped on the abolition bandwagon in 2007 when it figured out that the state could save $1.3 million on incarceration costs alone per condemned inmate by doing away with death row. What's more, the declining number of death sentences each year suggested that in an age of DNA testing, juries were more willing to opt for life without parole if it was available as an alternative. As one death penalty critic pointed out, "the death penalty turns out to be a very expensive form of life imprisonment,"[156] citing the fact that of the 3,279 prisoners on death row in 2009, only 52 were executed. Of course others will disagree, arguing that only evaluating the penalty from an economic perspective ignores the justice elements inherent in its use.

Historian Jill Lepore asserted that "among affluent democracies, the death penalty, like the U.S. homicide and incarceration rates marks an American exception."[157] No matter the advances in crime fighting and the research findings of legions of sociologists, criminologists, historians, and public officials, none have yet been able to explain why the United States still "has the highest homicide rate of any affluent democracy, nearly four times that of France and UK, and six times Germany."[158] One common theme has been the availability of firearms, which in 2008 were used in two-thirds of all murders in the United States. From an historical perspective, a number of European scholars have looked back over America's violent domestic history and suggested that the United States went through a different process of the "civilizing process." But American historian Randolph Roth recently opined that gun death statistics do not tell the whole story, suggesting that Americans have not necessarily intended to kill each other more often, they just have succeeded more often, noting that "three out of four people murdered before 1850 would probably survive today" if they had access to modern medicine, emergency response teams, trauma surgery, antibiotics, and wound care.[159]

However, one issue many observers can agree on was that exceptional high profile crimes – juvenile murders, mass murders, and terrorist attacks often lead to the creation of "**bad laws**." No crime in American history was as high profile and resulted in as much carnage as the attacks of 9/11 that left almost 3,000 dead on American soil. In its aftermath, the federal government introduced a number of new laws and crime fighting strategies that were controversial if not unconstitutional in some respects. Over the ensuing years, officials were able to reflect on what had transpired on 9/11 and that also meant revisiting the rushed legislation that followed. Within several years, many of these laws and strategies had been done away with by the Bush administration. Several Supreme Court decisions between 2004 and 2007 reversed White House policies despite attempts to increase executive authority in counterterrorism. These included allowing several enemy combatants to contest their arrest (2004); declaring the military tribunal system established at Guantanamo Bay, Cuba, illegal due to lack of congressional approval (2006); and a decision that prevents prosecution of U.S. citizens arrested in U.S. from being tried outside the criminal court system (2007). Likewise, California's three strikes laws, conceived too quickly in the aftermath of the Polly Klaas murder, have proven to be "bad law" as well. But it has taken the criminal justice system much longer to come to the realization and is only now dealing with it because of state prison budget issues.

In January 2010, President Barack Obama became the first African American president and "the first president to take office in the Age of Terrorism." He inherited two struggles – one with al Qaeda and its ideological allies and another that divides his own country over issues like torture, prosecutions, security, and what it means to be an American. "The first has proved to be complicated and daunting. The second makes the first look easy."[160] One journalist suggested that the new president "adopted the bulk of the counterterrorism strategy he found on his desk when he arrived in the Oval Office, a strategy that has already been moderated from the earliest days after 9/11."[161]

The history of America's criminal justice system proves that, if anything, no challenge to it is wholly new. The age of terrorism points to the fact that like other eras in history there is a "tradeoff" to be made between security and liberty. Prior chapters have demonstrated a number of lessons in American criminal justice history where the government took unpopular steps such as curbing civil liberties. Those previously covered included the Alien and Sedition Acts (1798), which punished free speech; President Lincoln's suspension of habeas corpus during the Civil War and the introduction of martial law; the prosecution of critics of World War I under President Woodrow Wilson; the internment of Japanese Americans during World War II; COINTELPRO at the height of the Vietnam War; and surveillance and bugging campaigns under Nixon and Hoover. These events echo in the current "war on terror," beginning with the Bush administration's call for military tribunals. The problem according to most critics in "striking a balance" between security and liberty is recognizing one "did not need to sacrifice one for the other."[162]

As of the beginning of 2010, the American criminal justice system continued to struggle with how to respond to the new era of crime and punishment. This was most glaring in the aftermath of the attempted Christmas Day 2009 bombing of a commercial airliner, when officials were unclear whether the Miranda warning extended to terrorist suspects. Despite being engaged in a campaign against domestic terror for more than a decade, the lines had not yet been firmly established on how to go about questioning a suspect. How does one differentiate between foreign and domestic terrorism cases? When can you conduct interviews? Where should suspected terrorists be imprisoned? Should terrorists be given their Miranda rights? These issues and others will surely be settled in the coming years, for American criminal justice is a work in progress that is constantly adapting to new challenges as history moves forward.

Point – counterpoint

The stand your ground defense

For more than a century, the American criminal justice system has grappled with how far someone can go in matters of self-defense. English common law established the doctrine of "duty to retreat." However, English law was transmogrified during the development of American jurisprudence and the doctrine evolved into the notion of "no duty to retreat." The duty to retreat doctrine was understood to mean that that individuals were expected to avoid physical conflict and let the courts peacefully decide the matter between the aggrieved parties. One was in fact expected to retreat from an enemy in any potential altercation until they were backed up against a wall. It was only at the point of "reasonably determined necessity," that one could physically protect themselves. In the event the aggressor was killed, courts would often decide it was an "excusable homicide" if all conditions satisfied the justice system. Richard Maxwell Brown, a historian of American violence, suggested that the law became Americanized, allowing an individual to stand their ground to kill in self-defense.[163]

*There were several Supreme Court and State Supreme Court cases in the nineteenth century that addressed the funda-
mentals of the self-defense doctrine. The first passage is taken from the 1895 case of **Beard v. United States**, revolving
around a homicide in the Oklahoma Territory after a dispute over a cow and a calf.[164] This court case expanded the
"castle doctrine" that permitted a person to kill someone inside the home without retreating, to also include outside the
premises. According to the historian, Brown, "it might have been this case that inspired" the term "hip-pocket ethics,"
due to the fact that Babe Beard claimed he stood his ground and smashed the skull of Will Jones when he feared that
he had a revolver in his hip-pocket.[165] It took two years for Beard to have his conviction overturned, winning acquittal under the "no duty to retreat" prerogative. The second passage is the 2017 Florida Justifiable Use of Force statute.*
Source: Beard v. US, 1895 case

The plaintiff in error, a white man and not an Indian, was indicted in the Circuit Court of the United States for the Western District of Arkansas for the crime of having killed and murdered in the Indian country, and within that District, one Will Jones, also a white person and not an Indian. He was found guilty of manslaughter and, a motion for a new trial having been overruled, it was adjudged that he be imprisoned in Kings County Penitentiary, at Brooklyn, New York, for the term of eight years, and pay to the United States a fine of $500. The principal question in the case arises out of those parts of the charge in which the court instructed the jury as to the principles of the law of self-defense.

There was evidence before the jury tending to establish the following facts:

An angry dispute arose between Beard and three brothers by the name of Jones – Will Jones, John Jones, and Edward Jones – in reference to a cow which a few years before that time, and just after the death of his mother, was set apart to Edward. The children being without any means for their support were distributed among their relatives, Edward being assigned to Beard, whose wife was a sister of Mrs. Jones. Beard took him into his family upon the condition that he should have the right to control him and the cow as if the lad were one of his own children, and the cow his own property. At the time Edward went to live with Beard he was only eight or nine years of age, poorly clad, and not in good physical condition. After remaining some years with his aunt and uncle, Edward Jones left the Beard house and determined, with the aid of his older brothers, to take the cow with him, each of them knowing that the accused objected to that being done.

The Jones brothers, one of them taking a shotgun with him, went upon the premises of the accused for the purpose of taking the cow away, whether Beard consented or not. But they were prevented by the accused from accomplishing that object, and he warned them not to come to his place again for such a purpose, informing them that, if Edward Jones was entitled to the possession of the cow, he could have it, provided his claim was successfully asserted through legal proceedings instituted by or in his behalf.

Will Jones, the oldest of the brothers, and about twenty or twenty-one years of age, publicly avowed his intention to get the cow away from the Beard farm or kill Beard, and of that threat the latter was informed on the day preceding that on which the fatal difficulty in question occurred.

In the afternoon of the day on which the Jones brothers were warned by Beard not again to come upon his premises for the cow unless attended by an officer of the law, and in defiance of that warning, they again went to his farm, in his absence – one of them, the deceased, being armed with a concealed deadly weapon – and attempted to take the cow away, but were prevented from doing so by Mrs. Beard, who drove it back into the lot from which it was being taken.

While the Jones brothers were on the defendant's premises in the afternoon, for the purpose of taking the cow away, Beard returned to his home from a town near by – having with him a shotgun that he was in the habit of carrying, when absent from home – and went at once from his dwelling into the lot, called the orchard lot, a distance of about 50 or 60 yards from his house and near to that part of an adjoining field or lot where the cow was, and in which the Jones brothers and Mrs. Beard were at the time of the difficulty.

Beard ordered the Jones brothers to leave his premises. They refused to leave. Thereupon Will Jones, who was on the opposite side of the orchard fence, ten or fifteen yards only from Beard, moved towards the latter with an angry manner and in a brisk walk, having his left hand (he being, as Beard knew, left-handed) in the left pocket of his trousers. When he got within five or six steps of Beard, the latter warned him to stop, but he did not do so. As he approached nearer the accused asked him what he intended to do, and he replied: "Damn you, I will show you," at the same time making a movement with his left hand as if to draw a pistol from his pocket; whereupon the accused struck him over the head with his gun and knocked him down.

"Believing," the defendant testified, "from his demonstrations just mentioned that he intended to shoot me, I struck him over the head with my gun to prevent him killing me. As soon as I struck him his brother John, who was a few steps behind him, started towards me with his hands in his pocket. Believing that he intended to take part in the difficulty and was also armed, I struck him and he stopped. I then at once jumped over the fence, caught Will Jones by the lapel of the coat, turned him rather to one side, and pulled his left hand out of his pocket. He had a pistol, which I found in his pocket, grasped in his left hand, and I pulled his pistol and his left hand out together. My purpose in doing this was to disarm him, to prevent him from shooting me, as I did not know how badly he was hurt. My gun was loaded, having ten cartridges in the magazine. I could have shot him, but did not want to kill him, believing that I could knock him down with the gun and disarm him and protect myself without shooting him. After getting his pistol, John Jones said something to me about killing him, to which I replied that I had not killed him and did not try to do so, for if I had I could have shot him. He said my gun was not loaded; thereupon I shot the gun in the air to show him that it was loaded."

Dr. Howard Hunt, a witness on behalf of the government, testified that he called to see Will Jones soon after he was hurt, and found him in a serious condition; that he died from the effects of a wound given by the defendant; that the wound was across the head, rather on the right side, the skull being crushed by the blow. He saw the defendant soon after dressing the wound, and told him that the deceased's condition was serious, and that he, the witness, was sorry the occurrence had happened. The witness suggested to the accused that perhaps he had better get out of the way. The latter replied that he was sorry that it had happened, but that he acted in self-defense and would not go away. Beard seemed a little offended at the suggestion that he should run off, and observed to the witness that the latter could not scare him, for he was perfectly justified in what he did. This witness further testified that he had known the defendant four or five years, was well acquainted in the neighborhood in which he lived, and knew his general reputation, which was that of a peaceable, law-abiding man.

The court stated at considerable length the general rules that determine whether the killing of a human being is murder or manslaughter, and, among other things, said to the jury: "If these boys, or young men, or whatever you may consider them, went down there, and they were there unlawfully – if they had no right to go there – you naturally inquire whether the defendant was placed in such a situation as that he could kill for that reason. Of course, he could not. He could not kill them because they were upon his place. . . . And if these young men were there in the act of attempting the larceny of this cow and calf and the defendant killed because of that, because his mind was inflamed for the reason that they were seeking to do an act of that kind, that is manslaughter; that, is all it is; there is nothing else in it; that is considered so far provocative as that it reduces the grade of the crime to manslaughter and no farther. If they had no intent to commit a larceny; if it was a bare, naked trespass; if they were there under a claim of right to get this cow, though they may not have had any right to it, but in good faith they were exercising their claim of that kind, and Will Jones was killed by the defendant for that reason, that would be murder, because you cannot kill a man for bare trespass – you cannot take his life for a bare trespass – and say the act is mitigated."

After restating the proposition that a man cannot take life because of mere fear on his part, or in order that he may prevent the commission of a bare trespass, the court proceeded: "Now, a word further upon the proposition that I have already adverted to as to **what was his duty** at the time. If that danger was real, coming from the hands of Will Jones, or it was apparent as coming from his hands and as affecting this defendant by some overt act at the time, was the defendant called upon to avoid that danger *by getting out of the way* of it if he could? The court says he was. The court tells you that he was. There is but one place where he need not retreat any further, where he need not go away from the danger, and that is in his dwelling-house. He may be upon his own premises, and if a man, while so situated and upon his own premises, can do that which would reasonably put aside the danger short of taking life, if he can do that, I say, he is called upon to do so by retreating, *by getting out of the way* if he can, by avoiding a conflict that may be about to come upon him, and the law says that he must do so, and *the fact that he is standing upon his own premises* away from his own dwelling-house does not take away from him the exercise of the duty of avoiding the danger if he can with a due regard to his own safety *by getting away from there* or by resorting to some other means of less violence than those resorted to. Now, the rule as applicable to a man of that kind upon his own premises, upon his own property, *but outside of his dwelling-house*, is as I have just stated." Again: "You are to bear in mind that the first proposition of the law of self-defense was that the defendant in this case was in the lawful pursuit of his business – that is to say, he was doing what he had a right to do at the time. If he was not he deprives himself of the right of self-defense, and, no matter what his adversary may do, if he by his own conduct creates certain conditions by his own wrongful conduct he cannot take advantage of such conditions created by his own wrongful act or acts. . . . Again, going to the place where the person slain is with a deadly weapon *for the purpose of provoking a difficulty or with the intent of having an affray*. Now, if a man does that, he is in the wrong, and he is cut off from the right of self-defense, no matter what his adversary may do, because the law says in the very language of these propositions relating to the law of self-defense that he must avoid taking life if he can with due regard to his own safety. Whenever he can do that he must do it; therefore, if he has an adversary and he knows that there is a bitter feeling, that there is a state of feeling that may precipitate a deadly conflict between himself and his adversary, while he has a right to pursue his usual daily avocations that are right and proper, going about his business, to go and do what is necessary to be done in that way, yet if he knows that condition I have named to exist and he goes to the place where the slain person is with a deadly weapon for the purpose of provoking a difficulty or with the intent of having an affray if it comes up, he is there to have it, and he acts for that purpose, the law says there is no self-defense for him. . . . If he went to the place where that young man was, armed with a deadly weapon, even if it was upon his own premises, with the purpose of provoking a difficulty with him, in which he might use that deadly weapon, or of having a deadly affray with him, it does not make any difference what was done by the young man, there is no self-defense for the defendant. The law of self-defense does not apply to a case of that kind, because he cannot be the creator of a wrong, of a wrong state of case, and then act upon it. Now, if either one of these conditions exist, I say, the law of self-defense does not apply in this case."

Later in the charge, the court recurred to the inquiry as to what the law demanded of Beard before striking the deceased with his gun, and said: "If at the time of this killing it be true that the deceased was doing an act of apparent or real deadly violence and that state of case existed, and yet that the defendant at the time could have avoided the necessity of taking his life by the exercise of any other reasonable means and he did not do that, because he did not exercise other reasonable means that would have with equal certainty saved his life, but resorted to this dernier remedy, under those facts and circumstances the law says he is guilty of manslaughter. Now, let us see what that requires. It requires, first, that the proof must show that Will Jones was doing an act of violence or about to do it, or apparently doing it or about to do it, but that it was an act that the defendant could have escaped from by doing something else other than taking the life of Jones, *by getting out of the way of that danger*, as he was called upon to do, as I have already told you, *for he could not stand there as he could stand in his own dwelling-house*, and he must have reasonably sought to avoid that danger before he took the life of Jones, and if he did not do that, if you find that to be Jones' position from this testimony, and he could have done so, but did not do it, the defendant would be guilty of manslaughter when he took the life of Jones, because in that kind of a case the law says that the conduct of Jones would be so provocative as to reduce the grade of crime; yet, at the same time, it was a state of case that the defendant could have avoided without taking his life, and because he did not do it he is guilty of the crime of manslaughter." Further: "If it be true that Will Jones at the time he was killed was exercising deadly violence, or about to do so, or apparently exercising it, or apparently about to do so, and the defendant could have paralyzed the effect of that violence without taking the life of Jones, but he did not do it, but resorted to this deadly violence when he could have protected his own life without resorting to that dernier remedy – if that be the state of case, the law says he is guilty of manslaughter, because he is doing that which he had no right to do. This great law of self-defense commands him at all times to do that which he can do under the circumstances, to wit, exercise reasonable care to avoid the danger *by getting out of the way of it*, or by exercising less violence than that which will produce death and yet will be equally effective to secure his own life. If either of these propositions exist, and they must exist to the extent I have defined to you, and the defendant took the life of Jones under these circumstances, the defendant would be guilty of manslaughter."

We are of opinion that the charge of the court to the jury was objectionable, in point of law, on several grounds.

There was no evidence tending to show that Beard went from his dwelling-house to the orchard fence *for the purpose* of provoking a difficulty, or with *the intent* of having an affray with the Jones brothers or with either of them. On the contrary, from the outset of the dispute, he evinced a purpose to avoid a difficulty or an affray. He expressed his willingness to abide by the law in respect to his right to retain the cow in his possession. He warned the Jones brothers, as he had a legal right to do, against coming upon his premises for the purpose of taking the cow away. They disregarded this warning, and determined to take the law into their own hands, whatever might be the consequences of such a course. Nevertheless, when Beard came to where they were, near the orchard fence, he did nothing to provoke a difficulty, and prior to the moment when he struck Will Jones with his gun he made no demonstration that indicated any desire whatever on his part to engage in an affray or to have an angry controversy. He only commanded them, as he had the legal right to do, to leave his premises. He neither used, nor threatened to use, force against them.

The court several times, in its charge, raised or suggested the inquiry whether Beard was in the lawful pursuit of his business, that is, doing what he had a right to do, when, after returning home in the afternoon, he went from his dwelling-house to a part of his premises near the orchard fence, just outside of which his wife and the Jones brothers were engaged in a dispute – the former endeavoring to prevent the cow from being taken away, the latter trying to drive it off the premises. Was he not doing what he had the legal right to do, when, keeping within his own premises and near his dwelling, he joined his wife who was in dispute with others, one of whom, as he had been informed, had already threatened to take 559*559 the cow away or kill him? We have no hesitation in answering this question in the affirmative.

The court also said: "The use of provoking language, or, it seems, resorting to any other device in order to get another to commence an assault so as to have a pretext for taking his life, agreeing with another to fight him with a deadly weapon, either one of these cases, if they exist as the facts in this case, puts the case in such an attitude that there is no self-defense in it." We are at a loss to understand why any such hypothetical cases were put before the jury. The jury must have supposed that, in the opinion of the court, there was evidence showing that Beard sought an opportunity to do physical harm to the Jones boys, or to some one of them. There was not the slightest foundation in the evidence for the intimation that Beard had used provoking language or resorted to any device in order to have a pretext to take the life of either of the brothers. Much less was there any reason to believe that there was an agreement to fight with deadly weapons.

But the court below committed an error of a more serious character when it told the jury, as in effect it did by different forms of expression, that if the accused could have saved his own life and avoided taking the life of Will Jones by retreating from and getting out of the way of the latter as he advanced upon him, the law made it his duty to do so; and if he did not, when it was in his power to do so without putting his own life or body in imminent peril, he was guilty of manslaughter. The court seemed to think if the deceased had advanced upon the accused while the latter was in his dwelling-house and under such circumstances as indicated the intention of the former to take life or inflict great bodily injury, and if, without retreating, the accused had taken the life of his assailant, having at the time reasonable grounds to believe, and in good faith believing, that his own life would be taken or great bodily harm done him unless he killed the accused, the case would have been one of justifiable homicide. To that proposition we give our entire assent. But we cannot agree that the accused was under any greater obligation, when on his own premises, near his dwelling-house, to retreat or runaway from his assailant, than he would have been if attacked within his dwelling-house. The accused being where he had a right to be, on his own premises, constituting a part of his residence and home, at the time the deceased approached him in a threatening manner, and not having by language or by conduct provoked the deceased to assault him, the question for the jury was whether, without fleeing from his adversary, he had, at the moment he struck the deceased, reasonable grounds to believe, and in good faith believed, that he could not save his life or protect himself from great bodily harm except by doing what he did, namely, strike the deceased with his gun, and thus prevent his further advance upon him. Even if the jury had been prepared to answer this question in the affirmative – and if it had been so answered the defendant should have been acquitted – they were instructed that the accused could not properly be acquitted on the ground of self-defense if they believed that, by retreating from his adversary, by "getting out of the way," he could have avoided taking life. We cannot give our assent to this doctrine.

****

The 2017 Florida Statutes

Title XLVI   Chapter 776
CRIMES   JUSTIFIABLE USE OF FORCE

776.013 Home protection; use or threatened use of deadly force; presumption of fear of death or great bodily harm. –

(1) A person who is in a dwelling or residence in which the person has a right to be has no duty to retreat and has the right to stand his or her ground and use or threaten to use:

(a) Nondeadly force against another when and to the extent that the person reasonably believes that such conduct is necessary to defend himself or herself or another against the other's imminent use of unlawful force; or

(b) Deadly force if he or she reasonably believes that using or threatening to use such force is necessary to prevent imminent death or great bodily harm to himself or herself or another or to prevent the imminent commission of a forcible felony.

(2) A person is presumed to have held a reasonable fear of imminent peril of death or great bodily harm to himself or herself or another when using or threatening to use defensive force that is intended or likely to cause death or great bodily harm to another if:

(a) The person against whom the defensive force was used or threatened was in the process of unlawfully and forcefully entering, or had unlawfully and forcibly entered, a dwelling, residence, or occupied vehicle, or if that person had removed or was attempting to remove another against that person's will from the dwelling, residence, or occupied vehicle; and

(b) The person who uses or threatens to use defensive force knew or had reason to believe that an unlawful and forcible entry or unlawful and forcible act was occurring or had occurred.

(3) The presumption set forth in subsection (2) does not apply if:

    (a) The person against whom the defensive force is used or threatened has the right to be in or is a lawful resident of the dwelling, residence, or vehicle, such as an owner, lessee, or titleholder, and there is not an injunction for protection from domestic violence or a written pretrial supervision order of no contact against that person; or

    (b) The person or persons sought to be removed is a child or grandchild, or is otherwise in the lawful custody or under the lawful guardianship of, the person against whom the defensive force is used or threatened; or

    (c) The person who uses or threatens to use defensive force is engaged in a criminal activity or is using the dwelling, residence, or occupied vehicle to further a criminal activity; or

    (d) The person against whom the defensive force is used or threatened is a law enforcement officer, as defined in s. *943.10*(14), who enters or attempts to enter a dwelling, residence, or vehicle in the performance of his or her official duties and the officer identified himself or herself in accordance with any applicable law or the person using or threatening to use force knew or reasonably should have known that the person entering or attempting to enter was a law enforcement officer.

(4) A person who unlawfully and by force enters or attempts to enter a person's dwelling, residence, or occupied vehicle is presumed to be doing so with the intent to commit an unlawful act involving force or violence.

(5) As used in this section, the term:

    (a) "Dwelling" means a building or conveyance of any kind, including any attached porch, whether the building or conveyance is temporary or permanent, mobile or immobile, which has a roof over it, including

> a tent, and is designed to be occupied by people lodging therein at night.
>
> (b) "Residence" means a dwelling in which a person resides either temporarily or permanently or is visiting as an invited guest.
>
> (c) "Vehicle" means a conveyance of any kind, whether or not motorized, which is designed to transport people or property.
>
> History. – s. 1, ch. 2005 – 27; s. 4, ch. 2014 – 195; s. 1, ch. 2017 – 77.
>
> Copyright © 1995 – 2018 The Florida Legislature

Key terms

Enron
Patriot Act Reauthorization
Department of Homeland Security
Commissioner Raymond W. Kelly
lone wolf provision
Eric Holder
military tribunals
black site prisons
subprime mortgage crisis
    Sarbanes-Oxley Law
Security Threat Groups prison
    gangs
"compassionate release"
    programs
Bernard Madoff
Virginia Tech Massacre
cybercrime
1996 Anti-terrorism Act
George Zimmerman

John Ashcroft
restitution
rendition
medical marijuana
Geneva Conventions
Robert Mueller
reinvestment
    movement
"stop and frisk"
restitution
deinstitutionalization
    movement
stand your ground
    defense
USA PATRIOT Act
    hawalas
USA PATRIOT Act
    Sunset Extension
    Act of 2009
"Gunshine State"

"National Security Letter"
    (NSL) provision roving
    wiretaps
Ker-Frisbie Doctrine *Hamdi v. Rumsfeld*
preventive detention Abu
    Ghraib
enhanced interrogation
Guantanamo Bay, Cuba
    Baze v. Reese
Roper v. Simmons
medical parole drug courts
Charles Ponzi Second
    Chance Act
9/11 Commission
predictive policing
Newark Experiment bad
    laws
Trayvon Martin
duty to retreat

Critical thinking questions

1 What impact did the terrorist attacks of 9/11, 2001, have on the various segments of the criminal justice system?
2 Is the death penalty declining in popularity? If so, why? If not, is it increasing or staying the same?

3 Has the role of the federal criminal justice system changed over the past several years? Discuss.

4 What are the biggest challenges to the American prison system?

5 What would America's earliest police and corrections reformers think about the state of the modern American criminal justice system?

6 What accounts for the growing influence of prison gangs in American prisons?

7 What have been the most controversial provisions of the USA PATRIOT Act?

8 How does the Point–Counterpoint section impact the understanding of the modern "stand your ground defense?" What insights do the two sections offer that better explains the result of the Trayvon Martin case?

Notes

1 Among the dead at the World Trade Center were 494 foreigners representing 91 countries, 17 percent of those killed.

2 Jeffrey Ian Ross, "'Post 9/11' Are We Really Safer Now?," in *Terrorism: Research, Readings and Realities*, ed. Lynne Snowden and Bradley C. Whitsel, Upper Saddle River, NJ: Pearson, 2005.

3 John P. Crank and Patricia E. Gregor, *Counterterrorism after 9/11: Justice, Security and Ethics Reconsidered*, Cincinnati: Lexis Nexus, 2005, p. 14.

4 Ibid., p. 12.

5 Al Baker, "In New York, Relief and Disappointment as 9/11 Trial Is Headed Elsewhere," *New York Times*, January 31, 2010, p. 19.

6 Peter Baker, "Obama's War on Terror," *The New York Times Magazine*, January 17, 2010, pp. 36–37.

7 Henry Weinstein, et al., "Civil Liberties Take Back Seat to Safety," *Los Angeles Times*, March 10, 2002, p. A28.

8 Quoted in Ibid., p. A1.

9 Lise Olsen, "Judging by the Judges," *Houston Chronicle*, December 13, 2009. District and circuit judges are appointed by the president for life and can only be replaced by an act of Congress. On the other hand, bankruptcy and magistrate judges serve finite terms.

10 Glenn Sulmasy and John Yoo, "Katz and the War on Terrorism," *University of California Davis Law Review*, 41(3), 2009, p. 1226.

11 J. J. Stambaugh, "Sneak and Peak Warrants Debated," *Knoxville News Sentinel*, August 13, 2007.

12 Lee R. Shelton and James Hall, "Patriot Act Another RICO?," 2002, www.enterstageright.com

13 David Stout, "FBI Director Admits Abuse of the Patriot Act," *Houston Chronicle*, March 10, 2007, p. A3.

14 Hawala originated in the early medieval commerce in the Near and Middle East. Traders used a system of money transfer based solely on trust and grounded in Islamic propriety. This allowed traveling merchants and others who traveled long distances to engage in business in foreign lands without having to actually carry the funds with them. It is still used today throughout much of South Asia and the Middle East. Since it does not leave a paper trail, hawalas are particularly popular for criminal and terrorist groups that need to transmit illegal funds.

15 Rachel L. Brand, "Reauthorization of the USA PATRIOT ACT," *The Federalist Society*, January 20, 2010. https://fedsoc.org/commentary/publications/reauthorization-of-the-usa-patriot-act

16 Charlie Savage, "Battle Looms over Patriot Act," *New York Times*, September 20, 2009.

17 Gus Martin, *Understanding Terrorism*, Los Angeles: Sage Publications, 2010.

18 Ryan M. Porcello, "International Bounty Hunter Ride-Along," *Vanderbilt Journal of Transnational Law*, 35, 2002.

19 Quoted in Jane Mayer, "The Secret History," *The New Yorker*, June 22, 2009, p. 56.

20 Ibid.
21 Crank and Gregor, 2005.
22 Quoted in Mayer, 2009, p. 56.
23 Darius Rejali, *American Torture*, Princeton, NJ: Princeton University Press, 2007.
24 Alfred McCoy, *A Question of Torture: CIA Interrogations from the Cold War to the War on Terror*, New York: Owl Books, 2006, p. 108.
25 Ibid.
26 Kristian Williams, *American Methods: Torture and Logic of Domination*, Cambridge, MA: South End Press, 2006, p. 18.
27 Ibid., p. 19.
28 Mayer, 2009.
29 Quoted in Williams, 2006, p. 17.
30 Ibid., p. 18.
31 Gus Martin, *Essentials of Terrorism*, Los Angeles: Sage Books, 2008, pp. 266–268.
32 Rhodri Jeffreys-Jones, *The FBI: A History*, New Haven, CT: Yale University Press, 2007, p. 237.
33 Ibid.
34 Quoted in David Cole, "The Grand Inquisitors," *The New York Review of Books*, July 19, 2007, p. 55.
35 David Cole, "Are We Safer?," *The New York Review of Books*, March 9, 2006.
36 Cole, 2007, p. 55.
37 Devlin Barrett, "Despite Recession, Crime Keeps Falling," *Houston Chronicle*, December 22, 2010, p. A14.
38 Ibid.
39 Allison Lowe, "Pot Arrests at Record High in U.S. Last Year, FBI Says," *Houston Chronicle*, September 21, 2008, p. A12.
40 Solomon Moore, "Dispensers of Marijuana Find Relief in Policy Shift," *Houston Chronicle*, March 22, 2009; Abby Goodnough, "Licensed to Sell Marijuana, But Still in the Shadow," *New York Times*, October 10, 2009.
41 Nick Gillespie, "Playing with Our Sins," *New York Times*, May 17, 2009.
42 Sarah Kershaw, "No. 2 Drug Fighter Brings History to Her Job," *Houston Chronicle*, April 27, 2009.
43 Ibid.
44 It was hoped this would bring to an end the repressive policies established by the Nixon administration in the 1970s and later adopted by Argentina's military dictators.
45 Michael Virtanen, "New York to Soften Laws on Harsh Drug Sentences," *Houston Chronicle*, March 28, 2009.
46 According to the 2007 Small Arms Survey, there were nine guns for every ten people in the United States with almost 270 million firearms in circulation.
47 Willard M. Oliver, *Homeland Security for Policing*, Upper Saddle River, NJ: Pearson, 2007, p. 103.
48 Mark S. Hamm, *Terrorism as Crime: From Oklahoma to Al-Qaeda and Beyond*, New York: New York University Press, 2007, p. 22.
49 Quoted in Kevin Johnson, "Police Chiefs Turning in Badges," *USA Today*, December 3, 2009, p. 3A.
50 Oliver, 2007, p. 103.
51 Jeffreys-Jones, 2007.
52 Moore, 2009.
53 Ibid.
54 Solomon Moore, "F.B.I. and States Vastly Expand DNA Databases," *New York Times*, April 18, 2009. https://www.nytimes.com/2009/04/19/us/19DNA.html
55 At this point, unlike the U.S., Great Britain has been taking DNA samples on arrest for years and out of a population of 61 million had 4.5 million profiles (as of 2008 almost one-fifth had no record). With the world's largest DNA database (7 percent of population), the racial

disparity of these profiles was most troubling, with almost 40 percent taken from black men. Similarly, in the United States blacks make up about 12 percent of the population but were overrepresented in the database at 40 percent.

56 "Politicians Watch Criminals Pack More Heat," *Houston Chronicle*, January 18, 2010.

57 Colleen Long, "Spike in Gun Deaths Frays the Thin Blue Line in '09," *Houston Chronicle*, December 14, 2009.

58 Jim Dwyer, "Mayor Turns Suddenly Shy About Money," *New York Times*, April 10, 2009. https://www.nytimes.com/2009/04/11/nyregion/11about.html

59 Al Baker, "The New York Police Department Is Holding the Line with a Smaller Force," *New York Times*, July 18, 2009.

60 Bradley Olson, "Data Show Crime Outpaces Officers," *Houston Chronicle*, August 3, 2009, p. A1.

61 Dan Frosch, "Helicopters Are Casualty in Cutbacks by Police," *New York Times*, December 25, 2009, p. A16.

62 Colleen Long, "For Some Stop-and-Frisk Gives Pause," *Houston Chronicle*, October 9, 2009.

63 Quoted in Ibid., p. A3.

64 Ibid.

65 Richard Gid Powers, *Broken: The Troubled Past and Uncertain Future of the FBI*, New York: Free Press, 2004, p. 1.

66 Jeffreys-Jones, 2007.

67 Powers, 2004, p. 24.

68 In the 2000 census, there were 1.3 million Arab Americans officially in the U.S., but only twenty-one FBI agents who could speak Arabic.

69 Philip S. Shenon and Eric Lichtblau, "Threats and Responses: The Inquiry; FBI is Assailed for its Handling of Terror Risks," *New York Times*, April 14, 2004. https://www.nytimes.com/2004/04/14/us/threats-responses-inquiry-fbi-assailed-for-its-handling-terror-risks.html

70 Powers, 2004, p. 26.

71 Richard Gid Powers, *Broken: The Troubled Past and Uncertain Future of the FBI*, NU: Free Press, 2004, p. 25.

72 Quoted in Powers, 2004, p. 26.

73 Powers, 2004, p. 26.

74 Ibid.

75 www.fbi.gov/priorities/priorities.com

76 Michael Grabell, "Policing the Air Marshals," *USA Today*, November 13, 2008, p. 1A.

77 Ibid.

78 Jim Webb, "We Must Fix Our Prisons," *Parade*, March 29, 2009.

79 Adam Liptak, "US Leads World in Prisoners," *New York Times*, April 23, 2008.

80 Steven Raphael and Raphael Stoll, eds., *Do Prisons Make Us Safer?*, New York: Russell Sage, 2009, p. 39.

81 Jeff Carlton, "US Prison Population Faces First Drop Since 1972," *Huffington Post*, December 30, 2009.

82 Cindy Horswell, "Texas Cuts Costs Amid Prison Reform," *Houston Chronicle*, December 15, 2009.

83 Quoted in Horswell, 2009, p. B3.

84 Ken Stier, "Another By-Product of the Recession: Ex-Convicts," *Time.com*, March 6, 2009.

85 Darryl Fears, "Demographics Shift for Drug Offenders in Prison," *Houston Chronicle*, April 16, 2009; Carlton, December 30, 2009.

86 C. West Huddleston III, et al., "Painting the Current Picture," *National Drug Court Institute, U.S. Department of Justice*, May 2008, p. 2.

87 Brooke Ninemire, "Drug Court Strives to Help Addicts Heal," *Areawide Media*, February 8, 2007. http://www.areawidenews.com/story/1429897.html

88 Stier, March 6, 2009.

89 George W. Bush, "Speech on the Signing of the Second Chance Act," 2008, http://blogs.suntimes.com/sweet/2008/04/rep_danny_davis_at_white_house.html

90 Mary Bosworth, *Explaining U.S. Imprisonment*, Thousand Oaks: Sage Publications, 2010, p. 181.

91 Melvin Delgado and Denise Humm Delgado, *Health and Health Care in the Nation's Prisons*, Lanham, MD: Rowman and Littlefield, 2009.

92 James Marquart, et al., "The Health Related Concerns of Older Prisoners," *Aging and Society*, 20, 2000.

93 Robynn Kuhlman and Rick Ruddell, "Elderly Inmates," *Californian Journal of Health Promotion*, 3(2), 2005, p. 51.

94 Delgado and Delgado, 2009, p. 6.

95 Laura M. Maruschak, *HIV in Prisons, 2007–08*, Bureau of Justice Statistics, Washington, DC, December, 2009.

96 Ibid.

97 Cara Buckley, "New York Law Has Little Impact on Early Release of Ailing Inmates," *New York Times*, January 30, 2010.

98 Alan Elsner, *Gates of Injustice: The Crisis in America's Prisons*, Upper Saddle River, NJ: Pearson, 2004, p. 85.

99 Ibid., p. 85.

100 Ibid.

101 Florida Department of Corrections, "Major Prison Gangs," n.d., www.dc.state.fl.us/pub/gangs/prison.html

102 Joseph T. Hallinan, *Going Up River: Travels in a Prison Nation*, New York: Random House, 2001, p. 96.

103 Edecio Martinez, "FBI: Despite Recession, Crime Keeps Falling," *CBS News*, December 22, 2009. https://www.cbsnews.com/news/fbi-despite-recession-crime-keeps-falling/

104 David O. Friedrichs, *Trusted Criminals: White-Collar Crime in Contemporary Society*, Belmont: CA: Wadsworth Cengage, 2010.

105 Mitchell Zuckoff, *Ponzi's Scheme*, New York: Random House, 2005; Donald Dunn, *Ponzi: The Incredible True Story of the King of Financial Cons*, New York: Broadway, 2004.

106 Richard B. Schmitt, "FBI Saw Threat of Loan Crisis," *Los Angeles Times*, August 25, 2008.

107 Paul Shukovsky, "FBI Saw Mortgage Fraud Early," 2009, www.seattlepi.com/national/397690_fbiweb

108 Laurence A. Urgenson and Peter A. Farrell, "Prosecution of Subprime: Mortgage Fraud," *Law Journal Newsletters*, September 2008.

109 Moises Mendoza, "Experts Fear Upswing in Hate Crimes," *Houston Chronicle*, July 16, 2009.

110 Ryan, 2008.

111 Mamta Badkar, "22 Chinese People Who Were Handed the Death Sentence for White Collar Crime," *Business Insider*, July 15, 2013.

112 Surprisingly, the state of Delaware actually has the highest per capita rate of executions in America. At the end of 2000, with a population 25 times that of Delaware, Texas had executed 193 people since 1991, compared to 11 in Delaware. The Texas state rate of execution stood at 0.106 per 10,000 residents compared to 0.137 in Delaware. See Jeff Barker, "Tiny Delaware Boasts Highest Per-Capita Execution Rate," *Houston Chronicle*, December 25, 2000.

113 Penry's case went back before the Supreme Court as his lawyers try to save his life on the grounds that his history as an abused child was not considered during the second trial and that the jury instructions on mitigation were fumbled. After thirty years on death row, Penry was resentenced to three life terms in 2008 and removed from death row.

114 States banning this practice include Arizona, Arkansas, Colorado, Connecticut, Florida, Georgia, Indiana, Kansas, Kentucky, Maryland, Missouri, Nebraska, New Mexico, New York, North Carolina, South Dakota, Tennessee, and Washington.

115 Deborah Hastings, "Cost Could Decide Execution Debate in Some States," *Houston Chronicle*, March 7, 2009.

116 Ibid.

117 Valium relaxes convict. Sodium pentothal makes him unconscious. Pavulon stops the breathing, and the addition of potassium chloride leads to cardiac arrest and death.

118 Bret Barrouquere, "Kentucky Ordered to Start Over on Lethal Injection," *Houston Chronicle*, November 26, 2009, p. A3.

119 Gilbert King, "Blood-Stained: Let's Move beyond Our Cruel and Unusual History," *Houston Chronicle*, April 27, 2008, p. E1.

120 Andrew Welsh-Huggins, "Judge: Ohio Inmates Appeal Has Limits," *Boston.com*, December 9, 2009. http://archive.boston.com/news/nation/articles/2009/12/09/ohio_killer_asks_judge_to_stop_2nd_execution_try/

121 Ian Urbina, "Ohio is First to Change to One Drug in Executions," *New York Times*, November 14, 2009.

122 Adam Liptak, "Weighing Life in Prison for Youths Who Never Killed," *New York Times*, November 8, 2009.

123 Ibid.

124 Twenty-two juvenile offenders had been executed in mostly Southern "death belt" states since court reinstated capital punishment in 1976.

125 Catherine Rampell, "How Old Is Old Enough?," *New York Times*, November 15, 2009, p. 5.

126 National Drug Intelligence Center, *National Drug Threat Assessment*, Department of Justice, Washington, DC, 2009.

127 Ibid.

128 Mark Scolforo, "Time to Pay Us Now, and Pay Later," *Houston Chronicle*, October 22, 2007.

129 Ibid.

130 Raphael and Stoll, 2009, pp. 62–63.

131 Ibid.

132 Jeff Mason, "Obama Blames 'Systemic Failures' in United States Security," *Reuters*, December 28, 2009. https://www.reuters.com/article/us-security-airline/obama-blames-systemic-failures-in-u-s-security-idUSTRE5BQ1AT20091229?feedType=nl&feedName=usmorningdigest

133 Quoted in Dan Eggen, "Violent Crime in U.S. Rises for Second Year in a Row, FBI Reports," *Houston Chronicle*, June 3, 2007.

134 Dan Eggen, "Violent Crime up for Second Year," *Washington Post*, June 2, 2007. http://www.washingtonpost.com/wp-dyn/content/article/2007/06/01/AR2007060102360.html?noredirect=on

135 Olson, 2009, p. A8.

136 Mendoza, 2009.

137 Hate Crime Statistics 2008, U.S. Department of Justice, November 2009. Almost two-thirds of those who were motivated by religious bias (65.7 percent) were anti-Semitic and 7.7 percent were anti-Islamic; almost three-quarters of racial bias incidents were directed against African Americans (72.6 percent) and the vast majority of sexual orientation–related hate crimes were directed at homosexuals.

138 Al Baker, "Homicide Rate in N.Y. Plummets," *New York Times*, November 24, 2007. In fact, the city was on track to have less than 500 homicides in 2007, the lowest number in a 12-month period since reliable NYPD statistics became available in 1963. Other official statistics were even more striking. Having only analyzed half of the killings, only 35 percent were committed by strangers; most were killed in disputes with friends and acquaintances, rival drug gang members, romantic partners, and family members. This continued a remarkable slide since 1990 when New York City recorded its greatest number of killings in a single year – 2,245, many between strangers (and averaging a little more than 1 killing per day compared to more than 6 per day 20 years ago). What's more, 77 percent of assailants had previous run-ins with the law, and 70 percent of the victims also had previous arrest histories.

139 "Homicide Soar in Second-Tier East Coast Cities," *NBC News*, June 29, 2007. http://www.nbcnews.com/id/19513374/ns/us_news-crime_and_courts/t/homicides-soar-second-tier-east-coast-cities/#.WyagHVVKiUk

140 Maryclair Dale, "Shortage of New Immigrants Blamed for Surge in Killings," *Houston Chronicle*, June 30, 2007.

141 David Porter, "New Jersey's Approach to Crime Seems to Work," *Houston Chronicle*, February 16, 2008.

142 Krissah Thompson and Scott Wilson, "Obama on Trayvon Martin: 'If I had a Son he'd look like Trayvon'," *Washington Post*, March 23, 2012. https://www.washingtonpost.com/politics/obama-if-i-had-a-son-hed-look-like-trayvon/2012/03/23/gIQApKPpVS_story.html?utm_term=.67062b3ea013

143 The law was first passed in 2005. In 2015, the Florida Supreme Court shifted the burden to defendants, requiring them to prove in pretrial hearings that they were defending themselves in order to avoid prosecution on charges for a violent act. Just two years later, a Florida judge ruled the updated law as unconstitutional. See also, "Florida's 'Stand Your Ground' Law Ruled Unconstitutional by Judge," *Fox News*, July 3, 2017.

144 This defense was first introduced by English common law and evolved over the centuries. In medieval England and for a number of centuries after, if an individual was attacked in a public place, he/she was expected to retreat posthaste to safety before using deadly force, that is, unless it was one's home that was being invaded. The law was designed in an age of low-tech weaponry, and except for the bow and arrow or a spear, there was little possibility of being victimized if one was able to run away fast enough. Fast forward to the gun-toting world of nineteenth- and twentieth-century America. Obviously, no one can outrun a bullet, so it was later understood that one could use deadly force if was thought warranted. So rather than turn tail and run, an individual could engage in a deadly confrontation to save one's life. Many other jurisdictions have moved away from the retreat provision of early common law.

145 Chelsea J. Carter and Holly Yan, "Why This Verdict? Five Things that Led to Zimmerman's Acquittal," *CNN*, July 15, 2013. https://www.cnn.com/2013/07/14/us/zimmerman-why-this-verdict/index.html

146 Alexandra Thomas, "Did Investigators Blow the Zimmerman Case?" *CNN*, July 12, 2013. https://www.cnn.com/2013/07/12/justice/zimmerman-trial-investigators/index.html

147 Ibid.

148 Patrik Jonsson, "Trayvon Martin Case: How Rachel Jeantel Went from Star Witness to 'Train Wreck'," *Christian Science Monitor*, June 29, 2013.

149 Quoted in Ibid.

150 Quoted in Ibid.

151 Jelani Cobb, "Rachel Jeantel on Trial," *The New Yorker*, June 27, 2013. https://www.newyorker.com/news/news-desk/rachel-jeantel-on-trial

152 Jelani Cobb, "Rachel Jeantel on Trial," *The New Yorker*, June 27, 2013.

153 Lawrence D. Bobo, "The Racial Double Homicide of Trayvon Martin," in *Deadly Justice: Trayvon Martin, Race, and the Criminal Justice System*, ed. Devon Johnson, Patricia Y. Warren and Amy Farrell, New York University Press, 2015, p. xii.

154 William J. Sabol, et al., *Prisoners in 2008*, Bureau of Justice Statistics, U.S. Department of Justice, 2009.

155 Kevin Johnson, "Budget Would Give Federal Prisons $528 Million Boost," *USA Today*, February 4, 2010.

156 Jeanne B. Stinchcomb, *Corrections: Foundations for the Future*, NY: Routledge, 2011, 2nd ed, p. 456.

157 Jill Lepore, "Rap Sheet: Why Is American History So Murderous," *The New Yorker*, November 9, 2009, p. 83.

158 Ibid., p. 79.

159 Quoted in Lepore, 2009, p. 80. See also Randolph Roth, *American Homicide*, Cambridge, MA: Harvard University Press, 2009.

160 Al Baker, "In New York, Relief and Disappointment as 9/11 Trial Is Headed Elsewhere," *New York Times*, January 31, 2010.

161 Ibid.

162 Peter Baker, "Obama's War Over Terror," *New York Times Magazine*, January 4, 2010. https://www.nytimes.com/2010/01/17/magazine/17Terror-t.html
163 Richard Maxwell Brown, *No Duty to Retreat: Violence and Values in American History and Society*, Norman: University of Oklahoma Press, 1991.
164 See *Beard v. United States*, 158 US 550 1895.
165 Brown, 1991, p. 29.

Sources

Abner, Carrie. 2006. "Graying Prisons: Sates Face Challenges of an Aging Inmate Population." *The Council of State Governments*, November/December, pp. 9–11. www.csg.org.

Aday, Ronald H. 2003. *Aging Prisoners: Crisis in American Corrections*. Westport, CT: Praeger.

Apuzzo, Matt. 2009. "Does Torture Work?" *Houston Chronicle*, April 22, p. A3.

Associated Press. 2005. "Elderly Prison Population Growing, Becoming More Costly." March 6. www.globalaging.org/elderrights/us/prison.htm.

Baker, Al. 2007. "Homicide Rate in N.Y. Plummets." *New York Times*, November 24.

———. 2009. "The New York Police Department Is Holding the Line with a Smaller Force." *New York Times*, July 18, p. A14.

———. 2010. "In New York, Relief and Disappointment as 9/11 Trial Is Headed Elsewhere." *New York Times*, January 31, p. 19.

Baker, Peter. 2010. "Obama's War on Terror." *The New York Times Magazine*, January 17, pp. 30–39, 46–47.

Barnes, Robert. 2008. "Justices Reject D. C. Ban on Handgun Ownership." *The Washington Post*, June 26.

Barrett, Devlin. 2009. "Despite Recession, Crime Keeps Falling." *Houston Chronicle*, December 22.

———. 2010. "2009 a Record Year for Terror Charges since 9/11." *Houston Chronicle*, January 18, p. A14.

Barrouquere, Brett. 2009. "Kentucky Ordered to Start over on Lethal Injection." *Houston Chronicle*, November 26, p. A3.

Biskupic, Joan. 2001a. "Feds Seek Right to Search in Probation Cases." *USA Today*, November 7.

———. 2001b. "Terror Attacks May Have Lasting Effects on Courts." *USA Today*, November 7.

Blumstein, Alfred and Joel Wallman, eds. 2006. *The Crime Drop in America*. Revised ed. New York: Cambridge University Press.

Borgeson, Kevin and Robin Valeri, eds. 2009. *Terrorism in America*. Boston: Jones and Bartlett.

Bosworth, Mary. 2010. *Explaining U.S. Imprisonment*. Thousand Oaks, CA: Sage Publications.

Buckley, Cara. 2010. "New York Law Has Little Impact on Early Release of Ailing Inmates." *New York Times*, January 30, pp. A14, A15.

Bush, George W. 2008. "Speech on the Signing of the Second Chance Act." http://blogs.suntimes.com/sweet/2008/04/rep_danny_davis_at_white_house.html.

Carlton, Jeff. 2010. "Once Criminal, Now Victim." *Houston Chronicle*, January 6, p. B2.

———. 2009. "US Prison Population Faces First Drop Since 1972." *Huffington Post*, December 30. www.huffingtonpost.com/2009/12/20/us-prison-population-drop.

Carry, David. 2001. "Death Sentence Predicted for Electric Chair's Future." *Houston Chronicle*, August 9.

Cole, David. 2004. "The Patriot Act Violates Our Civil Liberties." http://encarta.msn.com/sidebar_701713501/is_the_patriot_act_unconstitutional_html.

———. 2006. "Are We Safer?" *The New York Review of Books*, March 9, pp. 15–18.

———. 2007. "The Grand Inquisitors." *The New York Review of Books*, July 19, pp. 53–56.

Conley, John A. 1993. "Historical Perspective and Criminal Justice." *Journal of Criminal Justice Education*, 4(Fall):901–912.

Copeland, Larry. 2008. "Technology May Halt Hot Pursuit." *USA Today*, December 11, p. A1.

Crank, John P. and Patricia E. Gregor. 2005. *Counter-Terrorism after 9/11: Justice, Security and Ethics Reconsidered*. Cincinnati: Lexis Nexis.

Dale, Maryclaire. 2007. "Shortage of New Immigrants Blamed for Surge of Killings." *HC*, June 30, p. A25.

Delgado, Melvin and Denise Humm Delgado. 2009. *Health and Health Care in the Nation's Prisons*. Lanham, MD: Rowman and Littlefield.

Dickey, Christopher. 2009. *Securing the City: Inside America's Best Counterterror Force: The NYPD*. New York: Simon and Schuster.

Dunn, Donald. 2004. *Ponzi: The Incredible True Story of the King of Financial Cons*. New York: Broadway.

The Economist. 2008. "A Pointless Extinction." April 26, p. 46.

The Economist. 2008. "Can the Can." November 22, p. 91.

Eggen, Dan. 2007. "Violent Crime in U.S. Rises for Second Year in a Row, FBI Reports." *Houston Chronicle*, June 3, p. A8.

Elsner, Alan. 2004. *Gates of Injustice: The Crisis in America's Prisons*. Upper Saddle River, NJ: Prentice Hall.

Fathi, David. 2009. "Texas Increasingly Out of Step on Death Penalty." *Houston Chronicle*, May 24, p. B11.

Fears, Darryl. 2009. "Demographics Shift for Drug Offenders in Prison." *Houston Chronicle*, April 15, p. A6.

Florida Department of Corrections. n.d. "Major Prison Gangs." www.dc.state.fl.us/pub/gangs/prison.html.

Friedrichs, David O. 2010. *Trusted Criminals: White Collar Crime in Contemporary Society*. Belmont, CA: Wadsworth Cengage.

Frosch, Dan. 2009. "Helicopters Are Casualty in Cutbacks By the Police." *New York Times*, December 25, p. A16.

Gillespie, Nick. 2009. "Paying with Our Sins." *New York Times*, May 17, p. 14.

Goldsmith, Jack. 2007. *The Terror Presidency: Law and Judgment Inside the Bush Administration*. New York: Norton.

Goodnough, Abby. 2009. "Licensed to Sell Marijuana, But Still in the Shadow." *New York Times*, October 10, pp. A1, A10.

Grabell, Michael. 2008. "Policing the Air Marshals." *USA Today*, November 13, pp. 1A, 8A.

Hallinan, Joseph T. 2001. *Going Up the River: Travels in a Prison Nation*. New York: Random House.

Hamm, Mark S. 2007. *Terrorism as Crime: From Oklahoma City to Al-Qaeda and Beyond*. New York: New York University Press.

Hastings, Deborah. 2009. "Cost Could Decide Execution Debate in Some States." *Houston Chronicle*, March 7, p. A17.

Hate Crime Statistics 2008. 2009. U.S. Department of Justice, November, pp. 1–5.

Holland, Jesse. 2009. "Ruling Drops One Limit on Police Interrogations." *Houston Chronicle*, May 27, p. A9.

Horswell, Cindy. 2009. "Texas Cuts Costs Amid Prison Reform." *Houston Chronicle*, December 15, pp. B1, B3.

Huddleston III, C. West, Douglas B. Marlowe, and Rachel Casebolt. 2008. "Painting the Current Picture: A National Report Card on Drug Courts and Other Problem Solving Court Programs in the United States." National Drug Court Institute, U.S. Department of Justice, May, pp. 1–40, www.ndci.org/sites/default/files/ndci/PCPII1_web[i].pdf.

Jeffreys-Jones, Rhodri. 2007. *The FBI: A History*. New Haven, CT: Yale University Press.

Johnson, Kevin. 1999. "FBI Takes on Expanding Role." *USA Today*, June 8.

———. 2009. "Police Chiefs Turning in Badges." *USA Today*, December 3, p. 3A.

———. 2010. "Budget Would Give Federal Prisons $528 Million Boost." *USA Today*, February 4, p. 2A.

Kappeler, Victor E. and Karen S. Miller-Potter. 2004. "Policing in the Age of Terrorism." In *Controversies in Policing*, ed. Quint C. Thurman and Andrew Giacomazzi, pp. 27–40. Cincinnati, OH: Anderson Publishing.

Kershaw, Sarah. 2009. "No. 2 Drug Fighter Brings History to Job." *Houston Chronicle*, December 13, p. A29.

King, Gilbert. 2008. "Blood-Stained: Let's Move beyond Our Cruel and Unusual History." *Houston Chronicle*, April 27, pp. E1, E4.

Koch, Wendy. 2007. "Iris Scans Let Law Enforcement Keep Eye on Criminals." *USA Today*, December 5.

Kocieniewski, David. 2010. "New Jersey Lawmakers Pass Medical Marijuana Bill." *New York Times.com*, January 12.

Krebs, Brian. 2009. "Cyber-Gangs Attacking Small U.S. Businesses." *Houston Chronicle*, August 26, p. D3.

Kuhlmann, Robynn and Rick Ruddell. 2005. "Elderly Inmates: Problems, Prevalence and Public Health." *Californian Journal of Health Promotion*, 3(2):49–60.

Lake, Anthony. 2000. *6 Nightmares: Real Threats in a Dangerous World and How America Can Meet Them*. Boston: Little, Brown and Company.

Lavoie, Denise. 2009. "Police Find Texts Ideal for Crime Tips." *Houston Chronicle*, November 29, p. A4.

Lepore, Jill. 2009. "Rap Sheet: Why Is American History so Murderous." *The New Yorker*, November 9, pp. 79–83.

Lewin, Tamar. 2009. "School Gives New Meaning to Higher Ed." *New York Times*, November 29.

Liptak, Adam. 2008a. "More Than 1 in 100 Adults Are Now in Prison in US." *New York Times*, February 24, 2008, p. A14.

———. 2008b. "US Leads World in Prisoners." *New York Times*, April.

———. 2009. "Weighing Life in Prison for Youths Who Never Killed." *New York Times*, November 8, p. 4.

———. 2010. "A Busy Year for Judiciary, Roberts Says." *New York Times*, January 1, p. A19.

Long, Colleen. 2009a. "For Some, Stop-and-Frisk Gives Pause." *Houston Chronicle*, October 9, p. A3.

———. 2009b. "Spike in Gun Deaths Frays the Thin Blue Line in '09." *Houston Chronicle*, December 14, p. A9.

Lowe, Allison. 2008. "Pot Arrests at Record High in U.S. Last Year, FBI Says." *Houston Chronicle*, September 21, p. A12.

Marquart, James, Dot Merianos, and G. Doucet. 2000. "The Health Related Concerns of Older Prisoners: Implications for Policy." *Aging and Society*, 20, pp. 79–96.

Martin, Gus. 2008. *Essentials of Terrorism: Concepts and Controversies*. Los Angeles: Sage Publications.

———. 2010. *Understanding Terrorism: Challenges, Perspectives, and Issues*. 3rd ed. Los Angeles: Sage Publications.

Maruschak, Laura M. 2009. *HIV in Prisons, 2007–08*, Bureau of Justice Statistics, U.S. Department of Justice, December, pp. 1–12.

Mayer, Jane. 2009. "The Secret History." *The New Yorker*, June 22, pp. 50–59.

McCall, William. 2007. "Judge Slaps Down Two Provisions of the Patriot Act." *Houston Chronicle*, September 27.

McCoy, Alfred. 2006. *A Question of Torture: CIA Interrogations from the Cold War to the War on Terror*. New York: Owl Books.

Mears, Daniel P., Caterina G. Roman, Ashley Wolff, and Janeen Buck. 2006. "Faith-Based Efforts to Improve Prisoner Re-Entry: Assessing the Logic and Evidence." *Journal of Criminal Justice*, 34:351–367.

Mendoza, Moises. 2009. "Experts Fear Upswing in Hate Crimes." *Houston Chronicle*, July 16, p. B2.

Moore, Solomon. 2009. "Dispensers of Marijuana Find Relief in Policy Shift." *Houston Chronicle*, March 22, p. A6.

Morse, Dan. 2008. "Dog's New Tricks: Finding Cellphones." *Washington Post*, July 9.

"Museum Shooter Dies in Prison." 2010. *Houston Chronicle*, January 7, p. A8.

Napolitano, Andrew O. 2009. "The Case Against Military Tribunals." November 29. www.latimes.com/news/opinion/la-oe-napolitano29-2009nov29,0,3388576.

National Drug Intelligence Center (NDIC). 2009. "National Drug Threat Assessment, 2009." U.S. Department of Justice, December 2008.

"Okla: Governor Says Profiling Has Role against Terror." *Houston Chronicle*, February 3, 2007.

Oliver, Willard M. 2007. *Homeland Security for Policing*. Upper Saddle River, NJ: Pearson.

Olsen, Lise. 2009. "Judging by the Judges: Does a Secretive Process Let Errant Jurists Get Away with Breaking the Law?" *Houston Chronicle*, December 13, pp. A1, A10.

Olson, Bradley. 2009. "Data Show Crime Outpaces Officers." *Houston Chronicle*, August 3, pp. A1, A8.

Perkins, David B. 2004. "The Order vs. Freedom Debate after 9/11, 2001." In *Controversies in Policing*, ed. Quint C. Thurman and Andrew Giacomazzi, pp. 11–24. Cincinnati, OH: Anderson Publishing.

Pious, Richard M. 2006. *The War on Terrorism and the Rule of Law*. Los Angeles: Roxbury Publishing.

"Politicians Watch Criminals Pack More Heat." 2010. *Houston Chronicle*, January 18, p. A18.

Porcello, Ryan M. 2002. "International Bounty Hunter Ride-Along: Should U.K. Thrill Seekers Be Permitted to Pay to Experience a Week in the Life of a U.S. Bounty Hunter?" *Vanderbilt Journal of Transnational Law*, 35:953–987.

Porter, David. 2008. "New Jersey's Approach to Crime Seems to Work." *Houston Chronicle*, February 16.

Porter, David and Carla K. Johnson. 2009. "A World Where Kidneys Are Currency." *Houston Chronicle*, July 25, p. A3.

Posner, Richard A. 2007. *Countering Terrorism: Blurred Focus, Halting Steps*. Lanham, MD: Rowman and Littlefield.

Powers, Richard Gid. 2004. *Broken: The Troubled Past and Uncertain Future of the FBI*. New York: Free Press.

Rampell, Catherine. 2009. "How Old Is Old Enough?" *New York Times*, November 15, p. 5.

Raphael, Steven and Michael A. Stoll, eds. 2009. *Do Prisons Make Us Safer?: The Benefits and Costs of the Prison Boom*. New York: Russell Sage Foundation.

———. 2009. "Why Are So Many Americans in Prison?" In *Do Prisons Make Us Safer?: The Benefits and Costs of the Prison Boom*, ed. Steven Raphael and Michael A. Stoll, pp. 27–72. New York: Russell Sage Foundation.

Rejali, D. 2007. *American Torture*. Princeton, NJ: Princeton University Press.

Rosen, Jeffrey. 2010. "Could Keeping Convicts from Violating Probation or Their Terms of Release Be the Answer to Prison Overcrowding?" *The New York Times Magazine*, January 10, pp. 37–39.

Ross, Jeffrey Ian. 2005. "Post 9/11: Are We Really Safer Now?" In *Terrorism: Research, Readings, and Realities*, ed. Lynne Snowden and Bradley C. Whitsel, pp. 380–391, Upper Saddle River, NJ: Pearson.

Roth, Randolph. 2009. *American Homicide*. Cambridge, MA: Harvard University Press.

Sabol, William J., Heather C. West, and Matthew Cooper. 2009. *Prisoners in 2008*. Bureau of Justice Statistics, U.S. Department of Justice, December, pp. 1–46.

"San Jose Police to Don Helmet Cams." 2009. *Houston Chronicle*, December 20, p. A11.

Savage, Charlie. 2009. "Battle Looms Over the Patriot Act." *New York Times*, September 20, p. 25.

Savage, David G. 2009. "Life Terms for Teens on Docket." *Chicago Tribune*, September 27, p. 33.

Schmitt, Richard B. 2008. "FBI Saw Threat of Loan Crisis." August 25. http://articles.latimes.com/2008/aug/25/business/fi-mortgagefraud25.

Schwartz, Frederick A. O. and Aziz Huq. 2007. *Unchecked and Unbalanced: Presidential Power in a Time of Terror*. New York: New Press.

Schwartz, John. 2009. "Death Sentences Dropped But Executions Rose in '09." *New York Times*, December 18, 2009, p. A22.

Scolforo, Mark. 2007. "Time to Pay us Now, and Pay us Later." *Houston Chronicle*, October 22.

Shelton, Lee and James Hall. 2002. "Patriot Act Another RICO?" February 4. www.enterstageright.com/archive/articles/0202/0202patriot.htm.

Shukovsky, Paul. 2009. "FBI Saw Mortgage Fraud Early." www.seattlepi.com/national/397690_fbi-web28.html.

Sidel, Mark. 2004. *More Secure Less Free?: Antiterrorism Policy and Civil Liberties after 9/11*. Ann Arbor: University of Michigan Press.

Soros, George. 2008. "The Crisis & What to Do About It." *The New York Review of Books*, December 4, pp. 63–65.

Spelman, William. 2009. "Crime, Cash, and Limited Options: Explaining the Prison Boom." *Criminology and Public Policy*, 8(1), February:29–77.

Stambaugh, J. J. 2007. "Sneak and Peek Warrants Debated." *Knoxville News Sentinel*, August 13.

Stier, Ken. 2009. "Another By-Product of the Recession: Ex-Convicts." *Time*.com, March 6.

Stone, Brad. 2009. "Police Take Fight Onto the Web." *New York Times*, March 8, p. 3.

Stout, David. 2007. "FBI Director Admits Abuse of the Patriot Act." *Houston Chronicle*, March 10, p. A3.

Taxman, Faye S. and Liz Ressler. 2010. "Public Health is Public Safety: Revamping the Correctional Mission." In *Contemporary Issues in Criminal Justice Policy*, ed. Natasha A. Frost, Joshua D. Freilich, and Todd R. Clear, pp. 327–341. Belmont, CA: Wadsworth Cengage.

Transnational Records Access Clearinghouse (TRAC). 2007. "Criminal Terrorism Enforcement in the United States During the Five Years Since the 9/11/01 Attacks." http://trac.syr.edu/tracreports/terrorism/169/.

Urbina, Ian. 2009a. "Federal Hate Crime Cases at Highest Level Since '01." *New York Times*, December 18, p. A29.

———. 2009b. "Ohio Is First to Change to One Drug in Executions." *New York Times*, Nov. 14, p. A10.

Urgenson, Laurence A. and Peter A. Farrell. 2008. "Prosecution of Subprime-Mortgage Fraud: Will Congress Pay for It?" *Law Journal Newsletters*, September.

Van Dam, Andrew. 2009. "Elderly Prison Population Booming." *Hot Health Hotline*, November 17.

Virtanen, Michel. 2009. "New York to Soften Laws on Harsh Drug Sentences." *Houston Chronicle*, March 28, p. A17.

Webb, Jim. 2009. "Why We Must Fix Our Prisons." *Parade*, March 29, pp. 4–5.

Weinstein, Henry, Darren Briscoe, and Mitchell Landsberg. 2002. "Civil Liberties Take Back Seat to Safety." *Los Angeles Times*, March 10, November 15, p. A21.

Williams, Kristian. 2006. *American Methods: Torture and Logic of Domination*. Cambridge, MA: South End Press.

Wills, Gary. 2006. "A Country Ruled by Faith." *New York Review of Books*, November 16, pp. 8–12.

Woodard, Boston. 2005. "Seniors in the Cell Block: Why Elderly Prisoners Will Be the Next Big Problem Facing Our Prison System." www.fresnoalliance.com/home/magazine/2005/Oct2005/seniors_in_the_cell_block.htm.

Yoo, John. 2004. "The Patriot Act Is Constitutional." *Is the Patriot Act Unconstitutional?* www.encarta.msn.com/encnet/refpages/RefAuxArt.aspx?refid=701713501.

Zuckoff, Mitchell. 2005. *Ponzi's Scheme: The True Story of a Financial Legend*. New York: Random House.

2010	2010	2011	2012	2012	2014
Federal courts strike down Chicago ban on gun ownership	Obama signs Fair Sentencing Act	Gabrielle Giffords shot in Arizona	Massacre at Sandy Hook Elementary School leaves twenty students and six teachers dead	James Holmes kills twelve in Aurora, Colorado, movie theater massacre	Federal courts strike down ban on gun sales in Chicago

CHAPTER FIFTEEN

Crime and criminal justice in contemporary America (2010–2018)

Learning objectives

After reading this chapter students should understand and be able to discuss:

- The decline in American support for the death penalty
- The success and failure of criminal justice reforms during the Obama era
- The rising xenophobia that accompanied Donald Trump's ascendance to the presidency
- How a polarized Congress has prevented any meaningful criminal justice reform
- The waxing and waning of violent crime in certain parts of the country
- The support for plea bargaining and its impact on the criminal justice system
- The inequities of the cash bail system
- The federal and state conflict over the cannabis legalization movement
- The "Ferguson Effect" – its existence and its potential impact
- The debate over police use of deadly force
- The evolution of the ATF
- The criminal justice system response to mass murders
- The militarization of policing
- Hate crime in America
- The challenges of ending the current opioid epidemic

DOI: 10.4324/9781315148342-15

2014	2014	2013	2013	2013	2013
Recreational marijuana sales legalized in Colorado	State of Washington approves legal cannabis industry	Twelve employees murdered at Naval Sea Systems Command in Washington, DC	Gallup survey indicates 60 percent of Americans in favor of capital punishment (down from 80 percent in 1994)	Bite mark evidence disputed	Majority of NYPD officers are minorities (have been since 2006)

Introduction

In January 2009, President **Barack H. Obama** became the first African American president. In terms of criminal justice, President Obama worked to increase justice for "many of America's most dispossessed or forgotten citizens." Conversely, his administration did not prosecute "a single prominent banker or firm" for involvement in the subprime mortgage debacle that "nearly destroyed the economy."[1] During his years in office, "racial tensions across the country forced Obama to abandon his early reticence on race again and again."[2] Ultimately, he led a national conversation on race ignited by spasms of violence. Among his most significant efforts was his 2010 signing of the Fair Sentencing Act, which reduced penalties for crack cocaine offenses, and the 2014 independent Sentencing Commission that more equitably adjusted guideline ranges for drug crimes and applied the new penalties retroactively.

In July 2015, President Obama laid out his plans for fixing the American criminal justice system, focusing his speech to the annual NAACP annual convention on "communities, courtrooms, and cellblocks." As part of his week-long push for criminal justice reform, he also became the first sitting president to visit a federal correctional facility.[3] He visited the El Reno Correction Institution outside Oklahoma City, using this visit as a backdrop to layout his vision for the overhaul of the criminal justice system "in a way none of his predecessors have tried to do, at least not in modern times."[4]

Among the topics addressed at a national meeting of the NAACP was the restoration of voting rights for **felons** who had served their sentences as well as prohibiting employers from requiring a box to be checked related as to whether or not someone had a past conviction. The president announced that there would be a federal review of the use of solitary confinement and pressed Congress to pass some incarnation of a sentencing reform bill by the end of 2015.[5]

In his last years in office, he was eager to use his executive power to reduce harsh sentences, cut costs and correct disparities in the disproportionate burden on minorities. His intentions were piqued by series of disturbing incidents in Baltimore, New York City, and Ferguson that ignited tensions between law enforcement and urban minority communities. However, not everyone was on board with his goals. Indeed, since Congress implemented mandatory-minimum sentences for drug crimes, the federal prison system grew from 24,000 in the 1980s to over 214,000 in 2015.[6]

TIMELINE

2014	2014	2014	2015	2015	2015
Shooting of Michael Brown in Ferguson, Missouri	Missouri adds the firing squad to execution procedures	Congress passes Death in Custody Reporting Act	Twenty-eight executions nationwide	Nine African Americans killed in church in Charleston, South Carolina	Guns surpass auto deaths, leading cause of death for people under twenty-five years old

Ultimately, Obama, as a lame-duck president, was seeking to make common cause with the Republicans and Democrats who had come to realize that the nation had given too many punitive sentences to too many nonviolent offenders at "an enormous moral and financial cost to the country." Midway through 2015, more than 2.2 million Americans were housed behind the walls of federal and state prisons, seven times the number of just four decades earlier. With less than 5 percent of the world's population, the United States had more than 20 percent of its inmates. As one observer put it, this was the unintended consequences of the get-tough war on crime in the 1980s and 1990s, "born of the unfortunate U.S. penchant for applying simplistic answers to complicated questions . . . bumper sticker solutions have a way of bringing unintended consequences."[7]

When **Donald J. Trump** announced his candidacy for president in 2015, he referred to Mexican immigrants as criminals, drug dealers, and rapists. In June 2017, now President, Trump delivered equivocating comments following a white supremacist rally and counter-protest in Charlottesville, Virginia that left 1 dead and 17 wounded. His name was used as "a rallying cry" for "white supremacy, white nationalism or sense of triumphalism for taking back the country," a phenomenon unknown under previous modern presidents. Perhaps Pulitzer Prize winner Jon Meacham described this evolving "cult of personality" best, suggesting "It's saying we're American – and you're not."[8]

From an historical perspective, the United States, particularly its cities, is a remarkably safe place to live in 2018. Violent crime in 2016 was about half of what it was in 1991. However, violent crime did rise for the second straight year in 2017, driven by spikes in murders in several major cities. However, these rates still remained at historically low levels. Violent crime rose 3.9 in 2015 and 4.1 percent in 2016 compared to the years previously. Likewise, homicides increased 10 percent in 2015 and 8.6 percent in 2016. These increases served as fodder for the new administration, using it as proof that the country was in the midst of a dangerous crime wave that required a return to the more punitive punishments of drug offenders and tougher police tactics.

In 2016, less than half as many police officers were killed in the line of duty than in the mid-1970s. While Americans ranked "crime and lawlessness" as the most important domestic problem in 1968, in 2016, a Gallup poll ranked crime and violence below issues such as the economy, unemployment, racism, and race relations and dissatisfaction with the government. Nonetheless, during President Donald Trump's convention speech in 2016, he used the phrase "law and order" at least four times as he painted a bleak image of urban centers overrun by plundering gangs and murderous illegal immigrants. He went on to promise, "When I take the oath of office next year I will restore law and order to our country."[9] His vitriolic speech reverted to the lock-em up language of the 1980s and 1990s, not

2015	2015	2015	2015	2015	2016
White supremacist murders nine in a Charleston church	President Obama become first president to visit federal prison while in office	One quarter of world's prisoners in U.S. correctional facilities	*Montgomery v. Louisiana* Supreme Court case	Freddie Gray dies in a Baltimore police van	Applications for concealed carry permits hits record

just vilifying crime and criminals, but the disorder of the poor and marginalized, African Americans, street protesters, and dangerous immigrants.

As a postscript to the dawning of a new era in criminal justice policy, it did not go unnoticed that on the same night that Donald Trump became the president-elect, California, Maine, Massachusetts, and Nevada voted to legalize recreational marijuana, and three other states legalized it for medicinal purposes.

The lawgivers

From early in his administration, President Barack Obama made broad criminal justice reform a central goal of his tenure. In a 2013 landmark speech, he declared that too many people were in prison "for no good law enforcement reason."[10] He came out in favor of a 2010 law that eradicated divergent sentences for crimes involving crack and powder cocaine. In 2013, he went as far as ordering prosecutors to be more lenient toward low-level offenses and supported legislation that would reduce the mandatory-minimum sentences for many drug crimes.

But despite his strong leanings towards criminal justice reform, Obama made "a pragmatic calculation in January 2009 to be reticent in terms of race as America was beset by financial crisis." According to some accounts there was "fear inside the West Wing" that by advocating a "black agenda and aiming programs directly at African Americans at a time of widespread economic anxiety [it] would provoke a black backlash."[11]

No lawmaker was more prominent in the Obama era than Attorney General **Eric Holder**. His almost six year in that office proved to be "one of the most consequential" tenures in U.S. history.[12] Holder was, like President Obama, the first African American to serve in his position. As the country's top law enforcement official, he broke ground almost the moment he took office, even as he faced a hostile Congress. In 2011, he declared that the Justice Department would no longer defend the Defense of Marriage Act, which defined federal law as between a man and a woman. By most accounts, his decision was foreshadowed by the president's "evolution" on same sex marriage the following year and the 2013 Supreme Court decision invalidating an important part of the law. Since this court decision, nearly two dozen federal courts struck down state bans on same sex marriage across the country.

Not all of Holder's actions were as benign as his stance on marriage. He came under fire by civil libertarians and others for approving the targeted assassination of American civilians involved in foreign terrorist networks without judicial review, a fact the administration tried

TIMELINE

2016	2016	2016	2016	2016	2016
Debate over the so-called "Ferguson Effect"	Orlando Nightclub Massacre leaves forty-nine dead and fifty-eight wounded	President Obama sets one-day record for pardons	Chicago has more homicides than New York City and Los Angeles combined	64,000 drug overdoses in America	Murder rates rise in more than a quarter of 100 largest cities

to keep hidden for years. Moreover, the attorney general was zealous in plugging the leaks coming from his office and ended up bringing "more prosecutions under the Espionage Act than during all previous presidencies combined."[13]

Fair Sentencing Act of 2010

The Fair Sentencing Act was an example of what could be accomplished when Congressional bipartisanship took place. It reduced the disparity in sentencing for crack and powder cocaine, as crime levels receded to the lowest levels in forty years. As 2013 came to a close, Obama commuted the sentences of eight federal inmates convicted of crack offenses and who had been imprisoned at least fifteen years (six serving life). This was the

> First time retroactive relief was provided to a group of inmates who most likely would have received shorter terms if sentenced under current drug laws, sentencing rules and charging policies. . . . Commutations opened a new front in administration efforts to curb soaring taxpayer spending on prisons and correct inequality in the criminal justice system.[14]

Plea bargaining

Until the end of the Civil War, plea bargains were rare. Most defendants went on trial and either pleaded guilty or innocent. Judges had wide discretion to impose sentences deemed appropriate, without worrying about any barriers to passing sentence (which would come later with various mandatory sentencing provisions). According to one writer, conditions changed as a "result of the disruptions and dislocations that followed the war as well as greatly increased immigration and rising crime rates."[15] As a result, the criminal justice system was overburdened with caseloads. It was imperative to find a solution, and it came in the form of plea bargains.

Plea bargaining grew in popularity as the American criminal justice entered the twentieth century. During the 1920s Prohibition era, plea bargaining became more prominent following a rapid increase in the number of federal criminal offenses associated with the Volstead Act. In the following decade, the number of federal prosecutions under the Prohibition Act was eight times "the total figure for all federal prosecutions in 1914."[16] Although Prohibition was abolished in 1933, plea bargains continued.

2016	2017	2017	2017	2017	2017
Presidential candidate Donald J. Trump announces that crime "is out of control"	Drug overdoses leading cause of death among Americans under fifty years old	Las Vegas shooting leaves fifty-eight dead, deadliest mass shooting in U.S. history	Sutherland Springs, Texas, Church massacre leaves twenty-six people dead in worst church massacre	Rise in hate crimes	Nevada introduces legal recreational cannabis

In 1940, Attorney General Robert Jackson declared that "The prosecutor has more control over life, liberty, and reputation than any other person in America."[17] By 2014, prosecutors were more powerful than ever, thanks in part to the explosion in plea bargaining, where a suspect agrees to plead to a lesser charge in trade for having a more serious one dropped. During the early years of American criminal justice, plea bargaining was not available for defendants; today more than 95 percent of criminal cases end up in pleas rather than trials.

During the high crime 1980s, 19 percent of federal defendants went to trial. This decreased to 3 percent in 2010. At the state level, Georgia began using plea bargaining in 2004. Between 2005 and 2012 its use in convictions rose from 13 percent to 88 percent.[18] However, it became clear that, since 1970, when the Supreme Court approved plea bargaining at the state level, that it violated the intentions of its passage. When it was passed, it was with the tacit agreement that it would not be used to entice innocent defendants to plead guilty to crimes that they did not commit. Over the past decades, there have been numerous cases that have violated this understanding.

Psychiatrists and other mental health professionals have demonstrated the potential misuse of plea bargaining, including individuals confessing to crimes they did not commit rather than risk a trial and a potential longer sentence. In 2015, of the 149 cases in which individuals were cleared of crimes, 65 had pleaded guilty.[19] Moreover, the Innocence Project, which utilizes DNA evidence to reevaluate convictions, has overturned more than 300 sentences, most for murder and rape. In at least thirty of the cases, the defendants pleaded guilty. Suggesting the egregious use of this legal strategy, of all Americans absolved of murder between 1989 and 2012, one-quarter had originally confessed to the charges.[20]

Due to the proliferation of punitive mandatory-minimum sentencing rules and the lack of discretion afforded judges, for many defendants, taking a plea bargain seemed like a rational choice in lieu of trial. In most cases, making this choice ultimately was dependent on what charges the prosecution decided to file. For example, in a white-collar criminal case, a prosecutor has the power to charge the defendant for each e-mail as a separate case of wire fraud. Likewise, in a drug case, the prosecutor can choose how much contraband the defendant was caught with. The prosecutor has huge bargaining power. During the Obama administration, Attorney General Eric Holder attempted to curb federal use of mandatory-minimum sentences for nonviolent drug offenses. However, due to the anomalies of American criminal justice, it did not restrict these in state cases.[21]

Looking at the last thirty years, bargaining for much lower sentences while innocent of charges has become a common occurrence. Witnesses and criminal informants are open to the "same threats and incentives that push the innocent to plead guilty."[22] This will often lead criminal accomplices to testify against other criminals as a cooperating witness

2017	2017	2018	2018
Nebraska becomes first conservative state to abolish death penalty in forty years	Dallas Police use a robot to end deadly sniper rampage, first use of robot to kill civilian on U.S. soil	California begins recreational marijuana sales	Seventeen killed in Florida school shooting, the worst high school shooting in U.S. history

for a lighter term. Many juries are influenced by this type of testimony since they regard "snitches" as more knowledgeable about criminal activities.

As a result of the plea bargain panacea, of the 2.2 million inmates in American prisons in the mid-2010s, 2 million were the result of plea bargaining. By comparison, plea bargaining never found much of a reception in other countries and was considered "a kind of 'devil's pact'" by many observers.[23]

Alford pleas

One journalist declared the Alford plea as "an odd legal paradox."[24] Often plea bargaining includes giving up the right to challenge the conviction later. While plea bargains now account for almost 95 percent of final dispositions in felony cases, the Alford plea is exceptionally rare, only used in some 6 percent of all guilty pleas in state and federal courts. The Alford plea requires that a wrongfully convicted individual to formally plead guilty to a raft of lesser crimes, "but not admit actually committing them." This is just one tool that the prosecutor has to preserve the conviction on paper. It also eliminated the possibility of a second trial or face consequences for "bungling" the original one. It also protects the prosecutor from subsequently being sued. Nonetheless, for the defendant, the entire process results in a zero sum game, in that they still lose government benefits and the right to vote.[25]

The bail system

On January 1, 2018, New Jersey became the first state to almost completely eliminate the use of bail. This is just another example of how the American criminal justice system has always been a work in progress as it responds to new crimes and criminal justice trends. Traditionally, the amount of bail was determined "on hunches, or a fixed schedule matching bail amounts to crimes and lawyers' arguments to set bail." According to the new system, judges would begin using a "nine-factor algorithm" to determine whether a defendant was dangerous or likely to flee.[26]

There is still a lack of consensus over the feasibility of eliminating the current bail system. Those in favor have pointed "to a dramatic decline in the state's jail population, driven by a reduction in the number of poor, non-dangerous offenders who are incarcerated while waiting trial for no other reason than their inability to pay bail." In September 2017, New Jersey jails held 36 percent fewer people than they did two years earlier.[27] According to one account, there were almost 440,000 individuals detained awaiting trial "on any given day," representing about one-fifth of the total number of incarcerated Americans.[28] Those opposed cited the potential dangers of unleashing criminals back on the streets.

Other states have inaugurated related bail reforms. In New Orleans, a measure was approved that outlawed **cash bail** for misdemeanors. California and Connecticut have also instituted similar laws. Over the past two years, similar bail reforms have passed, reducing the use of cash bail in Illinois, Montana, New Mexico, and Alaska. Officials hope that these new steps will protect indigent defendants from pretrial incarceration. In a number of cities, lawsuits have been brought, arguing that "cash bail violated the 14th amendment's equal protection clause, sending people to jail purely because they cannot afford bail."[29] Recent studies of the impact of jailing poor misdemeanants who cannot make bail correlates with higher reoffending rates in the coming years.

Much of the debate surrounding this issue relates to the actual reason for bail, which is to make sure individuals return for court dates. The fact is that the vast majority return to court. Measures have been introduced to help make sure they do by haranguing defendants with a constant stream of reminders as to they were due in court. All indications are that New Jersey and other states that have reformed their bail systems are on the right side of history, especially as more and more jurisdictions eliminate cash bail.

The death penalty

During the second decade of the twenty-first century, there was a pronounced decline in support for the death penalty. While 60 percent of Americans supported capital punishment in a 2013 Gallup Survey, it still represented a decline from 80 percent in 1994. Between 2007 and 2013, six states repealed the death penalty. Of the thirty-two states that still used it in 2013, only fifteen had carried one out since 2010. The states of Texas, Virginia, Oklahoma, and Florida accounted for 60 percent of executions since 1976, with Texas accounting for 37 percent of them.

By all indications, capital punishment was becoming less popular and common than in the past. Studies have offered a variety of explanations for this shift, with most pointing to concerns about costs, its efficacy and controversy, racial discrimination, and execution methods. By most accounts, one of the most emotional arguments put forth by abolitionists is the fact that juries are quite capable of erring. During the first quarter of 2014, the country was on pace for the lowest number of executions since 1994. Indeed, it had dropped by two-thirds during the interregnum between 1998 and 1999. One of the more convincing interpretations of the data was the sharp decline in homicides (which augured for death sentences), from 10.2 per 100,000 in 1980 to 4.7 per 100,000 in 2012.[30]

Other factors cited for the declining rates include demographics, policing, culture, the job market, and the simple assumption that the death penalty has little effect on crime rates.[31] One important shift was in the power of juries to impose life sentences without parole in lieu of death. In 1972, when the Furman decision suspended capital punishment for the next four years, only seven states allowed life without parole. In 2017, every state except for Alaska gave juries this alternative to making sure a murderer is never released from prison.

While hundreds of murderers sit on death rows across the country, it is highly unlikely that they will ever see the inside of the death chamber. Yet they wait for decades in virtually solitary confinement. Death row prisoners are much more expensive to incarcerate than the general population since all of their meals have to be delivered to them, usually by multiple guards. Moreover, the years of appeals often engage more costly legal teams of attorneys.

Pardons

During his presidency, Barack Obama pardoned 148 citizens and shortened the sentences of 1,176 others (including 395 serving life). Pardons can range widely and might include forgiveness for a crime committed, the removal of voting restrictions on the right to vote or hold state and local offices, and the right to serve on a jury. These lessen the stigma arising from a conviction. In other cases, pardons were given for possession of counterfeit money, a felon in possession of a firearm and involuntary manslaughter. In another case, a serviceman dismissed from the military for conduct unbecoming (shoplifting) was pardoned.

In December 2016, President Obama gave "the greatest number of individual clemencies in a single day by any president."[32] These included the commutation of federal sentences for ninety-five prisoners and two pardons. This more than doubled the number he granted since he took office. Most of Obama's total number of clemencies were related to shortening sentences of convicted offenders rather than actual pardons. These included 78 pardons and the reduction of sentences of 153 others.[33]

The disenfranchisement of felons

In 2014, Attorney General Eric Holder sought to garner support for repealing the laws that barred felons from voting. This was just part of a strategy "to elevate issues of criminal justice and race in the president's second term and create a lasting civil rights legacy."[34] Although it was mostly symbolic, it touched a chord with civil rights activists, who pointed out how these laws so disproportionately affect minorities. African Americans made up almost a third of the almost 6 million people barred from voting. The U.S. was distinct among democratic nations for preventing so many people from voting. From an historical perspective, these laws were remnants of the late-nineteenth-century Jim Crow era, when states did what they could to stop blacks from exercising their right to vote. As expected, since this was a state's rights issue, it had little effect on existing policies. Nonetheless, Holder became the first attorney general to support repealing voting bans. Although Congress was empowered to pass a law guaranteeing felons the rights to vote, similar proposals had failed in the past

What often goes unremarked at election time is the fact that the disenfranchisement of felons in swing states such as Florida, Iowa, and Virginia can influence presidential elections.[35] According to one estimate, 1 out of every 40 American adults can't vote in the November election because state laws prohibit individuals with past felony convictions from voting. Not surprisingly, racial disparities in sentencing means that these laws have a "disproportionate effect on voting rights of blacks and Hispanics."[36] Of the more than

6 million barred from voting, only about 1.5 million were actually in prison, meaning that 4.5 million were either on parole, on probation, or had finished their complete sentences and were out of prison.

Florida is an excellent case in point, where 10 percent of the state's adults are ineligible to vote. Across the United States, an estimated 1 in 13 African American adults cannot vote due to a past felony conviction. In Florida, Tennessee, Kentucky, and Virginia, more than 1 in 5 cannot vote. But not all states are the same. Twelve states prohibit felons from voting even after completing their sentences. In fourteen states, a felon's voting rights are restored once released from prison. In Maine and Vermont, there are no restrictions on individuals with felony convictions, who are even allowed to vote while incarcerated.[37] In the case of a close election, the number of felons barred from voting can swing an election one way or another. For example, in the 2000 election, George W. Bush beat Al Gore in Florida by 537 votes out of a total of 600,000.

Currently, forty-eight states disenfranchise people who are incarcerated, while thirty-four disenfranchise people out of prison but on probation or parole. Conversely, in sixteen states, people who are on parole or probation can vote, including stalwart conservative states such as Indiana and Ohio, but *not* the more progressive-inclined states of California, Washington, and New Jersey.[38]

Cannabis laws

On January 1, 2014, recreational marijuana went on sale in Colorado, inaugurating the nation's first legal cannabis industry. (Although the smoking of marijuana had been legal in previous year, after Colorado voters in 2012 approved legal pot industry.) Likewise, Washington had its own version scheduled to begin in 2014.

On January 1, 2018, California kicked off recreational pot sales.[39] Initially, cannabis would be treated like alcohol, meaning, only individuals aged twenty-one and over could legally have one ounce of marijuana and grow six plants at home. When California legalized the sale of recreational cannabis, it joined the ranks of Alaska, Colorado (2013), Nevada, Oregon, and Washington (2013). By the end of 2018, Massachusetts and maybe Maine are expected to join the crowd. Meanwhile, medical marijuana has been partially legalized in twenty-nine states and Washington, DC.

According to one 2018 survey, 71 percent of Americans oppose federal government efforts to stop pot sales; an equally large majority think drug abuse should be treated as an addiction and mental health problem rather than criminal offense. But this hasn't stopped the government from spending more than $1 trillion over the past forty years on the failed drug war.

More Americans are arrested for pot possession than all the crimes that the FBI classifies as violent. But the real problem is opiate abuse. Overdoses and prescription sales of opioids have quadrupled since 1999. By some accounts, nearly 200,000 Americans have died from overdoses since 1999. One journalist has pointed out that only the Civil War and World War II had higher fatalities, comparing the anti-pot lobby to an "archaic moral crusade." Moreover, a new era prohibition will have the same effect as alcohol prohibition by creating "criminals [out] of nonviolent citizens."[40] Despite the evolution of drug policy on the state level, marijuana remains banned by the federal government and is classified in the same category as heroin.

Attorney General **Jeff Sessions** began 2018 by reversing Obama-era guidelines that effectively permitted states to develop legal cannabis programs without fear of federal interference. This shift threw into doubt the viability of the current multi-billion-dollar marijuana industry as the Trump administration "freed prosecutors to more aggressively enforce federal laws against drugs in states that have decriminalize its production and sale." Coincidentally or not, Sessions' vacillation on the issue of legalized marijuana coincided with its legalization in California, the most populous state. Sessions referred to the Obama policy as "unnecessary," as he zealously portrayed marijuana as a dangerous drug and a serious crime. This is just the latest drama over the states' rights conundrum on such issues as abortion, immigration, concealed weapons and drug possession. Usually the domain of the more conservative states, California's lieutenant governor Gavin Newsom proclaimed, "This brings states together around issues of freedom, individual liberty, states' rights . . . all of the principles that transcend red and blue [states]."[41]

Despite the intentions of the attorney general, marijuana use continued to be legalized. On January 10, 2018, the Vermont Senate gave final approval to a bill that would allow the recreational use of marijuana. This action would make Vermont the first state in the nation to legalize marijuana by an act of legislature rather than through a referendum of voters.[42] The vote made it legal for adults to possess and grow small amounts of cannabis. However, the state had still not set up a system of taxing and regulating its production, nor its sale. Its legalization would go into effect on July 1, 2018. Once it goes into effect, Vermont will become the ninth state (along with Washington, DC) to approve its recreational use. As of 2018, Vermont and the District of Columbia were the only jurisdictions without a tax and regulation structure as part of their legalization laws. As written, the Vermont law would permit adults aged twenty-one and over to possess up to one ounce of marijuana and have two mature marijuana plants or four immature plants.

At this writing, no crackdown or prosecution of marijuana-related businesses have taken place. Some observers suggest that the Sessions' directive was just a ploy to "sow doubt and slow growth in the semilegal industry."[43] By most accounts, it has been business as usual. Perhaps Colorado Governor John W. Hickenlooper (D) put it best when he noted that closing a marijuana dispensary should be low priority for prosecutors amidst a growing heroin epidemic, "What are you going to cut back on: heroin enforcement or sex trafficking, to shut down a little marijuana shop?" Conversely, opponents of legalization took great succor from Sessions' change of tact, castigating the hands-off approach fostered by the Obama administration that allowed the fledgling industry to flourish. As it stands, there are almost 4,500 medical and recreational shops in America. It remains to be seen if the genie can be put back in the bottle.

Like many previous claims, Sessions' mantra that cannabis poses a dangerous threat to society is not supported by any legitimate evidence. Survey data indicates that its legalization has not resulted in increased use among teenagers; in Colorado teen use is lower now than prior to legalization. Several studies have attempted to demonstrate a relationship between legalization and increased crime rates but found none. In fact, it is probably more verifiable that prohibition causes far more harm to society than cannabis itself, particularly after taking into consideration that cannabis laws have disproportionately impacted the poor and people of color by "saddling" tens of thousands with criminal records that often prevent them from landing a job or finding decent housing. What often goes unsaid is that, in states where the medical use of cannabis is legal, there are have roughly 1,800 fewer painkiller doses prescribed per physician than other states. Some studies have found a correlation between access to legal medical cannabis and lower rates of opioid use and overdose.[44]

Evolution of the exclusionary rule

1604	Castle doctrine in English common law
1791	Fourth Amendment against unreasonable search and seizure
1914	*Weeks v. United States,* evidence from illegal searches must be excluded from trials
1958	*Miller v. United States,* prior notice before police can force entry
1995	*Wilson v. Arkansas,* Police need not knock if risk of danger or potential destruction of evidence
1997	*Richards v. Wisconsin,* only "reasonable suspicion" of danger or evidence destruction required to force entry
2003	*United States v. Banks,* police can force entry fifty seconds after knocking
2006	*Hudson v. Michigan,* no suppression of evidence obtained from illegal searches[45]

Attorney General Jeff Sessions and the Justice Department

Hopes for criminal justice reform as the Obama administration pushed to conclusion were quickly dashed with the appointment of Jeff Sessions to the position of America's top cop. The former Alabama lawmaker had been the first Senate member to support candidate Trump. One recent article on Sessions described him as the "single most effective implementer of Trump's vision in the entire administration."[46] Going further, the article suggests that the current attorney general has not only "dramatically transformed" the Justice Department, but has caused it "to renege on its historic mission of defending civil rights." Nowhere is this better exemplified than in blatantly unconstitutional initiatives such as the anti-Muslim immigration ban. Moreover, it seems that Sessions had also reversed his long-standing support for state's rights. The case of *Masterpiece Cakeshop v. Colorado Civil Rights Commission* ruled in favor of the baker by a 7–2 vote in June 2018. Illustrating the administration's disdain for the rights of the LGBT community, Sessions came out in support of the rights of a baker to refuse baking a wedding cake for a same sex couple. According to one legal scholar, this is the first time in the history of the Justice Department that it "supported a constitutional exemption from a nondiscrimination law."[47]

As of 2018, it is not possible to forecast the future of the attorney general and the Justice Department. However, Sessions has made no secret of his plans to relaunch the war on drugs, especially marijuana, and expand the use of private prisons. Both notions clash with the previous administration's strategy toward reining in **mass incarceration**. His tough on crime attitudes predominated in the 1980s and 1990s. However, as continuing mass incarceration became untenable, especially as crime continued to decline, Sessions seemed to be swimming against the tide. This was made spectacularly clear in the bipartisanship agreement between politicians and lobbyists on the economic and social costs of imprisonment. This is perhaps best exemplified by the emergence of a consensus that included the Koch brothers, George Soros, the Tea Party, and the Center for American Progress, all of whom were convinced that the American criminal justice system was "needlessly harsh."[48]

Law enforcement

On July 17, 2014, Eric Garner, an unarmed New York City black man died while being arrested by several police officers. At the time, there were those who suggested that he perhaps died because of the broken-windows theory, which endorsed aggressively going after minor offenders, such as Garner, who was being arrested for selling loose, untaxed cigarettes. This theory has guided many an urban police force since the early 1990s. Conceptually, the theory entailed making arrests for panhandling, loitering, jaywalking, public intoxication, and so forth in order to protect community order. The issue of police strategies reached into the 2016 presidential election as candidates Hillary Clinton and Donald Trump debated the efficacy of stop-and-frisk policing. Then candidate Trump asserted that the tactic was not only constitutional, but had saved the lives of thousands of New Yorkers. Clinton countered that, besides being ineffective, a federal court had declared the strategy unconstitutional, and it would be necessary to develop new techniques to reduce urban violence.[49] While there is still much debate over police tactics, many civil libertarians suggest that past "siege-based tactics" used in cities like New York have come with a heavy cost. According to one editorial, "Broken-windows and its variants – 'zero tolerance,' 'quality of life,' 'stop and frisk practices' – have pointlessly burdened thousands of young people, most of them black and Hispanic, with criminal records."[50]

In the second decade of the twenty-first century, police were confronting a number of issues that few could have predicted a half century ago. Global terrorism, cybercrime, and financial crimes have left the FBI playing catch-up to the digital era. Traditional bogeymen such as the Mafia have been replaced by a new cast of characters. One major advance has been the increasing diversification of police forces. According to one source, since 2006, the majority of the NYPD were members of minority groups. However, there was still a decline in the number of black New York police officers. A litany of explanations have been offered, including demographic shifts of African American communities, the surge in new immigrant applications, or the publicity surrounding the reduction of police starting salaries in the previous decade (these have been increased). Others point to the racial tension over the aggressive stop and frisk policy or the ratcheting up of education requirements required to get into the police academy. Nonetheless, the greatest increases have been in the number of Hispanic and Asian patrolmen.[51]

By 2014, police deaths while on duty experienced a sharp increase over the prior year. In 2013, twenty-seven police were killed on duty, the lowest since 2005. However, this number almost doubled to fifty-one the next year (forty-five in accidents). Meanwhile, police departments were enthusiastic about any experiment that might decrease violent crimes. The use of predictive policing, for example, utilized intricate computer algorithms to try and identify which people were likely to become either victims or perpetrators. Predictive policing is built on several historical antecedents, combining rudiments of traditional polic-ing such as identifying crime hot spots and closely observing recent parolees.[52] Police forces in Los Angeles, Chicago, and Kansas City turned to predictive analytics to forecast crime trends. However, it has come under fire from civil liberties groups and has been criticized for reducing the waxing and waning of crime rates on a too limited number of factors.

America has been riven in recent years by a series of police shootings of unarmed suspects. By some estimates, American police kill close to 1,000 people each year. By comparison, Finnish police officers fired six bullets in 2017, the same number used by a Chicago police officer in a confrontation with a black teenager in 2014. While no rich country comes close to the United States in using firearms against civilians, a number of poorer countries make American police officers "look almost Nordic."[53] In Mathare, Kenya, a town of 250,000, for example, "killings by police are so common that they are considered normal."[54] Contrasted with strict American police reporting requirements, in this Kenyan town, police are not required to file a report and have even had the gall to charge relatives for the bullets used in killing. These killings, however, could not go on if not for the support from many corners. Many murders seem almost vigilante in nature, especially when it comes to thieves targeting downtrodden villagers living on the thin boundary of survival.

El Salvadoran police kill twenty-two times more people than their American counterparts. In fact, the Rio de Janeiro police, responsible for policing some 17 million inhabitants, killed more people in 2017 than all of the U.S. police combined.[55] A human rights activist in Nigeria suggested that "Police brutality is as common as water." The question arises as to why some police forces kill more than others. It seems that there is a correlation between the high homicide rates of a country and the number of deadly shootings, indicating that perhaps police in countries such as Kenya, Nigeria, and the Philippines feel less safe than their counterparts in richer countries. As one recent investigation pointed out, "American cops shoot more people than police in other rich countries largely because more people shoot at them."[56]

While a police involved shooting in America has many consequences for a police officer, in some countries police killings are lauded. In the Philippines, its current president Rodrigo Duterte openly urges his police officers to kill drug dealers with impunity. Since his administration began in 2016, it has been estimated that more than 12,000 people have been victims of "extrajudicial killings." Despite protests by human rights organizations it appears that almost three-quarters of the country's people support Duterte's approach. In Latin America, the so-called "iron-fist" approach, or *mano dura*, has led to a huge jump in police shootings in recent years. Three years ago, the vice president of El Salvador made it known that police could kill gang members without fear of consequences. Advocates of this policy suggest it is the only way to handle the rampant gang problem. Killings in India and Pakistan, known as "encounter killings," rose precipitously between 1997 and 2016. In Pakistan alone, there were 8,800 incidents where suspects died in shoot-outs with police.[57]

Is there a "Ferguson Effect?"

In 2014, Michael Brown, an unarmed black man, was the victim of a police shooting in the city of Ferguson, Missouri. Subsequently, this suburb of St. Louis was the scene of widespread rioting. In quick order, the nation was repulsed by the killings of two more unarmed black men, **Eric Garner** in New York City and **Freddie Gray** in Baltimore. The killing of **Michael Brown** in Ferguson and the subsequent rioting has been blamed in some quarters for creating what became known as the "Ferguson Effect," triggering rigorous debate over the state of American policing.

According to the theory of the "Ferguson Effect," which entered the criminal justice lexicon on the heels of a 2015 *Wall Street Journal* article, a rise in violent crime was the result of a series of videos of officer-involved shootings, which have become staples of YouTube and other social media. In response to the wave of criticism directed at police forces in general, it resulted in some police officers pursuing a less aggressive strategy in certain neighborhoods, fearing they might be put under the cellphone video microscope for any transgression. New York Police Commissioner William J. Bratton called it the "**YouTube Effect**." This notion was given some academic credence by a scholar at the Manhattan Institute named Heather McDonald.[58] Her thesis was that crime significantly declined since the 1990s due to the police use of aggressive techniques such as stop and frisk, "broken-windows," and just basically cracking down on public order infractions.

While there is still much debate over the nationwide crime decline, there is no doubt that crime did decrease significantly over the past twenty years. But according to McDonald and other proponents of this theory, in the wake of the Ferguson violence, police began eschewing the proactive strategies that seemed responsible for declining violent crime rates. As a result, exponents of the theory pointed to a spike in violent crime in 2015 and 2016. The "Ferguson Effect" is an intriguing notion. Indeed, when the FBI released its crime figures in September 2016, covering the previous year, it found a 3.9 percent increase in violent crime. Not only were robberies up 1.4 percent, but aggravated assaults rose 4.6 percent and homicides by 10.8 percent.[59]

Conservative advocates for tougher crime control blamed the rise in violent crime on protests against police brutality and racism in cities such as Ferguson. However, there were critics who argued that the increase in violent crime, rather than being a national phenomenon, was actually taking place in just a handful of urban communities. What's more, they argued, there was no evidence that protests had anything to do with it.

One study by a couple of sociologists tracked the number of reported crimes and arrests in Baltimore beginning with the 2014 civil disorder in Ferguson until after the death of Freddie Gray while in custody. They discovered that eight months after the Ferguson arrest, crime actually declined in Baltimore. However, following the Freddie Gray protests, arrests for low-level offenses in Baltimore decreased, as did the arrests for serious crimes, including murder and attempted murder. Between April and July 2015, nonfatal shootings rose 140 percent and homicides 92 percent. Several conclusions were derived from this study that lend credence to Macdonald's thesis above. While it is also possible that arrests for serious crimes declined since officers were too busy with other cases; more likely, reduced police activity in the wake of Freddie Gray's death probably contributed to the increase in violent and property crime. Other scholars have also asserted that the more the police were scrutinized there would be a higher likelihood of more crime.[60]

Use of deadly force

Over the past five years, the use of deadly force by police officers entered the American consciousness like never before after a series of high profile killings of unarmed black men. One of the major issues has been the lack of dependable official data on police shootings. One scholar asserted that 1,000 Americans die at the hands of police each year, double the number counted by the Department of Justice. What is perhaps most alarming is that out of these 1,000, only 1 police officer received a felony conviction. More troubling, was the fact that 400 of the victims were unarmed.[61] This form of violence seems to be an outlier in a time when police deaths are down along with violent crime in general, while violence by and against the police has skyrocketed. Criminologist Frank Zimring suggests that police killings of African Americans at more than double their share of the population is a "civil rights crisis that nobody had seen on the horizon."[62] It took the bystander video of the 2014 shooting of Michael Brown in Ferguson, followed by several other similar incidents for this phenomenon to register on the American consciousness.

Forensic evidence

During the second decade of the twenty-first century, a number of forensic science techniques have been brought into question. The use of **bite mark evidence**, first introduced in 1954, when a dentist in a small Texas town testified that that a bite mark left behind at a store robbery matched the teeth of a drunken man found with thirteen stolen silver dollars in pocket. Twenty years later, a bite mark left on a victim was used in a court case for the first time. But it wasn't until the trial of the notorious serial killer Ted Bundy in 1997 that "bite mark evidence hit the big time." Since 2000, DNA has been used to exonerate at least twenty-four men who had been convicted of rapes or murder due to bite mark evidence.[63]

Much of the debate over the validity of bite mark "science" occurred between 2013 and 2016, when a growing number of forensic scientists lambasted a small "mostly ungoverned group of dentists" who carry out bite mark analysis and find often key evidence in prosecutions "even though there is no scientific proof that teeth can be matched definitively to a bite into human skin."[64] Since DNA evidence has become the gold standard of identification, even the FBI has relegated its use to the past.[65]

It was not until 2016 that a scientific commission in Texas called for a halt to the use of what increasingly seemed was an antiquated and questionable procedure for obtaining evidence. This was the first time an official state or federal body recommended excluding its use in future trials. By most accounts, the repudiation of this form of evidence will affect hundreds of convictions, including a number of prominent murder, rape, and child abuse cases. Bite mark evidence now joins techniques such as microscopic hair comparisons as another technique called into question in recent years.[66] The technique of making hair matches was brought into question just the year before, when The Justice Department admitted that "nearly every examiner in an elite FBI forensic unit gave flawed testimony in almost all trials in which it offered evidence against criminal defendants over a more than two decade period before 2000."[67] This proved to be one of America's biggest forensic scandals, revealing the failure of the court system to prevent bogus scientific information from being presented in front of juries. Ultimately, there is "no accepted research on how often hair from different people may appear the same."[68]

Body cameras: a panacea?

While forensic science has undergone a number of challenges in recent years, law enforcement agencies have introduced a variety of technological advances to improve police safety, crime control and accountability. None has been the subject of more discussion than the body camera.[69] Following a spate of high profile shootings by police, beginning with the 2014 shooting of Michael Brown in Ferguson, Missouri, police departments across the country turned to this technology in order to document interactions between police and the public. By 2015, 95 percent of large police departments were either using them or were planning to adopt them.

Most observers expected their adoption would have a "civilizing effect" on officers and the citizens they encountered.[70] However, recent research has found that "they have almost no effect on officer behavior." According to an 18-month study of 2,000 officers in Washington, DC, researchers discovered that those "equipped used force and prompted civilian complaints at about the same rate as those who did not have them." In this study, 1,000 police officers were randomly selected to wear the cameras and the other thousand were not.[71] However, the results of the Washington, DC, study might not be applicable to most departments. Criminologists have argued that the Washington police already had a reputation for better than average training and supervision. Thus, it made sense that whether a cop wore one or not might not make any difference. Ultimately, it is too early to make these findings generalizable to all large cities.

Just as the body camera had become an accepted part of police gear, some police forces have begun to experiment with replacing them with cellphones. The Jersey City police became the first in the nation to experiment with a new smartphone app called CopCast. This allows officers to turn their "everyday cellphones" into body cameras. It has several advantages over the body camera. It is cheaper and allows supervisors to stream incidents and activities live to headquarters. All one needs to do is download the app on a smartphone as supervisors download a similar desktop variation. Once the officer straps the phone to his chest, all the officer has to do is push the start button to record video and audio. Not only will it show supervisors their exact location thanks to GPS technology, but at headquarters. the whole encounter can be saved automatically on a server. Body cameras, on the other hand, are not only more expensive but also require officers to wait until the end of their shifts to download all the video, which takes additional time reviewing and organizing before their superiors can view it.[72]

In Fresno, California, the use of gunfire sensors allowed police to quickly locate where and when gunshots were fired thanks to ShotSpotter technology. This technology relies on acoustic sensor mounted on lampposts and telephone poles, which then pick up the sound of gunfire and relay it to the police. The installation of numerous sensitive microphones allows computers and technicians at a California-based center to distinguish between gunfire and other noises. Similar to how cellphones are tracked through the triangulation of cell towers, the gunfire sensors can tell how many shots were fired and whether the location of gunfire had changed. The technology has been around since 2011 and is credited with helping end the rampage of a gunman who had just killed three people. The gunman was reportedly captured in just four minutes. ShotSpotter has been used in more than ninety U.S. cities including New York, San Francisco, Oakland, and Chicago. Fresno introduced it in 2015.[73]

Police DNA databases

In recent years, some police departments have begun amassing their own DNA databases. Critics have charged that this is more akin to subterfuge, with departments doing this to circumvent state and national databases "that restrict who can provide genetic samples" and how long they are held. In their defense, police chiefs claim that having their own DNA collection can solve cases faster and avoid backlogs that are typical with state and federal repositories. In many cases, it takes a state lab up to eighteen months to process DNA from a burglary; collecting on the local level has allowed forces to process DNA in less than one year. The Bensalem Township police in Pennsylvania created their database in 2010 and assert that the number of robberies and burglaries have declined due to their data collection efforts. While there are very few regulations at this point, it is expected that any local DNA collection should be correlated with a specific crime.[74]

Alcohol, Tobacco, and Firearms (ATF) in the twenty-first century

Recent reports indicate that the ATF "is on the verge of a crisis." The agency has not grown much since its founding in 1973 and, by some accounts, is about to confront a staffing shortage as it prepares to lose its tobacco and alcohol enforcement authorities. Since its founding, it has not grown significantly and by most accounts is on the verge of losing its tobacco and alcohol enforcement authorities.[75] President Trump has yet to nominate a director to oversee the agency, which has been without permanent leadership for eight of past twelve years. The White House has been pushing the ATF to the forefront of the fight against violent crime.

Since its inauguration in 1973, the ATF has been "overshadowed by more politically powerful law enforcement agencies such as the FBI."[76] When the ATF did attain any type of prominence, it was due to the illumination of its major failures, such as the deadly Branch Davidian siege in Waco, Texas, in 1993 and the "Fast and Furious" gunwalking scandal during the Obama administration.[77] In 2018, the Trump administration drafted plans to strip the ATF of its key authorities – fighting alcohol and tobacco[78] smugglers. Under the proposed plan, the Treasury Department would take over these tasks. If this occurs, the agency will need to change its name. Some have suggested possibly renaming it the Bureau of Arson, Explosives, and Firearms (AEF), but has not yet been determined.[79]

Following the mass shooting at Florida's **Parkland High School**, the federal government was pushing the ATF "to the forefront of its fight against violent crime."[80] This has presented a conundrum for the Trump administration, since the powerful gun lobby that supports him has endeavored to block the agency in efforts to regulate guns. This comes into conflict with the ATF mandate to fight violent gangs and illegal guns. As a result of this ideological conflict, as late as April 2018, the agency was still without a director. The power of the NRA and the gun lobby has not only crusaded against nominated directors but have sought to enact restrictions on the ATF's ability to regulate firearms and crimes. For example, one of the agency's funding provisions prohibits it from utilizing databases to trace guns to owners, forcing the ATF to rely on "a warehouse full of paper records." According to one ATF official, "It is beneficial to the NRA to have a smaller agency like the ATF in charge of gun regulation, rather than a larger, more politically powerful agency like the FBI."[81] In the meantime, the ATF is underfunded and understaffed and is on the verge of a major resource crisis. The agency has it made it clear that it "remains unable to fulfill even basic responsibilities, including inspections of firearms dealers – something the bureau says present a 'significant risk to public safety.'"[82]

National Integrated Ballistics Information Network (NIBIN)

Almost twenty years ago, the ATF equipped hundreds of law enforcement agencies and crime labs with ballistics imaging machines and began collecting photos of shell casings collected from crime scenes or test-fired from guns involved in investigations. However, its capabilities were never fully realized, due to a combination of budgetary issues, disinterest, and poor implementation, which at the local level ensured turnaround times took place at a glacial pace. In 2013, the ATF tried to reinvigorate the system by pouring millions of dollars into it. Currently, the **National Integrated Ballistics Information Network (NIBIN)** has improved exponentially, offering information in days rather than months. NIBIN allows firearms experts to match high resolution photos of marks left on bullet casings after being fired. Gun firing pins leave a mark that is unique to each gun and allows investigators to connect casings fired at different locations. As one police spokesperson put it, "Treating minor gun crimes as future homicides cut down violence."[83]

More recently, NIBIN has deployed a van that can "get emergency correlations back in as little as three hours."[84] The Houston Police Department, along with police forces in Chicago and Baltimore, have used the van. It was especially useful in Texas, which in 2016 led the United States in the number of fatal shootings, with 3,300 firearms-related deaths. Houston alone had more than 400 deaths from gunfire, including 160 suicides.

Militarization of policing

Innovation is part and parcel of modern policing. In 2016, for example, five members of the Dallas Police Department were killed and nine wounded after they were ambushed during a Black Lives Matter demonstration. Dallas already had a device used for bomb disposal called RoboCop. After negotiations with the shooter in a parking garage fell apart, it was decided to send the device in with an explosive attached to it. This was the first use of a robot to kill a civilian on U.S. soil.[85]

The use of the RoboCop, originally designed for the military is just another side of the trend of police forces adopting military equipment. By some accounts, since 2001, at least $5 billion worth of surplus army gear has been transferred to police forces for free. This includes 126 tracked armored vehicles, 138 grenade launchers, and 1,600 bayonets.[86] According to one criminologist, by the mid-2000s, 80 percent of police forces in cities containing 25,000 to 50,000 people had a military-style unit, compared to only 20 percent in the mid-1980s.[87]

Over the past decade, the so-called "war on terrorism" has had the unintended consequence of military hardware trickling down into the realm of law enforcement. In 2014, the public response of police using tear gas and BearCat armored trucks during the protests in Ferguson renewed a debate simmering for decades. In what type of situations should SWAT strategies and weaponry be deployed? Critics, not surprisingly, have compared SWAT to "occupying forces" acting "beyond their core mission."[88] SWAT was a product of a different era, introduced during the tumultuous 1960s. Although there have always been concerns over damaging community relations and frightening residents, "lax gun relations and strict national drug laws encouraged cities and towns to invest in weaponry."[89] Moreover, the "War on Drugs" that began in the 1980s encouraged police to use "militarized drug enforcement."

Corrections

By 2015, the United States, with less than 5 percent of the world's population, accounted for almost 25 percent of its prisoners. Of the more than 2.3 million people in prison, they were disproportionately from minority groups. Put another way, "No country in the world imprisons as many people as America does, for so long." According to one study, "At any one time, 1 American adult in 35 can expect to be locked up at some point." What's more, 1 in 9 African American children had a parent locked up. One of the more confusing aspects of these numbers is the fact that as the crime rate fell in the 1990s and 2000s, incarceration still increased.[90] The price for imprisoning so many at an average of $34,000 per year is staggering, costing taxpayers at least $80 billion each year.

Among the other challenges to the country's prison system was the fact that there are ten times as many mentally ill people in correctional facilities than in state mental health institutions. By most accounts, a combination of serious mental illness, the stigmatization of seeking treatment, and the lack of understanding mental illness has ended up with these mostly nonviolent offenders ending up in jails and prisons.[91]

The origins of today's mass incarceration dates back to at least the 1970s Nixon-era war on drugs. A recent study by the historian Elizabeth Hinton challenges the long-held contention that the country's mass incarceration problem began in the 1970s, tracing its evolution back further, to President Lyndon Johnson's social welfare program during the apogee of the civil rights movement.[92] When Johnson, according to Hinton, "first called for a 'War on Crime'" more than a half century ago, correctional facilities and law enforcement institutions began to function as a "central engine of American inequality."[93]

While it is true that in 1973 a number of states followed New York's lead by introducing mandatory sentences for drug crimes, one might be better served to go back and examine the 1965 Law Enforcement Assistance Act, which "empowered the national government to take a direct role in militarizing local police." In her cogent analysis, Hinton suggested that anticrime funding by the federal government "incentivized service providers to ally with police departments, courts, and prisons."[94] During the subsequent Nixon years and under his successors, "welfare programs fell by the wayside while investment in policing and punishment expanded."[95]

By the Reagan years of the 1980s, both the federal government and the states continued to pile on more punitive sentencing for crack cocaine dealers, imposing a strong racial bias in sentencing. Between 1980 and 1990 the proportion of offenders in prison whose primary offense was drug abuse had risen from 8 percent to almost 25 percent.[96]

Over the past several years, a bipartisan campaign to reduce mass incarceration has led to a significant decline in new inmates from large cities, diminishing the American prison population for the first time since the 1970s. Between 2006 and 2014, for example, annual prison admissions dropped in Indianapolis (–36 percent), Brooklyn (–37 percent), Los Angeles County (–69 percent), and San Francisco (–93 percent).[97] Unfortunately, these advances are not reflected in the American heartland, where the ongoing opioid/heroin epidemic has resulted in push back, meaning that smaller communities, concerned with public safety, are less inclined to divert drug users from prison into alternative programs. In fact, in counties with less than 100,000 people, prison admissions have continued to rise as crime declines.[98]

One recent study suggests that, only ten years ago, individuals from "rural, suburban, and urban areas were all equally likely to go to prison."[99] According to the authors of a recent study examining the current trend of locking up more people from smaller communities, the farther away a community is from Washington, DC. and state capitals, court prosecutors and judges "continue to wield great power over who goes and for how long." The journalists cite one Indiana prosecutor who recently stated, "I am proud of the fact that we send more people to jail than other counties . . . that's how we keep it safe here." He added the coda that this was how he kept his job.[100]

One explanation for this distinction involves taking a harder view of prosecutors. In rural locales, they face fewer obstacles in putting people in jail. Prosecutors typically control the local police force, which allows the prosecutor to both investigate and prosecute most of a county's most serious crimes. Moreover, there is usually more support for punitive measures from the rural inhabitants. By comparison, New York City prosecutors have been successful in reducing incarceration rates due to the availability of a wide assortment of diversion programs for drug offenses as the state continues to champion some type of alternative to incarceration. Ultimately, "Stark disparities in how counties punish crime show the limits of recent state and federal changes to reduce the number of inmates."[101]

According to federal data for 2015, the "number of adults locked up or on parole or probation fell to a level not seen since 2002 while overall crime continued to drop."[102] Reasons for the decline included new a federal prison system strategy that released thousands of nonviolent drug offenders in 2015. Additionally, states continue to seek ways to save money by enacting new policies to reduce the prison population. In 2014, for example, California voters approved California Prop 47, which retroactively reduced some drug and property crimes from felonies to misdemeanors; other states have expanded substance abuse treatment programs, have established specialty courts, and have directed more money toward reentry programs hoping to stem recidivism.

In 2015, the federal prison system was set to release 6,000 prisoners, "the largest ever one time release of federal prisoners" to ease overcrowding and relief for hard sentences given over the past thirty years. These early releases follow suggestions by the U.S. Sentencing Commission, which is an independent agency that sets sentencing policies for federal crimes.[103]

Texas tough or smart on crime?

As prisons became more and more overcrowded their quality declined as well. In Texas, where some prisons have no central air conditioning or heating, temperatures can reach 100 degrees for much of the year, while toilets sometimes froze in winter. Meanwhile, legions of drug addicts went without treatment. By the mid-2000s, the Texas criminal justice system budget had been stretched to the breaking point, leading the state to try cutting costs by "being smart on crime." Its success in reducing its prison population began in 2006 when corrections experts and several state politicians crafted alternatives to traditional incarceration, nixing a plan to add thousands of new beds. A number of alternatives included new in-patient and outpatient substance abuse programs and such alternatives as pretrial diversion programs that are meant to keep minor offenders out of jail. Thus far, dramatic results have been achieved as the Texas prison population decreased by about 5,000 inmates from its peak in 2010. In 2011, Texas closed a prison in Sugarland, the first time in 166 years that the state shut down a detention facility.[104]

Solitary confinement

It is estimated that, at any given time in the United States, there are more than 80,000 inmates serving sentences in solitary confinement. This usually means at least twenty-three hours a day alone behind bears. Harking back to the early nineteenth century, when Charles Dickens described the mind-numbing routine at Eastern State Penitentiary, by the twenty-first century, there was enough data to demonstrate that long-term isolation does indeed cause and aggravate mental illness. One of the greatest challenges for corrections system is how to house the most violent of the violent inmates. Physical isolation on Alcatraz and chain gangs have gone in and out of fashion. When Alcatraz closed in 1963, inmates were transferred to the maximum security lockup at the Marion Federal Penitentiary in Illinois. Twenty years later, after several guards were murdered there by members of the Aryan Brotherhood prison gang, it was "converted to the first modern all-lockdown facility," making the entire institution a solitary institution.[105] During the rest of the 1980s, California's Pelican Bay Prison and others began constructing "lockdown" prisons inspired by the Marion model. One recent study has linked this phenomenon to the era of mass incarceration and the almost nationwide closure of state-run mental health facilities.[106]

In 2014, Amnesty International castigated more than forty states for operating supermax facilities. Any personal interaction with someone outside the cell took place with either guards, psychologists, or clerical staff at the slot in the door where food received. One warden critiqued the supermax prisons as a "clean version of hell."[107]

In 2014, New York took steps to remedy prison conditions, prohibiting minors and the mentally ill from being placed in solitary. Colorado followed with a similar bill in 2015. Colorado was no stranger to prison reform. In 1890, the Supreme Court ruled against using solitary confinement on Colorado's death row. In September 2017, Colorado ended its solitary policy, limiting terms in isolation to fifteen days for serious violations. Additionally, inmates may also be required to undergo therapy or anger management classes after they get out of solitary. But at this juncture, this policy is unique to Colorado.[108] No place is more associated with solitary confinement than the death rows of America. One 2013 study revealed that 3,000 death row inmates in 35 states were held in solitary.[109] In 2017, inmates at the Louisiana Angola Penitentiary filed a federal class action lawsuit against the state. Of the Louisiana inmates on death row, fifty-six had been in solitary for more than ten years, forty-five for more than fifteen years and twenty for more than twenty years.

Juvenile confinement

Throughout American history, the criminal justice system has been challenged by the nature and punishment of juvenile offending, a conundrum dating back to the colonial era. During the so-called "**superpredator**" hysteria of the 1990s, a growing number of officials supported treating young criminals as adults. This was best reflected by the fact that, between 1990 and 2010, the number of juveniles in adult facilities rose 230 percent.[110] This meant that almost one-tenth of young offenders in confinement were either in an adult jail or prison. Not only was this costly (more than $30,000 per year), but research suggests that this practice turns juveniles into serious criminals. One study found that more than one-third of these young offenders were likelier to be rearrested than those tried only as juveniles.

The system of American criminal justice insures that punishment and sentencing depends on which state a juvenile commits a particular crime in. For example, any child accused of homicide in the state of Pennsylvania must begin in a state court. In Mississippi, a thirteen-year-old accused of any felony is tried in an adult court, while in neighboring Alabama, offenders are considered juveniles until they reach sixteen.[111] Likewise, in North Carolina and New York, sixteen-year-olds are always tried in adult courts. According to one Department of Justice study, when it comes to prosecutorial discretion, it is used unevenly, with African American youths 40 percent more likely to be charged as adults than whites.

Juveniles and life without parole

In 2010, the U.S. Supreme Court struck down mandatory life without parole for minors charged with crimes other than murder. Two years later, this ruling was extended to all juveniles. In *Montgomery v. Louisiana*, these new sentencing rules were challenged when the question came up in a particular murder case. Discussion hinged on whether these rules could be applied retroactively to the almost 2,000 inmates sentenced to die in prison for crimes committed before they were 18. This Supreme Court case resulted from the case of Henry Montgomery, who in 1963, at the age of seventeen, shot and killed a white police officer in Baton Rouge, Louisiana. It was an era of racial tensions, and almost from the start, the media portrayed Montgomery as a "wolfman." Not surprisingly, he was sentenced to death.[112] Just two years later, the Louisiana Supreme Court gave the case another look, acknowledging that KKK activity and cross burnings had created "an atmosphere . . . [that] prejudiced the defendant,"[113] and after another trial, he was resentenced to life without parole.

The 2012 the Supreme Court case of **Miller v. Alabama** once more put harsh juvenile sentencing under the spotlight. It coincided with the marked repudiation of the theory fostered by social scientists, that there would be hundreds of thousands of "superpredators" on the rampage by 2010. In early 1990s, when scholars and policy makers, such as John Dilulio, popularized the concept of superpredators, predictions of rampant bloodletting by young offenders led many states to begin toughening sentences, trying many juvenile offenders as adults and instituting life without possibility of parole.[114] *Miller v. Alabama* declared that juveniles convicted of murder may not be automatically given a life sentences and judges were expected to take into account each individual's circumstances, age, and background.[115]

In the early twenty-first century, Dilulio expressed regret for his prediction and relief that his predictions proved ill-founded. In fact, there was much data to indicate a sharp decline in juvenile crime. According to the Department of Justice, juvenile crimes peaked at 107,000 in 1999, and the number of minors in prison fell in the following years, until almost cut in half in 2013.[116]

Some observers pointed to the use of alternatives to incarceration tailored to reduce recidivism. Others noted better community policing or the utilization of "smaller institutions" in lieu of adult prisons, which were considered less effective at treating juvenile crime. In a major retreat from their earlier contentions, supporters of the superpredator hysteria found that the "alarm bells of the 1990s were muffled by reality" and "the myth of the ruthless juvenile was buried by its own creator,"[117] as John Dilulio joined the friend of the court brief in *Miller v. Alabama* to argue there "is no empirical basis for any concern" that juvenile crime would spike if mandatory sentences without parole were found to be unconstitutional. The 5–4 vote that followed was built on the foundation of earlier rulings that children "should be subject to neither capital punishment nor life sentences for crimes less than homicide."[118] Perhaps Supreme Court Justice Elena Kagan summed up the decision best when she noted, "Juveniles have diminished culpability and greater prospects for reform" and are "constitutionally different from adults."[119]

Women in prison

Between 2009 and 2015, America's female prison population in some states, such as Texas, increased by 10 percent (1,100 inmates) – this, at a time when the male prison population, at least in Texas, was down by 4 percent. Male prison populations had been falling across the United States by 5 percent during this time period. Although nationwide the number of women prisoners dropped by less than a half a percent, the female head count had actually increased by 700. According to the Prison Policy Initiative report, "Too often, states undermine their commitment to criminal justice reform by ignoring women's incarceration."[120] Texas was one of eight states experiencing the trend of increasing female incarceration between 2009 and 2015. In nineteen states, their numbers outpaced upsurges in male populations.

Prison reformers have suggested that "an increased reliance on probation" might explain the rise. In many cases, probation become a "net-widener" due to the fact that the conditions of probation are often onerous, requiring individuals to meet at difficult times. This becomes especially difficult when women are often taking care of children. Moreover, there are usually fewer diversion programs made available for women. With women making up such a small proportion of the overall prison population, not surprisingly, they are often overlooked or denied opportunities provided for men, including treatment programs and educational opportunities.[121]

Prison privatization

In 2018, the number of state inmates in privately operated prisons was once again on the increase. The Trump administration has made it clear that it intends to expand their use. Between 2000 and 2018, the number of individuals housed in private prisons increased 45 percent.

There has been a lack of a consensus over the value of private prisons for years. In 2016, a Justice Department report revealed that these institutions "were more violent than government-run institutions."[122] Violence affected both guards and inmates. During the Obama administration, there had been some indications that private prisons would be phased out at the federal level.[123] However, Attorney General Sessions recently overturned the ban.[124] Nonetheless, several states such as Michigan and Utah had already stopped using them due to security fears.

Private companies, such as the Geo Group, Corrections Corporation of America, and the Management & Training Corporation promoted their detention projects as low-risk and potential long-term solutions to budget problems in economically depressed towns and rural regions. The introduction of private prisons was seen as a stop-gap measure to deal with a rising inmate population and a decline in the number of correctional officers to police them. More than thirty years ago, Texas jumped on the privatization bandwagon. With its worst overcrowding in years, in the 1980s, the state prison system offered less than 40,000 beds and was under a federal court order not to exceed a 95 percent cap in occupancy.[125] By 1993, the state was trying to figure out where to put 60,000 state inmates with another 30,000 "backed up in county jails." By the time Texas went on a spending binge, investing $3 billion into prison expansion, private prisons were already filling the prison bed gap. One journalist captured the heyday of the private prisons in Texas, describing a "wild and wooly era of lightly supervised Texas private prison operators hawking beds to the highest bidder."[126] This arrangement was fraught with problems, including the escapes of murderers and violent sex offenders, prisoner abuse, and inadequate oversight.

Crime and punishment

The proportion of Americans who worried about crime has fallen dramatically since 2001. There are many reasons for this, including the significant decline of crime. However, many traditional criminal activities take place in anonymity. There is a remarkable amount of continuity between many of the crimes committed online and their counterparts in the pre-computer era. Although the tools are different, the motivation and intent remain the same. For example, bank robbers still physically rob banks, an increasingly dangerous avocation, while others have found it safer to simply hack into a bank's computer system and transfer money using electronic payment systems. Likewise, the burglar has been a stalwart under-world figure since there has been commodities of value to steal. Burglars have traditionally resorted to a handful of unsophisticated strategies such as kicking in doors or knocking on a door first to see if anyone is home. The high-tech incarnation works similarly online. According to one security expert, "the back door on a PC is opened through illegal hacker behavior, enabling viruses to spread easily and infect a machine."[127]

Commenting on the relationship between technology and criminality, several criminologists suggested that,

> In many respects, modern technology in the twenty-first century is no different from modern technology in the Middle Ages, and so forth: the invention and modification of tools continues to be applied to relieving victims of their money and/or property, and to moving property and money quickly.[128]

As illicit prostitution and gambling find new markets on the Internet, so too does the drug trade on the so-called "Dark Net." Dealing and buying drugs online on a secure provider means avoiding the dangers of the street, reducing the potential for physical violence for both the buyer and the dealer. While two of the largest Web drug markets were shut down in 2015, "one in seven drug users ordered their fix online."[129]

The drug trade has continued to flourish in the 2010s, as technology and globalization affect drug trafficking in the digital era. One recent case demonstrates the impact of globalization of the American marijuana trade. In April 2018, hundreds of federal and local police raided almost 100 Northern California houses purchased with money wired to the U.S. to grow massive amounts of pot illegally.[130] The plot was the brainchild of a crime organization based in China. If all went as planned, the houses would be set up as black market marijuana farms. The houses were located in suburban neighborhoods and valued at between $300,000 and $400,000.[131]

Prostitution has filled the coffers of organized crime groups in the U.S. for more than 150 years. As noted in an earlier chapter, mid-nineteenth-century America offered "a wide variety of commercial sexual activity."[132] Organized prostitution (and sex trafficking) have traditionally required a high level of organization, financing, and marketing. The era of the Internet has transformed the sex trade as it has many other forms of crime. The Internet has transformed the sex trade. It has made the sex trade easier to enter and safer to work in. For example, prostitutes and other sex workers have an almost anonymous venue to warn each other about violent clients, their backgrounds, and health checks before arranging a date.

Bank robberies

The decline in successful bank robberies in recent years suggests that this form of crime doesn't pay these days. Bank heists have been a staple of Hollywood movies and popular culture since the 1930s, when John Dillinger, Pretty Boy Floyd, and other social bandits made bank robbery the "quintessential American crime."[133] Traditional bank robberies have dropped 60 percent over the past twenty-five years, and those that continue to beat the banks are making off with much less lucre, for an average haul of about $6,500. Bank robbers, according to the FBI, are caught in greater numbers than any other criminals except for killers. By and large, it remains the crime of "the desperate,"[134] most likely to be committed as a crime of last resort for anyone that needs cash or a quick drug fix. Until the 1990s, banks spent little on updating obsolete security systems. Regarded as too costly to improve, by most accounts banks figured it was cheaper to absorb losses from robberies then to better equip thousands of banks. However, a tremendous increase in bank robberies in the early 1990s was beginning to cost banks money and result in lawsuits when customers were injured during the robberies. New measures included bullet-resistant "bandit barriers" designed for bank tellers, better security cameras and social media to feed the video to the public, metal detectors at entrances, and so-called "mantraps," entrances that can trap and hold robbers until police arrive.[135]

Hate crimes

As traditional crimes such as bank robbery rapidly decline hate crime continued to rise in 2017. Hate and bias crimes surged across the country for the second straight year, with more than 70 percent related to race or religion.[136] Members of Jewish, Muslim, and LGBT communities were especially targeted. In one of the most notorious incidents, white nationalists marched in the liberal college enclave of Charlottesville, Virginia, chanting "Jews will not replace us." During the first nine months of the year, incidents like these were clearly on the ascendant. According to the Anti-Defamation League, there was a 67 percent increase in physical assaults, vandalism, and attacks on Jews over the same period in 2016.[137] Some observers have suggested that the presidency of Donald Trump might have ignited a political firestorm in the wake of the Charlottesville violence when he commented that the violence that took one life and injured many others could be blamed "on both sides,"[138] which many people understood to mean white supremacists as well as their opposition.

Mass murder as hate crime

On June 18, 2015, Dylann Roof was arrested after he murdered nine black parishioners at the Emanuel African Methodist Episcopal Church in Charleston, South Carolina. His motivation was clear thanks to a message he left online which said, "I chose the city of Charleston because it is the most historic city in my state and at one time had the highest ratio of blacks to whites in the country."[139] In his screed left on a social networking site, he wrapped himself in a Confederate flag as he declared, "We have no skinheads, no real KKK, no one doing anything but talking on the Internet." His act of violence was intended to provoke a race war. Moreover, his embrace of the Confederate battle flag brought the debate over its use into the national spotlight like never before. Although Roof perpetrated the worst act of hate crime in the modern era, his actions had unintended consequences he surely did not plan for. Soon after the crime, South Carolina Governor Nikki Haley responded by initiating steps to take the Confederate flag down from its once hallowed position on the grounds of the state capitol. Her actions created a domino effect that only further inflamed white nationalist groups in the U.S. Mississippi and Alabama followed suit. Even the world of retail was impacted by this mass murder, with Amazon, Walmart, eBay, Sears, and Google pledging to quit selling that flag or any items branded with it. By all accounts, the swiftness of these changes were astonishing

Carjackings

Carjackings continue to plague American urban life. Some cities, such as Newark, New Jersey, have been hit harder than others. However, Newark and other cities saw the waxing and waning of this crime over the past decades. But in Newark it has "returned with a vengeance." By some accounts the crime has become so common in Newark it has been described as a "rideshare program" for criminals.[140]

Like other forms of criminality, there are a number of factors driving the proliferation of certain types of crime. Traditionally, carjackings were committed to use a car in a crime than dump it. In this case, it is partially related to the city's proximity to a major port in the current environment of globalization, offering car thieves the ability to move stolen cars quickly overseas. During the 1990s, as this crime became more common, maximum punishments were increased to thirty years in prison.

New technology has also played a role in the resurgence of the crime. In the past, it was not particularly difficult to steal a car – break out a window and hot wire the ignition – and you were off and running. Current automobiles are most likely to include sophisticated antitheft devices and measures such as computerized ignition systems that make it almost impossible to drive cars without keys. Conversely, the rise of the Internet has expanded the market for small-time thieves, who often hawk cars and car parts online.

In a small number of cases, organized crime rings have participated in schemes to send stolen cars to Africa. According to one 2013 report, one gang shipped stolen and carjacked cars to Africa to the tune of more than $1 million. Gang members who participated in carjackings would sell them to middlemen for as little as several $1,000. The cars were then transferred to individuals who specialized in cleaning VIN numbers and creating new ones. Once customers were identified, cars were shipped to western African countries of Nigeria, Sierra Leone, and Liberia.[141]

Executions

Over the past twenty years, there have been a number of controversies over the death penalty, particularly when it comes to Eighth Amendment protections against cruel and unusual punishments. The biggest hurdle for death penalty states became purchasing the drugs for injection. Until 2010, most lethal injections used a three-drug cocktail of sodium thiopental to induce unconsciousness, pancuronium to stop breathing, and potassium chloride to stop the heart. Due to the support for death penalty abolition in most of the developed world, it has become increasingly difficult for death penalty states to get all of the drugs for the combination. Opposition to the death penalty in Europe, where many of the drugs were produced, led to the drying up of supplies. In 2011, the only American producer of sodium thiopental ended production, concerned about a potential regulatory backlash in Europe if the drug was used in executions.[142] Meanwhile, federal regulations were put into place that prohibited the importation of drugs that did not meet certain standards. In addition, doctors and pharmacists increasingly sought to distance themselves from the process. As a result of the difficulties in getting all three drugs for lethal injection, some states have turned to less tested drugs with dreadful results. For example, in 2013, Oklahoma tried a drug cocktail using pentobarbital instead of sodium thiopental. During his execution the prisoner, Michael Wilson, was heard lamenting, "I feel my whole body burning."[143]

By 2015, the U.S. Supreme Court had upheld the constitutionality of lethal injection twice. In response, several states introduced backup methods in the event injection was not possible. Eight states offered electrocution; three had access to gas chambers; three offered the choice of hanging and two used firing squads, which Utah used in 2010 and 2013.[144]

In 2017, executions were on the decline, especially in the bellwether state of Texas. The prior year there were twenty executions nationwide, the fewest in a quarter century. Executions crested at ninety-eight in 1999. Nationally, the death penalty was certainly losing its luster as opposition, even in conservative states, continued. By 2018, few Americans could justify the death penalty, whether it was the waste of taxpayer dollars, religious reasons, or a host of other reservations. In May 2017, Nebraska, for a short time, became the 19th state and "the first conservative state in more than forty years to abolish the death penalty." If it was finally approved, Nebraska would have joined six other states that had abolished it since 2007.[145] But like many aspects of criminal justice throughout American history, the populace was never of one mind about almost anything. Since its move to abolish the death penalty in 2017, legal maneuvering in the higher echelons of state government ended what turned out to be a quixotic quest by abolitionists. In April of 2018, the state had set a date for its first execution since 1997.

In March 2018, Oklahoma prison officials announced they were planning to use nitrogen gas to execute inmates when the state resumes executions. The state had been unsuccessful in obtaining lethal injection drugs for months. This would be the "first time a U.S. state would use the gas" to carry out an execution.[146]

Drug-related

At the end of the first decade of the twenty-first century, cocaine use was on the wane. By one estimate, between 2006 and 2010, domestic cocaine use declined 37 percent. Numerous explanations have been given for this phenomenon, including increase in drug education and prevention programs, increased border seizures, and the fact that, as purity went down, the prices went up. The drug cartels, however, didn't miss a beat, entering new revenue streams ranging from marijuana and meth to counterfeit computer software and human smuggling.[147]

Heroin and opioids

Over the past decade, heroin use has surged, with a wave of addiction and overdoses closely related to the ongoing prescription drug epidemic. Overdoses quadrupled between 2002 and 2013 and in 2013 alone claimed 8,257 lives. These increases have been across all demographic groups, including women and people with private insurance and high incomes.[148] Much of the current drug crisis is attributable to the failure to regulate the pharmaceutical industry, leading to retail innovation on the black market.[149]

The opioid crisis has been linked to the recrudescence of heroin use. As the painkiller OxyContin was prescribed with virtually no oversight its abuse grew. By 2015, the majority of heroin addicts had formerly been hooked on Oxy, but switched to heroin because it was cheaper and more readily available on the black market. The states of Michigan, Ohio, and Indiana have been especially hard hit. The depressed corners of the rust belt have been hard hit by unemployment and poverty as factories closed and jobs disappeared. Many of the unemployed formerly held physically taxing jobs in heavy industry that have left many of them susceptible to injuries that could lead to prescriptions for painkillers. By 2017, Indiana had been one of the most affected states. With crackdowns on pill mills and doctor shopping, addicts robbed pharmacies to get their fixes. Between 2009 and 2016, more than 650 pharmacy robberies were reported in Indiana (with California next with 597).

No states have been hit harder by the current opioid crisis than the Midwestern states. One explanation is that the East and West Coasts faced drug epidemics as far back as the 1960s and were better prepared "to handle its resurgence." That said, the rural areas of the Midwest remain less aware and equipped to create strategies to fight drug trafficking, much of it emanating from Mexico by way of the transport hub of Chicago.[150]

New data on 2016 drug deaths indicated an acceleration of overdoses, mostly involving synthetic **opioids**, specifically, **fentanyl** and its analogues. In 2016, drug overdoses killed 64,000 people – put another way, as many as all of the American deaths from the Vietnam, Afghanistan, and Iraq wars combined. The first governmental account of nationwide drug deaths to cover all of 2016 indicated a 22 percent increase over the previous year. Some experts suggest that the deaths are to some degree the result of a reformulated version of Oxy released in 2010 that caused many to switch to heroin or other drugs.[151]

The DEA's Washington/Baltimore High Intensity Drug Trafficking Area Team (HIDTA) developed a smartphone app in 2016 that could be utilized by first responders to record the time and location of drug overdoses, which was then transmitted to a regional mapping database. This tool, OD-MAP, had been used by over 250 first responders, law enforcement agencies, and public health agencies in 27 states by the end of 2017.[152] By the end of 2017, this app was by most accounts the only tool designed to track overdoses (fatal and nonfatal) by location as they occur. Prior to the OD-MAP, few cities or states collected data on the collateral effects of the opioid epidemic, moreover, few states had been willing to share data with other states. The new app was considered the first to support a nationwide map of overdoses. As more and more jurisdictions use it, agencies can better track how the overdose epidemic moves from one neighborhood, county or state to another.[153]

Previously portrayed as a rural crisis, in 2016, the Center for Disease Control (CDC) broke down drug overdoses by geographic and racial lines. One unanticipated finding was that drug deaths among blacks in urban counties rose by 41 percent in 2016, "far outpacing any other ethnic group." In these same counties, deaths only rose 19 percent for whites. Driven in part by mounting drug deaths, life expectancy dropped for the second consecutive year, the first consecutive decline since 1963. More troubling was that overdoses, mostly from cocaine and heroin laced with fentanyl, outpaced heart disease as the leading cause of death for Americans under fifty-five years of age.[154]

The danger of just handling fentanyl has led some police forces to quit using field drug tests. It is widely known that, in order to quickly determine whether certain residue or powders are illicit drugs or not, it has been standard operating procedure to place the substances in a vial of liquid that will reveal a color that correlates with certain drugs such as heroin and cocaine. This is only an initial test with further testing confirmed in a crime lab. Just a minute amount of fentanyl can cause sickness and even death as it is either absorbed through the skin or inhaled. Over the past year-and-a-half, field testing has been banned by state police and the DEA in Oregon, Arizona, and Missouri as well as several big cities, including New York and Houston, Texas.[155]

Homicide

In 2015, homicide rates rose substantially in 25 out of the largest 100 cities, with half linked to just 7 cities, including Baltimore, Chicago, Houston, Milwaukee, Nashville, and Washington, DC.[156] It wasn't long until presidential candidate Donald Trump declared that crime was out of control. While it was true that violence had increased in a number of cities, most of the rise can be attributed to the aforementioned seven cities. By some accounts, homicide was "much more nuanced."[157] There was no consensus on why the spike occurred; however, more than three cities were embroiled in protests following police involved shootings of black males – Freddie Gray in Baltimore, Laquan McDonald in Chicago, and Tamir Rice in Cleveland.

Criminologists have suggested that the public "should not read too much into recent statistics." A better gauge of homicide rates is the fact that murders were unchanged in seventy cities and decreased significantly in five major cities.[158]

On September 25, 2017, the FBI released its annual crime numbers, demonstrating a 22 percent rise in murders between 2014 and 2016. During his inauguration speech that year, President Donald Trump made much hay out of what he described as "American carnage."[159] However, research suggests that the monthly murder numbers for America's fifty largest cities during this period and into the third quarter of 2017 indicated the murder rate was actually "flat."[160]

In 2018, Baltimore, with the highest murder rate in the country, selected its third police commissioner in five years. During the 30-month tenure of the former police chief (the 9th since 1994) almost 900 murders were recorded. A city of 615,000 mostly poor, minority residents, the city has been plagued by close to 300 homicides over each of the previous 3 years. By comparison, New York City has almost 10 times the number of residents but recorded less than 300 murders in each of the same years. Some have pointed to the lack of police on street. Baltimore has twice as many officers per capita as similar sized cities, but this is not reflected when considering the number of police on duty at any one time. When Darryl DeSousa became the new police commissioner, one of his first strategies to reduce violence was to "flood the streets with waves of officers" between 9 am and midnight.[161]

Chicago

Progress in reducing homicides in Chicago stalled out in 2004. It is instructive to compare its crime problem with New York City's. Several journalists have described this comparison as "a tale of two cities."[162] When the 1990s began, both diverse urban centers were dealing with historically high murder rates. However, there were some "significant differences in policing especially around the issue of guns."[163] When guns were not involved, Chicago's homicide rate was only slightly higher than New York's. That said, there was a huge disparity in the number of individuals shot, both fatally and not. According to a 2016 report, there was "a level of armed interaction" in Chicago that was not replicated in New York.[164]

Opponents of gun control of hung their hats on the argument that the Chicago still had high murder rates even though it had punitive gun laws. Thus, advocates for gun rights offer this as proof that gun regulation does not stem violence. However, most of these gun laws have been diminished in recent years. In 2010, the federal courts struck down its ban on handgun ownership and four years later its ban on gun sales. As a result, Chicago has become less retributive than New York when it comes to gun crimes, with a one-year minimum sentence for gun possession versus thirty months in New York. In 2013, movement was taken towards matching the New York law, but it was rejected by the Illinois legislature, which cited the widespread incarceration of young black men.

New York also hired more police officers in response to the crime problems of the 1990s and during its stop-and-frisk era in the 2000s sharply increased gun enforcement. This has led some observers to suggest that New York City has taken the so-called "arms race" more seriously than Chicago. Most homicide victims, perpetrators, and gang activity in both cities involve African Americans. Ultimately, the Chicago violence issue is related to the socioeconomic ills in the impoverished and segregated neighborhoods on the South and West sides of Chicago. According to one sociologist, "What predicts violent crime rates is concentrated poverty and neighborhood disadvantage, and what determines concentrated poverty is high levels of black segregation combined with high levels of black poverty."[165] By comparison, neighborhoods segregated by race are rare in New York City, making up less than 1 percent compared to Chicago's 12 percent. Although murder rates in most large cities declined in 2016, Chicago was one of several cities, including Milwaukee and Memphis, to experience spikes in murder rates.

Over the 2017 Memorial Day weekend in Chicago, forty-nine people were shot. This holiday weekend has historically been marked by carnage. Perhaps, said one journalist, Chicago "is oddly turning a corner in the fight against gun violence."[166] In any other developed country, this number of shootings would be outrageous. However, observers conceded that the five deaths and forty-four wounded between Friday and Monday represented an improvement over the previous year when seven were shot to death and sixty-one were injured.

Until relatively recently, the developing world accounted for about 3 percent of the world's reported serial killings. From a global perspective, between 1970 and 2000, almost three-quarters of the world's reported serial killings took place in the U.S., followed by 21 percent in Europe. But is serial murder really just a Western phenomenon, or is it just more likely to be reported? Some observers suggest that because industrialized countries have better crime reporting it skews the contrast between poor and rich countries. Others point to news censorship and underfinanced police systems more focused on political repression than common crime control. Moreover, poor countries have huge populations of impoverished, underprivileged, and "unwanted" people, the victims most at risk of being victimized. When looking at serial homicide as a numbers game, it is important to examine the correlation between the number of killers and the number of potential targets of opportunity. One need look no further than the increasing abundance of marginalized people in the developing world. Over the past decades, some of the world's most prolific serial killers have been arrested in less industrialized countries. Colombia's Pedro Alonso Lopez, for example, was estimated to have killed perhaps 300 girls in several countries before his capture in 1980. Javed Iqbal was sentenced to death in 2000 for the murders of almost 100 Pakistani children.[167] Famous American serial killers seem like amateurs, when it comes to numbers of victims.

For years, it has been de rigueur for communist countries to pass off serial murder as a Western phenomenon. If these crimes occurred in the former Soviet Union and China, they were seldom if ever reported. However, globalization and the increasing collaboration between journalists and officials around the world has led to some unexpected revelations, most recently in March 2018, when it was reported that, beginning thirty years earlier, Gao Chengyong went on a spree of rape murders in northwest China. On March 30, he was sentenced to death after an investigation that led authorities to individually sift through 230,000 sets of fingerprints. Gao was described as a "farmer, itinerant worker, and shopkeeper." When first arrested in 2016, his last murder had taken place in 2002, making his arrest even more surprising. However, his capture was more a combination of luck and advances in Chinese forensic science. Gao was able to elude suspicion for so long because he was just one of millions of rural peasants living a transient existence. He was lucky or adept enough to slip past city data checks. In 2011, local detectives acquired technology that could be used to trace DNA information. When one of Gao's relatives was implicated in some type of kickback scheme and his DNA was taken, it led investigators to the killer, who was now operating a small school store with his wife. Gao offered little in the way of a defense and according to police "knew that this day would come."[168]

Mass murder

The FBI defines a mass murder as the killing of four or more individuals, not including the shooter. In the United States, containing about 5 percent of the world's population, more than 40 percent own guns. This amounts to more than 265 million guns owned by 30 percent of the population. The debate continues on both sides why the number of mass shootings has risen sharply in recent years. Such incidents occurred 16.4 times each year between 2007 and 2013. By contrast, between 2000 and 2006, the average was 6.4.[169] By 2017, gun violence was claiming ninety-three victims on an average day in America. Of course, each time there is a mass shooting the question of gun control immediately comes up.

In December 2012, Adam Lanza stormed into the **Sandy Hook Elementary School** in Newtown, Connecticut, where he killed twenty children and six adults before taking his own life. Most advocates of gun control hoped this incident would become some type of tipping point. However, they were sorely disappointed after various bids to curb sales of the most powerful weapons and large capacity magazines stalled in Congress. Subsequently, Congress refused to expand the number of gun buyers checked for histories of crime and mental illness, although these steps were favored by the majority of Americans. In 2015, the Pew Research Center revealed that, for the first time in two decades, more Americans favored gun rights over gun controls.[170]

Over the past decade, America has become increasingly inured to mass shootings with little change in sight. With the highest rate of gun violence among developing nations, between 2014 and late 2017, gun violence took the lives of almost 40,000 and injured 200,000.[171] While mass murders have occurred sporadically over the twentieth century and are still rare, they occur with enough regularity that they fail to shock lawmakers into action. When the Columbine school shootings occurred in 1999, it left a new benchmark of thirteen dead for school shootings. By most accounts, it was treated as "a national calamity."

When Columbine occurred in the small rural Colorado town, it was the fifth deadliest mass shooting in America since World War II, only surpassed by mass murders at a Luby's restaurant in Killeen, Texas, in 1991 (twenty-three deaths); at a McDonalds in San Ysidro, California, in 1984 (twenty-one); at the University of Texas in 1966 (fifteen); and at a post office in Edmond, Oklahoma, in 1986 (fourteen).[172] However, by the end of 2017, none of these aforementioned shootings was even among the five deadliest. Previously, the top five took place over a period of thirty years. Sadly, four of the current top five have occurred over the past five years. The mass shootings at an **Orlando nightclub** in 2016 (forty-nine) and in Las Vegas in 2017 (fifty-eight) have ratcheted up the body count to unprecedented numbers. The year 2017 ended with the worst church mass murder in U.S. history following the shootings of twenty-six people in Sutherland Springs, Texas. In 2018, there were more to come.

Conclusions

As 2017 moved to conclusion, much had changed in American crime and criminal justice. Evolving notions of crime and retribution, deeply ingrained for centuries, indicated that many American criminal justice institutions were not engraved in stone and can indeed evolve over time. By all accounts, American support for the death penalty had dipped to its lowest ebb in more than forty years. Both sides of the political divide have affected the precipitous drop. The most recent Gallup poll indicated that 55 percent of U.S. adults support capital punishment for convicted murderers, a low that had not been reached since 1972.[173]

One of the more fascinating insights into the waning support for capital punishment is the fact that it has become less of a partisan issue, with close to one-third of sponsors of related legislation being members of the Republican Party. Much of the abolition activity has been taking place in "red" states, indicating an increase in conservative opposition to the death penalty. Indicative of this change is a report from Conservatives Concerned about the Death Penalty (CCATDP), which cited wrongful convictions, high costs, and pro-life concerns among the reasons for its abolition.

Although plea bargaining has reduced the number of trials, the consequences of using it are often "severe and long-lasting." In the United States, once felons are released, whether they plead guilty to a crime they did not commit or not, meant they would be permanently barred from voting, evicted from public housing, denied welfare benefits, or simply turned away at most job searches. By comparison, European countries typically expunge the criminal record, except for the most serious cases and provided one does not reoffend. However, there is usually a period of time when they cannot hold such sensitive jobs as teaching or public administration.[174] The huge number of disenfranchised voters became an important talking point since their voices might have changed the presidential voting results.

Criminologists, criminal justicians, policy makers, and social scientists have been trying to explain the great crime decline that began in the 1990s. Many of the explanations, such as police tactics, mass incarceration, and the end of the crack epidemic have been covered in the previous three chapters. It is a debate that continues to dominate the discourse on crime and criminal justice in American history. More recently, sociologist Patrick Sharkey suggested that scholars had been looking for the answers in the wrong places. In his insightful and compelling 2018 book, *Uneasy Peace: The Great Crime Decline, the Renewal of City Life, and the Next War on Violence*,[175] he gives credit to a host of uncredited urban actors, arguing that the decline in urban violence was a result of a team effort by local non-profits that responded to the disorder and violence by cleaning streets, building playgrounds, mentoring children, and employing young men.

President Trump's elevation of Alabama's Jeff Sessions to attorney general suggests, according to some observers, that this part of a current fixation of rolling back some of the reforms implemented by the recent Obama administration under Attorney General Eric Holder. By most accounts, prison reform advocates and officials had made great strides toward ending mass incarceration and excessive use of force by police. However, almost from the start Attorney General Sessions was inclined to do the opposite. He was zealous in supporting the return to the zero tolerance drug policies of the Reagan era, and despite historically low crime figures, he fed the impression that the country was in the midst of a crime wave. To that end, in May 2017, Sessions reversed the policy of President Obama's Justice Department, which urged prosecutors to avoid mandatory-minimum sentences for nonviolent drug offenses without gang ties, by instead advocating for prosecutors to tow a more draconian line when it came to low-level drug offenses.

No criminal justice issue seemed more pressing in recent years than the current opioid abuse epidemic, the deadliest drug scourge in recent history. In 2017, drug overdoses became the leading cause of death among Americans under fifty years old. One pragmatic official commented that the country could not "arrest our way out of this." This was particularly true when only one in ten addicts were able to get treatment.[176]

Contrary to the prevailing fears of superpredators prowling the streets of urban America, as the 2010s moved to conclusion, the national trend away from the harsh punishment of juveniles continued. Over the past several years, the U.S. Supreme Court banned the death penalty and mandatory life sentences without parole for juveniles. By 2016, sixteen states prohibited life without parole for juveniles. Over the past two decades, the criminal justice system has come to grips with juvenile sentencing, recognizing that sending them to adult prisons was not the correct approach, and has moved away from tough mandatory sentencing and treating them as adults.

While crime decreases as does the prison population, there are other stark reminders of American exceptionalism when it comes to guns and drugs. Gun violence, drug overdoses, and car accidents continue to claim more than 100,000 lives each year at a rate in each category higher than other comparable nations.[177] This is most glaring when it comes to guns. Research into better firearms safety has been hamstrung by a congressional ban on federal grants for such studies. What's more, the National Institutes of Health did not even fund a study on childhood firearms injuries between 2005 and 2014, although firearms were the second leading cause of death for Americans between one and nineteen years old, after car crashes.[178]

In December 2017, the Centers for Disease Control and Prevention (CDC) released its annual report on American mortality. Its conclusions were disheartening. For the second year in a row, life expectancy decreased. The last time it fell in successive years was in 1963–1964. Its statistics suggest the trend is the result of the opioid epidemic, which has become deadlier. Of the more than 63,000 lives lost to drug overdoses in 2016, two-thirds were from opioids.[179] The leading causes of death remained heart disease and cancer. In third place was the category of "unintentional injuries" which includes drug overdoses (only percent of deaths). In order to prevent a third successive year of life expectancy decline, it is incumbent on the new administration to take steps to control the scourge. In 2016, while stumping for the presidency, Trump promised to make the opioid crisis a priority. However, after a year in office, the administration has no strategy and is still without a new drug czar. Moreover, the new regime has not even asked Congress to allocate the much needed billions of dollars to treat the estimated 2 million opioid addicts.[180]

Key terms

Jeff Sessions
Ferguson Effect
Freddie Gray
Fair Sentencing Act
  plea bargaining
YouTube Effect
Alcohol, Tobacco, and
  Firearms (ATF)
superpredators
Donald J. Trump
fentanyl
Eric Garner

cash bail
body cameras
Parkland High School
  shooting
Miller v. Alabama
Barack Obama
opioids
Michael Brown Sandy
  Hook Elementary
  School Orlando
  Nightclub
  Massacre

felon disenfranchisement
  cannabis
deadly force
National Integrated
  Ballistics Information
  Network (NIBIN)
prison privatization
Eric Holder
Alford plea
bite mark evidence
police militarization
mass incarceration

Critical thinking questions

1 What impact did the Obama administration have on criminal justice reform?
2 What are some of the most convincing explanations for the crime drop?
3 How has the Trump White House distanced itself from the current administration in terms of criminal justice reform?
4 What are some of the best explanations for the decline in the popularity of capital punishment?
5 What seems to be the most pressing problems facing the contemporary criminal justice system?
6 How has the publicized shooting of unarmed black men by police officers affected relations between the police and the urban communities that they serve? Is there a "Ferguson Effect?"
7 What can explain the increase in hate crimes?
8 What can be done to end the current opioid crisis? Does it have anything to do with the marijuana legalization movement?

Notes

1 "Eric Holder's Legacy," *New York Times*, September 26, 2014, p. A26.
2 Michael D. Shear and Yamiche Alcindor, "Finding Michael His Voice on Race," *New York Times*, January 15, 2017, pp. 1, 18.
3 Peter Baker, "Obama Takes Reform Message Behind Bars," *New York Times*, July 17, 2015.
4 Ibid.
5 Josh Lederman, "Obama Urges Criminal Justice Reforms," *Houston Chronicle*, July 15, 2015, p. A2.
6 Ibid.
7 Leonard Pitts Jr., "American Justice System Not Worthy of the Name," *Houston Chronicle*, July 23, 2015, p. B9.
8 Dan Barry and John Eligon, "A Rallying Cry or Racial Taunt Invoking the President: 'Trump!',", *New York Times*, December 17, 2017, pp. 1, 14.
9 Text of Donald Trump's Speech to GOP Convention, July, 21, 2016. http://www.thestate.com/news/politics-government/article91203222.html
10 "Eric Holder's Legacy," September 26, 2014.
11 Shear and Alcindor, 2017, pp. 1, 18.
12 "Eric Holder's Legacy," September 26, 2014, p. A26.
13 Ibid.
14 Charlie Savage, "Obama Curbs Sentences of 8 in Crack Cases," *New York Times*, December 20, 2013, pp. 1, A16.
15 Jed S. Rakoff, "Why Innocent People Plead Guilty," *New York Review of Books*, November 11, 2014, pp. 14–18.
16 "A Deal You Can't Refuse," *The Economist*, November 11, 2017, pp. 53–54.
17 "Kings of the Courtroom," *The Economist*, October 14, 2014, p. 33.
18 "A Deal You Can't Refuse," November 11, 2017.
19 Ibid.
20 Ibid., National Registry of Exonerations.
21 "Kings of the Courtroom," October 14, 2014.

22 "The Kings of the Courtroom," *The Economist*, October 4, 2014. https://www.economist.com/united-states/2014/10/04/the-kings-of-the-courtroom

23 Rakoff, 2014.

24 Alan Feuer, "After 28 Years in Prison, A Rare Plea Deal Frees a Connecticut Man," *New York Times*, November 23, 2017. https://www.nytimes.com/2017/11/23/nyregion/rare-alford-plea-wrongful-conviction-rape-connecticut.html

25 Alan Feuer, 2017.

26 "Outing Bail," *The Economist*, November 25, 2017, p. 29.

27 According to American law, those in custody awaiting trial or serving short prison stints wait in "jails"; most others who have already been convicted go to "prison."

28 "Outing Bail," November 25, 2017, p. 29.

29 "Replacing Bail with an Algorithm," *The Economist*, November 25, 2017. http://media.economist.com/news/united-states/21731631-new-jersey-has-bold-experiment-reduce-number-people-jail-awaiting

30 "The Slow Death of the Death Penalty," *The Economist*, April 26, 2016, pp. 27–29.

31 Ibid.

32 Not all were carte blanche. Some would not be commuted immediately and would have to wait until 2018; others had to participate in drug treatment program first.

33 Kevin Freking, "Obama Sets One-Day Mark for Clemencies," *Houston Chronicle*, December 20, 2016, p. A10; Julie Hirschfield Davis and Peter Baker, "Obama Issues Largest Block of Commutation Yet," *New York Times*, December 19, 2015, p. A11.

34 Matt Apuzzo, "Holder Urges State to Lift Bans on Felons," *New York Times*, February 12, 2014, p. A17.

35 These three states have some of the nation's most punitive felon laws. These can range from a lifetime ban on voting to the restoration of voting rights on a case-by-case basis by a governor or court.

36 K. K. Rebecca Lai and Jasmine C. Lee, "10 Percent of Florida Adults Are Ineligible to Vote: Why," *New York Times*, October 7, 2016, p. A12. https://www.nytimes.com/interactive/2016/10/06/us/unequal-effect-of-laws-that-block-felons-from-voting.html

37 K. K. Rebecca Lai and Jasmine C. Lee, 2016.

38 Daniel Nichanian, "The Case for Letting Felons Vote," *New York Times*, February 23, 2018, p. A23.

39 The path to legalization in California began in 2016 when voters approved Proposition 64.

40 Timothy Egan, "From the Department of Injustice, More Prohibition," *New York Times*, January 6, 2018, p. A18.

41 Charlie Savage and Jack Healy, "Justice Dept. Shift Threatens Legal Marijuana," *New York Times*, January 5, 2018, pp. A1, 15.

42 Wilson Ring, "Vermont Set to Enact Legal Pot Via Legislature," *Houston Chronicle*, January 11, 2018, p. A10. Historically, Vermont does not allow referendum votes like the other states that have legalized it.

43 Charlie savage and Jack Heaky, "Trump Administration Takes Step That could Threaten Legalization Movement," *New York Times*, January 4, 2018. https://www.nytimes.com/2018/01/04/us/politics/marijuana-legalization-justice-department-prosecutions.html

44 Katherine Neill Harris, "Why Sessions' War on Weed Won't Work," *Houston Chronicle*, January 1, 2018, p. A2.

45 Adapted from Kevin Sack, "Door Busting Raids Leave Trail of Blood," *New York Times*, March 19, 2017, pp. 16–18.

46 David Cole, "Trump's Inquisitor," *New York Review of Books*, April 19, 2018, p. 16.

47 Ibid.

48 Ibid.

49 Michael D. White and Henry F. Fradella, *Stop and Frisk: The Use and Abuse of a Controversial Policing Tactic*, New York: New York University Press, 2016.

50 "Broken Windows, Broken Lives," *New York Times*, July 26, 2014, p. A18.

51 J. David Goodman, "More Diversity in City's Police, But Blacks Lag," *New York Times*, December 27, 2013, pp. A1, 3.

52 John Eligon and Timothy Williams, "On Police Radar for Crimes They Might Commit," *New York Times*, September 25, 2015, pp. A1, 23.

53 "Why They Do Tt," *The Economist*, March 10, 2018, p. 62.

54 "Cops Who Kill," *The Economist*, March 10, 2018, p. 61.

55 "Why They Do It," March 10, 2018, p. 62.

56 Ibid.

57 Ibid.

58 Heather MacDonald, *The War on Cops: How the New Attack on Law and Order Makes Everyone Less Safe*, New York: Encounter Books, 2016.

59 Neil Gross, "Is There a 'Ferguson Effect'?" *New York Times*, October 2, 2016, p. 9.

60 Ibid.

61 Frank E. Zimring, *When Police Kill*, Cambridge, MA: Harvard University Press, 2017.

62 Frank E. Zimring, *When Police Kill*, Cambridge: Harvard University Press, 2017, p. ix.

63 "Last Gasp for Bite Mark 'Science,'" *Houston Chronicle*, June 17, 2013, p. A5.

64 "Last Gasp for Bite Mark 'Science,'" 2013, p. A5.

65 Recent studies suggest that human skin is so malleable that wound patterns from the same teeth can differ and change over time.

66 Erik Eckholm, "Texas Panel Calls for an End to Criminal Identification via Bite Mark," *New York Times*, February 13, 2016, p. A10.

67 Spencer S. Hsu, "FBI Admits to Flawed Forensic Hair Matches," *Houston Chronicle*, April 19, 2015, p. A3.

68 Spencer S. Hsu, "FBI Admits Flaws in Hair Analysis Over Decades," *Washington Post*, April 18, 2015. https://www.washingtonpost.com/local/crime/fbi-overstated-forensic-hair-matches-in-nearly-all-criminal-trials-for-decades/2015/04/18/39c8d8c6-e515-11e4-b510-962fcfabc310_story.html?utm_term=.a3d7c472b223

69 Body cameras are sold by Axon, formerly Taser International. It has sold more than 300,000 worldwide, or about three-quarters of the business in the United States. David Gelles, "Company Known for Stun Guns Corners the Market on Body Cameras for Police," *Houston Chronicle*, July 14, 2016, p. B10.

70 Amanda Ripley and Timothy Williams, "Body Cameras Watch Officers with Little Effect, Study Finds," *New York Times*, October 21, 2017, pp. A1, 11.

71 Ibid.

72 Alan Gomez, "Police Cellphones May Replace Body Cameras," *USA Today*, June 26, 2017, p. 3A.

73 Scott Smith, "Gunfire Sensors Cited for Swift Arrest in Fresno Attack," *Houston Chronicle*, April 21, 2017, p. A12.

74 Michael Balsamo, "Police Databases Stir Debate," *Houston Chronicle*, March 5, 2017, p. A18.

75 Ali Watkins, 2018, p. A12.

76 Ali Watkins, "How the NRA Uses Its Influence to Hobble Federal Gun Regulators," *New York Times*, February 23, 2018, p. A12.

77 Ali Watkins, 2018, p. A12.

78 Tobacco investigations were prioritized by the ATF at one time. Cigarette smuggling is a lucrative criminal enterprise throughout the world. In the United States, it hinges on the ability of smugglers to purchase cigarettes in low tax states, such as Virginia, which charges $3 per carton. Meanwhile, in New York taxes were $43.50 per carton. Not surprisingly, it is estimated that more than half of the cigarettes in New York have been purchased from the black market. See Ali Watkins and Matt Apuzzo, "White House Envisions a Revamped A.T.F., Minus Two Letters," *New York Times*, January 20, 2018, p. A17.

79 Watkins and Apuzzo, January 20, 2018, p. A17.

80 Ibid.

81 Cited in Watkins, February 23, 2018.

82 Watkins, 2018.

83 St. John Barned-Smith, "Network Is New Weapon vs. Gun Crimes," *Houston Chronicle*, June 25, 2017, pp. A1, A8.

84 Cited in John St. John Barned-Smith, "Mobile Lab to Speed Up Police Work," *Houston Chronicle*, April 20, 2018, pp. A1, A8.

85 Dane Schiller, "Use of Rolling Robot to Take Out Sniper Breaks New Ground for Law Enforcement," *Houston Chronicle*. https://www.houstonchronicle.com/news/houston-texas/houston/article/RoboCop-used-to-kill-suspect-marks-a-first-for-8349013.php

86 "Arms Race," *The Economist*, September 2, 2017, pp. 24, 26.

87 James Faggone, "Swatted," *The New York Times Magazine*, November 29, 2015, pp. 33–37, 60; "Cops or Soldiers?" *The Economist*, March 22, 2014, pp. 27–28.

88 Ibid.

89 Jason Fagone, The Serial Swatter," *The New York Times Magazine*, November 24, 2015. https://www.nytimes.com/2015/11/29/magazine/the-serial-swatter.html

90 "Jailhouse Nation," *Economist*, June 20, 2015, p. 11; "The Right Choices," *The Economist*, June 20, 2015, pp. 23–26.

91 James Volpe, "Jail is No Place for People with Mental Illness," *Washington Post*, September 27, 2015, pp. A1, A13.

92 Elizabeth Hinton, *From the War on Poverty to the War on Crime: The Making of Mass Incarceration in America*, Cambridge, MA: Harvard University Press, 2016.

93 Ibid., pp. 1–26.

94 Ibid.

95 Elizabeth Hinton, *From the War on Poverty to the War on Crime: The Making of Mass Incarceration in America*, Cambridge: Harvard University Press, 2016. https://scholar.harvard.edu/elizabethhinton/war-poverty-war-crime

96 "Jailhouse Nation," June 20, 2015, pp. 23–26.

97 Josh Keller and Adam Pearce, "As Crime Falls, Small Counties Fill the Prisons," *New York Times*, September 2, 2016, pp. A1, 10.

98 Ibid.

99 Josh Keller and Adam Pearce, "A Small Indiana County Sends More People to Prison than San Francisco and Durham, North Carolina Combined. Why?," *New York Times*, September 2, 2016. https://www.nytimes.com/2016/09/02/upshot/new-geography-of-prisons.html

100 Ibid.

101 Ibid.

102 Timothy Williams, "Correctional Population Hit 13-Year Low in 2015," *New York Times*, December 30, 2016, p. A16.

103 "Feds Plan Record Early Releases of about 6,000 Drug Offenders," *Houston Chronicle*, October 7, 2015, p. A14.

104 Reid Wilson, "Texas for Cutting Crime Rates and Prison Costs," *Washington Post*, July 7, 2014.

105 Mark Binelli, "This Place Is Not Designed for Humanity," *New York Times Magazine*, March 29, 2015, p. 39.

106 Ibid.

107 Ibid., p. 40.

108 Rick Raemisch, "Putting an End to Long-Term Solitary," *New York Times*, October 13, 2017, p. A23.

109 Liam Stack, "Death Row Inmates Sue Over Solitary Confinement," *New York Times*, March 31, 2017, p. A18.

110 "Children in Adult Jails," *The Economist*, March 28, 2015, p. 36.

111 However, judges in Alabama have the authority to send those as young as fourteen to a criminal court.

112 "Parsing Sentence," *The Economist*, October 17, 2015, pp. 31, 34.

113 "Parsing Sentence," *The Economist*, October 15, 2015. https://www.economist.com/united-states/2015/10/15/parsing-sentence

114 See, for example, James Traub, "The Criminals of Tomorrow," *The New Yorker*, November 4, 1996; *Body Count*.

115 Dave Phillips, "Iowa Court Says Parole Must Apply for Juveniles," *New York Times*, May 28, 2016, p. 13.

116 "Parsing Sentence," October 17, 2015, pp. 31, 34.

117 "Parsing Sentence," *The Economist*, October 15, 2015. https://www.economist.com/united-states/2015/10/15/parsing-sentence

118 "Parsing Sentence," *The Economist*, October 15, 2015. https://www.economist.com/united-states/2015/10/15/parsing-sentence

119 Ibid.

120 Keri Blakinger, "Texas Female Prison Population Rises as Male Population Decreases," *Houston Chronicle*, January 12, 2018. https://www.chron.com/news/houston-texas/article/Report-Texas-female-prison-population-rises-male-12490462.php

121 Keri Blakinger, "Texas' Female Inmates on Rise," *Houston Chronicle*, January 12, 2018, pp. A3, A6.

122 Timothy Williams, "Inside a Private Prisons: Blood, Suicide and Poorly Paid Guards," *New York Times*, April 3, 2018. https://www.nytimes.com/2018/04/03/us/mississippi-private-prison-abuse.html

123 Charlie Savage, "U.S. to Start Phasing Out Use of Private Prisons to House Federal Inmates," *New York Times*, August 19, 2016, p. A11.

124 Timothy Williams, "Glimpse Inside Private Prisons is a Disturbing View," *Houston Chronicle*, April 4, 2018, p. A9.

125 John MacCormack, "Prison Bust Spreads Across Rural Texas," *Houston Chronicle*, August 23, 2015, p. B2.

Don Thompson, "Marijuana 'Grow Houses' Tied to Criminals in China," *Houston Chronicle*, April 5, 2018, p. B9.

126 John MacCormack, "Private Prison Boom Goes Bust," *San Antonio Express News*, August 23, 2015. https://www.expressnews.com/news/local/article/Private-prison-boom-goes-bust-6459964.php

127 McAfee, "McAfee Virtual Criminology Report, 2005," www.mcafee.com.

128 Kip Schlegel and Charles Cohen, "The Impact of Technology on Criminality," in *The New Technology of Crime, Law and Social Control*, ed. James M. Byrne and Donald J. Rebovich, Monsey, NY: Criminal Justice Press, 2007, p. 23.

129 "The Net Closes," *The Economist*, April 11, 2015, p. 59.

130 Thompson, April 5, 2018, p. B9.

131 Ibid.

132 Timothy Gilfoyle, 1992, p. 18.

133 Justin Jouvenal, "Crime Doesn't Pay at Least When You Rob Banks Nowadays," *Houston Chronicle*, October 17, 2016, p. B3.

134 Ibid.

135 Ibid.

136 St. John Barned-Smith, "Groups Fear Hate Crime in Texas Go Unreported," *Houston Chronicle*, November 14, 2017, p. A3.

137 "Anti-Semitic Incidents on Rise," *Houston Chronicle*, November 5, 2017, p. F8.

138 Mark Landler, "Trump Resurrects His Claim that Both Sides Share Blame in Charlottesville Violence," *New York Times*, February 22, 2018. https://www.nytimes.com/2017/09/14/us/politics/trump-charlottesville-tim-scott.html

139 "At Half Mast," *Economist*, June 27, 2015, p. 21.

140 Marc Santora and Michael Schwirtz, "An Epidemic of Carjacking Afflicts Newark," *New York Times*, December 29, 2013, pp. 1, 24.
141 Ibid.
142 "The Slow Death of the Death Penalty," April 26, 2014, pp. 27–29.
143 Ibid.
144 Kevin Johnson and Richard Wolf, "Is the Death Penalty Dying?," *USA Today*, September 14, 2015, pp. 1A, 6A.
145 Julie Bosman, "Nebraska Abolishes the Death Penalty," *Houston Chronicle*, May 28, 2017, p. A4.
146 Sean Murphy, "Oklahoma Officials Plan to Use Nitrogen Gas for Executions," *Houston Chronicle*, March 18, 2018, p. A10.
147 Dan Freedman, "Cocaine Losing Its Allure in US," *Houston Chronicle*, December 19, 2011, p. A1.
148 Lisa Girion, "Heroin Use, Addiction Surging in U.S.," *Houston Chronicle*, July 8, 2015, A14.
149 Sam Quinones, *Dreamland: The True Tales of America's Opioid Epidemic*, London: Bloomsbury, 2015.
150 "A Hydra-Headed Scourge," *The Economist*, September 9, 2015.
151 Josh Katz, "New Count of 2016 Drug Deaths Shows Accelerated Rate," *New York Times*, September 3, 2017, p. 14.
152 Christine Vestal, "App Maps Overdose Epidemic in Real Time," *Houston Chronicle*, November 19, 2017, p. A19.
153 Ibid.
154 Josh Katz and Abby Goodnough, "Opioid Deaths Rising Swiftly Among Blacks," *New York Times*, December 22, 2017, pp. A1, A15.
155 "Potent Opioids Force Police to Abandon Drug Field Tests," *Houston Chronicle*, February 25, 2018, p. A17.
156 Haeyoun Park and Josh Katz, "Murder Rates Rose in More Than a Quarter of the Nation's 100 Largest Cities," *New York Times*, 9/11, 2016, p. 14.
157 Haeyoun Park and Josh Katz, "Murder Rates Rose in a Quarter of the Nation's 100 Largest Cities," *New York Times*, September 9, 2016. https://www.nytimes.com/interactive/2016/09/08/us/us-murder-rates.html
158 Ibid.
159 Conor Friedersdorf, "American Carnage," *The Atlantic*, February 15, 2018. https://www.theatlantic.com/politics/archive/2018/02/trump-carnage/553424
160 "Counting Murders," *The Economist*, September 30, 2017, p. 28.
161 Richard A. Oppel Jr. and Jonah Engel Bromwich, "Baltimore, Its Murder Rate Sky High, Fires Police Commissioner," *New York Times*, January 20, 2018, pp. A1, 18.
162 Nicole Gelinas, "A Tale of Two Cities: New York and Chicago," June 12, 2016. https://www.manhattan-institute.org/html/tale-two-cities-new-york-vs-chicago-8976.html
163 Ford Fessenden and Haeyoun Park, "Chicago's Murder Problem," *New York Times*, May 27, 2016. https://www.nytimes.com/interactive/2016/05/18/us/chicago-murder-problem.html
164 Haeyoun Park and Ford Fesenden, "Chicago's Murder Problem," *New York Times*, May 28, 2016, p. A9.
165 Douglas S. Massey, Quoted in Ibid. See also Robert J. Sampson, *Great American City: Chicago and the Enduring Neighborhood Effect*, Chicago: University of Chicago Press, 2013 edition.
166 Aamer Madhani, "Chicago Persists in Its War on Street Violence," *USA Today*, May 31, 2017, p. 8A.
167 Peter Vronsky, *Serial Killers: The Method and Madness of Monsters*, New York: Berkley Books, 2004.
168 Chris Buckley, "Murderer of 11 Women in China Gets Death Penalty," *New York Times*, March 31, 2018, p. A7.

169 Julie Turkewitz, "After Virginia Mass Shooting: A Complex Grief for a Widow," *New York Times*, July 2, 2017, pp. 1, 4. These FBI figures to not include episodes of domestic violence or gang related killings.

170 "Why the Gun Lobby Is Winning," *The Economist*, April 4, 2015, p. 31.

171 Shreela V. Sharma, "Gun Violence Is Leaving Us Desensitized to Bloodshed," *Houston Chronicle*, October 13, 2017, p. A17.

172 Maggie Astor, "Horrifying and Tragic, But Not a Surprise," *New York Times*, November 11, 2017, p. A12.

173 Keri Blakinger, "Support for DP Lowest in Decades," *Houston Chronicle*, October 30, 2017, p. A5.

174 "A Deal You Can't Refuse," November 11, 2017.

175 Patrick Sharkey, *Uneasy Peace: The Great Crime Decline, the Renewal of City Life, and the Next War on Violence*. New York: W.W. Norton and Company, 2018.

176 Sam Quinones, "A New Kind of Jail for the Opiate Age," *New York Times*, June 16, 2017, pp. 1, 7.

177 These deaths include suicide by guns and drugs (illicit and legal).

178 "Three Reasons Why Americans Die Younger," *Houston Chronicle*, February 10, 2016, p. A8.

179 Also included in opioid deaths are those related to synthetic drugs such as fentanyl and tramadol. Both are rather difficult to control and result in accidental overdoses as they become more popular among illegal drug users.

180 "Not Great, Again," *The Economist*, January 6, 2018, p. 16.

Some concluding thoughts and observations

A number of themes have been repeated throughout the text. From the earliest days of the American Republic to the present, no era has been without some debate or concern about rising crime, the perils of immigration, xenophobia, or trying to solve perceived social problems with various ill-conceived prohibitions. But few issues drive the public discussion on crime and the criminal justice system in the second decade of the twenty-first century than the American love affair with the gun.

When no meaningful firearms legislation came after the 2012 Newtown Elementary School shooting that left twenty children and six teachers dead, gun control advocates chalked it up to the intransigence of politicians beholden to their supporters back home. Over the past 18 years, firearms have killed 26,000 American youths under the age of 18, making injuries with firearms the third leading cause of death for children ages 1–17. Even more disturbing is the fact that the United States accounts for 91 percent of all firearms deaths of children under the age of fifteen in the developed world.[1] According to the Center for Disease Control (CDC), teenagers bore the brunt of gun violence, particularly those between ages thirteen and seventeen, representing 85 percent of child firearms deaths.[2]

In 2017, foreign gun tourism was booming in the United States. In China, where guns are so harshly restricted that the mere possession of an air rifle or toy gun can land one in jail for years, there are still a large number of gun enthusiasts. It has been estimated that tens of thousands of wealthy Chinese gun aficionados travel to the U.S. each year to shoot to their hearts content at firing ranges. However, there was a time when China was awash in guns. Chinese weapons laws date back centuries, but after World War II, following a violent resistance campaign against the Japanese occupation, firearms were commonplace. Weapons were also widely available during the subsequent Chinese Civil War. But after the communist victory in 1949, tight controls were put into place, and in 1996, Chinese residents were formally prohibited from owning guns. In 2008, restrictions were tightened

DOI: 10.4324/9781315148342-16

to include replica weapons as well. What goes unsaid is the fear that widespread gun owner-ship might lead to rebellion or more violent crime. To foster support for its punitive laws, China often publicizes mass shootings[3] in the United States. There are no official figures for gun crime in America (nor in China). For the lucky few, there are Chinese gun ranges with weapons permanently fixed to benches.[4]

*****

Often unspoken when the topic of firearms is discussed is the large numbers of gun-assisted suicides. Between 2012 and 2016, 108,100 suicides were recorded and 63,000 shot by others. Never of one mind on guns, there are numerous variations in gun laws. Some states, such as Texas, have liberalized its gun laws, inaugurating concealed carry in the state's colleges. Other states have responded to gun violence by increasing the scrutiny given to gun purchases at gun shows and on the Internet. As of April 2018, six states (California, Washington, Oregon, Connecticut, Indiana, and Florida) had passed "extreme risk protection order laws." Under these statutes, police are permitted to petition court to remove guns temporarily from individuals thought to pose a risk to themselves or others. California, Washington, and Oregon allow family members to fill out a petition.[5]

As the finishing touches are being applied to this manuscript, the 2018 Florida Parkland High School deaths of fourteen teenagers and three teachers might have signaled a turning point in the debate over gun control, at least in American schools, although it is much too early to tell. But in the wake of the tragedy, student-led marches targeting gun violence in schools took place across the country. The polls that followed indicated that the majority of American gun owners and half of Republicans favored new laws to address gun violence after the Parkland killings. Almost 70 percent of Americans now favor stricter gun mea-sures, an increase from 61 percent in October 2016 and 55 percent in 2013.[6]

Another theme throughout the text is the fact that the American criminal justice sys-tem is always evolving. In a diverse nation with divergent views on everything from soda consumption to gun ownership, the criminal justice system has developed in response to changes in American society. Much of the blame, when there are hotly debated issues, is placed on the historically partisan Congress. However, recent events have cast a spotlight on the pragmatism of the criminal justice system and its ability to rights wrongs when there is *less* partisanship and *more* partnership between the political parties and the U.S. Congress that makes the rules.

In an era, where even facts come under fire, it is more and more imperative for Americans to become historically cognizant of the nation's past and its relationship with the present. This text was conceived as an attempt to illustrate these links through a comprehensive examination of the development of the American criminal justice system and the various crimes that helped make it. Although the means for committing crimes are quite different in the digital world, the goals and motivations of criminals and the criminal justice system remain firmly rooted in their historical antecedents.

I will end this section of the conclusion with a brief example of how a lack of grasp on past events can affect any understanding of the present. While being interviewed by Bob Schieffer on CBS's *Face the Nation* on April 27, 2014, the former presidential candidate Rick Santorum suggested there were few gun crimes in the Old West. He supported, what turns out be an ill-informed historical assertion this way, "You know everybody romanticizes the O.K. Corral and all the things that happened. But gun crimes were not very prevalent back then. Why? Because people carry guns."[7] The senator perhaps should be excused for his ahistorical comments, since like most other consumers of television, movies, and popular culture, he was innocent of the fact that many frontier communities, on the cusp of civilization, actually had strict gun laws that were usually enforced. The legendary cattletown of Dodge City, Kansas, for example, was swarming with young men, horse thieves, gunmen, and all varieties of desperadoes in the 1870s, that is, until the iconic lawmen Wyatt Earp and the brothers Jim and Bat Masterson were hired to establish the rule of law. They enforced laws that prohibited horses or other animals inside saloons and no guns allowed north of the "Dead Line," which essentially was "the railroad-tracks separation between the respectable section of the city. . . . and the anything goes section."[8]

One typical scenario went like this: Wyatt Earp spotted a man walking down the street north of the Dead Line, carrying a six-shooter. When he refused to give up the gun, Earp smashed him over his head with his pistol barrel, a strategy that became known as "buffaloing."[9] "In the history of western expansion," according to one chronicler, "there were very few face-to-face gunfights." Holsters were used mostly out on the trail, "a non-lawman wearing a gun belt was such a unique sight that he would cause comment" in towns.[10]

Much in the way Victorian-era police officers in America honored the so-called "Victorian compromise,"[11] which allowed vice in proto-zoned sections of various cities but outlawed it beyond its limits, the Dodge City peace officers preferred to keep guns out of the more respectable parts of the city, by establishing a "Dead Line." In some cases, even peace officers policed without firearms. Thomas "Bear River" Smith came to prominence in Abilene, Kansas, for his proclivity to eschew gunplay and making it a crime to carry firearms in the city limits.[12] Contrary to popular notions, the lawmen of the day would typically try and reason with a man rather than kill him, particularly if he was unarmed. Moreover, there was an unwritten understanding that, when they were forced to shoot, at least in Dodge City, they would try to wound rather than kill a man.[13]

All of this leads to Mr. Santorum's Gunfight at the OK Corral analogy. Further scrutiny of his claims sheds light on both the *actual* and imagined ubiquity of firearms on the streets of "Wild West" towns. First of all, officials in most cowtowns and mining communities "passed laws that prohibited carrying guns inside city limits."[14] On October 26, 1881, tensions had been building all day beginning when a group of "cowboys," violated the town ordinance that required "newcomers" to check their guns. By most accounts, the gunfight was actually sparked by efforts to enforce town Ordinance No. 9: "It is hereby declared unlawful to carry in the hand or upon the person or otherwise any deadly weapons within the limits of said city of Tombstone, without first obtaining a permit in writing." Carrying guns within city limits was generally prohibited in growing frontier towns. These prohibitions usually began against concealed carry before expanding to concealed carry.[15] So, contrary to the Hollywood West, gun homicides were rather rare, especially as towns making the transition from frontier to civilization recognized that towns that disarmed young men typically demonstrated lower levels of personal and mortal violence.

Rising nativism and hate crime

During the heyday of the 1960s, the black power advocate H. Rap Brown pronounced "violence is as American as cherry pie."[16] If he had thought long and hard on it, he might have added nativism to his proclamation. The theme of American nativism and xenophobia resonates throughout this text and American criminal justice history. The handwringing over its recent increase is only surprising to those unfamiliar with American history. A straight line can be drawn from the Protestant treatment of Irish-Catholic immigrants in the 1820s to recent policies geared toward preventing Muslim immigration from certain countries.

A pillar of President Donald J. Trump's campaign speeches was his contention that undocumented workers posed a threat to public safety and national security. However, there are several studies that actually indicate immigrants are less likely to commit crimes than native-born Americans. The data just doesn't support this widely held belief that the undocumented commit a disproportionate number of crimes. An analysis of census dates between 1980 and 2010 shows that among men between the ages of 18 and 49, immigrants "were one to one-fifth as likely to be incarcerated as those born in the United States."[17] Conversely, federal prisons incarcerate a higher share of noncitizens (22 percent). However, this is a very small fraction of the nation's inmates. By most accounts, noncitizen inmates represent an unusual population, since almost one-third of noncitizen federal inmates are behind bars for immigration offenses. Typically, these include attempting to reenter the country illegally after having been deported (not covered by state law).[18]

In January 2017, the president signed an executive order directing the Department of Homeland Security to publish a comprehensive weekly "list of criminal actions committed by aliens and any jurisdiction that ignored or otherwise failed to honor any detainers with respect to such aliens." Unfortunately the chief executive order "blurs the line between who is or wasn't a serious criminal." Undocumented immigrants had crime rates somewhat higher that those here legally, but much lower than citizens.

There has been a rise in hate and bias crimes in recent years. Targets have included Jews, Latinos, Arabs, trans-people, whites, and Muslims. Many observers correlate this trend with the toxic xenophobic rhetoric that accompanied the recent presidential election. Indeed, the antagonistic 2016 presidential election "gave oxygen to hate."[19]

According to an analysis of FBI crime data by the Center for the Study of Hate and Extremism at California State University, San Bernardino, there was a 26 percent increase in bias incidents during the last quarter of 2016, the "heart of the election season" compared to the same time the prior year. This trend continued into 2017. As the year moved to conclusion, the most recent partial data for the five most populated urban centers showed a 12 percent increase, with anti-Muslim incidents doubling since 2014. This could probably be chalked up to the fact that there had been more so-called "mega rallies" by white nationalists over the past two years than in the previous twenty.[20]

Several American historians were quick to point out that "the invocation of the president's name as a jaw-jutting declaration of exclusion, rather than inclusion, appears to be unprecedented."[21] Historian Jon Meacham, author of a Pulitzer Prize-winning biography of

Andrew Jackson,[22] declared that "If you are hunting for historical analogies, I think you're in virgin territory."[23]

Following the election, the Southern Poverty Law Center published a report entitled, "The Trump Effect: The Impact of the 2016 Election on Our Nation's Schools." Its findings were startling. The survey of 10,000 educators detailed an increase in incidents involving the use of swastika, Nazi salutes, and Confederate flags. Conversely, it has not been uncommon for anti-Trump supporters to attack supporters wearing Trump-touting "Make American Great Again" hats and shirts.[24]

*****

In November 2017, President Trump called the American criminal justice system a "laughing stock" and "a joke," after a truck mowed down cyclists in Manhattan. The president claimed that the criminal justice system was too weak to deter terrorism and too slow to mete out punishment. However, experts responded that the U.S. is actually "tougher on terrorism than most other nations."[25] It is worth noting that attackers in deadly terror plots are rarely captured alive. The attackers were killed in incidents believed inspired by Islamic extremists in 2002 at LA International Airport; 2015 in Chattanooga, Tennessee; and in San Bernardino. Suspects who have survived have actually been dealt with swiftly and severely in federal courts. After the 2013 Boston Marathon bombing, the surviving Tsarnaev brother was sentenced to death in 2015. Other plotters whose plots never reached fruition have been sentenced to life in prison. Between 9/11, 2001, and the year 2015, the Justice Department reported a total of 627 terrorism-related cases. In most cases, convictions were brought within two years after the indictments issued. One expert noted, "My impression is that the US has higher conviction rates and higher sentences for terrorism charges than the UK, Australia or Canada." Moreover, he stated, "I cannot think of another country, except perhaps China, that would have higher convictions and longer sentences in terrorism cases than the United States."[26]

*****

Criminal justice reform comes slowly, often after society pays great costs in terms of figuring out the correct balance between punishment and good intentions. Louisiana is a case in point, a state that has traditionally locked up its people at twice the American average. But this did little to make the state safer. The state remains one of the poorest in the nation and, what's more, has the highest murder rate in the U.S. By most accounts, the tremendous resources used to lock up the state's malefactors could be better spent on improving conditions. One of the more consistent patterns in American criminal justice history is the sectional variations in crime and punishment that began during the colonial era. For example, Louisiana is "more than twice as likely to imprison persons for nonviolent crimes as southern states with similar crime rates."[27] More recently, there has been a rare bipartisan attempt to relieve that state's prison overcrowding, which is mostly due to the state's comparatively long prison sentences. However, as the race for governor beckons in 2019, two Republican candidates pushed back almost immediately by cherry picking several boogeymen who committed crimes shortly after early release. The two candidates dubbed the bipartisan push, the "Louisiana Prisoner Release and Public Safety be Damned Act."[28]

*****

On October 1, 2017, the bump stock gun accessory entered the American consciousness after the worst mass shooting in American history. The devices briefly became a talking point in the national gun control debate. This device, as was widely reported, essentially turned a semiautomatic weapon into a fully automatic machine gun. In Maryland, several high profile gun measures were expected to be signed into law by its Republican governor. One required gun owners to surrender their weapons if judges found them to be an "extreme risk." The other banned the bump stock in the state. One Maryland gun safety advocate suggested that, if both bills pass, this would be the most "progress on gun violence bills since 2013."[29] As worded, the bump stock ban meant a "near-total prohibition on owning, manufacturing, selling or purchasing" the device, otherwise known as the "rapid fire trigger activator," making the Maryland law the strongest of this nature in the entire country.[30]

In April 2018, Slide Fire Solutions, based in a small Texas burgh and the leading maker of bump stocks, announced it was no longer taking orders after May 20 and would shut down its website soon after.[31]

*****

Each generation has had an increased lifespan over the previous one, with decreased life expectancy mostly tied to Third World countries. However, recent data from the Centers for Disease Control and Prevention (CDC) "should rock us out of our complacency."[32] Average life expectancy in the U.S. declined in 2016 for the second consecutive year. This hasn't happened in more than a century. Especially troubling was the fact that, at the same time, life expectancy was going up in other developed countries. Deaths caused by "unintentional injuries" were a key factor. Drug overdoses, especially from opioids, increased by 21 percent between 2015 and 2016.

By the end of 2017, crime had dropped in the country's thirty largest cities. As one observer noted, several decades of safer urban centers "has cleared the way for major changes in the nation's criminal justice system," exemplified by a decrease in incarceration, shorter prison sentences, and more pardons.[33] The criminal justice system is changing more quickly than ever before and should be considered a work in progress as the new information era adds new crimes and threats to the criminal justice system. What was once a slow evolution based on experimentation and innovation has turned into a dynamic and proactive attempt to contain and suppress criminal behavior that was almost unthinkable in years past. No one can forecast what the next chapter in this saga will hold.

Notes

1 Christopher Ingraham, "Since 1999, Firearms Have Killed 26,000 U.S. Teens, Kids," *Houston Chronicle*, March 18, 2018, p. A29.

2 Ibid.

3 I teach at a police college for several weeks each year. My university has an exchange program that allows English-speaking Chinese students to come to America and study for a year. When I ask the class of more than fifty students how many will come to the U.S. the following year (they can also choose South Korea), it seems the numbers dwindle each year. In an informal survey with

students, the overwhelming response for choosing South Korea instead was that they were afraid of being shot in America.

4 Hannah Gardner, "'Gun Tourism' Booms in the United States," *USA Today*, April 10, 2017, pp. 1–2A.

5 "What Works," *The Economist*, March 24, 2018, pp. 26–27.

6 Emily People and Emily Swanson, "Support Is Soaring for Tougher Laws on Guns, Poll Shows," *Houston Chronicle*, March 25, 2018, p. A29.

7 Glenn Kessler, "Santorum's Misguided View of Gun Control in Wild West," *Washington Post*, May 4, 2014, p. A7.

8 Tom Clavin, *Dodge City: Wyatt Earp, Bat Masterson, and the Wickedest Town in the American West*, New York: St. Martin's Press, 2017, pp. 134–135.

9 Ibid., p. 245.

10 Jeff Guinn, *The Last Gunfight: The Real Story of the Shootout at the O.K. Corral: And How It Changed the American West*, New York: Simon and Schuster, 2011, p. 18.

11 Lawrence M. Friedman, *Crime and Punishment in American History*, New York: Basic Books, 1993, p. 127.

12 Joseph G. Rosa, *The Gunfighter: Man or Myth?*, Norman, OK: University of Oklahoma Press, 1969.

13 Clavin, 2017, pp. 134–135.

14 Guinn, 2011, p. 19.

15 Adam Winkler, *Gunfight: The Battle Over the Right to Bear Arms in America*, New York: W.W. Norton and Company, 2013.

16 Steve Chapman, "Political Violence is 'As American as Cherry Pie'," *Chicago Tribune*, June 16, 2017. http://www.chicagotribune.com/news/opinion/chapman/ct-political-violence-america-history-perspec-chapman-20170616-column.html

17 Richard Perez-Pena, "Migrants Less Likely to Commit Crimes," *New York Times*, January 17, 2017, p. A14.

18 Ibid.

19 Dan Barry and John Eligon, "Trump, Trump, Trump!' How a President's Name Became a Racial Jeer," *New York Times*, December 16, 2017. https://www.nytimes.com/2017/12/16/us/trump-racial-jeers.html

20 Dan Barry and John Eligon, "A Rallying Cry or Racial Taunt Invoking the President: 'Trump!'," *New York Times*, December 17, 2017, pp. 1, 14.

21 Ibid.

22 Jon Meacham, *American Lion: Andrew Jackson in the White House*, New York: Random House.

23 Cited in Dan Barry and John Eligon, "Trump, Trump, Trump!' How a President's Name Became a Racial Jeer," *New York Times*, December16, 2017. https://www.nytimes.com/2017/12/16/us/trump-racial-jeers.html

24 Barry and Eligon, December 17, 2017, pp. 1, 14.

25 Linda Qiu, "Trump Calls Trial Process 'a joke,' Despite Hundreds of Convictions," *New York Times*, November 2, 2017. https://www.nytimes.com/2017/11/02/us/politics/fact-check-trump-terror-convictions.html

26 Linda Qiu, "Is Terrorism Trial Process 'A Joke'? Experts Say No," *New York Times*, November 3, 2016, p. A27.

27 "In Louisiana Criminal-Justice Reform is badly Needed," *The Economist*, April 15, 2018. https://www.economist.com/united-states/2018/04/05/in-louisiana-criminal-justice-reform-is-badly-needed

28 "Don't Throw Away the Key," *The Economist*, April 7, 2018, p. 24.

29 Michael Dresser, "Bump Stocks Banned Under Maryland Bill," *Houston Chronicle*, April 5, 2018.

30 Ibid.

31 Michael Balsamo, "Largest Maker of Bump Stocks Closing Up," *Houston Chronicle*, April 19, 2018. It should be noted here that this was reversal of a 2010 decision by the ATF to permit

the sale of bump stocks, declaring that they "did not amount to machine guns and could not be regulated unless Congress amended existing firearms laws or passed a new one."

32 "Editorial: Decline in Life Expectancy Should Shock Politicians Into Action," *Houston Chronicle*, December 27, 2017. https://www.houstonchronicle.com/opinion/editorials/article/Editorial-Declining-life-expectancy-should-shock-12456295.php

33 Jose Del Real, "The US Has Fewer Crime: Does That Mean It Needs Fewer Police?," January 7, 2018.

GLOSSARY

Abjuration   Process by which a fugitive takes exile from a country.

Abolitionists   Zealous opponents of slavery prior to emancipation.

Abu Ghraib   This prisoner abuse scandal involved Iraqi detainees held at the Abu Ghraib Prison near Baghdad between October and December 2003.

Adultery   Refers to sexual relations between a married person and someone other than his or her lawful spouse.

Alcatraz Prison   Prison of last resort; considered the original supermax prison until its closure in 1963.

Alien and Sedition Acts   Early international scandal in 1797–1798 that led to legislation that led to debate on constitutional freedoms.

American Indian Movement (AIM)   Radical Native American organization founded in 1968 by Dennis Banks and Clyde Bellecourt.

National Prison Congress   In 1870, 130 delegates from around the world convened in Cincinnati to discuss principles of prison reform. The National Prison Congress provided the nucleus for what would become the American Correctional Association.

Anarchists   Individuals who sought to promote violence or revolt against established law, rule, or custom.

Angles   A West German people who migrated to Britain in the fifth century.

Antebellum period   Years of sectional tension leading up to the Civil War (1861–1865).

Anti-Drug Abuse Act of 1986   America's first mandatory-minimum sentence for drug offenders was passed in the wake of the cocaine overdose of college basketball star Len Bias that same year.

Anti-terrorism and Effective Death Penalty   This 1996 bill, which includes provisions for the death penalty and for designating private groups as terrorist organizations, is regarded as the country's "first counterterrorism legislation."

Apalachin Conference   When authorities stumbled on a meeting of organized crime figures in upstate New York in 1957, federal law enforcement was forced to concede its existence and make it a high priority in the war on crime.

Approvers   Criminal informants in the Middle Ages.

Army disease   Refers to morphine addiction that often plagued ex-soldiers when they returned home after the Civil War.

Ashurst-Summers Act   In 1935, this legislation strengthened prohibitions on prison industries first implemented under the Hawes-Cooper Act in 1929.

Assize of Arms   In 1181, freemen in England were encouraged to own arms and armor according to their station and means.

Assize of Clarendon   Established trial by grand jury in 1166.

Assize of Northhampton   Divided England into six circuits traveled periodically by the king's judges. These judges superseded local courts.

Attica Prison   The bloodiest prison riot in American history took place at this New York State prison in 1971.

Auburn prison system   New York prison system that relied on the silent system and allowed convicts to work in a congregate setting at day but at night were kept in solitary cells.

Bailiff   Created by the Statute of Winchester, initially responsible for tracking strangers in medieval towns after dark.

Barathron   A prominent place of execution in ancient Athens.

Barons Highest level of Norman lords.

Baze v. Rees   Between 2007 and 2009 the legitimacy of lethal injection as a humane form of capital punishment was at the center of several court appeals that brought a seven-month de facto nationwide moratorium on the process. On April 16, 2008, in a 7–2 ruling, the Supreme Court in *Baze v. Reese* upheld the use of lethal injection for capital punishment giving the go-ahead for the forty executions that had been put on hold until this issue was decided.

Benefit of clergy   Members of the clergy were given an exemption from secular punishments during the Middle Ages.

Bertillon system   In the 1890s, this complicated identification system of measurements was created in France to identify recidivist offenders. It was eventually replaced by fingerprint identification.

Bestiality   Sexual relations between a person and an animal.

Bier rite   A Germanic ordeal in which the suspect was ordered to touch an alleged victim of a homicide. If the corpse bled or frothed at the mouth, the suspect was pronounced guilty.

Bigamy   The crime of marrying while one has a husband or wife living and where no valid divorce has been affected.

Big House prisons   In the 1920s, huge capacity prisons were constructed that led to social divisions among inmates at such prisons as San Quentin, California, and Stateville, Illinois.

Black codes   Southern states instituted laws to replace the old slave codes following the Civil War.

Black Death   One of the worst pandemics in world history.

Black Hand gangs   Gangs of Sicilian extortionists who preyed on fellow immigrants.

Black site prisons   Rendition has received its harshest criticism for its affiliation with black sites (secret detention centers), operated by the CIA outside U.S. territory and jurisdiction, where many allegations of abuse and mistaken identities and abductions of "alleged unlawful enemy combatants" have taken place.

Blasphemy   Irreverent behavior toward anything held sacred, such as cursing or reviling God.

Bobbies   In respect to Sir Robert Peel, refers to policemen on the London Metropolitan Police.

***Body of Liberties* (1641)**   Early Massachusetts colony law code inspired by Mosaic Law.

Bounty jumping   An early organized crime racket. During the Civil War, individuals would collect bounties from individuals seeking to escape the draft. Once the bounty was collected, the individual would desert and repeat this sequence elsewhere.

Bow Street Runners   A specially formed group of constables created by Henry Fielding who were expected to run to the aid of crime victims and pursue criminals.

Bradwell v. Illinois   This 1873 Supreme Court decision temporarily ruled that the equal protection clause of the Fourteenth Amendment protected only men.

Brady Handgun Violence Prevention Act   The 1993 Brady Bill was approved by Congress in 1991 but not approved by President Bush until the waiting period for purchases was decreased from seven to five days.

Branch Davidians   Cult led by David Koresh in Waco, Texas. The deaths of more than eighty members during a federal raid led to congressional hearings in 1995.

Bridewells   Houses of corrections; forerunner of modern prison.

Brinks robbery   This 1950 heist was the biggest robbery in American history up to that time.

Broken-windows model   According to this theory, neighborhood disorder, such as broken-windows, send out crime-promoting signals. If police target these environments and gain the cooperation of citizens, they can more effectively fight crime.

Bulla   Charm worn by Roman boys to ward off evil spirits.

Canon law   Church law, with the pope as the supreme legislator; originally superseded the law of England.

Carroll Doctrine   In 1925, the Supreme Court ruled in *Carroll et al. v. United States* that police can conduct a search of moving vehicles without a warrant.

Celtic   An ancient people now represented by the people of Ireland, Wales, Scotland, and Britain.

Cherry Hill Prison   Better known as Pennsylvania's Eastern State Penitentiary.

Child Savers   Politically active women at the turn of the twentieth century who tried to protect children from lives of crime.

Christopher Commission   In 1991, following the beating of motorist Rodney King by police officers, this Los Angeles commission was convened to investigate the LAPD. Its report called for reform and ultimately led Police Chief Daryl Gates to resign.

COINTELPRO   A clandestine FBI program established along the lines of a "department of misinformation" to create a climate of confusion among left-wing organizations in the 1960s. The Black Panther Party was a special target.

Coldbath riots   In 1833, the London Metropolitan Police gained the support of the public by suppressing a riot with few serious injuries.

College cops   As police chief of Berkeley, California, August Vollmer insisted that his officers attend college in the early 1900s.

Community policing   Beginning in the 1980s, this philosophy demonstrated a transition to a more proactive approach in policing.

Comprehensive Crime Control Act   Rising crime concerns of the 1980s led Congress to pass this act in 1984, creating the U.S. Sentencing Commission and signaling a transition from a rehabilitative model to a punitive one in sentencing.

Compstat   Shorthand for "computer statistics," it was used as part of a strategy of the NYPD in the 1990s and credited with contributing to the city's historic crime drop.

Compurgation   Method of determining guilt or innocence under the Anglo-Saxons.

Comstock Law   Passed by Congress in 1873, it prohibited the transmission of obscene materials through the mail.

Coneymen   Early American counterfeiters.

Constable   Formerly the "head of the stables," this position became identifiable with peacekeeping after the Norman Conquest.

Constantinople   Formerly Byzantium and now Istanbul, Turkey; Emperor Constantine established this city as the new capital of the eastern Roman Empire following its decline in the West.

Convict hulks   Often called "floating hells" or "hell holds," the British used these broken-down warships anchored in rivers and bays as floating prisons.

Convict leasing   The convict leasing system was used as an alternative to imprisonment after the Civil War. During the 1870s and 1880s, the leasing of convicts under contract to private contractors dominated southern penology.

Cop or copper   Pejorative term for police officer. There is no consensus as to the origin of either word.

COPS program   Community Oriented Policing Services program.

Coroner   Position originated in England in 1194 to investigate suspicious deaths.

Corpus Juris Civilis   Continental legal system that developed out of Roman law.

Court of Areopagus   Established by Greek lawgiver Draco for trying murder cases and other serious offenses.

Credit Mobilier scandal (1872)   One of the greatest congressional scandals of the nineteenth century.

Criminology   The study of crime and criminals.

Curfew   Traditionally used by the upper class to limit movements of the lower classes. Normans ruled that fires had to be out by eight o'clock to keep subversive Anglo-Saxons from congregating.

Dale's Laws   Martial law code in colonial Virginia.

Danelaw   Region of England controlled by the Danes stretching from the Thames River to Liverpool.

Daubert guidelines   According to these rules established in 1993, new questions would have to be answered before fingerprints were entered into evidence.

"DC Snipers"   Domestic terrorism struck urban America in 2002 when traveling snipers Lee Boyd Malvo and John Allen Muhammed, known as the DC Snipers, shot sixteen individuals, killing ten in a shooting spree that lasted from September to October, paralyzing holiday shoppers in the Washington, DC, corridor.

Decemvirs   Group of ten men who wrote Roman law at its earliest stages.

Declaration of Principles   Their adoption at the 1870 National Prison Congress represented a great stride toward progressive prison reform.

De jure   Officially sanctioned.

Demon rum   Early temperance groups targeted the popularity of rum as the main cause of social disorder in the Jacksonian era.

Department of Homeland Security (DHS)   Just one month after the 9/11 attacks, President George W. Bush signed Executive Order 13688, creating the Office of Homeland Security and Homeland Security Council. The creation of the new cabinet position – the Department of Homeland Security – was supposed to reorganize the American security community. More than half of the agencies under the DHS have police powers.

Desmoterion   Ancient Athenian prison, or "place of chains."

District attorney   This county attorney or prosecutor was an important colonial modification of the English criminal justice system.

Domesday Book   A comprehensive survey or census of the English land tenure system.

Dooms   Earliest written Anglo-Saxon laws.

Draconian   In homage to the ancient Greek legislator Draco; synonymous with "harsh."

Drug Enforcement Administration   Created in 1973 to enforce federal drug statutes and investigate major drug traffickers.

Dyer Act   In 1919, the National Motor Vehicle Act, or Dyer Act, made the transportation of stolen automobiles across state lines a federal crime.

Eastern State Penitentiary   When it was completed in 1829, it was the largest public building in America and a showplace for prison reform.

Ecclesiastical courts   Church courts presided over by the clergy.

Eddings v. Oklahoma **1982**   Court decision ruling that courts must take into account the age of juvenile offenders during capital sentencing.

Eighteenth Amendment   Congress approved the Volstead Act in 1919, and it was ratified in 1920, making it illegal to manufacture, import, distribute, or sell alcoholic beverages in the United States.

Eighth Amendment   Prohibits cruel and unusual punishments.

Elmira Reformatory   Originally set up in New York State in 1876 for youths aged sixteen to thirty serving their first prison terms. Emphasis was on trade training and academic education.

Enlightenment   A philosophical movement of the seventeenth and eighteenth centuries characterized by a belief in the power of human reason. This movement had great impact on the development of criminal justice, particularly in the birth of the penitentiary.

Enron scandal   Once the country's seventh largest corporation, by the end of 2001, the former energy trading giant Enron had filed for Chapter 11 bankruptcy protection. This was the largest bankruptcy in American history up to that time.

Ergastulum   Ancient Roman prison cells.

Espionage Act of 1917   Criminalized certain unpopular political views.

Eugenics   Pseudoscience that attempted to "improve" human genetic stock through such controversial methods as forced sterilization.

Ex parte Milligan   Supreme Court ruled in 1866 that only the legislative branch had the power to suspend the writ of habeas corpus.

Faith-based initiatives   The concept dates back to the eighteenth-century prison reform efforts of Pennsylvania Quakers. Shortly after taking office in 2001, President Bush created a special White House Office of Faith-Based and Community Initiatives leading to a number of crime prevention efforts linking various religious communities with the goal of preventing and reducing crime.

Federal Bureau of Narcotics   Established in 1930.

Federal Bureau of Prisons   Created in 1929.

Federal Crimes Act of 1790   Federal crime act that defined seventeen crimes and prescribed death by hanging for six crimes.

Felony   Since the Norman Conquest in 1066, this has referred to serious crimes.

Female Prison and Reformatory Institution for Girls and Women   In 1874, Indianapolis, Indiana, opened the first separate prison devoted solely to women.

Feudalism   Class system of mutual obligation brought to England by Normans.

Fifth Amendment   Guarantees that no person shall be compelled to testify against himself or herself and ensures due process in capital cases.

Fingerprinting   The adoption of fingerprinting in the late 1890s gave crime investigators the first reliable proof of an individual's presence at a crime scene.

First Amendment   Affirmed rights of freedom of religion, freedom of speech, freedom of the press, and the right to assemble peacefully and to petition the government for a redress of grievances.

Five Points   New York City district where five streets intersected; known as a breeding ground for crime in the early nineteenth century.

Flagrante delicto   While the crime or act is being committed.

Flood and frisk   Refers to saturating hot zones of crime with plainclothes police and detectives followed by uniformed police, looking for legal excuses to stop and question suspicious individuals.

Fornication   Voluntary sexual relations between two unmarried persons or two persons not married to each other.

Fourteenth Amendment   Gave blacks citizenship and equal protection under the law in 1868.

Fourth Amendment   Prohibits arbitrary search and seizure.

Fourth Lateran Council   In 1215, this meeting of church officials diminished the importance of trial by ordeal.

***Frame of Government* (1682)**   William Penn's "Great Law," the first criminal code of Pennsylvania.

Freedom Summer   In the late 1960s, civil rights activists went to the South to register black voters.

Fugitive Slave Act of 1850   By prohibiting alleged runaway slaves from testifying in court, this escalated sectional tensions leading to Civil War.

Furman v. Georgia   In 1972, the Supreme Court voted that the death penalty constituted cruel and unusual punishment.

Gaol fever   A form of typhus often prevalent among early prisoners, particularly on convict hulks.

Gates v. Illinois   In 1983 the Supreme Court ruled that police could obtain a search warrant on the basis of an anonymous tip.

Geneva Conventions   In the aftermath of 9/11 and the USA PATRIOT Act, the United States came under fire for violating the Geneva Conventions. The Third and Fourth Geneva Conventions were written and ratified following the civilian carnage that accompanied World War II. Their stated purpose was to codify international norms and offers special protections to captured soldiers and civilians living under military occupation.

Gideon v. Wainwright   In 1963, the Supreme Court ruled that all felony defendants were entitled to legal representation.

G-men   Government men; used as moniker for FBI agents beginning in the 1930s.

Golden Rule policy   Advocated dealing more informally with juvenile offenders through diversion programs to avoid stigmatization.

Great Depression   Economic crisis that began with 1929 stock market crash and continued through the 1930s.

Gregg v. Georgia   This case upheld the death penalty, leading to a return of capital punishment in 1976.

Habeas Corpus Amendment of 1679   Prohibited the secret confinement of prisoners and required that an individual accused of a crime be present in court at time of trial.

Hamdi v. Rumsfeld The U.S. Supreme Court ruled in June 2004 that the president did not have the power to order individuals considered enemy combatants locked up for an indefinite period. In *Hamdi v. Rumsfeld*, the Court "reaffirmed the principle of habeas corpus." What this meant was that non-U.S. citizens detained at Guantanamo Bay could now contest their captivity in U.S. courts (but did not apply to foreign detainees held elsewhere). Furthermore, anyone in U.S. custody, whether they were citizens or foreigners, has the right to challenge the basis for their incarceration.

Harrison Narcotic Act In 1914, the federal government passed its first antidrug legislation by requiring a doctor's prescription for the sale of controlled dangerous substances.

Hawalas Since it does not leave a paper trail, this informal money transfer system that originated in the Middle Ages in the Middle East is particularly popular for criminal and terrorist groups that need to transmit illegal funds today.

Hawes-Cooper Act In 1929, Congress allowed states to ban the sale of goods made in another state's prison within its borders.

Hemlock This poison was sometimes used as a form of execution in ancient Greece.

Heresy Opinion or doctrine at variation with accepted church doctrine; once considered the worst religious crime.

House Un-American Activities Committee (HUAC) Created in the 1930s, its activities were most prominent in the 1940s and 1950s during Senator Joseph McCarthy's "American Inquisition" of American Communist Party members.

Hue and cry A call for help in apprehending an offender in the Anglo-Saxon era.

Hundreds Shires were divided into these territorial subdivisions.

Indentured servant A person who came to America and was placed under contract to work for another person for a specific period of time (usually seven years).

Indeterminate sentencing Sentencing reform in which convicts could earn marks for good behavior leading to earlier release from prison; precursor to parole.

Infanticide The act of killing an infant.

Innocence Project Created in 1992 to help exonerate the wrongly accused with the help of modern forensic technology.

Inns of Court London guilds for lawyers learning the common law.

In re Gault In 1967, the Supreme Court extended the *Gideon* ruling to juvenile delinquency proceedings.

Inquisition Special tribunals or official investigations, often political or religious in nature, established in the thirteenth century; originally engaged in combating and punishing heresy.

Institutes Law textbook published under the reign of Justinian in 533 making the Twelve Tables obsolete.

International Association of Chiefs of Police (IACP) National police association that since the 1890s; has been influential in one form or another in implementing various police reforms.

International Association of Policewomen (IAP) Established in 1915 in an effort to include more women in policing.

Jacksonian America This era coincided with the so-called Age of the Common Man and the presidency of Andrew Jackson, which lasted from 1828 to 1836. Many historians suggest that it was also the period when Americans first perceived crime as a threat to the security of the Republic, extending the era from 1820 to 1850.

Jim Crow   A practice or policy of segregating African Americans in public places, employment, and so on.

Judiciary Act of 1789   Created the federal courts system, including the Supreme Court, and the positions of U.S. marshal and attorney general.

Justice of the peace   Beginning in 1361, this unpaid peacekeeping position became the cornerstone of British law and order.

Jutes   Germanic tribe that invaded Britain in the fifth century.

Kansas City Massacre   After four law enforcement officers were killed in an ambush in 1933, anticrime legislation enlarged the crime fighting powers and jurisdiction of the FBI.

Kansas City Preventive Patrol Experiment   Reported in 1974 that police patrols, whether absent or present, had no significant impact on crime.

Katz v. United States   In 1967, the Supreme Court limited the use of electronic eavesdropping because of concerns about invasion of privacy.

Ker-Frisbie Doctrine   The doctrine enabling modern rendition, based on two U.S. Supreme Court decisions in 1886 and 1952.

Kerner Report   This 1969 report was the first federally funded examination of race relations in the United States.

Kinship groups   A form of extended family.

Knapp Commission   Independent citizens' commission established to investigate New York City police corruption in the early 1970s.

Know-Nothing Party   Nativist and anti-Catholic political party in the 1850s.

Ku Klux Klan   White supremacist group created by ex-Confederate soldiers in Tennessee in 1866.

Law Enforcement Assistance Administration (LEAA)   Created in 1968 by Congress as its centerpiece in a "national war on crime."

Law of the goring ox   Early Mosaic law pertaining to the law of liability.

Lawes Divine, Morall, and Martiall   Also known as "Dale's Laws," a harsh law code used to keep order in the Virginia Colony. It instituted capital punishment for a wide range of offenses.

Leatherheads   Slang for 1820s New York City night watchmen who wore leather helmets.

Leavenworth Prison   America's first federal prison; opened its doors in Kansas in 1897.

Lethal injection   The latest trend in sanitizing executions.

Levellers   Outspoken reformers who argued for a simplification of the legal system, a bill of rights, and prohibition of debt imprisonment.

Lexow Committee   This 1894 investigation revealed widespread corruption on the New York City Police Department.

Lindbergh Law   The kidnapping and murder of aviator Charles Lindbergh's son led Congress to pass legislation in 1932 that elevated kidnapping to a capital offense and earlier FBI involvement in cases where the victim was taken across state lines.

Liveried lackeys   Early police officers opposed wearing uniforms because it would make them resemble uniformed servants.

Lynchings   This term evolved from its colonial era meaning as punishment not sanctioned by law, but not necessarily fatal, to the unlawful execution of persons of color in the 1890s.

Magna Carta   The Great Charter of 1215 had a great impact of on subsequent developments in constitutional law and political freedom.

Mandatory sentencing   Fixed sentences that take sentencing discretion out of the hands of judges.

Manor   Landholdings of Norman barons.

Manslaughter   In early sixteenth century, murder without premeditation became distinct from murder with malice aforethought.

Mapp v. Ohio   The Supreme Court ruled in 1961 that evidence secured by the police through unreasonable searches must be excluded from trial.

Marijuana Tax Act   In 1937, the recreational use of marijuana was made illegal.

Mark system   A method of earning early release from prison; considered a precursor to parole.

Mayflower Compact   Drawn up by the Pilgrims, this document is considered the first charter of laws ever framed by English common people.

McCleskey v. Kemp   The Supreme Court case that tested the constitutionality of the death penalty. In its decision, the Court ruled that an inmate's treatment did not violate the Eighth Amendment.

Medical marijuana   The expansion of medical marijuana has become one of the more contentious debates over the last decade. It has been the subject of the long-simmering controversy over the legality of state laws permitting medical marijuana use, although it is still classified under the 1970 Federal Controlled Substances Act as a drug in the highest category for potential abuse. Despite numerous studies testifying to its therapeutic qualities by patients and doctors, federal prosecutors refused to budge from their prohibition approach until the end of the Bush administration in 2008.

Medieval   Refers to the Middle Ages; originated in sixteenth century as a way to designate the era between early Christianity and the Protestant Reformation as well as the period between classical antiquity and the Renaissance.

Megan's Law   In 1994, New Jersey passed this law after young Megan Kanka was raped and murdered by a neighbor. Area residents had no idea that the perpetrator who lived among them had two prior convictions for sex offenses. Under the new law, on release from prison, sex offenders were required to register with the police.

MIBURN   In 1964, the FBI launched "Mississippi Burning," or MIBURN, following the abduction and murder of three civil rights workers in Mississippi.

Military tribunals   In November 2001, President George W. Bush issued an executive order authorizing the creation of military tribunals to try noncitizens on charges of terrorism. In these trials, a panel of military judges has the latitude to decide guilt or innocence without a unanimous vote and can even impose the death penalty. Once defendants are sentenced, they have little recourse, being barred from appealing to a higher court. A verdict of a military tribunal can be overturned only by the president or the secretary of defense.

Militia groups   Militant anti-government groups that sprouted up in America's heartland in the 1980s and 1990s.

Miranda v. Arizona   The 1966 Supreme Court decision that ruled that defendants must be made aware of their right to counsel and that anything they say can be used against them in a trial.

Molly Maguires   Predominantly Irish-Catholic secret organization that waged a campaign of terror against mine owners in northeastern Pennsylvania in the 1860s and 1870s.

Monotheistic religion   Belief in only one God.

Mount Pleasant Female Prison   In 1835, New York established this institution run exclusively by female prison matrons for women.

Muckrakers   Investigative journalists who chronicled the social abuses of the Progressive era.

Murdrum   Murder fine introduced by Normans; the word "murder" might have been derived from this term.

Mutual Welfare League   Prison reform experiment initiated at Sing Sing Prison by Thomas Mott Osborne in 1914.

Nativism   The policy of protecting the interests of the native-born inhabitants against those of immigrants.

Neck verse   During the Middle Ages, if one could successfully read Psalm 51, a defendant could be saved from hanging. This test became more obsolete when reading became more widespread.

Newgate Prison   Opened in New York in 1797, it was the first prison modeled on the Pennsylvania model.

New penology   In the 1920s and 1930s, many northern states implemented concepts of diagnosis and classification and added specialized personnel in psychology to the prison environment.

New York City draft riot   This 1863 anti-draft riot is regarded as one the worst urban riots in American history.

Night watch   Prior to the advent of modern policing, amateur night watchmen patrolled the streets in a peacekeeping capacity.

9/11 attacks   On 9/11, 2001, a concerted attack on America by nineteen Arab airplane hijackers on four planes left almost 3,000 dead. It was the second-bloodiest day in American history (next to the Civil War battle of Antietam in 1862). In the aftermath of the attacks, the criminal justice system faced reorganization and challenges unparalleled in its 200-plus-year history.

Normans   Inhabitants of northern France who were descended from the Northmen, better known as Vikings.

Nullification Controversy   In 1833, South Carolina's John Calhoun proclaimed the right of his state to nullify any federal legislation that it disapproved of.

***On Crimes and Punishments* (1764)**   Beccaria's celebrated indictment of the eighteenth-century criminal justice system.

Ordeals   A primitive method of determining guilt or innocence by subjecting the accused to fire, water, or other serious dangers; the result was regarded as a divine judgment.

Outlawry   Beginning in the 800s, individuals could be placed outside the protection of the law if they refused to attend court or tried to evade justice.

***Oyer and Terminer*, Court of**   Specialized courts in colonial America convened to handle serious complaints involving slaves.

Parliament   Originally designated a meeting of shire knights to discuss new taxes. By 1295, its representative nature had been established.

Parricide   The killing of a parent by a child.

Patricians   Members of the Roman aristocracy.

Patronage system   The distribution of jobs and favors on a political basis.

Peine forte et dure   Pressing to death with an accumulation of weights.

Peelers   Nickname for Robert Peel's London Metropolitan police officers.

Penny presses   Cheap newspapers in the 1830s and 1840s considered precursor to today's tabloids, using sensational and lurid crime stories to sell newspapers.

Pentateuch   From the Greek meaning "five books," as in the first five books of the Bible, which contain the Ten Commandments.

Perjury   The willful utterance of a false statement under oath during a legal inquiry.

Peterloo Massacre   In 1819, British troops fired into a crowd while trying to end civil unrest, killing eleven and wounding hundreds.

Petty treason   The killing of a master by a servant.

Pilgrims   Religious separatists that refused to conform to the Church of England and eventually arrived in America on the Mayflower in 1620.

Pinkertons   America's most prominent private detective/police organization in the nineteenth century.

Plan for Preventing Robberies within Twenty Miles of London   John Fielding's 1755 pamphlet detailing his strategy for suppressing highway robbery.

Plebeians   Refers to the common people of Rome.

Plessy v. Ferguson   In 1896, this Supreme Court decision essentially condoned racial segregation by approving the "separate but equal" doctrine, which held sway until 1954.

Ponzi scheme   Named after early twentieth-century fraudster Charles Ponzi, on the face of it, the scheme was rather simple, as twenty-first-century practitioners such as Bernard Madoff have found out. Ponzi would pay the high returns to early investors as new money came in from others. As long as the funds mounted, he could continue to pay interest on old accounts, whose owners could vouch for his sincerity. Ponzi never had to actually invest any of his own money, and he spent most of the money on his dandified lifestyle while paying off early investors.

Posse comitatus   Power of the county.

Praetorian Guard   Elite soldiers used for law enforcement by Augustus Caesar.

Precipitation   Ancient Athenian execution practice in which individuals were thrown from high cliffs to their deaths.

Prison privatization   To reduce some of the costs of essentially warehousing inmates in the 1980s, a number of prisons turned to the private sector, and by the mid-1990s, at least thirty states were contracting out prison labor to private companies.

Probation   Considered the oldest form of non-institutional corrections, its development in the United States is credited to the efforts of John Augustus in Boston in the 1840s.

Progressive era   Era characterized by reform, urbanization, industrialization, and immigration between 1890 and 1920.

Prohibition era   Inaugurated by the ratification of the Eighteenth Amendment, it lasted from 1920 to 1933.

Punitive   Concerned with inflicting punishment.

Pure Food and Drug Act   Imposed federal standards on the patent-medicine industry.

Puritans   A religious movement that sought to purify the Church of England.

Quakers   A radical religious sect that emerged in seventeenth-century England. They would play an important role in various criminal justice reform efforts in America beginning in colonial Pennsylvania.

Rampage killings The 1990s witnessed a dramatic rise in such killings, in which one or two individuals went on killing sprees that would not end until they ran out of bullets or were killed or taken prisoner.

Rattle watch Early Dutch peace officer in New Amsterdam.

Reconstruction era Refers to the years 1866–1877.

Red Hannah Delaware's whipping device.

Red Scare Following the Bolshevik Revolution in Russia and post-World War I labor unrest in 1919, the Justice Department embarked on a campaign to suppress radical views in America.

Reeve Anglo-Saxon official who was forerunner of the sheriff.

Reformatory movement An experiment in prison reform in the late 1860s that emphasized education, indeterminate sentencing, trade training, and parole.

Regulators America's first vigilante organization appeared in South Carolina in 1767.

Renaissance Era in European history between the fourteenth and the seventeenth centuries marking the transition from the medieval world to the modern one.

Rendition This controversial tactic entails apprehending suspects in any part of the world and then transporting them back to the United States where they will be forced to appear before state or federal court. (See also "black site prisons.")

Report on the Prisons and Reformatories of the United States and Canada This 1867 publication by Enoch Wines and Louis Dwight led the movement for the central control of state prisons.

Republic A state in which the supreme power rests in the body of citizens entitled to vote and is exercised by representatives who are chosen.

Restitution In 2004, almost one-fifth of all felons convicted in the United States were given an additional penalty of restitution. Nationwide unpaid court-ordered restitution was estimated in the billions of dollars. States are beginning to back up these judgments and even turning to outside collection agencies to supplement their own in-house efforts.

Restorative justice Although it is considered a recent trend, it has a timeworn legacy dating back perhaps as far as the ancient world, when the community played a pivotal role in the healing and retributive processes after a crime had been committed.

RICO statute The Racketeer Influenced and Corrupt Organizations (RICO) statute was created under the 1970 Omnibus Crime Control and Safe Streets Act. It is considered the most significant piece of legislation targeting organized crime.

Roaring Twenties The era of the 1920s.

Robber barons Nineteenth-century industrialists reputed to have become wealthy by exploiting natural resources, corrupting lawmakers, and other unethical actions.

Roper v. Simmons The Supreme Court ruled in 2005 that executing convicts for offenses committed before the age of eighteen was unconstitutional. The jurists cited such factors as immaturity, irresponsibility, and susceptibility to peer pressure and potential for turning lives around.

Roving wiretaps The USA PATRIOT Act permits the use of wiretaps that allowed the surveillance of individual telephone conversations on any telephone anywhere in America.

Ruby Ridge, Idaho Scene of an eighteen-month standoff between the Weaver family and federal peace officers in 1990–1991.

Sacrilege The violation of anything held sacred.

St. Valentine's Day Massacre   The biggest gangland murder of the Prohibition era.

Salem witchcraft trial   Notable 1692 trial in Salem, Massachusetts.

San Francisco Committee of Vigilance   Forced to contend with a growing crime problem and lack of professional policing in San Francisco during the gold rush years, citizens organized vigilance committees in the 1850s to maintain order.

Sanctuary   Fugitives could be protected in churches under certain circumstances in the Anglo-Saxon era.

Saxons   They migrated to England from what is now northern Germany after the Romans left in the fifth century.

Schout   Early Dutch peacekeeper in New Amsterdam.

Scold   A woman who is constantly scolding, usually in loud, abusive language.

Scorcher squads   Bicycle-mounted police initiated by New York City police commissioner Theodore Roosevelt in the 1890s.

Scotland Yard   Original headquarters of the London Metropolitan Police.

Scottsboro trials   Between 1931 and 1937, despite spurious charges, nine black youths fought for their lives in a series of Alabama court battles.

Second Amendment   Protects the right of states to form militias and is currently at the center of the debate on gun control.

Second Chance Act   In 2008 President Bush signed the Second Chance Act, designed to address the reintegration of legions of ex-convicts back into society and lower recidivism rates. Its goal was to improve reentry programs for adult and juvenile offenders and develop new and better ones.

Security Threat Groups   Today, a number of prison officials and police organizations refer to some prison gangs as Security Threat Groups (STGs).

Sedition   Any action promoting discontent or rebellion.

Sedition Act of 1918   Made it a federal offense to criticize the U.S. Constitution, the U.S. government, the American uniform, or the American flag.

Shafer v. South Carolina   In 2001, the Supreme Court reversed the death penalty for a man who was condemned by jurors who were confused about the meaning of the phrase "life imprisonment."

Shaming   An ancient form of exhibitory punishment that can include letter wearing or public humiliation. Several judges have used this as an alternative to prison sentences.

Shire   Somewhat equivalent to a county, England in the Anglo-Saxon period was subdivided into these.

Simsbury Prison   Connecticut prison opened in an abandoned copper mine in 1773.

Sing Sing Prison   Infamous New York state prison opened in 1825.

Sixth Amendment   Promises an impartial jury in all criminal prosecutions.

Skinner v. Oklahoma   The Supreme Court ruled in 1942 against sterilizing criminals.

Social Darwinism   Theory that individuals should depend on individualism and competition to get ahead rather than depend on social cooperation and reform.

Society for the Prevention of Pauperism   In 1817, this New York group became the first to call attention to neglected children.

Sophists   Professional philosophers, such as Socrates, in ancient Athens.

Speakeasy   Place where alcoholic beverages are illegally sold.

Special Weapons and Tactics (SWAT)   During the 1960s, Philadelphia and Los Angeles police forces created special units in response to new trends in criminal violence.

Spoils system Practice in which public offices are at the disposal of the victorious party for its own purposes.

Stamp Act This 1765 tax was the first direct or internal tax that Parliament ever imposed on American colonies.

Star Chamber Court of Introduced in fifteenth century to punish wealthy supporters of criminal activity. Since there was no jury, this court was prohibited from imposing capital punishment or other serious punishments.

Star police Refers to first New York City police officers who wore copper badges to identify themselves as officers prior to the acceptance of uniforms.

State of the Prisons John Howard's 1777 report on the abuses of European prisons and suggestions for reform.

States' rights Rights belonging to the various states. Using a very strict interpretation of the U.S. Constitution, all rights not delegated by the Constitution to the federal government belong to the states.

Statute of Winchester One of the most important pieces of criminal justice legislation to come out of the Middle Ages. Established watch and ward system of day and night watch.

Subprime mortgage crisis The current financial crisis is widely considered the country's worst since the Great Depression. Most observers assert its roots are firmly planted in the subprime mortgage crisis that began in 2006. It was caused by several factors including unprincipled lending practices in the mortgage industry, deceptive credit ratings, and years of deregulation and loose mortgage standards.

Sumptuary laws Laws that restricted certain fashions among the Puritan colonists.

Supermax prisons Super-maximum prisons. The first was opened at Alcatraz in 1934. The trend of building these escalated in the 1980s.

Sûreté Highly professional French detectives; originated in the 1830s.

Scythians Captured warriors from the north; the Athenians employed them as town guards.

Taboo A prohibition of something; a system or practice whereby things are set apart as sacred or forbidden under threat of being ostracized.

Tammany Hall One of the most powerful urban political machines in American history. It dominated Democratic politics in New York City from 1855 to the 1930s.

Tarpein Cliff High cliff used for precipitation by the Romans.

Teapot Dome scandal In 1924, this scandal led to the first imprisonment of a cabinet officer (1929) and entered the American lexicon as a synonym for government graft.

Telephone pole design In the 1950s, this penitentiary design flourished. This design better accommodated treatment programs, maintained security, and offered a new openness to inmates.

Temperance groups Moral reformers dedicated to the prohibition of alcohol sale, manufacture, and consumption.

Teutonic Pertaining to people of northern European ancestry, including Germanic, Scandinavian, and British peoples.

Texas Rangers The first statewide law enforcement agency, created in 1823 (but not officially called Texas Rangers until 1874).

Thief takers Early bounty hunters.

Things   Local assemblies or courts convened by the Danes. Some consider this a precursor to the English jury system because twelve freemen swore an oath not to convict an innocent man.

Thirteenth Amendment   Abolished slavery in 1865.

Thompson v. Oklahoma   In 1988, the Supreme Court ruled that executing an individual who committed a crime before the age of sixteen violated the Eighth Amendment.

Three strikes policy   This sentencing policy originated in California after the abduction and murder of Polly Klaas in the 1980s. The rallying cry, "Three strikes and you're out" became a slogan for get-tough politicians.

Tithings   Anglo-Saxon self-policing in which ten men belonged, each responsible for the others' behavior.

Trailbaston   Commissions convened beginning in 1304 to counter the escalation of organized criminal activities.

Transportation   England used this method to banish convicts to its colonies in America and later Australia.

Treatise on the Police of the Metropolis   Patrick Colquhoun's 1797 concepts on police reform.

Trial by battle   Judicial duels used to determine guilt or innocence.

Trustees   Until the 1970s, most prisons empowered trusties to help control the inmates.

Twelve Tables   Considered the first written laws of Rome.

Twinkie defense   This insanity defense has been identified with the case of Dan White, who murdered the mayor of San Francisco and City Supervisor Harvey Milk in 1978. However, its centrality to the trial has been largely discredited as myth.

Uniform Crime Reports **(UCR)**   Crime statistics disseminated by the FBI beginning in 1930.

United States Secret Service   Originally established in 1865 to handle the counterfeiting problem.

Untouchables   Prohibition agents led by Eliot Ness.

Urban Cohort   Daytime peacekeepers in Rome under Augustus Caesar.

USA PATRIOT Act   On October 26, 2001, President George W. Bush signed the USA PATRIOT Act into law. From a purely criminal justice perspective, its passage eliminated some of the barriers that formerly prevented law enforcement agencies from collaborating, created new money laundering crimes, while increasing penalties for existing money laundering violations.

Usury   Practice of lending money at an exorbitant rate of interest.

Vigiles   Composed mostly of freed slaves, they patrolled Roman streets and fought fires at night under Augustus Caesar.

Virginia Tech Massacre   On April 16, 2007, a senior at Virginia Polytechnic Institute and State University (Virginia Tech) went on a campus rampage that left thirty-two students and faculty dead and twenty-five wounded in what became known as the "Virginia Tech Massacre." It was the nation's worst mass murder.

Volstead Act   Its passage inaugurated the Prohibition era in 1919.

Waco Branch Davidian Siege   Four federal agents were killed at the Branch Davidian compound in Waco, Texas, in 1993. A fifty-one-day standoff ensued that ended with the deaths of eighty-five cult members.

Walnut Street Jail   Opened in Philadelphia in 1790, it was considered the "cradle" of the American penitentiary.

Wayward Sisters   Refers to female criminals in late nineteenth century.

Weeks v. United States   Landmark case that established the exclusionary rule.

Wergild   Form of compensation designed to replace the blood feud among Germanic tribes.

White Slave Traffic Act   Better known as the Mann Act, this 1910 legislation was the culmination of Progressive reform efforts to legislate morality.

Wickersham Commission   Between 1929 and 1931, the National Commission on Law Observance and Enforcement, chaired by George Wickersham, examined criminal justice in America. Its conclusions were published in two volumes and recommended a number of procedures for improving due process and eliminating corruption.

Wilkerson v. Utah   This 1879 Supreme Court decision upheld the constitutionality of execution by firing squad.

Witan   Considered by some a precursor to Parliament; an assembly of major landlords in Anglo-Saxon England.

Wobblies   Members of the International Workers of the World (IWW) labor union, often targeted by the government for subversive activities.

Xenophobia   An unreasonable hatred or fear of foreigners.

Zero tolerance policy   Draconian rules that take discretion out of the hands of administrators and other officials. Following several school shootings, these policies were aimed at schools, calling for the expulsion of students who carried anything that could be construed as a weapon.

Zoot-Suit riots   Anti-Hispanic riots in 1940s Los Angeles.

WHO'S WHO IN CRIMINAL JUSTICE HISTORY

Adams, John (1735–1826)   American lawyer, patriot, and future president who defended the British soldiers accused of the Boston Massacre, demonstrating his belief that the accused has the right to a vigorous defense.

Aethelbert of Kent (ca. 552–616)   Responsible for the first extant Anglo-Saxon laws drawn up after the example of the Romans.

Anslinger, Harry (1892–1975)   During his tenure as commissioner of the Bureau of Narcotics, he waged an unrelenting war against illegal drug use.

Ashcroft, John (b. 1942)   Attorney general in the administration of President George W. Bush.

Augustus Caesar (63 B.C.–A.D. 14)   Introduced three separate organizations for policing Rome and its provincial towns.

Augustus, John (1785–1859)   Boston cobbler who became a leading proponent of probation.

Austin, Stephen (1793–1836)   In 1823, Austin created what would later become known as the Texas Rangers.

Baldwin, Lola (prominent in early 1900s)   Hired by the Portland, Oregon, Police Department, she was an early pioneer in women's law enforcement.

Barrow, Clyde (1909–1934)   Partner with Bonnie Parker in a series of robberies and murders during the late 1920s.

Bates, Sanford (1884–1972)   While leading the Federal Bureau of Prisons in the 1930s, Bates improved officer training, enhanced prison education programs, and adopted the "telephone pattern" for prison construction.

Battle, Samuel J. (1883–1966)   As the first African American on the New York City police force in 1910, he was subjected to a year of silent treatment by fellow officers.

Beccaria, Cesare de (1738–1794)   His theories laid the foundation for the reform of the European criminal justice system.

Bentham, Jeremy (1748–1832)   Advocate of legal reform and founder of the philosophy of utilitarianism, which argued that law must be used for the "greatest good of the greatest number" of people.

Bertillon, Alphonse (1835–1914)   While employed by the Paris police, he created Bertillon identification system, leading to his reputation as the "father of modern detection."

Bias, Len (1963–1986)   The cocaine-related death of this college star in 1986 proved a catalyst for more punitive drug laws such as the 1986 Anti-Drug Abuse Act.

Bonnie and Clyde See Barrow, Clyde; Parker, Bonnie.

Borden, Lizzie (1860–1927)   The alleged perpetrator of one of the most famous American murder cases. She was eventually acquitted of killing her father and stepmother.

Bradwell, Myra (1831–1894)   Prominent in the women's suffrage movement, her efforts at legal reform eventually led Illinois to become the first state to pass a law allowing women to practice any profession.

Brady, James (b. 1936)   Brady was wounded in 1981 during the assassination attempt on President Ronald Reagan. Subsequently, he has become a leading advocate for gun control.

Bratton, William (b. 1947)   While serving as New York City police commissioner beginning in 1994, his crime control strategies were given much of the credit for the city's dramatic drop in crime in the 1990s.

Brockway, Zebulon (1827–1920)   Prison reformer who came to national prominence after his participation in the Prison Congress of 1870. Later appointed superintendent of the Elmira Reformatory.

Brooks, Charles (1942–1982)   Texas death row inmate who became first person executed by lethal injection. He was also the first African American executed after the death penalty was reinstated in 1976.

Brown, John (1800–1859)   Violent abolitionist and insurrectionist who was executed following his capture of the armory at Harper's Ferry.

Burns, Robert Elliott (1890–1965)   World War I veteran who escaped from a Georgia chain gang in 1922. During his years of freedom, he publicized the barbaric conditions on the Georgia chain gangs.

Burns, William John (1861–1932)   Established Burns Detective Agency before being selected to head the Bureau of Investigation in 1921.

Burr, Aaron (1756–1836)   Killed Alexander Hamilton in an 1804 duel and three years later was tried for treason for plotting to create his own empire west of the Appalachian Mountains.

Byrnes, Thomas F. (1842–1910)   Chief of the New York City Detective Bureau in the 1880s, he rose to prominence for his photographic "rogues' gallery."

Calhoun, John C. (1782–1850)   Tested the rights of states during the 1833 Nullification Controversy in South Carolina.

Capone, Al (1899–1947)   Public enemy number one during the 1920s, he was finally brought to justice by the Internal Revenue Service.

Charles I (1600–1649)   Best known for suspending Parliament for eleven years and for his execution in 1649. The reliance on the antiquated watch system during his reign inspired the sobriquet "Charleys" for watchmen.

Charles II (1630–1685)   King of Great Britain, 1660–1685.

Chessman, Caryl (1921–1960)   California's infamous "Red Light Bandit." During his twelve years on death row before his execution, he became an articulate opponent of the death penalty.

Colquhoun, Patrick (1745–1820)   Created the Thames River Police and was a campaigner for police reform in London prior to the creation of the London Metropolitan Police.

Comstock, Anthony (1844–1915)   Led crusade against obscenity and vice.

Constantine I (ca. 288–337)   Roman emperor who converted to Christianity and legally sanctioned the practice of the religion.

Crofton, Walter (1815–1897) Applied Maconochie's parole ideas to the Irish prison system.

Curtis, Edwin (1861–1922) Boston police commissioner who provoked a police strike in 1919.

Cutpurse, Moll (real name Mary Frith) (ca. 1584–1659) An English highway robber and fence.

Darrow, Clarence (1857–1938) One of America's greatest criminal defense lawyers and staunch opponent of the death penalty. Among his most prominent death penalty cases was the 1924 Leopold and Loeb trial.

Darwin, Charles (1809–1882) English naturalist, best known for his theory that the origin of species is the result of natural selection of those best adapted to survive in the struggle for existence.

Davis, Katherine Bement (1860–1935) Progressive era penologist and social worker.

Dewey, Thomas E. (1902–1971) Special prosecutor in New York City in the 1930s.

Diallo, Amadou (1975–1996) Became a martyr for crusade against police brutality after his killing by NYPD police.

Dickens, Charles (1812–1870) Novelist who wrote a critique of the solitary prison system after visiting Eastern State Penitentiary in 1842.

Dillinger, John (1903–1934) Midwestern bank robber and public enemy number one during the Great Depression.

Dix, Dorothea (1802–1887) Early prison reformer who championed the rights of mentally ill prisoners.

Dorr, Thomas (1805–1854) Harvard-educated attorney who organized a campaign to abolish voting restrictions.

Douglas, William O. (1898–1980) Served as Supreme Court justice longer than any other (thirty-six years). Remembered as a steadfast supporter of civil rights.

Draco (ca. 600 B.C.) First to put Athenian laws into writing. He introduced laws dealing with homicide and other offenses. He is remembered for the severity of his code of laws.

Dwight, Louis (1793–1854) A supporter of the Auburn prison system, he organized the Prison Discipline Society of Boston in 1825.

Eddy, Thomas (1758–1827) Quaker prison reformer regarded as the "Father of New York State prison" and a leading advocate of the separate-cell system.

Edward the Confessor (ca. 1002–1066) Last Anglo-Saxon king of Britain.

Fall, Albert (1861–1944) Secretary of the Interior and central figure in the Teapot Dome scandal of 1924. He became the first cabinet officer jailed for crimes committed in office.

Faulds, Henry (1843–1930) Pioneer in fingerprint identification.

Fawkes, Guy (1570–1606) English conspirator executed for attempting to blow up Parliament and King James I.

Fielding, Henry (1707–1754) Introduced the Bow Street Runners and was an early advocate for professional, full-time police in London.

Fielding, John (1721–1780) Half-brother of Henry; despite being blind from birth, the "Blind Beak" could reportedly identify hundreds of criminals by voice alone.

Forsyth, Robert (d. 1794) First law enforcement officer killed in America following the birth of the Republic.

Fosdick, Raymond (1883–1972) His studies of police systems in Europe and America led to reform in American policing prior to World War I.

Fouche, Joseph (1759–1820)   He created a centralized police force in France and served as its director under Emperor Napoleon.

Freeh, Louis (b. 1950)   Led the FBI through some of its most controversial years, including the debacles at Waco and Ruby Ridge.

Fuld, Leonhard (1883–1965)   Author of *Police Administration*, the first comprehensive study of American police administration.

Galton, Francis (1822–1911)   Author of *Fingerprints* and founder of the eugenics movement in early twentieth century.

Garrison, William Lloyd (1805–1879)   Massachusetts abolitionist.

Gates, Daryl (b. 1926)   Los Angeles police chief from 1978 to 1991 and proponent of the SWAT team concept.

Gilmore, Gary (1940–1977)   Utah murderer who became the first American executed after the return of capital punishment in 1976.

Giuliani, Rudolph (b. 1944)   During the 1980s he proved the nemesis of New York City's five Mafia crime families. As New York City mayor in the 1990s, he was given some of the credit for reducing crime in the city through the implementation of controversial tactics such as "flood and frisk."

Glueck, Sheldon (1898–1972) **and Eleanor** (1896–1980)   Criminologists and pioneers in modern research criminology who collaborated on a number of juvenile delinquency studies.

Goddard, Calvin H. (1891–1955)   Forensic expert and pioneer in ballistics testing.

Goetz, Bernard (b. 1947)   Came to prominence in 1984 as the "subway vigilante," shooting four young African American men in crime-plagued New York City.

Gonzalez, Alberto (b. 1955)   In 2005, replaced John Ashcroft as attorney general. He became controversial for his support of practices such as waterboarding and extraordinary rendition and his willingness to violate the Geneva Conventions.

Grant, Ulysses S. (1822–1885)   President who declared martial law in parts of the South during the 1870s.

Hammurabi (ca. 1792–1750 B.C.)   Best remembered for his great law code detailed in cuneiform (pictographic) writings on a stone slab.

Hauptmann, Bruno Richard (1899–1936)   German-born kidnapper executed for death of aviator Charles Lindbergh's infant son.

Hays, Jacob (1772–1850)   Served a half century as New York City's first high constable and is credited with introducing the police tactic of patrolling in pairs.

Heirens, William (b. 1929)   Suspected of several unsolved murders, as a teenager, he became the first person questioned under the "truth serum" sodium pentothal.

Hennessey, David (1857–1890)   The murder of this New Orleans police chief led to the mob killings of eleven Italian prisoners in the city jail.

Henry, Edward Richard (1850–1931)   A career civil servant, he perfected the fingerprinting system in 1896 by developing a more practical method of filing prints. The so-called Henry system was implemented in the United States and Europe.

Henry, Patrick (1736–1799)   Politician, lawyer, and revolutionary firebrand who demanded national independence and vigorously opposed the Stamp Act.

Henry II (1133–1189)   British law made great strides under his reign between 1154 and 1189. He transformed civil and criminal law as the king's law became national in scope.

Henry VIII (1491–1547)   Made the transition from "Defender of the Faith" to cutting all ties with Rome and creating a schism within the Church of England.

Herschel, William J. (1833–1917)   Fingerprinting pioneer who discovered the unique "signature" nature of individual fingerprints.

Hinckley, John W. (b. 1955)   Attempted to assassinate President Ronald Reagan. Found not guilty by reason of insanity.

Holder, Eric (b. 1951)   Appointed U.S. attorney general by President Obama, becoming the nation's first African American to hold that position. In 2009, he announced that the U.S. Justice Department would not enforce federal laws that conflicted with state laws on marijuana possession nor prosecute medical marijuana distributors that complied with state laws.

Holmes, Oliver Wendell (1841–1935)   The Supreme Court's leading champion of civil rights during the Progressive era.

Hoover, John Edgar (1895–1972)   Controversial director of the FBI from 1924 to 1972.

Howard, John (1726–1790)   Early English prison reformer whose writings led Parliament to pass the first Penitentiary Act in 1779.

Jackson, Andrew (1767–1845)   Served as president at a time when Americans began to first perceive crime as a threat to the order and security of the Republic.

John (king of England) (ca. 1167–1216)   Son of Henry II and signer of the Magna Carta in 1215.

Johnson, Jack (1878–1946)   World heavyweight boxing champion arrested for violating the Mann Act in 1912.

Julius Caesar (ca. 100–44 B.C.)   Roman statesman and general.

Justinian (483–565)   Under his direction, Roman law was codified.

Kanka, Megan (1986–1994)   The rape and murder of this seven-year-old by a convicted sex offender inspired "Megan's Law."

Kefauver, Estes (1903–1963)   Led the Kefauver Committee hearings, the first significant investigation of organized crime in America.

Kelly, Raymond W. (b. 1941)   Selected as NYPD commissioner in 1992, he has received credit for revamping the department into what is perhaps the nation's best counterterrorist operation and for increasing the number of officers devoted to it from fewer than 24 (pre-9/11) to close to 1,000 today.

Kemmler, William (d. 1890)   New York ax murderer and first person to be executed in the electric chair.

Kennedy, John F. (1917–1963)   His assassination is one of the most chronicled murders in American history.

Kennedy, Robert F. (1925–1968)   As attorney general in his brother John's administration, he intensified efforts in the war against organized crime.

Kerner, Otto (1908–1976)   Illinois governor who chaired the 1967 National Advisory Commission on Civil Disorders.

King, Martin Luther Jr. (1929–1968)   America's leading civil rights figure assassinated in Memphis, Tennessee, by James Earl Ray.

King, Rodney (b. 1965)   The eighty-one-second tape of the beating of this black motorist by several LAPD officers after an early morning car chase in 1991 led to an investigation of police brutality in the force by the Christopher Commission. It became a catalyst for black rage that led to the Los Angeles riots (1993) and the resignation of the city's Police Chief Daryl Gates.

Klaas, Polly (1981–1993)   Her kidnapping and murder by a career criminal led to the passage of the three strikes law in California.

Kohler, Fred (1869–1933)   Cleveland police chief who implemented diversion programs for minor offenses.

Latrobe, Benjamin Henry (1764–1820)   Architect of Richmond, Virginia, Penitentiary.

Leopold, Nathan (1906–1971), **and Loeb, Richard** (1907–1936)   Two outstanding university students who were caught after a murder that they thought would be the perfect crime.

Lincoln, Abraham (1809–1865)   One of the greatest American presidents, he was criticized for suspending the constitutionally guaranteed writ of habeas corpus during the Civil War.

Locke, John (1632–1704)   English philosopher and political theorist, he advocated religious toleration and that government should be based on the consent of the governed.

Lombroso, Cesare (1835–1909)   Founder of the positivist school of criminology and "father of modern criminology."

Louima, Abner (b. 1966)   This Haitian immigrant was brutalized by members of the NYPD following his arrest outside a nightclub in 1997. In 2001 the case ended in a settlement in the millions of dollars, the largest police brutality settlement in New York City history.

Lovejoy, Elijah (1802–1837)   Abolitionist murdered in 1837, he became a martyr for the antislavery crusade.

Luciano, Charles "Lucky" (1897–1962)   Prominent New York gangster credited with helping organize the national crime syndicate.

Lynch, Charles (1736–1796)   Best remembered for his participation in vigilante activities in colonial Virginia.

Lynch, William L. (1724–1820)   Led a 1780 vigilante movement in Virginia.

Lynds, Elam (1784–1855)   Credited with establishing Auburn Prison's silent system.

Maconochie, Alexander (1787–1860)   Considered the "father of parole" after his experiment with indeterminate sentencing at the English prison colony of Van Diemen's Land.

Madoff, Bernard (b. 1938)   In 2009, admitted to operating what is believed to be the largest Ponzi scheme in history costing investors' losses in the billions of dollars. He was sentenced to 150 years in prison.

Maple, Jack (1952–2001)   As executive assistant and chief strategist to NYPD Chief William Bratton in the 1990s, he introduced a groundbreaking computer map system dubbed "Compstat." His strategies have been credited with contributing to the crime drop in NYC and other cities.

Marshall, John (1755–1835)   Chief justice of the Supreme Court from 1801 to 1835.

Marshall, Thurgood (1908–1993)   The grandson of slaves, he rose to national prominence during the civil rights struggle in the 1950s. In 1967, he became the first African American Supreme Court justice.

Mayne, Richard (1796–1868)   Served as commissioner of the London Metropolitan Police for almost forty years.

McCarthy, Joseph (d. 1957)   Wisconsin senator whose name has become synonymous with anticommunist hysteria during the 1950s.

McCormick, Austin (1893–1979) Noted prison educator and pioneer in correctional reform. When he retired in 1940, he was considered one of the nation's greatest prison executives.

Montesquieu, Charles Louis de (1689–1755) Leading French Enlightenment philosopher and author of *The Spirit of the Laws*.

More, Sir Thomas (1478–1535) One of the earliest to theorize on crime and punishment and to lobby against the death penalty. He was executed for treason under the rule of Henry VIII.

Mueller, Robert (b. 1944) Became the director of the FBI just one week before the 9/11 attacks, replacing Louis Freeh.

Nast, Thomas (1840–1902) Cartoonist and social commentator.

Ness, Eliot (1902–1957) Rose to prominence as head of Chicago's "Untouchables" during the Prohibition era.

Obama, Barack (b. 1961) In 2008, this former senator from Illinois became the first African American to win a presidential election. He was also the first president "to take office in the Age of Terrorism."

O'Connor, Sandra Day (b. 1930) In 1981, she became the first woman appointed to the Supreme Court.

Osborne, Thomas Mott (1859–1926) Sing Sing Prison warden, prison reformer, and champion of the Mutual Welfare League experiment.

Palmer, A. Mitchell (1872–1936) Attorney general who initiated a federal attack on radical activists in 1919.

Parker, Bonnie (1911–1934) Partner of Clyde Barrow in bank robbing and murder spree in early 1930s.

Parker, William H. (1902–1966) An advocate of police professionalism, he served a controversial sixteen years as Los Angeles police chief.

Peel, Robert (1788–1850) As home secretary, he helped pass the Metropolitan Police Act of 1829, creating a uniformed police force along military lines, which included being better disciplined and trained.

Penn, William (1644–1718) Pennsylvania Quaker leader who championed law and criminal justice reform in the early colonial period.

Pinkerton, Allan J. (1819–1884) Founder of what would become Pinkerton's National Detective Agency.

Ponzi, Charles (1877–1949) After orchestrating one of the most famous frauds in American history in 1919, his name has become forever linked to a scam that persisted into the twenty-first century and was made notorious by Bernard Madoff.

Prosser, Gabriel (ca. 1776–1800) A Virginia slave executed for conspiring to lead a slave insurrection.

Ragen, Joseph Edward (1896–1971) Rose to prominence as a reform-minded warden of the Illinois State Penitentiary at Joliet.

Redfield, Horace (1845–1881) Journalist who publicized the high homicide rate in the South.

Rehnquist, William (b. 1924) Chief justice of the Supreme Court.

Reno, Janet (b. 1938) During the Clinton administration, she became the first female attorney general in America.

Ridge, Tom (b. 1945)   In 2003, he resigned as governor of Pennsylvania and became the first secretary of Homeland Security. He resigned the following year.

Riis, Jacob (1849–1914)   New York City social reformer who chronicled the immigrant plight of the late nineteenth century.

Roberts, John (b. 1955)   Was appointed chief justice of the U.S. Supreme Court in 2005.

Rogers, Mary (1820–1841)   Her sensational murder and the subsequent investigation led to reform in the New York City Police Department in the 1840s.

Roosevelt, Franklin D. (1882–1945)   During his terms as president, federal crime control went through unprecedented growth.

Roosevelt, Theodore (1859–1919)   Prior to his ascendance to the presidency, he served as a reform-minded New York City police commissioner between 1895 and 1897.

Rosenberg, Julius (1918–1953), **and Ethel** (1915–1953)   Executed for espionage during the communist hysteria of the 1950s.

Rousseau, Jean Jacques (1712–1778)   French philosopher and social reformer.

Rowan, Charles (1783–1852)   Served as co-commissioner of London Metropolitan Police with Richard Mayne until 1850.

Rudolph, Eric (b. 1966)   American far-right domestic terrorist who committed a series of bombings in southern states between 1996 and 1998, including the Olympic Park bombing in Atlanta.

Rush, Benjamin (1746–1813)   Statesman and penal reformer during the American Revolution era.

Sacco, Nicola (1891–1927), **and Vanzetti, Bartolomeo** (1888–1927)   Italian anarchists executed for double murder during a payroll robbery in Massachusetts.

Scheck, Barry (b. 1949)   Lawyer came to prominence as a member of the O. J. Simpson defense team as the director and cofounder of the Innocence Project.

Schultz, Dutch (real name Arthur Flegenheimer) (1902–1935)   New York bootlegger and racketeer who was killed after threatening to kill Thomas Dewey.

Scott, Dred (ca. 1790s – 1858)   Slave who initiated groundbreaking Supreme Court case after he sued for his freedom in a Missouri state court.

Serpico, Frank (b. 1936)   New York City police detective who fought corruption but was shunned by colleagues for violating the "blue curtain" of silence.

Shakespeare, William (1564–1616)   English poet and dramatist who introduced early night watchmen and constables as ineffective comic foils.

Sheppard, Sam (1924–1970)   Ohio doctor accused of killing wife in a controversial murder case that inspired the television series The Fugitive.

Siegel, Benjamin "Bugsy" (1906–1947)   American gangster and founder of the Las Vegas Flamingo Hotel and Casino.

Simpson, O. J. (b. 1947)   This former football great and television pitchman's 1995 trial and acquittal in the murders of his ex-wife and a friend in 1994 transfixed America and demonstrated the racial divide that still existed. It also brought up a number of issues related to cameras in the courtroom and the utility of jury trials.

Smith, Bruce (1892–1955)   Police consultant and criminologist who became the nation's leading expert on police operations.

Smith, John (1580–1631)   English colonizer who introduced military discipline and martial law at the Jamestown Colony.

Socrates (ca. 469–399 B.C.)   Athenian philosopher and public figure who was a central participant in the city's intellectual debates in late fifth century B.C.

Solon (ca. 638–558 B.C.)   Athenian statesman and lawgiver who replaced Draco's harsh laws, except those dealing with homicide.

Sotomayor, Sonia (b. 1954)   In 2009 she became the first Hispanic woman nominated to the U.S. Supreme Court.

Surratt, Mary E. (1817–1865)   Executed for her role in Lincoln assassination conspiracy. She was the first woman hanged by the federal government.

Sutherland, Edwin H. (1883–1950)   Prominent criminologist who coined the term "white-collar crime" and developed concept of differential association.

Taney, Roger (1777–1864)   Succeeded John Marshall as chief justice of Supreme Court in 1836.

Till, Emmett (1941–1955)   His murder in Mississippi in 1955 reinforced black fears of racially motivated violence in the South.

Torrio, John (1882–1957)   Mentor to Al Capone and Chicago crime boss.

Toussaint Louverture, Pierre Dominique (1743–1803)   Former Haitian slave who led the first large-scale slave uprising in the Americas in 1791.

Tukey, Francis (b. 1814)   Serving in a variety of capacities and with a penchant for the dramatic, Tukey was an unremarkable Boston law enforcement official in the 1840s and 1850s.

Turner, Nat (1800–1831)   Led first actual slave revolt in the United States in 1831.

Tweed, William Marcy (1823–1878)   New York City Tammany Hall boss who exemplified the corruption of urban America in the 1860s.

Vidocq, Eugene (1775–1857)   Former French criminal, often considered the world's first private detective.

Vollmer, August (1876–1955)   Police reformer and father of modern professional policing.

Warne, Kate (1833–1868)   Became America's first female detective after joining the Pinkertons in 1856.

Warren, Earl (1891–1974)   Former governor of California, his tenure as chief justice of the Supreme Court was marked by judicial activism that made the Court an active participant in the crusade for social change.

Weaver, Randy (b. 1948)   He was at the center of the Ruby Ridge confrontation with the FBI in 1992.

Wells, Alice Stebbins (prominent in 1910–1920s)   Considered by many to be the first full-time policewoman in America.

Wells-Barnett, Ida B. (1862–1931)   African American journalist and advocate for racial justice and women's suffrage who led a crusade against lynching in the 1890s.

Wickersham, George (1858–1936)   As chair of the National Commission on Law Observance and Enforcement, his name became synonymous with police reform during the crisis decades.

Wild, Jonathan (1682–1725)   Led a posse of thief catchers who got higher prices for stolen goods by returning them to the original owners after they were "found."

William I (1027–1087)   Following his victory at the Battle of Hastings, William the Duke of Normandy became the first Norman king of Britain.

Williams, Alexander "Clubber" (1839–1910)   A symbol of New York City police corruption during the 1890s.

Wilson, Orlando W. (1900–1972)   Author of influential *Police Administration* (1963), as police chief in Wichita, Kansas, and later Chicago, Wilson was an advocate of police professionalism.

Wines, Enoch (1806–1879)   Prison reformer who publicized deplorable conditions of several northeastern penitentiaries.

Wolfgang, Marvin (1924–1998)   A pioneering criminologist who conducted an early academic study of homicide in Philadelphia.

Wood, Fernando (1812–1881)   Regarded as a tool of Tammany Hall, this New York City mayor was reluctant to suppress vice in the 1850s.

Wood, William P. (1819–1903)   First chief of the U.S. Secret Service.

Woods, Arthur (1870–1942)   As New York City police commissioner, he established the first school for patrol officers.

Yates, Andrea (b. 1964)   After drowning her five children in 2001, the insanity defense was put on trial during an appeals process that increased awareness about postpartum depression and psychosis.

Zenger, John Peter (1697–1746)   American journalist, printer, and publisher whose exoneration in a seditious libel suit became a major step in achieving freedom of the press in the colonies.

APPENDICES

Appendix A: Leaders of the Bureau of Investigation and the FBI

Stanley Wellington Finch	July 26, 1908
A. Bruce Bielaski	April 30, 1912
William E. Allen	February 10, 1919
William J. Flynn	July 1, 1919
William John Burns	August 22, 1921
John Edgar Hoover	May 10, 1924
Clyde Anderson Tolson	May 2, 1972
Louis Patrick Gray III	May 3, 1972
William D. Ruckelshaus	April 27, 1973
Clarence Marion Kelley	July 9, 1973
William H. Webster	February 23, 1978
John Otto	May 26, 1987
William Steele Sessions	November 2, 1987
Floyd Clarke	July 19, 1993
Louis J. Freeh	September 1, 1993
Thomas J. Pickard (Acting)	June 25, 2001
Robert S. Mueller III	September 4, 2001
James B. Comey	May 9, 2013
Andrew McCabe (Acting)	May 9, 2017
Christopher Wray	August 2, 2017

Appendix B: New York City Police Department commissioners, 1901–2018

Michael C. Murphy	2/22/1901–1/1/02
John N. Partridge	1/1/02–1/1/03
Francis V. Greene	1/1/03–1/1/04
William McAdoo	1/1/04–1/1/06
Theodore A. Bingham	1/1/06–7/1/09
William F. Baker	1/1/09–10/20/10
James C. Cropsey	10/20/10–5/23/11
Rhinelander Waldo	5/23/11–12/31/13

Douglas I. Mckay	12/31/13–4/8/14
Arthur Woods	4/8/14–1/1/18
Frederick H. Bugher	1/1/18–1/23/18
Richard Edward Enright	1/23/18–12/30/25
George V. McLaughlin	1/1/26–4/12/27
Joseph A. Warren	4/12/27–12/18/28
Grover A. Whalen	12/18/28–5/21/30
Edward P. Mulrooney	5/21/30–4/12/33
James S. Bolan	4/15/33–12/31/33
John F. O'Ryan	1/1/34–9/24/34
Lewis Joseph Valentine	9/25/34–9/14/45
Arthur W. Wallander	9/23/45–2/28/45
William P. O'Brien	3/1/49–9/25/50
Thomas E. Murphy	9/26/50–7/5/51
George P. Monaghan	7/9/51–12/31/53
Francis W. H. Adams	1/1/54–8/1/55
Stephen Patrick Kennedy	8/2/55–2/22/61
Michael J. Murphy	2/23/61–6/6/65
Vincent I. Broderick	6/7/65–2/21/66
Howard R. Leary	2/22/66–10/8/70
Patrick V. Murphy	10/9/70–5/12/73
Donald E. Cawley	5/13/73–1/11/74
Michael Codd	1/12/74–12/31/77
Robert J. McGuire	1/1/78–12/29/83
William Devine	12/30/83–12/31/83 (interim position only)
Benjamin Ward	1/1/84–10/22/89
Richard J. Condon	10/23/89–1/21/90
Lee Patrick Brown	1/22/90–9/1/92
Raymond W. Kelly	9/1/92–1/9/94
William J. Bratton	1/10/94–4/15/96
Howard Safir	4/15/96–2000
Bernard Kerik	8/21/2000–9/2/2001
Raymond W. Kelly	1/1/2002–12/31/2013
William J. Bratton	1/1/2014–9/16/2016
James P. O'Neill	9/16/2016–present

The New York City Police Department has been under the direction of a single police commissioner since February 22, 1901. Prior to that time, the department was jointly run by a board made up of four to six police commissioners, one of whom would act as the president of the board. The most famous president of the board was Theodore Roosevelt who served from May 6, 1895, to April 19, 1897.

Source: NYPD homepage, July 12, 1999, available at: www.ci.nyc.ny.us/html/3100/ commish.html, Internet.

Appendix C: Los Angeles police chiefs, 1876 – 2018

Jacob T. Gerkins	12/18/1876–12/26/77
Emil Harris	12/27/77–12/5/78
Henry King	12/5/78–12/11/80
George E. Guard	12/12/80–12/10/81
Henry King	12/11/81–6/30/83
Thomas J. Cuddy	7/1/83–1/1/85
Edward McCarthy	1/2/85–5/12/85
James W. Davis	12/22/85–12/8/86
John K. Skinner	12/13/86–8/29/87
P. M. Darcy	9/5/87–1/22/88
Thomas J. Cuddy	1/23/88–9/4/88
L. G. Loomis	9/5/88–9/30/88
Hubert H. Benedict	10/1/88–1/1/89
Terrence Cooney	1/1/89–4/1/89
James E. Bums	4/1/89–7/17/89
John M. Glass	7/17/89–1/1/1900
Charles Elton	1/1/1900–4/5/04
William A. Hammell	4/6/04–10/31/05
Walter H. Auble	11/1/05–11/20/06
Edward Kern	11/20/06–1/5/09
Thomas Broadhead	1/5/09–4/12/09
Edward F. Dishman	4/13/09–1/25/10
Alexander Galloway	2/14/10–12/27/10
Charles E. Sebastian	1/3/11–7/16/15
Clarence E. Snively	07/17/15–10/15/16
John L. Butler	10/16/16–07/16/19
George K. Home	7/17/19–9/30/20
Alexander W. Murray	10/01/20–10/31/20
Lyle Pendegast	11/1/20–7/4/21
Charles A. Jones	7/5/21–1/3/22
James W. Everington	1/4/22–4/21/22
Louis D. Oaks	4/22/22–8/1/23
August Vollmer	8/1/23–8/1/24
R. Lee Heath	8/1/24–3/31/26
James Edgar Davis	4/1/26–12/29/29
Roy E. Steckel	12/30/29–8/9/33
James E. Davis	8/10/33–11/18/38

D. A. Davidson	1l/19/38–6/23/39
Arthur C. Hohmann	6/24/39–6/5/41
Clarence B. Horrall	6/16/41–6/28/49
William A. Worton	6/30/49–8/9/50
William Henry Parker	8/9/50–7/16/66
Thad F. Brown	7/18/66–2/17/67
Thomas Reddin	2/18/67–5/5/69
Roger E. Murdock	5/6/69–8/28/69
Edward M. Davis	8/29/69–1/15/78
Robert F. Rock	1/16/78–03/27/78
Daryl F. Gates	3/28/78–5/31/92
William L. "Willie" Williams	6/1/92–8/21/97
Bayan Lewis	1997
Bernard Parks	8/22/97–present
Bayan Lewis	5/18/97–8/12/97
Bernard Parks	8/12/97–5/4/2002
Martin H. Pomeroy	5/7/2002–10/26/2002
William J. Bratton	10/27/2002–10/31/2009
Michael Downing	11/1/2009–11/16/2009
Charlie Beck	11/16/2009–present

Source: Arthur W. Sjoquist (historical text by), *Los Angeles Police Department Commemorative Book, 1869–1984*, 1984.

▎ Appendix D: Chicago police chiefs, 1855 – 2018

Cyrus P. Bradley	1855–1863
Jacob Rehm	1863
Cyrus P. Bradley	1864
William Turtle	1864–1865
Jacob Rehm	1866–1871
W. W. Kennedy	1871–1872
Elmer Washburn	1873–1874
Jacob Rehm	1874–1875
Michael Hickey	1875–1878
V. A. Seavey	1878–1879
Simon O'Donnell	1880
William McGarigle	1880–1882
Austin Doyle	1882–1885
Fred Ebersold	1885–1888
George W. Hubbard	1888–1889
Fred Marsh	1890–1891
Bob McCullough	1891
Robert W. McClaughry	1892–1893

Michael Brennan	1893–1895
John J. Badenoch	1895–1897
Joseph Kipley	1897–1901
Francis O'Neill	1901–1905
John M. Collins	1905–1907
George M. Shippy	1907–1909
LeRoy T. Steward	1909–1911
John McWeeny	1911–1913
James J. Gleason	1913–1915
Charles Healey	1915–1916
Herman Schuettler	1917–1918
John J. Garrity	1918–1920
Charles C. Fitzmorris	1920–1923
Morgan Collins	1924–1927
Michael Hughes	1927–1928
William F. Russell	1928–1930
James Allman	1931–1946
John C. Prendergast	1946–1950
Timothy J. O'Connor	1950–1960
Orland W. Wilson	1960–1967
James B. Conlisk Jr	1967–1973
James M. Rochford	1974–1977
James E. O'Grady	1978–1979
Richard Brzeczek	1980–1983
Fred Rice Jr.	1983–1987
Leroy Martin	1987–1992
Matt L, Rodriguez	1992–1997
Terry G. Hilliard	1998–2003
Philip J. Cline	2003–2007
Jody P. Wells	2008–2011
Garry McCarthy	2011–2015
Eddie T. Johnson	2016–present

Sources: Raphael W. Marrow and Harriet I. Carter, *In Pursuit of Crime: The Police of Chicago*, 1996; John J. Flinn, *History of the Chicago Police*, 1887; rev. ed., 1973.

Appendix E: Attorneys general of the United States, 1908–2018

Charles Joseph Bonaparte	December 17, 1906–March 4, 1909
George W. Wickersham	March 5, 1909–March 5, 1913
James C. McReynolds	March 5, 1913–August 29, 1914
Thomas Watt Gregory	August 20, 1914–March 5, 1919
A. Mitchell Palmer	March 5, 1919–March 5, 1921

Harry M. Daughtery	March 4, 1921–March 28, 1924
Harlan Fiske Stone	April 7, 1924–March 2, 1925
John T. Sargent	March 17, 1925–March 5, 1929
William D. Mitchell	March 5, 1929–March 3, 1933
Homer S. Cummings	March 4, 1933–January 2, 1939
Frank Murphy	January 2, 1939–January 18, 1940
Robert H. Jackson	January 18, 1940–July 10, 1941
Francis Biddle	September 5, 1941–June 30, 1945
Tom C. Clark	July 1, 1945–August 24, 1949
J. Howard McGrath	August 24, 1949–April 7, 1952
James P. McGranery	May 27, 1952–January 20, 1953
Herbert Brownell Jr.	January 21, 1953–November 8, 1957
William P. Rogers	November 8, 1957–January 20, 1961
Robert F. Kennedy	January 21, 1961–September 3, 1964
Nicholas D. Katzenbach (Acting)	September 4, 1964–February 11, 1965
Nicholas D. Katzenbach	February 11, 1965–October 2, 1966
Ramsey Clark (Acting)	October 3, 1966–March 2, 1967
Ramsey Clark	March 2, 1967–January 20, 1969
John N. Mitchell	January 21, 1969–March I, 1972
Richard G. Kleindienst (Acting)	March 2, 1972–June 12, 1972
Richard G. Kleindienst	June 12, 1972–May 24, 1973
Eliot L. Richardson	March 25, 1973–October 20, 1973
William B. Saxbe	January 4, 1974–February 3, 1975
Edward H. Levi	February 5, 1975–January 20, 1977
Griffin Bell	January 26, 1977–August 16, 1979
Benjamin Civiletti	August 16, 1979–January 19, 1981
William French Smith	January 23, 1981–February 1985
Edwin Meese III	March 25, 1985–August 12, 1988
Richard Thornburgh	August 12, 1988–August 15, 1991
William Barr	November 20, 1991–August 15, 1991
Janet Reno	March 12, 1993–January 20, 2001
Eric Holder (Acting)	January 20, 2001–February 2, 2001
John Ashcroft	February 2, 2001– February 3, 2005
Alberto Gonzales	February 3, 2005–September 17, 2007
Paul Clement (Acting)	September 17, 2007– September 18, 2007
Peter Keisler (Acting)	September 18, 2007–November 9, 2007
Michael Mukasey	November 9, 2007–January 20, 2009
Mark Filip (Acting)	January 20, 2009–February 3, 2009
Eric Holder	February 3, 2009–April 27, 2015
Loretta Lynch	April 27, 2015–January 20, 2017
Sally Yates (Acting)	January 20, 2017–January 30, 2017
Dana Boente	January 30, 20017–February 9, 2017
Jeff Sessions	February 9, 2017–present

Source: Athan G. Theoharis, ed., *The FBI: A Comprehensive Reference Guide*, 1999

Appendix F: Chronology of American policing

1631   First night watch established in Boston
1704   First of the slave patrols established in the South
1710   Publication of *The Constables Pocket-Book*
1767   Emergence of the Regulators, a South Carolina vigilante group
1789   U.S. Marshals Service established
1823   Texas Rangers established
1829   The first modern police force established, in London
1838   Boston introduces first American police force
1845   The first twenty-four-hour unified police force in America established
1845   New York City Police Department created
1850   Pinkerton National Detective Agency created in Chicago
1851   Chicago Police Department created
1853   New York City police become first American police to adopt wearing uniforms
1867   Publication of Allan J. Pinkerton's *General Principles of Pinkerton's National Police Agency*
1870   William Johnson of the Jacksonville, Florida, police force becomes first African American police officer killed in line of duty
1871   First National Police Convention is held in St. Louis, Missouri
1874   John Philip Clum establishes the first Indian police force
1878   First police matrons hired
1886   Eight Chicago police officers killed in Haymarket Riot bombing
1887   George Washington Walling publishes *Recollections of a New York City Chief of Police*
1890   Publication of George M. Roe's *Our Police: A History of the Cincinnati Police Force from the Earliest Period until the Present-Day*
1893   Marie Owens* is hired by the Chicago Police Department
1894   Lexow Committee on police com1ption (headed by Clarence Lexow) convenes in New York City
1895   Theodore Roosevelt hired as New York City Police commissioner
1902   U.S. uses fingerprinting for first time
1905   Lola Baldwin hired by Portland, Oregon, Police Department
1905   Pennsylvania State Police becomes first state police agency
1908   Police cars introduced in Louisville, Kentucky
1908   Bureau of Intelligence created
1909   MI5 in England created as Secret Service Bureau
1909   Publication of *Police Administration* by Leonhard Felix Fuld
1910   Washington, DC, police superintendent Richard Sylvester addresses the International Association of Chief of Police concerning the use of the third degree
1911   Berkeley, California, Police Department chief August Vollmer puts entire police force on bicycles
1912   August Vollmer introduces motorcycle patrols
1914   Berkeley, California police department becomes the first to have all patrol officers using automobiles

1919   Publication of *Policeman and Public* by Arthur Woods; Boston Police Strike of 1919

1920   Publication of *American Police Systems* by Raymond Blaine Fosdick

1921   August Vollmer adopts the first lie detector in a police laboratory

1921   Vollmer introduces police car radios in patrolling

1921   John Larson invents lie detector

1923   LAPD becomes first police department to create crime lab

1924   John Edgar Hoover appointed director of the Bureau of Investigation (see Federal Bureau of Investigation [FBI], origins of)

1930   Bureau of Investigation placed in charge of *Uniform Crime Reports*

1930   310 police officers killed in line of duty, deadliest year for police

1931   Wickersham Commission releases *Report on Police* (see Wickersham, George Woodward)

1935   Bureau of Investigation renamed Federal Bureau of Investigation (FBI); FBI establishes National Police Academy

1950   Publication of *Police Administration* by Orlando Winfield "O. W." Wilson; William Henry Parker* appointed Los Angeles Police Department (LAPD) chief

1961   *Mapp v. Ohio*

1966   *Miranda v. Arizona*

1968   Publication of James Q. Wilson's *Varieties of Police Behavior*; Indianapolis, Indiana, Police Department becomes the first American police department to assign women on routine patrol duty

1968   Betty Blankenship and Elizabeth Robinson of the Indianapolis, Indiana, police department become first female foot patrol officers

1970   RICO statute enacted

1972   Knapp Commission convenes

1974   Washington, DC, police officer Gail Cobb becomes for African American female killed in line of duty

1974   Police start wearing soft-body armor against potential handguns attacks

1982   Publication of "Broken-Windows" by James Q. Wilson and George Kelling

1986   Dr. Alec Jeffreys uses DNA to arrest and convict rapist murderer

1991   Rodney King beating

1992   Christopher Commission delivers report on LAPD

1993   Four ATF agents killed in Waco, Texas, raid on Branch Davidians

1994   Publication of David H. Bayley's *Police for the Future*

1994   Violent Crime Control and Law Enforcement Act

1995   Bombing of Alfred P. Murrah Federal Building in Oklahoma City

1999   New York City police shoot unarmed Amadou Diallo

1999   First challenge to Daubert guidelines for fingerprinting

1999   Columbine High School shooting

2001   9/11 terrorist attacks on America leave almost 3,000 dead

2001   New York settles $8.75 million lawsuit for police torture of Abner Louima

2015   Freddie Gray dies in Baltimore police van

2016   Debate over the so-called "Ferguson Effect"

2017   Dallas Police use a robot to end deadly sniper rampage, first use of robot to kill civilian on U.S. soil

Sources: Bryan Vila and Cynthia Morris, eds., *The Role of Police in American Society*, 1999; William G. Bailey, ed., *The Encyclopedia of Police Science*, 1995.

Appendix G: American State Police Organizations – date and name of first state agency

Alabama	1919	Special Force
Alaska	1941	Highway Patrol
Arizona	1901	Arizona Rangers
Arkansas	1929	State Road Patrol
California	1929	Highway Patrol
Colorado	1917	Department of Safety
Connecticut	1903	State Police
Delaware	1898	State Detectives
Florida	1939	Department of Public Safety
Georgia	1917	Home Guard
Hawaii		Each island has its own police force
Idaho	1919	State Constabulary
Illinois	1921	Highway Patrol Officers
Indiana	1921	Deputies
Iowa	1915	Special Agents
Kansas	1933	Traffic Inspectors
Kentucky	1932	Highway Police
Louisiana	1928	Highway Police
Maine	1917	Special Constables
Maryland	1916	Motorcycle Deputies
Massachusetts	1865	State Police
Michigan	1917	State Troops
Minnesota	1929	Highway Patrol
Mississippi	1938	Highway Patrol
Missouri	1931	Highway Patrol
Montana	1935	Highway Patrol
Nebraska	1919	Special Assistants
Nevada	1908	State Police
New Hampshire	1937	State Police
New Jersey	1921	State Police
New Mexico	1905	Mounted Police
New York	1917	State Police
North Carolina	1929	Highway Patrol
North Dakota	1935	Highway Patrol
Ohio	1933	Highway Patrol
Oklahoma	1937	Highway Patrol
Oregon	1921	Field Deputies
Pennsylvania	1905	State Police
Rhode Island	1917	Constabulary
South Carolina	1868	State Police
South Dakota	1917	State Constabulary
Tennessee	1915	State Constabulary
Texas	1835	Texas Rangers

Utah	1923	Traffic Patrols
Vermont	1925	Traffic Enforcement Officers
Virginia	1924	Motor Vehicle Inspectors
Washington	1921	Highway Patrol
West Virginia	1919	Department of Public Safety
Wisconsin	1939	Traffic Inspectors
Wyoming	1935	Department of Law Enforcement

Source: H. Kenneth Bechtel, *State Police in the United States: A Sociohistorical Analysis*, 1995.

Appendix H: Chicago police chiefs, 1855–1933

Cyrus P. Bradley	1855–1863
Jacob Rehm	1863
Cyrus P. Bradley	1864
William Turtle	1864–1865
Jacob Rehm	1866–1871
W. W. Kennedy	1871–1872
Elmer Washburn	1873–1874
Jacob Rehm	1874–1875
Michael Hickey	1875–1878
V. A. Seavey	1878–1879
Simon O'Donnell	1880
William McGarigle	1880–1882
Austin Doyle	1882–1885
Fred Ebersold	1885–1888
George W. Hubbard	1888–1889
Fred Marsh	1890–1891
Bob McCullough	1891
Robert W. McClaughry	1892–1893
Michael Brennan	1893–1895
John J. Badenoch	1895–1897
Joseph Kipley	1897–1901
Francis O'Neill	1901–1905
John M. Collins	1905–1907
George M. Shippy	1907–1909
LeRoy T. Steward	1909–1911
John McWeeny	1911–1913
James J. Gleason	1913–1915
Charles Healey	1915–1916
Herman Schuettler	1917–1918
John J. Garrity	1918–1920
Charles C. Fitzmorris	1920–1923
Morgan Collins	1924–1927

Michael Hughes	1927–1928
William F. Russell	1928–1930
John H. Alcock	1931
James Allman	1931–1933

Sources: Raphael W. Marrow and Harriet I. Carter, *In Pursuit of Crime: The Police of Chicago*, 1996; John J. Flinn, *History of the Chicago Police*, 1887; rev. ed., 1973.

Appendix I: Year of first African American police appointments in selected cities

Chicago	1872
Pittsburgh	1875
Indianapolis	1876
Boston	1878
Cleveland	1881
Philadelphia	1881
Columbus, OH	1885
Los Angeles	1886
Cincinnati	1886
Detroit	1890
Brooklyn, NY	1891
St. Louis	1901
New York City	1911

Source: W. Marvin Dulaney, *Black Police in America*, 1996.

Appendix J: Police origins worldwide

Afghanistan	1880s
Algeria	1962
Andorra	Andorran Police, 1931
Angola	People's Police Corps of Angola, 1978
Anguilla	Anguillan Police, 1972
Antigua and Barbuda	Antigua and Barbuda Police, 1886
Argentina	federal police, 1880
Australia	1788
Austria	City Guard, 1569
Bahamas	Royal Bahamas Police Force, 1840
Bahrain	Bahrain Police, 1926
Bangladesh	provincial police, 1861
Barbados	Barbados Police Force, 1835
Belgium	gendarmerie, 1795

Belize	British Honduras Police Force, 1885
Bermuda	1879
Bolivia	1886
Botswana	Bechuanaland Mounted Police, 1884
Brunei	Straits Settlement Police, 1905
Burundi	judicial police, 1967
Cameroon	Cameroon National Gendarmerie, 1960
Canada	Quebec, 1651
Chad	Sûreté, 1961
Chile	Queen's Dragoons, 1758
China	"runners," Confucian China; public security, 1949
Columbia	1858
Congo	National Gendarmerie, 1961
Cyprus	1960
Denmark	Copenhagen, 1590
Dominican Republic	National Police, 1936
Ecuador	municipal police, 1830
El Salvador	National Guard, 1912
Ethiopia	1935
Finland	"servants of the town," 1700s
France	*commissaire-enqueteurs*, 615; *marichausee*, 1544
Gambia	River Police, 1855
Germany	1732
Ghana	Gold Coast Militia and Police, 1844
Gibraltar	Gibraltar Police, 1830
Greece	Gendarmerie (Khorofylaki), 1833
Grenada	Grenada Militia, 1783
Guyana	Guyana Police Force, 1891
Honduras	Special Security Corps, 1963
Hong Kong	Royal Hong Kong Police Force, 1841
India	Sind constabulary model, 1843
Indonesia	Dutch Alegmeene Politie, pre-1947
Iran	Gendarmerie, 1911
Iraq	Iraqi Police Force, 1919
Ireland	provincial police, 1822
Israel	Palestine police force, 1926
Italy	Carabinieri, 1814
Ivory Coast	Gendarmerie, 1854
Jamaica	Jamaica Constabulary Force, 1867
Japan	1871
Jordan	1956
Kampuchea	1970
Kenya	1886
Korea, South	paramilitary constabulary, 1945
Laos	1945

Lesotho	Lesotho Mounted Police, 1872
Liberia	Liberian National Police Force, 1924
Liechtenstein	Princely Liechtenstein Corps, 1933
Luxembourg	*marechausee*, seventeenth century
Malawi	Malawi Police Force, 1921
Malaysia	British police force, 1806
Malta	Malta Police Force, 1814
Mauritius	Mauritius Police Force, 1859
Monaco	1867
Mozambique	Public Security Force, 1975
Nepal	Raksha Dal, c. 1952
Netherlands	1795
New Zealand	armed constabulary, 1846
Nigeria	Lagos Police Force, c. 1890s
Norway	local police, twelfth century; first chief constable appointed, 1686
Oman	*askars* tribal police, no date; Muscat Police Force, 1931
Panama	Corps of National Police, 1904
Paraguay	Paraguayan Police, 1951
Peru	Civil Guard, early twentieth century
Philippines	Philippines Constabulary, 1901
Poland	National Police, 1918
Portugal	sixteenth century
Puerto Rico	Civil Guard, 1868
Qatar	Qatar Police, 1948
Russian Federation	The Cheka, 1917
St. Helena	constabulary, 1865
St. Lucia	St. Lucia Police, 1834
Senegal	National Gendarmerie, 1843
Seychelles	1775
Sierra Leone	Sierra Leone Police Force, 1829
Singapore	Singapore Police Force, 1827
Somalia	armed constabulary, 1884
South Africa	Cape Constabulary and similar forces, nineteenth century
Spain	Carabineros, 1829
Sri Lanka	Vidanes, 1806
Sudan	Sudan Police Force, 1898
Suriname	Armed Police Corps, 1865
Tanzania	British East Africa Police, 1919
Thailand	*tamruat*, sixteenth century
Trinidad and Tobago	Trinidad Constabulary Force, early 1900s
Turkey	Jandarma, 1845
Tuvalu	Gilbert and Ellice Islands Armed Constabulary, 1892
Uganda	Armed Constabulary, 1900
United Arab Emirates	1974
United Kingdom	tithings, A.D. 800; New Police, 1829

United States   *schout fiscal*, 1640s
Uruguay   National Police of Uruguay, 1829
Vatican City   Swiss Guard, 1506
Western Samoa   Western Samoan Police, 1900
Yemen   Aden Police Force, 1937

Sources: George Thomas Kurian, *World Encyclopedia of Police Forces and Penal Systems*, 1989; James Cramer, *The World's Police*, 1964.

Appendix K: Prison history time line

c. 1900 B.C.   References made to the "Great Prison" of ancient Egypt.
c. *500* B.C.   *Desmoterion,* or "the place of chains," described in Greek play by Aeschylus.
451 B.C.   Rome's Twelve Tables mention imprisonment for debt.
399 B.C.   Plato discusses imprisonment in his *Apology* and in the trial of Socrates.
64 B.C.   Rome's Mamertine Prison built beneath city sewer system.
428   Theodisian Code notes separation of prisoners by sex.
817   Meeting of Benedictine priors at Aix-la-Chapelle set standards for punishment and torture.
1066   King William I begins construction of Tower of London.
c.1100   England begins imprisoning debtors.
1166   Assize of Clarendon requires sheriffs to build jails in each county until the arrival of justice of the peace.
1200   Best known early French prison in operation at the Chatelet in Mont-Saint Michel.
1298   Marco Polo imprisoned in Genoa.
1370   Groundwork laid for the Bastille in Paris.
1460s   Antonio Averlino describes a progressive prison regime in his *Treatise on Architecture.*
1495   Dungeons built under the Kremlin's Trinity Tower.
1500s   Use of galley servitude popularized in France, Spain, and Italian states.
1539   Lazaretto of San Pancrazio, Italy, designed.
1556   London's Bridewell opened.
1575   Cervantes enslaved by Barbary pirates for five years.
1596   Amsterdam incorporates house of correction known as the *rasphuis.*
1601   John ("No Man is An Island") Donne imprisoned.
1627   The Malefizhaus built for sinners and witches in Bamberg, Germany.
1633   Italian scientist Galileo sentenced to house arrest.
1635   Joseph Furttenbach describes cellular confinement in his *Architectura Universalis.*
1660   John Bunyan sentenced to Bedford Prison, County Gaol.
1677   Hospice of San Filippo opened in Florence for delinquent boys.
1682   William Penn's Code introduces important penal reform to Quaker colony of Pennsylvania.

1703	Author Daniel Defoe sentenced to prison for libel.
1704	Pope Clement XI opens house of correction for criminal boys at San Michele.
1718–1722	France transports convicts to Louisiana.
1718	England begins transportation to America.
1720	English statute rules that houses of correction be used to house criminal offenders.
1734	Iceland introduces imprisonment (in Danish prisons) as punishment.
1757	Benjamin Rush advocates classification of prisoners.
1764	Cesare Beccaria's *On Crimes and Punishment* published.
1769	London's Newgate Prison erected.
1771	Iceland opens prison in Reykjavik.
1773	Walnut Street Jail opens as local and county prison.
1773	John Howard appointed High Sheriff of Bedfordshire.
1773	John Howard begins tour of British prisons.
1776	Britain ends transportation of convicts to America.
1776	England begins using convict hulks to house prisoners.
1776	Belgium's Vilvorde Prison completed.
1779	English Penitentiary Act of 1779.
1785	Francesco Milizia distinguishes between civil and criminal architecture in *principi di Archiettura Civile*.
1787	The Pennsylvania Prison Society is created.
1787	England resumes transportation, this time to Australian penal colonies.
1788	First British convicts arrive in Australia.
1789	Publication of John Howard's *Account of the Principal Lazarettos in Europe*.
1790	John Howard dies from "gaol fever" in the Crimea.
1790	Philadelphia's Walnut Street Jail introduces the penitentiary and Pennsylvania system to America, when it becomes state penitentiary.
1790	Jeremy Bentham's first plan for the Panopticon submitted to British Parliament
1791	Bentham's *Panopticon Postscript* published.
1797	New York prison reformer Thomas Eddy oversees construction of Newgate Prison on the Hudson River.
1800	Virginia opens prison in Richmond based on the panopticon design.
1809	Dartmoor Prison completed.
1815	First use of striped uniforms in American prisons.
1816	England's Millbank Prison opens.
1817–1819	New York's Auburn Prison receives its first prisoners.
1818	Maidstone Prison opens.
c. 1820	England introduces treadmill.
1824	Early Italian reform prison opened in Padua in the Kingdom of Lombardy and Venice
1825	New York's Sing Sing Prison accepts its first prisoners.
1825	Switzerland's Geneva penitentiary completed.

1825	New York City opens house of refuge to handle juveniles.
1826	The Society for the Improvement of Prison Discipline publishes *Remarks on the Form and the Construction of Prisons with Appropriate Designs* in Great Britain.
1829	Eastern State Penitentiary receives its first prisoner.
1830	Coldbath Fields Prison opens.
1830s	Australia opens Berrima jail, one of its first professionally designed prisons.
1831	Magistrates Gustave de Beaumont and Alexis de Tocqueville visit American prisons.
1835	Kingston Prison opens, Canada's first penitentiary.
1835	Manuel Montesinos becomes director of Spain's Valencia Prison.
1836	Eastern State Penitentiary completed.
1836	John Haviland's Trenton State Prison opens.
1836	Paris's Petite Roquette Prison completed.
1836	Alexander Maconochie arrives in Australia.
1837	Joshua Jebb appointed England's first surveyor-general of prisons.
1838	Debtors' prisons banned under federal law. Replaced with bankruptcy laws.
1838	The Haviland-designed Tombs Prison opens in New York City incorporating Egyptian revival motifs.
1840	Alexander Maconochie experiments with convict reform on Norfolk Island.
1841	Victoria Prison opens in Hong Kong.
1842	Great Britain opens Pentonville Prison, becoming one of the most copied prisons in the world.
1844	Construction begins at Berlin's Moabit Prison based on Pennsylvania system.
1844	Reading County Gaol opens.
1845	Elizabeth Fry dies.
1846	First international prison congress convenes in Frankfurt.
1847	Sweden's earliest departmental prison opens at Gavle.
1849	Holloway Prison opens.
1849	Novelist Fyodor Dostoyevsky sentenced to Siberian gulag.
1850	Early Spanish reform prison at Valladolid opens.
1851	Oslo, Norway, opens cellular prison.
1853	Denmark's Horsens Prison built on Auburn model.
1854	Sir Walter Crofton inaugurates Irish system, or mark system.
1861	Spain completes its first cell prison in Vitoria.
1866	Convict leasing begins
1867	McNeil Island Territorial Prison opens.
1870	First National Prison Association meets.
1870	Declaration of Principles adopted at National Prison Association meeting.
1870	Britain ends transportation of convicts to penal colonies.

1873	Opening of the Indiana Women's Prison, marks appearance of first separate women's prison in the United States.
1876	Elmira Reformatory opens.
1876	Bogota, Colombia, opens model prison on Auburn plan.
1883	Panopticon in La Paz, Bolivia, is first national prison for men.
1884	Prison reform in Egypt begins under the first director general of prisons.
1884	Three panopticon prisons open in Holland, at Arnhem, Haarlem, and Breda.
1885	Construction on Uruguay's first penitentiary begins.
1891	U.S. Congress approved Three Prisons Act leading to construction of three federal penitentiaries.
1891	Wormwood Scrubs Prison opens, considered first telephone pole style prison.
1896	Howard League Founded.
1898	Fresnes-les-Rungis, based on telephone pole plan, completed outside Paris.
1905	England opens its first Borstal in Rochester, Kent.
1906	Leavenworth Federal Penitentiary opens.
1907	Penal Reform League founded.
1914	Thomas Mott Osborne becomes warden of New York's Sing Sing Prison.
1918	Bertrand Russell imprisoned.
1921	Howard Association and Penal Reform League join forces to become the Howard League for Penal Reform.
1925	Opening of Illinois's Stateville Prison marks the construction of America's last panopticon-style prison.
1926	Cuba opens national prison on the Isle of Pines.
1927	First federal women's prison opens in Alderson, West Virginia
1928	Alabama becomes last state to outlaw convict leasing
1929	America's Federal Bureau of Prisons organized.
1930	Ohio State Penitentiary fire on Easter Monday kills 320 inmates, America's deadliest prison disaster as of 2018
1930	United States establishes Federal Bureau of Prisons.
1932	Publication of *I Am a Fugitive om a Georgia Chain Gang!*
1934	Alcatraz Prison opens.
1946	French penal colony of Devil's Island closed.
1948	World's first use of boot camps method of "shock incarceration" demonstrated in England.
1948	England Outlaws penal servitude and hard labor.
1955	Deinstitutionalization of mentally ill begins. Jails and prisons eventually take up the slack.
1963	Weekend incarceration, a form of periodic detention, introduced in Auckland, New Zealand.
1963	Storied Alcatraz Prison closed.
1971	Attica Prison Riot results in thirty-nine deaths.

1975	Publication of Michel Foucault's *Surveiller et punir: La Naissance de la prison*, or *Discipline and Punish: The Birth of the Prison*.
1980	New Mexico State Prison Riot
1982	Lethal injection used for first time
1982	English Borstals replaced by youth custody.
1983	Use of electronic monitoring inaugurated in Albuquerque, New Mexico.
1983	Supreme Court rules that people cannot be incarcerated for failing to pay debts.
1983	Corrections Corporation of America, the first and largest of contemporary private prisons founded.
1984	Sentencing Reform Act recommends mandatory minimums and eliminates judicial discretion.
1985	Marion County, Kentucky, the site of the modern world's first privately owned and operated prison for adult felons.
1986	Passage of Anti-Drug Abuse institutes 100:1 disparity, requiring a minimum sentence of five years without parole for possessing five grams of crack cocaine and five years for possession of 500 grams of powder cocaine.
1986	Polls suggest than less than 2 percent of public believe illegal drugs are major problems facing the U.S.
1988	Polls show that a majority of Americans believe illegal drugs are a major problem.
1990	Australia's Borallon Prison becomes the nation's first privately managed prison.
1992	England opens its first privately managed prison at Wold's Prison, Humberside.
1993	Washington State passes the nation's first three strikes law (Initiative 593).
1993	First execution by hanging since the 1960s (Washington State's Westley Allan Dodd).
1994	American federal government opens its first super-maximum prison in Florence, Colorado.
1994	California passes nation's most punitive and used three strikes law.
1994	Violent Crime Control and Law Enforcement Act includes provisions for more prisons and bans prisoners from receiving Pell Grants for college.
1995	Alabama reintroduces the chain gang.
2002	American prison population reaches 2,166,260.
2002	100th prisoner freed because of DNA testing.
2004	Iraq's Abu Ghraib Prison scandal erupts.
2010	Federal Fair Sentencing Act reduces 100:1 disparity between crack and powder cocaine to 18:1.
2012	California passes Proposition 36 in order to reform its three strikes law.
2014	Missouri adds the firing squad to execution procedures.
2014	Congress passes Death in Custody Reporting Act.

2015	*Ashker vs. Governor of California* dramatically reduces number of people held in solitary in California prisons; sets limits on how and for how long people can be incarcerated.
2015	President Obama becomes first president to visit federal prison while in office.
2017	Nebraska becomes first conservative state to abolish death penalty in forty years.

Sources: Morris and Rothman, eds., *The Oxford History of the Prison*, 1995; Greg Newbold, "A Chronology of Correctional History," in *Journal of Criminal Justice Education* 10, no. 1 (Spring 1999), pp. 87–100; Johnston, *Forms of Constraint*, 2000; A Handbook for Jewish Communities Fighting Mass Incarceration, www.truah.org.

Appendix L: National Prison Congress Declaration of Principles (1870)

1 Establishing reformation, not vindictive suffering, as the purpose of penal treatment
2 Making classifications on the basis of the mark system, patterned after the Irish system
3 Rewarding good conduct
4 Helping prisoners realize that their destiny is in their own hands
5 Removing the chief obstacles to prison reform, namely: the political appointment of prison officials and the instability of management
6 Providing job training for prison officials
7 Replacing fixed sentences with indeterminate sentences; removing the gross disparities and inequities in prison sentences and demonstrating the futility of repeated short sentences
8 Establishing religion and education as the most important agencies of reformation
9 Using prison discipline that gained the will of prisoners and conserved their self-respect
10 Making industrious freemen rather than orderly and obedient prisoners as prison's aim
11 Urging full provision for industrial training
12 Abolishing the system of contract labor in prison
13 Establishing small prisons and separate institutions for different type of offenders
14 Laws striking against the so-called "higher-ups" in crime, as well as against the lesser operatives
15 Indemnifying prisoners who later were discovered to be innocent
16 Revising laws relating to the treatment of insane criminals
17 Making more judicious exercise of pardoning power
18 Establishing a system for the collection of uniform penal statistics
19 Developing more adequate prison architecture, providing sufficiently for air and sunlight, as well as for prison hospitals, schoolrooms, and such
20 Establishing central prison management within each state

21 Facilitating the social training of prisoners through proper associations and abolishing the silence rule
22 Making society at large realize its responsibility for crime conditions
23 "In the official administration of such a [prison] system and in the voluntary cooperation of citizens, therein, the agency of women may be employed with excellent effect."

Source: This is a summary, or abridgement, of the Declaration of Principles adopted at the National Prison Congress meeting in Cincinnati in 1870.

Appendix M: The Mutual Welfare League

1 The League is a prison system not imposed arbitrarily by the prison authorities, but one, which is desired and requested by the prisoners themselves.
2 There must be no attempt on the part of the prison administration to control the result of the League elections.
3 Membership in the League must be common to all prisoners; any other basis is false and will not attain the desired object-universal responsibility.
4 Under the League better discipline is secured because the prisoners will cooperate with the authorities when precious privileges are granted through the League.
5 Under the League all privileges are utilized as means of obtaining responsibility for the good conduct of the prison community.
6 The open courts of the League mean better conduct and fewer punishments.
7 The League has proved to be the most effective agent of stopping the drug traffic and combating unnatural vice.
8 The League, when properly handled by prison authorities, can largely increase the output of work and improve its quality.

Source: Osborne, *Prisons and Common Sense*, 1924.

INDEX